LAW AND BUSINESS

LAW AND BUSINESS

Douglas Whitman

University of Kansas

F. William McCarty

Western Michigan University

Frank F. Gibson

Ohio State University

Thomas W. Dunfee

*University of Pennsylvania,
The Wharton School*

Bartley A. Brennan

Bowling Green State University

John D. Blackburn

Ohio State University

RANDOM HOUSE
BUSINESS DIVISION
NEW YORK

First Edition

987654321

Copyright © 1987 by Thomas W. Dunfee, F. William McCarty, Frank F. Gibson, Douglas Whitman, John D. Blackburn, and Bartley A. Brennan.

Portions of this work were originally published in *Modern Business Law.*

Library of Congress Cataloging-in-Publication Data

Law and business.
  Includes index.
  1. Business law — United States.   I. Whitman, Douglas.
KF889.L387   1987   346.73′07   86 – 26097
ISBN 0 – 394 – 33962 – 2   347.3067

Manufactured in the United States of America.

Cover photo: Bohdan Hrynewych/Stock, Boston
Cover and Book Design: Glen M. Edelstein

PREFACE

In today's dynamic, fast-paced business environment, no one can afford to be ignorant about the fundamentals of business law. Practically every aspect of our everyday lives involves business transactions of one kind or another, and all of these have legal implications. Whether you're buying a house, setting up shop, entering a partnership, borrowing from the bank to pay off a creditor, or simply trying to cash a check, you need to be well-informed about the legal implications of every financial transaction you enter into in order to avoid being duped, going bankrupt, losing your health, and worse, even your life. Business people, students, professors, and lay people everywhere will find this book a clear, concise, and sensible guide through the complex issues that befuddle most of us when we are confronted by the subtleties of the law.

STRUCTURE OF THE BOOK

Business law is not simple; it cannot be reduced to tidy formulas and clear-cut solutions. Yet it has a basic structure with sound, fundamental principles. *Law and Business* provides its readers with a clear understanding of that structure and its basic principles. Since its goal was to meet the particular needs of beginning business law students, the text presents succinctly a wide range of traditional business law topics while providing extensive coverage of the law as it relates to contracts, commercial transactions, business organizations, property law, and government regulations. To help professors cover a broad range of topics in one or two semesters, the text has been designed to minimize the number of introductory chapters, enabling a professor to move rapidly into business topics after a brief coverage of the legal system.

Each chapter is designed to emphasize the basic rules of law without going into every nuance concerning these rules. Thus professors who wish to hit the high points concerning business law without going into unnecessary detail will find the text compatible with their philosophy of teaching. All the basic rules of law and fundamental topics business students must know, along with background on the context from which laws evolved, are included.

CHAPTER HIGHLIGHTS

Considerable time and attention was devoted to features that will make the book enjoyable for both students and professors to use. Each chapter is arranged in a readily-assimilated format and contains features that students and professors will find extremely valuable. These are:

- *Learning Objectives* stated at the outset of each chapter to acquaint the students with the particular issues they will be dealing with in the chapter.
- *Short, briefed cases* used throughout the text, and in context, to illustrate quickly and concisely the concepts of business law. These are arranged in a facts/issue/decision format throughout that is simple to read and comprehend. These were

specially chosen for their teachability and student appeal as well as to illustrate precisely the point of law discussed in the text.
- *Marginal definitions* for key terms and concepts, which are indicated in boldface type in the text. These marginal definitions reinforce and clarify the terms for students as they come across them and, again, in context.
- *Chapter summaries* that review the material covered in the chapter in a clear, complete, and unified context and provide the student with a quick, substantive chapter survey.
- *End-of-chapter review materials,* which include:
  - simple, self-testing chapter review questions and case problems
  - more challenging questions and problems based on real legal cases for class analysis, discussion, and assignments
- *Abundant examples, figures, and charts,* used throughout the text for instructors who feel that students gain a better understanding of the rules of law if they are illustrated by business examples and forms in addition to the cases.

ADDITIONAL MATERIAL

The text is generously supplied with helpful backmatter. *Appendices* on the U.S. Constitution, the current version of the Uniform Commercial Code, the Uniform Partnership Act, the Uniform Limited Partnership Act, and the Model Business Corporation Act are included. There is an extensive *glossary* that supplies definitions to key terms and concepts discussed in the text. There is also a *case index,* which enables a reader to locate quickly any case cited in the text, and a *subject index.*

ANCILLARIES

We have worked together to produce an Instructor's Manual which includes teaching objectives, lecture notes, answers to the end-of-chapter questions and case discussions with case questions. To supplement the briefed cases in the texts, the instructor's manual also includes longer case opinions in the language of the court. These longer cases can be made available to students for their further study and analysis.

A Study Guide has been prepared by Angela M. Cerino of Villanova University. Dennis Kuhr, also of Villanova University, has prepared the Test Bank which is available both in print form and as a computer disk.

ACKNOWLEDGMENTS

No project, of course, is the product of a single person. All the authors have contributed their authoritative knowledge and teaching expertise, with additional insights from their students and colleagues. In particular, the structure, content and design of this text were immeasurably influenced by a number of professors who read the numerous drafts of this text and offered their suggestions on ways to improve the rough drafts. We appreciate the thoughtful comments they made. They are: Frederick L. Baker, Columbus Technical Institute; Zohreh S. Behbehani, Johnson County College; Jere L. Crago, Delgado Community College; Eugene B. Culberson, Illinois Central College; Frank J. Del Bene, SUNY at Farmingdale; Paul F. Desseault, Herkimer County Community College; Floranna Miller, Fashion Institute of Technology; Craig C. Milnor, Clark College; Violet E. Molnar, Riverside Community College District; Jim Lee Morgan, West Los Angeles College; William E. Ringle, Queensborough Community College; Brian S. Terry, Johnson and Wales College; Richard E. Vizard, Manchester Community College.

We also gained insight for the development of this text from various people willing to share their experience and ideas with us by responding to phone calls and questionnaires. They are: Tom Dent, St. Louis Community College; Templeton Briggs, Fullerton College; George Katz, San Antonio College; Jerry Lasselle, Portland College; Marilyn Menack, Westchester Community College; Jesse Walker, Gadsden State Junior College; James Rowe, Mercer County Community College; Tom Lang, St. Petersberg Jr. College; Jim Nipps, Sheridan College; Ralph Washington, Hinds Jr. College; Jackie McKinney, Georgia Southwestern College; Douglas Jensen, Ft. Steilacoom Community College; Al Johnson, Indian River Community College; Marvin Newman, Rollins College; Gerald Saunders, Massachusetts Bay Community College; Dick Adams, College of the Redwoods; Paul Morrison, Central Valley Community College; John Wooten, Kellogg Community College; Richard Mills, Cypress College; James Wellman, Jamestown Community College; Harris Rollins, Jr., Grambling State University; D. A. Dalka, Carthage College; Gale Heiman, Aims Community College; Mike Kauffman, Linn-Benton Community College; Javier Garcia III, Ashland College; Tom Curry, Shelby State Community College; Leon Sherman, New Mexico Jr. College; R. Newcomb, Broome Community College.

We wish to particularly mention Carole Beard of the Word Processing Center, College of Business Administration, Bowling Green State University, for the typing of the manuscript and Sandra Cully, graduate assistant, for proofreading the copy and galleys.

We welcome comments from users of this book, both instructors and students. Our aim is to please users of *Law and Business* in every possible way. Please send us your suggestions for improvement.

We also wish to thank the many people at Random House who contributed so much to this text. In particular, we wish to express our thanks to Susan Badger, Anne Mahoney, Valerie Raymond, Lisa Mitchell, Neils Aaboe, and Beena Kamlani.

Douglas Whitman
F. William McCarty
Frank F. Gibson
Thomas W. Dunfee
Bartley A. Brennan
John D. Blackburn

CONTENTS

Chapter 22: Commercial Paper: Liability and Defenses   371

Chapter 23: Commercial Paper: Checks   388

Chapter 24: Secured Transactions   405

Chapter 25: Bankruptcy   429

PART I

THE LEGAL ENVIRONMENT OF BUSINESS

CHAPTER 1

An Introduction to Law

CHAPTER OBJECTIVES

After reading this chapter, you should be able to:

1. Explain the nature of law.

2. Discuss the sources of American law.

3. List the alternatives to settling a dispute by going to court.

4. Explain why the law is adversarial in nature.

5. Discuss how the law is classified.

INTRODUCTION

People in business, whether they own, manage, or simply work for someone else, must be familiar with the law. Every day people in business do things that may result in serious legal consequences for their employers or themselves. When a person plans on entering into an agreement with another person, he or she needs to know the formalities necessary to create an enforceable agreement. Businesspeople are called upon to sign a wide variety of forms and need to understand the nature and consequences of the documents they are signing. An employer who hires workers needs to be aware of the law governing employment relationships. People contemplating entering into a business relationship with someone else need to be aware of the types of business entities used in the United States.

Of course, businesspeople do not need to be lawyers in order to engage in business. However, the client who understands the law can avoid many legal problems. Sometimes businesspeople end up in court because they have entered into a transaction without first consulting with a lawyer. Knowing when to call a lawyer is very important.

One of the functions of this text is to introduce the student to various topics in law important to businesspeople, to familiarize the student with common problems, and teach the student when to consult with an attorney before taking any action. A second function of this text is to teach students how to communicate meaningfully with an attorney. Concepts and terminology used by lawyers will be clearly presented. Of course, no one is a walking encyclopedia of the law. For this reason, it will probably be useful for you to keep this text after you have completed your law courses. When a problem arises, you can refer to the text to refresh your memory of the legal terminology. For that matter, if you read an article in the *Wall Street Journal,* a business magazine (*Business Week, Fortune,* or *Forbes,* for example), or a book on business, you may find it helpful to refer back to some of the material in this text.

THE NATURE OF LAW

People often say, "You can't do that. It's against the law!" Exactly what do they mean when they use the word *law*? Many definitions of law have been suggested. We define **law** as the entire body of principles that govern conduct and can be enforced in the courts.

Everyone in society is subject to a variety of rules. Not all of these rules are laws. For example, many religions set rules of behavior. Violating these rules, however, does not mean that a person has violated the law. If a group of men gets together one afternoon to play a game of baseball, certain rules govern the conduct of the game. These rules are not laws. If four people sit down at a card table to play bridge, an elaborate set of rules governs the players. These rules are not laws. If a boy and girl go out on a date and their parents tell them to be in by midnight, the parents are enforcing rules but not laws. In all of these cases, the rules are not laws and cannot be enforced in court.

If a person does violate a law, in the event a court finds him or her in violation of the law, the court generally imposes some form of penalty, called a **sanction.** Typically sanctions require a person to do or to not do something; to pay money to someone else; or impose a prison sentence on someone. For example, if a man agrees to purchase a guitar and takes possession of it, he may be sued for whatever amount of money he agreed to pay for the guitar. A court, if it finds that the person agreed to pay $300 for the guitar, may order the person to pay the seller $300. If a married couple splits up, and the wife has custody of the children, a judge can order the husband to pay her for child support. If a thief robs a convenience store, a judge may sentence the thief to prison.

In the next section we discuss the various ways in which the law may be classified.

Law principles that govern conduct and can be enforced in the courts

Sanction a penalty or punishment provided as a means of enforcing obedience to the law

HOW LAW IS CLASSIFIED

Substantive and Procedural Law

Substantive Law   includes the laws that create, define, and regulate rights and obligations. Substantive law regulates rights and duties. If a student agrees to rent an apartment during the school year, the legal rights and obligations of the student to the apartment are determined by the law that governs the relationships between the owner of the apartment and the student.

Procedural Law   specifies the methods of enforcing rights and obligations created by substantive law. If the student in the example above feels the apartment owner has somehow violated the student's rights, she may file suit in court. The laws that determine in which court the case should be filed, how the trial is conducted, and how a court judgment is enforced are all part of procedural law. For the most part, this text deals with substantive law, although some procedural law is discussed.

Public Law and Private Law

Public law deals with the rights and powers of the government. An example of public law is criminal law. Suppose that the owner of an apartment and a student get into an argument and the student hits the owner with a baseball bat. By engaging in such behavior, the student probably has violated the criminal laws of the state she is living in. Criminal law is discussed in Chapter 3.

Private law is administered between private citizens. If the student fails to pay her rent, the landlord may file suit to collect it. The case will be governed by private law, because the government is not involved.

Civil Law

Civil case a case brought by a private individual trying to enforce a private right

Plaintiff a person who brings a lawsuit

Defendant a person being sued

Civil law deals with violations against an injured party. In a **civil case,** a private party, the **plaintiff,** files suit against the **defendant** to recover for the injury the plaintiff has sustained as a result of the defendant's conduct. To win the suit, the plaintiff must establish his or her case by a preponderance of the evidence. That is, the court must find that more evidence favors the plaintiff's position in the case than supports the defendant's position. The purpose of a civil lawsuit is to compensate the injured person.

Suppose that Bob purchased a new motorcycle from a dealer for $2,500. The dealer delivered the motorcycle to Bob, who agreed to pay the dealer $75 per month. After Bob got the motorcycle, he refused to make payments. In this situation, the dealer could file a civil suit against Bob either for $2,500 or to force Bob to return the cycle to the dealer. The dealer would be the plaintiff, and Bob would be the defendant. The dealer would have to convince the court that Bob agreed to purchase the cycle for $2,500. If the court agreed and Bob had no defense, the court would order Bob to pay the $2,500 or to return the cycle to the dealer.

FIGURE 1-1   Classification of Law

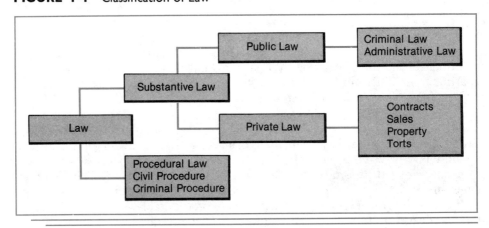

FIGURE 1-2 Comparison of Civil and Criminal Law

	Civil Law	**Criminal Law**
Who files suit:	Private individual (plaintiff) sues	Government prosecutes
Burden of proof:	Preponderance of the evidence	Beyond a reasonable doubt
Principal sanctions:	Monetary damages	Death
	Equitable remedies	Imprisonment
		Fines

Criminal Law

Criminal law establishes the duties people owe to society. If a person violates any of these duties, he or she has committed a wrong against society. **Criminal cases** are brought by the government (local, state, or federal) against the defendant. The prosecutor files the case on behalf of the government. To win the suit, the prosecutor must establish, beyond a reasonable doubt, that the defendant committed the crime which the prosecutor asserts he or she committed. In a criminal case, but not in a civil case, a judge may impose a sanction against a criminal as punishment for violating the law. Such sanctions are either:

Criminal case a case brought by the state against a defendant who has violated a law enacted to protect society from harm

1. money, which in most cases must be paid to the government, or

2. prison sentences.

In some states, if a person is found guilty of murder, he or she may be executed. It should be noted that juveniles, defined in most states as people under the age of 18, are tried in a separate court, juvenile court, for violations of criminal law.

SOURCES OF AMERICAN LAW

One myth accepted by many people is that all laws can be found in nicely indexed, officially published books. All a person has to do to learn about law is to find the right page in the right book, and there the law will be in clear black letters. Unfortunately this is not true. Although some laws are found in books, others are created by judicial opinions.

To learn about law, people must consult these sources:

Constitutions

Treaties

Statutes

Ordinances

Administrative rules and orders

Judicial opinions

Each is discussed briefly in the following pages.

Constitutions

A constitution is the fundamental law of a nation. The men who wrote the United States Constitution gathered in Philadelphia 200 years ago with specific goals in mind. They wrote the Constitution so that the three branches of government — the legislative, the executive, and the judicial — had checks over one another to prevent an abuse of power by any one branch of government. The Constitution also created a system of checks and balances between the powers of the states and the federal government.

Separation of Powers   The separation of powers doctrine thus involves the division of the authority of government among legislative, judicial, and executive branches and contemplates that none of the three shall exercise any of the powers belonging to the others. Chief Justice John Marshall described the end result of the doctrine as follows: "The difference between the departments undoubtedly is, that the legislature makes, the executive executes, and the judiciary construes the law."[1]

The Constitution gave the legislative power to the United States Senate and the United States House of Representatives (collectively referred to as "Congress"). It gave Congress the power to control federal spending and to pass laws, for example. The executive power was granted to the president. The judicial power was given to the courts. The courts have the power to strike down laws that conflict with the provisions of the Constitution.

The Federal System   The genesis of the American federal system is the Constitution. It is actually a compact between the individual states and the federal government. As a result of this compact, each state — a sovereign entity in its own right — has delegated certain powers to the federal government. When the federal government acts within the framework of these **delegated powers,** its actions are supreme. Similarly, the actions of each state are supreme when the state acts on the basis of a **retained power.** At the same time, some powers are concurrent, in the sense that they can be asserted by both state and federal governments. The power to tax is an example. Both state and federal governments have this authority.

An interesting feature of the United States legal system is that the federal government and the 50 state governments all have certain powers. In effect, we really have 51 different legal systems. However, the supremacy clause of the Constitution states that laws passed by Congress are the supreme law of the land. That is, if there is a conflict between a federal and a state law, the federal law is supreme.

Every state also has a constitution. State constitutions are similar to the United States Constitution. Laws passed in each state must conform to the requirements of both that state's constitution and the United States Constitution.

Delegated powers the powers the states constitutionally delegated to the federal government

Retained powers those powers that the states did not delegate to the federal government

The Commerce Clause   One of the powers that the states delegated to the federal government was the power "to regulate commerce with foreign nations, and among the several states. . . ." Over the years "the commerce clause," as this grant of authority is called, has been subject to varying interpretations by the United States Supreme Court. Today it is largely through the use of this power that the federal government regulates many aspects of American economic life.

The different interpretations of the commerce clause over nearly 200 years of constitutional history provide an example of the manner in which the legal system responds to economic, political, and social change. In *Gibbons* v. *Ogden,* the most famous of the early cases interpreting the clause, both *commerce* and *regulate* were given broad meanings. These insured that the national government and not the states would have authority to control navigation on public waterways, even those wholly within a state. The decision thus met the needs of expanding national economic interests for an efficient means of moving goods that could not be restricted by local pressures. At the same time, the decision reflected the rise of national spirit in much of the nation at the time.

Although the commerce clause has been interpreted in various ways since *Gibbons* v. *Ogden,* since the 1930s the U.S. Supreme Court has interpreted it very broadly. This broad interpretation has permitted a great deal of federal legislation. Much of this **legislation** deals with topics of concern to people in business, such as labor relations laws and consumer protection laws.

Legislation laws made by a legislative body

Treaties

The Constitution declares that treaties are the supreme law of the land. That means that if a conflict arises between the provisions of a treaty and a law passed either by Congress or a state legislature, the federal or state law is invalid. Treaties are negotiated by the president of the United States and must be ratified by a two thirds vote of the Senate.

Statutes

A **statute** is a law passed by a legislative body. The Constitution gives Congress the power to pass federal statutes. These statutes are subject to veto by the president. State constitutions give their state legislatures the power to pass state statutes. These statutes are subject to veto by state governors. Many statutes have been passed by both the federal government and the states. Many require businesses to do certain things; many require businesses to refrain from doing other things. Many areas of the law today are largely statutory. That is, the answer to whether a business can do something is spelled out by statute. Criminal law, the law of the sale of goods, and many other areas of law are extensively dealt with by federal and state statutes.

Statute a law

Model statutes may be proposed by scholars and practitioners. State legislatures and Congress may use the models as bases for enacting statutes. The Uniform Commercial Code is a good example of such a model statute. A product of the Uniform Commissioners on State Law, the code is an effort to make the law on certain business issues uniform across the United States. For example, Article 2 of the code deals with sales laws. Every state except Louisiana has adopted Article 2 in more or less the same form. Because we have 50 different states, and because many organizations conduct business in a number of states, the need for uniformity is great. The code has been adopted in virtually all states.

Statutory Interpretation   Most statutes are broadly written, indicating only the outlines of legislative policy. Before the meaning of a statute is established, it often has to be interpreted or, as lawyers say, "construed" by the courts. Thus in many situations, when a person needs to know what the law is, he or she looks first at the statutory provision and then at cases in which it has been applied. These cases indicate what the statute actually means.

Does it make sense for the courts to explain what the legislature actually meant? The process makes good sense, for it allows the meaning of the law to be filled in by the courts. They are better equipped than the legislature to respond to specific problems and less affected by the political pressures of the moment. Although having the courts interpret statutes is not without risk, courts in the United States have consistently stated that, in interpreting statutes, their primary function is to determine and give effect to the intention of the legislature.

Because legislatures seldom have specific intents, statutory interpretation is an imperfect science. To improve the process, courts have developed principles of statutory interpretation to determine legislative intent.

In applying these principles, a court must take into consideration the general purpose of the legislation, its historical background, the evils at which the statute is directed, and its evident objectives. The principles of construction, which include looking at the plain meaning of terms, contextual analysis, and examination of the statute's legislative history, must yield if they conflict with clear evidence of the legislative will.

Ordinances

Laws are also passed by local — city and county — governments. These laws are like the statutes passed by state legislatures and Congress. Although ordinances apply in only relatively small geographical areas, businesspeople must be aware of the ordinances that apply where they operate. San Francisco has passed an ordinance, for example, that people who do not smoke must be provided a smoke free environment. Businesses operating in San Francisco must comply with the ordinance; businesses operating outside of San Francisco do not have to comply. Cities pass a wide range of such ordinances, many of which have a major impact on business decisions. Rent control ordinances, building ordinances, and local sales taxes are examples of local laws.

Administrative Rules and Orders

Agencies play important roles in local, state, and national affairs. Many have the authority to adopt rules and regulations that have the force of law. Frequently business managers as well as private citizens must be aware of these rules when making decisions.

One example of a business in which an agency's rules and regulations are significant is the sale of securities. In 1934 Congress passed the Securities Exchange Act to insure fairness in securities transactions. This act established the Securities and Exchange Commission (SEC). On the basis of authority granted to it, the SEC has adopted numerous rules that regulate issuing and trading securities. Although the rules are not made by a legislative body, a person or firm violating them is subject to penalties such as the revocation or suspension of the privilege to market a new security or possible criminal prosecution. Other important administrative agencies with rule-making authority are the Federal Trade Commission (FTC), the National Labor Relations Board (NLRB), and the Environmental Protection Agency (EPA).

In addition to the authority to make rules, administrative agencies often have the authority to hear cases and issue orders. This is referred to as administrative **adjudication.** When hearing cases, the agency frequently must interpret a statute. Although these agency interpretations are subject to limited review by the courts, the interpretations are an important indication of the law. Courts generally respect an agency's interpretation of the statute that it administers. Presumably the administrators have the specialized knowledge that judges do not have.

Adjudication the pronouncing of a formal judgment for one party or the other in a lawsuit

Judicial Law

Common Law   A distinguishing feature of Anglo-American law is its reliance upon previously decided cases as a primary source of law. Reliance on judicial decisions is known as case law or **common law.** The term, common law, originated in England and referred to a body of law that was *common* throughout England. Another source of law in England was the court of the chancery (also called the court of equity).

Common law law derived from court decisions

Equity   Many years ago, the courts in the United States were divided into courts of law and courts of **equity** like British courts. Today in the United States a single court hears both law and equity matters.

Generally, people who went to law courts wanted monetary damages. People who desired some remedy other than money went to the equity courts. Today whenever monetary relief is not an adequate remedy, the courts grant some form of equitable relief. For example, a person enters into a contract to purchase a particular painting. The buyer wants the painting, not money. If the seller refuses to deliver the painting to the buyer, the buyer may file suit. In this situation, the court requires the defendant to honor the contract and deliver the painting. The order is an example of an equitable remedy.

Common law is based in part on the concept of **stare decisis.** Stare decisis, which is Latin for "to abide by or to adhere to decided cases," reflects the policy that, once a court applies a particular principle of law to a certain set of facts, that same legal principle should govern all future cases in which the facts are substantially the same. The major problem in applying the doctrine of stare decisis arises because there are often conflicting **precedents** that can be compared to the case under consideration.

Equity fairness and justice, as opposed to statutory or case law, as a basis for a decision

Stare decisis the doctrine that courts follow principles derived from previous cases involving similar facts

Precedent a previous decision relied upon by a court for authority in making a current decision

Opposing attorneys argue that the facts of a present case are similar to those of cases in which different results were reached.

Factual Distinction   Even if a statement in a prior case is considered to be precedent for later cases, the facts of a later case may be different from those of a prior case.

For example, suppose in a New York case that a New York court held that if the owner of an apartment allows ice to accumulate on the sidewalks, the owner will be liable to anyone injured on the sidewalks. In July, Mary is walking along the sidewalk in front of an apartment, and she slips on some paint that painters spilled on the sidewalk. Is Mary entitled to collect damages in light of the earlier New York case? It is possible that a court could distinguish between the two situations: one involves ice and the other involves paint. The court could create a different rule to govern Mary's case because the facts are different from those in the earlier case.

When major factual distinctions exist between a case under consideration and a supposed precedent, the cases are said to be distinguished. Stare decisis does not apply to cases that can be distinguished from the relevant precedents.

Changed Conditions   On occasion courts do refuse to follow previous decisions, even though such decisions are based on similar facts, because conditions have changed significantly. The changes may involve new technology or novel economic, social, or political circumstances. The concept of a change of conditions is illustrated by the case of *Flagiello* v. *Pennsylvania Hospital*.

Flagiello v. Pennsylvania Hospital

Supreme Court of Pennsylvania
208 A. 2d 193 (1965)

FACTS   Plaintiff Mary Flagiello fell and broke her ankle while a patient at defendant Pennsylvania Hospital. The fall was caused by the negligence of two hospital employees. Mrs. Flagiello sued the hospital for medical expenses, pain and suffering, and loss of earnings resulting from the fall. The hospital did not deny that its employees were negligent but argued that as a charitable hospital it was not liable under Pennsylvania law for the employees' acts. The trial court dismissed the suit. It agreed with the hospital's argument, which was based on well accepted law.

ISSUE   Should the court follow the well established case law which holds that a charitable hospital is not liable for the negligence of its employees?

DECISION   No. The appellate court ruled that where justice, reason, and fair play call for changes in judge-made law, the courts must make them. The court noted that over 90 percent of today's charitable hospital patients pay for their care. Charitable hospitals no longer serve almost exclusively patients who cannot pay for their care.

The court also rejected the hospital's argument that if changes in the law are to be made, they must come from the legislature. The court stated that because charitable hospital immunity was a judge-made rule, the court could abolish it.

> The dissent stated that consistency in following judge-made law provides certainty
> and stability in the law. When judge-made law is not followed, no one knows from
> week to week what the law is or what one's rights and responsibilities are.

DISSENT

Dicta   Not all the statements of the court in a previous case must be followed in subsequent cases. Those statements from previous cases required by the facts and directly related to the result are precedent to which the doctrine of stare decisis is applicable. Other statements, which are not necessary to determine the decision in the case, are referred to as **dicta** and need not be followed in subsequent court decisions.

In the earlier example concerning Mary, suppose that the judge had stated that apartment owners should not permit children to leave toys in yards. Because this statement was not necessary for resolving the case — Mary slipped on paint on the sidewalk, not a toy in a yard — the statement is dicta and need not be followed in a later case.

Dicta statements made by a court in a prior case that later courts need not follow because the statements were not necessary to the result

Scope of Precedent   Each state has its own sources of law, its own constitution, laws, administrative rulings, and judge-made precedent. The courts of one state do not have to follow decisions from other states. If the Supreme Court of Ohio decides a case, all lower courts in Ohio must follow its rule. However, the courts in other states are not obligated to follow the rule. Thus, a Kansas court need not concern itself with the decisions of the Ohio court. Of course, decisions from other states may be consulted for reference. Courts sometimes consult decisions from other states when there are no previous decisions on the point in question from the state where the case is being heard. Reasons given by other state courts for adopting new policies also may be considered.

Courts in each **jurisdiction** — federal or state — are grouped in a particular order. In this order, **appellate courts** are generally considered higher courts, **trial courts** lower courts. Every federal or state trial court is "under" an appellate court. Precedent flows down from higher to lower courts.

All courts are bound by decisions of the U.S. Supreme Court. In each state, lower trial and appellate courts must abide by decisions of state courts. Trial courts only need follow precedent from the appellate court covering their jurisdiction. Thus the U.S. District Court for the Southern District of New York — a federal trial court — is not bound by a decision of the Ninth Circuit Court of Appeals, a federal appellate court whose geographic control is limited to the West Coast.

Jurisdiction the geographic area, persons, and subject matter over which a particular court has the power to make decisions

Appellate court a court that reviews the decisions of a lower court

Advantages of Precedent   By following the doctrine of stare decisis, the courts make the law predictable. If a previous case has been based upon a certain principle, that principle will be used in a later case. Predictability is very important to people in business. When they are planning courses of action, they need to know in advance what the courts will consider the law to be. By examining earlier court decisions, a businessperson can determine the law that applies in a given situation. Because of the

Trial court the court in which evidence is presented and witnesses testify

principle of stare decisis, judicial decisions affect the parties to a lawsuit and all parties involved in similar suits in the future.

Disadvantages of Precedent   The needs of society change over time. If courts rigidly follow the doctrine of stare decisis, situations may arise in which it would be unjust to follow precedent. In such situations, courts may create new rules in the interest of justice. Although for many years cases were the chief source of Anglo-American law, statutes were also important as a source both in England and the United States. For many reasons, during the past 150 years statutory law has increased in importance. In addition, much of the judge-made law of previous centuries has been enacted by legislative bodies into statute. This process is called **codification.** Today, a person trying to determine the law in a particular field probably would first look for a statute covering the question.

Codification the process of enacting judge-made law into statute

Statutory law law based upon statutes enacted by government bodies

Distinctions between Statutory and Judicial Law   **Statutory law,** in contrast to judge-made law, is usually more directly responsive to political, social, and economic conditions. Judges are aware of social forces, and their opinions generally are filled with references to the social conditions underlying a case. But judge-made law responds slowly to society's needs.

Other differences between statutory law and law based on judicial decision are also significant. In general, statutes apply to many people, and they change or add to the existing law from their effective date. Thus they affect actions yet to occur. But judicial decisions apply to one or a few individuals and to actions that have taken place.

Ordinarily legislators enact a law to address issues involving a substantial portion of the population. However, a judicial decision is limited to the specific facts and the legal dispute between specific parties. Nevertheless, because of stare decisis, some judicial decisions do establish principles that are followed later in similar cases.

ALTERNATIVE DISPUTE RESOLUTION

One of the principal functions of the legal system is to provide a forum for settling disputes. During the last 50 years, more and more people have turned to the courts to resolve their differences. In 1982, 206,000 civil cases were filed in federal district courts, compared to 35,000 in 1940. Most of the growth occurred in the last few years. Additionally, 12 million cases were filed in state courts, or one lawsuit for every 13 adults.

Litigation contested legal action

The cost of this **litigation** to the public treasury is enormous. It costs $2.2 billion each year to process civil cases and an additional $4 billion to process criminal cases. Even with this extensive use of public funds, long delays often exist in litigation. In some metropolitan areas, plaintiffs must wait from two to three years before their cases are heard. Direct costs to individuals in time and money are substantial. Because of these costs and delays, both individuals and business are increasingly looking to alternative means of resolving disputes.

Alternative dispute resolution (ADR) techniques generally are intended as alternatives to the traditional court process. They usually involve impartial people who are referred to as "third parties" (no matter how many parties are involved in the dispute) or "neutrals." Some of these techniques are arbitration, mediation, fact finding, and conciliation.

Arbitration

Arbitration is widely used in settling commercial and labor–management disputes. In many industries, arbitration is the standard method of settling conflicts between firms. The use of arbitration to resolve consumer complaints recently has increased dramatically. Currently, consumers can use arbitration for complaints against automobile manufacturers, most new car dealers, appliance manufacturers, movers, and some funeral directors. In 1984 the Better Business Bureau's national arbitration program listed as participants 17,000 local businesses, ranging from carpet shops to auto repair shops. Arbitration involves the submission of the dispute to a third party who hears arguments, reviews evidence, and then renders a decision. Arbitration is not so formal, complex, or time consuming as a court proceeding. In binding arbitration, the most common form used in commercial disputes, the parties select the arbitrator and are bound by the decision (called an "award"). In some instances, the award is binding upon the parties because of a statute. But in most instances, the parties agree to accept the award before they submit to arbitration. Agreeing on an arbitrator is sometimes difficult. One common practice is to have a panel of three arbitrators. Each party selects one of the arbitrators, and those two select the third.

In labor–management disputes, arbitration traditionally has been used to resolve grievances. Almost all collective bargaining contracts contain an arbitration clause. This clause generally outlines a grievance mechanism. If an issue cannot be resolved by the parties, the arbitration clause provides a method for selecting an arbitrator and outlines the arbitrator's authority. Generally, this authority is extensive, with the arbitrator being authorized to decide all disputes regarding the interpretation and application of the agreement.

Last offer arbitration is a relatively recent development. In last offer arbitration, the arbitrator is required to choose between the final positions of the two parties. In major league baseball, for example, last offer arbitration is used when a player and club owner cannot agree on the player's salary.

A final form of labor–management arbitration, interest arbitration, has been used when collective bargaining breaks down in the public sector, where strikes may be unlawful.

Mediation

Mediation is the involvement of a neutral third party in a dispute to help the disputing parties resolve it. Mediation is usually an informal, voluntary process that is designed to move the parties toward a mutually satisfactory agreement. Although the mediator participates in the discussion or negotiations, the mediator does not decide the dispute. Experience with mediation programs in Atlanta, Chicago, New

York, San Francisco, Tulsa, Oklahoma, and Columbus, Ohio, has demonstrated that it is an effective way of resolving landlord–tenant disagreements, domestic disputes, neighbors' disputes, damages for minor theft, vandalism, and other minor criminal incidents.

Fact Finding

Fact finding is another alternative mechanism for dispute resolution. This process is primarily used in public sector collective bargaining. The fact finder, drawing on information provided by the interested parties and independent research, recommends a written solution to each outstanding issue. The recommended solution is never binding, but often it paves the way for further negotiation and mediation.

Conciliation

Conciliation is an informal process in which the third party tries to bring the disputing parties together in hopes of lowering tensions, improving communication, helping to interpret issues, providing technical assistance, exploring potential solutions, and bringing about a negotiated settlement, either informally or, in a subsequent step, through formal mediation. Conciliation frequently is used in volatile conflicts and in disputes where the parties are unable, unwilling, or unprepared to come to the table to negotiate their differences.

In summary, alternative dispute resolution can be characterized as the seeking of a simple but equitable form of dispute settlement with the least expenditure of money and time. It is likely that alternative dispute resolution programs will continue to grow throughout the country.

SPECIFIC TASKS OF LEGAL SYSTEMS

Early in our study, we need to consider some of the specific tasks of the legal system as it helps resolve the hard questions that society faces. At the same time, other social institutions play important roles in solving some of these same problems. Western societies appear to rely most heavily upon their legal systems to resolve these problems.

Maintain Order

Probably the most important function of the legal system, certainly the one most frequently mentioned, is maintaining order within the community. Laws define the manner in which society expects people to act so that they can live together with a minimum of friction. In the absence of order, people must spend substantial amounts of time and energy dealing with problems that might disrupt the community. A means for orderly solution of social issues is especially important in an era such as ours, when technology causes rapid changes in people's lives.

Bring about Social Change

Although maintaining order is an important function of even relatively primitive legal systems, legal systems also have been used to fulfill other societal needs and to help the community attain other objectives. As an important agent for accomplishing change, the legal system is effective because of the many sanctions that it can employ and because the courts and the law are impersonal but respected powers. Antitrust, civil rights, and environmental protection statutes are examples of the legal system operating to accomplish social change.

The Constitution, too, is involved in this process of change, as the following case illustrates.

_____ *Shelley v. Kraemer* _____

United States Supreme Court
334 U.S. 1 (1947)

Shelley, a black man, purchased property from Fitzgerald. The property was part of an area in the city of St. Louis. Thirty owners of property in the area, including the former owner of the parcel purchased by Shelley, had signed an agreement restricting, for a 50-year period, occupancy of their property "by people of the Negro or Mongolian Race." Kraemer and a number of other residents who had signed this agreement sued, asking the court to restrain Shelley from taking possession of the property, divesting Shelley of title, and revesting title in Fitzgerald.   FACTS

The trial court denied this relief, but the Supreme Court of Missouri reversed. The Supreme Court of Missouri held that the agreement did not violate the federal Constitution, because it was a private agreement and the Constitution only prohibits unequal treatment by state and federal government. Shelley appealed to the U.S. Supreme Court.

Was the U.S. Constitution violated?   ISSUE

The Supreme Court held that it is a violation of the equal protection clause of the Fourteenth Amendment for state courts to enforce restrictive agreements of this nature. Although the private agreements themselves did not violate the U.S. Constitution, the Court stated as follows: DECISION

We hold that in granting judicial enforcement of the restrictive agreements in these cases, the States have denied petitioners the equal protection of the laws and that, therefore, the action of the state courts cannot stand. We have noted that freedom from discrimination by the States in the enjoyment of property rights was among the basic objectives sought to be effectuated by the framers of the Fourteenth Amendment. That such discrimination has occurred in these cases is clear. Because of the race or color of these petitioners they have been denied rights of ownership or occupancy enjoyed as a matter of course by other citizens of different race or color.

Other Functions

In addition to performing the aforementioned tasks, legal systems have several other functions. They provide a forum in which disputes can be settled without violence. They also protect expectations so that people can plan for the future. This aspect is especially important to business. Finally, the legal system helps to maintain the established government.

THE ADVERSARY PRINCIPLE

Adversary principle the principle that places the responsibility for developing or defending a case upon the parties and not on some designated legal official

In the United States, civil and criminal litigation are characterized by the **adversary principle.** This principle places the responsibility for developing and proving cases upon the parties rather than upon some designated legal official, with the court serving primarily as a referee. Because of the complexities of litigation, ordinarily the parties hire lawyers to represent them and to argue for them.

The rationale for the adversary principle is that truth and justice will most effectively be attained by making each litigant responsible for his or her case. Litigants have more incentive than outsiders to see that the evidence, legal arguments, and other factors are presented in the best light.

The adversary principle has been subject to considerable criticism, especially in criminal cases. Some argue that in an adversary system, winning or losing often depends upon the skill of the attorneys instead of the merits of the case. Others claim that in a criminal case, the resources of the state are so much greater than those of the defendant that the defendant is placed at a disadvantage. Another objection is that, because each party's primary interest is to win, each has an incentive to distort or hide facts unfavorable to his or her position.

During the past 50 years, the impact of the adversary principle has been lessened as a result of several developments. The legal system had adopted a number of procedural reforms that help the individual search out information to support his or her case. Courts have become more willing to bring in witnesses and to rely upon experts. Litigants with limited resources are furnished legal aid. Finally, new processes have been developed to substitute for traditional courtroom litigation.

SUMMARY

A legal system consists not only of laws but also of processes and structures for making and carrying out these laws. Legal systems perform a number of important functions. They help maintain order so that people can live together with a minimum of conflict. They help to bring about social change, provide a forum in which disputes can be settled, protect expectations, and help to maintain the established government.

A person who needs to know what the law is must often examine a number of sources. A constitution is one source of law. Both state and federal governments have constitutions. They are fundamental sources of law. Treaties, in some cases, also state the law that controls a given situation. Judicial decisions are also important sources of law. Because of the doctrine of stare decisis, courts follow prior decisions based on similar facts. Thus an earlier judicial decision will be followed unless a good reason exists for not doing so.

Although for many years, judicial decisions were the chief source of law, today statutory law is more important. However, statutes often have to be interpreted by courts before people know exactly what the statutes mean. As a result, an examination of judicial decisions often is necessary if a person wants to know what the law is. When dealing with local governments, a person must also examine ordinances. Administrative rules and orders are also sources of law. Administrative rules are like statutes, but they have been made by an administrative agency and not an elected legislature. Administrative orders are similar to court decisions. Because administrative rules and orders have the force of law, they have a major impact on how businesses operate.

People who do not wish to take their cases to court may use a variety of alternatives, including arbitration, conciliation, fact finding, and mediation.

When people do go to court, they are responsible for developing their own cases. A judge does not develop cases for them.

REVIEW PROBLEMS

1. What policy is reflected by the concept of stare decisis? Does this policy seem logical?

2. Compare and contrast statutory and judge-made or common law.

3. Does the concept of law apply to the rules of play in a tennis game?

4. What are the various ways of classifying the law?

5. Explain the difference between criminal law and civil law.

6. What is meant by equity?

7. What are the various alternatives to settling a case by filing suit?

8. What are the functions of the legal system?

9. What do lawyers mean when they say that our legal system is an adversary system?

10. Smith was injured while working in a plant owned by the Big Bang Company, an explosives manufacturer. The explosives industry was regulated by a statute which in part stated, "In case of an employee injury resulting from a violation of this act, a right of action against the employer shall accrue to the injured party." The company did not follow required safety measures and so had violated the act. Is the statute substantive or procedural law? Explain.

11. The attorney general of Oklahoma, in which the Big Bang plant was located, brought an action against the company for violation of the safety measures. Is this a civil or criminal case? Support your answer.

12. Smith lost his action in the trial court. He then took his case to the Oklahoma appellate court, arguing that the trial court judge had incorrectly excluded certain evidence. To support his argument he cited rulings by the Supreme Court of Nebraska and the Supreme Court of Ohio. Both the Ohio and Nebraska cases involved facts that were similar to those in Smith's case. Does the Oklahoma court have to abide by decisions from Nebraska and Ohio? Discuss.

13. Becker was seriously injured when he slipped and fell through an untempered glass shower door in the apartment he rented from the IRM Corporation. Becker sued IRM for negligence. When his case was dismissed on grounds that IRM did not know the shower door was of untempered glass, Becker appealed, and the appellate court reversed the decision. In reversing the trial court, the appellate court stated that IRM was negligent, as a careful inspection of the property would have revealed that the shower doors were of untempered glass. In addition, the court stated that a landlord is liable to a tenant if the tenant is injured because of a defect on the premises, even if the defect is one that neither the tenant nor the landlord could discover. In a later case could a tenant injured because of an undiscovered defect use the appellate court's opinion as precedent? Discuss.

NOTES

1. Wayman v. Southhard, 10 Went. 1 (1825).

CHAPTER 2

Legal Systems

CHAPTER OBJECTIVES

After reading this chapter you should be able to:

1. Define common terms such as *judgment, answer, petition, summons, garnishment,* and *verdict.*

2. Compare and contrast the functions of trial and appellate courts.

3. Outline the jurisdiction of the federal courts.

4. Indicate the purpose of:
   a. full faith and credit clause.
   b. privileges and immunities clause.

5. Briefly outline the steps in the typical civil case.

This chapter examines the structure of the legal system. It discusses the basic procedure that is followed from the time a case is filed in court until the final appeal has been made.

When an attorney decides to file suit on behalf of a client, the attorney must decide whether to file suit in federal or in state court. The first part of this chapter discusses the major considerations behind this decision. Suppose, for example, that the attorney represents Laura Smith from Illinois. While on vacation in Florida, Mrs. Smith was hit by a car driven by Albert Jones. Jones lives in Georgia. Mrs. Smith was seriously injured in the accident and has hired the attorney to file suit against Jones. One of the first questions her attorney considers is whether to file suit in federal court.

FEDERAL COURTS

Jurisdiction

To file suit against Mr. Jones in federal court, the attorney must learn whether the federal court has the power to hear the case and to decide the dispute. This power is referred to as its jurisdiction. Two types of cases may be filed in federal court:

1. those cases involving a **federal question** and

2. those cases in which there is **diversity of citizenship** between the parties.

Federal questions are matters dealing with the U.S. Constitution, federal statutes, treaties, and federal regulations. For example, a person who has been denied the right to vote may bring suit in federal court, because the Constitution guarantees all

Federal question a case in which the result depends upon interpretation of the Constitution, a federal statute, treaty, or federal regulation

citizens the right to vote. If a chemical company dumps mercury into a river, and the mercury floats into other states, a suit could be brought against the chemical company in federal court for violating federal statutes that prohibit polluting rivers.

In Mrs. Smith's case, probably no federal law has been violated. It is doubtful that a federal court would assert jurisdiction on the basis of a federal question. But she may file in federal court on the basis of diversity of citizenship. Diversity cases are those cases in which the parties to the dispute are citizens of different states. In this case, Mrs. Smith is a citizen of Illinois, and Mr. Jones is a citizen of Georgia. The only limitation on the power to file in federal court in this situation is that the amount in controversy must exceed $10,000. Therefore, for Mrs. Smith to file suit, she must claim damages in excess of $10,000.

Certain types of cases must be filed in federal court. For example, cases involving patents and copyrights must be filed in federal court.

Diversity jurisdiction power of federal courts to hear cases in which opposing parties are residents of different states

Trial Court

In the federal system, trial courts are called *district courts.* There evidence is presented and witnesses testify. The nation is divided into 94 districts, and each

FIGURE 2-1   United States District Courts: Types of Civil Cases Commenced

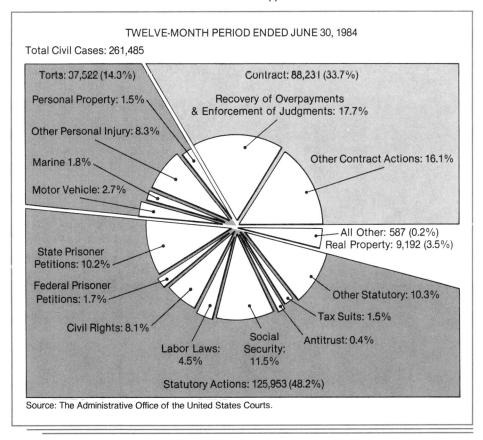

TWELVE-MONTH PERIOD ENDED JUNE 30, 1984

Total Civil Cases: 261,485

Torts: 37,522 (14.3%)

Personal Property: 1.5%

Other Personal Injury: 8.3%

Marine 1.8%

Motor Vehicle: 2.7%

Contract: 88,231 (33.7%)

Recovery of Overpayments & Enforcement of Judgments: 17.7%

Other Contract Actions: 16.1%

All Other: 587 (0.2%)
Real Property: 9,192 (3.5%)

State Prisoner Petitions: 10.2%

Federal Prisoner Petitions: 1.7%

Civil Rights: 8.1%

Labor Laws: 4.5%

Social Security: 11.5%

Antitrust: 0.4%

Tax Suits: 1.5%

Other Statutory: 10.3%

Statutory Actions: 125,953 (48.2%)

Source: The Administrative Office of the United States Courts.

FIGURE 2-2   United States District Courts: Civil Cases Commenced

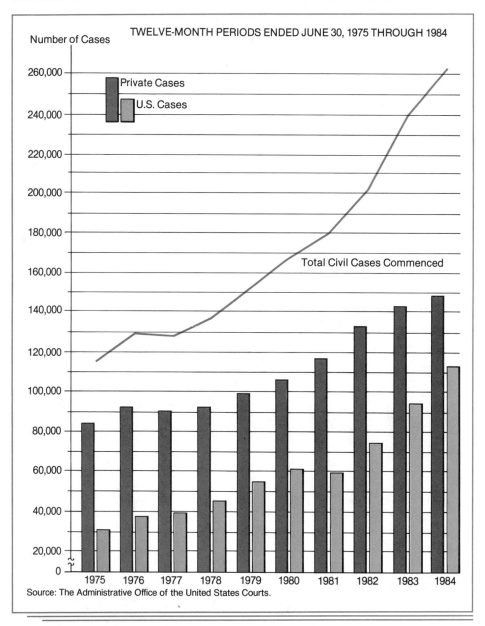

Source: The Administrative Office of the United States Courts.

district has a single district court. Thus every state in the nation has at least one U.S. District Court; many states have more than one.

If Mrs. Smith decides to file in federal court, her case will actually be tried in a federal district court. If she loses the case, she may decide to appeal the decision to the next level in the federal system, the court of appeals, or appellate court.

Court of Appeals

When a person appeals a case from a trial court, the person must assert that the trial court made some error. For example, if the trial judge refused to permit Mrs. Smith's attorney to introduce certain evidence, she might appeal on the basis that the failure to let her introduce that evidence at trial was an error. No witnesses appear at this stage of an appeal. An appellate court receives written **briefs** from the parties to the case and sometimes hears oral arguments from the attorneys. The court makes its decision on the basis of the briefs and the oral arguments.

Briefs written documents presenting the legal arguments

Federal appellate courts are called U.S. Courts of Appeals. The United States is currently divided into 12 geographic circuits (see figure 2-3), with a court of appeals

FIGURE 2-3   Federal Judicial Circuits

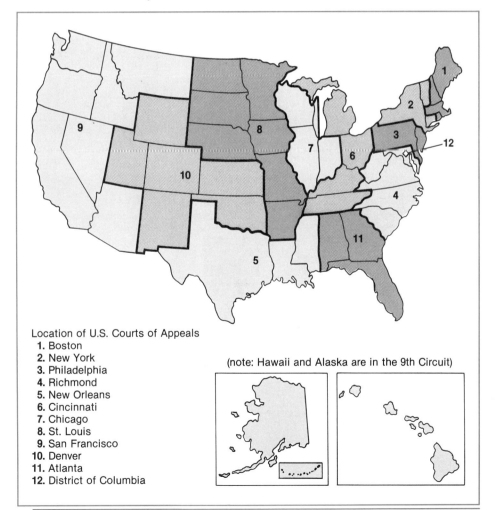

Location of U.S. Courts of Appeals
1. Boston
2. New York
3. Philadelphia
4. Richmond
5. New Orleans
6. Cincinnati
7. Chicago
8. St. Louis
9. San Francisco
10. Denver
11. Atlanta
12. District of Columbia

(note: Hawaii and Alaska are in the 9th Circuit)

FIGURE 2-4 United States Judicial Structure

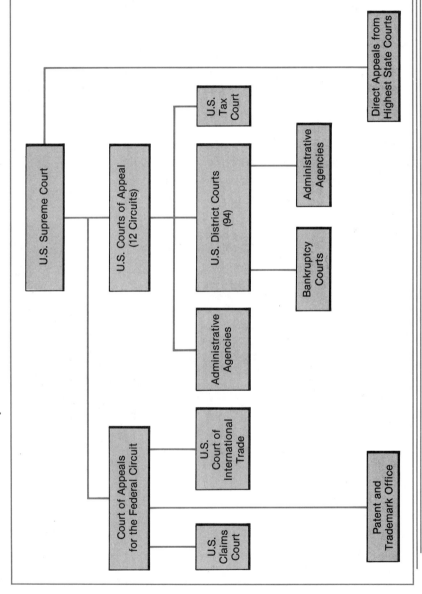

for each circuit. These courts hear appeals from federal district courts and from many federal administrative agencies.

In addition to the 12 regional courts of appeal, in 1982 Congress created a Court of Appeals for the Federal Circuit. This court has nationwide jurisdiction defined by subject matter. It handles appeals of patent matters, appeals of claims against the federal government, and other cases in which the United States is a defendant. The court is located principally in Washington, D.C., but it may hold court anywhere that a U.S. Court of Appeals sits.

Many cases are decided by panels of three judges. In very important matters, all the judges of the circuit court consider the case. These decisions are referred to as *en banc*.

The Supreme Court

The U.S. Supreme Court is the highest court in the United States. Although it is highly unlikely, Mrs. Smith could try to take her case to the U.S. Supreme Court. Only a few cases are appealable to the U.S. Supreme Court as a matter of right. In all other cases, the party unhappy with the federal circuit court decision must first ask the Supreme Court to hear the case. The party petitions for an order of ***certiorari***. If the Supreme Court wants to hear the case, it will grant the petition. Most petitions for *certiorari* are denied.

Certiorari a judicial procedure in which a higher court directs a lower court to send up the record of a case for appellate review

STATE COURTS

Rather than filing her case in a federal district court, Mrs. Smith may choose to file in a state court.

Jurisdiction

Mrs. Smith can file in state court because state courts have jurisdiction to hear most types of disputes (except those that the Constitution specifies must be resolved in federal courts, such as patent and copyright disputes, as we have mentioned). Most criminal and civil cases are decided in state courts. Divorces, will contests, matters of contract, and torts (see Chapter 3) also are largely concerns of state courts. Many more cases are tried in the state courts than in federal courts.

All states have a number of trial courts of **limited jurisdiction.** These courts can decide only those cases in which the plaintiff is seeking monetary damages of a limited amount. Their criminal jurisdiction is limited to petty offenses. It is impossible to make general statements about these courts because of the wide variety of tasks that have been assigned to them in different states. In some areas, these lower trial courts have extensive monetary jurisdiction and are manned by a number of full time, legally trained judges with large staffs. These courts often play significant roles in the administration of justice. In other areas, these courts hear only the most trivial cases and are presided over by part-time judges. Some have no legal training.

Mrs. Smith probably would not want to file suit in such a court, because she has

Limited jurisdiction a court that has the power to hear only certain types of cases

been seriously injured. She probably wants to recover more money than she could recover in a lower court.

An example of such a court is the small claims court. These courts have been created in most states to permit people to resolve disputes without attorneys. If a student had a dispute with his or her landlord that involved only a few hundred dollars, he or she could file suit in small claims court without hiring an attorney. Cases in small claims courts are handled much like regular trials, but the procedures followed are less formal. A person who is unhappy with a decision of a small claims court generally has a right to appeal the matter to a trial court. This appeal is called a ***trial de novo.*** It is a completely new trial of the case, unlike most appeals discussed in this text.

Trial de novo a
new trial

Trial Courts

**General
jurisdiction** the
power of a court to
hear all types of
cases

Each state has trial courts of **general jurisdiction** throughout the state. In Ohio they are called *courts of common pleas;* in New York, *supreme courts.* Probably the most common designation is *county court.*

Although the titles differ from state to state, these general trial courts have some common characteristics. Usually they are organized on a county basis. They have the power to hear a wide variety of cases, both criminal and civil, and there are ordinarily no upper limits on their monetary jurisdiction. Only in these courts do parties in civil cases have a right to trial by jury.

In heavily populated areas, many courts of general jurisdiction specialize in domestic relations, juveniles, and estates. In some states, an independent court handles decedent estate matters. In a number of states, specialized courts are independent of trial courts. It is also a common practice to separate the courts that hear criminal cases from those that hear civil cases.

Intermediate Appellate Courts

State intermediate appellate courts are found only in the heavily populated states. In half the states, no intermediate level of review exists. These courts operate in much the same manner as federal courts of appeals.

Litigants parties
to a lawsuit

To petition to
request to a court
to consider a matter

Although intermediate courts are not the highest appellate courts, for most appeals they are the court of last resort. There are two principal reasons for this. First, an appeal is a very expensive process. Most **litigants** cannot afford even an initial review, much less the cost of the two appeals necessary to argue their case before the highest appellate court. Second, in most states, the highest court reviews only those cases that it considers important. A person appealing from the intermediate level must **petition** the high court. Most petitions are rejected because the high court is satisfied that justice has been accorded by the intermediate court.

The Highest State Courts

At the top of the pyramid in each of the 50 state judicial systems is a court that decides almost all cases appealed within the jurisdiction. This court usually is called

FIGURE 2-5   Ohio Judicial Structure

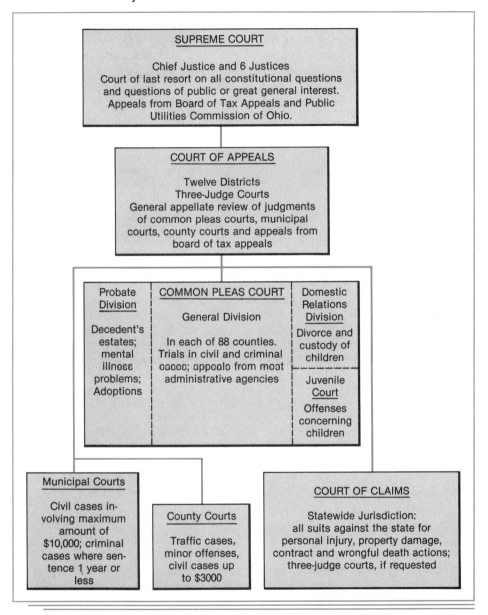

the *supreme court,* as in the federal system. Ordinarily a party whose case is heard at this level in a state system can appeal the case no further. If Mrs. Smith filed her case in a state court, the final review probably would be in the highest state court.

Full Faith and Credit Clause

Full faith and credit clause a provision in the Constitution requiring each state to recognize the judgments, public acts, and records of every other state

Several problems could arise even after Mrs. Smith has a final decision from the highest court in Illinois. First, if she wins a judgment against Mr. Jones in Illinois, will the courts in Georgia, the state in which Mr. Jones lives, enforce the judgment? The answer is yes, because the U.S. Constitution requires every state to recognize the judgments of every other state.

The **full faith and credit clause** permits someone who wins a judgment in one state to take this judgment into the courts of another state, which must accept it as binding. Of course, someone who loses a case in the courts of one state cannot bring it in another state. The full faith and credit clause does not apply to criminal cases.

Conflict of Laws

If Mrs. Smith files suit in the state of Illinois, which law shall the Illinois court apply — that of Illinois, Georgia, Florida, or some other state? State courts often are called upon to settle disputes involving activities that have occurred in other states. In these situations, the question that must be asked is: What state law applies?

Due process fundamental fairness in administration of justice

Although we would expect that a state court would apply its own state's law in all cases, it doesn't always do so. Often a state court applies the laws of a sister state. Public policy considerations underlie this choice. Both legislature and courts recognize that in a legal dispute, the controlling law should be that which the parties reasonably would expect it to be. In addition, the U.S. Supreme Court has held that **due process** is violated if a state court applies its own laws to transactions in which the parties have more substantial contacts with other states. Because even small businesses often operate across state lines, the business administrator must be aware of the applicable laws of each relevant state.

Privileges and Immunities Clause

Privileges and immunities clause a provision in the Constitution prohibiting states from adopting legislation that discriminates against citizens of other states

A constitutional provision of interest to people in business is the **privileges and immunities clause.** This clause guarantees that a business firm operating in a state, even if it is chartered elsewhere, is treated like firms of the home state. State laws may not discriminate against people *because* they are citizens of another state. State laws may discriminate for valid reasons. In one case, a Virginia statute denied out-of-state firms the right to harvest oysters in Virginia waters. The statute was held valid on the grounds that oyster beds were common property held in trust by the state for its citizens and that the state was merely trying to conserve this natural resource.

BASIC CONDITIONS OF DISPUTE RESOLUTION

The legal resolution of a dispute requires that four problems be solved:

Tribunal court

1. There must be a **tribunal** to find out what differences exist between the parties and to separate these from areas of agreement.

2. There must be a means for determining the facts, events, and circumstances in a particular case. Questions of this kind may be the only differences between the parties.

3. Because parties often disagree about the law, some means for determining the applicable law must be provided. In litigation, disputes about law are called "issues of law," and disputes about events and circumstances are called "issues of fact."

4. Legal procedures must meet standards of fairness acceptable to the community.

PRETRIAL PROCEDURES

The mechanisms that have evolved to meet the conditions listed above provide the framework for civil litigation. Although civil and criminal litigation are similar, differences exist in procedures, especially in the pretrial stages.

Jurisdiction over the Person

Just as court must have jurisdiction over the subject matter of the case, it also must have jurisdiction over the parties to the case. A court obtains jurisdiction over a plaintiff as a result of the plaintiff filing suit. The real problem is obtaining jurisdiction — **personal jurisdiction** — over the defendant.

If a defendant is physically present within a state when certain papers are presented to him or her, the state has no problem asserting personal jurisdiction over the defendant. However, consider a case like that brought by Mrs. Smith in Illinois after an accident in Florida, against Mr. Jones from Georgia. By filing suit in Illinois, Mrs. Smith cannot present the papers to Mr. Jones that are necessary to start the case. What is she to do?

Personal jurisdiction power of a court to hear a case involving a specific defendant

Long-Arm Jurisdiction   To permit plaintiffs like Mrs. Smith to bring suit against nonresident drivers causing injury like Mr. Jones, a number of states in the 1920s adopted legislation that gave local courts **long-arm jurisdiction** over nonresidents driving within the state. This procedure, although challenged as a violation of due process, was held constitutional by the U.S. Supreme Court. During the 1930s, this "long-arm" theory was extended to cover not only nonresident drivers but also various business activities carried on within a state. In 1945 the Supreme Court ruled that defendants who have certain "minimal contacts" with a state may be sued in that state. Due process is not violated, and the courts of the plaintiff's state have jurisdiction. In Mrs. Smith's case, therefore, the Florida long-arm statute forces Mr. Jones to defend the case in Florida.

Long-arm jurisdiction power a state court acquires over a nonresident defendant who has done business in the state or who has certain other "minimal contacts" with the state

Pleadings

When a person goes to an attorney, one of the first things the attorney requests is for the person to sign a contract of employment (see Figure 2-6). After the attorney discusses the case with the client and makes a general investigation of the facts, the attorney usually asks the client to sign such an agreement. At that point, the attorney prepares papers that start the case or respond to a case that has already started.

FIGURE 2-6 Contract of Employment

I, <u>John D. Blackburn</u>, hereby agree to employ the law firm of Frank F. Gibson to represent me and act on my behalf and in my best interest in presenting a claim for any and all damages including personal injury, which arose out of an accident occurring on or about August 31, 1985, near Portland, Oregon.

I agree to pay to said law firm a sum equal to 30 percent of any and all sums collected by way of settlement or legal action. In the event of trial (determined as of the time a jury is impaneled), I agree to pay said firm a sum equal to 50 percent of any sums received.

Said law firm agrees to act on client's behalf with all due diligence and in client's best interest at all times in prosecuting said claim.

It is understood that no settlement will be made without consent of client.

It is understood that if nothing is obtained on client's behalf that client owes nothing to said law firm, except for the expenses associated with handling this case.

DATED this _____ day of _____, 19____

_____
John D. Blackburn, Client

FRANK F. GIBSON
By: _____

The first stage in a civil case is called the **pleadings.** In this stage, the parties exchange legal documents in which they outline their claims and defenses. The basic pleadings are the **petition** or **complaint** and the **answer.** Copies of each document of the pleadings are filed with the court.

Pleadings the first stage in a civil case

The Summons   A lawsuit actually begins when the defendant is served with a **summons.** The summons informs the defendant that action is being brought and that a judgment against the defendant will be entered if no appropriate response is made (see Figure 2-7). Summonses tell the defendants little or nothing about the claims against them. Traditionally, the law has required that a summons be handed to the defendant. But most states today allow a summons to be published, mailed, or delivered to a defendant.

Petition (complaint) a document outlining the plaintiff's claim; part of the pleadings

Answer a document outlining the defendant's defense; part of the pleadings

The Complaint   The complaint details the nature of the claim. In many jurisdictions, the summons and the complaint are served together. The statements in the complaint are factual. The rules of one state direct that the statements be "plain and concise" and "sufficiently particular to give the court and parties notice of the transactions, occurrences . . . intended to be proved. . . ."

Summons a document that notifies the defendant that an action is being brought against him or her

The Answer   Most defendants answer that all or some of the claims in the complaint are not true. This answer is called a **denial.** Some defendants answer that facts not mentioned in the complaint constitute a defense. For example, a defendant might respond to a complaint for money owed that payment had been made. An answer of this kind is called an **affirmative defense.** The defendant may also **counterclaim,** assert that he or she has a claim against the plaintiff that could be the basis for an independent action. A sample complaint and answer are shown in Figures 2-8 and 2-9 (on pages 35 and 36, respectively).

Denial an answer that asserts that some of the claims in the complaint are not true

Affirmative defense an answer that asserts that plaintiff has no legal claim

Reply   If the defendant states an affirmative defense or counterclaim, the plaintiff responds in a document called a *reply.*

Counterclaim an answer that asserts that defendant has a claim against the plaintiff

Functions of Pleadings   The pleadings serve different purposes. They notify the parties of each other's claims. In many jurisdictions, this is their chief purpose. This provides for fairness in the litigation. Pleadings also determine what differences exist between the parties and how each sees the facts and understands the law. In answering, if the defendant does not deny a statement that the plaintiff has made in the complaint, the court assumes that no dispute exists regarding that particular fact. If the defendant does deny a statement made in the complaint, an issue of fact exists that must be resolved. In some instances, parties dispute the law that applies to the case, a dispute that also must be resolved.

FIGURE 2-7 Summons

```
                  United States District Court
                 for the Southern District of Ohio

                        Civil Action, File Number 85-1234



      John D. Blackburn, Plaintiff ⎤
                       v.          ⎬
      Douglas Whitman, Defendant   ⎦


      To Above Named Defendant _____ SUMMONS _____

         You have been sued by the person(s) named ''plain-
      tiff'' in the court stated above.

         The nature of the suit against you is stated in
      the complaint which is attached to this document. It
      also states the demand which the plaintiff has made
      and wants from you.

         You must answer the complaint in writing, by you
      or your attorney, within twenty (20) days, commencing
      the day after you receive this summons, or judgment
      will be entered against you for what the plaintiff has
      demanded. You have twenty-three (23) days to answer if
      this summons was received by mail. Such Answer Must Be
      Made in Court.

         If you have a claim for relief against the plain-
      tiff arising from the same transaction or occurrence,
      you must assert it in your written answer.

      Date _____    _____
                                    Clerk (Seal)


      _____
      Frank F. Gibson, Attorney for Plaintiff
      Mulberry Building
      Newark, Ohio 43201
      _____

      Telephone
```

FIGURE 2-8 Complaint

```
              United States District Court
              for the Southern District of Ohio

                      Civil Action, File Number 85-1234


John D. Blackburn, Plaintiff⎫
              v.              ⎬  Complaint
Douglas Whitman, Defendant   ⎭


1. Plaintiff is a citizen of the State of Ohio and
defendant is a citizen of the State of Kansas. The
matter in controversy exceeds, exclusive of interest
and costs, the sum of ten thousand dollars.
2. On August 31, 1985, in Mountain View, a public
park in Portland, Oregon, defendant negligently drove
a bicycle against plaintiff, who was jogging on a
public way in said park. As a result plaintiff was
thrown to the ground and had his arm and leg broken
and was otherwise injured, was prevented from carrying
out his business, suffered great pain in body and
mind, and incurred expenses for medical attention and
hospitalization in the sum of $2500.
3. Wherefore plaintiff demands judgment against de-
fendant in the sum of $15,000 and costs.


                           Signed: Frank F. Gibson
                           Attorney for Plaintiff
                           Address: Mulberry Building
                           Newark, Ohio 43201
```

Motions   Defendants also may respond with motions. Simply stated, a **motion** is an application to the court for an order of some kind. A wide variety of motions can be made. They are important at every stage of litigation. During the trial, motions are generally made orally. Before or after trial, motions are generally made in writing. In most instances, parties must notify each other that they are making a motion, and the court provides an opportunity for each to argue for or against the motion.

Motion an application to a court for an order

FIGURE 2-9   Answer

```
                United States District Court
             for the Southern District of Ohio

                         Civil Action, File Number 85-1234



John D. Blackburn, Plaintiff ⎫
                v.             ⎬  Answer
Douglas Whitman, Defendant  ⎭


1. Defendant admits the allegation contained in para-
graph 1 of the complaint.
2. Alleges that he is without knowledge or information
sufficient to form a belief as to the allegations
contained in paragraph 2 of the complaint; and denies
each and every other allegation contained in the com-
plaint.


                         Signed: Bartley A. Brennan
                         Attorney for Defendant
                         Address: 81 Main Street
                         Bowling Green, Ohio 43264
```

Discovery procedures methods for obtaining information about a case from an opposing party

Deposition an attorney's interrogation of a person sworn to tell the truth

Interrogatories written questions answered under oath

Discovery   Parties obtain further information about a case with **discovery proce-dures.** Further information tends to reduce the facts about which the parties disagree. Discovery procedures also tend to reduce the possibility of surprise during the trial and to add fairness to the litigation process. With discovery procedures, parties can obtain particulars about the opposition's case, sworn statements from hostile or friendly witnesses, and information about the prospective testimony of particular witnesses. Books, papers, and items relevant to the litigation can be examined, and under certain circumstances, a party can be required to submit to physical or mental examination.

Information may be obtained through the interrogation under oath of parties to the lawsuit and witnesses. This discovery technique is called a **deposition.** Another discovery tool is written questions to be answered under oath. The written questions are called **interrogatories.** In some cases, an attorney simply asks a person to sign a written statement and swear that the statements in it are true. This statement is called an **affidavit.**

Pretrial Conference   Most courts use **pretrial conferences** to speed litigation. In some courts, the pretrial conference is a formal affair; in others, it is informal. Often the parties themselves attend, but sometimes only attorneys and judge meet. In large metropolitan courts, one or two judges are assigned to supervise the pretrial calendar, but in rural areas the judge assigned the case usually directs the conference.

At the conference, the parties try to narrow and simplify the factual and legal issues. They also may consider the number of expert witnesses who will testify, changes in the pleadings, and the date for the trial.

Pretrial conferences help to eliminate surprise at a trial. In many pretrial conferences, the parties consider the possibilities of settling the case. If the parties are not too far apart, the judge may try to persuade—but not force—them to reach a settlement. A forced settlement denies people their right to trial.

Affidavit a written statement of fact sworn to be true by the person who signs it

Pretrial conference a meeting presided over by a judge in which parties try to eliminate problems that might arise at trial

THE TRIAL

Litigation often results because parties cannot agree about what the facts are. The purpose of the trial is to process the information that will be used to determine the facts. Most civil cases use the **petit jury**—a group of laypeople—to decide these important questions. Parties may waive their right to a jury trial. In that case or when parties do not have the right to a jury trial, a trial judge decides the facts.

Petit jury a jury, traditionally of 12 people, used for the trial of a civil or criminal case

The Jury System

Although the jury system has many critics, it continues to be important in American law. For many decades, Americans have looked upon the jury as a bulwark of democracy. It is an institution in which citizens participate directly, and it is often seen as a protection against the power of government. These sentiments stem primarily from the use of juries in criminal cases, but parties in civil cases generally prefer to have their claims determined by juries rather than judges.

Traditionally, the civil jury consisted of 12 persons. Over the past 25 years, the trend has been toward smaller trial juries. Many jurisdictions now allow juries of fewer than 12 in most civil cases. Traditionally, the civil jury's verdict was required to be unanimous, but today in more than half the states, unanimous verdicts are no longer required. These changes have been made primarily to shorten trials.

One of the first steps in the jury trial is the selection of the jurors. Lists of prospective jurors are made from various sources, depending upon the jurisdiction. The names are to be chosen at random from these sources and represent a fair cross section of the community.

In spite of random selection, many people chosen for jury duty have biases. These biases may influence their decisions. To insure greater fairness, the parties have the right to exclude certain jurors by **challenge.** Each side has a limited number of **peremptory challenges** by which it may exclude a prospective juror without giving any reason whatsoever. In addition, any prospective juror may be challenged and excluded for cause.

Challenge the right of parties in a lawsuit to object to a particular person serving as a juror; usually must be for a reason

Peremptory challenge the right of parties in a lawsuit to object without giving a reason to a particular person serving as a juror

Trial Stages

Opening Statement   Once the jurors have been selected, the attorneys present their opening statements. The purpose of the opening statement is to give the jurors a broad overview of the case that they will be listening to during the trial. After the plaintiff presents an opening statement, the defendant generally remarks about evidence to be presented.

Presentation of the Case   Once the opening statements have been presented, the plaintiff presents its case by asking people to testify under oath. The plaintiff's attorney asks questions of witnesses, which the witnesses answer under oath. The defendant is then provided the opportunity to question witnesses, called *cross examining* the witness. The purpose of cross examination is to permit the opposite party to test what has just been stated by the witness. After the defendant's attorney concludes the cross examination, the plaintiff then can conduct a redirect examination of the witness. This process continues throughout the trial, with the plaintiff's attorney continuing to call one witness after another to the witness stand. After the plaintiff has concluded its case, the defendant may call a series of witnesses to the stand to establish its case.

After the plaintiff's witnesses have testified, the defendant frequently moves to dismiss the case on the grounds that the plaintiff has failed to prove all the facts necessary to establish a case. If the court agrees, it can end the case at this point. A similar motion is often made by one or both of the parties after all the evidence has been presented. This motion often is referred to as a **motion for a directed verdict.** If granted, the case is in effect taken from the jury and determined by the judge.

Motion for a directed verdict a request by one party that a court order a verdict in its favor because the other party has failed to prove facts necessary to win its case

Instructions to the Jury   After all the evidence has been submitted and the lawyers have summed up their cases, the judge explains to the jury the law that applies to the case. This process, which is called **instructing** or **charging** the jury, presents the jury with:

1. information about the essential facts that each party must prove to support its position

2. the relationships between the evidence presented and the legal issues involved.

Basically, the instructions present the legal result of each possible factual finding the jury might make. Suppose that in litigation involving Joe, a defendant, and Mary, a plaintiff, the single contested fact is whether Joe made a statement to Mary with the intention of deceiving her. Legally, if he did intend to deceive he will be liable; if he did not, the case against him will be dismissed. The judge might charge the jury as follows: "If you determine that the defendant made the statement with the intention of deceiving the plaintiff, you must find for the plaintiff. If, however, you determine that the defendant's statement was made with no intention of deceiving the plaintiff, you must find for the defendant."

Another important function of the judge's instructions is to explain to the jury the complex legal rules regarding which side has the **burden of proof** on each issue in the case. This task is especially important, because often the decision about which side

Burden of proof the necessity of proving certain facts in dispute on an issue

FIGURE 2-10   The Litigation Process

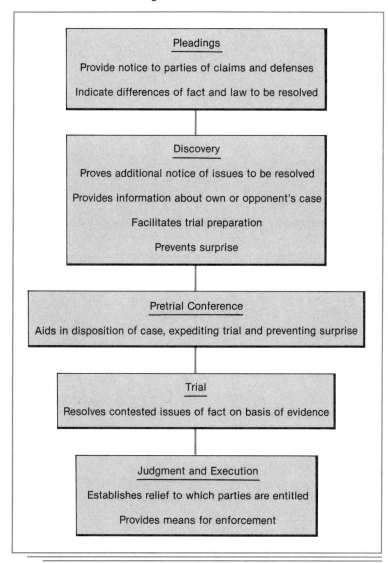

Pleadings

Provide notice to parties of claims and defenses

Indicate differences of fact and law to be resolved

Discovery

Proves additional notice of issues to be resolved

Provides information about own or opponent's case

Facilitates trial preparation

Prevents surprise

Pretrial Conference

Aids in disposition of case, expediting trial and preventing surprise

Trial

Resolves contested issues of fact on basis of evidence

Judgment and Execution

Establishes relief to which parties are entitled

Provides means for enforcement

has the burden of proof determines the outcome of the case. In civil cases, for example, the plaintiff usually must prove each element of the case by a preponderance of the evidence. There may, however, be situations where the defendant will bear the burden of proof.

The Verdict   A trial is usually concluded when the jury brings in a **verdict,** an answer to the questions that the court has submitted to it. In a civil action, the verdict

Verdict a jury's answer to the questions of fact that the court has submitted to them

FIGURE 2-11 Journal Entry

United States District Court
for the Southern District of Ohio

Civil Action, File Number 85-1234

John D. Blackburn, Plaintiff ⎤
             v.   ⎬
Douglas Whitman, Defendant ⎦

<u>JOURNAL ENTRY</u>

Now on this _____ day of _____, 19____, the above captioned matter comes regularly on for trial. The plaintiff appears in person and by his attorney, Frank F. Gibson. The defendant, Douglas Whitman, appears in person and by his attorney, Bartley A. Brennan. The parties announce they are ready for trial.

WHEREUPON, a jury of twelve citizens of the state of Ohio is selected, empanelled and duly sworn to try the cause.

WHEREUPON, the parties make their opening statements and the plaintiff commences the introduction of evidence on his behalf and at the conclusion of same rests, and

WHEREUPON, the defendant introduces evidence in his behalf and at the conclusion of same rests his case, and the plaintiff offers no rebuttal evidence and rests his case, and

WHEREUPON, the Court instructs the jury and the parties make their closing arguments and the case is submitted to the jury on _____, 19____, and

WHEREUPON, the jury retires to deliberate and after deliberation advise the Court they have a verdict, and

WHEREUPON, the foreman of the jury announces a verdict in favor of the defendant and at the plaintiff's request, the jury is polled and the twelve jurors state that they are in agreement with the verdict.

```
    IT IS CONSIDERED, ORDERED, AND ADJUDGED that the
judgment on the verdict in favor of the defendant for
his costs should be and the same is hereby rendered
herein.

    IT IS FURTHER CONSIDERED, ORDERED, AND ADJUDGED
that this Journal Entry shall be effective on the date
it is filed with the Clerk of the District Court for
the Southern District of Ohio.



APPROVED AS TO FORM         _____
                            Judge of the District Court

_____
Attorney for Plaintiff

_____
Attorney for Defendant
```

is either general or special. In a **general verdict,** the jurors determine the issues either for the plaintiff or the defendant. If the jury finds for the plaintiff, the amount of damages also is stated. In a **special verdict,** the jury writes answers to specific questions of fact that the court has submitted to it. The court uses these answers to apply the law and resolve the issues in dispute between the parties.

When an attorney prevails at trial, and the judge finds for his or her client, certain papers must be filed with the court that reflect what happened at trial. The attorney prepares what is called a **journal entry** (see figure 2-11). It is signed by the attorneys in the case and by the judge. This journal entry then is filed with the court.

Judgment and Execution   The **judgment** establishes the relief to which the parties are entitled. If the jury finds for the defendant, the judgment dismisses plaintiff's suit. If the plaintiff wins the case, ordinarily the judgment awards him or her a sum of money. When a monetary award does not furnish the plaintiff adequate relief, the court may order relief of another sort.

If the plaintiff has won a monetary judgment, the court locates the defendant's assets, prevents defendant from disposing of these assets, and may order the sale of the assets. A sheriff may seize and sell the assets. The proceeds of the sale are used to pay the award. The defendant often is referred to as a **judgment debtor.** If the judgment debtor's assets are in the hands of a third party, the court can order the third party to turn the property over to the plaintiff. This procedure, referred to as **garnishment,** is sometimes used to get an employer to turn over to a creditor some of the wages of an employee who is a judgment debtor.

Sometimes a judgment debtor has assets that produce income. Under these circumstances, the court can appoint someone to operate the property and pay the proceeds to the creditor.

General verdict a verdict in which the jury finds either for plaintiff or defendant

Special verdict a verdict in which the jury answers specific questions of fact submitted to it by the court

Journal entry official document reflecting what happened at trial

Judgment the decision of a court about the rights and claims of litigants

Judgment debtor a defendant against whom a judgment has been rendered which remains unsatisfied

Garnishment a legal proceeding in which a debtor's assets, held by another person, are applied to pay a debt

THE APPELLATE PROCESS

The appellate court reviews the legal rulings that one or both of the parties think the trial court judge made incorrectly. In an appeal, a determination of facts is unnecessary, because factual issues are decided at trial. Oral testimony of witnesses and other types of evidence, direct and cross examination of witnesses, and rules of evidence are eliminated. Discovery and motions for summary judgment also are eliminated.

When deciding if a legal error has been committed, the appellate court gets considerable information. It gets a record of the trial, called a *transcript*. Additional input is supplied by the parties, who, in our adversary system, are responsible for either pointing out the errors or supporting the rulings of the lower court. In fact, if one or both of the parties does not argue that some substantial legal error has been made, the appellate court has no power to review a trial.

The input from the parties generally consists of oral arguments before the court supported by written briefs. Briefs inform the appellate court judges about the facts of a case, errors allegedly made by the trial court, and a long section on the law relating to the case. The appellate court judges, especially in the higher courts, make their decisions based upon the oral arguments, the briefs, and their own research and group discussion. Many appellate courts publish written opinions.

Another difference between the trial and appellate process is the number of judges involved. Appeals are heard by a number of judges; a trial is heard by a single judge. In a trial the judge is not the important decision maker, unless the parties have waived a jury or are not entitled to one. The trial judge makes legal decisions, primarily to see that the trial is conducted properly and with reasonable speed. A single judge can more efficiently carry out these tasks.

Appellate courts are made up of a number of judges who are the primary decision makers. They deal only with legal questions. Because their answers to these legal questions influence the entire system, it is reasonable to have several experts make decisions.

Important similarities exist between the appellate and trial processes. Both are characterized by formal, clearly articulated procedures designed to insure a solution that not only *is* just but *appears* just. Both are characterized by time-consuming deliberation and significant input from the parties, and the results of each are open to public scrutiny.

If an appellate court decides that a trial court correctly decided a case, it affirms the decision of the trial court. If it decides that the trial court made a material error, it may reverse the decision of the trial court, or it may reverse and send the case back to the trial court—*remand* it—for further consideration.

SUMMARY

Each state and the federal government has its own system of courts. Federal courts hear cases involving a federal question and those involving citizens of different states. In a federal question case, the result depends on the interpretation of the Constitution, a federal statute, or a treaty. Diversity of citizenship cases, which involve plaintiffs and defendants who live in different states, also require the amount in controversy to exceed $10,000.

A case may go through various stages in the federal system of courts, starting with a trial in a district court and going all the way up to a review by the United States Supreme Court. Most cases are heard by the Supreme Court only if the Court grants an order of *certiorari*.

Most cases in the United States are litigated in the state courts. Trials are held in trial courts and then are subject to review by state appellate courts. Only in rare instances can a decision of a state's highest court be reviewed by the United States Supreme Court.

Because each state retains the powers not delegated to the federal government, state laws influence business. To reduce conflict among states, the Constitution requires each state to give full faith and credit to the judgments, public acts, and records of the other states. States cannot adopt statutes that discriminate against the citizens of other states unless some substantial reason exists for the discrimination. State courts often have to settle disputes involving activity that has taken place in other states with different laws. In these conflict of law cases, the state court applies the law of the other state, if that is what the parties reasonably would expect.

The primary purpose of litigation is to resolve a dispute. Several stages exist in the litigation of civil cases. In the pleading stage, parties exchange legal documents in which they outline their claims and defenses. At the end of the pleadings, if the only difference between the parties is a legal question, the trial court judge can resolve the issue. If the difference is a dispute over the facts, the case must proceed to trial.

The purpose of the trial is to provide the information necessary to determine the facts. A jury is often used to decide the facts, but the parties may waive the right to a jury and let the trial court judge decide. After a jury has been selected, the principal steps in the trial are the attorneys' opening statements, the presentation of evidence, the attorneys' closing statements, the judge's instructions to the jury, the verdict, and the judgment. The judge instructs the jury about what facts each party must prove to support its position and, usually, about alternative legal results of the factual findings the jury can make. The jury's verdict and the judgment based upon it conclude the trial. The legal system provides plaintiffs who have won monetary judgments means for collecting it.

If either party feels that a legal error has been made during the trial, an appeal may be taken. The appellate process differs from the trial process as the only questions are of law not of fact. No jury is required. To decide if a legal error has been made, an appellate court may review the record of the trial, read briefs submitted by the parties, and hear oral arguments by attorneys representing the parties.

REVIEW PROBLEMS

1. Explain the purpose of the following in civil litigation:

   1 ☐ pleadings

   2 ☐ long-arm statutes

   3 ☐ motion for directed verdict

4 ☐ full faith and credit clause

5 ☐ peremptory challenge

2. Are most cases appealable to the U.S. Supreme Court?

3. If a plaintiff who lives in Kansas sues a defendant who lives in Ohio for $15,000 for injuries arising out of an automobile accident, may this suit be filed in federal court?

4. To start a lawsuit, what documents must be served on the defendant? What is the nature of these documents?

5. How does a jury know what law applies in a case it is hearing?

6. If a person loses a case, what are the options open to him or her?

7. Donald Yee, who lives in Pennsylvania, enters into an agreement to construct a building for Malone Company, a New York corporation. The contract price is $125,000. The building is to be built on land owned by Malone Company in Pennsylvania. The agreement was signed in Yee's office in Philadelphia. Yee defaults, and Malone sues in federal court. Does the federal court have jurisdiction? Support your answer.

8. Sam Falcone owns a house in a predominantly Italian neighborhood. His neighbor, Tony Fatio, tells Falcone that the Fatios are going to sell their home. Believing that the ethnic character of the area is changing, Falcone also contracts to sell his home. Fatio then tells Falcone that the Fatios have decided not to sell. Falcone is upset and hires an attorney to sue Fatio. What legal steps should Fatio's attorney take if Fatio is served with a complaint? Why?

9. Clements purchased a boat from Barney's Sporting Goods, an Illinois corporation. Signa, the manufacturer of the boat, is an Indiana corporation with no offices in Illinois. Clements sued Signa Corporation for breach of warranty in the Illinois courts. Signa advertises in boating magazines which had been received by Clements, and Signa's boat was displayed at a Chicago boat show. Barney's Sporting Goods also displayed the boat in Illinois. Barney's gave Clements a written warranty issued by Signa. Do the Illinois courts have jurisdiction over Signa? Support your answer.

10. Smith and Barney were involved in a dispute involving the legal meaning of a clause in their contract. Smith's attorney stated that the only difference between the parties was a difference of law. Neither party would concede, and litigation was contemplated by Barney. Would his case be brought in a trial court or in an appellate court? Support your answer.

CHAPTER 3

Crimes and Intentional Torts

CHAPTER OBJECTIVES

After reading this chapter, you should be able to:

1. Explain the types of crimes and identify protections created by the U.S. Constitution.

2. Define white collar crime and distinguish between crimes that are malum in se and crimes that are malum prohibitum.

3. Identify intentional wrongdoing, negligence, and strict liability as the major classifications of tort law.

4. Describe the kind of intent required for an intentional tort.

5. Identify the torts of battery, assault, false imprisonment, defamation, invasion of privacy, and intentional infliction of emotional distress as torts that protect personal dignity; and to further be able to identify the requirements of each tort, as well as the available defenses.

6. Identify the torts of trespass and conversion as torts that protect interests in private property, and be able to further identify the requirements of each tort, and the available defenses.

7. Identify the torts of unfair competition, appropriation of trade secrets, interference with contractual relations, and disparagement as torts that protect competition, and be able to further identify the requirements of each tort, and the available defenses.

CRIMES

Crime an act or failure to act that the government has made punishable by imprisonment, fine, or death

A **crime** is an act or omission for which a jail sentence, fine, or even death may be imposed by a judge. Crimes are wrongs not only against the injured parties but also against society.

Criminal cases are brought by a prosecutor in the name of the government. Federal crimes are prosecuted by a federal prosecutor. Cases that involve actions that violate state criminal laws are brought by state prosecutors.

Felony the most serious category of crime

The most serious crime is called a **felony.** A felony is generally punishable by imprisonment for more than one year in jail and, in some cases, a fine. A typical felony is theft of property worth more than a specified amount of money, for example, $100. Other felonies are murder and rape.

Misdemeanors crimes that are less serious than felonies

Most crimes that are not felonies are classified as **misdemeanors.** Misdemeanors are punishable by up to one year in jail. A fine also may be imposed. Theft of property of small value is an example of a misdemeanor (see Table 3.1).

TABLE 3-1   Examples of Crimes

Felonies	Misdemeanors
1. Murder	1. Theft of property worth under a specified
2. Rape	amount
3. Theft of property worth over a specified	2. Giving a worthless check of small value
amount	3. Littering
4. Kidnapping	4. Unlawful hunting

Today criminal law is largely governed by statutes. The government decides the types of behavior to prohibit and passes a statute outlawing it. Congress and the state legislatures are not free to pass any statute they desire, because the U.S. Constitution and state constitutions place limits upon the law. For example, the Fifth Amendment to the U.S. Constitution prohibits the government from compelling people to be witnesses against themselves. It would be illegal for police to beat a confession out of a criminal suspect.

How Much Evidence of Guilt Must Be Introduced at Trial?

The United States legal system is somewhat different from legal systems in other parts of the world. In the United States, a person accused of a crime is presumed to be innocent. A prosecutor must introduce enough evidence at trial to convince the judge or jury that a crime has been committed and that the accused has committed the crime.

Furthermore, a prosecutor must establish this evidence beyond a reasonable doubt. If, at the end of a trial, the jury or the judge still has reasonable doubts about the guilt of a person accused of a crime, the accused is not to be convicted. This principle holds true even if judge or jury thinks that a great deal of evidence suggests that the defendant might in fact be guilty. It has long been the belief in the United States that it is better to let a guilty person go free than to convict an innocent person. This rule helps to prevent innocent people from being convicted of crimes they did not commit.

A prosecutor also must establish that a statute has outlawed a certain behavior and that the accused person had the capacity to form a criminal intent. People are presumed to have this capacity, and so the accused's attorney must convince the court that the accused lacked such a capacity. For example, a person accused of murder might allege that he or she was insane at the time the crime was committed.

Criminal Procedure

The first ten amendments of the U.S. Constitution contain many provisions that protect a person accused of a crime. The Fourth Amendment, for example, prohibits unreasonable searches and seizures. Before police may search through a person's

Search warrant
a written court
order that gives po-
lice the right to
search a particular
place

home, in most instances they first must obtain a **search warrant** from a judge to permit the search. The Fifth Amendment also creates a number of safeguards to protect people from being prosecuted unfairly. For example, it prohibits the government from trying a person twice for the same offense. The Sixth Amendment guarantees people the rights to a speedy and public trial, to be informed of the charges against them, and to have an attorney.

White Collar Crimes

**White collar
crime** crime com-
mitted in
commercial
context, often by
managers and
professionals

White collar crime describes crime committed in a commercial context, often by managers and professionals. Examples include employee theft, antitrust violations, income tax evasion, and securities fraud.

White collar crime costs the economy billions of dollars every year, yet often it seems less evil than "traditional" crime, perhaps because white collar crime often is impersonal, with no specific victim besides an impersonal government agency or a large institution. White collar criminals rationalize their actions by claiming that they "didn't hurt anyone," merely "beat the system."

In fact, everyone pays for white collar crime in higher prices. In addition, white collar crime damages the ability of our industrial system to produce goods, to grow, to cope with international changes, and to distribute wealth more fairly. Similarly, fraud committed against government agencies adds substantially to the cost of running the government. White collar crime increases the probability that less desirable systems will evolve — systems selected for their ability to control abuse rather than for their ability to serve the public interest.

**Crimes *malum
prohibitum***
crimes that do not
require criminal
intent

**Crimes *malum in
se*** crimes that
require conscious
wrongdoing

Most white collar crimes are considered ***crimes malum prohibitum,*** as opposed to ***malum in se.*** Crimes *malum in se* are those like murder and rape that are considered by reasonable people to be "naturally wrong." Crimes *malum in se* require *mens rea* (a guilty mind), or criminal intent. Crimes *malum prohibitum* are considered wrong only because a statute declares them to be so. Crimes *malum prohibitum* do not require a guilty mind. They are criminal even in the absence of criminal intent. Driving on the left side of the road or, in some states, selling furniture on Sunday may be criminal acts under *malum prohibitum* statutes.

In the following case, the U.S. Supreme Court addressed the issue of whether criminal violations of the federal Food, Drug, and Cosmetic Act (FDCA) are crimes *malum prohibitum* or crimes *malum in se.*

United States v. Park

U.S. Supreme Court
421 U.S. 658 (1975)

FACTS   The United States brought a criminal proceeding against Acme Markets and John Park for violation of the federal Food, Drug, and Cosmetic Act. Acme and Park were charged with the unsanitary storage of food in Acme's Baltimore warehouse. Acme pleaded guilty, but Park contested the charge. Evidence at the trial indicated that Park, Acme's chief executive officer and president, had been advised by letter at least twice of heavy rodent infestation at the warehouse. Park testified that he identified those responsible for sanitation and was assured that the Baltimore division vice president "would be taking corrective action." The criminal suit was brought when inspection indicated continued unsanitary conditions.

May a criminal conviction be obtained under FDCA solely upon a showing that the defendant was the president of the offending company, or is conscious wrongdoing by the defendant required?

In upholding Park's conviction, the Court ruled that conscious wrongdoing by a corporate executive was not required for a criminal conviction under FDCA. Rather, corporate employees who have a responsible relation to the situation by virtue of their position are subject to criminal conviction. This is because the statute does not make criminal liability turn on awareness of wrongdoing. Rather, a criminal conviction may be based on the fact that "the defendant had, by reason of his position in the corporation, responsibility and authority either to prevent or promptly correct the violation and that he failed to do so."

TORT LAW: AN INTRODUCTION

A **tort** is a civil wrong, other than a breach of contract, for which a court will provide a remedy. The term "tort" is a French word meaning injury or wrong; it comes from the Latin *tortus,* which means "twisted," as in conduct that is twisted, or not straight.

Tort a civil wrong other than a breach of contract

Torts fall into three categories: intentional torts, negligence, and strict liability. In intentional torts, the defendant intends to engage in conduct that interferes with the socially protected interest of the plaintiff. Negligence does not involve the presence of wrongful intent but rather the failure of the defendant to conform to a standard of reasonable conduct. Strict liability assesses liability without regard to either the unreasonableness of the defendant's intent or the unreasonableness of his conduct; it is liability without fault. The rest of this chapter focuses on intentional torts; Chapter 4 discusses negligence and strict liability.

People who file suit to recover money to compensate them for injuries inflicted by someone else may request two kinds of damages:

1. compensatory damages

2. punitive damages

Compensatory damages are awarded by courts to return people to their positions before the injury. If a motorcycle rider collides with a car, the motorcyclist may ask for money for medical bills, damage to the motorcycle, and any loss of earnings caused by the accident. If the behavior of the defendant was particularly bad, a court also may award the motorcyclist punitive damages over and above the actual damages. Punitive damages are awarded to punish the defendant for wrongful actions.

Interestingly, the same behavior that the law treats as criminal also may result in civil liability. Thus the state may prosecute a person for a crime, and the injured party

TABLE 3-2   Intentional Torts

Torts Against the Person	Interference with Property Rights	Competitive Torts	Trends in Torts
1. Assault 2. Battery 3. False imprison- ment 4. Defamation 5. Invasion of privacy 6. Intentional infliction of emo- tional distress	1. Trespass to land 2. Trespass to personal property 3. Conversion	1. Unfair competi- tion 2. Appropriation of trade secrets 3. Interference with contractual relations 4. Disparagement	1. Wrongful dis- charge

also may file a civil suit for damages. If a person slashes another person's face in a knife fight, this behavior violates state criminal laws. It also violates civil law. (As will be seen later in the chapter, it is the tort of battery.)

INTENTIONAL TORTS

The difference between intentional torts and other torts is that in intentional torts, the plaintiff must establish that the defendant intended the act in question. For example, suppose that a bank permits customers to enter its vault to examine their safe deposit boxes. At the end of the day, the guard carelessly forgets that a customer is in the vault, and the guard shuts the door. The customer is confined to the vault against his or her will. But the guard did not lock the customer in the vault intentionally, so no intentional tort has been committed. As is discussed under false imprisonment later in this chapter, it is improper intentionally to confine people to a certain place against their will.

Several intentional torts are discussed briefly below. For convenience, they are classified into four categories: torts against the person, torts against property interests, competitive torts, and trends in torts (see Table 3-2 for examples of each).

TORTS AGAINST THE PERSON

Several torts protect people from intentional interference with their bodies or minds. Starting with the tort of assault, this section discusses the torts that provide redress for the intentional infliction of bodily or mental harm.

Assault

A person who intentionally does something that causes another to expect to be harmed immediately or touched offensively has committed an *assault*. Most courts state that words alone are not enough for assault. Assault also requires an act, such as a threatening gesture, as well as hostile words. Suppose that after winning a football game with their archrivals, State University, the members of the State College team go to a local tavern to celebrate their victory. While at the bar, a student from State U. gets into an argument with a student from State College over the merits of the two teams. The State U. student becomes angry and says: "If you weren't bigger than me, I'd hit you." This threat is not an assault. First, it is just words. Second, a reasonable person would not expect to be touched immediately.

If the State U. student waves his fist and says, "I'll get you next week," that is not an assault either. Statements concerning something that will happen in the future are not assaults, because no immediate touching is likely.

Battery

Just as people expect not to be threatened, they expect not to be touched by others. *Battery* is the intentional touching of another person in a harmful or offensive manner, without that person's consent. Battery does not require that a person be seriously harmed. Any touch that is offensive to a person of ordinary sensibilities may be a battery. Suppose, for example, that during class, Professor Smith remarks that he finds Janice extremely attractive, and in front of the class he leans over and kisses Janice on the lips. Under these circumstances, Janice may argue that the kiss was offensive — a battery. But now suppose that a person gets on a subway car in New York City during rush hour and a person bumps him. That kind of jostling is to be expected in a big city. Even if the person were offended, a person of ordinary sensibilities would not have been offended, and so the act is not a battery.

It is not necessary actually to touch a person. Merely touching something closely associated with the person is sufficient to make a case for battery. Suppose that Professor Smith, rather than kissing Janice, reaches over and pulls Janice's blouse. Even though he never actually touches Janice, Professor Smith has violated the law.

In some situations, even though a person has been touched physically, there has been no battery. In these situations, the person consented to the behavior. For example, when a person steps into a boxing ring, even though he never expressly says to the other boxer, "You may hit me," his actions are in effect a consent. Similarly, before a physician operates on a patient, the physician must obtain the patient's consent to the operation. If the patient consents, he or she cannot sue for battery, even though the physician certainly touched him or her.

Generally, a person can meet force or the threat of force with similar force without liability. If a person hits a man, the man may respond by hitting back. The amount of force that may be used in defending property is dealt with in the next case.

_____ *Katko* v. *Briney* _____

Supreme Court of Iowa
183 N.W.2d 657 (1971)

Katko, a trespasser, broke into an unoccupied, boarded up farmhouse intending to   FACTS
steal old bottles and fruit jars, which he considered antiques. When Katko opened the

bedroom door, a 20 gauge shotgun, rigged to the doorknob with wire, discharged and shot Katko in the right leg. Katko lost much of his leg and was hospitalized 40 days. He sued Briney, owner of the farmhouse, for battery. Briney argued that the law permits use of a spring gun in a dwelling or warehouse for the purpose of preventing the unlawful entry of a burglar or thief.

ISSUE   Is the defense of justification available under the circumstances?

DECISION   No. The court ruled that Briney's use of a 20 gauge shotgun exceeded the lawful use of reasonable force necessary to protect property, even though the injured party acted in violation of the law. The law values human safety more than property rights and requires the use of force to be reasonable under the circumstances. The use of force likely to inflict great bodily harm or death is prohibited except to prevent felonies of violence and to protect human life. Neither condition had been present here.

False Imprisonment

False imprisonment is the act of forcing a person to stay in a certain place against that person's will and without just cause. This tort protects a person's freedom of movement. If it is possible for a person to leave, the person has not been falsely imprisoned. But if to escape a person would have to expose him- or herself to some unpleasant situation, the person has been falsely imprisoned. Suppose that Mary goes to her favorite sports store, where she has purchased sportswear in the past. Mary owes some money, and the owner wants to be paid immediately. When Mary goes to try on some garments, the owner slips into the dressing room and takes all of her clothes. The owner refuses to give Mary back her clothes until she pays her bill. Although Mary could leave the store, a court would not expect her to leave under these circumstances. She has been forced to stay against her will.

The tort of false imprisonment comes up quite often in the context of the retail store. Retail stores in America have a serious problem with people who come to steal goods, called *shoplifting*. Shoplifting is a common crime. Businesses need to protect themselves from shoplifting, or they would soon be stripped of all their merchandise.

Because shoplifting is a major social problem, costing the consuming public billions of dollars through inflated prices, the law in most states resolves the conflict between the storekeeper's property interest and the consumer's rights by conferring a limited privilege on the storekeeper to detain those he or she reasonably suspects of shoplifting. In exercising this right, the storekeeper must act reasonably. Suppose that a clerk suspected a customer of slipping something into her purse. Would it be reasonable to shout across the store, in the presence of other customers, "Stop, thief!" and then rush to the woman and block her exit from the store? Although retail merchants have a right to question and detain customers suspected of shoplifting, they may not do so in this manner.

Although one might think of false imprisonment as confining a person within walls, the tort has a much broader application, as the following case illustrates.

National Bond & Investment Company v. Whithorn

Court of Appeals of Kentucky
123 S.W.2d (1939)

National Bond & Investment Company claimed to have a conditional sales contract on a car that Whithorn possessed. Claiming that payments due under the contract had not been made, two of the company's employees attempted to repossess the car. They followed Whithorn, then approached his car and presented their demands. Whithorn was uncooperative and remained in his car. The employees then called a tow truck and disconnected the car's distributor wire to prevent it from being driven. One employee got in the car with Whithorn, against his protests, and remained there as the tow truck began pulling the car. Whithorn tried to prevent the truck from towing the car, but the employees succeeded at repossessing the car. Whithorn sued the company for false imprisonment. The company argued that Whithorn had been free to leave at any time.
FACTS

Assuming that a valid contract had existed, were the employees within their right to repossess the car, or did their actions amount to false imprisonment?
ISSUE

The court rules that in towing the car while Whithorn was in it, against his protest, the employees restrained and detained him in a manner that amounted to false imprisonment. Although Whithorn himself was not prevented from leaving the scene, he had a legal right to remain in the car, and the employees did not have a right to enter it. Assuming a valid contract claim existed, the company's employees had the right to peaceably repossess the car. They had no right to restrain Whithorn or to use force against him in repossessing the car.
DECISION

Defamation

Defamation is the communication of untrue statements about someone to a third party. The statements in question must injure the victim's reputation or character. For example, if Jack tells his friends that Mary is a prostitute, when in fact she is not, Jack has defamed Mary.

There are two categories of defamation: slander, or oral defamation, and libel, or written defamation. In most states today, plaintiffs must establish that they have been damaged, for example, by a loss of customers, business, or a particular contract.

One form of defamation, defamation **per se**, eliminates the necessity of establishing such damages. Four categories of defamation fall under the per se rule. Defamation per se exists when the plaintiff alleges that the defendant:

Per se Latin for "by itself," something forbidden in and of itself

1. accused the plaintiff of having committed a serious crime, such as murder

2. stated that plaintiff has a loathsome disease, such as a venereal disease

3. asserted that the plaintiff was professionally incompetent, for example, calling a surgeon "a butcher," or

4. stated that the plaintiff was an unchaste woman.

Several defenses may be asserted in a defamation case. Truth is an absolute defense. Thus if Jack calls Mary a prostitute and Mary in fact is a prostitute, Jack has a good defense. It is also necessary that someone other than the person defamed hear the defamatory statement. If someone angrily shouts a defamatory remark about someone else, but no one hears it, there can be no suit for defamation. Another defense against a charge of defamation is **privilege.** If defamation occurs in a privileged context, no legal relief is available to the victim of the defamation. A privilege may be either an absolute privilege or a qualified privilege. An absolute privilege exists for judges, legislators, lawyers, and parties and witnesses acting in their official capacities or in the roles for which the privilege exists. A qualified privilege exists for communications where it is in the public interest to promote the communication. For example, if one employer asks another to comment on the character of a former employee, the former employer enjoys a qualified privilege to do so. The qualified privilege is lost if the plaintiff can establish malice on the part of the speaker.

Privilege a particular benefit or advantage held by a person over and above the rights held by others

Invasion of Privacy

A person's dignity and right to be left alone are protected by the tort of *invasion of privacy.* Suppose that a person goes on vacation, and in his or her absence, the next-door neighbor searches the empty home. This search is an invasion of privacy. Many movie stars have filed suit against advertisers who have used their pictures without permission.

Placing someone in a false light in the public eye also has been treated as an invasion of privacy. Suppose that a person lives next door to a country club, and members of the club are making a great deal of noise. If the person calls the club repeatedly to complain but gives another person's name, the caller violates the other person's rights.

Finally, the public disclosure of private facts about a person may be an invasion of privacy. Suppose that a merchant receives a bad check from a customer. The next day, the merchant posts a picture of the customer at the checkout counter with a label stating, "Joe Smith writes bad checks." This act may be regarded as an invasion of privacy.

Intentional Infliction of Emotional Distress

A person's interest in emotional tranquility is protected. Intentional infliction of emotional distress is a separate tort. The tort may be defined as the intentional causing of severe mental suffering in another by means of extreme and outrageous conduct. The defendant's conduct must be what the average community member would consider outrageous. The plaintiff's emotional distress must in fact exist, and it must be severe. Minor offenses, such as name calling, may wound a person's feelings and cause some degree of mental upset. But they are not torts. A person cannot recover merely because of hurt feelings. The law is not concerned with trifles and cannot provide a civil remedy for every personal conflict in a crowded world.

The following case discusses a situation in which the court decided against the plaintiff.

Slocum v. Food Fair Stores of Florida

Supreme Court of Florida
100 So.2d 396 (1958)

Slocum was a customer in a Food Fair store. She approached an employee who was marking and shelving items, and she asked the price of an item. The employee replied, "If you want to know the price, you'll have to find out the best way you can. You stink to me." Slocum sued Food Fair, seeking money damages for emotional distress, an ensuing heart attack, and aggravation of preexisting heart disease. She claimed that she had suffered these ills from the employee's insulting language. She asserted that the employee's remark had been intended to inflict great mental and emotional disturbance to her.

FACTS

Did the employee's insult justify the customer's claim to the tort of intentional infliction of emotional distress?

ISSUE

No. In deciding that Slocum had failed to allege facts sufficient to claim the intentional infliction of emotional distress, the court stated:

DECISION

> So far as is possible to generalize from the cases, the rule which seems to be emerging is that there is liability only for conduct exceeding all bounds which could be tolerated by society, of a nature especially calculated to cause mental damage of a very serious kind. . . . A study of [the tort's] factual applications shows that a line of demarcation should be drawn between conduct likely to cause mere "emotional distress" and that causing "severe emotional distress."

INTERFERENCE WITH PROPERTY RIGHTS

The right to use and enjoy **property** without interference by others is an important right. Those who interfere with a person's property rights can be successfully sued.

Property a bundle of rights that people have in the things they own

Trespass to Land

Trespass to land may be defined as intentionally entering upon the land of another without permission or the right to do so. A person may be held liable for trespass even if he or she caused no harm by trespassing on the land. For example, suppose that some hunters are in search of quail. They see some quail on a farmer's land. They stop their car and walk onto his fields. They are trespassing, even if they cause the farmer no harm by their activities. Had the farmer given them permission to hunt on his property, however, there would have been no trespass. But if a fire breaks out in the farmer's barn, and the firefighters drive a fire engine to his barn, there has been no trespass because they have a right to enter the property under these circumstances.

Trespass to land also may occur where a person intentionally remains on another's land. If the owner of an apartment orders the tenants to leave because they have not paid their rent, and the tenants refuse to leave, the tenants may be held liable for trespass. People also may be charged with trespass if they fail to remove objects that they are under a duty to remove.

Trespass to Personal Property

Personal property moveable property; all property other than land

If a person takes or damages another's **personal property,** he or she has committed the tort of trespass to personal property. If Jack leaves his motorcycle parked outside of school, and another student takes it for a ride, this is a trespass. If the student damages the cycle, that is a trespass also. But if Jack had given the student permission to ride the cycle, there would have been no trespass.

Conversion

Conversion is the tort of controlling personal property in a way that interferes with another person's right of possession. Torts of trespass to personal property and conversion differ in their amounts of damages. In trespass to personal property, damages equal the diminished value of the personal property because of any injury to it. In conversion, the damages equal the full value of the property at the time it was converted. Because of the larger damages, conversion is limited to interferences with the right of possession serious enough to justify requiring the defendant to pay its full value. For example, suppose that the student who took Jack's motorcycle without permission not only rode it but sold it to another person. The student has converted the cycle and is liable to Jack for the full value of the cycle.

COMPETITIVE TORTS

The American economy relies primarily upon the free market for the allocation of resources. Legal opinion generally supports the proposition that the market assures the most efficient allocation of goods and services while preserving economic, social, and political freedom. Nevertheless, limited government intervention has been deemed necessary to prevent competition from taking socially undesirable and destructive forms. To assure fair and honest competition and to award damages against unfair trade, the courts have applied tort theory.

In the following discussion, special attention is given to the torts of unfair competition, appropriation of trade secrets, disparagement, and interference with contracts. Several federal statutes that protect against the infringement of patents, copyrights, trade names, and trademarks are not discussed because of their specialized nature.

Unfair Competition

Because of the high value placed on competition, the law recognizes a qualified privilege to engage in business in good faith. Someone who causes another person to lose business merely by doing business in good faith is not liable for the loss. The theory is that, in the long run, competition promotes efficiency and general economic welfare, and to penalize a person for competing prevents competition. However, the privilege is lost if a person acts in bad faith. It is lost if a person does business primarily to cause another to lose business and go out of business. "Bad faith" usually takes the form of predatory business practices.

The following case illustrates how the tort of unfair competition favors competition as a social good.

Tuttle v. Buck

Supreme Court of Minnesota
119 N.W. 946 (1909)

FACTS

Tuttle was a barber in a small town in Minnesota until he was forced to close for lack of business. He sued Buck, a banker, alleging that Buck had set up a rival barbershop, not for his own legitimate purpose, but for the sole purpose of driving Tuttle out of business.

ISSUE

Has Tuttle stated a valid claim?

DECISION

The court ruled that Tuttle did state a valid claim. Generally, a businessperson can legitimately offer goods and services at lower prices to attract the customers of a business rival. This practice is justified as fair competition. If, however, one opens a rival business only to drive a competitor out of business and intends to remain in business only until the competitor is out of business, then a tort has been committed.

Appropriation of Trade Secrets

Someone who discloses or uses another's trade secret and has no privilege to do so may be liable for the damages caused. The information obtained must qualify as a trade secret. That is, it must be information not generally known in an industry. Absolute secrecy is not required.

The information also must have been obtained or used in a wrongful manner. Obtaining trade secrets wrongfully includes the practice of industrial espionage, in which one firm hires an agent to spy upon and discover the secrets of a competitor. Consider the following case.

_____ *E.I. duPont De Nemours & Co., Inc. v. Christopher* _____

United States Court of Appeals, Fifth Circuit
431 F.2d 1012 (1970)

FACTS Rolfe and Gary Christopher were hired by a third party to take aerial photographs of a duPont plant under construction. The plant was designed for a highly secret yet unpatented process for producing methanol. Because the plant was under construction, parts of the process were exposed to view from overhead. The pictures could be used by a skilled person to discover the process. DuPont sued the Christophers for damages and an order preventing them from taking other pictures of the plant. DuPont claimed that one who improperly discovers, discloses, or uses another's trade secret, without a privilege to do so, is liable to the other. The Christophers contended that because they flew in public airspace and did not trespass or engage in other illegal conduct, their discovery had not been made by improper means.

ISSUE Does "improper means" embrace more than merely illegal conduct?

DECISION The court ruled in favor of duPont. "Improper means" is a dynamic concept used to enforce higher standards of commercial morality in the business world. If the holder of a trade secret takes reasonable precautions to ensure secrecy and does not voluntarily disclose the secret, a competitor must discover it through independent research. The court indicated that the proper way to get a competitor's secret process is to create a duplicate through reverse engineering.

Interference with Contractual Relations

Someone who prevents another person from performing a contract with a third person is liable for the resulting harm. Suppose that Smith contracts with Acme Construction for the construction of a high rise office building. Work is to begin on May 1. Soon thereafter, a giant corporation, Zoom Corporation, determines that it must build an office building in the same city. Zoom is fully aware of Smith's contract and knows that Acme cannot build two office buildings at the same time. Zoom offers Acme $1 million to break the contract with Smith and to begin a building at once for Zoom. Acme breaks the contract with Smith. In this situation, Smith may sue Zoom for any damages he sustains as a result of its actions.

Over the years, courts have been willing to extend this tort to situations in which someone has interfered wrongfully with another's reasonable expectation of a contractual relation. Thus liability for inducing someone to break a contract is not the only situation this tort applies to.

Disparagement

A person who makes false statements about the quality of a company's products or services or the company's ownership of those goods may be sued for disparaging the other company. The injured company must show that it has suffered actual damages. Suppose, for example, that a toothpaste producer advertises that Brite Smile, a competitor's toothpaste, makes a person's teeth fall out. If this claim were not true, the disparager could be successfully sued.

_____ TRENDS IN TORTS _____

The Emerging Tort of Wrongful Discharge

As we mentioned at the beginning of this chapter, tort law is not stagnant. New torts often are recognized by the courts. The tort of wrongful discharge is such a new tort. It has developed in response to particular social concerns.

In states where the tort of wrongful discharge is recognized, a fired employee may sue a former employer if the firing is against public policy. The employee must prove that it is in the public interest to protect the employee from termination. For example, it is the tort of wrongful discharge for an employer to fire someone for serving on a jury, because to allow such a termination would undermine the jury system.

In states that do not recognize the tort of wrongful discharge, either employer or employee may end a job of indefinite duration, unless a contract or a statute exists to the contrary. An example of such a contract would be a contract with a labor union that contains a clause prohibiting discharges except for cause. An example of a statute would be Title VII of the Civil Rights Act, which forbids discharges based on an employee's race, sex, religion, or national origin. In the absence of a contract or statute, an employer may discharge an employee for cause or no cause, in good faith or maliciously.

In the following case, the court recognizes the tort of wrongful discharge.

_____ *Tameny v. Atlantic Richfield Company* _____

Supreme Court of California
164 Cal. Rptr. 839 (1980)

Gordon Tameny was discharged by his employer, the Atlantic Richfield Company (ARCO), after 15 years of service. He sued ARCO, alleging that he was discharged because he refused to participate in a scheme to fix retail gasoline prices. Tameny contended that ARCO wrongfully discharged him for refusing to commit a criminal act. He sued for compensatory and punitive damages under normal tort principles. ARCO asked the court to dismiss Tameny's complaint. It contended that Tameny's allegations, even if true, did not state a cause of action in tort. The trial court accepted ARCO's argument and dismissed the complaint. Tameny appealed to the California Supreme Court. FACTS

Did ARCO's discharge of Tameny subject ARCO to liability in tort? ISSUE

DECISION   Yes. In reversing the trial court dismissal of Tameny's suit, the California Supreme Court stated:

> We conclude that an employee's action for wrongful discharge subjects an employer to tort liability . . .
> We hold that an employer's authority over its employee does not include the right to demand that the employee commit a criminal act to further its interest, and an employer may not coerce compliance with such unlawful directions by discharging an employee who refuses to follow such an order. An employer engaging in such conduct violates a basic duty imposed by law upon all employers, and thus an employee of such discharge may maintain a tort action for wrongful discharge against the employer.

SUMMARY

Crimes are acts or omissions for which a sentence, fine, or, in some cases, death may be imposed by a judge. Criminal cases are brought by prosecutors who represent the government. Most crimes today are statutory. One category of crime of interest to people in business is white collar crimes. These crimes cost the public billions of dollars and generally are committed by nonphysical means.

A tort is a civil wrong other than a breach of contract. Torts fall into three categories: intentional torts, negligence, and strict liability. Intentional torts are different from negligence and strict liability in that in intentional torts, defendants must have had a voluntary intent to do the act in question to be found liable.

This chapter examines four types of intentional torts: torts against the person, interference with property rights, competitive torts, and emerging torts, such as the tort of wrongful discharge. Torts against the person include assault, battery, false imprisonment, defamation, invasion of privacy, and intentional infliction of emotional suffering. Interference with property rights include trespass to land, trespass to personal property, and conversion. Competitive torts includes unfair competition, appropriation of trade secrets, interference with contractual relations, and disparagement.

REVIEW PROBLEMS

1. What is the difference between crimes that are *malum in se* and crimes that are *malum prohibitum*?

2. What are the three classifications of tort law?

3. What kind of intent is required for an intentional tort?

4. What two defenses are available for most intentional torts?

5. What are the classifications of crimes?

6. Mrs. Marion Bonkowski, accompanied by her husband, left Arlan's Department Store in Saginaw, Michigan, about 10:00 A.M. on December 18, 1962, after making several purchases. Earl Reinhardt, a private policeman on duty that day in Arlan's, called to her to stop as she was walking to her car about 30 feet away in the adjacent parking lot. Reinhardt motioned to Mrs. Bonkowski to return to the store. When she had done so, Reinhardt said that someone in the store had told him that Mrs. Bonkowski had put three pieces of jewelry into her purse without having paid for them. Mrs. Bonkowski denied having taken anything unlawfully, but Reinhardt told her he wanted to see the contents of her purse. Standing on a cement step in front of the store, Mrs. Bonkowski emptied the contents of her purse into her husband's hands. Mr. Bonkowski produced sales slips for the items she had purchased, and Reinhardt, satisfied that she had not committed larceny, returned to the store. Mrs. Bonkowski brought suit against Earl Reinhardt and Arlan's Department Store, claiming that, as a result of defendants' tort, she suffered psychosomatic symptoms, including headaches, nervousness, and depression. Who wins? Explain.

7. On leaving a restaurant, X by mistake takes Y's hat from the rack, believing it to be his own. When he reaches the sidewalk, X puts on the hat, discovers his mistake, and immediately reenters the restaurant and returns the hat to the rack. Has X committed either trespass to personal property or conversion?

8. Mr. Harris obtains a credit card in his name only from Slick Oil Company and uses it in making purchases at Slick gas stations. Mrs. Harris, a secretary at Cow College, handles family finances. She tells her husband (but not Slick) that she will not make further payments on the account, and the account becomes delinquent by $200. Slick sends a letter to the personnel director at Cow College asking for help. The letter claims that Mrs. Harris is Slick's customer, has incurred expenses, and requests Cow College's help in interviewing Mrs. Harris. Did Slick commit any intentional torts?

9. Anderson, a wholesaler of gasoline and motor oil, who does not operate and does not intend to operate any retail stations, demands that Baker, the proprietor of a retail gasoline station, carry Anderson's oil exclusively. Baker refuses. Anderson determines to drive Baker of out business. Anderson leases a vacant lot next to Baker's station for six months and daily sends a gasoline truck to the lot to sell gasoline directly from the truck. Is Anderson liable to Baker under any tort theory?

10. Brents, an exasperated creditor, puts a placard in the show window of his garage, on the public street, which states "Dr. W. R. Morgan owes an account here for $49.67. This account will be advertised as long as it remains unpaid." Morgan sues Brents for the tort of invasion of privacy. Who wins? Explain. Could Brents hold the authors of this text liable for invasion of privacy because they have published the incident in this text? Explain.

11. A.L. Stephens and Carl Stephens have arranged to bury their brother, George Stephens, at the Goodbye Cemetery, with the permission of the owners of the cemetery. At 7:30 A.M. on the day of the burial, Bud Waits comes to the cemetery and informs A.L. Stephens that Stephens is trespassing on Waits's lot. Bud Waits goes home to get papers proving his ownership of the lot and sends his

wife, Ora Waits, to the cemetery to prevent the funeral. At 12:30 P.M., the vault to line the grave is brought to the cemetery. Mrs. Waits seats herself on the vault, takes up an iron pick, and threatens to strike anyone who tries to place the vault in the grave. From 2:30 P.M. until 3:30 P.M., funeral services are held in the church next to the cemetery. When the body is brought to the grave, Ora Waits refuses to allow anyone to move the vault on which she is seated or to place it in the grave. A.L. Stephens seeks a justice of the peace, who persuades Ora Waits to get off the vault so that George Stephens's body can be put into it. A.L. and Carl Stephens sue Bud and Ora Waits, alleging that the Waitses committed the tort of intentional infliction of emotional distress. Who wins and why?

CHAPTER 4

Negligence and Strict Liability

CHAPTER OBJECTIVES

After reading this chapter, you should be able to:

1. Define negligence.

2. Identify duty, its breach, injury, and actual and proximate cause as the elements of negligence.

3. Recognize the procedural doctrines of negligence per se and res ipsa loquitur.

4. Recognize the defenses of contributory negligence and assumption of risk and be able to apply them.

5. Evaluate the trend toward comparative negligence.

6. Explain how dangerous animals and abnormally hazardous activities give rise to the imposition of strict liability.

7. Explain recklessness.

8. Evaluate the application of strict liability to the manufacture and sale of defective and dangerous products.

9. Define vicarious liability and its application to employee torts.

10. Explain workers' compensation and no fault automobile insurance.

NEGLIGENCE

Suppose that a hunter is stalking a deer in the forest. He sees some leaves rustle, and without being able to see anything other than the movement of the leaves, he fires a shot. Another hunter, not a deer, falls into the clearing. Because the hunter did not intend to shoot another hunter, he is not guilty of an intentional tort. But he is liable to the injured hunter. In this case, the injured man sues to recover for his injuries based on a claim of negligence.

Elements of Negligence

Negligence
conduct that creates an unreasonable risk of harm to another; a tort; a civil wrong

To establish **negligence,** the plaintiff must establish five elements. These are:

1. The defendant owed a *duty of care* to the plaintiff. The plaintiff must establish that the law obliges the defendant to protect the plaintiff against an unreasonable risk of harm.

FIGURE 4-1
Elements of a
Negligence Suit

1. Duty of Care
2. Breach of Duty
3. Injury
4. Actual Cause
5. Proximate Cause

2. The defendant *breached this duty.*

3. The plaintiff sustained an *injury.*

4. The defendant caused the plaintiff's injury. This is known as *cause in fact* or *actual cause.*

5. The defendant's conduct was the *proximate* or *legal cause* of the plaintiff's injury.

Duty of Care   To avoid liability for negligence, a person must avoid injuring others. In judging whether a person acted reasonably to avoid injuring others, a court measures the person's conduct against how a reasonable and prudent person would have acted under similar circumstances. This reasonable person is a hypothetical, not an average, person. A court examines all the facts of a case before determining whether a person acted reasonably.

Suppose that a customer enters a grocery store, and while pushing a shopping cart, slips on some jelly that has fallen from a shelf. The customer breaks her leg when she slips. Did the store act reasonably under these circumstances in letting jelly fall to the floor where it might injure a customer? To answer this question, a court must look at all the facts:

Was the jar knocked to the floor by a customer?

How long was the jelly on the floor?

Did the store employees know of the jelly on the floor?

Did the customer see the jelly on the floor before stepping on it?

In some cases, a person owes no duty of care to another person. For example, Doctor Anderson, a surgeon, sees the man walking in front of her at a shopping center collapse on the sidewalk. Doctor Anderson suspects that the man is having a heart attack. Does she have an obligation to stop and help the man? The answer in nearly all states is no. Dr. Anderson is not responsible for this man's collapse and has no duty to stop and give aid.

Breach of Duty   In deciding whether a defendant breached his or her duty to a plaintiff, a judge compares the behavior of the defendant with what a reasonable person would have done in a similar situation. If the defendant's conduct does not conform to this ideal standard, the court rules that the defendant *breached his or her duty* to the plaintiff.

Suppose that Dr. Anderson, the surgeon, decides to stop and help the man who has collapsed on the sidewalk. Courts in this situation rule that, although a doctor has no duty to stop and help, if the doctor chooses to do so, he or she must act as a reasonable doctor would act under the circumstances. For example, Dr. Anderson examines the man, asks someone to call an ambulance, and sits beside the man for a few minutes. Suddenly, she glances at her watch and remembers that her husband is waiting for her at a nearby store. Knowing that her husband has a volatile temper, Dr. Anderson rushes off to meet him, leaving the man alone on the sidewalk. Under these circumstances, a court is likely to rule that Dr. Anderson has acted unreasonably and may be liable for any injuries caused by her actions.

The following case presents the reasonable and prudent person in some very unusual circumstances.

Cordas v. Peerless Transportation Company

City Court of New York, New York County
27 N.Y.S.2d 198 (1941)

FACTS   While being chased for committing a robbery, a man jumped into a Peerless taxi and ordered the driver to follow his commands. The robber's gun made the driver obey until, fearing for his life, the driver slammed on the brakes and leaped from the taxi. The taxi continued rolling, however. It ran onto the sidewalk and injured Cordas and her two children, though not seriously. Cordas sued the taxi company for damages.

ISSUE   Was the taxi driver negligent in abandoning the taxi under these circumstances?

DECISION   The court ruled in favor of Peerless. The driver did not act negligently in protecting his own life. Negligence, the failure to exercise that caution that a reasonable and prudent person ordinarily would exercise under like conditions, is always relevant to conditions of time, place, or person. Someone acting in an emergency created by another is not held to the same standard of mature judgment that applies to other deliberate actions.

Injury   The plaintiff must establish that he or she sustained an injury. If the grocery store customer who slipped on jelly spilt on the store floor is not injured, she cannot recover any damages because she suffered none.

Actual Cause   The plaintiff must establish that his or her injury was caused by the defendant's act. Suppose that when the woman slipped on the jelly, a person four aisles away, and totally unaware of the accident, had had a heart attack. Because there is no connection between the store's possible breach of duty in leaving jelly on the floor and the customer's heart attack, the store is not liable for the heart attack.

Proximate Cause   To determine actual cause is to determine the cause-and-effect relationship between the defendant's conduct and the plaintiff's injury. Proximate cause is different from actual cause. Assuming that actual cause exists, determining proximate cause is a finding of whether the defendant is responsible for all the events that actually occurred.

The issue of proximate cause arises in situations where the defendant's original negligence leads to unforeseen consequences. Because one act of negligence should not subject a defendant to unlimited liability for all the consequences that could possibly result, the doctrine of proximate cause limits the defendant's liability to those events that are reasonably foreseeable. A defendant is liable only for the natural, probable, foreseeable, and thus avoidable consequences of his or her conduct, not for all consequences, however remote. The doctrine of proximate cause recognizes the fact that a particular wrong may set off a chain of events so completely unforeseeable, and resulting in an injury so remotely related to the wrong itself, that common sense suggests that the defendant should not be liable for it. The doctrine of proximate cause is a principle of law and policy that limits liability to foreseeable injuries.

Procedural Doctrines

The plaintiff has the burden of proving that he or she is entitled to a recovery. This burden of proving the defendant's negligence is placed upon the plaintiff because it is the plaintiff who is asking the court for relief. In certain cases, the plaintiff may have the burden of proof lightened by two procedural doctrines: *negligence per se* and *res ipsa loquitur.*

Negligence Per Se   Under the doctrine of *negligence per se,* a plaintiff may use the defendant's violation of a criminal statute to establish the defendant's negligence. For the doctrine of negligence per se to apply, the statute must be relevant to the case. The court must determine whether the statute applies as a standard of civil liability.

Courts determine whether a statute was intended to apply in the case at hand by determining whether the plaintiff falls within the class of people the statute was intended to protect, and whether the injury to the plaintiff falls within the class of injuries the statute was intended to prevent. If the court finds that these two conditions are met, the plaintiff may claim negligence per se.

For example, suppose that a statute makes it illegal to sell an explosive substance to a person under the age of 16. A retail store sells gunpowder to a 15-year-old, who in turn seriously injures a person when the gunpowder explodes. The seller is negligent per se and can be held liable to the injured party.

Res Ipsa Loquitur   In some cases, it is difficult to prove negligence. It is especially difficult when the thing causing the injury is in the exclusive control of the defendant.

Res ipsa loquitur
Latin for "the thing speaks for itself"; legal doctrine permitting establishment of an inference of negligence from the evidence of the act itself

In such a case, it may be possible for the plaintiff to rely upon the doctrine of *res ipsa loquitur.* The plaintiff must establish:

that the injury is a type that does not ordinarily occur without negligence and

that the defendant was in exclusive control of the thing that caused the injury.

This evidence creates an inference of negligence. The defendant must introduce evidence to prove that he or she was not negligent or lose the case.

Suppose that a farmhand is walking in front of a barn when a hay bale falls from the second story, striking the farmhand. In that the barn is in the exclusive control of the farmer, and hay bales normally do not fall in the absence of negligence, the farmhand may rely upon the doctrine of res ipsa loquitur to establish a case of negligence. If the farmer fails to introduce evidence that proves he was not negligent, he will be held liable to the farmhand.

The following case illustrates the application of the res ipsa loquitur doctrine.

Rose v. Melody Lane of Wilshire

Supreme Court of California
247 P.2d 335 (1952)

FACTS   At about 11:00 P.M., Rose and a friend entered the Melody Lane cocktail room for a drink on their way home from a lodge meeting. Almost immediately after sitting down, Rose's chair separated from its base, and he fell backward to the floor, sustaining an injury. There is no question of intoxication; the injury was sustained before any liquor was consumed.

ISSUE   May plaintiff rely upon the doctrine of res ipsa loquitur to establish his case?

DECISION   Yes. This type of accident would not ordinarily occur in the absence of negligence. The bar had exclusive control over the bar stool, which caused the injury to Rose. Seats do not ordinarily collapse without negligence in their construction, maintenance, or use. The inference of negligence created by these facts was not overcome by evidence introduced by the cocktail lounge that it had not been negligent. The court found for Rose.

Defenses

There are two basic defenses to a negligence action: contributory negligence and assumption of the risk.

Contributory Negligence   Someone who has failed to exercise reasonable care for his or her own safety and thus has contributed to his or her injury is guilty of

contributory negligence Someone found guilty of contributory negligence cannot recover damages for the injury from a defendant. Suppose that two cars come to a four-way stop sign. Both drivers fail to stop and collide in the intersection. If one driver sues the other, the second driver may argue that the first driver ran the stop sign and was thus contributorily negligent.

Because the tort of negligence bases liability on fault, proof of contributory negligence formerly prevented a person from recovering any damages at all. Because of the harshness of this rule, the concept of **comparative negligence** developed as an alternative. Comparative negligence is now followed by most states. This defense weighs the relative negligence of the parties. Then it either reduces the award of damages in proportion to the plaintiff's negligence or bars recovery only if the plaintiff's negligence was greater than the defendant's.

Comparative negligence removes the "all or nothing" rule of contributory negligence and replaces it with a rule that allows a jury to apportion damages to reflect the relative fault of the parties. Suppose that a case is litigated in a state that follows the doctrine of comparative negligence. The jury decides that the defendant was 75 percent at fault for an accident and the plaintiff 25 percent at fault. In a state that followed the doctrine of contributory negligence, the plaintiff would have received nothing. In this state, however, the plaintiff will recover 75 percent of the damages. If the jury finds that the plaintiff was damaged to the extent of $100,000, it will award him $75,000.

In the following case, the Supreme Court of California adopted comparative negligence.

Contributory negligence a defense to a negligence claim that states conduct by the plaintiff contributed to the plaintiff's injury

Comparative negligence a defense that weighs the relative negligence of the parties and adjusts the award accordingly

_____ *Li v. Yellow Cab Company of California* _____

Supreme Court of California
532 P.2d 1226 (1975)

Nga Li, a motorist, sued the Yellow Cab Company and its driver for personal injuries sustained by her when her car collided with a taxi in an intersection. The jury found that Li was contributorily negligent, and the judgment was for Yellow Cab. Li appealed the judgment.

FACTS

Does Li's contributory negligence prevent her from recovering any damages caused by the accident?

ISSUE

The court ruled in Li's favor and replaced the "all-or-nothing" rule of contributory negligence, as it existed in California, with comparative negligence. The fundamental purpose of comparative negligence is to assign responsibility and liability for damage in direct proportion to the amount of negligence of each of the parties. The doctrine of contributory negligence operates inequitably because it fails to assign responsibility in proportion to fault.

DECISION

Assumption of Risk   The defense of assumption of risk exists when a plaintiff actually had or should have had knowledge of a risk and voluntarily exposed himself or herself to it. In such a situation the defendant, although negligent, is not responsible for the resulting injury.

Suppose that Bart goes to a roller skating rink. During an intermission, the manager polishes the floor. After finishing the job, the manager realizes that he has put too much wax on the floor and that it is dangerous to skate on. The manager tells Bart not to skate on the slippery floor, but Bart ignores his warning and skates anyway. Soon after entering the rink, Bart falls down and injures himself. Bart assumed the risk of the injury.

RECKLESSNESS

Recklessness
intended harm, but
harm more serious
than the defendant
expected

Recklessness exists when someone knows that the act he or she intends to commit is harmful, but he or she fails to realize that it will produce the extreme harm which it in fact produces. Recklessness differs from an intentional tort in that the person does not intend to cause the *extreme* harm that results from it, although the person did realize that there was a strong probability that some harm would occur. Recklessness differs from negligence in that the defendant *intended* to commit the act, which he realizes may be harmful.

Suppose that a student is walking down a hall at school and encounters a student whom he dislikes. He punches the other student in the back, intending not to harm him seriously, just to push him around some. The second student, however, sustains a neck injury. The injured student may bring suit based on recklessness.

STRICT LIABILITY

Strict liability
tort theory that
permits liability
without regard to
fault

Up until now, the discussion of tort law has focused on situations in which liability is based on fault: intentional wrongdoing (discussed in Chapter 3) or negligent conduct. However, the law imposes liability in some situations even if the defendant is not guilty of intentional wrongdoing and even if the defendant has exercised reasonable care. This standard is known as **strict liability.**

The strict liability standard has been applied in situations where the defendant's conduct creates an unusually high risk of harm, even if due care is exercised. In such situations, injury is highly probable, and to require the plaintiff to prove negligence is to require him or her to bear the risk inherent in the defendant's dangerous conduct. Although the law could simply prohibit such conduct on the part of the defendant, some hazardous conduct is socially beneficial, such as blasting done during the construction of buildings. According to the strict liability standard, people may engage in risky activities but must bear the inherent risk of loss. The result is that those who are injured are compensated by the party who caused the injury. In turn, they must consider such liability a cost of engaging in risky activity.

Strict liability was early applied to the keepers of dangerous animals. A dangerous animal is one that is known by its keeper to be likely to inflict injury, such as a lion, a tiger, or a poisonous snake. For strict liability to apply, a keeper must know or have reason to know of the animal's dangerous propensities.

Strict liability was later applied to extremely hazardous activities. Common examples are blasting operations, public fireworks, and storing gasoline dangerously near property.

There are limits to the extent of strict liability. The defendant must be aware of the abnormally risky activity and voluntarily engage in it. Further, liability is limited to the reasonably expected consequences of such risky conduct. For example, liability would not extend to damage done by a rock hurled an unusual distance by a blasting operation.

A defendant is not liable to a plaintiff who voluntarily and unreasonably encounters a known danger. For example, a person cannot claim strict liability who agrees to work with poisonous snakes.

During the past 20 years, strict liability has been applied to injuries caused by products made unreasonably dangerous by defects in their condition or design. The following case illustrates the application of strict liability to cases involving defective products.

Dunham v. Vaughan and Bushnell Manufacturing Company
Supreme Court of Illinois
247 N.E.2d 401 (1969)

FACTS

Dunham, a farmer, bought from Belknap Hardware a claw hammer manufactured by Vaughan and Bushnell Manufacturing Company. Eleven months later, while he was using the hammer to drive a pin connecting his tractor to a manure spreader, a chip from the beveled edge of the hammer broke off and struck him in the right eye, destroying its sight. Dunham sued both Belknap and Vaughan and Bushnell, citing the standard of strict liability.

ISSUE

Under these circumstances, should the standard of strict liability be imposed on the manufacturer and the seller of the hammer?

DECISION

The court upheld a jury verdict in favor of Dunham. For strict liability to be imposed on a manufacturer, it must be shown that the product was defective and therefore unreasonably dangerous to the user. Whether a product is "defective" depends on whether the product as sold meets the reasonable expectation of the user about its safety. Hammers have an increasing propensity to chip with continued use. A new hammer is not expected to chip, although at some point in its use the possibility of chipping becomes a reasonable expectation of how the hammer is likely to perform. While acknowledging that problems arise in the middle range, the court concluded that the evidence supported the jury's conclusion that the hammer was defective.

The court also decided that strict liability, applied to the manufacturer of the hammer, extends as well to the seller, despite the fact that the box in which the hammer was packaged passed unopened through the seller's warehouse:

The strict liability of a retailer arises from his integral role in the overall producing and marketing enterprise and affords an additional incentive to safety.

Vicarious Liability

Under the doctrine of vicarious liability, an employer is liable for negligence of employees acting within the scope of their employment. The doctrine is also known as *imputed negligence* or **respondeat superior** ("let the superior respond"). It is an application of strict liability theory, meaning that for policy reasons liability is imposed regardless of the employer's fault or blame.

Respondeat superior Latin for "let the superior respond"; legal doctrine by which an employer is held liable for the torts of an employee committed within the scope of employment

Scope of Employment Limitation   Only when an employee is negligent in the scope of employment — that is, when the injury is caused by the employee's wrongdoing incidental to the work — is the employer liable under respondeat superior.

This limit on the employer's liability is more easily stated than applied. Determining if an employee acted within the scope of employment often is difficult because employees may temporarily be performing a personal errand, or working and serving a personal purpose simultaneously, or working in a forbidden manner.

No Fault Insurance Systems

In two areas, state-mandated insurance compensation systems have replaced the traditional tort litigation system as a means of determining damages. These are the areas of workers' compensation and no fault automobile insurance.

Workers' Compensation   The defenses of contributory negligence, assumption of risk, and the fellow-servant rule (which provided that an employer was not liable for a worker's injury where the injury resulted from the negligence of a fellow worker), made it extremely unlikely that an employee could hold an employer liable for on-the-job injuries. In response to the growing number of job-related injuries and political pressure from labor groups, early in this century state legislatures enacted workers' compensation laws. By 1949, every state had some form of workers' compensation. Although the laws vary, they have certain common features.

Workers' compensation statutes apply the standard of strict liability instead of negligence to job-related injuries. Fault is immaterial. Employees are entitled to benefits despite their negligence and despite their employer's freedom from fault.

Injuries that arise out of and during the course of employment are compensable under workers' compensation laws. This standard is similar to the scope-of-employment test of the respondeat superior doctrine discussed previously.

Under workers' compensation, employers are required either to contribute to a state-administered workers' compensation fund or, as in most states, to procure workers' compensation insurance from private insurers.

Claims for workers' compensation are administered by a state agency, usually called the Industrial Commission or Workers' Compensation Bureau. If the employer contests the claim, the agency holds a hearing and determines if the injury is compensable under the statute. Because employers contribute to the state fund or pay insurance premiums according to the employer's experience rating, the employer has an economic incentive to contest doubtful claims.

Workers' compensation is computed according to a schedule of compensation for various types of injury and disabilities.

No Fault Automobile Insurance   Many negligence cases involve automobile accidents. Because courts devote so much time to these cases, states have passed laws that, to varying degrees, remove automobile accidental injury cases from the courts to administrative agencies. These statutes provide an injured party with an automatic but minimal award rather than a day in court and the chance for a greater award. The laws differ from state to state. Basically, they provide that the injured party need not prove negligence in the traditional way, only that the no fault insurance statute applies to the case. As long as the amount claimed by the injured party is below a prescribed maximum, his or her own insurance pays the claim without regard to fault. This process is analogous to the change from the use of negligence to workers' compensation insurance for recovery by injured employees.

SUMMARY

Negligence is conduct that creates an unreasonable risk of harm to another. The elements of negligence are duty, breach of duty, injury, actual cause, and proximate cause. Courts determine the existence of a duty by balancing several factors, primarily the risk and foreseeability of harm versus the social utility of the actor's conduct. The standard for determining whether a duty has been breached is whether the actor's conduct is consistent with that of a reasonable and prudent person under the same or similar circumstances. A person's conduct is said to have been a cause of another's injury when it is a substantial factor in bringing about the injury. A person's conduct is said to be the proximate cause of another's injury when the injury is a foreseeable, natural, and probable result of such conduct.

Two procedural doctrines lighten the burden that plaintiffs face in proving negligence. These are the doctrines of negligence per se and res ipsa loquitur. Two defenses against negligence are contributory negligence and assumption of the risk.

The tort of recklessness involves a defendant who committed an act that he or she knew might cause harm, but which caused harm that was more extreme than anticipated.

Strict liability is another standard of tort law. Strict liability is imposed in certain situations without regard to fault. Traditionally, strict liability has been imposed for injuries resulting from dangerous animals and unusually hazardous activities. In such cases, liability is imposed even if the defendant acted with all due care. Strict liability also has been used in cases involving defective products. In such cases, plaintiffs must prove that the product was defective and therefore unreasonably dangerous to them.

The concept of strict liability also can be seen in the concept of vicarious liability, no fault systems of workers' compensation, and no fault automobile insurance. Vicarious liability is a concept in which an employer is held liable for those torts of its employees falling within the scope of the employees' employment. Systems of workers' compensation and no fault automobile insurance substitute an administrative compensation system for traditional tort litigation.

_____ REVIEW PROBLEMS _____

1. Define negligence, and describe each of its elements.

2. What procedural doctrines are available to plaintiffs in a negligence case, and what defenses are available to defendants?

3. What is strict liability, and in what types of cases has it been applied?

4. What is vicarious liability, and when is it applied?

5. Breisig operated an automobile repair shop. Roberts took his car to Breisig's shop for repairs. When Roberts asked when the car would be ready, Breisig said the car probably would be ready by the end of the day. If so, Breisig said, he would park the car in his shop's parking lot so that Roberts could pick it up that evening. At about 7 P.M., Breisig finished the work and parked the car in the lot, leaving the keys in the ignition. Soon thereafter two teenage boys stole the car and drove it around town. They picked up two friends and left the car on a street overnight. The next day one of the friends, Williams, returned to the car. While driving negligently, he struck George, who suffered serious injuries. George sued Breisig, claiming that leaving the keys in an unattended car was negligence, particularly because Breisig's shop was located in a deteriorating neighborhood. Breisig denied liability. Who wins? Explain.

6. A passenger was running to catch one of the Long Island Railroad Company's trains. A railroad employee, trying to help the passenger to board the train, knocked a package out of his arms, and it fell on the rails. The package contained fireworks, which exploded with some violence. The explosion overturned some scales, many feet away on the platform, and they fell upon Palsgraf and injured her. Palsgraf sued the Long Island Railroad Company, claiming that it was liable for her injuries as a result of its employee's negligence. Long Island Railroad disclaimed any liability. Who wins? Explain.

7. A driver for the Coca Cola Bottling Company delivered several cases of Coca Cola to the restaurant where Escola worked as a waitress. She stacked the cases on the floor, under and behind the counter, where they remained for over 36 hours. Escola picked up the top case and set it on a nearby ice-cream cabinet in front of and about 3 feet from the refrigerator. She then took the bottles from the case with her right hand, one at a time, and put them into the refrigerator. After she had placed three bottles in the refrigerator and had moved the fourth bottle about 18 inches from the case, it exploded in her hand. The bottle broke into two jagged pieces and inflicted a deep 5-inch cut, severing blood vessels, nerves, and muscles of the thumb and palm of her hand. Escola sued Coca Cola, relying on the doctrines of res ipsa loquitur and strict product liability. Does Escola succeed under these theories? Explain.

8. A dead mouse is found baked inside a loaf of bread from the Continental Baking Co., and Doyle is injured by eating the bread. Continental introduces evidence from many witnesses that all possible care was used in the bakery and that the precautions taken made it impossible for mice to get into the product. Continental makes a motion for a directed verdict in its favor. Will the court grant the motion?

9. On a stormy night, the owner of a tractor truck left it parked without lights in the middle of the road. The driver of a car in which Hill was a passenger saw it in time to turn and avoid hitting it but negligently failed to do so. Hill is injured. Who is liable to her?

10. A fireman develops lung cancer after some years of inhaling smoke from fires and also from cigarettes. The fireman files a claim for workers' compensation. Will the fireman recover benefits? Explain.

11. The Kosmos Portland Cement Company failed to clean oil residue out of an oil barge, which was tied to a dock. Lightning struck the barge, the vapor in the barge exploded, and workers on the dock were injured. Is Kosmos liable to the workers for their injuries? Explain.

12. Anthony and Jeannette Luth were driving south on the Seward Highway in Alaska when their car collided with another driven by Wayne Jack. The accident occurred when Jack tried to pass another vehicle going north. On the day of the accident and for the previous six weeks, Jack was employed by Rogers and Babler Construction Company as a flagman on a road construction project. At the time of the accident, he was returning home to Anchorage from his job. Because he did not live near the job site, Jack commuted approximately 25 miles to work by car every day. The Master Union Agreement under which Jack worked provided for additional pay of $8.50 a day for work at sites a considerable distance from Anchorage. However, all of the firm's employees on this particular construction project received the $8.50 extra whether they commuted from Anchorage or lived near the job site. The Luths sued Rogers and Babler Construction, claiming that the company was responsible under the doctrine of respondeat superior for their injuries. Is the company liable? Explain.

PART II

CONTRACTS

CHAPTER 5

Introduction to the Law of Contracts

CHAPTER OBJECTIVES

After reading this chapter, you should be able to:

1. Explain how contracts are used.

2. Identify the elements of a contract.

3. Describe the source of contract law.

4. State how contracts are classified.

As we shall see in the following chapters, contracts are everywhere in our daily lives. For instance, the law of contracts governs a boarding agreement with a university, renting an apartment, buying books at a bookstore, agreeing to lend a roommate money, and buying beer at the local store.

THE UTILITY OF CONTRACTS

Contract law can be viewed in several ways. Some see the freedom of individuals and organizations to contract as fundamental to the free enterprise system.[1] Contracts between sellers and buyers implement the law of supply and demand. Contract law protects both seller and buyer against the possible bad-faith conduct of the other. Without this protection, people might breach contracts at will. If the law of contracts did not provide a remedy for the breach of contracts, sellers would have to require deposits or entire purchase prices before they would release goods. Transaction costs would rise, and the flow of goods in our economy would be impaired.[2]

Another view of a contract is as a tool by which people — often assisted by their lawyers — establish private rules to govern a particular business or personal relationship. From a lawyer's perspective, a contract is a device by which a situation may be defined and controlled. The expectations of the contracting parties are made known and serve as guides for future behavior.

For example, in a real-estate purchase contract, a seller promises to sell a house and lot to a buyer. In the contract, a number of the parties' expectations are spelled out. Such expectations include:

1. when the buyer may take possession

2. what kind of document of title the seller is to provide the buyer

3. what articles the seller may remove from the house and yard

4. how the taxes owing are to be split among the parties

5. how the risk of loss is to be allocated among the parties, and so on.

With the contract, buyer and seller create their own set of rules to govern the sale. In a sense, their agreement embodies a private legal system.

Not surprisingly, many questions about the operation of government legal systems also come up in the context of private agreements. For example, what is to be done if the parties in the agreement just described fail to provide for responsibility in case of loss and the house is destroyed by a meteor after the contract is signed but before the buyer takes possession? What happens if one of the parties blatantly disregards one of the clearly established private rules — for example, by refusing to provide the required evidence of title?

In the first case (a house destroyed by a meteor), the expectations of at least one party cannot be met. Either the buyer must buy damaged property, or the seller must give up a sale he or she thought was closed and final. How can this issue be resolved when the parties have not dealt with the problem themselves and insurance does not cover the loss? For commonly occurring situations of this sort, the courts and legislatures have established guidelines, and general legal principles have been issued.

The second case (refusing to provide required evidence of title) goes to the heart of contract law. The parties are not to enforce their contract by private means. Our legal system does not tolerate the use of threats or force to induce faithful observance of the terms of private agreements. Instead, it allows the parties to enforce the terms through civil suits.

The intervention of the legal system when private parties disagree raises many questions. Should all private agreements be enforced — for example, an agreement by two bank robbers to split the proceeds of a holdup 55 percent to 45 percent? What relief should be provided for someone injured as a result of the other's failure to observe the terms of the agreement? Can a university compel a professor who has just won $1 million in a lottery to teach the last academic year of a three-year contract? Should the legal system enforce only "fair" contracts? If so, what constitutes a fair contract? Should unwritten contracts be enforceable?

Because the case below involved actor Lee Marvin and received extensive media coverage, it provides an interesting introduction to the law of contracts.

_____ *Marvin v. Marvin* _____

Supreme Court of California
555 P.2d 106 (1976)

Plaintiff and defendant lived together for seven years without marrying. All property acquired during this period was taken in the defendant's name. Plaintiff alleged that she was entitled to half of the property and to support payments because of an oral contract between the parties. The plaintiff alleged that they had agreed to hold themselves out to the public as man and wife and she would serve as companion, homemaker, housekeeper, and cook to the defendant. The defendant alleged that the contract should not be enforced because it involved an illicit relationship and therefore was an unlawful contract.   FACTS

If the contract exists, is it enforceable?   ISSUE

The court ruled that if the plaintiff could establish the existence of such a contract, it should be enforced. Adults who voluntarily live together and engage in sexual relations   DECISION are competent to contract. They cannot lawfully contract to pay for the performance of sexual services, because such a contract is an agreement for prostitution and unlawful for that reason. This contract, however, was not a contract for prostitution and therefore might be enforced.

CONTRACT DEFINED

Contract an agreement that courts will recognize and enforce

We need to define a contract. The simplest, most accurate definition is: A **contract** is an agreement that the courts will recognize and enforce. What do the courts require before an agreement will be recognized and enforced? The following list represents the elements of enforceability for most types of contracts in most jurisdictions.[3]

1. a valid offer

2. a proper acceptance

3. sufficiency of consideration

4. absence of fraud, force, or legally significant mistake

5. legal capacity of parties

6. consistency with general public policy

7. observance of proper legal form

8. consistency with special rules governing the type of agreement involved

Several basic points regarding the true nature of contracts must now be made. First, almost all contracts are voluntarily carried out by the parties to their mutual satisfaction, so the judicial system never becomes involved. Second, the mere fact that one has a legal right to sue for breach of contract does not mean that it is a sound business decision to do so. Before suit is filed, factors such as likelihood of again doing business with the other party, industry attitudes about businesses that often file suit, relative economic strength of the parties, and alternative private means of resolving the dispute should be considered. Third, although we will be discussing basic rules about contracts in general, many specific categories of contracts have laws that apply specifically to them.[4]

SOURCES OF CONTRACT LAW

The principles of contract law are found in judicial decisions of cases involving contractual disputes. Courts follow earlier decisions involving similar situations. Only Louisiana has a comprehensive state contract law.

Many state laws spell out special rules for certain types of contracts. For example, state laws regulate insurance contracts. The most important of the state laws affecting

FIGURE 5-1   Sources of Contract Law

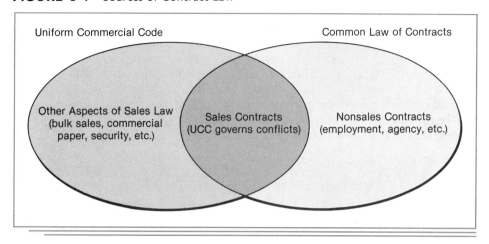

contracts is the Uniform Commercial Code (UCC). The UCC, which has been adopted at least in part by the legislatures of all 50 states, establishes a series of rules dealing with all aspects of sales transactions. One part of the UCC, Article 2, contains rules governing sales contracts. (Article 2 is included in full in Appendix B.) If the. UCC does not rule on an aspect of a sales contract, the general common law of contracts controls. If there is a UCC rule, it governs sales contracts even when the common law rule is to the contrary. This relationship is shown in Figure 5-1.

CLASSIFICATION OF CONTRACTS

We offer the following classification of contracts to help readers analyze problems related to contracts in later chapters.

Express, Implied, and Quasi Contracts

An **express contract** is one formed by the words of the parties, either oral or written. If a seller agrees to sell her home and a buyer agrees to buy it, and the parties express their intention to contract in a written contract that includes all the necessary terms of the sale, such a contract is called an express contract. An express contract can be oral. If Jack agrees to sell his textbook to Lois for $20, and Lois agrees to buy it for $20, an express contract has been formed. A **contract implied in fact** is inferred from actions of the parties. Going to a doctor, describing symptoms, and accepting treatment establishes a contract implied in fact. The test is whether a reasonable person would intend to contract by engaging in such actions.

Express contract a contract formed by the oral or written words of the parties

Contract implied in fact a contract created by the actions of the parties

Contract implied in law a contract created by a court although the parties never intended to contract

A *quasi contract,* also known as a **contract implied in law,** differs from express and implied in fact contracts in that the parties did not intend to make a contract. In creating the legal fiction of a quasi contract, the courts are trying to be fair. Suppose, for example, that a doctor performed valuable services upon a patient who had suddenly become unconscious in the doctor's waiting room. Clearly, no express contract exists. Further, many courts would refuse to recognize a contract implied in fact because no intention could be inferred from the actions of the patient. A quasi contract could be recognized by a court, however, that would require the patient to pay the reasonable value of the services rendered.

For courts to recognize a quasi contract, there must be:

1. a benefit or unjust enrichment to the benefited party

2. no other legal recourse for the "victim" of the benefit.

The victim is entitled to recover only the reasonable value of the benefit — not what would have been a likely contract price. The case that follows presents an implied in law contract.

County of Champaign v. Hanks

Court of Appeals of Illinois
353 N.E.2d 405 (1976)

FACTS

Hanks was accused of a crime. He claimed at the time of his arrest that he had no money to hire an attorney to defend himself. This statement was in fact false, because he owned real estate worth over $50,000. In relying on these false statements, the state provided a free attorney to Hanks. When it discovered that the statements were false, it sued to recover the cost of providing an attorney to Hanks for defending him in the criminal trial.

ISSUE

Is there a contract between the state and Hanks that requires Hanks to pay for the legal services provided to him by the state?

DECISION

Hanks must pay the reasonable value of the legal services provided to him. A quasi contract does not depend upon the intention of the parties. Hanks received benefits from the state under circumstances in which it would be unfair for Hanks to retain those benefits without paying for them. Under these circumstances, the law implies a promise by Hanks to compensate the state. The measure of damages for an implied in law contract is the amount by which the defendant has been unjustly enriched or the value of the actual benefit received by the defendant. Hanks must therefore pay the reasonable value of the legal services provided to him.

Executed and Executory Contracts

Executed contract a contract that has been fully performed

An **executed contract** is one in which all required performances have been rendered. A goes to B's garage, picks up a new tire, and pays B. The contract has been fully performed. Nothing remains to be done by either party. An **executory contract** is one in which some of the required performance remains to be done. A and B enter an agreement whereby B agrees to repair A's car in two weeks, and A agrees to pay B $100 upon completion. Because neither has performed his part of the agreement, it is executory in nature.

> **Executory contract** a contract that has not been fully performed

Valid, Void, and Voidable Contracts

A **valid contract** is one that is perfectly good and that may be enforced by all parties to it. A **void contract**, on the other hand, is not good; it is not enforceable by anyone. A void contract is a contradiction in terms in that it is not really a contract under our definition. For example, if Ames contracts with Brown to kill Ames's wife, Brown's failure to perform will not be grounds for a suit by Ames, because a legally enforceable contract never existed. Their contract is a void contract. A **voidable contract** has an in-between status. It is currently valid, but one or more of the parties has the power to render the contract unenforceable. For example, Mark, a minor, contracts with Mrs. Ross, who is of legal age, to paint her house. The contract is voidable by Mark, because under certain circumstances, a minor has the right to get out of a contract.

> **Valid contract** a contract in which all the elements necessary to create a contract have been complied with

> **Void contract** a contract that is not enforceable by anyone

Bilateral and Unilateral Contracts

A contract may involve an exchange of promises in which two parties agree that each will perform in a certain way in the future. Player promises to abide by the team rules and be available to play baseball for the coming season. Team promises to pay Player $85,000 for the year. At the moment the contract is signed, neither party starts performing. Instead, the agreed upon performance will take place in the future. The exchange of a promise for a promise is known as a **bilateral contract.**

Suppose Team promises to pay Player $2,000 for every home run over 30 during the season. Player has not promised to hit more than 30 home runs and will not be in breach of contract for failing to do so. Instead, Team has made a promise that performance will be forthcoming in exchange for an act. This is an offer of a **unilateral contract** that can be accepted only by performance of the act. Most commercial contracts are bilateral. The case that follows illustrates the importance of distinguishing between unilateral and bilateral contracts.

> **Voidable contract** a contract that may not be enforceable under certain circumstances

> **Bilateral contract** a contract involving an exchange of promises

> **Unilateral contract** a contract that involves a promise in return for action

Cook v. Johnson

Supreme Court of Washington
221 P.2d 525 (1950)

Johnson made an offer on December 20, 1947, for Cook to clean a drainage ditch on Johnson's property. On December 23, 1947, Cook accepted Johnson's offer. Cook agreed to clean the ditch by the end of January unless there were extreme weather conditions. Thereafter, Johnson sold the property to Fink. Cook completed the work in question and billed Johnson for it. Johnson refused to pay. He contended that after

FACTS

Cook learned of the sale of the property to Fink, Cook first should have contacted Johnson before proceeding with the work.

ISSUE   Must Johnson pay for the work performed by Cook?

DECISION   The court ruled that when Cook accepted Johnson's offer, an enforceable bilateral contract was created. Cook had no obligation to contact Johnson after learning of the sale of the property. Johnson should have contacted Cook to have the contract rescinded.

SUMMARY

A valid contract requires that the following elements be present: a valid offer; a proper acceptance; sufficiency of consideration; the absence of fraud, force, or legally sufficient mistake; legal capacity of the parties; observance of proper legal form; and consistency with any special rules governing the type of agreement involved.

Contract law comes from two main sources, the common law of contracts and the Uniform Commercial Code. The UCC controls cases involving the sale of goods.

Contracts are classified as: express, implied, quasi, valid, void, voidable, bilateral, and unilateral.

REVIEW PROBLEMS

1. What elements must be present before the courts will enforce a contract?

2. What is meant by the statement that contracts is a "common law field"?

3. What contracts are governed by the UCC?

4. How does a contract implied in law differ from one implied in fact?

5. Cone has a house in a development that looks very similar to his neighbor's house. The neighbor orders landscaping done. The landscaper arrives and starts working on Cone's house. Cone sees the landscaper and does nothing until the lawn has been leveled and several attractive bushes have been planted. Landscaper sues Cone. Result?

6. Suppose that Cone had been gone all day and that Cone did not like the work done. Would that change the outcome in the case?

7. A seller lists a house for sale with a real estate broker, thereby promising to pay a 7 percent commission if the broker finds a buyer ready, willing, and able to buy the house for $75,000. What kind of contract is this?

8. John Doe requests that Jack Maverick paint his house, promising that he will pay

him $1,200 when Maverick finishes. Maverick paints the house. What type of contract is this?

9. Smith wrote Lowe a letter in which she offered Lowe $500 to watch her house while she was away for the summer on business. Lowe watched Smith's house for the summer, although he never wrote back to Smith. What type of contract did Lowe's actions create?

10. May a voidable contract ever be enforced?

11. Donna entered into a contract for the sale of her car to Diane. Donna gave the car to Diane. Diane paid Donna for the car. What type of contract is this?

12. John made an appointment for a dental checkup. On the day of the appointment, he arrived at the office. The dentist checked his teeth and told John that they looked healthy. Neither the dentist nor John ever discussed the question of John's obligation to pay for the dentist's services. Must John pay the dentist?

 NOTES

1. See Lawrence Freedman, *Contract Law in America,* 1965, pp. 20–24.
2. See Richard Posner, *Economic Analysis of Law* (2nd ed.), 1977, p. 42.
3. There is no universally accepted, written-in-stone list of the elements of enforceability. Textbooks vary greatly in how these elements boil down to their simplest, most basic levels of enforceability.
4. See Grant Gilmore, *The Death of Contract,* 1974.

CHAPTER 6

Offer and Acceptance

CHAPTER OBJECTIVES

REQUIREMENTS FOR AN OFFER

Intent to Contract / Definite and Certain Terms / Communication of the Offer

TERMINATION OF THE OFFER

Lapse of Time / Revocation by the Offeror / Rejection by the Offeree / Destruction of the Subject Matter

ACCEPTANCE

INTENT TO ACCEPT

COMMUNICATION OF ACCEPTANCE

Bilateral or Unilateral Agreement / Means of Communication

SATISFYING TERMS OF THE OFFER

PROBLEMS WITH ACCEPTANCE

Silence as Acceptance

CANCELLATION OF ACCEPTANCE

SUMMARY

REVIEW PROBLEMS

CHAPTER OBJECTIVES

After reading this chapter, you should be able to:

1. List the essential elements of a valid offer.

2. Explain the importance of intent and communication.

3. State the terms to be specified in an agreement.

4. Identify problems in fine print offers and in exchanging contradictory printed forms.

5. Explain how offers may be terminated.

6. Explain how option contracts work.

7. Explain the "mailbox rule."

8. List the requirements for proper acceptance of an offer.

9. Discuss whether or not silence communicates acceptance.

People usually do not imagine taking legal action to enforce their agreements (or to recover damages if the other party has not performed as agreed). Yet people want the assurance that they can reasonably expect the law to stand behind their agreements.

The law of contracts defines and determines which agreements will be recognized and enforced. Because contract law requires a valid offer to have been made if an agreement is to be recognized as enforceable, we begin with this requirement.

REQUIREMENTS FOR AN OFFER

For a valid offer to exist, contract law requires the offer to:

1. Manifest the intent to enter into a contract

2. Be definite and certain regarding the essential terms of the proposed contract

3. Be communicated to the party (known as the **offeree**) for whom the offer is intended.

Offeree one who accepts an offer

Even though a valid offer has been made initially, it is necessary to determine that it still exists prior to acceptance. Offers may terminate prior to acceptance for a variety of reasons. If the offer has expired, a purported acceptance fails to establish a contract. Many cases have been litigated over the questions of whether or not an offer has been validly made and whether or not an offer has expired prior to acceptance. The rest of this section discusses the rules of law that determine these issues.

Intent to Contract

Determining Intent   How should a person's intent be determined? Consider the following situations. Suppose that you are at a used car lot. The price of a car you like is listed as $3,995. You ask the salesperson what he'd take for the car. He doesn't answer, but asks what you would offer. If you say, "I wouldn't pay the list price, but I might pay $3,000 if I could finance it," have you made an offer—and become an **offeror**? Did you intend by that statement to commit to a contract?

Offeror one who makes an offer

An auctioneer selling home furnishings announces at the start of the auction that anyone who wants to bid on an item should simply raise his or her hand when a certain price is called. If you, in gesturing to a friend with whom you are talking, raise your hand while the auctioneer is asking for a $500 bid for a couch, have you offered to buy it? Are you intending to contract?

To answer these questions, we must first consider how a person's intent is ascertained. A person's actual intentions are very difficult to ascertain, and a person's subjective mental state is not susceptible to discovery or verification. Instead, the law seeks to determine intent entirely by objective standards. What would a reasonable person, watching and listening to the offeror, conclude about the offeror's intentions of entering into a contract? The evidence of the offeror's intent comes from actions and words as perceived by a reasonable person.

Social Invitation, Excitement, or Jest   The law presumes social invitations do not imply intent to contract. An invitation to a wedding, even one requesting a reply, is not considered an offer to contract. Similarly, an invitation to the movies or dinner is not an offer to contract, and an acceptance does not impose a contractual obligation on the inviter.

Suppose that someone makes a statement in the midst of an exciting event. As I watch my favorite basketball team fall behind in the playoffs, I announce to you and to everyone else who can hear me, "I am disgusted with this team. For two cents, I'd sell my tickets to the finals." Should the law treat my statement as an offer that invites your acceptance?

If it was apparent to you that I was upset, and you should have known that I did not really intend to contract, the necessary sign of intent is lacking. Factors to be considered in determining whether I signaled intent include the correlation between the "offer" price and the value of the object, the witnessing of the precipitating incident (here, the temporary taking of the lead by the opposing basketball team), whether I appeared excited and upset, and whether we had discussed the sale of the tickets at some previous time.

When a statement is made in jest, there is no manifestation of the intent to contract. Informal bets often fall into this category: "I'll bet you a hundred dollars you can't throw the ball through the hoop," or "The Mets will win more games than the Yankees this year; I'll bet my house on it." Similarly, the prankster who says, "I'd pay $1,000 to anyone who gives my boss an exploding cigar," cannot be taken seriously. Yet the jester must be careful if the joke relates to a situation where the other party might take the joke seriously, as the following case illustrates.

Lucy v. Zehmer

Supreme Court of Appeals of Virginia
84 S.E. 2d 516 (1954)

In December 1952, W. O. Lucy met Zehmer at a restaurant and once again at-   FACTS
tempted to buy Zehmer's farm. While both men were drinking liquor, Lucy bet that
Zehmer wouldn't take $50,000 for the farm. Zehmer asked if Lucy would give him
$50,000 for the farm. Lucy said yes. Although Zehmer later claimed that his offer was
made in jest and that he "was high as a Georgia pine" during the transaction, he and his
wife signed the back of a guest check and wrote, "We hereby agree to sell to W. O.
Lucy the Ferguson Farm for $50,000 complete." Zehmer refused to give over title, and
Lucy sued for specific performance of the contract by which it was alleged that the
Zehmers had sold the farm.

Did Zehmer's words and actions manifest an intent to sell his farm to Lucy?   ISSUE

The court ruled in favor of Lucy. Although an agreement, or mutual assent, is   DECISION
essential for a valid contract, the law infers that a person's intention corresponds to the
reasonable meaning of his words and acts. Because Zehmer's words and acts, judged by
a reasonable standard, manifested an intention to agree, it is immaterial what the real
but unexpressed state of his mind might have been. There was enough evidence that the
contract was a serious business transaction rather than a casual jest.

Advertisement of Goods for Sale   Do advertisements in the newspaper constitute
offers? If they do, the reader can go into the store and say "I accept" and thereby
create a contractual obligation for the store. If five people or 50 or 5,000 accept, the
store would have to fulfill all acceptances or else be liable for breach of contract.

Courts have interpreted the law as not imposing such an unfair burden on each
business advertiser. Thus, as a general principle, advertisements do not constitute
offers. However, if the advertiser uses language in the advertisement that, to the
reasonable reader, expresses a commitment to contract, the courts will enforce a
contract resulting from the offeree's acceptance of the seller's advertisement. The
case below illustrates an exception to the general rule of law, although it has become a
classic involving the possible interpretation of advertisements as offers.

Lefkowitz v. Great Minneapolis Surplus Store

Supreme Court of Minnesota
86 N.W. 2d 689 (1957)

On April 6, 1956, the Great Minneapolis Surplus Store published the following   FACTS
advertisement in a local newspaper:

**Saturday 9 A.M. Sharp
3 Brand New Fur
Coats Worth to
$100.00
First Come First
Served
$1
Each**

The following week, the defendant store published a similar advertisement in the same newspaper which mentioned the intention to sell "1 Black Lapin Stole for $1." When plaintiff Lefkowitz responded to each advertisement by being the first to present himself at the store, Great Minneapolis refused to honor its advertisement. It stated on the first visit that by a "house rule" the offer was intended for women only and sales would not be made to men, and on the second visit that plaintiff knew defendant's house rules. Lefkowitz brought suit against Great Minneapolis to enforce a contract he claimed to have accepted to buy the fur offered for sale in the newspaper advertisement.

ISSUE   Was a contract formed when Lefkowitz presented himself at the store and indicated he was purchasing the stole?

DECISION   The court ruled in favor of Lefkowitz. Whether a newspaper advertisement is an offer (rather than an invitation to make an offer) depends on the legal intention of the parties and the surrounding circumstances. The test of whether a binding obligation may originate in advertisements addressed to the general public is whether the facts show that some performance was promised in positive terms in return for something requested. The newspaper advertisement was a clear, definite, and explicit offer of sale by defendant. The plaintiff, who fulfilled the terms of the offer by appearing first to be served at defendant's place of business, was entitled to have the defendant perform the contract or to receive damages from the defendant.

Definite and Certain Terms

The second requirement of an offer is that it be definite and certain regarding the essential terms of the proposed contract. As the court in *Lefkowitz* concluded, when the offeror's statement is clear, definite, and explicit and leaves nothing open for negotiation, an offer (not merely an invitation to make an offer) has been made. What terms must be expressed in order for a statement to be construed as an offer?

If I offer to sell you my 1985 Ford Fiesta and you agree, do we have a contract? In this example, the obvious problem is that we have omitted the most basic element of an agreement — the price. Would a court seek to complete our agreement for us? A court has no ready reference point to use to enforce this agreement. Because a court does not wish to make a contract where the parties themselves have failed to do so, it would conclude that no offer was made by me when I proposed to sell you my car. Therefore, your agreement in response was not an acceptance of an offer. No contract resulted.

An offer must define the essential terms of performance by both the offeror and offeree. One of the essential terms in an offer is the subject matter of the proposed transaction. Is the offeror going to sell a car? What car? Does the sale of the car include the sale of the ski rack on top of the car? The offer must reasonably identify the subject matter.

A second essential term that an offer must include is the quantity of items being offered. A farmer proposing to sell wheat to a bakery must specify how much wheat he wants to sell. A furniture dealer's agreement to sell you ''bedroom furniture'' for $500 would be too vague unless it specified how many items were included in the offer.

Finally, as we have seen, the price of the item offered for sale must be specified. The price is specified if it is either fixed or easily determinable. My offer to lend you $1,000 at the prime interest rate in effect at Continental Illinois National Bank is specific. Although the offer does not state the exact rate of interest, the rate is determinable.

Communication of the Offer

General Rule   The third requirement that a valid offer must meet is to be communicated to the party for whom the offer is intended. The communication may be expressed or implied. For example, if the offeree learns of an offer from a third person who is not the offeror, and the offer is a general one which may be accepted by anyone who learns of it, the offeree would have the power to accept the communicated offer. Communication is usually not a problem with offers.

The Reward Offer   A reward is an offer for a unilateral contract. It is not unusual for someone to perform the act bargained for in the reward offer without knowing about the reward. If that occurs, then under the technical rules of contract law, the party performing the act is not entitled to the reward. But that does not represent sound policy when viewed in the context of the reasonable expectations of our society. Most people expect that rewards will be paid if their terms are met. As a consequence, many state laws provide that rewards are enforceable regardless of whether the person performing the specified act first learned of the offer of a reward.

The Fine Print Offer   Consumers often are asked to sign contracts that contain fine print provisions, many of which are quite harsh. For example, a clause may increase the contracted price of a car before delivery. Most consumers signing such contracts are unaware of the existence or the legal effect of such clauses. Some courts have refused to enforce them on the theory that they were not really communicated to the consumer. Consider the following case.

Green's Executors v. Smith

Special Court of Appeals of Virginia
131 S.E. 845 (1926)

FACTS
Plaintiff Howard Smith sued Mrs. A. D. Green to recover damages he had been compelled to pay to John L. Moore for injuries inflicted in an automobile accident. Smith owned a garage where Mrs. Green contracted for the storage of her car and for its delivery between her home and the garage. In October 1918, Mrs. Green's car injured Moore while it was being driven to the garage by one of Smith's employees. Smith contended that he was not liable, because he had sent Mrs. Green a "folder" with her monthly bill. The folder listed garage fees and contained a paragraph that absolved him of liability for negligence by his employees in the act of moving cars to or from the garage. Mrs. Green responded that the parties had no such contract. The lower court ruled in favor of Smith and ordered Green to repay him for the damages he had paid to Moore. Mrs. Green having died, the case was appealed by those responsible for her estate.

ISSUE
Had Green entered into a contract absolving Smith of liability?

DECISION
The court ruled in favor of Green's estate. Mutuality of assent — the meeting of the minds of the parties — is an essential element of a contract. Before one can be held to have accepted the offer of another, there must have been some form of communication of the offer. Otherwise there can be no assent and in consequence no contract. Whether Mrs. Green agreed to and was bound by the terms of the folder depended on whether Smith communicated the terms to Mrs. Green. The court ruled that there was nothing on the face of the folder, nor in its form or character to indicate that it contained a contract that Mrs. Green should read carefully and consider herself bound by. A person cannot be considered to be bound by conditions of which he is ignorant, even though they are contained in a written document, unless the person knows or should have known that the document contains such terms.

TERMINATION OF THE OFFER

An offer may be terminated before its acceptance. The termination of an offer may occur in a variety of ways, as the following sections of this chapter indicate.

Lapse of Time

The offer itself may provide that it will terminate within a specified period. Once that period expires, the offer is terminated. Thus an offer that states "This offer is good until May 30" would terminate after that date. The offeror should carefully specify the duration of the offer.

Even if the offeror does not provide for a specific termination date, the offer will lapse after a "reasonable time." How long is a reasonable time? The answer must vary with the circumstances surrounding the offer. An offer to sell real estate such as a home or an office building will probably last for weeks or months. An offer to buy stocks or commodities may be open for acceptance for only minutes.

Further, the definition of reasonable time is affected by the context in which an offer is made. If you seek to buy souvenir pennants to sell outside the Super Bowl, your offer to the supplier would probably terminate on the day of the game. The timing of any prior dealings between the offeror and offeree are relevant in determining what is a reasonable time for an offer to remain open.

The case which follows is one illustration of a court's consideration of reasonable time.

Ward v. Board of Education of Harrison Township Rural School District

Court of Appeals of Ohio
173 N.E. 634 (1930)

On June 4, 1928, the Board of Education accepted Ina Ward's application to teach school in its district. The Board decided that Ward would have until July 2 to accept its employment offer by signing a contract. Ward received the contract in the mail on June 18. She signed it and returned it to the Board on July 5. In the meantime, on July 2, the Board had hired another teacher for Ward's position. Ward claimed that she had not been notified of the deadline. There was evidence to suggest that she had waited until another employment application had been denied before she responded to the Board's offer. Ward sued the Board for the amount she claimed was due her under the employment contract.   FACTS

Had Ward responded to the Board's offer within a reasonable time?   ISSUE

The court ruled in favor of the Board. Accepting Ward's contention that she had not been notified of the deadline, the law would allow her reasonable time to accept an offer made by mail. The law would require, however, that she act with "due diligence" to respond to the offer within that reasonable time period. If Ward unduly delayed her acceptance of the offer, the Board would not be bound by that acceptance. The court decided that Ward did not use "due diligence" in responding to the Board's offer and that her acceptance did not bind the Board to employ her. The court supported its finding with the evidence that Ward did not return the Board's contract until she had been denied employment elsewhere.   DECISION

Revocation by the Offeror

General Rule   A **revocation** is a withdrawal of an offer by the offeror. The law requires that an effective revocation be communicated to the offeree. Generally, the revocation must be received by the offeree before he or she has effectively accepted   **Revocation** recall of an offer by the offeror the offer. Although an offeror generally can revoke the offer at any time prior to its acceptance, there are several exceptions to this rule.

Even if the offer states that it will remain open for a specified time, the rule allowing the offeror to revoke at any time prior to acceptance usually applies. For example, if an offeror wrote on February 27 that the offer would expire in ten days but decided on March 2 to revoke the offer before the end of the ten-day period, can he or she do so after promising to hold the offer open for ten days? The general answer is yes, as long as no acceptance of the offer has been made by the offeree. There are, however, several situations in which the offeror may not revoke an offer.

Option contract a contract which mandates that an offer be kept open for a set period of time

Limitations   If someone enters into a contract with an offeror to keep an offer open for a certain time, that **option contract** will be enforced. The offer cannot be revoked for the period specified in the contract. For example, a school board offers to sell a school that it no longer uses to Acme Development Corporation for $100,000. Acme is thinking of buying the school if it can interest several businesses in renting space there after the building has been remodeled. Acme might agree with the school board to enter into an option contract, by which, in consideration of a payment of $5,000, the school board gives Acme 90 days to accept or reject the offer. During those 90 days, the school board cannot sell to someone else, nor can it revoke its offer to Acme.

Firm offer an offer that cannot be revoked for a certain time

Second, the Uniform Commercial Code (Section 2-205) provides that if an offer to buy or sell goods contains a promise that it will be held open for a specific time, it cannot be revoked by the offeror during that time. This **firm offer** rule requires that the offeror be a merchant in the kind of goods being offered and that the offer must be in writing and signed by the offeror. Finally, the time during which the offer is irrevocable is limited to three months. This rule does not apply to offers that are not made by merchants or that do not involve the sale of goods. Nevertheless, most commercial transactions (other than those for services or for real estate) fall within the terms of the firm offer rule.

Third, if the offer requires that an act be performed in order for acceptance to occur, the law limits the offeror's power to revoke the offer while the offeree is in the process of performing the requested act of acceptance. In recent years, the trend of many decisions has been to suspend the offeror's right of revocation until the offeree has had a reasonable time to complete the act called for in the offer.

Finally, to avoid unfairness, courts usually limit a person's right to revoke if an offer is made in such a way that the offeree reasonably expects that the offer will not be revoked. The courts usually require:

Promissory estoppel doctrine used to insure fairness in situations in which one party has justifiably relied on the promise of another

1. that the offeror expected the offeree to rely on the statement

2. that the offeree in fact does rely on the statement, and

3. that the offeree who has relied on the statement is harmed by doing so. The principle of protecting those who reasonably rely on the promises of others is called **promissory estoppel**. Promissory estoppel is discussed in detail in Chapters 7 and 11.

Rejection by the Offeree

An offer ends when it is rejected by the offeree. A person may reject an offer either by directly stating so or by responding with a counteroffer that seeks to change the terms of the offer. But a person who merely seeks information about the terms of the offer (Must I pay cash? What credit terms are available? Is that your lowest price?) is neither accepting nor rejecting the offer.

In short then, if a person responds to an offer with an acceptance, the parties have made a contract. If the response is a rejection, the offer terminates and the parties must begin new negotiations. If the response is an inquiry, the offer remains for the offeree's review. When the response is a counteroffer, the original offer terminates. In its place is a new offer that may be accepted and turned into a contract.

Destruction of the Subject Matter

Hoper offers to sell his Porsche to Allen, who is familiar with the car. Although neither knew it, five minutes after the offer was made a landslide destroyed Hoper's garage and the car. Such destruction of the subject matter of the offer by an "act of God" terminates the offer.

Suppose instead that Farmer offers to sell 10,000 bushels of apples to Processor and that Farmer's apples are destroyed by an act of God, such as a tornado. A court is likely to conclude that the offer is terminated because the subject matter of the offer (Farmer's apples) has been destroyed. However, if Processor could prove that Farmer had offered to sell 10,000 bushels of apples *in general* rather than apples raised specifically on Farmer's property, then the offer would still be valid. In that case, Farmer could buy apples from someone else; the fact that Farmer's apples had been destroyed would not mean that all apples were unavailable.

ACCEPTANCE

A valid offer gives the person to whom it is offered the power to accept it. To result in a contract, the acceptance of the offer must meet three basic criteria. First, like the offer itself, the acceptance must be made with an intent to form a contract. Second, the person accepting must communicate the acceptance to the person making the offer. Third, the acceptance must satisfy all conditions and terms established by the offeror. Any change in the terms of the offer usually results in a rejection that terminates the offer.

INTENT TO ACCEPT

The law is not concerned with an offeree's state of mind. Instead, it asks what the person accepting an offer said or did to indicate to a reasonable person his or her intent.

Actions alone (without verbal or written expression) on the part of the offeree can constitute an acceptance. For example, Widget Company sends Gizmo Incorporated five dozen widgets, with an invoice stating their purchase price. Gizmo says nothing but uses the widgets. It has shown by its action an intent to accept Widget's offer to sell.

The following case shows a court determining that a person's actions can constitute an acceptance of an offer, even if that person argues that he did not "express" any acceptance.

_____ _Crouch v. Marrs_ _____

Supreme Court of Kansas
430 P.2d 204 (1967)

FACTS   Crouch wished to buy a silica processing plant from Purex. Crouch received a letter from Purex, signed by Frank Knox, indicating that Purex would sell the plant for $500. Crouch thought that $500 was too much and on March 19 wrote to Knox asking him to consider taking $300. This letter was not answered. On April 26, Crouch again wrote to Knox, offering to pay $500 and enclosing a check for that amount. The check was endorsed by Knox and deposited.

Meanwhile, on April 17 Purex, through Knox, sold the silica plant to Martin Asche, who in turn sold it to defendant Roy Marrs. On April 27, Knox sent Crouch a telegram stating that Crouch's counteroffer of April 26 was unacceptable and that the check had been deposited by mistake. Knox later sent a $500 check to reimburse Crouch. Plaintiff Crouch brought this action against Marrs in order to prevent him from interfering with the property which Crouch claimed to have purchased.

ISSUE   Did Knox's actions constitute an acceptance of Crouch's offer to buy the plant?

DECISION   The Court ruled in favor of Crouch, saying that Knox's endorsement and deposit of the check constituted an acceptance of the offer to buy the plant. An offer may be accepted by performance of a specified act as well as by an affirmative answer. When the offeree acts as though he or she owns the thing offered (in this instance, the check), this act is evidence of acceptance. Therefore, Knox's action constituted an acceptance of the offer even though he did not actually "express" or subjectively intend an acceptance.

COMMUNICATION OF
ACCEPTANCE

An acceptance must be communicated to be effective. A person may use any means to communicate acceptance.

Bilateral or Unilateral Agreement

If the offer is a promise for an act (a unilateral contract), the offeree must perform the requested act. For example, the promise, "I'll pay you $10 if you type my paper by tomorrow night," requires the offeree to type the paper by tomorrow night to accept the offer to pay $10. A person making an offer also may seek the offeree's **forbearance** in not doing something that the offeree might otherwise do. Thus the statement "I promise to pay you $100 if you don't smoke cigarettes for a year" asks the offeree unilaterally to forbear from an act that he or she might otherwise do.

Forbearance an agreement to refrain from something that a person could otherwise do

To accept an offer, a person needs only to perform the specified act. The person does not need first to communicate to the offeror that he or she intends to perform the requested act. The person only needs to communicate that the act has been done.

In contrast, if the offer is one to enter into a bilateral contract, in which each party makes a promise ("I'll promise to sell you my 1980 Trans Am if you promise to pay me $300 cash"), the offeree must communicate his or her promise in order to accept the offer. If there is uncertainty about what the offer requires of an offeree, most courts interpret agreements as bilateral promises that require a communication from the offeree.

Means of Communication

Most kinds of communication that notify the person making an offer of the offeree's intent to accept the offer are effective. But the offeree also must comply with all the terms of the offer. If the offer dictates that the person accepting must communicate by certain means, or at a certain time, or place, the person must comply.

When an offer specifies the means by which a person is to communicate his or her acceptance, the acceptance takes effect when the person complies. If an offer states, "You may mail in your acceptance," the acceptance is effective at the moment the offeree deposits a letter of acceptance with the postal service, even if the letter is delayed or lost. The offeree has effectively communicated acceptance by delivering it to the authorized agent. Even if the offer does not expressly authorize a particular means of communication, the way in which the offer was communicated is an acceptable way in which to respond. A mailed offer implies that the person can accept by mail. Under the "mailbox rule," the acceptance takes effect when mailed.

If a person making an offer does not specify a particular means of communication, most courts rule that the person accepting may use any "reasonable means of communication" in accepting the offer. Reasonableness depends on the subject matter of the offer, the custom in a particular business, and the prior conduct of the parties. For example, if it is customary in a business to mail acceptances, or if the parties have mailed other contracts, an acceptance would be effective when mailed. If an acceptance is sent by another means, it takes effect only upon receipt.

Pribil v. Ruther

Supreme Court of Nebraska
262 N.W. 2d 460 (1978)

Defendant Ruther listed property for sale with Thor, a real estate broker. On April 12, plaintiff Pribil made an offer to purchase the property for $68,000. The offer was made on a form known as a Uniform Purchase Agreement, which included a space for written acceptance of the offer. Mrs. Ruther and her husband signed the acceptance and

FACTS

asked one of Thor's office employees to send a copy to Pribil. This copy was post-marked "April 15, P.M." and was received by Pribil on April 16.

Meanwhile, Mrs. Ruther became dissatisfied with the transaction when she discovered that a test well had been drilled on the property. She testified that she called Thor, the real estate agent, the next morning (April 14) and said that she was going to "terminate the contract." Thor testified that Mrs. Ruther had the date wrong and that the conversation took place at 11:42 A.M. on April 15 and that he immediately contacted plaintiff Pribil.

Pribil sued to enforce the contract whereby Pribil agreed to buy real estate owned by Ruther.

ISSUE   Did Ruther's acceptance become effective before her change of mind about selling the property was communicated to Pribil?

DECISION   The Court ruled in favor of defendant Ruther. An express contract is proved by evidence of a definite offer and an unconditional acceptance. When the offer requires a promise on the part of the offeree, a communication of the acceptance is essential. The signing of the acceptance on the Uniform Purchase Agreement by the defendant did not make the contract effective. Instead, it was necessary that there be some communication of the acceptance to the plaintiff. There must be an irrevocable action, such as depositing the acceptance in the mail, so that it is placed beyond the power or control of the sender before the acceptance becomes effective and the contract is made. Delivery to the agent of the defendant (Thor's office) was not delivery to the plaintiff as it did not put the acceptance beyond the control of the defendant. There is no evidence that the acceptance was deposited in the mail before Thor called the plaintiff and informed him that the defendant would not sell the property. Therefore, the acceptance did not become effective before the defendant rejected the offer.

SATISFYING TERMS
OF THE OFFER

Generally, an acceptance must *mirror* the terms of the offer. But in some situations, the law or facts imply terms that may not have been expressed in the offer. For example, if you offer to sell me your house for $75,000 and in response I state, "I accept your offer, subject to my attorney checking that you have good title to the property," my response is considered an acceptance. The law implies that the person offering to sell a house guarantees that he or she has a good title to it. My response has not changed the terms of your offer. Similarly, suppose that it is customary in an industry that an offer to sell goods for a stated price implies that the buyer has "thirty days, same as cash" to pay for them. The buyer who expresses in an acceptance "I'll accept your offer if the normal credit terms are extended" is not varying the terms of the offer. Those credit terms were an unexpressed part of the original offer.

The general rule that any response that varies the terms of an offer cannot be considered an acceptance has proved unworkable in commercial transactions where each party has form documents that it sends in response to inquiries. The "battle of the forms" arises because each party wants to be the one whose form controls the transaction.

For example, the buyer's form to the seller might say:

> We offer to buy 500 widgets from you at $100 each. The goods are to be shipped to us F.O.B. our plant. They must be packaged in cartons of 50 each. Payment will be due from us 60 days after receipt of the widgets. No arbitration. No variation in the terms of this offer can be made without our written consent.

Seller has received a definite offer. It wants to sell the widgets, but on slightly different terms, and responds with its own form:

> We have received your offer and are glad to contract with you. Our goods will be shipped to you F.O.B. your plant. They will be packaged in cartons of 100 each. Disputes will be submitted to arbitration. Payment will be due from you 30 days after receipt of the widgets. Thank you for your order.

Do the parties have a contract? Clearly, there is an offer, but have the terms of the offer been accepted? Under common law, if the terms of the offer are not mirrored by the terms of the acceptance, no contract results. But suppose the parties act as if there is a contract, sending and accepting the goods without protest. Later a dispute arises over the terms of payment. The seller argues that the dispute must be submitted to arbitration.

Whether the seller is correct that the dispute must be submitted to arbitration depends on how the forms are treated. Under common law, the seller's form would be considered a counteroffer that was accepted by the buyer's actions in taking the goods. This is called the **last shot doctrine,** because the last document exchanged before the parties perform controls the transaction. Under that rule, the seller's form controls, and abritration is required.

last shot doctrine the principle that the last document exchanged before performance contains the terms of the contract

The Uniform Commercial Code (Section 2-207) establishes a different rule for the battle of the forms. The UCC rule is important because it applies to most situations in which buyers and sellers each use their own forms. (Consumers rarely use their own forms.) The UCC provides that when two merchants use forms, any additional or different terms found on the acceptance form become part of the contract. This rule lists the following exceptions:

1. The offeror has stated in the offer that he or she will agree only on the basis of his or her terms.

2. The variant terms materially alter the existing contract.

3. The offeror has objected or objects within a reasonable time to the variant terms.

In effect, the UCC rule allows changes in a contract offer only if the changes are not substantial. But even minor changes fail to become part of the contract if the offeror objects to them before or after getting them. The result is a contract based essentially on the offeror's terms.

In our widget example, the buyer's form was the offer. The seller's form, which proposed arbitration, was the acceptance. Thus arbitration would become part of the contract unless it materially altered the contract. Many courts have found arbitration to be a material change. Given that interpretation, arbitration materially changed the terms of the offer. The seller's form would not become part of the contract, and there would be no arbitration.

The following case involves a dispute over a clause in a form that limits a manufacturer's liability for defective products.

Air Products and Chemical, Inc. v. Fairbanks Morse, Inc.

Supreme Court of Wisconsin
206 N.W. 2d 414 (1973)

FACTS   Air Products and Chemical, Inc., bought large electric motors from defendant Fairbanks Morse, Inc. The motors turned out to contain defective parts. Defendant had sent plaintiff an "acknowledgment of order" form. It contained the following printed at the bottom of the front page in reasonably bold type:

> YOUR ORDER . . . SHALL BE GOVERNED BY THE PROVISIONS ON THE REVERSE SIDE HEREOF UNLESS YOU NOTIFY US TO THE CONTRARY WITHIN 10 DAYS OR BEFORE SHIPMENT WHICHEVER IS EARLIER

The reverse side of the form stipulated:

> The Company nowise assumes any responsibility or liability with respect to use, purpose, or suitability, and shall not be liable for damages of any character, whether direct or consequential, for defect, delay, or otherwise, its sole liability and obligation being confined to the replacement in the manner aforesaid of defectively manufactured guaranteed parts failing within the time stated.

Fairbanks contended that the provision became part of the contract, because Air Products did not notify them of an objection to it. Air Products contended that its right to rely on the implied fitness of the engines and consequential damages if the engines did not operate as reasonably expected were not limited by the provision on the back of the form because it was never assented to and therefore never became part of the contract.

ISSUE   Did Fairbanks's printed disclaimer of liability become part of the final contract?

DECISION   The court ruled in favor of Air Products. The UCC (Section 2-207) states that in dealings between merchants, "additional terms" shall become part of the contract unless "they materially alter it." The court found that the disclaimer contained in Fairbanks's "acknowledgment of order" materially altered the agreement. If terms materially alter what would otherwise be confirmed by acceptance of an offer, they do not become part of the contract unless the buyer expressly agrees to them. The disclaimer for consequential loss was material enough to require express conversation between the parties over its inclusion or exclusion in the contract.

PROBLEMS WITH ACCEPTANCE

In many situations, the offeror controls the form and manner of the acceptance, because the acceptance must conform to the terms of the offer. Thus the person who makes an offer often has the power to change many of the rules discussed in this chapter. The person making the offer simply adds certain requirements. For example, he or she may specify that the offeree's silence will constitute acceptance.

Silence as Acceptance

Inaction and silence usually are not regarded as manifestations of agreement. However, some exceptions to this rule occur, usually because of the terms suggested in the offer. Book clubs, record clubs, wine clubs, and gourmet clubs often make agreements under which someone who receives merchandise is considered to have accepted the "monthly offer" if that person is silent and does not tell the club that he or she does not want the merchandise. The exceptions recognized by the law usually occur in one of three situations:

1. If the past transactions of the parties show their intent to regard silence as an acceptance, that intent becomes a part of their future transactions. Here, the *course of dealing* between the parties in past transactions is the basis for finding their present intent to have silence constitute acceptance.

2. The *initial agreement* between the parties constitutes the basis for treating silence by the offeree as acceptance. Thus the member of the book, record, or wine club signs a written agreement stating that the member who does not send in the card or notice rejecting the monthly offering agrees to pay for the items received. The member agrees that he or she does not have to affirmatively express his or her acceptance each month. Silence on the part of the member is a method of accepting the club's monthly offering.

3. If the offeree *uses the goods,* the courts consider the actions and silence to constitute acceptance. This problem occurs most often with magazines and newspapers sent to people who didn't order them. Courts usually consider that, because the offeror is in business and does not intend a gift, the person who receives them and reads them is assumed to have agreed to pay for them. However, most states now have statutes that allow the recipient of unsolicited merchandise, particularly merchandise sent through the mail, to treat it as a gift. The Postal Reorganization Act provides that mailing unsolicited merchandise is an unfair method of competition unless the product is marked "sample" or is sent by a charity. The act also provides that the recipient may treat the received merchandise as a gift.

CANCELLATION OF ACCEPTANCE

If someone has accepted an offer, the offer no longer can be revoked by the offeror because it has become part of a contract. Similarly, an offeree who has accepted an offer generally is not free to reject the offer later on. Neither party can reverse its original position.

Even so, statutes in many states allow one of the contracting parties to cancel an acceptance (or to terminate an offer) in certain circumstances. For example, a Michigan law grants to the buyer of goods or services costing more than $25 who has accepted an offer the right to revoke within three business days from the date of the transaction. The law applies only to sales made at a buyer's home, and only the buyer may cancel the acceptance. The law is intended to protect consumers from high pressure salespeople who force them to act in ways they might not with more time and less pressure. The three-day period is a "cooling-off period" when the buyer can reconsider.

SUMMARY

A valid offer must manifest contractual intent; provide a reference for determining the essential terms of the contract, and be communicated to the offeree. The existence of contractual intent is determined by objective standards. Social invitations and statements made obviously in jest or excitement are not enforceable offers. Advertisements generally are not considered offers unless they expressly state the contrary.

Offers must contain a clear statement of the subject matter and must provide a basis for determining the quantity of any item being sold and the sale price. The offer must be communicated to the offeree either directly, indirectly, or by publication. Problems sometimes arise with the communication of rewards or the fine print provisions on forms.

Offers may be terminated by lapse of a reasonable or stated time, revocation by the offeror, rejection by the offeree, or by the destruction of the subject matter of the offer. Both a revocation and a rejection must be communicated. An offeror loses the power to revoke when a firm offer is made, or payment is received to keep the offer open.

A valid acceptance must manifest contractual intent, must be communicated, and must be consistent with and satisfy all terms of the offer. In accepting a unilateral offer, the offeree must perform the requested act. In accepting a bilateral offer, the offeree must promise to perform as requested.

If the offeree replies by an authorized mode of communication or by the same one used in making the offer, the acceptance is effective when the offeree delivers the response to the communication agency. This rule is known as the implied agency, or "mailbox rule."

Under common law, acceptance must mirror the terms of the offer. But because merchants exchange printed forms in setting up transactions, the UCC has modified common law so that new terms in the acceptance document become part of the contract unless they materially affect the terms of the contract or are objected to by the offeror. The general rule is that silence is not acceptance, but there are a few special circumstances in which a failure to reply results in a contract.

Many states allow a consumer to cancel a contract in which he or she is sold goods or services at home, provided that the consumer acts within a designated time.

REVIEW PROBLEMS

1. What is the importance of a party's intent in a suit for a breach of contract?

2. Give examples of terms essential to an offer if it is to be considered "definite and certain."

3. Under what circumstances can an acceptance be considered to be communicated to the offeror before he or she has actual notice of it?

4. Explain the three basic situations in which the law recognizes exceptions to the rule that silence does not create acceptance.

5. Rofra, Inc., bid for plumbing work to be done for the board of education. The bid was sent in response to a "Solicitation for Connection of Building Sewer to the Public Sewer at Sunatsville Senior High School." Attached to that notice was a statement of "Contract General Provisions" that included a section reserving to the board the right "to reject any and all bids, in whole or in part." Rofra was the second low bidder for the work. The lowest bidder did not employ a master plumber, as the solicitation required. Plaintiff sued to enforce the contract, which it claimed existed as a result of the school board's solicitation offer and its own bid, which was the lowest bid conforming to the offer. Defendant claims no contract exists. Is plaintiff right?

6. Employer issued a booklet to employees stating that it had been customary for the company to make year-end bonus payments to employees, the amount depending on earnings and the discretion of the board of directors. An employee who read the booklet and continued working for the employer contends that by working, he has accepted the offer of a year-end bonus. Do you agree?

7. An antinuclear protest group, the Clamshell Alliance, sought permission to rent the National Guard armory in Portsmouth, New Hampshire, for the night of April 29, 1978. In response to that request, the Adjutant General on March 31 mailed an offer to rent the armory and specified the terms that had to be met. The offer specified that a signed acceptance be returned to the office of the Adjutant General. Cushing, a member of the alliance, received the offer on April 3. On that same date, he signed the acceptance on behalf of the alliance and placed the letter in the office's outbox. At 6:30 P.M. on April 4, Cushing received a telephone call from the Adjutant General revoking the offer. Cushing replied that he had already accepted the offer. The procedure followed in the alliance office indicates that letters placed in the office outbox one day usually are put in the mailbox before 5:00 P.M. the following day. The letter of acceptance sent by Cushing was received by the Adjutant General's office on April 6; the postmark on the letter was April 5. Was the acceptance effectively communicated before the offer was revoked?

8. In September 1969, Buske, an insurance agent, sent Roberts a renewal of an automobile liability policy that was a renewal of one defendant's father had previously held. Roberts accepted the policy and paid the premium. In September 1970, just prior to the expiration date of the policy, Buske sent a renewal notice to Roberts. The notice stated that if Roberts did not wish to accept it, he must return it or be liable for the premium. Roberts made no response to that notice or to subsequent ones sent to him. Roberts had in fact purchased a policy from another company, but Buske did not learn of that fact until December. The insurance agent says the Roberts's silence constituted his acceptance of the offer to renew the policy. Do you agree?

9. On December 15, Patrick wrote to Kleine about the lot she owned. Patrick's letter said: "If you have not sold, I, of course, am the logical purchaser. ˙. . . I hope I shall have the pleasure of hearing from you soon." On December 16,

Kleine responded by letter to Patrick and said: "If you should be interested in my lot, I would be glad to hear from you. The size of the lot is 20 × 100. Price $1,000 (One thousand dollars)." On December 18, Patrick telegraphed Kleine: "Will accept your proposition of $1,000 dollars for lot 35 in block 7906. Will get contract and check to you within a day or so." On December 19, Patrick followed with a letter: "Enclosed find contracts in the usual form and also my check for $100 as evidence of good faith. Please sign and return one copy so the title company can institute its search." On December 23, Kleine returned Patrick's $100 check and the contract and stated in her letter that the property had been sold. Patrick sues to enforce his contract with Kleine. Does he have a valid contract?

10. Scheck in writing offered to sell real estate to a specified prospective buyer and agreed to pay a percentage of the sales price as a commission to the broker. The offer fixed a six-day time limit for acceptance. Scheck then revoked the offer. On the morning of the sixth day, the broker received notice of Scheck's revocation. Later that day, the offeree accepted the offer that the broker had given to him. Does the revocation by Scheck to the offeree also revoke the broker's power to act on behalf of Scheck? If the broker had already begun to perform the offer to sell the property to the prospective purchaser, would the offer then be considered irrevocable?

11. Employee sues an employer to enforce an alleged contract to pay the employee a bonus and commission. The agreement provided that the amount of bonus and commission would be determined three months later, after marketing operations for a new product had begun. However, no later agreement appears to have been made. Is there an offer capable of acceptance by the employee?

12. Westside & Hurble entered into an agreement on April 5, 1963, wherein Hurble, for $50, was given a 60-day option to purchase certain real estate. The option provided that the offer by Westside to sell the real estate at an agreed upon price was irrevocable. On May 2, 1963, Hurble sent Westside a letter stating that Hurble exercised its option and also noting that "as additional inducement for Hurble to exercise its option, you have agreed that all utilities, gas, water, sewer, and electricity, will be extended to the property prior to the closing date. The contract of sale is hereby amended to provide seller shall extend all utility lines to the property before the closing date. Please sign this letter to indicate your acceptance of the amendment." On May 14, Hurble sent Westside another letter instructing it to disregard the proposed amendment in the letter of May 2 and that it now was exercising its option without amendment. Has Hurble accepted Westside's offer so as to create a contract?

13. Systems Engineering offered to sell equipment to Golden Dept. Co. Its proposal stated that a 25 percent down payment would have to be submitted with any order. It further required the proposal, signed by the purchaser, be submitted to and accepted by Systems Engineering to be effective. Golden telephoned Systems Engineering and stated that the proposal by Systems to sell its equipment to Golden was approved and that Systems should begin work. Systems responded, "We'll get on it immediately." Subsequently, a mistake in the quoted price was found by Systems Engineering, and it notified Golden. Golden said that it had a contract at the price quoted in the proposal of Systems. Do you agree?

14. During a two-year period, plaintiff, Carpet Mart, purchased a variety of carpeting from the defendant, Collins & Aikman. After checking that the terms agreed to in conversations were met, defendant sent an acknowledgment form to plaintiff for each of its orders. The following provision was printed on the acknowledgment form:

"The acceptance of your order is subject to all of the terms and conditions on the face and reverse side hereof, including arbitration, all of which are accepted by buyer; it supersedes buyer's order form, if any. It shall become a contract either (a) when signed and delivered by buyer to seller and accepted in writing by seller, or (b) at seller's option, when buyer shall have given to seller specification of assortments, delivery dates, shipping instructions, . . . or instructions to bill and hold as to all or any part of the merchandise herein described, or when buyer has received delivery of the whole or any part thereof, or when buyer has otherwise assented to the terms and conditions hereof."

Is the arbitration agreement on the back of the acknowledgment form sent to the Carpet Mart by Collins & Aikman a part of the contract between them?

CHAPTER 7

Consideration

CHAPTER OBJECTIVES

After reading this chapter, you should be able to:

1. Explain why consideration is required before a contract is enforced.

2. Explain how legal detriment differs from economic and social costs and benefits.

3. Distinguish between adequacy and sufficiency of consideration.

4. State why an illusory promise is not enforceable.

5. Describe the typical cases of insufficient consideration.

6. Describe UCC rules regarding consideration.

7. Describe the role of consideration in bargaining.

8. Explain promissory estoppel as a way to enforce contracts.

No legal system enforces all promises. For example, a promise to undertake a social obligation — to come for dinner or to attend a wedding — would not be enforced by any court. The mere fact that one person promises something to another creates no legal duty and makes no remedy available if the person does not carry out the promise. The problem before the courts has been to determine which promises should be enforced and which should not.

The preceding chapter examined the requirements of a valid offer and acceptance as the essential elements of an agreement. Although agreement is essential to the formation of a contract, not all agreements are contracts. This chapter focuses on the additional element that is generally necessary if an agreement is to rise to the level of a contract. This element is the consideration.

Consideration is the exchange element of a contract. It is what induces the parties' agreement. It is what one party must give to another to make the other party legally obligated to perform its promise; the quid pro quo of the agreement. If there is no consideration there is no contract, and this is true even if there has been a valid offer and acceptance.

Consideration is the legal obligation that a person takes on. This person is a **promisee.** A promisee bargains with someone who makes a promise — the **promisor.** This bargained exchange is the consideration.

Society benefits from the fair enforcement of promises. A society that refused to enforce any promise would place people in risky positions. A promisor's word would be only as good as his or her reputation for performance. But no society can enforce all promises. Some promises are unreasonable or harmful. The existence of consideration is treated as evidence that the promisee's expectation is reasonable and that nonperformance would injure the community.

Consideration a legal obligation incurred as the bargained exchange for a promise

Promisee a person who receives a promise

Promisor a person who makes a promise to a promisee

TABLE 7-1   Consideration in a Contract

Situation	John carelessly runs into David's car	
Agreement	John promises to pay $500	David promises not to sue over car accident
Bilateral contract	promise	promise
Consideration	through promise incurs obligation	through promise gives up right

The concept of consideration can be illustrated by a simple example. John carelessly drives his car into David's. David's car is damaged and he has a right to sue John. John promises to pay David $500 and David promises that he will not sue over the car accident. The contract is supported by consideration. John has undertaken a new obligation — to pay David. David has given up a legal right — to sue John. The agreement is illustrated in Table 7.1.

The following discussion examines two components of consideration: the legal detriment of the promisee and the bargained exchange for the promise.

LEGAL DETRIMENT

Legal detriment
legal obligation
stemming from a
contract agreement
to take on a duty
or give up a right

A person incurs **legal detriment** by voluntarily agreeing to assume a duty or to give up a right. A person must do or promise to do what he or she was not legally obligated to do, or the person must promise not to do what he or she has a right to do.

A *legal* detriment is not the same as real detriment or loss. In deciding whether someone has incurred a legal detriment, the courts do not focus on whether that person suffered economic or physical loss. The courts focus on whether the person agreed either to assume a *duty* or to relinquish *right*. The following case illustrates the distinction between the two kinds of detriments.

Hamer v. Sidway

Court of Appeals of New York, Second Division
27 N.E. 256 (1891)

FACTS   In March 1869, William E. Story, Sr. promised his nephew the sum of $5,000 if the nephew would refrain from drinking, smoking, swearing, and gambling until his 21st birthday. In January 1875, the nephew had reached his 21st birthday. Having satisfied all of the necessary conditions, he wrote to his uncle claiming the $5,000. The uncle replied that the nephew would get that money. But he asked to be allowed to hold it in the bank until he felt the nephew was capable of taking care of it. In 1879, the nephew turned over his claim to the $5,000 to his wife. In turn, she turned it over to the plaintiff. When the uncle died, plaintiff claimed the $5,000. But the executor of the estate denied the claim. The executor argued that the $5,000 was without consideration, because the nephew had benefited from the actions necessary to receive the reward.

Was the nephew's abstinence from drinking, smoking, swearing, and gambling consideration for a valid contract?

The court ruled in favor of the plaintiff. Consideration is necessary for a contract to be enforceable; the critical question in this case is what constitutes consideration. The court said:

> "Consideration" means not so much that one party is profiting as that the other abandons some legal right to the present, or limits his legal freedom of action in the future, as an inducement for the promise of the first.

Therefore, it is unimportant whether the nephew's action physically benefited him. The fact that he restricted his lawful freedom of action on the basis of his uncle's agreement to pay him $5,000 is sufficient consideration.

Adequacy vs. Sufficiency of Consideration

When deciding whether a contract is supported by consideration, it is important to distinguish between the **adequacy** of the consideration and the **sufficiency** of the consideration. Although the semantic distinction between these terms is small, the legal distinction between them is significant. So watch your language!

Adequacy
economic value of a consideration

The term "adequacy" refers to the quantity or value of the consideration. Courts do not generally inquire into the adequacy of the consideration; they are concerned only that there is a legally sufficient consideration, meaning that the promisee incurred a legal detriment in exchange for the promise. Thus any legal detriment constitutes valuable consideration no matter how economically inadequate it may be.

Sufficiency
presence of a legal detriment in exchange for a promise

For example, suppose that for $1 Penelope gave to Ring Telephone Company the right to install and maintain telephone wire over her land. Later Penelope finds out that other property owners have received much more money for giving the same rights to Ring. Penelope cannot later refuse to allow Ring on her land by arguing that she received an inadequate consideration for her promise to Ring. For Ring to obtain enforcement of Penelope's promise, Ring must show that Penelope received sufficient consideration for her promise. Ring would be able to obtain enforcement because, by paying $1 to Penelope, Ring relinquished the right it had to keep its money. Thus Ring incurred a legal detriment in exchange for Penelope's promise. A court would enforce her promise because the economic value of the consideration is not relevant in determining whether there is a valid consideration.

Courts do not inquire into the adequacy of consideration, because they should not be required to police the marketplace to protect people from their own imprudence. This policy of judicial self-restraint in dealing with economic matters is consistent with the common law notion that the courts do not make contracts for people. However, the rule assumes that the parties have freely entered into their agreement. Where this assumption is questioned, the courts *do* take into account the adequacy of consideration. If someone argues that a contract was made through fraud, misrepresentation, duress, undue influence, or mistake, a court will examine the adequacy of the consideration as evidence of the existence of those factors.

The only other circumstance in which a court examines the adequacy of consideration is in the equal exchange of interchangeable goods or the equal exchange of money. Goods that are *fungible* are indistinguishable and interchangeable. One carload of wheat cannot be distinguished from another; the carloads of wheat are thus fungible goods. Under the **fungible goods** doctrine, a contract calling for an exchange of equal amounts of wheat is not supported by consideration. Similarly, people who put a clause in their agreement that each has given the other $1 as consideration for the agreement will find that they have no contract because there is no consideration.

Unlike adequacy of consideration, sufficiency of consideration is readily examined by the courts. If what was given in exchange for a promise is insufficient to constitute consideration, there is no contract. Consideration requires a legal detriment bargained for and given in exchange for a promise. When what is given is not a legal detriment, then it is not sufficient to constitute consideration, and there is no contract.

Fungible goods
goods that are indistinguishable and interchangeable

Illusory Promises

Illusory promise
one which makes performance entirely discretionary for the promisor

Any promise that leaves it up to the promisor whether to perform is **illusory.** A person who promises to do something ''if I feel like it'' has not promised anything at all and has incurred no legal detriment. Even though people use promissory language, if the person making the promise is not required to do anything, the promise is illusory. An illusory promise is not sufficient consideration because nothing has been promised.

Although the rule that an illusory promise cannot serve as sufficient consideration is logical, the result of such a rule can be harsh. Two categories of promises illustrate this problem: cancellation of termination clauses and output/requirements contracts. We turn to those now.

Cancellation or Termination Clauses   Contracts often let one or both parties cancel obligations under certain circumstances. Suppose that two enter into a contract in which one promises to buy and the other promises to sell 500 widgets a month. The buyer has the right to cancel ''at any time without notice.'' That clause means that there is no contract. Lack of consideration makes the buyer's promise illusory. Because the buyer has the right to terminate the agreement at will and is not required to perform, the buyer has not actually assumed a duty to buy. If a cancellation clause allows a party to avoid an obligation at will, the contract is voidable. A contract that is voidable at the will of one of the parties is illusory.

However, the situation is different if the buyer is required to notify the seller that he or she is terminating the contract. Most courts hold that with a termination clause requiring notice ahead of time, the promisor incurs a legal detriment.

Additionally, many courts have held that when a termination clause contains no notice requirement, the requirement of a reasonable notice of termination is assumed. This assumption is made when it is clear that both parties intended to enter into a binding contract. This approach seeks to preserve the intent of the parties and reflects legislative and judicial reluctance to strike down an otherwise valid agreement on a technicality.

Output/Requirements Contracts   An **output contract** is an agreement to sell one's entire production of goods to a purchaser. A **requirements contract** is an agreement to purchase all one's requirements for a given product from the seller. Such contracts are useful, especially for new businesses. However, many courts once held that such agreements are illusory because they provide no specifications of how much of the product is to be sold or bought. The seller might choose not to produce to full capacity and the buyer might choose not to buy the product at all.

The UCC (Section 2-306) has legitimized output/requirements contracts by providing standards required for enforcement. It imposes an obligation to act in good faith on the party who determines the quantity. This good-faith obligation constitutes a sufficient consideration for any output or requirements contract.

The illusory promise problem is illustrated in the following case. Determine whether the court made the best decision in terms of both the law and business ethics. The decision predates the UCC.

Output contract one in which a producer agrees to sell the entire production of an item to a particular buyer

Requirements contract one in which a buyer agrees to purchase all of its requirements for an item from a particular supplier

---

Streich v. General Motors Corporation

Appellate Court of Illinois
126 N.E.2d 389 (1955)

Streich alleged that General Motors had entered into a contract with him to buy all of its requirements for air magnet valves between September 1, 1948, and August 31, 1949. During that time, General Motors ordered only 12 valves. Streich claimed that he had originally been led to believe that 1,600 or more valves would be needed and that therefore he had spent a great deal of money, time, and effort gathering the materials needed for production of the valves. General Motors contended that it did not promise to buy 1,600 valves in its purchase order.

FACTS

Did General Motors agree to purchase 1,600 valves from Streich?

ISSUE

The court ruled in favor of General Motors. The formal document involved here is merely an agreement by the seller to furnish a certain valve, at a certain price, in quantities designated by the buyer when and if it issues a purchase order for the same. No contract exists until the buyer orders a specified number of items. Until that time, the buyer has made no promise to do anything, and any implied promise in the original agreement is illusory. The court admitted that the agreement was deceptive (perhaps even unethical) but ruled that contract law required a decision in favor of defendant General Motors.

DECISION

The Preexisting Duty Rule

When people promise to do something that they are already obligated to do, they have not incurred a legal detriment. This is known as the **preexisting duty rule.** For example, people cannot promise not to commit crimes in return for payment

Preexisting duty rule the rule by

detriment is
incurred if a party
already is obligated
to perform by an
earlier contract or
law

because they have a preexisting duty not to commit crimes or torts. Thus some preexisting duties are created by law. Similarly, public officials cannot collect rewards for performing their duty. If a shopkeeper offers a $5,000 reward for the arrest and conviction of the person who burglarized his or her store, the police officer who diligently pursues and jails the offender may not collect that reward. The officer is already required by law to catch criminals and therefore has incurred no new legal detriment that would entitle him or her to enforcement of the promise of reward.

A preexisting duty also may be created by contract. When the promise of one party is merely a repetition of an existing promise and no additional duties are imposed, the promise does not constitute consideration. For example, suppose that Penelope hires Julius to repair her garage door. Julius and Penelope agree that the price of the repair will be $150. However, after starting work, Julius reconsiders his costs and asks Penelope to pay him $200. She agrees. Upon completion of the repair, Julius is entitled to only $150. Because Julius was already under contract to repair Penelope's door for $150, he has incurred no legal detriment in exchange for her promise to pay $50 more. Julius has merely agreed to finish the repair, which he was under a contractual duty to do already.

The preexisting duty rule is often criticized as illogical. In the above example, Penelope appears able to avoid the enforcement of her promise. But the reason for the rule is the concern that enforcement of the second promise would encourage coercion. In most of the cases where the preexisting duty rule is invoked, the second bargain was coerced. For example, a contractor might threaten a homeowner that unless she pays an extra $150, he will leave her roof half fixed. Where the facts do not show coercion, the courts have stretched doctrine to reach a more desired result.

For example, if in consideration for Penelope's promise to pay $50 more, Julius had agreed to do something, however slight, that was not called for in the original contract, Julius would have incurred a legal detriment. A court, searching for a way to enforce Penelope's promise, would seek to discover if Julius had agreed to undertake something not called for in his original contract in exchange for Penelope's promise. The addition of a new duty in exchange for Penelope's promise makes the promise enforceable without any conflict with the preexisting duty rule.

Another device for getting around the preexisting duty rule is for the parties to agree to rescind their old contract and make a new one. Contracts may be canceled and new ones made when the people involved mutually consent to the cancellation of the contracts. Furthermore, the cancellation itself is a contract and must be supported by consideration. In this case, the consideration usually takes the form of the parties' agreement to release each other from their obligations. When people rescind their earlier agreement and enter into a new one, there are actually three contracts: the original contract, the rescission contract, and the new contract.

Unforeseen
difficulties unan-
ticipated factors
that substantially
change expecta-
tions under a
contract

Some courts recognize an exception to the preexisting duty rule in cases where the second promise results from substantial **unforeseen difficulties** in performance. For example, if a contractor agreed to build a house and a tornado destroyed the half-built house, some courts would hold that an owner's subsequent promise to pay the contractor more is binding, even though the contractor has not agreed to do anything more than was called for by the original contract. The suspicion of coercion by the contractor is not present, and the owner might be criticized for promising to pay more to induce the contractor to continue but later disavowing the promise.

The following case illustrates some of the issues in the preexisting duty rule.

Levine v. Blumenthal

Supreme Court of New Jersey
186 A. 457 (1936)

FACTS

On April 16, 1931, William Levine agreed to lease a business site to Anne Blumenthal. Rent for the first year was to be $2,100, payable in monthly installments of $175 in advance. The second year the rent was scheduled to increase to $2,400, payable in monthly installments of $200. In April 1932, approximately one year into the lease term, Blumenthal told Levine that, due to adverse business conditions generally resulting from the Great Depression, she would be unable to pay the increased rent of $200. She asserted that if Levine insisted on the extra $25 a month, she would have to leave the building and perhaps go out of business altogether. Blumenthal claimed that Levine agreed not to demand the extra $25 a month until business improved. Levine claimed that he agreed to accept the reduced rent "on account." Blumenthal paid rent of $175 for 11 months of the second year of the lease and then vacated the premises. Levine sued to recover the unpaid rent for the last month of the lease and the unpaid balance of $25 per month for the preceding eleven months.

Was Levine's promise not to demand the increased rent supported by consideration? ISSUE

The Court ruled in favor of plaintiff Levine. It stated that to impose a contractual obligation, the second agreement (by which Levine continued to accept the lower rent) would have had to be supported by a new and independent consideration. The fact that Blumenthal feared she would be put out of business by the second year's higher rent was not the same thing as agreeing to forgo bankruptcy proceedings (which would be adequate consideration). By the same token, partial payment was not regarded as satisfaction of the whole because the partial payment was not part of an agreement supported by consideration. DECISION

The drafters of the UCC cut through the maze of the common law and established a different rule for goods transactions. The UCC (Section 2-209) states simply: "An agreement modifying a contract within this Article needs no consideration to be binding." For example, suppose that a supplier agrees to deliver goods at $1 a unit. Later, due to market conditions, the supplier calls the buyer and asks if the buyer will agree to pay $2 a unit for the same goods. Under the preexisting duty rule, the buyer's promise to pay the higher price would not be enforceable for lack of consideration. However, under the UCC, if the buyer agrees to pay the higher price, the promise is enforceable. Note that the buyer still has to _agree_ to pay the higher price. The buyer can refuse to accept the price change and hold the supplier to the original contract or recover for its breach. Once they have agreed to the modification, they cannot later disavow their promise.

Compromise of Debts   The preexisting duty rule also comes into play in agreements between debtors and creditors to compromise on payments of debts. The delinquent debtor is a perennial problem for creditors. On the theory that a bird in the hand is worth two in the bush, creditors often accept less than the amount owed on the debt. But sometimes such arrangements are not enforceable for lack of consideration. If a creditor later seeks to recover full payment on the original debt, a debtor may not be able to enforce the creditor's promise to accept only partial payment. If the creditor's promise is not supported by consideration, because the debtor has not incurred any new legal detriment, the debtor may not be able to enforce the promise.

For example, suppose that a student owes State College $1,000. State College agrees to accept $300 as full payment. State College's promise to release the student from all claims is not supported by consideration. Because the student was already under a duty to pay $300, plus an additional $700, the student has not incurred any additional legal detriment.

However, to avoid causing people severe hardship or discouraging honesty and fair dealing, the courts have tried to find new consideration of some kind to support such compromises. Thus when a debtor gives partial payment on a loan before the loan is due, or when a debtor gives a combination of money and property as satisfaction of the debt, courts may hold that the new consideration supports a modification of the original contract.

Under bankruptcy laws, once someone is declared bankrupt, the person is no longer required to pay his or her creditors. The debts are discharged by court order. But in some circumstances, it is advantageous to the bankrupt debtor to reaffirm some old debts and keep paying them. The courts usually hold that the consideration is the refusal of the debtor to use the defense of bankruptcy against the creditor. Debtor and creditor then are free to reach a settlement in which the debtor satisfies the debt with only partial payment.

Composition agreement an agreement between a debtor and many creditors to reorganize debt payments

A slight variation of this device involves what are called **composition agreements.** These are used when debtors are in financial difficulties and fear being unable to pay their creditors in full. To avoid bankruptcy, one creditor may call other creditors to convince them to accept less than what is owed. The expenses of declaring bankruptcy and the likelihood that some creditors may wind up with nothing sometimes are enough incentive for creditors to consent to such an agreement. For example, if Julius thinks that he can pay 40 percent of his total debts, he may seek to enter into a composition agreement with his creditors. In such a case, each creditor may agree to accept 40 percent of the amount due from Julius.

The consideration in such agreements is the promises of the creditors to forgo part of their claims, the debtor's payment of the assenting creditors in equal proportions, the debtor's securing the assent of the creditors, or the part payment made to other creditors. Courts want to encourage these agreements between creditors and debtors, because they discourage litigation.

Accord and satisfaction a contract with new consideration to discharge an earlier contract

Accord and Satisfaction   When a legitimate dispute exists about the existence or size of a debt, the preexisting duty rule gives way to the doctrine of **accord and satisfaction.**

An accord and satisfaction is the offer of something different from what was provided for in the original contract (the accord) and an agreement to accept it (the satisfaction). Partial payment of an unliquidated debt, offered as full satisfaction of the obligation, is supported by consideration and discharges the obligation.

For example, suppose that Julius hires Penelope, a marketing consultant, to advise him about where to locate his business. Penelope performs the service and delivers a bill for $10,000. Julius believes that her fee is much too high for the services rendered. He maintains that a more reasonable fee would be $3,000. Together they settle their dispute by agreeing on a fee of $4,000. Here, the debt is in dispute; the amount owed is uncertain; the debt is unliquidated. By agreeing to pay $4,000, Julius is assuming a duty to pay $1,000 more than he in good faith believes is owed. By agreeing to take $4,000, Penelope is relinquishing her right to collect $6,000 more, which she in good faith believes is owed her. Each party has incurred a legal detriment in exchange for the other's promise. Their agreement is supported by consideration.

Forbearance to Pursue a Legal Right   If people bargain, and one side agrees to give up a legal right, that surrender is adequate consideration to support a contract. This situation arises most frequently in insurance cases, when an insurance company promises to pay an agreed upon settlement amount in return for a claimant's promise not to file suit to recover for the alleged injury. If the insurance company refuses to make the payment after it has agreed to do so, the claimant is no longer bound by the contract and may file suit. However, the claimant may choose instead to file suit against the insurance company for breach of contract, seeking the promised settlement and any other damages.

The law in this area becomes muddied when the insurance company responds that the claimant did not have a valid claim from the outset. Because one cannot surrender what one does not have a right to in the first place, the insurance company argues that in surrendering or not asserting an invalid claim, the claimant has suffered no legal detriment and therefore any promise of settlement made in return by the insurance company is not supported by consideration.

Courts have generally not accepted this argument. Many courts have held that if the claim was made in good faith and a reasonable person could believe that the claim was well founded, surrender or forbearance would provide sufficient consideration. Other courts have held that good faith alone is sufficient. Still other courts have accepted claims when there is objective uncertainty of the validity of the claim. The trend appears to be that if the claim is neither patently ridiculous nor corruptly asserted, then the court will view surrender or forbearance as adequate consideration.

This area of law resembles the doctrine of accord and satisfaction. Agreeing not to pursue a legal claim constitutes a legal detriment, because a person is relinquishing a right to bring suit. The requirement that the claimant believe in good faith that the claim is valid is similar to the requirement of a good faith dispute for an accord and satisfaction.

BARGAINED EXCHANGE

A person who receives a promise can incur all kinds of legal detriment, and even much real detriment for good measure, but it will not serve as sufficient consideration unless it is the bargained exchange for the promisor's promise.

Bargain

The requirement that the parties bargain is not so much a requirement that they actually sit down and dicker over the consideration as it is a requirement that the consideration be something that the promisor requested in return for being bound by the promise. An example of an unbargained-for promise is a promise to make a gift. Sometimes a person attaches conditions to making a gift, things that the promisee must do to accept the gift. For example, Jennifer promises to give her tape collection to her sister, Shannon, if Shannon will come over to pick up the tapes. Jennifer is not bargaining for Shannon to come over, and there is no consideration for the promise to give the tapes. The critical factor in distinguishing a promise to make a gift on condition from a promise supported by consideration is the motive of the promisor.

Another example of a promise that is not supported by a bargained-for consideration is a promise to do something because of something the promisee has done in the past. **Past consideration** is no consideration because it was not bargained for in exchange for the promisor's promise. Past consideration cannot be used to support a new promise, because the legal detriment was neither bargained for nor given in exchange for the promise. Because every new contract requires new considerations, past consideration cannot be used to create an enforceable obligation.

Past considera-tion the bargained-for performance has already occurred

The reasoning of the courts in refusing to enforce promises based upon past consideration stems not so much from a lack of legal detriment as from a lack of bargained exchange. The present promise is induced by a past consideration; the past consideration was not given in exchange for the present promise.

Likewise, a promise by one party made to another that is based on only a moral duty generally does not constitute consideration. Technically speaking, if the promisor has received a material benefit that prompts the making of a promise, there is no consideration. For example, if A pulls B from a burning building, saving B's life, and a week later B promises to give A $5,000 "in consideration for saving my life," B's promise is not enforceable because A's conduct was not induced by B's promise.

Exchange

Two parties may sign a written agreement in which one party agrees to do something in exchange for the other party's promise to pay a sum. For example, one person may promise something in exchange for "$1 in hand paid, receipt of which is acknowledged." The dollar is what is bargained for and given over in exchange for the promise.

If the stated consideration is a pretense, there is no consideration. If the stated consideration is not actually exchanged, there is no consideration. Just saying that they have agreed to a price of $1 does not constitute consideration. If the consideration is nominal, perhaps $1 in exchange for a valuable promise, courts examine whether that $1 was bargained for and given in exchange for the promise. The dollar must be both bargained for and actually exchanged for the promise to be supported by sufficient consideration. Some courts hold that an untrue **recital of consideration** operates as an implied promise to pay the recited sum and that this implied promise satisfies the consideration requirement.

Recital of consideration a statement of what the consideration is and an indication that it has been given in exchange

PROMISSORY ESTOPPEL

The requirement that a contract be supported by consideration is part of classic contract law. Legislative dissatisfaction with the doctrine has been expressed by the UCC. In addition, many courts have criticized the results of this requirement and courts have established a substitute for consideration, the doctrine of **promissory estoppel.**

Promissory estoppel doctrine used to insure fairness in situations in which one party has justifiably relied on the promise of another

The doctrine permits a remedy based on reliance upon a promise. Under this theory, someone who makes a promise is "estopped" (meaning "made to stop") from denying the existence of the promise in cases where the promisee has justifiably relied upon the promise and has suffered harm. Thus a promise that induces detrimental reliance on the part of the promisee may be sufficient to bind the promisor, even though the detriment was not bargained for and given in exchange for the promise, so long as the promisor had reason to expect some act of reliance by the promisee.

Under promissory estoppel, four elements must be established by the promisee. These elements are:

1. A promise. Not just any promise will do. The promise must be the type of promise that the promisor should reasonably expect the promisee will rely upon. The promise must generally be expressed. However, silence may constitute an implied promise where the promisor is under a duty to speak.

2. The promisee must in fact rely upon the promise. The reliance must be justifiable.

3. Substantial economic detriment to the promisee.

4. Injustice can be avoided only by the enforcement of the promise.

For example, consider the case of an employer who promises to pay an employee an annuity for the rest of the employee's life. The employee resigns from a profitable job, as the employer expected the employee would. The employee receives the annuity for several years. In the meantime, the employee becomes disqualified from working. The employer's promise would be enforced under the doctrine of promissory estoppel. Now suppose that the employee had been able to work. In that event, the third and fourth elements of promissory estoppel would not be met. The following case illustrates the application of promissory estoppel.

Hoffman v. Red Owl Stores

Supreme Court of Wisconsin
133 N.W.2d 267 (1965)

Hoffman contacted a representative of Red Owl Stores in November 1959 about the possibility of obtaining a Red Owl franchise. Hoffman told the representative that he could invest no more than $18,000. In 1961, Red Owl selected a site for Hoffman in the town of Chilton. In consequence, Hoffman sold his bakery, bought and sold a small

FACTS

profitable grocery store, made a down payment for the Chilton property, and rented a home for his family in that city. In 1962, Red Owl told Hoffman that he had to contribute $34,000. Of this amount, $13,000 was to come from Hoffman's father-in-law as an "absolute gift." Negotiations broke down. Hoffman sued to recover the amounts spent by him in reliance on the various promises made by Red Owl.

ISSUE   Did Red Owl have a legal obligation to fulfill its promises to Hoffman?

DECISION   The court ruled in favor of Hoffman. According to the doctrine of promissory estoppel, a promisee's acts of reliance can provide a substitute for consideration. In this instance, even though Hoffman's actions in preparation for franchising a Red Owl Store were not part of a legal bargained-for exchange, they are clear evidence that he relied on Red Owl's promises to his own detriment. Injustice would result if he were not granted relief because of Red Owl's failure to keep its promises.

SUMMARY

Consideration is the exchange element of a contract and distinguishes binding agreements from promises to make gifts. Consideration is a person's legal obligation incurred in bargained exchange for a promise. A person incurs a legal detriment when he or she takes on a legal obligation or gives up a legal right.

The courts rarely decide on the adequacy of consideration: they do not evaluate the economic or social value of consideration. Instead, they test whether legal detriment has been incurred in exchange for a promise, that is, whether there is sufficient consideration.

The courts do not find sufficient consideration when a promise is so qualfied as to be illusory. In that case, the promisor incurs no legal detriment. But courts find sufficient consideration in output and requirements contracts because they define the obligation to perform.

Problems with consideration arise when people, in exchange for a new promise, merely agree to do what they already are committed to do by law or by prior agreement. The doctrine of consideration guards against people forcing others to change contract terms. Some courts enforce changes that are in response to unforeseen difficulties.

In the compromise of debts, a creditor says that he or she will accept partial payment for the entire debt. Courts enforce the creditor's promise if the creditor gets something new or if the amount owed is in legitimate dispute. Composition agreements, which are informal reorganizations of debts, are enforced as a matter of public policy, as are charitable subscriptions.

Under certain circumstances, the doctrine of consideration might produce unjust results. Therefore the doctrine of promissory estoppel is applied. It results in the enforcement of certain promises, even though they are not supported by consideration.

1. Explain the difference between adequacy and sufficiency of consideration.

2. List three types of situations in which the preexisting duty rule creates legal difficulties.

3. Briefly explain the two basic components of consideration.

4. Explain the doctrine of promissory estoppel.

5. The Boston Redevelopment Authority (BRA) took over the buildings owned and operated by the Graphic Arts Finish Company. Graphic's president agreed with BRA that Graphic would receive its "total certified actual moving expenses" from BRA in return for leaving the premises peacefully and quickly and relocating elsewhere. Graphic alleges it performed these promises and demands the $54,069.11 still owed by BRA for moving expenses. Result?

6. While Hurley worked for Marine Contractors, he accumulated $12,000 in a retirement trust plan. The plan provided that when an employee left the company for reasons other than disability or retirement at age 65, the employee's share would be held by Marine for five years before distribution to the employee. Marine's president agreed to pay Hurley his $12,000 share immediately if Hurley would not compete with Marine within 100 miles for five years. Hurley agreed and received his money. But less than a year later Hurley was in active competition with Marine. Was the agreement valid?

7. Keen's mother died, leaving Keen an interest in property the mother had owned jointly with her husband, Keen's stepfather. Keen agreed not to claim her mother's interest in return for a promise from her stepfather that he would leave the entire property to her upon his death. He died without a will, and the state claimed that it was the rightful owner as there had been inadequate consideration in the contract between Keen and her stepfather. Result?

8. Sons, Inc., had leased premises from W&T for over 3½ years and wished, contrary to the terms of the lease, to leave. W&T was bound by the terms of the lease at least until April 30 of the year following its execution. It could terminate after that on 90 days' notice to Sons. Sons had no such option, and W&T intended to enforce the lease against it for the full 10-year term. Could Sons terminate?

9. The Office of Milk Industry (OMI) of New Jersey established set minimum prices for gallon and half-gallon containers of milk and prohibited the giving or lending of anything of value to any customer by a retail establishment. Garden State Farms, a milk dealer, began distributing refund certificates to purchasers of milk, authorizing a small refund for each purchase payable "(o)n the day on which retail milk controls . . . are abolished in New Jersey or declared void by the court." Had Garden State violated the regulations?

10. Gill had performed plumbing work for Black Canyon Construction but had not been paid fully. In October 1971, the stockholders of Black Canyon sold the company and agreed to assume various liabilities the company then had. Gill

sued the stockholders in March 1972 for his accumulated debt, but he agreed to dismiss his suit in return for continued work and total payment due. Gill completed the new work and soon found himself back in court trying to collect his money. The court ruled that he was not a beneficiary of the October sale and could not collect for work done prior to then. Could he enforce the rest of the later agreement?

11. Carmichael, a shoe store owner, owed International Shoe Company $5,318.92 for shoes sold to him. When his debt had earlier been $12,272.51, Carmichael had agreed to pay International Shoe $8,000 immediately and the balance at $50 a week in return for receipt on account of an additional $2,000 worth of shoes. Carmichael was making payment according to this schedule when suddenly International Shoe Company brought suit for the balance of money owed. Result?

12. Polinger pledged $200,000 to the United Jewish Appeal (UJA), a nonprofit group that raises funds for various charities. He died shortly afterward, leaving an unpaid balance of $133,500. The UJA sued to recover the unpaid balance from Polinger's estate. UJA used Polinger's announcement of his pledge to induce others to pledge large amounts, although the effect of Polinger's pledge on the decisions of other solicited contributors was not known. What additional information would you require to determine whether the UJA should recover, and how should this information affect the outcome?

13. Plaintiffs each had put down a $1,000 deposit toward the purchase of condominium units. Each receipt contained an agreement providing that the deposit was to insure the buyer the "first option" to purchase a specified unit at a specified price, and if the sales contract eventually drawn up by the seller proved unacceptable to the buyer, the deposit would be refunded with interest. The seller later notified each buyer that the units would be priced 16 percent above the agreed upon price. Plaintiffs sued for breach of contract. Were the contracts to give the buyers the option of buying their units at the original price supported by sufficient consideration?

14. Buyer signed an order for the purchase of three sprinklers to be installed before May 1, 1974. The sprinklers were to be paid for upon delivery. The agreement permitted the buyer to cancel by notifying the seller 30 days before the delivery date. Seller delivered only two of the three sprinklers. Buyer paid for them and sued for breach of contract for failure to deliver the third. Seller argued that buyer's option to cancel the order rendered buyer's promise to pay for the sprinklers illusory and that there was thus no consideration for the seller's promise to deliver the sprinklers. What result and why?

CHAPTER 8

Genuine Assent

CHAPTER OBJECTIVES

FRAUD

Misrepresentation of Fact / Materiality / Knowledge of Falsity and Intent to Deceive / Reliance / Injury or Damage

DURESS

UNDUE INFLUENCE

MISTAKE

Bilateral Mistake / Unilateral Mistake / Knowledge of Mistake / Mistake of Material Fact

SUMMARY

REVIEW PROBLEMS

CHAPTER OBJECTIVES

After studying this chapter, you should be able to:

1. Identify four problems in genuine assent to a contract.

2. Understand how the law defines fraud.

3. Define duress.

4. Understand the circumstances under which undue influence occurs.

5. Differentiate unilateral from bilateral mistakes.

6. Distinguish the kinds of contract mistakes that are given relief by the courts.

In the preceding chapters, the elements necessary for the formation of a contract were discussed. Almost all contracts that include those elements are enforced. But in some situations, the required elements appear to be present but in reality are not. For example, a store owner who accepts a gang leader's offer to protect his property from gang violence in exchange for owner's agreement to pay the gang $100 a month is not genuinely assenting to the terms of a contract. Similarly, a buyer who relies on a used car salesperson's claim that a car has a rebuilt engine and has never been in an accident does not genuinely assent to buy if the salesperson knew the claims to be false. Assent to a contract must be given voluntarily and knowingly by each of the parties. If it is not, there is no genuine assent and thus no contract between them.

This chapter discusses situations involving agreements that lack genuine assent. Fraud, duress, undue influence, and even mistake may cancel a person's assent to a contract and entitle that person to relief.

FRAUD

A person who has been induced to enter into a contract as a result of fraud may cancel or rescind the contract. In addition, because fraud is an intentional tort, the victim of the fraud can sue for monetary damages to compensate for any loss. Punitive damages are also allowed if it can be proved that the intention to commit the fraud was malicious.

Literally thousands of acts may be fraudulent. Realizing that it would be impossible to list all possible fraudulent acts, courts have defined fraud in general terms. The essence of **fraud** is misrepresentation. One party misrepresents certain facts to another person, who, relying on the misrepresentations, assents to enter into a contract. If the person who misrepresents the facts clearly intends the misrepresentation and the resulting deception of the other, fraud results. But a misrepresentation of facts

Fraud intentional misrepresentation of fact

may be unintentional. In that case, there is no fraud. It is important to note, however, that in either case, a person who has contracted as a result of misrepresented facts may cancel the contract. The victim of an intentional misrepresentation not only can cancel the contract but also can sue for damages to compensate for any loss incurred. The victim of unintentional misrepresentation can only cancel the contract.

Because fraud requires an intentional misrepresentation of fact, it is difficult to prove. But many court rulings have established the elements that must be proved in a case of fraud. Fraud exists where there is:

1. a misrepresentation of a fact

2. the misrepresentation is material

3. the misrepresentation is made with knowledge of its falseness and with intent to deceive the other party

4. someone who reasonably relies on the misrepresented statement

5. someone who suffers injury as a consequence of the reliance.

Misrepresentation of Fact

To misrepresent is to actively conceal a material fact. A person may misrepresent expressly or implicitly, in writing, orally, or through conduct. Silence can constitute a misrepresentation in situations where the law imposes a duty to speak.

Active Concealment of Fact   An active concealment of a fact is the most obvious type of misrepresentation. If the seller of a used car turns back the odometer to conceal the number of miles the car has been driven, fraud has occurred.

Lies also constitute fraud. Partially misleading statements as well as outright lies constitute fraud. If a company that wants to borrow money supplies a balance sheet and profit-and-loss statement to a bank but does not disclose important information about its liabilities or the true nature of its assets, it has only partially disclosed the truth and is guilty of a misrepresentation.

Silence and the Duty to Disclose Information   On occasion silence constitutes a misrepresentation of fact leading to fraud. For silence to be the basis for fraud, the silence must be interpreted as an intentional misrepresentation.

Generally, mere failure to disclose information to another party does not constitute even an unintentional and innocent misrepresentation, because the law does not impose a duty of disclosure.

There are, however, a number of exceptions to this rule. The Truth in Lending Act requires disclosure of actual finance charges in contracts for the loan of money. Similarly, many courts recognize a seller's duty to disclose known defects in a new house.

Suppose that a prospective seller of land knows of a hidden defect in the property, one that cannot be observed through inspection. If the seller fails to inform the purchaser of the defect, the seller may be held liable for fraud because the silence was intended to mislead the purchaser into assuming there was no defect. The following case exemplifies this type of fraud.

Sorrell v. Young

Court of Appeals of Washington
491 P.2d 1312 (1971)

FACTS   In May 1968, Sorrell contracted to buy land from Young with the intention of building a house on it. To get a building permit, plaintiff Sorrell had a soil test made. He found the soil unstable and unsuitable for construction because it contained fill. Sorrell sued to rescind the contract, and to recover money he had already paid to Young, money paid for taxes, and other expenses. Sorrell claimed fraud because Young had intentionally misrepresented the condition of the property by stating "You could build a house on the lot."

ISSUE   Did Young's failure to disclose the use of fill dirt to Sorrell constitute fraud?

DECISION   Yes. The court agreed with Sorrell that Young had committed fraud. Because the condition of the land was not readily observable through a reasonable inspection, defendant Young's failure to inform plaintiff Sorrell of the existence of the fill dirt was considered fraudulent. Young's knowledge of the fill dirt, Sorrell's unawareness of it, and the material effect of the fill dirt on the value of the property entitled Sorrell to rescind the contract and to recover damages for the fraud committed by Young.

Fiduciary relationship a relationship based on trust or confidence

A person in a **fiduciary relationship** with another must disclose all known information concerning the subject of that special relationship. An agent owes this duty to a principal, a partner owes it to another partner, and an attorney owes it to a client. A physician must tell a patient of the risks of surgery before the patient can consent to the surgery. Silence and nondisclosure under such circumstances may be considered fraud.

A Fact Must Be Misrepresented   False statements that are merely opinions cannot be considered the basis for fraud, because an opinion is not a fact. Whether a statement is one of fact or opinion is a matter that must be determined in each particular case. In general, an opinion is a statement of one's expectations about future events or one's personal beliefs. A merchant who sells goods may state that the product will last "a long time," or that the "sale price is reasonable," or that the manufacturer of the goods has "an excellent reputation." Usually, such a statement is known as **puffing** and constitutes a matter of opinion. But the car dealer's statement that a used car has been driven only 25,000 miles and was purchased by the present seller from the original owner for $3,000 are considered statements of fact. Statements of fact relate events that did or did not take place. Their truth or falseness can be proven.

Puffing mere sales talk

Beierle v. Taylor

Supreme Court of Montana
524 P.2d 783 (1974)

Edwin and Agnes Beierle, husband and wife, bought a motel from defendants Robert and Wanda Taylor, hoping that it would provide them with income in their retirement years. For the Taylors, a real estate agency gave the Beierles a brochure containing an appraisal, an expense and income statement, and an analysis of projected income and expenses. The brochure stated that the motel could produce an income of $27,648. Before the purchase, the Beierles had several meetings with the realtor, who showed them that in fact the motel had operated at a loss for the previous three years. The Beierles sought to rescind their purchase contract.   FACTS

Were the statements made in the brochure given to them by the Taylors' real estate agent fraudulent?   ISSUE

No. The court found that any misrepresentations made were opinions, not fact. It held that a statement about possible or probable future income is only an estimate or opinion. False statements that are merely opinions cannot be considered the basis for fraud, because an opinion is not a fact. The fact that the income statements showing past losses were made available to the Beierles should have given them adequate notice that the brochure's statements of future income were based on possibilities (opinions), not on past history (fact).   DECISION

Materiality

The question of whether a fact is a material — significant — fact is determined on a case to case basis. The test is to determine whether the person would have entered into a contract if he or she had known of the misrepresentation. The policy of the law is to distinguish between insignificant and significant, or material, facts. A person cannot review a complex contract, find one minor misrepresentation of fact, and then sue for fraud. Misrepresentation of a material fact exists only if the fact in question was one of the important reasons for entering into the contract.

Knowledge of Falsity and Intent to Deceive

The third requirement for fraud is that the misrepresentation of a material fact be made with knowledge of the falsity and with intent to deceive. The law does not require proof that the person who committed fraud had an evil or malicious motive. The question is whether that person knew the facts and then misrepresented them. As with other areas of the law in which intent must be determined, a person is deemed to have intended the natural consequences of an action. It is no excuse for the person making a misrepresentation of a material fact to say that he or she did not intend to take advantage of the other party. Neither can a person say that he or she did not know the true facts if he or she recklessly disregarded the facts that were available. Knowledge of the facts is inferred if a person makes a statement with reckless disregard for its truth.

The intent to deceive is found in the intent to create a false impression. Because fraud requires this intent, mere negligence or carelessness cannot constitute fraud. The professional accountant, lawyer, or doctor who fails to disclose certain facts or makes half-true statements is clearly negligent and unprofessional. But for there to be fraud, an active intent to deceive, to cover up known facts, must exist.

Reliance

The fourth element to be proved in a case of fraud is that the misrepresentation of a material fact was relied upon by the person to whom it was made. A person who does not pay attention to a misrepresented fact or who conducts his or her own investigation to determine whether a fact is true is not relying upon what the other party has said or done. In that case, even if there is a misrepresentation of a material fact, because there is no reliance there is no fraud.

Suppose that a person acts foolishly in relying on a fraudulent statement. Will the law protect that person? Although there is some conflict among court decisions as to what constitutes "unreasonable" reliance, where there is an intentional misrepresentation, relief generally is granted even though the defrauded party was foolish or negligent. In balancing the interests of the foolish person against those of the person intentionally misrepresenting a material fact, the law generally seeks to protect the victim of the fraud.

Injury or Damage

The fifth element required to prove fraud is that an injury occurred as a result of the fraud. The party who relied upon a misrepresentation of a material fact must prove that some damage was caused by the fraud. If the purchaser of a car relies on a statement that a car has been driven only 25,000 miles, and it is later proved to have been driven 60,000 miles, what damage has the purchaser suffered? The basic standard is the difference in value between that which was promised and relied upon and that which in fact was received. If there is no difference, there is no injury. If there is a difference, the defrauded party is compensated. If the person committing fraud acted with malice, extreme carelessness, or recklessness, the defrauded person can recover punitive damages as well.

Review how each of the elements of fraud is addressed in the following case.

_____ *Greene v. Gibraltar Mortgage Investment Corporation* _____
488 F.Supp. 177 (D.C.D.C., 1980)

FACTS   Rosa Greene lived in a single family home which she had bought in 1966. She had obtained a $26,000 mortgage from the Carey Winston Company. In the spring of 1979, Mrs. Greene fell behind in her mortgage payments. She called Gibraltar Mortgage

Investment Corporation, and met with its president, Mr. Willis Kemper. Mr. Kemper told Mrs. Greene that she could not get a loan unless it was for a "business purpose." He discussed converting her single family home to a rooming house and encouraged her to apply for a rooming house license as proof of her business purpose. Mrs. Greene gave Kemper $40.00 to process the loan application. The loan was to be for approximately $3,000.

In mid-June 1979, Mrs. Greene got a letter from the Carey Winston Company, the holder of the first mortgage, threatening to foreclose on her home unless she paid them all amounts due by June 21, 1979. On June 20 and 21, 1979, in exchange for its agreement to lend her the money she needed to pay Carey Winston, Mrs. Greene signed a promissory note, secured by her property, to Gibraltar.

Mrs. Greene later discovered her note to Gibraltar was for $5,800, not the $3,000 earlier discussed. Of this $5,800, Gibraltar deducted $2,800 as a broker's fee and $290 in settlement fees. Gibraltar sent $1,582 to the Carey Winston Company. Mrs. Greene received only $1,128 and was to pay $117.62 a month for five years, or $7,000, for the use of $2,710.

In September 1979, Mrs. Greene became unemployed and fell behind in her payments on both mortgages. When Gibraltar sought to foreclose, Mrs. Greene claimed her contract was voidable due to its fraud.

Is the contract between Mrs. Greene and Gibraltar voidable due to fraud?　　　ISSUE

Yes. A contract is voidable for fraud when a party misrepresents facts about essential terms of the proposed contract. Gibraltar failed to disclose material facts to plaintiff in the negotiations that led to the promissory note and deed of trust. Gibraltar did not disclose that it charged a fee for brokering the loan, which, in this instance, amounted to more than the actual proceeds of the loan. Gibraltar knew when Mrs. Greene arrived at its office on the afternoon of June 21, 1979, that she was faced with the threat of imminent foreclosure. Gibraltar took advantage of the fact that plaintiff was faced with the unpleasant alternative of signing the papers as they were offered or losing her home. The court concluded that Gibraltar's actions rendered the contract void for fraud.   DECISION

DURESS

A second factor nullifying a party's assent to a contract is duress. Few areas of the law of contracts have undergone such radical changes in the twentieth century as the law governing **duress**. Relief from an agreement on the grounds of duress is clearly available if a person is deprived of liberty or property through physical force. Even the threat of physical force constitutes duress. Yet duress is not limited to these situations.

The essence of duress is lack of free will or voluntary consent. Any wrongful act or threat that overcomes the free will of the consenting party constitutes duress. Economic coercion, threats to a person's family and loved ones, and other uses of moral or social force which put a person in such fear that his or her act is not voluntary

Duress an unlawful use of acts or threats by one person to force another person to perform an act (i.e., make a contract) that he or she otherwise would not have performed constitute duress. For example, if the supplier of an item that is critical to a purchaser threatens to stop supplying that item unless a specific contract is made, the purchaser's assent to the terms of the contract could be the product of duress. Thus, the supplier of key parts to a machine shop or hard-to-find spices to a specialty restaurant might use duress in forcing a contract on these purchasers.

In determining whether a contract can be voided because of duress, it is necessary to determine:

1. whether the acts or threats were wrongful and

2. whether it was the acts or threats, and not the free will of the party, that induced the required contractual assent.

Duress cannot be limited to the fear that might overcome an ordinary person. If a contracting party, whether brave or timid, is actually coerced into assenting to a contract, duress has occurred. Thus the state of mind of the person who is being threatened must be examined. Did one party involuntarily accept the terms of the other party? Were the circumstances such that there was no real alternative? Were those circumstances due to the coercive acts of the other party?

The following case exemplifies duress caused by economic coercion.

Totem Marine T. & B. v. Alyeska Pipeline, Etc.

Supreme Court of Alaska
584 P.2d 15 (1978)

FACTS   In June 1975, Totem contracted with Alyeska to ship pipeline construction materials from Texas to Alaska by a required date. Problems arose that delayed delivery. Alyeska terminated the contract and took the materials off a ship in California. Totem sent a bill to Alyeska for costs and charges incurred, but Alyeska suggested that it might be months before it paid. Alyeska knew that Totem was in serious financial difficulty; it forced Totem to release Alyeska from further payment obligation in exchange for Alyeska's prompt payment of one third of its bill. Six months later, Totem filed suit to rescind its settlement contract and to recover the balance allegedly due on the original contract.

ISSUE   Was Totem's agreement to release Alyeska from its obligation to pay the full bill in exchange for prompt partial payment voidable due to Alyeska's coercion?

DECISION   Yes. The Alaska Supreme Court found that if Totem involuntarily accepted the terms proposed by Alyeska because it had no alternative and because Alyeska had coerced it, economic duress would exist. Because expert testimony showed that even slight delays in payment can seriously threaten a firm's financial status, Totem may have had no choice but to agree to Alyeska's terms or else face serious financial hardship. Under such conditions, its assent to the agreement was neither voluntary nor genuine.

UNDUE INFLUENCE

Undue influence exists when one person coerces another mentally . Many cases involve an elderly, sick, or senile person who is unduly influenced by another person. The essence of **undue influence** is that the influenced person's own judgment and free will are subjected to those of the dominating person. Thus the assent given by the person influenced is not genuine.

In examining cases involving undue influence, the courts usually follow a two-step approach. First, they seek to determine if a relationship of trust and confidence has existed between the two parties. The law presumes that a trusted party can dominate the other. When a contract between them benefits the dominating person, the law presumes undue influence. The lawyer who benefits from a contract with a client and a doctor who is given property by a terminally ill patient must prove that they did not use undue influence. If they cannot, the contract may be cancelled by the other party.

In the following case, questions about fraud, duress, and undue influence arise.

Undue influence the wrongful persuasion of a person to do something that he or she would not do if left to act alone.

Odorizzi v. Bloomfield School District

California Court of Appeals
54 Cal. Rptr 533 (1966)

During 1964, Donald Odorizzi was employed as a teacher by the Bloomfield School District and was under contract to teach the following year as a permanent employee. On June 10, he was arrested on criminal charges. After Odorizzi had gone through a process of arrest, questioning, booking, release on bail, and 40 hours without sleep, the superintendant and the principal of his school came to his apartment. They suggested that if he were to resign immediately, his record would not be tarnished when he sought employment in other schools. Failure to resign, however, would bring suspension, dismissal, and humiliation. On June 11, Odorizzi resigned. In July, the criminal charges against him were dismissed. In September, Odorizzi's attempt to resume employment with the district was refused. He filed suit to rescind his agreement to resign.

FACTS

Was Odorizzi's agreement to resign voidable due to duress, fraud, or undue influence?

ISSUE

Although the court found no case of duress or fraud, it held that the possibility of undue influence was a cause of action for voiding the contract between Odorizzi and the school district. The court considered Odorizzi's claim that he was under severe mental and emotional strain when he was approached by the school officials and that this strain when he signed prevented him from freely and competently judging the problem before him. Because undue influence involves the use of excessive pressure to persuade one vulnerable to such pressure and pressure by a dominant person to a subservient one, the question of undue influence arose. Odorizzi was granted a full trial to determine if his resignation was the product of undue influence or of his genuine assent.

DECISION

MISTAKE

Mistake is generally defined as a state of mind not in accord with the facts. In contract law, mistake refers to a mental attitude coupled with an act that has legal significance, such as the execution of a contract. Parties to contracts can make many kinds of mistakes. They can make a mistake in the performance or execution of the contract. They can make a mistake in judgment or a mistaken assumption about the subject matter of the contract, its legality, or its tax effects. Mistakes in typing up a contract can occur.

In most situations, the law grants no relief to the mistaken party. The legal significance of any mistake depends on who made the mistake, the kind of mistake, and its effect on the contract. Did both parties make a mistake and act on it? Was it a serious mistake? If a serious mistake was made by one party, does that mean that the other party should have known of the mistake? If both parties to a contract make a mistake, it is a **bilateral mistake.** If only one of the parties makes a mistake, then it is a **unilateral mistake.**

Bilateral Mistake

People can make several kinds of bilateral mistakes about contracts. For example, both may make a mistake about a material fact on which the contract is based. Suppose that you agree to buy my lakefront summer cottage in northern Michigan and I agree to sell it. We decide to enter into a contract for purchase and sale when we return to the city from visiting the cottage. But unknown to us, a fire has destroyed the cottage. Mistakenly believing the cottage to be standing, we have contracted for its purchase and sale. Bilateral mistakes often happen when the subject matter of the contract has, unknown to both parties, been destroyed prior to the agreement of the parties.

Our mistake is a bilateral mistake of an important material fact. We both believed that the cottage still existed. When a bilateral mistake about the subject matter of the contract occurs, the courts grant relief to the parties and allow the contract to be rescinded. It was not the fault of either party that their assumptions were mistaken. Obviously, if the parties had known the true facts, they would not have entered into their contract.

Bilateral mistakes may also occur if there is some ambiguity in the terms of the contract and each party interprets the ambiguous terms differently. In the *Volpe* case, presented below, the partners were mistaken about one of the provisions of their partnership agreement. The mistake concerned whether their individual franchises were to have been contributed to the partnership as assets. Because the judge found that one of the parties thought that the franchises were to have been contributed by each of the parties, while the other party thought that the franchises were not to have been contributed, the parties really did not agree on the terms for the partnership. Each had a different understanding, and each mistakenly assumed that its understanding was shared.

Volpe v. Schlobohm

614 S.W.2d 615 (1981)
Court of Civil Appeals of Texas

Originally, three partners owned a franchise business. Partner Schlobohm believed that the individual franchises were not to become a part of the partnership's assets. Partner Volpe believed that the franchises were to become part of the partnership's assets. When partner Wright withdrew from the partnership, Schlobohm bought Wright's franchise. Because Volpe believed that all three franchises had been included in the partnership, he demanded to buy his share of the Wright franchise. Schlobohm refused and sued to rescind the partnership agreement with Volpe.

Did the parties make mistakes about the inclusion of the franchises in the partnerships so that their agreement to become partners was voidable?

Yes. The court ruled in favor of Schlobohm. The partnership agreement could be rescinded because of the mistakes made by the parties. Its decision was based on both parties' misunderstanding of whether the franchises were to be a part of the partnership. Rescission of a contract may be granted when a mistake prevents the parties from ever reaching a meeting of minds. Each party had different assumptions about the inclusion of the franchises in the partnership. Further, each partner mistakenly assumed that all partners shared his assumptions.

FACTS

ISSUE

DECISION

Unilateral Mistake

A unilateral mistake is a mistake made by only one of the contracting parties. If one person makes a careless or negligent mistake in negotiating or in performing a contract, the law generally does not grant that person relief from the mistake. There are, however, several exceptions to this rule. Even when a mistake is made by only one party, courts generally grant relief if refusing to do so would impose undue hardship or expense on the person who made the mistake.

In other words, the courts seek to balance the scales of justice. They examine the relative consequences to both parties of a decision to grant or deny relief for a unilateral mistake. What burden would be imposed on the one person if relief is granted to the mistaken person? What hardship would be suffered by the mistaken person if no relief is granted? Either a slight burden on the innocent party or a great burden on the mistaken party generally is grounds for granting relief.

Knowledge of Mistake

If a mistake was made by only one of the contracting parties, but the other party knew or should have known of the mistake, the courts generally do not allow the other party to take advantage of the mistake by enforcing the contract. Suppose that several contractors are asked to submit bids for construction work on a hospital addition. The bid from one contractor is significantly lower than the others. If the bid was lower due to the contractor's unilateral mistake in calculation, and the error was so great that the hospital had reason to know of the mistake before accepting the bid, the contractor would be granted relief from the obligation.

The following case exemplifies this type of mistake.

_____ *M. J. McGough Company v. Jane Lamb Memorial Hospital* _____

United States District Court S. D. Iowa
302 F.Supp. 482 (1969)

FACTS   McGough, a contractor, submitted a bid for construction on the Jane Lamb Memorial Hospital. The bid figures were relayed to McGough by a representative at the opening. McGough was immediately concerned over the 10 percent difference between his low bid and the next lowest bid. Realizing that he may have made a serious mistake in his bid, he immediately called his representative and ordered him to withdraw the bid while the hospital board was still analyzing the bids received. A hospital official requested that McGough submit in writing the circumstances of the error and a request to withdraw the bid. After discovering an error in the amount of $199,800 due to an employee's transposition of a figure, McGough sought to rescind his bid due to his mistake. The hospital refused and stated it intended to accept the bid and hold McGough to the contract.

ISSUE   Was McGough entitled to rescind its contract due to its mistake?

DECISION   Yes. The court held that the contractor was entitled to have its bid rescinded on the basis of unilateral mistake. McGough's bid was low due to a simple clerical error, which was promptly communicated to the hospital authorities, in fact before the hospital's acceptance of the bid. The error was so great that the hospital should have noticed it. Because the hospital had suffered no loss and McGough had made every possible effort to explain the circumstances of the mistake, the court decided that the hospital could not take advantage of McGough's unilateral mistake.

Another type of unilateral mistake is one concerning a person's identity. We have seen in the chapters on offer and acceptance that an offer may be accepted only by the person to whom it is made. But what if the offeror receives an acceptance from someone whom he or she mistakenly believes to be the offeree? If offeror Book Club intends to deal only with Mrs. Jones, but Mrs. Jones's daughter accepts the offer, there is no contract between Book Club and the daughter. The daughter never received an offer from the book club and thus must have known that the book club was mistaken in identifying her as a person who could accept its offer.

A mistake about the identity of a person can also be made as a result of fraud. A person can forge identification papers and pass as someone else. Such a situation would be a combination of fraud and mistake. Consequently, there would be double reason to allow the protected person to avoid the contract. The forger has committed fraud on the protected person, and the protected person has made a unilateral mistake regarding the forger's identity, a mistake which was known to the forger.

However, if a person makes an offer to someone who occupies a certain capacity — for example, the manager of the ABC store — any person who is in that capacity can accept it. If the offeror does not know that a new manager has been appointed, the offeror cannot plead mistake because he or she thought that a personal friend, the former manager, was still there. In this case, the offer is made to any person in the position, not to the individual who was mistakenly thought to be there. There is no mistaken identity in this situation, only a mistaken assumption.

Mistake of Material Fact

Finally, in determining the legal significance of a factual mistake, a court evaluates the importance of the mistake. The court must find that the mistaken fact at least partly induced the person now seeking relief to have entered into the contract. The law is reluctant to undo contracts. Only the most significant and important mistakes of fact are grounds for undoing them.

A related question is the risk assumed by the parties. If either of the contracting parties has made a mistake in judging risk, the court does *not* grant relief.

The following case exemplifies the court's attitude toward granting relief to people for their mistaken assumptions.

___ *Friedman v. Grevnin* ___

Supreme Court of Michigan
103 N.W.2d 336 (1960)

In April 1956, the Grevnins bought land from the Friedmans for development pur-   FACTS
poses. As early as 1953, one of the Grevnins asked the city engineer about the adequacy of the sewers and was told that a pump or lifting station would be necessary to accommodate the lots. Before the purchase, the Grevnins sought to make the sale conditional on both a satisfactory agreement with the city for sewers and an approval by the Federal Housing Administration. Both conditions required adequate sewer facilities.

The Friedmans refused to agree to the conditions, and the Grevnins offered to purchase the land without the conditions. The Friedmans accepted that offer, and a contract was made. In September 1956, the Grevnins learned that the sewers were overloaded and that alterations were necessary. The Grevnins sued to rescind the contract and recover the sums paid.

Is the contract between the Friedmans and the Grevnins voidable because there was a   ISSUE
mutual mistake of fact?

No. The court found that the Grevnins had assumed the risk with full knowledge that   DECISION
the Friedmans had made no guarantee about the sewers. There was no mutual mistake. Instead, there was a unilateral mistake by the Grevnins, who knew of the uncertainty, made inquiries, and took their chances. The Grevnins' unilateral mistake was not subject to relief.

SUMMARY

Even though the elements of offer, acceptance, and consideration needed for a valid contract are present, if one party's assent to the contract is not genuine, the law allows that party to cancel it. Contracts that lack genuine assent are voidable contracts. Genuine assent is lacking if there has been fraud, duress, undue influence, or certain types of mistake.

Fraud exists where one party intentionally misrepresents material facts to the other party who, relying on the misrepresentation, enters into a contract. Although fraud is difficult to prove, even an innocent misrepresentation can be the basis for rescinding a contract. Duress occurs when a person's free will is replaced by threats or wrongful acts of another party. Economic and physical duress make a contract voidable.

Undue influence is present when someone who is in a position of trust so dominates another person's exercise of free will that a contract between them, which benefits the dominant party, lacks genuine assent. Because of the close relationship between the parties, undue influence is presumed when a contract benefits the dominant party. The contract is voidable unless the dominant party can prove the existence of genuine assent.

Mistakes made by one or both parties to a contract generally do not allow either to cancel that contract. However, if both parties make a mistake about the subject matter of their contract, the contract lacks genuine assent. Further, if one party makes a mistake that the other should be aware of, the mistaken party may rescind the contract if doing so does not unduly burden the other party.

REVIEW PROBLEMS

1. If someone misrepresents a fact and another person is injured because of reliance on that misrepresentation, has fraud been committed?

2. What is meant by the statement that few areas of the law of contracts have undergone such radical changes as the law governing duress?

3. What is the importance of distinguishing between the bilateral and unilateral mistakes of contracting parties?

4. How does undue influence differ from duress?

5. Andersen agreed to sell a portion of his waterfront property to Vermette, who had made a visual inspection of it and was satisfied. After settling with Andersen, Vermette drew up plans for the construction of a home on the lot and began to build. The project was halted when a county building inspector found evidence of potential soil slippage. After examining the foundation footings and considering the recent landslide on a nearby lot, the inspector issued an order suspending activities until a soil expert certified the land as being sufficiently stable for the construction of a house. Vermette discharged the contractor and sued to rescind the sale. Will he succeed?

6. Greber suffered from a weight problem. After trying free treatment at the local Slenderella Salon, she immediately agreed to take a weight-reducing course consisting of 150 treatments at a total cost of $300. Greber also had long suffered a back ailment and informed the Slenderella Salon manager of this before signing the agreement. The manager did not discourage Greber from entering into the contract. She thought the treatments would do her back some good. Several days later, before taking any of the paid treatments, Greber's back hurt so much that she consulted a doctor, who advised her against taking the Slenderella program. Now Slenderella is suing for the money Greber agreed to pay, but she wants to rescind the contract. What result?

7. Usry leased two ice-making machines from Poag, an agent for Granite Management Services (GMS). Prior to the execution of the contract, Poag drew a separate purchase order, signed by Usry, that contained the following: "Customer own[s] equipment at end of lease" and "free service until lease ends." The lease agreement itself contained no such language, but said: "the contract constitutes the entire agreement between the lessor and lessee and . . . no representation or statement made by any representative of lessor or the supplier not stated herein shall be binding." When the machines failed to perform properly and Usry was refused free service, he discontinued making lease payments. GMS brought suit, but Usry claimed he was induced into signing the agreement by the fraudulent misrepresentation of Poag. Will Usry be able to rescind the contract?

8. While Avallone was employed as a manager in Elizabeth Arden's Boston beauty salon, she and other individuals made plans to open their own salon right next to the Arden salon. After officers of the Arden corporation discovered Avallone's intentions, they summoned her to the executive headquarters in New York City, ostensibly to discuss new hair dyes. In fact, she was scheduled to meet with several corporate officers, who asked her whether the information about her future plans were true. Avallone denied any intentions to open her own salon and at the officers' request signed a contract that restricted her from competing with the Arden corporation. Back in Boston, she had second thoughts about what she had just done and sued to void the agreement due to duress. Result?

9. A doctor informs his patient that in his opinion costly weekly treatments at the doctor's office for one year are necessary to cure an illness. After treatment for one year, the patient learned that the doctor in fact had known that such treatments had been unnecessary. The patient sued to cancel the contract and to get back the money he paid for the treatment. The doctor claimed the contract was valid and that he had no obligation to repay because the patient used the doctor's services and treatment. Who is right and why?

10. John buys a new car from Al's lot because Al tells him it's the lowest price in town for that type of car. After purchasing the car from Al, John finds a similar car at another lot that costs $400 less than the car he purchased from Al. John claims that Al's statement was false. Can John cancel his contract with Al on the basis of Al's statement?

11. International Underwater Contractors contracted with New England Telephone to assemble and install certain conduits under the Mystic River for $150,000. Due to delays caused by the telephone company, the contractor incurred addi-

tional costs of approximately $800,000, largely because it had to perform the work in the winter rather than in the summer, making the equipment originally specified unusable. The telephone company agreed to pay the additional costs. But once the work was completed, it offered only $575,000 and did so after refusing to make any payments for a period of a year. The contractor claims its financial difficulties forced it to accept the telephone company's settlement. If the contractor was in fact in dire financial condition, do these facts show economic duress such that its assent to the release was not genuine?

12. Aetna Life Insurance Company issued a disability insurance policy for James Boyd, who was married to Christine Boyd, the beneficiary named in the policy. After she and Jones separated, she continued to make payments on the policy for several years. Then, not knowing anything about the health of her husband, James Boyd, she surrendered the policy to Aetna and received a very small sum of money equal to the cash value of the policy. Later, Christine found that James had in fact been disabled six months before she returned the policy to Aetna. When he died a year after she had surrendered the policy, she requested Aetna pay her the death benefits as well as the unpaid disability benefits which were to have been paid to her husband during his life. She claimed the cancellation of the policy, made when she surrendered it to Aetna, was a mistake since both she and Aetna believed at that time that James was not disabled. Does Christine's mistake allow her to rescind her cancellation of the policy?

13. Frank owns 10 acres of vacant farmland worth about $50 an acre. He induced Jane to buy the farmland for $200 an acre by falsely stating that neighbors had discovered gas and mineral deposits on nearby property. After Jane bought the land, she discovered oil under it. Frank sued Jane to have his sale to her set aside due to the false and fraudulent statements he had made to her at the time of the sale. Is the contract between Frank and Jane voidable due to fraud?

14. Farmer Jones found an odd looking stone in his field and took it to Harry, the local jeweler. Harry examined the stone and said that he thought it might be an emerald. He offered to pay Jones $100 for it. Jones accepted the $100 and gave the jeweler the stone. After talking with several other jewelers, Harry found out that the stone was probably a diamond. He took it to an appraiser (who charged Harry $75 to appraise the stone) who valued it at $2,000. Farmer Jones claims that he was defrauded by Harry, who is an expert, and seeks to recover the value of the stone, less the $100 he has already received. Can he?

15. Russ was negotiating the purchase of a lodge and real estate owned by Brown. The parties discussed the water rights that went with the property being sold. Brown did not tell Russ that an adjoining landowner had disputed the water rights to the property and that parts of the dispute still existed. Russ sued to rescind the contract due to Brown's failure to disclose the dispute over the property's water rights. Should the contract be rescinded.?

16. John and Mary had been married for 12 years when John began to have mental health problems. He was hospitalized for several months and suffered recurring episodes over a period of years. He was diagnosed as suffering from schizophrenia and manic depression. When John's illness recurred, Mary had an attorney

prepare a separation agreement for both John and Mary to sign. John didn't want a separation but signed the separation agreement without speaking to her attorney, without having read it, and without being represented by counsel. When he signed, he was committed to the hospital but allowed to attend to his job and affairs during the day. At night he received treatment and medication for his illness. John claims that the agreement is voidable by him. Do you agree? Why?

CHAPTER 9

Capacity to Contract

CHAPTER OBJECTIVES

CONTRACTS OF PEOPLE WHO MIGHT BE MENTALLY INCOMPETENT

Mental Competency and Mental Illness / Mental Competency and the Use of Intoxicants and Drugs

LEGAL INCOMPETENCY AND MINORS

Disaffirmance of Contracts by Minors / Ratification / A Minor's Contracts for Necessaries / A Parent's Liability for a Minor's Contracts

SUMMARY

REVIEW PROBLEMS

CHAPTER OBJECTIVES

After studying this chapter, you should be able to:

1. Discuss how a person's mental or legal competency can affect the legal capacity to make a valid contract.

2. Identify the legal options of a person whose contract is considered voidable.

3. Explain how the law defines and classifies mental competency.

4. Understand disaffirmance and ratification of contracts made by minors.

5. Discuss necessaries and their relationship to the liability of minors and their parents.

A person's capacity to contract is determined by two different issues. The first is mental competency. Mental competency is an issue with people who generally can enter into valid contracts but whose state of mind prevents them from making specific contracts. When their mental facilities have recovered, they may make valid contracts. Although the law used to be concerned primarily with those people legally determined to be insane, today the law applies the issue of mental competency to people who are senile or feebleminded. People who are legally intoxicated or under the influence of drugs also may lack the mental competency to enter into valid contracts.

The test of mental competency is not whether a person's mind is impaired or unsound nor whether the person has understood all terms of the contract. Instead, the test is whether that person can comprehend the nature of the transaction at hand and understand its consequences. If a person who is not mentally competent to contract does enter into a contract, the law protects that person by letting him or her cancel the contract. The contract of this person is voidable. Although it can be upheld as a valid contract, the protected party also may choose to make it void.

The second issue of contractual capacity concerns a person's legal competency. Most legal competency problems today concern minors. They lack the capacity to contract because the law tries to protect minors from making unwise contracts with more mature adults.

The law does not presume that any person lacks the capacity to contract. A person who acts senile, is intoxicated, or is a minor when a contract is made is presumed able to make a valid contract. To void that contract, a person must do something to indicate that he or she wants to exercise the option the law allows and make the contract voidable.

CONTRACTS OF PEOPLE WHO MIGHT BE MENTALLY INCOMPETENT

Mental Competency and Mental Illness

As medical science has come to recognize different degrees of mental illness, the courts have become concerned with the contracts of people who might be incompetent even though not legally insane. Instead of declaring contracts made by such persons to be void, the modern rule is generally to treat contracts made by people suffering from mental illness as voidable. The following case illustrates this principle.

Cundick v. Broadbent

U.S. Court of Appeals, Tenth Circuit
383 F.2d 157 (1967)

FACTS   Irma Cundick, guardian for her husband, Darwin Cundick, sued Broadbent to have set aside a contract between her husband and Broadbent made on September 2, 1963. She claimed that her husband was incompetent to contract, that Broadbent knew of her husband's incompetency, and that the contract was voidable. Darwin Cundick, 59 years old, was a sheep rancher who agreed to sell his lambs to Broadbent. After a one-page contract was signed by both parties, the Cundicks took it to their lawyer, who refined it. Cundick and Broadbent later resigned it.

In 1960, Cundick was diagnosed by his family physician as suffering depressive psychosis, a mental illness, and was referred to a psychiatrist. Several physicians examined Cundick in 1961 and 1965. They all testified that he was not capable of entering into the 1963 contract because of confusion and poor judgment. In 1965, Cundick suffered further mental problems.

ISSUE   Is the 1963 contract made by Mr. Cundick voidable because of his mental illness?

DECISION   No. The court found that Mrs. Cundick had not proved that at the time of the transaction, her husband was mentally incapable of managing his affairs. In regard to the contract, Cundick's acts were those of a person competent to manage his affairs. Cundick's lawyer testified that the contract had been explained in detail and that all parties apparently understood it. There was no record of medical treatment or consultation regarding his condition between 1961 and 1965. Despite some medical and **lay testimony** tending to show that Cundick might have been incompetent on the contract date, there was also evidence that Cundick knew the extent and condition of his property, how he was disposing of it, to whom, and upon what consideration. Thus he did not lack the mental capacity to contract.

Lay testimony
testimony given by
a nonprofessional
person; for
example, a person
who is not a
psychiatrist testifies
about someone's
mental condition

The court usually examines the fairness of allowing a protected person to void a contract. If the result were unfair, no right to cancel the contract would be granted. Finally, as we have noted, the person claiming mental incompetence must prove that at the time of making the contract, he or she did not understand the nature and effect of the transaction that resulted in the contract.

If a person has been judged legally incompetent after a court hearing and a guardian or conservator has been appointed by the court, the contracts of that person usually are regarded as void. In this case, the guardian or conservator has the capacity to make contracts on behalf of the protected person. If the guardian does not buy certain necessities for the protected person, the person may have the capacity to contract for those items.

But without a court determination of legal incompetency, insanity, or inability to manage one's affairs, the law presumes that a person is legally competent to enter into valid contracts.

Mental Competency and the Use of Intoxicants and Drugs

A person who is intoxicated may be unable to understand the nature and effects of contracts that he or she makes while intoxicated. Generally, the law treats as voidable the contracts made by people who are intoxicated and do not know what they are doing. Intoxication by alcohol and other drugs is treated much like incompetency from mental or physical illness.

Fairness and Fraud   However, several differences exist between the capacities to contract of people under the influence of drugs or alcohol and people who are mentally ill. Some states only allow people to void contracts they made while intoxicated or drugged if they can show that those with whom they contracted knew of their condition and took advantage of it.

Those who are responsible for intoxicating people with whom a contract is made and those who take unfair advantage of the intoxication, whether or not responsible for causing it, often are not allowed by the courts as a matter of fairness to enforce the contract. Instead, the intoxicated person is allowed to cancel the contract.

The courts are generally less concerned with the intoxication that affects someone's capacity to contract than with the conduct of the person with whom he or she contracts. Intoxication or impairment of judgment, coupled with fraudulent action or deceit by the other person contracting, may give the intoxicated person grounds to void the contract.

Degree of Intoxication   If a person has been legally judged incompetent because of habitual drunkenness, that person no longer has any capacity to contract. (His contracts are considered void, not voidable.) But when a person has not been judged legally incompetent due to drunkenness, a court must determine if the degree of drunkenness allows the person to void contracts by disaffirming them.

Generally, in the absence of fraud or special circumstances, if a person is slightly under the influence of alcohol or is partially intoxicated, contracts made by that person are considered valid. Intoxication that causes some impairment of judgment or a feeling of exhilaration generally is not sufficient to render contracts voidable.

Instead, as the following case indicates, intoxication must deprive a person of reason and the ability to understand the consequences of his or her actions.

People too intoxicated to contract competently usually are allowed to disaffirm their obligations. But if they cannot return the consideration that they have received, in the absence or fraud by the other party, they may not disaffirm their contracts. Furthermore, if the contracts are for necessaries, intoxicated people are held liable for the reasonable value of the items.

Olsen v. Hawkins

Supreme Court of Idaho
408 P.2d 462 (1965)

FACTS   Olsen sued to collect proceeds as beneficiary to Turner's life insurance. Turner, Olsen's stepfather, died in 1960. Until 1957, Olsen was named as Turner's beneficiary. Olsen claimed that Turner was intoxicated and therefore incompetent when he changed his beneficiary from Olsen to Hawkins, in March 1960. Following Mrs. Turner's death in 1956, Mr. Turner became a heavy drinker. He had been arrested while intoxicated in 1957 for various offenses. In May and October 1957, he entered the state hospital for treatment of chronic alcoholism. He was discharged in May 1958.

Hawkins claimed that Turner was entirely competent at the time he changed beneficiaries. Three witnesses testified to Turner's sobriety during the several months surrounding March 1960.

ISSUE   Does Turner's history of intoxication make his 1960 contract to change the beneficiary on his life insurance voidable due to intoxication?

DECISION   No. The court found no substantial evidence that Turner was incompetent when he changed his beneficiary. A contract made in a sober interval by a chronic alcoholic who has neither been adjudged incompetent nor suffered a permanent mental impairment is valid, at least in the absence of undue influence or fraud.

LEGAL INCOMPETENCY
AND MINORS

The legal capacity to enter into contracts is not the same as the capacity to commit a crime or a tort. The law often holds minors responsible for crimes and torts but usually not for contracts. The higher standard for contracts arises because contracts generally involve bargaining with another person. A minor who bargains with an adult needs to be protected from making unwise or foolish contracts. For the same reason, the standard of capacity is also generally higher for contracting than for making a gift or a will, because neither involves bargaining with others.

Historically, the law has provided special protection to minors who enter into contracts. They are considered privileged because of their assumed immaturity and inexperience in commercial transactions.

Common law has treated people under the age of 21 as minors. But since the enactment of the Twenty-sixth Amendment to the U.S. Constitution, which lowered the voting age to 18, most states have lowered the **age of majority** from 21 to 18. (Although most of the cases that follow concern people who are minors because they are under 21, in most states now only those under 18 are considered minors.) At the age of majority, the legal incapacity of the minor disappears, and a person has full legal competence to enter into valid contracts.

Age of majority
the age at which a person attains legal competency and loses minor status

The law allows minors the choice of carrying out a contract or seeking to avoid its provisions. A minor avoids a contract by any act that shows the minor intends not to be bound by the contract any longer. Since most contracts entered into by minors can be avoided, they are generally referred to as voidable contracts. The contracts are valid unless the minor, by disaffirming them, seeks to avoid their provisions. Statutes in many states specify that certain contracts cannot be disaffirmed by a minor. Contracts of this type are considered valid, not voidable. Examples of such contracts, which are valid even though made by minors, are contracts:

1. to enlist in the armed forces

2. to borrow money from an institutional lender or the government to finance the minor's education

3. to adopt a child

4. to participate in a professional sport

5. made as an employee or purchaser of a business not to compete with the business of the employer or seller

6. to borrow mortgage money from a lender who secures the loan with a mortgage on property

7. to buy or sell land.

Contracts for necessaries are usually exceptions to the general rule allowing minors to avoid their contracts. **Necessaries** are determined by the needs of each individual concerned, but generally, food, clothing, and shelter suitable to the minor's station in life are regarded as necessaries. The law generally holds minors liable for the reasonable value of the necessaries. If a 16-year-old agrees to pay $100 for a jacket with a reasonable value of only $70, the 16-year-old's liability is only $70.

Necessaries
items which, based on a minor's station in life, are required for his or her general welfare

In summary, although minors may disaffirm most contracts, a court trying to decide whether a minor may disaffirm a contract must answer the following questions:

1. Do any statutes specify that this type of contract may not be disaffirmed?

2. Is the subject of this contract a necessary?

3. If the contract may be disaffirmed, has the minor done something that in fact amounts to disaffirmance?

Several other questions about holding a minor liable for contracts are noted later in this chapter.

Fisher v. Cattani

District Court, Nassau County, 3rd District
278 N.Y.S. 420 (1966)

FACTS   Fisher, an employment agency, sued Cattani, a minor, to recover the balance due on a contract. In September 1962, when Cattani was 19 years old, she contracted with Fisher, who agreed to find work for Cattani in exchange for her promise to pay for this service. Fisher found work for Cattani. Cattani resigned one month after accepting the position. In November 1962, Cattani notified Fisher by registered mail of her intent as a minor no longer to be bound by the contract made in September. The total fee due Fisher was $146.25. Because Cattani had paid $45, Fisher sued for the $101.25 balance.

ISSUE   Can a contract for employment be disaffirmed? Did defendant properly notify plaintiff of her intent to disaffirm the contract?

DECISION   Yes. The court held that Cattani's disaffirmation of the contract was effective because notice was adequate, promptly given, and happened when she was a minor. Further, the court said that a contract of this nature does not fall within any statutory exception that prohibits a minor from voiding a contract. Therefore, the court ruled that as a minor Cattani properly disaffirmed her contract.

Disaffirmance of Contracts by Minors

Unless state statutes expressly exempt the particular contract, or its subject matter is considered a necessary, the law generally treats any contract made by a minor as voidable.

Time of Disaffirmance   Minors may avoid any contract that is subject to disaffirmance during their minority and for a reasonable period of time after attaining the age of majority. The law thus gives minors time to review and reflect on contractual agreements made during minority. What constitutes a reasonable time depends on the complexity of the transaction, its subject matter, and the circumstances peculiar to each agreement.

Methods of Disaffirmance   A minor may disaffirm a contract in many ways. The minor can simply inform the other party (whether an adult or minor) that he or she intends to disaffirm their contract. The minor can clearly indicate by some action that he or she has such an intent. A minor who has agreed to sell goods to one person but instead sells them to another disaffirms the contract with the first person. A minor who takes legal action to avoid a contract's obligations also acts to disaffirm the contract.

Disaffirmance and Restitution of Property   Although the law seeks to protect the minor from unwise or imprudent contracts, court decisions disagree on the rights of the parties if a minor cannot return the property he or she received. Most decisions hold that the minor may disaffirm a contract and get back any consideration given, even if the minor cannot return what he or she has received. A minority of decisions require the minor to return the consideration to disaffirm the contract. If the minor cannot return the property received (or its equivalent value), the minor may not disaffirm the contract.

Compare the decisions in the following cases.

Central Bucks Aero, Incorporated v. Smith

Superior Court of Pennsylvania
310 A.2d 283 (1973)

Central Bucks Aero sued Smith, a minor, to recover for damage to the airplane. While a minor, Smith leased an airplane from Central. In landing it, Smith damaged the airplane and landing field. After Central filed suit, Smith disaffirmed his contract with Central. Central then asked the court to overturn the common law doctrine that a minor, by disaffirming a contract, can avoid liability under the contract and thereby leave plaintiff without a remedy.

FACTS

Should Smith be prevented from disaffirming his contract with Central?

ISSUE

No. The court stated that if it were to hold Smith legally responsible, the minor would be deprived of his "shield of protection." The law's policy is that a business has a chance to protect itself by asking whether it is dealing with a minor. If the person is a minor, then the business can either refuse to deal with the minor or require that an adult join in the contract. Because Central did not ask whether Smith was a minor, it has only itself to blame for not taking such precautions. Smith was allowed to disaffirm the contract.

DECISION

Haydocy Pontiac, Incorporated v. Lee

Court of Appeals of Ohio
250 N.E.2d 898 (1969)

On August 22, 1967, Haydocy Pontiac sold Lee a 1964 Plymouth Fury automobile. At the time of the sale, Lee was 20 years old but told the seller that she was 21. The total amount due on the automobile after the sale was $2,016.36, including insurance and finance charges. A certificate of title named Lee as the owner. Later Lee gave the car to a friend. The friend had repairs made on it, and it was held by the repairing garage for nonpayment. Thus neither Lee nor Haydocy can now recover possession of the car.

Haydocy sued Lee to recover the $2,016.36. Haydocy claimed that Lee is liable on

FACTS

the contract because she entered into it through her falsehood and deceit, while Haydocy had contracted in honesty and good faith. Lee claimed that her minority allowed her to avoid the contract and released her from any obligation to pay Haydocy.

ISSUE   Can Lee disaffirm this contract with Haydocy even if she lied to Haydocy about her age?

DECISION   No. The court held Lee liable for the fair value of the car, as long as that value did not exceed the purchase price. The court said that if a minor were allowed to avoid a transaction entered into falsely and deceitfully and were not required to restore the consideration received when it had been used and disposed of by the minor, the other party would suffer undue hardship. To hold for the minor in a case like this would allow the person's status as a minor to be used not as a shield of defense but as a weapon of injustice. Thus a minor who falsely represents her age and who cannot return the consideration she received is liable for a contract made with a party who has contracted in good faith.

Disaffirmance and Misrepresentation of Age   A minor's right to disaffirm a contract also can be influenced by misrepresentations made by the minor. When minors misrepresent their age and others rely on the misrepresentation and enter into a contract, a conflict between legal policies results.

On the one hand, the law seeks to protect minors from being victimized by wiser and more mature adults. On the other hand, if a person is the victim of fraud, the law generally allows the victim to cancel the contract. What should be done if the minor commits the fraud and the adult is the victim? The response to these questions has not been uniform; the court decisions are split.

The following case discusses the question: Is a minor who appears to be of legal age or who has signed a form stating that he or she is of age entitled to disaffirm a contract?

Kiefer v. Howe Motors, Incorporated

Supreme Court of Wisconsin
158 N.W.2d 288 (1968)

FACTS   On August 9, 1965, Kiefer made a contract with Howe Motors, Inc. Kiefer paid the contract price of $412 and took possession of a 1960 station wagon. Kiefer had difficulty with the car that he claimed was caused by a cracked engine block. He contacted Howe Motors and asked that the car be taken back. After Howe Motors refused, Kiefer's lawyer wrote a letter in which he declared the contract void, offered to return the car, and demanded repayment to Kiefer of the purchase price. Howe did not respond, so Kiefer sued to recover the $412 purchase price.

At the time of the sale, Kiefer was 20 years old, married, and the father of one child. Howe Motors claimed the contract was not voidable because Kiefer stated that he was an adult. Furthermore, the contract Kiefer signed stated that he represented himself to be 21 years old, and Howe Motors said that it relied upon that representation. It also claimed that a minor older than 18 should be legally responsible for his contract or else should be held liable for damages for misrepresenting his age.

Should the minor Kiefer be allowed to disaffirm a contract which was made while he was married and which stated that he was of legal age? **ISSUE**

Yes. The court decided for Kiefer. Merely because Kiefer was married did not mean **DECISION** he was more wise or mature than his single counterpart. Because Kiefer was a minor at the time of the contract, he could disaffirm his contract for a nonnecessary item. The letter from Kiefer's attorney to Howe Motors established effective disaffirmance.

The elements of fraud by the minor were not proved. Because Howe Motors never took any affirmative steps to determine whether Kiefer was in fact 21, it was not justified in relying only on Kiefer's signature on the contract.

Ratification

The effective surrender of the power of disaffirmance is **ratification**. Minors cannot ratify contracts. But once people reach the age of majority, they can ratify contracts made while they were still minors. First, the minor may fail to make a timely disaffirmance. Because the minor has the right to disaffirm only for the period of his or her minority, plus a reasonable time after reaching majority, the minor who does not disaffirm within that time ratifies contracts made during minority. Second, the minor can expressly *state,* orally or in writing, that he or she intends to ratify the contract. If the statement is clear, unambiguous, and made after attainment of the age of majority, the contract is ratified. Once a contract is ratified, it may not be disaffirmed. Finally, a person may *act* in a way that shows an intent to ratify a contract made while a minor.

The *Bronx Savings Bank* case illustrates this concept.

Ratification the later approval of a prior act performed by a person, or by another person on his or her behalf, which was not authorized or binding on that person when originally done

Bronx Savings Bank v. Conduff

Supreme Court of New Mexico
430 P.2d 374 (1967)

On December 14, 1964, Conduff sold a home to Dalton, a minor, who promised to **FACTS** pay the mortgage owed by Conduff to Bronx Savings Bank. Dalton, who reached the age of majority in June 1965, remained in possession of the home until September 1965. During that time, he made only five partial payments through payroll deductions which Dalton had authorized while a minor.

In January 1966, the bank sued Conduff for the mortgage payments. Conduff contended that despite Dalton's minority at the time of the sale, Dalton should have been held liable for the mortgage payments. Conduff claimed that the mortgage payments Dalton made after he reached the age of majority expressed his intent to ratify the contract with Conduff. Dalton claimed that he did not ratify the contract but disaffirmed it.

ISSUE   Do the mortgage payments made by Dalton constitute his ratification of the contract?

DECISION   No. The court found no proof of ratification nor the intent to ratify the contract. The court noted that Dalton made only part of the payment due to Conduff after Dalton reached his majority. Furthermore, the part payments were made simply by continuing the payroll deductions started while Dalton was a minor. Those actions, said the court, did not show Dalton's express promise nor intent to ratify the contract. No other action by Dalton occurred after he reached the age of majority, and it is only then that ratification can occur. Conduff did not prove that Dalton had ratified the contract made during his minority. Accordingly, Conduff was the only person liable to the bank for the mortgage, and it was entitled to foreclose against Conduff for his nonpayment of the mortgage.

A Minor's Contracts for Necessaries

As we have noted, minors generally are liable for the reasonable value of necessaries, such as food, clothing, and shelter, for which they have contracted. Minors who are not dependent for financial support on their parents ("emancipated") can be held liable for buying necessary items. With the lowering of the age of majority in most states to 18, few minors are likely to be emancipated, self-supporting, or totally independent from their parents or guardians. For minors who are dependent on their parents for financial support and therefore for their necessaries, parents who can furnish those necessaries are liable for doing so. In either case, a merchant can recover from the minor or the parent the value of necessary items furnished to a minor.

A Parent's Liability for a Minor's Contracts

Most businesspeople are aware of the law's desire to protect minors. They therefore seek to make contracts with adults whose contracts are not subject to disaffirmance. Businesspeople who contract with 16- or 17-year-olds are likely to do so only if a parent or other adult is expressly committed to abide by the terms of the contract. Banks, for example, usually require an adult cosignor for any loan made to a minor. Merchants check that charge cards are issued in the name of an adult and that minor children have the express permission of that adult to charge purchases. School authorities require parents' permission and approval, as well as the children's consent, before children may take part in extracurricular activities or special programs.

Parents who cosign contracts and loans are liable even though minors can avoid most contracts. But even when a merchant does not have an express contract with a parent and furnishes necessaries to a minor, the merchant may be able to hold the parent liable. Because most states require parents to furnish their minor children with necessaries, if a merchant can prove that a minor agreed to purchase necessaries, which were not but could have been furnished by a parent, the parent can be held liable. The contract between the parent and the merchant is implied by the provisions of the law.

What if minors buy nonnecessaries that were authorized by parents? For example, a child uses a parent's charge account to charge a life-sized stuffed bear. Because it is the parent's account with the merchant, the store can look to the parent as liable on the charge account contract with the store. The child in this instance is merely the agent of the parent and may not be held liable.

SUMMARY

A person may lack either the mental or legal competency required by law to make valid contracts. A person's mental competency is determined when a court looks to see whether the person understands the nature of the transaction engaged in and its legal consequences. People who are mentally ill or so intoxicated that they cannot understand the nature of a transaction lack the mental competency to contract. Mental competency is presumed, and the burden of proving the lack of such competency is on the person asserting it.

The minor, a person under the age of majority, lacks the legal competency to make valid contracts. Instead, most contracts made by minors are voidable. The minor may choose that a contract be either valid or void. Minors can disaffirm most contracts if the disaffirmance is proper and timely. But, if minors want to have the contract treated as valid, they can ratify the contract after attaining the age of majority.

When a minor contracts for necessaries, the minor is liable for their reasonable value. Because a parent has the legal obligation to furnish a minor with necessaries, the parent also may be held liable for necessaries a minor buys. If a minor purchases nonessential items, the minor may be able to disaffirm the contract. The minor's parent is liable only if the minor had been authorized by the parent to make the purchase.

REVIEW PROBLEMS

1. What is the test of a person's capacity to make a contract?

2. Are all contracts of minors voidable? Explain.

3. Are most contracts made by people who are intoxicated voidable by them?

4. Pelham, 17 years old, bought a car from Howard Motors for $2,075.60, paying $500 down. In the bill of sale, Pelham certified that he was 18 or older, and he told the salesman he was 19. Pelham took the car home but brought it back the next day for repairs. When Howard failed to correct the problems, Pelham had his attorney write the company, repudiating the contract and demanding return of the down payment. Should Pelham prevail?

5. Horton, age 17, rented three furnished rooms from Johnson. He and his wife occupied the rooms for five months. When Horton moved out, Johnson brought suit for one week's rent, "one week of notice in lieu of intent to terminate tenancy," and damages to furnishings. Could Horton be held responsible?

6. Stewart and Curry were partners in a paving contracting business. Curry began to drink heavily and once was hospitalized for alcoholism. During this time Curry contributed very little to the paving business. For several months Stewart and Curry talked about their business problems. An agreement dissolving the partnership was prepared by Stewart and given to Curry. Two weeks later Curry returned the signed agreement. Stewart also signed. Several other documents relating to the dissolution of the partnership were also signed by both Stewart and Curry. Three months later, Curry filed suit. He claimed that he was still recovering from his alcoholism, under the influence of sedatives, and therefore was entitled to avoid the dissolution agreement because he lacked the capacity to contract. Do you agree?

7. Bowling, age 16, bought a used car from Sperry for several hundred dollars. He paid the full amount in cash. After one week, he found the main bearing had burned out. He returned the car to Sperry and asked that it be repaired; Sperry said the repair would cost Bowling $80. Bowling said he wouldn't pay $80 and left the car with Sperry. The next week, he wrote to Sperry that he wanted to disaffirm his purchase contract. He asked for his money back. Sperry refused, and Bowling sued. Can Bowling disaffirm this contract? How would you decide if this car is a necessary for Bowling?

8. Jack Jones, a 16-year-old high school student, lives with his parents. He works part time but depends on his parents for most of his support. Jack buys the items listed below. He then notifies each of the sellers that he is a minor, is renouncing his contract, and will not return the merchandise. Further, he wants his money back. What should happen regarding his purchase of:

1 □ drugs at a drugstore which were prescribed for his asthma

2 □ food at a local restaurant bought after school and before going to his part-time job

3 □ a winter jacket costing $60 to keep him warm in the Michigan winter

4 □ $400 in photography equipment for his hobby of three years

9. James Taylor, a minor, bought a used car when he was one year under the age of majority and began making payments on it to the bank that financed it. Then he went into the service and made no more payments on the car. He told his father to have the bank pick up the car. It did so and sold it for salvage. When Taylor returned from the service, the bank claimed that he had not disaffirmed his contract because he did not ask for the return of his payments. Do you agree? Why?

10. Parent, a minor, made a compromise settlement with Mazurek, an adjuster representing the insurance company that underwrote workmen's compensation for the state. The agreement was based on compensation due Parent for a back injury he sustained while employed at Midway Toyota. Mazurek represented Midway Toyota during the settlement negotiations and negotiated directly with Parent and his mother, who was present when he signed the agreement. Parent's mother did not object to the signing. Neither she nor any other adult cosigned the agreement. Since Parent was the sole contracting party with Mazurek, is he now entitled to disaffirm the agreement? Why or why not?

11. Halbman, a minor, agreed to buy a 1968 Oldsmobile from Lemke for $1,250. Lemke was the manager of L & M Standard Station, and Halbman was an employee at L & M. At the time of the agreement, Halbman paid Lemke $1,000 cash and took possession of the car. Halbman was to pay $25 a week until the balance was paid, at which time title would be transferred. About five weeks after the purchase agreement, and after Halbman had paid $1,100, a connecting rod on the car's engine broke. Halbman sought to disaffirm his contract, but Lemke claimed that Halbman was responsible for the damage to the car. Does a minor who has disaffirmed a contract to buy a nonessential item and who has returned the property to the seller have to make restitution for damage to the property before the disaffirmance?

12. A minor owns property which is managed for him by a legal guardian. The legal guardian filed an accounting with the court about how the property was being managed. The minor objected to that accounting and hired an attorney to represent him before the court. The attorney was successful in having some change made in the guardian's accounting. Could the contract between the minor and the attorney be disaffirmed by the minor?

13. Mrs. Schmaltz was a passenger in an automobile which was struck by a truck driven by Walder. She was injured, taken to the hospital, and treated for possible internal injuries, abrasions, and bruises. She was also given pain killers and tranquilizers. She made appointments for checkups with an internist and with her own doctor. Several days later, an insurance agent, representing the truck driver, came to discuss a settlement with her. When he offered her $2,000, she discussed it with her husband, and quickly accepted. Before the agent's visit, Mrs. Schmaltz was upset, thinking constantly about how close she had come to more serious injuries. She asserts that her nervous tension and anxiety impaired her capacity to contract. Is her settlement with Walder and his insurance company voidable due to her lack of mental capacity?

14. William Schiller, a widower 67 years old, has a gangrenous right foot which needs to be amputated. Schiller also has organic brain damage and is considered incapable of understanding his condition or the amputation of his leg as a means of saving his life. Can the hospital operate on Schiller without his consent?

CHAPTER 10

Illegality

CHAPTER OBJECTIVES

After reading this chapter, you should be able to:

1. Understand the variation in law regarding contracts' illegality.

2. Understand that statutes and court decisions establish the conditions under which contracts are illegal.

3. Identify four or more types of contracts frequently declared illegal by the legislature.

4. Identify four or more types of contracts frequently declared illegal by the judiciary.

5. Understand that not all contracts found illegal are treated alike.

A contract may include all the elements necessary to be valid, but if its purpose is illegal, the contract may not be enforced. Illegal contracts are generally referred to as **unenforceable contracts.**

The most obvious example of an illegal contract is an agreement to commit a crime. Television detective shows have made us all familiar with the expression, "to put a contract out on someone." No one would argue seriously that the people who kill by contract should be aided by the courts in securing the agreed contract price for their services.

Contracts to commit crimes and torts are clearly illegal and unenforceable. Further, most states have laws that declare other transactions illegal, and contracts that violate these laws generally cannot be enforced. Some states prohibit the sale of firecrackers; others do not. Some states prohibit gambling; a few states allow and, in fact, promote some kinds of gambling.

Because a state's public policy may be declared by the legislature or by the courts, both statutory and common law must be examined for agreements considered illegal. Although the lists of such contracts vary from state to state, this chapter examines a few of the most common regulations of illegal agreements.

Unenforceable contract an agreement that is valid but which may not be enforced because it is illegal

STATUTES AND ILLEGAL CONTRACTS

A variety of contracts may be pronounced illegal by statute. Because contracts generally are regulated more by state than by federal law, our focus here is on state law. As we have noted, states vary significantly in contract regulation. Nevertheless, at least four areas often are dealt with by state laws: wagering, usury, blue laws, and licensing laws.

Statutes and Wagering Agreements

Wagering contract an agreement to pay a designated amount of money or property when the uncertain outcome of an event is determined

A **wagering contract** is one in which the parties promise to pay a designated sum of money or to transfer property upon the determination of an uncertain event or a fact in dispute. Bets on a horse race, football game, or roll of the dice are all wagers. The public policy regarding wagering agreements varies from state to state. Although most states prohibit many wagering agreements, most permit such schemes as raffles, bingo, and the awarding of door prizes.

Many states have recognized that gambling generates money and have instituted state lotteries. Charitable organizations also may be licensed to conduct raffles, to give millionaires' parties, or to sponsor bingo games. In a few states, wagering agreements that do not involve substantial amounts are permitted. Thus a friendly bet on the local football game might be permitted in some states but prohibited in others. A poker game among senior citizens in Florida received national attention when a local prosecutor decided to enforce the state's gambling laws. Although the enforcement of these laws is usually sporadic, it is wise for people to check the statutes in their state and to be aware of the possibility (if not the probability) that contracts violating these statutes not only may be unenforceable but also may result in criminal sanctions.

Not all contracts that reward each party differently depending on a future event are wagers. An insurance policy or a contract for the sale or purchase of commodities that will be harvested in the future are both speculative. These agreements, however, involve items of value that are bought and sold. The parties are not merely speculating on the outcome of a future event. The insured has a substantial interest in his or her life or property, and the commodity purchaser agrees to accept the commodity being bargained for. Because these agreements are not wagers, they are legal and enforceable.

Statutes and Usury Contracts

Usury contracts contracts which are illegal because the amount of interest charged for the use of money exceeds the amount permitted by law

State statutes often limit the amount of interest that a lender may charge. Any contract by which the lender receives more than the permitted interest is illegal. A **usury contract** is one in which the lender of money receives more interest on the loan than is permitted by law. Civil and criminal penalties usually are placed on those who lend money at usurious rates. In most states, the lender is denied the right to collect any interest on a usurious contract. Some states also prohibit the lender from collecting the principal due on a usurious loan. A few states allow the lender to collect the interest permitted by law and prohibit only the excess, illegal interest. Lenders usually may recover expenses and fees incurred in preparing loan documents.

Often many different usury statutes exist in a state. Some statutes apply only to certain lenders, such as small loan associations, others to specific transactions, such as installment loans. Loans made to businesses are often totally exempt from usury statutes. Most states permit interest rates charged by those who issue credit cards and those who lend money to finance homes and cars to exceed the basic rate. Finally, almost all states permit small loan companies to charge interest rates of up to 36 percent so that the borrower who cannot go to conventional financial institutions has a legitimate source from which to borrow.

The primary objective of usury statutes is to protect the borrower from being forced to pay an excessive amount for the use of money. Usury has been illegal since biblical times, and the usurious lender often has been a moral outcast. Yet the effect of usury statutes often has been to penalize those most in need of funds. The statutes reduce consumers' options rather than increasing their bargaining power with the lender. Indeed, some lenders have refused to make loans in certain states. Others, including some major New York banks, have transferred some of their operations to other states because of the effect of usury laws on their business.

Statutes and Blue Laws

Some states have statutes that forbid "all secular labor and business on the Sabbath." **Blue laws,** named for the color of the paper they once were printed on, outlaw certain sales and transactions on Sundays. In some states, all contracts made on Sundays are illegal and unenforceable, at least so long as they remain unperformed, or executory (see Chapter 5). Other states prohibit only certain types of transactions or the sale of certain goods on Sunday. For example, laws prohibiting the Sunday sale of merchandise such as hammers, oars, beer, and socks are common in some southern states. Many state statutes and municipal ordinances prohibit the sale of alcoholic beverages on Sundays. The Sunday sale of automobiles and other consumer products also may be prohibited to regulate competition among sellers and to provide a day of rest from commercial activity.

In interpreting blue laws, courts typically seek to avoid the harsh effects that could result if the agreements were totally unenforceable. Instead, if some part of the agreement is made or performed on some day other than Sunday, the contract is usually enforced. Thus a contract that would have been illegal because it was made on a Sunday is legal if the parties later negotiate or approve their agreement. For this reason, blue laws generally have little effect on business transactions. However, active enforcement of these laws varies significantly from one place to another.

Blue laws laws that outlaw certain sales or transactions on Sundays

Statutes and Licensing Regulations

Statutes in all states require that licenses, certificates, permits, or registrations be obtained to perform certain acts. For example, the Michigan Department of Licensing and Regulation includes many boards and commissions, such as the Board of Accountancy, the Board of Registration for Architects, the Athletic Board of Control, the Board of Barber Examiners, the Builders Residential and Maintenance and Alteration Contractors Board, the Board of Chiropractic Examiners, the Professional Board of Registration for Community Planners, the Board of Dentistry, the Professional Board of Registration for Engineers, the Board of Registration for Foresters, the Board of Horology, the Board of Regulation for Land Surveyors, etc. Each board and commission is charged with regulating some activity of interest to the state, frequently by issuing licenses or permits to those persons who meet qualifications established for the regulated activity.

In some cases, state statutes merely require a fee be paid for a license. These licensing laws are known as **revenue statutes,** because they are primarily concerned

Revenue statutes licensing laws requiring a fee for a permit; primarily concerned with raising revenue

with raising revenue, even though some application procedure may have to be completed. Usually, anyone can obtain a fishing license or a minnow and wiggler dealer license. Such licensing laws do not usually subject the licensee to any significant regulation by the state.

Regulatory statutes licensing laws requiring a fee for a permit to engage in a business or activity; primarily concerned with regulating permit seekers

In contrast, the primary purpose of **regulatory statutes** is to regulate those obtaining a license. The state wants to insure that its nurses, doctors, real estate brokers, plumbers, lawyers, and others who serve the public are competent to engage in their profession or business. Although regulatory statutes are concerned chiefly with protecting the public, a fee is often assessed to cover administrative costs. There are several consequences for people who do not comply with the requirements of state licensing statutes. The consequences may be criminal charges or disciplinary action taken by a panel, board, or professional association.

Our primary concern here is the civil law consequences to those who have made a contract that does not comply with licensing requirements. If a state requires you to have a license to be an architect, may you contract with someone to provide architectural services if you do not have the required license? Will the state enforce your contract? If you are not paid by the other contracting party, may you sue to recover the money you were to be paid? The answer to these questions depends on the wording of the applicable licensing statute.

Many statutes specify that any agreements made by people who do not comply with their terms will be unenforceable. When the statute is silent on the enforceability of such agreements, the courts frequently look to the purpose of the statute. Contracts made without a license that violate revenue statutes usually are enforceable. Thus a farmer who should but does not have a license to sell his produce at a city market can enforce contracts with those who buy the produce. Although the farmer has violated a licensing statute intended to raise revenue for the city, that violation does not affect contracts made by the farmer.

However, if the purpose of the licensing statute is primarily regulatory, courts will not help those who perform services or deliver goods without complying with the licensing provisions to enforce contracts with the purchasers of the goods or services. The *Silver* case exemplifies this principle.

Silver v. A.O.C. Corporation

Court of Appeals of Michigan
187 N.W. 2d 532 (1971)

FACTS   A.O.C. Corporation is an apartment management company that had become the manager of an apartment building in Detroit. Silver, a journeyman electrician, had been employed by A.O.C.'s predecessor to repair lights at the apartment building. He was not licensed as an electrical contractor under state law or city ordinance. Those laws require that anyone who performs electrical work for payment get a license, unless the work is worth less than $50.

After the caretaker's wife called Silver to fix a short circuit in the caretaker's apartment and to fix one or two hallway lights, Silver found that the wires in the hallway were burned by oversized bulbs. When he found the same condition in all the lights in the building, he replaced and rewired all the defective wiring. He worked during a four-month period. Silver spent 125 hours on the job and used $143 worth of his own materials. After completion, he submitted a bill for $893 to the defendant. A.O.C. refused to pay Silver, and Silver sued. A.O.C. claimed that because Silver was not licensed as provided for in the licensing statute and municipal ordinance, he could collect nothing for his work.

Should Silver be able to collect money due him for performing electric work when he was not a licensed electrician?   ISSUE

No. The court found that Silver's work was well in excess of $50 and therefore would not fall under the "minor repair work" exception to the licensing requirement. Silver had entered into a contract to perform services in violation of a licensing statute enacted to protect the public health, morals, and safety. Because the licensing statute imposed a penalty if it was violated, it was clearly intended to prohibit unlicensed work. Accordingly, Silver's contract in violation of the statute was unenforceable.   DECISION

THE COMMON LAW AND ILLEGAL CONTRACTS

This section reviews contracts that are illegal because they restrain trade, relieve one party from some liability to another party, include unconscionable provisions, or involve other acts that conflict with public policy.

Agreements in Restraint of Trade

The law does not favor agreements in which one person agrees not to compete with another. Such agreements impose too great a restraint on the individual and adversely affect competition. Unless such agreements are part of other lawful contracts and are limited to reasonable terms, the courts do not enforce them.

Agreements not to compete often appear in contracts to buy and sell a business. The purchaser wants to insure that the seller, who has built up the good will of the business, will not compete with the purchased business. Agreements not to compete also appear in employer–employee contracts. An employee may be working in a vital segment of the employer's business. The employer wants to insure that the employee does not establish a competing business based partly on the valuable information learned from the employer.

A noncompetitive agreement generally is examined to determine if it is reasonable to the concerned parties and to the public. Agreements that restrict competition between the seller and buyer of businesses are generally viewed favorably by the courts. A court usually focuses on whether a contract provision restraining the seller is reasonable in time and area. Thus a provision restricting the seller from working in or opening a business that is competitive with the buyer is reasonable in specifying several years but not 10 or 20 years. The restraint ordinarily cannot prohibit the seller from opening a similar business in the next state or in a distant community. The geographic area of the restraint must be limited to that in which the purchaser's need for protection is dominant.

Agreements between an employer and employee that restrict the employee's right to compete with the employer are usually examined more closely by the courts than agreements between seller and purchaser. Unlike the purchaser of a business, the employee generally is not in an equal bargaining position with the employer. In the sale of a business, the purchaser almost always wants to protect the good will of the business. But the employer has less need to protect the business's good will against the employee. Employees are less likely to be able to take an employer's good will to their own use. In employment cases, the courts examine not only the need for protection by the employer but also the relative hardship imposed on the employee. The employee's lack of bargaining power often is a decisive factor. The public interest in the restraint also is examined, particularly if vital services or goods would be withheld from the public if restraint were enforced.

After the reasonableness of the restraint has been determined, the court must decide several questions about the agreement's enforceability. If the restraint is unreasonable, should the court rewrite the restraint so that it is reasonable and enforce it, or should it leave one party free from restraint? Similarly, if an agreement contains a provision that unreasonably restrains the seller, can that provision be separated from other provisions in the agreement? If one part of a contract is illegal and unenforceable, can any other part of the contract be enforced?

Knoebel Mercantile Company v. Siders

Supreme Court of Colorado
439 P.2d 355 (1968)

FACTS   Siders was a salesman for Knoebel Mercantile Company. At the time he was hired, June 1, 1964, Siders signed an employment contract with a clause preventing him from working for any of Knoebel's competition in a seven-state area for two years after he stopped working for Knoebel. Siders worked for Knoebel until September 1966. He then took a position as a salesman with John Sexton and Company, a competitor of Knoebel. Knoebel sued Siders, seeking to restrain him from working as a salesman for John Sexton, as their contract provided. Siders claimed that the restriction was unenforceable.

ISSUE   Should the restriction in the contract be enforced?

DECISION   No. The court refused to enforce the restriction covenant because it was too broad. The court found that Siders was not in a position to control where Knoebel's customers did business. Further, Siders's services were not unique in character. Finally, if the contract restriction were enforced, it would force Siders to move from the region in which he had spent most of his adult life or to abandon the type of work in which he was most experienced. Because the test of whether a restriction will be enforced is the reasonableness of the restriction, the court's determination that the restriction was unreasonable led to its finding for Siders.

Contracts with Exculpatory Clauses

Exculpatory clauses in a contract relieve or limit the liability of one of the parties if that party does not perform. The law does not view such clauses favorably. The law holds that damages caused by one party's nonperformance of contract terms should be available to the injured party. The courts, as well as some state statutes, have declared exculpatory clauses unenforceable, illegal, and contrary to public policy. For example, most jurisdictions have statutes that deny the enforceability of some exculpatory clauses in apartment leases prepared by landlords for tenants.

Exculpatory clause provision that relieves or limits a party's liability for nonperformance of a contract

Exculpatory clauses that are unenforceable can be classified under two main headings: 1. those limiting liability of someone who regularly sells goods or services to the public and 2. those limiting an employer's liability for negligence that causes injury to an employee. With clauses of the first type, the law notes that there rarely is equality of bargaining power between the consumer and the dealer. The public interest is best served if people whose contracts with the public are not subject to bargaining or negotiation are liable for their own negligence. With clauses of the second type, the policy of the law is to discourage negligence by making wrongdoers pay damages. If an employer causes injury to anyone, even an employee, the injured party should be able to recover damages. Furthermore, an employee is generally not in an equal bargaining position with an employer. For these reasons, such clauses are not favored and will not be enforced.

Some exculpatory clauses are enforced. Some states allow contracting parties the freedom to contract under the broadest possible terms. In these states, freedom of contract outweighs concern over exculpatory clauses. Two factors are particularly important in these instances: the bargaining power of the parties and the degree to which the law otherwise regulates the agreement. If both parties are business firms, the courts are likely to allow one party to limit its liability. Similarly, if one of the businesses already is significantly regulated by the state, that regulation may permit the business to limit its liability in certain contracts.

One of the most common situations in which people seek to limit their liability concerns those who have been given the right to possess property. The restaurant checkroom, the downtown parking lot, and the airport baggage counter usually post signs or print statements on their receipts and claim tickets that limit their liability, even for their own negligence, if a customer's property is lost or damaged. While there are some exceptions, most of these clauses generally are enforceable.

Unconscionable Contracts

Closely related to the problem of determining whether a contract is illegal because it contains an exculpatory clause and therefore violates public policy is the problem of determining whether a particular contract is illegal because it is unconscionable. An **unconscionable contract** is one that is so unfair, unjust, or unreasonable that it shocks the conscience of a court asked to enforce it. If a contract is too oppressive or one-sided, the courts do not enforce it. The basis for most of the litigated cases today is the Uniform Commercial Code (Section 2-302). It provides:

Unconscionable contract an agreement that shocks the conscience and is so unfair and unreasonable that it should not be enforced

1. If the court as a matter of law finds the contract or any clause of the contract to have been unconscionable at the time it was made, the court may refuse to enforce the

contract, or it may enforce the remainder of the contract without the unconscionable clause, or it may so limit the application of any unconscionable clause as to avoid any unconscionable result.

2. When it is claimed or appears to the court that the contract or any clause thereof may be unconscionable, the parties shall be afforded a reasonable opportunity to present evidence as to its commercial setting, purpose, and effect to aid the court in making the determination.

Several factors are important in the determination of what makes a contract unconscionable. What is the relative bargaining power of the parties? Is one party economically stronger than the other? Does each party have options? Can the seller sell to others? Is there only one source of supply? How reasonable are the terms? According to the UCC:

The basic test is whether, in the light of the general commercial background and the commercial needs of the particular trade or case, the clauses involved are so one-sided as to be unconscionable under the circumstances existing at the time of the making of the contract.

Contracts which give to only one party the right to cancel or significantly alter its terms may be unconscionable. A contract between a large industrial firm and one of its suppliers may be unconscionable if the number of units to be purchased and the duration of the contract are to be decided solely by the large firm. A contract will not be unconscionable if it merely allocates risks between the contracting parties. Frequently, one party receives greater benefit from a contract than the other party because that party has assumed a greater risk. For example, neither the selling manufacturer nor the purchasing store contracting for "Cabbage Patch" dolls eight months before the Christmas season knows how well the dolls will sell. In this case the purchasing store assumes a greater risk by committing to purchase X number of dolls far ahead of the selling season. Thus, the manufacturer would not be able to claim that the bargain price it had agreed to was unconscionable just because the dolls became a successful gift item and subsequently commanded a higher contracted price.

Contracts against Public Policy

A contract or one of its provisions may be declared contrary to public policy if it injures the public interest or interferes with the public's general welfare, health, safety, or morals. But what constitutes "public policy"? The term itself is vague and uncertain. Today's public policy may be repudiated tomorrow. For instance, in *Henningsen* v. *Bloomfield Motors,* the New Jersey Supreme Court held that a provision in a printed contract used by all large automobile companies that disclaimed virtually all guarantees of performance or service was contrary to public policy. The court stated:

Public Policy is a term not easily defined. Its significance varies as the habits and needs of a people may vary. It is not static and the field of application is an ever increasing one. A contract, or a particular provision therein, valid in one era may be wholly opposed to the public policy of another.

Public policy is based in constitutions, statutes, and court decisions. It is influenced by political, economic, and historical events. There really is no limit on the sources a court may use in determining public policy. An analysis of court decisions on public policy invariably produces conflicting results.

In the *Western Cab* case, which follows, the Supreme Court of Nevada examined a contract Western Cab made with a businessman who agreed to testify on behalf of the taxicab company.

Western Cab Company v. Kellar

Supreme Court of Nevada
523 P.2d 842 (1974)

FACTS Kellar owned all the stock of Western Cab Company, and agreed to transfer his stock to Crockett. Crockett, one of the Company's founders, was seeking to reorganize the business. Later, the local taxicab authority reviewed the reorganization and change of ownership. Kellar threatened to testify before the authority that he had never transferred his ownership to Crockett, but instead had transferred it to his wife. Crockett, acting on behalf of Western, agreed to pay Kellar $6,000 in cash plus 500 shares of stock if Kellar would testify in support of Western's application and would not claim ownership in Western. Western's payment to Kellar depended on the success of its application to reactivate the company. Kellar testified as agreed at the authority hearing. When he was not paid as agreed, he sued to enforce the contract.

ISSUE Is the contract between Western Cab Company and Kellar unenforceable?

DECISION Yes. The court held that the contract between the two parties was contrary to public policy and therefore unenforceable. Contracts that involve payment for testifying, coupled with the condition that the witness's right to compensation depends upon the result of the suit in which the testimony is given, tend to lead to perjury and the perversion of justice. As such, their contract, which was contrary to public policy, was unenforceable.

Dissenting Opinion: The dissenting judge would allow the contract to be enforced, because Kellar (who once owned all the company's stock), still had a claim to an ownership interest in the corporation. For this reason, his agreement to testify at the Taxicab Authority hearing was not solely for the benefit of Crockett. He was in part protecting his own interest in the company and was not merely testifying in a certain way in exchange for money.

EFFECTS OF ILLEGALITY

Not all contracts found illegal are treated alike. For example, we have seen that contracts violating revenue licensing provisions are treated differently from those contradicting regulatory licensing requirements. A violation of the revenue statutes generally does not adversely affect a contract as does a violation of regulatory statutes.

The general policy of the law is not to enforce an illegal agreement. But refusing to enforce an agreement is different from saying that no agreement has been made. If no agreement has been made, neither party should keep what the other may have given as consideration. If an unenforceable agreement has been made, the party who has done something illegal should not be able to enforce the agreement. However, if one party has not done anything illegal, that party may be able to keep the consideration he or she received. These parties to an unenforceable agreement have still made a contract, even though the courts usually aid neither of them to enforce its provisions.

What about an agreement that has both legal and illegal provisions? Can the legal provisions be enforced while the illegal provisions are denied? The answer to this question depends on how easily one may separate the two. If the essence of the entire contract is illegal, probably none of its provisions can be enforced. But if the legal provisions can be separated from the illegal ones, the legal provisions may be enforceable. Suppose that a seller and buyer of a business agree illegally that the seller will not compete with the buyer in any business, in any area, for a long period of time. The fact that the restraint on the seller is unreasonable and unenforceable probably generally does not make illegal and unenforceable the remaining terms for the transfer of the business.

Finally, if the court refuses to enforce some or all of the contractual provisions the parties have agreed to, it must determine whether either party can seek some other remedy in the courts. Does the unenforceability of the contract extend to other actions that one of the parties might bring against the other?

This question is discussed in the *Glyco* case that follows. Although in this case, the parties' contract is not enforced, the tenant still must pay for the benefit he has received. It is *as if* there had been a reasonable contract, and that contract, not the one the parties actually made, is to be enforced.

Glyco v. Schultz

Municipal Court of Sylvania, Ohio
289 N.E.2d 919 (1972)

FACTS   Plaintiff Glyco rented a house and 30 acres of land to defendants Schultz. The house had not been maintained in accordance with the local housing code regulations. When the Schultzes moved in, the electrical system was in disrepair and woefully underserviced. The furnace was faulty, the steps were deteriorating, and the upstairs floor was weak. These conditions continued throughout the Schultzes' stay and greatly inconvenienced them, damaged their personal property and cost them money for repairs. After the Schultzes notified Glyco of the violations by letter on at least three occasions and Glyco did not fix them, the Schultzes stopped paying the rent.

ISSUE   Is a contract that provides defective housing enforceable so that the tenant still has to pay the rent?

DECISION   No. The court determined that the contract was illegal because the house was in substantial violation of the county housing code, both when the lease was signed and throughout the Schultzes' stay. It also determined that in this contract, both parties were not equally at fault. The Schultzes had no real choice but to participate in the contract's illegality. Because the contract was illegal and unenforceable, the Schultzes could recover any rent they had paid that was more than the reasonable rental value of the defective property.

ILLEGALITY AND CONFLICTS OF LAW

As we have seen, both statutes and common law determine certain contracts to be illegal and unenforceable. Because contracts are governed almost totally by state laws, those state laws determine which contracts are illegal. What happens if a contract is made in one state and performed in another? What if one party signs a contract in New York and the other party signs it in Georgia? Does New York law or Georgia law control? What if that contract is to be performed in Missouri?

The rules that states use to answer questions like these are **conflict of law rules.** When a conflict exists between the laws of several states or nations, courts use general principles to determine which state's or nation's rules should be applied.

Sometimes courts use general rules: Apply the law where the contract is to be performed. Follow the law selected by the parties. Sometimes courts look to the effect or the policy of the law. In the *National Starch* case, which follows, the court examines a contract that restrains trade. Some states will not enforce such a contract because it is contrary to public policy. Other states do enforce such an agreement if its provisions are reasonable.

Conflict of law rules general principles used to determine which laws should be referred to when a conflict exists between the laws of several states or nations

National Starch and Chemical Corporation v. Newman
577 S.W.2d 99 (Mo. Ct. App., 1979)

National Starch and Chemical is a Delaware corporation that manufactures and sells industrial adhesives nationwide. It has, among others, an established market in states comprising its sales district administered from offices in Kansas City, Missouri. Theodore A. Newman started work with National as a sales representative in New York in December 1958. Since 1965, he was responsible for sales in the Kansas City district. Newman signed an employment agreement on April 1, 1965, in Atlanta, Georgia. The agreement was signed by National in New York City. The agreement provided that Newman would not take customers from National for two years after he stopped working for National.

When he was with National, Newman learned about its activities, methods of operation, and sales methods, and met many customers.

In 1975, National asked Newman to sign a revised employment agreement which would have protected against disclosure of National's trade secrets. Newman did not sign that agreement but gave notice of his intent to stop working for National. National

FACTS

responded by reminding Mr. Newman of the postemployment provision in the 1965 agreement.

In 1976, Newman and several others formed the Missouri River Company to manufacture and distribute adhesives in Missouri, Kansas, Ohio, Illinois, and Colorado.

ISSUE   Do the laws of Missouri and not those of New York or Georgia determine the legality of the contract between Newman and National Starch?

DECISION   Yes. The court found the laws of Missouri to be controlling. The contract did not delineate the place of Newman's performance. At all times, Newman performed in the states of his sales territory. Newman performed in Georgia for some seven months but in the Kansas City district for 10½ years. Newman lived and established his competing business in Kansas City and solicited most of National's customers in Missouri.

Therefore, Missouri's relationship to the parties and the transaction is superior to that of any other state. The policy of Missouri is to enforce reasonable restrictive clauses to protect Missouri businesses from unfair competition by former employees and to protect individuals engaging in business in Missouri from unreasonable restraints. Because the court found the restrictive clauses to be reasonable under Missouri law, the contract as a whole was legal and enforceable.

SUMMARY

Contracts that are otherwise valid may be unenforceable if they are illegal. The illegality of contracts is a matter of state law and so varies from state to state. Nevertheless, the types of contracts noted in this chapter are illegal in most states.

Statutes prohibit wagering agreements as contrary to the promotion of the people's general welfare. The states also limit the interest that a lender of money can charge to a borrower. Contracts that provide for higher than allowed interest rates are usurious and illegal. While blue laws are not enforced throughout the United States, in some communities contracts to provide certain services on a Sunday are illegal and unenforceable.

A violation of a state licensing law or regulation may also be illegal. Frequently, it is critical to determine if the licensing was intended to regulate or only to raise revenue. While a violation of the former will frequently result in an illegal and unenforceable contract, no such result generally occurs if only a revenue licensing statute is involved.

Court decisions in the states have made other types of contracts illegal. Contracts that restrain trade by restricting the mobility of a businessperson or his or her ability to compete with a former employer can be illegal if they are too pervasive. Contracts that limit a person or firm's liability for negligence or that are so one-sided as to shock the court's conscience are also illegal.

Finally, the public policy in a state may make illegal other contracts, such as those to provide certain testimony in a lawsuit in exchange for a fee. While a variety of contracts can be found to be illegal, not all such contracts are unenforceable. Generally the law refuses to aid either contracting party who desires to enforce an illegal contract. Instead it leaves the parties where they are. Occasionally, however, the law is aimed at protecting one of the parties and an illegal contract will still be enforceable by that one party.

REVIEW PROBLEMS

1. Are all illegal contracts unenforcable?

2. When are contracts that include provisions that restrain trade or that limit a person's ability to compete unenforceable?

3. What is an exculpatory clause?

4. What determines if a clause in a contract is unconscionable and therefore unenforceable?

5. Tovar, a physician practicing in the state of Kansas, wrote the Paxton Hospital in Illinois to inquire about obtaining a position as a full-time resident. In his letter and in a subsequent personal interview, Tovar fully described the nature and extent of his education, training, and licensing as a physician. The hospital assured him that his professional credentials were satisfactory and hired him. Soon thereafter Tovar, who had relocated to Illinois, was discharged by Paxton Hospital for failure to hold a license to practice medicine in Illinois as required by a state statute. Tovar sues the hospital. What result?

6. Weaver, a high school dropout, signed a service station lease with American Oil Company containing a clause in fine print that released the oil company from liability for its negligence and compelled Weaver to pay American for any damage incurred through negligence. Weaver never read the lease, nor was it ever explained to him. During the course of business, a visiting American Oil employee negligently sprayed gasoline over Weaver and his assistant, causing them to be burned and injured. American disclaimed liability on the basis of the contract clause. Is this correct?

7. Hiyanne worked as a contact lens grinder and fitter for the House of Vision from 1959 until 1964 in branch stores, several in different cities. His employment contract said that when he stopped working for House of Vision, he would never engage in similar business anywhere within a 30-mile radius of any of the branch stores in which he had worked. Hiyanne resigned in 1964 and began working for a competitor 150 feet away from a House of Vision store where he had once worked. The House of Vision seeks to enforce the restrictive clause in the employment contract. What result?

8. Sweazea, a building owner, contracted with Measday for water and gas plumbing work. A local statute provides that a permit be applied for before plumbing work is begun. The intent of the regulation is that work done for which a permit is required is to be inspected for compliance with professional standards. Measday failed to apply for a permit until he had substantially completed the job. Now Sweazea has refused to finish paying him, and Measday claims a breach of their contract. Sweazea says the contract cannot be enforced because it is illegal due to the statutory violation. Does the violation make the contract illegal?

9. A retail store owner contracted with the Wisconsin Telephone Company to place an advertisement in the Racine, Wisconsin, yellow pages. The advertisement was to include the company's name in large print, followed by information on its location, products, and telephone number. The contract the store signed with the telephone company stated that the company would not be liable for errors in the directory beyond the price it charged for the advertisement. When the directory was published, the advertisement omitted the company's name. The telephone company agreed to refund part of the fee for the advertisement, but the store claimed other damages due to its loss in profits. The telephone company claims its contract provision validly limits its liability. The store claims the contract provision is unconscionable and the contract unenforceable and illegal. Who is correct?

10. Henry was an unemployed widower with two children who received public assistance from the county. He rented an apartment from Marin Corporation. The lease stated:

    owner shall not be liable for any damage or injury to Tenant or to any other person on the premises or any part thereof and Tenant agrees to hold owner harmless from any claims for damages no matter how caused.

    Henry fractured his wrist when he tripped over a common stairway leading to his and other apartments on the upper levels of the apartment building. When he sued to recover damages, Marin claimed the contract provision effective. Is it?

11. Thorpe, a licensed real estate broker, agreed to find a buyer for Carte's property. Subsequently, Thorpe agreed to share his commission with a person who would find a buyer for Carte's property. The finder who located a buyer for Carte was not licensed to sell real estate. Does Thorpe's contract to share his commission with an unlicensed finder make Thorpe's contract with Carte unenforceable?

12. A corporation borrows money from a bank. The loan specifies the payment of 10 percent interest (the maximum allowed under usury laws) and also specifies that the principal amount of the loan will be adjusted for inflation. May this agreement become usurious if interest rates go over 10 percent?

13. Tom Welch operated a business under the name "Tom Welch Accounting Services." He did bookkeeping for client Roger Walby, for which he charged Walby $1,400. Welch was not licensed, and the state law required that public accountants be licensed. Can Welch collect from Walby?

14. Best-Way Transportation Corporation, a transport trucking firm, contracted to transport truckloads of steel products from San Francisco to Phoenix for the Mountain States Bolt, Nut, and Screw Company. Mountain States withheld part of the payment due under its contract with Best-Way, claiming that part of the transportation route was not authorized under Best-Way's Arizona license. Does the fact that Best-Way's license did not authorize transportation over part of the route excuse Mountain States from paying Best-Way?

15. The Brovermans, as owners of the Taylorville landfill, contracted with the city of Taylorville to receive the city's garbage and waste matter. The city withheld part of the payment due under its contract with the Brovermans because the landfill

did not have the operating permit required by the Environmental Protection Act. The Brovermans sued to recover the unpaid amount due them. Can they recover from the city?

16. Hendrix, an electrical engineer, entered into a two-year employment contract with McKee, an Oregon manufacturer of "gaming" devices, to design a "pull tab" machine for McKee. Hendrix, who specialized in designing gambling devices used in Nevada, knew the contract was for the design of an amusement device which was illegal when used in Oregon. Hendrix worked for McKee for one year. Then McKee fired Hendrix. Can Hendrix recover damages because McKee terminated his employment after only one year?

CHAPTER 11

Legal Form

CHAPTER OBJECTIVES

STATUTE OF FRAUDS

Contracts Required to Be in Writing / What Constitutes a Writing / Problems with the Rule

CONTRACTS WITHIN THE STATUTE OF FRAUDS

Contracts in Consideration of Marriage / Executor's Promise to Pay the Debts of the Deceased / Promise to Pay the Debt of Another / Sale of Land or an Interest in Land / Promises Not Performable in One Year / Sale of Goods for $500 or More / Equitable Estoppel and Promissory Estoppel

THE PAROL EVIDENCE RULE

Requirements / Exceptions / UCC Parol Evidence Rule / The Effect of Consumer Protection Statutes

INTERPRETATION OF CONTRACTUAL PROVISIONS

SUMMARY

REVIEW PROBLEMS

CHAPTER OBJECTIVES

After reading this chapter, you should be able to:

1. Explain why certain contracts must be in writing to be enforceable.

2. Describe the type of writing required as evidence of a contract.

3. Explain how the Statute of Frauds may work to the disadvantage of consumers.

4. Describe how the courts have modified the Statute to protect consumers.

5. State which contracts for the sale of goods must be in writing and why.

6. Describe when side agreements or promises may be added to a written contract.

7. Describe the rules for interpreting contracts when the parties disagree about terms.

Many people assume that contracts must be written to be enforceable. In fact, oral contracts are also enforceable. Only a few types of contracts must be written. This chapter identifies those that must be written and then covers legal principles about the interpretation of contracts.

STATUTE OF FRAUDS

Contracts Required to Be in Writing

The English Parliament in 1677 enacted a Statute for the Prevention of Frauds and Perjuries. This Statute of Frauds attempted to prevent fraud about the existence of contracts by requiring that certain important contracts be written and signed before they could be enforced. Today all states in the United States have enacted similar statutes requiring that certain contracts be in writing to be enforceable. These contracts, discussed in detail later, include:

1. Contracts involving a promise by an executor to pay the debts of the deceased out of the executor's own funds

2. Contracts to pay the debt of another

3. Contracts for the sale of land or an interest in land

4. Contracts not to be performed within one year

5. Contracts for the sale of goods priced at $500 or more

6. Contracts in consideration of marriage (prenuptial agreements)

Some states require that certain other contracts — for example, real estate brokerage agreements — be written to be enforceable.

Although the statutes were designed for the broad purpose of preventing fraud and perjury, they serve three more specific purposes. First, the presence of a written contract reduces the chance that a court and jury will be misled about the existence or terms of the contract. Second, people are more likely to think about what they are getting into if they are required to sign something. They are less likely to act rashly. Finally, requiring a writing serves as a channeling device, distinguishing between those contracts that are enforceable and those that are not.

What Constitutes a Writing

Within the Statute required by the Statute to be in writing

A legal term, *within,* is used throughout this chapter. If a contract must be in writing, it is called **within the Statute.** If it does not have to be in writing, it is called "without" the Statute. Oral contracts that are required to be in writing are considered unenforceable in most states, though they are otherwise valid. Thus, if someone fails to raise the defense of the Statute of Frauds, that person is legally bound by the contract.

What must a contract that must be written include? To be enforced, such a contract must be evidenced by a document describing the basic agreement signed by the person being sued on the contract. In general, the document must identify the parties, the subject matter of the contract, and the performance obligations of the parties.

Problems with the Rule

The rule that certain contracts must be written has on occasion worked to the disadvantage of consumers. The experience of a former student provides a ready example. The student signed a contract for the purchase of a motorcycle for $1,200. The merchant then contacted the student and told him that the dealership could not sell the cycle for less than $1,350. The student produced the contract form. It had never been signed by the merchant. The student could not sue to enforce the agreement.

In similar situations, a contract may be signed by a salesperson who has not agency authority to sign. At best, there are several legal hurdles that must be overcome to enforce such an agreement. At worst, the consumer, thinking that he or she has a "deal," discovers at the end that there is no legal recourse.

The example of the student and the motorcycle also demonstrates a second problem with the Statute. The student could not sue the merchant. But could the merchant sue the student? The surprising answer is yes — because the student had signed the contract. Because of this problem of one-way enforceability, the Statute has been partially modified by the UCC in regard to agreements between merchants [2-201(2)]. Even greater strides have been made with the recent development of consumer protection laws at both state and federal levels. These laws will be discussed later in this chapter.

A final problem arises from the technical application of the rule. The purpose of the Statute is to insure that there is in fact an underlying contract between the parties. Yet some courts have refused to enforce oral agreements that fall within the scope of the Statute that everyone concedes were made. Modern courts have responded to this unfortunate tendency by emphasizing the rule's exceptions. When it comes to applying the Statute, it is important to recognize that the exceptions are as important as the rule.

CONTRACTS WITHIN THE STATUTE OF FRAUDS

Contracts in Consideration of Marriage

Contracts in consideration of marriage involve property settlements in exchange for a promise to marry. Such prenuptial agreements are used mainly when two well-to-do people, both with children of their own, decide to marry late in life. Mutual promises to marry do not have to be written.

Executor's Promise to Pay the Debts of the Deceased

When a person dies, it is almost certain that there will be some unpaid bills. It is also certain that creditors will demand payment before any other assets are distributed. To wind up the deceased's affairs, the executor of the estate is required to pay the debts. Generally, the executor is not personally liable for paying the debts. If the deceased has left no assets, the creditors lose. But in some situations, the executor may promise personally to satisfy the obligations of the deceased. For example, the executor who is also a family member may want to prevent creditors from seizing and selling family heirlooms, some of great sentimental value, to satisfy the debts. To be enforceable, the Statute of Frauds requires such promises to be in writing.

When you consider that a bereaved relative who is also serving as an executor may be extremely vulnerable emotionally, the rationale behind the writing requirement becomes obvious. To protect such people, any contracts by executors to satisfy personally debts of the deceased must be in writing.

Promise to Pay the Debt of Another

Promises by an executor to be personally liable for debts of a deceased and promises by one person to be liable for the debts of another are somewhat similar. The difference is that promises to pay the debts of another are not usually given in states of emotional distress, and all the parties are living.

Primary and Secondary Liability   The basic way to determine whether a person's promise to pay another's debt must be written is to ask whether the person making the promise is primarily or secondarily liable. **Primary liability** exists when the creditor can proceed directly against the person making the promise. **Secondary liability** exists when the creditor must look first to the original debtor before proceeding against the promisor. Promises involving secondary liability are within the Statute and must be in writing to be enforced.

Primary liability condition in which a promisor is directly liable to a creditor

Secondary liability condition in which a promisor is liable only after the original debtor has defaulted

For example, Charles is the owner of a local hardware store. Martin, a recent college graduate, has gone into business for himself as a building contractor. Martin comes into Charles's store seeking building supplies because he has just landed his first building contract. Charles, however, is unwilling to let Martin have the goods on credit, essentially because Martin hasn't had time to establish a credit rating. Martin, prepared for this, has his father, Martin, Senior, a well-known local businessman, call Charles and guarantee Martin's creditworthiness. Martin, Sr. promises that if Martin, Jr. defaults, Martin, Sr. will cover Charles's losses. Martin, Sr.'s promise is covered by the Statute of Frauds. Martin, Sr. has not made an absolute promise to pay Martin, Jr.'s debts; rather, Martin, Sr. has made a *conditional* promise to pay only if Martin, Jr. defaults. Charles must *first* look to Martin, Jr., not to Martin, Sr., for payment. Martin, Sr. is secondarily liable. His promise must be in writing.

However, assume that Martin, Jr. has won the building contract from Martin, Sr., his father. This time, when Martin, Sr. calls Charles, he tells Charles to give Martin, Jr. all the supplies he needs and to send the bill to him, Martin Sr. In this case, the father is primarily liable. His oral promise is enforceable. Charles must look to the father for payment.

Main purpose doctrine policy that states when the promisor benefits from accepting secondary liability, an oral promise is enforceable

Main Purpose Doctrine   In addition to the primary – secondary liability distinction, the courts also limit the application of the Statute with the **main purpose doctrine**. Under this doctrine, an oral promise creating secondary liability is nonetheless enforceable if it is made mainly to benefit the person making the promise. Assume, for example, that a franchisor of a tool rental business learns that one of his franchisees in a key location is about to be evicted for not paying rent on time. Franchisor calls the landlord and says, "I'll pay the rent if Franchisee doesn't pay you what he owes you. Don't evict him right now." That oral promise would be enforceable, because Franchisor's main purpose in making the promise is his own benefit. The franchise system depends for its success upon a strong distribution system, and the franchisor usually receives direct periodic payments from each operating franchisee. Thus, Franchisor has a personal motive for promising to effectively keep the franchised outlets operating.

Sale of Land or an Interest in Land

For our purposes, land is considered earth and the things permanently attached to it. The most common real estate transactions, such as the sale of residential or commercial property, clearly fall under this rule and must be written. But what constitutes an *interest* in land?

Assume that I promise to sell to you the right to cross my property for a particular purpose. This is known as an **easement**, and it constitutes an interest in land. Thus my promise, if only oral, is not enforceable. An option to buy is considered an interest in land, as is a lien or security interest given against the land. In many states, leases are within the Statute, although some states require that only leases for an extended term (for example, more than one year) must be in writing.

A generally recognized exception to the provision about real estate is the doctrine of **part performance.** This doctrine is used in circumstances where one party promises to sell land in return for certain actions by the buyer. For example, Owner of real property may promise to sell part of it to Tenant if Tenant improves the entire property and works it for Owner. After Tenant does the work, Owner refuses to sell and raises the Statute of Frauds as a defense. If the parties have acted as though they had entered into a contract for the sale of certain land and if failing to recognize an oral agreement would defraud Tenant, the courts enforce the oral agreement. The part performance must be substantial and in reliance on the oral promise to sell.

Easement a right to make limited use of the land of another

Part performance condition in which an oral agreement is enforceable if one party already has taken substantial action in reliance on the promise of another

Promises Not Performable in One Year

If a contract cannot be performed within a year, it must be put in writing. For example, a three-year contract for the services of a professional athlete must be written.

Assume that no date is set in a contract. Instead, the arrangement is to continue until some event occurs or until one of the parties cancels the agreement. Such contracts do not have to be written if the event could possibly occur within one year or if there is no limitation on the right to cancel during the first year. For example, an agreement to provide service to a person until death usually need not be written because death could occur within one year.

One final problem arises with contracts involving construction projects. Determining whether these contracts must be written becomes a question of fact. Is there any possibility that if everything goes perfectly (no strikes, good weather) the job can be completed within a year? If so, the contract need not be written.

The case that follows demonstrates several important facets of the Statute of Frauds, including the manner in which the courts interpret the one-year rule.

Buttorff v. United Electronic Laboratories, Incorporated

Court of Appeals of Kentucky
459 S.W.2d 581 (1970)

Buttorff contends that in February 1961, it entered into an oral contract with United Electronic Laboratories (U.E.L.), a manufacturer of surveillance cameras. Under the terms of the oral contract, Buttorff was to develop a market for the cameras and establish distributorships under its exclusive agency. Buttorff claims that the oral contract was to govern its relationship with U.E.L. until the two parties could negotiate a formal written agreement. U.E.L. contends that no such oral contract had ever been reached and that because Buttorff only sold cameras for U.E.L. between May 1961 and May 1962, any agreement between them would have to be in writing. Buttorff charges U.E.L. with breach of an oral contract.

FACTS

ISSUE   Is the agreement required to be in writing because it is within the Statute of Frauds?

DECISION   The court ruled in favor of part of the claim by plaintiff Buttorff. It pointed out that although the Statute of Frauds has consistently been applied to those contracts which could not possibly be completed within one year, oral contracts of uncertain duration historically have been enforced. The problem here is that, although the entire agreement could not be carried out within a year (establishing distributorships), part of it could (the sale of cameras). The court ruled that because the parts of the contract were divisible, the part not within the Statute could be enforced. Therefore Buttorff was entitled to recover the agreed compensation for selling cameras before the agreement was terminated.

Sale of Goods for $500 or More

The UCC Statute of Frauds [section 2-201] states:

1. Except as otherwise provided in this section a contract for the sale of goods for the price of $500 or more is not enforceable by way of action or defense unless there is some writing sufficient to indicate that a contract for sale has been made between the parties and signed by the party against whom enforcement is sought or by his authorized agent or broker. A writing is not insufficient because it omits or incorrectly states a term agreed upon but the contract is not enforceable under this paragraph beyond the quantity of goods shown in such writing.

2. Between merchants if within a reasonable time a writing in confirmation of the contract and sufficient against the sender is received and the party receiving it has reason to know its contents, it satisfies the requirements of subsection 1 against such party unless written notice of objection to its contents is given within ten days after it is received.

3. A contract which does not satisfy the requirements of subsection 1 but which is valid in other respects is enforceable
   a. if the goods are to be specially manufactured for the buyer and are not suitable for sale to others in the ordinary course of the seller's business and the seller, before notice of repudiation is received and under circumstances which reasonably indicate that the goods are for the buyer, has made either a substantial beginning of their manufacture or commitments for their procurement; or
   b. if the party against whom enforcement is sought admits in his pleading, testimony or otherwise in court that a contract for sale was made, but the contract is not enforceable under the provision beyond the quantity of goods admitted; or
   c. with respect to goods for which payment has been made and accepted or which have been received and accepted.

Subsection 1 establishes the general rule that a contract for the sale of goods for $500 or more must be evidenced by "some writing" to be enforceable. The writing must be signed by the party against whom enforcement is sought. The writing requirement may be satisfied by more than one document. One case has held that a signed memo *without* terms referring to an unsigned document with terms established an enforceable contract.

TABLE 11-1   Contracts within the Statute of Frauds

Non Goods	Goods
Executor's promise to pay debts of deceased	Sale of goods for $500 or more
Promise to pay the debt of another	
Sale of land or an interest in land	
Promises not performable in one year	

The rest of the section limits the general rule. Subsection 2 modifies the one-way enforceability result in the case of merchants. Assume that Jones and Smith, both merchants, orally agree to a contract. The next day Jones sends a signed letter to Smith detailing the terms of the agreement. Smith does not respond for ten days. The contract is enforceable against Smith on the basis of Jones's letter even though Smith has never signed anything.

The three exceptions established in Subsection 3 have a common element: in the situations defined, there is persuasive evidence that a contract has in fact been made. Under (b) there is an outright admission by the defendant that a contract exists. It would be contrary to the basic purpose of the Statute to allow a defense in such a circumstance. Under (c), one can assume that a buyer will not accept goods unless a contract is intended. Note that the contract is enforceable only in regard to the quantity of goods that has been accepted. Similarly, a seller will not accept payment unless a contract is intended. A down payment may satisfy the exception in Subsection 3, paragraph c. This is simply a version of the part-performance exception to the Statute of Frauds, which, until the UCC, applied only to contracts involving an interest in land. The specially manufactured goods in (a) must be shown to have a reasonable connection with the buyer. Again there is external evidence that a contract has been made.

The case that follows involves the application of the UCC Statute of Frauds.

Southwest Engineering Company v. Martin Tractor Company

Supreme Court of Kansas
473 P.2d 18 (1970)

FACTS

Southwest Engineering Company was preparing to submit a bid to the U.S. Army Corps of Engineers for construction of runway lighting facilities. On April 28, Southwest met with Martin Tractor Company to negotiate the price of a standby generator and accessory equipment to be used for the project. At this meeting, the agent for Martin Tractor noted each required item and its price on a memorandum which he then gave to Southwest's agent. Martin's agent did not sign the memorandum but hand printed his name and that of his company in the upper left corner. On May 24, Martin Tractor wrote to Southwest refusing to supply the generator and equipment. Southwest repeatedly tried to convince Martin Tractor to supply the equipment, until September 6, when it got the required items from another supplier at a cost of $6,041 more than the figures listed by Martin Tractor on the memorandum. Southwest filed suit for breach of contract.

ISSUE   Was the agreement between the parties enforceable under the UCC?

DECISION   Yes. The court ruled in favor of the plaintiff, Southwest Engineering Company, saying that the April 28 meeting between plaintiff and defendant had resulted in an agreement which was enforceable under the provisions of the Uniform Commercial Code. The question hinged on whether the memorandum, particularly because it was not signed, constituted an enforceable agreement. The court ruled that the memorandum prepared by the defendant satisfied the three essential requirements of the statute: it evidenced a sale of goods, was authenticated by the defendant, and specified quantity. Southwest was awarded damages of $6,041.

Equitable Estoppel and Promissory Estoppel

As we have noted, courts have become increasingly sensitive to the use of the Statute of Frauds to perpetrate fraud. They have tried to minimize fraud by using the doctrines of equitable estoppel and promissory estoppel.

Equitable estoppel general legal doctrine used to achieve fairness by holding a party to an act that someone has justifiably relied on

Equitable estoppel, a doctrine as old as the Statute itself, is used in situations where applying the Statute would result in a substantial injustice. The part-performance exception to the Statute discussed earlier in this chapter is basically an application of the doctrine of equitable estoppel.

Promissory estoppel is a more specific application of the principles of equitable estoppel. As indicated in Chapter 7, promissory estoppel has been used primarily to make exceptions to the rule that all contracts be supported by consideration.

If the person making the promise should have known that the promise would induce the person being promised something to rely on the promise to his or her detriment, the promisor may find that he or she is obligated to comply with the contract, even if the contract itself does not satisfy the Statute of Frauds.

For example, consider how promissory estoppel might apply to a contract governed by the Statute of Frauds in the following case. Assume that Rogers is a police captain who will be eligible for retirement in two years. The retirement package includes a pension of full salary, paid medical insurance, life insurance, and other benefits. In addition, the city's contract with the police union provides that no one, union member or not, may be discharged except for cause. Sullivan, chair of the board of a large corporation, induces Rogers to quit his job as a police officer in exchange for an extremely lucrative ten-year employment contract with Sullivan's company. Sullivan further promises to put the contract in writing when she returns from Europe. Unfortunately, Sullivan is killed while traveling, and the other board members are reluctant to honor Sullivan's promise of employment to Rogers.

Under traditional Statute of Frauds principles, the contract would be unenforceable. Because it is an offer of employment for ten years, the contract falls within the requirement that it be put in writing. Rogers, having already quit his job as a police captain, would be without a remedy and without a job. Fortunately for Rogers, most courts today do not tolerate such an inequitable result. It is apparent that Sullivan knew and intended that her promise of employment would induce Rogers to quit his current job in reliance on the promise. Because he has been induced to quit his prior job, and because injustice cannot otherwise be avoided, Sullivan's fellow board members are bound by the contract. They are, in essence, "estopped" from asserting the Statute of Frauds as a defense.

The result would have been different had the policeman not yet quit his job at the time of Sullivan's death and the refusal of the other board members to honor the contract. All jurisdictions have required that the promisee be in danger of suffering "unconscionable injury" if the contract is not enforced. When people have relied to their detriment on other people's promises, and when enforcing a contract is the only way to prevent either substantial injury or injustice, the contract is to be enforced.

When deciding whether to use promissory estoppel as a means for avoiding the Statute of Frauds, it is important to consider the aspect of damages. In an action for breach of contract, a plaintiff can generally recover compensatory damages to the extent that they can be proven. However, this is not true when recovery is based on promissory estoppel. The courts have held uniformly that when promissory estoppel is used as a means of avoiding the Statute of Frauds, only restitutional damages (that is, out-of-pocket expenses) can be recovered. In these cases, the plaintiff generally is not entitled to the benefit of the bargain; instead, he or she will only be restored to the position he or she was in before acting in reliance on the defendant's promise.

The following case illustrates the types of circumstances a court must consider in applying promissory estoppel to the Statute of Frauds.

_____ McIntosh v. Murphy _____

Supreme Court of Hawaii
469 P.2d 177 (1970)

In April 1964, McIntosh received a telephone call from the general manager of   FACTS
Murphy Motors stating that a job as sales manager was available in Honolulu. McIntosh accepted the offer and notified Murphy Motors by telegram that he would arrive in Honolulu on April 26. On April 25, Murphy Motors telephoned McIntosh to say that his duties as assistant sales manager would begin on April 27. McIntosh was surprised that the position had changed from sales manager to assistant sales manager but decided to go to Honolulu anyway. He moved from Los Angeles to Honolulu and gave up employment opportunities on the mainland. However, approximately 2½ months after beginning his new job, McIntosh was let go, allegedly because he could not close deals or train new salespeople. McIntosh seeks to recover damages from defendant Murphy for the breach of an alleged one-year oral employment contract.

Is McIntosh entitled to enforcement of the oral contract?   ISSUE

Yes. The court ruled in favor of the plaintiff, McIntosh, and awarded him $12,103.40   DECISION
(the equivalent of one year's salary). The court referred to the law governing situations where there has been reliance on an oral contract and the use of promissory estoppel to avoid the Statute of Frauds is sanctioned. Courts have considerable discretion in implementing the true policy behind the Statute of Frauds, which is to prevent fraud or any other type of unconscionable injury. As a result of his reliance on defendant's promise, plaintiff found himself living in Hawaii without a job. Plaintiff's reliance was such that injustice could be avoided only by enforcing the contract for one year's salary.

_____ **THE PAROL EVIDENCE RULE** _____

Parol evidence rule a rule that excludes as unenforceable terms or promises not contained in a final and complete written contract

Even if people have to reduce an agreement between them to writing, and even if the writing satisfies all the requirements of the Statute of Frauds, there are bound to be some disputes over the meaning of the language in the contract or allegations that the contract has been modified or does not include *all* the terms of the agreement. To solve these problems, it is often helpful to turn to what is known as the **parol evidence rule.**

Parol evidence has nothing to do with shortening the prison terms of convicted felons. In contract situations, "parol" evidence is made up of statements or writings that do not appear in the written contract document. Parol evidence can be either written or oral.

The parol evidence rule is based upon a simple principle. The simple principle is: When contracting parties draw up a document of their agreement that appears both complete and final on its face, it is appropriate to conclude that the parties have put everything into that document. The contracting parties may not use earlier or concurrent agreements to contradict the written document.

The parol evidence rule is similar to the Statute of Frauds in that it imposes a technical, formal requirement on the way contracting parties write their agreements. Unfortunately, the parol evidence rule is also similar to the Statute of Frauds in that it often results in harm to consumers and small-business operators. The rule can make promises that were made but not written into the contract unenforceable.

Requirements

The parol evidence rule applies only to written contracts that are final and apparently complete. If the written contract is obviously incomplete or states that certain terms are to be filled in later, the rule does not apply. (The parol evidence rule does not require that the parties use a writing. Only the various Statutes of Frauds do that. Instead, the parol evidence rule affects the manner in which the contract terms may be established once a final and complete writing has been used.)

Attorneys have responded to the rule by putting clauses similar to the following in written contracts:

> This contract is the final and complete agreement between the parties. All prior negotiations and/or agreements are merged into this contract and all additions to or alterations or changes in this contract must be in writing and signed by both parties.

Integration agreements clauses stating that all previous negotiations are merged into the final contract

Such clauses are known as **integration agreements,** because they are intended to integrate all earlier agreements of the parties into the contract document. The hope is that an integration agreement will make it extremely difficult to introduce evidence of earlier agreements. Whether the final document integrates earlier documents is really a question of fact that must be resolved by considering the particular circumstances of the contract negotiations. In addition, an ambiguous provision of a written contract may be cleared up by parol evidence. But parol evidence that *contradicts* the written agreement is inadmissible.

These two issues — whether the document is a final integration and whether its terms are ambiguous — give the courts leeway to limit the application of the rule.

Many courts have used this opportunity to make rulings hostile to the rule. Why such hostility? Doesn't the basic principle underlying the parol evidence rule make sense? The answer is that the principle is flawed and often produces an unfair result.

The parol evidence principle assumes a contract fully negotiated between equals or near equals. But, as we have seen, many written contracts, particularly those entered into by consumers, do not meet that standard. Instead, consumers are handed form contracts to sign. Invariably these contain a clause stating that the form represents the final agreement between the parties and that there are no other understandings between them. It is not uncommon for a salesperson to make oral statements such as, "We'll extend the warranty 30 extra days," or "Of course, we'll provide free service for a year," or "Although it's not our usual policy, we will deliver your purchase free of charge." Relying on these statements, consumers sign contracts and then are prevented by the parol evidence rule from trying to show the "other understandings" that the consumer assumed were part of the deal.

Further, form contracts are drafted for the standard or typical deal. Any customized deal causes problems with the form. Salespeople, office managers, and consumers are not likely to be familiar with the legal consequences described in legal jargon in the form. In these cases, a merchant may use the parol evidence rule as a shield against liability.

The case that follows shows how courts have tried to soften the parol evidence rule.

_____ *Masterson v. Sine* _____

Supreme Court of California
436 P.2d 561 (1968)

FACTS

Rebecca Masterson and her husband, Dallas, together owned a ranch. On February 25, 1958, they deeded it to Medora and Lu Sine. The deed "reserved unto the grantors herein [the Mastersons] an option to purchase the above described property on or before February 25, 1968." Defendant Medora was Dallas Masterson's sister. After the deed was given, Dallas became bankrupt. Rebecca and his trustee (the person in the bankruptcy proceeding responsible for collecting assets and paying claims) sued to enforce the option to purchase the ranch. The Sines offered evidence showing that the parties wanted the property kept in the Masterson family, and because the option was personal, it could not be exercised by the trustee in bankruptcy. The trial court found that the parol evidence rule prevented admission of the new information from the Sines and ruled that the option could be exercised. Defendants Medora and Lu Sine appealed.

ISSUE

Does the parol evidence rule exclude the Sines's information that the option could only be exercised by a family member?

DECISION

The court ruled in favor of the defendants, Medora and Lu Sine. It stated that when only part of the agreement is integrated, parol evidence may be used to prove other elements of the agreement not reduced to writing. The option clause on the deed in this case did not explicitly provide that it contained the complete agreement, and the deed was silent on the question of assignability. Thus the trial court erred in excluding the new evidence.

Exceptions

A number of logical exceptions follow directly from the basic premise of the parol evidence rule. The fact that on a particular day two people sign a formal agreement does not mean that they have intended to bind themselves forever to those particular terms. As a consequence, parol evidence is always admissible to prove a *later modification* of the contract. The major legal problem with modification, as discussed in Chapter 7, is with sufficiency of consideration.

Parol evidence is admissible to clear up an *ambiguity* in the contract terms. It is also admissible to prove fraud, alteration, mistake, illegality, duress, undue influence, or lack of capacity. If any of these things can be shown, then the document does not represent a valid contract. It would be very poor legal policy to allow the parol evidence rule to protect a defrauding party or to prevent the showing of duress or mistake. For example, fraud may be perpetrated when one party alters the document or signs it by, say, using a carbon and a second sheet with different terms. Similarly, a mistake may occur as the document is prepared. These occurrences may be proved by parol evidence.

UCC Parol Evidence Rule

The UCC (Section 2-202) has a special parol evidence rule on the sale of goods. This rule is more liberal than the common law rule. Usage of trade and course of dealing or performance are always admissible, whether or not the contract terms are found to be ambiguous. The only way by which such factors would be inadmissible would be by an express contract term to that effect.

Further, unless it is quite clear that the document represents an exclusive statement, noncontradictory *additional* terms may be admitted into evidence. There is no presumption that a written document is considered by the parties as a complete, exclusive statement of their agreement.

The Effect of Consumer Protection Statutes

Consumer protection laws can affect the use of the parol evidence rule. Most states have adopted such laws in the last few years, and they add an interesting twist to the rule. Many such laws make it illegal for suppliers to *fail* to integrate all earlier agreements, oral or otherwise, into the final contract document. Thus if a car salesman makes a variety of performance and warranty guarantees to a car buyer, but the manufacturer's warranty that comes with the car or the bill of sale does not reflect these guarantees, the salesman has violated such consumer laws. Further, because of these laws, the salesman may not argue his guarantees should not be binding because of the parol evidence rule. Carrying this even further, once evidence of the agreements is used to prove their existence for purposes of showing violations of the consumer laws, their existence also has been proved for purposes of enforcing the guarantees themselves.

INTERPRETATION OF
CONTRACTUAL PROVISIONS

When people who have made a contract dispute its terms, the courts use specific, established rules of interpretation to resolve the disputes. Problems typically arise because:

1. In using prepared form documents, the parties:
   a. add language that contradicts other provisions in the form
   b. do not intend that all of the form provisions apply to their agreement, or
   c. add contradictory or ambiguous language.

2. In using negotiated, specially prepared documents, the parties:
   a. use ambiguous language,
   b. fail to anticipate a problem that arises during performance, or
   c. compromise without coming to precise understandings of certain terms.

In interpreting the particular language used in a written contract, the courts are primarily concerned with correctly learning the intention of the contracting parties. The intentions of the parties cannot be learned by simply asking the people what they intended because, obviously, if they had agreed on such an issue they would not be in court. Consequently, the courts use the following specific rules designed to ascertain the objectively viewed intention of the parties:

1. Words are to be given their plain and ordinary meanings so long as such an interpretation does not result in a clearly unique or strange result.
   a. The meaning of words may be varied by the prior usage between the parties. The parties are governed by their course of dealing.
   b. Technical words and terms are to be given technical meanings unless it is clear that the parties intend some other definition. (This rule tends to be important in contracts for the sale of land because of the large number of technical terms used in real property law.)
   c. Trade usage may supply a basis for the interpretation of terms.

2. Writings are to be interpreted as a whole, and language is not to be taken out of context.

3. Special circumstances under which a contract was made may be used to show the actual understanding of the parties.

4. Legal and reasonable interpretations are preferred over illegal and unreasonable alternatives.

5. Specific provisions control general provisions.

6. Generally, handwritten provisions prevail over typed provisions, and typed provisions prevail over printed provisions. In applying this rule, the courts assume that the material most recently added by the parties represents their true intention.

7. In commercial contracts, the UCC supplies many implied terms. Usually the UCC terms are applicable unless the parties provide otherwise in their agreement.

SUMMARY

The original Statute of Frauds required certain contracts to be in writing to be enforceable. In the United States, the following contracts must be written to be enforceable:

1. sales of goods for $500 or more

2. sales of interests in land

3. promises not performable within one year

4. promises to pay the debts of another

5. promises by executors personally to pay debts of deceased

6. promises in consideration of marriage.

Such contracts are said to be *within* the Statute and must be written and signed by the party against whom enforcement is sought.

Unfairness may result when one party signs a document and the other does not. Then the agreement may be enforceable only against one party. The UCC modifies this result in contracts between merchants. The courts have applied the doctrines of equitable and promissory estoppel to minimize unfairness.

Under the parol evidence rule, an agreement that appears to be final and complete cannot be contradicted by evidence relating to other agreements. For the rule to apply, it must be clear that the parties intended the written document to be a complete integration of their agreement. Outside evidence may be used to clear up ambiguities in the written agreement or to prove fraud, duress, or lack of capacity.

The courts use several rules to interpret language in contracts. The basic objective of the courts is to ascertain the intent of the parties.

REVIEW PROBLEMS

1. List the types of contracts which must be in writing.

2. Explain how the doctrines of equitable estoppel and promissory estoppel minimize possibly unjust results of the Statute of Frauds.

3. Describe the general circumstances under which the parol evidence rule does *not* apply.

4. How may the Statute of Frauds and the parol evidence rule work to the detriment of consumers?

5. Pope & Cottle sold lumber to Blakely, to be used in building a garage for Wheelwright. Blakely failed to pay, and Wheelwright told Pope & Cottle that he would pay Blakeley's debt "from such funds as might be in his hands due the said Blakely." Pope & Cottle than formally released Blakely and demanded payment of the $1,478.63 from Wheelwright, who refused to pay. Pope & Cottle sued Wheelwright on the promise. Decision?

6. Barney Sorrenson owed Security $1,400. Barney's mother, Ragnhild Sorrenson, wanted to borrow $200 from Security. Security agreed to make the loan if

Ragnhild "would secure up the debts of Barney." Security made the loan and the question arose whether Ragnhild's estate was liable for Barney's debts. Is it?

7. Dragage & Co. contracted with Pacific Gas to remove and replace the cover of a steam turbine. Dragage agreed

> to indemnify Pacific against all losses, damage, expense, and liability resulting from . . . injury to property, arising out of or in any way connected with the performance of this contract.

During the work, the cover fell and injured the turbine. Pacific sued Dragage for the $25,144.51 it spent on repairs. Dragage offered to prove by the testimony of employees of both firms that the parties had understood that the indemnity clause was meant to cover only third parties. Is such proof allowable?

8. Mitchell agreed by a written contract to purchase a farm from Lath. Mitchell contended that in return for her agreement to purchase the farm, Lath agreed to remove an icehouse that she found objectionable. The icehouse was not removed, and Mitchell sued to compel its removal. Decision?

9. Harris contracted to sell cotton to Hine Cotton Co., and both signed the following document:

> This agreement is entered into this date wherein Hine Cotton Company, 103 East Third Street, Rome, Georgia, agrees to buy from H. E. Harris and Sons, Route 1, Taylorsville, Georgia, all the cotton produced on their 825 acres. The rate of payment shall be as follows:
>
>> 1 □ All cotton ginned prior to December 20, 1973, and meeting official U.S.D.A. Class will be paid for at 30¢ per pound. Below Grade Cotton at 24½¢ per pound.
>>
>> 2 □ All cotton ginned on or after December 20, 1973, will be paid for at the rate of 1,000 over the CCC Loan Rate with Below Grades being paid for at 24½¢ per pound. Settlement will be made on net weights on Commercial Bonded Warehouse Receipts with U.S.D.A. Class cards attached with $1 per bale being deducted from the proceeds of each bale.

During the time that the cotton was growing its market value more than doubled, and Hine Co. wrote and asked assurance of Harris that he would perform. Harris repudiated by return letter. Hine Co. sued for the $140,000 difference between the contract price and the market price. Result?

10. Beanblossom sold 1,000 bushels of soybeans to Lippold at $4.42 per bushel. Lippold then brought suit claiming that the 1,000 bushel transaction was partial performance of an oral contract by which Beanblossom was to sell 7,000 bushels of soybeans at $4.42 per bushel. Beanblossom denies that any oral contract was ever made. Decision?

11. A representative of Mid-South, a plastic supplier, and Fortune Furniture Manufacturing entered into an oral agreement by which Mid-South would provide Fortune with plastic needed in the latter's manufacturing process. As a consequence the following letter was sent and received:

Mr. Sidney Whitlock, President
Fortune Furniture Manufacturers, Inc.
Okolona, Mississippi 38860

Dear Sid:

This is to confirm the agreement entered into this date between myself and Phil Stillpass on behalf of Mid-South Plastic Co. Inc. and you on behalf of Fortune Manufacturing Co. Inc.

We agree to maintain expanded and 21 oz. plastic in the warehouse of Mid-South Furniture Suppliers, Inc. in sufficient amounts to supply all of the plastic for your plant's use, and if for any reason we do not have the necessary plastic you will be at liberty to purchase the plastic from any other source and we will pay the difference in price paid the other source and our current price.

We also agree to pay Fortune 2% rebate on the gross sale price of our plastic as an advertisement aid to your Company which rebate to be paid at your request.

We assure you that all fabrics you need will be in our warehouse at all times and we appreciate your agreeing to buy all of your plastics from us.

Very truly yours,

W. E. Walker, President
(Mid-South)

Mid-South was unable to supply all of Fortune's needs and Fortune had to buy from other suppliers at a higher price. Does Fortune have a cause of action against Mid-South?

12. Cohen bought a farm jointly owned by Luca Rienzo and his eight brothers and sisters. After the Cohen purchase, Luca, who had lived there for 30 years, made improvements on the buildings, rented part of the farm, and cultivated the rest. After eleven months Cohen asserted his interest in the property. Luca's wife claims that there was an oral agreement between her and Cohen that, after Cohen acquired the property, he would reconvey it to her. Decision?

13. Cohn advertised in the *New York Post* that his 30-foot sloop was for sale. Fisher checked over the boat, phoned Cohn, and they agreed to the sale of the boat for $4,650. They met the next day. Fisher gave Cohn a check for $2,325 and wrote on it "deposit on sloop, *D'Arc Wind,* full amount $4,650." Fisher then contacted Cohn and said he would not close the deal. Fisher stopped payment on the check. Cohn then sold the boat for $3,000 to another and sued to enforce the contract with Fisher. Is Fisher liable for damages for breach of contract?

14. Williams entered into a home construction contract with the Johnsons. The Johnsons signed the contract that had an integration clause and further stated, "There are no verbal agreements or representations in connection therewith." Williams sought to enforce the contract against the Johnsons, and they defended that they had signed thinking that it was an estimate and that they had told Williams that their signing was contingent upon the approval of financing by their bank. Can Williams enforce the contract?

CHAPTER 12

Rights of Third Parties

CHAPTER OBJECTIVES

PRIVITY OF CONTRACT

Expansion of Third-Party Rights

ASSIGNMENT AND DELEGATION

Assignment / Delegation / Assignment of Monetary Rights / Assignment of Nonmonetary Rights / Prohibitions of Assignment / Rights of the Assignee / Notice to the Obligor / Form of Assignment / Transfer by Negotiation / Delegation of Duties / Assignment under the UCC

CONTRACTS FOR THE BENEFIT OF A THIRD PARTY

Donee Beneficiary / Creditor Beneficiary / Incidental Beneficiary / Intended Beneficiary

SUMMARY

REVIEW PROBLEMS

CHAPTER OBJECTIVES

After studying this chapter, you should be able to:

1. Explain the difference between assigning and delegating a contract.

2. Predict reasonably well when contract rights are not assignable nor contract duties delegable.

3. Discuss how the Uniform Commercial Code has changed common law on the assignment of contract rights and the delegation of contract duties.

4. Distinguish between those third-party beneficiaries who can enforce a contract's provisions and those who cannot.

PRIVITY OF CONTRACT

Privity of contract the concept that only parties to a contract may use the contract as a basis for suit

Originally, a plaintiff could maintain a contract action only against the party with whom the contract had been made. Over the years this limiting doctrine, which is generally referred to as **privity of contract**, or privity, has lost most of its importance. Today there are several situations in which a person who is not a party to a contract can use the contract as the basis for suit. The following are some examples:

1. The person suing, often called the *third party,* has acquired another's contract right by purchase or gift. For example, Smith agrees to sell his house to Jones. Jones decides she does not want the house. She transfers her right to Martin. In most cases, Martin would have a right to sue Smith if Smith refused to sell the house to Martin.

2. The original contract was made for the benefit of a noncontracting third party who is the plaintiff. For example, Brown insures his life with Capital Insurance Company. He names Green as beneficiary. If the company refuses to honor the agreement to pay benefits to Green when Brown dies, Green ordinarily has a right to sue.

3. A person other than the purchaser of a product may be able to sue on the contract made between the purchaser and seller, if the product causes injury to that person.

The primary focus of this chapter is on the first two situations. The third is treated in Chapter 18, on sales remedies.

Expansion of Third-Party Rights

Over the last 150 years, courts grudgingly began to allow suits by a person who was not a party to a contract. Many state legislatures also made laws to a similar effect. As the economy of the United States became more credit-oriented, effective financing required that a party to whom a debtor's obligation had been transferred be able to use it as the basis for suit. Economic need helped to bring about a change in the law.

The expansion of the rights of third parties has also been influenced by technological developments. In most American jurisdictions today, a person who is injured by a defective product may sue the seller, even though the injured party is not a party to the contract of sale. As the number of costly injuries from complex products increased, society accepted the idea of **enterprise liability.** The manufacturer or seller of a defective product is now legally responsible to the consumer injured because of the defect.

Today, when a person is injured as a result of product failure, most states do not require the plaintiff to establish privity of contract with the defendant. However, some theories of recovery still require proof of this contractual relationship for the plaintiff to recover. These are discussed in greater detail in Chapter 19, which covers products liability.

Enterprise liability the principle that the manufacturer or seller of a defective product is responsible to the consumer injured because of that defect

ASSIGNMENT AND DELEGATION

Assignment

Assignment is the transfer by one person to another of benefits that a person is entitled to under a contract. Contract benefits are generally referred to as *rights.* A person or firm transferring contract rights is called an **assignor.** The recipient of these rights is the **assignee.** The party responsible for performing is the **obligor,** while the person receiving the performance is the **obligee.**

An example emphasizing the basic relationships among parties to a contract often helps to clarify this terminology and some of the legal problems that arise when contract rights are transferred.

Each party to a contract acquires rights as a result of the agreement. Each also acquires obligations. If a farmer promises to sell 1,000 bushels of wheat to a feed mill for $2,200, the farmer has a duty to transfer title to the wheat to the mill. The mill has a duty to pay the farmer $2,200. The mill's duty is the farmer's right, just as the farmer's duty is the mill's right (see Figure 12-1).

If the farmer chose to transfer his right to the $2,200 to his bank, he could do so by assignment. The farmer would be the assignor, the bank the assignee, the mill the obligor (see Figure 12-2). Of course, the mill also could assign its right to the wheat to someone else. The mill would then be the assignor, the recipient of the right the assignee, and the farmer the obligor.

Assignment the transfer of rights or benefits of a contract

Assignor the person transferring a contract's rights.

Assignee the person receiving a contract's rights

Obligor has the duty of performing so that someone (assignor or assignee) will have a contract right

Obligee receives the performance of the obligor

Delegation

In some instances, the law allows a person to transfer the duties or obligations that have been assumed by the contract. This transfer is called a **delegation.** The farmer in the previous example might be able to delegate his duty to deliver the 1,000 bushels of wheat to someone who had agreed to perform for him (see Figure 12-3).

Businesspeople often wish to transfer an entire contract — both rights and obliga-

Delegation the transfer of contractual duties

FIGURE 12-1 Both parties have contractual duties and rights. Further, one party's duty is the other party's rights.

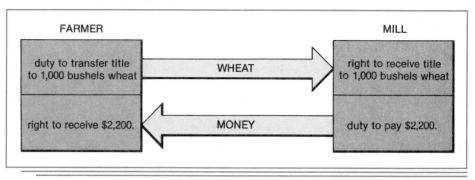

tions. For example, suppose that the mill that purchased the 1,000 bushels of wheat from the farmer sold the contract to a new owner. The entire contract, both duties and rights, might be transferred to the new owner (see Figure 12-4). Unfortunately, this transfer is also referred to as an *assignment,* even though the new owner acquires both rights and duties. Sometimes when businesspeople are negotiating the transfer of an entire contract, they are interested in the rights involved, not the duties. Because they have given little thought to who will perform the duties, their agreement generally does not cover this responsibility. The problem of whether the assignee who has acquired the rights is also responsible for the duties must be faced at a later time.

FIGURE 12-2 Farmer is *assignor* because he had the contract right and transfers it to a third party. Bank is *assignee* because it is a third party and is receiving a right from one of the contract parties. Mill is *obligor* because it has the duty or obligation to pay under the contract. If properly notified, its obligation is to bank, not to farmer. If not properly notified, its obligation is to farmer. If mill's obligation is to bank, bank can sue if mill does not perform its obligation.

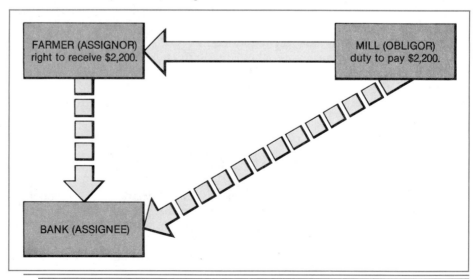

FIGURE 12-3 Here, farmer remains obligated to transfer title to wheat *until* the delegatee (farmer's friend) makes his delivery of 1,000 bushels of wheat to mill *and* mill accepts that wheat in substitution for the wheat farmer promised to deliver.

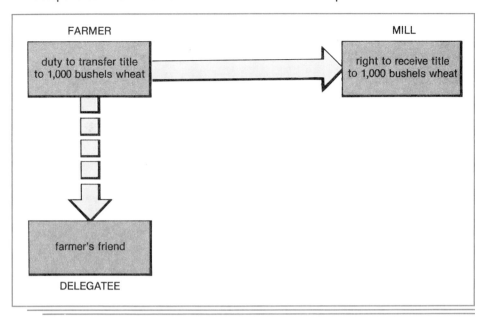

FIGURE 12-4 Transfer of Contract, Both Rights and Duties, Held by One Party (Mill) to a Third Party (New Owner)

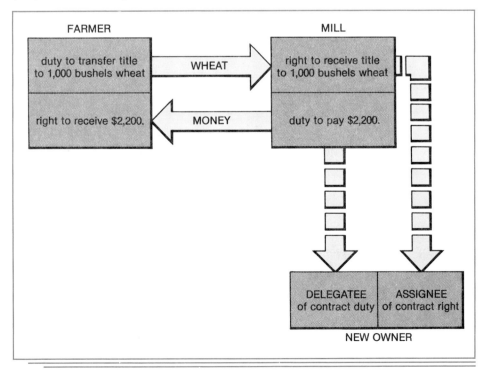

―――― *Hurst v. West* ――――

Court of Appeals of North Carolina
272 S.E. 2d 378 (1980)

FACTS   A client, Hurst, sued his attorneys, West and Groome, for breach of contract. The lawyers had contracted with Hurst to represent him on a criminal case. In return, Hurst gave them an interest in some property he owned. The contract between the parties permitted the attorneys to sell the property and apply the proceeds against their fees. The attorneys succeeded in getting the criminal charges against Hurst dropped. Thereafter, they assigned their interest in the contract to a third party.

ISSUE   Should West and Groome be allowed to assign their contract to a third party?

DECISION   Yes. The court held for the attorneys and allowed the assignment. The general rule is that unless expressly prohibited by statute or some principle of public policy, all ordinary business contracts are assignable. Exceptions to the rule occur when the contract expressly provides that it is not assignable or when performance of some term of the contract involves an element of personal skill or credit.

The contract between Hurst and West and Groome did not expressly prohibit assignment. Although the duty of the attorneys to defend Hurst had involved an element of personal skill and would not have been assignable to a third party, those obligations were fulfilled and discharged when the criminal charges against Hurst were dismissed. The remaining obligation of the lawyers under the contract, that they sell the property at a reasonable market value if their option to purchase was not exercised, was not personal in nature. Thus no breach occurred merely by West's and Groome's assignment of the contract to the third party.

Assignment of Monetary Rights

In this credit oriented society, the contract right most frequently assigned is the right to receive a sum of money. It is the legal basis for several types of financing. For example, many people buy cars on "time." The dealer, however, to maintain its inventory and to pay business expenses, must often have cash immediately. To obtain this cash, the dealer might assign its right to the buyer's money to a financial institution at a small discount. The financial institution, now the owner of the right, notifies the buyer and orders the buyer to make payments to it.

Accounts receivable financing the financial lender advances money secured by accounts receivable

Factoring the financial lender advances money and purchases the firm's accounts receivable

Accounts Receivable and Factoring   The assignment is also the basis for accounts receivable financing and factoring. In **accounts receivable financing,** a financial institution advances funds to a business that are secured by the accounts receivable of the business. In accounts receivable financing, the debtor usually continues to pay the original seller and creditor who guarantees in turn to repay the loan amount to the financing agency. In **factoring,** the firm advancing funds makes an absolute purchase of outstanding accounts that are assigned to it. The debtor is instructed to pay the factor (financial institution) directly. If the factor is unable to collect, it ordinarily suffers the loss.

For example, Highland appliances sells some of its appliances on credit, allowing purchasers to make installment payments over time. Highland's right to receive these payments an Account Receivable. If it wants the purchaser to pay the installments to Highland, it could still use the Accounts Receivable to borrow money from First Bank. The bank would have a security interest in the accounts to insure its loan is paid by Highland. If Highland didn't repay the loan, the bank could notify the purchasers to pay directly to First Bank. In this Accounts Receivable financing, Highland owns the accounts and is paid by the purchaser. Or Highland may sell these accounts to First Bank, which would then own the accounts. The purchaser makes payments directly to the bank, which in this case is called the factor. In factoring, the risk of nonpayment by the purchaser is on the bank, while in Accounts Receivable financing, the risk is on Highland Appliance.

Few limitations have been placed upon assignment of money rights. In fact, the UCC provides that a contractual term limiting the right to assign a money right is ineffective. However, many states, for public policy reasons, either prohibit or limit wage assignments.

Wage Assignments   States may regulate and restrict the assignment of wages. Legislatures hope to protect wage earners through such statutes. Some states have prohibited the assignment of future wages. In other states, statutes limit the right to make assignments of future earnings to a specific time period.

In the absence of such a statute, the general rule is that future earnings under an existing contract of employment may be assigned. But people who assign their earnings must be employed when they do so, or the assignment normally is invalid. Generally, employees need not get their employers' consent before assigning wages under an existing contract of employment.

Assignment of Nonmonetary Rights

Monetary rights are almost always assignable because it really does not make much difference to whom the debtor pays the money.

In determining whether other types of rights are assignable, the guiding principle is whether the transfer materially changes the obligor's duty. The payment of money, the obligation to sell goods or land, and the obligation to do a job to particular specifications are all freely transferable. If, however, the nature of the assignment or the circumstances are such that the assignment materially changes the obligor's responsibility, the assignment is ineffective.

Prohibitions of Assignment

Sometimes the parties try to prohibit assignment by a contractual provision. Many courts have refused to recognize restrictions of this nature. Their justification is that a contract right is property, and the owner should be free to transfer it if he or she wishes.

Most states would probably enforce a contractual clause restricting assignment. As one New York court stated:

> [W]e think it reasonably clear that, while the courts have striven to uphold freedom of assignability, they have not failed to recognize the concept of freedom to contract. . . . When "clear language" is used, and the "plainest words . . . have been chosen," parties may limit the freedom of alienation of rights and prohibit the assignment.

Rights of the Assignee

Defenses Good against Assignor and Assignee   Although assignment is an integral element of much business financing, the assignee, ordinarily a financial institution advancing funds, is subject to some legal risk. All that the assignee acquires are the rights possessed by the original assignor. If the obligor has defenses that can be asserted against the assignor, these same defenses can be asserted against the assignee. For example, if the original transaction was voidable because of fraud or failure of consideration, the obligor can assert these defenses against the assignee to the same extent that it could have asserted them against the assignor. If the underlying transaction is voidable because the obligor lacked the capacity to contract, this defense can also be asserted by the obligor against the assignee.

With recourse an assignment that commits the assignor to repurchase the right that was the subject of the assignment; ultimate burden of collection is on the assignor

Practically, this means that when a financial institution or individual advances funds upon the basis of an assignment, the value of what is acquired is determined by the original transaction. This is true even when the assignee takes in good faith and has no knowledge of what took place in the original transaction. An assignee can protect itself from this risk to a degree by asking the obligor if it has defenses against performance. If the obligor gives assurances that no defenses exist, the obligor may not at a later time assert defenses that are inconsistent with these assurances.

Suppose that First National Bank wishes to purchase a note signed by a home-owner. The homeowner agreed to pay Acme Home Improvement $500 for work done on the home. If the bank, prior to taking the note, asks the homeowner (the obligor on the note) if Acme did the work, and the homeowner says yes, the home-owner may not assert the failure of Acme to do the work as a reason to refuse to pay the bank after it takes the note.

Without recourse an assignment that does not give the assignee any right or recourse to the assignor if the obligor does not pay his or her account; burden of collection is on the assignee

With and without Recourse   An assignee can also protect itself by extracting from the assignor a commitment to repurchase a claim that is uncollectible. This is usually referred to as an assignment **with recourse.** If the assignee takes **without recourse,** it assumes the risks of collection.

Guarantees Made to Assignee   Even in situations in which an assignment is made without recourse, the assignor by the very act of assigning makes certain warranties to the assignee. Although collection is not guaranteed, the assignor does guarantee that any document evidencing the right is genuine and that the right is not subject to any undisclosed defenses of which he or she is aware. In addition, the assignor guarantees that he or she will do nothing to defeat or impair the assignment. If he or she were to collect the debt, he or she would thus violate this last guarantee.

The following case discusses an assignment of all of a corporation's rights to collect assessments on lots in a subdivision.

Chimney Hill Owners Association v. Antignani

Supreme Court of Vermont
392 A. 2d 423 (1978)

Eastern Woodworking Company acquired 11 lots from Chimney Hill Corporation. A standard deed, filed with the local town clerk, provided that each lot was to be assessed an annual charge for the use of common land that contained a clubhouse, pools, tennis courts, roads, and a water system for the community. The duty to pay the annual charge was imposed upon each lot owner. In addition to the standard sales agreement, which included the clause to pay the annual charge for the common land, the Chimney Hill Corporation agreed in writing to charge Eastern only a single assessment on one lot rather than eleven separate assessments. (Antignani, the successor to Eastern's interests, is not referred to in this case except in the title.)

The corporation then conveyed the common land and facilities to the Chimney Hill Owners' Association and assigned to it the right to collect the assessments due from the lot owners. When the Chimney Hill Owner's Association billed Eastern for a separate assessment on each lot it owned, Eastern claimed that the agreement of the (assignor) Corporation to charge it for only one lot was binding on the (assignee) Association.

FACTS

Is the Association bound by the Corporation's agreement with Eastern?

ISSUE

Yes. The Court concluded that Eastern had received a valid release from Chimney Hill Corporation concerning the ten unimproved lots. Eastern's release from the assignor corporation constituted a valid defense to the association's claim for a separate assessment on each of the 10 lots. When the association acquired the common lands and facilities from the corporation, it was aware that some multiple lot owners were being charged for only one assessment. As such, the association as an assignee of the corporation had to abide by the agreement made by its assignor with Eastern.

DECISION

Notice to the Obligor

Assignment to One Person   For several reasons the assignee should notify the obligor of the assignment as soon as possible. Suppose that Mary owes $100 to Betty. Betty then assigns her right to receive the $100 to John. Betty is thus the assignor and John the assignee of a contractual right to receive money. What if John never instructs Mary to pay him rather than Betty? In that situation, because Mary is unaware of the assignment, she could pay the entire sum to Betty. This would completely discharge Mary of any obligation under the contract. John's only recourse in this situation would be against Betty. John could sue Betty for not observing the implied warranty that she would do nothing to prevent John from obtaining performance from Mary.

In most states, after proper notice is given, the person who must perform can no longer assert counterclaims or defenses against the person getting the contract rights unless these arise out of the transaction that gave rise to the assignment. Additionally, until the person who must perform gets notice of the assignment, he or she may perform to the assignor. Once, however, the person who must perform has notice of the assignment, he or she can honor the contract only by performing to the assignee. If the right assigned is a debt, the debtor is discharged only by payment to the assignee. A debtor who pays the original creditor after notice of assignment would have to make a second payment to the assignee.

Assignment to Two or More People   Notice is also important if the assignor fraudulently or mistakenly assigns the same right to two different parties. For example, if Mary owes $100 to Betty, Betty could assign her right to receive the $100 to John. If John fails to notify Mary, this would give Betty the opportunity to assign this same debt to Tom. In most states, because John was the first assignee, he has the right to collect. However, in some states, if Tom notified Mary of the assignment before John did, Tom would be entitled to collect. John's only recourse in that situation would be against Betty.

Form of Assignment

Although people may validly assign rights orally, for a number of reasons they should do so in a writing and sign the document. The principal reason is to provide clear evidence that a transfer of the right has taken place. In addition, many states have statutes that require certain types of assignments to be in writing to be effective. One common example is the wage assignment. The UCC also requires that certain commercial assignments must be in writing to be effective.

The document should describe the right that is being transferred and identify who has the duty to perform. A typical assignment of a contract right might be worded as follows:

> For value received, receipt of which is hereby acknowledged, Betty Blaine does hereby assign to John Smith all her right, title, and interest in a contract between Mary Morris and Betty Blaine, dated February 28, 1987, which contract obligates Mary Morris to pay to the undersigned $10,000 on or before October 31, 1987.
>
> The undersigned further guarantees payment of and agrees that if default be made, she, Betty Blaine, will pay the full amount to John Smith upon demand.
>
> Dated July 20, 1987.
> Signed by _____
>   Betty Blaine

Transfer by Negotiation

The principal legal risk of being assigned a contract right is that the person is subject to defenses that the person who must perform may raise against the person who transfers the rights. From very early in its development, the business community has required a means of transferring the right to receive money that frees the recipient from defenses that arise out of the agreement that created the right. This need is especially pressing today, in an economy in which a large percentage of business is done on credit.

A manufacturer that sells $100,000 worth of goods on 90-day credit has a valuable contract right. If everything goes well, the firm is paid in 90 days. But the firm may need immediate cash to meet its own obligations. It might get the cash by selling at a slight discount its right to receive the $100,000. But a bank or finance company is not likely to pay much for this right if it has to worry about the risk of nonperformance or improper performance by the manufacturing firm on the underlying contract. In a transfer by assignment, the financial institution has to take this risk. If assignment were the only method available to transfer contract rights, our credit economy would operate less efficiently.

The need for an easy, safe means of transferring monetary rights gave rise to the legal concept of transfer by **negotiation** and to instruments such as the check, promissory notes, and drafts. Negotiation involves only rights to receive money. The claim to the right to receive money must appear in particular written instruments known as **negotiable instruments.** If these instruments — checks, IOUs, drafts — are in the proper form and are transferred properly, the person acquiring them, known as a holder in due course, is not subject to many defenses that might exist between the original parties. A holder in due course is often in a better legal position than the party who has sold the instrument.

The use of a negotiable instrument in a typical business transaction makes this clear. Alice and Ben have entered into a contract in which Ben has promised to sell to Alice 100 molds at $50 per mold. Alice has given Ben in payment a promissory note for $5,000, payable in 30 days. Ben, in need of cash to meet his payroll, has sold this note at a small discount to his bank.

If the note is in the proper form and has been transferred properly, the bank has a right to collect the note in 30 days even if Ben has breached the contract by shipping molds that do not meet the specification of the agreement. If Ben, however, had kept the note, he would not be able to collect the full value because he had breached the contract. The damage to Alice arising from the failure of the molds to meet contract requirements would be set off against the $5,000. If Ben had assigned his claim to a bank instead of using a promissory note, the bank also would be unable to collect the full value of the note, because it would be subject to the defense that Alice had against Ben.

Because the holder in due course of a negotiable instrument can require the debtor to make payment even when the debtor would not have to pay the original creditor, the law requires that negotiable instruments meet exacting standards. They must contain words that amount to an order or promise to pay. A written instrument in which Arthur states that he owes Sam $5,000 and promises to pay Sam is not negotiable because Arthur promises only to pay Sam, not to pay anyone whom Sam orders be paid. (Holders in due course are discussed in more detail in Chapter 21.)

Negotiation the transfer of an instrument to a third party

Negotiable Instrument an instrument in writing and signed, containing an unconditional order or promise to pay a specific amount of money to order or bearer at a definite time or on demand

An instrument also must be negotiated properly if the taker is to be a holder in due course. If the bank in the previous example had known of the breach of contract by Ben, the bank would not be a holder in due course. To be in this preferred position, the holder must not know of a defense existing between the original parties.

In summary, if a person is assigned a contractual right to receive money, he or she "steps into the shoes" of the person assigning the right. He or she is subject to any claims or defenses existing between the original parties to the contract. A holder in due course of a negotiable instrument generally takes possession free of defenses and claims of the original obligor of that instrument. The holder in due course is thus in a better position than the person from whom he or she took the instrument.

Delegation of Duties

Novation an agreement in which a third party agrees to perform the duties of one contracting party, so that the replaced party no longer has any contract obligation

Although someone who assigns a right generally does not guarantee that the new owner will be able to collect, the person who transfers a duty makes a different commitment. He or she generally remains liable for performance. But in some situations, the person for whom the obligation must be performed releases the original obligor from responsibility. This is called a **novation**. If a novation is carried out properly, the original obligor is released from a duty to perform, and the third party now has the entire obligation (see Figure 12-5).

Delegable Duties   Most obligations or duties incurred as a result of most business contracts can be transferred. But although contract duties are delegable, a delegation does not cancel the obligation of the original contracting party. If the person to whom the duty was delegated fails to perform, the person who assigned the duty is responsible for performing it.

FIGURE 12-5   Novation

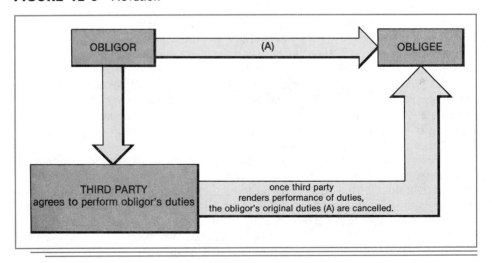

Construction contracts are good examples of the type of contract in which people may delegate duties. Ordinarily people understand that a general contractor does not personally perform all the work. Much of it is done by subcontractors, although the general contractor remains responsible for all of their obligations agreed to with the property's owner.

Nondelegable Duties   A duty may not be delegated under these conditions:

1. The performance by the person to whom the duty is delegated would be significantly different from that of the person bound by contract to perform. Johnny Cash may not honor Liza Minnelli's singing contracts.

2. The person who originally made the contract has a substantial interest in using the personal services of the other contracting party. Even though another designer or apprentice might be able to do just as good a job for me in designing a chair, if I contract with a master craftsman to do it for me, I don't want the craftsman to delegate his duty to an apprentice.

What if, in a contract between Smith and Jones, Jones delegates his duties to Brown, and informs Smith that he will no longer be responsible for the performance of the contract? Smith may treat Jones's action as a breach of contract. However, if Brown does perform and Smith accepts Brown's performance, Jones's obligation to perform is extinguished. In this case, a novation has occurred. The person for whom the third party performs no longer has any obligation under the original contract.

In a situation such as that among Smith, Jones, and Brown, the courts disagree as to whether Jones can force such an agreement on Smith without Smith's consent. Some courts permit Smith to take Brown's services, and still sue Jones for breach of contract. Other courts treat Smith's acceptance of Brown's services as a consent by Smith to extinguish Jones's liability under the contract.

Assignment under the UCC

Delegating Duties   The UCC (Section 2-120) has its own provisions covering assignments. It permits a party to delegate his or her duties if there is no contrary provision in the contract — unless the other party has a substantial interest in having the original promisor perform. In any event, that someone delegates his or her duties does not relieve that person of any duty to perform or any liability for breach. Suppose that Acme Contracting enters into a contract with Stewart Sand for delivery of sand to Acme's job site. May Stewart delegate its duty to perform to Lignite Sand? Unless there is a contrary agreement, and unless Acme has a substantial interest in having the original party perform, the UCC's answer is yes.

What if Stewart was a very dependable seller, but Lignite was not? The UCC recognizes that the original party, such as Acme, has a stake in the reliability of the person with whom he or she originally contracted. It therefore provides that if a party feels insecure, it may demand assurances of performance from the party assuming the obligation. Acme may demand assurances of performance from Lignite, and the demand does not prejudice Acme's rights against Stewart (see Figure 12-6).

Assigning Rights   The UCC also distinguishes between rights and duties. The UCC provides that unless there is a contrary agreement, all rights of buyers and sellers may be assigned. This provision holds unless the assignment would materially change the duty, burden, or risk imposed on the other party.

Clauses Barring Assignment of Rights   The UCC states that unless there is a contrary agreement, a contract provision which prohibits assigning the contract only bars the delegation of *duties* by either of the contracting parties. This provision reflects the UCC's general opposition to clauses that prevent the assignment of *rights*. If the contract between Acme and Stewart had stated, "There may be no assignment of this contract," the courts would interpret it to mean that the duty of performance may not be delegated to a third party such as Lignite. But the clause does not prevent Stewart from assigning its right to receive money.

Assigning a Contract   The UCC distinguishes between a normal assignment, in which people transfer both rights and duties, and a financing assignment, in which people transfer only rights. In a normal business assignment, when someone assigns "the contract" or "all my rights under the contract," both rights and duties are

FIGURE 12-6   Assigning a Contract

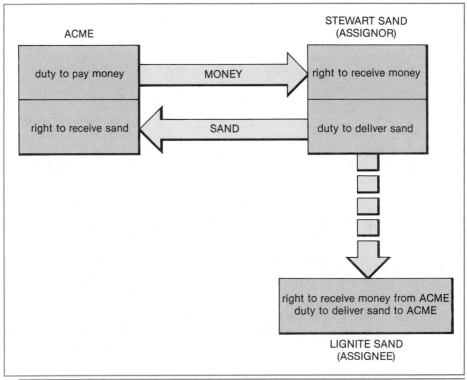

transferred. Acceptance by the assignee of the assignment also constitutes a promise to perform the duties that were delegated.

If Stewart assigns its contract with Acme to Lignite and uses language such as "all my rights under the contract," Lignite acquires all of Stewart's rights under the contract (the right to receive money) as well as all of Stewart's duties under the contract (the duty to deliver sand to Acme). Before a company takes an assignment of a contract, it should understand its rights and obligations under the contract. Otherwise it may end up obligated to perform duties it had not anticipated.

Defenses   In many cases, when someone who has been assigned a contract attempts to collect, the person finds the party who is bound to perform asserting a defense. What if Stewart assigned its right to receive money from Acme to its bank? When the bank attempts to collect from Acme, Acme refuses to pay because Stewart has somehow failed to live up to its obligations under the contract. Is there any way the bank can protect itself from the possibility of being confronted by these defenses?

Yes. One method the bank (or any assignor) might use is to include a waiver of defenses clause. This clause in the original contract states that the party obligated to pay agrees to assert any defenses against *only* the party originally obligated to perform. The original contract between Stewart and Acme might state that Acme agrees it will not assert any defenses it might have against Stewart against anyone to whom Stewart assigns the contract.

Generally, the UCC allows people to use waiver of defenses clauses, unless another law establishes a different rule for those who buy or lease *consumer* goods. Many statutes, such as the Uniform Consumer Credit Code and the Truth in Lending Act, restrict the use of such clauses in consumer contracts. The Federal Trade Commission's holder in due course rule also prohibits the use of such clauses in consumer credit contracts.

CONTRACTS FOR THE BENEFIT OF A THIRD PARTY

In many instances, a third party benefits from the performance of a contract. Some contracts are made deliberately to benefit the third party. For example, life insurance policies, which are contracts between an insured and an insuring company, provide benefits for a third party (the beneficiary) when the insured dies.

Donee Beneficiary

The beneficiary of a life insurance policy is a third party who benefits from a gift. This relationship makes the person a **donee beneficiary**. The insured purchased the policy with the intent to benefit the third party, and if the insurance company refuses to pay, the donee beneficiary may sue the company for the amount of the insurance policy. The donee beneficiary may sue even though he or she has no direct contract with the company and has not given anything to the insurance company.

Donee beneficiary a third party whose benefit from a contract is a gift from the promisee

FIGURE 12-7   Donee Beneficiary

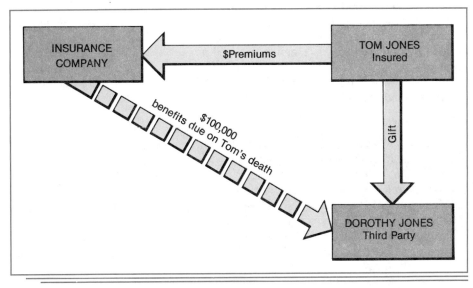

Not only may a donee beneficiary sue the party who contracted to perform (the promissor), but the promisee also may sue. In our example in Figure 12-7, it is not just the donee beneficiary who could sue the insurance company. The representative of Tom Jones's estate could also sue since the insurance company did not perform a promise it made to Tom (to pay Dorothy). However, since it is Dorothy, not Tom's estate, who has not received the $100,000, Tom's estate would probably recover only nominal damages from the insurance company.

Creditor Beneficiary

Creditor beneficiary a third party whose benefit from a contract is in payment of a legal duty owed by the promisee

If someone makes a promise to discharge an obligation that the promisee owes or believes he or she owes to the beneficiary, the third party is called a **creditor beneficiary.** In the case of a donee beneficiary, the person who makes a contract for the benefit of a third party intends to make a gift to that party. In the case of a creditor beneficiary, that person wishes to discharge a debt owed to the third party (creditor) beneficiary. Suppose that Tina already owes Cindy $1,000 when Tina sells her automobile to Sam. Tina then asks Sam to pay the $1,000 not to her, but to Cindy, so that the debt between Tina and Cindy will be discharged. When Sam agrees, Cindy is a creditor beneficiary of Sam's promise. She has an enforceable claim against Sam for $1,000.

Incidental Beneficiary

If a contracting party neither intends to confer a gift on the third party nor is trying to discharge an obligation to the third party, the third party is called an **incidental**

beneficiary. He or she has no rights under the contract. Suppose that McDonald's contracts to build a store next to Louise's Dress Shop. Because the McDonald's would attract many people to the area, Louise anticipated she would do more business than ever. The contract between McDonald's and the builder was not intended to benefit Louise. If the builder breaches the contract, and the McDonald's is never built, does Louise have a cause of action against the builder? No. This contract was not intended to benefit Louise in any way. She would have no cause of action against the builder even though, had the store been built, her business might have increased.

> **Incidental beneficiary** a third party whose benefit from a contract is not intended by the contracting parties

Intended Beneficiary

Sometimes courts do not use the terms *donee* or *creditor beneficiary,* but instead substitute the term **intended beneficiary** to describe any beneficiary who receives rights under a contract.

> **Intended beneficiary** any third party who receives rights under a contract

Whichever terms are used, courts frequently have had to decide whether a third party who benefits from an agreement has a right to sue if the agreement is not carried out. This question is especially troublesome when the parties to the contract did not contemplate benefiting another or if it were not their primary concern.

Although the law varies from state to state, most states allow the third party to sue. Even though the third party did not make the agreement, the legal system generally recognizes that it is both just and practical to allow an outsider to recover if it is clear that this action carries out the intentions of the contracting parties. A third party who has a right to sue is an intended beneficiary. Incidental beneficiaries do not have a right to sue. To determine if a party is an intended beneficiary, the courts first look at the intention of the parties. If it is clear that the parties intended to benefit the outsider, a right to sue is recognized. This is the case whenever the promisor has agreed to perform directly to or for the third party.

The third party also may have a right to sue as long as the main purpose of the contract is for his or her benefit, even if the contracting parties also benefit. The cases that follow raise issues about intended and incidental beneficiaries.

United States v. Ogden Technology Laboratories

U.S. District Court
406 F. Supp. 1090 (1973)

FACTS

The United States alleges that through its agent, the Atomic Energy Commission, it entered into a contract with Minnesota Mining and Manufacturing Company (3M) for the development and testing of certain thermoelectric power supply systems. In turn, 3M subcontracted with the Linde Division of Union Carbide Corporation to design, fabricate, and perform certain analytical work. Linde then contracted with Ogden to laboratory test some prototype units. Ogden was to test the units with prescribed shocks and vibrations. A test of one of the units severely damaged it.

The U.S. claims that the unit was damaged because Ogden improperly administered a shock far greater than specified in its contract with Linde. The U.S. claims that Ogden did not report to Linde the reason for the damage to the unit. As a consequence, the

U.S. did not know about the excess shock. Instead, it believed that the design of the units might have been faulty. Accordingly the U.S. spent $500,000 to have 3M and Linde reevaluate the design and determine the cause of damage to the units. It seeks to sue Linde on the contract between Linde and Ogden.

ISSUE   Is the United States a beneficiary entitled to enforce the contract between Ogden and Linde?

DECISION   Yes. The court found that the terms of the agreement between Linde and Ogden showed the U.S. to be more than just an incidental beneficiary of Ogden's obligations to test the units and report the results. The court found it unimportant whether the duty of Ogden (the promisor) to the U.S. (third party beneficiary) arose from a bargain between them or was created by its assumption of some duty. Because Linde was obligated to report to the U.S., although by way of an intervening contract with 3M, the U.S. was entitled to state a claim as a third-party beneficiary to the contract.

Martinez v. Socoma Companies, Incorporated

Supreme Court of California
521 P.2d 841 (1974)

FACTS   Plaintiffs claimed that Socoma Companies and others failed to perform contracts with the United States government. The contracts provided that Socoma and the other companies would provide job training and at least one year of employment to certain disadvantaged unemployed people in exchange for the government's agreement to pay each defendant a stated sum. Although the government paid part of the contracted sum to Socoma and to other companies, almost all of the companies failed to perform as provided under their respective contracts.

ISSUE   Are the disadvantaged and unemployed plaintiffs third-party beneficiaries who may sue defendants for Socoma's nonperformance of its contract with the U.S. government?

DECISION   No. The court did not allow the plaintiffs to sue on the contract. Clearly, plaintiffs were among those whom the government intended to benefit through their contract with the defendants. However, the fact that a government program for social betterment confers benefits upon individuals, who are not required to render contractual consideration in return, does not necessarily imply that those benefits are intended as gifts.

The contracts did not show that either party intended that the defendants pay damages to compensate plaintiffs or other members of the public for their nonperformance of the contracts. To the contrary, the contracts' provisions show that the U.S. intended to retain control over the determination of all contractual disputes. Further, the contract shows the U.S. sought to limit the defendants' financial risks in undertaking the contract. These provisions indicate the U.S. government intended to exclude granting to the plaintiffs the direct right to assert claims for nonperformance of Socoma's contract with the U.S.

SUMMARY

The rights of third parties to enforce contracts made by others has changed dramatically in recent years. The requirement that one person have a contractual relationship with another person to enforce a contract is no longer the law in most situations. The assignment of contract rights to third parties generally is permitted. The only exceptions concern the assignment of rights which are personal in nature. Duties under a contract cannot be assigned but can be delegated. Thus a third party's performance of duties generally discharges the obligation of the party to the contract who is delegating the duties. The Uniform Commercial Code has made some changes in the assignment of contract's rights and duties.

A person who is not assigned rights under a contract still may be able to enforce its provision if that person was intended to benefit from the contract. Thus a creditor and a donee beneficiary can enforce a contract's provision, but an incidental beneficiary cannot. The intent of the contracting parties is often critical in determining a third party's right to sue to enforce their contract.

REVIEW PROBLEMS

1. What is the difference between an assignment and a delegation?

2. Do parties to a contract delegate duties more often than they assign rights?

3. If a bank or financial institution is an assignee of a contract right (such as the right of a seller of a product to receive a sum of money from the purchaser at a specified later date), may the assignee sue the assignor if the money due to it is not paid?

4. What is meant by the statement, "Duties can't be assigned"? What type of contract duties may not be delegated?

5. Bull Dog Insurance issued a policy of insurance to D'Alassano against loss by theft of an automobile. The automobile was stolen and never recovered. D'Alassano assigned his claim under the policy to Ginsberg. The policy provided that "no assignment of interest under this policy shall be or become binding upon the association unless the written consent . . . is endorsed thereon and an additional membership fee is paid." Present arguments supporting Ginsberg's right to collect under the policy.

6. Dooley contracted with Rose to provide enough stone to meet Rose's business requirements for ten years at favorable listed prices. In return, Rose promised

not to compete with Dooley in the rock-crushing business. Later, Dooley assigned the contract to Vulcan Materials Co. Is Vulcan required to supply stone to Rose at the original contract prices?

7. McDonald's granted a franchise in the Omaha-Council Bluffs area to Copeland, a reputable and highly successful businessman. *In a separate agreement,* Copeland was granted a right of first refusal, that is, the right to receive the first offer of additional McDonald's franchises to be developed in the area. Subsequently, Copeland assigned his franchise contracts to Shupack, with McDonald's consent. When McDonald's later offered a new area franchise to someone else, Shupack sued, claiming that the right of first refusal was included in the assignment from Copeland so that he should have been offered the new restaurant first. McDonald's had previously written Shupack stating that the right was personal to Copeland and had not passed to Shupack. Was the right assignable? How can you determine whether it was personal to Copeland?

8. Cunningham played basketball for the Cougars, a professional team owned by Southern Sports Corp. His contract prohibited assignment to another club without his consent. When Southern Sports assigned the Cougars franchise and Cunningham's contract to Munchak Corp., Cunningham protested, claiming that his contract was personal and therefore not assignable. Is the assignment of Cunningham's contract effective?

9. Upon the separation of Robert and Jane Lingle, Robert agreed to leave one half of his estate to his daughters, Sandy and Laura. (The separation agreement was signed by both parties and made a part of the court's order regarding the legal separation of Robert and Jane.) When Robert died, his will left his entire estate to his second wife. Sandy and Laura seek to enforce the separation agreement made on their behalf by their father. Can they?

10. The New Orleans Basketball Club (Jazz), a partnership, signed a contract with HMC Management Corporation (HMC), the corporation operating the Louisiana Superdome in New Orleans, to play their home games there. When the Jazz broke their contract with HMC by moving their team and its home games to Salt Lake City, Utah, the city of New Orleans sued on the contract. The city claims it clearly benefits under the contract of the parties and that the parties to the contract intended it to benefit. Can the city enforce the contract or seek damages caused by the Jazz's nonperformance of its terms?

11. Lenox Homes built a house for the Buengers in 1972. In 1974, the Buengers sold the house to the Coburns. The Coburns occupied the house and found that the septic system installed by Lenox was faulty. The Coburns sued Lenox and claimed that they were beneficiaries of the contract made between Lenox and the Buengers. Do you agree?

12. Mrs. Lara entered the Kern County hospital to give birth. She died shortly after her child was born, and the hospital was not paid for the medical services it provided to her child. Under state law, her husband, a part-time farmworker, was billed by the hospital. Can the hospital assign its right to receive money from Mr. Lara to a collection service?

13. Smith purchases a new automobile from the Warren Oldsmobile dealer. One of

the terms of the purchase is that the dealer perform certain specified warranty work on the car for two years without further charge. A year after Smith's purchase, the chief mechanic at Warren quits, and Warren notifies Smith that all future warranty work will be performed by the Ace Garage. Warren contracts with the Ace Garage to provide this service to Smith. May Warren do this? Explain.

14. Asphalt Paving Company contracted with the city of Flint to pave certain streets. A clause in that contract provided that Asphalt would be liable for damages to any property resulting from the paving work. In moving one of its bulldozers, Asphalt struck a gas main, which exploded and seriously damaged the house of Leo Stevenson. Stevenson sued Asphalt and relied on the contract between Asphalt and the city of Flint. Can Stevenson use that contract in his case?

CHAPTER 13

Performance and Discharge of Contracts

CHAPTER OBJECTIVES

After reading this chapter, you should be able to:

1. Define and distinguish condition precedent and condition subsequent.

2. State the rules of law that apply when a party's duty of performance is conditional upon approval or satisfaction.

3. Describe the substantial performance doctrine.

4. Describe material breach of contract and compare to substantial performance of contract.

5. Compare and contrast the perfect tender rule to the substantial performance doctrine.

6. State the rules about time of performance for contracts.

7. Define and describe discharge of a duty of performance.

8. Define and distinguish strict impossibility of performance, commercial impracticability, and frustration of purpose.

9. Define and describe anticipatory breach of contract.

The discussion of contract law to this point has been concerned with the issues of whether or not a valid contract has been entered into by the parties. Now the focus shifts to what happens after the contract has been made: the consequences of performance and nonperformance of the contractual obligations.

PERFORMANCE DEPENDENT UPON CONDITIONS

Conditional Promises

Sometimes the parties to a contract condition their respective performances upon the occurrence of an event. For example, a seller may condition its duty to deliver ordered goods upon the buyer's making a specified down payment. Similarly, the buyer may condition its payment on getting financing for the purchase, being satisfied with the delivered merchandise, or both. In these examples, the contract does not create a duty to perform unless and until some event occurs. Such promises are *conditional*.

Similarly, a duty to perform may be conditioned upon the nonoccurrence of an

Condition precedent a clause in a contract that provides for the happening of some event or the performance of some act before the contract becomes binding

Condition subsequent a clause in a contract that provides for the release or discharge of an obligation upon the happening of a certain event

event. An example is "I promise to cut the lawn if it does not rain on Saturday." Rain on Saturday removes the mower's present duty to cut the lawn. Conversely, when the buyer makes the down payment it creates a duty in the seller to deliver the merchandise.

An event that must occur to create a duty to perform is a **condition precedent**. An event that removes a duty to perform is a **condition subsequent**. If the condition precedent — the necessary event — does not occur, a person is excused from performing. If the condition subsequent happens, a person is excused from performing whatever hinged on that condition. In both cases, the nonperformance is excused, and the person is not liable to the other party for breaking the contract. But if the condition precedent — the necessary event — happens to be the other party's performance, and that party does not perform, the party relying upon that condition may claim that the other has broken the contract. In such a case, the party who was relying on the condition is excused from performing, and the other party remains liable for breaking the contract.

Approval or Satisfaction

Contracts sometimes require that one party's performance be approved by the other party or by a person who is not a party to the contract. In such cases, the approval is a condition to the performance of one of the parties to the contract.

A common example of a contract requiring the approval of a third party is the typical construction contract. Construction contracts often require outside approval of the work before the owner is obligated to pay. Usually the job must be inspected by an architect or an engineer who issues a certificate for payment if the construction is satisfactory, meaning that the construction has met the specifications contained in the architect's or engineer's building plans. Until this certificate is issued, the owner has no obligation to pay, because the architect's or engineer's certificate is a condition precedent to performance by the owner.

A party's duty to perform also may be conditioned upon its own satisfaction with the other's performance. One party may bargain that its performance will satisfy the other party. Although there is considerable risk to the person or firm making this kind of commitment, it is relatively common. Contracts for the sale of goods often give the buyer the right to return the goods if not satisfied. Employment contracts sometimes allow an employer to let employees go if their work does not satisfy the employer within a specific period of time.

Because of the potential for abuse in such contracts, courts generally have interpreted these provisions narrowly. They have consistently held that the dissatisfaction or refusal to approve must be in good faith and not left to the will or quirks of the interested party. The dissatisfaction must be valid and genuine.

For example, suppose that an artist agrees to paint a portrait of Penelope to her satisfaction. Any dissatisfaction expressed by Penelope must be made in good faith. That is, it must be an honest dissatisfaction. Proving Penelope's bad faith may be difficult because her dissatisfaction is a subjective state involving artistic taste and personal feeling. But suppose that the artist can show that Penelope expressed dissatisfaction with the portrait only after she had suffered severe financial problems. The artist might succeed in arguing that Penelope was really responding to her finances rather than to the quality of the artist's work.

When performance can be measured against an objective standard — for example, whether a reasonable person would be satisfied — the party to the contract also must be satisfied. Suppose that Bigdome, Inc., contracts to buy certain tools from Ace Tool that are to be satisfactory to Bigdome. If Ace can establish that the tools meet certain standards in Bigdome's industry — for example, that they have been calibrated according to industry standards — Bigdome's dissatisfaction does not excuse its nonpayment for the tools.

The following case shows a court confronting a situation involving approval as a condition to performance.

Aztec Film Productions Incorporated v. Prescott Valley, Incorporated

Supreme Court of Arizona
626 P.2d 132 (1981)

Aztec Films contracted in May 1974 with Prescott Valley, an Arizona land developer, to produce a film, "Why Arizona," to be used in marketing land in other states. Prescott Valley paid one third ($6,250) of the total contract price ($18,750) when the agreement was signed. The contract provided that the film was to be completed within 90 days after Prescott Valley approved the film's script. The contract further provided that such approval "be given expeditiously and not unreasonably withheld."

When the script was submitted, Prescott Valley refused to approve it because some of the script's factual statements were not documented, as required by states where Prescott Valley was marketing its land. Aztec argued that many of the undocumented facts did not need to be documented. The parties agreed to let a real estate investigator for Minnesota look at the script, and this investigator stated that the script was unacceptable.

Aztec sued Prescott Valley for breach of contract, seeking payment. Prescott Valley countersued for the return of the $6,250 paid under the contract. Aztec claimed that Prescott Valley's refusal to approve the script was unreasonable, because the script would have satisfied a reasonable Arizona land developer.

FACTS

Did Prescott Valley unreasonably withhold approval of the Aztec script?

ISSUE

No. The court found in favor of Prescott Valley, stating that the contract required Prescott Valley to be "objectively dissatisfied" with the script. The facts supported a conclusion that, under the objective test of reasonableness, Prescott Valley's withholding of approval was not unreasonable.

DECISION

SUBSTANTIAL PERFORMANCE AND MATERIAL BREACH

Most contracts are fully performed, and the relationships among the parties to the contract end. But when one party fails to perform, the injured party must determine what remedy is available.

Substantial Performance

The most satisfactory way to perform contractual obligations is for both parties to perform exactly as promised. However, one party may perform incorrectly as a result of misinterpreting the contract. Exact performance may be prevented by circumstances that cannot be controlled. Clearly, a party is entitled to the promised performance. Just as clearly, justice dictates that the injured party should not be unjustly enriched by the penalty imposed on the defaulting party.

When one party fails to render a part of the promised performance, the following questions may arise:

1. May the other party refuse to perform his or her duty in return?

2. Is the other party discharged from its contractual duty?

3. Can the other party sue for damages, regarding the breach as "total"?

4. Can the other party sue for damages for a "partial" breach?

Substantial performance a state in which all material terms of an agreement have been met, and only insignificant matters remain

Under older common law, an express contract had to be completed to the last detail before a party could enforce the performance of the other party. Under the newer concept of **substantial performance,** a party who has failed to perform to the last detail may nevertheless enforce the performance of the other party if there was:

1. substantial performance of the contract

2. an honest effort to comply fully with the contract's requirements, and

3. no willful or intentional departure from the terms of the contract.

The reason for what is often called the *substantial-performance doctrine* is that justice does not demand full, literal fulfillment of contractual obligations, only substantial fulfillment.

Breach the full or partial violation of the terms of a contract

When one contracting party has substantially performed its contractual duties, it may enforce performance by the other party. That is, the injured party may not refuse to render a reciprocal promised performance. It is not discharged from its duties. But the party that rendered substantial performance nevertheless has broken the contract. The violation — a **breach** — is partial, not material, but it remains a violation. When a contract has been violated, the injured party may sue and recover damages. Thus although the injured party is not excused from its promised reciprocal performance, it is entitled to recover damages for the other party's failure to perform exactly as promised. If the injured party's promised performance is payment, it is entitled to deduct from the contract price the amount that compensates for the damages.

Material Breach

When someone fails substantially to perform a contractual obligation, the person has *materially* breached the contract and is liable to the injured party for damages. A material breach also carries a further legal consequence. The injured party is excused from its part of the bargain. The injured party may consider its contractual duties discharged. Its nonperformance is excused, and it may sue for damages resulting from the material breach.

When is a violation of a contract considered material and substantial? The test of substantial performance is whether the performance met the essential purpose of the contract and whether the nonperformance was willful. Someone who wants to rely on the substantial performance doctrine must show that the departure from the contract was slight and unintentional.

In the following case, the court wrestles to balance a policy against unjust enrichment with a policy of enforcing a contract.

Plant v. Jacobs

Supreme Court of Wisconsin
103 N.W.2d 296 (1960)

Plant contracted with Frank and Carol Jacobs to construct a house according to plans and specifications. The specifications were standard printed forms with some modifications and additions written in by the parties. Although the house had essentially been completed, the Jacobses refused to pay the full price because Plant had misplaced the wall between the kitchen and the living room, thus narrowing the living room by more than one foot. Plant sued Jacobs to recover the unpaid balance of the contract price.   FACTS

Did Plant substantially perform the contract?   ISSUE

Yes. Plant's performance met the essential purpose of the contract and therefore amounted to substantial performance, even though the Jacobses were dissatisfied with their house. Something less than perfection is the test of substantial performance, unless all details are made the essence of the contract. Having substantially performed, Plant is entitled to recover the contract price less damages caused by the incomplete performance.   DECISION

Sale of Goods

In contracts for the sale of goods, the doctrine of substantial performance does not apply. The seller must make *perfect tender.* The goods must be perfect.

The Uniform Commercial Code (Section 2-601) states:

> If the goods or the tender of delivery fail in any respect to conform to the contract, the buyer may (a) reject the whole; or (b) accept the whole; or (c) accept any commercial unit or units and reject the rest.

Several other provisions of the UCC, however, soften the harsh effect of this rule. The buyer who rejects goods must explain the nature of the defect to the seller. The seller is entitled to "cure the defect" within a reasonable time. If the buyer accepts goods, it cannot revoke that acceptance if there has been substantial performance in good faith. Similar rules apply to installment contracts.

Time of Performance

Contracts often state a time by which performance must be completed. A common example is a contract for goods that states the date upon which delivery will be made. Sometimes the time of performance is important to the parties. Sometimes performance by a particular time, even though stated in the agreement, really does not make much difference.

Ordinarily, unless performance by an exact date is vital, lateness does not discharge the duty of the other party. Contracts for the sale of real estate usually come within this rule. If a real estate contract scts a **closing** date of February 15, the inability of the buyer to close because the necessary financing has not been approved does not excuse the seller from performing. The buyer may enforce the contract later, and the seller is entitled to interest on the purchase price from February 15 as well as actual damages, if any could be proved.

Closing the final steps in a sale of real estate, when the buyer pays for the property and the seller delivers the deed

If performance by a particular time is important to one or both parties, they should include a provision in the contract that clearly indicates this. Ordinarily they may do this by stating, "Time is of the essence." Statements of this kind often are included in contracts. To bc of any value, the statement must indicate clearly which part of the performance is the heart of the agreement.

If the parties do not agree specifically that time is of the essence, determining whether it is essential requires consideration of the particular circumstances. A wholesaler who promises delivery to a retailer before April 1 and knows that the retailer plans a major advertising campaign to begin April 1 would have to perform on or before that date, even though the contract did not include a "time is of the essence" clause.

DISCHARGE OF
CONTRACTUAL OBLIGATIONS

Discharge to release a party from obligations in a contract

When a contract is **discharged,** it usually means that the legal duty of one of the parties has been terminated. A party who is under a legal duty by virtue of his or her contract may assert that the duty has been "discharged" by some event that has occurred since the contract was made.

Contract duties may be discharged in a variety of ways. Some of these have already been discussed, although not in the context of discharge. The following discussion focuses on the primary methods of discharge.

Discharge by Complete Performance

The most obvious method of discharge of a contractual duty is by complete performance. Most contracts are discharged in this way. Complete performance means full and exact performance — not only of the character, quality, and amount required, but also within the time agreed upon.

Discharge by Occurrence of a Condition Subsequent

As mentioned earlier, a condition subsequent is an event that terminates a present duty to perform. If a condition subsequent occurs, it discharges the duty. Because of their potentially harsh effects, conditions subsequent in contracts are narrowly interpreted by the courts.

Discharge by Mutual Agreement

Rescission   A contract still to be executed by both sides may be discharged by an express agreement that it shall no longer bind either party. Such an agreement, called mutual **rescission,** is itself a contract. Its purpose is to restore the parties to the positions they were in before they made the first contract.

Rescission cancellation or abrogation of an agreement

Substitution of New Contract   A contract may be discharged by the substitution of a new contract. A contract may be discharged when a new contract is expressly substituted or when a new contract is made that is inconsistent with the old one, with new terms agreed upon by both sides.

Discharge by Impossibility of Performance

After a contract is made but before full performance, an event may occur that makes performance by one of the parties difficult, unprofitable, impractical, or impossible, or that frustrates the very purpose for which one of parties entered into the contract. Under such conditions, the party who views its own performance as no longer desirable may be expected to not perform its contractual obligation. But the other party may be expected to sue, claiming breach of contract. The party being sued may defend itself on the basis that events made its performance impossible or that the purpose for which it made the contract had become frustrated.

Strict or Objective Impossibility   If, after a contract has been formed, but before it is fully performed, some unforeseeable event occurs that makes performance objectively impossible, the promising party's duty to perform ends. By *objectively* impossible, the courts mean that no person could legally or physically perform the contract. But if the event that arises makes performance impossible only for that particular promising party, it is merely a *subjective* impossibility and is insufficient to cancel the promisor's duty to perform. Objective **impossibility** has been found in the following three circumstances:

Impossibility a doctrine in contract law that allows for a cancellation when a contract becomes legally impossible to perform

1. the death or serious illness of a promisor whose personal performance is required,

2. a change of law, making the promised performance illegal, and

3. the destruction of the subject matter of the contract.

Commercial Impracticability and Frustration of Purpose   The trend in the law is toward enlarging the definition of impossibility. As a result, a fourth circumstance has been frequently allowed in recent years. Impossibility now may be due to the fact that a certain state of affairs has come about, but the contracting parties assumed that this state of affairs would *not* come about. "Impossibility" is probably an inappropriate word to use here. Thus courts have used the terms **commercial impracticability** and *frustration of purpose* to describe such a circumstance. The two concepts are different but closely related.

Commercial impracticability the doctrine that may allow for cancellation of a contract when it becomes commercially impracticable to perform

The concept of commercial impracticability describes a situation where a party claims that some circumstance has made its own performance impractical. Performance may be impractical because extreme and unreasonable difficulty, expense, injury, or loss to one of the parties will occur. A severe shortage of raw materials or of supplies, due to war, embargo, local crop failure, unforeseen shutdown of major sources of supply, or the like, which either causes a marked increase in cost or prevents performance altogether may constitute impracticability.

The concept of frustration of purpose deals with a situation that arises when a change in circumstances makes one party's performance virtually worthless to the other, frustrating its purpose in making the contract. Frustration of purpose differs from commercial impracticability in that there is no impediment to performance by either party. For the concept of frustration of purpose to excuse a party's nonperformance, the purpose that is frustrated must have been a principal purpose of the party in making the contract, the frustration must be substantial, and the nonoccurrence of the frustrating event must have been a basic assumption on which the contract was made.

The Second Restatement of Contracts has endorsed both the concept of commercial impracticability (Section 261) and the concept of frustration of purpose (Section 265). The revisers of the Restatement were influenced by the UCC (Section 2-615), which excuses a seller from making timely delivery when the seller's performance has become commercially impracticable:

> by the occurrence of a contingency the nonoccurrence of which was a basic assumption on which the contract was made.

The following case concerns the application of the UCC rule (Section 2-615).

Mishara Construction Company v. Transit Mixed Concrete Company

Supreme Judicial Court of Massachusetts
310 N.E.2d 363 (1974)

FACTS   Mishara Construction Company was the general contractor for a construction project. It contracted with the Transit Mixed Concrete Company to supply all the ready-mixed concrete needed for the project. Under the contract, Mishara was to specify the dates and amounts of deliveries. In April 1967, a labor dispute stopped work on the project. Work resumed in June, but the workers maintained their picket line for two more years. Transit Mixed Concrete made few deliveries during the two-year period, and Mishara had to get concrete from other sources. Mishara sued for damages as a result of Transit's delays and the higher cost of purchasing concrete elsewhere. Transit defended on the basis of impossibility of performance.

Can a labor dispute ever constitute an excuse for nonperformance?

Yes. Where at the time of contracting the probability of a labor dispute appears to be
practically nil, and where the occurrence of such a dispute provides unusual difficulty,
the excuse of impracticability is applicable. Commercial impracticability under the UCC
(Section 2-615) does not require scientific or actual impossibility, just some extreme or
unreasonable difficulty or expense. The requirement that the contract be made on the
assumption of the nonoccurrence of the contingency is a practical response to the use
of contracts for risk distribution, where parties exchange the elimination of some risks
for others. Commercial impracticability presents an excuse when the risk apportionment is beyond the scope of the contract, was not bargained for, and has made
performance of the promise vitally different. The foreseeability of a contingency is thus
an important consideration.

Discharge by Breach of Contract

A contract is breached when a party under a duty to perform fails to perform. As
already discussed, a material breach of contract by one party discharges the injured
party from any further duty of performance. A partial or minor breach of contract
does not operate as a discharge but does render the breaching party liable for the
injuries sustained by the innocent party as a result of the breach.

Anticipatory Breach   In most instances, breach of contract occurs only after
performance is due. But sometimes a party to a contract repudiates a commitment to
perform before the performance is required. This is known as an **anticipatory breach**.
An anticipatory breach raises the questions of whether the other party is immediately
discharged from its contractual obligations and whether it can seek a remedy immediately.

Repudiation must be clear and unequivocal. A statement by one of the parties
indicating doubt about its ability to perform or even doubt about whether it wants to
perform is not an anticipatory breach. Repudiation does not have to be verbal. An act
is sufficient, if it clearly indicates an intent not to perform in the future. A party who
prevents another from performing an act that is necessary to carrying out the agreement has committed an anticipatory breach. Some courts have held that voluntary or
involuntary bankruptcy is the equivalent of anticipatory breach.

When the other party to a contract has repudiated before it has performed, a firm
has several options. It may treat the entire contract as broken and sue immediately
for damages without complying further with its own obligations. Assume that a
homeowner and a contractor have entered into an agreement in which the contractor
agrees to move a house for the homeowner. The homeowner has promised to pay the
contractor $3,000 for the job and to get all necessary permits and road clearances. If
the contractor repudiates the agreement, it is not necessary for the homeowner to get
the permits and clearances before bringing suit.

The firm may choose to ignore the repudiation and wait until performance is due
before taking any action, or it may rescind the agreement and sue to recover anything

**Anticipatory
breach** the
breaking of an
agreement before
the duty of
performance

it has furnished under the contract. If the contract can be specifically enforced, an immediate action requiring performance can be brought.

In goods transactions, reasonable grounds for insecurity give rise to the right to demand assurance of performance, and the failure to give such assurance is a repudiation according to the UCC (Section 2-609). The repudiation may be treated as an immediate breach.

SUMMARY

A condition is an event that serves either to create a duty of performance or to eliminate a duty of performance. A condition precedent is an event which serves to create a duty of performance. A condition subsequent is an event which serves to extinguish a duty of performance.

Contracts sometimes contain provisions requiring that a party's performance be approved by the other party or by a person who is not a party to the contract. In determining whether someone's disapproval serves to discharge contract obligations, the courts use an objective standard of reasonableness if possible. If not, they use a subjective standard of good faith.

In cases where one of the contracting parties has substantially performed its obligations but has committed a minor breach in the process, the courts apply the substantial performance doctrine. This doctrine allows the party who has substantially performed to hold the innocent party to its duty of performance under the contract. The innocent party thus may not treat its return obligation as discharged. The innocent party is entitled to recover damages for the breach, however. In determining whether a party has substantially performed its contract duty, a court examines whether the essential purpose of the contract has been fulfilled.

Where a party has failed to substantially perform its contract duties without excuse, it has materially breached the contract. In such a case, the innocent party may treat its return duty of performance as discharged and may seek damages.

Where a breach of contract takes the form of delay, the courts apply the substantial performance doctrine and hold that reasonable delays do not relieve the innocent party of its duty to perform. If the parties have made time the essence of their agreement, a delay does result in a discharge.

A party may discharge its duties by complete performance, by occurrence of a condition subsequent, by mutual agreement, by impossibility of performance, or by the material breach of the other party. Traditionally, courts have made it difficult for parties to assert impossibility as a ground for the discharge of their contract duties by requiring that performance be strictly or literally impossible. The trend is to allow parties to assert that unforeseen circumstances making performance commercially impracticable serve as a basis for the discharge of a contracting party's duty of performance.

REVIEW PROBLEMS

1. What is the difference between a condition precedent and a condition subsequent?

2. What is the substantial performance doctrine? When does performance qualify as substantial under the doctrine?

3. When does a delay in the performance by one party result in the discharge of the innocent party's contractual duty of performance?

4. What is impossibility of performance?

5. Taylor contracted to make a suit of clothes to Smith's satisfaction. Smith promised to pay $400 for the suit if he was satisfied with it when it was completed. Taylor completed the suit using materials ordered by Smith. The suit fit Smith perfectly, but Smith told Taylor that he was not satisfied with it and refused to accept or pay for it. Must Smith pay Taylor the price of the suit?

6. Ace contracted with Jones to do certain remodeling work on the building owned by Jones. Jones supplied the specifications for the work. The contract price was $70,000. After the work was completed, Jones was dissatisfied and had Clay, an expert, compare the work done to the specifications provided. Clay testified that the work had been done improperly by Ace and that it would cost about $6,000 to correct the mistakes of Ace. If Jones refuses to pay any amount to Ace, what recourse, if any, does Ace have against Jones? Explain.

7. Julius agreed to purchase land and office buildings from Herschel. The contract provided that Herschel was to furnish good title to the property. The contract expressly made Julius's liability dependent upon his ability to obtain a $120,000 loan at 11 percent interest. Explain the legal consequences that result if

    1 ☐ Herschel is unable to furnish a good title to Julius, or

    2 ☐ Julius is unable to get the loan at 11 percent interest.

8. Seller agreed to sell 800 bags of Number 1 goose down to Buyer at $10 a bag. Seller planned to obtain the down from geese housed on two large farms she owned. Buyer was not informed of this, although Buyer did know that Seller raised geese on the two farms. The main barn on one farm was struck by lightning, and all the geese were destroyed. The geese on the other farm became diseased through no fault of Seller, and none of the down was delivered to Number 1. At the time of scheduled delivery, the market price of down is $13 a bag. Discuss Seller's liability, if any, to Buyer.

9. On January 4, General Contractors, Inc., contracted with Julius and Penelope Jones to construct a house fit for occupancy by June 1. What is the legal consequence if General Contractors fails to complete the house by June 1, but does finish it by June 20? What would be the consequence if it were stated that, with regard to the June 1 deadline, "Time is of the essence"? Suppose further that by May 10, no work has been started by General Contractors. When contacted by Julius, General Contractors's president states that due to other projects still pending, he is unable to build the house until late November. What legal recourse, if any, do Julius and Penelope have against General Contractors?

10. Frank and Flo Gibson enter into a contract with Ace Home Builders for the construction of a house. After construction is complete, the Gibsons discover several cracks in the foundation, which cause flooding in the basement. What recourse do the Gibsons have against Ace, if any?

11. Anderson, a carpenter, contracted with Baker to shingle the roof of Baker's house. Anderson had partially completed the work when a hurricane destroyed a large part of the house, including the roof. Baker repaired the house, except for the roof, and demanded that Anderson honor his agreement. Is Anderson responsible?

12. Smith owned and operated a large motel in Phoenix, Arizona. To increase room occupancy, he contracted with a local tennis club to extend membership privileges and the use of its courts to guests of the motel. The agreement was to last for two years, and the motel was to pay the club $500 a month. Seven months later, the motel was destroyed by fire. Smith refused to continue the monthly payments. The tennis court sued. What result? Why?

13. The Aluminum Company of America (ALCOA) sued for relief from a burdensome contract under which it converted alumina into molten aluminum for the Essex Group, Inc., the supplier of the raw material. ALCOA sought a judgment that its nonperformance of the contract was excused as a result of commercial impracticability and frustration of purpose. For relief, it sought a reformation or modification of the contract.

    Under the terms of the contract, entered into December 26, 1967, Essex would supply ALCOA with alumina, which ALCOA would convert into molten aluminum at its Warrick, Indiana, plant. Essex then would pick up the aluminum for further processing into aluminum wire products. The contract contained a complex price formula, with escalators pegged to the Wholesale Price Index — Industrial Commodities (WPI — IC), a government price index, and to the average hourly labor rates paid to ALCOA employees at the Warrick plant. The adjusted price was subject to an overall ceiling of 65 percent of the price of a specified type of aluminum, sold on specified terms, as published in a trade journal.

    The price formula was designed to reflect changes in nonlabor and labor costs. ALCOA selected the WPI — IC as a pricing element after assuring itself that the index had closely tracked ALCOA's nonlabor production costs for many years in the past and was highly likely to continue to do so in the future. However, the formula had failed to account for burgeoning energy costs. Beginning in 1973, increased oil prices and unanticipated pollution control costs greatly increased ALCOA's electricity costs. Electrical power is the principal nonlabor cost factor in aluminum conversion, and the electrical power rates rose much more rapidly than did the WPI — IC. ALCOA complained that if it were compelled to perform the unexpired term of the 16-year contract, it would lose over $75 million. Essex counterclaimed for damages and specific performance of the contract, arguing that ALCOA had breached the contract. Who wins? Explain. If you decide in favor of ALCOA, should the court be allowed to reform the contract by writing a wholly new price term for the parties? If so, how would you reform the price formula? If you decide in favor of Essex, should the court award the remedy of specific performance?

CHAPTER 14

Remedies for Breach of Contract

CHAPTER OBJECTIVES

After reading this chapter, you should be able to:

1. Explain the types of damages that may be recovered after a breach of contract.

2. Identify the standards that must be met to collect money damages and nonmonetary damages.

3. Identify liquidated damage clauses.

4. Describe punitive damages as applied to contract law cases.

5. Describe the application of remedies such as specific performance, injunction, rescission, and restitution in breaches of contracts.

As we have noted in earlier chapters, a major function of contract law is to assure that people's expectations based on commitments made by others are met. Businesses must be able to plan future operations effectively. Private individuals also, in our complicated world, must plan for the future if they are to live satisfactory lives. Because both business and personal planning often are based on commitments from others, methods of inducing people to honor their agreements are of major importance to society.

Recourse a turning to or a seeking of aid

Legal remedies are available to enforce legal promises. Even if the parties pay little conscious attention to what will happen if a promise is broken, the underlying threat of legal **recourse** has an impact. In this chapter, we explore some of the remedies provided by the law to induce contractual performance. (See Table 14-1 for a summary of these remedies.)

The courts usually do not require a party actually to perform a breached promise. They offer several reasons for this reluctance. First, because agreements often are for long periods of time, the courts feel that continuous supervision of performance would be a difficult, if not impossible, burden. Second, the courts fear that they would become involved in disputes over whether the terms of the agreement were being met. A party *ordered* to perform might do as little as it could get away with. The other party would raise objections to this minimal performance, with the court being required to settle recurring differences. Finally, in some cases, a court decree ordering a person to perform would verge on involuntary servitude.

DOLLAR DAMAGES

As a result of judicial reluctance to order actual performance, contract law attempts to compensate the injured party by requiring monetary damages from de-

TABLE 14-1

Contractual Remedies	When Available
Money	Generally Available
Specific Performance	Only if the payment of monetary damages is not an adequate remedy
Injunction	In personal service contracts, if a person agreed to exclusively serve the plaintiff and to enforce ancillary agreements
Rescission	In cases involving fraud, duress, undue influence, and mistake
Restitution	If a contract has been canceled, a party has been unjustly enriched or benefited from an unenforceable contract, and if there has been mistaken payment of money

faulting parties. The general objective of damages is to place the injured party in the position it would have been in had the agreement been carried out. For example, if a firm has contracted to buy 1,000 units at $6 for delivery on January 15, and the units are not delivered, the buyer has a right to obtain the units elsewhere. If the market price is now $6.50, the buyer may be awarded damages of $500, the additional amount that had to be paid to obtain 1,000 units. Then the buyer is placed in the position it would have been in under the contract. In both instances, the buyer has to pay at least $6,000, so this amount is not part of its damages.

In most cases, damages cover reasonably anticipated losses and expenses as well as any gains and profits that might have been made. This rule, although easily stated, is often complex in application and leads to many legal problems.

The Reasonable Anticipation Standard

The defaulting party is responsible for those damages that a reasonable person could foresee at the time the contract was made. In the often cited English case of *Hadley* v. *Baxendale,* a mill was shut down because of a broken shaft. The mill owner delivered the shaft to a cartage (transportation) company that promised to return it in three days. When the shaft was not returned in three days as promised, the mill owner sued for the profits lost during the additional period that the mill was closed. The appellate court refused to allow the plaintiff to recover the lost profits, contending that it was not reasonable to anticipate that a mill would be closed completely because of a broken shaft.

Although the defendant is responsible for only reasonably foreseeable losses, anticipation of a *particular* loss is unnecessary. Responsibility extends to that which a reasonable person would know in the ordinary course of events. It also extends to knowledge of special circumstances that could result in larger than ordinary loss.

Certainty

Closely related and often overlapping the rule that an injured party is entitled to compensation only for losses that could reasonably have been foreseen is the additional requirement that damages be certain, not speculative nor uncertain. The plaintiff must establish that a particular loss was caused by the breach and that the amount lost actually can be calculated.

A problem about the certainty of the relationship between breach and loss arises when the defendant can show that intervening factors might have been responsible for plaintiff's loss. Ordinarily, the relationship is a known fact. If a jury finds that the breach was the "primary" or "chief" cause of the loss, the loss is part of the damage award.

Difficult problems also arise out of the need for certainty in the actual calculation of damages. Courts generally have not equated *certainty* with *absolute exactness*. In fact, they appear to have been more concerned with the need for certainty in allowing an award of damages than they are with certainty in calculating the actual amount to be awarded. Over the years, courts in commercial cases have increasingly admitted the testimony of expert witnesses who analyze business records and market summaries to satisfy the certainty requirement. One difficult question for the courts has been whether a defaulting defendant should be responsible for the loss of future profits stemming from a particular contract. Although most jurisdictions allow an injured party to collect anticipated profits if a contract is breached with a business in operation, the rule appears to be different when the business is new or being planned. In these cases, the plaintiff is not entitled to anticipated profits.

Mitigation of Damages

A person injured by breach of contract has a right to recover losses that are reasonably predictable and relatively certain. The injured party, however, must limit these losses as much as possible. An injured party cannot allow damages to accumulate and then collect all that has been lost. The injured party cannot continue to perform when the other party is in default and then recover the full contract price.

Mitigation the obligation to lessen damages

The obligation of the injured party to keep losses as low as possible is known as **mitigation** of damages. If opportunities to mitigate damages are available and plaintiff has not taken advantage of them, the court subtracts from any award the amount by which the plaintiff could have minimized his or her own losses.

The mitigation requirement forces the injured party to make many decisions if the contract is breached. An employee who has a contract but is fired must secure comparable employment elsewhere if possible. This requirement raises several questions. Is any employment paying the same amount comparable? Suppose a potential job involves moving to an area that the injured party does not like. Is the employment comparable?

A difficult mitigation decision for a manufacturer occurs when a buyer repudiates an agreement during the manufacturing of special items. The manufacturer-seller may have invested heavily in parts and materials necessary for the job. Managers must decide if the buyer's losses will be less if the firm immediately halts production and sells the partially completed merchandise for salvage or if it completes the contract and sells the finished merchandise on the market. The UCC allows the manufacturer to do either as long as it uses "reasonable commercial judgment."

The following case illustrates some of the possible ramifications of mitigation decisions.

_____ *Parker v. Twentieth Century Fox Film Corporation* _____

Supreme Court of California
474 P.2d 689 (1970)

Shirley MacLaine Parker, a well-known actress, was under contract with Twentieth Century Fox Film Corporation to play the female lead in the film company's musical *Bloomer Girl.* Parker was to be paid a minimum "guaranteed compensation" of $750,000 for a 14 week period. Before beginning production, Twentieth Century Fox notified Parker of its decision not to produce the movie and offered her instead the lead role in a western, *Big Country, Big Man.* Unlike *Bloomer Girl,* which was to be filmed in California, *Big Country, Big Man* was to be filmed in Australia. Additionally, the right of approval over the director and screenplay, which was granted to Parker under her original contract, was to be omitted from any contract that she would sign to work in *Big Country, Big Man.* Parker refused the offer and sued to recover the agreed compensation.

FACTS

In rejecting Twentieth Century Fox's offer of substitute employment, did Parker unreasonably refuse to mitigate damages?

ISSUE

No. Twentieth Century Fox's substitute offer could not be used to mitigate damages. Thus Parker did not unreasonably refuse to mitigate. Employment in *Big Country, Big Man* was not comparable, or substantially similar, to the original employment of which Parker was deprived. A straight dramatic role in a western in Australia is different from a musical review in Los Angeles involving dancing as well as acting. Also, the elimination or impairment of employee rights under a new contract makes the substitute offer inferior to the original contract.

DECISION

Liquidated Damages

Some contracts include a provision in which the parties agree on an amount of compensation for the injured party if there is a breach. This is known as a **liquidated damages clause.** Generally, when negotiating, the parties do not concern themselves with the effects of a breach. They are primarily interested in performance and its costs and benefits. But in some instances, the results of a breach are an important part of the bargain. This consideration often is important in contracts involving large sums of money, in those in which the time of completion is highly important, or when the amount of loss in the event of breach is unclear.

In other cases, one of the parties may think that liquidated damages will force the other to perform. If that party has superior bargaining power, the other party might agree to pay damages that would exceed any likely loss. When liquidated damages are not reasonably related to loss, they are not damages, but a penalty that violates the underlying concept of damages — that is, to place the injured party in the position it would have been in had the contract been performed. Courts therefore have been

Liquidated damages clause
a clause that specifies the amount that will be paid if a party breaches a contract

unwilling to accept liquidated damage provisions that penalize the defaulting party. They do not recognize a provision that is not reasonably related to losses.

The UCC (Section 2-718) provides:

Nonfeasibility
impracticability

> Damages for breach by either party may be liquidated in the agreement but only at an amount which is reasonable in the light of the anticipated or actual harm caused by the breach, the difficulties of proof of loss, and the inconvenience or **nonfeasibility** of otherwise obtaining an adequate remedy. A term fixing unreasonably large liquidated damages is void as a penalty.

Punitive Damages

Punitive or exemplary damages are those that exceed the injured party's loss. In tort cases, they are often a substantial portion of the plaintiff's recovery. The primary purpose of punitive damages is to deter the defendant and others from the type of act that caused the loss. Punitive damages are seldom awarded in contract cases. In those few instances in which they have been awarded, plaintiffs have been able to prove something akin to fraud, recklessness, or malice.

Recently some courts have allowed punitive awards in contract cases in which the plaintiff was a consumer, or at least a "little guy" with limited bargaining power, and the defendant, a party with greater bargaining power, acted outrageously or oppressively.

Wright v. Public Savings Life Insurance Company

Supreme Court of South Carolina
204 S.E. 2d 57 (1974)

FACTS   In 1963, Mamie Lee Wright acquired life, health, and accident insurance policies from Public Savings Life Insurance Company. Beginning in 1971, Wright was engaged in employment of such a nature that the agent collecting for the insurance company had trouble contacting Wright at home. To avoid problems, Wright started making payments to the local office of the insurance company, where the agent would later pick up the payments and credit her account. On May 3, 1971, the local office reported to the home office that Wright's policies had lapsed for nonpayment of premiums. On May 13, an application for a revival of her policies was filed. This form included an acknowledgment, purportedly by Wright, that the policies were properly lapsed. The signature on this form, however, was forged, and Wright had no knowledge of its preparation. Finally, on May 28, the local office informed Wright of the lapsing of her policies, offered her a refund of one month's premiums, and requested her signature on a receipt. Wright refused. Wright sued to recover actual and punitive damages.

ISSUE   Is Wright entitled to punitive damages?

DECISION   Yes. The breach of a contract, committed with fraudulent intent, and accompanied by a fraudulent act, or acts, entails liability for punitive as well as actual damages.

SPECIFIC PERFORMANCE

Although Anglo-American law generally awards damages to a party against whom there has been a breach, under some circumstances the courts require the defaulting party actually to perform the promised act. This remedy for breach is referred to as **specific performance.** The governing principle is that specific performance is required when payment of damages would not adequately or completely compensate the injured party. A contract promise to pay money ordinarily is not enforced specifically because the damage remedy is considered adequate.

Specific performance judicially compelled fulfillment of exact terms of contract

Whether or not the damage remedy is adequate depends to a large extent on the facts of the particular case. The courts generally have held that damages are inadequate in two types of cases. First are those cases in which the subject matter of the contract is unique. Unusual items of personal property, such as antiques and original paintings, clearly fall into this category. Money is not considered an adequate replacement for a prized heirloom. Second are cases involving the sale of real estate. Because of land's economic importance, the courts historically have assumed that every piece of land is unique. As a result, contracts for the sale of real estate almost inevitably can be enforced specifically. Real estate agreements are the subject matter most commonly involved in actions for specific performance.

Other types of agreements that courts have considered unique pervade economic activity. They include contracts to sell a business, to issue a policy of insurance, to repurchase corporate stock, to act as a **surety,** to execute a written instrument, and even, in some instances, to lend money. In these and similar cases, if the defendant can show that plaintiff has an adequate remedy at law, specific performance is not granted.

Surety one who undertakes to pay money or to do any other act, in the event that his or her principal fails to do so

The UCC (Section 2-716) provides that in goods transactions, "Specific performance may be decreed where the goods are unique or in other proper circumstances." The Official Comment on this section states:

> The present section continues in general prior policy as to specific performance. . . . However, without intending to impair in any way the exercise of the court's sound discretion in the matter, this article seeks to further a more liberal attitude than some courts have shown in connection with the specific performance of contracts of sale.

Under the UCC, if a buyer cannot readily find substitute goods in the market, the buyer is entitled to an award of specific performance, although the goods may not be "unique." The code allows a court to award specific performance "in other proper circumstances."

INJUNCTION

An injunction is a remedy sometimes used in contract cases. But like specific performance, its use has been limited. Injunctions have been used in employment contracts to prevent a party from performing the contract service for someone else. In a leading English case, an opera singer had contracted to sing exclusively for a particular company. When she refused to do so, the court forbade her from singing for any other company. The court felt that it could not compel her specifically to perform her contractual obligation but that economic pressure might move her to honor it.

American courts generally follow a similar rule in personal service contracts where the defendant refuses to perform. If the defendant's services expressly or by clear implication have been promised exclusively to the plaintiff, the courts forbid service for anyone else. An injunction, however, is not granted if the injured plaintiff could be compensated adequately by damages. As a result, injunctions are granted in personal service contracts only if the individual is a person with unique skills. Professional athletes who refuse to honor their contracts with one employer are often forbidden to perform for another.

Ancillary agreements agreements that are attendant to or aid the principal agreement

The injunction is also used to enforce **ancillary agreements** not to compete. As discussed in Chapter 7, this type of agreement is permissible under certain circumstances. These generally involve the sale of a business and its accompanying good will, an employment contract in which the employee agrees not to work for a competitor or compete with the employer after leaving the job, or an employment contract in which the employee has access to customer lists or trade secrets that could be used by a business rival. Injunctions are also used to enforce **covenants** that limit land use. A rental or ownership agreement may contain a provision limiting the premises to residential use. If the tenant or owner uses the property for some other purpose, someone injured by the improper use may get an injunction.

Covenants binding agreements to do something

RESCISSION AND RESTITUTION

Many situations exist in which a party has the right to rescind or cancel a contract. Rescission (see Chapter 13) is available in cases involving fraud, duress, undue influence, and mistake. During the past decade, many laws have given consumers the right to cancel contracts under certain circumstances. One example is the home solicitation or door to door sales contract. Many states and a Federal Trade Commission rule allow a buyer three days to cancel certain types of agreements that have been solicited and made in the buyer's home. These laws also generally require the seller to notify the buyer in writing of this right. The three day period does not start until notification is given. The right to cancel a home solicitation sales contract does not depend on any wrongdoing by the seller.

Restitution the return of whatever one has received under terms of an agreement

When a contract is canceled, both parties must, if possible, return any benefits received under the agreement. This return is known as making **restitution**. Restitution may involve returning specific items or compensating for benefits conferred. The principle of restitution applies even for cancellation due to fraud. The defrauded plaintiff is entitled to the return of benefits conferred because of fraud; but the law requires the defrauded plaintiff, if possible, to return the wrongdoer to the **status quo.** The defrauded plaintiff may, of course, choose to enforce the contract and sue for damages.

Status quo the existing state of things

Restitution is a remedy also available in cases in which one person has been unjustly enriched at another's expense. Unjust enrichment is a fundamental concept affecting several legal areas, the theory being that justice is violated if a person is allowed to retain benefits that enrich him or her unfairly at another's expense. As a result, the courts may order restitution of those benefits or their value. Before the courts order restitution, they must be convinced not only that retention of the benefits enriches the person but that the enrichment is unjust.

Restitution is ordered by the courts when money has been paid by mistake or when a person has benefited from a contract that turns out to be unenforceable. The restitution rule applies if one party keeps the benefits from a broken contract when these could have been returned easily.

SUMMARY

Money damages as a remedy for breach of contract generally are awarded by a court when complete performance of a contract has not taken place—that is, when the contract has been breached. The court requires that the damages were reasonably anticipated by the defendant at the time of entering into the contract; that there is some certainty in determining the amount of damages; and that the plaintiff has made a reasonable attempt to mitigate, or lessen, the dollar damages.

Liquidated damages are those dollar damages set out in a clause of the contract as a reasonable amount which would compensate one of the parties in the event of a breach. Punitive damages are a form of dollar damages not often awarded in breach of contract cases unless there is a factual situation where a "little guy" is being victimized by a "big guy" who had superior bargaining power when the contract was entered into.

Nonmonetary remedies include injunction, specific performance, rescission, and restitution. These remedies generally are awarded when dollar damages are insufficient to redress the grievance of the plaintiff in breach of contract situations.

REVIEW PROBLEMS

1. What is the standard a court uses to award dollar damages when lost profits are involved?

2. When are liquidated damage clauses considered penalties and thus not enforced?

3. Why should a party who has not breached a contract be required to mitigate the damages of the breaching party?

4. Why are compensatory damages preferred as a remedy for a breach contract, over the remedy of specific performance?

5. Smith inherited a substantial sum of money, a portion of which she used to make the following purchases: an antique piano, the first foal sired by Spend-A-Buck, a new Mercedes, a riding horse, and a farm. In each case, the seller refused to deliver the item. In which instances, if any, could Smith obtain a decree of specific performance? Explain.

6. Milstead, a contractor, sued the Evergreen Amusement Company for the balance due on a contract to clear and grade a site for the company's first drive-in movie theater. The court awarded Milstead the balance due less damages to the

amusement company for delay in completing the work. These damages were based on the rental value of the site during the delay ($4,500). Defendant argued that the damages for delay should have been based on loss of profit during the delay ($12,500). Who is correct? Explain.

7. Helen Gonzales, the chief accountant for a small New York City firm, had a 12-month contract with the company. The contract ran from April 1 to March 31 at a salary of $1,100 per month. On December 1, 1974, Gonzales's employer wrongfully terminated the agreement. Gonzales was immediately offered a job as a bookkeeper at $800 per month. She did not accept this job. On February 1, 1975, Gonzales was offered a job as a chief accountant at $1,100 per month in Atlanta. The company also offered to pay moving expenses. Gonzales also refused this job, because her family lived in New York. She finally went back to work on February 1, 1976, as a chief accountant. Her salary was $1,150. Gonzales sued her original employer for breach of contract. Her employer argues that she failed in her duty to mitigate damages. May she recover? Explain.

8. Plaintiff's husband died. Plaintiff contracted with an undertaker, who agreed to furnish a casket and a watertight vault, to conduct the funeral, and to inter the body. About three months after the funeral, plaintiff visited her husband's grave and found that very heavy rain had forced a corner of the vault to rise above the ground. Defendant undertaker, notified about the problem, met cemetery authorities and plaintiff at the grave for the purpose of reinterring the body. When the vault was raised, it was discovered that water and mud had entered the vault because it had been improperly locked at one end. Angered at this and other complications, the undertaker said, in plaintiff's presence, "To hell with the whole damned business. It's no concern of mine." Plaintiff sues for breach of contract and requests punitive damages for mental anguish. On what grounds might defendant defend? Who would be successful? Discuss.

9. A contractor agreed to build a skating rink for plaintiff at a price of $180,000. The rink was to be completed by December 1 and was designed to replace a similar but older rink that plaintiff rented for $800 per month. A clause in the contract awarded the plaintiff "$100 per day in liquidated damages" for each day after December 1 that the rink was not completed. Was this a valid liquidated damage clause? Explain.

10. On April 15, Don Construction contracted to build a house for Jessup. The contract price was $55,000. The agreement contained a provision stating that the builder would deduct $1,000 a day from the contract price for each day the house was not completed after August 15. It was not completed until September 15. Don Contruction refused to deduct $30,000 from the contract price. Jessup refused to sue. Don Construction sued, claiming the $1,000 a day was a penalty clause, not a liquidated damage clause. What result? Explain.

11. Julius W. Erving ("Dr. J") entered into a four-year contract to play exclusively for the Virginia Squires of the American Basketball Association. After one year, he left the Squires to play for the Atlanta Hawks of the National Basketball Association. The contract signed with the Squires provided that the team could apply for an injunction to prohibit Erving from playing for any other team.

Erving sued to have his contract set aside for fraud. The Squires counterclaimed seeking injunctive relief pending arbitration. Who won? Explain.

12. Berke entered into an employment contract with Bettinger to become a sales manager. The contract provided that if Berke terminated employment he would not work for any employment agency for at least one year within 50 miles of Philadelphia. Berke left Bettinger and opened his business immediately within a 50-mile radius. Bettinger seeks an injunction claiming irreparable harm. What result? Explain.

13. Invester entered into a contract with Family Pools, Inc., for installation of a pool in his backyard. After it was installed, the pool became defective and could not be filled with water. Family Pools attempted to solve the problem but could not. Invester sued for damages based on a breach of contract theory. Family Pools defended, claiming that Invester had a duty to mitigate the total damages by repairing the defects and then suing for the cost of repairs. Who won? Explain.

14. Contractor contracted to repair the roof of homeowner's house. Contractor removed part of the roof but negligently failed to cover the open space. Rain caused damage to the interior of the house. Homeowner sued for damages to the house and its contents. He also sought punitive damages for emotional distress resulting from the contractor's breach. What result? Explain.

PART III

COMMERCIAL TRANSACTIONS

CHAPTER 15

Sales Law: Formation and Terms

CHAPTER OBJECTIVES

After reading this chapter, you should be able to:

1. Describe the duty of good faith for negotiating transactions.

2. State when title to a good may be passed as agreed upon by buyer and seller.

3. Define goods.

4. Identify conditions for acceptance of an offer.

5. Explain the place of indefinite terms in sales contracts.

GENERAL CHARACTERISTICS OF THE UCC

Duty of Good Faith

Nullify to treat an act or proceeding as not taking place or having no legal effect

Extortion conduct which seeks to compel or coerce payments in an unlawful manner

The UCC (Section 1-203) states that every contract and duty imposes an obligation of good faith in its performance or enforcement. Good faith is factual honesty in conduct and transactions. No direct sanction is imposed for failure to act in good faith. Instead, it is a general principle that courts may follow. For example, the courts may modify or **nullify** unconscionable contracts and terms. Good faith may be used as a guideline in determining whether certain aspects of a commercial transaction may be considered unconscionable. The good faith principle also may be used on its own — for example, to disallow a contract that is tantamount to **extortion**, such as when a buyer has become so dependent on a seller for the supply of a commodity that the buyer cannot effectively resist the seller's demand for a higher price.

The following case offers an illustration of the good faith principle.

Baker v. Ratzlaff

Kansas Court of Appeals
564 P. 2d 153 (1977)

FACTS   Ratzlaff entered into a contract with Baker to sell in 1974 his total crop of popcorn at $4.75 per hundred weight. Under the agreement Ratzlaff was to deliver at a specific time, and if Baker failed to pay upon delivery, Ratzlaff could sell his popcorn to anyone. After Ratzlaff delivered two loads of popcorn, Baker's agent, who was authorized to make payment, failed to pay. Ratzlaff did not demand payment. When Baker later requested more deliveries of popcorn, Ratzlaff refused, claiming illness of an employee. Shortly thereafter Ratzlaff sent Baker note of termination of their agreement and sold his popcorn at $8 per hundred weight. Baker sued Ratzlaff for a breach of contract. Ratzlaff argued that under UCC Section 1-203 he was not under a "good faith" obligation because termination of a contract is not "performance" or "enforcement" of a contract as called for by that section. Further, he argued that even if "termination" falls under 1-203, he has shown good faith.

Must Ratzlaff show "good faith" in terminating a contract?   ISSUE

The court ruled in favor of Baker, stating that the defendant, Ratzlaff, must act in good faith in terminating the contract pursuant to sections 1-203 and 1-201(19) of the Uniform Commercial Code. The court did not agree with the defendant's arguments, stating that his right to terminate the contract cannot be separated from enforcement of the agreement. The court therefore refused to exempt the defendant's exercise of the termination clause from the good faith obligation. A breach of good faith was shown by Ratzlaff's failure to demand payment upon delivery and his quick resale of the popcorn to another buyer at close to double the contract price of $4.75.   DECISION

Merchant Standards

Merchants generally are held to higher standards under the UCC than nonmerchants. For example, **implied warranty of merchantability** applies only to merchants. (Implied warranties are discussed in Chapter 19.) Only merchants are bound by firm offers, and only merchants may be bound, without agreement, by additional terms in an acceptance. There are many other examples of the higher standards applied to merchants.

Why hold merchants to higher standards? Several justifications can be given. Merchants can reasonably be expected to be more sophisticated regarding the legal rules pertaining to their profession. They should know when to seek legal advice and are, in fact, often guided by legal advice. Many merchants enter into sales transactions day after day. A nonmerchant seller, in contrast, may make one major sale every two or three years. If we view the special rules for merchants from consumers' perspective, it seems appropriate that consumers should be held to a less rigorous standard.

Who is a merchant? The UCC defines a merchant in three different ways. A merchant may be a person who deals in goods of the kind in question. If a person in the hardware business sells a hammer, he or she is a merchant for purposes of the sale of the hammer because a hardware store regularly deals in goods such as hammers. The second group classified by the UCC as merchants are those who by their occupation represent themselves as having knowledge or skill peculiar to the practices or goods involved in the transaction. Suppose that a mechanical contracting firm installed cooling equipment. With respect to the sale of the cooling equipment, it would be regarded as a merchant. Finally, people may be classified as merchants who employ someone who qualifies as a merchant, under the first two definitions, to act on their behalf. If Mary hired a jeweler to represent her in the sale of her diamonds, the UCC treats *her* as a merchant because she employed a merchant.

Implied warranty of merchantability a promise made by a merchant's conduct in selling a good that the product is fit for the ordinary purposes for which it is used

The *Decatur* case discusses the farmer as merchant. Some courts view farmers as merchants. But others reject this view, as the following case illustrates.

_____ *Decatur Cooperative Association v. Urban* _____

Kansas Supreme Court
547 P. 2d 323 (1976)

FACTS   Urban allegedly entered Into an oral contract for sale of 10,000 bushels of wheat with the plaintiff, a grain elevator named Decatur Cooperative Association. He is a resident of Decatur County and was a member of the Cooperative throughout 1973. He is engaged solely in farming. During a phone conversation, Urban allegedly agreed to sell to the Cooperative 10,000 bushels of wheat at $2.86 per bushel, to be delivered on or before September 30, 1973. A written memorandum of sale was prepared and later sent to Urban. Urban received the confirmation within a reasonable time, read it, and gave no written notice of objection to its contents within ten days after it was received. On August 13, 1973, Urban notified Decatur that he would not deliver the wheat. The price of wheat at the Cooperative on that date was $4.50 per bushel.

ISSUE   Can the Decatur Cooperative enforce the oral agreement under the UCC (2-201[2]) against the farmer, Urban?

DECISION   The court ruled that Decatur could not enforce the agreement. The court stated that a merchant is deprived of the defense of the Statute of Frauds against an oral contract with another merchant if he fails to object to the terms of the written confirmation within ten days of its receipt. The court said that Urban did not qualify as a merchant, and this was not a sale between merchants because the UCC contemplates knowledge and skill of professionals on each sale of the transaction in defining merchant status. Urban sold only the products he raised, on a cash basis, to local grain elevators, and thus he did not have the skill of a professional. The court implied that if the transaction had been more than just Urban's crops, and they had been sold to others beyond the local Cooperative, his status would have risen to that of a merchant.

Modified Concept of Title

Title the right to possess goods

Unallocated not distributed or assigned

The UCC deemphasizes the concept of **title**. Sometimes a person receives a written paper from the state called a *title*—for example, when a person buys a car. (See Figure 15-1.) Under prior law, title had been used as a basic determinant of other legal rights and interests, including **unallocated** risk of loss, security, and insurability. Before these other rights could be determined, the title to the goods had to be established. This was a very indirect way of approaching the real question of who, for example, should bear the risk of any loss of the goods. The policy implications of who most appropriately should bear the risk of loss were difficult to consider. Everything was determined by the possession of title, which assigned not only risk of loss but several other important rights as well.

FIGURE 15-1   Certificate of Title

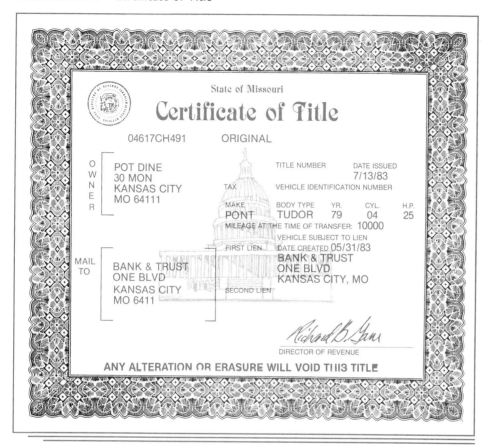

The UCC now has separate sections dealing with rights related to risk of loss, insurable interests, and security interests. All matters of rights and obligations of parties to a contract apply without regard to title to goods, except where a UCC provision specifically refers to the question of title.

The UCC (Section 2-401) determines when the buyer obtains title to goods covered by a contract. It states that title may not pass before identification of the goods. When the goods are identified in the contract, the buyer acquires certain rights in them, called a special property interest in the goods. **Identification** means that specific goods are somehow identified (by a mark or by being set aside or described) as the object of the particular transaction. For example, Buyer agrees to purchase a color TV. When Seller selects a particular TV in the warehouse as the one that Buyer is to get, that TV becomes identified in the contract. In a sense, before identification of specific goods, there is nothing on which a title can be passed.

Generally, people are free to arrange explicitly for the transfer of title to existing goods in any manner and on any conditions. If they fail to specify when title is to pass, it passes when and where the seller delivers the goods.

Identification
marking of goods as objects of a particular transaction

Origin Contract   Suppose that a buyer in Oklahoma City wants to buy a lawn mower from a seller in Chicago. The seller's only obligation under the contract is to put the mower on board a truck in Chicago bound for Oklahoma City. Title to the mower remains with the seller only until he or she delivers the goods to the trucking company. This is called an **origin contract**. The principle is that if the seller intends to send the goods to the buyer, but the contract does not require the seller to deliver the goods to a destination, title to the goods passes to the buyer at the time and place of shipment.

Destination Contract   Suppose that the contract just described requires the seller actually to deliver the lawn mower to the buyer in Oklahoma City (as opposed to merely delivering it to the trucking company in Chicago). In this situation, title to the mower remains with the seller until the seller gives it to the buyer. If the goods arrive in Oklahoma City, and the shipper, at a reasonable time, offers to deliver the mower to the buyer's place of business, a tender has been made and title passes to the buyer — whether the buyer actually takes delivery of the goods or not. This is called a **destination contract**.

If the seller is obligated under the contract actually to deliver the goods to the buyer, the title to the goods does not pass to the buyer until they are tendered to the buyer at the destination specified in the contract.

The comments of the UCC (Section 2-503) make it clear that the seller is not obligated to deliver to a named destination unless he or she has specifically agreed to such a delivery. In other words, there is a presumption that the parties intended an origin, not a destination, contract. Unless the contract calls for the seller to deliver goods at a particular destination, his or her only obligation is to deliver them to a carrier.

Documents of Title   If delivery is to be made without moving the goods, two other rules control (2-401[3]). If the seller is to deliver a document of title, it passes at the time and place the seller delivers it. Suppose that the lawn mower in our example has been stored in a public warehouse. When the seller left the goods, the warehousemen gave the seller a document of title called a *warehouse receipt*. If the receipt is negotiable, anyone in possession of the receipt has the power to receive the goods from the warehouseman. If the contract signed by the buyer and seller specifies that a delivery may take place without moving the goods from the warehouse, whenever the seller gives the buyer the negotiable warehouse receipt, title to the mower passes to the buyer.

No Documents   If the goods are already identified to the contract (the seller has specified certain goods will be given to the buyer) and no documents are to be delivered, then title to the goods passes at the time and place of contracting. In the earlier example, suppose that the seller had the lawn mower in his or her own plant. The seller intended for the buyer to pick up the mower at the seller's plant. He or she identified a certain mower as the buyer's prior to signing the contract. In this situation, title to the mower passes to the buyer at the time of contracting.

Origin contract
an agreement in which seller is responsible for delivering the goods from seller's place of business

Destination contract an agreement in which seller is responsible for delivering goods to the buyer's city

Security interest
A pledge by a debtor of property or other materials of value to make his or her promise of payment under a contract enforceable by a creditor in the event of a breach

The next case illustrates the point that when a seller sells goods to a buyer, the seller may not retain title to the goods. Any attempt to retain title in the contract of sale is construed by courts as a mere reservation of a **security interest** in the goods.

Commonwealth v. Jett

Pennsylvania Superior Court
326 A. 2d 508 (1974)

The defendants purchased an organ from Menchey Music Service on December 24, 1970. After making a down payment and three monthly installments, they defaulted on their payments in April 1971, and never made any further payments. The property could not be recovered, because the appellants had sold it. A criminal action was brought against the Jetts by the state of Pennsylvania, charging fraudulent conversion of the organ because Menchey Music Service had retained title. The defendants alleged that under Section 2-401 of the UCC, title cannot be retained by the seller after delivery of the goods. FACTS

Could Menchey Music Service retain title to the organ after delivery to the buyer and thus make the defendant guilty of fraudulent conversion by selling it following defendant's default on installment payments due? ISSUE

The court ruled that Menchey Music Service could not retain title after delivery of the organ and thus the defendant is not guilty of conversion. The court reasoned that were the seller able to retain title to goods delivered to the buyer under an installment sales contract, it would be superfluous for him to file a financing statement to perfect a security interest. His retention of title would establish his priority over all creditors or even a trustee in bankruptcy. In limiting the effect of a retention of title clause, the UCC Code drafters sought to protect subsequent creditors of the buyer who altered their positions in reliance upon the buyer's title to the collateral. Thus, the court stated that a reservation of title clause in an installment sales contract is inoperative. The Jetts had title to the organ when they sold it, so the sale could not have constituted a fraudulent conversion. DECISION

Transfer of Title to Third Person

Section 2-401 determines when the buyer receives title to goods from the seller. Once the buyer receives goods, he or she may choose to convey them to a third party. Section 2-403 determines the title of the third person who receives goods from the original buyer.

If the buyer receives title to the goods (Section 2-401), he or she has the power to transfer the good title to goods to a third person. But what if the buyer, for example, gives the seller a bad check? Does the buyer have the power to transfer good title to a third person? Section 2-403 answers this question.

FIGURE 15-2   In this situation, the third party must return the goods to the owner.

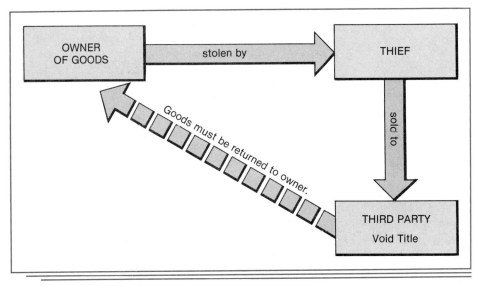

Void Title   A purchaser gets title to all that the transferring person had or had power to transfer (Section 2-403). Suppose that a person steals goods from someone, and the thief resells the goods to an innocent third party who knows nothing of the theft. The third party in this situation acquires a **void title.** That is, if the original owner demands the goods back from him or her, the third party must surrender the goods. The thief had no title to the goods and had no power to transfer title to anyone else (see Figure 15-2).

Voidable Title   Certain people acquire a mere **voidable title.** In the case of an original owner and a buyer with a mere voidable title, the owner may reclaim his or her goods. Suppose that Mary gave Alice a bad check in return for Alice's dress. As long as Mary has the dress, Alice can get it back. Mary got a mere voidable title by giving a bad check.

But if the buyer with voidable title transfers the goods to a third person, in certain instances the third person may keep the goods (see Figure 15-3). The third person must establish several things to keep the goods. This person must prove that he or she was a good faith purchaser. Essentially, the third person must establish that he or she acquired the goods by paying a reasonable price and that, in doing so, the person acted in good faith. Assuming that the third person establishes that he or she meets these standards, the person also must establish that the person from whom the third party acquired the goods had a voidable title.

The UCC sets out several transactions that give rise to a voidable title. If a case does not resemble one of these four transactions, courts must refer to the cases and statutes to determine whether the third person's title is voidable. The four transactions that give rise to a voidable title are:

1. when the transferor of the goods was deceived about the identity of the purchaser;

2. when the purchaser acquired the goods by giving a bad check;

3. when title was not to pass until the seller was paid;

4. when the goods were gotten through criminal fraud.

This provision works as follows. Suppose Alfred is in the business of selling typewriters. Sam robs Alfred and takes a typewriter. Sam sells this typewriter to Alice. Alice acquires a void title. Alfred may reclaim the typewriter from Alice even if she took the typewriter in good faith, without any knowledge of the theft, and paid a reasonable price for the typewriter.

Let's change these facts somewhat so that Sam gives Alfred a check that later bounces. Sam sells the typewriter to Alice, who purchases it for a reasonable price and is unaware of the bad check. Alfred now demands the typewriter back from Alice. May Alice keep the typewriter? Yes, she acquired the typewriter from a person, Sam, with a *voidable* title. Sam acquired a voidable title, because he gave Alfred a check that subsequently bounced. As between Alfred and Sam, as long as Sam kept the typewriter, Alfred was able to get it back from Sam. Once Sam transferred the typewriter to Alice, a good faith purchaser who has paid a reasonable price, Alfred lost his right to reacquire the typewriter. The same result would occur if Sam deceives Alfred about his (Sam's) identity, or if Sam agrees to pay cash for the typewriter at some later date, or if Sam acquires the typewriter through criminal fraud. If Sam acquires a voidable title by any of these devices, or any other transfer recognized as voidable by state law, Sam has the power to transfer a title good against the original seller to a good faith purchaser who has paid a reasonable price.

FIGURE 15-3 In this situation, the third party does not have to return the goods to the original owner.

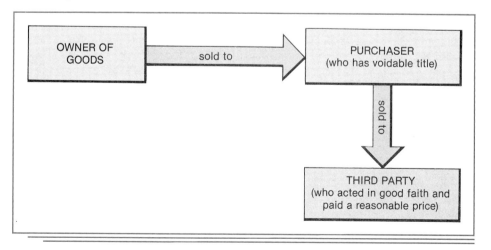

Purchasers from Someone with Good Title   The UCC protects anyone who purchases from a person who acquires a good title. Suppose that Sam gives a check to Alfred that subsequently bounces, and Sam resells the goods to Alice, a good faith purchaser. Alice now has the power to transfer all title she has. Because she has a title good against even Alfred, she can transfer a good title to Linda — even if Linda knows that Sam acquired the goods from Alfred by passing a bad check! Linda cannot qualify as a good faith purchaser, but she still acquires a good title because she takes it through Alice. The following case offers a further example of this.

R. H. Macy's New York, Inc. v. Equitable Diamond Corp.

New York Civil Court
34 U.C.C. Rep. 896 (1982)

FACTS   Draper purchased a 2.25 carat diamond ring for $9,142.50 from the plaintiff, Macy's department store. Her check made in payment was returned because of insufficient funds. Draper sold the ring to Equitable Diamond Corp. on November 18, 1981, for $2,500. Equitable sold the ring for $4,000 to Ideal Cut Diamonds on December 7, 1981. On December 8, 1981, Ideal sold it to a customer for $4,900. Macy sued Equitable and Ideal to recover the value of the ring, claiming Draper was a thief and that Equitable never obtained title to the ring. Macy argued that Draper was not a good faith purchaser for value, and Equitable should have known this, because the ring was in excellent condition and obviously worth more than $2,500. Equitable and Ideal argued that Draper had voidable title, and because she was a good faith purchaser for value, they had full title, thus their motion for dismissal should be granted.

ISSUE   Was Draper a good faith purchaser for value under UCC 2-403(1)?

DECISION   The court ruled that Draper was not a good faith purchaser for value and refused to grant the motion to dismiss. The court stated that UCC 2-403(1) provides that if passage of title is conditioned upon the performance of an act, then title is voidable, and full title can be transferred to a third party who is a "good faith purchaser" for value. Passage of title from Macy's to Draper was conditioned upon payment of her check. She had only voidable title and could transfer full title only if a third party (Equitable) qualified as a "good faith purchaser" for value. The court found that if a merchant takes advantage of a low price at which an item is being sold, the unusually low price puts the merchant on notice of possible defective title, and he purchases at his peril with the protection of UCC 2-403(1). In this case, it appeared to the court that if a diamond dealer (Equitable) purchased a ring for $2,500, sold it for $4,000 to another dealer (Ideal), who in turn sold it to his customer for $4,900, the good faith requirement of UCC 2-403(1) became an issue of fact for a trial jury to resolve.

Entrustment
delivery and
acceptance of goods

Entrustment   It is also possible for a merchant who deals in goods of the kind entrusted to him or her to transfer all title of the person entrusting the goods (the entruster) to a buyer in the ordinary course of business. **Entrustment** is broadly

FIGURE 15-4 In this situation, the third party may keep the goods because the owner entrusted the painting to a merchant who deals in goods of this kind (paintings) and the buyer is a buyer in the ordinary course of business.

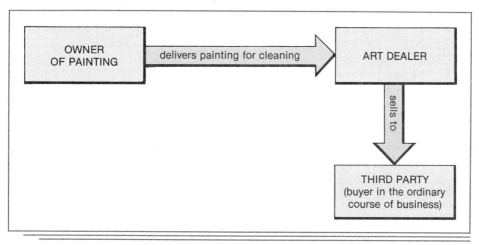

defined as any delivery and any acquiescence in retention of possession (See UCC 2-403[2] and [3]).

Such a transfer might occur when an art dealer accidentally mixes a painting left for cleaning with his or her regular stock and sells it to a customer by mistake (see Figure 15-4). Another situation in which this applies is when a manufacturer sells goods to a retailer. If the manufacturer attempts to take a security interest in the goods held by the retailer for resale, the retailer may still cut off the manufacturer's security interest by selling the goods to a customer. The buyer acquires a clear title if he or she qualifies as a buyer in the ordinary course of business.

To obtain a title superior to that of the previous owner of the goods, the buyer must establish several facts. The goods must have been entrusted to a merchant who regularly deals in goods of that kind. In the case of the jeweler, the jeweler regularly deals in watches, so he qualifies as a merchant. (Note that the definition of merchant here is narrower than that in Section 2-104.) The jeweler has the power to transfer all rights of the entruster to a buyer in the ordinary course of business. A *buyer in the ordinary course of business* is a person who, in good faith and without knowledge that the sale to him or her is in violation of the ownership rights or security interest of a third party, buys from a person in the business of selling goods of this kind. Whether a person is a buyer in the ordinary course depends on the facts and circumstances of the case. In the case of the art dealer who mixes the painting with his other stock, the dealer has the power to transfer good title to a person who purchases the watch.

SCOPE OF ARTICLE 2

Article 2 of the UCC covers all transactions involving a **sale** in which title passes from the seller to the buyer for a price. It also covers contracts for sale, which include

Sale passing of title from seller to buyer of goods

FIGURE 15-5 Bill of Sale

> Know all men by these presents that John Doe of Kansas City, Missouri, for and in consideration of the sum of $7,000.00 (Seven Thousand Dollars), to him in hand paid by Doris Smith of Leavenworth, Kansas, the receipt of which is hereby acknowledged, by these presents does bargain and sell unto the said Doris Smith all of the following described goods and chattels, now remaining and being in Kansas City, Missouri, to wit: a 1982 Datsun 280 Z automobile.
>
> TO HAVE AND TO HOLD THE SAME, Unto the said Doris Smith, heirs and assigns forever, and that John Doe will warrant and defend the title to the said goods and chattels hereby sold unto the said Doris Smith, heirs and assigns, forever, against the lawful claims and demands of all persons whomsoever.
>
> IN WITNESS WHEREOF, the said Janice Brooks, notary public, has hereunto set her hand and seal, this 10th day of September, 1986.
>
> SEAL   _____
>   John Doe
>
> STATE OF KANSAS
> COUNTY OF LEAVENWORTH
> Before me, a notary public in and for said county, this day appeared the undersigned, to me known to be the person described in and who executed the foregoing instrument, and acknowledged that he executed the same as his free act and deed and who, being by me first duly sworn, on his oath says that he is the owner of all said property herein described and that the same is unencumbered, except as herein stated.
>
> _____
>
> Subscribed and sworn to before me this 10th day of September, 1986. My Commission expires June 30, 1989.
>
> _____
> Notary Public

both a present sale and a contract to sell at a future time. In a present sale, the making of the contract and the completion of the sale (passing of title) occur at the same time. In a future sale, the making of the contract and the completion of the sale occur at different times.

Often when people sell goods, such as an automobile or a motorboat, they use a written document called a bill of sale. A bill of sale is illustrated in Figure 15-5.

Goods

Unless the sale involves the sale of **goods,** the contract is not controlled by Article 2. Section 2-105(1) of the UCC defines goods as "all things . . . which are movable at the time of identification to the contract for sale." For an item to qualify as a good, it must meet two requirements:

1. the item must be tangible (have a physical existence)

2. the item must be movable

The UCC definition of goods also includes the unborn young of animals, growing crops, and other things attached to property that eventually are to be **severed.** A contract for the sale of growing crops, timber to be cut, or other *severables* is a contract for the sale of goods. If the contract covers goods that are not yet existing and identified, the goods are future goods. The sale of future goods operates as a contract to sell.

Goods tangible, movable items

Severed separated or divided from property (land or anything permanently attached to it)

Contracts Not Covered

Contracts that are not covered by Article 2 are those involving the sale of land or things permanently attached to it, such as buildings, real property, personal property that is net goods (for example, a contract for the sale of an investment security), or services. Where a contract involves both goods and services, the court may apply Article 2 even though the contract is not a pure *goods* contract.

The sale of mixed goods and services has created a number of complex cases. Suppose that you go to a dentist. If the dentist fills one of your teeth with silver, is the transaction a sale of goods? What if a plumber comes to your house and installs a new pipe? Is the transaction a sale of goods? In both of these examples, it is most likely that a court would consider the transaction a service contract, because goods are only incidentally involved in the performance of the service contract. In other words, because the service aspect of the transaction predominates, the transaction is not covered by the UCC.

Conversely, an item might be sold along with a minor service. Suppose that you went to a restaurant at which a waiter or waitress brought food to the table. Courts are likely to construe this situation as predominantly a sale of goods and therefore covered by the UCC. Not all situations are as clear cut as these examples, and the mixture of goods and services gives courts some trouble in deciding whether the UCC or the common law of contracts should control a situation.

ACCEPTANCE

Method of Acceptance

Several important changes from the common law rules of offer and acceptance appear in the UCC. The UCC makes it easier for a person offered a promise to determine in what manner he or she must accept an offer when the offer itself does not make clear how it must be accepted. The UCC (Section 2-206[1]) provides that:

> unless otherwise unambiguously indicated by the language or circumstances . . . an offer to make a contract shall be construed as inviting acceptance in any manner and by any medium reasonable in the circumstances.

For example, when faced with an offer made by telegram, one might accept by mail unless the circumstances warranted a more immediate reply. If the offeror has specified a particular mode of acceptance, however, even under the UCC the offeree must accept in that manner.

Shipment   Subsection b of Section 2-206(1) permits a seller to accept an order or offer to buy goods:

> either by a prompt promise to ship or by the prompt or current shipment of conforming or nonconforming goods.

Conforming the quality of meeting the exact specifications and quantity agreed upon by the parties

This provision in effect allows for both bilateral and unilateral contracts (see Chapter 5). If the seller chooses to accept the offer by the prompt shipment of goods, an acceptance occurs whether **conforming** or nonconforming goods are shipped. The seller no longer can argue when the buyer receives nonconforming goods that there has been no acceptance of the offer, and therefore no breach of contract, because nonconforming goods were shipped in response to the buyer's order. When there has been a shipment of nonconforming goods in response to an order, there is both an acceptance of the offer and a breach of contract.

Accommodating Shipment   Of course, situations may arise where the seller is unable to supply the exact item ordered by the buyer but is in the position to ship something very similar and perhaps equally acceptable to the buyer. If the seller wishes to ship the goods to the buyer on the condition that the buyer may return them if he or she does not want them, the seller may ship nonconforming goods to accommodate a buyer. Section 2-206(1)(b) provides that:

Seasonably within an appropriate time based on industry standards

> such a shipment of nonconforming goods does not constitute an acceptance if the seller **seasonably** notifies the buyer that the shipment is offered only as an accommodation to the buyer.

If the buyer finds the good unacceptable, he or she may return them, but the accommodating shipment is *not* treated as a breach of contract.

Beginning Performance   It is also possible under the UCC to accept an offer by beginning performance. The offeree, rather than responding to an offer with an acceptance, may choose to perform the requested act. The UCC recognizes this as a method of acceptance where it is "a reasonable mode of acceptance," but it places an important limitation on the offeree's power to accept in this manner:

Lapse a passage of time within which a party has a right to exercise a right

> An offeror who is not notified of acceptance within a reasonable time may treat the offer as having **lapsed** before acceptance.

The silence of the offeree is not treated as an acceptance. Where the offeror in New York offers to purchase lawn mowers from a company in Los Angeles, the company in Los Angeles may begin to produce the mowers, but it must also notify the New York purchaser of its acceptance. If it fails to do so, the New York company may treat the offer as having been rejected. The Los Angeles company has only a reasonable time from the time it begins performance to notify the buyer of the acceptance. If the offeror doesn't hear from the offeree within a reasonable time, he or she may safely make other arrangements to get the lawn mowers without fear of being held to the contract.

Form of Acceptance

The common law requirement that the acceptance be a mirror image of the offer and the resulting "battle of the forms" problem were discussed in Chapter 7. The explanation of the UCC (Section 2-207) modification of the common law rule appears in Chapter 6 and should be reviewed at this point.

CREATION OF SALES CONTRACTS

The UCC makes it relatively easy for a court to find that a contract for the sale of goods has been made. If the court determines that the parties intended an agreement because of something they wrote or said or because of their conduct, it can find that a contract for sale of goods has been made even though the moment of its making is uncertain. Section 2-204(3) states the principle pertaining to "open terms" adopted in the UCC. The contract is not set aside for indefiniteness merely because one or more terms have been left open, as long as the parties intended to make a contract and there is a reasonably certain basis for giving an appropriate remedy. The more terms the parties have left open, the more difficult it is for a court to conclude that the parties intended to make a binding agreement. For the court to have a reasonably certain basis for giving an appropriate remedy, the parties must specify in the contract the quantity of goods sold.

Indefiniteness

Before the UCC was adopted, courts sometimes refused to enforce contracts because parties failed intentionally or unintentionally to cover all the terms necessary for the contracts to be considered valid and enforceable. A contract might not have clearly specified the price to be paid or certain delivery or payment terms. Rather than fill in the missing terms for the parties, the courts simply refused to enforce the agreement. The UCC, in Part 3 of Article 2, provides a number of statutory terms that may be used by a court in the event the contract fails to specify particular terms. We discuss these terms in the following sections.

Price   Section 2-304 states that the price can be made "in money or otherwise." A contract does not fail simply because it does not make the price payable in money. The price can be paid in money, goods, buildings, land, or "otherwise."

But what if the parties leave the price term open? Section 2-305 covers this situation. It is not necessary for the contract to include the price term. If it has not been agreed upon at the time the contract is executed, then the price is whatever a reasonable price is at the time of delivery. Any price set later must be set in good faith. If the buyer has the right to set the price later, and the buyer sets an unreasonably low price in light of the market conditions and surrounding circumstances, then the price declared does not control, because the buyer acted in bad faith. If one of the parties to a contract has the duty to fix a price, and he or she fails to do so, the other party may cancel the contract or may set a reasonable price.

But a contract fails for indefiniteness if the price term is left out and if the contract clearly states that the parties do not intend to be bound by the agreement if the price is not subsequently fixed and agreed upon. Unless the contract very clearly indicates that the parties do not wish to be bound if the price cannot be agreed upon, the court may end up setting a price for them.

Delivery   A contract that does not contain directions for the time, place, or method of delivery still does not fail for indefiniteness. If the time for delivery has not been specified in the contract, Subsection 2-309(1) states that the time for shipment or delivery shall be a reasonable time. What is reasonable depends on the circumstances. If the contract calls for successive performances but does not specify when the contract terminates, it is valid for a reasonable time but may be terminated at any time by either party upon reasonable notice. If the contract does not specify whether the delivery is to be in one lot or in several lots, the goods must be handed over in a single delivery, and payment is due at that time.

Section 2-308 makes the seller's place of business or, if he or she has no place of business, the seller's residence the appropriate place for delivery of goods in the absence of a specified place of delivery. If the contract is for the sale of identified goods that the parties know are located at some place other than the seller's place of business or residence, the place where the goods are located is the place for delivery.

Quantity   The only term that absolutely *must* be stated in a contract for the sale of goods is the quantity. Section 2-201 of the Statute of Frauds states:

> A writing is not insufficient because it omits or incorrectly states a term agreed upon but the contract is not enforceable . . . beyond the quantity of goods shown in such writing.

If the contract is one that must be in writing to be enforceable, and the writing omits the quantity term, there is no enforceable contract. If the writing incorrectly states the quantity term, there may be an enforceable contract — at least to the extent of the quantity stated in the writing.

Thus the UCC reflects the philosophy that a contract for the sale of goods should not fail, even though one or more terms have been left open, as long as the parties intended to enter into a contract and "there is a reasonably certain basis for giving an appropriate remedy" (Section 2-204[3]).

Course of Dealing, Usage of Trade, Course of Performance

In interpreting a contract, courts must take into consideration more than the literal language of the contract and the meaning normally associated with its words. The UCC requires courts to examine the course of dealing, usage of trade, or course of performance between the parties. (These terms are defined in the following sections.)

Whenever possible, the express terms of the agreement and any course of dealing, usage of trade, and course of performance must be considered consistent with one another. When such an interpretation is unreasonable, the written terms control the situation. Sections 2-208(2) and 1-205(4) make it apparent that conflicts between the express and implied terms are to be resolved in the following manner:

1. Express terms prevail over course of dealing, usage of trade, and course of performance if they cannot be reasonably construed together.

2. Course of performance prevails over both course of dealing and usage of trade.

3. Course of dealing prevails over usage of trade.

Course of Performance   The UCC (Section 2-208[1]) states:

> Where the contract for sale involves repeated occasions for performance by either party with knowledge of the nature of the performance and opportunity for objection to it by the other, any course of performance accepted or acquiesced in without objection shall be relevant to determine the meaning of the agreement.

Course of performance involves situations where more than one performance is contemplated by a contract.

Course of performance situations in which more than one performance is contemplated by a contract

Course of Dealing   Course of performance relates to conduct *after* the execution of an agreement, whereas **course of dealing** relates to conduct between the parties *before* the execution of an agreement.

> A course of dealing is a sequence of previous conduct between the parties to a particular transaction which is fairly to be regarded as establishing a common basis of understanding for interpreting those expressions and other conduct (Section 1-205[1]).

Course of dealing a sequence of previous conduct between parties to a transaction

Because the conduct that is material to a course of dealing occurs before the execution of an agreement, course of dealing cannot be used to modify or waive a written contract.

Usage of Trade   Section 1-205(2) states:

> A **usage of trade** is any practice or method of dealing having such regularity of observance in a place, vocation or trade as to justify an expectation that it will be observed with respect to the transaction in question. The existence and scope of such a usage are to be proved as facts. If it is established that such a usage is embodied in a written trade code or similar writing the interpretation of the writing is for the court.

Usage of trade the regular and usual method of dealing in a place, vocation, or trade

Usage of trade is not the same as custom, because the practice or method of dealing may be of recent origin or may be followed only in a particular part of the country. It simply must be observed with such regularity "as to justify an expectation that it will be observed with respect to the transaction in question." Like course of dealing, usage of trade can be used to give meaning to the particular language selected by the parties in their contract.

Hegyblade-Marquleas-Tenneco, Incorporated v. Sunshine Biscuit, Incorporated

California Court of Appeals
131 Cal. Rptr. 183 (1976)

FACTS   A contract was entered into between Hegyblade-Marquleas-Tenneco (HMT) and Bell Brand, a subsidiary of Sunshine Biscuit. HMT was to supply Bell Brand with potatoes for making snack foods such as chips and french fries. In 1971, Bell Brand's sales declined, thus reducing their need for potatoes. By the end of September 1981, Bell Brand was able to buy only 60,105 hundredweight sacks of potatoes out of the 100,000 that HMT had estimated. HMT sued Bell Brand for the difference. Bell Brand claimed that estimating the number of hundredweight sacks, as opposed to using exact numbers, was customary in the potato processing industry. They further argued that evidence of such usage and custom should be admitted by the court to explain the numbers in the contracts.

ISSUE   Should the court have admitted evidence of usage and custom in the potato processing industry to explain the numbers in the contract?

DECISION   The court ruled that usage and custom in this industry should be allowed to be admitted into evidence. It stated that persons carrying on a particular trade are assumed to be aware of customs that apply to their industry. Because potatoes are a perishable commodity dependent upon a fluctuating market, and contracts are signed eight or nine months in advance of the harvest season, the court stated that quantity should be dictated by both growers (HMT) and processors (Bell Brand). The court further stated that as a matter of law it cannot be said HMT was ignorant of the trade custom, thus the evidence of usage of trade was properly admitted by the trial court.

Filling in Terms   The UCC sets up a system for filling in the terms missing from an agreement between parties. When a term is fully expressed in writing or by a valid oral statement, this term controls the agreement, unless it conflicts with a mandatory provision of the UCC. In the absence of a particular term in a written agreement, the court fills it in by first looking to course of performance, then to course of dealing, and finally to usage of trade to supply the missing information. If none of these enable the court to fill in a missing term, the court examines the statutory terms in Part 3 of Article 2 of the UCC to fill in the missing information. If the UCC does not specify the term to be filled in, then the contract is enforced even though the court is unable to fill in the missing term — as long as the contract indicates that the parties intended to be bound and there is a reasonably certain basis for giving an appropriate remedy.

SUMMARY

A duty of good faith — honesty in dealing — binds those involved in the transaction of goods under the UCC. Merchants are generally held to a higher standard by the courts than are nonmerchants, because they enter into many agreements and are more sophisticated than a nonmerchant.

The UCC has deemphasized the concept of title as a basis for determining other legal rights and interests such as risk of loss and insurability. Under the code title cannot pass to the buyer before identification of the goods, but the parties are free to agree when title will pass. If they fail to specify, title generally passes at the time and place the seller delivers the good. If a buyer wishes to transfer title to a third person, the code gives that person all title that the buyer-transferor had. If the buyer passes a void title to the third party, the original seller may demand the good back.

Article 2 of the UCC defines goods as items that are tangible and movable. It includes unborn animals, growing crops, and other things attached to realty that can be severed. This is an important definition, because *only contracts for the sale of goods* are covered by the UCC. State law usually governs contracts for the sale of real and personal property as well as service contracts.

Under the UCC, an offer for the sale of goods may be accepted by any reasonable medium, and an effective acceptance has taken place. This differs greatly from the common law requirement that an acceptance must "mirror" the offer, as discussed in Chapter 7.

Contracts for the sale of goods under the UCC are created even though terms are left open or are indefinite about price and quantity. The courts interpret the parties as intending a contract if their writings, words, course of dealings, and conduct in the trade indicate such.

REVIEW PROBLEMS

1. Why does the UCC distinguish between merchants and nonmerchants? Explain.

2. How does the UCC define *goods*?

3. What contracts are not covered by Article 2 of the UCC?

4. Define the *usage of the trade.* Is it the same as *custom*?

5. In April 1973, Val, a con artist, borrows a $25,000 Utrillo painting from Porter to hang in his townhouse pending a decision whether to buy it. At this time, Porter does not know that Val is a con artist. While the Utrillo is in his possession, Val sells it to a gallery. After two subsequent sales, the painting ends up in

South America. Porter now sues everyone who has possessed or purchased the painting. Does Section 2-403(2) apply?

6. Weaver's contracts with Casual Slacks for the sale of teenage clothing, the order calling for delivery during "June–August." The shipment is made in August and is incomplete. Weaver's refuses to pay the full invoice price because the shipment is received so late as to miss the major part of the preschool marketing period, making it necessary to mark the clothing from one third to one half off the usual retail price to sell it. Weaver's contends that the use of the term "June–August" has a trade meaning of delivery of a substantial portion of the goods in June, a similar delivery in July, and the balance in August. Casual Slacks contends that use of the terminology "June–August" is unambiguous and means that delivery may be made at any time during the period from June 1 to August 31. Weaver's introduces parol evidence (oral evidence) of the meaning in their trade of "June–August" at trial. Does the term "June–August" have a meaning given it by usage in the trade that would explain or supplement the express terms of the written agreement, and is this testimony admissible?

7. Dravo and Key enter into an oral contract for Key to sell to Dravo up to 143,000 pounds of 2-inch or smaller steel punchings. No price is specified. Key provides part of the goods under the contract, but Dravo refuses to pay. Dravo contends that the contract is invalid for lack of a specified price term. Who wins?

8. Harbach, a farmer, orally contracts in February with Continental to sell 25,000 bushels of soybeans at $3.81 a bushel, delivery and payment deferred until October, November, and December. There is some question about whether Continental sent Harbach a written confirmation of the contract. Harbach contends that he did not receive such a confirmation. Harbach then refuses to make delivery, contending that no contract exists and, even if there were a contract, that the Statute of Frauds prevents enforcement. Further, Harbach claims that he, as a farmer, was not a merchant at the time of the transaction and therefore the merchant exception to 2-201 does not apply. At trial, evidence is admitted tending to show that Harbach has been engaged in farming for over 25 years and, in particular, has raised and sold grain, primarily corn, but including some small quantities of soybeans, on the type of contract here in issue for several years. It is known that Harbach is familiar with the operations of the grain market on which both corn and soybeans are traded. Is Harbach, who is a farmer, also a merchant under the Uniform Commerical Code?

9. A and B were public welfare recipients. A salesman of Company C sold them a refrigerator for $900 which had a unit retail value of $300. With insurance credit charges, credit life insurance, and sales tax, the total cost was $1,234.80. When A and B were sued by a credit collection corporation, their defense was that the contract should be nullified because it was unconscionable under Section 2-302 of the Uniform Commercial Code. Who won?

10. Loeb and Company, Inc., bought cotton from farmers and resold it. It entered into an oral contract with Schreiner, a farmer with 10 years experience, for 150 bales of cotton. Loeb sent a written confirmation of the oral agreement. Defendant did not object. The price of cotton doubled several months later, and Schreiner refused to sell. Loeb sued, claiming that both were merchants under

2-201(2) and thus the oral agreement as confirmed in writing was enforceable. Was the farmer a merchant? Was the contract enforceable?

11. Lane was in the business of selling boats and trailers. He sold a boat motor and trailer to a person who said he was John W. Wills and who wrote a check of $6,285 in payment. The check bounced, and one John Garrett, who obtained possession of the boat motor and trailer in an unknown manner, sold the goods to Honeycutt. Lane filed suit against Honeycutt to recover the goods. Honeycutt's defense was that he was a "good faith purchaser for value" under 2-403 of the Uniform Commercial Code. Was he correct?

CHAPTER 16

Sales Law: Risk of Loss, Insurable Interest, Bulk Transfer

CHAPTER OBJECTIVES

After reading this chapter, you should be able to:

1. Explain the significance of bearing the risk of loss.

2. Explain the allocation of risk of loss in a destination contract.

3. Explain the allocation of risk of loss in an origin contract.

4. Define standard commercial terms such as *C.I.F.* and *F.O.B.*

5. Describe the effect of a breach of contract on risk of loss.

6. Explain when a party to a sales contract can take out insurance on the goods.

7. Identify the special rules that apply when goods are sold in bulk not in the ordinary course of business.

Sometimes goods are damaged or destroyed by occurrences such as fire, floods, chemical leaks, or ordinary accidents. An unexpected loss of goods which are in the process of being sold may be catastrophic from the viewpoint of the parties involved. It may also raise complex legal issues.

The question of who bears the risk of loss and who may insure the goods in a contract of sale is the primary focus of this chapter. The chapter closes with an analysis of the legal ramifications that arise when a retailer or other seller disposes of inventory in bulk, rather than through ordinary sales channels.

RISK OF LOSS

The Uniform Sales Act, which governed the law of sales prior to the adoption of the UCC, forced the courts to struggle with the question of who held title to the goods in order to determine which party bore the risk of loss. The UCC greatly simplifies the determination of who bears the risk of loss by treating risk of loss separately from the issue of title.

There are a number of factors that will influence the determination of who bears the risk of loss to the goods in a contract of sale. Typically, the parties will use standard merchant terms such as "F.O.B.," "C.I.F." or "No arrival, no sale." These terms are defined in the UCC (and later in this chapter) and will have an important impact on how risk of loss is allocated.

Sometimes parties expressly agree about how risk of loss is to be allocated. If the parties have made such an agreement, it is the determining factor in most circumstances. Another factor that influences risk of loss is whether one of the parties has breached the contract. A party who has breached often bears the risk of loss.

Risk of loss cannot pass to the buyer until the goods are identified to the contract. Section 2-501 states that, in the absence of a contrary agreement, identification occurs: when the contract is made if the goods are existing and identified; or if the goods are future goods, when the goods are shipped, marked, or otherwise designated by the seller as goods to which the contract refers.

Agreement

In general, the UCC reflects the philosophy that the parties may determine the details of a contract. The parties may arrive at an agreement on risk of loss contrary to that specified in the UCC. The agreement may shift the allocation of risk of loss, or it may divide the risk between the parties. The only restraints on the modification of the risk-of-loss provisions in the UCC are that such modifications be made in good faith and not be unconscionable.

If a seller intends to shift the risk of loss to the buyer, the contract must clearly state the manner in which risk of loss will be allocated. This is especially true when the seller tries to shift the risk of loss to the buyer before he or she takes possession of the goods.

In Hayward v. Postma, 188 N.W.2d 31 (1971), the seller argued that the risk of loss for a 30-foot Revel Craft Playmate Yacht worth $10,000 that was destroyed by fire while it was still at the seller's premises should fall on the buyer. Neither the seller nor the buyer had an insurance policy covering the boat. The seller claimed that he had transferred the risk of loss to the buyer by a clause in the security agreement signed by the parties. (See Chapter 24 for an explanation of security agreements.) The court acknowledged that a risk of loss could be transferred to the buyer in this fashion, but it observed that the agreement in this case was not sufficiently clear and prominent to apprise the buyer that he bore the risk of loss on the yacht.

The court noted that the usual rule in such cases was for the risk of loss to fall on the merchant-seller unless he or she had physically delivered the goods to the buyer. The rationale for this rule was that the buyer had no control over the goods and that it would be extremely unlikely that the buyer would carry insurance on goods not yet in his possession. The seller might transfer this risk to the buyer only if he or she clearly brought this matter to the buyer's attention.

Merchant Terms

When contracting, merchants frequently use mercantile terms or symbols as abbreviated methods of stating the delivery duties of the seller. The UCC defines these mercantile terms in Sections 2-319 to 2-325. Unless the parties to a contract specify another meaning, the UCC definitions of these terms controls.

F.O.B. free on board a carrier, typically a truck or train

F.A.S. free alongside a ship

F.O.B.   The terms **F.O.B.** (free on board a carrier, typically a truck or train) and **F.A.S.** (free alongside a ship) are defined in Section 2-319. If the contract states "F.O.B. St. Louis" and the seller is in St. Louis, then it is a shipment or origin contract (see Chapter 15). The seller must, unless otherwise agreed:

1. put the goods in the possession of the carrier

2. make a proper contract for transportation of the goods (for example, meat must be refrigerated) on behalf of the buyer

3. obtain and deliver or tender to the buyer any documents necessary for the buyer to obtain possession of the goods

4. promptly notify the buyer of the shipment

If the contract states "F.O.B. New York" and the seller is in St. Louis and the buyer in New York, then the seller pays the freight and bears the risk of loss under Section 2-319(1)(b). This is a destination contract (see Chapter 15). The seller must at his own risk and expense transport the goods to New York and tender them to the buyer in New York. Section 2-503 requires the seller to put and hold conforming goods at the buyer's disposition and to give the buyer reasonable notification in order to enable him or her to take delivery. The tender must be at a reasonable hour and the goods must be available for a reasonable period of time.

Presumption of Origin Contract   Through an examination of the contract and the surrounding circumstances, it generally will be possible to determine whether the seller must send the goods to the buyer and whether the parties contemplated an origin or a destination contract. If the contract fails to clearly cover this point, the presumption is that the parties intended an origin contract.

C.I.F.   The term **C.I.F.** stands for the words cost, insurance, and freight. When this term is used, it means that the price includes the cost of the goods, the cost of insuring the goods, and freight to a named destination. The seller must at his own expense put the goods into the possession of a carrier at the port for shipment, and obtain a negotiable bill of lading covering the entire transportation to the named destination.

C.I.F. term meaning that price of goods includes insurance and transportation

C. & F.   According to Section 2-320(1 and 3), when a contract includes the term **C. & F.,** the price includes cost and freight to the named destination. The seller need not obtain insurance under a C. & F. term. The term has the same effect and imposes upon the seller the same obligations and risks as a C.I.F. term, except for the obligation to insure. The risk of loss under C.I.F. or C. & F. is on the buyer once the seller has delivered the goods to the carrier.

C. & F. term meaning that price of goods includes transportation only

Ex-Ship   In a sale **ex-ship** (which means from the carrying vessel) the seller must cause the goods to be delivered to the buyer from a ship which has arrived at the port of delivery. The seller must pay freight to the named port and furnish the buyer with a direction that puts the ship under a duty to deliver the goods. The risk of loss does not pass until the goods are properly unloaded from the ship.

Ex-ship term meaning that seller pays freight to designated port where buyer obtains the goods

No arrival, no
sale term
meaning that seller
retains risk of loss
during shipment
but is not liable for
accidents in transit

No Arrival, No Sale   The term **no arrival, no sale** is used when the parties execute a destination contract by which the risk of loss remains on the seller during shipment. Under this term, however, the seller is not liable for breach of contract if the goods are not delivered through no fault of the seller. The parties may arrive at a different understanding, but the seller is free of liability if goods conforming to the contract fail to arrive due to the hazards of transportation.

UCC Allocation of Risk

If the contract between the buyer and the seller fails to specify how risk of loss will be allocated between the parties, Section 2-509 controls if there is a loss but no breach of contract. Section 2-510 applies if there has been a loss and a breach of contract.

The policy underlying these provisions is to place the loss on the party most likely to have insured against it. The person in possession of the goods normally is able to prevent a loss from occurring in the first place. For this reason, the risk of loss usually falls on the party in possession of the goods.

Section 2-509 divides risk of loss into three categories: 1. Goods shipped by carrier, 2. Goods held by a bailee that are to be delivered without being moved, and 3. All other cases.

Shipment by Carrier   When the parties enter into an origin contract and agree to delivery by carrier, risk of loss shifts to the buyer when the seller puts the goods in the possession of a carrier, makes a reasonable contract for their transportation, obtains all documents necessary for the buyer to obtain possession of the goods, and notifies the buyer of the shipment.

If a destination contract is involved, whereby the seller agrees to ship the goods to the buyer by carrier, risk passes to the buyer when the seller has put and held conforming goods for the buyer at the destination point and given the buyer any notification and documents reasonably necessary to take delivery of the goods.

Suppose a paint manufacturer sells 500 cans of paint to a retail paint store. If the parties agree for the seller to ship the goods to the buyer's store at 1011 Main, Oklahoma City, and the goods are lost in transit after the seller loads them on a common carrier (e.g., a railroad, truck, or airline), who bears the risk of loss? It must first be determined if the parties entered into an origin contract or a destination contract. Bear in mind that the UCC views an origin contract as the typical contract.

The seller does not bear the risk of loss after placing the goods on the carrier unless he or she has specifically agreed to bear the risk of loss to the destination point. In this case, the courts probably would treat the agreement as an origin contract and place the risk of loss on the buyer. The term "ship to," attached to the goods with an address, has no significance in determining who bears the risk of loss.

On the other hand, language such as "F.O.B. buyer's plant" or "Ship to buyer, risk of loss remains on seller until tender by carrier to buyer" clearly contemplates a destination contract, and the risk does not pass to the buyer until the goods are tendered to the buyer at the place of destination.

The risk of loss will not pass unless the seller makes a proper contract for transportation and ships conforming goods.

Goods Held by a Bailee   If the goods are not to be shipped by carrier but are in possession of a **bailee** and are to be delivered without being moved, Section 2-509(2) controls. If the bailee has issued a negotiable document of title, the risk of loss passes to the buyer when he or she receives it. Risk of loss also passes to the buyer after his or her receipt of a nonnegotiable document of title, but not until the buyer has had a reasonable opportunity to present the document to the bailee. If the bailee refuses to honor the nonnegotiable document of title, risk of loss does not pass. If a nonnegotiable document of title has been issued, risk of loss passes to the buyer when the bailee acknowledges the buyer's right to the possession of the goods.

> **Bailee** one who holds goods under the instructions of the owner

Other Cases   All other cases *not* involving a breach of contract are covered by Section 2-509(3). This section covers the situation where the seller intends to deliver the goods to the buyer in the seller's truck or the buyer intends to pick up the goods at the seller's place of business.

Subsection 3 sets out two rules, one of which covers a merchant-seller and the other applies to a nonmerchant-seller. In the case of the merchant-seller, risk of loss remains on the seller until the buyer actually takes physical possession of the goods. If the seller is not a merchant, risk of loss passes to the buyer on tender of delivery. Tender means putting and holding conforming goods at the buyer's disposition and giving the buyer any notification reasonably necessary to enable him to take delivery. The tender must be at a reasonable hour and kept available long enough for the buyer to take possession.

Suppose that Acme Glass agrees to sell fifteen panels of glass to a building contractor. Nothing is said about who bears the risk of loss in the contract. If the glass is destroyed prior to the time the contractor picks up the glass, who bears the risk of loss? As Acme Glass deals in goods of this kind, it is a merchant under Section 2-104. Acme must actually deliver physical possession of the glass to the contractor. The risk of loss is on Acme.

But suppose Elmo sells fifteen panels of glass to his next-door neighbor and tenders them to his neighbor. The neighbor fails to pick up the glass, and after a week passes a fire destroys Elmo's home and the glass. Who bears the risk of loss? Because Elmo is not a merchant, and he tendered the glass to his neighbor, the risk of loss falls on his neighbor.

Note that a merchant-seller who retains physical possession of goods after selling them retains the risk of loss. This is true even after title has passed and the seller has received his or her money for the goods, as is illustrated by the following case.

Martin v. Melland's, Incorporated

Supreme Court of North Dakota
283 N.W. 2d 76 (1979)

On June 11, 1974, Martin entered into a written agreement with Melland's, a farm   FACTS
implement dealer, to purchase a truck and attached haystack mover for the total
purchase price of $35,389. Martin was given a trade-in allowance of $17,389 on his old
unit, leaving a balance owing of $18,000 plus sales tax of $720 or a total balance of

$18,720. The agreement provided that Martin "mail or bring title" to the old unit to Melland's "this week." Martin mailed the certificate of title to Melland pursuant to the agreement, but he was allowed to retain the use and possession of the old unit "until they had the new one ready."

Fire destroyed the old truck and the haymoving unit in early August 1974, while Martin was moving hay. The parties did not have any agreement regarding insurance or risk of loss on the old unit. Plaintiff (Martin) argued that since he did not have title to the truck, the haymover defendant should bear the loss. Defendant argued that although plaintiff executed title to the haymover, he did not relinquish possession, thus he was the owner of the truck at the time the fire occurred, and should bear the loss.

ISSUE   Does Martin bear the risk of loss from the fire because he retained possession after passing title to the defendant?

DECISION   The court ruled that Martin was responsible for the loss. It stated that under Section 2-509, the question of loss is no longer related to title. A party must show that a tender of delivery took place in the manner, time and place determined by the agreement. The court held that because Martin did not tender delivery of the trade-in truck and haystack mover to Melland in accordance with 2-509, Martin must bear the loss.

Risk of Loss When Contract Is Breached

Section 2-510 addresses the problem of risk of loss when there has been a breach of contract by either the seller or the buyer. If for any reason the goods delivered by the seller fail to live up to the requirements of the contract, the risk of loss does not pass to the buyer.

Breach by Seller; Buyer Rejects   Section 2-510(1) covers the situation where the seller tenders or delivers goods not conforming to the contract under circumstances that give the buyer the right to reject (refuse to accept) the goods. In this case, the risk of loss remains on the seller until the buyer accepts the goods or the seller replaces the nonconforming goods with conforming goods (referred to as a "cure" by the seller).

Suppose a seller ships paper goods to the buyer. Because the goods fail to meet the standards set forth in the contract, the buyer rejects the goods. Buyer holds the goods, and while in his possession they are destroyed by fire. In this case, seller bears the risk of loss. What if the buyer accepts the paper in spite of its nonconformity? The risk of loss is then on the buyer. Likewise, if the seller takes back the nonconforming paper and substitutes conforming paper, and then the paper is destroyed, the risk of loss is on the buyer since the seller has "cured" the defective performance.

Breach by Seller; Buyer Revokes   Section 2-510(2) sets forth the buyer's rights upon revoking an acceptance. When the buyer rightfully revokes an acceptance, the risk of loss is treated as having remained on the seller from the beginning, to the extent of any deficiency in the buyer's insurance.

Suppose a seller ships groceries, which the buyer accepts. Thereafter, the buyer finds some defect in the groceries that gives grounds to revoke the acceptance. When the buyer revokes the acceptance, risk of loss is treated as having been on the seller from the beginning. If the goods are destroyed while in the buyer's possession, after the buyer's revocation, the loss falls on the seller entirely if the buyer has no insurance.

What if the buyer has $500 worth of insurance, but the fire destroys $2,000 worth of groceries? In this case $500 of the loss falls on the buyer's insurance company, and the other $1,500 falls on the seller. We are assuming in these examples that the goods are destroyed through no fault of the buyer or the seller—in a fire, for example.

Breach by Buyer   The final subsection of 2-510 puts the risk of loss on the buyer who breaches the contract before the risk of loss passes to the buyer. In this case, the seller may, to the extent of any deficiency in his or her insurance coverage, treat the risk of loss as resting on the buyer for a commercially reasonable time. The seller must meet several conditions to put the loss on the buyer:

1. The seller must have had conforming goods

2. The goods must have been identified to the contract

3. The buyer must have breached the contract before the loss passed to the buyer

4. The loss must not have been covered, at least in part, by the seller's insurance

5. The loss must have occurred within a commercially reasonable time

Suppose that on June 1 the parties enter into a contract for a delivery scheduled for June 15. On June 10, the seller segregates conforming goods and identifies them to the contract. Normally, the risk of loss remains on a merchant-seller, assuming the buyer plans to pick up the goods at the seller's place of business, until the goods are delivered to the buyer (subsection 2-509[3]). On June 12, the buyer repudiates the contract. On June 14, the goods are destroyed while in possession of the seller. If the seller has no insurance, the whole loss falls on the buyer.

What if the seller keeps the goods in storage until March of the next year, at which time they are destroyed? The buyer might argue that the loss did not occur within a commercially reasonable time. Such an argument probably would be successful.

In the following case a buyer breached the contract, and the goods were destroyed by fire.

Multiplastics, Incorporated v. Arch Industries, Incorporated

Supreme Court of Connecticut
328 A. 2d 618 (1974)

The plaintiff, Multiplastics, agreed with the defendant on June 30, 1971, to manufac-   FACTS
ture and deliver 40,000 pounds of brown polystyrene plastic pellets for nineteen cents a pound. The pellets were specially made for the defendant, who agreed to accept delivery at the rate of 1,000 pounds per day after completion of production. The defendant's confirming order contained the notation "make and hold for release.

Confirmation." The plaintiff produced the order of pellets within two weeks and requested release orders from the defendant. The defendant refused to issue the release orders, citing labor difficulties and its vacation schedule. On August 18, 1971, the plaintiff sent the defendant a letter stating that it had warehoused the product for forty days as agreed and requested shipping instructions. On September 22 the plaintiff's plant and warehouse pellets were destroyed. When the insurance did not cover the pellets, the plaintiff sued for breach of contract.

ISSUE   Is defendant Arch Industries liable to pay for the destroyed plastic pellets?

DECISION   The court ruled in favor of Multiplastics. Section 2-510(3) applied because Arch Industries breached the contract by failing to provide delivery instructions in response to plaintiff's legal tender of delivery in its August 18, 1971, letter. The court also found that August 20 – September 22 was a commercially reasonable period to shift the risk of loss to Arch Industries because it had repeatedly agreed to transmit delivery instructions to the plaintiff and the goods were specifically made for Arch Industries.

Sale or Return and Sale on Approval

Sale on approval term for goods intended for use by the buyer but that may be returned

Sale or return term for goods intended for resale by the buyer but that may be returned

Section 2-326(1) states that if goods are delivered primarily for use and may be returned by the buyer to the seller even though they conform to the contract, the transaction is a **sale on approval.** If the goods are delivered to a buyer who is entitled to return conforming goods and the buyer intends to resell the goods, the transaction is a **sale or return.** In order to determine whether conforming goods that may be returned to the seller have been sold on sale or return or sale on approval terms, the court must examine whether the buyer intended to use the goods or to resell them.

When goods are purchased on sale on approval, the buyer may wish to try out the goods before accepting them. If he or she uses the goods to try them out, it does not constitute acceptance. The risk of loss and title remain with the seller until the buyer accepts the goods. Acceptance can occur automatically if the buyer fails to notify the seller of his or her election to return the goods within a reasonable time. Acceptance of any part of the goods is acceptance of the whole — if the goods conform to the contract. If the buyer elects to return the goods, the return is at the seller's risk and expense. If the buyer is a merchant, he or she must follow any instructions provided by the seller.

Under sale or return terms, the buyer can return all or part of the goods shipped as long as they are substantially in their original condition. But the buyer must elect to return them within a reasonable time and must do so at his or her own risk and expense.

Risk of loss is summarized in Table 16-1.

INSURABLE INTEREST

The UCC, in Section 2-501, specifies who has an **insurable interest** in goods. The buyer obtains an insurable interest in existing goods as soon as they are identified to

TABLE 16-1   Risk of Loss

Terms of Agreement	Who Bears the Loss
Written Agreement	Depends on terms of agreement
Terms	
F.O.B. Origin	On buyer when goods delivered to the carrier
F.O.B. Destination	On buyer when goods tendered to buyer at destination
No agreement/No Breach of Contract 2-509	
Ship by Carrier Destination Contract	On buyer when goods tendered to buyer
Ship by Carrier Origin Contract	On buyer when goods delivered to carrier
Goods Held by Bailee Negotiable Document of Title	When buyer receives documents
Goods Held by Bailee Nonnegotiable Document of Title	When bailee acknowledges right of buyer to goods
All Other Cases if Merchant Seller	When goods are delivered to the buyer
All Other Cases if Nonmerchant Seller	When goods are tendered to the buyer
No Agreement/Breach of Contract 2-510	
Breach by Seller; Buyer Rejects	Risk on seller until buyer accepts
Breach by Seller; Buyer Revokes	Risk on seller to the extent of any deficiency in buyer's insurance
Breach by Buyer	Risk on buyer to the extent of any deficiency in seller's insurance
Sale or Return 2-326	Risk on seller until buyer accepts goods
Sale on Approval 2-236	Buyer to return goods at buyer's risk

the contract. The buyer obtains an insurable interest even though the goods identified are nonconforming.

However, if the contract is for the sale of future goods, that is, goods that are not yet in existence and identified, the buyer obtains an insurable interest in the future goods when they are shipped, mailed, or otherwise designated by the seller as goods to which the contract refers.

The seller has an insurable interest in goods so long as he has title to the goods or any security interest in the goods.

Insurable interest the right to insure against a loss of goods (or, in some cases, human life)

BULK TRANSFERS

Article 6 of the UCC covers **bulk transfers.** Section 6-102 defines these as:

> any transfer in bulk and not in the ordinary course of the transferor's business of a major part of the materials, supplies, merchandise or other inventory . . . of an enterprise.

Bulk transfer a sale in bulk, not in the ordinary course of business

When a substantial part of the equipment of an enterprise is transferred, it will be a bulk transfer only if it is made in connection with a bulk transfer of inventory.

All businesses whose principal business is the sale of merchandise from stock, including businesses who manufacture what they sell, are covered by Article 6. The purpose of Article 6 is to prevent a fraud on the creditors of a going business.

Creditors may extend credit to a business based on its inventory. Article 6 prevents a merchant from selling his or her inventory all at once without taking care of creditors.

Requirements

Inventory may be sold in bulk without violating Article 6 if the merchant adheres strictly to the provisions of the article. A bulk transfer is not effective against any creditor of the transferor unless:

1. the buyer gets a list of the seller's creditors

2. the parties prepare a schedule of the property to be transferred

3. the schedule of property and list of creditors are preserved for six months following the transfer and are made available to any creditor of the transferor

4. the seller signs and swears to the list of creditors.

Section 6-104(3) makes the seller responsible for the completeness and accuracy of the list of the creditors. The transfer is not rendered improper because of errors and omissions unless the buyer knew of these errors or omissions.

Notice

The buyer must notify all creditors on the list of the bulk transfer, or the transfer is ineffective against those creditors not receiving notice of it. This notice must be given at least ten days before the buyer takes possession of the goods or pays for them, whichever happens first. The purchaser does not need to provide notice of the transfer when the sale is by auction. This responsibility is transferred by Section 6-108 to the auctioneer. Some states have adopted optional Section 6-106, which specifies that the proceeds of the sale are to be applied to the debts of the seller. Other states merely require notice to the creditors.

Failure to Comply

If the buyer fails to comply with the provisions of Article 6, the transfer of goods is ineffective. In other words, the creditors of the seller can reach these goods even though the buyer has paid for them. But if the buyer in turn sells these goods to a good faith purchaser for value, the power of the creditors to reach the goods is cut off. Creditors of the seller have six months after the date on which the transferee took possession of the goods to take action (unless the parties concealed the transfer).

SUMMARY

Several UCC rules determine who bears the risk of loss when goods are destroyed by acts beyond the control of the parties. The parties may expressly allocate the risk of loss among themselves by a contract term. Unless otherwise provided, the form of the contract determines risk of loss. In an origin contract — in which the seller delivers the goods at the seller's place of business — the risk of loss is on the buyer after the goods are delivered to a carrier. In a destination contract — in which the seller delivers goods to the buyer's city — the risk of loss remains on the seller until the goods are placed at the buyer's disposal. Generally, a party who breaches a contract bears the risk of loss. Risk of loss depends on possession of a document of title when the goods are held by a bailee.

The term *C.I.F.* indicates whether the price includes the cost, insurance, and freight. A *sale on approval* arises when the goods are intended for use by a buyer who has a right of return. Risk of loss is on the seller until the goods are accepted. A *sale or return* is involved when goods are intended for resale by a buyer who has a right of return. Risk of loss is on the buyer.

A buyer may insure goods at the moment that they are identified to the contract. A seller may insure the goods so long as the seller retains title or has an insurable interest in the goods.

A bulk transfer involves the sale of a major part of the goods of a business, not in the ordinary course of the business. To protect creditors of the business who may have a security interest in the goods, the seller must provide the buyer with a signed and sworn list of creditors along with a schedule of the transferred property. The buyer then must notify the creditors on the list, or the sale is not good against them.

REVIEW PROBLEMS

1. Why is the allocation of risk of loss between the parties so important?

2. What is an insurable interest?

3. Can both seller and buyer have an insurable interest in the same goods at the same time?

4. Define the terms *F.O.B.*, *C.I.F.*, *C. & F.*, *Ex-ship*, and *No Arrival, No Sale*.

5. Detwiller purchases a new truck from Stevens Dodge. The truck is then shipped to Bob, a dealer closer to Detwiller's home town, for pick up. After Detwiller pays Stevens Dodge, documents of title are sent to Detwiller. Before he receives them, the truck is destroyed by fire on Bob's lot. Detwiller and Stevens Dodge have no agreement regarding the risk of loss. Where does the risk of loss lie?

6. Eberhard agrees to sell and ship certain goods to Brown. The contract does not contain any F.O.B. terms, nor is there any agreement on who bears the risk of loss. Certain goods are placed on board a common carrier by Eberhard but apparently are lost in transit. Eberhard sues Brown for the price of the goods. Brown contends that the risk of loss remains with Eberhard. Is Brown's contention correct?

7. Adrian Corporation is a creditor of Larry. Larry sells his business in bulk to Will, who later sells it to Climax. At the time of closing, Larry furnishes an affidavit stating he has no creditors; Climax also inquires of Larry's attorney to learn if

there are any creditors and is assured that there are none. Adrian now sues to have the sale declared ineffective, as it had received no notice of the sale as required by Section 6-105. Under the UCC Section 6-104, is the sale effective against Adrian?

8. White delivers a truck to Bronx pursuant to a purchase agreement. After delivery, but before White assigns title to Bronx, the truck is stolen. Bronx contends that because it did not have a proper title to the truck, the risk of loss is on White. Is Bronx correct?

9. New Jersey Pipeco imported three shipments of steel from Japan. The shipments were subject to import duties. The Federal Insurance Company (Federal) had been engaged by New Jersey Pipeco to guarantee its payment of duties to the federal government. New Jersey Pipeco failed to pay certain amounts owed to the federal government, so Federal was required to pay. New Jersey Pipeco thus became legally obligated to reimburse Federal for the payments. New Jersey Pipeco, in a bulk transfer, sold some of its assets to Delaware Pipeco (no relation). Delaware Pipeco was furnished a list of New Jersey Pipeco's creditors, as required by UCC Section 6-104(1)(a), but Federal was not on the list. Because New Jersey Pipeco was unable to make good on its obligation, Federal sued to collect from Delaware Pipeco. Although Delaware Pipeco had no actual knowledge of New Jersey Pipeco's obligations, Federal argued that because Delaware Pipeco knew that New Jersey Pipeco was an importer, it should have investigated to see if it owed any import duties to the federal government. An investigation would have uncovered New Jersey Pipeco's obligation to Federal, and Delaware Pipeco would then have been able to notify Federal before the sale (as provided by UCC Section 6-105) and allow Federal to protect its interest. What result?

10. Crump signed a "conditional sales contract" to purchase a television antenna system from Lair Distributing Company, a merchant. The contract provided that until the purchase price was fully paid, Lair could retain title and Crump could not remove the system from his premises without Lair's consent. After the system was installed on Crump's property but before it was fully paid for, it was damaged by lightning. Crump argued that because of the contract's terms, he was not really in possession of the system when the damage occurred. Does the question of Crump's possession of the system have any bearing on whether he or Lair must shoulder the risk of loss under UCC Section 2-509? Who bore the risk of loss at the time of the accident?

11. Ramos signed a contract to purchase a motorcycle from Wheel Sports Center in New York City. The contract called for delivery to Ramos by June 30. Ramos paid for the motorcycle in full, registered the motorcycle, and purchased liability insurance for it. Before receiving delivery, however, Ramos notified the Wheel salesman that he was going on vacation and would pick up the cycle upon his return. On July 11, while Ramos was still on vacation, New York was hit by a power blackout. Ramos's cycle was stolen from the Wheel Sports Center by looters. Under the UCC, is the loss borne by Ramos or the Wheel Sports Center? Hint: See UCC Sections 2-509 and 2-103(1)(c).

12. Morauer contracted with Deak and Company, a currency dealer, to purchase $5000 worth of various foreign silver and gold coins for investment purposes.

To avoid District of Columbia taxes, the parties agreed that the gold coins would be mailed from Deak's D.C. office to Morauer's suburban Maryland home. Morauer paid for all of the coins, and Deak mailed them to him in two packages, obtaining postal receipts. Morauer received only one package of coins; the other was lost in the mail. Who must bear the loss of the missing coins?

13. Lakeview Mobile Homes contracted to sell a mobile home to Moses and to install it. On February 9, Lakeview delivered the mobile home, set it on cinder blocks, removed the tires and axles, and connected the plumbing. Moses pointed out to Lakeview that a window was broken, a water pipe was damaged, and that he had no door keys to the home. On the next day, when Lakeview's crew had planned to return to complete its work, the home was destroyed in a windstorm. Who bears the risk of loss?

14. Fox, a retail jeweler, requested that Baumgold, a wholesale jeweler, send it certain diamonds for examination by a potential purchaser. The contract, supplied by Baumgold, stated that the "merchandise . . . is delivered to you . . . upon the express condition that all such merchandise . . . shall be returned on demand, in full, in its original form." Baumgold sent the diamonds by registered mail and insured the risk of loss during shipment. Fox never received the diamonds. What is the common term to describe the contract between Fox and Baumgold? Who must bear the loss?

CHAPTER 17

Sales Law: Performance

CHAPTER OBJECTIVES

After reading this chapter, you should be able to:

1. Explain the basic performance obligations of seller and buyer.

2. Explain the basic requirements for proper delivery of goods.

3. Describe how and when goods must be paid for.

4. Identify acceptance of goods in a sales transaction and when a buyer may unintentionally accept goods.

5. Explain how goods may be properly rejected.

6. Define the circumstances in which an acceptance may be revoked by the buyer.

7. Identify the special rules for performance under an installment contract.

8. Explain when a worried party is entitled to an assurance of performance and what constitutes an adequate assurance.

9. Describe how a party can repudiate a contract before performance is required and the consequences for the aggrieved party.

10. Detail the circumstances under which the UCC allows a contract to be discharged on grounds of impossibility.

The formation and interpretation of sales contracts are discussed in the preceding chapters. This chapter focuses on the performance obligations that parties incur when they contract for the sale of goods. The student should review Chapter 13, which deals with these matters in regard to contracts in general.

PERFORMANCE

The basic duty of the seller is to deliver or make available the goods purchased by the buyer. The buyer's basic responsibility is to pay for the goods. The obligations of the seller and buyer are discussed in turn.

Delivery

The UCC (Section 2-307) makes it the duty of the seller to transfer and deliver goods according to the terms of a contract. But how must the seller deliver the goods?

Must all goods be delivered at one time? Unless the contract indicates a contrary agreement, all the goods must be delivered at one time. The buyer is entitled to reject a delivery that has been improperly delivered in lots — subject to the right of the seller to make good the improper offer of goods.

Place of Delivery   What is the proper place for delivery? If the parties have agreed to or have authorized delivery by carrier, the seller's duties are determined by whether the agreement is a destination or origin contract. In both cases, the seller actually delivers the goods to a carrier such as a trucking firm, railroad, or airline.

If delivery by carrier is neither required nor authorized by the contract, the proper place for delivery is the seller's place of business or (if he or she has no place of business) the seller's home. If the contract is for the sale of identified goods that are known by both parties to be at some other place, that place is the proper place for delivery of the goods.

Time for Delivery   If the time for shipment or delivery has not been agreed upon, it is assumed to be a reasonable time. What is reasonable depends on the nature, purpose, and circumstances of the action to be taken. If the time for delivery has not been specified, neither party may demand or offer delivery at an unreasonably early time.

Delivery of Nonconforming Goods   What happens if the seller delivers at the proper place and time but the goods do not conform to the contract? Although a delivery has been rejected by the buyer because of **nonconforming goods,** the buyer does not necessarily have a right to sue for breach of contract. If the time for performance has not yet expired, the seller may seasonably notify the buyer of his or her intention to make a conforming delivery within the contract time. Thus if the seller is to deliver goods on December 1 and delivers nonconforming goods, which the buyer rejects, on November 1, the seller may notify the buyer of an intention to make good and deliver conforming goods any time until December 1.

A different problem occurs when the seller sends nonconforming goods which he or she reasonably believes will be acceptable to the buyer. If the seller did not anticipate the buyer's rejection of the nonconforming goods and does not have time to deliver conforming goods before the specified date, the seller has a "reasonable time" to **substitute performance** (Section 2-508[1]).

Suppose that a seller has agreed to deliver green, red, and blue swimsuits by December 1 and sends green, red, and yellow suits because no blue suits are in stock. The buyer may be able to reject the goods as nonconforming if color is a significant characteristic. If the goods arrive on November 29, the seller may not have time to change them and may try to rely on Section 2-508(2) to get a reasonable time after the expiration date to substitute performance.

Reasonable grounds for believing that a buyer will accept goods may be found in the earlier course of dealing, course of performance, usage of trade, and the circumstances of the making of the contract. If the buyer has accepted a substitute color before, that is reasonable grounds for believing that the buyer will accept one again. The buyer may obtain protection against the seller's "reasonable grounds" claim by including a **no-replacement clause** in the contract.

Nonconforming goods goods which differ from specifications of a contract

Substitute performance change actions so as to meet contract requirements

No-replacement clause a term in a contract stating that no variances are acceptable

Cash or Check   Unless the parties have agreed to the contrary or the goods are sold on credit, payment is due at the time and place of delivery (Section 2-310[a]). The buyer usually may pay by check, unless the seller demands cash. If the seller accepts the buyer's check, the payment is conditional on the bank's honoring the check. If the bank does not do so, the buyer must still pay for the goods.

If the seller demands cash, the buyer must be given a reasonable time to get it. The purpose for allowing this time is to prevent the buyer from being unprepared because he or she planned to pay by check or on credit. This provision prevents the seller from treating the buyer's inability to pay in cash at the time for payment as a breach of contract.

Right to Inspect   Before payment or acceptance, the buyer generally has a right to inspect the goods at any reasonable place and time and in any reasonable manner. The right of inspection is important to the buyer because, without it, one cannot tell if goods that have been shipped in containers are conforming.

The buyer does not have a right of inspection when the goods are shipped C.O.D. (cash on delivery). In this case, the goods must be paid for even if they do not conform to the contract, unless the nonconformity is visible without inspection (Section 2-512[1]). But the buyer still has the right to inspect after paying and is not considered to have accepted the goods until there has been an opportunity to inspect them.

Delivery by Documents of Title   If delivery is authorized and made by documents of title, payment is due at the time and place at which the buyer is to receive the documents, regardless of where the goods themselves are to be received. Although the goods must be paid for when the appropriate documents are received, the buyer retains the right to inspect. No acceptance occurs until the buyer has had the opportunity to inspect the goods.

If a buyer purchases goods C.O.D. and receives the proper documents, he or she must pay for the goods even though they are still in transit. When the goods arrive, the buyer may inspect them and exercise the right to accept or reject.

ACCEPTANCE

A buyer accepts goods in one of three ways: by an express statement, by inaction, or by an act which is inconsistent with the seller's ownership (Section 2-606).

Express Statement of Acceptance

The buyer accepts the goods if, after a reasonable opportunity to inspect them, he or she indicates that the goods are conforming or that he or she will take the goods even if they are not conforming.

Suppose that a buyer orders 100 blue and red swimsuits. If the seller delivers 100 blue and green swimsuits, the buyer, after inspecting them, accepts the goods by indicating that he or she will take them even though they are not blue and red. Bear in mind that because this delivery was not conforming, the buyer could have rejected the swimsuits.

Inaction

An acceptance also may occur as a result of inaction by the buyer, that is, by the buyer's failure to effectively reject the goods after a reasonable opportunity to inspect them. Now suppose that the blue and green swimsuits arrive on January 1 but, rather than opening the box immediately to inspect the goods, the buyer puts the box in the storeroom. The buyer could have inspected the goods on January 1, determined that they were not conforming, and rejected them. On April 15, the buyer opens the box. The buyer now wants to reject the suits. Because of the buyer's inaction, however, it is too late to reject them because a reasonable time has expired.

Act Inconsistent with Seller's Ownership

The third method of acceptance is an act on the part of the buyer that is inconsistent with the seller's ownership. Suppose the buyer receives the blue and green swimsuits, puts them on the shelves in the store, and sells a number to the public. Selling the suits amounts to an act inconsistent with the seller's ownership.

Knowledge of Defects   In considering that a buyer has accepted when he or she has acted in a way that is inconsistent with the seller's ownership (Section 2-606[1]), the courts distinguish between cases where the buyer knows of a defect and those where he or she does not know of it. In the example in the preceding paragraph, the buyer knew the goods were nonconforming, made no attempt to reject them, and sold them to third parties. This is an act inconsistent with the seller's ownership. The same would be true if the seller attempted to reject the suits but then sold them to third parties.

Sometimes it is impossible for the buyer to avoid using the product even after rejecting it. Suppose a homeowner purchases a wall-to-wall carpet that is glued to the floor. In this situation, the homeowner may call the seller, reject the carpet, and continue to use it.

A more difficult case is the continued use of a car or mobile home after a rejection. Whether the continued use constitutes acceptance is not easy for the courts to resolve. In general, it is dangerous to use goods after rejection, because a court may interpret this use as an acceptance. This matter is discussed later in this chapter.

Another difficult situation arises when the buyer is aware of a defect but uses the goods before rejecting them. If the buyer and the seller are trying to straighten the problem out, and this is why the buyer has delayed rejecting the goods, the use of the product should not be regarded as an acceptance. The policy of the UCC is to encourage parties to work out their differences.

Similarly, the buyer's use of a product while unaware of a defect does not constitute an acceptance. Suppose our buyer purchases a car, drives it for two days, and then the transmission fails. The UCC gives the buyer the right to inspect goods and a reasonable time to reject them. Using the car for two days and then learning of the defect does not constitute an acceptance.

The following case illustrates acceptance through actions inconsistent with the seller's ownership.

Pettibone Minnesota Corporation v. Castle

Supreme Court of Minnesota
297 N.W.2d 52 (1976)

Castle ordered a particular brand of machinery used in processing gravel, an 880 Crusher, from Pettibone. Pettibone substituted a Pitmaster Crusher and delivered it to Castle. Castle signed a purchase order for the Pitmaster Crusher and never tried to return it. Castle insured the crusher and then sold it to a third party. Pettibone sued Castle for the purchase price, and Castle counterclaimed for damages, citing breach of the contract to deliver the 880 Crusher.   FACTS

Did Castle accept the Pitmaster Crusher from Pettibone?   ISSUE

The unexplained retention and later sale of the crusher were acts "inconsistent with the seller's ownership" and amounted to a purchase of the item. Castle failed to prove that the Pitmaster Crusher was accepted only until the 880 Crusher was reconditioned, as it had claimed. Having acted inconsistently with the seller's ownership, Castle was liable for the purchase price.   DECISION

REJECTION

Perfect Tender Rule

The UCC (Section 2-601) gives the buyer of goods who has received an improper delivery the right to reject the goods "if the goods or the tender of delivery fail in any respect to conform to the contract." This is called the **perfect tender rule.** It does not apply to installment contracts, which are discussed later in this chapter, and it is limited by the seller's right to make good on the error, or cure.

The perfect tender rule has been rendered less significant because of the manner in which the courts interpret the UCC. A buyer may reject goods only when they fail substantially to conform to the contract. Trivial defects do not give the buyer a right to reject.

Perfect tender rule policy by which goods that fail to conform in any respect may be rejected by the buyer

Commercial Units

A **commercial unit** is defined in Section 2-105(b) of the UCC as:

> a single whole for purposes of sale and division of which materially impairs its character or value on the market or in use. A commercial unit may be a single article (as a machine), or a set of articles (as a suite of furniture or an assortment of sizes), or a quantity (as a bale, gross, or carload) or any other unit treated in use or in the relevant market as a single whole.

If the buyer chooses to accept part of a commercial unit, he or she must accept the entire unit (Section 2-606). But the buyer does not need to accept goods that do not conform to the contract. If the seller delivers nonconforming goods, the buyer may (Section 2-601):

1. reject all the goods

2. accept all the goods or

3. accept any commercial unit(s) and reject the rest.

Assume that shoes are typically sold to retailers in 100-pair batches. If the seller delivers 100 pairs of men's shoes and 100 pairs of women's shoes, the buyer may accept all 200 pairs of shoes, reject the 100 pairs of women's shoes and accept the 100 pairs of men's shoes, or reject all the shoes. If the buyer elects to accept the 100 pairs of men's shoes, a commercial unit, he or she must pay at the contract rate for the shoes accepted.

Notice of Rejection

If the buyer wants to reject a delivery of nonconforming goods, he or she must notify the seller of the specific grounds for rejection within a reasonable time. Failure to make an effective rejection may constitute an acceptance.

Suppose that Acme Lawn Equipment sends a sprinkler system to Johnson's Lawn Supply on March 1. When the sprinkler system arrives, Johnson determines that it fails to conform to the contract description. Johnson must reject the goods within a reasonable time after receiving them and must notify Acme that he has done so.

Suppose that Johnson receives the sprinkler system on March 5. If he sends a letter to Acme on March 10 rejecting the system and specifying his reasons, he has probably complied with the requirements of the UCC (Section 2-602). Because Johnson is a merchant, he must follow any instructions he receives from Acme with respect to the sprinkler system. After rejecting the goods, he must be careful not to take any action inconsistent with Acme's ownership, such as selling the sprinkler to a customer. If Johnson sells the sprinkler, the courts would find that he has accepted the sprinkler, even though he rejected it earlier.

State the Defect   It is not enough for the buyer merely to tell the seller that he or she rejects the goods. To be safe, the buyer must state specifically the particular defect on which the rejection is based. This act gives the seller an opportunity to make good or cure the defect. If the buyer rejects the goods and fails to specify the defect, and the defect is of a nature that the seller could have corrected, the buyer cannot rely on this unstated defect as a basis for rejection or to establish a breach of contract.

It is not necessary that the buyer be absolutely precise. A quick informal notice of the defects will suffice. A buyer must state the particular defect if both the buyer and the seller are merchants and if the seller has made a written request for a full and final written statement of all defects on which the buyer proposes to rely as justification for a rejection of the goods (Section 2-605[1][b]). If the buyer fails to list certain defects in the written statement, he or she cannot rely on these defects as grounds for rejection in a later trial.

Timing of Notice   Actions are taken seasonably if they are taken at or within the time agreed or, if no time is agreed, within a reasonable time (Section 1-204[3]). If the buyer acts too slowly in rejecting the goods, he or she is deemed to have accepted them. To determine whether the buyer acted within a reasonable time, the court considers the surrounding circumstances. The following case illustrates the types of circumstances a court considers.

Jones v. Abriani

Court of Appeals of Indiana
350 N.E.2d 635 (1976)

Abriani ordered a mobile home from Jonesy's Mobile Home Sales and left a $1,000 down payment with Jones. When the home arrived, Abriani inspected it but was dissatisfied with the quality of the home's construction and furnishings. When he tried to reject the home, Abriani was told by Jones that he must take the home or lose the down payment. Not able to afford a $1,000 loss, Abriani took the home on condition that Jones would take care of the problems. Abriani rented space on a lot owned by Jones, and throughout the next year continued to complain about the problems that arose in the mobile home. Complaints were made about crooked doors, inferior carpeting, leaking bathtubs, a gas leak, wiring troubles, and other various problems. No attempt was made to remedy any of these defects. Finally, Abriani sued to recover the down payment made on the mobile home.   FACTS

Has Abriani effectively rejected the mobile home, so that he is entitled to a return of the down payment?   ISSUE

Yes. Abriani made a valid rejection. The seller's threats to withhold the down payment were not justified under law. Rejection of the mobile home was valid under UCC 2-601, the perfect tender rule. The court found substantial defects in the home and variances from the contract terms that would amount to imperfect tender. Although the seller had the right to cure minor defects after proper notice, the evidence demonstrated that no such response was forthcoming within the contemplated time of performance or at any time.   DECISION

Duties after Rejection

Once a buyer has given notice of rejection within a reasonable time, he or she must take care not to give the appearance of exercising ownership over the goods. If the goods are in the possession of a buyer who is not a merchant, his or her only duty is to hold them after reasonable care for a long enough time for the seller to take possession.

If the buyer is a merchant, his or her duties with respect to rejected goods are set out in Section 2-603. In general, the buyer must follow any reasonable instructions from the seller with respect to the goods.

In the absence of such instructions, the merchant-buyer must make reasonable efforts to resell the goods for the seller if they are perishable or may quickly decline in value. The buyer is entitled to reimbursement from the seller for expenses incurred in caring for or selling the goods.

A buyer in possession or control of nonperishable goods or goods that do not decline quickly in value has several options if the seller fails to give instructions within a reasonable time after learning of the buyer's rejection. At the seller's expense, the buyer may:

1. store the goods

2. reship them to the seller or

3. resell the goods (Section 2-604).

REVOCATION

As we noted in the section on rejection, once a buyer has accepted goods, he or she has lost the right to *reject* them. However, the buyer still may in certain circumstances *revoke* his or her acceptance and compel the buyer to take the goods back.

A buyer cannot revoke unless he or she meets one of three conditions (Section 2-608):

1. The buyer knew of the defect but accepted because he or she reasonably believed the nonconformity would be corrected, and it was not seasonably cured

2. The buyer did not discover the defect before accepting, because the defect was difficult to discover

3. The buyer did not discover the defect before accepting, because the seller assured the buyer that there were no defects.

If any of these three conditions applies, and the nonconformity substantially impairs the value of the goods to the buyer, the buyer may revoke the acceptance. Revocation is available only under these circumstances.

Reasonable Time

For the revocation of acceptance to be effective, it must occur within a reasonable time after the buyer discovers or should have discovered the grounds for revocation.

The buyer must act within a reasonable time to give the seller a chance to cure or make good. A revocation of acceptance is not effective until the buyer notifies the seller of the defect.

Substantial Change

The revocation must occur before there is any substantial change in the condition of the goods beyond that caused by the initial defects. If the buyer does something to the goods to change them from their original condition and cannot restore them to their original condition, an acceptance cannot be revoked. But if the condition of the materials (perishables, for instance) changed because of their own defects, the buyer may revoke an acceptance.

Suppose that Mrs. Smith purchased a trailer home from the Lemon Corporation. When she received the trailer on February 15, she inspected it. The carpet in the trailer was missing. When she inquired about the missing carpet, the seller told her he would see that she received a carpet at once. Mrs. Smith moved into the trailer. During the next six weeks, Mrs. Smith called the seller several times about the carpet, and each time the seller assured her that he would deliver it. On April 10, she sent a letter to the seller revoking her acceptance because of the failure to supply the carpet. She locked the trailer, turned the keys over to Lemon, and moved out on April 10. Mrs. Smith's revocation is effective. She accepted the trailer only because the seller assured her that the nonconformity (the absence of carpet) would be cured. It was not cured within a reasonable time, and the absence of the carpet substantially impaired the value of the trailer to her.

What if Mrs. Smith did not move out on April 10 but continued to occupy the trailer until December 1, at which time she attempted to revoke her acceptance? It is very likely that a court would refuse to let Mrs. Smith revoke because she failed to do so within a reasonable time.

Suppose that Mrs. Smith inspected the trailer on February 15, failed to detect any defects, and moved in on February 16. On February 17, she realized that a hat rack in the closet was missing. She then wanted to revoke her acceptance based on the theory that the defect was difficult to discover. In this case, Mrs. Smith may not revoke, because any nonconformity must substantially impair the value of the trailer to her. Although the absence of a hat rack might lessen the value of the trailer by a few dollars, it clearly fails to constitute a substantial impairment of value. Mrs. Smith would, however, have a right to sue the seller for the value of the hat rack.

Schumaker v. Ivers

Supreme Court of South Dakota
238 N.W.2d 284 (1976)

FACTS

On December 11, 1972, Mrs. Schumaker bought an organ from Ivers's store for $1,119.71. Within two weeks, one of the bass pedals failed to play. Soon a second bass pedal and two keys also stopped working. Schumaker promptly notified Ivers, who did not come to service the organ until March 13, 1973. Following this visit, the problems with the organ multiplied, and on May 11, 1973, Schumaker requested a refund of the purchase price. She agreed, however, to accept a replacement on condition that it operate satisfactorily. The rhythm system on this second organ malfunctioned shortly after Schumaker received it, and Ivers was unable to remedy the problem. On August 3, 1973, Schumaker sued for a rescission (cancellation) of the contract and the return of her purchase price.

ISSUE   Did Schumaker rightfully revoke her acceptance of the organ?

DECISION   Yes. Schumaker rightfully revoked her acceptance. Notice of her desire to revoke the acceptance was adequate. Even if her revocation of acceptance had been waived by her accepting delivery of the second organ, the waiver was based on the condition that the replacement organ operate satisfactorily, a condition that failed to materialize. Notice was equally prompt following the inoperability of the second organ.

INSTALLMENT CONTRACTS

The rule governing the buyer's rejection of nonconforming goods is different if the contract the parties have entered into is an installment contract. An installment contract requires or authorizes the delivery of goods in separate lots to be separately accepted (Section 2-612[1]).

If the parties enter into an installment contract, how may a nonconforming delivery affect one of the installments? In general, the standard applied when one of the parties breaches an installment contract is not so rigorous as the standard applied when there has been a breach of a contract requiring delivery to take place at one time (Sections 2-612[2] and [3]). The reason is that it would be unfair if a breach on an installment always could be used as grounds for canceling the entire contract.

Rejection of an Installment

In general, an installment delivery of nonconforming goods must be accepted if the nonconformity can be fixed and if the seller gives adequate assurance of doing so (Section 2-612, Comment 5). Thus a buyer may only reject a nonconforming installment if the nonconformity:

1. substantially impairs the value of that installment and cannot be cured, or

2. involves a defect in the required documents (such as a title).

These conditions differ from those governing an ordinary contract, in which goods may be rejected if they fail to conform in any respect.

Cancellation of Entire Contract

In certain circumstances, the nonconformity of one or more installments may be so great that the entire contract's value is impaired. If so, the entire contract may be canceled (Section 2-612).

ASSURANCE OF PERFORMANCE

Sometimes a party to a contract will not or cannot perform, and the other party to the contract is threatened with losing what was bargained for — performance. The seller who faces a buyer unable to pay or the buyer who questions whether the seller really will make good a delivery of nonconforming goods wants some guarantee that the obligations of the contract will be fulfilled. This guarantee is called **assurance of performance**.

An **aggrieved party** to a contract may require adequate assurance of performance from the other party (Section 2-609). What constitutes "adequate" assurance of due performance depends on the facts. If a seller of good repute gives a promise that a defective delivery will be straightened out, this promise normally is sufficient. But if an untrustworthy seller makes the same statement, the statement alone might not be enough.

When merchants have contracted, the question of the adequacy of any assurance offered is judged by commercial rather than legal standards. For example, if a reasonable merchant believes that a buyer will not pay, this belief is regarded as satisfactory grounds for insecurity.

The following case illustrates questions that can arise about assurances of performance.

> **Assurance of performance**
> legal promise that party will carry out a contract

> **Aggrieved party**
> one who is the victim of another's repudiation

AMF, Incorporated v. McDonald's Corporation

Seventh Circuit Court of Appeals
536 F.2d 1167 (1976)

McDonald's was interested in computerizing its fast food restaurants. It contracted with AMF to install a prototype computerized cash register in a McDonald's in Elk Grove, Illinois. Shortly thereafter, McDonald's ordered 16 additional systems. Problems then developed with the Elk Grove system, including lengthy breakdowns. McDonald's officials met with AMF to discuss the problems at Elk Grove and to discuss the fact that AMF was late in delivering the additional units. McDonald's representatives visited AMF's main plant and found that none of the systems was being assembled. When progress had not been made six weeks later, McDonald's notified AMF that the contract was canceled. AMF argued that demands for adequate assurance of performance must be made in writing.   **FACTS**

Can McDonald's cancel the contract?   **ISSUE**

Yes. McDonald's did have reasonable grounds to cancel. The prototype was not working, and it was clear from the visit to the AMF factory that AMF did not have the engineering talent to deal with the problems in the system. It was clear from AMF's internal memos that it knew that McDonald's was concerned about their ability to perform. Written notice is not a prerequisite for McDonald's to cancel when the other party is aware of all the facts.   **DECISION**

ANTICIPATORY REPUDIATION

Anticipatory repudiation notification, before the fact, of an intention not to perform

In addition to situations of uncertain ability or willingness to perform, parties to contracts may face a direct repudiation. If one of the parties has indicated that he or she will not perform at some date in the future — an **anticipatory repudiation** — must the other party wait until that date to see whether performance actually will take place?

Suppose that two people enter into a contract to be performed on August 1. If the seller says on June 1 that goods will not be delivered on August 1, what can the buyer do? (See the general discussion in Chapter 13 of anticipatory breach. Contracts for the sale of goods are covered by Sections 2-610 and 2-611 of the UCC.) If either party to the contract foreshadows nonperformance at some time in the future, and the failure to perform would substantially impair the value of the contract, the aggrieved party may:

1. simply wait a reasonable time for performance or

2. treat the contract as broken and seek any available remedy.

These provisions hold true even if the aggrieved party has urged the other to retract the repudiation. In any event, the aggrieved party's own performance may be suspended.

If the aggrieved party chooses the first option, the repudiating party may retract the repudiation unless the aggrieved party has canceled the contract, materially changed position, or indicated that the repudiation is considered final (Section 2-611). Although a retraction is possible by any method that clearly indicates to the aggrieved party that the repudiating party intends to perform, the repudiating party must give the aggrieved party whatever assurances of performance are demanded (consistent with Section 2-609).

What if two parties enter into a contract calling for delivery of goods on May 15, and on January 1 the seller tells the buyer that the goods will not be delivered as the contract specifies? The buyer may treat the contract as having been breached on January 1, get the goods elsewhere, and bring a suit for damages against the seller. The buyer need not wait until May 15 to see if the seller changes his or her mind. But the buyer also may wait a commercially reasonable time for the seller to perform. The question of what is a commercially reasonable time is discussed in the following case.

Whewell v. Dobson

Supreme Court of Iowa
227 N.W.2d 115 (1975)

FACTS   On September 4, 1970, Dobson contracted to purchase 400 Christmas trees from Whewell for $3.75 a tree. Payment was due upon delivery on or about December 1, 1970. Whewell then ordered the trees from a Michigan firm for $3.25 a tree. Near the end of September, Whewell received Dobson's copy of the tree order with the word "cancel" written across its face. On October 2, Whewell received a letter from Dobson repeating his intent to cancel the order. Whewell was unable to cancel his order with the Michigan firm and thus received the trees. Between October 30 and November 6,

Whewell and Dobson exchanged communications that confirmed Dobson's refusal to accept delivery. Whewell then attempted to find other buyers for the trees. Ultimately, Whewell was able to dispose of 124 of the trees at $3 a tree, but he incurred additional expenses of $85 in the process. Dobson's defense to Whewell's suit for damages was based on the Official Comment to UCC 2-610, which states, "If the aggrieved party awaits performance beyond a commercially reasonable time he cannot recover resulting damages which he should have avoided."

In view of the rapid rate at which cut Christmas trees decline in value, was Whewell's effort to resell the trees within a commercially reasonable time? **ISSUE**

Yes. Whewell's attempt to resell the trees was within a commercially reasonable time under the circumstances. This was so even though Dobson's repudiation became effective in September, at the time of the first "cancellation." Whewell thus satisfied his duty under the UCC. What is a "reasonable" time depends upon the nature of the goods, the condition of the market, and other circumstances of the case. Its length cannot be measured by any legal yardstick or divided into degrees. **DECISION**

IMPOSSIBILITY

Sometimes a party to a contract cannot perform because the goods identified to the contract have been destroyed. In this case, both parties may escape from the contract (Section 2-613). If the goods have been only partially destroyed or have deteriorated so as no longer to conform to the contract, the buyer has the option either to (1) treat the contract as void or (2) accept the goods with due allowance for the deterioration or the deficiency in quantity but without further right against the seller.

Goods Must Be Identified

For the rule on impossibility to apply, the goods must be identified when the contract is made. A seller who promises to deliver any 100 lawn mowers to the buyer cannot rely on the rule on impossibility. But a seller who specifies 100 lawn mowers from his or her plant, which then burns to the ground along with all the mowers, may rely on the defense of impossibility.

Impracticality

Sometimes performance is not impossible, but nonetheless is very difficult. The seller is excused from a timely delivery of goods when unforeseen circumstances make performance impractical (Section 2-615). The mere fact that costs go up does not excuse performance; that is the type of business risk assumed in signing a contract. But a severe shortage of raw materials or supplies because of a war, embargo, or unforeseen shutdown of major sources of supply, which causes the goods to be significantly more expensive or impossible to obtain, is the type of situation covered.

Part Performance

Partial perform-ance carrying out as much of the contract as is possible under the circumstances

When unforeseen circumstances make complete performance impossible, the seller must fulfill the contract to the extent possible (Section 2-615[b]). Such **partial performance** usually involves the allocation of production and deliveries among customers. This allocation must be fair and reasonable, and all affected buyers must be seasonably notified.

A buyer, upon receipt of notification of a delay or an allocation, may either terminate the contract or agree to take the available allocation (Section 2-616). The buyer must agree to this modification within a reasonable time, not to exceed 30 days, or the contract for any deliveries lapses.

SUMMARY

The seller's basic obligation is to deliver conforming goods in the manner specified by the contract. The buyer's basic obligation is to pay for the goods properly at the time and place of delivery.

The buyer has a right of reasonable inspection before paying unless the goods are shipped C.O.D. or delivery is made by documents of title. Acceptance of goods may occur by an express statement, by inaction, or by an act inconsistent with the seller's ownership. To reject the goods, the buyer must notify the seller of specific grounds for rejection within a reasonable time. Failure to reject effectively often results in an acceptance. After rejecting, the buyer must hold the goods for the seller, and a merchant buyer must follow reasonable instructions provided by the seller.

A buyer may revoke an acceptance when the buyer reasonably expected that the problem with the goods would be cured, or the defect was latent, or the seller assured the buyer that there were no defects. The revocation must be within a reasonable time, and the defect must substantially impair the value of the goods.

In an installment contract, a buyer may reject only when the nonconformity substantially impairs the value of the installment. This rule is an exception to the requirement of literal performance. The entire contract is canceled if the nonconformity of the installment impairs the value of the entire contract.

A party may repudiate a contract in advance of the duty to perform. The aggrieved party may wait and hope for performance, or instead may sue immediately for breach of contract. The UCC uses a test of commercial impracticality to determine when a contract is discharged because of some event not foreseen by the parties.

REVIEW PROBLEMS

1. What must a buyer do to effectively reject nonconforming goods under the UCC?

2. Describe the difference between rejection and revocation.

3. What test of impossibility is adopted by the UCC?

4. When must the buyer pay for the goods if the contract is silent concerning the time, place, and method of payment?

5. Pace ordered a large quantity of lumber from Sagebrush. On delivery, it was discovered that there were two truckloads of materials that had not been ordered. Pace allowed them to be unloaded without objection but wrote "not ordered" on his copy of the invoice. Pace then attempted to correct the situation but was unable to contact Sagebrush. The nonordered lumber items were then placed in Pace's inventory, offered for sale to the public, and a portion was sold. Pace also made a part payment on the order and made no attempt to return the unordered lumber. Did Pace accept the unordered lumber?

6. Fablok purchased ten knitting machines of a certain type from Cocker, the sole domestic manufacturer of these machines. Shortly after delivery of the first two machines, Fablok notified Cocker of defects in the machines. Cocker assured Fablok that the defects were correctable, and Cocker tried to correct the defects for about two years. Cocker failed to correct the defects. Fablok then notified Cocker of its revocation of acceptance. Was Fablock's revocation of acceptance made within a reasonable time?

7. White contracted with Continental for 20 carloads of plywood to be delivered in separate lots. Upon receipt of the first carload, White determined that it did not meet the contract specifications. White decided to cancel the contract. White then notified Continental. In the meantime, however, Continental had shipped another carload under the contract. Upon arrival of the second car, both parties agreed to an inspection according the a U.S. government standard, per the original contract, which provides that a 5 percent variance from the specifications is too great. The second carload, however, was within the allowed variance. White paid for the first carload, but refused to pay for any others. Continental then sued for breach of contract. May White cancel the entire contract?

8. Davis bought a mobile home from Colonial Mobile Homes. Davis paid cash. Upon delivery, Davis noticed that one tire was flat and was told by Colonial's employee that the driver had pulled it to the site on the flat tire "all the way" from the plant where it had been manufactured. Davis had to wait three weeks to inspect the interior, because no keys were delivered with the mobile home. Upon inspection, severe problems were discovered. The cabinets were out of line, the doors and windows would not shut, it leaked when it rained, the floors were buckled, and there were other defects. None of these defects was visible on inspection when Davis purchased the mobile home. After living in the home for three months, Davis moved out. Prior to his vacating, his attorney sent a letter to Colonial demanding replacement or refund. Davis had attempted to make repairs before the lawsuit was filed. Did Davis's payment in cash for the mobile home impair his right of inspection upon delivery?

9. Mrs. Kelly's father bought a color television set. When the set was turned on shortly after delivery, the picture was marred by a reddish tinge. The seller's service representative, who came to examine the set four days after delivery, told Mrs. Kelly that he would have to take the chassis back to the shop for further

inspection. Mrs. Kelly refused to allow the repairman to take the chassis, insisting that the seller supply a new set instead. Mrs. Kelly later demanded that the purchase price be refunded. The seller refused but again offered to make any necessary adjustments or repairs and to replace the set if such work proved unsuccessful. Mrs. Kelly's father sued for the purchase price. What result?

10. Fairchild, who owned a refuse hauling business, needed to replace an engine in one of his trucks. He bought an engine from National. The engine delivered by National was not of the type requested by Fairchild and was not suitable for Fairchild's truck. Fairchild so informed National's president, who told Fairchild that his money would be refunded when he returned the engine. Fairchild then repaired the original engine, which he had intended to replace with the National engine. About two months later, Fairchild's father returned the engine to National. National refused to refund Fairchild's money but instead offered Fairchild credit toward the purchase of other National products. Fairchild sued to have his money refunded. National argued that, even though the engine was properly rejected for nonconformance, the UCC gave National the right to attempt to make good, which it tried to do by offering credit. What result?

11. United Air Lines ordered a flight simulator from Conductron Corporation. The contract provided that the simulator would not be accepted by United unless and until it met the specifications of United and the Federal Aviation Administration (FAA). The contract provided that title to the simulator would nonetheless pass to United upon delivery. Because of delays in the completion of the simulator, the parties modified the contract to provide for testing of the simulator at United's flight training center rather than at Conductron's plant. Before the simulator was delivered to United, United employees notified Conductron of over 600 deficiencies in the device. The modified contract entitled United to cancel the agreement if all of the deficiencies were not corrected by November 1, 1969. Conductron subsequently delivered the simulator, which United used for training purposes. United could not use the machine formally as an aircraft flight simulator because it had not yet been approved by the FAA. On April 18, 1969, after the simulator had been tested for ten hours by United test pilots, it was destroyed by a fire of unknown origin. United sued Conductron for breach of contract, claiming that Conductron had failed to deliver an acceptable simulator by the agreed upon date. Conductron claimed that United had accepted the simulator through its use and possession of it and thus had waived its right to object to the nonconformities it had noted before delivery. What result? (See UCC Sections 2-606 and 1-102.)

12. In February 1980, Wickliffe Farms signed a contract with Owensboro Grain Company by which it agreed to deliver 35,000 bushels of white corn to Owensboro between December 15, 1980, and January 31, 1981. The contract said nothing about where the corn was to be grown, although there was evidence that the parties expected Wickliffe to grow the corn on its own farmland. A severe drought made it impossible for Wickliffe to grow and deliver the full 35,000 bushels. If Owensboro were to sue Wickliffe for damages resulting from the failure to deliver the full 35,000 bushels, should Wickliffe be able to raise the defense of impracticality (Section 2-615)?

13. Gallin, who owned an electronics components business, bought several mate-

rials from Surplus Electronics Corporation between July and September 1977. Surplus guaranteed the usability of its products and provided that unacceptable items could be returned for full refund. Gallin had not paid for any of the purchases by January 1978, and Surplus sued for the adjusted purchase price of $6,170. Gallin admitted to owing $2,656 but claimed that he was in the process of testing the balance of the components for usability and would, when he was finished, return the unacceptable goods in one shipment. This testing process had apparently not been completed when the trial commenced in April 1980. What result?

14. Max Bauer was under contract to supply frozen pork roasts to the military. The parties had agreed to the following inspection procedure: military officials would examine 20 roasts from each day's lot, and if more than three contained more than ¼ inch of surface fat, the lot was unacceptable. Bauer would have the right to rework and obtain reinspection for any lot deemed unacceptable. As a practical matter, however, it was impossible to rework or inspect pork roasts once they had been frozen. Bauer's usual practice was to ship one truckload of the daily lot to a freezer storage company around noon and a second truckload around 6 P.M. A single daily military inspection, as agreed to by Bauer, occurred at the freezer storage company shortly after the second truckload arrived. During one such inspection, seven roasts were found to have unacceptable levels of surface fat. The inspecting officer recommended rejection of the lot when he concluded his inspection at 7:30 P.M. At that time, the roasts delivered at noon were frozen and could thus not be reworked or inspected; the roasts delivered at 6 P.M., however, had not yet frozen. The inspecting officer did not receive authority from his superiors to reject the entire lot until after 10 P.M. By that time, all of the roasts were frozen. Bauer sued the U.S. government for losses resulting from the military's rejection of the lot. Did the military properly reject the lot (under UCC Section 2-602)? Should the noon shipment and the evening shipment be considered separately?

CHAPTER 18

Sales Law: Remedies

CHAPTER OBJECTIVES

REMEDIES

Statute of Limitations

SELLER'S REMEDIES

Cancel the Contract / Withhold Delivery of Goods / Demand Return of Goods in Buyer's Possession / Resell the Goods / Recover the Price of the Goods / Recover Damages

BUYER'S REMEDIES

Cancel the Contract / Cover / Obtain Specific Performance / Resell the Goods / Recover Damages

LIMITATION OR ALTERATION OF REMEDIES

SUMMARY

REVIEW PROBLEMS

CHAPTER OBJECTIVES

After reading this chapter, you should be able to:

1. Explain how the statute of limitations affects breach of contract cases.

2. Identify the basic remedies available to a seller when a buyer breaches a sales contract and how sellers choose among alternative remedies.

3. Explain how a seller may deal with an insolvent buyer.

4. Explain how damages are calculated when a sales contract has been breached.

5. Identify the basic remedies available to a buyer when a seller breaches a sales contract and how buyers choose among available remedies.

6. Identify the UCC rules on contract terms that try to limit or alter remedies.

REMEDIES

The preceding chapter dealt with the obligations of the parties to a contract for the sale of goods. This chapter focuses on what happens when either seller or buyer fails to live up to those obligations. In these situations, the victims often have more than one form of relief available. Some of the remedies are mutually exclusive, and others involve limiting factors such as a specific number of days within which people must act. When a breach of an important sales transaction occurs, it is important that the victim immediately contact a lawyer to insure that the right to seek a remedy is not inadvertently lost.

Statute of Limitations

A person who wants to bring an action for breach of a sales contract must do so within four years after the action has occurred — unless the parties have agreed to a shorter period of time. But they may not agree to reduce the **statute of limitations** to less than one year. A party to a contract who fails to bring suit within the time stipulated in the agreement (or, if no time is specified, within four years) is barred from ever bringing suit by the statute of limitations even though the claim is otherwise perfectly valid. Ordinarily the four years start to run from the date the breach of contract occurs, whether the victim knows of the breach or not.

Breach of Warranty   The time limit for a breach of **warranty** begins to run when delivery is made, except when the warranty extends to the future performance of

Statute of limitations
statutes establishing time within which legal action must be begun

Warranty
guarantee that a product is free from certain defects

goods. In that case, the time limit runs from the time the breach is or should have been discovered.

If, for instance, Sam purchases an air conditioner that is warranted for three years, the three years begins to run from the date when Sam discovers or should have discovered the breach. If he tries the air conditioner on May 1 and learns of the breach, the statute of limitations begins to run on that date. But if he fails to turn it on all summer, the statute begins to run sometime at the beginning of the summer — the date when he should have discovered the breach of warranty. If Sam never turns on the air conditioner and so never learns of the breach, the time period starts to run anyway on the date he should have discovered it. This rule encourages purchasers to be diligent in discovering defects in items they buy.

Diligence in reporting defects is important, because it lets the seller try to remedy the defect and helps to minimize the buyer's damages.

SELLER'S REMEDIES

If the buyer wrongfully rejects goods, improperly revokes his or her acceptance, fails to make a payment due, or repudiates part or all of the contract, the aggrieved seller has a number of remedies. The UCC (Section 1-106[1]) states:

> The remedies provided by this Act shall be liberally administered to the end that the aggrieved party may be put in as good a position as if the other party had fully performed.

The purpose of the remedies is not to punish the wrongdoer but simply to make whole the victim, to put the victim in the position he or she would have been in had the contract been performed.

The UCC (Section 2-703) provides the aggrieved seller with a number of possible remedies:

1. cancel the contract

2. withhold delivery of goods

3. demand return of goods in buyer's possession

4. resell the goods

5. recover the price of the goods

6. recover damages

Remember that these remedies are not necessarily mutually exclusive. In some situations, an aggrieved seller has only one available remedy. In other situations, a combination of remedies applies. We turn now to these remedies.

Cancel the Contract

When a seller becomes the victim of a buyer's breach of contract, the simplest and most obvious remedy is to cancel the contract. This remedy is easily applied to an executory contract, one in which neither of the parties has begun performance (see Chapter 5). But if the seller already has begun performing the duties called for under the contract, simply canceling the contract may not be enough to restore the seller to his or her position before performance began. In such a case, the seller must apply one or more of the other remedies.

Withhold Delivery of Goods

If a buyer becomes **insolvent**, the seller's ability to collect damages is impaired. A judgment against a buyer with no money is of little practical value to a seller. For this reason, the UCC provides special remedies for situations in which a buyer is insolvent (Section 2-702).

Insolvent the financial condition of a person or business that cannot pay its debts as they become due

The seller who discovers that a buyer has become insolvent may refuse to deliver the goods except for cash. If the buyer owes the seller for goods already delivered, the seller also may demand payment for those goods before making any further deliveries. The mere fact that the seller withholds delivery of goods does not mean that he or she cannot later go after any other remedy available for damages.

Goods Held by Carrier or Bailee   If goods already have been delivered to a carrier or other bailee (see Chapter 16) when the buyer's insolvency is discovered, the seller may wish to stop delivery. The seller can stop delivery until the buyer has received the goods, until the documents of title have been negotiated to the buyer, or until the carrier or other bailee gives notice that the goods are being held for the buyer. The seller must give enough notice to allow a reasonably diligent bailee to stop delivery. If the notice does arrive in time, the bailee must hold and deliver the goods according to the seller's directions.

In Re Murdock Machine & Engineering Company of Utah

Tenth Circuit Court of Appeals
620 F.2d 767 (1980)

Ramco Steel sold steel on credit to Murdock, delivery F.O.B. Buffalo, the place of shipment. After the steel was shipped from Buffalo, Ramco learned that Murdock was insolvent and Ramco stopped delivery of the steel. Murdock had purchased the steel pursuant to a contract with the United States government, which provided that "immediately upon the date of this contract, title to all . . . materials acquired . . . by [Murdock] and properly chargeable to this contract . . . shall forthwith vest in the government." The United States argued that its claim on the goods through the title clause of its contract with Murdock was superior to Ramco's claim.

FACTS

Can Ramco stop delivery of the steel when the buyer's contract provides that the government obtains title immediately?

ISSUE

DECISION   Yes. The case is governed by state law. The UCC provides that the seller's right to stop goods in transit (Section 2-702[1]) is not limited by a right to title or by the rights of good faith purchasers. Whenever a buyer becomes insolvent, the seller may stop the delivery of goods, regardless of the rights of any third party to the transaction.

Delivery by carrier also may be stopped for reasons other than insolvency — for instance, breach of contract. But in this case, the size of the shipment must be relatively large (a carload or more). This provision was adopted because it is a burden on carriers to stop delivery.

Demand Return of Goods in Buyer's Possession

What happens when a buyer has received the goods but has not yet paid for them? If the buyer received the goods on credit while insolvent, the seller is entitled to the goods if a demand is made for their return within ten days (Section 2-702[2]).

But for an insolvent buyer to receive goods on credit amounts to fraud — a misrepresentation of solvency by the buyer. If the buyer misrepresented his or her solvency to the seller in writing within three months of the time the buyer received the goods, the ten-day rule does not apply. In that event, the seller may claim actual fraud by the buyer and reclaim the goods.

Resell the Goods

The UCC considers the seller's principal remedy as resale. When a buyer has rejected goods wrongfully, revoked an acceptance improperly, failed to make a payment, or repudiated all or part of a contract, the seller may resell the goods in question. If the resale fails to cover the contract price of the goods plus expenses, the seller is entitled to the difference in price, plus expenses of reselling, less expenses saved.

To assure that the resale takes place fairly, the UCC (Section 2-706) sets standards for how it is to be conducted. Of course, the parties may agree between themselves on details, but the method of resale still must be fair. In the absence of such an agreement, the resale may be public or private, as long as every aspect of the sale is commercially reasonable and as long as the buyer is notified.

The aggrieved seller also has certain rights to unfinished goods. When the buyer breaches the contract, the seller can associate with the buyer any completed conforming goods and may either: (1) stop work on unfinished goods and sell them for their scrap or salvage values, or (2) using reasonable commercial judgment, complete the unfinished goods and identify them to the contract (Section 2-704). The seller has this option to minimize the buyer's damages. If the seller chooses to complete finished goods, the burden is on the buyer to show that it was unreasonable for the seller to do so. The seller then may proceed to resell (Section 2-706) or, if resale is not practical, sue for the price (Section 2-709).

Recover the Price of the Goods

Because the seller is in the business of selling goods, it is customary for the seller to resell goods to minimize losses from the buyer's breach. But the seller may recover the price of the goods from the buyer under certain circumstances: when resale is impractical, when the buyer has accepted the goods, or when the goods were destroyed or lost within a reasonable time after the risk of loss had passed to the buyer (Section 2-709).

The seller may try to recover the price of the goods only after a "reasonable effort to resell" them at a reasonable price. But the seller need not try to resell if it is not possible to sell them at a reasonable price. Suppose that a manufacturer custom designed a rolling steel door for a buyer. If the steel door does not fit any other building, the buyer is liable for the price of the door. In this case, reselling the goods would be impractical.

The UCC also lets the seller recover the price of the goods if the buyer has already accepted them. Whether a buyer has accepted does not depend on the passage of title or on the date set for payment. Acceptance takes place if one of the events listed in Section 2-606 occurs (see Chapter 17). Suppose that the seller delivers goods to the buyer, and the buyer states that he or she will take them. The buyer's statement constitutes an acceptance and creates liability for the price (Section 2-709).

Likewise, if goods are lost or damaged within a commercially reasonable time after the risk of loss has passed to the buyer, the buyer is liable for the price. A seller who ships goods "F.O.B. seller's plant" need only deliver the goods to the carrier. Once the goods are in the possession of the carrier, the risk of loss passes to the buyer. If the goods are destroyed while in the possession of the carrier, the buyer is liable for the price of the goods.

Recover Damages

Sometimes the remedies described above do not do enough to return an aggrieved seller to the same position as if the buyer had not breached the contract. In these circumstances, the seller is entitled to some form of damages.

Generally, if the seller resells the goods in good faith and in a commercially reasonable manner, he or she may recover the difference between the resale price and the contract price together with any incidental damages, but minus any expenses saved as a result of the buyer's breach (Section 2-706[1]).

Incidental Damages   The UCC (Section 2-710) states that **incidental damages** to the seller include:

> any commercially reasonable charges, expenses or commissions incurred in stopping delivery, in the transportation, care and custody of the goods after the buyer's breach, in connection with return or resale of the goods or otherwise resulting from the breach.

Incidental damages expenses resulting from handling of goods made necessary by other party's breach

These are the typical expenses for sellers. But the UCC allows a seller to recover all commercially reasonable expenses.

For instance, if a seller incurs $29.50 in expenses by reselling goods, that amount

Market price
cost of a good at a
particular place and
time

can be charged to the buyer or added to any loss brought about by differences in **market price** or profit.

Market Price   The UCC (Section 2-708[1]) states that the seller's damages for nonacceptance or repudiation by the buyer are the

> difference between the market price at the time and place for tender and the unpaid contract price.

In addition, the seller may recover for incidental damages but must deduct any expenses saved as a result of the buyer's breach. A seller might use this rule to keep goods that a buyer had refused to accept. It is not mandatory that a seller resell goods to establish damages although, as we have noted, most sellers try to do so.

The market price is measured at the time and place the goods are due. To take a straightforward case, if the buyer agreed by contract to pick up goods at the seller's place of business on June 15, and the buyer does not meet the terms of the contract, the seller may collect the difference between the contract price and the market price for the goods in the town of the seller's business. If the buyer agreed to pay $1,000 for the goods, and they are now selling for $800 in the seller's town, the seller collects $1,000 minus $800, or $200, plus incidental damages and minus any expenses saved.

Profit   In the event that the market price measure of damages is inadequate to put the seller in as good a position as performance would have done, the seller may collect the profit (including overhead) that would have been made had the contract been performed, plus any incidental damages.

Take, for example, the lost-volume seller. Suppose that a retailer agrees to sell a couch for $500 to Mrs. Jones. If Mrs. Jones breaches the contract, the retailer is entitled to the difference between the contract price ($500) and the market price ($500). This solution leaves the retailer with no damages as long as all the couches in stock can be sold. But what if the supply of couches exceeds the demand? In that case, because Mrs. Jones breached the contract, the seller sells one less couch. In this situation, the seller may recover the profit (including overhead) that he or she would have made on the Jones contract.

The following case illustrates some of the questions a court must consider in applying seller's remedies.

Wolpert v. Foster

Supreme Court of Minnesota
254 N.W.2d 348 (1977)

FACTS   Wolpert owned a firm that sold fishing equipment. Foster owned Strike Master, Inc., a firm that made and sold fishing tackle and ice fishing equipment. Foster had trouble getting supplies, and Wolpert agreed to buy merchandise for Foster at a 10 percent markup. Foster had trouble paying, and Wolpert extended credit until Foster owed $55,000. Shortly thereafter Foster ended the agreement and did not pay what he owed. Wolpert resold as much of the merchandise as he could and sued for the contract price for the rest. The resale did not meet the requirements of UCC 2-706, which provides the seller's basic remedy for resale.

Is Wolpert entitled to the contract price for the goods he couldn't resell?   ISSUE

Yes. Wolpert is entitled to the contract price. Wolpert was exercising his rights   DECISION
under UCC 2-709, which allows a suit for the price of goods if they cannot be resold through a reasonable effort. The requirements of UCC 2-706 do not apply, because this section deals only with the *resale* of goods. Wolpert is not seeking to recover damages on the goods that he did sell and has acted reasonably under the circumstances.

BUYER'S REMEDIES

Of course, sometimes a seller does not honor a contract, and the buyer needs legal help to avoid loss. When a seller fails to make delivery, or repudiates the contract, or when the buyer rightfully rejects or revokes an acceptance, the UCC provides the buyer with several remedies:

1. cancel the contract

2. cover

3. obtain specific performance

4. resell the goods

5. recover damages

We will discuss each of these in turn.

Cancel the Contract

The simplest recourse for the wronged buyer is to cancel the contract. Cancellation often must include recovering any money already paid to the seller. But as with seller's remedies, merely canceling the contract often is not enough to place the buyer in a fair position. Then the buyer must seek other remedies. Cancellation may not be available to a buyer in certain circumstances, as the following case demonstrates.

Plateq Corporation v. Machlett Laboratories

Supreme Court of Connecticut
456 A.2d 786 (1983)

Machlett ordered two lead-covered steel tanks to be specially built by Plateq. The   FACTS
tanks were to be radiation proof, according to federal standards. Plateq had trouble

building the tanks and was late in performing. When the tanks were finished, Machlett's engineer inspected them, noted some deficiencies, asked that they be corrected, and indicated that a truck would be sent to pick the tanks up. Instead, Machlett later sent a telegram stating "This order is hereby terminated for your breach. . . . We will hold you liable for all damages incurred by Machlett including excess cost of reprocurement." Plateq sued for wrongful cancellation.

ISSUE   Was Machlett entitled to cancel the contract?

DECISION   No. Machlett inspected the tanks when Plateq indicated they were finished and accepted by stating they would pick up the tanks. Machlett could not simply cancel the contract, but instead would have to show grounds for revoking its acceptance, which it was unable to do.

Cover

Cover obtain goods to substitute for those not delivered

The remedy most buyers use is to **cover.** Covering involves buying goods to substitute for those the seller has been unable or unwilling to deliver.

When a seller fails to make a delivery, the buyer is left without material needed to conduct business. To remedy this situation, the UCC allows the buyer to purchase goods in substitution for those covered in the contract (Section 2-712). If the buyer acts in good faith and without unreasonable delay, he or she may establish damages as the difference between the cost of cover and the contract price.

The court does not second guess a buyer about the reasonableness of actions. It merely examines whether the buyer's actions were reasonable for the time and place. If it later turns out that a cheaper or more effective means of cover had been available, the conclusion is not necessarily that the buyer acted unreasonably, as demonstrated in the following case.

_____ *Laredo Hides Company, Incorporated v. H&H Meat Products, Incorporated* _____

Court of Civil Appeals of Texas
513 S.W.2d 210 (1977)

FACTS   H&H is a meat processing company that sells cattle hides as a byproduct of its business. Laredo Hides buys hides and ships them to tanneries. The two parties contracted for Laredo to buy all of H&H's hides for the rest of 1972. The contract set a price of $9.75 per hide. The market price of hides rose steadily the rest of the year. In April, H&H wrongfully tried to cancel the contract as a result of a dispute over the payment for a single shipment of hides. Thereafter, H&H refused to sell to Laredo, and Laredo had to buy hides from other sources at prices ranging up to $33 per hide. Laredo sued for breach of contract. Laredo introduced evidence that it had paid $142,254 over the contract price in buying the substitute hides from other sources and had incurred transportation costs of $1,435 and handling costs of $2,013 in making the alternate purchases.

Can Laredo recover the full cover price when it paid over three times the contract price for some of the purchases?

ISSUE

Yes. The court ruled in favor of Laredo. Although H&H argued that the cover price was too high, H&H did not offer proof to show that the cover was not reasonable. H&H's argument that Laredo should have bought all the hides at once when it saw that the price was going up was incorrect because Laredo did not have facilities to store the hides. The presumption is that Laredo acted reasonably on the basis of the information presented. Laredo is entitled to the increased cost of cover plus the transportation and handling charges less any expenses saved because of the breach by H&H.

DECISION

Obtain Specific Performance

Specific performance judicially compelled fulfillment of exact terms of contract

The buyer who cannot cover with substitute goods may want to get the goods that were part of the breached contract. The UCC (Section 2-716) gives the buyer the right to **specific performance** and **replevin** in certain circumstances. The buyer may obtain specific performance of the contract when "the goods are unique or in other proper circumstances." What is "unique" depends on the circumstances. In any event, if a buyer cannot cover, it is good evidence of other proper circumstances that merit specific performance of the contract.

Replevin legal process of obtaining property that is in another's hands

Resell the Goods

In some circumstances, a buyer does not learn of a seller's breach until after goods have been delivered. If the buyer rightfully rejects goods or revokes their acceptance, the buyer gets a security interest (see Chapter 15) in the goods that he or she possesses or controls (2-711[3]). The buyer may hold and resell these goods if a part of the price has been paid or if expenses have been incurred for the inspection, receipt, transportation, care, and custody of the goods. The buyer who resells must comply with Section 2-706 and must forward the balance of the amount received (beyond what was paid on the goods and expenses) to the seller.

Recover Damages

As we saw in the case of cover, if the seller has failed to deliver goods in accordance with a contract or has repudiated the contract, a buyer may establish damages by purchasing substitute goods. But a buyer need not cover to establish damages. Instead the buyer may choose to recover damages (under Section 2-713), even if other goods have been bought. The buyer has no duty to use the price of the goods bought in establishing damages and, in fact, may not want to do so if a better deal came of buying the goods than the original contract allowed for.

Ordinarily, the dollar amount of the damages owed the buyer is determined by an assessment of one or more of the following: incidental damages, consequential damages, market price, and value as warranted. We discuss each of these below.

Incidental Damages   Incidental damages include, but are not limited to, "expenses reasonably incurred in inspection, receipt, transportation and care and custody of goods rightfully rejected, any commercially reasonable charges, expenses or commissions in connection with effecting cover and any other reasonable expense incident to the delay or other breach" (Section 2-715[1]).

Consequential damages losses that are an indirect result of a contract breach

Consequential Damages   **Consequential damages** do not flow directly from the seller's breach of the contract (as do incidental damages). Instead they are an indirect result of the breach. For instance, if the buyer is forced to breach a different contract because he or she expected to get the materials necessary to perform it from the seller, damages accruing from the loss of the second contract may be assessible against the seller.

Consequential damages include all losses to the buyer that the seller had reason to know of at the time of contracting and that could not reasonably have been prevented by cover or otherwise. It is not necessary that the buyer establish damages with mathematical precision, but the buyer does bear the burden of proving the loss. Proof is harder to establish than with incidental damages, because the loss is indirect.

Market Price   As we have seen, the measure of damages is the difference between the market price at the time the buyer learned of the breach and the contract price. The buyer also can collect any incidental and consequential damages incurred, but must credit the seller with any expenses saved as a result of the seller's breach.

The market price will be determined by examining the current market price (when the buyer learned of the breach) at the place for tender or, if the buyer rejected the goods after they arrived or revoked acceptance, by examining the current market price (when the buyer learned of the breach) at the place of arrival. Thus the UCC (Section 2-713) uses as a guideline the market in which the buyer would have gotten cover had he or she attempted to do so.

If the seller was to have tendered goods to the buyer in Los Angeles, the market price to be used would be the prevailing price in the Los Angeles market at the time the buyer learned of the breach. If the buyer had attempted to cover, presumably this would have been the price he or she would have paid.

Value as Warranted   When the buyer has accepted goods and the time for revocation has passed, he or she still is entitled to damages if the seller fails to perform properly (according to 2-714[2]). The buyer's damages are the difference between the value of the goods accepted and the value they would have had if they had been as warranted. The buyer may also credit incidental and consequential damages. For example, if the purchaser of an automobile determines that the car has a defective horn, a court might award him as damages the cost of repairing or replacing the defective horn.

The following case illustrates some of the questions that can arise in assessing damages in a suit for breach of warranty.

Chatlos Systems v. National Cash Register Corporation
Third Circuit Court of Appeals
670 F.2d 1304 (1982)

Chatlos ordered a computer system that was to be able to perform designated tasks from National Cash Register (NCR). NCR provided a warranted NCR 399/656 computer system for $46,020. The system did not perform as expected and Chatlos sued NCR for breach of warranty. An expert witness testified that a computer system capable of doing what Chatlos required would be worth much more than the contract price. **FACTS**

Can the damages in a breach of warranty case exceed the contract price? **ISSUE**

Yes. The plaintiff is entitled to the benefit of the bargain in a suit for a breach of warranty. The award should be based on the value of the system had it been capable of performing as warranted. The court found that value to be $207,826, subtracted $6,000 for the value of the hardware that Chatlos retained, and awarded damages of $201,826. **DECISION**

LIMITATION OR ALTERATION OF REMEDIES

The UCC does not require parties to a contract to follow these rules on remedies. The parties to a contract are free to shape their own remedies. They may add remedies not covered in the UCC, or they may choose to substitute different remedies for those provided in Article 2. If the parties to a contract wish to specify that one particular remedy must be used exclusively, the contract must clearly indicate that that remedy is the exclusive remedy available to the aggrieved party.

Damages recoverable under Article 2 also may be limited or altered. Rather than leave the determination of damages to the court, the parties may agree in advance what the measure of damages will be in the event that one of the parties to the contract breaches. When damages have been specified in the contract, they are referred to as **liquidated damages.**

A court enforces the amount of liquidated damages only if it is reasonable in light of all the circumstances. If it is unreasonably large, it is void as a penalty. This leaves the court free to award damages as seem appropriate under the circumstances (Section 2-718). Thus, if the buyer would normally sustain $500 a day in damages in the event the seller fails to deliver on time, a provision awarding the buyer $10,000 a day for every day the seller is late in delivering the goods would be void as a penalty.

Likewise, attempts to fix other types of remedies in advance may be scrutinized by the courts. All attempts to modify and especially to eliminate the remedies provided under Article 2 are subject to the test of unconscionability — the quality of shocking the conscience (Section 2-302). Some minimum remedy must be available to an

Liquidated damages those which are specified in a contract

aggrieved party. If the remedy provisions in a contract are found to be unconscionable or to deprive either party of a substantial value of the bargain, the court may strike them and apply the remedies found in Article 2.

Prima facie
determined to be
so without more
information needed

The UCC (Section 2-719[3]) permits consequential damages to be limited or excluded unless such an exclusion would be unconscionable. But when consumer goods are involved, a limitation of consequential damages for injury to a person is *prima facie* unconscionable. Limitations of damages in cases of commercial loss are judged individually.

The following case raises some of these questions.

Equitable Lumber Corporation v. IPA Land Development Corporation

New York Court of Appeals
344 N.E.2d 391 (1976)

FACTS   Equitable Lumber contracted to supply IPA with lumber and building materials required for several construction projects. The written contract provided as follows:

> If the buyer breaches . . . the buyer agrees to pay, in addition to all of Seller's expenses, a reasonable counsel fee; and in the event the matter turned over is the collection of monies, such reasonable counsel fee is hereby agreed to be THIRTY (30%) PERCENT.

IPA took delivery of lumber and materials that it used and then refused to pay.

ISSUE   Under what circumstances, if any, would the liquidated damages provision be enforceable by Equitable?

DECISION   The clause is enforceable if it is reasonable with respect to the harm that the parties anticipate at the time of contracting or with the actual harm sustained. On these facts, the test would be whether attorneys generally would be expected to charge 30 percent for work of this sort or whether the actual arrangement here between Equitable and its attorney was for that amount and was not a disproportionate fee for such services.

SUMMARY

Unless the parties otherwise agree, the statute of limitations for the breach of a sales contract under the UCC is four years. The seller's possible options when the buyer breaches a contract for the sale of goods include: canceling the contract; withholding delivery of goods; demanding return of goods; reselling goods; or suing for damages or the price of the goods. The principal remedy is resale, with the seller recovering from the buyer the difference between the contract price and the resale price, plus the expenses of resale, less costs saved. The seller may recover the full contract price when resale is impractical, when the buyer has accepted the goods, or when the goods have been destroyed or lost after risk of loss has passed to the buyer.

The buyer's possible options when the seller has breached the contract include the following: canceling the contract; covering by buying comparable goods elsewhere; suing for specific performance of the contract; reselling goods in the buyer's possession; and suing for damages. The primary remedy is cover, whereby the buyer acts reasonably to purchase comparable goods elsewhere and then recovers from the seller the difference between the contract price and the cover price, plus any costs incurred in covering, less expenses saved. A buyer may recover consequential damages resulting from circumstances that the seller had reason to know of at the time of the contract and which the buyer could not reasonably prevent after the breach. A court enforces reasonable liquidated damages that are not punitive. The parties may limit or substitute remedies so long as they do not act unconscionably. Consequential damages cannot be limited for injury to a person.

_____ REVIEW PROBLEMS _____

1. What is considered the seller's principal remedy under the UCC?

2. What is cover, as used in the UCC?

3. How is market price determined in a suit for breach of contract under the UCC?

4. When is a buyer entitled to specific performance under the UCC?

5. Describe the difference between incidental and consequential damages.

6. Waites constructs certain cabinets to Thrift's order for use in a motel under construction. The cabinets are shipped to Thrift, who, upon receipt, notifies Waites that they cannot be used because of an error in the construction plans. Thrift wants to return them. Waites refuses to take them back but offers to find an outlet for them. After not hearing from Waites for many months, Thrift ships the cabinets back to Waites, without Waites's authority. Thrift has made no payments to Waites. Can Waites recover the price of the goods from Thrift?

7. Jimlar contracts to purchase certain boots and shoes from Armstrong to be resold by Jimlar. Armstrong does not deliver the boots and shoes. The purchase was particularly attractive to Jimlar, because the boots and shoes were offered at a price considerably below market. The market price allegedly is above the price at which Jimlar contracts to resell the boots and shoes. What damages may Jimlar recover?

8. Hirst buys a metal casket manufactured by Elgin, which is warranted in writing as being leakproof. Approximately three months after the burial of Hirst's father, the body is disinterred for a second autopsy. Upon opening, the casket is found to contain water. There is no evidence that the casket has been mistreated. Hirst sues for damages caused by mental suffering. May Hirst recover these damages from Elgin?

9. Sun Maid contracts to buy 1,800 tons of raisins from Victor Packing Company and Pyramid Packing Company. The packing companies should have been aware that Sun Maid's practice was to resell the raisins at a profit. The packers

repudiated their contracts by refusing to deliver the last 610 tons of raisins. Is Sun Maid entitled to recover from the packers the profit it would have made on the resale of the 610 tons of raisins? How would these damages be characterized under the UCC? Which Section, if any, grants such a remedy?

10. The Sedmaks orally contract with Charlie's Chevrolet in Missouri to buy a certain Corvette for $15,000. The car is a limited edition, manufactured by Chevrolet to commemorate the Corvette's selection as the Indianapolis 500 pace car. Six thousand such special cars are manufactured, and each dealer is allotted only one. The Sedmaks ordered specific options on the car, which differentiated it from most others in the limited edition. Charlie's subsequently receives offers for the car of $24,000 and $28,000 from Hawaii and Florida, respectively. When the car arrives, Charlie's notifies the Sedmaks that they may not have it for $15,000 but will have to bid for it. The Sedmaks, alleging that they can acquire an identical car, if at all, at great difficulty, expense, and inconvenience, sue Charlie's for specific performance of the contract. Do you think that the Sedmaks are entitled to specific performance under UCC Section 2-716?

11. McGinnis purchases a 1978 El Camino from a local Chevrolet dealer. Before delivery, McGinnis is promised that certain defects will be repaired. McGinnis discovers several more defects after delivery. She revokes her acceptance of the car and sues the dealer for a refund. The trial court finds that the car is a "lemon" and that McGinnis is justified in revoking her acceptance of it. In addition to the purchase price, McGinnis also seeks to recover the cost of putting the car in storage after the dealer refused to take it back, fees and interest paid on the loan used to finance the car, and the cost of renting a substitute car. Which, if any, of these expenses should she be allowed to recover? How would these expenses be characterized under the UCC?

12. Modern Merchandising contracts to buy 3,000 photocopiers from Copymate Marketing for $55 a machine. Copymate is to acquire the copiers by exercising its option to buy them from one Dowling for a total of $51,750. The machines have been in storage in Canada for nine years, and there has been no active market for them. Modern Merchandising repudiates the contract, and Copymate cancels its order to purchase the copiers from Dowling. Is Copymate entitled to recover from Modern Merchandising? If so, what is the correct measure of damages? Should Copymate have been required to mitigate its damages by seeking another buyer?

13. Palmisciano contracts to buy a Jeep from Tarbox Motors. He pays $1,120 in cash and $6,000 by check. After picking up the vehicle, Palmisciano notices that the window sticker, floor mats, and bumper guards are missing and that the hood is dented. He telephones Tarbox to complain, and Tarbox promises to look into it. Before Tarbox has the chance to correct the situation, Palmisciano returns the Jeep to Tarbox and directs his bank to stop payment on the check. Palmisciano demands a refund, and Tarbox refuses. In subsequent litigation, the court determines that Palmisciano wrongfully denied Tarbox the opportunity to remedy the defects, and that Tarbox was therefore entitled to the purchase price. Tarbox argues that it is entitled to the interest that would have accrued on Palmisciano's check if it had been able to invest the funds in a savings certificate at the time of purchase. Should Tarbox be able to recover this interest? Should it be required to

establish that Palmisciano's check would indeed have been used to purchase an interest-bearing saving certificate and not to cover expenses?

14. Sharon Steel contracts to buy a total of 30,000 metric tons of steel slabs from Associated. The contract provides that the slabs be delivered in several shipments and requires Sharon to pay for each shipment within 15 days of receipt. Sharon is late with many of its payments, although it eventually receives and fully pays for all 30,000 tons of steel. Associated claims that Sharon's failure to pay on time caused Associated to incur financing expenses. Associated sues Sharon for interest on the late payments. Assuming that interest is within the scope of incidental damages (as discussed in UCC Section 2-710), does the UCC provide relief for the type of injury alleged by Associated? Restrict your search to UCC Sections 2-706(a), 2-708(a), and 2-709(a).

CHAPTER **19**

Warranties and Products Liability

CHAPTER OBJECTIVES

TYPES OF WARRANTIES

Express Warranties / Implied Warranties / Warranty of Title

EXPRESS WARRANTIES

Basis of the Bargain / Affirmation of Fact / Description / Sample or Model

IMPLIED WARRANTIES

Implied Warranty of Merchantability / Implied Warranty of Fitness for a Particular Purpose

WARRANTY OF TITLE

UCC Provisions / When There Is No Warranty of Title

EXCLUSION OR MODIFICATION OF WARRANTIES

Express Warranties / Implied Warranties / Limitation of Remedies

FEDERAL TRADE COMMISSION WARRANTY RULES

Products Covered / Information that Must Be Disclosed / Full or Limited Warranty / Disclaimer of Implied Warranty

PRODUCT LIABILITY THEORIES

Warranties / Negligence / Strict Liability / Misrepresentation

SUMMARY

REVIEW PROBLEMS

CHAPTER OBJECTIVES

After reading this chapter, you should be able to:

1. Recognize the difference between express and implied warranties for sales of goods.

2. Define warranty of title.

3. List the three ways to create an express warranty.

4. List the three types of warranties implied by law.

5. Describe contract provisions that exclude or modify warranties for sales of goods.

6. Compare and contrast the warranty, negligence, and strict liability theories used in product liability cases.

This chapter discusses warranties and product liability law. As we discussed in Chapter 18, a warranty is a guarantee that the product being sold meets certain standards. Warranties may be expressed by a seller or implied by law. Because warranty claims are often the basis of product liability cases, we begin this chapter by exploring several aspects of warranty law.

Warranty cases are among the most common cases involving sales of products. For many years, the law favored the seller. The prevailing doctrine was caveat emptor: let the buyer beware. Since the 1960s, a consumer movement has pressed the courts and legislatures to strengthen the rights of purchasers. Today, the seller, not the buyer, must beware of the way the law treats sales.

A second theory used in product liability cases is that of negligence. Negligence occurs when a duty to someone, such as the buyer of a product, is not met and the consequence causes injury (see Chapter 4).

In tort a strict liability theory permits liability without regard to fault. Because strict liability frequently is easier to prove than the existence of a warranty or negligence, it accounts for a growing number of recoveries by injured users of defective products.

Finally, **misrepresentation** may be a basis for recovery if a seller's promotional literature states untruths about a product being sold. This theory of recovery is less common than the others we have mentioned.

Misrepresentation words or conduct that misleads others as to the material facts of a situation

TYPES OF WARRANTIES

A warranty is made when a seller makes a representation as to the character, quality, or title of the goods as part of the contract of sale and promises that certain facts are as represented. A seller who assures or guarantees a buyer that the goods conform to certain standards may be liable for damages if the goods fail to meet those standards.

Express Warranties

Express warranty a guarantee regarding the quality, character, or suitability of goods that arises by action or words of the seller

Sometimes a seller creates an **express warranty.** Suppose that Acme Machines states in a brochure that a lifting device lifts loads of up to 1,000 pounds. Because this statement is a representation of fact, Acme creates an express warranty. If a buyer later learns that the machine is only able to lift 400 pounds, the buyer can sue Acme for breach of an express warranty.

Implied Warranties

Implied warranty of fitness for a particular purpose a guarantee by a seller who knows both the particular purpose for which the purchaser needs the goods and that the purchaser is relying on the seller to select goods for that purpose

Not every warranty arises out of the words or actions of the seller. Two warranties arise out of a sale automatically by operation of law—the implied warranty of merchantability (see Chapter 15) and the **implied warranty of fitness for a particular purpose.**

In the example mentioned earlier, suppose that the manufacturer designed and sold the lifting device for use in loading railroad boxcars. If the machine fails to function properly when used in the loading of boxcars, the manufacturer has breached the implied warranty of merchantability. The machine was not merchantable because it was not fit for the ordinary purpose for which such goods are sold.

Assume instead that the purchaser of this machine told the seller what his requirements were. The buyer states that he needs a machine capable of lifting very dense packages weighing around 2,000 pounds and relies on the seller's skill and judgment to select a suitable machine for that purpose. These facts create an implied warranty that the machine selected by the seller will be fit for the particular purpose noted by the purchaser.

Warranty of Title

Warranty of title a guarantee that the owner has good title to the goods as against all other people

A third warranty also automatically arises from a sale, the **warranty of title.** It guarantees title to the goods being sold. If the buyer of the Acme lifting device learns that it has been stolen, the seller has breached the implied warranty of title.

Article 2 of the UCC applies only to sales of goods. Title must pass from seller to buyer for a price for a sale to take place. The UCC does not cover gifts because a gift is not a sale of property for a price. Some courts also apply Article 2 to leases even though the parties do not intend to transfer title. Similarly, some courts have found that there should be warranties for the sale of a home or the sale of personal services even though goods are not involved. Thus, UCC Article 2 sometimes applies even though there is no sale or no goods being sold.

EXPRESS WARRANTIES

Three situations create an express warranty. The UCC (Section 2-313) provides that:

1. Statements of fact and promises made by seller to buyer about the goods and which become part of the basis of the bargain create an express warranty that the goods shall conform to the statement or promise.

2. Any description of the goods that becomes part of the basis of the bargain creates an express warranty that the goods shall conform to the description.

3. Any sample or model that becomes part of the basis of the bargain creates an express warranty that the whole of the goods shall conform to the sample or model.

Basis of the Bargain

Exactly what is meant by the phrase, "the basis of the bargain"? The drafters of the UCC intended for the courts to examine the actual agreements between parties. "Basis of the bargain" is much like reliance. Suppose that the seller of a used car states, "The tires on this car are brand new radials and cost over $500." The buyer responds, "In that case, I'll take the car." If the tires turn out to be bias-belted retreads with 7,500 miles on them, the seller has breached an express warranty because the seller's statement of fact had created a warranty. The seller's statement would be treated by a court as a basis of the bargain.

Do advertisements for products create express warranties? They do if the advertisement is part of the basis of the bargain between the parties. For example, a man bought a hammer after he read in a promotional brochure that the hammer was "excellent for repair work since it has plenty of beef to handle heavy tires. Also can be used for many other jobs such as straightening frames, bumper brackets, bumpers, puller work, etc." The man was struck in the eye by a chip from the hammer. He sued the hammer manufacturer for breach of express warranty, but he lost because there was no evidence that he had been influenced by the catalogue description when he purchased the hammer. Without evidence that a plaintiff has been influenced by an advertised statement, the plaintiff is unlikely to establish an express warranty.

Affirmation of Fact

Although a specific statement of fact creates a warranty, a statement about the value of goods or a seller's opinion of the goods does not create a warranty (Section 2-313 [a]). Buyers must reasonably expect sellers to speak favorably about the products they are selling. A buyer should expect the salesman at Al's Used Car Lot to declare, "That car is the best deal in town." The buyer may not later rely upon such a statement to claim breach of warranty. As we mentioned in Chapter 8, these general statements by which sellers promote their products are known as puffing.

In determining whether a statement is fact or opinion, a court looks to see how specific the statement is and whether it is oral or written. The most commonly cited rule on this question holds that:

> The decisive test for whether a given representation is a warranty or merely an expression of the seller's opinion is whether the seller asserts a fact of which the buyer is ignorant or merely states an opinion or judgment on a matter of which the seller has no special knowledge and on which the buyer may be expected also to have an opinion and to exercise his judgment. . . . General statements to the effect that goods are "the best" . . . or are "of good quality," or will "last a lifetime" and be "in perfect condition" . . . are generally regarded as expressions of the seller's opinion or "the puffing of his wares" and do not create an express warranty. (*Royal Business Machines* v. *Lorraine Corp.,* 633 F. 2d 34 [1980]).

Description

Descriptions of goods that are made as a part of the basis of the bargain between parties also create express warranties. The description may be words, technical specifications, blueprints, and other forms.

Sample or Model

Samples or models that form part of the basis of the bargain also create express warranties. A sample is an item a seller draws from the bulk of goods that is the subject matter of the sale. A model is a demonstration item offered for inspection. The seller who shows a sample or a model to a buyer expressly warrants that the goods being bought will conform to the sample or model.

IMPLIED WARRANTIES

The Uniform Commercial Code provides for three warranties which are implied with a sale of goods. The implied warranty of merchantability, found in Section 2-314, and the implied warranty of fitness for a particular purpose, found in Section 2-315, relate to the quality and fitness of the goods. The third implied warranty, the warranty of title, concerns the ownership of those goods. This warranty, found in Section 2-312, is discussed in the next section of the text.

Implied Warranty of Merchantability

The UCC states:

1. Unless excluded or modified (Section 2-316), a warranty that the goods shall be merchantable is implied in a contract for their sale if the seller is a merchant with respect to goods of that kind. Under this section the serving

for value of food or drink to be consumed either on the premises or elsewhere is a sale.

2. Goods to be merchantable must at least be such as
   a. will pass without objection in the trade under the contract description; and
   b. in the case of fungible goods (see Chapter 7), are of fair average quality within the description; and
   c. are fit for the ordinary purposes for which such goods are used; and
   d. will run, within the variations permitted by the agreement, of even kind, quality and quantity within each unit and among all units involved; and
   e. are adequately contained, packaged, and labeled as the agreement may require; and
   f. will conform to the promises or affirmations of fact made on the container or label if any.

3. Unless excluded or modified (Section 2-316) other implied warranties may arise from course of dealing or usage of trade.

Generally, courts try to determine if goods are fit for the ordinary purposes for which such goods are used. For example, a seller who delivers shoes that come apart when the buyer walks around in them clearly has breached the warranty of merchantability. Shoes should be fit for ordinary walking.

But the warranty of merchantability applies only when the seller is a merchant. If the seller is not a merchant, no such warranty arises. For example, a plaintiff who had purchased an old saw from a man in the sawmill business and who was injured while operating the saw was not allowed to recover based on the implied warranty of merchantability.

In determining whether food is fit for consumption (merchantable), some courts follow the "foreign-natural" test. That is, a given food is fit if it contains elements natural to the product. A consumer who breaks a tooth on a cherry pit while eating cherry pie may not recover under this test. Other courts follow the "reasonable expectation" test. That is, only those things that we reasonably expect to be in the food should be in it. The consumer who breaks a tooth on a cherry pit in a piece of pie might be able to recover under this rule.

Implied Warranty of Fitness for a Particular Purpose

The UCC provides:

> If the seller knows at the time of contracting the particular purpose for which the buyer wants the goods and the buyer relies on the seller's skill or judgment to select or furnish suitable goods, there is an implied warranty that the goods will be fit for the purpose the buyer specifies at the time of contracting.

A *particular* purpose differs from the ordinary purpose for which goods are used. If a buyer wants climbing shoes and asks the seller to select a pair, the seller breaches this warranty if he or she sells the buyer shoes used only for ordinary walking. It is not necessary for a buyer to specify exactly how a product is to be used as long as the circumstances make the seller aware of the needs of the buyer.

That goods are fit to be sold does not necessarily mean they are fit for the buyer's particular purpose. If a buyer wants a furnace to heat a house of 2,000 square feet, the seller who has been told of the buyer's need breaches the implied warranty of fitness for a particular purpose if the furnace sold is adequate only for a house of 1,200 square feet, even though it operates properly.

Unlike the implied warranty of merchantability, the warranty of fitness for a particular purpose applies to both merchants and nonmerchants. Of course, when buyers specify to sellers exactly which shoes and which furnaces they want, there is no *reliance* by the buyer on the seller's skill. Therefore there would be no breach of this warranty even if the seller knows the purpose for which the goods are used.

Consider the *Gates* case as it relates to the implied warranty of fitness for a particular purpose.

Gates v. Abernathy

Court of Appeals of Oklahoma
11 U. C. C. 491 (1972)

FACTS   Gates wanted to buy some clothes as his wife's Christmas present. Because he knew that his wife frequently shopped at "Penelope's," a store owned by Abernathy, and that Abernathy knew her sizes, Gates went there and asked for items of the proper size and type for Mrs. Gates. The items selected by Abernathy and sold to Mr. Gates were too big, and when Mrs. Gates tried to exchange them she couldn't find anything suitable in her size. She asked for her money back and was refused.

ISSUE   Has defendant Abernathy breached the implied warranty of fitness for a particular purpose in the sale of clothes to Mr. Gates?

DECISION   Yes. The court ruled in favor of the Gates, saying that it was hard to imagine a case which fit the outline of Section 2-315 as well as this one. In this case, the buyer clearly was relying on the judgment of the seller to furnish the kind of goods that he wanted, and there is no question that the seller knew that her skill was being relied on by the buyer. Plaintiff did not sue because the clothes were unfit for sale or use. Instead, he claimed that they were not usable for the particular purpose for which they had been bought.

WARRANTY OF TITLE

UCC Provisions

When someone buys goods, receipt of good title is expected. The law acts on this expectation by imposing the warranty of title. The UCC states (Section 2-312[1]) that the seller of goods warrants that:

1. the title conveyed is good and its transfer rightful

2. the goods are free of any security interest or other encumbrance that the buyer does not know of

The requirement that the title conveyed be good protects the buyer. If a seller conveys stolen property to a buyer, the seller has breached the warranty of title. A title also is not good if it unreasonably exposes the buyer to a lawsuit. For example, if a third party claims ownership of a car being sold, so long as that claim is not frivolous, the buyer may sue the seller for breach of the implied warranty of title. The seller's questionable title has exposed the buyer of the car wrongfully to a lawsuit. The second provision is violated if there is a **lien** on goods being sold that the buyer does not know about. For example, if a person selling a watch still owes money to a jeweler who has just repaired the watch, that jeweler may have a security interest in the watch. If the seller sells the watch without alerting the buyer of the jeweler's interest, the seller may be breaching the warranty of title.

Lien a security interest in property of another

The following case illustrates one application of the warranty of title provisions.

Ricklefs v. Clemens

Supreme Court of Kansas
531 P. 2d 94 (1975)

On March 26, 1971, Ricklefs bought a Corvette Stingray from Clemens. Clemens signed a certificate of title warranting the title to be free from all liens and encumbrances. Ricklefs drove the automobile until December 1, 1971, when he was notified by an FBI agent that the car was stolen and that he might be arrested if he continued to drive It.

FACTS

Has Clemens breached the implied warranty of title?

ISSUE

Yes. The court ruled in favor of the plaintiff, Ricklefs, citing the judicial decision in an earlier case involving similar circumstances:

DECISION

> The purchaser of goods which are warranted as to the title has a right to rely on the fact that he will not be required, at some later time, to enter into a contest over the validity of his ownership. The mere casting of a substantial shadow over his title, regardless of the ultimate outcome, is sufficient to violate a warranty of good title.

In this case, the notice of the FBI agent and the warning that Ricklefs may be arrested are enough to cast a shadow over the plaintiff's title and breaches the warranty of title.

When There Is No Warranty of Title

In some cases, there is no warranty of title in a sales contract. The buyer may know that the seller does not claim to hold title or that the seller purports to sell only the rights and title that the seller or a third person may have. For example, when people buy goods at a sheriff's sale, from an executor, or from a creditor who is selling a

TABLE 19-1 Types of Warranties

Types	How Created
Express warranties	By affirmation of fact or promise
	By description of the goods
	By sample or model
Implied warranty of merchantability	Automatically created by law
Implied warranty of fitness for a particular purpose	Automatically created by law
Warranty of title	Automatically created by law

debtor's property, the seller does not warranty the title. Specific language may exclude or alter the warranty of title and alert the buyer that the sale offers no warranty of title. Specific language to this effect must be included in the sales contract, because even when a seller excludes all other warranties, a buyer usually expects a warranty of title.

EXCLUSION OR MODIFICATION OF WARRANTIES

Express Warranties

Express warranties, as we have noted, can be created by a statement of fact or promise by the seller, by a description, or by a sample or model that becomes a basis of the bargain between the parties. Once an express warranty has been created, it is very difficult to disclaim.

Conflict between Warranty and Disclaimer   Any language in a contract suggesting that express warranties have been disclaimed creates a conflict between the warranty and the disclaimer. If it is possible to read the warranty and disclaimer as consistent, the court must do so; but if such a reading is unreasonable, then the express warranty prevails over the disclaimer. The drafters of the UCC were trying to protect the buyer from hidden disclaimers by negating any language inconsistent with the express warranty. For example, if a seller shows a buyer a sample but tries to exclude "all warranties, express or implied" in the contract, the express warranty created by the sample will not be disclaimed.

Suppose that a person signs a contract for the purchase of steel pipe. The contract explicitly states that the pipe will withstand temperatures to 30 degrees below zero. This statement is an affirmation of fact and constitutes an express warranty. The contract also attempts to exclude "all warranties, express and implied." A court must read the warranty and disclaimer as consistent, if possible. But such a reading would not be possible here. The express warranty and the exclusion directly conflict. Therefore, the express warranty has not been excluded.

Problems of Proof   It is important to note that the UCC (Section 2-316) subjects express warranties to the provisions on parol, or extrinsic, evidence (Section 2-202).

Although the parties have agreed upon a particular express warranty, if they have not inserted their agreement into the final written contract the evidence of their warranty may not be admissable at trial.

Suppose that the pipe salesman *tells* the buyer that the pipe will withstand temperatures to 30 degrees below zero. But the contract they sign expressly *states* that the seller does not guarantee the performance of the pipe in temperatures below zero. The contract also states that it is intended as the final agreement of the parties and is a complete and exclusive statement of the terms of the agreement. Because this contract is neither silent nor ambiguous about the pipe's ability to withstand temperatures, the court does not allow introduction of the salesman's statement to alter or vary the explicit terms of this written contract. Instead, the more limited, written warranty is effective.

Implied Warranties

Implied Warranty of Merchantability   The implied warranty of merchantability may be disclaimed if the disclaimer mentions the word "merchantability" and, in case of a writing, is conspicuous. Explicitly stating in a written contract, "There is no implied warranty of merchantability," in larger type than the rest of the contract, calls a buyer's attention to the exclusion of this warranty.

Implied Warranty of Fitness for a Particular Purpose   To exclude the implied warranty of fitness for a particular purpose, the exclusion must be in writing and conspicuous. It can be disclaimed by the language: "There are no warranties which extend beyond the description on the face hereof." Note that Subsection 2 of 2-316 does not specifically require that language excluding the implied warranty of fitness use the phrase "implied warranty of fitness." A seller might exclude this warranty in a contract by stating: "all implied warranties are excluded in this sale." If this appears in larger type than the rest of the contract, it calls the buyer's attention to the exclusion of this warranty.

Implied Warranty of Title   Special language must be used to exclude the implied warranty of title. A buyer expects this warranty when buying goods, and a seller must comply with the provisions of Section 2-312(2), as discussed earlier, to exclude the warranty of title.

See Table 19-2 for a summary of how different types of warranties are excluded.

Limitation of Remedies

An attempt to exclude or modify a warranty is different from an attempt to limit the remedies of a buyer (under Section 2-719 or 2-718). Buyers' remedies often are limited by liquidated damage provisions and exclusion of liability for consequential damages.

As we discussed in Chapter 18, liquidated damages are damages agreed upon by the parties and specified in a contract. Such provisions are enforceable only if the contract provides for an amount that is reasonable. The parties may agree in advance that

TABLE 19-2 Exclusion of Warranties

Type of Warranty	How Excluded
Express warranty	By words or acts that negate this warranty
Implied warranty of merchantability	By a conspicuous writing that uses the word *merchantability*
	By using the phrases *as is* or *with all faults*
Implied warranty of fitness for a particular purpose	By a conspicuous writing
	By using the phrases *as is* or *with all faults*
Warranty of title	By specific language brought to the attention of the buyer

the seller will pay the buyer a particular sum in case of breach of warranty, as long as that sum is reasonable. Consequential damages include indirect losses from breaches of contract. They generally are lost profits that a seller knows a buyer might suffer if the seller breaks the contract. The UCC (Section 2-719) allows the parties in some cases to modify or limit the remedies usually available to buyers. The UCC generally recognizes clauses that limit or exclude consequential damages, unless they are shocking to the conscience. (See Chapter 10 for a discussion of unconscionability.) If a seller tries to limit consequential damages to a person injured by consumer goods, the clause is considered unconscionable.

Contracts may exclude or modify implied warranties of quality by stating, "There are no implied warranties of merchantability or fitness for any purpose."

Phrases such as bought "as is" or "with all faults" also may exclude implied warranties (Section 2-316 [3]). The seller need not use these exact phrases, but the language must "in common understanding call the buyer's attention to the exclusion of warranties and make plain that there is no implied warranty." By using the phrases provided, a seller can be certain of protection. Although the rule does not specify that the disclaimer be conspicuous, a cautious seller should make sure that it is conspicuous.

To make disclaimers conspicuous, a seller should use type larger and darker than that in the rest of the contract, and the disclaimer should appear on the first page of the contract. A doubly cautious seller might print the disclaimer in a contrasting color and have the buyer initial the paragraph containing the disclaimer. If this course is followed, there can be little doubt that the buyer knew of the disclaimer of all warranties.

The following case discusses why the term "as is" should be conspicuous.

Fairchild Industries v. *Maritime Air Services, Limited*

Court of Appeals of Maryland
333 A.2d 313 (1975)

FACTS   Maritime exercised an option to buy a helicopter which it had been leasing from Fairchild for almost a year. The parties entered into a purchase agreement which consisted of a printed form, furnished by Fairchild, on which relevant provisions were inserted by typewriter. Among those typewritten provisions, each of which was typed in lower case letters, was the following:

> It is specifically understood and agreed by the parties that the Aircraft is sold in an "as is" condition. Seller makes no representation or warranties express or implied whatsoever except Warranty of Title. Buyer acknowledges that before entering into this agreement he has examined the Aircraft as fully as he desires.

Maritime alleged that Fairchild had breached its implied warranties of merchantability and fitness for a particular purpose.

Does the quoted provision of Fairchild's contract with Maritime adequately exclude warranties under the UCC?   **ISSUE**

No. The court ruled in favor of Maritime. It rejected Fairchild's argument that implied warranties had been excluded effectively by use of the phrase "as is." The court found that the phrase "as is" was not conspicuous enough to bring the warranty exclusion to the buyer's attention because it was typed in lower case rather than capital letters.   **DECISION**

FEDERAL TRADE COMMISSION WARRANTY RULES

In the Magnuson-Moss Warranty-Federal Trade Commission Act, Congress expanded the power of the Federal Trade Commission (FTC), specified minimum standards for what written consumer product warranties must disclose, and set certain minimum standards for those warranties. The act can be enforced by the FTC, by the U.S. Attorney General, or by a private party. It gives consumers a chance before they buy to learn the nature of the warranty and provides for effective enforcement of the warranty in case of breach. But the act does not require any warranties on consumer products.

Products Covered

The act applies to any consumer product accompanied by a written warranty. **Consumer goods** are formally defined as any tangible, personal property normally used for personal, family, or household purposes. Service contracts also are covered by the act. Goods that are purchased for commercial or industrial purposes or for resale in the ordinary course of business are not covered by the FTC warranty rules.

The FTC warranty rules require compliance only if the consumer product costs $15 or more and is accompanied by a written warranty. If a company does not wish to be bound by the act or the FTC rules, it should not offer a written warranty on its consumer products. Oral warranties are not covered by the act.

Consumer goods any tangible, personal property normally used for personal, family, or household purposes

Information that Must Be Disclosed

A written warranty must be in terms easily understood by the average consumer. It must disclose to consumers before the sale such information as:

1. The name and address of the warrantor

2. The products or parts covered

3. A statement of what the warrantor will do, at whose expense, and for what period of time

4. The step by step procedure that the consumer should follow to enforce the warranty

Full or Limited Warranty

The act requires that a product be labeled as having either a "limited" or a "full" warranty. This labeling system allows a consumer to compare products before making a final purchase. Before the act, consumers often found out what type of warranty a product carried at home, after opening the box.

Full warranty a warranty that meets all of the standards imposed by the FTC act

A written **full warranty** must provide that:

1. Any defects, malfunctions, or inability to conform to the terms of a written warranty must be corrected by the warrantor without charge and within a reasonable length of time

2. The warrantor cannot limit the period within which the implied warranty is effective for the consumer product

3. The warrantor cannot limit or exclude consequential damages on a consumer product unless noted conspicuously on the face of the warranty

4. The warrantor must allow the consumer to choose between a refund of the purchase price or replacement of the defective product or part after a reasonable number of attempts to remedy the defect or malfunction

Limited warranty any warranty covered by the FTC act that does not meet the standards for a full warranty

Note that a **limited warranty** does not give the consumer these guarantees. A product must be clearly and conspicuously labeled as having a limited warranty if a written warranty is provided and the full warranty conditions are not met. (See Figure 19-1).

Disclaimer of Implied Warranty

With both a full and a limited warranty, the warrantor is prohibited from disclaiming any implied warranty. The act also prohibits the disclaimer or modification of an implied warranty to a service contract with a buyer within 90 days after the sale. A full warranty may not disclaim, modify, or even limit the basic implied warranties. Although a limited warranty may not be disclaimed or modified either, the implied warranties can be limited in duration to that of the written warranty, as long as the limitation is reasonable, conscionable and conspicuous.

FIGURE 19-1   Limited Warranty

This product has been manufactured under the highest standards of quality and workmanship. We warrant to the CONSUMER all parts of this product against defects in material and workmanship for TEN (10) YEARS from date of purchase. Any defective part will be replaced FREE OF CHARGE, excluding labor or service charges. We will not be responsible for any product damage due to installation error, product abuse, or product misuse whether performed by a contractor, service company, or yourself. Use of other than Acme factory parts may void this warranty.

This warranty applies only TO THE CONSUMER USE of the product and any inquiries regarding warranty claims are to be directed to:

Acme Corporation
100 Main Street
Anytown, Missouri 66066

This warranty gives you specific legal rights and you may also have other rights which vary from state to state.

PRODUCT LIABILITY THEORIES

If a plaintiff establishes a breach of warranty and proves that as a result of the breach he or she was injured, a case may be pursued against the seller. Today, persons who are injured through the use of a defective product can base a suit seeking compensation for their injuries on several different legal theories. In addition to suing for a breach of warranty, an injured consumer may use negligence, strict liability in tort, and misrepresentation as a bases for holding a manufacturer, distributor, or seller of a product liable. These personal injury suits collectively are known as **product liability cases.** In the sections that follow, we discuss the law applying to such cases.

Product liability cases cases involving defective products, whether based on warranty, misrepresentation, strict liability or negligence theories

Over the past few decades, there has been a trend toward increased consumer protection. Society faces the question of whether a person who is injured by a dangerous product should bear the loss or whether the loss shold be borne by a manufacturer, distributor, or seller. The scales appear to have tipped in favor of the consumer.

The UCC does not rule on suits against someone more remote in the distributive chain than the buyer's immediate seller. If a homeowner is injured by a defective mower, he or she may sue the retailer who sold the mower. But the UCC takes no position on whether the homeowner may sue the wholesaler or manufacturer of the mower. Most courts today allow injured parties to sue both manufacturers and wholesalers. Injured parties typically try to sue manufacturers, because manufacturers often are in a better position to pay than are local retailers.

The UCC (Section 2-607[3]) provides that a buyer must give notice of the breach of warranty. Within a reasonable time after consumers discover or should have discovered any breach of warranty, they must notify sellers of the breach, or else they may not collect damages.

Warranties

Someone injured by a product may use warranties to establish a personal injury claim. If that person can establish that the defendant made a warranty, failed to live up to the warranty, and that as a result of the breach the plaintiff was injured by the product, plaintiff may be able to collect damages.

Today the trend is away from requiring the plaintiff in a warranty case to establish privity of contract with the defendant. Privity is a direct contractual relationship between parties. Most states have adopted a policy on the necessary relationship between an injured party and seller by which the buyer or any natural person in the buyer's family or household, or a guest in the buyer's home may sue the seller directly for injuries sustained. This provision does not help everyone injured by a defective product—for example, a bystander. If a homeowner is mowing the lawn, and the mower blade flies off and strikes the next-door neighbor, the neighbor may not sue the seller of the product on the basis of breach of implied warranty.

The following landmark case broke through the privity requirement and began a new era in product liability. Note that this suit was based on the breach of an implied warranty.

_____ *Henningsen v. Bloomfield Motors, Incorporated* _____

Supreme Court of New Jersey
161 A. 2d 69 (1960)

FACTS   Henningsen bought a Plymouth from Bloomfield Motors. The sales contract contained an express warranty obligating Chrysler, the manufacturer, to replace any defective parts for 90 days or 4000 miles. Other wording in the contract disclaimed any other warranty, express or implied, by Chrysler or Bloomfield Motors.

Mrs. Henningsen was injured as a result of a defect in the car. The Henningsens sued Chrysler and Bloomfield Motors for breach of an implied warranty of merchantability. Chrysler defended on the grounds that no privity existed between it and the plaintiff. Bloomfield Motors argued that it was not liable to Mrs. Henningsen because its contract was with Mr. Henningsen. Both defendants claimed that the implied warranty of merchantability had been waived in the contract signed by Mr. Henningsen.

ISSUE   Is privity of contract required in a product liability suit based on breach of implied warranty? Is a contract provision that disclaims the implied warranty of merchantability effective if it is not brought to the buyer's attention?

DECISION   The court answered no to both questions. It held that privity is not required in an action based on implied warranty and that the disclaimer was ineffective.

The court stated that Mrs. Henningsen was entitled to sue because she was reasonably expected to use the automobile. The court also held the disclaimer void as a matter of law, because it was not fairly obtained. The consumer did not have the bargaining power to obtain a modification of the contract. The court found the wording of the warranty was such that no reasonable person would conclude that he or she had relinquished all personal injury claims that might occur due to a defect in the automobile.

Negligence

A second type of product liability case is based on negligence, the breach or nonperformance of a legal duty, which through neglect or failure to use ordinary care, causes damage or injury to another. In essence, a plaintiff must establish that a defendant failed to exercise due care in manufacturing or handling a product. The plaintiff need not have purchased the product from the defendant. But the plaintiff must establish that his or her injury is a result of a breach of duty on the part of the defendant. The defendant's duty is to exercise that degree of care that would be exercised by a reasonably prudent person under the same circumstances.

The main problem in suing for negligence is the substantial burden of proof that falls on the plaintiff. Defendants may be able to establish that they exercised all due care possible under the circumstances. If so, they are not held liable.

Manufacturer's Negligent Design   Unlike negligence in production, which may affect one or a few products, a defective design may affect an entire class of products and may involve potential liability to thousands of individuals. Several federal agencies charged with regulating certain types of products increasingly use mandatory recalls to correct defective products.

A manufacturer may be held liable for injuries caused by a product poorly designed, improperly built, or improperly assembled. Suppose that a manufacturer adopts an unsafe design — for example, an electric fan that does not have a screen to protect users from the rotating metal blades. A young child sticks a hand into the path of the blades and loses fingers. The manufacturer may be liable for the child's injuries because it failed to exercise reasonable care in the design of the fan.

Today manufacturers must design products that will be safe when they are used improperly as well as properly — if the improper use is foreseeable. For example, a car manufacturer's design must reasonably protect passengers from the effects of collisions. Cars are not designed for the purpose of colliding. But because collisions are readily foreseeable results of the way cars are normally expected to be used, manufacturers' designs must take collisions into account.

Manufacturer's Duty to Inspect, Test, and Warn   The manufacturer generally must exercise due care to make certain a product placed on the market is safe. It must run reasonable tests and inspections to discover present or hidden defects before putting a product on the market. For example, the manufacturer of a chair was held liable when it failed to find a defect that it could have found by inspecting the chair.

A manufacturer must not only test and inspect a product. It also has a duty to warn the public that a product may be dangerous.   Suppose that the manufacturer of a chemical knows that the chemical is highly caustic and that users may not be aware of that fact. The manufacturer must take reasonable care to inform users of the danger. One way to do so is to put a prominent warning on containers of the chemical. If the manufacturer fails to supply any warning, it is liable to anyone injured by the chemical who the manufacturer might have expected would use it, such as someone transferring the chemical from one container to another.

Proximate cause the direct and natural sequence between the breach of duty and injury

The defect in the product must be the **proximate cause** of the injury. A connection must exist between the defect in the product and the injury sustained. If a chemical in a drum explodes when exposed to heat, but a worker is injured by a drum falling on his or her foot, the dangerousness of the chemical is *not* the actual cause of the worker's injury.

The law holds the manufacturer liable only if it can foresee that the product may be dangerous in duty-to-warn cases. Must the manufacturer warn consumers not only of dangers inherent in the proper use of the product but also of dangers inherent in its misuse? Many courts have said yes.

A warning must be clear and intelligible. Even if a warning makes clear the dangers inherent in using or misusing the product, it still faces the problem of where to put the warning. Suppose, for example, that a warning appears in literature supplied by a manufacturer to buyers of its products but not directly on the dangerous products themselves. The cautious manufacturer puts warnings where they will be seen by everyone who might be endangered by the product. For example, the seller of a lawn mower may warn users not to put their hands in the mower's exhaust chute while the mower is in operation by putting the warning in the operating instructions *and* on the exhaust chute itself, where it is more likely to be seen. A number of statutes and regulations (for example, the Food, Drug, and Cosmetic Act and the Federal Hazardous Substances Act) require warnings to be placed on certain products.

Negligence of Assemblers and Submanufacturers   Many products are composed of parts manufactured by several companies. To what extent is a company that uses the products of another company in making its own product liable if a component part malfunctions? Take the case of an airplane company. If a malfunctioning altimeter causes the plane to crash, can the manufacturer escape liability by pointing to the altimeter manufacturer?

Generally, the answer depends on whether the manufacturer could have discovered the defect by making a reasonable inspection of the incorporated part. Of course, regardless of whether or not the airplane company is negligent, the manufacturer of a component is liable for its negligence.

Negligence of Retailers   Negligence generally is not effective in suits brought against retailers. (But see the discussion of strict liability.) When retailers get products from manufacturers, they may know little more about them than buyers know. Many products are packaged when retailers receive and sell them. Because retailers have little control over products' design and fabrication, they rarely are held liable for negligence due to faulty design or construction of products.

Ordinarily retailers need not inspect or test the items they sell if they do not know nor have reason to know that the products are dangerous. The courts tend not to impose a duty to inspect or test under these circumstances. But if retailers should have known that a product was dangerous and could have inspected or tested the product, they may be liable. A retailer who knows that a product is dangerous and that a buyer is unlikely to discover the danger has a duty to warn the buyer of the danger.

Many companies market under their own names products manufactured by others. Sears, Roebuck, for example, sells floor scrubbers manufactured by another company but labeled *Kenmore,* the Sears trade name. Retailers that advertise, label, or package products so that it appears that they are the manufacturers are held to the same standards as the actual manufacturer.

Statutory Violations as Proof of Negligence   Some federal and state statutes, such as the Federal Food, Drug, and Cosmetic Act, specify a certain standard of conduct. If someone injured by a product can show that a statute or regulation has not been complied with, the person may have a statutory right of action. A manufacturer who ignores the safety standards of a government agency leaves the company open to liability. For this reason, companies must keep well informed of government statutes and regulations about the products they manufacture.

Defenses Available in Negligence   A number of defenses are available to a company in a product liability suit. One defense frequently urged in such suits is **contributory negligence.** Contributory negligence is conduct that falls below the standard of care that reasonably prudent people would exercise over their safety and that contributes to their injury. For example, a press operator who fails to use all available safety equipment contributes to his injury and may not recover damages. Some states have replaced the doctrine of contributory negligence with that of comparative negligence (see Chapter 3).

Contributory negligence a defense to a negligence claim that states conduct by the plaintiff contributed to the plaintiff's injury

Although contributory negligence bars recovery by the plaintiff, comparative negligence does not. When a court applies the comparative negligence doctrine, it weighs the relative negligence of the parties and reduces the amount of recovery in proportion to the plaintiff's negligence. It bars recovery only if the plaintiff's negligence was proportionally greater than the defendant's. For example, suppose that a jury decided that the employer was 80 percent responsible for a given injury but that the employee was 20 percent responsible. If the court followed the doctrine of *contributory* negligence, the plaintiff would recover nothing. But if the court applied the doctrine of *comparative* negligence, the jury would determine how much the plaintiff's injuries were worth (for example, $100,000) and then reduce this amount by 20 percent, the extent of the plaintiff's responsibility for the accident. The plaintiff therefore would receive $80,000.

In some cases, manufacturers and other sellers assert that an injured party acted voluntarily, with full knowledge, and with full appreciation of the risk. In short, the injured party **assumed the risk.** For example, a farm worker might be injured by a corn grinding machine that must be fed by hand when corn is wet. In such a case, a court might hold that the farm worker knowingly assumed the risk and not award damages.

Assumption of risk the voluntary exposure to a known and appreciated danger

In general, contributory or comparative negligence and assumption of risk are available to dependants in product liability suits based on negligence. For this reason, negligence is less appealing for plaintiffs than other defenses.

Strict Liability

As we have seen, the doctrine of strict or absolute liability imposes liability regardless of a user's reasonable care. Strict liability in the products liability area began in the 1960s. It does not make the seller of a defective product absolutely liable. An injured party must demonstrate that a product was defective and that it was the proximate cause of injury. But that liability generally is easier to prove than negligence. The only defense commonly accepted in strict liability cases is that the injured person knowingly assumed the risk involved.

This defense appears in the following case.

Karabatsos v. Spivey Company

Appellate Court of Illinois (1977)
364 N.E.2d 319

FACTS   On June 26, 1970, Karabatsos, a conveyor belt attendant, lost his right arm while lifting boxes as they were diverted off a conveyor belt by a diverter and placing them on a top conveyor belt. Karabatsos sued Spivey, who installed the conveyor in 1963, alleging that his injury had resulted because no screens had been placed on the machine.

It was Karabatsos's job to put packages that had been kicked onto a catwalk back onto the top belt. It appears that, at the time of the accident, it had become the practice to try to reach packages that jumped over the diverter before they were caught in rollers. The evidence was conflicting on whether Karabatsos had been told not to go for the packages unless he turned the belt off and on whether he knew how to turn the belt off. He testified that he did not know how and that no one had told him not to put his hands near the conveyor while it was on. But "he knew it was dangerous" because he had often seen a supervisor take packages which had been caught in the belt.

ISSUE   Did the plaintiff assume the risk of injury, so that he cannot recover against Spivey, the installer of the equipment?

DECISION   No. The court noted that although contributory negligence is not a defense in a products liability action, assumption of risk is. The burden of proof therefore is on the defendant. In this case, the jury found that the defendant had failed to prove that the plaintiff had assumed the risk of injury. The jury concluded that although Karabatsos knew that he would be hurt if his hands were caught in the rollers, he was not aware that he could be injured if he reached for a package several feet away from the rollers.

Unlike the plaintiff in a negligence case, the plaintiff in a case of strict liability in tort need not prove that a defendant's actions were unreasonable. Manufacturers may be held liable even though they exercise all possible care in the preparation and sale of their products. Product liability cases based on strict liability require the plaintiff to prove that:

1. The defendant is a merchant

2. The product was expected to and reached the injured party without substantial change in the condition in which it was sold

3. The product was defective

4. This defect made the product unreasonably dangerous to the user

5. The defect caused physical harm to user or property

Strict liability applies whether or not a user has entered into a contract with the seller. An injured party may sue retailers, distributors, manufacturers of component parts, and general manufacturers. The only seller an injured buyer may not collect from is a seller who is not engaged in the business of selling such a product.

Although the law clearly holds manufacturers and sellers liable to ultimate users, states vary on whether they are liable to other people as well. Some courts extend strict liability to bystanders.

What if a manufacturer produces a product that, although carefully manufactured, could cause injury to a person because of some hidden danger? For example, suppose a drain cleaner could not safely be used with liquid bleach — two articles a person might commonly use in housecleaning — but the manufacturer failed to warn users of this fact. Manufacturers must label dangerous products or be held liable because the product was in a "defective condition unreasonably dangerous to the user or consumer."

The following case illustrates the problems of inadequate warning.

Jackson v. Coast Paint and Lacquer Company

U.S. Court of Appeals, Ninth Circuit
499 F. 2d 809 (1974)

Jackson, a journeyman painter, was assigned by his employer to paint the inside of some tank cars with Copon EA 9, a product manufactured by Reliance Universal, Incorporated. While Jackson was painting, a fire started, and he was severely injured. The fuel of the fire consisted of paint fumes that had accumulated in the tank car. **FACTS**

The label on the paint warned of its toxicity if ingested and also stated the following:

Keep away from heat, sparks, and open flame. USE WITH ADEQUATE VENTILATION.

Jackson testified that although he had not known of the possibility of fire from paint fumes, he had known of the danger from breathing these fumes. There was evidence that some people in his company did know of the fire danger.

Was the manufacturer's warning adequate in view of the fact that people in the company knew of the existence of the danger from fire? **ISSUE**

No. The manufacturer's duty to warn runs directly to the painter who was using the product. The fact that the hazard was known to plaintiff's employer does not lessen the manufacturer's duty to warn him, because the seller's duty is to the ultimate user or **DECISION** consumer. In the case of paint sold in labeled containers, the adequacy of warning must be measured according to the knowledge and understanding common to painters who will use the paints.

In strict liability cases, plaintiffs must establish that products were defective, that the defects caused the injuries in question, and that the defendants are responsible for the defects. Sellers are not liable when they deliver safe products, and later mishandling or other causes make them harmful by the time they are consumed. In determining the source of the defect, courts commonly examine the consumers' expectations of a product and then determine whether the injured consumer had been surprised by the danger of the product.

Strict liability theory also requires an injured person to establish that the danger posed by the product was unreasonable — that is, more dangerous than would be contemplated by an ordinary consumer. This requirement is imposed because some products are defective yet not unreasonably dangerous. A stove that gets foods too hot may be defective but not necessarily unreasonably dangerous. A new car delivered with greasy upholstery is defective but not dangerous.

Misrepresentation

Sellers sometimes say or write things about their products that are inaccurate. The buyer who is injured by the product may sue based on the misrepresentation. The misrepresentation must be of a material fact, one a buyer has taken into consideration in deciding to buy.

Sellers often defend themselves from charges of misrepresentation by claiming that the misrepresentation was innocent. They may claim that a statement was mere puffery, not fact. If they prove this claim, a plaintiff may not recover damages.

To recover on grounds of innocent misrepresentation, the buyer also must prove that he or she justifiably relied on the factual misrepresentation. If the buyer had been unaware of the misrepresentation or indifferent to it, or if the statement did not influence the purchase or the buyer's later conduct, the buyer may not recover. The misrepresentation must have been a substantial factor in inducing the purchase or use of the product.

The following case provides an example of innocent misrepresentation.

Klages v. General Ordinance Equipment Corporation

**Superior Court of Pennsylvania
367 A. 2d 207 (1976)**

FACTS   Klages was employed as a night auditor at a motel. After being held up, he purchased a Mace pen for protection. The promotional literature for the pen states

Rapidly vaporizes on face of assailant effecting "instantaneous incapacitation" . . . an attacker is subdued instantly.

When Klages was held up soon thereafter, he squirted the Mace, hitting the intruder right beside the nose. He immediately ducked behind the cash register, but the intruder shot him in the head. He completely lost the sight in his right eye. Klages sued both the manufacturer and retailer of the Mace pen, claiming that they were liable due to their misrepresentation.

Do the statements on the promotional literature constitute a misrepresentation of material fact relied on by the plaintiff?   **ISSUE**

Yes. Both defendants were held liable. The court stated that the promotional litera-   **DECISION**
ture was material, because a consumer was expected to rely on it in making a purchase. The statements were not puffing but specific data on the capability of the product. The purchaser specifically purchased the product for protection from harm under extremely dangerous conditions.

_____ SUMMARY _____

Warranties are guarantees that products being sold will meet certain standards. Express warranties may arise from actions, conduct, oral expressions, or written brochures or documents promoting the product. Although a seller or manufacturer need not make any express warranties, FTC rules impose some requirements on written warranties that are made by manufacturers of consumer goods. Implied warranties are created by the law and are imposed regardless of the conduct of seller or manufacturer of a product. The warranty of title guarantees that the seller of the goods has title to them; such a warranty is expected to be a part of almost all sales. Under certain specific circumstances, both express and implied warranties can be excluded or limited.

Product liability laws involve warranties and cases based on negligence, strict liability, and misrepresentation. The negligence case requires the injured party to prove that the manufacturer or seller of a product did not use reasonable care and that the lack of reasonable care caused the party's injury. The strict liability case requires proof that a product was defective and dangerous and that these conditions caused the injury. The misrepresentation case requires that the seller or manufacturer misstate a material fact about a product and that the misstatement be relied on by the injured party. These different theories may be combined within any one case.

The requirements for proof and the defenses that may be used vary with the theories used in a particular case. Contributory or comparative negligence may be used in negligence cases but not in strict liability cases. It is important that readers understand the requirements and defenses of each theory.

_____ REVIEW PROBLEMS_____

1. What are the three implied warranties that automatically arise out of the sale of a good?

2. List how an express warranty may be created.

3. If you were a merchant who wanted to exclude all implied warranties in your transaction with a consumer, what would you do to make sure the exclusion would hold up in court?

4. Explain the differences and similarities between product liability actions based on negligence and on strict liability.

5. Autzen contracted to buy a used 50-foot boat from Taylor for $100,000. After agreeing on the price, but during the process of negotiating, Autzen was assured that the boat was in good condition. Taylor's agent had the boat inspected for dry rot before Autzen's purchase, although Autzen felt it was unnecessary to do so. The inspector concluded that the hull was sound and that the boat was well suited for its intended purpose. Autzen gave Taylor's agent $10,000 and took possession. About two months later, Autzen discovered that parts of the boat's flying bridge had been weakened by dry rot. A further inspection of the boat revealed an enormous amount of dry rot and insect infestation. Had an express warranty been made about the condition of the boat? Explain.

6. Louis ordered a quantity of enamel lined steel pipe from Key for an Alaskan construction project. The pipe was delivered in March, a time of extremely low temperatures. In April, Louis began laying the pipe. By early May, some 5,000 feet of the pipe had been installed. An inspection showed that portions of the enamel lining had cracked and were hanging off in sheets. Louis sued for breach of the implied warranty of fitness for a particular purpose (under Section 2-315). Was there an implied warranty of fitness for a particular purpose?

7. Christopher bought a motor home from Larson for $16,000. Christopher was assured by Larson's salesman that the motor home would meet the requirements Christopher expressed to the salesman. Christopher therefore purchased the motor home. On the back of the contract was a disclaimer of warranties, including the implied warranty of merchantability, among other fine print provisions. This disclaimer was never called to Christopher's attention. Christopher and his family took a trip in the motor home, which proved to be defective in a number of ways. Some repairs were needed to make it back home. Was the disclaimer of warranties effective?

8. George purchased a 1971 Mustang from Pettigrew, a retail Ford dealer. Browder, George's mother-in-law, is injured when the right front wheel of the Mustang collapses. Ford Motor Company, the manufacturer of the Mustang, validly disclaimed all implied warranties as to George. Browder sues Pettigrew and Ford for, among other things, breach of the implied warranties, alleging her status as a third-party beneficiary. Was Browder a third-party beneficiary of any implied warranties?

9. Cantrell was injured while using a ladder that had come in a cardboard box bearing the following message:

GOOD QUALITY; LIGHT, STRONG, SAFE; RATED LOAD 200 LBS.; FOR SAFETY'S SAKE BUY ME. I'M LIGHT AND STRONG; FIVE-YEAR GUARAN-TEE . . . The manufacturer guarantees the ladder, under normal use and service, to be free from defects in material and workmanship, for five years from the date of purchase.

Cantrell weighed only 165 pounds. The ladder had not been misused or abused. It collapsed as it was being used on a clean cement floor with all braces properly extended and locked. The front legs of the ladder buckled inward, throwing plaintiff to the cement floor. Cantrell sued Amarillo Hardware, the wholesaler, and Werner, the manufacturer, for breach of warranty. The defendants argued that there was no evidence indicating that any component, design feature, or material in the ladder was defective, and without product defect they are not liable. Do you agree?

10. Smith purchased an electric floor polisher-scrubber from Sears. The polisher was manufactured by Regina but sold under the Sears' trade name "Kenmore." When Smith plugged the appliance in for its initial use, he received a violent electric shock that threw him across the room, causing a severe back injury. Smith sued Sears and Regina.
     Sears defended alleging that since it was not the manufacturer of the defective polisher, it is not liable for Smith's injuries. Is a retailer who sells as his own a product manufactured by a third party responsible for injuries resulting from defects in the course of manufacture?

11. Chappuis was injured in the eye by steel chip from the edge of an already chipped hammer. Neither Chappuis nor anyone else on the job had known about the previous chipping. Sears, the seller, and Vex, the manufacturer, knew that once the hammer was chipped, it had to be discarded, because it was likely to chip again. The hammer was sold with a label stating that safety goggles should be worn while a person was using the hammer, that the hammer should be used only to drive and pull common nails, and that the hammer would chip if used for other purposes. Chappuis was using the hammer for its intended purposes when he was injured. Are Sears and Vex strictly liable for Chappuis's injuries?

12. Moody was injured when he fell from a defective aluminum ladder sold by Sears under its trade name. The ladder in fact was manufactured by Wex, but there was nothing connected with the sale to show that anyone but Sears was involved. The defect in the ladder was a latent one. May Moody recover from Sears for his injury? What legal theory, if any, would impose liability on Sears?

13. Greenman was injured when using a power tool, manufactured by Yuba as a lathe, when the piece of wood he was turning suddenly flew out of the machine and struck him in the forehead. The machine had been a gift to Greenman from his wife. Examination of the machine revealed that inadequate set screws had been used in its construction, permitting wood to fly out of the lathe. Yuba's brochure attested to the tool's ruggedness and the high quality of construction. On what theories may Greenman seek recovery of damages from Yuba? May

Greenman actually recover? If so, under which theory is recovery easiest, and why?

14. Simpson was a passenger in a car equipped with a bench seat. He was sitting in the middle of the seat when the car collided head on with another vehicle. The automobile was equipped with a floor shift, manufactured by Hurst, that had been installed by a previous owner. Simpson, who was not wearing any seatbelt or other restraint, was impaled on the shift. Simpson sued Hurst, claiming that Hurst was negligent in failing to warn of the danger of installing the shift in an automobile with a bench seat. Will Simpson prevail in her action against Hurst? On what grounds might the court find for Hurst on the issue?

15. Spruill, a 14-month-old infant, died of chemical pneumonia as a result of ingesting a small quantity of furniture polish manufactured by Boyle. Spruill had been left alone for a few minutes by his mother in a room in which she had been polishing furniture. The infant reached the bottle, opened it, and drank from it. On the label, red letters 1/8-inch high warned of the combustible nature of the product. Several lines below this, brown letters 1/32-inch high warned that the product was harmful if swallowed, especially by children. In fact, ingestion of 1 teaspoonful by an infant is fatal. Did the accident in question arise from the normal use of the product? Was the accident foreseeable by the manufacturer? Was the manufacturer's warning sufficient about the harmful effects of the polish if swallowed?

16. Brown bought a helicopter from Brontley Corporation for business use. In promotional literature, the helicopter was described as "safe, dependable, not tricky to operate" and one that "beginners and professional pilots alike agree is easy to fly." Brown had never flown a helicopter, but he did have an airplane pilot's license. The third time up in the helicopter, Brown encountered a fairly heavy wind, was unable to control the machine, and was killed when it crashed. Brown's heirs sued on the basis of the "misrepresentations made by the Brontley Corporation in its literature." Should Brown's heirs recover?

CHAPTER 20

Commercial Paper: Introduction and Negotiability

CHAPTER OBJECTIVES

After reading this chapter, you should be able to:

1. Identify documents of title.

2. Explain why people use commercial paper.

3. List the types of commercial paper.

4. State how commercial paper is transferred.

5. State the requirements that must be met for an instrument to be classified as negotiable.

Article 3 of the UCC deals with people's written promises and obligations to pay certain sums of money. Article 4 covers bank deposits and collections. For the most part, the material covered in this and the following chapters on commercial paper deals with provisions of Article 3, although Article 4 is mentioned in places.

Commercial paper written promises or obligations to pay money

This chapter deals primarily with the basics of **commercial paper** and the law dealing with the transfer of such paper. Before examining the law on checks, drafts, notes, and certificates of deposit, we first cover another important type of document used in commercial transactions — documents of title.

DOCUMENTS OF TITLE

When a business sells goods, it frequently ships the goods to the buyer by a carrier, such as a trucking firm or railroad. In other cases, a seller stores goods in a warehouse, where the buyer picks them up. In both cases, the business temporarily gives up possession of the goods.

Bill of lading a document of title issued by a carrier

The carrier or the warehouse, upon receiving the goods, gives the business a receipt for the goods. When the business ships goods by carrier, the receipt in question is called a **bill of lading.** When the business stores goods in a warehouse, the business receives a **warehouse receipt.** Bills of lading and warehouse receipts are **documents of title.** A title establishes who is en*title*d to the goods described in the document. These documents usually are issued by professional bailees who are in the business either of delivering or storing goods. As we discussed in Chapter 16, a bailee is someone who takes temporary possession of the property of another for a particular purpose.

Warehouse receipt a document of title issued by a warehouse

Document of title an instrument indicating the holder's right to obtain possession of the goods covered

Documents of title are of two basic types: negotiable and nonnegotiable. A document of title is negotiable if by its terms the goods are to be delivered to the bearer or to a named person. For example, a document of title that specifies "Deliver to Bearer" or "Deliver to the order of John Jones" is negotiable. If a document of title is

FIGURE 20-1 Order Bill of Lading

ORDER BILL OF LADING
ACME TRANSPORT COMPANY

Received, subject to the classifications and tariffs in effect on the date of issue of this Bill of Lading, the property described below, in apparent good order (except as noted) marked, consigned, and destined as indicated below, which company agrees to carry to its place of delivery at said destination. It is mutually agreed that every service to be performed hereunder shall be subject to all the conditions not prohibited by law herein contained, which are hereby agreed to by the shipper and accepted for himself and his assigns. The surrender of this ORIGINAL ORDER BILL OF LADING properly indorsed shall be required before the delivery of the property.

Car Initial	Car Number	Length/Capacity of Car		Weight in Tons		Waybill Date	Waybill No.
		Ordered	Furnished	Gross	Tare		

STOP THIS CAR AT	FOR	CONSIGNEE AND ADDRESS AT STOP
AT	FOR	

ORIGIN   STATE

FULL NAME OF SHIPPER

ADDRESS:

Bill of Lading Date	Bill of Lading No.	Invoice No.

CONSIGNED TO ORDER OF:

Destination:

Shippers Special Instructions (Include Icing, Ventilation, Heating, Weighing, Etc.)

No. Pkgs.	Description of Articles	Weight	Rate	Freight	Advances	Prepaid

negotiable, it may be freely exchanged among people. The person in possession of a negotiable document of title is entitled to take possession of the goods the document describes.

A person who acquires possession of a nonnegotiable document of title does not necessarily acquire title to the goods covered by the document. A nonnegotiable document of title does not state by its terms that the goods are to be delivered to bearer or to the order of a named person. If a nonnegotiable document of title is used, the bailee must follow the instructions of the **bailor** and must deliver the goods to the party specified by the bailor. Nonnegotiable documents of title are widely used.

Bailor the owner of bailed property

FIGURE 20-2 Warehouse Receipt

ACME WAREHOUSE
A PUBLIC WAREHOUSE

Date of Issue:

This is to certify that we have received in our warehouse located at 100 Tree Street in the city of Kansas City, Kansas for the account of _____

_____ in apparent good order except as noted hereon the following property, subject to all terms and conditions contained herein and on the reverse side hereof, such property to be delivered to the order of _____

_____ upon payment of all storage, handling and other charges and the surrender of this document bearing proper indorsement.

Lot #	Quantity	Said to Be or Contain	Storage per Month		Handling In and Out	
			Rate	Per	Rate	Per

ACME Warehouse Company claims a lien for all lawful charges for storage and preservation of the goods described above, as well as for all lawful claims for monies advanced, interest, insurance, transportation, labor, weighing, and all other charges and expenses in connection with the goods. Except as may otherwise be required by law, the ACME Warehouse Company has not insured the goods described above for the benefit of the depositor against fire or other casualty.

ACME WAREHOUSE COMPANY

By: _____

Its:

The goods listed below are hereby released from this receipt for delivery. Any unreleased balance of the goods is subject to lien for any unpaid charges and advances on the released portion, in addition to the lien as aforedescribed.

Date	Lot #	Quantity Released	Signature	Quantity Due on Receipt

COMMERCIAL PAPER

People use commercial paper all the time. When people go to the grocery store for food, quite often they give the store employee a check. If a person wants to buy a car, he or she may borrow the money to pay for it from a bank. The banker requires the borrower to sign a note in which the borrower agrees to pay the money back. Both the note and the check are forms of commercial paper. We use commercial paper as a substitute for money and as a credit device.

The law dealing with assignments, as discussed in Chapter 12, affects many aspects of commercial paper. In particular, the law of assignments governs any instrument that fails to qualify as a negotiable instrument.

Contracts and Commercial Paper

A person may enter into a contract with another person for the payment of money. Suppose Smith agrees to pay Jones $100, and they enter into a contract that reflects Smith's obligation to pay $100 to Jones. In general, Jones's right to receive $100 may be assigned by Jones to a third person. Jones in this case is referred to as the assignor or transferor, and the person to whom he has transferred this right to receive money is referred to as the assignee or transferee. There is nothing improper about assigning a contractual right to receive money to a third party.

Rather than sign a contract to pay $100, Jones instead might ask Smith to sign a negotiable instrument in which Smith agrees to pay the $100 to Jones. Jones then may transfer the instrument to a third person. When a negotiable instrument is given by Smith to Jones, the UCC refers to the transfer as an **issuance** of the instrument. If Jones properly transfers the instrument to a third party, the UCC calls this a **negotiation.**

A right to receive money may be created by contract and *assigned* to a third party, or it may be created by a negotiable instrument and *negotiated* to a third party. In either case, the third party may collect.

Issuance the first delivery of an instrument to a holder

Negotiation the transfer of an instrument to a third party

TYPES OF COMMERCIAL PAPER

Promissory Notes

A promissory note is a written promise to pay money. It must contain an unconditional promise to pay a certain sum in money. It must be payable on demand or at a definite time. It must be payable to order or to the bearer. It must be signed by the person making the promise.

There are two parties to the instrument: 1. the **maker,** who agrees to pay a certain sum of money; and 2. the **payee,** the person whom the maker promises to pay.

A *demand* note is one that is payable on demand. A *time* note is one that is payable at some definite time. If a note states that it is payable on demand, the person in possession of the instrument knows that he or she may collect on the instrument immediately by demanding payment from the maker. If the note states that it is payable 90 days after date, the person in possession of the instrument knows that the maker must pay 90 days from the date on the note.

In the note in Figure 20-3, Douglas Whitman, the maker, promises to pay a certain sum of money to Thomas Dunfee, the payee. The payee knows that he will be able to demand payment on this instrument two years from January 1, 1987. Because this instrument is not payable on demand, it is a time note.

Suppose that Thomas Dunfee wishes to transfer this instrument to Bartley Bren-

Maker the party to a note who promises to pay a sum of money

Payee the person to whom an instrument originally is issued

FIGURE 20-3 Promissory Note

$100.00   Kansas City, Kansas January 1, 1987
Two (2) years after date I promise to pay to the order of Thomas Dunfee
One Hundred and no/100 _____ dollars
Payable at the First National Bank of Kansas City

                                                    Douglas Whitman
                                                    SAMPLE

nan. Dunfee may transfer his rights under this note to Brennan by endorsing it, usually on the back of the instrument, and delivering it to Brennan. In this case, Dunfee is called the *endorser* (or transferor) and Brennan is referred to as the *endorsee* (or transferee).

Drafts

Draft a written order to pay money

Drawer the person who orders a drawee to pay a draft

Drawee the person to whom an order to pay a draft is directed

A **draft** is a written *order* to pay money. It is a written, unconditional order by one person addressed to another person, signed by the person giving the order, requiring the person to whom it is addressed to pay a certain sum in money, on demand or at some specific time, to the order of the bearer or some specific person. The person giving the order is called the **drawer.** The person to whom the order is addressed is the **drawee.** The person who is to receive the money is the *payee.* The drawer may name himself or herself as the payee.

In the draft shown in Figure 20-4, John Blackburn, the *drawer,* orders William McCarty, the *drawee,* to pay a sum of money to Frank Gibson, the *payee.* It is an unconditional order, in writing, signed by John Blackburn (the party who gives the order), to William McCarty. It orders William McCarty to pay a certain sum in

FIGURE 20-4 Draft

$100.00   January 1, 1987
                                               SAMPLE

Thirty days after date _____
Pay to the order of Frank Gibson
One Hundred and no/100 _____ dollars
To: *William McCarty*   Charge the same to the
      Kalamazoo, Michigan   account of *John Blackburn*

money ($100) to the order of a specific person, Frank Gibson. The draft in this case is not payable immediately, as it would be in the case of a demand instrument. This draft is a time instrument, as opposed to a demand instrument, because it is not payable until 30 days after January 1, 1987.

While John Blackburn has ordered William McCarty to pay $100, McCarty is not obligated to pay anything until McCarty agrees to pay this draft. If he agrees to pay the draft, he becomes an **acceptor.** A drawee becomes an acceptor of a draft by signing his or her name across the face of the draft. The acceptor may write also on the instrument the date on which he or she accepted the instrument as well as the place where it will be paid. Once the drawee has accepted the draft, he or she is obligated to pay it when it becomes due.

Acceptor a drawee who has agreed to pay a draft when it is due

As was the case for the note, if Frank Gibson, the payee, wants to transfer this instrument to Tom Dunfee, he may do so. Gibson may transfer his rights under this draft to Dunfee by endorsing the draft and delivering it to Dunfee. In this case, Gibson is called the endorser (or transferor) and Dunfee is called the endorsee (or transferee).

Checks

A **check** is a special form of draft that is written by a depositor (drawer) directing a bank (drawee) to pay a designated sum of money on demand to a third party (payee).

Check a special form of draft drawn on a bank

The check in Figure 20-5 is payable on demand. Whenever the person named on the check presents it for payment, he or she is entitled to payment of the $100. (See Chapter 23, "Checks," for an extensive discussion of the law relating to checks.) The drawer of the check is Bartley Brennan, who signed it. The drawee is the First National Bank of Chicago. The payee is Douglas Whitman. Clearly, this check contains an unconditional order directed to the bank to pay a certain sum in money, at a definite time, to the order of a specific person.

A special form of check called a *cashier's check* is a check drawn by a bank on itself.

Certificates of Deposit

A **certificate of deposit** (CD) represents an acknowledgment by a financial institution of the receipt of a designated sum of money plus a promise to repay this sum at an agreed rate of interest.

Certificate of deposit (CD) an instrument acknowledging that a bank has received money and promises to repay it

FIGURE 20-5 Check

```
SAMPLE                                           No. 101
                                           January 1, 1987
                                                  $100.00
         Pay to the order of Douglas Whitman
         One Hundred and no/100 _____ dollars
         The First National Bank of Chicago    Bartley Brennan
```

PARTIES TO COMMERCIAL PAPER

Accommodation Party

Accommodation party a person who lends his or her name and credit to an instrument

An **accommodation party** is one who signs an instrument in any capacity for the purpose of lending his or her name and credit to another party to the instrument. An accommodation party may sign as a maker, acceptor, drawer, or endorser.

Why would a person need to have an accommodation party sign an instrument? The person taking the instrument wants an assurance that he or she will be paid and refuses to accept the instrument without the signature of an accommodation party. Suppose that a student wants to buy a motorcycle, but because he has not yet developed a satisfactory credit history, the bank refuses to lend him the money. The bank might agree to lend him the money if his parents agree to cosign a note. In this case, the bank is assured that it will get its money back either from him or his parents. There is some risk in signing as an accommodation party. The accommodation party may end up paying off someone else's debts, although he or she has the right to be reimbursed by the party accommodated, who in this example is the maker.

Guarantor

Guarantor a person who agrees to pay an instrument under certain circumstances

A **guarantor** is a person who signs an instrument and agrees to pay the instrument under certain circumstances. Usually, the guarantor does this by signing, in addition to his or her name, "payment guaranteed," "collection guaranteed," or similar words.

USING COMMERCIAL PAPER

Commercial paper generally is used in several ways: to borrow money, to substitute for money, or to create evidence of a debt.

To Borrow Money

If Brown goes to the bank to borrow money, the bank will probably ask Brown to sign a note in which Brown promises to repay the money over a certain period of time at a stated rate of interest. Suppose that Brown wants to buy a car with the proceeds of the loan. The bank will ask him to sign a note and a security agreement. (See Chapter 24, "Secured Transactions," for a discussion of security agreements.) The note obligates Brown to repay the money to the bank over a period of time or on a fixed date. The security agreement gives the bank an interest in the car Brown intends to buy. If Brown fails to comply with his obligations under the note, the bank will exercise its rights under the security agreement. The bank may repossess the car, resell it, and pay off the note with the proceeds of the sale.

To Create Evidence of a Debt

In the example just discussed, the note signed by Brown serves as written evidence of Brown's obligation to the bank. The fact that Brown signed a note simplifies the bank's burden of establishing that a debt exists between Brown and it. The note constitutes proof that Brown in fact owes the bank a certain amount of money, which must be repaid at a certain time.

As a Substitute for Money

Commercial paper also serves as a substitute for money. When a person goes into a store to buy something, he or she might pay for it by presenting a check to the store. If someone is buying a very expensive item, he or she probably pays by check, because it eliminates the need to carry a large sum of money. It also provides a record of payment.

Negotiability

The UCC seeks to encourage the free transfer of negotiable instruments. The holder in due course device is the basic method by which such transfer is encouraged. A **holder in due course** of a negotiable instrument is given preferred status. A holder in due course is a person with good title to an instrument, who took the instrument in good faith, for value, and without notice of any claims or defenses against it.

For example, a merchant buys goods from a manufacturer and signs a negotiable promissory note. Manufacturer negotiates the note to a bank. Merchant never receives the goods and raises that fact as a defense against the bank. Because the bank is a holder in due course, the merchant cannot successfully raise the defense of failure of consideration and refuse to pay the bank. Instead, the merchant's only recourse is to sue the manufacturer for breach of contract.

Some modifications of the rule on the holder in due course doctrine have been made in the area of consumer transactions. Some states have adopted the Uniform Consumer Credit Code, which prohibits promissory notes in the purchase of consumer goods. A major modification of the holder in due course device in consumer transactions was created by a Trade Regulation Rule adopted by the Federal Trade Commission. This rule is discussed in Chapter 21.

Holder in due course a holder of an instrument who took it in good faith, for value, and without notice of any claims or defenses against it

REQUIREMENTS OF NEGOTIABLE INSTRUMENTS

The requirements of a negotiable instrument are formal, and considerable emphasis is placed upon the use of special words. The courts look to the document itself to determine whether it is negotiable. The UCC requires that the document:

1. be signed

2. be written

3. contain an unconditional promise or order to pay

4. the promise relates to a "sum certain" of money

Further, the document must:

5. contain no other promise or order

6. be payable on demand or at a certain time

7. be payable to order or to the bearer (or words of similar meaning)

Reexamine the promissory note in Figure 20-3. Does it meet all the requirements of negotiability?

1. The instrument is signed by the maker (Doug Whitman).

2. The instrument is in writing.

3. The instrument contains an unconditional promise to pay.

4. The maker promises to pay a sum certain of money.

5. The instrument contains no other promise or order.

6. The instrument is payable at a certain time.

7. This instrument is payable to order.

Because all the elements of negotiability are present, this note qualifies as a negotiable instrument.

If some of these elements are missing, the instrument could still be transferred, but it would *not* be governed by the rules in Article 3 of the UCC. Such an instrument is nonnegotiable. It would be governed by the law of contracts and, in particular, by the law relating to assignments.

Writing

To be negotiable, an instrument must be in writing. An instrument fulfills this requirement if it is handwritten, typed, or printed. The code does not require the writing to appear on any particular material. For example, it may be written on an envelope.

Signed

To be negotiable, an instrument must be signed by the maker or drawer. An instrument need not be signed in handwriting. A signature may be made by printing, stamping, writing, or initialing. To qualify as a valid signature, the symbol on the instrument must have been executed or adopted by the person who signed the instrument with the intention of authenticating the writing.

Most people sign instruments by writing their signatures on them. But others print the name of a person or business on a check. This signature is also valid.

Agent   A person need not sign an instrument personally. A person may designate an agent or representative to sign for him or her.

In the following case, the owner of a business permitted his agent to write checks on the business account. The name of the business was printed on the check, but the agent merely signed his name.

Jenkins v. *Evans*

New York Supreme Court
295 N.Y.S.2d 226 (1968)

Albert Stickler wrote a check on the Glass Lake House account, on which he was authorized to write checks. He gave his check to Payne, who transferred it to Jenkins. Evans, the owner of the Glass Lake House, was sued by Jenkins to recover the face amount of the check. Evans claimed he was not liable because neither his signature nor the words "Glass Lake House" appeared on the signature line of the check. Jenkins satisfied the requirements for a holder in due course of the check.   FACTS

Is Evans liable on this check?   ISSUE

The court held that neither the words "Glass Lake House" nor Evans's signature was required to appear on the signature line. The fact that Evans's name and address were printed at the top of the check indicate that it was not necessary for Stickler to note that he was signing in a representative capacity. Because Stickler's name was authorized by Evans as a proper signature, then there was nothing to indicate that his capacity to sign the check was limited to business rather than personal purposes. Jenkins took the check without notice of any defense. Evans was obligated to pay the check.   DECISION

Capacity of Signer   A person may sign an instrument in a number of capacities — as a drawer of a draft, as an acceptor of a draft, as a maker of a note, or as an endorser of an instrument.

A person who signs a *note* in the lower righthand corner is presumed to be a maker. A person who signs a *draft* in the lower righthand corner is presumed to be a drawer. When the drawee of an instrument signs his or her signature across the face of the draft, the signature is regarded as an acceptance. If a person's signature is ambiguous, it is treated as an endorsement. Usually, an endorsement appears on the reverse side of an instrument.

Signature of a Representative   Although it is true that a person's signature must appear on an instrument before he or she has any liability on the instrument, the required signature may be made by someone on behalf of that person.

An agent must sign an instrument properly, or else he or she may be liable under certain circumstances for the face amount of the instrument. The correct way for a person to sign an instrument on behalf of another is as follows:

Jack Jones
by Alice Jackson, Agent

Principal a person who agrees to let an agent act on his or her behalf

A signature in this manner clearly indicates to any person taking it that the agent signed on behalf of the **principal** and did not intend to incur any personal liability on the instrument. If an officer of the corporation is signing on behalf of the corporation, he or she should sign the instrument as follows:

Boob Corporation
by Doug Whitman, President

This signature clearly indicates that Whitman signed on behalf of the corporation and intended to bind *only* the corporation and not himself. This practice becomes significant when a corporation cannot pay its debts. Usually shareholders and officers are not liable for the debts of a corporation. But when a corporation cannot pay its debts, the holders of instruments may attempt to enforce the instruments against anyone whose signature is on them. A small corporation owned by the person who signed a note might go bankrupt. In that case, the holder of the note may sue the officer who signed the note. If that person failed to sign the note in the manner suggested above, he or she might end up paying a debt of the corporation.

A very dangerous way to sign an instrument is to sign as an agent but fail to name the person represented or the fact that the agent has signed in a representative capacity. If Alice Jackson signs an instrument on behalf of Jack Jones, but the only signature appearing on the instrument is "Alice Jackson," Jack Jones is not liable. Alice Jackson is liable.

In the following case, the president of a corporation signed notes on behalf of the corporation without indicating that he was signing in a representative capacity.

Rotuba Extruders, Incorporated v. Ceppos

Court of Appeals of New York
385 N.E.2d 1068 (1978)

FACTS   Kenneth Ceppos signed seven notes so that his corporation, Kenbert Lighting Industries, Inc., could receive goods from Rotuba. Rotuba had requested that one of the owners of Kenbert guarantee payment personally. When Kenbert filed a bankruptcy petition, Rotuba sued Kenneth Ceppos on the notes. The signature line of each note contained Ceppos's signature. Above that were the words "Kenbert Lighting Ind. Inc." There was no indication that Ceppos signed in a representative capacity.

Was Ceppos personally liable on the notes?   ISSUE

Yes. Generally, Section 3-403 of the UCC does not permit resort to proof other than   DECISION
the instrument itself to establish the limited liability of the signer. There is an exception
when it is "otherwise established between the immediate parties." The signer must
establish that some agreement, understanding, or course of dealing existed, indicating
that the instrument was signed in a representative capacity only. The court held that the
undisclosed intention of Ceppos, without more, to sign in such a representative capacity
does not satisfy this burden. Ceppos had to accept personal liability on the notes.

If a person signs a check that does not mention the party represented anywhere on
the check, the signer is quite likely to be held personally liable. A more difficult case
comes up from time to time when people sign checks with their signatures alone, and
without signing the names of the parties represented nor the capacity in which they
are signing the checks, but the checks have the names of the principals printed on
them.

The UCC (Section 3-403[2][b]) clearly indicates that except as otherwise established between the parties to an instrument, an authorized representative who signs
his or her own name to an instrument is personally liable if the instrument names the
person represented but does not show that the representative signed in a representative capacity. The UCC does allow an exception to this rule if the person taking the
instrument was fully aware that the signer signed in a representative capacity, even
though the instrument does not so indicate.

The following case illustrates the approach of many courts faced with this situation.

Colonial Baking Company of Des Moines v. *Dowie*

Iowa Supreme Court
35 U.C.C. Rep. Ser. 874 (1983)

The president and sole stockholder of Fred Dowie Enterprises, Inc., ordered 325,000   FACTS
hot dog buns from Colonial Baking. He paid for the buns with a check for $28,640. The
check showed the name of the corporation and its address in the upper lefthand corner.
The signature on the check was "Frederick J. Dowie." Dowie did not sign the corporation's name nor write the word "President" after his name. Colonial sued Dowie in his
personal capacity as signer of the check. Dowie did not introduce any evidence of an
agreement, understanding, or course of dealing between the parties to the effect that
when he signed he did so as a representative of the corporation.

Is Dowie personally liable on this check in light of the fact that the corporation's name   ISSUE
was imprinted on the check?

Yes. Dowie was personally liable. A drawer of a check is personally liable if there is no   DECISION
evidence, other than the fact the corporate name was printed on the check, that the

check was signed in a representative capacity. The fact that he alleged that Colonial knew it was dealing with a corporation was not in itself sufficient for him to escape liability on the check. Dowie merely relied upon the fact that the name of the corporation was printed on the check. In that no information was introduced by Dowie that there was an agreement or understanding between himself and Colonial that he was not to be personally liable on the check, the court held Dowie liable.

Although not every court has held drawers of checks liable in a situation like this one, the *Colonial Baking* case illustrates the need to be very careful in signing a check.

Unconditional Promise or Order

To be negotiable an instrument must contain an unconditional promise or order to pay. Notes and certificates of deposit must contain an unconditional *promise* to pay. Drafts and checks must include an unconditional *order* to pay. If the language in an instrument states that the obligor *promises* to pay someone, the instrument cannot be a draft or check.

Suppose that John Doe wrote out the following statement on a piece of paper: "I.O.U. $100 [signed] John Doe." This piece of paper clearly has some elements of a negotiable instrument. But it lacks one important element: a promise or an order to pay. Although John Doe acknowledges his obligation to pay a debt of $100, he does not promise to pay it or order someone else to pay it. This missing element renders the IOU nonnegotiable. In the typical note, a statement appears such as "I promise to pay." In a draft, some language must appear that orders someone or some institution to pay.

The negotiability of an instrument must be determinable by an examination of the face of the instrument itself. If an instrument is negotiable, someone who wants to take it should not have to refer to any other document.

To determine whether the negotiable instrument includes an unconditional promise or order to pay, one need only examine the instrument itself. Oral statements do not affect the negotiable character of an instrument. Suppose that McGrew tells Allison at the time she executes a promissory note that she will pay the note only if Allison delivers a 1979 Ford to her. This statement has no effect on the negotiable character of the instrument. A party examining the face of the instrument would be unaware of the oral condition put on the instrument by McGrew when she executed the note. If the instrument states that it is subject to or governed by any other agreement, it is not negotiable. If the instrument merely refers to a separate agreement or states that it arises out of such an agreement, it is negotiable.

For example, if a note contains the statement, "Payment is subject to the terms of the contract entered into between the parties," it is not negotiable. To determine the terms of the note, a person who wishes to take it would need to examine a document other than the instrument. But a simple notation, such as, "A contract was entered into at the time of executing this note," is a mere reference to the contract and does not subject the note to the terms of the contract. A note with such a notation is negotiable.

Take the case of Allison and McGrew again. If the note McGrew signs indicates that McGrew is giving this note to Allison in consideration for the 1979 Ford, or if it indicates that the note is being transferred because Allison sold her 1979 Ford to McGrew, McGrew's promise to pay Allison is *not* rendered conditional. Such recitals only explain why the note is issued — but the note stands regardless of the recitals. But if McGrew writes into the note that the terms of the note are subject to or governed by the contract signed between McGrew and Allison for the sale of the 1979 Ford, the promise to pay is rendered conditional. The instrument would be nonnegotiable.

Sum Certain in Money

To be negotiable, an instrument must also contain a sum certain in money. If it is possible for a holder to determine at the time of payment the amount payable merely by examining the instrument itself, the amount payable is certain. If it is necessary to make computations in order to determine the amount payable, the sum is certain if the computation can be made from the instrument itself without reference to any outside source. The fact that the sum is payable with stated interest or with different rates of interest before and after default does not make the note nonnegotiable. All of this information can be determined from the face of the instrument. But if the note is payable "at the current rate," the instrument is not negotiable, because the holder would not know the current rate by examining the instrument itself.

An instrument is payable in money if the medium of exchange in which it is payable is money at the time the instrument is made. The promise to pay may be stated in foreign currency rather than in dollars. But an agreement to pay "one cow" is not payable in money. The instrument therefore is not negotiable.

Payable on Demand or at Certain Time

To be negotiable, an instrument must be payable on demand or at a definite time. In essence, someone examining the instrument must be able to determine when it is payable. An instrument is payable on demand if it is payable at sight, or on presentation, or if it contains no time for payment. It must be paid whenever the holder presents it for payment.

An instrument payable at a definite time must state the date on which it is payable. The note in Figure 20-3 is payable two years after its date — that is, two years after January 1, 1987.

According to the UCC (Section 3-109), an instrument is payable at a definite time if by its terms it is payable:

1. on or before a stated date or at a fixed period after a stated date

2. at a fixed period after sight

3. at a definite time subject to acceleration

4. at a definite time subject to extension at the option of the holder

5. at a definite time subject to extension to a further definite time at the option of the maker or acceptor or automatically upon or after a specified act or event.

The instrument in Figure 20-3 is payable at a fixed period after a stated date. A draft payable "30 days after sight" is also payable at a definite time. When the holder presents it to the drawee, and the drawee accepts it (thereby becoming the acceptor of the draft), the 30-day period begins to run.

Acceleration clause a clause that advances the date for payment

The time for payment must be determinable from the face of the instrument. An instrument may contain an **acceleration clause,** which, in an instrument payable at a definite time, permits the entire draft to become due immediately upon the option of one of the parties or the occurrence of some specified event. A clause in an instrument that reads "payable June 1, 1988, but the entire sum is due and payable immediately in the event the maker dies" is a valid acceleration clause. The payee of this instrument knows that he or she will be paid on June 1, 1988, at the latest, or earlier if the maker dies before that time. An instrument also can be written so that the holder may accelerate the time for payment. However, the holder must reasonably believe that the prospect of payment or performance has been impaired.

If the instrument is payable only upon the event of an uncertain occurrence, the instrument is not payable at a definite time even though the act or event has occurred. For instance, if the note is payable "upon the marriage of my daughter," and the daughter now has married, the note is still not payable at a definite time. It must be possible to determine, at the time a person takes the instrument, whether the instrument is payable at a definite time or on demand. The specified event (the daughter's marriage) may never occur. She may never marry, or she may die before the note comes due. In such cases, the instrument never would be payable. No one would want to take an instrument unless he or she was certain that it would be paid either immediately or at some definite time in the future.

The following case concerns a note that the court determines is not negotiable because it was not payable on demand or at a definite time.

Barton v. Hudgens Realty and Mortgage, Incorporated

Court of Appeals of Georgia
222 S.E.2d 126 (1975)

FACTS

Barton signed a promissory note with Hudgens Realty which was to become due and payable once an "acceptable permanent loan" had been arranged by Hudgens and had been accepted by Barton. The note was signed by Barton. Hudgens got a loan of $290,000. Barton nevertheless alleged that an acceptable permanent loan had not been made because he had not accepted the loan. Barton argued that the note was not due and payable as Hudgens argued. Hudgens brought suit on the note to require payment of the $3,000 loan origination fee under the terms of the note.

ISSUE

Is this instrument a negotiable instrument?

DECISION

No. The court held that the case was not governed by the UCC but rather by the general law of contracts. To be a promissory note, the instrument must be payable on demand or at a definite time. If payable upon an act or event uncertain in time, a note is not payable at a definite time and therefore is not negotiable. Had the note been negotiable, the UCC would have allowed a judgment for Hudgens based on the admission by Barton that he signed the note. The court found the note to be a contract to pay money if a loan were secured by Hudgens. In that Hudgens successfully secured a permanent loan, the fee had been earned by Hudgens. Barton was obligated to pay the $3,000 called for in the contract if a loan were arranged by Hudgens.

To Order or Bearer

To Order   To be negotiable, an instrument also must be payable to order or to the bearer. An instrument payable to the order of a person is called an **order instrument**. A check payable "to the order of John Jones" is negotiable. The courts interpret this requirement strictly: a check "payable to John Jones" is not negotiable because it does not say "to the order of John Jones." The printed checks issued by banks have "to the order of" printed on them. An instrument alternatively might state "to John Jones or order" or "to John Jones or assigns."

An instrument must specify a particular person or organization so that it will be clear who is entitled to payment. It can be made payable to more than one person. For example, an instrument can be "payable to the order of John Doe and Acme Car Repair." In this case, the instrument may be properly negotiated to a third party only if *both* parties to the instrument endorse it and if the instrument is delivered to the appropriate party. An instrument made payable to two parties in this fashion may not be properly negotiated if *only* John Doe *or* Acme Car Repair endorses it. People often use this device when they want to make certain that all parties to whom they are obligated have been paid. But if an instrument is made payable to the order of "John Doe *or* Acme Car Repair," the signature of *either* party as an endorser, along with a delivery of the instrument, will result in a proper negotiation.

> **Order instrument** an instrument payable to the order of a specified person

To Bearer   Even though an instrument fails to qualify as an order instrument, it is negotiable if it is payable to bearer. An instrument payable to bearer is called **bearer paper.** If an instrument is payable "to order of bearer" or "cash," it is bearer paper. Anyone who gets possession of this instrument has the power to negotiate it. Instruments containing phrases like "Pay cash," "Pay to the order of cash," "Pay bills payable," or others that do not designate a specific payee are treated as instruments payable to bearer.

> **Bearer paper** an instrument not payable to the order of a specified bearer

Incomplete Instrument   An instrument that merely states "to the order of" followed by a blank space is an *incomplete* order instrument. The following case illustrates what may happen if the instrument fails to specify a payee.

Gray v. American Express Company

Court of Appeals of North Carolina
239 S.E.2d 621 (1977)

Gray received an order from Ernie's Truck Stop for about $4,900 worth of cigarettes. Gray delivered them to the manager, who turned them over to Faillance, a

FACTS

customer of Ernie's. Faillance issued $4,800 in American Express Travelers Checks for the purchase, which he signed, but he did not date or make them payable to anyone. The manager gave the checks to Gray but did not endorse them. Gray turned the checks over to a local bank, still blank as to date and payee, and was refused payment on the grounds that they were stolen, even though the signature and countersignature matched. Gray was again refused payment by Chase Manhattan Bank.

ISSUE   Must American Express honor the check?

DECISION   No. The court held that a travelers check is a negotiable instrument under Article 3 of the UCC and that Section 3-114 permits an instrument to be undated without affecting its validity or enforceability under Section 3-115. But the name of the payee is an essential element (Section 3-104). Under the UCC, a note payable neither to order nor to bearer is incomplete and nonnegotiable. Both the manager and ultimately Gray had the authority to complete the payee's name, but in that neither did so, the instrument remained incomplete and unenforceable.

An incomplete instrument is payable neither to order nor to bearer and is not negotiable. No one can become a holder in due course of such an instrument.

No Other Promise, Order, Obligation, or Power

Even if an instrument is a signed writing containing an unconditional promise or order to pay a sum certain in money, payable on demand or at a definite time, and payable to order or bearer, it still may not be negotiable if the maker or drawer gives any other promise, order, obligation, or power except as authorized by Article 3.

Certain additional information may be given in an instrument without impairing its negotiability. A statement that collateral has been given to secure the obligation does not impair the negotiability of an instrument. For example, a person obtaining a loan to buy a car signs a note for the bank indicating that the maker is using the car as collateral. That is, if he or she fails to make the payments specified under the note, the bank may repossess the car. (See Chapter 24, "Secured Transactions," for a discussion of collateral.) Merely mentioning this information does not impair the negotiability of the instrument. Similarly, the note may indicate that the maker must protect the collateral. (Other information that may appear in a note without impairing its negotiability appears in UCC Section 3-112).

The negotiability of an instrument is not affected by the omission of the place where the instrument is drawn and payable (Section 3-112).

Date

In most cases, the negotiability of an instrument is not affected by the fact that it is undated. But if an instrument states that it is "payable 15 days after date," the instrument is not negotiable if it is undated. It is an incomplete instrument. The instrument may be completed as authorized (Section 3-115). The instrument is not negotiable until the date is filled in.

An instrument also is not rendered nonnegotiable because it is dated some time in the past (an antedated instrument) or at some time in the future (a postdated instrument).

RULES OF CONSTRUCTION

The UCC (Section 3-118) lists several rules that apply if the writing is ambiguous or leaves out certain information. When one is in doubt as to how to interpret an instrument, these rules should be consulted: If there is doubt whether an instrument is a note or a draft, the holder may treat the instrument as either. Handwritten terms control typewritten and printed terms, and typewritten control printed. Words generally control figures, but if the words are ambiguous, the figures control.

SUMMARY

People use documents of title when goods are temporarily transferred to another party for shipping or storing.

Some types of commercial paper contain promises to pay: promissory notes and certificates of deposit. There are two parties to a note, the maker and the payee. Other types of commercial paper contain orders to pay: drafts and checks. Checks are simply a special form of draft on which the drawee is a bank. There are three parties to a draft: the drawer, the drawee, and the payee.

For an instrument to qualify as a negotiable instrument, it must satisfy nine requirements: it must be signed, in writing, contain a promise or order to pay, which is unconditional, relates to a sum certain, the sum being in money. The instrument must not contain any other promise or order, it must be payable on demand or at a certain time, and it must be payable to order or to bearer.

That an instrument is negotiable does not mean that the person holding the instrument may collect whatever sums are due under the instrument. An instrument may be negotiable but not collectible.

REVIEW PROBLEMS

1. What is a document of title?

2. What advantages are associated with taking a negotiable instrument as opposed to a simple contract to receive money?

3. Ross agrees to pay his cousin Mary $300. He signs a piece of paper that states: "IOU $300 [signed] Ross James." Is this a negotiable instrument?

4. Anderson signs a demand note for $200, payable to the order of Bailey. The note states that it was given in exchange for the sale of a bicycle by Bailey to Anderson. The note also states that it is governed by the terms of the contract entered into between Bailey and Anderson for the sale of the bicycle. Do either of these provisions render the note nonnegotiable?

5. Erwin enters into a contract with Singer for the purchase of some machinery. Erwin promises to pay Singer $2,000 for the machinery. Erwin signs a note that specifies, among other things, that the note will be paid by Erwin in British pounds sterling. The note also states that it is "payable 6 months after sight, but the entire sum is due and payable immediately if Erwin dies." Is this instrument negotiable?

6. Prentice entered into a contract with Moore. Prentice signed the following note "January 1, 1986, 30 days after date, pay to Bill Moore the sum of one hundred and no/100 dollars [signed] Mary Prentice." Is this instrument negotiable?

7. An instrument contains the following information: "January 1, 1986, thirty (30) days after date I promise to pay to the order of John Frank the sum of one Hundred and no/100 Dollars [signed] Peter Graves." Identify what type of instrument this is.

8. An instrument reads as follows: "January 1, 1986, on demand, pay to the order of Alice Smith the sum of one Hundred and no/100 Dollars [signed] Jack Jones." In the lower lefthand corner, it also states, "to Bill Ford, Kansas City, Missouri." What type of instrument is this? Who is liable on this instrument in its current form?

9. Michelle Clark was asked by her brother, David Clark, to act as his representative while he was out of the country. David gave Michelle the authority to sign instruments on his behalf until he returned to the country. Michelle was asked to sign a note on behalf of David. What is the proper way for her to sign this note?

10. Davis Aircraft Engineering, Inc., entered into a loan agreement with Bank A. On the face of each note was printed: "This note evidences a borrowing made under, and is subject to, the terms of the loan agreement." There is nothing in the loan agreement that would impose any contingency upon the obligation to pay. Davis contends that there is not an unconditional promise to pay. Will Davis win?

11. Hotel Evans contracted with A. Alport & Son to construct a hotel and in return gave Alport certain promissory notes. The notes contained the notation "with interest at bank rates." At the time of payment, the bank wrote "8½%" above the words "bank rates." Are the notes negotiable?

12. Defendant executed and delivered two promissory notes to Consumer Foods, Inc., who subsequently assigned the notes to Aetnor Acceptance Corporation. The notes simply stated in part, "Buyer agrees to pay to Seller . . ." In light of this wording, are these promissory notes negotiable?

13. Max Williams signed and delivered a note to Glenn W. Cooper that, among other things, contained the following statement: "At the earliest possible time after date, without grace, for value received, I promise to pay to the order of

Glenn W. Cooper, payable at Seymour, Texas, Five Thousand Dollars.'' Is this a negotiable instrument in light of this language?

14. Knoxville Casket Co. entered into a loan agreement with Acme Metals. On the face of the note appears the following provision: ''90 days after date, for value received, Knoxville Casket Co. promises to pay to the order of Acme Metals the face amount of the note.'' The signature of the president of Knoxville Casket Co. appears on the face of each note without designating that he is president or agent for Knoxville Casket Co. Acme asserts that the president is personally liable for debt. At the trial, there is testimony that the president intended to sign only in his representative capacity and that Acme knew of his intentions. Is the president held liable?

15. Griffin, the president of Greenway Co., signs checks to pay for a project for the company. The company's name and address appear on the check. There is nothing on the check to indicate Griffin's office or capacity to sign for the corporation. Should he be held personally liable?

CHAPTER 21

Commercial Paper: Transfer, Negotiation, and Holder in Due Course

CHAPTER OBJECTIVES

After reading this chapter, you should be able to:

1. Explain when an instrument has been issued.

2. Explain what it takes to negotiate an instrument.

3. Define the meaning and consequences of the various types of endorsements.

4. Define holder in due course.

5. Define holder through a holder in due course.

6. Explain the consequences of a holder in due course dealing with a party.

7. Explain the FTC's modification of the holder in due course rule.

As noted in the preceding chapter, several conditions must be met for a person to qualify as a holder in due course:

1. The person must have a *negotiable* instrument (as explained in Chapter 20).

2. The instrument must be issued or *negotiated* to the holder.

3. The person in possession of the negotiable instrument validly issued or negotiated to him or her must also *comply with Section 3-302* of the Uniform Commercial Code.

When these three conditions are met, the person becomes a holder in due course. This chapter examines the concepts of negotiation and holder in due course.

TRANSFER AND NEGOTIATION

Issue

When a negotiable instrument has been drawn up and signed by the parties, one more step must take place for the instrument to become enforceable: It must be **issued** by the maker or drawer to the holder. In the typical transaction, issuance occurs when the maker or drawer of the instrument hands the instrument to the payee. This delivery of the instrument by the drawer or maker to the payee is called an *issuance* of the instrument.

Issue delivery of an instrument by the drawer or maker to the payee

The maker or drawer of an instrument is *not* liable on an instrument until he or she delivers or issues it. Delivery of an instrument simply means its voluntary transfer. Transfer may be achieved either by physical delivery or, in rare instances, by constructive delivery of the instrument. Constructive delivery occurs when the maker or drawer performs a symbolic act representing the transfer. For example, delivering the keys to a safe containing the instrument may constitute a constructive transfer.

Transfer

Once the original maker or drawer of an instrument has signed and issued the instrument, the instrument may be transferred to a third party. If the transfer qualifies as negotiation, the person to whom the instrument is transferred becomes a **holder** of the instrument. If the transfer fails to qualify as a negotiation, the person to whom the instrument is transferred (the assignee) never attains the status of a holder in due course. Such a person takes the instrument by **assignment** (as opposed to taking it by negotiation) and therefore may not become a holder of the instrument. A person must be a holder of an instrument to qualify as a holder in due course. This is true even if the instrument assigned qualifies as a negotiable instrument under Section 3-104(1).

The transfer of an instrument by assignment is governed by common law contract rules. The rights of the person acquiring an instrument by assignment are no greater than those of the person from whom he or she acquired the instrument.

Holder a person to whom an instrument has been negotiated

Assignment the transfer of rights or benefits of a contract

Negotiation

How does one become a holder? The person in possession of an instrument must in some cases have:

1. the **endorsement** of the prior holder of the instrument and

2. delivery of the instrument.

In other cases, the delivery of the instrument alone is enough to negotiate the instrument. If the instrument qualifies as an **order instrument,** the former is required, but a **bearer instrument** may be negotiated by delivery alone. As we have noted earlier, an order instrument generally is one made payable to the order of someone. A bearer instrument is one made payable to bearer or cash.

Suppose that Smith writes a note but makes it payable to bearer, as shown in Figure 21-1. Smith now physically delivers the note to Jones. The act of transferring the note to Jones is an *issuance* of the instrument. What if Jones now wants to transfer this note to her daughter, Mary? What must she do to validly negotiate the note so that Mary becomes a holder of the instrument? All Jones must do is deliver the note to Mary, because this is a bearer instrument, which may be negotiated by delivery alone.

Suppose instead that this note was made payable to the order of Mrs. Jones, as in Figure 21-2. If Jones merely delivers this instrument to Mary, she has not negotiated the instrument. This note must be endorsed on the back by Jones and delivered to Mary to negotiate it, because it is an *order instrument.*

Because they may be negotiated by delivery alone, instruments that are payable to bearer are risky. What if Smith signed the first note, which was payable to bearer, and a thief stole it from him? There is no delivery of the instrument to the thief because a

Endorsement the signature of an endorser written for the purpose of transferring an instrument

Order instrument an instrument payable to the order of a specified person

Bearer instrument an instrument not payable to the order of a specified person

FIGURE 21-1

$100.00   Chicago, Illinois, January 1, 1987
On demand I promise to pay to the order of *bearer*
One hundred and no/100 _____ dollars
Payable at First National Bank, Chicago, Illinois

John Smith
SAMPLE

delivery is a *voluntary* transfer of possession. No negotiation takes place, and the thief does not acquire an interest in the note. But the thief may transfer this instrument to a subsequent innocent purchaser. The UCC permits such a person taking bearer paper to become a holder of the instrument. In other words, although the thief may not acquire title to stolen bearer paper, the thief has the power to transfer good title to a third party. A party who is unaware of the theft may become a holder of the instrument and may enforce the instrument against the original maker.

Although bearer instruments expose the maker or drawer to some risks, order instruments do not. Take the note illustrated in Figure 21.2. It is payable to the order of Jones and therefore qualifies as an order instrument. Suppose that a thief or finder comes into possession of this instrument. If the thief signs Jones's name and transfers the instrument to an innocent third party, Quinn, does Quinn become a holder of the instrument? No. This instrument was drawn payable to the order of Jones. To negotiate it, there must be a delivery of the instrument, and the instrument must be endorsed by Jones. The *forged* endorsement by the thief is ineffective. No title to the instrument passes to Quinn. She does not become a holder. The note has not been negotiated to Quinn, because she lacks Jones's endorsement. Because Quinn holds the instrument through a forged endorsement, when she presents it to Smith for payment, Smith may refuse to pay the instrument if he detects that Jones did not sign it. Not only does Quinn not qualify as a holder of the instrument, but anyone Quinn transfers the instrument to also does not become a holder. No one may qualify as a holder under a forged endorsement of an order instrument.

FIGURE 21-2

$100.00   Chicago, Illinois, January 1, 1987
On demand I promise to pay to the order of Grace Jones
One hundred and no/100 _____ dollars
Payable at First National Bank, Chicago, Illinois

John Smith
SAMPLE

ENDORSEMENTS

Negotiable instruments are endorsed for two reasons:

1. the endorsement may be necessary for negotiating the instrument and
2. the endorsement may be required to obligate the endorsee to pay the instrument (under circumstances discussed in the next chapter).

Blank Endorsement

Blank endorsement an endorsement that does not specify a particular payee

A **blank endorsement** specifies no particular endorsee and may consist of a mere signature. It is the most common type of endorsement. How would Jones endorse in blank the note in Figure 21-2 that was payable to her order? On the reverse side of the note she would sign as shown in Figure 21-3. When Jones signs the instrument in this fashion and delivers it to another person, the note has been negotiated. The person to whom she transfers the note becomes a holder of the note. Jones has transferred title to the instrument to the third person. By endorsing the instrument in this fashion, she also promises to pay the instrument, under certain circumstances.

When an instrument is payable to order and it is endorsed in blank, it becomes payable to bearer and may be negotiated by delivery alone. Just as in the case of an instrument originally payable to bearer, an instrument that is endorsed in blank may be negotiated by delivery alone. The same risks associated with an instrument that is originally payable to bearer also apply to an instrument that is endorsed in blank.

Special Endorsements

Special endorsement an endorsement that specifies to whom or to whose order an instrument is payable

A **special endorsement** specifies the person to whom or to whose order an instrument is payable. Jones could endorse the note discussed earlier as shown in Figure 21-4. The note in question was originally payable to the order of Jones and therefore

FIGURE 21-3

FIGURE 21-4

was an order instrument. When Jones endorses the note in this manner it becomes payable to the order of the special endorsee (Mary Jones) and may be further negotiated only by Mary Jones's endorsement and delivery of the note to a third person. A note remains an order instrument when it is endorsed with a special endorsement.

Jones also could have endorsed the note with the words "Pay to the order of Mary Jones, [signed] Grace Jones" or "Pay to Mary Jones or order, [signed] Grace Jones." In other words, it is not necessary to include the words of negotiability in the special endorsement. Although it is true that an instrument originally must be payable to order or to bearer to be negotiable, the special endorsement need not include the words of negotiability.

It is possible to convert an instrument endorsed in blank into a special endorsement by writing over the signature of the endorser in blank words such as "Pay to Mary Jones." If Mary's mother simply endorsed the note over to Mary by signing "Grace Jones" on the reverse side, Mary could convert the endorsement into a special endorsement by writing the words "Pay to Mary Jones" above her mother's signature. The instrument then would need to be endorsed by Mary Jones and delivered to someone for there to be a valid negotiation of the instrument.

By specially endorsing bearer paper and thereby converting it to order paper, the person taking possession of the instrument avoids the risks associated with bearer paper. If a thief steals the instrument, the thief must forge the signature of the special endorsee to whose order the instrument is payable. Because a forged endorsement is ineffective, the special endorsee has protected himself or herself.

The following case illustrates the use of special endorsements.

Klomann v. Sol K. Graff & Sons

Appellate Court of Illinois
317 N.E.2d 608 (1974)

Robert J. Graff, one of the partners of Sol K. Graff & Sons, executed three promissory notes naming Fred Klomann as payee on each note. Fred Klomann held the notes for a time and then specially endorsed them to his daughter, gave them to her for inspection, and later placed them in safekeeping. Still possessing the notes, Fred later scratched out his daughter's name and inserted his wife's name, after which he delivered them to Mrs. Klomann. She brought suit for the value of the notes against Robert Graff and Sol K. Graff & Sons. Graff contended that she had no right, title, or interest in the notes and refused to pay.   FACTS

Is Mrs. Klomann entitled to enforce these notes?   ISSUE

No. Under Section 3-204 of the UCC, once an instrument has been specially endorsed, it requires the endorsement of the special endorsee to be further negotiated. Merely scratching out the special endorsee's name and inserting Mrs. Klomann's name was insufficient to negotiate the note to her. Once Fred Klomann endorsed the notes to his daughter, he had no more interest in them and had no power to negotiate the notes further.   DECISION

Qualified Endorsements

The two endorsements discussed above, in blank and special, are also *unqualified* endorsements. The in blank or special endorser promises to pay the holder of the instrument under certain circumstances. For example, suppose that Jones receives the $100 note from Smith. Jones then endorses the note in blank and delivers it to Mary Jones. If Mary attempts to collect from Smith when the note comes due, but Smith refuses to pay, Mary could sue Jones for the $100 because Jones endorsed with an unqualified endorsement. The unqualified endorser in effect guarantees payment of the instrument if the holder is unable to collect from the maker, drawer, or acceptor when the instrument comes due.

A person who wishes to sign as a qualified endorser does so by adding "without recourse" or similar words to the endorsement, as in Figures 21-5 and 21-6. The endorsement in Figure 21-5 is a qualified, in blank endorsement. The endorsement in Figure 21-6 is a **qualified,** special **endorsement.** When Jones signs in either of these ways, she eliminates her secondary or conditional liability as an endorser. The conditional or **secondary liability** is the agreement of an unqualified endorser to pay the instrument if the party primarily obligated to pay fails to pay the instrument when it comes due.

Both a qualified and an unqualified endorser, however, give certain warranties to the people to whom they transfer their instruments. This warranty liability is not excluded by signing an instrument with a qualified endorsement.

Qualified endorsement an obligation of the unqualified endorser to pay an instrument if the party primarily obligated to pay fails to pay when the note comes due

Secondary liability a condition in which a promisor is liable only after the original debtor has defaulted

Restrictive Endorsements

In addition to in blank, special, and qualified endorsements, the UCC also creates a category of endorsements called restrictive endorsements. The UCC creates several types of restrictive endorsements.

FIGURE 21-5

FIGURE 21-6

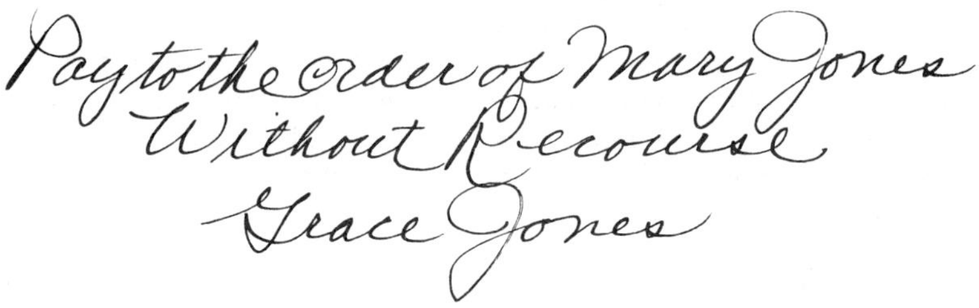

Conditional Restrictive   If the endorsement imposes a condition on the right of the endorsee to collect, it is a **conditional restrictive endorsement**. Suppose that Jones, when she received the note from Smith payable to her order, endorsed the note over to her daughter Mary in the following fashion: "Pay to Mary Jones when she delivers her 1957 Ford to me, [signed] Grace Jones." This actually is a conditional restrictive endorsement. Jones then hands the note to Mary.

Why would Jones endorse the note in this manner? She wants to make certain that she receives the 1957 Ford before Mary is paid. In effect, she is putting a restriction on the ability of Mary to collect on this note. Once Mary delivers the Ford to her mother, she may collect on the note but not before.

Restrictive endorsements, including conditional restrictive endorsements, do not prevent the further transfer or negotiation of the instrument. Conditional restrictive endorsements are not common.

Prohibit Further Transfer   Endorsements that try to bar further transfer of an instrument are not common. Such an endorsement might read: "Pay to Mary only." The endorser is trying to bar further transfer of the instrument. But such an endorsement does *not* prevent the further transfer or negotiation of the instrument.

For Deposit or Collection   The most common restrictive endorsement includes words such as "**for collection**," "**for deposit**," "pay any bank," or other terms signifying a purpose of deposit or collection. For example, if Smith gave Jones a check for $100, she might endorse the check, "For deposit, [signed] Grace Jones." Hers is an in blank, restrictive, unqualified endorsement.

The endorsement "pay any bank" specifies that only banks are to receive the proceeds of the instrument. When a person deposits a check to his or her bank account, the bank may restrictively endorse the check in this manner. Only a bank then may become a holder of an instrument so endorsed, unless a bank specially endorses the check to someone who is not a bank. A bank might use such an endorsement when putting a check through the collection process.

To the extent that a transferee pays or applies any value given by the transferee consistently with the endorsement, he or she becomes a holder for value. If the transferee otherwise complies with Section 3-302, he or she qualifies as a holder in due course. If Jones's bank credits her account for the $100, it has applied the value consistent with the "For deposit" endorsement and is therefore a holder. When the payor bank pays the intermediary bank, it has paid the check consistent with the "For collection" or "Pay any bank" endorsement, and the payor bank qualifies as a holder.

Trust Endorsements   A restrictive endorsement that states that it is for the benefit or use of the endorser or another person is a **trust endorsement**. It is the fourth type of restrictive endorsement recognized under Section 3-205. Such an endorsement might read "Pay Lance only in trust for Mary." In this case, Lance, the restrictive endorsee, is acting as a representative of Mary and holds any money paid on the instrument in trust for Mary. To the extent that Lance applies the proceeds consistent with the terms of the endorsement, he qualifies as a holder.

Conditional restrictive endorsement an endorsement that Imposes a condition on the right of an endorsee to collect

For deposit endorsement an endorsement that uses the words "for deposit"

For collection endorsement an endorsement that uses words such as "for collection" or "pay any bank"

Trust endorsement an endorsement that states that it is for the benefit or the use of the endorser or another person

As with the three other types of restrictive endorsements, a trust endorsement does not prevent the further transfer or negotiation of the instrument.

Restrictive Endorsements Generally   Most restrictive endorsements require the endorsee to take some action on the proceeds of an instrument, such as holding it in trust for someone or depositing it to someone's account.

HOLDER IN DUE COURSE

To become a holder in due course of a negotiable instrument, a holder must take the instrument:

1. for value

2. in good faith

3. without knowing that the instrument is overdue, dishonored, or has any defense against or claim to it (Section 3-302).

Even assuming a person in possession of an instrument fulfills these three requirements, he or she still may not qualify as a holder in due course. A person wishing to claim that status also must establish that he or she holds a *negotiable* instrument and that he or she is a *holder* of the instrument.

The mere fact that a person holds a nonnegotiable instrument does not mean that he or she may not recover. As we noted earlier, the right to receive money generally is assignable to third persons. The only problem for the assignee is that he or she steps into the shoes of the assignor. That is, the assignee acquires only the rights the assignor had. If a defense existed between the original parties to a contract to pay money, that defense may be asserted against the assignee of the contractual right to receive money.

Assuming that the note is negotiable and the person attempting to enforce it is a holder, that person may qualify as a holder in due course if he or she otherwise complies with Section 3-302. The following material discusses these requirements.

For Value

Executory promise a promise that has not yet been fulfilled

Executory Promise   An **executory promise** to give value is not value. Thus if an attorney is given a note for $200,000 for $10,000 in legal services already rendered, with the rest of the services to be rendered in the future, the attorney would be a holder in due course of the note only to the extent of $10,000. The promise of the attorney to perform services could serve as consideration to support a contract, but a promise to perform services does not qualify as giving value. Had the attorney in this case already performed services worth $200,000, he or she would have given value.

Suppose that Smith executes the $100 note payable to Jones. What if Jones gives the note to Mary, who promises to pay her mother $100 in return for the note? May Mary qualify as a holder in due course? No. Mary has not given value in exchange for the note. Hers is a mere executory promise to give value. Until Mary pays the $100, she has not given value. If she sues Smith before she pays the $100 to her mother, Smith may assert any defense he has on the instrument against Mary, because Mary is not a holder in due course.

In some instances, an executory promise may be regarded as value. Section 3-303(c) states that a holder takes an instrument for value when he or she "gives a negotiable instrument for it or makes an irrevocable commitment to a third person." Giving an instrument for an instrument constitutes value.

Suppose that Jones transfers Smith's $100 note in return for Mary's check for $100. When Mary gives the check to her mother, she has given value for the note.

Any irrevocable commitment by the holder to a third party also is treated as value. Suppose that a company gives its bank a $1,000 note. In return, the bank issues a letter of credit in which it promises to pay a seller from whom the company wants to buy goods. Because a letter of credit constitutes an irrevocable commitment by the bank to the seller, the bank has given value for the $1,000 note.

In the following case, the court found an executory promise to constitute value.

Saka v. Mann Theatres

Supreme Court of Nevada
575 P.2d 1335 (1978)

Mann Theatres rented a theater to Affinity Pictures for two weeks at a cost of $5,442 per week. Saka, on behalf of Affinity, issued two checks, each for $5,442. The first was honored, but the second check did not clear the bank. Mann Theatres sued for payment of the second check. Saka argued that Mann Theatres was not a holder in due course, as required by Section 3-302 of the UCC. Saka's argument was based on the fact that the second check was offered and accepted for the second week's showing of the film by Affinity, so that Mann Theatres merely gave an "executory promise to give value," rather than "value" as required by Section 3-302 to be a holder in due course. · FACTS

Did Mann Theatres give value for the check? · ISSUE

Yes. The court held that one is considered to be a holder in due course to the extent that such an executory promise is actually performed. The check did not return until after performance was begun, so Mann Theatres qualified as a holder in due course, and Saka was liable on the second check. · DECISION

What happens if a person who gives an executory promise learns of a defense or claim to the instrument before he or she performs the promise? The person may become a holder in due course only to the extent that he or she has fulfilled the promise. In the case mentioned earlier, in which Mary promises to pay her mother $100 for Smith's note, suppose that Mary pays her mother $50 on June 1. On June 2, Mary learns from Smith that her mother defrauded him. May Mary enforce the note? Mary is a holder in due course only as to the amount she has already paid her mother—$50. As to the other $50, she cannot collect if Smith establishes his defense of fraud by Mary's mother. What if Mary on June 3 pays her mother the other $50? Could she then claim to be a holder in due course for the entire sum of $100? No. Paying off the executory promise at this point is too late, because she already has learned of a defense against the instrument. Mary takes the instrument for value only to the extent that the agreed consideration has been performed before she learns of any claims or defenses.

Banks and Value   When a person receives a check from someone and deposits it to his or her account, the bank credits the depositor's account. Probably the check was written on an account at another bank, so the depositor's bank acts as an agent for purposes of collection. Does the mere fact that a customer deposits a check to his or her account, and the bank credits the account, mean that the bank has given value for the check? No. The mere crediting of an account by a bank does not constitute the giving of value. Only to the extent that the depositor draws against an instrument has the bank given value. If the bank otherwise complies with Section 3-302, it qualifies as a holder in due course of this check.

Most depositors have some money in their accounts when a check is deposited. If the bank lets depositors write checks on the account, how do we know whether the bank is permitting the customers to draw against the deposited checks? To simplify this matter, the UCC rules that "credits first given are first withdrawn." In other words, the UCC adopts a "first in, first out" rule (Section 4-208).

Suppose that Alice gives Frank a check for $100. Frank takes the check to his bank and deposits it on June 1. Frank already has $200 in his account. On June 2, Frank receives another $100 check from Alice, which he deposits to his account that day. On June 3, Frank withdraws $200 from his account. At this point, has the bank given value for either of Alice's checks? No. Because the UCC applies a first-in, first-out rule, the $200 is treated as a withdrawal of the $200 initially in Frank's account. On June 4, Frank withdraws another $100. Now the bank has given full value for Alice's first check, which was deposited to Frank's account on June 1. If the bank otherwise complies with Section 3-302, it is treated as a holder in due course of Alice's first check, deposited June 1. On June 5, Alice notifies the bank of a defense on the second check. On June 6, the bank lets Frank withdraw the final $100 from his account. Has the bank given value for Alice's second check? No. Applying the first-in, first-out rule, Frank's final $100 withdrawal is treated as a withdrawal against Alice's second check. Because the bank gave value *after* it learned of Alice's defense, it has not given value for the second check and cannot qualify as a holder in due course of the second check.

Negotiable Instrument as Security   If a person acquires a security interest in an instrument (other than by legal process), he or she takes the instrument for value.

Suppose that Jane agrees to buy some goods from a business. The business has some doubts about Jane's capacity to pay for the goods. Jane has a note from Linda, in which Linda agrees to pay her $100. If the business sells goods to Jane for $100 and takes the note from Linda to Jane as security for the debt, it has given value for Linda's note. If Jane does not pay for the goods, the business may collect the $100 from Linda, because it gave value for Linda's note by taking it as security for the debt Jane owed it.

Instrument in Payment or as Security for Antecedent Claim   The final category in which a person is treated as having given value is when the person

takes the instrument in payment of or as security for an antecedent claim against any person whether or not the claim is due (Section 3-303[b]).

Suppose that Alice purchases some goods from Jane in March for $100. Several months pass. In May, Alice gives Jane a $100 note. Jane is treated as having given value for the note. But what if Jane merely asked for some security in May, and Alice gave Jane a $100 note executed by Tom? The UCC treats Jane as having given value for Tom's note, even though she does not extend the time in which Alice must pay her or make any other concession to Alice. If Alice fails to pay Jane, Jane may try to collect on the note from Tom. Jane is treated as having given value for Tom's note, even though she took it as security for an earlier claim against Alice, and even though she made no additional concessions to Alice when she took Tom's note. If Jane otherwise has complied with Section 3-302, she is treated as a holder in due course of Tom's note and takes the note free of certain defenses Tom might have been able to assert against Alice.

Good Faith

To be a holder in due course, the holder of the instrument also must have taken the instrument in good faith. The drafters of the UCC, in defining good faith as honesty in fact, left judges fairly wide discretion in determining what is an acceptable level of behavior. However, they clearly selected a *subjective* test, not an objective test. The UCC thus does not adopt the standard of the behavior of a reasonably prudent person acting under the same circumstances. Instead, it adopts a standard that examines the actual behavior of the person taking the instrument. To determine if a person took an instrument in good faith, the court must determine if he or she acted honestly, even though his or her actions were not those of a reasonable person. A person who, for example, takes an instrument under suspicious circumstances has not necessarily acted in bad faith. If this person acts honestly, although perhaps not reasonably, he or she qualifies under the UCC definition of good faith.

Whether an individual took an instrument in good faith is determined at the time of taking the instrument. If a person acted in good faith at that time, and then *later* learns of facts that make him or her suspicious, he or she still is regarded as having taken the instrument in good faith.

The question of good faith is dealt with in the following case.

Manufacturers & Traders Trust Company v. Murphy

U.S. District Court, Western District, Pennsylvania
369 F. Supp. 11 (1974)

Murphy gave Brownsworth a personal check for $15,000 in consideration for certain   FACTS
money he expected Brownsworth to derive from investing the money. Brownsworth took the check to Manufacturers and exchanged it for a cashier's check. Manufacturers contacted Murphy's bank, was told that there were enough funds, and issued the new

check. Later Murphy, unaware of this exchange, became suspicious of the transaction and placed a stop payment order on his check. Brownsworth later exchanged the cashier's check for cash and four smaller checks at a branch, which he later cashed. Manufacturers then sued Murphy on the original personal check issued to Brownsworth, claiming holder in due course status. Murphy contended that Manufacturers was not a holder in due course, citing a lack of good faith by Manufacturers. Manufacturers claimed good faith, because it had contacted Murphy's bank to verify the account and the sufficiency of funds and had no notice of the stop-payment order because it was not made until later.

ISSUE   Did Manufacturers take this check in good faith?

DECISION   Yes. The court rejected Murphy's contention that Brownsworth had to be a regular customer of Manufacturers to satisfy the requirement of good faith, in general, because the bank's investigation went beyond mere formality. Manufacturers became liable upon originally issuing the first cashier's check, becoming a holder in due course at that particular moment regardless of later events. Murphy was therefore liable on the check he had issued because Manufacturers was a holder in due course.

Without Notice

We now know that a person, to qualify as a holder in due course, must be the holder of a negotiable instrument who took the instrument for value and in good faith. To qualify as a holder in due course, this person must establish one last element (as set forth in Section 3-302[a][c]). He or she must establish that the instrument was taken without his or her knowing that it was overdue, dishonored, or had been defended against or claimed by any person. The holder of an instrument must take it without notice of four things:

1. that the instrument is overdue
2. that the instrument has been dishonored
3. a defense by any person
4. any claim to it by any person

Assuming that the holder does *not* have notice of any of these four points, he or she may qualify as a holder in due course. But what did the drafters of the UCC mean when they wrote that the holder must take "without notice"?

Notice   The UCC defines *notice* in Section 1-201. Section 1-201(25) states that a person has notice of a fact when he or she has actual notice of it; or if he or she has received notice or notification of it; or if from all the facts and circumstances known to the person at the time in question, he or she has reason to know a fact exists.

Notice Instrument Overdue   By examining the face of an instrument a person may learn important information. One of the most critical things revealed by the face of the instrument is whether the instrument is **overdue.**

Basically, there are two types of instruments: demand instruments and time instruments. The latter is payable at a specific time — for example, a note "payable June 1, 1988." A demand instrument is one that is payable "on demand," "at sight," "on presentation."

A taker of a negotiable instrument is denied status as a holder in due course if he or she takes an instrument that is overdue. The very fact that the instrument is still in circulation after it is payable should make anyone taking it suspicious. When instruments are due, one assumes that the party entitled to collect will attempt to collect.

An instrument that is payable at a definite time, such as one payable June 1, 1988, is overdue at the beginning of the day after it is due. In this case, the instrument is overdue on June 2, 1988.

A person is considered to have notice that an instrument is overdue in several situations (Section 3-304[3]). One of these is when he or she is taking a demand instrument after demand has been made or *more than a reasonable length of time after its issue.* The UCC sets forth a relatively clear rule about checks: a reasonable time for presentation of a check for collection is 30 days. Suppose that Linda issues a check to Alice on September 1. Alice has 30 days from the date of issue to present the check. Anyone taking the check later than 30 days after issue may not qualify as a holder in due course.

Demand instruments other than checks create more of a problem in defining when they are overdue. The UCC merely states that a person has notice that such an instrument is overdue if he or she takes it more than a reasonable length of time after its issue. It is not possible to state a clear cut rule about when such an instrument is overdue.

Notice Instrument Dishonored   In general, a **dishonor** of an instrument occurs when a demand for payment or acceptance has been made and the party expected to pay or accept refuses to do so. Suppose that a note payable September 1, 1988, is presented by the payee to the maker on that date. If the maker refuses to pay at that time, there has been a dishonor of the instrument. (See the next chapter for a full discussion of the issue of dishonor.)

A person who takes an instrument knowing of such a dishonor cannot qualify as a holder in due course. In many cases, a simple examination of the instrument reveals that it has been dishonored. For example, a check that has been dishonored by a bank might be stamped "insufficient funds." Clearly, a person taking such a check would have notice of the dishonor.

But in some cases, the instrument does not indicate on its face that it has been dishonored, and the transferor may not tell the transferee of the dishonor. In such cases, the courts must determine whether there is any other evidence that the transferee had notice of the dishonor. If it finds that the transferee had such notice, he or she does not qualify as a holder in due course.

Notice of Claim or Defense   A purchaser has notice of a claim or defense if the instrument is incomplete; appears to have been forged or altered or is so irregular as

Overdue an instrument that has not been paid by its maturity date

Dishonor a refusal to accept or to pay after a proper request

to call into question its validity, terms, or ownership; creates an ambiguity as to the party to pay. The purchaser also may have notice of a claim or defense if he or she has notice that the obligation of any party is voidable or that all parties have been discharged.

A *defense* to an instrument typically is something that is asserted as a reason not to pay it. A *claim,* in contrast, is an argument asserted by a person claiming the instrument.

Some defenses or claims are obvious from the face of the instrument, such as a crude alteration or a forgery. If such an alteration or forgery calls into question the validity, terms, or ownership of the instrument, a person holding the instrument may not qualify as a holder in due course.

It does not follow that merely because the holder knew that an instrument was incomplete that the holder also knew about any defense or claim unless the holder had notice of an *improper* completion. An instrument might be blank as to some unnecessary fact, might contain minor erasures, or might even have an obvious change, such as a change of date. For example, "January 2, 1987" could have been changed to "January 2, 1988" without exciting suspicion. If a check had no date, the holder would not have notice of a defense or claim merely because the transferor filled in the date.

So long as an instrument is blank, it is incomplete, and the taker may not qualify as a holder in due course. Any person taking such an incomplete instrument takes it subject to any defenses or claims. But an instrument may be completed as authorized, and once it is completed, it is effective.

Is there anything about the check in the following case that would lead the taker to know that it was overdue, or had been dishonored, or that any defense against or claim to it had been made?

Jaeger & Branch, Incorporated v. Pappas

Supreme Court of Utah
433 P.2d 605 (1967)

FACTS
Pappas bought carpet from Allo. To get Allo to release the materials, Pappas gave Allo a check, which Allo gave to Jaeger. Jaeger had spoken to Pappas before Pappas issued the check, but Jaeger did not state whether Allo owed money to him. In any event, after Pappas issued the check to Allo, Pappas informed Allo that he would stop payment if Allo shortchanged him. Jaeger was not told of this condition on payment by either Pappas or Allo. The check was endorsed to Jaeger by Allo and deposited by Jaeger. In the meantime, the carpet was released and received by Pappas. Four days later Pappas issued a stop-payment order for "overpayment." The check not having cleared, it was dishonored by the bank. Jaeger then sued on the check.

ISSUE
Did Jaeger take this check with notice of any claim or defense?

DECISION
No. The court held that although good faith requires one who takes a negotiable instrument to be alert for facts indicating the existence of a defense, the opposite also is true. In the absence of anything to warn a holder to the contrary, he or she may assume that people with whom he or she deals are themselves acting honestly and in good faith.

There is no requirement that a holder must inquire into the satisfactory performance of the obligations of prior holders. Jaeger was unaware of any conditions Pappas had imposed on Allo by the use of the check and was therefore not bound by these conditions. Jaeger qualified as a holder in due course and took the check free of any personal defenses.

Holder through a Holder in Due Course

Although a person who holds an instrument may not qualify as a holder in due course, he or she may have all the rights of a holder in due course. The so-called "shelter provision" of the UCC (found in Section 3-201[1]) states that the "transfer of an instrument rests in the transferee such rights as the transferor had therein." The drafters of the UCC adopted this provision to encourage the free transfer of negotiable instruments. A person who for one reason or another knows that he or she cannot qualify as a holder in due course may take an instrument if the transferor is a holder in due course or if any earlier person qualified as a holder in due course. If the transferor is a holder in due course or if any earlier person qualified as a holder in due course, the transferee has the *rights* of a holder in due course.

For example, suppose that on June 5 Briscoe offers to sell a note "payable on June 1" to Knott. Knott cannot qualify as a holder in due course, because she knows that the instrument is overdue — it is payable June 1. But she may safely take the note if Briscoe is a holder in due course. In that case, Knott has all the rights of her transferor.

Holder through a holder in due course someone who takes a negotiable instrument after a holder in due course has possessed it

STATUS OF HOLDER IN DUE COURSE

A holder in due course occupies a very special position. The holder in due course generally takes the instrument free from all defenses of any party to the instrument *with whom the holder has not dealt.* This point is illustrated by the following case.

Wilmington Trust Company v. Delaware Auto Sales

**Supreme Court of Delaware
271 A.2d 41 (1970)**

Hoopes bought a used car from Delaware and paid for it with a personal check drawn on the Wilmington account. The next morning, dissatisfied with the car, which he later returned, Hoopes stopped payment on the check at 8:35 A.M. At about 9:15 A.M. Kutner, the owner of Delaware, went to another branch of the bank and exchanged the personal check for a cashier's check, unaware of the stop payment order. At 9:24 A.M., the account was charged with a hold in the amount of the check. When Kutner later presented the check for payment, the stop payment was noted, and the check was canceled. Wilmington alleged want or failure of consideration and mistake as defenses

FACTS

to payment. Delaware contended that it was a holder in due course and not subject to these defenses.

ISSUE   Can Wilmington assert a personal defense against Delaware if Delaware qualifies as a holder in due course?

DECISION   Yes. The court held that under Section 3-305, personal defenses are available between the immediate parties. The status of holder in due course only protects the holder from defenses of parties to the instrument with whom the holder has not dealt. Because the bank received the stop payment order before it issued the cashier's check, it had no right to charge Hoopes's account, resulting in a complete failure of consideration as between Wilmington and Delaware. The bank thus had a valid defense against payment of the check.

Abuses of Holder in Due Course Doctrine

Although designed to encourage the transfer of commercial documents, the holder in due course doctrine has hurt consumers. Fly by night businesses have induced consumers to sign contracts obligating them to pay installments over several years in return for the businesses' promises to deliver goods over time. The businesses then negotiate the consumers' promissory notes to financial institutions, the businesses are abandoned, and the consumers are left with no legal defense against the financial institution and no recourse against the defunct merchants. The following case is a classic involving a situation of this type and shows how a few courts have sought to protect consumers.

——— *Unico v. Owen* ———

Supreme Court of New Jersey
232 A.2d 405 (1967)

FACTS   Owen bought a record changer and 140 record albums from Universal, to be received over five years and one third. Payment was to be made monthly over a three-year period. Universal discounted the note to Unico on its face and apart from the contract between Owen and Universal. Included in the contract was language intended to bar any defense against Unico (an assignee) for Universal's (the seller's) default. Owen received the record changer and the first 12 records but nothing further, even though Owen continued making payments. After 12 months, Owen stopped making payments. As it turned out, Universal had become insolvent. Unico insisted upon payment. Owen defended on the ground that Unico was not a holder in due course and took the note subject to the default of Universal and the consequent failure of consideration.

ISSUE   Is Unico a holder in due course?

No. The court held:

> Where the seller's performance is executory in character and when it appears from the totality of the arrangements between dealer and financer that the financer has had a substantial voice in setting standards for the underlying transaction, or has approved the standards established by the dealer, and has agreed to take all or a predetermined or substantial quantity of the negotiable paper which is backed by such standards, the financer should be considered a participant in the original transaction and therefore not entitled to holder in due course status.

As a result, Unico took the note subject to the default of Universal and the consequent failure of consideration and was not a holder in due course.

Some state courts tried to help purchasers by finding that holders of instruments failed to qualify as holders in due course. Other states adopted the Uniform Consumer Credit Code, which gives consumers more protection. On the whole, the state approach had not been uniform. What was needed was a sweeping, uniform rule that applied everywhere in the United States. Thanks to the Federal Trade Commission, we now have such a rule for consumer-credit contracts.

FTC Modification of the Doctrine

The FTC adopted a Trade Regulation Rule effective May 14, 1976, which virtually eliminated the problem of consumers' being forced to pay on an obligation when a seller fails to live up to his or her part of a bargain. The FTC rule provides that:

In connection with any sale or lease of goods or services to consumers, in or affecting the Federal Trade Commission Act, it is an **unfair** or deceptive act or **practice** within the meaning of Section 5 of that Act for a seller, directly or indirectly, to:

Unfair trade practice an act in violation of the Federal Trade Commission Act

a. take or receive a consumer credit contract which fails to contain the following provision in at least ten point, bold face, type:

NOTICE
ANY HOLDER OF THIS CONSUMER CREDIT CONTRACT IS SUBJECT TO ALL CLAIMS AND DEFENSES WHICH THE DEBTOR COULD ASSERT AGAINST THE SELLER OF GOODS OR SERVICES OBTAINED PURSUANT HERETO OR WITH THE PROCEEDS HEREOF. RECOVERY HEREUNDER BY THE DEBTOR SHALL NOT EXCEED AMOUNTS PAID BY THE DEBTOR HEREUNDER.

or,

b. accept, as full or partial payment for such sale or lease, the proceeds of any purchase money loan (as purchase money loan is defined herein), unless any consumer credit contract made in connection with such purchase money loan contains the following provision in at least ten point, bold face, type:

NOTICE

ANY HOLDER OF THIS CONSUMER CREDIT CONTRACT IS SUBJECT TO ALL CLAIMS AND DEFENSES WHICH THE DEBTOR COULD ASSERT AGAINST THE SELLER OF GOODS OR SERVICES OBTAINED WITH THE PROCEEDS HEREOF. RECOVERY HEREUNDER BY THE DEBTOR SHALL NOT EXCEED AMOUNTS PAID BY THE DEBTOR HEREUNDER.

This amendment was designed to protect the rights of consumers who purchase on credit and thereby incur obligations to financial institutions by preserving the consumers' claims and defenses.

Consumer credit contract an instrument that shows or embodies a debt by a consumer, arising from a purchase money loan

Note that the act bars *sellers* from taking a **consumer credit contract** or proceeds of a **purchase money loan**, unless the consumer credit contract contains the above-cited provision. This provision takes care of the situations where a seller arranges for financing a sale or where a seller refers a buyer to a finance company to get a loan for the seller's goods. In a purchase money loan, a consumer gets a cash advance. In exchange for the cash, the consumer pays a finance charge. The consumer uses the cash to buy goods and services from a seller who:

1. refers the consumer to the creditor or

2. is affiliated with the creditor by contract or business arrangement.

Purchase money loan a cash advance to a consumer in exchange for which the consumer pays a finance charge; the cash is used to buy goods.

A consumer credit contract is an instrument that evidences or embodies a debt arising from a purchase money loan or a sale in which credit is extended to a consumer.

This rule does not apply to people buying goods for use in their businesses but to people who buy goods for personal, family, or household use. These consumers now may buy goods on credit, and if a defense, either real or personal, arises that may be asserted against the seller, this defense may be asserted against the holder of the consumer credit contract even though the holder qualifies as a holder in due course.

The FTC rule does not apply to credit card transactions. But the Fair Credit Billing Act protects buyers who use credit cards. There are two requirements: the merchandise must cost more than $50, and the consumer must live within 100 miles of the place where the original transaction took place. If both conditions are met, the consumer need only make an effort to return the item and ask for a refund or replacement. The consumer then can wait to pay the credit card company's bill until the problem is ironed out with the retailer. The FTC rule also does not apply to consumer purchases by check. It applies only to consumer credit purchases.

SUMMARY

When an instrument is originally delivered by the maker or drawer to a third party, the transfer is called an *issue*. A negotiation is the transfer of the instrument so that the transferee becomes a holder.

When instruments are transferred, often they are endorsed. There are a number of types of endorsements: blank, special, qualified, and restrictive.

Assuming that a negotiable instrument has been properly negotiated to a third party, that party may qualify as a holder in due course if he or she took the instrument for value, in good faith, and without notice of any defenses against or claims to the instrument.

The FTC enacted a rule designed to protect consumers from the holder in due course rule. The rule permits any consumer who enters into a consumer credit contract to assert any defense he or she has against the holder of the consumer credit contract.

REVIEW PROBLEMS

1. What must a person do to negotiate a negotiable order instrument and a negotiable bearer instrument?

2. What is a special endorsement? How does a person negotiate an instrument with a special endorsement?

3. How if at all has the FTC altered the holder in due course doctrine?

4. On June 1, Morris takes a note payable to the order of Katz. Katz, a holder in due course of the note, endorsed and delivered the note to Morris. At that time, Morris was aware that the note was overdue. Is Morris a holder in due course?

5. If a person takes an instrument under suspicious circumstances, can the person be a holder in due course of that instrument?

6. Talbot has $500 in his checking account at the First National Bank as of July 1. Talbot deposits a check from Smith for $250 to his account on July 2. On July 7, the bank allows Talbot to withdraw $200 from his account. On July 8, the bank allows him to withdraw $300 from his account. On July 9, it allows Talbot to withdraw the remaining $250 from his account. When, if ever, did the bank give value for Smith's check?

7. Smith signs a note for $1,000 payable to the order of Kennedy. Kennedy in turn transfers the note to Clark, who gives Kennedy a check for $1,000 in return. Has Clark given value for the note?

8. Hughes endorses the back of an instrument payable to his order as follows: "Without recourse, Christian Hughes." What type of endorsement is this, and why would a person endorse an instrument in this fashion?

9. A note is executed as follows: "Boston, Massachusetts, January 1, 1987. On demand I promise to pay to the order of Randy Davidson One Hundred and no/100 Dollars. Payable at the First National Bank of Boston [signed] Pamela Hyde." Pamela issues this note to Randy. Randy in turn endorses the note on the back as follows: "Pay to the order of Rose Davidson [signed] Randy Davidson." He then delivers the note to his wife, Rose Davidson. Identify this endorsement, and explain the consequences of using such an endorsement.

10. Lowe signs the following note: "San Antonio, Texas, January 1, 1987. On ,demand I promise to pay to the order of Donna Sylvester One Hundred and no/100 Dollars. Payable at the First National Bank of San Antonio [signed] Yvonne Lowe." Lowe issues this note to Sylvester. Soon thereafter a thief steals

the note and sells it to an innocent purchaser. Does the thief get a good title to this instrument? Does the innocent purchaser get a good title to this instrument? Would it make any difference if the note had been payable to bearer rather than to the order of Donna Sylvester?

11. Stuckey signs a note in which he agrees to pay Hempel $500. It qualifies as a negotiable instrument. But when Hempel transfers it to Anderson, the transfer is executed improperly and does not qualify as a proper negotiation of the instrument. Stuckey now argues that because the instrument was not properly negotiated to Anderson, Anderson has no rights in the instrument. Is Stuckey correct?

12. Barrett issues a check for $1,500 drawn on his joint banking account with his wife to the order of Aquatic Industries. His bank pays the check even though Aquatic fails to endorse the check. The bank debited his account for $1,500. No stop payment order has been issued by Barrett prior to payment. He is now suing the bank for unauthorized payment of the check. Should he prevail in light of the fact that Aquatic did not endorse the check?

13. Korzenik is an attorney for Southern New England Distributing Corporation. Southern obtains by fraud some notes from Supreme Radio. Southern then endorses the notes over to Korzenik as a retainer for future legal services. Supreme Radio discovers the fraud and demands the notes back from Korzenik. Korzenik claims he is a holder in due course. Supreme Radio claims he is not, because he has given no value in exchange for the note. Who wins?

14. Pazol draws a check on Fulton National bank for payment to Eidson. Eidson deposits the check into his account at Sandy Springs Bank. On the same day, Eidson withdraws the amount of check from his account. On the next day, Sandy Springs discovers the dishonorment of this check. Sandy Springs claims it is a holder in due course and demands payment from Pazol. Pazol claims Sandy Springs does not qualify as a holder in due course because it gave no value for the check. Is Sandy Springs a holder in due course?

15. Villa has a corporate account under the name of Villa Auto Sales. The manager of the bank is personally acquainted with Villa. Corporate authority stating that Villa is authorized to sign or endorse any check held by the corporation is on file on the bank. Villa cashes two checks given to him by Leo Used Cars. These checks are written on another bank. The checks are cashed by the teller at Industrial and sent through the bank collection procedure. The teller does not follow the bank's set procedure of obtaining a manager's approval before cashing a corporate check. Meanwhile, Leo Used Cars stops payment on the checks because Villa has sold them defective used cars. The bank now claims that it is a holder in due course and not subject to the claims against Villa Auto Sales. Is the bank's claim valid?

CHAPTER 22

Commercial Paper: Liability and Defenses

CHAPTER OBJECTIVES

After reading this chapter, you should be able to:

1. Explain the basic liability of each party to commercial paper.

2. Define and compare primary and secondary liability.

3. Describe how commercial paper may be dishonored.

4. Explain which legal defenses may be asserted against a holder in due course.

5. Explain which legal defenses may not be asserted against a holder in due course.

6. Describe the role of commercial paper as a substitute for money in our economy.

Chapters 20 and 21 have discussed different types of commercial paper and the legal doctrines that support commercial paper as a vital component of the economy of the United States. This chapter investigates further the liability of businesspeople who use commercial paper and the defenses against honoring commercial paper.

TYPES OF LIABILITY

Unconditional or Primary Liability

The makers, drawers, drawees, and endorsers of commercial paper all incur appreciably different kinds of liability. The liability of the maker of a promissory note is the most easily understood. A note, as indicated in Chapter 20, is a two-party instrument. The maker of a note assumes an unconditional responsibility based upon the instrument's promise to pay. This responsibility is often referred to as **primary liability.** Potentially, the drawee of a draft also assumes a similar liability, but the way this arises is more complicated. Remember that a draft is a three-party instrument in which a drawer orders a drawee to pay a payee. When the drawee accepts this order, the drawee becomes the acceptor, assuming a liability comparable to that of the maker of a note.

Primary liability an unconditional obligation to pay according to the terms of commercial paper

Both the maker of a note and the acceptor of a draft contract to pay the instrument according to its terms at the time they become parties. Neither is excused from paying even if the holder presents the instrument long after it becomes due. As a primary party, the maker or acceptor is bound to pay, and the holder need resort to no one else first. This obligation continues until the statute of limitations prevents the holder from recovering.

Until the drawee's **acceptance** — that is, his or her signed agreement to honor the draft as presented (Section 3-410[1]) — the drawee has no liability on the instrument. Upon acceptance, unconditional liability is established. A common example of acceptance is the certification of a check by a bank. By accepting, the drawee agrees to honor the instrument according to its terms as presented. The mechanics of acceptance were discussed in Chapter 20.

Acceptance a drawee's agreement to honor a draft, resulting in primary liability

Although it is not an advisable practice, a drawee sometimes accepts an incomplete instrument. When doing so, the drawee accepts liability on the completed instrument to the extent that he or she authorized completion. But if the instrument is completed in an unauthorized manner and is transferred to a holder in due course, the acceptor's liability may increase if the holder in due course enforces the instrument as completed (Section 3-407[3]).

Secondary Liability

Drawers and endorsers of commercial paper may incur **secondary liability** on commercial paper. Under certain circumstances, the holder of the commercial paper can turn to them for payment if the party that is primarily liable fails to pay. The responsibility of drawers and endorsers for payment depends upon certain events taking place. Accordingly, the UCC refers to endorsers and drawers as *secondary parties* (Section 3-102[1][d]). A secondary party is not expected to pay the instrument in the ordinary course of events, but a primary party is.

Secondary liability conditional commitment to pay commercial paper only after the party primarily liable fails to pay

Drawer's Commitment   Recall that a drawer initiating a draft is ordering the drawee to pay. The drawer expects the drawee to do so. This expectation is generally based upon a contractual relationship between the two. By accepting, the drawee agrees to be bound as ordered.

Endorser's Commitment   When commercial paper is transferred by endorsement, the endorser expects that the primary party, the drawee/acceptor or maker, will pay. The endorser's commitment, like that of the drawer of a draft, is to pay only if the primary party fails to do so.

Dishonor   The trigger for establishing secondary liability is a dishonor. As we have discussed in Chapter 21, an instrument is dishonored if it is properly presented for acceptance or payment, and the party to whom it is presented refuses to comply (Section 3-507[1][a]). A draft is dishonored by the drawee's refusal to accept or refusal to pay, but a note is dishonored only if the maker refuses to pay.

ESTABLISHING SECONDARY LIABILITY

Generally, the following events must occur to establish the secondary liability of endorsers and drawers of a draft:

1. presentment

2. dishonor and

3. notice of dishonor.

A fourth step called *protest* is required in some situations.

Presentment

Presentment
submission of
commercial paper
for acceptance or
payment

Presentment describes the procedure in which the holder of commercial paper or the holder's agent submits the instrument to the drawee or maker for acceptance or payment. For many drafts, presentment is made twice — once for acceptance and once for payment. A note is not presented for acceptance, because the party who is liable for payment has already promised to do so.

Presentment for Acceptance   Presentment for acceptance often is a critical step in a transaction involving a draft. At first presentment for acceptance is necessary for establishing the drawee's primary liability. Then the secondary liability of the drawer and endorsers often depends on a proper presentment for acceptance.

According to the UCC, presentment for acceptance is required in three instances. It must be made when the draft so provides, when it is payable at some place other than the drawee's residence or place of business, or where the time of payment depends upon the acceptance date (Section 3-501[1][a]). But the holder may present any draft payable at a stated date for acceptance. A common example is the trade acceptance, which is discussed in Chapter 20.

Presentment for Payment   A holder of commercial paper must present the instrument to the proper party to collect. Presentment for payment is also necessary to establish the liability of secondary parties if the instrument is dishonored. Unless presentment is done correctly, all endorsers are discharged completely, and drawers are discharged to a limited extent if the drawee becomes insolvent during any delay in presentment (Section 3-502[1][b]). In the following case, the drawer of a number of checks argues that he is discharged because the checks were not presented for payment for several months.

Kaiser v. Northwest Shopping Center, Incorporated

Court of Civil Appeal of Texas
544 S.W.2d 785 (1976)

FACTS   Kaiser leased retail space for his drugstore from Northwest Shopping Center, Inc. The lease provided that Kaiser's would be the only drugstore in the shopping center. Kaiser was granted the option of extending the lease on the same terms, except that the monthly rent would be raised from $500 to $750. In January 1974, Northwest informed Kaiser that because he had not acted to extend the lease, he would be considered a month-to-month tenant at $600 a month. Kaiser claimed that he had in fact extended the lease by tendering monthly rent checks of $750. From January until October 1974, Northwest held Kaiser's $750 monthly rent checks without cashing them while it negotiated with another tenant who wanted to open a drugstore. After these negotiations failed, Northwest recognized Kaiser's lease extension and presented the accumulated rent checks to his bank. The bank refused to honor some of the checks because they were too old or because Kaiser's account lacked sufficient funds. By the time Northwest again presented the dishonored checks two days later, Kaiser had stopped payment on them. Northwest sued Kaiser for the unpaid rent and won in trial court. Kaiser appealed.

Does the length of time that Northwest held the checks discharge Kaiser's obligation to pay the rent money?   ISSUE

No. The court ruled in favor of Northwest Shopping Center. The court ruled that Northwest's retention of Kaiser's checks—even if for an unreasonable time—discharged neither the checks nor the underlying debt. Kaiser also cited the UCC (Section 3-503[b][1]), which provides that all instruments be presented within a reasonable time. The court ruled, however, that the payee's undue delay in presenting an instrument does not discharge the drawer's liability on the instrument. According to the UCC, such a delay discharges the drawer's liability on a stale check only when the bank on which the check was to have been drawn has since become insolvent.   DECISION

If an instrument indicates the date on which it is due, presentment for payment is due on that day. An accepted draft payable a specified number of days after acceptance is due at that time. To fix the liability of secondary parties when a note is payable on demand, presentment for payment is due within a reasonable time after the party becomes liable (Section 3-503[1][e]). A "reasonable" time is determined by the nature of the instrument, customs of the trade, and the facts of the particular case (Section 3-503[2]).

Presentment for payment and acceptance must be made at a reasonable hour. If presentment is required at a bank, the presentment must be made during the banking day (Section 3-503[4]). If presentment is due on a day that is not a full business day for either party, presentment is due on the next day that is a full business day for both parties (Section 3-503[3]). Presentment may be made by mail, through a clearing house, or at the place of acceptance or payment specified in the instrument. When nothing is specified, presentment may be at the home or place of business of the party who is to accept or pay (Section 3-504[2][1]).

People to whom presentment is made may require the presenter to:

1. show the instrument

2. identify themselves

3. sign a receipt on the instrument for any partial payment

4. surrender the instrument upon full payment (Section 3-505[1])

If these requirements are not met, the person upon whom presentment is made may refuse to accept or pay without dishonoring.

Dishonor

Dishonor, as we have mentioned, is the refusal of a party upon whom a proper demand for payment or acceptance is made to comply within the required time. Payment of an instrument may be deferred without dishonor so that the person who must pay can examine it to determine if it is properly payable (Section 3-506[2]). But the person must pay before the close of business on the day of presentment (Section 3-506[2]). Subject to any required notice of dishonor and protest, a holder has upon dishonor an immediate right of recourse against the drawers and endorsers. (Section 3-507[2]). In the following case, the holder of an improperly dishonored check loses a suit against the drawee bank.

Stewart v. The Citizens and Southern National Bank

Court of Appeals of Georgia
225 S.E. 2d 761 (1976)

FACTS   Stewart received a check for $185.48 from a client as payment for services. The check was made out by a corporation to the client, who endorsed it and delivered it to Stewart. Stewart presented the check to the corporation's bank, Citizens and Southern National Bank. The bank, through its branch manager, refused to honor the check, despite the facts that there was enough money in the corporation's account and the check was otherwise proper. Stewart sued the bank for the $185.48 value of the check and for $50,000 in punitive damages.

ISSUE   Was the bank obliged to honor the check?

DECISION   No. The court ruled in favor of the defendant bank. Because a check is a draft, the court ruled that the bank could not be held liable on the check unless it had accepted the instrument. The court further ruled that the bank had no duty to Stewart, contractual or otherwise, to accept the check. Because the bank did not accept the check, plaintiff had a cause of action against the endorser and/or the drawer — in this case the client and the corporation, respectively — but not against the bank.

Notice of Dishonor

In most cases, the final step in establishing the liability of secondary parties is to provide notice that the instrument has been dishonored. A holder has until midnight of the third business day after dishonor to notify his or her immediate transferor of the dishonor. Earlier holders are required to give notice before midnight of the third business day after they have gotten notice of dishonor (Section 3-508[2]). A bank is required to give notice before midnight of the banking day following the banking day on which it has gotten the item or notice of dishonor (Sections 3-508[2], 4-104[1][h]).

Although the time within which notice must be provided is relatively short, other requirements for notice are more liberal. Notice of dishonor may be spoken in person or over the telephone. But both of these practices should be avoided, because the party providing notice later may have to prove that it was given. Oral notice should be followed by written notice within the time limit.

The most common type of notice of dishonor is the check that has been returned through a clearinghouse because the drawer has insufficient funds or has stopped payment. But notice of dishonor is frequently given by mail or telegram. The UCC allows notice of dishonor in any reasonable manner as long as the instrument is identified and the fact of dishonor clearly indicated.

Notice of dishonor does not have to be given in any particular order. Usually the holder notifies the person who transferred the instrument to him or her. This notice triggers that person's liability. That person in turn notifies the person from whom the instrument was received, and so on down the line. The holder might, however, notify other transferors to initiate their responsibility if collection from the immediate transferor fails. Once a party has been notified of dishonor, no further notice need be given, for the notice operates for the benefit of all parties who have rights on the instrument (Section 3-508[8]).

EXTENT OF SECONDARY LIABILITY

As we have noted, an endorser's liability is secondary. This liability is conditioned upon the instrument's being dishonored when properly presented and notice of dishonor being provided the endorser. Unless excused, a holder's failure to meet these conditions discharges an endorser completely and immediately (Section 3-502[1][a]).

The liability of the drawer of a draft is also secondary, because it depends on certain conditions being fulfilled. But a critical difference exists between the position of the drawer of a draft and that of an endorser. The drawer usually receives a consideration from the payee. This is the reason that the drawer has ordered the drawee to honor the instrument. To allow a drawer to escape liability because the holder fails to make due presentment or provide notice of dishonor would result in the drawer receiving an unjustifiable gain. As a result, if the drawee refuses to accept or pay, policy generally dictates that the drawer be liable. But if the drawer were to suffer a loss because the holder fails to make proper presentment or provide notice of dishonor, that loss should be the holder's.

The drawer suffers a loss if it leaves funds on deposit with the drawee to cover a draft and the drawee becomes insolvent. If the drawee's insolvency occurs after the draft is due, the drawer's loss is a result of the holder's failure to make the necessary presentment or to give notice of dishonor in a timely manner. With this in mind, the UCC limits the drawer's liability on the draft to the extent that the drawee's insolvency deprives the drawer of funds. This result is accomplished by providing the drawer with a right to obtain a discharge of liability by assigning his or her right against the drawee to the holder (Section 3-502[1][b]).

LIABILITY BASED ON WARRANTY

The UCC implies certain warranties when a negotiable instrument is transferred or presented. The person presenting or transferring the instrument may incur liability for breach of warranty even though he or she did not sign or endorse the instrument. A person transferring a negotiable instrument for consideration warrants to the transferee that:

1. he or she has good title or is authorized to act on behalf of someone holding good title

2. all signatures are genuine or authorized

3. the instrument has not been materially altered

4. no defense of any party is good against him or her

5. he or she knows of no insolvency proceedings involving the maker, acceptor, or drawer of an unaccepted instrument.

If the transferor endorses, then the warranty extends to any holder who later takes the instrument in good faith. If the endorsement is "without recourse," then the transferor only warrants having no knowledge of any defenses good against him or her.

A party presenting an instrument for payment warrants that:

1. he or she has good title or is authorized to act on behalf of someone with good title

2. he or she does not know that the signature of the maker or drawer is unauthorized

3. the instrument has not been materially altered.

UNIVERSAL DEFENSES

Commercial paper is a substitute for money. Although not as widely acceptable as currency, checks, drafts, and promissory notes transfer readily in the economy. In some situations, commercial paper is preferable to money. Individuals and businesses pay many obligations with checks because to do so is safer and more convenient than to use currency.

The doctrine of holder in due course is the major reason that commercial paper is readily acceptable in most transactions. With limited exceptions, a holder in due course takes the instrument free of defenses of any party to it with whom he or she has not dealt.

Defenses that may be asserted against a holder in due course are called **universal** or *real* **defenses**. These defenses are recognized because they are based on public policies so important that they override the need for free transfer of commercial paper. As a matter of public policy, we protect infants and prohibit outrageous fraud and duress. Further, if an action has prevented an agreement from being formed in the first place, then no liability should follow. Negotiable instruments are a form of contract. If no contractual liability has been assumed, the instrument is meaningless.

A note upon which the maker's signature is forged is an example. Even if the instrument is proper in form and duly negotiated to a holder in due course, the victim of the forgery should not be liable. A similar result follows when an instrument is materially altered after being executed. The party liable is not responsible for the instrument in its altered state, because it is not the same contract the party actually agreed to.

Other universal defenses include infancy; certain other types of incapacity; duress and illegality when these render the underlying transaction void; discharge in bankruptcy; and certain types of fraud.

Universal defenses defenses that may be asserted against a holder in due course

Forgery

A person whose signature is used on a negotiable instrument without authority is not liable on it. But if the person's negligence substantially contributed to the use of the unauthorized signature, he or she may not assert the lack of authority against a holder in due course (Section 3-406).

K & K Manufacturing, Incorporated v. Union Bank

Court of Appeals of Arizona
628 P.2d 44 (1981)

FACTS

K & K Manufacturing and its president, Bill J. Knight, sued Union Bank to recover funds paid from their respective accounts on checks with Knight's forged signature. The forgeries were performed by Eleanor Garza, the firm's bookkeeper. Garza used her forgeries to take $49,859.31 from K & K's account and $11,350 from Knight's personal account. The trial court, relying on UCC 4-406(2)(b), held that K & K and Knight could only recover those funds paid by the bank before May 20, 1977, which was 14 days after Knight first received a bank statement containing forged items. Plaintiffs were thus able to recover only $5,500 from Knight's account and nothing from the K & K account. Plaintiffs appealed.

ISSUE

Should K & K recover all the funds paid out on account of the forgeries or only those paid out before they could have been aware of them?

DECISION

The appeals court affirmed the trial court's ruling that plaintiffs could recover no funds paid out after May 20. UCC 4-406 imposes a duty on a bank customer to use reasonable care to examine account statements and accompanying items sent by the bank. The court concluded that if Knight had properly examined the bank statement and canceled checks that he received on May 6, he would have discovered the forgery. Section 4-406(2)(b) provides that if a customer fails to spot a forgery for lack of due care, the bank generally is not liable for good faith payments to the same forger made after the customer has had reasonable time — up to 14 days — to detect the forgery.

Material Alteration

Material alteration a later change of commercial paper that significantly changes the contract of a party

A **material alteration** is one that changes the contract of any of the parties. Changes that do not affect the agreement of the parties are not considered material. For example, adding a co-maker is a material alteration (Section 3-407, Comment 1).

A holder in due course who takes after a material alteration may enforce the instrument but only according to its original terms (Section 3-407). If a person who is obligated on the instrument is negligent and that negligence contributes substantially to the instrument's being materially altered, the holder in due course may enforce the instrument in its altered form (Section 3-406).

In protecting the rights of a holder in due course, the UCC treats an incomplete instrument as it treats one that has been materially altered. A holder in due course may enforce the instrument as it has been completed, even though it was completed in an unauthorized manner (Section 3-407[3]). A check signed by the drawer in blank and stolen or lost is enforceable by a holder in due course against the drawer as it has been completed by a thief or finder.

Fraud in the Execution

Fraud in the execution fraud so basic that a victim never actually assented to a contract

The basis of this defense is similar to that underlying forgery and material alteration. A holder in due course attempting to recover on a forged instrument is not allowed to recover because the defendant never agreed to be bound. When a material alteration has occurred, the defendant's liability is limited, because he or she did not agree to the instrument's terms as they now appear. In **fraud in the execution,** also called *fraud in the factum,* the party defending escapes liability because he or she was misled about what was being signed.

This kind of fraud might happen in a number of ways. Extreme cases exist in which a promissory note was cleverly hidden under another document that a person signed. When the cover document is removed, the signature is on the note, which the payee then negotiates. More often a buyer signs a promissory note or some other type of commercial paper, being assured by the seller that the instrument is merely an authorization to conduct a credit investigation or a receipt. In these situations, because the signer never intended to make a promise, no liability exists. For this defense to be successful, the defendant must be able to show that no reasonable opportunity existed to discover what was actually being signed. If the defendant acted carelessly, either in not reading the instrument being signed or in some other manner, the defense fails.

Fraud in the execution differs from the false statement made to induce a person to enter into a contract. The latter is called *fraud in the procurement* or **fraud in the inducement**. Fraud in the inducement is not a defense against a holder in due course. Although it is a defense in a contract case, contractual defenses of this kind may be asserted only against ordinary holders. These defenses are examined in some detail later in this chapter.

Fraud in the inducement
fraud in the material facts that causes a victim to assent to a contract

Infancy

As indicated in Chapter 9, a minor has the right to rescind most contractual obligations. The extent of this right depends on state law. Under the UCC, a minor may raise the defense of infancy — minor status — against a holder in due course to the same extent that infancy is a contractual defense according to state law governing the transaction (Section 3-305[2][a]). For example, in most states a minor purchasing a stereo is allowed to disaffirm the contract, because the item is not a necessity. If the minor signs a note as payment for the stereo, the note is not enforceable even if transferred to a holder in due course who has no knowledge of the maker's minority.

Other Incapacity

In some cases, mental incapacity and drunkenness may be used as defenses against a holder in due course. Incapacity is available against a holder in due course if applicable state laws "render the underlying obligation a nullity" (Section 3-305[1][b]). In effect, the underlying contract must be void, not just voidable, if incapacity is to be used successfully against a holder in due course. In most states, contracts by mental incompetents are void only if the incompetent has been judged insane. A similar rule applies to drunkenness. If the promisor was so drunk (or drugged) that he or she could not have intended to contract, the agreement is void. In a similar situation, a person obligated on commercial paper has a good defense against the holder in due course.

Void contract a contract that is not enforceable by anyone

Voidable contract a contract that may not be enforceable under certain circumstances

Duress and Illegality

The UCC treats duress and illegality as it does incapacity (Section 3-305[1][b]). In both instances, if applicable state law renders the contract void, duress or illegality may be asserted against a holder in due course. In most states, a contract secured by duress is voidable, not void. Thus duress generally is unavailable as a defense against a holder in due course. But if the duress is so extreme that the agreement is void from the beginning, duress is a good defense. Illegality is treated comparably.

The case that follows is an example of how negotiable instruments used in consumer transactions can injure unsophisticated buyers. Many states have adopted statutes requiring that notes executed in connection with a retail installment contract be labeled "Consumer Note" and that such notes *not* be negotiable. The FTC also has adopted a rule limiting the use of negotiable instruments in consumer transactions.

New Jersey Mortgage & Investment Corporation v. Berenyi
Superior Court of New Jersey, Appellate Division
356 A.2d 421 (1976)

FACTS   In May 1964, the Superior Court of New Jersey barred Kroyden Industries, Incorporated, from using certain practices in the sale of carpeting. In August, a Kroyden employee offered to give defendants Andrew and Anna Berenyi free carpeting for referring prospective customers to Kroyden. Relying on this employee's representations, the Berenyis signed a negotiable promissory note for $1,521. This arrangement violated the injunction against Kroyden. The note was negotiated to the plaintiff, New Jersey Mortgage and Investment Corporation, who sued the Berenyis for its value.

ISSUE   Must the Berenyis pay the mortgage company even though Kroyden's actions were in violation of an injunction?

DECISION   Yes. The court ruled in favor of the New Jersey Mortgage and Investment. The court held that under New Jersey law, a holder in due course takes free from the illegality defense unless otherwise stated by statute. Because plaintiff was a holder in due course, and because no statute stated that a note issued in violation of an injunction was unenforceable by a holder in due course, the mortgage company could recover.

Discharge in Bankruptcy

Providing individuals and firms that are insolvent with an opportunity to make a fresh start has long been an important public policy. When a holder in due course is a creditor of the bankrupt, and for some reason the claim of the holder in due course is not asserted until the bankrupt is discharged, the discharge provides a good defense.

LIMITED DEFENSES

An ordinary holder of commercial paper is entitled to payment unless a signature necessary to liability is missing or the obligor establishes some defense. The ordinary holder is subject to all the universal defenses as well as to many other claims and defenses. These additional defenses are usually referred to as limited or **personal defenses.**

Personal defenses defenses that cannot be asserted against a holder in due course

Limited defenses differ from universal defenses in that they are based on legally acceptable reasons for not performing a contract whereas universal defenses are based on the idea that no contract ever existed. For example, fraud in the execution is a universal defense good even against a holder in due course because the defendant never intended to execute a negotiable instrument. But fraud in the procurement is merely a personal defense. It is not good against a holder in due course but is good against an ordinary holder because the defendant intended to contract, although the defendant was induced wrongfully to do so.

Under the UCC, an ordinary holder of commercial paper is subject to all valid claims against it as well as the following defenses:

1. breach of contract

2. lack or failure of consideration

3. nonperformance of a condition precedent (see Chapter 13)

4. nondelivery

5. acquisition of the instrument through theft by any person

Although these are the chief personal defenses, other defenses also may be asserted against the ordinary holder.

The fact that many defenses can be raised against a holder does not appreciably limit the usefulness of commercial paper. In most instances, the obligor has no defense, and the holder collects. Because the status of holder in due course is relatively easy for the person who takes commercial paper in good faith to attain, business people generally are willing to use commercial paper.

IMPOSTERS AND FICTITIOUS PAYEES

Checks are occasionally drawn to the order of a person posing as someone else or to a fictitious payee. The UCC provides special rules designed to protect subsequent holders in these situations and to impose liability upon the makers of the checks.

Assume that a Bruce Springsteen lookalike walks into a pawn shop and pawns a stolen electric guitar. The pawn shop draws a check for $200 payable to Bruce Springsteen. The imposter then signs the back of the check "Bruce Springsteen" and uses it to buy running shoes at the Fleet Foot Store. The UCC provides (Section 3-405[1][a]) that an endorsement by anyone of the name Bruce Springsteen is effective and that the maker of the check cannot use as a defense that the endorsement is forged. Fleet Foot would be able to recover on the check against the pawn shop, leaving the shop with the difficult task of hunting down the imposter and recovering against him.

On first reading the rule appears to condone the actions of the imposter, but its real purpose is to impose the responsibility on makers so that they will be cautious in dealing with potential imposters. The maker cannot avoid liability and therefore has an incentive to check identities.

The fictitious payee rule involves similar policy considerations. A common way of embezzling funds is for an employee who has the authority to write checks to draft checks in the name of someone who does not exist. The employee then endorses the check in the name of the fictitious person and takes the money. Again, the UCC provides (Section 3-405[1][b] & [c]) that the endorsement is effective. In this situation, too, a holder can recover against the maker, whose only recourse is to find and recover against the disloyal employee. The maker's potential liability will encourage caution and the exercise of control over the actions of employees who have authority concerning the issuance of company checks.

SUMMARY

Unconditional or primary liability means that a party has an unconditional obligation to pay according to the terms of an instrument. The maker of a promissory note immediately incurs primary liability. The drawee of a draft is primarily liable after accepting the draft. Secondary liability involves a conditional commitment to pay if the party primarily liable fails to pay. Drawers and endorsers of commercial paper may incur secondary liability. To establish secondary liability, there must be: a proper *presentment* for acceptance or payment; a *dishonor* by refusing to accept or pay; and *notification* of the dishonor by any reasonable means to the party having secondary liability.

A party transferring or presenting a negotiable instrument makes certain implied warranties to the transferee, payor, or acceptor. Liability may be based upon breach of these warranties even though the transferor or presentor did not sign the instrument.

A holder in due course of commercial paper is not subject to personal defenses such as breach of contract, nondelivery, or failure of consideration. The reason is to maintain the easy transferability of commercial paper. Certain defenses are seen as so important that they are good against a holder in due course. Called universal or real defenses, they include infancy, certain other forms of incapacity, duress, and illegality sufficient to render the transaction void, discharge in bankruptcy, forgery, material alteration, and fraud in the execution.

The UCC provides special rules that protect holders of commercial paper drawn to the order of imposters or fictitious payees. In both situations the holder could recover from the maker of the checks, whose potential liability should induce caution.

REVIEW PROBLEMS

1. List the steps required for a holder to establish secondary liability. What parties can be subject to secondary liability?

2. What are the major policy justifications for limiting the defenses available against a holder in due course?

3. Can the holder in due course doctrine result in unfairness to certain parties? How?

4. List the major universal defenses available against holders in due course. In light of your answer to question 2, explain the policy justifications for recognizing these defenses.

5. Henry Jaroszewski and his wife agreed to purchase frozen food from Merit Food Corporation, to be delivered in three batches. When they entered into this agreement, they signed a "purchase and sales agreement." They also signed a form titled, "Request for a personal loan." The second page was a promissory note, the third page was a credit application, and the fourth authorized the bank

to pay the proceeds of the loan ($1,850) to Merit. The purchasers became dissatisfied with the food after receiving $200 worth, and they refused to accept further deliveries. The bank meanwhile had paid Merit the $1,850. The purchasers now claim that Merit's representatives fraudulently represented the nature of the forms they were signing. They also claim that the bank knew of Merit's misconduct because it had dealt with Merit on similar transactions in the past. Must the Jaroszewskis pay the bank?

6. Linda Mesnik opened a checking account with the Hempstead Bank in the name of Linda Mesnik Agency. During the next 18 months, approximately $60,000 was deposited and paid out by checks. The account then was closed. Mesnik claims that the signatures on many of the checks were not hers but unauthorized forgeries, and the checks were cashed as part of a conspiracy between her husband and a bank employee. The bank contends that Mesnik's claim is barred by the statute of limitations because she did not report the unauthorized signatures within one year. Mesnik's response is that the statements were intercepted by her husband. Would Mesnik be successful? Discuss.

7. Bergfield contracted to sell Kirby real estate for $352,560. The contract called for a $20,000 payment at the closing. The closing was completed in the office of Bergfield's attorney, and all necessary documents were executed by both parties. All of the documents except the check were kept by Bergfield's attorney until Bergfield could find out whether the check was good. The following day, Bergfield went to his bank and requested the cashier to phone Kirby's bank to determine if there were sufficient funds in Kirby's account to cover the check. The person who answered the phone indicated that Kirby's account did not contain sufficient funds. Unknown to this person, the bank's president had arranged with Kirby to cover the check when it was presented. Because the contract contained a "time is of the essence" clause, Bergfield treated the contract as breached and refused to allow his attorney to deliver the deed. He also retained Kirby's deposit. Kirby now sues for specific performance. Would he be successful?

8. About 9:30 A.M. on July 17, 1952, Evern Jones got his mail at the post office in the City of Jackson. One letter contained a payroll check of American Book Company in the sum of $432.53, payable to the order of Jones. He wrote his name on the back of the check in the post office and started across the street to a nearby bank. He had several other pieces of mail in his hands. A strong wind blew the mail out of his hands. Passersby helped him, but he could not catch his check. He immediately reported his loss to the bank and asked the Book Company to stop payment. This was done.

   Between 2 and 3 o'clock that afternoon, Mrs. Tommie Davis, an employee of the White System of Jackson, Inc., took a telephone call ostensibly from Leon Orman, at Five Point Service Station, who advised that one of their customers, with a check larger than they could handle, wished to buy some tires, and inquired if the System would cash it. She asked Mr. White, the president, what to do, and he advised her, if it was a company check, to cash it. About 30 minutes later, a man came into the office and presented the check.

   Mrs. Martha Lewis, another employee, took the check, and Mrs. Davis explained the previous telephone conversation. In addition to the name Jones, there purported to be an endorsement of Five Point Service Station and Leon Orman. Mrs. Lewis thought the man was Leon Orman. Because of the size of the check, she asked Mr. Taylor, the office manager, about it. He told her to get Mr. White's approval. The White System frequently accommodated people by cashing checks for them, and generally the checks were brought into the office by errand boys or employees.

White System seeks to recover the amount of the check on which American Book Company had stopped payment. Would White System be successful? Explain.

9. Central Jersey Bank kept several blank checks in its locked vault. Some of those checks were stolen. Brogan Cadillac-Oldsmobile received one of the checks when it was used to pay for a car. Forged signatures of Central Jersey's officers appeared on the check, which was made out for $22,000. When Brogan found out that the check was forged, it sued Central Jersey for payment. Central Jersey argued that it was not liable because the check was materially altered and the signatures were forged. What would Brogan counterargue? What result?

10. Kelly, representing himself to be an aluminum siding salesman, visited Mr. and Mrs. Burchett. He offered to install aluminum siding on the Burchetts' home at a certain price, under an arrangement by which they would allow their home to be a demonstration model for prospective customers. As compensation for making their home available for demonstration purposes, the Burchetts would receive $100 credit for every aluminum siding contract sold in their area. In this way, Kelly assured them, the Burchetts would get their aluminum siding for free. The Burchetts agreed, and Kelly gave them a contract to read. While they were reading, Kelly prepared other forms for them to sign. The Burchetts signed these other forms without reading them, assuming that they were identical to the contract that they had just read. What the Burchetts actually signed were promissory notes and mortgages, with no mention of the credits. Aluminum siding was subsequently installed on their home unsatisfactorily. The notes and mortgages that they signed were negotiated to Allied, which took as a holder in due course. In an action on the notes and mortgages, can the Burchetts assert the defense provided in UCC Section 3-305(2)(c)? Should your answer depend on the Burchetts' level of education, sophistication, or familiarity with the English language?

11. Betty Ellis, as comaker with her husband, executed a $2,800 note payable to Standard. In a later action by Standard to enforce the note, Betty claimed that it was void because she had signed it under duress. The duress allegedly consisted of periodic physical beatings and psychological pressure from her husband for at least three years before the note's execution. In considering her defense, the court looked to the official comment to Section 174 of the Restatement (Second) of Contracts: "The essence of [the type of duress which makes a contract void] is that a party is compelled by physical force to do an act that he has no intention of doing. He is . . .'a mere mechanical instrument.' " Do you think that Betty can successfully assert the duress defense against Standard? Assuming that Standard dealt with Betty in the note's execution, does it matter whether Standard was a holder in due course?

12. Michael Heymann executed an $8,000 promissory note, payable to Gaffin. The note was endorsed by Paul Heymann, Michael's father. After Michael had stopped making payments, Gaffin unsuccessfully tried to locate Michael through his father and through the telephone directory. Long after the note had come due, Gaffin sent notice of dishonor to Paul Heymann and demanded payment. What defense might Paul raise under UCC Section 3-502? Could Gaffin successfully counter this defense? See UCC Section 3-511(2).

CHAPTER 23

Commercial Paper: Checks

CHAPTER OBJECTIVES

After reading this chapter, you should be able to:

1. Explain the relationship between a bank and its customers.

2. Detail the consequences if a customer fails to endorse a check, creates an overdraft, or postdates a check and describe a bank's obligations when checks are presented to it.

3. Explain what happens when a customer stops payment on a check.

4. Define certification of a check.

5. Understand the importance of reporting to a bank unauthorized signatures and alterations.

6. Describe the customer's rights if his or her signature is forged on a check.

7. Explain the enforceability of a check that has been materially altered or improperly completed.

8. Describe what happens if a bank pays a check with a forged endorsement.

A check is a special type of draft, which is an instrument ordering one person to pay another. The drawer of a check orders a bank to pay someone on the drawer's behalf. Thus a check is a draft drawn on a bank and payable on demand.

CHECKS

The Bank and Its Customers

The relationship between the bank and its customers is generally controlled by Article 3 of the UCC. In certain circumstances, controversies between banks and depositors are resolved by the rules in Article 4 of the UCC.

Section 4-104(1)(e) of the Uniform Commercial Code defines a customer as:

> any person having an account with a bank or for whom a bank has agreed to collect items and includes a bank carrying an account with another bank.

Thus a customer can be someone other than a depositor. Generally, though, a customer is thought of as a depositor.

The Bank as Debtor   Ordinarily, when a person makes a deposit to his or her checking or savings account, the bank becomes a debtor of the depositor, who is then a creditor of the bank.

As a debtor of the general depositor, the bank is bound by an implied contract to repay the deposit on the depositor's demand or order. The relationship between the bank and its depositor is determined by the terms of the deposit agreement, which is an express contract between the parties and is binding on them. An example of such a contract is the signature card signed by a depositor when opening his or her account at the bank. The debtor–creditor relationship begins immediately after the depositor makes a deposit. (Note that the provisions of Article 4 may be varied by agreement, but no agreement can disclaim a bank's responsibility for its own lack of good faith or failure to exercise ordinary care.)

The Bank as Agent   Even though the bank is a debtor, in discharging its obligations to the depositor the bank is also his or her agent and is bound by the rules of principal and agent. In this situation, the bank is the agent, and the customer the principal. This relationship arises, for example, when the bank pays checks drawn upon it. Thus the bank's relationship to a depositor is twofold: debtor–creditor and principal–agent.

Another situation where a principal–agent relationship arises between a bank and its depositor is when the bank seeks to obtain collection of an item for its depositor, who is the owner of the check. It should be noted that the status as agent is only a presumption and may be contradicted by evidence that a party clearly intended otherwise.

Death or Incompetence of a Customer

In light of the principal–agent relationship between a bank and its customer, one might conclude that the bank's authority to act ends on the death or declaration of **incompetence** of the principal. Because of the large number of items handled by a bank and the possible liability of the bank for a wrongful dishonor, the UCC instead relieves a bank of liability for paying any instrument before it has notice of the death or incompetence of the drawer. The bank may pay (and another bank consequently may accept) an item until it knows of the death or the adjudged incompetence and has a reasonable opportunity to act on it.

Incompetence a declared inability to perform a required duty

Even if the bank knows of the death of a customer, the UCC permits the bank to pay or certify a check drawn on it for ten days after it receives notice. The bank may pay or certify a check unless a person claiming an interest in the account orders the bank to stop payment during this ten-day period. Suppose that Smith writes a check on March 10, and someone presents it for payment on March 15. Even if Smith dies on March 11, and the bank knows it, the bank may honor the check. But if an interested party notifies the bank to stop payment of the check, the bank must comply.

CHECKS GENERALLY

Failure to Endorse

If a customer deposits a check written by someone else, the bank credits the customer's account for the amount of the check, but only subject to the bank's actually collecting the amount due from the drawer of the check. The bank (called a *depository bank*) then tries to collect the check from the drawee bank (the bank on which the check was written). The customer could, of course, go directly to the drawee bank and cash the check, but this probably would be very time consuming. By depositing checks, customers authorize banks to collect checks for them.

What if the customer fails to endorse the check? Must the bank get the customer's signature? An order instrument must be endorsed for a proper negotiation to occur. Because we all make mistakes, the UCC has a special rule for this situation. Generally, the depository bank simply may supply the customer's endorsement. This rule eliminates the need to call the customer back to the bank to endorse the check.

Not an Assignment of Funds

Merely because one receives a check from someone else does not mean that one is entitled to the funds in the other's account. A check does not operate as an assignment of funds in the hands of the drawee. A bank is not liable on a check until it accepts it. As for the holder of the check, he or she has no recourse against the bank when it fails to accept a check. The holder of a check that has been dishonored must try to collect from the drawer of the check or from one of the endorsers.

Overdrafts

If the bank decides to honor a check, it may do so even though the charge creates an **overdraft.** A customer who writes a check for $550 but who has only $500 on deposit has in effect authorized the bank to pay $550 to the payee. By implication, the customer has agreed to repay the bank for the other $50. The bank has no obligation to honor such a check because it creates an overdraft. At most banks, the customer soon discovers that his or her check has "bounced."

Overdraft a check written for an amount of money in excess of the amount on deposit

Postdating

Sometimes a customer **postdates** a check. He or she issues the check before the date on the check has arrived. For example, the customer may give a check to the payee on March 1 but date it March 15. People postdate checks when they do not intend checks to be presented before the date on the check (and very likely do not have sufficient funds in their accounts to cover the check).

The time when a postdated check is payable is determined by the stated date on the instrument. If a customer writes a check on March 1 dated March 15, it is not payable until March 15. This rule is true even though a check generally is payable on the

Postdated the condition of a check delivered before its date

demand of the payee or other holder of the instrument. Unfortunately, postdating checks is dangerous.

First, if the check goes through before March 15, and there are no funds to cover it, the drawer has issued a check for insufficient funds. Although a bank should not honor a check before its stated date, the check is negotiable before the date and need not be affected by postdating. The check may be negotiated to the bank before the stated date.

Second, the drawer might be prosecuted. The prudent practice is to not write checks until one has sufficient funds in an account to cover them. The Fair Debt Collection Practices Act makes it illegal for a debt collector to take a postdated check.

Failure of the Bank to Honor a Check

Proximate the quality of being a direct and natural sequence between a breach of duty and an injury

What if a bank fails to pay a check written by the drawer when it ought to have done so? The bank is liable to the drawer for any damages **proximately** caused by a wrongful dishonor of the check. If the bank merely made a mistake, its liability is limited to actual damages proved. The UCC explicitly recognizes damages for arrest, prosecution, and other consequential damages proximately caused by the wrongful dishonor. If a drawer writes a check that a bank wrongfully fails to honor, the drawer may be prosecuted. (In most states, the drawer is not likely to be arrested. Most states require that notice of the dishonor and an opportunity to make the check good be given to the drawer. The drawer probably can straighten the matter out with the bank.)

The following case deals with the wrongful dishonor of checks by a bank.

––––––––––––––– *Twin City Bank v. Isaacs* –––––––––––––––

Arkansas Supreme Court
672 S.W.2d 651 (1984)

FACTS   Isaacs discovered the loss of his checkbook on May 13. On May 14, he reported the loss to his bank. He later learned that the bank had honored two forged checks totaling $2,050, on May 11 and May 12. The bank suspected Isaacs of having something to do with the forgeries, and so it froze the remaining $2,000 in his account. On May 30, the police notified the bank that Isaacs had had nothing to do with the forgeries and brought forgery charges against someone else. Nonetheless, the bank kept the $2,000 frozen in the account for the next four years. Isaacs sued for wrongful dishonor of his checks, caused by the bank's action in freezing the remaining $2,000 in his account as well as for the wrongful withholding of his funds. Isaacs claimed that as a result of the bank's action, he lost two cars on which he could not make payments, that his credit was damaged, that he lost the use of the $2,000 for four years, and that he suffered marriage difficulties.

ISSUE   Is the bank liable for the wrongful dishonor of these checks?

DECISION   Yes. The court awarded $18,500 in compensatory damages and $45,000 in punitive damages. Isaacs had a number of clearly established losses, among them the loss of his

$2,000 wrongfully withheld by the bank for four years and the loss of two vehicles worth $2,200. But he also asserted losses relating to the mental suffering caused by his loss of credit, inability to buy a home, and marriage problems. Although such damages could be regarded as speculative, the court let him recover for them. The court ruled that Section 4-402 implicitly recognizes mental suffering and other intangible injuries as recoverable when a bank wrongfully dishonors a check. Punitive damages are recoverable because the UCC limits awards to actual damages in wrongful dishonor cases only when the wrongful dishonor happens by mistake.

Stale Checks

A bank also has no obligation to its checking account customers to honor uncertified checks presented more than six months after date. Such a check is referred to as a **stale check**. But the bank may honor such a check if it acts in good faith. If one receives a dividend check from GM on August 1 but neglects to cash it until March 1 of the following year, the check is stale. Nonetheless, it would seem reasonable to cash such a check, because GM presumably wants the check to be paid.

Before cashing a check that is more than six months old, a bank probably should consult with the drawer. Otherwise the drawer might argue that a failure to consult before cashing a stale check violates the bank's obligation to act in good faith.

> **Stale check** a check presented more than six months after its date

STOP PAYMENT

Right to Stop

Section 4-403 of the UCC gives a bank customer the right to stop payment of a check. Subsection 1 requires the customer to notify the bank in a way and time that give the bank a reasonable opportunity to act on the stop payment order. The order must be received by the bank before it has paid a check in cash, accepted the check, or certified it.

Under Section 4-403(2), an oral order is effective for 14 days. A written order is effective for six months. A written stop payment order can be renewed for extra periods of six months. If a check is paid despite a binding stop payment order, the burden is on the bank's customer to establish any loss resulting from payment of the check.

Defenses

Even though the drawer of a check has the right to stop payment, he or she remains liable to any holder of the instrument unless the drawer has a defense good against the holder. The drawer of a check cannot issue a check to someone and expect to escape liability simply by stopping payment on the check. The drawer must establish a defense that can be successfully asserted against the holder of the instrument — for example, failure of consideration. If one writes a $450 check to an appliance store for a refrigerator, but the store never delivers the refrigerator, one could stop payment on the check. If the store sued, one could successfully assert failure of consideration as a defense against the store. The store could not sue the bank for refusing to honor the check, because a check is not an assignment of funds in the account of the drawer.

If the drawer of a check is unfortunate enough to be in the situation of the person whose refrigerator never appeared, and the check is transferred to a holder in due course or to someone having the rights of a holder in due course, he or she may be liable on the check even if he or she stopped payment on it. The defense of failure of consideration is a personal defense and therefore may not be asserted successfully against a holder in due course. But a real defense may be asserted against a holder in due course. (See Chapter 22 for a discussion of these defenses.)

Payment Despite Stop Payment Order

What if the bank pays a holder in due course despite a stop payment order? Section 4-407(a) gives the bank the rights of the person it pays. Because the drawer has only a real defense against that person, the bank can collect the amount paid from its customer, even though the check was paid over a stop payment order. (Note that the burden of establishing a loss is on the customer.)

Conversely, if the bank reimburses its customer when it pays a check over a stop payment order, it receives any rights of the drawer against the payee or any other holder of the check with respect to the transaction out of which the check arose.

What if someone issues a check to a store for a refrigerator but the store never delivers the refrigerator? If the bank honors the check over a stop payment order, the bank may proceed against the store for the amount it received under the check.

The following case discusses the issue of stop payment orders.

Thomas v. Marine Midland Tinkers National Bank

**Civil Court of the City of New York
381 N.Y.S.2d 797 (1976)**

FACTS   Thomas contracted to buy two rugs from Gallo. He paid $2,500 of the $10,500 price with a postdated check drawn on Marine Midland and took one of the rugs. On the morning the check became current, Thomas requested a stop payment order. The next day, Gallo presented the check for payment at the bank and received cash. The same day, Thomas returned the rug to Gallo, rescinding the contract. Thomas discovered that the check had been cashed when he received his monthly bank statement. He demanded that Gallo refund the $2,500. Gallo refused, as did Marine Midland Bank, to refund or credit the amount.

ISSUE   Must the bank repay Thomas for cashing the check?

DECISION   Yes. A day and one half was more than reasonable to enforce the stop payment order on the check, presented at the very same branch where the order was issued.

The plaintiff needed only to show that adequate notice and a reasonable opportunity to act had been given to the defendant to make out a *prima facie* case. At that point, it was up to the defendant to produce evidence negating the plaintiff's case and proof of loss, which the bank did not do.

CERTIFICATION

As clearly stated in Section 3-411, **certification** is an acceptance. A bank has no obligation to certify a check in the absence of a specific agreement to do so. But once a bank has certified a check, it is obligated to honor it. When it certifies a check, the bank becomes primarily liable on the instrument. The drawer may not stop payment of a certified check.

Certification of a check by a bank at the drawer's request does no more than affirm the genuineness of the drawer's signature and indicate that funds will be on deposit to pay the item when the check is presented for payment. If the drawer obtains certification of his or her check, the drawer remains secondarily liable, although the bank is primarily liable.

The holder of a check also may have the check certified. The drawer and all prior endorsers are released from liability if the holder takes this action. Of course, a holder may present the check for payment in this situation. It therefore is reasonable to release the drawer and endorsers from liability.

A certified check may be endorsed after the bank has certified it. In this instance, the certification remains effective, and the endorser has all the duties imposed by Section 3-414.

Certification a guarantee by a financial institution to pay an instrument when presented

UNAUTHORIZED SIGNATURES AND ALTERATIONS

Customer's Duty to Discover and Report

The customer of a bank has a duty to discover and report to the bank forgeries and alterations on his or her checks. This duty arises once the bank has sent its customer both a statement of his or her account and the checks honored by the bank (Section 4-406[1]). The customer must exercise "reasonable care and promptness" in examining the statement and checks to discover unauthorized signatures or any alterations. If he or she discovers an improper signature or an alteration, the next step is to notify the bank promptly. The customer must contact the appropriate person at the bank so that the bank may take action on the check. Thus after a customer receives a statement and checks honored by the bank, he or she must review them.

If the customer fails to comply, he or she may not later assert an unauthorized signature or any alteration as a defense against the bank if the bank establishes that it suffered a loss as a result of the customer's failure to comply with Section 4-406(1).

Consider the following case. On March 1, Pete gets his checks and statement from the bank. Rather than examining them, he throws them on his desk. After several months, Pete decides to examine the checks. He discovers a forgery of a check. If the bank establishes that it suffered a loss as a result of his failure to notify it promptly, the loss is Pete's.

Acts by the Same Wrongdoer

Once a customer has received a statement and a check with an unauthorized signature or alteration, a second rule comes into play that covers additional acts by the same wrongdoer. This rule covers endorsements as well as unauthorized signatures of the customer and alterations. A customer has a reasonable period of time but not more than 14 calendar days to notify the bank of any unauthorized signature or alteration. If the customer fails to notify the bank, any loss caused by an unauthorized signature or alteration by the same wrongdoer after this 14-day period falls on the customer.

The burden clearly is on the customer to police his or her account so that a wrongdoer cannot continue. Once a customer notifies the bank of any such unauthorized signature or alteration, the risk of loss shifts back to the bank. Then the bank must guard against other unauthorized signatures or alterations by the wrongdoer.

Consider the following case. Mary receives her checks and statement on June 1. Her signature had been forged on a check that had been returned to her on June 1. Susan, an acquaintance of Mary, forged the check. On June 5, Susan forges another check on Mary's account. Mary receives the second check along with her statement and other checks on July 1. On July 18, Susan forges another check. The third check is returned to Mary on August 1. On August 3, Mary discovers all the checks forged by Susan. She notifies the bank that day and asks the bank to credit her account.

The UCC gives Mary 14 days from the time she learns of the first forgery to notify the bank. The bank must credit her account for the first two checks. But it need not credit her account for the third check, because it was honored after the date by which Mary was obligated to notify the bank of the forgery—June 15. The bank may charge Mary's account for any check honored by the bank after June 15 up to the time it receives notice of the forgeries from Mary. If the bank honors a forgery by Susan after Mary notifies the bank on August 3, the bank is not acting reasonably, and it may not charge her account for any check it honors after August 3.

The following case illustrates a customer's duty to examine his or her checks.

Zenith Syndicate, Incorporated v. Marine Midland Bank

Civil Court, New York County
23 UCC Rep. 1267 (1978)

FACTS Zenith kept an account with Marine Midland Bank on which either the president or vice president of Zenith was authorized to sign checks. In 1972, between February and November, Zenith's bookkeeper drew 20 fraudulently signed checks. Marine Midland paid these checks and charged them to Zenith's account. Each month Marine Midland sent the statements and checks from the account to Zenith for inspection. Each month, the bookkeeper received the statements and canceled checks and approved the debits.

In November, the wrongdoing was discovered. Marine Midland was unable to recover $4,279 of the amounts paid on the checks and refused to credit Zenith's account for this loss. Zenith sued Marine Midland to compel such action.

Must Marine Midland recredit Zenith's account?   ISSUE

No. The UCC (Section 4-406) requires that the customer exercise reasonable care   DECISION
and promptness in examining the monthly statement and canceled checks to discover unauthorized signatures and must notify the bank promptly after the discovery. If this is not done, then the customer may not assert this unauthorized signature against the bank nor later unauthorized signatures by the same wrongdoer, unless the bank did not satisfy its own duty of ordinary care. According to the court, the fact that the book-keeper concealed the forgery does not free Zenith of its responsibility to exercise reasonable care in examining its own bank statement. Because the plaintiff could not establish that Marine Midland failed to exercise ordinary care, the court held that the bank did not have to credit Zenith's account in the amount of the unrecovered loss.

Bank's Burden of Proof

Before a bank may charge its customer's account (under either Section 4-406[2][a] or [b]), the bank must establish that the customer failed to exercise reasonable care and promptness in examining his or her statement and checks and that the customer failed to notify the bank promptly. But even if the bank does establish this, the risk of loss shifts back if the customer proves that the bank was less than ordinarily careful in paying an item (Section 4-406[3]).

If the bank loses the suit against its customer on an unauthorized drawer's signature, it may proceed against anyone who broke the presenter's warranty that he or she had no knowledge that the drawer's signature was unauthorized (Section 4-207).

FORGED SIGNATURE OF THE DRAWER

Signature of the Drawer Required

For an instrument to be negotiable, it must be signed by the maker or drawer. Section 3-401(1) clearly indicates that no one is liable, even to a holder in due course, on an instrument without his or her signature. Only if a customer's authorized signature appears on a check may the bank charge his or her account.

The UCC assumes that the bank recognizes the signatures of its customers and does not honor forgeries. Suppose for example, that Stan steals one of Robert's checks without Robert learning of the theft. Stan makes the check payable to himself and forges Robert's signature. The bank charges Robert's account. When Robert receives his checks and statement, he discovers the forgery. Robert immediately notifies the bank. Assuming that Robert was not negligent, the bank must recredit his account.

Other People Liable

Assuming that a bank paid a check, and a customer establishes that his or her signature was unauthorized, the bank may not charge his or her account. But the bank may be able to collect from someone other than its customer.

One possibility is for the bank to bring suit for breach of warranty. The bank might try to recover its loss from the person who presented the check to it for payment. To recover from this person the bank must establish that the person *knew* of the forgery when the check was paid. But, if the person did *not* know of the forgery, the bank cannot recover its loss from that party.

Another possibility is to sue the forger. Section 3-404(1) states that, even though an unauthorized signature does not bind a customer of the bank, it operates as the signature of the unauthorized signer in favor of any person who in good faith pays the instrument or takes it for value.

Of course, if a customer okays an unauthorized signature, the bank may charge the customer's account.

Negligence by Customer

The bank also may charge a customer's account if the customer was negligent. If a customer's negligence results in a check's being materially altered or signed by someone unauthorized, the customer may not assert the lack of authority against a bank that pays the instrument in good faith and in accordance with reasonable commercial standards.

Banks once examined each check to determine if the drawer's signature matched the bank's signature card. If the bank employee who examined the signature card were careless, a bad check might be honored by the bank. Even if the customer had been negligent, the bank also would have failed to observe reasonable commercial standards and would have no right to charge its customer's account for the check.

Today one of the most obvious cases of negligence is the drawer who uses an automatic signing device and is negligent in looking after it. Alice, for example, uses a mechanical check writer. She leaves the check writer and her checks on her desk at all times. An employee of Alice's takes a check and uses the check writer to make a check out to himself. Because Alice was negligent, she cannot require the bank to recredit her account if it honors the check.

The following case illustrates a bank not acting according to reasonable commercial standards.

Medford Irrigation District v. Western Bank

Oregon Court of Appeals
676 P.2d 329 (1984)

FACTS   Medford Irrigation District's bookkeeper forged the name of the district's manager on several checks drawn on the district's account at the Western Bank. Western paid the checks and charged the district's account. The district admitted that it had been negligent in not supervising the bookkeeper and in not reviewing its bank statements. It conceded that its negligence had substantially contributed to the forgeries. But district argued that Western could not charge its account, in spite of the district's negligence, because the bank had failed to follow reasonable banking standards and had failed to exercise ordinary care in paying the checks. The district alleged that Western's practice of automatically paying all checks for a face amount under $5,000 without first inspecting the signatures barred the bank from relying on the defense of the district's negligence, because the bank had not followed proper procedures.

Did the bank improperly charge the district's account?   ISSUE

Yes. The court held as a matter of law that by automatically paying all checks under $5,000, the bank had failed to exercise ordinary care and that this procedure was not a reasonable commercial practice. A bank must adopt some means of reviewing checks that reasonably relates to the detection of unauthorized signatures. Automatically paying all checks under $5,000 did not meet this standard. When it is determined that a bank has been negligent, the defense of a customer's negligence is not available, and the bank is strictly liable for improperly charging its customer's account.   DECISION

Today most banks automatically process checks by computer. They do not inspect every check, because the costs of inspection are high. This case shows that banks must choose some manner of reviewing checks that is a reasonable way to detect unauthorized signatures.

ALTERED CHECKS

Material Alteration

As we discussed in Chapter 22, any alteration of an instrument is material if it changes the contract of any party. If someone were to come into possession of a check and improperly raise the amount of the check, he or she would have materially altered the instrument.

For example, suppose that Susan writes out a check for $10 and makes it payable to Doris, signs, and gives the check to Doris. Doris alters the amount to read $110 and she alters the words on the check to read "One Hundred Ten Dollars." If the bank pays the check, it may charge Susan's account for only $10.00 — the amount of the original check Susan wrote.

The following case concerns an instrument that was allegedly altered by its holder.

Bluffestone v. Abrahams

Court of Appeals of Arizona
607 P.2d 25 (1979)

David and Pearl Bluffestone held a $5,000 note signed by Gary Abrahams. Following David's death, Pearl's son in law, Alan Gilenko, helped Pearl to settle the estate. Gilenko   FACTS took the demand note and added monthly payments and a provision for attorney's fees. Gilenko induced Bert and Lee Abrahams, Gary Abraham's brother and father, to sign the note with full knowledge of the changes. Gary, Bert, and Lee all contended that they were not liable because the note had been materially altered.

ISSUE   Were Gary, Bert, and Lee liable for these instruments in light of the fact the checks had been altered?

DECISION   Yes. Bert and Lee Abrahams were liable because they had full knowledge of the changes Gilenko made to the note when they signed. The court held that consent to an alteration of an instrument may be implied by the acts of the parties, but the circumstances creating the implication must be plain and unambiguous. In that Gary Abrahams neither expressly or implicitly consented to the alterations in the $5,000 note, he was not personally liable for the changes. The attorney's fees and monthly payments could not be enforced against Gary Abrahams.

If a customer's negligence results in an alteration, the bank may enforce the instrument as altered. Although the UCC does not define negligence, it indicates that negligence has been found when spaces are left in the body of the instrument so that it is possible to insert words or figures.

When a drawer receives his or her checks, even though he or she was not negligent, the drawer has an obligation to inspect the checks for alterations and to notify the bank promptly of any alterations. If the drawer fails to notify the bank promptly, he or she may not be able to use the defense of alteration against the bank.

Improperly Completed Checks

Payment in Good Faith of Improperly Completed Check   If a check was improperly completed, rather than altered, the bank may enforce it according to the amount of the check as completed. The bank may do so even though the bank knows that the item was completed, unless the bank has notice that the completion was improper.

Suppose that a drawer of a check casually dates and signs a check, making it payable to cash, but fails to fill in the amount. This check eventually falls into the hands of a holder in due course. In the meantime, someone has filled in the amount of the check as $500. The holder in due course presents the check to the drawer's bank, and the bank cashes the check. May the bank charge the drawer's account for $500? Yes, the bank may charge the account of its customer according to the amount of the completed check. Of course, the bank must not know that the completion was improper. This section of the UCC gives the bank rights like those of a holder in due course who takes an item that has been completed without authorization.

Bank's Rights Against Others

Simply because a bank is unable to collect from the drawer of the instrument does not mean that it must bear the loss for a check. A bank may at this point try to collect from anyone who broke the presenter's warranty.

PAYMENT ON A FORGED ENDORSEMENT

For a drawee bank properly to charge a drawer's account when it honors one of his or her checks, the bank must pay only a holder of the check. With respect to bearer paper, this does not create a problem. But what if the drawer wrote a check to a specific payee whose endorsement was forged or unauthorized? No one who comes into possession of the check can be a holder because of the forged endorsement. (Because no one could become a holder of the check, no one could become a holder in due course of the check.) Therefore it would be improper for the bank to charge its customer's account. The bank in turn could sue its transferors for breach of warranty of title or genuineness of signatures.

For example, Bill writes a check to Glenn. The check is stolen from Glenn by Richard. Richard forges Glenn's endorsement and cashes the check at Bill's bank. The bank charges Bill's account. In the meantime, Glenn tells Bill that the check has been stolen. When Bill receives the check from the bank, he calls Glenn, who assures him the endorsement was forged. If Bill notifies his bank within a reasonable time after learning of the forged endorsement, the bank must recredit Bill's account.

SUMMARY

A bank is obligated to its checking account customers both as an agent and as a debtor of the customers.

Many rules about checks are discussed in this chapter. Of particular importance is the rule relating to stop payment orders. In general, a customer may stop payment on a check. But this action is only useful if the customer has a defense good against the person presenting the check. A check also may be certified by a bank. When a bank certifies a check, it becomes primarily liable on the instrument.

In general, a customer has a duty to examine his or her statement and checks after they are returned by the bank. If a customer fails to notify the bank promptly of any forgeries or alterations, the bank may be able to charge the customer's account for a forged or altered check. In the absence of negligence by a customer or a failure to timely notify the bank, a bank usually may not charge a customer's account for checks with forged endorsements or forged signatures of the drawers. In general, a customer who promptly notifies the bank and was not negligent is only liable for the original amount of his or her checks, even if they were later improperly altered. But if a check is improperly completed, the bank may enforce it against its customer for the amount specified in the check as completed.

REVIEW PROBLEMS

1. What if anything should a customer do when he or she receives a statement and checks from a bank?

2. Under what circumstances if any are people liable for checks when their signatures, as drawers of the checks, have been forged?

3. Under what circumstances if any could a bank charge its customer's account for a check it honored even though the customer had given the bank a stop payment order on the check?

4. Must a bank certify a check presented to it? How does certification affect a drawer's obligation on the check?

5. Colburn had an account with the First National Bank. He wrote a number of checks the week of June 1, and on June 10, he died. Many of his checks had not been honored by the bank at the time of his death. May the bank now honor these checks?

6. Williams received a check from Acme Automobiles drawn on the First National Bank. Williams deposited the check to his account, and the bank presented Acme's check to the First National Bank. First National refused to honor the check because there were no funds in the Acme account to cover the check. Can Williams force First National to honor the check?

7. Wade wrote a check for $250 on September 30 to pay his October rent. The check was dated October 10. He gave the check to the manager at the Villa Apartments. The manager assured Wade that he would not deposit the check until October 10. Mark did not have enough money in his account on September 30 to cover the check, but he planned to deposit his paycheck on October 1. Mark's employer failed to pay him on October 1. In the meantime, the manager of the Villa Apartments accidentally deposited the check to the Villa account. If the check is presented to Mark's bank, may it honor the check?

8. Mather wrote a check on his account on July 1, 1986. This check was presented for payment on February 1, 1987. What is the term for a check presented so long after it was written? Can the bank honor it?

9. Lorenzi ordered a washing machine from the Acme Department Store. She issued a check to Acme for $450 to pay for the machine. When the machine was delivered, it was defective. Lorenzi called her bank and stopped payment on her check. Three days later the bank overlooked the stop payment order and paid First National Bank, a holder in due course of the check. First National was acting on behalf of its customer, Acme Department Stores. Acme refused to fix the defect in the machine. May Lorenzi force her bank to recredit her account for $450?

10. Clark received his checks and statement on September 1. His signature had been forged on a check that was returned to him on September 1. An acquaintance of Clark's had forged the check. On September 20 another check on Clark's account was forged. This check was returned to Clark on October 1. On October 3, Clark discovered the forgeries and notified his bank. On October 15, the bank honored another forged check on Clark's account. May Clark force the bank to recredit his account for these checks?

11. When Wallace received his monthly statement and checks from the bank, he discovered the forgery of his signature on one of the checks. He immediately notified the bank. May Wallace force the bank to recredit his account for the amount of the check it honored? If so, from whom will the bank be able to collect its loss?

12. Roberts signed a number of blank checks just before lunch. He left these partially completed checks on his desk while he was at lunch. His office was left open all this time. The janitor came in, stole a check, filled it in, and cashed it. The bank charged Roberts's account for the face amount of the check. May Roberts force the bank to recredit his account?

13. Gardner wrote a check payable to the order of Andrew Jones. This check was stolen from Jones, and the thief cashed the check. The thief forged Andrew Jones's signature on the back of the check. Gardner's bank then honored the check and charged her account. Soon thereafter, Jones informed Gardner of the theft. Gardner notified the bank of the forgery immediately. Must the bank recredit her account?

14. Murphy operated a restaurant. His bookkeeper wrote a series of checks on his account by forging his name on the checks. When the checks were returned to the restaurant, the bookkeeper reviewed the checks and the statement. Several months later, Murphy learned of the forgeries and notified his bank. He demanded that the bank recredit his account. The bank argued that Murphy's negligence had substantially contributed to the forgeries. What could Murphy argue even if he admitted that he had been negligent?

15. Kidwell had a checking account with Exchange Bank, upon which the president of Kidwell was authorized to draw. Smith, the corporate secretary of Kidwell, forged the president's signature on 65 checks made payable to her over a three-year period. These forgeries were not reported by Kidwell to Exchange Bank until after the end of the three-year period. The quality of the forgeries ranged from crude to fair. Exchange Bank handled a larger volume of checks than other banks and may not have compared all the signatures on the checks against the signature card bearing the signature of Kidwell's president. Will Kidwell's failure to report the forgeries to Exchange Bank excuse any liability of the bank for improper payment? Will Exchange Bank be liable at all for the improper payments?

16. Nu-Way had a checking account with Merchantile Bank. Nu-Way hired Jones, a former convict, as night manager. Among Jones's duties was ordering automotive parts from parts companies. Smith, the president of Nu-Way, occasionally dated, signed, and filled in the name of the parts company on checks for payment of parts used by Jones. The president left the amount blank for Jones to fill in as needed. Jones altered the seven checks to substitute his own name as payee and cashed the checks for his own benefit. The alterations were obvious. Merchantile Bank cashed the checks, charging Nu-Way's account for them. Nu-Way sued Merchantile Bank for the wrongful payment of the altered checks. What will be the result in this case? Assume that it took Nu-Way several months to notify Merchantile Bank of the alterations. Does this have any effect on your answer? Explain.

17. A welfare check drawn on Franklin Bank was issued to Smith in the amount of $13.50. After it was issued, and before it was cashed, the amount of the check was raised to $313.50, in which amount it was cashed at Westbury Bank, and then paid to Westbury Bank by Franklin Bank. In what amount may Franklin Bank charge the drawer's account? Who, if anyone, will be liable for the amount by which the check was altered, i.e., $300?

18. McKay issued a postdated check to Smith in connection with a building contract. The bank accepted the check for deposit three days before the date on the check. The check was returned to the bank by McKay's bank with a stop payment notation on it. McKay had issued a stop payment order on the check because of some difficulties he and Smith had had with the contract. The bank demanded payment of the check from McKay, who refused. Between whom is a stop payment order effective? Does the stop payment order have any effect on the bank's rights against McKay?

CHAPTER 24

Secured Transactions

CHAPTER OBJECTIVES

ARTICLE 9

Background of Article 9 / Terminology of Article 9 / Scope of Article 9 / Purpose of Article 9

ESTABLISHING AN ENFORCEABLE SECURITY INTEREST

The Security Agreement / Additional Requirements

PERFECTION OF A SECURITY INTEREST

Methods of Perfecting a Security Interest / Perfection by Filing / Perfection by Possession

PRIORITY

The Unperfected Security Interest / Conflicting Security Interests / Purchase Money Security Interest / Chattel Paper and Instruments / Protection of Buyers of Goods / Statutory Liens / Security Interests in Fixtures / Accessions and Commingled or Processed Goods

ASSIGNMENT

Rights of an Assignee / Waiver of Defenses

DEFAULT

Secured Party's Right to Possession after Default / Disposition of Collateral / Liability of Secured Party for Noncompliance

SUMMARY

REVIEW PROBLEMS

CHAPTER OBJECTIVES

After reading this chapter, you will be able to:

1. Define secured creditor, collateral, security agreement, financing statement, perfection, and purchase money security interest.

2. Explain how a security interest attaches and the legal consequences of attachment.

3. Explain the legal purpose for perfecting a security interest.

4. List the methods for perfecting a security interest, describing each briefly.

5. Describe a floating lien and indicate how it and a future advance clause help in the financing of inventory.

6. Explain how the waiver of defense clause enhances a seller's ability to finance the sale of goods.

Secured creditor a creditor who acquires a security interest in personal property

Collateral property securing a debt or obligation

Personal property movable property; all property other than real property

Sometimes providing credit for individuals and businesses subjects lenders to considerable risk because of the possibility that they will not be repaid. This risk is reduced if lenders can obtain an interest in property as assurance that debtors will meet their obligations. When a creditor establishes a valid security interest and the debtor fails or refuses to pay, the creditor can take the property or have it sold and the proceeds applied against the debt. A creditor who acquires a security interest in personal property is known as a **secured creditor.** The property providing the security is called **collateral.**

This chapter discusses the nature and scope of security interests in personal property and fixtures. Chapter 38 deals with transactions in which real property is the collateral. Much of the law dealing with secured transactions in which **personal property** is the collateral is based on Article 9 of the Uniform Commercial Code.

ARTICLE 9

Background of Article 9

Article 9 of the UCC provides a comprehensive scheme for administering the many different types of financing using personal property as security. Before Article 9 was adopted, secured financing in the United States was carried out in a variety of ways, causing confusion and expense. The rights of the parties were often adversely influenced by legal technicalities arising from the differences in the methods used to establish the creditor's rights to the security.

The major objective of the drafters of Article 9 was to provide a uniform and simple system by which creditors establish a **security interest**. Article 9 eliminates the traditional distinctions that existed among security devices such as chattel mortgages, conditional sales, trust receipts, factor's liens, and assignments of accounts receivable. For these devices, the drafters substituted the single term **security interest**.

Security interest an interest in personal property or fixtures which secures payment of an obligation

Terminology of Article 9

In addition to security interest, a number of other terms have specific meanings as they are used in Article 9. The following are important for understanding how creditors protect their interests in property. Most of these are discussed in greater detail as they relate to particular provisions of Article 9.

Purchase Money Security Interest   Under the UCC, a purchase money security interest (PMSI) arises in two types of transactions. A PMSI is acquired by a seller who keeps an interest in the property sold to secure all or part of the purchase price. For example, if a retailer sells goods and retains a security interest in these goods, it is a PMSI. The term also is used when a person advances funds to a buyer who uses the funds to acquire property with the newly purchased property serving as collateral for the funds advanced. Thus a PMSI may exist if a bank makes a loan to a person to buy a boat and the funds are used to buy the boat. Under the UCC, purchase money obligations often have priority over other obligations.

Secured Party   A secured party is a lender, seller, or other person in whose favor there is a security interest, including a person to whom accounts or chattel paper have been sold (Section 9-105[m]).

Security Agreement   This is an agreement that creates or provides a security interest (Section 9-105[2]).

Security agreement an agreement that creates or provides a security interest

Financing Statement   This is a document that gives notice to all people searching the records that the secured party claims an interest in certain collateral owned by the debtor (Section 9-402). Subject to requirements to be discussed later, the security agreement may be filed instead of a separate financing statement.

Although the UCC no longer retains distinctions based on form, for purposes of filing the financing statement in the appropriate place it is extremely important to understand what type of collateral is involved. If the secured party improperly classifies the collateral, he or she may file the financing statement in the wrong place and lose whatever protection the secured party might have had against other creditors of the debtor.

Financing statement a publicly recorded document that indicates a secured party's interest in collateral

Fixtures personal property that has become real property through attachment to real estate

Goods   "Goods" are defined in Section 9-105(h) as all things that are movable at the time the security interest attaches or those things that are **fixtures.** Goods become fixtures when they become so related to particular real estate that an interest in them arises under real estate law (Section 9-313[1][a]).

Goods are classified in one of four categories: consumer goods, equipment, farm products, or inventory. The classification of goods depends on their use, but goods cannot be classified in more than one category in any single transaction.

Consumer goods, as we discussed in Chapter 19, are used primarily for personal, family, or household purposes. Equipment is goods used in business. An example is machinery used in manufacturing. Inventory is goods held for sale, lease, or to be furnished under service contracts. Inventory also includes raw materials, work in progress, and materials used and consumed in the manufacture of a product. Farm products are crops, livestock, and supplies used and produced by a person engaged in farming operations.

Although goods cannot be classified in more than one category in any single secured transaction, the classification may change as the goods move in commerce. For example, eggs in the hands of a farmer are farm products, but when the farmer sells those eggs to a grocery chain, they become inventory.

Negotiable instrument an instrument in writing and signed, containing an unconditional order or promise to pay a specific amount of money to order or bearer at a definite time or on demand

Instrument   According to Section 9-105(i), *instrument* means a **negotiable instrument** (as defined in Section 3-104, e.g., a note), or a **security** (as defined in Section 8-102, e.g., stocks), or any other writing that evidences a right to the payment of money and is not itself a security agreement or lease and is of a type that is, in the ordinary course of business, transferred by delivery with any necessary endorsement or assignment.

Security an instrument or transaction in which people invest in a common enterprise in expectation of profits derived solely from the efforts of a promoter or third party

Document of Title   A document of title is a written instrument issued by or addressed to a person who holds goods for another. It identifies those goods unless they are fungible, that is, part of an identifiable mass (Section 1-201[15]). For example, an order from a farmer who has stored corn addressed to the storage facility to deliver 10,000 bushels of the corn to a railroad is a document of title. Other documents of title are bills of lading, dock warrants, dock receipts, and warehouse receipts.

Chattel paper writings that evidence both a money debt and a security interest

Chattel Paper   Writings that evidence both a monetary obligation and a security interest in or a lease of specific goods is **chattel paper.** If the transaction consists of a security agreement or a lease and an instrument or a series of instruments, the *group* of writings taken together constitutes chattel paper.

When a merchant sells goods to a consumer, the merchant may retain a security interest in the goods sold. Suppose that a retail merchant sells a television set to a consumer and retains a security interest in it. The contract by which the merchant retains a security interest in the TV is a security agreement: the merchant is the secured party; the buyer is the debtor; and the TV is the collateral. If the merchant wishes to finance operations, the merchant may sell a number of such contracts to a bank. With respect to the bank, these contracts are collectively referred to as *chattel paper.* The retail dealer is a debtor with respect to the bank, and the bank is the secured party. The customers are referred to as *account debtors.*

Account   An **account** is any right to payment for goods sold or leased or for services rendered that is not evidenced by an instrument or chattel paper, whether or not it has been earned by performance (Section 9-106). Accounts are not evidenced by writing. This term covers the ordinary **account receivable.** If a clothing store sells clothes to customers on an open account and gives them 30 days to pay, the accounts of the customers can be sold to a financer. The financier would be a secured party, the clothing store the debtor, and the customers the account debtors.

Account a right to payment for goods sold or leased or for a service

Account receivable a claim against a debtor for goods sold or services rendered

General Intangibles   These are any personal property other than goods, accounts, chattel paper, documents, and money (Section 9-106). The term covers the various contractual rights and personal property that are used as commercial security — for example, good will, trademarks, and patents.

Scope of Article 9

Article 9 applies primarily to security interests in personal property and fixtures arising out of agreements. The article does not apply to **statutory liens** such as the mechanic's or artisan's lien. These liens are created by legislation to protect contractors and others who provide improvements to real property. But Article 9 does cover priority problems between statutory liens and secured transactions (Section 9-310). The article also applies to transactions involving the sale of accounts and chattel paper.

Statutory liens a claim created by statute to secure payment of a debt

Although Article 9 applies to consumer transactions, its provisions do not replace other state legislation such as small loan acts, retail installment sales statutes, and other regulatory measures applicable to consumer financing.

The major exclusion from Article 9 coverage is security interest in real estate. Fixtures, however, are covered, and in some circumstances real estate and Article 9 transactions are connected. For example, if Jones owns a promissory note and a real estate mortgage that secure funds he has advanced to Smith, Jones may use them as collateral when borrowing from Brown. Section 9 also applies to transactions in which the collateral is minerals, standing timber, or growing crops.

Purpose of Article 9

To limit risk in secured financing, the creditor has two major objectives. First, he or she needs assurance that security rights in the collateral are protected if the debtor defaults. This goal is accomplished if the creditor obtains an enforceable security interest. Second, the creditor needs protection against third parties establishing superior rights in the collateral. To prevent this, the creditor must take steps in addition to those required to establish rights against the debtor. But in both cases, the first step is to establish a security interest.

ESTABLISHING AN ENFORCEABLE
SECURITY INTEREST

Attachment the
procedure through
which a secured
party establishes a
security interest in
collateral against a
debtor.

Three events must take place before a creditor obtains a security interest in the collateral. These events do not have to occur all at once or in any particular order. Once they have occurred, the secured party's right in the collateral is said to *attach*. **Attachment** establishes the secured party's right to the collateral against the debtor, if the debtor defaults.

The secured party's right attaches when:

1. the parties agree that the secured party has a security interest

2. the debtor receives value

3. the debtor has rights in the collateral.

The Security Agreement

As we have discussed, a security agreement creates or provides a security interest (Section 9-105[1]). Unless the collateral is in the possession of the secured party, the security agreement must be in writing. The agreement must contain a description of the collateral and must be signed by the debtor. A description that reasonably identifies the collateral is sufficient. But care should be taken to describe the collateral adequately, because inadequate identification can lead to litigation.

Matter of Charles O. Cooley, Bankrupt

United States Court of Appeals
624 F. 2d 55 (1980)

FACTS   Cooley borrowed funds from the First National Bank of Louisville to finance his business. Cooley and his wife executed a security agreement, a financing statement, and a promissory note for $10,000 plus interest.

When Cooley became bankrupt, the trustee in bankruptcy argued that the security agreement was unenforceable because it did not disclose the amount of the loan or the maturity date. The trustee also argued that it was invalid because the description of the collateral was insufficient.

ISSUE   Is the security agreement enforceable?

DECISION   Yes. The security agreement is enforceable. The UCC sets forth the requirements of a valid security agreement, and there is no requirement that the amount secured or the date of maturity be shown. The flexibility intended by the UCC would be severely limited by a requirement that a security agreement state a fixed amount and maturity date. The collateral was adequately described in the security agreement. It was adequate because the borrower was a going business, and the listing of collateral, described in categories, included all the usual assets that a business would need to operate.

FIGURE 24-1

SECURITY AGREEMENT

Debtor (last name first) and addresses	Secured Party(ies) and addresses	For Filing Officer

DEBTOR, whether one or more, for consideration, hereby grants to Secured Party a security interest in the following property and any and all increase, additions, accessions, substitutions, and proceeds thereto or therefore (hereinafter called the Collateral):

The Debtor hereby grants a security interest in all similar property owned by Debtor during the time the obligations are outstanding, although such property may be acquired or be natural increase after the date hereof, and should the secured party deem any collateral inadequate or unsatisfactory, or should the value of the security decline the secured party shall have the right to call for additional security to its satisfaction.

The Debtor shall, so long as no event of default has occurred, have the right in the regular course of business, to process and sell inventory only, but the security interest shall attach to all product and proceeds of all Collateral.

If the security interest is in commercial paper, or assigned accounts, or contract rights, the secured party is authorized to notify the Debtor or others of the assignment of their accounts, or rights to the secured party, and to call upon such parties to make payment directly to the secured party.

If any of the collateral has been attached to or is to be attached to real estate, or if the Collateral includes crops or oil, gas or minerals to be extracted or timber to be cut, a description of the real estate is as follows:

and the name of the record owner of the real estate is _____

This and all allied instruments are executed to secure payment of the indebtedness evidenced hereby and by Debtor's note(s) of even date herewith, and also any and all liability of the Debtor, direct or indirect, absolute or contingent, now existing or hereafter arising, of the Debtor, payable to Secured Party. Total amount of this loan to be repaid in scheduled installments as follows:

Principal Amount of Loan Excluding Charges $_____	Rate of Charges per $100 per year $_____	Amount of charges for additional time permitted over 30 days to make first payment $_____	Total Dollar Amount of Charges $_____
Amount charged or collected for insurance and included in principal amount: $_____	For Life Insurance $_____	Health and Accident Insurance $_____	Other Insurance — describe _____	$_____

Filing and Other Fees charged or collected and added to indebtedness (describe) _____ $_____

together with the covenants in this agreement, such additional sums as may at the option of the Secured Party be advanced to Debtor, such advances as shall be made by Secured Party under this agreement for the protection of the Collateral, any and all other amounts as shall in any manner be due from Debtor to Secured Party and all costs and expenses incurred in the collection of same and enforcement of rights of Secured Party hereunder, including a reasonable attorney's fee and legal expense, all of the foregoing being collectively called the Obligations.

DEBTOR AGREES THAT HE HAS READ THIS AGREEMENT AND THAT THIS AGREEMENT INCLUDES AND IS SUBJECT TO THE KANSAS UNIFORM COMMERCIAL CODE AND THE ADDITIONAL PROVISIONS SET FORTH BELOW AND ON THE REVERSE SIDE HEREOF, SUCH ADDITIONAL PROVISIONS BEING INCORPORATED HEREIN BY REFERENCE, WITHOUT LIMITATION BECAUSE OF ENUMERATION.

Although the formal requirements of a security agreement are minimal, most also contain references to the following items.

After-Acquired Property   This is collateral that becomes the subject of a security interest after the parties have reached an initial agreement. One example is a retailer's inventory purchased to replace goods subject to the original security agreement. When an after-acquired property clause is included in a security agreement, the secured party acquires a "continuing general lien" in property acquired to replace the original inventory.

Future Advances   Security agreements may include a clause covering advances of credit made by the secured party after the agreement is signed. This kind of clause is necessary if the advance is to be secured by the original agreement. The clause might read:

> This security agreement shall include future advances or other indebtedness that debtor may owe to secured party during the time that the security agreement is in force, whenever incurred.

Rights of the debtor established by an after-acquired property clause and a future advance clause are often referred to as a **floating lien** (Section 9-204, Comment z). Combining the after-acquired property and future advances clauses helps in the financing of inventory and accounts receivable when the collateral is goods being retailed or raw materials being manufactured.

Floating lien a secured party's lien in both present and future property acquired by the debtor

A number of other subjects are covered in most security agreements. They include, but are not limited to, the following:

1. amount of the debt
2. terms of payment
3. responsibility for care and maintenance of the collateral
4. acceleration of payment rights
5. right to additional collateral

Additional Requirements

In addition to a valid security agreement, two other conditions must be met before the creditor can obtain a security interest in the collateral. First, the debtor must receive value. If the secured party extends credit, makes a loan to the debtor, or provides the debtor any consideration sufficient to support a simple contract, this requirement has been fulfilled. Second, the debtor must have rights in the collateral. The debtor does not have to have title to the collateral. A purchaser acquiring property under an agreement in which the seller retains title has rights in the collateral sufficient to support a creditor's security interest.

PERFECTION OF A
SECURITY INTEREST

A security interest that has attached may be enforced by the secured party against the debtor. The secured party also needs protection against claims to the collateral that others might assert arising out of their transactions with the debtor. To secure this protection, the secured party must **perfect** his or her security interest in the collateral. By perfecting the security interest, the secured party puts the world on notice that he or she claims a special interest in the collateral. Other people dealing later with the debtor may realize that the secured party has a superior interest in the property that may well be used to satisfy the debt.

Perfection the process by which the secured party establishes priority in the debtor's collateral against the competing claims of third parties.

Methods of Perfecting a Security Interest

In a few transactions, a security interest may be perfected automatically. It exists merely because the interest was created. The purchase money security interest (PMSI) is the most important example. In most other transactions, the secured party may perfect the security interest by either of the following methods:

1. filing a financing statement in the appropriate public office

2. taking possession of the collateral

Whether the secured party may perfect by filing, by taking possession, or by relying upon automatically obtaining a perfected security interest largely depends on the type of collateral involved. For example, if a person borrows money from a bank and uses corporate stock as collateral, the borrower has to deliver possession of the stock to the bank. The bank has a perfected security interest in the stock, because the stock is in its possession. This type of transaction is generally referred to as a *pledge*.

Perfection by Filing

The most common method of perfecting a security interest is by filing a financing statement. This document, when properly filed, gives the public notice of the secured party's interest in the collateral. Public notice needs to be provided so that other creditors or transferees of the debtor may learn of the creditor's claims to the collateral.

The Financing Statement   A financing statement must give the names of the debtor and the secured party and their respective addresses, must be signed by the debtor, and must contain a statement indicating the types — or describing the items — of collateral. A financing statement is effective even if it contains minor errors.

When the financing statement covers crops, timber to be cut, minerals, or goods that are to become fixtures, the financing statement must describe the real estate involved. Usually a standard form is used for the financing statement. But under the

FIGURE 24-2   Financing Statement (Approved Form UCC Sec. 9-402)

> This financing statement is presented to a filing officer for filing pursuant to the Uniform Commercial Code.
>
> Name of Debtor (or Assignor)_____
>
> Address_____
>
> Name of Secured Party (or Assignee)_____
>
> Address_____
>
> 1. This financing statement covers the following types (or items) of property:
>
>   (Describe)_____
> 2. (If collateral is crops) The above described crops are growing or are to be grown on:
>
>   (Describe Real Estate and specify Name of Record Owner)_____
> 3. (If collateral is goods which are or are to become fixtures) The above described goods are affixed or to be affixed to:
>
>   (Describe Real Estate and specify Name of Record Owner)_____
> 4. (If proceeds or products of collateral are claimed) Proceeds — Products of the collateral are also covered.
>
>   Signature of Debtor (or Assignor) _____
>
>   Signature of Secured Party (or Assignee)_____

UCC, a copy of the security agreement may be used if it contains all of the information listed above and is signed by the debtor.

Place of Filing   The place of filing depends on the type of collateral covered by the security agreement. If the secured party improperly classifies the collateral and files in the wrong office, secured status of the described collateral does not exist.

For collateral related to land such as fixtures, goods that are to become fixtures, timber to be cut, or minerals, filing generally is required in the county where the land is located. For other types of collateral, the states have different rules on the proper place to file. Many states direct that filing take place in the county of the debtor's residence or, if the debtor is not a resident of the state, in the county where the goods are kept. A minority of states take the position that filing is most effective when centralized within a state. This system reduces costs and speeds the acquisition of credit information. These states generally require that filing, except for land related collateral, be done in the office of the Secretary of State, located in the state capital. Connecticut, Georgia, Iowa, Oregon, and Washington are among the states requiring centralized filing.

Time and Duration of Filing   A financing statement can be filed at any time, even before a security agreement is made or before a security interest attaches to the collateral (Section 9-402[1]). A secured party might want to file before attachment because it may aid in getting a higher priority than other parties claiming an interest in the same collateral by filing.

A filed financing statement is effective for five years from the date of filing. To assure its continuing validity after five years, the secured party must file a **continuation statement.** Otherwise, the security interest becomes unperfected. A continua-

Continuation statement a document publicly filed to renew a financing statement

FIGURE 24-3 Continuation Statement

This STATEMENT is presented to a filing officer for filing pursuant to the Uniform Commercial Code:

1. Debtor(s) (Last Name First) and address(es)	2. Secured Party(ies) (or assignee and address(es):	For Filing Officer: (Date, Time, Number and Filing Office)

3. This statement refers to original Financing Statement bearing File No. _____

Filed with _____ Date Filed _____ 19 _____

4. ☐ A. Continuation The original Financing Statement bearing the above file number is still effective.

☐ B. Termination The Secured Party of record no longer claims a security interest under the Financing Statement bearing the above file number.

☐ C. Release From the collateral described in the Financing Statement bearing the above file number the Secured Party of record releases the collateral below.

☐ D. Assignment The Secured Party of record has assigned the Secured Party's rights in the property described below under the Financing Statement bearing the above file number to the Assignee whose name and address are shown below.

☐ E. Amendment The Financing Statement bearing the above file number is amended as set forth below:

5. This area for description of collateral, release, collateral if assigned, amendment, or description of real estate, if necessary.

By: _____
(Signature(s) of Debtor(s) (necessary only if item E is applicable)

By: _____
Signature(s) of Secured Party (or assignee)

White: Filing Officer — Alphabetical
Green: Filing Officer — Numerical
Canary: Filing Officer — Acknowledgment
Pink: File Copy — Secured Party(ies)
Gold: File Copy — Debtor(s)
Form K-UCC-2 Kansas Uniform Commercial Code.

Form approved by

Secretary of State

tion statement may be filed by the secured party within six months before the expiration of the five-year period. The continuation statement makes the original statement valid for an additional five years. Succeeding continuation statements may be filed. The continuation statement need be signed by only the secured party.

Once all the obligations of the parties have been completed under the security agreement, the secured party must file a termination statement with each filing officer with whom the financing statement was filed.

Perfection by Possession

For most types of collateral, an alternative to perfection by filing is for the secured party to take possession of the property. Article 9 permits a secured party to perfect a security interest in goods, negotiable documents, or chattel paper by taking possession of them. But the secured party may choose to perfect an interest in these items by filing a financial statement. A security interest in money or in negotiable instruments can be perfected only by the secured party's taking possession.

A secured party in possession of collateral must use reasonable care in keeping and preserving it. The secured party must keep the collateral identifiable unless it is fungible, in which case it may be mixed in with the fungible (interchangeable) goods. The secured party responsible for a loss to the collateral through failure to use reasonable care bears that loss, but the security interest is retained. Reasonable expenses incurred to preserve the collateral and insurance costs are borne by the debtor.

PRIORITY

In some situations, other people besides the secured creditor claim an interest in the collateral. A secured creditor may have to compete with someone who has purchased the collateral from the debtor, holders of statutory liens, general creditors, secured creditors, and even the government. Because of the different interests involved, many state and federal statutes influence the solution to these conflicts.

Article 9 of the UCC provides the rules for resolving many of them.

The Unperfected Security Interest

As a general rule, Article 9 establishes a priority for the holder of a perfected security interest against other creditors and transferees from the debtor. Although the key to the secured creditor's protection is perfection of the security interest, an unperfected security interest gives limited protection. The unperfected security interest does enjoy priority over general creditors of the debtor who have established no lien on the collateral.

But general creditors have little difficulty in overcoming this priority. Because it is so easy for a general creditor to establish a priority over an unperfected security interest, the careful secured creditor always perfects.

Conflicting Security Interests

When two or more people claim security interests in the same collateral, the general rule of priority is stated in Section 9-312(5)(a) as follows:

> Conflicting security interests rank according to priority in time of filing or perfection — *Priority dates from the time a filing is first made covering the collateral or the time the security interest is first perfected,* whichever is earlier, *provided* that there is no period thereafter when there is neither filing nor perfection [emphasis added].

Purchase Money Security Interest

The UCC places the holder of a PMSI in a beneficial position. Article 9 provides a claimant with a PMSI priority over a conflicting security interest in the same collateral if the PMSI is perfected within ten days of the time the debtor takes possession of the collateral (Section 9-312[4]). Priority for a PMSI may be justified on grounds that the party who supports the purchase of property deserves to be protected.

A PMSI provides protection for the seller in the following situation, although a perfected security interest already exists in the collateral. First State Bank advances funds to Jones Manufacturing and perfects a security interest in all the firm's equipment. The security agreement has a provision extending the bank's interest to any after-acquired equipment. Later Jones buys a new machine on credit from Smith Machine Company. As long as Smith Machine files a financing statement within ten days of the machine's delivery, its security interest has priority over that of First State Bank.

Consumer Goods   The holder of a PMSI in most types of consumer goods has extensive protection. Perfection is automatic for the retailer who obtains a security agreement from a customer. No filing is necessary to establish the seller's priority. One exception to this rule is automobile financing. To perfect a security interest in an automobile, the secured party must file a security agreement or comply with a state's certificate of title law.

Inventory   A PMSI in inventory has priority even though another creditor has previously perfected a security interest in the debtor's inventory if the following events occur (Section 9-312[3]):

1. The PMSI is perfected when the debtor gets possession of the inventory

2. The purchase money secured party gives written notice to the holder of the conflicting security interest if the holder had filed a financing statement covering the same types of inventory (i) before the date of the filing made by the purchase money secured party or (ii) before the beginning of the 21-day period when the PMSI is temporarily perfected without filing or possession.

3. The holder of the conflicting interest gets notice within five years *before* the debtor gets possession of the inventory

4. The notice states that the person giving notice has or expects to acquire a PMSI in inventory of the debtor, describing such inventory by item or type.

Problems arising under Section 9-312(3) usually involve a conflict between a secured party claiming interest in certain collateral under an after-acquired property clause and a person claiming a PMSI in the same collateral. The rationale for this section is that a secured party typically makes advances on new inventory or releases of old inventory as new inventory is received. If the inventory financier learns of the PMSI in particular inventory, he or she may not make an advance against it.

Chattel Paper and Instruments

When chattel paper is sold to a secured party, the secured party may choose to have the retail merchant collect the accounts, or the secured party may collect the accounts. The secured party may leave the chattel paper with the dealer, or the secured party may take possession of the paper. As we have noted, an interest in chattel paper may be perfected either by filing or by taking possession of it. Leaving it in the hands of the retail merchant is dangerous. If the secured party leaves the paper in the hands of the merchant and perfects an interest by filing, a later secured party who takes possession of this chattel paper may gain priority over the secured party who merely files to perfect. Certain purchasers of chattel paper left in the debtor's possession take free of the security interest that has been perfected by filing. This is one of the limitations on the otherwise protected status of a party with a perfected security interest.

In general, the rules applicable to chattel paper also apply to the purchase of instruments. However, a security interest in instruments generally can be perfected only by possession. The only other types of perfected security interest that can arise in an instrument are the temporary 21-day perfection provided for in Section 9-304(4) and (5) or the ten-day perfection of Section 9-306. If a security interest is temporarily perfected under either of these sections, a person taking possession of them during this period without knowing that they are subject to a security interest has priority over the conflicting security interest (Section 9-308[a]).

Protection of Buyers of Goods

The UCC protects some buyers of goods against perfected security interests. When a person in good faith and without knowing that the sale to him or her violates the ownership rights or security interest of a third party in the goods buys in ordinary course from a person in the business of selling goods of that kind (excluding pawnbrokers), that person qualifies as a "buyer in ordinary course of business." A buyer in the ordinary course of business takes free of a security interest created by the seller, even if it is perfected and the buyer knows this (Section 9-307[i]).

This rule lets the ordinary consumer buy goods from a retail merchant without being liable to a secured party of the merchant who claims a security interest in the goods the consumer has bought. Usually, of course, a security agreement lets a merchant sell from inventory. This rule therefore applies to the situation in which the security agreement between the seller and the secured party does not permit such sales.

A special rule exists for purchase of consumer goods. Remember that a PMSI in consumer goods can be perfected without filing. (Other security interests in consumer goods must be filed.) As long as the buyer buys without knowledge of the security interest for his or her own personal, family, or household purposes before a financing statement is filed, he or she takes free of even a perfected security interest (Section 9-307[2]).

If a person buys goods from someone not in the business of selling goods of that kind, he or she is *not* a buyer in ordinary course of business. The rule covering the buyer in the ordinary course of business stated in Section 9-307(1) does not apply. Suppose that a finance company lends money to a retail merchant and gets a perfected security interest in the merchant's equipment. Because the merchant is not in the business of selling equipment, but rather is in the business of selling inventory, someone who purchases this equipment from the merchant is *not* a buyer in the ordinary course of business.

Cunningham v. Camelot Motors, Incorporated

Superior Court of New Jersey
351 A. 2d 402 (1975)

Cunningham bought a Triumph automobile from Camelot Motors. He paid in full, FACTS
took possession, and got a temporary registration certificate. Although Camelot promised to get the required certificates of ownership, it could not deliver these documents. The certificates were being held by Hudson United Bank, which had a security interest in Camelot's inventory. Because Camelot had failed to make required payments to Hudson, Hudson refused to surrender the certificate to Camelot or to Cunningham. Cunningham argued that Hudson's perfected security interest was invalid toward him because he was a buyer in the ordinary course of business.

Is a buyer in the ordinary course of business free of a security interest in the collateral? ISSUE

Yes. The UCC protects purchasers who buy goods from a merchant's inventory in DECISION
the ordinary course of business. To meet the conditions imposed by the UCC, plaintiff must show only that he bought the car in good faith; without knowledge that the sale was in violation of Hudson's security interest; from a person in the business of selling goods of that kind; and for present value, that is, for cash or a present exchange of other property. The facts establish that Cunningham takes free of Hudson's security interest in the automobiles.

An order was entered directing Hudson to surrender the certificates to Camelot and directing Camelot to execute and deliver the certificates to Cunningham.

Statutory Liens

If a person furnishes services or materials in the ordinary course of business, any lien on goods in his or her possession that is granted by state law takes priority over a perfected security interest (Section 9-310). When a mechanic repairs a vehicle, if state law gives him or her a lien on the car for services rendered, this lien takes precedence over that of a bank that has a security interest in the car.

Security Interests in Fixtures

Goods are fixtures when they become so attached to a particular piece of real estate that an interest in them arises under real estate law (Section 9-313[1]). Article 9 recognizes three categories of goods:

1. Those that retain their *chattel* character entirely and are not part of the real estate, which should be perfected by filing in accordance with the rules on personal property

2. *Ordinary building materials* that have become an integral part of the real estate, which should be perfected by recording a real estate mortgage

3. *Fixtures* that are perfected by making a "fixture filing," a financing statement filed in the office where a mortgage on the real estate would be filed or recorded, covering goods that are or are to become fixtures (Section 9-313[1][b]).

A fixture filing gives to the fixture security interest priority over other real estate security interests created on the principle that the first to file or record prevails. This is the usual rule with respect to conflicting real estate interests. An additional requirement is that the debtor must have an interest of record in the real estate or be in possession (such as a tenant). This later requirement restricts a valid fixture filing when the creditor is a contractor.

An exception to the first to file rule exists for a PMSI in a fixture. This interest has priority over previously recorded real estate interests as long as the security interest is perfected by a fixture filing before the goods become fixtures or within ten days afterwards (Section 9-314[4][a]).

Another exception to the first to file rule covers readily removable factory or office machines or readily removable replacements of home appliances that are consumer goods. If an interest in these goods is perfected by any method in Article 9 before they become fixtures, the fixtures filing prevails over a conflicting interest of most claims that are acquired in the real estate or the conflicting interest of the owners.

The final exception to the first to file rule for filing gives a perfected security interest in fixtures priority over a conflicting interest that is a lien on the real estate obtained by legal or fair proceedings after the security interest was perfected (Section 9-313[4][c]).

Accessions and Commingled or Processed Goods

A secured party who claims an interest in goods installed or affixed to other goods ("accessions") is entitled to priority, with certain exceptions, over anyone else claiming an interest in the whole goods, if the security interest attaches before the goods are installed or affixed to other goods (Section 9-314[1]).

If a security interest in goods is perfected and the goods subsequently become part of a product or mass and their identity is lost in the product or goods, the security interest continues in the product or mass (Section 9-315).

ASSIGNMENT

A common business practice is for a seller of goods holding an installment contract with an accompanying security interest to transfer these to a finance company. In return, the finance company advances funds that the seller uses to operate its business.

Rights of an Assignee

When an installment contract and security interest are sold to a finance company, the finance company becomes the secured party. Because this transaction usually is an **assignment,** the finance company is often referred to as the **assignee.** The original seller, who is the **assignor,** is now a *debtor,* because it has received an advance from the finance company. The original purchaser is referred to as an **account debtor.** In general, the UCC does not let the original buyer restrict the assignment of an installment contract (Section 9-318[4]). Even if the parties include a provision restricting assignment in the installment contract, the contract may be assigned.

Assignment the transfer of rights or benefits of a contract.

In the absence of a contrary provision, the rights of an assignee are subject to all terms of the contract between the account debtor and assignor and any defense or claim. The assignee takes the contract subject to any claims the account debtor has against the assignor that arise independently of the contract and accrue *before* the account debtor receives notification of the assignment (Section 9-318[1][a] and [b]).

Assignee the person receiving a contract's rights

Assignor the person transferring a contract's rights

Waiver of Defenses

Often a seller, anticipating that the documents will be used in financing, asks the buyer to sign an installment contract and security agreement containing words similar to the following:

> Buyer hereby agrees to waive as against any assignee of this contract all claims or defenses buyer may have against secured party to the full extent permitted by law.

Account debtor an installment purchaser whose contract has been assigned to a finance company by the seller

This clause makes easier the seller's assignment of the installment contract to a financer, for the buyer has waived its rights to sue and set up defenses against the financer (assignee). If a buyer accepts this phrasing, it must settle any dispute arising over the goods with the seller, although the seller has transferred all its rights to a finance company. The UCC permits waiver of defense clauses as long as the assignee takes the assignment for value, in good faith, and without knowing of a claim or defense.

A waiver of defense clause is effective against the account debtor unless his or her defense is one that could be asserted against a holder in due course of a negotiable instrument (see Chapter 22) or a statute or decision establishes a different rule for consumer goods. A Federal Trade Commission rule abolishes such clauses in consumer contracts everywhere in the United States, but the clause is still effective in business transactions.

DEFAULT

When the debtor defaults under a security agreement, a secured party has the rights and remedies provided in Article 9 and whatever rights and remedies the security agreement itself gives the secured party — subject to certain limitations specified in Section 9-501(3). In general, the secured party may reduce the claim to a judgment, foreclose, or otherwise enforce the security interest by any available judicial procedure. The secured party may choose to reduce the claim to a judgment and then levy on the collateral. In this case, the judgment lien relates back to the date of perfection of the security interest (Section 9-501[5]). When there is a judicial sale following judgment, execution, and levy, the judicial sale is a foreclosure of the security interest, but the sale is not governed by Article 9.

Secured Party's Right to Possession after Default

In the absence of a contrary agreement, if the debtor defaults, the secured party has a right to possession of the collateral. Section 9-503 lets a secured party take possession of the collateral if it may be done without breach of the peace. The secured party may go to the place where the collateral is and take possession of it. Although the UCC permits this kind of repossession, the process is not without legal risk. One problem involves the meaning of the term "breach of peace," which is used in the statute but not defined. If the secured party commits a breach of the peace in repossessing the collateral, he or she is subject to tort liability. Generally, courts have construed this term broadly in a manner that protects the debtor, as the following case indicates.

General Electric Credit Corporation v. Timbrook

Supreme Court of Appeals of West Virginia
291 S.E. 2d 383 (1982)

FACTS   Timbrook bought a mobile home from Winchester Mobile Home Sales, Incorporated. She fell behind in her payments, and although she tried to arrange an agreeable payment schedule, she could not. A short time later, Timbrook found a note on her door requesting her to call Winchester's collection department. She bought a new lock for her front door, but the following day while she was at work, representatives of Winchester broke the lock to release a household pet, removed her home from its cinderblock foundation, and towed it away. Timbrook got an injunction to prevent the sale of her home, but after a full hearing the trial court dissolved the injunction, ruling that the repossession was proper because there had been no breach of the peace.

Was the repossession proper?   ISSUE

No. The repossession was not proper. A creditor's common law right to self-help   DECISION
repossession has been codified (Section 9-503):

> Unless otherwise agreed a secured party has on default the right to take possession of the collateral. In taking possession a secured party may proceed without judicial process if this can be done without breach of the peace.

We have never defined what a breach of peace is; that would weaken a self-help repossession. Tortious activity incites or tends to incite breaches of the peace. The use or threat of violence impairs the tranquility to which our citizens are entitled in their homes and possessions. We agree with those courts that have recognized breakings and unauthorized entries of debtors' dwellings to be breaches of the peace that deprive creditor or repossessors of self-help default remedies.

A creditor has a legitimate interest in getting collateral from a defaulting debtor. But that strong interest must be balanced against a person's right to be free from invasions of his or her home. If creditors cannot repossess without peace breaching, they can sue. In this case, the unauthorized entry into the debtor's dwelling was a breach of peace. The trial court erred in finding that the peace had not been breached.

Disposition of Collateral

After default the secured party may sell, lease, or otherwise dispose of the collateral. The disposition may be by public or private proceedings — but every aspect of the disposition, including the method, manner, time, place, and terms, must be commercially reasonable. Before public sale, the secured party usually must notify the debtor of the time and place of the sale. If it is a private sale, the debtor must be notified of the time. If nonconsumer goods are involved, the secured party must also notify any other secured party from whom he or she has received written notice of a claim of an interest in the collateral.

As a general rule, the secured party may retain the collateral in satisfaction of the obligation. If a secured party wishes to do this, the debtor and other appropriate parties, such as those with security interests in the collateral, must be notified. In the absence of objections within 21 days from the date of notification, the secured party may keep the collateral. If objections are received, he or she must dispose of the collateral as directed by the UCC.

If the collateral is sold, the proceeds are distributed in the following order: The reasonable expenses incurred in repossessing and disposing of the collateral are deducted. Next, the secured party collects the unpaid debt and other lawful charges agreed to in the security agreement. Finally, if the secured party receives written demand from any subordinate security interests, these are paid. Any remaining funds go to the debtor.

These issues are raised in the following case.

Citizens State Bank v. Hewitt

Court of Appeals of Georgia
279 S.E. 2d 531 (1981)

FACTS   On July 24, 1975, Hewitt executed and delivered a note and security agreement in favor of Citizens State Bank. These documents created a security interest in a 1975 Dodge pickup truck. On October 7, 1976, he executed similar documents to the same bank creating a security interest in a boat, motor, and trailer. Some time later Hewitt defaulted in his payments on the truck, boat, motor, and trailer, and these items were repossessed by the bank.

On July 12, 1978, the bank sent Hewitt a standard form letter indicating that it would sell the automobile "to recover the amounts owed . . . plus any expenses allowed by law." The letter also indicated that if the proceeds were insufficient to pay the amount due, the bank intended to pursue a deficiency claim against Hewitt. No mention was made in the letter of the boat, motor, and trailer. All four items were sold by the bank. But $4,225 remained outstanding on Hewitt's debt, and the bank sued for this amount. Hewitt argued that he had not been notified in a commercially reasonable manner of the sale of the boat, motor, and trailer.

ISSUE   Was the notification of the sale of these three items commercially reasonable?

DECISION   No. Both trial and appellate court agreed that the notice concerning the boat, motor, and trailer were insufficient. The court stated that the UCC must be strictly construed. The court eliminated the bank's claim for $2,731, the deficiency on the loan secured by the boat, motor, and trailer.

The appellate court stated that the UCC

> sets forth in detail the secured party's right to dispose of the collateral after default. As to the effect of the disposition . . . paragraph (3) states clearly that the disposition may be by public or private proceedings . . . (with) reasonable notification of the time and place of any public sale or reasonable notification of the time after which any private sale or other intended disposition is to be made . . . sent by the secured party to the debtor. The secured party, in failing to comply with the statutory law with reference to reasonable notification . . . cannot recover the deficiency.

Liability of Secured Party for Noncompliance

If the secured party is not performing as required by the UCC, he or she may be restrained from disposing of the collateral. If the disposition has already occurred, the secured party is liable for any loss caused by a failure to comply with Part 5 of Article 9.

Of particular significance is the penalty when consumer goods are used as collateral. If the secured party fails to meet the requirements of the UCC in this instance, he or she is liable for an amount not less than the finance charge plus 10 percent of the principal.

SUMMARY

Article 9 of the UCC applies primarily to agreements that create security interests in personal property and fixtures. Article 9 substituted the term *security interest* for the various security devices that existed before the code was drafted.

For a secured party to establish a security interest in collateral, three events must occur. The parties must agree that a security interest exists, the debtor must receive value, and the debtor must acquire rights in the collateral. If the debtor defaults after these events have occurred, the secured party has rights in the collateral. A written document called a *security agreement* is instrumental in indicating the debtor's consent to a security interest in the collateral.

Perfection of a security interest establishes the secured party's rights in the collateral against other people dealing with the debtor. Perfection is usually accomplished when the secured party publicly files a financing statement. Filing alerts third parties of the secured party's interest in the collateral. For some types of goods, perfection can be accomplished by the secured party taking possession of the collateral.

If a secured party's interest in the collateral conflicts with an interest claimed by someone else, a priority problem exists. Article 9 provides rules for resolving many priority problems. The general rule is to give preference to the party that has first perfected the interest.

Several exceptions exist to this general rule. One exception protects a seller who has a purchase money security interest in the collateral. Another exception exists when a purchaser obtains possession of chattel paper left in the debtor's possession.

Sometimes a buyer purchases goods that are subject to a perfected security interest. If the purchase is from a seller in the business of selling goods of that kind, the buyer is a "buyer in the ordinary course of business." This type of buyer takes free of a security interest created by the seller.

Sellers who own installment accounts secured by security interests in the goods sold often assign the contracts covering these accounts in return for financing. The finance company that the accounts have been transferred to is subject to the terms of the installment contract between the original buyer and seller. The original buyer has surrendered this protection if the installment contract contains a waiver of defense clause.

If a debtor defaults under a security agreement, the secured party has several remedies. The usual remedy is to foreclose against the security and have the proceeds of the foreclosure sale applied against the debt. Another remedy is to take possession of the collateral, so long as this can be done without breaching the peace.

REVIEW PROBLEMS

1. Explain the twofold purpose of Article 9 in the UCC.

2. Define attachment and indicate the conditions that must occur for a security interest in collateral to attach.

3. Briefly indicate why a security interest must be perfected. Explain how this process occurs.

4. What is a purchase money security interest? How does it benefit the holder?

5. On August 10, Barbie's Beauty Salon borrows $20,000 from Third Bank. The loan is to be secured by equipment. Third Bank files a financing statement declaring that its collateral is "all equipment now owned and that to be acquired by Barbie's Beauty Salon." On August 13, Barbie's acquires additional equipment from the Newbold Co. Barbie's pays 50 percent of the purchase price, and Newbold retains a security interest in the equipment for the balance. The equipment is delivered on August 18. Newbold files a financing statement on August 24. If Barbie's cannot pay for the equipment, who has the priority, Third Bank or Newbold? Support your answer.

6. Lancaster Equipment Exchange and the Union Bank enter into an agreement in which the bank agrees to finance Lancaster's entire inventory of farm machinery. The bank files a financing statement and later advances funds. Lancaster agrees to purchase several pieces of farm equipment from the John Deere Company. The equipment is for Lancaster's inventory. Deere is to retain a security interest in the equipment. What must the company do to perfect this interest? Discuss.

7. MacKenzie, the owner of a clothing store, buys several display cases and stock racks to improve service. He borrows money from the Graiot Bank to pay for these items, and the bank perfects a security interest in the equipment. MacKenzie decides that he has bought too much equipment and sells some to Fiacre. When MacKenzie becomes bankrupt, the bank attempts to obtain the equipment from Fiacre. Fiacre contends that the bank has no right to the equipment as she is a purchaser in the ordinary course of business. Is her contention correct? Support your answer.

8. Irwin owns a car that needed extensive repairs. GMAC has a perfected security interest in the car. Irwin takes the car to the Sleepy Hollow Garage to be repaired. The bill is not paid. State law allows an unpaid repair facility to have the car sold and the proceeds applied against the debt. Sleepy Hollow advertises a public auction of the automobile. GMAC attempts to enjoin the sale. Will it be successful? Support your answer.

9. A plant owned by Di-a-bol, Inc., is mortgaged to Carolina Bank. The plant needs a new heating unit. The Varmdaze Company has agreed to supply the unit and install it for $23,000. Di-a-bol is to pay half the purchase price upon installation of the unit and the balance over a five-year period. The heating unit is to be the collateral. Explain the steps Varmdaze must take to protect its security interest in the unit.

10. Carso buys a small grocery business from Lake. Because Carso cannot pay the entire purchase price immediately, Lake agrees to accept the balance over the next three years. It also is agreed that Lake will have a security interest in a cash register, three display cabinets, and two refrigerators. This agreement is oral but made in the presence of two witnesses. A financing statement is filed covering "all equipment now owned by Lake necessary to operate the grocery store

located at 97 Mohawk St." The two people who were present at the closing are willing to testify that Carso agreed to give Lake a security interest in the items. Is Lake's security interest enforceable? Discuss.

11. Norton buys a used tractor from Hodges for $12,500, giving Hodges a security interest in the tractor to secure the unpaid portion of the purchase price. Three months later, after paying $370, Norton defaults and returns the tractor. Hodges then sells the tractor at a public auction for $2,500 and sues Norton for the balance.

    At the trial there is evidence that Hodges's attorney posted a notice of the auction on the courthouse door as required by state law. This notice was posted two weeks before the sale. No notice of the sale was sent to Norton, nor was there any evidence of additional publicity. When returned, the tractor has been subject to ordinary wear and tear. The UCC requires that a creditor's disposition of the collateral be done in a commercially reasonable manner. Is Hodges entitled to a judgment for the unpaid portion of the purchase price? Discuss.

12. Bristol, Incorporated, enters into an agreement leasing a store premises to the Commonwealth of Pennsylvania. Two years later, Bristol borrows from Girard Trust and as security assigns its interest in the lease to Girard. Girard does not record its security interest under Article 9 or make any other public record of the assignment. The following year Bristol files for bankruptcy. A receiver is appointed. The receiver keeps all rentals from the store and applies them to Bristol's business operations. Girard Trust thereupon files a petition with the bankruptcy court to recover the rentals paid to the receiver under the lease that has been assigned. Should the petition be granted? Discuss.

13. Peco leases an electronic cutting machine to Hartbauer for 36 months for a rental of $26,399.96. The rental includes an $8,000 "lease deposit" to be paid by work performed by Hartbauer for Peco, with the balance in regular monthly installments of $511.11 each. The lease gives Hartbauer an option to buy the equipment at any time after the 36 months, if not then in default, for $1,000. Peco never records a financing statement. Within the 36 months, Hartbauer, being insolvent, executes an assignment for the benefit of creditors to Dodge. Dodge intends to sell the machine leased by Peco to Hartbauer at an auction. Peco brings a suit to enjoin the sale. There is proof that at the end of the lease the value of the machine would be $10,000. Would the injunction be granted? Explain, indicating the issue involved.

14. F buys a mobile home from L, executing an installment contract and a security agreement. The security agreement gives L a purchase money security interest in the mobile home. L eventually sells this to M. On the date that F purchased the mobile home, he acquired title. But because of an understanding with L, F leaves the mobile home on L's lot. The trailer is to be picked up later, at which time F will make the down payment. In the meantime, R, who financed L's purchase of inventory and holds a security interest in it, seizes all of L's inventory, including F's trailer, because L has defaulted. R eventually sells the mobile home to another. F, upon returning to L's lot, finds the mobile home gone and refuses to pay M. M asserts its right to the mobile home as a secured creditor of F. For M to prevail, the security interest under F's security agreement must have attached. Had the security interest in fact attached? Discuss. What effect, if any, did the

fact that the mobile home was left on L's lot have on any attainment of the security interest?

15. R gets a judgment against M. In trying to seize a herd of cattle to pay the judgment, R discovers that M's interest is subject to a security interest in favor of a third party. The financing statement on file in the county courthouse lacks the signature of the secured party and the addresses of both M and the secured party. R challenges the validity of the security interest, for it otherwise has priority over the judgment lien. All parties involved are residents of the same small town. R knows M and the secured party and where they each lived. Is the failure of the secured party to sign the financing statement fatal to his or her security interest? Is the omission of the secured party's and M's address fatal to the security interest?

CHAPTER 25

Bankruptcy

CHAPTER OBJECTIVES

After reading this chapter, you should be able to:

1. Compare the main features of the three types of bankruptcy proceedings.

2. Outline the major steps in a straight bankruptcy proceeding.

3. Define after-acquired property, preference property, priority claims, estate exemptions, and discharge.

4. Determine what from a basic bankruptcy estate is distributed to creditors with general and priority claims and what remains with the bankrupt.

Approximately 350,000 bankruptcies are filed each year in the United States, 80 percent of them personal bankruptcies. Bankruptcy laws provide relief and protection to debtors while fairly distributing debtors' assets among creditors. The United States Constitution provides that Congress shall have the power to establish "uniform laws on the subject of bankruptcies throughout the United States." Thus bankruptcy laws are entirely federal. States do not have the power to enact them. But state laws do play a role in bankruptcy proceedings because they define the nature of liens, secured transactions, and other property interests.

THE BANKRUPTCY ACT OF 1978

The Bankruptcy Reform Act of 1978 is the source of present law on bankruptcies. It reformed previous law and created a separate system of federal bankruptcy courts presided over by bankruptcy judges. Previously bankruptcy cases had been heard in federal district courts.

Bankruptcy Courts

A bankruptcy judge does not administer a debtor's estate. That power is given to a **trustee in bankruptcy.** A temporary trustee is initially appointed by the bankruptcy judge. Later the creditors select a permanent trustee. The trustee represents the debtor's estate, administers it by collecting property, investigating the debtor's financial status, and reporting to the court about the distribution of the estate.

Types of Bankruptcy Proceedings

Liquidation   The bankruptcy laws provide for three kinds of proceedings. The **liquidation,** or straight bankruptcy proceeding, is the most common and is the

FIGURE 25-1   Bankruptcy Petitions Commenced

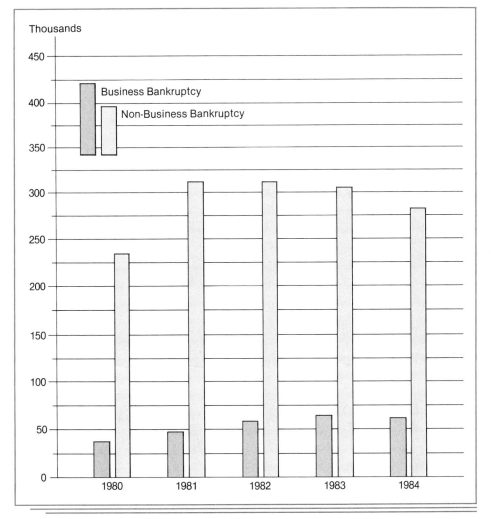

Source: *Statistical Abstract of the United States, 1986.* U.S. Department of Commerce, Bureau of the Census.

Trustee in bankruptcy someone who represents a debtor's estate by collecting property, investigating the debtor's financial status, and reporting to the court about its distribution

Liquidation a bankruptcy proceeding that erases all debts of the bankrupt after all of his or her property has been collected and distributed to claimants

Reorganization a bankruptcy proceeding that allows a business debtor to stay in business while reorganizing its debts; some portion of outstanding debts are paid to creditors while the remainder are erased

primary focus of our discussion. In the liquidation proceeding, the debtor's assets are collected into the estate and distributed to claimants. At the end of the bankruptcy, outstanding debts of the bankrupt are discharged or canceled.

Reorganization   A **reorganization** is a type of bankruptcy proceeding often used by corporate debtors. It allows debtors to stay in business rather than liquidate. Debtor and creditors agree on a plan by which the debtor pays a part of its debts and is discharged from paying the rest. We will discuss this form of bankruptcy near the end of the chapter.

Regular Income   A third type of bankruptcy proceeding, provided for in Chapter 13 of the bankruptcy laws, permits the adjustment of debts of an individual with a **regular income.** This **proceeding,** referred to as either a *Chapter 13* or *regular income plan,* relieves the person with a regular income but does not bankrupt the person. We discuss the regular income plan briefly at the end of this chapter.

THE BANKRUPTCY PROCEEDING

Regular income proceeding allows individuals with regular incomes to readjust debts without being declared bankrupts; any plan to repay the debts in full or in part must be approved by the court

A liquidation proceeding is either voluntary (started by the debtor) or involuntary (started by the creditors). The debtor may be an individual, a corporation, or a partnership (for definitions of types of business organizations, see Chapter 28) that has a residence, domicile, place of business, or property in the United States. Corporations subject to extensive regulation by administrative agencies — such as insurance companies, banks, savings and loan associations, and similar institutions — are not subject to the bankruptcy laws. Railroads are subject to the reorganizations referred to at the end of this chapter. Municipal corporations can seek adjustment of their debts under another section of the bankruptcy laws if state laws authorize such action.

Beginning of the Proceeding

Voluntary Proceeding   The filing of a voluntary proceeding automatically subjects the debtor and its property to the jurisdiction and supervision of the bankruptcy court. Once a petition is filed, creditors cannot start a suit or seek the enforcement of an existing judgment against the debtor. The filing of the petition acts as a **stay** upon other legal proceedings. (Criminal proceedings and the collection of alimony and child support are not stayed.)

Stay of proceedings the effect that a filing for bankruptcy has in freezing other legal proceedings involving the debtor; those proceedings stay as they were at the time the petition in bankruptcy is filed

Involuntary Proceeding   Creditors may file an involuntary proceeding against any debtor who may file a voluntary proceeding, with two exceptions: farmers and nonprofit corporations. If a debtor has 12 or more creditors, at least three must join in filing the petition. If there are fewer than 12 creditors, one may file the petition. Regardless of how many creditors file, their unsecured claims against the debtor must total at least $5,000.

If the debtor does not challenge the creditors' petition, the debtor's property is subjected to the supervision of the bankruptcy court. But if the debtor does challenge the petition, the creditors must prove that the debtor has not been paying his or her debts or that the debtor's property has been placed in receivership or assignment for the benefit of the creditors within 120 days before the petition was filed. Once the creditors prove either requirement, the debtor's property is subjected to the court's supervision. But if neither requirement is proved, the creditors' petition is dismissed.

The Role of Creditors

Within a reasonable time after a petition in bankruptcy has been filed, the debtor must file with the court a schedule of assets and liabilities, a statement of financial affairs, and a list of creditors. The creditors listed by the debtor then are notified of the bankruptcy petition. Those who have claims against the debtor file proofs of claims with the court. The court generally allows the claims unless they are objected to by the debtor or other creditors. The creditors who are claimants in the bankruptcy proceeding generally are **unsecured creditors.** An unsecured creditor is a person whose claim must be paid from the general property of the debtor. This creditor has no right or legal interest to any specific property of the debtor.

If a creditor has a claim secured by a security interest or other lien on specific property of the debtor, that creditor, and only that creditor, may use the property to pay off the debt. If the value of that property is equal to the value of the debt, the creditor need not be concerned with the debtor's remaining assets and liabilities.

After the claims of the creditors have been filed and allowed, the court calls a meeting of the unsecured creditors. The judge cannot appear at the creditors' meeting, but a temporary trustee appointed by the judge does attend. At their first meeting, the creditors usually do several things. First, they elect a permanent trustee. Then they examine the debtor, who is placed under oath and asked questions by the creditors and the trustee. The questions concern the debtor's assets and the discharge of the debtor's debts.

Unsecured creditor a person who has no claim on any specific property of the debtor and who is paid from the general assets that are not tied to any specific debts

THE DEBTOR'S ESTATE

Property in the Estate

The trustee is responsible for administering the debtor's estate. He or she collects all the property in the estate, reduces the property to money, and closes the estate after distributing the money according to the priorities established by the bankruptcy law. The debtor's estate consists of all property owned by or on behalf of the debtor as of the date of the filing of the bankruptcy petition. The following case involves the question of whether employee benefits should be included in a debtor's estate.

Matter of Turpin

5th Circuit Court of Appeals
644 F.2d 472 (1981)

Turpin filed a voluntary petition in bankruptcy on December 16, 1976. On April 6, 1977, the trustee in bankruptcy filed a complaint against Turpin and City National Bank of Austin in the bankruptcy court. The complaint asserted that the bankruptcy trustee was entitled to certain funds held for Turpin by the bank as trustee of a profit sharing plan and a pension plan created by Turpin's employer as retirement benefits. When the bankruptcy petition was filed, Turpin had been employed for seven years, and his

FACTS

employer had contributed $66,931.82 to the profit sharing plan and $42,780.56 to the pension plan on Turpin's behalf.

ISSUE   Does Turpin's interest in the profit sharing and pension plans constitute property that should pass to the trustee of his bankruptcy proceedings?

DECISION   No. The court agreed with Turpin that his interest in the pension and profit sharing plans were not property to be turned over to the bankruptcy trustee. The scope of the term *property* must be determined by the distinct purposes of the Bankruptcy Act. Although the primary purpose of the act is to secure for creditors everything of value that the bankrupt may possess, the act also is designed to leave the bankrupt free after the date of his petition to accumulate new wealth in the future and to make a fresh start.

The law provides that future wages may not be garnished to pay past obligations. Pension and profit sharing benefits received in the future, even though they may be the product of prebankruptcy contributions to a pension fund, are a substitute for future wages. Thus these funds should pass to the bankrupt free of the claims of prebankruptcy creditors.

Property Added to the Estate

After-Acquired Property   Certain property a debtor acquires after the petition has been filed is added to the debtor's estate. Specifically, property acquired within 180 days after the date the petition is filed is added to the estate. The property must have been acquired by inheritance, through a property settlement or divorce decree with the debtor's spouse, or as a beneficiary on a life insurance policy.

Preference Property   The trustee has the right under some circumstances to void or recall certain property transfers made by the debtor. If the debtor unfairly transferred property to one creditor rather than others when the debtor was insolvent, the property transferred sometimes may be recovered and added to the debtor's estate. The transfer must have been made within 90 days before the filing of the bankruptcy petition and must have given the creditor more than the creditor would have received through the bankruptcy proceeding. Thus not all transfers of property to creditors before the filing of the petition are **preferences.** But if the transfer does constitute a preference, it may be added to the debtor's estate.

Preference the payment of money or transfer of property to a creditor that gives a creditor priority over other creditors

Lien creditor a creditor with a claim against specific property in the debtor's estate

Lien Creditor's Property   A third type of property that may be added to the debtor's estate is that obtained by the trustee acting as a **lien creditor.** If the debtor had given to a creditor a lien on certain property, and if that lien had not been perfected or had not become effective as of the date of the filing of the petition, the trustee could add that property to the debtor's estate.

When the petition is filed, the trustee has the status of a lien creditor. If that status gives the trustee a better claim than other lien creditors to some of the bankrupt's property, that property is added to the bankrupt's estate for eventual distribution. The creditor who thought that he or she had a valid lien then becomes merely a general creditor, unable to look to specific property to satisfy the debt owed by the bankrupt.

The following cases illustrate the conflict between lien creditors and the trustee in bankruptcy, acting as another lien creditor.

_____ Matter of Hamlin _____

United States Bankruptcy Court, E.D. Michigan, S.D.
34 B.R 673 (1983)

Sears, Roebuck & Company installed an air conditioning system in the home of FACTS Michael and Barbara Hamlin. The work began on June 11, 1982, and ended on March 11, 1983. On March 23, 1983, 12 days later, Michael and Barbara Hamlin filed a petition for bankruptcy. On April 26, 1983, Sears filed a claim of lien on the home of the debtor. Although the lien was filed after the debtor's bankruptcy petition, Sears claimed that under state law, its lien is valid as of the date it finished installing the air conditioner. Michigan law provides that a contractor or laborer:

who provides an improvement to real property shall have a construction lien upon the interest of the owner or lessee who contracted for the improvement to the real property.

But the lien conferred by this section ceases:

unless, within 90 days after the lien claimant's last furnishing of labor or material for the improvement . . . a claim of lien is recorded in the office of the register of deeds.

Sears had recorded its lien within the 90 days provided by law. The trustee in bankruptcy claimed that the filing of the bankruptcy stays Sear's lien in its unrecorded form.

Can the trustee of bankruptcy stay the lien of Sears in its unrecorded form even if ISSUE state law allows 90 days for the lien to be recorded and thus perfected?

No. The court ruled that to do otherwise would destroy the state law and would DECISION deprive a mechanic's lien claimant of the very protection the statute was designed to provide. Accordingly, the bankruptcy law does not preclude Sears, Roebuck from recording its lien after the beginning of the bankruptcy case. The lien, having been recorded within the time permitted by law, is voidable neither by trustee nor debtor.

_____ Matter of Schalk _____

8th Circuit Court of Appeals
592 F.2d 993 (1979)

The trustee for the estate of Robert Schalk sought to compel the Belle-Bland Bank to FACTS turn over a 1972 mobile home trailer to the trustee. The trustee claimed that its rights as a lien creditor, whose lien was perfected as of the date (1976) of the filing of Schalk's petition in bankruptcy, gave it a better ownership claim to the property than that of the bank. Schalk had acquired an interest in the trailer by paying $1,000 and by agreeing to pay the bank the balance owed by Limberg, the original purchaser of the trailer. As of that date (1973), the bank had a secured interest in the trailer. The bank claimed that because Limberg never transferred a certificate of title to Schalk, as required under state law, Schalk did not have title to the trailer on the date the petition was filed. Thus it claimed that the trustee could not claim the property as a lien creditor of Schalk.

ISSUE   If the debtor's right to a trailer when bankruptcy is filed is subject to the bank's security interest in the trailer, can the bankruptcy trustee claim the trailer as a part of the debtor's property?

DECISION   No. The court found for the bank and held that the bankruptcy trustee did not have title to the property on the date Schalk filed his petition. Under Missouri law, a buyer's failure to get an assigned certificate of ownership in connection with his purchase of a registered motor vehicle or trailer in the state prevents title from passing to him and voids the sale. The Missouri courts consistently have held that absolute technical compliance with this law is required. Although the bankruptcy trustee has the rights of a lien creditor whose lien was perfected as of the date of bankruptcy, here the bank had perfected its security interest in the trailer by 1973, well before the 1976 date of the bankruptcy. Thus the bank's interest in the trailer has priority over the trustee's lien.

Voidable Transfers   The trustee also may restore to the debtor's estate property transferred by or for the debtor to third parties. First, any transfer by or for the debtor made after the filing of the bankruptcy petition may be voided within two years after the transfer or before the bankruptcy case is concluded, whichever is first. Second, the trustee may void any transfer made by the debtor within one year before the petition was filed if the transfer was fraudulent or made to hinder, delay, or defraud a creditor. Finally, a trustee may restore to the debtor's estate any property that has been taken by someone else's fraud, mistake, duress, or undue influence.

Exemptions from the Estate

A private individual who has filed for bankruptcy can claim certain exemptions that corporations and partnerships may not claim. The exempt property is not included in the debtor's estate and is not distributed to creditors. The debtor is allowed to keep the exempt property and still be discharged from the debts and liabilities he or she has listed.

The Bankruptcy Reform Act of 1978 gave all debtors a list of federally exempt properties. But debtors need not rely on that list and may choose the exemptions available under the laws of the states where they live. The bankruptcy laws also let states *require* that debtors use the exemptions listed under the state law.

Federal Exemptions   The list of federally exempt properties includes:

1. The debtor's residence, up to a value of $7,500

2. The debtor's interest in a motor vehicle, up to $1,200

3. The debtor's interest in household furnishings, clothes, appliances, books, musical instruments, animals, or crops held for personal, family, or household use, up to $200 for each item

4. Up to $500 in jewelry

5. The debtor's interest in implements, tools of the trade, or professional books

6. Any unmatured life insurance policy owned by the debtor, except for credit life policies

7. Prescribed health aids

8. The debtor's right to certain public benefits, including unemployment compensation, Social Security, veteran's benefits, and disability benefits

9. The debtor's right to certain private benefits, including alimony, child support, pension and profit sharing plans to the extent reasonably necessary for the support of the debtor or the debtor's dependents

10. The debtor's interest in any other kind of property up to a value of $400 plus any amount not used under the first exemption listed. (Thus if a debtor does not own a residence, he or she may exempt $7,900 of property under this exemption.)

State Exemptions   Properties exempt from bankruptcy vary according to state laws. Some states exempt items that are not specifically exempted by federal law. Some states also are more liberal than the federal law.

In the following cases, state exemptions are taken up.

Matter of Samuel

United States Bankruptcy Court, E.D. Virginia
Richmond Division
36 B.R. 312 (1984)

FACTS

Before 1982, Samuel was exclusively engaged in the home construction and remodeling business. In 1982, Samuel grossed approximately $49,000 and netted approximately $13,000 from this home business. In 1982 as well, he had gross sales of $4,500 and a net loss of $4,164 from a crabbing business. As part of the crabbing operation, he owned a truck, a boat, and about 220 crabpots. Before 1982, Samuel had had no experience in crabbing. He had been in the home building business since 1966. Samuel claimed that in 1982, he spent 90 percent of his time in the crabbing business. Samuel also claimed that he is a fisherman and that under Virginia law is entitled to exempt $1,500 of the value of his boat. Virginia law provides that in addition to the estate of $5,000 or less, a debtor may exempt — "in case of an oysterman or fisherman his boat and tackle," of not more than $1,500 in value.

ISSUE   Can a person who is a building contractor and a fisherman claim the exemption that state law allows for a fisherman's boat?

DECISION   No. In light of the respective income, shown by his 1982 tax return for his home building business and his crabbing, it appears patently absurd that Mr. Samuel would have spent 90 percent of his effort at what he considered his primary occupation during 1982. The legislature did not intend that a party could engage in several trades or occupations to claim multiple exemptions. For purposes of the exemption statutes, a debtor may claim occupationally related exemptions only in his or her principal occupation. A debtor may claim only one principal occupation.

Belcher v. Turner

10th Circuit Court of Appeals
579 F.2d 73 (1978)

FACTS   Carl and Esther Belcher filed a voluntary petition for bankruptcy in which they claimed as exempt property the duplex which they owned. The claim was made under the homestead exemption of the state law on bankruptcy that specifies:

> A homestead to the extent of one hundred and sixty (160) acres of farming land, or of one acre within the limits of an incorporated town or city, occupied as a residence by the family of the owner, together with all the improvements on the same, shall be exempted from forced sale under any process of law.

Each unit in the duplex has a separate entrance, driveway, garage, and address. The Belchers had lived in one unit since buying the property and had always leased the other unit. The trustee claimed that only the half occupied by the Belchers was exempt. The Belchers sought to have the entire duplex exempted.

ISSUE   Can the entire value of a duplex of a debtor who lives in only one half be considered exempt property?

DECISION   No. The court found that only one half of the duplex was exempt property. Clearly, the Bankruptcy Act makes available to bankrupts those exemptions prescribed by state law. The Kansas courts have interpreted their homestead exemption laws so that the test for determining whether a structure is a homestead is determined by its use or occupancy as a residence. An "incidental" departure for business purposes does not deprive it of its homestead character.

But in this case, half of the duplex always has been rented out and was never intended or expected to serve as the Belchers' residence. The unit was intended to produce income. The purpose and intent of the Bankruptcy Act is to protect the residence of the debtor. Exempting the half of the duplex in which the Belchers reside fully achieves that purpose.

DISTRIBUTION OF DEBTOR'S ESTATE

Priority Claims

After the trustee has collected all the debtor's property and reduced it to money, the money is distributed to the creditors. Some claims are given a higher priority than others, and claims are paid in order of priority. Each class of claims is paid in full before the next lowest class of claims is paid. If there is not enough money to pay fully all claims in any class, the money available is prorated among the creditors in that class.

The highest priority is assigned to the costs and expenses involved in administering the bankruptcy proceeding. These include legal fees, accountants' fees, trustee fees, and court costs. The next class of claims pertains only to involuntary proceedings: ordinary business or financial expenses incurred after filing but before appointment of the trustee. The third class consists of claims for wages, salaries, or commissions earned by employees within 90 days before the filing of the petition or the end of the debtor's business, whichever occurs first. Claims in this class have priority up to $2,000 a person.

Three other categories of claims have some priority over general claims. The fourth class is claims for contributions to an employee benefit plan arising from services rendered within 180 days before the filing of the petition or the cessation of the debtor's business. The limit per claimant in this category is also $2,000, and no individual can receive more than $2,000 from a combination of claims falling in the third and fourth priority classes. The fifth class is for claims for deposits made on consumer goods or services that were not received; the limit for claims in this class is $900. The sixth class consists of tax claims by government units.

General Claims

If a claim exceeds the amount allowed as a priority, the excess becomes a general claim. After all classes of priority claims have been paid, any remaining property in the estate is distributed on a pro-rata basis to all unsecured creditors with general claims. Often general claimants get little if anything. Creditors therefore try to have their claims classified as priority claims, as the following case illustrates.

Matter of Adams

United States Bankruptcy Court, E.D. Pennsylvania
34 B.R. 352 (1983)

FACTS   On March 25, 1981, Harry and Catherine Adams filed a petition for bankruptcy. On July 14, 1981, the city of Philadelphia filed a priority proof of claim in the amount of $1,215.32. The Adamses objected to the priority claim of $220.82 for past water and sewer rents. The city argued that water and sewer charges should be treated as a priority claim. The debtors claim that the city cannot tax for a private function, which defendant believes includes providing of water and sewer, as It can for public functions that promote the general welfare.

ISSUE   Are debts owed to a city for water and sewer charges considered taxes under the Bankruptcy Code and therefore entitled to priority status?

DECISION   Yes. Interpreting earlier bankruptcy law, the United States Supreme Court stated that whether an obligation is a "tax" entitled to priority within the meaning of the statute is a federal question. Nothing in the language of the bankruptcy law nor its legislative history suggests that it should vary by state. The Supreme Court has indicated what is a tax under the provisions of the prior bankruptcy laws; there is nothing in the 1978 act that should lead this court to charge that determination. Since water and sewer charges owing to the city of Philadelphia are practically indistinguishable in their nature and effect from property taxes, these charges are entitled to priority status under the bankruptcy law.

DISCHARGE OF DEBTS

After the debtor's estate has been liquidated and distributed among creditors, the bankruptcy court conducts a hearing to determine if the debtor should be discharged from remaining debts. A discharge may be granted to an individual petitioner, but a partnership or a corporation must instead seek to reorganize (under Chapter 11 of the federal bankruptcy laws) or seek to liquidate under state laws.

Exceptions to Discharge

In some cases, courts deny debtors a discharge. Then the debtors remain liable for the unpaid portion of the creditors' claims. A debtor is denied a discharge more than once every seven years. A debtor is denied discharge for intentionally concealing or transferring assets to hinder, delay, or defraud creditors up to one year before and any time after filing for bankruptcy.

Other reasons for refusing to discharge a debtor include the debtor's concealment, destruction, falsification, or failure to keep financial records. A debtor who fails to adequately explain the loss of assets, refuses to obey the bankruptcy court, or makes fraudulent statements during the bankruptcy case also may be denied the discharge of unpaid debts, as the following case shows.

_____ *Matter of Horton* _____

9th Circuit Court of Appeals
621 F.2d 968 (1980)

FACTS Horton sought a discharge of his debts in bankruptcy and was refused by the bankruptcy judge in December 1974. Horton appeared in the bankruptcy court like clockwork every seven years. He was granted discharges in 1960 and again in 1967. This latest petition in bankruptcy was filed in 1974. The reason for refusing discharge was Horton's unjustified failure to keep adequate books of accounts or financial records. Such records are required. Horton claims that his records, when considered along with those of his daughter, are sufficient for purposes of the bankruptcy laws.

ISSUE If a bankrupt does not keep sufficient records of his financial transactions, can records kept by his daughter be considered? If the combined records are not sufficient, can he be denied a discharge in bankruptcy?

DECISION Although the court reviewed the records of Horton's daughter as well as his own, it found both insufficient and therefore denied him a discharge. The Bankruptcy Act provides that a discharge cannot be granted if the bankrupt has failed to keep sufficient records of his financial transactions. Horton dealt almost exclusively in cash, keeping few or no verifiable records, and could not show where his salary was spent.

The court also examined Horton's contention that certain of his daughter's records provide the necessary information. First, the court said that legally Horton had a duty to maintain his own records, even if his daughter's records were complete. Even so, the court found that the daughter's records also were insufficient. Her records did not differentiate between payments made to Horton for his own time and labor in building a house for her and payments made to him to reimburse the suppliers who furnished materials he had used. Once the trustee shows that the bankrupt's records are inadequate, the burden shifts to the bankrupt to justify the nonexistence of these records. This he did not do.

Nondischargeable Claims

A discharge relieves debtors from having to pay the debts that they incurred before filing the petition. But for some claims debtors continue to be liable. These are known as **nondischargeable claims.** These include:

Nondischargeable claims claims for which a debtor remains liable even after other claims are discharged

1. claims for back taxes accrued within three years before the bankruptcy

2. claims arising out of the debtor's embezzlement, fraud, or larceny

3. claims based on the debtor's willful or malicious torts

4. claims for alimony or child support

5. unscheduled claims

6. certain fines and penalties payable to government units

7. educational loans that became due and payable less than five years before the filing of the bankruptcy petition.

Reaffirmations   Debtors may agree to reaffirm or reassume certain debts after the bankruptcy proceeding. But because debtors may be under pressure from creditors to reaffirm the discharged debts, the bankruptcy laws make the reaffirmation of debts somewhat difficult. A **reaffirmed debt** is one that is reinstated after it has been legally discharged by a bankruptcy proceeding. A simple promise made by the debtor, even in writing, is not sufficient for a valid reaffirmation.

For a valid affirmation, first the court must conduct a hearing at which the debtor is informed of the consequences of reaffirming a debt. Second, the debt usually must be approved by the court as not imposing an undue hardship on the debtor and as being in the debtor's best interest. If these conditions are not met, the reaffirmation of the debt is invalid, and it remains discharged.

> **Reaffirmed debt** an agreement that a debt, having been legally discharged in bankruptcy, is again legally valid

BUSINESS REORGANIZATION

Instead of filing a petition for liquidation, a business may elect to file for reorganization under Chapter 11 of the Bankruptcy Act. As in a liquidation proceeding, a petition for reorganization may also be filed by the creditors. Most of the rules that apply to a liquidation proceeding also apply to a reorganization. (Railroads are not subject to liquidation because the public depends on their services.) Reorganization allows a financially troubled firm or railroad to continue to operate while its financial resources and obligations are put in order.

Under Chapter 11 reorganizations, the court must appoint a creditors committee. This committee usually consists of the seven largest unsecured creditors and is appointed as soon as possible after the order for relief has been entered by the court. The committee examines the affairs of the business and decides whether the business should continue in operation. It also usually determines whether to request of the court that a trustee take over management of the business. The committee may hire attorneys, accountants, and others to help it.

Generally the debtor or any other interested party may file a plan for reorganization. Although only the debtor may file a plan during the first 120 days after the petition has been filed (unless a trustee has been appointed), the debtor's plan usually is developed in consultation with the creditors. A debtor who files a plan within the 120 days has another 60 days to have the plan approved by the creditors. The court can extend or reduce these time periods. If the debtor does not meet the deadline or cannot get the creditors' consent, a creditor or the trustee may propose a plan.

The plan that is proposed must classify claims and ownership interests. It must specify the treatment of each class of claims and must provide for the same treatment for everyone within a class unless someone agrees to less favorable treatment. The plan also must provide adequate means for carrying out the plan's payment terms. If the debtor is a corporation, the plan must also protect stockholders and creditors.

The plan may modify the rights of some creditors. It may specify that some property be transferred to other creditors, that some creditors be paid over an extended time, and even that some creditors not be paid at all. The only requirement is that all claimants receive as much as they would have received in a liquidation proceeding.

Those who hold claims or interests in the debtor's property are allowed to vote on the proposed plan. If creditors representing more than one half of the claimants and at least two thirds of the value of the claims in a class vote in favor of the plan, that class of creditors has accepted the plan. Usually plans are not approved unless all those whose claims or interests have been impaired (those whose rights have been altered or who are to receive less than the full value of their claims or interests) have agreed. But a court may confirm a plan if it finds that everyone in a particular class is treated fairly, even when those with **impaired claims** do not consent.

In the following case, the court approves a plan despite its nonacceptance by some of the creditors. When a court confirms a plan, it binds the debtor and all the creditors. The property of the debtor is then released from the claims of the creditors, and the debtor is given a Chapter 11 discharge. It must make payments to the creditors as provided by the plan, but no other payments are required for the debtor's obligation to be discharged.

Impaired claim a claim that would receive less than full value under a reorganization plan

---

Matter of Poly Therm Industries, Incorporated

United States Bankruptcy Court, W.E. Wisconsin
33 B.R. 412 (1982)

Some of the creditors of the bankrupt did not accept the plan for reorganization of debts.   FACTS

Can the court confirm the plan despite their nonacceptance?   ISSUE

Yes. The court made the following finding on the debtor's plan: DECISION

1. The plan has been proposed in good faith and not by any means forbidden by law.

2. A. All payments made or promised by the proponent, by the debtor, or by anyone issuing securities or acquiring property under the plan have been disclosed.
   B. All payments are reasonable or subject to the approval of the court as reasonable.

3. A. The identity and affiliations of individuals proposed to serve as a director, officer, or voting trustee of the debtor, an affiliate of the debtor in a joint plan, or a successor to the debtor under the plan have been disclosed.
   B. The proponent of the plan has disclosed the identity of any **insider** that will be employed or retained by the reorganized debtor and the nature of any compensation for such insider.

Insider someone with information not available to people outside the corporation concerning the value of a corporation's securities

4. In that the large majority of class (A) holders of claims have accepted the plan but that certain classes and creditors of the secured creditors have not accepted the plan, the court applies the doctrine of the "cram down" theory of law and so finds that the plan has presented the necessary approval as to number and amounts.

CHAPTER 13 REGULAR INCOME PLANS

Chapter 13 proceedings are used by people with regular incomes who owe debts and want to pay them without harassment by creditors. Any person except a stockbroker or commodity broker who has a regular income from wages, investments, Social Security, or pensions, unsecured debts of less than $100,000, and secured debts of less than $350,000 may use Chapter 13. Unlike liquidation or reorganization, Chapter 13 proceedings may be begun only by a voluntary petition.

When a debtor files under Chapter 13, an automatic stay stops creditors from taking action against the debtor. The debtor then proposes a plan for applying future income to debts. That income is controlled by a trustee. The plan must provide that all priority claims are paid in full unless they agree to accept less than the full amounts of their claims. Unsecured claims may be divided into classes, but all claims within any class must be treated alike. Claimants may be paid in full or paid no less than they would get in a liquidation proceeding. Usually plans provides for payment over three years or less, although courts may extend the period of payment to five years. Secured creditors vote on accepting the plan. If they do not accept the plan, but either retain their liens or receive the properties securing their claims, the court confirms the plan. Unsecured creditors do not vote on the plan, but they must receive at least the amounts they would have received in a liquidation proceeding.

ALTERNATIVES

People increasingly seek the advice of credit counselors on their financial troubles. Most clients have suffered a temporary setback, such as a job loss or serious injury, that interrupted their normal source of income. But an increasing number are managers and professionals with relatively high incomes who cannot handle their debts. Credit counselors generally review a person's cash flow, establish a budget, and advise on whether a person can handle his or her bills or needs a debt repayment plan such as those noted below.

About half of the clients need only one session with a counselor, because they determine they can solve their own financial problems. Over one third of clients work out a plan to pay their debts. The regular income plan provided under Chapter 13 is one such alternative. The straight bankruptcy proceeding usually is a last resort, because it tarnishes the debtor's credit record for many years and can make it difficult for a person to find work.

In a composition agreement (see Chapter 7), each creditor agrees to take less money than is owed. The debtor immediately pays the creditors. They in turn agree to cancel the entire debt. Composition contracts are viewed not only as agreements between the debtor and each creditor but also as agreements among creditors. Two or more creditors therefore must agree for the courts to view such a contract as being supported by appropriate consideration.

In an **extension agreement**, each creditor agrees to a longer repayment period. The debtor agrees to pay the debt in full. As in the composition agreement, more than one creditor must join before such an agreement is considered valid.

Extension agreement an arrangement wherein a creditor agrees to a longer repayment period and the debtor agrees to pay the debt in full

SUMMARY

Bankruptcy laws provide relief and protection to a debtor while fairly distributing the debtor's assets among creditors. There are three types of bankruptcy proceedings available under federal laws in the United States: straight, or liquidation, bankruptcy; the business reorganization proceeding; and the Chapter 13 regular income plan. A liquidation bankruptcy proceeding may be voluntary or involuntary. The bankruptcy trustee is charged with collecting the debtor's assets for the estate. Some property that may have been disposed of by the debtor may be returned to the estate. Items regarded as preference property, voidable transfers, and property that the trustee as lien creditor can obtain also belongs to the estate. Exempt property belongs to the debtor and is not distributed to creditors. Although there are both priority and general claimants, general claimants usually get little from a bankrupt's estate. Most debts are discharged through a bankruptcy proceeding, but some claims are nondischargeable, and a debtor who commits fraud is denied a discharge.

A business may file for reorganization. A plan for repayment of the outstanding debts must be submitted to the creditors. All creditors must receive as much as they would have received in a liquidation plan. Most plans are agreed to by all creditors, but a court can confirm a plan even in the absence of such consent.

A regular income proceeding may be filed by any individual with a regular income who wants to pay debts without harassment from creditors. For the regular income plan to be confirmed, all priority claimants must receive full payment, to the extent funds are available, unless they agree to accept less. Unsecured creditors must receive at least the amount they would receive under a liquidation proceeding.

REVIEW PROBLEMS

1. Compare and contrast the uses and consequences of the three kinds of bankruptcy proceedings.

2. What is the purpose of the bankruptcy law?

3. What are exemptions? Give several examples of exemptions in bankruptcy.

4. Who receives the property of the debtor that is not exempt?

5. Assume that an individual debtor has a regular income, owns a small ($20,000) business, and has $30,000 of property, $75,000 of unsecured debts, and $225,000 of secured debts. The debtor wants to stay in business but cannot pay her debts. Which of the bankruptcy proceedings is available for and might help this debtor?

6. The bankrupt, Keidel, borrowed $3,500 from the bank to finance the purchase of a mobile home from Mitchell. Keidel signed a security agreement with the bank and gave it her promissory note. The bank gave her a check, issued to her and to Olin Employees' Credit Union, the prior lienholder. The bankrupt was advised to get a new certificate of title showing that she, instead of the seller Mitchell, had the title to the mobile home.

    Keidel began to apply for a certificate of title, but did not complete her application. Five months later, she filed a petition in bankruptcy. One month after that date, the bank applied for and obtained a new certificate of title, showing Keidel's ownership of the mobile home and the bank's lien interest. Under the state law, the bank had a security interest in the mobile home as of the date of its loan to Keidel. However, that security interest was not perfected until the date the bank applied for the new certificate of title. Does the trustee in bankruptcy, standing in the position of a lien creditor, prevail over the bank that had a security interest created prior to the date of the petition in bankruptcy, but perfected after that date?

7. The defendant filed a voluntary proceeding in bankruptcy. Six weeks later, his mother died and he became entitled to money from a trust fund. After his mother's death, the debtor filed a disclaimer, which under state law disclaimed his interest in that money and passed it instead to his children. The trustee in bankruptcy claims that the property that the debtor was entitled to was part of his estate and that the state law allowing him to disclaim it is inconsistent with and subject to the federal bankruptcy law. Is the trustee correct?

8. Sotello was the principal officer and major stockholder of a corporation that was liable to withhold employees' wages for payment of taxes. The Internal Revenue Code states that any person who is required to but fails to pay withholding taxes is penalized the amount of taxes due. Sotello, his wife, and the corporation were all adjudged bankrupt. Sotello claims that the amount owed to the IRS is a corporate debt for which he is not liable. He further claims that even if he is liable, the amount owed is a penalty, not a tax, and therefore is a debt from which his bankruptcy discharges him. The IRS says that because he has always been the corporation's president, director, and majority stockholder, he "has a duty to collect, account for and pay over the taxes" due from employees. Furthermore, it says that the amount owed by him to the IRS is a tax that is not dischargeable under the bankruptcy laws. Is the IRS correct?

9. Petitioners are claims adjustors and attorneys who provided professional services to an insurance company that has been liquidated under state law. The statutory scheme for distributing assets of an insolvent insurance company gives priority status, after expenses of administration are paid, to claims owed to employees. The language of the state law is very similar to that in the federal

bankruptcy statutory provision. The other general creditors claim that the attorneys and claims adjustors are not employees but are independent contractors. Thus amounts owed to them are not due as "wages" and are not entitled to priority status. Assume that this provision in the state law is interpreted in the same way as is the provision in the federal bankruptcy laws. Should the claims adjusters' and attorneys' claims, or a part of them, be granted priority status?

10. Review the federal exemptions in bankruptcy listed on page 437 and the *Samuels* and *Belcher* cases which follow. Assume the following facts and answer these questions: 1. Assume Samuels is in fact a fisherman whose boat has a value of $5,000 and Belcher's duplex is valued at $75,000 — $40,000 for the portion he resides in and $35,000 for the rental portion (it is not maintained as well as his residence). If the courts followed federal law rather than state law in the debtor's use of their exemptions, how would the court's decision in these two cases differ from the versions presented in the text?

11. Feenstra got a loan to pay his son's college tuition for his first year of college. The bankruptcy act provides that educational loans are not dischargeable in bankruptcy unless these were due for more than five years or would produce hardship. Feenstra was 49 years old and had five dependents, a wife and four children whose ages ranged from 15 to 21. Three of the children were recovering drug addicts, and Mr. Feenstra was a recovering alcoholic. Mr. Feenstra was employed mixing chemicals at the Olin Corporation. Is a government-guaranteed educational loan made to a student's parent subject to discharge when the parent becomes a debtor in bankruptcy if the loan would impose an undue hardship on the debtor and his dependents?

12. Shannon filed a petition for bankruptcy in 1980. She omitted from her schedule of assets and claims against other people the child support owed her from her former husband. Because she did not list the claim, it was not listed as an exemption. The former husband claims because it was not exempted, it was discharged. Do you agree? Explain.

13. Brenda purchases a refrigerator, stove, and air conditioner from Freddie's Appliance Store. She paid Freddie $1,000 and signed a contract to take delivery of the appliances in two weeks. One week after her purchase of the appliances, Freddie filed a straight bankruptcy. What will be Brenda's status as a claimant? Is she entitled to any priority?

14. Pan American Paper Mill was required by state law to pay premiums to a state insurance fund to provide workman's compensation benefits to injured employees. The law provides that if the payments are not made by employees, the fund still provides insurance for the injured employees, but it will have a claim against the employer for all unpaid insurance premiums plus the costs paid out to employees of that employer. Pan Am failed to pay its premiums for several years. These premiums amounted to $68,000. The fund paid out insurance benefits to Pan Am employees of $50,000. Pan Am files for bankruptcy. What is the status of the state's claims for repayment of funds due from its bankruptcy estate?

15. The bankrupt was a contractor who built basic (shell) homes. He admitted that he made false statements when he filed a written document with a lumber

company for the purpose of obtaining a loan. When the contractor filed for bankruptcy and sought a discharge of his debts, the lumber company objected to the granting of the discharge. Should the discharge be denied?

16. Conn filed a bankruptcy petition on September 30, 1980. He admitted making 3 payments to the Ohio National Bank between August 1 and September 10 of that year; those payments amounted to approximately $440. These were car payments on an Oldsmobile, on which the bank had a $4,000 secured debt as of October 1979. The car had a value of $3,500 on September 1980. Do the payments to the bank on the car loan constitute a voidable preference that can be avoided by the trustee?

PART IV

BUSINESS ORGANIZATIONS

CHAPTER 26

The Agency Relationship

CHAPTER OBJECTIVES

After reading this chapter, you should be able to:

1. Define the agency relationship.

2. Identify the necessity of control in the agency relationship and distinguish between an agent and an independent contractor.

3. Explain how an agency relationship is established.

4. Identify when an agent is entitled to compensation.

5. Explain the fiduciary duty of loyalty of agent to principal.

6. Compare and contrast the agent's duties of obedience, exercising skill and care, and informing and rendering account to the principal.

The purpose of an agency is to allow one person to accomplish results through another person's activities. Despite modern advances in communication and transportation, a person is limited by certain basic physical features: he or she has only one pair of hands to work with, one mouth to speak from, and can be in only one place at a time. When the time arrives that more hands and mouths are needed, or when it becomes necessary to transact business at the same time in various and remote places, the businessperson must turn to someone for assistance and representation. That someone is the agent.

AGENCY DEFINED

Agency a legal relationship in which one person, an agent, is authorized to act for another, a principal

Agent a person authorized to act for another in a legal relationship

Principal a person who agrees to let an agent act on his or her behalf

Agency is the name given to the legal relationship created when two people agree that one of them, called the **agent,** is to represent the other, called the **principal,** subject to the principal's right to control the agent's conduct in the delegated activity. Agency relates to commercial or business transactions conducted between the principal and third parties through the agent. In agency relations, the principal confides to the agent the management of some business that the principal may lawfully do in person. The result is to legally bind the principal to third persons as though the principal personally transacted the business. The agent is merely the medium. When the dealings are completed and the dust finally clears, it is the principal and the third person who are legally bound to each other. It is the agent who has tied the bond.

TYPES OF AGENTS

Agents are classified as either general agents or special agents. The *general* agent is more or less continuously employed by the principal to conduct a series of transactions. He or she may be the manager of the principal's business or the lowliest of clerks. The *special* agent is hired for one particular transaction or occasion. There is no continuity in the special agent's employment. He or she is hired on a one-shot basis. Realtors and investment brokers are examples of special agents. The distinction between general and special agents is primarily a matter of degree, depending upon the agent's continuity of employment.

TYPES OF PRINCIPALS

Principals are classified as either disclosed or undisclosed. In the usual agency transaction, the third person knows that the agent is acting for a principal and the principal's identity. The principal's identity may be important because the third person may be relying on the principal's credit and reputation. The agent's identity is unimportant because the transaction is between the principal and the third person, and the agent is not a party to the deal. When the third person knows the principal's identity, the principal is referred to as a **disclosed principal.**

Sometimes a principal may not wish to reveal his or her identity and the existence of the agency relation to the third person. When the third person has no knowledge that the agent is working for the particular principal, the principal is called an **undisclosed principal.** In these situations, the agent's identity becomes more important than the principal's identity. Because the agent purports to be acting on his or her own, the agent is a party to the contract along with the principal. Undisclosed principals really are not sinister. People frequently have honest reasons for not wishing their connection with a transaction known. In some dealings, the principal's identity simply is unimportant. For example, buyers and sellers of stock usually are unaware of the identity of the other, each knowing only his or her broker in the deal.

Disclosed principal a principal whose existence and identity are known to the third party

Undisclosed principal a principal whose existence is unknown to the third party

AGENCY DISTINGUISHED

There are many relationships in which one person acts for the benefit of another that are distinguished from agency. It is important to distinguish an agency relationship from something else. If it is an agency, certain legal consequences attach. If it is some other relation, significantly different legal consequences may attach.

In determining whether a relationship is an agency, the name the parties give it is not controlling. The *substance* of the relationship is controlling. Whether a relationship is an agency does not depend on clever draftsmanship. Otherwise, people could label their relationships to avoid liability.

What distinguishes agency from other similar relations is the power of control retained by the principal over the agent's activities. Relations usually distinguished from agency may become agency relations if this power of control is present. Frequently called the "power of control" test, the concept is more a useful tool than an acid test for the existence of agency.

Because they render services while pursuing independent occupations, *independent contractors* usually are not agents. When working for employers, these contractors agree only to accomplish certain results and are responsible only for their final products. Employers hire them by the job and do not control the details of performance. This relationship differs from the principal-agent relationships, because principals control their agents' contractual dealings. Because independent contractors usually are not agents, their employers are not liable to the contractor's creditors nor to persons harmed by the contractor's negligence. But an individual contractor may become an agent or servant if the employer retains control over the details of performance. Whether an independent contractor becomes an agent depends on the degree and character of the control retained by the employer over the work done, and no absolute dividing line can be drawn between the two. An employer who hires an independent contractor to perform dangerous work or to take on duties which by law cannot be delegated to others remains liable for injuries caused by the contractor.

The following case shows the importance of analyzing whether a relation is an agency.

Columbia Broadcasting System, Incorporated
v. Stokely-Van Camp, Incorporated

U.S. Court of Appeals
522 F.2d 369 (1975)

FACTS   Lennen & Newell, Incorporated, a so-called full service advertising agency, had handled Stokely's account for over 17 years on the basis of an unwritten arrangement. Lennen produced television commercials, with Stokely's approval, out of an advertising budget approved by Stokely. Stokely did not know what contracts, if any, were made by Lennen with the media. Stokely simply paid Lennen on its invoices. CBS sold time for Stokely commercials under network contracts which stated that Lennen was "acting as agent for" and purchasing "in behalf of" Stokely. CBS billed Lennen for the cost of the advertising time less 15 percent, the standard commission in the trade for an advertising agency. Under the contract, Stokely was to be ultimately responsible for payment and had the right to terminate upon a breach by CBS. Lennen went bankrupt. Although Stokely had paid Lennen, CBS had not been paid. CBS sued Stokely for payment under the contract. CBS alleged that Lennen had express or apparent authority or "power arising from the agency relation" to bind Stokely.

ISSUE   Was Lennen acting as an agent for Stokely or as an independent contractor?

DECISION   Lennen was acting as an independent contractor. To determine the extent of an authorization, a court looks to the accompanying circumstances, including the situation of the parties, their relations to one another, and the business in which they are engaged; the general usages of the business in question and the purported principal's business methods; the nature of the subject matter and the circumstances under which the business is done. As to authorization to contract, it may be inferred from authority to conduct a transaction if the making of the contract is incidental to the transaction, usually accompanies such a transaction, or is reasonably necessary to accomplish it. No evidence exists that advertising agencies generally execute contracts binding their clients. No actual or apparent authority exists from Stokely to Lennen to bind Stokely to pay CBS. Therefore, there was no agency relationship.

CREATION OF AGENCY RELATIONS

Capacity

Any person having **capacity** to consent can become a principal or an agent. A principal only has capacity to appoint an agent to perform activities that the principal may lawfully perform. A person is not allowed to accomplish through an agent what he or she is not allowed to accomplish alone. A statute may restrict a person's capacity to be an agent. Licensing statutes may limit the capacity of someone to act as an agent by requiring a license to engage in a particular business. For example, most states require real estate brokers to be licensed before they may lawfully engage in the practice of buying and selling real estate for others.

Capacity the ability or competence to do something at law

Formalities

Generally, no formalities are required to create an agency. Payment need not be promised or made to the agent for representing the principal. Uncompensated agents are called *gratuitous* agents. The transactions they conduct are as binding on their principals as dealings conducted by *paid* agents. For example, if Penelope, knowing that her roommate is going by the bookstore after classes, asks her roommate to stop and buy a book on Penelope's account, the bookstore is entitled to payment from Penelope.

Usually it is not necessary to create an agency relation in writing. But written authorization often is desirable. Careful businesspeople spell out their agency relations in carefully drafted written instruments. Written authorization, sometimes called a **power of attorney,** is necessary in a few situations. (For more on power of attorney, see Chapter 27.)

Power of attorney written authorization creating an agency

RIGHTS AND DUTIES BETWEEN PRINCIPAL AND AGENT

Agent's Right to Compensation

Unless it appears that the agent's services are intended to be gratuitous, the agent is entitled to compensation for the general value of his or her services. The agent's right to compensation usually is provided by contract, with matters of interpretation determined according to the ordinary rules of contract law. An important issue ordinarily is whether the agent performed the services specified in the contract. Because the contract's terms and conditions governing the agent's compensation often are a source of disputes between the parties, these provisions should be established between the parties clearly in writing. The matters to be considered vary with each agency, but parties to most agencies ordinarily should consider the amount and the basis of compensation. For example, whether the compensation is to be by salary, wages, commission, a share of profits, bonuses, or in a form other than money should be expressly provided in writing. The agent also should consider including some provision to compensate for extra services and to reimburse expenses. The principal should consider including conditions governing the right of compensation. For example, he or she may wish to provide that the agent is to achieve certain results or render specified services before becoming entitled to compensation. Both parties should consider providing for compensation in the form of **liquidated damages** in the event of a breach of contract or other misconduct.

Liquidated damages those which are specified in a contract

Agencies involving practices peculiar to a trade require special attention to avoid misunderstanding. For example, sales agents may wish to stipulate that commissions are earned in the event the principal fails to fill orders, or if the customer rejects delivery, or has not paid for ordered merchandise. Principals of sales agents may wish to provide that commissions are earned when orders are either obtained, accepted, delivered, or paid for.

In the absence of an agreement, there is an implied obligation on a principal to pay for services rendered by the agent when the services are customarily paid for. If the agency contract does not provide compensation, a promise to pay is inferred from the fact that the agent's services are rendered at the principal's request or have been accepted by the principal.

When customary and practical, the principal is obligated to keep and render accounts of the compensation owed to the agent. This allows the agent to know what he or she is entitled to and serves to implement the agent's right to compensation. Like the right to compensation, this right to an accounting depends on custom and usage. For example, principals employing traveling sales agents whose compensation is based on completed sales are in the better position to maintain sales records. Therefore, they customarily keep the accounts. When this custom exists, an individual principal is required to maintain the records. But agents such as real estate brokers and lawyers, who own their own businesses and have complete knowledge of all transactions, ordinarily keep their own accounts. Principals employing them are relieved of accounting responsibilities. But principals may be required to maintain certain records for tax purposes. The parties also may state in their agency contract who is to maintain and render accounts.

As another incident of the principal's obligation to compensate the agent, the principal is obligated to assist and cooperate with the agent and to do nothing that unreasonably prevents the agent's performance. This duty of the principal to refrain from unreasonably interfering with the agent's work allows the agent to render performance and be compensated. If the principal unreasonably interferes with the agent's performance, the agent is entitled to the compensation that would have been earned if he or she had been permitted to perform as originally requested. Only the principal's unreasonable interference is prohibited, and what is "unreasonable" depends on the circumstances. Unreasonable interference may be improper commands to the agent or the principal's conduct toward third persons. The parties also may specify what constitutes an unreasonable interference. For example, ordinarily nothing is said by the parties about competition by the principal, and the principal is allowed to compete with the agent because competition is not considered unreasonable. But if the parties provide that the principal is not to compete either directly or by hiring other agents, competition by the principal is an unreasonable interference and constitutes a material breach of the agency agreement. An example of this type of agency contract is an exclusive real estate listing contract between a homeowner and a real estate broker, providing that the owner not compete against the broker by attempting to sell the property through his or her own efforts or by listing the property with other brokers.

In addition to compensating the agent for services rendered, the principal is obligated to indemnify or reimburse the agent for any authorized expenses or losses suffered by the agent while acting for the principal. An **indemnity** is an obligation or duty resting on one person to make good any loss or damage incurred by another while acting for his or her benefit. It is simply the shifting of an economic loss to the person primarily responsible for it. The guiding principle is that the true benefactor should bear the burden of payment. In agency relations, the agent customarily has expenses for the principal. The agent is exposed to claims as a result of being designated an agent by the principal. Because the principal originally put the agent in this position, the principal bears the financial burden.

Indemnity reimbursement

The agent's right to indemnity usually is provided in the agency agreement, and the parties may provide that the agent bears the risk of loss and the expenses of performance of his or her duties. But if no provision is made for indemnity, the right is inferred when the agent incurs an expense, suffers a loss, or assumes a liability while acting in an authorized manner. For example, the agent is entitled to reimbursement from the principal for any authorized payment that is necessary to the agent's performance. This right to reimbursement does not arise until payment is made.

When the principal is liable to the agent for compensation, reimbursement, or indemnity, the agent is permitted a lien or security interest in the principal's goods or money lawfully possessed by the agent. This lien only extends to the amount of the agent's compensation or indemnity and entitles the agent to retain possession of the property of the proceeds from its sale until the agent is paid what is owed.

Agent's Fiduciary Duty of Loyalty

Because the agent acts solely for the principal's benefit in all matters connected with the agency, the principal–agent relation is called a *fiduciary relationship,* and the agent is referred to as the principal's fiduciary. A **fiduciary** is simply someone who acts for someone else or holds property for the benefit of another. An agency relation is just one form of fiduciary relation. Other examples are executors and administrators of estates as well as trustees.

Fiduciary a person holding a legal relationship of trust in which he or she acts primarily for the benefit of another in certain matters

The important element of the fiduciary relation is that the fiduciary acts for another person. Because someone else puts trust and confidence in the fiduciary, the fiduciary is held to very high standards of conduct. Certain fiduciary duties are imposed for the protection of the other person's property and interests, and the courts do not tolerate any change of these duties without the consent of the other person. A fiduciary is under a general duty to act for the other person's benefit on matters within the relationship. The agent, therefore, is under a fiduciary obligation to act solely for the principal's benefit in all matters affecting the agency relation.

As part of the fiduciary duty, the agent must give undivided loyalty to the principal. Such fidelity is fundamental to the agency relation, because without it there would be no assurance that the principal's interests would be promoted. The agent must act with the utmost good faith solely for the principal's benefit with no adverse or competing interests on his or her part. The agent must not allow his or her personal interests to conflict with the principal's. He or she may not compete directly with the principal without permission or indirectly by working for the principal's competition without the principal's consent.

Because the agent is bound to act solely for the principal, the agent must forward all agency profits to the principal. All benefits resulting from the agency relation belong to the principal. The agent may not secretly profit from his or her performance. All profits belong to the principal. The agent may not use the principal's property for his or her own benefit without the principal's consent. Furthermore, the agent may not take advantage of an opportunity rightfully belonging to the principal. For example, a purchasing agent, authorized to buy property for the principal, cannot buy for him or herself any property that the principal would be interested in buying. Any such property bought belongs to the principal even though held by the agent.

It follows that the agent cannot deal with the principal as an adverse party, unless the principal consents to such a transaction. For example, a sales agent authorized to sell the principal's property to third persons cannot buy the property for himself or herself without the principal's consent. Even if the agent pays a fair price, the principal may cancel the sale and recover the property or obtain any profits made by the agent in any resale of the property to an innocent purchaser.

Because the agent cannot deal with the principal as an adverse party, the agent also cannot represent an adverse party in a transaction with the principal unless both parties are fully informed and agree to the arrangement. Such dual agencies, involving the agent representing two adverse parties, have a great potential for fraud. Any transaction negotiated by a double agent is voidable at the option of the party having no knowledge of the agency.

The agent's duty of loyalty also extends to the use of confidential information, such as the principal's trade secrets and customer lists. The agent may not use or communicate information confidentially given to him or her by the principal.

The following case illustrates the application of an agent's fiduciary duty of loyalty to the principal.

Desfosses v. Notis

Supreme Court of Maine
333 A.2d 83 (1975)

FACTS   Desfosses owned and operated a corporation engaged in selling mobile homes and developing mobile home parks. He employed Notis, a licensed real estate broker, to acquire land for development as mobile home parks. Desfosses requested Notis to negotiate the purchase of a tract of land suitable for the company to develop as a mobile home park. When Notis related that the land was available, Desfosses directed Notis to purchase the land and then to convey the land to Desfosses. While Notis was negotiating the purchase of the land, he repeatedly told Desfosses that the land would cost $32,400, although he knew the land could be bought for $15,474.62. Notis made these false statements to induce Desfosses to deliver to him the sum of $32,400. Relying on Notis's statements, Desfosses delivered $32,400 to Notis, intending to deliver only the amount necessary to make the purchase. Using Desfosses's money, Notis paid the owner of the land $15,474.62, took title in his own name, and promptly conveyed the land to Desfosses. Notis kept the balance of the $32,400. Desfosses later learned of Notis's actions and brought suit to recover his money. He also refused to pay Notis any commission for his efforts. Notis claimed that Desfosses was only entitled to a cancellation of the resale contract, thereby entitling Notis to the return of the land in exchange for the money.

Has Notis breached his fiduciary duty to Desfosses, and if so, what are the consequences?   ISSUE

Yes. Notis violated his duty of loyalty when he failed to deal fairly with his principal,   DECISION
Desfosses. The secret profits Notis made belong to Desfosses. The Supreme Court of Maine decided that cancellation of the contract was not required. Desfosses was entitled to retain the benefit of his bargain (the land) and also was entitled to his money back.

Agent's Duty to Obey

Because the principal's control over the agent's activity is an important element of the agency relation, the agent must obey any reasonable instruction from the principal regarding the agent's performance. The "reasonableness" of an instruction depends on ethical and legal considerations. For example, a sales agent need not obey an order to misrepresent the quality of merchandise, for such an order is illegal and unethical.

If the principal issues an ambiguous instruction, the agent should seek clarification while giving it a reasonable interpretation consistent with trade practice and prior dealings. Reasonable instructions that are clear, precise, and imperative must be strictly followed, or the agent is liable for any losses resulting from the obedience. Any violation of such a clear directive is not excused by custom or usage in the business. Furthermore, the agent's motives are immaterial to his or her liability. The fact that the agent disobeys in good faith, intending to benefit the principal, does not relieve the agent of liability for any resulting loss. But the agent may disobey instructions to respond to an emergency that the agent did not create, if communication with the principal is impractical.

Agent's Duty to Use Skill and Care

The agent must use whatever skill and care is required to perform the principal's business. If the agent fails to exercise reasonable skill and care, the principal may recover for any loss or damage resulting from the agent's negligence. The principal is permitted to rely on the agent to properly perform the assigned responsibilities, and the agent is in the better position to know whether he or she possesses the qualifications to perform the job. The duty of skill and care arises from what is commonly accepted as the customs and experience in everyday living. If someone hires another to perform a job, he or she usually expects that the job will be done skillfully and carefully. Thus the agent should possess and exercise the necessary skill and care to perform the principal's business. For example, an insurance broker should know something of the trade, the form of policy, the nature of the risk, the solvency of the underwriter, and all general matters affecting the contract, or the broker is liable for negligently failing to provide adequate insurance protection for the insured.

The agent is only required to exercise reasonable and ordinary skill and care in the performance of the agency objectives. He or she is held to a standard of skill and care ordinarily possessed by persons engaged in the same business or occupation. However, if the agent claims certain special skills, he or she is held to a higher standard of care that is commensurate with the claimed specialization.

The following case shows the duty of diligence in a contemporary setting.

Bucholtz v. Sirotkin Travel Limited

District Court, Nassau County, New York
343 N.Y.S.2d 438 (1973)

FACTS   Bucholtz engaged Sirotkin Travel to arrange a trip to Las Vegas. The agency made hotel reservations and arranged flights. However, these were not confirmed. The flight was changed and the reservation unavailable. Bucholtz was forced to stay in a motel one half mile out of town. This resulted in both additional expense and inconvenience. Bucholtz sued the travel agency for $106 for damages resulting from his inconvenience and discomfort.

ISSUE   Does the travel agency owe a duty to the traveler to verify or confirm the plane and hotel reservations such that the agency is liable in negligence for its failure to exercise reasonable care in making the reservations?

DECISION   Yes. The travel agent deals directly with the traveler, is paid by the traveler, and must be charged with the duty of exercising reasonable care in securing appropriate reservations. Where, as here, the agent is selected because he is supposed to have some special fitness for the performance of the duties to be undertaken, the traveler is entitled to rely on the judgment and discretion of that agent as well as his honesty and financial responsibility.

Agent's Duty to Inform and Account

It makes sense that parties in agency relations should communicate with each other. Therefore, a duty is imposed on the agent to communicate to the principal on anything affecting the principal's interests. The agent must make a reasonable attempt to inform the principal of matters relating to any agency transaction that the agent should realize the principal would want to know about. For example, a real estate agent who is authorized to sell the principal's property at a specified price and on specified terms should inform the principal if he or she knows of someone who will pay a higher price or agree to better terms. Furthermore, the agent should disclose any information that disqualifies the agent from effectively promoting the principal's interests. If the agent is unable to undertake the principal's interests, he or she must inform the principal. Even if the agent is merely ill for a day, the agent's duty to inform requires the agent to notify the principal of the fact so that the principal may make other arrangements.

It follows that if the agent must communicate with the principal, he or she also must keep and render an account of money or other property which the agent receives. This account includes anything received from the principal as well as anything obtained from third persons for the principal. The agent is liable to the principal if he or she does not properly account for all funds coming into the agent's possession during the agency relation. Although it is ordinarily the principal's duty to keep his or her own accounts, the duty shifts to the agent if the agent is entrusted with funds or property or is required to make collections and expenditures. The manner of accounting need not be formal or meet technical accounting requirements. The method of bookkeeping depends on what is normally done in the business or is accepted by the principal.

Implicit in the duty to account is the agent's duty not to mix the principal's money or property with his or her own. The reason for this requirement is to make any accounting more accurate. Thus the agent may not put the principal's money in his or her own bank account or in a joint account unless the principal agrees to such an arrangement. To allow otherwise would make it difficult to determine whether it was the principal's or the agent's money that was deposited.

Consider the following case.

McKeehan v. Wittels

Missouri Court of Appeals
508 S.W.2d 277 (1974)

McKeehan, looking for investment opportunities, dealt directly with Malcolm and Jacob Wittels of Wittels Investment Company and was assured by them that they would take care of her investments. In response to the Wittels's urging, McKeehan entrusted $28,813 to them. The Wittelses invested this money in various types of investment securities. After the investments matured, McKeehan repeatedly demanded that her funds be returned. The Wittelses, who knew of McKeehan's instructions, disregarded them. The Wittelses renewed the investments without her consent and against her expressed wishes. Additionally, tax liens existed on all properties in the investments, and there was strong evidence that the Wittelses were aware of these tax liens. McKeehan sued the Wittels for damages alleging that they breached their duty to her.

FACTS

Did the Wittelses breach their duty to McKeehan?

ISSUE

DECISION   Yes. The failure to follow McKeehan's instructions and the nondisclosure of material facts regarding her investments are sufficient to constitute a breach of the Wittelses' duty to McKeehan. An agent cannot ignore the directions by the principal about how the business put into the agent's hands shall be transacted. Also an agent is obligated to disclose fully all material facts to the principal, to strictly avoid misrepresentation, and in all respects to act with the utmost good faith.

SUMMARY

Agency is the legal relationship created when two people agree that one of them, the agent, is to represent the other, the principal, subject to the principal's right to control the agent's conduct concerning the delegated activity. Agents are classified as either general or special. Principals are either disclosed or undisclosed.

What distinguishes agency from other, similar relations is the power of control retained by the principal over the agent's activities. Because they render services while pursuing independent occupations, independent contractors usually are not agents. Because independent contractors usually are not agents, their employers are not liable to the contractor's creditors nor to persons harmed by the contractor's negligence.

Anyone having capacity to consent can become a principal or an agent. A principal only has capacity to appoint an agent to perform activities that the principal may lawfully perform. A statute, such as a licensing statute, may restrict a person's capacity to be an agent.

Generally, no formalities are required to create an agency. Written authorization, sometimes called a power of attorney, is necessary in a few situations.

An agent is entitled to compensation for his or her services. The agent's right to compensation is usually provided by contract. In the absence of an agreement, there is an implied obligation on a principal to pay for services when the services are customarily paid for. The principal is obligated to keep and render accounts of the compensation owed the agent, and the principal is obligated to assist and cooperate with the agent and to not prevent the agent's performance. The principal also must reimburse the agent's authorized expenses.

The agent is under a fiduciary duty of loyalty to the principal. The agent must forward all profits from the agency to the principal. The agent cannot take advantage of an opportunity belonging to the principal. The agent cannot deal with the principal as an adverse party, nor can the agent represent an adverse party to the principal without the principal's consent. The agent is under a duty to obey any reasonable instruction given to the agent by the principal. The agent must use reasonable skill and care when performing the principal's business. Failure to use skill and care may result in the agent becoming liable to the principal for the resulting injury.

The agent is under a duty to inform the principal about all matters concerning the agency. The agent must keep and render account of money or other property which the agent receives. The agent also must not mix the principal's money or property with his or her own.

1. What is an agency relationship? Who is the principal and who is the agent?

2. What distinguishes an agent from an independent contractor?

3. Why is an agency relationship a fiduciary relationship?

4. What duties does a principal owe an agent? What duties does an agent owe a principal?

5. Porter had been employed by the Brinn & Jensen Company for many years as a traveling salesman and had been assigned to cover a definite territory. Porter used his own automobile as a means of transportation and covered his territory once every five weeks. He worked on commissions but had a drawing account with the company, which was treated as an advance on commissions earned. He also made collections for the company and performed other services when so directed by the home office. The company could discharge Porter any time it became dissatisfied with the manner in which he was doing his work. The company required Porter to furnish an automobile to be used in covering his territory, and he would not have been retained if he could not have provided one. It was generally left to Porter to determine the route to be used in covering his territory, but the company retained the right to direct him to go within the territory if it desired to do so. Porter was required to make personal calls on customers and send in his orders daily. The company instructed him about the merchandise to be pushed. He was required to devote all of his time to company business. While driving on company business, Porter was killed when his automobile crashed into another automobile driven by Peterson, who was seriously injured. At the time of the accident, Porter had with him a sample case, forms, catalogues, and a number of orders signed by customers. Peterson sued the company, claiming that Porter was its agent. The company claimed that it had no liability, because it did not control the physical movements of the automobile being driven by Porter. Who is right?

6. Arthur Murray, Incorporated, licenses people to operate dancing studios using its registered trade name and its method of dancing. Burkin, Inc., obtained such a license for a dancing school in San Diego. The agreement between Arthur Murray and Burkin provided that Arthur Murray would:

1 □ fix minimum tuition rates

2 □ designate the school's location and layout

3 □ make pupil refunds and charge the amounts to Burkin and

4 □ collect 5 percent of the school's weekly gross receipts to be used to pay any suits against Arthur Murray's.

The agreement also provided that Burkin would:

1 □ obey Arthur Murray's rules regarding the qualifications and conduct of instructors and discharge any employee found unacceptable to Arthur Murray

2 □ submit advertising for Arthur Murray's approval

3 □ maintain and manage the school according to Arthur Murray's general policies and

4 □ submit weekly financial records to Arthur Murray.

Gertrude Nichols entered into several contracts with the San Diego school and made prepayments for lessons that were never furnished because Burkin discontinued its operations. Nichols brought suit against Arthur Murray, Inc., claiming that the San Diego school was its agent. Is she right?

7. Penelope had inspected equipment to be sold at an auction. She planned to go to the auction and try to buy three pieces of equipment. On the day of the auction, her friend Andrew gratuitously offered to go to the auction for Penelope and to bid on the equipment for her. Penelope authorized Andrew to bid up to $10,000 for each of the three pieces she wanted. Andrew acquired the first piece for Penelope for $9,000. He bid on the second piece on his own behalf and bought it for $9,500. Andrew left the auction before the third piece was offered. It was sold for $7,000. Is Andrew the agent of Penelope? Explain. If so, has Andrew violated any of the duties that an agent owes a principal? Explain.

8. Owner orally authorized Agent to sell his house. Agent completed a sale of the house to Buyer. When Buyer attempted to enforce the contract against Owner, Buyer was told that the contract was not enforceable because Owner's agency relation with Agent was not in writing. Must Owner have given Agent written authorization?

9. Owner listed his house with Penelope, a real estate broker, granting Penelope an exclusive right to sell Owner's house. Penelope entered negotiations with Buyer, who seemed interested in purchasing the property. Buyer found the price agreeable. But he insisted on including a clause in the sales contract giving him the right to cancel the contract if he could not get a loan to finance his purchase. At the closing, Buyer exercised his right to cancel, giving as his reason the inability to procure a loan. Penelope turned to Owner and claimed that she was entitled to her commission even though the sale did not go through. Must Owner pay Penelope a commission?

10. Julius and Olga Sylvester owned an unimproved piece of land near King of Prussia, Pennsylvania. They were approached by Beck, a real estate broker, who asked if they were willing to sell their land, stating that an oil company was interested in buying, renting, or leasing the property. The Sylvesters said that they were only interested in selling, and they authorized Beck to sell the property for $15,000. Several weeks later, Beck phoned the Sylvesters and offered to buy the property for himself for $14,000. Olga asked, "What happened to the oil company?" and Beck responded, "They are not interested. You want too much money for it." The Sylvesters sold the property to Beck. A month later, Beck sold the property to Epstein for $25,000. When the Sylvesters learned that Beck had realized a huge profit in a quick resale of the property, they sued Beck, claiming that he owed them the $9,000 profit. Does Beck owe the Sylvesters the money?

11. Peter authorized Arnon, a grain broker, to buy for Peter at the market 20,000 bushels of wheat. Arnon had in storage at the time 5,000 bushels belonging to John, who had authorized Arnon to sell for him. Arnon also had 15,000 bushels which she owned. Arnon transferred these 20,000 bushels to Peter's name and charged Peter the current market price. Shortly thereafter and before Peter had used or sold the wheat, the market price declined sharply. Peter refused to pay for the wheat and tried to cancel the contract. Can Peter do this? Explain.

12. The Hagertys decided to spend a week in Hawaii. They went to the Ace Travel Agency, secured reservations at the Ritz Hotel, and were issued round trip tickets on Kamikaze Airline to and from Hawaii. When they arrived at the airport on the date of departure, they found that an airline employee had failed to record their reservation properly. They could not be accommodated on the assigned flight. The Hagertys managed to secure a reservation on a flight which left several hours later. They arrived later that day at the Ritz Hotel and checked in. Two days before their scheduled checkout date, the Hagertys were asked by the management to leave the hotel to make room for a convention checking in that day. When they refused to comply with the request, the hotel authorized its employees to enter their room and remove their belongings. When Mr. Hagerty resisted eviction, he was knocked to the floor and suffered a broken arm. The Hagertys left the hotel, spent the remaining two days of their vacation at a nearby motel, and then returned home on the assigned flight. Worn and harassed by the preceding events, the Hagertys sued the Ace Travel Agency for medical expenses incurred by Mr. Hagerty, for mental anguish, and for the additional expenses resulting from these occurrences. The Hagertys claim that Ace breached its fiduciary duties as the Hagertys' agent. Ace claims that it was not the Hagertys' agent. Who is right?

CHAPTER 27

The Effect of Agency Relations

CHAPTER OBJECTIVES

After reading this chapter, you should be able to:

1. Distinguish among the express, implied, and apparent authority of an agent.

2. State how a principal may ratify the unauthorized acts of an agent.

3. Explain the effect of an agent's knowledge on the liability of the principal.

4. Compare the rules for agents' liability when the existence of the agency relationship is disclosed to the third party with those when the existence of the agency relationship is undisclosed.

5. Explain the rules for an agent's liability in unauthorized transactions.

6. Describe the legal principle making a principal liable for the torts of its agent.

7. Describe the agent's liability to third parties in torts.

8. State the rules for ending an agency.

9. State the rules for notifying certain third parties if an agency relationship ends.

10. Identify irrevocable agency.

Chapter 26 examined the nature of the principal–agent relation by focusing on how the two parties create their relation and the rights and duties they owe each other. But there is more to the agency relation. The principal hires the agent to interact with others as the principal's representative. This interaction is the essence of the agency. It is the reason the agent is hired. The agent interacts with others in two ways:

1. by making contracts for the principal with third persons and

2. by committing torts during the agent's employment that harm others.

When the agent acts in these ways, the legal picture adds a third dimension. The legal consequences of this interaction attach not only to the principal and the agent, but to the third person, affecting the rights and duties of each person toward the others. This chapter explores how these legal consequences affect all three individuals. The chapter also examines the ending of the agency relation and how it affects the rights of the parties.

CONTRACTUAL DEALINGS:
PRINCIPAL AND THIRD PARTIES

The contracts made by an authorized agent for a principal are as binding on the principal as they would have been had the principal entered into them in person.

An agent's authority is conferred by various methods. The principal may expressly authorize the agent's action. The principal may indicate to the agent by conduct that the agent has authority to undertake certain transactions. Authority is established also if others can reasonably infer from the principal's conduct that the principal authorizes the agent's activity. Even when the principal does not authorize someone to act as an agent, a third party may establish authority if the principal later authorizes transactions done for him or her.

Actual Authority

Actual authority is the power of an agent to affect the principal's legal relations by acts done according to the principal's show of consent to the agent. The principal may consent by any means that causes the agent to understand what the principal wants the agent to do. If the agent's actual authority is stated in words, it is referred to as *express* authority. If the agent's actual authority is communicated by the principal's conduct toward the agent, it is called *implied* authority. The legal effect of the two is the same: the agent is empowered to change the principal's legal relations with third persons. For example, if a businessperson tells a secretary to accept customer payments, the secretary has express authority to collect payments as instructed. If the secretary also buys office supplies and the principal pays without objection, the secretary or the seller may reasonably infer that the principal authorizes continued

FIGURE 27-1   Scope of Authority

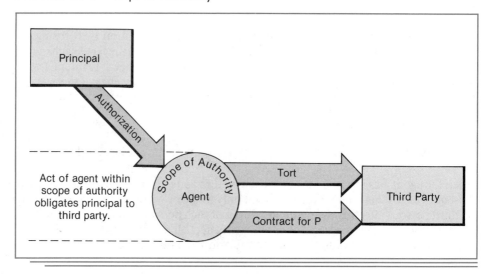

purchases of office supplies. In both situations, the principal is obligated to others by the secretary's actions.

Express Authority   The clearest example of express authority is the **power of attorney.** A power of attorney is a formal written instrument conferring authority upon an agent. Powers of attorney often are used because a third person entering into a specific, major transaction with an agent may require evidence of the agent's authority. In these situations, the authority may be set forth in a form that is familiar and convenient to people in the business. The acts authorized usually require the execution of specifically described documents. For example, banks and other professional lenders that deal regularly with borrowers' agents have standard forms for the purpose of assuring themselves of the authority of agents to borrow on their principals' credit. Because of absence, sickness, age, or lack of interest, people widely delegate the management of their affairs to others. Interpretation of the activities included in these powers often is a problem.

Informal written expressions of authority often are included in standard form contracts that the agent negotiates with third persons. Known as merger, integration, or **exculpatory clauses,** these statements serve explicitly to limit an agent's authority to make only those agreements contained in the standard form contract. A typical merger clause is:

> It is hereby further agreed that there are no prior writings, verbal negotiations, understandings, representations or agreements between the parties not herein expressed, and no agent of Seller is authorized to make or enter into on Seller's behalf any writings, verbal negotiations, understandings, representations or agreements not here expressed.

Unauthorized transactions made by the agent with a third person who has notice of this limitation on the agent's authority are not binding on the principal. Obligations undertaken in violation of this express limitation of authority are the agent's.

The following case illustrates the rules governing limitations on an agent's authority.

Power of attorney written authorization creating an agency

Exculpatory clause a provision that relieves or limits a party's liability for nonperformance of a contract

---

Dembrowski v. Central Construction Company

Supreme Court of Nebraska
185 N.W.2d 461 (1971)

Central Construction Company was in the home improvement business. It sold materials and furnished labor for that purpose. It also employed a number of salesmen on a commission basis. One of Central's salesmen called on Dembrowski and induced him and his wife to sign a contract for the purchase and installation of new siding, aluminum doors, and windows on their home. The contract provided:

FACTS

> There are no representations, guarantees, or warranties except such as may herein be incorporated. Contractor does not make, and no agent of Contractor is authorized to make, any agreement with Owner(s) either concerning the use of the Owner(s) premises as a "model home" or concerning any payments, credits or commissions to be received by Owner(s) for referrals of prospective customers.

The Dembrowskis were aware of this provision, objected to it to the agent, but nevertheless executed the contract in reliance upon the agent's representations that they would not have to pay anything on the contract because their house was to be used as a model home, and a percentage of other sales made on the strength of it would be credited to them in sufficient amounts to pay the contract in full. The agent told them that the contract provision mentioned did not apply to them and would be disregarded. The Central Construction Company had no knowledge of the fraudulent conduct of its agent until after the materials and labor called for in the contract had been furnished by the company.

ISSUE Is Central Construction Company entitled to the contract price for the work done to the Dembrowskis' home?

DECISION Yes. The court decided that the Dembrowskis must pay for the work. A principal may limit the authority of its agent, and if such limitations have been brought to the attention of the party with whom the agent is dealing, the power to bind the principal is defined by the limitation of authority. Clearly, a limitation by the principal of the agent's authority, communicated to a third party, is effective to excuse the principal from liability to that third party for acts by the agent in excess of the limit. A person dealing with an agent must use reasonable diligence and prudence to learn whether the agent is acting within the scope of his or her powers. The principal is not bound if the third person dealing with the agent knows or should know the limitations placed by the principal on the agent's authority and that the agent is exceeding it.

Implied Authority In most agency relations, it is impossible to express every detail of the agent's authority. For example, if a storeowner hires someone to manage the business, it is impossible to describe every single management function. For the sake of flexibility, the agent is allowed additional implied authority to perform activities that he or she or a third party might reasonably infer are incidental or necessary to carry out the principal's instructions.

Several factors determine whether implied authority exists. The circumstances generally considered by courts are customary trade usages, the principal's practices with other agents in similar situations, and earlier experiences of the principal and the particular agent. For example, a question of whether a particular salesperson has the implied authority to extend warranties on merchandise sold to third persons may be answered by examining what similar salespeople in the trade usually do, what other salespeople employed by the principal usually do, and what the principal has permitted that particular salesperson to do in the past.

Although the principal implicitly authorizes the agent to do whatever is ordinarily required to accomplish the job, sometimes as the job progresses the agent confronts an emergency. In such an emergency, the agent can reasonably infer that the principal consents to the agent's undertaking whatever is required to protect the principal's interests. Authorization of the agent's activity is implied in these situations. This implied authority exists only when the threat to the principal's business is sudden and unexpected and when contact with the principal or superior officer is impractical. It extends only to activities that the emergency makes necessary.

FIGURE 27-2 Scope of Authority

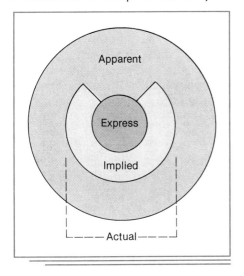

Apparent Authority

Authority also exists if the principal's conduct causes third persons reasonably to believe that the agent is authorized. This rule permits third parties to rely upon the principal's manifestation in dealing with an agent. This type of authority is called *apparent authority.* Its effect on the principal's liability to third persons is the same as actual authority, because both types empower the agent to affect the principal's legal relations with others. The adjectives "actual" and "apparent" denote only the viewpoints used in interpreting the principal's conduct. Actual authority is determined from the agent's viewpoint. Apparent authority is determined from the third person's viewpoint.

The agent's apparent authority may arise in various ways. It may result from the principal's statement to a third person or from the principal's allowance of the agent's activities. It may be established from the principal's permission to the agent to do something under circumstances creating a reputation of authority in the area in which the agent acts. Earlier dealings between the agent and third persons might lead a third person reasonably to infer that the agent is authorized. For example, a customer might reasonably believe that a salesperson in a department store is authorized to transact business in an adjacent department. But apparent authority cannot be established by the agent's statements alone. If it could, anyone might confer upon himself or herself authority to obligate others simply by acting and talking like an agent.

Ratification of Unauthorized Activity

Authorization of the agent need not occur before the agent transacts the principal's business. If the principal earlier has not authorized someone to act as an agent, the principal may supply the authority later by ratifying the transaction. As we discussed in Chapter 9, ratification is the later approval by the principal of an earlier, unauthorized act by someone claiming to act as an agent. Ratification may occur when the agent exceeds his or her original authority and enters into unauthorized transactions or when a stranger supposedly acts as another's agent. The difference between the principal's liability created by ratification rather than by earlier authorization is the timing of the principal's consent to be bound. In actual or apparent authority, the principal shows consent before the agent conducts any business. In ratification, the principal's consent comes after the business is conducted.

Because ratification treats the transaction as if it had been originally authorized, only those acts that could have been authorized originally may later be ratified. For this reason, the ratifier must have been competent to be a principal at the time the transaction took place. Only those acts undertaken for the principal may be ratified. No ratification can occur for acts done by someone acting on his or her own.

Any act of a principal that shows complete, knowledgeable affirmation of the agent's acts can constitute a ratification. Any acts, words, or conduct reasonably indicating an intent to ratify may constitute a ratification. For example, a principal who benefits by an agent's unauthorized bargain or sues to enforce a contract made by a false agent may constitute a ratification. But the principal's affirmation must be complete. He or she cannot affirm part of a transaction but disaffirm the rest.

Effect of Agent's Knowledge

An important consequence of the agency relation is that the principal is charged with knowing everything about the agency that the agent knows. The agent must communicate to the principal information about agency matters. Presumably the agent tells the principal everything relating to the agent's performance. Whether this actually is done is unimportant, because the reason for imputing the agent's knowledge to the principal is to protect innocent third persons. When determining the principal's liability to innocent third persons, the principal and not the third person bears the risk of the agent's failure to inform.

Notification is the act of informing an agent, which has the same legal effect as if the principal had received it. For example, filing a claim with an insurance company's claims agent is a form of notification to the company. To be effective, notification must be made to an agent authorized to receive it. Frequently the terms of a contract specify the person authorized to receive notice, but the agent also may be implicitly or apparently authorized to receive notification. Notice to an agent not authorized to receive it is not effective notification to the principal unless the principal later ratifies its receipt.

A principal is not assumed to know what an agent knows when the agent and a third party conspire to cheat or defraud the principal or when the agent otherwise acts against the principal's interests. In these situations, the principal's knowledge is not assured because it cannot be presumed that the agent communicates the information to the principal. For example, an insurance company may rescind an insurance contract when there is collusion between the insured and the company's agent to defraud the company.

The following case illustrates the exception to the general rule that an agent's knowledge is binding upon the principal.

Maryland Casualty Company v. Tulsa Industrial Loan and Investment Company

U.S. Court of Appeals for the Tenth Circuit
83 F.2d 14 (1936)

The directors of the Tulsa Industrial Loan and Investment Company instructed the **FACTS**
secretary-treasurer to prepare the documents necessary to indemnify the company for
losses that might be caused by the employees' embezzlement. The secretary-treasurer
did so, signing the application for the company. The application included a statement
that to the best of the company's knowledge and belief, all employees who would be
covered by the agreement had always performed their duties faithfully and that the
company knew of no acts to the contrary. Before the application was signed, the
secretary-treasurer, in collusion with other agents, had embezzled substantial amounts
from the company. Upon discovering this, the company filed a claim to collect under its
indemnification policy. The insurer refused payment, stating that the company misrepresented facts in its application. The insurer argued that because the secretary-treasurer
was the company's agent and he knew of the embezzlement, his knowledge was
imputed to the company, making its statement in the application a knowing misrepresentation.

Is the company entitled to payment? **ISSUE**

Yes. The company is entitled to payment. The court recognized that the general rule **DECISION**
that an agent's knowledge is imputed to the principal is subject to an exception when
the agent acts against the principal's interest. The reason for this exception is that there
Is no reason to expect the agent to inform the principal of such activities.

CONTRACTUAL DEALINGS:
AGENTS AND THIRD PARTIES

Contractual liability depends on whether a person is a party to the contract.
Generally, an agent who negotiates an authorized contract for a principal is not a
party to the agreement and therefore is neither liable on the contract nor able to
enforce it against the third person. The agent may agree to become a party, but in
most situations the agent acts only for the principal. But even if not a party to the
agreement, an agent is responsible for unauthorized dealings, based upon an implied
warranty of authorization to act for the principal.

Undisclosed Agency

When the agent acts for an undisclosed principal, the third person has no notice of
the agency relation or the principal's identity. From the third person's viewpoint, the
person negotiating the contract is the party to the contract. For this reason, an agent

purporting to act alone, but in fact acting for an undisclosed principal, becomes a party to the contract, along with the principal. However, while outwardly appearing to be a party, in reality the agent is still acting for another. This relationship transforms the agent into a peculiar form of contracting party with special rights and duties. For example, if the agent enforces the contract against the third person, the principal is entitled to any proceeds or performance, because that is what the principal and agent originally agreed. Once the undisclosed principal's identity is revealed, the agent may force the third person to choose which party is responsible for performance. If the agent is forced to perform, he or she is entitled to reimbursement from the principal.

Disclosed Agency

The agent who contracts in the name of a disclosed principal does not become a party to the contract unless he or she personally agrees to do so. The principal and third person are directly liable to each other, and the agent is not involved. An agent seeking to avoid personal liability under a contract must fully disclose the principal's identity.

The agent for a disclosed principal must exercise care when a negotiated agreement is put in writing. When the names of both the principal and the agent appear on the written contract, to avoid liability the agent should make certain that his or her signature indicates the agency relation and identifies the principal. For example, "Peter Principal by Arthur Adams, his agent" is sufficient. Extrinsic (parol) evidence may be used to explain an ambiguous signature. Currently the courts do not uniformly interpret a signature in the form of "Arthur Adams, agent." The trend is to treat the signature as sufficiently ambiguous to permit parol evidence to explain whether the agent was intended to be a party. However, some states still prohibit any explanation and hold the signer personally liable.

The following case illustrates the need for agents to disclose their agency relationship to avoid liability on the contracts that they negotiate.

--- *Bio-Chem Medical Laboratories, Incorporated* v. *Harvey* ---

Louisiana Court of Appeals
310 S.2d 173 (1973)

FACTS   From May 17, 1973, to June 1973, Harvey was employed by the Magnolia Health Center as a laboratory technician. While at Magnolia, Harvey ordered laboratory testing services from Bio-Chem Medical Laboratories. Harvey left Magnolia on June 13, 1973, to assume an administrative position with another clinic. Later that month, he received a bill from Bio-Chem for the testing services he ordered while at Magnolia. Harvey claimed that he contracted for these services in a representative capacity for his employer and therefore was not obligated to pay the bill.

ISSUE   Is Harvey liable as a party to the contract, or did sufficient disclosure of his agency relation occur to protect him from liability on the contract?

The court awarded judgment against Harvey, holding him personally liable to pay Bio-Chem for the laboratory testing services. A person contracting for services in a representative capacity must disclose that fact to avoid personal liability under the contract. But this disclosure is unnecessary if the circumstances surrounding the contract reasonably informed the creditor that he or she was dealing with the person in a representative capacity. The court stated:

> In the present case, Harvey ordered the testing and failed to disclose he was merely an employee of the contracting party. For all Bio-Chem knew at the time the services were ordered, Harvey could have operated a sole proprietorship under the trade name of Magnolia Health Center. Furthermore, the record does not divulge any circumstances to indicate Bio-Chem would be unreasonable in so believing. We therefore conclude from the record Harvey was the contracting party and became personally liable for the cost of the services. Perhaps his employer, Magnolia, received the benefits of the services and is also liable for the charges, but this does not affect a creditor's right to recover from the agent of the undisclosed principal.

Agent's Warranty Liability

The agent for a disclosed principal may be liable to a third person even without becoming a party to the contract. If the agent purports to act with authority but actually exceeds this authorization, the principal is not bound on the transaction unless it is ratified. However, the agent is not a party to the contract because he or she purported to contract for someone else. While not liable as a contracting party, the agent is responsible for damages to the third person for breach of an implied warranty of authority. The agent is better able to know the limits of his or her authorization, and a third person is permitted reasonably to rely on the agent's representation of authority. The agent may avoid liability by informing the third person that he or she makes no warranty or is unsure of his or her authority.

AGENT'S TORTIOUS ACTIVITY

Besides performing contract negotiations, the agent's activity may involve a tort against others. This tort may be intentional or negligent. Either way, the innocent victim may recover damages for the resulting injury. Damages may be recovered from the agent, because every person is responsible for his or her own torts unless acting under the benefit of a legal immunity. The principal also is sometimes financially responsible for the agent's torts. The result is that the victim gets a windfall in the form of an additional responsible party.

Doctrine of *Respondeat Superior*

The principal is liable for any torts the agent commits during the agent's employment. As we discussed in Chapter 4, this concept, called the doctrine of *respondeat*

Vicarious liability indirect liability; used in agency law to describe a principal's tort liability to third parties

superior ("let the superior respond"), is imposed regardless of the principal's fault or blame. Strict liability is used in other areas of tort law where significant policy reasons require discarding traditional fault ideas in favor of no-fault liability. However, unlike other applications of strict liability, the principal's liability is based on some original fault of the agent. Thus the principal's responsibility is often referred to as **vicarious.**

Scope of Vicarious Liability

While *respondeat superior* is recognized because it is believed desirable and expedient to make the principal responsible for injuries inflicted by the agent, the principal is not made responsible for every tort the agent commits. Only when the agent commits a tort in the scope of employment is the principal liable under respondeat superior. The phrase "scope of employment" indicates the limits of the principal's liability for another's wrongdoing. The principal is liable only for accidents that are incidental to agency purposes. To make the principal responsible for acts that are in no way connected with agency goals would be unfair. The principal can be expected to bear only those costs that are closely associated with the business.

This limit on the principal's liability is easier to state than to apply. Determining if the agent is acting within the scope of employment often is difficult because the agent may temporarily be performing a personal errand or doing the principal's work while also serving a personal purpose, or the agent may be performing the principal's work in a forbidden manner. No precise formula exists to determine whether at a particular moment a particular agent is engaged in the principal's business. Whether the agent is inside or outside the scope of employment is often a matter of degree. Since the scope of employment test determines whether respondeat superior applies, as a guide courts often refer to the policy purposes that respondeat superior is supposed to serve.

The following case shows just how far an agent's scope of employment may extend.

Mauk v. Wright

U.S. District Court, M.D. Pennsylvania
367 F.Supp. 961 (1973)

FACTS   Denise Mauk was driving her 1969 Volkswagen shortly after midnight on July 31, 1971, when she was involved in an accident with a 1968 Lincoln Continental driven by Stephen Wright, a professional football player for the Washington Redskins. Wright had just picked up a girlfriend to give her a ride from her place of work to her home in Carlisle, Pennsylvania. Carlisle was the site of the Redskins' annual training camp, operated from July 10 until Labor Day.

Wright had spent the day before the accident in football training exercises. After dinner, the team viewed training films until mid-evening. Then they watched the annual College All Star football game, which began at 9:00 P.M. on July 20. That night the players were given a curfew of 30 minutes after the end of the televised game.

Wright watched the game at a local "beer joint," then went to a local cocktail lounge where his girlfriend worked. Several minutes after midnight, Wright and his girlfriend left the cocktail lounge and were shortly thereafter involved in the collision.

Mauk sued the Washington Redskins as well as Wright, seeking compensation for her injuries. The Washington Redskins argued that Wright's leisure-time activity fell outside the scope of his employment with the Redskins.

Are the Washington Redskins vicariously liable for Wright's tortious conduct?   ISSUE

Yes. The concept of respondeat superior requires that the employee's actions benefit   DECISION
the employer in his business relation. The court stated:

> This court finds the employment relationship between Wright and the Redskins to be so unique as to be without parallel. For the fixed period of the football training camp the players' time is accounted for seven days per week and all but two or three hours per day. During that limited "free time" the conduct, dress and associates of the players are circumscribed to the extent that a player can be barred from employment for improper conduct "regardless of whether it is directly connected with the team. . . . " There is sufficient evidence that the Redskins did "control" the players during free time.

Agent's Liability to Third Parties

In conducting the principal's business, the agent may, of course, harm third persons. The fact that the agent acts in a representative capacity does not make the agent immune from tort liability to third persons. Although the doctrine of respondeat superior extends the principal's liability by making the principal liable to third persons for the agent's torts, the doctrine does not affect the agent's liability. An agent's tort liability to another is the same as if the agent were not employed. The doctrine of respondeat superior does not repeal the law of torts, which makes individuals liable for the torts they commit. Respondeat superior makes both the principal and the agent liable to the victim. Thus the agent's tort liability differs from the agent's usual liability in contract. Because the agent for a disclosed principal usually is not a party to the agreement, the agent is not liable on the contract.

TERMINATION OF AGENCY

Probably a majority of agencies end when the objective for which the agency was created is met or when the time allotted for completing performance expires. But the agency can end in many other ways. It may be ended by events or conditions that destroy the agent's power to act for the principal. An example is the bankruptcy of the principal or of the agent, if the agent's financial status is important to the relationship. Another example is the destruction of the subject matter. In addition, because the agency relationship is consensual, either party may end the agency at any time by withdrawing his or her consent. The death or incompetence of the principal also ends the agency. But some states permit the relationship to continue after the principal's incompetence if a power of attorney expressly so provides or if the power of attorney is approved by the court.

The following case shows a court following the traditional rule with regard to the effect of the principal's death upon an agency relationship.

Charles Webster Real Estate v. Richard

California Court of Appeals
98 Cal. Rptr. 559 (1971)

FACTS   On May 26, 1967, Dr. Moore and his wife executed an exclusive listing contract with Warde D. Watson Realty Company, giving the broker an exclusive and irrevocable right to sell a 156-acre vineyard at a stated price of $234,000, for a term ending December 31, 1968. The agreed commission was to be 5 percent of the selling price, to be paid to the broker if the property were sold during the term of the listing by the broker, by the owner, or through any other source. The agreement also provided that if the owner withdrew the property from sale or if it were transferred or leased during the term, he would pay the specified commission to the broker.

On March 18, 1968, the listing was transferred from Warde D. Watson Realty to Webster Real Estate. Dr. Moore and his wife consented in writing to the transfer. The stated price was reduced to $187,200. Dr. Moore died on June 19, 1968, and the probate court appointed someone to administer the terms of Dr. Moore's will. In November 1968, this person sold the vineyard for $152,000, independently of any efforts by Webster Real Estate. Upon learning of the sale, Webster Real Estate demanded a 5 percent commission on the sale price of $152,000.

ISSUE   Was Webster Real Estate entitled to the commission?

DECISION   No. The appellate court decided that the exclusive right to sell terminated, by operation of law, upon Dr. Moore's death, with no contractual liability under the agreement falling to the administrator of the will. The death of the principal automatically terminated the agency relation as a matter of law.

Notifying Agent of Termination

Before an attempted termination is effective, the other party to the relation ordinarily must be notified of the termination. Thus, if the principal wishes to fire the agent, notice to the agent of the termination is required to revoke the agent's authority. Notification may be made in any way that tells the agent that his or her services are no longer desired. For example, if a realtor who has been hired by a homeowner to sell the owner's house hears that the owner has sold the house on his or her own, the realtor should realize the agency relation has been terminated. In this way, revocation of an agent's authority is like revocation of an offeror's contract offer. Actual notice is needed, but no particular form of notice is required. All that is needed is for the agent to realize that the agency is over.

Notifying Third Parties of Termination

Although revocation of the agent's real authority may be accomplished by notifying the agent, third parties also must be notified. If they do not know of the termination, they may think that the agency still exists and continue to transact business with the agent and hold the principal responsible. To revoke the agent's apparent authority, the principal must give suitable notice of the agent's termination to third parties.

What constitutes "suitable" notice depends on the circumstances. In some cases, no notice need be given at all. Generally, no notice need be given to third parties when the principal ends the employment of a special agent, such as a realtor, because this type of agency gives notice to third parties of its limited authority. People dealing with special agents should seek assurance of the agent's continued authority. Usually this may be done by seeking written authorization. Principals giving their agents written authority should invalidate the writing upon ending the agency.

When the principal ends a general agency, the principal generally must actually notify everyone whom the principal has dealt with through the agent. This may require consulting appropriate records for determining the agent's customers, although sometimes it is impossible to notify every person who has dealt with the agent. Others who might rely upon the agency relationship deserve to know that the agency has ended. In these situations, reasonable notice requires some compromise between the principal's duty to notify third parties and the difficulty of doing so. Suitable notice is any means reasonably designed to reach all third parties. Publication in a newspaper is a typical method. After publication, all persons except those who dealt with the agent on a regular basis are considered to have been notified of the termination.

A number of changes in circumstances automatically terminate the agent's authority. These include events such as the loss or destruction of the subject matter, the bankruptcy of the principal or, under some circumstances, the bankruptcy of the agent, and the death or incompetence of the principal. When the agency is terminated because of changes of this nature, generally neither the agent nor the third party need be notified of the termination. The courts entertain the fiction that these events are facts known to all. Because everybody in the world knows about the event all at once, its occurrence automatically revokes the agent's authority. This results in excusing the principal from liability to anyone and in making the agent liable to the third party for breach of the agent's warranty of authority.

A sizeable minority of states allows the agent's authority to continue after the principal dies or is declared incompetent until the agent or the third party learns of the death or incompetence. In these states, the agent can bind the estate of a dead or incompetent principal and can avoid any warranty liability. In the case of banks, the UCC provides that neither the death nor the incompetence of the customer revokes a bank's authority to accept, pay, or collect an item until the bank knows of the death or the judgment of incompetency and has a reasonable opportunity to act on it.

Irrevocable Agency

In some agency relations, the principal cannot revoke the agent's authority because the agent has an interest in continuing the relation. Courts sometimes say the agent possesses a property right in the relation or has an *agency coupled with an*

Irrevocable agency an agency which cannot be ended by the principal

interest. Actually, these are not true agencies. Usually an agency exists to allow the principal to accomplish something through the agent. An **irrevocable agency** is designed to allow the agent to do something for himself or herself.

An irrevocable agency is like a contract that must be specifically performed. Someone breaching a contract must perform the agreed undertaking if money is no substitute for performance. Similarly, if the agent must continue performing as an agent to protect an interest because money will not pay for the principal's breach of a promise not to revoke, the agency is irrevocable. An example of an irrevocable agency is when a debtor borrows money, giving property as collateral by granting the creditor authority to sell the property in event of default. The creditor is the debtor's agent. Money cannot substitute for continuing the agency relation because the agency has been created to protect the creditor against the debtor's financial default.

SUMMARY

An agent interacts with others by making contracts and, in some cases, committing torts. Both types of interaction affect the rights and liability of all three individuals: the principal, the agent, and the third party. Contracts made by an agent acting within his or her authority are binding on the principal. An agent's authority to bind the principal may be either actual or apparent.

Actual authority is authority that the principal has manifested to the agent. Actual authority may be either express, as in a power of attorney, or implied. Implied authority is authority granted to the agent either by some conduct of the principal or the circumstances of the agency relationship. An agent, by law, has implied authority to do what is reasonable and necessary to carry out the purposes of the agency. When the principal's conduct makes it appear to others that the agent has been authorized, the agent is considered to possess apparent authority to bind the principal to contracts. If the agent's conduct with third parties was not authorized, the principal may nevertheless be liable if the principal ratifies the agent's act. Any conduct by the principal indicating its complete, knowledgeable consent to the agent's conduct constitutes a ratification. Another way that an agent may impose liability on a principal is through the acquisition of knowledge. The principal is charged with the agent's knowledge.

Generally, an agent who negotiates an authorized contract for the principal is not a party to the contract. Whether an agent becomes a party to the contract depends on whether the existence of the agency relationship has been disclosed to the third party. If the agency is disclosed, the agent does not become liable unless the agent agrees to become a party to the contract. If the agency is undisclosed, the agent is liable. An agent may become liable to a third party even when the agency is disclosed, if the agent has exceeded his or her authority. The basis of the agent's liability is a warranty implied in law that the agent is authorized to make the contract for the principal. This is known as the agent's *warrant of authority.*

Under the doctrine of *respondeat superior,* a principal is liable to third parties for the torts of the agent that are committed while the agent is acting within the scope of his or her employment. But the doctrine does not relieve the agent of tort liability to the injured party.

Termination of an agency relationship occurs by events or conditions that destroy the agent's authority to act on behalf of the principal. For termination to be effective, notification must be given to the other party. Notification also must be given to third parties to terminate an agent's apparent authority. Adequate notification for third parties depends on the circumstances. Generally, actual notification must be given to third parties who have dealt with the agent. When an agency is "coupled with an interest," the principal cannot terminate the agent's authority, because the agent has an interest in continuing the relationship.

REVIEW PROBLEMS

1. How can an agent affect a principal's liability to third parties in contractual transactions?

2. How can an agent affect the principal's tort liability to third parties?

3. When does an agent who negotiates contracts on behalf of a principal become liable to the third party?

4. Why is notification important in ending agency relations?

5. Profit Corporation authorized Anderson, an employee, to find a buyer for used equipment that Profit intended to sell. Anderson believed that he had authority to contract for the sale of the equipment, but in fact he did not have such authority. Anderson found a prospective buyer, Caveat Corporation, and contracted with Caveat on behalf of Profit for the sale of the equipment to Caveat. In this contract, Anderson warranted that the equipment was fit for Caveat's particular needs. A responsible officer of Profit read the contract and directed that the equipment be shipped to Caveat. The equipment did not meet the special needs of Caveat, and Caveat refused to pay for it. Profit sued Caveat for the contract price. Who wins and why?

6. Mrs. Terry, dealing with Alice, a clerk in Peters Department Store, sees a cashmere sweater she likes, but she notices that it is slightly soiled. Alice, pushing for a sale, agrees to mark it down from $55 to $40, which she has no authority to do. Mrs. Terry consents, asks that the sweater be delivered, and promises to pay C.O.D. The manager of Peters sees the item being wrapped, corrects the bill, and sends it out to Mrs. Terry. On seeing her sweater accompanied by a bill for $55, Mrs. Terry calls and is told by Peters that Alice had no authority to knock down the price. Mrs. Terry is told that she should either pay the bill or return the sweater. Is Mrs. Terry entitled to the bargain? Why or why not?

7. Anderson and Boyd planned to form Capable Corporation to market a new product. Anderson told Portaro that he was president of Capable Corporation and contracted with Portaro to lease a retail store building. Anderson signed the lease as follows: "Capable Corporation by Anderson, President." When Capable Corporation was chartered (given legal existence), it did not ratify the contract. Portaro sued Capable Corporation, Anderson, and Boyd for breach of the contract to lease. What result and why?

8. Principal Corporation owns a chain of jewelry stores. All stores are owned completely by Principal, but each store is operated under the name of the person who is the store manager. Ambrose manages one of Principal's stores. Xenia sold merchandise to Ambrose for sale in the store. The merchandise was to be delivered within ten days, and payment was to be made 30 days after delivery. Ambrose signed the contract in his own name. Xenia did not know of the agency relationship between Principal and Ambrose. If Xenia fails to perform the contract, what are the rights and liabilities of Principal, Ambrose, and Xenia among themselves? Explain. If Xenia delivers the merchandise and is not paid within 30 days, what are the rights and liabilities of Principal, Ambrose, and Xenia among themselves? Explain.

9. Harold, the owner of Harold's Department Store, directed Julius, his stock-handler, to arrange a display containing lightbulbs. Julius arranged the display in a negligent manner. Penelope, a purchaser, was injured when the display fell over, causing the lightbulbs to explode. Penelope brought suit against both Harold and Julius for damages. Harold went bankrupt before the case went to court. Julius claimed that he should not be liable because he had acted under Harold's direction. Is Julius right? Explain.

10. Paul, the sole owner of a small manufacturing plant producing special equipment, employed Arnon as a traveling sales representative. On March 1, Paul's plant was damaged by fire. On March 2, Arnon contracted with Terry for the sale of certain equipment to be manufactured at Paul's plant. Neither Arnon nor Terry knew of the fire. On March 3, Paul died of a heart attack. On March 4, Arnon contracted with Frank for the sale of equipment to be manufactured at Paul's plant. Neither Arnon nor Frank knew of the fire or Paul's death. What are the rights and liabilities of Paul, Arnon, Terry, and Frank among themselves? Explain.

CHAPTER 28

Business Organizations

CHAPTER OBJECTIVES

After reading this chapter, you should be able to:

1. Define the three major forms of business organizations.

2. Explain the advantages and disadvantages of each as a method of doing business.

3. Identify the five special forms of doing business.

SINGLE PROPRIETORSHIP

Estate the interest that a person has in real or personal property

A single proprietorship is usually a small business in which one or two people operate and control the business. Usually the owner receives all the profits and assumes full liability for the debts of the business. The owner's personal property or **estate** (upon death) is liable for all the business debts.

PARTNERSHIP

Partnership an association of two or more people to carry on as co-owners of a business for profit

A **partnership** is a form of business organization in which two or more individuals agree, either implicitly or through an expressed agreement, to carry on a business as co-owners for the purpose of making profits. The partners are held personally liable. If there is not an expressed agreement between the partners, the Uniform Partnership Act (UPA), which has been adopted in 48 states, determines the responsibilities and liability of the partnership. A partner's share of the profit from the partnership is taxed as ordinary income both at the federal and state levels. The partnership's profit in contrast is taxed only at the state level in the state in which it is doing business. Law firms, accounting firms, and engineering firms take the form of partnerships.

Limited partnership an agreement between a general partner, who will conduct a business daily, and one or more special partners who will contribute capital but not participate in management, and not be held liable for the debts of the partnership

A **limited partnership** is an agreement between two or more people to operate a business. One partner is a general partner who actively runs the business and usually has contributed the largest amount of investment capital. Usually one or more limited partners play no active role in the management of the business and have contributed smaller amounts of investment capital. Limited partners usually are responsible for losses up to the amount of their capital contributions unless otherwise specified in the agreement. General partners are personally liable for all debts. Partnerships are discussed in greater detail in Chapters 29 through 31.

CORPORATION

Corporations are business entities created for the primary purpose of making profits. A **certificate of incorporation** must be registered with the Secretary of State of the state where the entity is to be incorporated. A corporation requires one or more officers, a board of directors, and shareholders. The shareholders invest money in a business and receive certificates of ownership in return. They elect boards of directors, who in turn elect officers or management to carry on the daily operation of the corporation. Shareholders usually are liable only to the extent of the money they have invested. The board of directors usually is not liable for the debts of the corporation unless they can be shown to have exercised bad business judgment based on a reasonably prudent person's standard for people in their positions. Shareholder derivative suits are more frequent today. These suits request courts to order directors or officers to return funds to the corporations from their personal assets because they have violated the business judgment rule. In Chapter 34 the business judgment rule is discussed in more detail.

Corporation business entity created for the primary purpose of making a profit

Certificate of incorporation an instrument by which a private corporation is formed; generally must be filed with the Secretary of State of the state a company is to be incorporated in

FACTORS TO BE WEIGHED IN SELECTING A FORM OF BUSINESS ORGANIZATION

Managerial Control

One of the major factors to be considered by an individual in choosing a form of business organization is how much control he or she wants over the business entity. For a family owned or closely held business that needs to raise capital to expand and compete, the decision about degree of control is an important one. If owners intend to incorporate and sell shares, they must weigh the degree of control over operations that they will give up and also the possibility of a takeover by shareholders (as discussed in Chapter 33).

Extent of Personal Liability

When choosing a form of business organization, the extent of personal liability for a sole proprietorship or a limited partnership is likely to be greater than that for a corporation. This matter of liability is significant, because even if an individual dies, his or her estate is liable for the debts of a partnership or single proprietorship. As discussed in Chapters 30 and 31, partners are liable personally for the debts of a partnership. Shareholders in a corporation are not.

Transferability of Interest

As discussed in Chapters 30 and 33, a partnership interest may be assigned (transferred to another), but assignees generally do not have the same partnership rights as parties to the partnership agreement. Shares in a corporation generally are transferable by shareholders.

Taxation

Distributed
actually paid out as
dividends

A single proprietorship pays federal and state taxes on the business profits as ordinary income. Each partner is taxed on his or her proportional share of the partnership's income, whether **distributed** or not. Only state taxes are paid by the partnership. A corporation pays state and federal tax on net profits. Shareholders also pay federal and state tax on dividends they receive.

Legal Status

In most states, a single proprietorship is not a separate legal entity divorced from its owners, and thus the business is dissolved when the owner dies. In the case of a corporation, even if the officers, directors, or a shareholder dies, the corporation continues in legal existence. See Table 28-1 for a comparison of business organizations according to the five factors discussed here.

ADVANTAGES AND DISADVANTAGES OF EACH MAJOR FORM OF BUSINESS ORGANIZATION

Single Proprietorship

Advantages   Managerial control in a single proprietorship is kept in the hands of a single owner, and all profits are retained by him or her. It is the easiest form of business to start, because it does not require a partnership agreement or incorporation papers. The sole proprietor pays only ordinary personal income taxes and does not pay corporate income taxes. As discussed in Chapter 33, corporate income taxes may be lower than those on a single proprietorship because of a lower rate of taxation and tax breaks that lower the taxable income of a corporation.

Disadvantages   A sole proprietorship has unlimited personal liability for all debts of the business. All of the owner's personal assets and those of the family are subject to contractual, tort, and other forms of liability. Sole proprietors can only expand operations with their personal wealth or with what can be borrowed.

Partnership

Advantages   An expressed or implied agreement between two or more individuals to carry on a business for the purpose of making a profit enables each to raise capital

TABLE 28-1 Comparison of Major Business Organizations

Characteristics	Single Proprietorship	Partnership	Corporation
Managerial control	Controlled by single individual only	Controlled by partners each with equal vote, unless partnership agreement directs otherwise	Controlled by shareholders, who elect directors, who appoint managers
Extent of personal liability	Unlimited personal liability	Unlimited liability except in case of limited partnerships, where only general partners have unlimited liability	Limited liability of shareholders for debts of corporation as well as managers and directors, unless corporate veil is "pierced"
Transferability of interest	Interest can be sold or assigned at any time	Interest of partnership can be assigned but not partnership rights unless approved by partners	Shares of stock in a corporation can be transferred
Taxation	Owner's profits taxed as personal income tax	Partners pay pro rata share of income taxes on net profits of partnership, whether distributed or not. Does not pay federal income tax, but some states levy taxes	Corporation income tax paid at federal and state levels; dividends of shareholders taxed at federal and state levels
Legal status	Not a separate legal entity, terminated upon death of owner	Not a separate legal entity in most states, dissolved upon death of a partner unless partnership agreement states otherwise	A separate legal entity with perpetual existence in the event of death of a shareholder, officer, or director

more easily than one can do and to spread liability among a greater number of individuals. There are certain tax advantages for partnerships. Partners do not pay Social Security taxes but do pay a self-employment tax. In some states, the partnership's net profits are not subject to state income taxes, although each partner pays a pro rata share of income taxes on his or her share.

Disadvantages   A partnership is mainly disadvantaged by the fact that a creditor may hold each partner personally liable. Even if a partner has not personally signed a contract, he or she may be held liable because all partners in a partnership generally become legal agents of the partnership. Further, a partnership is dissolved when one of the partners dies unless the partnership agreement states otherwise. Managerial control and profits are spread among all the partners in proportion to their investment or according to the terms of the partnership agreement. Lawyers, doctors, engineers, and retail establishments that formerly chose the partnership form of doing business now are incorporating to obtain federal tax advantages (lower rate of taxation) and tax exempt pension and profit-sharing plans.

Corporation

Advantages   A corporation's major advantage is that it can raise capital and expand by selling shares (stocks). There is no personal liability for its shareholders. Its shares are easily transferable on the stock market if it is a publicly owned corporation (see Chapter 33). The corporation has a separate legal status divorced from its ownership, and so its owners, managers, and directors are protected from personal liability unless the corporate "veil is pierced." As noted in the case below (and in Chapter 34), a court may hold managers and officers personally liable if the corporate form is a fiction and is being used to avoid the law.

Gartner v. Snyder-Westerlind Enterprises

United States Court of Appeals, Second Cir.
607 F.2d 582 (724)

FACTS   Gartner sued Westerlind Enterprises for a breach of contract when it failed to deliver a home contracted for by a certain date. Enterprises was one of three corporations owned by Snyder. It had no capital, books, files, or office distinct from Snyder's. Gartner claimed that these facts showed that Enterprises was being used in a fraudulent manner by Snyder to get a higher price for houses sold.

ISSUE   Was the fact that Enterprises was undercapitalized grounds for piercing the corporate veil and holding Snyder personally liable?

DECISION   No. The appeals court disagreed with the lower court. It said that the court was wrong because Snyder's disregard of Enterprises, as one of three corporations he owns, does not prove that Snyder used Enterprises purely to conduct his own personal business. Though Enterprises was thinly capitalized, that alone was not sufficient ground under New York law for disregarding the corporate form.

Disadvantages   The corporate form of business organization involves a great deal of paperwork in the incorporation process. Double taxation is involved, because corporations pay a federal and state income tax on their profits, and shareholders pay the same on their dividends. Managerial control is lost when shareholders are widely scattered. Management and boards of directors are subject to state and federal securities regulation (Chapter 33) as well as other forms of regulation (Chapters 41, 42) if the corporation sells its shares on recognized stock exchanges.

SPECIALIZED FORMS OF BUSINESS ORGANIZATIONS

In addition to the three major forms of business organizations discussed thus far in this chapter, there has been a growth in several less-well-known ways of operating a business. For businesses involved in retailing of food or shoes (McDonald's or Athlete's Foot) franchising may be the best method of organization and marketing. For two corporations, such as General Motors and Toyota, a joint venture may be the best means of pooling resources to compete in the marketplace. The major goals of these special forms of business organization are to raise capital quickly, mass produce goods and services, and market them in the least costly manner. Although corporations and partnerships are founded on state law, most specialized forms of business are based on private contractual arrangements.

Joint Venture

A joint venture exists when individuals or corporations agree to pool their capital and labor for the purpose of producing and selling goods, securities, or commodities for a limited period of time. The joint venture agreement, unlike that of a partnership, generally is limited to a definite period or to a defined number of transactions. Major joint venture agreements like that of General Motors and Toyota spell out in considerable detail the rights and duties of each party, the nature of the decision-making process, and how labor relations will be carried on.

In some states, joint ventures may sue and be sued. In most states, the lack of a legal status means that both corporations and individuals involved in joint ventures may be sued as individuals.

Cooperative

A cooperative is a nonprofit business organization formed by individuals in a private agreement. Its aim is to market products at the best prices. The most common form of cooperative is a farmers' cooperative in which farmers agree to pool their crops to obtain the best market prices. Any profits made by the cooperative are returned to its members in the form of dividends. Unlike a corporation's shareholders, who receive dividends based on the amount of capital they have invested, dividends of a cooperative are paid out in proportion to the amount of business the members have conducted with the organization yearly.

Unincorporated cooperatives are generally treated as partnerships in most states.

TABLE 28-2   Specialized Forms of Business

Type	Characteristics
Joint Venture	A group of people or businesses that pool capital and labor
Cooperative	A nonprofit business created to market products
Syndicate	An investment group created for the purpose of financing a purchase
Joint Stock Company	A partnership in which partners agree to stock ownership in exchange for partnership liability
Franchising	A method of marketing goods in which the franchisee is given the right to use the franchisor's trademark or copyright

In contrast, an incorporated cooperative is governed by separate state statutes enacted to cover nonprofit corporations.

Syndicate

Syndicates, often referred to as *investment groups,* are individuals, partnerships, or corporations who make a private agreement to associate with each other to finance a purchase which individual members could not make alone. Syndicates usually are involved in commercial transaction such as buying hotels or sports teams. The advantage of this type of business association is that it can quickly raise large amounts of capital. The disadvantage is that members of a syndicate may later find themselves held individually liable for a breach of contract or tort if a third-party plaintiff is successful in a suit against them.

Joint Stock Company

Joint stock company unincorporated association that has many characteristics of a corporation but is treated as a partnership at law

A **joint stock company** generally is a partnership arrangement in which partners agree to stock ownership in exchange for partnership liability. It resembles a corporation in that members own transferable stock shares. But it is usually treated as a partnership in that all goods or property owned are held in the name of the members, and each partner is held personally liable when successfully sued by a third party. Unlike a partnership, each member is not an agent for the other in terms of making enforceable contracts.

Franchising

Trademark a distinct mark of authenticity by which a product of a manufacturer may be distinguished from all others

Franchising is often referred to as a method of marketing goods whereby a corporation, partnership, or individual (franchisor) enters into a private contractual agreement with another individual, corporation, or partnership (franchisee) giving the franchisee the right to use a **trademark** or **copyright** for a specific purpose for a limited period of time. McDonald's Corporation allows its franchisees to use its trademark and logo, under the conditions outlined in its agreement, for the purpose of selling specific types of foods provided by McDonald's. Terms and conditions of the franchisor's agreement may include:

- the hours a franchisee's store will be open,

- the products to be sold,

- the percentage of gross profits to go to the franchisor,

- the health and sanitary conditions that will prevail,

- and the grounds for terminating the franchisor – franchisee relationship.

Further, when involved in a franchisor – franchisee agreement, the franchisor may require the franchisee to buy only its own product in exchange for the use of its brand name. These provisions are often referred to as **tying** or **tie in agreements.** They have been scrutinized by courts for possible restraints of trade (Section 1 of the Sherman Antitrust Act), because the franchisor is refusing to allow its franchisee to buy from any competitors of the franchisor. The case below illustrates a successful defense by a franchisor when an antitrust complaint was filed by one of its franchisees.

Copyright a right granted by statute to an author or originator of a literary or artistic production whereby the author is invested for a limited time with the right to sell or license to sell his or her creation.

Tying agreement in antitrust law, a refusal by a manufacturer to sell a primary product (tying) unless the retailer or franchisee agrees to buy a secondary product (tied)

Principle v. McDonald's Corporation

United States Court of Appeals (4th Cir.)
631 F.2d 303 (1980)

FACTS   Principle (franchisee) sued McDonald's (franchisor) for tying its willingness to lease its stores and use its brand name to a $15,000 security deposit and 8½ percent of its gross sales or rent. Principle argued that McDonald's is selling three distinct products: franchise, leases, and security deposit. It argues that this is a violation of the antitrust laws because a prospective franchisee must agree to all three to obtain the franchise, thus restricting its ability, for example, to lease another building not built by McDonald's or to build its own stores. McDonald's argues that it is not selling three distinct products but one system of selling hamburgers, using its name in exchange for royalties. It seeks to bring quality control to the location of its stores, their management, and the products sold by virtue of its franchise agreements.

ISSUE   Is the requirement by McDonald's in its franchise agreements a violation of Section 1 of the Sherman Act?

DECISION   No. The court said that McDonald's operated a single system, not three distinct products. Thus a tying agreement did not exist. Further, the court pointed out that the system of franchising set out by McDonald's was necessary to maintain quality control over its franchised store and the integrity of its name in the eyes of the public.

Government Regulation of Franchising   Because many franchisors overpromised potential sales to franchisees and did not disclose fairly all the terms of their agreement, the Federal Trade Commission enacted regulations that provided that certain franchisors must disclose details of their operation to franchisees ten days before entering into an agreement. In addition, if the franchisor makes any earning predictions, it must show the basis of the predictions. Violations of these rules may lead to civil fines of up to $10,000.

SUMMARY

Single proprietorship, partnerships, and corporations are the three major forms of business organizations. Their advantages and disadvantages should be weighed based on several factors: managerial control, extent of personal liability, ability to raise capital, and tax considerations. Additionally, there are specialized forms of business, generally based on private contractual agreements, which should be looked at. They include:

1. joint ventures

2. cooperatives

3. syndicates

4. joint stock companies, and

5. franchising.

REVIEW PROBLEMS

1. What are the advantages of a corporate form of organization?

2. What factors should be weighed in determining whether a partnership or corporation is the better form of business organization in a particular case?

3. What features does a joint stock company have that make it like a partnership?

4. What advantage does a single proprietorship have over a corporation?

5. Why do individuals enter into cooperatives?

6. What terms of agreement often are included in a franchisor–franchisee agreement?

7. What tax considerations make incorporation of a business disadvantageous?

8. A, the owner of a brokerage house, signed a limited partnership agreement with B, C, and D, who contributed $10,000 each. When a client sued A for mishandling of her investment portfolio, causing a $500,000 loss, and won, A's assets and those of the partnership could not cover the loss. Do B, C, D have to cover what A and the partnership assets cannot? Explain.

9. A franchisor of ice cream stores requires its franchisees to buy only from approved suppliers. A franchisee sues claiming that this requirement is a tying

agreement which violates Section 1 of the Sherman Antitrust Act. Does it? Explain.

10. A was the owner of a scrap iron business. B loaned A money to purchase scrap under an informal agreement that when A sold the scrap, B would be repaid with interest. A dispute arose, and B claimed that this was a joint venture, and he should receive a portion of A's profits. What result? Explain.

11. State the differences between a limited partnership and a partnership.

12. Are corporations doubly taxed? Explain.

13. When do courts "pierce the corporate veil" of a corporation and hold officers personally liable?

14. A and B entered into an agreement to buy a professional baseball club and share profits and losses equally. A was to be the only active party to the agreement. What form of business organization had they formed? Explain.

15. Three people entered into an agreement to purchase shares in a corporation that they control and manage. A fourth person sues them each individually for a breach of contract. Does the suit succeed? Explain.

CHAPTER OBJECTIVES

After reading this chapter, you should be able to:

1. Define and compare general partnership and limited partnership.

2. Define partnership as an entity and distinguish that from partnership as an aggregate.

3. Describe the essential elements of partnership in Section 6 of the Uniform Partnership Act.

4. State and apply the "profit sharing" test of partnership in Section 7 of the Uniform Partnership Act.

5. Identify profit-sharing situations that do not qualify as partnerships.

6. Describe what is required to establish partnership by estoppel.

7. Describe the formalities for creating general partnerships and limited partnerships.

NATURE OF PARTNERSHIPS

Known to the ancients, the partnership is the oldest form of business association. The partnership concept is traceable from Babylonian sharecropping, through classical Greece and Rome, to the enterprise of the Renaissance. Today the partnership still is an important form of business organization, especially in areas outside of manufacturing.

Sources of Partnership Law

The Uniform Partnership Act (UPA) and the Uniform Limited Partnership Act (ULPA) are the main sources of partnership law. The two acts have been enacted in virtually every state and are referred to throughout the text.

Partnership Defined

The UPA defines a partnership as "an association of two or more persons to carry on as co-owners a business for profit" (Section 6[1]). This statutory definition governs whether a partnership exists. Anyone entering a relation satisfying this definition incurs the liability of a partner to the firm's creditors.

Types of Partnerships   Partnerships are either general or limited. A *general* partnership is the ordinary partnership governed by the UPA. To constitute a general partnership, nothing more is needed than to satisfy the definition of a partnership provided by Section 6(1). All the participants in a general partnership incur unlimited personal liability to partnership creditors.

A *limited* partnership carries many characteristics of a general partnership except that the liability of some members is limited. Governed by the ULPA, it offers some of the benefits of both partnerships and corporations and may be used to attract investors willing to put up money but unwilling to risk personal liability. A limited partnership protects a special partner by exempting him or her from personal liability. It consists of one or more general partners who conduct the business and are personally liable to creditors, as in an ordinary partnership. It also includes one or more limited partners who contribute capital and share in profits but who do not participate in the firm's management or operation and who assume no liability beyond a fixed amount, usually their capital contribution.

Aggregate and Entity Nature of Partnerships

There are two conceptions of partnerships: one that it is an aggregate of people who associate to share its profits and losses, owning its property and liable for its debts, the other that it is an artificial being, a distinct entity, separate in rights and responsibility from the partners who compose it. The first conception is referred to as the aggregate theory of partnership, and the second is called the entity theory.

Aggregate Theory   The aggregate theory considers the partners to be co-owners of the enterprise and the property used in it, each owning an individual interest in the partnership. The consequence of this is to hold each partner personally liable for partnership debts. Creditors can reach each partner's personal assets if partnership assets are insufficient to discharge a debt.

Entity Theory   The entity theory treats the partnership as a separate legal entity, distinct from the individual partners. This theory holds that the partnership is a "person" for legal purposes. Because the partnership is a separate legal person, individual partners may enter into transactions with the firm, such as lending it money or equipment. Accountants and businesspeople generally regard and treat a partnership as a business, separate and distinct from its individual partners.

UPA Approach   The UPA strikes a balance between the two theories. Generally speaking, under the UPA a partnership is an aggregate, but in certain limited circumstances it is treated as an entity. For example, the UPA recognizes the partnership as an entity for owning its own property by authorizing conveyances of real estate to or by the partnership in the partnership name and by creating the presumption that all property acquired with partnership funds is partnership property. Thus the UPA adopts both the aggregate and entity theories of partnership, depending upon the particular problem involved.

In the following case, the court considers whether a partnership is to be treated as an entity or as an aggregate.

McKinney v. Truck Insurance Company

Missouri Court of Appeals
324 S.W.2d 773 (1959)

Truck Insurance Company issued a workers compensation policy to "Ralph McKinney & Paul McKinney dba Acme Glass Co.," which was described in the policy as a "co-partnership" whose "operations" were classified as "glass merchants." Davis, a man employed by Paul McKinney in connection with the operation of McKinney's 167-acre farm, was injured while working on activities wholly unrelated to the business conducted by Acme Glass. Davis filed a claim for benefits against McKinney, as employer, and Truck Insurance, as his insurer. After successfully defending against Davis's claim, Paul sued Truck Insurance to recoup his expenses incurred in the defense. Paul theorized that "a partnership cannot be considered as a separate entity." It is an aggregate of individuals, and the effect of the policy was to fully insure all workers compensation obligations of the two individuals named. **FACTS**

Is Paul correct that the partnership must be considered as an aggregate? **ISSUE**

No. Although the UPA only partially modifies the aggregate or common law theory of partnership, judicial recognition is given to the partnership entity as it is contemplated by the contracting parties. In construing and giving effect to contracts made by and with partnerships, it may appear from the subject matter or otherwise that the parties dealt with and treated the partnership as if it were an entity. Here the parties intended and expressly provided that the policy was for Acme Glass Company. In the policy, the partnership entity of Acme Glass was recognized as the employer with whom Truck Insurance contracted. **DECISION**

PARTNERSHIP FORMATION

No particular steps are required to form a general partnership. Although customarily each partner's rights and responsibilities are established in an instrument called the *partnership agreement* or the *articles of partnership*, usually this is not required. A partnership may result from any arrangement of facts fulfilling UPA Section 6(1)'s definition of a partnership.

Factors Establishing Partnership Existence

To understand how the UPA (Section 6[1]) determines partnership existence, the meaning of each phrase of the definition must be examined. The following paragraphs dissect the definition of a partnership and explain the reasons for the words used.

"An Association"   *Association* denotes the voluntary nature of the partnership arrangement. Because a partnership is a voluntary association, the participants must intend to enter into a partnership. Whether or not a partnership is created depends on the intent of the participants to create one. Their intent is the primary test of partnership existence. This intent may be expressed by either a written or an oral agreement, or it may be inferred from conduct. As with contractual intent, partnership intent is measured objectively. Subjective intent is not material.

"Of Two or More Persons"   One person alone cannot form a partnership. A sole proprietor cannot convert his or her sole proprietorship into a partnership by drafting articles of partnership or otherwise conducting the business as a partnership. It takes two to tango, and it takes at least two to partner. Although a minimum number of two is required, the UPA imposes no maximum limit on the number of people who may form a partnership. A thousand people may create a partnership.

The intention of one person alone cannot create a partnership. When someone wishes to join an existing partnership, all the partners must consent to the new member's admission.

Section 2 states that a *person* "includes individuals, partnerships, corporations, and other associations." Thus the definition of a partnership provides that any of these entities may form a partnership. Any individual having contractual capacity may become a partner. By including partnerships as persons in Section 2, the UPA permits one partnership to be a member of another partnership. Similarly, two corporations ought to be able to form a partnership. But there is some disagreement on this point. The courts are divided on whether a corporation may become a partner. The prevailing view is that without some statutory authorization by a state corporation code, a corporation may not become a partner. The trend recently has been for such codes to permit this. Many contemporary corporation codes allow corporations to become partners. Some states permit a corporation to become a partner only if it is allowed to do so by the corporation's charter or articles of incorporation.

"To Carry On"   It is often said that "the carrying on" of a business, not an agreement to carry on business at a future date, is the test of partnership existence. The official comment to UPA Section 6 indicates that this is not the intended meaning of the phrase "to carry on." Section 6(1) does not provide that persons are not partners until they participate in the carrying on of the business. The words "to carry on," not "carrying on," are used.

"As Co-Owners"   To form a partnership, the associates must *co-own* the business. Co-ownership distinguishes partnership from nonpartnership relations such as employment. For example, if a general manager is not a co-owner of the enterprise, he or she is an employee, not a partner.

Co-ownership describes the community of interest each partner shares in the firm's operations. It includes the power of ultimate control each partner possesses in the firm's management. For an association to consist of co-owners, the associates must have equal rights in the decision-making process. Section 18(e) of the UPA states that "all partners have equal rights in the management and conduct of the partnership business." Factors reflecting co-ownership include giving instructions, hiring and firing employees, and determining how money is spent. But Section 18 permits partners to agree to delegate their managerial rights to a managing partner.

"A Business"   Co-ownership of property by itself does not establish a partnership. The co-ownership required by Section 6(1) is co-ownership of a *business.* A partnership must be formed as a business. Section 2 states that a business includes "every trade, occupation, or profession." If two people together inherit real estate that remains unimproved and idle, they are co-owners, but not of a business. However, if they improve the property by erecting an apartment complex, their actions constitute a business.

"For Profit"   A partnership must be formed as a business *for profit.* Nonprofit organizations cannot be formed as partnerships under the UPA. Courts require only an expectation, not the actual making, of profit for the existence of a partnership. Profit motive, not profit making, is the test.

The importance of profit sharing to the determination of partnership existence is reflected in UPA Section 7(4)'s declaration:

> The receipt by a person of a share of the profits of a business is prima facie evidence that he is a partner in the business.

Protected Relations

While providing that profit sharing presumes partnership existence, Section 7(4) enumerates certain situations in which profit sharing does not create a partnership. These include situations in which profits are:

1. received to discharge a debt

2. received as wages or rent

3. paid to a widow or an estate as an annuity

4. paid for the purchase of a partnership asset

This protection against the risk of unwanted partnership formation can be lost if the protected party becomes too involved in the firm's operation. Frequently an uneasy creditor or landlord, unsatisfied with simply a share of the profits, seeks to protect his or her interests by controlling the firm's operations. If the control reserved over business operations is merely that necessary to protect the creditor's or landlord's interests, the relation remains protected from becoming a partnership. But if the control goes beyond what is necessary to protect the creditor's or landlord's interests, the risk of unwanted partnership formation increases. No clear-cut rule exists for determining when protected status is lost and partnership status is gained. A sliding scale, not a rigid rule, is the measure. The greater the participation in the business and the greater the degree of unnecessary control, the greater the risk of partnership formation. In the following case, the court considers whether the parties created a partnership.

P & M Cattle Company v. Holler

Supreme Court of Wyoming
559 P.2d 1019 (1977)

FACTS
In 1971, Holler was looking for someone to pasture cattle on his land. He entered into a written agreement with Bill Poage and L. W. Maxfield, the two partners of the P & M Cattle Company. The agreement specified that Holler was to furnish the grass, and P & M would furnish money for cattle, trucking, and salt. It was agreed that net profits from the sale of the livestock would be split in half. No mention was made in the contract of what would happen if the cattle sold at a loss. Following successful operations, the parties orally renewed the agreement in 1972, 1973, and 1974. In 1974, however, a cash loss of $89,000 resulted. P & M insists that Holler is bound to pay it $44,500, representing one half of the loss, because he was its partner.

ISSUE
Did the parties create a partnership?

DECISION
No. Although the UPA states that the sharing of profits is presumptive of partnership existence, this may be rebutted by a showing that the parties intended the profits as payment of rent or as payment of a debt. When a partnership is not expressly created by the agreement, the intent of the parties controls. A court looks to the conduct, surrounding circumstances, and the transactions between the parties. Here the parties never referred to their agreement as creating a partnership, and their income tax treatment of related expenses reflects this fact. The division of profits was only a standard of payment in discharge of a debt for services and grass or in payment for rent.

Partnership Established by Representation

The existence of a true partnership depends on the intent of the parties to associate as partners. But in certain situations, people who actually are not partners are liable to third parties as though they were. People who represent themselves to be partners or consent to others' representing them as partners are liable as partners to third parties who rely upon those representations in their dealings with the purported partnership. This arrangement is called partnership by **estoppel**. Represented partners are called *partners by estoppel* or *ostensible partners.* The statutory basis for this doctrine is provided by UPA Section 4(2), and Section 16's more detailed declaration that:

> When a person . . . represents himself or consents to another representing him to any one as a partner . . . he is liable to any such person to whom such representation has been made, who has, on the faith of such representation, given credit to the apparent partnership.

Liability is imposed on the represented partner in these situations, because he or she is in a better position to avoid injury to others by correcting the misconception. Liability rests on the person most capable of preventing any loss from occurring. Two elements are the essence of estoppel: representation and reliance.

Representation   Partnership by estoppel results either from someone representing himself or herself as a partner or from consenting to such a representation by another. A signature on a letter or check can constitute a representation. Liability resulting from someone's own representation simply is another application of the principle, well established in contract law, that a person is responsible for the apparent or objective manifestations of intent. Someone behaving like a partner is liable as a partner. It is not material that a person may secretly deny all connection with the partnership or even be unaware of the significance of the behavior.

Liability also results from someone consenting to being represented as a partner by another. But it is not enough that a person knows that he or she is being portrayed as a partner. UPA Section 16 imposes liability *only* where there is some *consent* to the other person's representation.

Reliance   Someone seeking to hold another liable as a partner by estoppel must have extended credit in reliance upon the representation of that person as a partner. UPA Section 16 requires that the duped person must have "on the faith of such representation, given credit to the actual or apparent partnership." Thus not every creditor of the purported partnership relation may hold the false partner responsible as a partner by estoppel. Only creditors who have suffered economic loss by relying on the represented partnership may require payment from the ostensible partner.

A creditor's reliance must be reasonable under the circumstances. This requirement of reasonable reliance may impose upon a creditor a duty to investigate the relationship before assuming the existence of a partnership. In certain circumstances, a creditor may have no obligation to inquire further, such as when the representations of partnership are made directly to the creditor by one of the purported partners.

The following case illustrates the nature of the consent requirement.

Estoppel term which refers to the inability of an individual based on justice and fairness to assert legal rights, especially when another individual has been induced to act based on conduct or silence of the former's representation

---

Cox Enterprises Incorporated v. Filip

**Court of Civil Appeals of Texas
538 S.W.2d 836 (1976)**

A newspaper publisher, Cox Enterprises, Incorporated, doing business as the *Austin-American Statesman,* sued Richard Filip for payment for newspaper advertising services

FACTS

furnished to Trans Texas Properties. Filip defended on the ground that he had no financial interest in Trans Texas Properties and was not liable for the debts of that business. The evidence showed that to obtain credit for Trans Texas, its employee, Tracey Peoples, represented to Cox Enterprises that Filip was an owner of the business. Peoples had no authority to make that representation, and Cox made no effort to verify it. As for Filip, he did not hold himself out as having an ownership interest in Trans Texas.

ISSUE   Is Filip liable to Cox for the debts of Trans Texas under the UPA as a partner by estoppel?

DECISION   No. The court held that Filip is not liable because Cox failed to prove that Filip consented to Peoples's representation of him as a partner in Trans Texas. Section 16 of the UPA imposes a duty on a person to deny that he is a partner once he knows that third persons are relying on representations that he is a partner. But it does not create an affirmative duty on one to seek out all those who may represent to others that he is a partner. Here, because Filip did not know of the representation to Cox, he is not bound by it.

Formalities

Although under the UPA no formalities are required to create a general partnership, some may be required by other statutes. Certificates, licenses, and permits may have to be obtained. A name should be selected and in some cases must be registered. Although not usually required, the execution of a partnership agreement often is advisable. Technical formalities do accompany the formation of limited partnerships.

License, Permit, and Certificate Requirements   Partnerships engaging in certain types of activity usually do need to obtain state or local licenses to do business. Occupational licensing is a well known fact of professional life among doctors and lawyers. License requirements also fall on those in other callings. Certified public accountants, real estate brokers, and construction contractors are only a few of the many businesspeople required to obtain licenses. Failure to obtain the necessary licenses and permits may deprive a partnership of the ability to enforce its contracts. Here is another application of the rule of contract law to the nonenforcement of illegal agreements.

Name Selection and Registration   It is customary, but not necessary, to use a firm name for a partnership. A partnership should have a business name because of the goodwill that may develop from its use. As a practical matter, a name may be required for the opening of the partnership's bank account.

Unless prohibited by statute, the partners may use any name they desire so long as fraud, trade name infringement, and unfair competition are not involved. Thus the partnership cannot use a name that is deceptively similar to the name of another business.

Most businesses operate under fictitious names. A fictitious name is one that does not disclose the surnames of all the firm's owners. For example, if Julius Jones and Penelope Smith operate a cafe under the name of "The Bottoms Up Bar," their business name is fictitious. By statute in most states, fictitious names must be registered so that creditors of the partnership can enforce their rights against all the firm's members. A nonfictitious name is one containing the surnames of all the partners and does not have to be registered. Any form of expression may be used for the fictitious name. But some states prohibit use of the word "Company" or any other word that might confuse the partnership with a corporation.

Registration provides public notice of the names and addresses of all partners. It usually involves the filing of a certificate with the county recorder where the partnership is located and, in some states, in each county in which partnership real estate is situated. A few states, such as California, require the information supplied on the certificate to be published in a local newspaper for a designated period. A new certificate or amendments to the old certificate must be filed for every change in the firm's composition.

Noncompliance usually results in the partnership's inability to sue on its contracts until the registration requirement is satisfied. Registration is easily done and does not usually result in hardship to the partnership. Fines and penalties are also authorized but seldom levied because prosecutors and police usually have more important matters to look after than pursuing nonregistered partnerships.

Partnership Articles   Although not usually required, it is customary to define the rights and duties of the members of a partnership in an instrument called *the partnership agreement* or *articles of partnership.* There are advantages to a writing. A written partnership agreement avoids the problem of later proving that the agreement to enter into partnership was actually made. Drafting articles of partnership with the help of a good lawyer can focus the parties' attention on potential problem areas in their relationship. The written agreement also helps to avoid future disagreements by clarifying the parties' relationship.

The partnership agreement usually takes the form of a series of numbered paragraphs addressing important aspects of the parties' relationship. Partnership agreements range from fairly simple instruments to rather complex documents, depending on the nature of the business and the number and character of the associates.

Written partnership articles are necessary if the partnership agreement qualifies as a contract coming under the Statute of Frauds, which requires a written memorandum signed by the party against whom enforcement is sought for certain contracts. If a partnership is to continue for longer than one year or involves the transfer of an interest in real estate to or by the partnership, written articles must be executed.

Limited Partnerships   The UPA does not require formalities to form general partnerships, but technical formalities do accompany the formation of limited partnerships. Formation of limited partnerships is governed by the ULPA. Drafted in 1916, the ULPA is positive law in 27 states. In 1976, the Commission on Uniform

State Laws substantially revised the ULPA to reflect modern usage. As of the date of this book's publication, 22 states have adopted the Revised ULPA.

Under ULPA Section 2, those forming limited partnerships must file a certificate of limited partnership with a designated government official, usually the county clerk or recorder. The certificate provides public information about the general and limited partners and the nature of their firm, including the partnership name and the character of the business, the names and addresses of all general and limited partners, and information regarding each limited partner's capital contribution (ULPA Section 2). The certificate must be amended to reflect any changes in the character or composition of the limited partnership. Although technical defects in the certificate do not defeat the formation of a limited partnership, a limited partner may lose the protection of limited liability if he or she knows of any false statements contained in the certificate. Under Section 6, any person detrimentally relying upon false statements in the certificate may hold liable any party to the certificate who knew that the statement was false. To avoid liability as a general partner in this situation, the limited partner must promptly renounce his or her interest in the profits of the business upon learning of the mistake.

Filing the certificate restricts the limited partner's liability to his or her capital contribution, which may be cash or other property but not services. If the limited partner contributes capital in the form of services or takes part in the control of the business, he or she becomes liable as a general partner. Under the 1976 revision, present contributions of service and promises to make future cash payments, property contributions, or performances of service are permissible forms of capital contribution. Accordingly, the services or promise must be accorded a value in the certificate of limited partnership, and that value determines the limited partner's liability.

Under the ULPA, the surname of a limited partner cannot appear in a limited partnership's name unless that name is also the name of a general partner or unless the partnership operated under that name before that person became a limited partner. The ULPA also provides:

> A limited partner whose name appears in a partnership name . . . is liable as a general partner to partnership creditors who extend credit to the partnership without actual knowledge that he is not a general partner.

Many firms avoid this liability by including, wherever the firm's name is printed, the notation "limited partner" or "ltd." after the limited partner's name. By so designating the limited partner, the firm tells creditors that the person is not a general partner.

Under the 1976 revision of the ULPA, the name of each limited partnership has to contain without abbreviation the words "limited partnership," and also "may not contain any word or phrase indicating or implying that it is organized other than for a purpose stated in its certificate of limited partnership." To make it easy to choose a name, the revised ULPA provides for the reservation of the intended partnership name. Anyone intending to form a limited partnership may apply to the Secretary of State for the desired name. If the name is available, it may be reserved for exclusive use by the partners for 120 days while the partnership is being formed.

The following case shows the loss of limited liability when a limited partner asserts control over the business. The case also discusses the power of corporations to enter partnerships.

_____ *Delaney v. Fidelity Lease Limited* _____

Supreme Court of Texas
526 S.W.2d 543 (1975)

In February 1969, Delaney entered into an agreement with the limited partnership, Fidelity Lease Limited, to lease a fast food restaurant to the partnership. Fidelity's sole general partner was a corporation, Interlease, Inc. Delaney built the restaurant, but Fidelity failed to take possession or pay rent. Of Fidelity's 22 limited partners, three were officers, directors, and shareholders of Interlease. Delaney sued these three individuals. He claimed that they were personally liable because they had become general partners by participating in the general management and control of the limited partnership. The corporation had no function except to operate the limited partnership, and the three involved were obligated to their other partners to operate the corporation so as to benefit the partnership.   FACTS

Did the three individuals become general partners of Fidelity and therefore become personally liable to Delaney?   ISSUE

Yes. The court ruled in favor of Delaney. Personal liability, which attaches to a limited partner when he or she takes part in the control and management of the business, cannot be evaded merely by acting through a corporation. Strict compliance with the statute is required if a limited partner is to avoid liability as a general partner. Otherwise the statutory requirement of at least one general partner with general liability in a limited partnership can be avoided through the use of a corporation with minimum capitalization and therefore minimum accountability. If these three individuals took part in the business, their doing so in the capacity as officers of Interlease does not protect them from personal liability.   DECISION

_____ SUMMARY _____

A partnership is an association of two or more people to carry on as co-owners a business for profit. There are two types of partnerships: the general partnership, which is governed by the Uniform Partnership Act (UPA), and the limited partnership, which includes at least one general partner and one or more limited partners. The latter is governed by the Uniform Limited Partnership Act (ULPA).

There are two conceptions of partnership: as an aggregate of persons sharing in profits and losses and as a distinct entity, separate in rights and responsibility from the partners who compose it. Under the UPA, a partnership is generally treated as an aggregate, but in certain limited circumstances it is treated as an entity.

The essential elements of partnership existence are provided in the definition of a partnership in Section 6 of the UPA, which defines a partnership as "an association of two or more persons to carry on as co-owners a business for profit."

Under Section 7 of the UPA, the receipt by a person of a share of the profits of a business creates a presumption that that person is a partner in the business. That presumption can be rebutted by showing that the parties did not actually intend to create a partnership. Section 7(4) expressly provides that profits received to discharge a debt, or received as wages or rent, or paid to a widow or an estate as an annuity, or paid for the purchase of a partnership asset are not to be treated as creating the presumption of partnership existence.

Partnership liability to a partnership's creditors may arise as a result of someone being represented as a partner in a business. When a person represents himself or herself or consents to another representing him or her to anyone as a partner, he or she is liable to any such person to whom such representation has been made and who has, on the faith of such representation, given credit to the apparent partnership.

Generally speaking, no formalities are required to form a general partnership. Certain licenses, permits, and certificates may need to be obtained. If a fictitious name is used, it may need to be registered. Usually a partnership agreement is drafted to define the rights and responsibilities of the partners. Greater formality is followed in the formation of limited partnerships. Those forming a limited partnership must file a certificate of limited partnership, which sets forth information about the limited partners and the capital structure of the limited partnership.

REVIEW PROBLEMS

1. What is a partnership? How is the general partnership different from the limited partnership?

2. What is meant by treating the partnership as an entity? As an "aggregate"? When is a partnership treated as an entity? When is it treated as an aggregate?

3. What are the essential elements of partnership existence under Section 6 of the Uniform Partnership Act? What test of partnership existence is provided in Section 7 of the Uniform Partnership Act?

4. What is required to establish partnership by estoppel (under Section 16 of the Uniform Partnership Act)?

5. Seller operates a store in a building he rents from Owner. Creditor, who dealt with Seller, wants to hold Owner liable for the debt as Seller's partner. May Owner ignore the obligation on the basis that both Seller and Owner had mutually agreed that their relationship was not a partnership? Suppose that Owner and Seller had an agreement which reads: "The parties do not intend by this agreement to form a partnership of any kind, but rather a landlord–tenant relationship." Is this language conclusive on the issue of partnership liability?

6. Can-Do Corporation and Cannot Corporation wish to form a partnership. Can they?

7. Penelope and Julius inherit joint ownership rights in a house. Are they partners? Suppose that they decide to lease the house to Renter. Are they then partners?

8. Penelope and Julius decide to go into the business of making widgets, but instead of making profits they lose money. Are they liable to creditors as partners?

9. United Foods, a food broker, was an authorized buyer of produce from Minute Maid. It realized profits by purchasing Minute Maid inventories at bargain prices. United entered into an agreement with Cold Storage as follows: Cold Storage would lend money to United to purchase produce. The produce would be collateral for the loans. A special account would be established and managed by Cold Storage. The books were to be credited with advances by Cold Storage and debited by advances made by Minute Maid. At the year's end the books were to be closed and the profits divided. Over the year, United became overextended and indebted to Minute Maid, which sued Cold Storage rather than United because it was a more attractive defendant, alleging that Cold Storage was United's partner. What result?

10. Ralph Presutti approached his father, Claude, in April 1969, saying, "Dad, if you put up the money, we'll go partnership in a gas station." However, because the oil company whose station they were to operate frowned on partnership stations, Ralph explained that Claude could not sign any dealer agreements or leases or any other partnership documents, such as tax returns. Claude agreed to the arrangement. He withdrew $8,000 from his bank account, which he and Ralph used to open a joint account under the service station's trade name. From time to time, Claude drew checks upon the account for payment of merchandise at the station. In July, Ralph returned $2,000 to Claude. In September, Claude began working at the station and continued for one year. For these services, Claude drew salary of $125 each week. Occasionally he received additional sums that were from partnership profits, as well as free gas, tires, and automobile accessories. During his one-year tenure, Claude managed the station whenever Ralph was away and participated in such policy decisions as whether they should buy a truck and whether they should distribute trading stamps. After a year, Ralph still refused to sign a written partnership agreement, so Claude stopped working at the station. Despite this, he continued to receive payments of money and car repairs from the station until January 1972. As of January 1972, Claude had received approximately $17,000 as salary, partial return of his capital contribution, and distribution of profits. When Ralph finally refused to affirm the partnership's existence, Claude filed suit for an accounting of his share of the partnership profits. What result?

11. A barbershop owner executed two separate but similar partnership agreements with two barbers in his shop. Under the agreements, the owner provided the barber chair, supplies, and licenses while the others provided the tools of their trade. Upon dissolution, ownership of these items was to revert to the party providing them. Income was divided 30 – 70 percent between the owner and one barber and 20 – 80 percent between the owner and the other barber. The agreements further required the owner to hold and distribute all receipts and stated the work hours and holidays of the two barbers. The agreements provided that all policy was to be decided by the shop owner, and it also forbade any assignment of the agreement without the owner's permission. By state law, employers are to file an assessment report with the state employment commission and make unemployment compensation contributions. But partnerships are not subject to un-

employment compensation assessment when no nonpartner employees are involved. Must the barbershop owner file the forms and make the assessed contributions?

12. Francis and Thelma Gosman were an ambitious and industrious young couple, married in 1945 when he was 21 and she was 18. He drove a milk truck and she was a clerk-typist. After several years of marriage, when their first child was expected and Thelma could no longer keep her job, she began to raise chickens at home and planted a garden to supplement the family income — selling chickens, eggs, and garden produce from the house. The sale proceeds were deposited in the Gosmans' joint bank account, which was subject to the order of either of them. Ultimately, Francis gave up his milk route, and his participation in the family business increased while Thelma's decreased. This was followed by the removal of the business from their home to a business complex, where the business ultimately became a grocery store, a liquor store, a restaurant, and a night club, which grossed almost $500,000 in 1969, close to $600,000 in 1970, and over $600,000 in 1971. Francis managed the enterprise and, although Thelma's duties were less onerous, she continued stocking grocery shelves, waiting tables in the restaurant and night club, bartending, counting money and making bank deposits, managing the club when Francis was sick or out of town, decorating the building interior, and running errands. In 1972 Francis filed for divorce against Thelma, and she counterclaimed, seeking a divorce and alleging that, because she was a "partner" with Francis in the family business, her property rights should be determined pursuant to the Partnership Act, awarding her 50 percent of the partnership's fair market value and 50 percent of the balance of the checking account. What result?

CHAPTER 30

Operation of Partnerships

CHAPTER OBJECTIVES

PROPERTY RIGHTS IN PARTNERSHIPS

Partnership Property / Partner's Interest in the Partnership / Limited Partnerships

RELATIONS AMONG PARTNERS

Partners' Fiduciary Duties / Profits and Compensation / Management / Information / Limited Partners

RELATIONS WITH THIRD PARTIES

Contracts / Torts / Admissions, Knowledge, and Notice / Withdrawing and Incoming Partners

SUMMARY

REVIEW PROBLEMS

CHAPTER OBJECTIVES

After reading this chapter, you should be able to:

1. Identify partnership property and partners' personal assets.

2. Define tenancy in partnership.

3. Define interest in the partnership and state the rules for assignment of a partner's interest, creditors' rights, and inheritance.

4. Distinguish property rights in limited partnerships from those in general partnerships.

5. State the rules for partners' fiduciary duty to each other, right to profits and compensation, right to manage the partnership, and right to information about the partnership, and compare these rules with those applying to limited partnerships.

6. Explain how partners may contractually bind the partnership with third parties.

7. Identify when the partnership becomes liable for the torts of a partner.

8. Recognize the effect of a partner's admissions, knowledge, and notice on the partnership.

9. State the rules for the liability of withdrawing and incoming partners.

This chapter explores the rights and duties of partnerships. It first focuses on the property rights created by the partnership relation. Partnerships generally involve the use of property, either furnished by the partners or acquired by the firm. The partnership, its partners, and creditors both of the partnership and of the individual partners may acquire rights in this property.

This chapter also examines the rules governing the relations among partners and their relations with those who deal with the partnership. Once the partnership starts operating, it sometimes is necessary to settle managerial disputes among partners. These issues may be covered by a partnership agreement. The Uniform Partnership Act and the Uniform Limited Partnership Act address the solution of disputes when they are not covered by the partnership agreement. The UPA and ULPA further regulate the rights and liabilities resulting from dealings with third persons.

PROPERTY RIGHTS IN PARTNERSHIPS

UPA (Section 24) defines the property rights of partners as:

1. their rights in a specific partnership property
2. their interest in the partnership, and
3. their right to participate in the management.

The following paragraphs discuss the first two types of property rights. The partner's right to participate in the firm's management is discussed in the material on the rules about a partner's managerial rights and responsibilities.

Property rights in partnerships pose two problems:

1. distinguishing partnership property from an individual partner's personal assets and
2. distinguishing partnership property from the related type of property known as the partner's interest in the partnership.

Partnership property is property that the partners agree belongs to the partnership and must be used for partnership purposes. It differs from a partner's personal assets because it belongs to all the partners as tenants in partnership. Partnership property differs from a partner's interest in the partnership, which is the partner's share of the profits and surplus. In ordinary language, a partner's interest is commonly called a *partner's share.*

Partnership property property that belongs to the partnership as opposed to property that belongs to a partner in his or her individual capacity

Partnership Property

Most partnerships require property for their operation. This property may be either **real property** (land) or **personal property** (movable items). Usually the partnership acquires its original property from individual partners as their capital contributions. The partners may contribute specific assets to the firm, such as land, equipment, or patents, or they may contribute money used to purchase assets. These assets, including money, usually become partnership property.

Partners may have property that is not partnership property. This property may remain the sole property of an individual partner even though it is used by the firm. For example, an individual partner's real estate may be used by the firm for its business premises without becoming the partnership's property if the partner providing it intends only to lend it to the firm. Similarly, nothing prevents a partner from lending equipment to the firm while retaining ownership of it.

Real property land or anything permanently attached to land

Personal property movable property; all property other than real property

What Constitutes Partnership Property   Although a partner's personal assets may be vulnerable to partnership obligations, distinguishing partnership property from a partner's personal assets is essential for several reasons. If property belongs to the partnership, its use by individual partners is restricted. If it is sold, any **capital gain or loss** is distributed to each partner in the same proportion as profits, unless otherwise

Capital gain or loss profit or loss resulting from the sale or exchange of a capital asset

agreed. If the property must be applied to satisfy creditor claims, partnership creditors have priority over an individual partner's personal creditors. But if the property is an individual partner's personal asset, his or her use of it is unrestricted. The entire capital gain or loss from its sale belongs to the partner and is subject to personal income taxes. If the partner dies, the property belongs to his or her estate.

The controlling criterion for deciding if certain property is the partnership's is the partners' *intent* that it belong to the firm and be devoted to its purposes. The partners' intent is the primary consideration. They may decide among themselves what will be owned by all as partnership property and what will be retained by each as his or her own.

One measure of the partners' intent is the way the property is acquired. Property bought with the firm's money is considered the partnership's. If it is bought with individual funds, it is considered that individual's property. Additional factors may strengthen this presumption. Repairing and improving the property at partnership expense, paying insurance premiums from partnership accounts, or listing the property on partnership financial statements may reinforce this presumption. But the presumption can be explained away if an intention of individual ownership appears.

One way for the partners to explain away the presumption is to establish their intent at the outset in their partnership agreement. The partnership agreement generally governs, because it is the clearest indication of intent. Usually the statement describes the partnership property and its agreed upon value in a separate schedule incorporated by reference into the agreement. Property used by the firm but owned by an individual partner also may be identified in this way. When an individual partner's property is loaned to the partnership, a copy of the lease may be attached to the agreement and incorporated by reference. The partnership agreement can provide that acquired property be recorded as partnership property in the partnership accounts. A well-kept set of books identifies the partnership's assets, and the property listed there will be considered partnership property.

In the following case, the court confronted the question of what is partnership property.

Brouillette v. Phoenix Assurance Company

Louisiana Court of Appeals
340 S.2d 667 (1977)

FACTS   Ranton Brouillette and his brother, Vinnie, owned pieces of real estate as partners. Ranton moved the frame of his house onto one of the lots and started to build and make improvements on it. Because of hard feelings between the brothers, Vinnie drove a bulldozer into the house. Ranton filed a claim with his insurer. The insurer refused to pay the claim on the ground that the property was no longer Ranton's but belonged to the partnership.

ISSUE   Had Ranton's house become the property of the partnership, thereby preventing him from collecting on his insurance policy claim?

DECISION   No. The court held that the house did not become the property of the partnership simply because the land itself was owned by the partnership. Ranton had a right as owner of the house to collect proceeds under the policy, insuring him against vandalism by anyone, including his brother, even though they were a partnership with respect to their business dealings.

Tenancy in Partnership   Assuming that certain property belongs to the partnership, the UPA describes the nature of a partner's ownership rights in it. "A partner is a co-owner with his [or her] partner of specific partnership property as a tenant in partnership." This tenancy in partnership is a unique property concept created by the UPA especially for partnerships. It recognizes that a partner's co-ownership rights in specific partnership property differ from other types of co-ownership. For example, many of the details of land ownership do not fit the needs of partnerships. The UPA's tenancy in partnership recognizes that the rights of a partner as a co-owner of specific partnership property should depend on the needs of the partnership relation.

The special needs of the partnership relation require that an individual partner's ownership rights in specific partnership property be restricted. Although the partners are co-owners of partnership property, they have limited ownership rights. Generally, a partner cannot sell specific partnership property or dispose of it by will. The theory is that the partnership property is to remain intact. It reflects recognition of the business primacy of the partnership relation.

Under the UPA,

> A partner . . . has an equal right with his partners to possess specific partnership property for partnership purposes, but he has no right to possess such property for any other purpose without the consent of his partners.

A partner's use of partnership property is limited to partnership purposes. He or she may not use partnership property for personal or other nonpartnership purposes unless all the other partners agree. Their agreement may be implied by continued acceptance of the individual partner's personal use of partnership property, or the partners may expressly provide their consent in their partnership agreement.

Because a partner cannot possess partnership property for personal purposes, he or she cannot claim that specific partnership property as part of his or her home and thereby free it from seizure by creditors in a bankruptcy proceeding.

The UPA further restricts a partner's power to assign his or her rights in specific partnership property. A partner cannot assign his or her rights in partnership property unless it is an assignment of the rights of all the partners in the same property. For example, a partner cannot **mortgage** specific partnership property for a personal obligation. This aspect of the tenancy in partnership is necessary because partnerships are voluntary, personal relations. If the law recognized the possibility of individual assignments, the assignee would become a partner in the firm with the rights to possess the property for partnership purposes. But partnerships are voluntary relations, and people cannot have partners forced on them.

Mortgage an interest in property created by a writing providing security for the payment of a debt

Creditors may not force an involuntary assignment through a judicial seizure of the property. Thus a partner's rights to partnership property are not subject to creditor claims, except upon a claim against the partnership.

When a partner dies, his or her ownership of specific partnership property passes to the surviving partners. It is not included in the deceased partner's estate. This is

Survivorship the right of a person to property by reason of having survived another person who had an interest in it

called the right of **survivorship.** It fits nicely the needs of the partnership, because it permits the partnership to be dissolved without interference from the dead partner's estate. Because a deceased partner's ownership rights in specific partnership property are not distributed to the heirs or beneficiaries, a partner may not include it in a will.

Partner's Interest in the Partnership

The UPA states that "a partner's interest in the partnership is his [or her] share of the profits and surplus, and the same is personal property." This interest is an intangible economic right. Its value appears on the partnership's balance sheet as each partner's capital account. Unlike specific partnership property, which belongs to the firm and is collectively held by the partners, each partner's interest belongs to him or her individually. Because it is each partner's individual property, a partner's interest has most of the ownership qualities that are denied to a partner in specific partnership property: it is assignable; it may be seized by creditors; and, when a partner dies, it becomes a part of the estate.

Assignment of Partner's Interest   Partners may convey their interest to another. An attempted assignment by a partner of his or her ownership in specific partnership property is regarded as valid. The person the partner transfers the interest to does not become a partner in the firm but only receives a right to share in the firm's profits. The assignee does not enjoy the usual rights and privileges of partners. He or she may not interfere with the firm's management, require information about firm transactions, or inspect the partnership books. But if the partnership is dissolved, the assignee may require an accounting of the interest from the date it was acquired. These restrictions place the assignee of a partner's interest in an insecure position and effectively make it difficult to find a buyer.

Creditor's Rights   Unlike specific partnership property, which is shielded from attack by a partner's personal creditors, a partner's interest in the partnership may be seized by his or her individual creditors to satisfy a debt resulting from a transaction outside of the firm business. In that a partner may voluntarily assign his or her interest to creditors, it follows that the partner's personal creditors should be able to force an involuntary assignment by a judicial seizure of the interest. The creditors

Charging order a court order given to a judgment creditor so that a partnership will stand charged with paying a partner's debt out of the partner's interest

may accomplish this by seeking a **charging order,** which is similar to the garnishment of someone's wages. Under the charging order, a personal creditor may reach the partner's interest without interfering with firm business.

The charging order attaching the partner's interest is the exclusive remedy for a partner's personal creditors. It is available only to a partner's personal creditors, those who have obtained a judgment against the partner. UPA (Section 28) provides that a court "may charge the interest of the debtor partner with payment of the unsatisfied amount of such judgment debt."

A creditor also may ask a court to appoint a receiver, an independent person who receives the partner's share of profits for the creditor. The receiver enters into the partnership and acts as a partner. The receiver may make:

> orders, directions, accounts and inquiries which the debtor partner might have made, or which the circumstances of the case may require.

From the other partners' perspective, the appointment of a receiver is not desirable. They may redeem the charged interest and get rid of the receiver by paying off the judgment creditor. They also can use partnership property to do this, provided there is approval among all the partners whose interests are not subject to the charging order.

Inheritance   When a partner dies, his or her interest in the partnership passes to the heirs or beneficiaries of his or her estate. Because a partner individually owned the partnership interest while living, it follows that it should become a part of the estate upon death. A partner may convey the interest by will. This may be done by a specific **bequest** of the interest to a particular beneficiary. But because a partner's interest is personal property, a bequest of all a partner's personal property includes a transfer of the partnership interest.

Bequest a gift by will of personal property

In addition to transfers by will, a partner may provide in the partnership agreement that his or her interest in the partnership will pass to one or more surviving partners. Usually this is done by a buy-sell provision in the partnership agreement. Under a **buy-sell agreement,** the partners agree that the survivors will buy the deceased partner's interest by paying the representative of the deceased partner the value of the deceased's interest in the firm. This payment may be either in a lump sum or in installments, and it may be backed by insurance. The partnership agreement may state that partnership proceeds be used to purchase life insurance for each partner covering the value of each partner's interest. The insurance proceeds then are used to pay the value of the deceased partner's interest to the deceased's representative.

Buy-sell agreement an agreement among partners to buy the interest of any partner who withdraws from the partnership

Limited Partnerships

A limited partner's property rights are similar to a general partner's, except there is no right to participate in the management of the limited partnership. Distinguishing partnership property from a limited partner's individual property is seldom a problem. The nature of a limited partner's interest in a limited partnership is similar to the general partner's. But the assignee of a limited partner's interest may become a substitute limited partner, enjoying more protection than the assignee of a general partner's interest.

Partnership Property   Confusion over the distinction between partnership property and a limited partner's personal assets is not likely, because the certificate of limited partnership must describe and state the agreed value of the property that each limited partner contributes to the firm. A limited partner also may lend money to and transact other business with the partnership. If additional property belonging to the limited partner is used by the firm, the presumption is that it has been loaned to the firm.

Limited Partner's Interest   A limited partner's interest in a limited partnership is the same as a general partner's. It is the partner's share of the profits of the limited partnership and the right to receive distributions of partnership assets. Like the interest in a general partnership, it is personal property, assignable and subject to a charging order. When the limited partner dies, it is included in the estate.

The assignee of a limited partner's interest acquires whatever rights the limited partner had to the firm's profits and the return of the partner's capital contribution. This arrangement differs from the assignment of a partner's interest in a general partnership under the UPA, in which the assignee acquires only the partner's share of the profits.

The assignee of a limited partner's interest in the partnership potentially has more protection than the assignee of a general partner's interest. Although the assignee of a general partner's interest is denied the inspection and accounting privileges enjoyed by partners, the assignee of a limited partner's interest may become a **substitute limited partner.** A substitute limited partner acquires all the rights and privileges enjoyed by the assignor. This arrangement may come about only if it is authorized by the certificate of limited partnership and if all the partners consent to the substitution. Once the substitution occurs, the certificate must be amended to reflect the change. If an assignee does not become a substitute limited partner, his or her inspection and accounting rights remain restricted.

Substitute limited partner
a person who takes the place of a limited partner

RELATIONS AMONG PARTNERS

The UPA contains rules governing the relations of the partners to each other. These rules reflect the partners' presumed intent regarding their relationship. In providing general rules for determining the rights and obligations of the partners, the UPA states:

> the rights and duties of the partners in relation to the partnership shall be determined, *subject to any agreement between them,* by the following rules [emphasis added].

The phrase *subject to any agreement between them* lets the partners alter or waive the rules governing their relationship when that is their actual intent. They usually make these changes in the partnership agreement, in that its function is to express the intentions of the partners about law and tax considerations. When no partnership agreement exists, or when an existing agreement is silent, the UPA provisions are implied. Thus the UPA serves as a backdrop and as a point of departure for the drafting of the partnership agreement.

As we have noted earlier, smart businesspeople appreciate the advantages of a written partnership agreement. Because a partnership is an intimate relationship, perhaps the greatest potential problem is the risk of future disagreement among those who start out with the highest mutual regard. This risk may be diminished by reducing the partners' relation to a written instrument. By focusing attention on potential trouble spots, a carefully drafted partnership agreement may avoid future disagreements and litigation. Because the UPA provides the basic rules governing the partners' relation to each other and also provides that these rules may be varied by the partners, the following paragraphs discuss these rules and the extent to which they may be altered by agreement. In short, the UPA defines: the fiduciary duties of partners, their rights to compensation, their management rights, and their right to information. Special rules exist for limited partners, reflecting the differences between the limited and general partnership relations.

Partners' Fiduciary Duties

The UPA provides that partners owe a fiduciary duty to each other. The fiduciary duties of agents were discussed in Chapter 27. In that the UPA provides that "every partner is an agent of the partnership for purposes of its business" and further states that "the law of agency shall apply under this act," it follows that partners share fiduciary duties similar to those of agents. A partnership is just a special type of agency, and partnership law is simply the application of agency principles to partnerships.

The intimate nature of the partnership also makes the application of the fiduciary rule to partnerships appropriate. Someone should not have to deal with his or her partners as if they were opposing parties. A partner should be able to trust his or her partners, to expect that they are pursuing a common goal and not working at cross purposes.

The partner's fiduciary duty requires loyalty to his or her partners. In a partnership, each partner is the confidential agent of his or her other partners. Therefore, no one may act at his or her partners' expense. The fiduciary relation prohibits all forms of trickery, secret dealings, and selfishness in matters relating to the partnership. For example, a secret profit may not be made to the exclusion of other partners.

The duty of loyalty resulting from a partner's fiduciary position is such that the severity of a partner's breach is not questioned. The question is whether there has been any breach at all. The required degree of loyalty must be maintained at all times. From the first exploratory discussions, through formal association in partnership, to final severance of the relationship, partners are required to exercise scrupulous loyalty and good faith. A partner's duty of loyalty usually operates in two areas:

1. instances in which a partner engages in transactions with other partners and the firm and

2. instances in which partnership opportunities are presented to a partner.

Nothing prohibits partners from dealing with each other at arm's length, as ordinary businesspeople, when negotiating a nonpartnership transaction. But when a transaction concerns any aspect of the partnership relation, the requisite degree of loyalty must be maintained. Transactions of this type include one partner's purchase of the partnership share of another and one partner's sale of personal property to the partnership.

Whenever a person buys the partnership share of another partner, the purchasing partner must inform the selling partner fully of any information he or she has that would affect the value of the partnership share. The purchaser may not conceal or fraudulently represent material facts to his or her partner. Similarly, when a partner sells his or her own property to the partnership, there must be no misrepresentation to the firm nor concealment of the seller's identity.

The same high standards of loyalty apply when partners are presented with a partnership opportunity. Occasionally third parties refuse to deal with the partnership and offer a partnership opportunity to a partner in his or her individual capacity. A partner may not accept such an offer while still a member of the firm, unless his or her partners grant permission.

When partners learn of or are offered any opportunity in their capacity as member of a partnership, they may not appropriate this opportunity for personal benefit without first offering it to the firm. A partner may not, for example, purchase the rights to manufacture a product that would fit into the firm's product line. When the firm is presented with a business opportunity, a partner may take the opportunity for himself or herself if the partnership does not have enough money to take advantage of the opportunity or simply fails to take action on it. Otherwise, a partner may take advantage of a partnership opportunity only when it has been completely abandoned by the firm.

Because a partner is a fiduciary, he or she is held accountable for profits made in competition with the business. But a partner may engage in additional enterprises for personal benefit so long as they are not within the scope of the partnership and are undertaken in good faith. When litigation develops, it is not always easy to determine what the partners intended as the scope of the business. For example, partners in real estate may intend to retain some freedom to deal on their own accounts. Failure to delineate the scope of the partnership business in a partnership agreement invites quarrels. This problem is usually avoided by the inclusion of a purpose clause in the partnership agreement. A closely allied problem is the amount of time each partner must spend on firm business. If outside interests of one or more partners are to be permitted, a partnership agreement can provide for this.

The classic case of *Meinhard* v. *Salmon* demonstrates the high degree of loyalty required from a partner.

Meinhard v. Salmon

Court of Appeals of New York
164 N.E. 545 (1928)

FACTS   Salmon secured a 20-year lease to the Hotel Bristol, at 42nd Street and Fifth Avenue, in New York City. The lease provided that he alter the hotel to make it suitable for shops and offices. Needing capital for the work, he enlisted the financial help of Meinhard. Under a joint venture agreement, Meinhard was to furnish one half of the cost of alteration, upkeep, and repair in return for half of the profits. Losses were to be shared equally. Salmon retained sole management responsibility and authority. The project was highly successful. Four months before the end of the 20-year term, the lessor made a new lease, having renewal provisions up to 80 years, with the Midpoint Realty Company, which was owned by Salmon. Salmon, as Midpoint Realty Company, was to develop the hotel property and adjoining lots on both streets and construct a larger, $3 million building. About one month later, Meinhard learned of the project and demanded that the lease be held in trust for the joint venture, which had not yet expired. When Salmon refused, Meinhard sued.

Does Meinhard have any rights to the new lease?

Yes. The opportunity for the new lease, offered to Salmon as the visible owner and
manager of the old lease, was an incident of the joint venture and could not be
appropriated by Salmon in secrecy and silence. Joint adventurers, like partners, owe to
one another the duty of the finest loyalty while the enterprise continues. At a minimum, Salmon was under a duty to concede to Meinhard the opportunity to bid for the
new lease. The opportunity for the new lease belonged to the joint venture because the
subject matter of the new lease was nothing more than an extension and enlargement
of the subject matter of the old lease.

Profits and Compensation

Unless there is an agreement to the contrary, under the UPA partners share equally
in the profits. This equal sharing in profits results regardless of unequal contributions
of capital, skills, or services by the partners.

Without an agreement stating otherwise, a partner is not entitled to compensation
for services rendered for the firm's business. What a partner does for the firm's
business is presumed to be in his or her own interest. It is ordinarily expected that
each partner devote himself or herself to the promotion of the firm's business without
compensation. This expectation holds even when one partner performs more than
the others. This rule rests on the presumed intent of the partners. If a provision for
compensation is included in the partnership agreement, it is enforced.

From an economic perspective, the rules governing profits and compensation are
sound when partners have contributed equally to the venture. To the extent that
contributions are unequal, different rules are needed. For example, the senior
partner in an accounting firm may demand more of the earnings than the other
partners on the basis of his or her experience and reputation. Contributions to a
manufacturing enterprise may vary widely in terms of equipment, goodwill, and
time. By fixing the percentages of each partner's share of the profits in the partnership
agreement, some of these differences may be taken into account. If the chief variation
in contribution is the amount of capital, the proportion of capital contributed may
determine the proportion of the profits received. But in many situations it is wise to
base salaries on economic contributions, as for example when one partner contributes managerial talent. The important point is that, unless the partners want the
UPA's rules governing equal sharing of profits and no compensation to apply, the
partnership agreement should specify the partners' intent.

Management

Under the UPA, all partners have equal rights in the management and conduct of
the partnership business. From this concept of equality, it follows that a majority of
the partners may decide ordinary partnership matters, provided that no agreement
between them makes a different rule. A majority of the partners may determine firm

action in ordinary affairs regardless of each partner's comparative investment in the firm. A majority governs over a minority in such matters as borrowing money, hiring and firing employees, collecting debts, and determining when and how profits are to be divided.

Individual partners and those in a minority are protected from majority oppression by two exceptions to the general principle of majority rule in management matters:

1. No partner may be excluded from participating in the firm's management.

2. The majority must act in good faith for the firm's interest and not out of self-interest.

Because each partner has an equal right to take part in the management of the firm's business, it makes sense that one partner may not exclude another partner from his or her full share in the management of the partnership. The requirement that the majority act in good faith and not for private advantage springs from the fiduciary duty of loyalty each partner owes to the other. Practically speaking, fairness requires consulting with the minority before taking action.

Individual partners and minorities are also protected by the requirement of unanimous approval on extraordinary matters, admission of incoming partners, and changes in the partnership agreement. Because the UPA permits majority rule regarding *ordinary matters* connected with the partnership business, majority control does not extend to unusual or extraordinary transactions. These require unanimous approval. For example a majority cannot engage the firm in a different business nor change the firm's location if any partner objects.

The UPA provides that no one may become a member of a partnership without the consent of all the partners. This rule reflects the intimate nature of partnership. No person should have a partner forced on him or her. Each partner may choose his or her associates.

Nothing contradicting the partnership agreement may be undertaken without unanimous approval. This rule is just another application of contract law, in that an act contravening the partnership agreement constitutes a breach of contract, and any modification of a contract requires agreement among all parties. Both majority and unanimous actions may be taken with complete informality, such as an exchange of letters or a telephone call.

Because either majority or unanimous approval usually govern the firm's operations regardless of each partner's contribution, the partners may prefer to specify a different rule in the partnership agreement. For example, majority rule may be replaced by a provision in the partnership agreement leaving ordinary business decisions to a "majority in interest" of either the earnings or the capital contributions of the partners. The partners who together are entitled to more than half the profits or who together contributed more than half the capital would make ordinary business decisions under this provision. A major contributor may insist on complete control, and the partnership agreement may allow it. When the partners contemplate that one of them will assume most of the managerial duties, the partnership agreement may designate a "managing partner," specifying the responsibilities entrusted to him or her. When a firm has many partners, such as a large, national accounting firm, provisions for centralizing management in an executive committee may be considered. If there is an even number of partners, the agreement may provide for arbitration to resolve deadlocks.

The UPA provides

> Partners shall render on demand true and full information of all things affecting the partnership to any partner or to the legal representative of any deceased partner or any partner under legal disability.

Thus each partner has the right to all information concerning partnership affairs. Although the UPA conditions the duty to render information on a demand, the courts hold that partners must perform a duty of disclosure regardless of demand. The duty to inform springs from the partners' fiduciary duty of loyalty. As part of this duty, partners must not conceal information from each other.

A partner's right to information continues even if a partner lets others manage the firm. To protect his or her investment and to guard against exposure to potential liability, a partner needs access to all partnership information whether or not the partner actively participates in the firm's management.

The UPA requires

> The partnership books shall be kept, subject to any agreement between the partners, at the principal place of business of the partnership, and every partner shall *at all times* have access to and may inspect and copy *any* of them [emphasis added].

Although the UPA does not specify what type of books and records are to be kept, federal income tax regulations require a detailed balance sheet, statements of partnership income and each partner's share of income and deductions, and a reconciliation of the partners' capital accounts. A partner need not be a bookkeeper or an accountant to maintain the records, nor need he or she follow standard accounting practice. But partners may be wise to hire a competent accountant or bookkeeper when they lack these skills themselves. If keeping partnership records at the principal place of business and making them available at all times seems inconvenient, the partnership agreement may provide for a different location and specify times when records may be inspected.

To protect a partner's right to partnership information further, the UPA gives each partner the right to a formal accounting of partnership affairs. A formal accounting is a comprehensive, court ordered investigation of partnership transactions by a court appointed investigator. The UPA gives the right to an accounting when specific circumstances justify it even though there is no dissolution of the partnership. Under the UPA, a partner may seek an accounting without dissolving the partnership when:

1. he or she is wrongfully excluded from partnership business

2. a partner withholds profits from a secret transaction

3. it is provided for in the partnership agreement

4. other circumstances render it just and reasonable.

Except in these situations, one partner does not have a right to an accounting from his or her partners unless the partnership is dissolved. The partner already has access to the firm's books and property.

A partner's only recourse against his or her partners for breaching a duty owed under either the UPA or the partnership agreement is to bring an action for an accounting. A partner cannot otherwise sue his or her partners or the partnership for claims arising out of the partnership's affairs because the partner would be both plaintiff and defendant in the case. Outside of an action for an accounting, a partner can sue his or her partners only when the problems at issue have nothing to do with partnership affairs or when an accounting has already taken place and the partner's share has been determined.

Limited Partners

Limited partners are not subject to the same rules as general partners. Limited partners owe no fiduciary duties, have different rights to compensation, and may not participate in the management of the partnership. But generally they have the same rights to information as general partners. The law on the relations between general and limited partners is in transition. The Revised ULPA has been recommended by the Conference on Uniform State Laws. But it has been adopted by only 22 states. The following paragraphs discuss both the ULPA and the Revised ULPA.

Unlike a general partner, a limited partner owes no duty of loyalty and may, for example, operate a business in competition with the partnership.

Under the ULPA, a limited partner may receive any profits or compensation stipulated in the certificate of limited partnership. But the ULPA fails to provide any basis for profit sharing in the absence of agreement. The Revised ULPA provides that, in the absence of agreement, profits be allocated according to the value of each partner's contribution to the partnership.

The limited partner's management rights are less than those of a general partner. The trade-off for obtaining limited liability is the surrender of any right to participate in the management of the partnership. This arrangement prevents a creditor from mistaking a limited partner for one of the general partners with full liability. Under the ULPA, a limited partner loses the protection of limited liability if he or she takes part in the control of the business. Difficulty in determining when the control line is crossed has created substantial uncertainty over when the rights of review, consultation, and veto become participation in the firm's management. Under the Revised ULPA, if a limited partner's participation in the control of the business is not substantially the same as the exercise of the powers of a general partner, he or she loses the limited liability "only as to persons with actual knowledge of his participation in control." Under this rule, a limited partner may participate in the firm's management so long as he or she refrains from exercising all the powers of a general partner and avoids direct dealings with third parties. To further provide safe harbor for limited partners, the Revised ULPA lists certain activities — such as consulting, being a contractor, or being an agent of the firm — that a limited partner may perform without being considered to take part in the control of the business. The Revised ULPA expands and clarifies the permissible participation of limited partners in the management of the firm.

Although limited partners may not participate in the firm's management as fully as general partners, their passive position requires that they have access to information to protect their investment. Under the ULPA, a limited partner may demand:

> true and full information *of all things affecting the partnership* and a formal account of partnership affairs whenever circumstances render it just and reasonable [emphasis added].

Furthermore, the limited partner has the right to have the partnership books kept at the principal place of business of the partnership, and *at all times* inspect and copy *any of them*. The Revised ULPA conditions the right to information "from time to time upon reasonable demand" and limits the available information to records on the state of the business and the financial condition of the limited partnership, tax returns, and other information about the partnership as is just and reasonable.

The Revised ULPA also states what records are to be kept by the partnership. Although it does not require a standard form of financial report, it does require that certain basic documents, including the certificate of limited partnership and any partnership agreement, be kept along with tax returns and other financial statements.

RELATIONS WITH THIRD PARTIES

Because partnerships exist to do business, partners need to interact with third parties who deal with the partnership. This interaction may be in making contracts or committing torts. The problem is to what extent a partner's conduct binds the firm and fellow partners.

As mentioned earlier, partnership law is a particular application of agency law. A partner's power to bind the firm in dealings with third parties is determined by the general rules of agency law as provided in the UPA. Because each partner is an agent of the partnership for the purpose of its business, his or her acts may result in the firm's being: liable for contracts made and torts committed by a partner; bound by a partner's admissions; and charged with the knowledge of or notice to a partner. Agency rules provided in the UPA also apply for determining the liability of incoming and withdrawing partners for obligations incurred by the partnership. A limited partner is not an agent of the partnership and therefore has no authority to act for the firm and bind it to third parties.

Contracts

The power of a partner to bind the partnership to contracts with third parties may be either actual or apparent. The partner may have actual authority as expressly provided in the partnership agreement. If no actual or express authority is provided there, the partner may have apparent authority. When a partner's acts are unauthorized, they may be ratified by a majority of the partners and made binding on the firm. Thus the power of a partner to bind the firm by contract to third parties may be found either in the partnership agreement or, by implication, in his or her conduct or the conduct of the partners.

The UPA provides that any act of a partner is binding on the partnership if it is "for apparently carrying on in the usual way the business of the partnership." This is just a restatement of the agency rule regarding apparent authority. Partners have apparent authority consistent with the nature of the partnership business. The usual authority possessed by partners in similar businesses is the measure of a particular partner's apparent authority. The UPA further provides that any:

act of a partner which is not apparently for the carrying on of the business of the partnership in the usual way does not bind the partnership unless authorized by the other partners.

For acts unrelated to the partnership's business, a partner needs actual authority, whether informal or given in the partnership agreement.

Sometimes a partnership agreement restricts a partner's authority to bind the partnership. For example, a partnership agreement may provide that no partner shall incur any debt for the firm of over $500. What effect should this have on third parties? Under the UPA, third parties are not limited nor bound by secret restrictions of a partner's authority or by restrictions in a partnership agreement, unless they know of them. Thus any contracts made by a partner for the firm and related to its business are binding on the partnership despite any secret restrictions on the partner's authority if they are unknown to the third party.

In the following case, the court examines to what extent a partnership is liable on the contracts entered into by the partners.

_____ *National Biscuit Company v. Stroud* _____

Supreme Court of North Carolina
106 S.E.2d 692 (1959)

FACTS   In March 1953, Stroud and Freeman entered into a general partnership to sell groceries under the name of Stroud's Food Center. Thereafter, the National Biscuit Company (Nabisco) sold bread regularly to the partnership. In October 1955, Stroud advised an agent of Nabisco that he personally would not be responsible for any additional bread sold by Nabisco to Stroud's Food Center. From February 6, 1956, to February 25, 1956, Nabisco, through this same agent, at the request of Freeman, sold and delivered bread in the amount of $171.04 to Stroud's Food Center. Stroud and Freeman by agreement dissolved the partnership at the close of business on February 25, 1956. Stroud paid all of the partnership obligations, amounting to $12,014.45, except the amount of $171.04 claimed by Nabisco. To pay the partnership obligations, Stroud exhausted all the partnership assets. Nabisco sued both Stroud and Freeman seeking to recover the $171.04. Stroud claimed that he was not liable to Nabisco.

ISSUE   Can a partner restrict the power of his or her partners to enter into contracts for the firm?

DECISION   No. The court awarded judgment for Nabisco against both Stroud and Freeman. The court stated: There is nothing . . . to indicate or suggest that Freeman's power and authority as general partner were in any way restricted or limited by the articles of partnership in respect to the ordinary and legitimate business of the partnership. Certainly, the purchase and sale of bread were ordinary and legitimate business of Stroud's Food Center during its continuance as a going concern. . . . Stroud, his copartner, could not restrict the power and authority of Freeman to buy bread for the partnership as a going concern, for such a purchase was an "ordinary matter connected with the partnership business,". . . for the purpose of its business in the very nature of things, Stroud was not and could not be, a majority of the partners. Therefore,

> Freeman's purchases of bread from [Nabisco] for Stroud's Food Center as a going
> concern bound the partnership and his copartner, Stroud.

Torts

Under the UPA, the partnership is liable for the torts of any partner acting in the ordinary course of the business of the partnership or with the authority of his or her partners. All members of a partnership are liable for a partner's torts committed within the scope and course of the partnership business. This liability also extends to absent partners who did not participate in, ratify, or know about the tort. The determining factor for invoking partnership liability is whether the tort was committed within the reasonable scope of and on behalf of the partnership business. If the wrongful conduct was clearly outside the scope of the partnership business, the nonparticipating partners may still be liable if they authorize, ratify, or consent to the tort. Consent, scope, and course of business provide the principal channels through which liability attaches to a partnership for a partner's torts. Liability usually attaches when a partner's negligence injures a third party. In comparison to negligent conduct, a willful and malicious tort is generally held not to be within the scope of an ordinary partnership, and the partnership is not liable unless the nonparticipating partners authorize, ratify, or consent to their partner's willful tort. For example, if a partner in a tavern assaults a customer without provocation, liability would not extend to the absent partner who had neither consented to nor authorized the attack.

The following case demonstrates the potential tort liability of partners.

Kelsey-Seybold Clinic v. Maclay

Supreme Court of Texas
466 S.W.2d 716 (1971)

FACTS

For several years, John Dale Maclay and his wife and children had been under the medical care of the Kelsey-Seybold Clinic, including treatment by a pediatrician, Dr. Brewer, who was a partner in the clinic. Claiming that Dr. Brewer was engaging in conduct designed to alienate the affections of his wife, Maclay notified Dr. Kelsey, a senior partner at the clinic, of the alleged tortious relationship. Maclay claimed that in spite of such notice, the physician's relationship with Maclay's wife continued. Maclay brought suit against Dr. Brewer and the clinic for the tort of alienation of affection.

ISSUE

Under these circumstances, is the clinic, as a matter of law, liable to John Maclay for the conduct of its partner?

DECISION

Yes. Although Dr. Brewer was acting outside of his authority and there was no consent to his authority to do the act for the partnership, the clinic was under a duty to exercise ordinary care to protect its patients from harm resulting from tortious conduct of people on the premises. A negligent breach of that duty could thus subject the clinic to liability without regard to whether the tortious conduct was that of an agent or was in the ordinary scope of the partnership business. The court stated:

> If and when the partnership received information from which it knew or should have known that there might be a need to take action, it was under a duty to use reasonable means at its disposal to prevent any partner or employee from improperly using his position with the clinic to work a tortious invasion of legally protected family interests.

Admissions, Knowledge, and Notice

Agency rules make the partnership responsible for the admissions or representations of any partner about partnership affairs within the scope of his or her authority. As in agency law, knowledge or notice to any partner of matters relating to partnership affairs is assumed to extend to all the partnership. Thus notice to a partner about a matter of firm business — for example, a prior mortgage on property acquired by the firm — is notice to the partnership and all its members. But knowledge or notice is not assumed when the partner acquires it while acting fraudulently or adversely to the firm, or when the knowledge was acquired by the partner before joining the firm.

Withdrawing and Incoming Partners

Partners often withdraw or retire from firms and are replaced by incoming partners. Partners must take care to consider how the change in membership will affect the liabilities of each. A retiring partner remains liable to third parties unless he or she notifies third parties who know of the partnership and have extended credit to it. This notice may be given informally by letter or phone, or by a novation, substituting the incoming partner for the retiring partner as responsible to the partnership's creditors (see Chapter 12). Constructive notice, such as publication in a newspaper, is essential to adequately notify third parties who know about the partnership but never extended credit to it.

An incoming partner is liable for all partnership obligations arising before his or her admission, just as if the incoming partner had been a partner when such obligations were incurred. But this liability may be satisfied only out of the partnership property. A judgment for such an obligation may not be satisfied out of the incoming partner's individual property. An incoming partner may promise the partners that old creditors will be paid. When this happens, the promise can be enforced by the creditors as third-party beneficiaries to the contract and may subject the incoming partner's individual property to satisfy the debt. Another way to accomplish the same result is for the creditors to enter into a novation, substituting the incoming partner for any withdrawing partner.

SUMMARY

The property rights of a partner are the partner's rights in specific partnership property, the partner's interest in the partnership, and the partner's right to participate in the business. Partnership property is property that the partners agree belongs to the partnership. In determining what constitutes partnership property, the primary consideration is the partners' intent. Property bought with partnership funds is presumed to be partnership property. All of the partners own partnership property as "tenants in partnership." This special type of property ownership, created by the UPA, limits the rights of partners to use partnership property only for partnership purposes and further restricts a partner's right to sell, assign, or dispose of the partnership property through inheritance. Surviving partners obtain the partner's ownership of partnership property.

A partner's interest in the partnership is the partner's right to a share of the profits and surplus of the partnership. Because the partner's interest is considered a personal asset of the partner, it may be sold, assigned, and transferred by a will. Judgment creditors of an individual partner can seize a partner's interest by obtaining a court-ordered charging order.

A limited partner's property rights are similar to a general partner's, except that there is no right to participate in the management of the partnership. Distinguishing partnership property from a limited partner's individual property is seldom a problem, because the certificate of limited partnership must set forth the property each partner contributes to the partnership. A limited partner's interest is the same as a general partner's. An assignee of a limited partner's interest may acquire all of the rights of the limited partner by becoming a substitute limited partner.

Under the UPA, partners owe a fiduciary duty of loyalty to each other. The fiduciary duty requires full disclosure by partners when they deal with each other. It also requires that a partner must offer any opportunity that falls within the partnership business first to the partnership. Unless otherwise agreed, the partners share equally in partnership profits. Partners also share equal rights to participate in the management of the partnership. The concept of majority rule applies to ordinary partnership matters, unless the partners otherwise agree. Unanimous approval is required for extraordinary matters and those that contradict the partnership agreement. Partners have a right to information about the partnership. Limited partners are not subject to the same rules as general partners. Limited partners owe no fiduciary duties, have different rights to compensation, may participate in the management of the partnership, but generally have the same rights to information as general partners.

The principles of agency law apply to interactions between partners and third parties. All members of a partnership are liable for a partner's torts committed within the scope and course of the partnership business.

REVIEW PROBLEMS

1. What is the difference between partnership property and a partner's interest in a partnership?

2. In the absence of a partnership agreement, how are profits distributed among partners?

3. In the absence of a partnership agreement, how are ordinary partnership matters to be decided by the partners?

4. How is a partner's power to bind the partnership similar to an agent's authority to bind a principal?

5. Julius and Penelope formed a partnership to operate under the name The Swish Toilet Company, which would manufacture and sell contour toilet fixtures. Julius applied for a personal loan at the Hard Luck Loan Company. The intended purpose of the loan, as disclosed by Julius to Hard Luck, was to purchase a new car for his wife, Fifi. Hard Luck refused to lend Julius the money unless the firm signed as guarantor, guaranteeing Julius' repayment. Julius signed his name on the loan contract and then signed the Swish Toilet Company name, as guarantor. All this was done in the presence of the Hard Luck agent. If Julius fails to pay back the loan and is insolvent, can Hard Luck hold the Swish Toilet Company liable as guarantor of the loan? Explain.

6. Assume the same facts as in Question 5. Can Hard Luck obtain Julius's partnership interest in the Swish Toilet Company? Explain.

7. Again assume the same facts as in Question 5, except that now Julius has died. What are Penelope's rights with regard to the partnership property? Explain.

8. Assume the same facts as in Question 7. What are Fifi's rights with regard to the partnership property?

9. Doug Whitman, Bill McCarty, and Bartley Brennan formed a partnership, the Ace Cosmetic Company, which manufactured cosmetics for women. They did not enter into either a written or an oral partnership agreement. Whitman and McCarty each contributed $200,000 to the capital of the partnership. Brennan contributed $50,000. For the first year of operation, Brennan managed the business. Profits for the first year amounted to $300,000. How should the profits be distributed among the three partners? Explain.

10. Assume the same facts as in Question 9. Brennan now wants the partnership to bring out a new line of cosmetics for the older woman. Whitman and McCarty think that this is a bad idea. How should the issue be decided if the partners maintain their positions? Explain.

11. Julius owned and operated a sawmill. One day his daughter, Penelope, introduced him to Frank, who had recently moved into the area and who had met Penelope at a social function. Frank had previously managed a sawmill in another state. Julius asked Frank if he would be interested in going into the mill business as his partner. Frank looked the sawmill over and agreed to go into partnership with Julius. It was agreed that Frank would pay $60,000 for a half interest. He would pay $20,000 down, $10,000 in 30 days, and the rest at $1,000 a month. Things went smoothly for a month, but the mill was forced to close down when loggers refused to deliver logs due to the failure of the mill to pay on past accounts. It was then that Frank took his first look at the mill's books. There he discovered that the mill's liabilities exceeded its assets. The only cash in the bank was the money Frank had contributed. The mill owed over $300,000 to creditors. Its chief assets were its premises and its equipment. But Frank discovered that the First National Bank held mortgages on the land, the building, and the equipment. What are Frank's rights and liabilities with regard to the mill's creditors and Julius? Explain.

12. Curtis Cyrus wrote to his brother Cecil in North Dakota asking him to come to Minnesota to form a partnership in a resort venture. Curtis had recently bought 60 acres of land in Minnesota with his own money and in his own name. Cecil, a skilled carpenter, agreed. He moved his family to Minnesota, built a cabin on the property, and moved his family into it. Cecil built six other cabins on the property and operated them as a resort. The building expenses were paid out of the resort's earnings. Cecil received his family's living expenses out of the resort's earnings. He and his family contributed their labor to the resort. Curtis remained in Minneapolis and contributed his labor to the resort only during vacations at the resort. Each year the brothers divided the profits equally between them. When Cecil died several years later, his wife decided to move back to North Dakota. She asked Curtis to pay her one half of the value of the resort, including the fair market value of the land. Curtis claimed that the land was his. What are the rights of the parties? Explain.

CHAPTER 31

Partnership Dissolution

CHAPTER OBJECTIVES

PARTNERSHIP DISSOLUTION

Dissolution, Winding Up, and Termination / Causes of Dissolution / Winding Up the Partnership Business / Distribution of Assets / Continuing the Partnership Business

SUMMARY

REVIEW PROBLEMS

CHAPTER OBJECTIVES

After reading this chapter, you should be able to:

1. Define partnership dissolution, winding up, and termination.
2. Identify acts of partners that may cause dissolution of partnership.
3. Identify how a partnership may be dissolved by operation of law.
4. Compare causes of dissolution of limited and general partnerships.
5. Define winding up the partnership business and who may do it.
6. State the order of distribution of assets for general and limited partnerships.
7. Describe the doctrine of marshaling of assets.
8. Describe how the partnership business may be continued after the partnership has been dissolved, and further describe the effect of continuing the partnership business on both existing and later liabilities.

PARTNERSHIP DISSOLUTION

The day may come when the partnership is dissolved. The partners may wish to withdraw from the firm or simply to change to the corporate form. The partnership may be bankrupt. There are many reasons for **partnership dissolution.** Unlike corporations, partnerships lack continued existence. Like humankind, they are mortal. But with a little wizardry, the partnership business may be born again and continue its commercial course in a new guise. This chapter visits the deathbed of the partnership, views its "dissolution," and witnesses its "winding up." It concludes on a happier note, with how the business may be continued.

Partnership dissolution the relation caused by any partner ceasing to be associated in the carrying on of the partnership business

Dissolution, Winding Up, and Termination

The UPA distinguishes among a partnership's dissolution, winding up, and termination, which are the three phases of ending a partnership. The first phase, the partnership's dissolution, represents when the partners cease being associated with one another as partners. It has nothing to do with the discontinuation of the partnership *business* but refers only to a change of *relation* among the partners. The partnership does not automatically stop doing business upon dissolution. A partnership continues after dissolution until the business is liquidated and the partnership terminated, unless continued by agreement or pursuant to the UPA. The second phase is

Winding up the process of terminating and liquidating the partnership business

the winding up of partnership affairs. **Winding up** is the process of bringing the partnership business to an end. The third phase is the partnership's termination. Upon termination the partnership is legally and functionally dead.

Dissolution   The UPA defines dissolution as the change in the relation of the partners caused by any partner's ceasing to be associated in the carrying on, as distinguished from the winding up, of the business. Dissolution is a legal event, a point in time when partners stop doing business together. The partnership has technically dissolved.

Winding Up and Termination   The UPA cautions that "on dissolution the partnership is not terminated, but continues until the winding up is completed." The winding up, otherwise called by businesspeople *liquidation,* is the process of ending partnership affairs. It is the process through which termination is reached. It is the administration of assets to discharge the firm's obligations to its creditors and members. When that process is complete, the partnership is terminated.

Causes of Dissolution

Partnership dissolution is caused by the acts of the partners or by operation of law.

Acts of the Partners   Any partner may dissolve the partnership at any time, and each partner has the power to dissolve the partnership. But the distinction between the *power* to dissolve and the *right* to dissolve should be carefully noted. A power is the ability to affect the legal status of another — for example, a partner's ability to alter his or her associates' status as members of a partnership by dissolving the firm. A person may incur a liability for exercising a power wrongfully. But with a right to do something, there is no liability for its exercise. A partner may have the power to dissolve but not the right. Although a partner can cause a dissolution of the partnership at any time, if the dissolution is wrongful, the guilty partner may be liable to his or her partners for the misconduct.

Whether the partner has the right to dissolve is determined by the agreement among the partners. It may show consent to future dissolution. It may confer the right to dissolve the firm upon a partner, or it may withhold the right under certain circumstances. Any act by a partner that causes the firm's dissolution is rightful if it complies with the agreement. Any act by a partner that causes the firm's dissolution is wrongful if it contradicts the agreement. Under the UPA, dissolution is caused without violating the agreement between the partners:

1. when the partnership term expires, which may be upon the completion of a specified time period or a particular project

2. if no definite time or particular undertaking is specified, at the express will of any partners

3. by agreement of all the partners or by less than all when one or more of the

partners has assigned his or her interest or it has been subjected to a **charging order**

Charging order
a court order given to a judgment creditor so that a partnership will stand charged with paying a partner's debt out of the partner's interest

4. by expelling a partner according to the terms of the partnership agreement.

When a dissolution contradicts the partnership agreement, the remaining partners may recover damages from the guilty partner. This provision is another application of the contract law principles regarding the rights of contracting parties in the event of a breach. The UPA also protects the remaining partners from wrongful dissolution by permitting them to continue the partnership without the errant partner. To do so, the remaining partners must pay to the dissolving partner the value of his or her interest in the partnership, less damages, and must indemnify (repay) him or her against all partnership liabilities.

Operation of Law   Dissolution of a partnership also may be caused by operation of law. Under the UPA, dissolution is caused by operation of law in the following ways:

1. by any event that makes it unlawful to carry on the partnership business

2. by the death of any partner

3. by the bankruptcy of any partner or the partnership

4. by court decree under the UPA

The UPA allows dissolution by a court when a partner applies for it on one of the following grounds:

1. when a partner is incapable of performing as a partner

2. in the case of improper conduct detrimental to the business, such as continual breaches of the partnership agreement

3. if the business can only be carried on at a loss

4. when circumstances and equities show that dissolution is necessary

In the following case, the court considers whether a partnership has been dissolved.

Ramseyer v. Ramseyer

Supreme Court of Idaho
558 P.2d 76 (1976)

From approximately 1959 to 1969, Homer Ramseyer and his sons, Duane and Donald, conducted a cattle ranching business as equal partners pursuant to an oral agreement. The partnership, Ramseyer Cattle Company, owned and operated two ranches, Antelope Springs Ranch and Grassy Hills Ranch. On June 12, 1969, Homer executed a deed conveying to his sons his interest in the Antelope Springs Ranch. He also sold them his partnership interest in the cattle. On the same date, Duane and Donald executed a deed conveying Grassy Hills to Homer and orally agreed to pay $20,000 to Homer's daughter. Duane and Donald also assumed certain partnership

FACTS

debts. After June 12, 1969, Duane and Donald continued to operate a cattle ranching business as a partnership under the name of Ramseyer Cattle Company. Homer no longer participated in the management of the Antelope Springs Ranch, no longer used the partnership checking account, and no longer shared in the partnership's profits or losses. In October 1973, Homer sued his sons, seeking a judicial dissolution of the old partnership and an accounting for transactions since 1969 involving the assets of the old partnership.

ISSUE   Did the transactions of June 12, 1969, constitute a dissolution of the partnership and a winding up of the partnership affairs?

DECISION   Yes. Under the UPA, Homer's "ceasing to be associated in the carrying on . . . of the business" was uncontradicted evidence of the dissolution of the partnership, and the agreed settlement and disposition of the partnership accounts and obligations accomplished a winding up of partnership affairs. The dissolution was by mutual agreement, evidenced by the express will of all the partners, and was thus within one of several specific nonjudicial causes of dissolution. The fact that Duane and Donald continued to conduct a similar operation under the same name did not prevent dissolution, because the new partnership's assets were not the same as those of the old partnership. All of the partnership's assets were divided, so far as the record showed, the partner's respective interests were settled, and agreement was reached on the assumption of outstanding partnership liabilities by Duane and Donald.

Limited Partnerships   The causes of dissolution of limited partnerships are much the same as ordinary partnerships. For example, a limited partnership is dissolved by the completion of its term or undertaking. But some differences arise from limited partners' narrow roles. Although in an ordinary partnership the ceasing of a partner to carry on the business may bring about dissolution, this is not true with limited partners. The death, incapacity, bankruptcy, or withdrawal of one of the limited partners does not dissolve a limited partnership.

Winding Up the Partnership Business

The winding up is the process by which the partnership business is brought to an end. After the partnership relation has dissolved, the partnership's affairs must be wound up if business is to be terminated. This winding up of firm affairs is the process of reducing assets to pay creditors and members of the partnership. During winding up, all uncompleted transactions are finished, debts are settled or paid, claims and accounts owed are collected or settled, and the remaining assets are either sold or distributed along with any surplus to the partners. During this process, the partnership continues for the limited purpose of liquidation, and the partners retain only those powers that are incidental to winding up the business.

Right to Wind Up   The surviving partners who are not bankrupt and who have not wrongfully dissolved the partnership have the right to wind up the affairs of the partnership. When the partners agree to a dissolution, or when the partnership's term expires, all the partners have the right to wind up the firm's affairs. Partners often designate a fellow partner to be in charge of winding up the business. This person is usually called the **liquidating partner** or liquidator. The partners may appoint the liquidating partner by agreement in the articles of partnership.

If the partnership is dissolved because of the bankruptcy or death of a partner, the remaining or surviving partners are entitled to wind up the partnership. Under the UPA, a surviving partner is entitled to reasonable compensation for winding up the business. Only if the last surviving partner dies before the business is wound up does the legal representative of a deceased partner have the right to participate in the winding up. If dissolution is by court order, a court appointed receiver winds up the firm.

> **Liquidating partner** The partner chosen by other partners to oversee the winding up of the business

Partners' Powers during Winding Up   Two needs arise upon dissolution of the partnership:

1. the need to wind up the firm affairs and
2. the need to protect third parties who do business with the firm without knowing of its dissolution.

Both needs are satisfied by two agency law concepts: actual and apparent authority.

To prevent partners from engaging in any new business that might delay winding up, a partner's actual authority upon dissolution is limited to what needs to be done to end the business. A partner may do only what is necessary and incidental to winding up the firm's affairs.

Whether a transaction is necessary and incidental to winding up the partnership depends on the circumstances. Generally, the partners who are winding up the partnership may sell partnership property to liquidate firm assets, take payment for obligations owed to the partnership, and enter into compromises with creditors to release the partnership from its obligations. Actions that at first seem inappropriate actually may be appropriate if they are necessary and incidental to the partnership's winding up.

The concept of apparent authority protects third parties who deal with a partner without knowing about the partnership's dissolution and winding up. A partner's apparent authority may serve to bind the firm to a transaction that would have been binding before dissolution when a third party deals with a partner without knowledge or notice of the dissolution. The UPA incorporates the concept of apparent authority by providing that after dissolution a partner may still bind the partnership to transactions with those who formerly extended credit to the firm if the former creditor has no notice of the dissolution. People who never extended credit to the firm are considered to have notice of the dissolution if the fact of dissolution has been advertised in a newspaper of general circulation.

In the following case, the court considers what constitutes the winding up of partnership affairs and the extent of a surviving partner's authority.

_____ *King v. Stoddard* _____

California Court of Appeals
104 Cal Rptr. 903 (1972)

FACTS   Lyman Stoddard, Sr., his wife, Alda, and their son, Lyman, Jr., operated a partnership which published a newspaper, the Walnut *Kernel*. After Lyman, Sr., and Alda died, Lyman, Jr., continued operating the paper as the sole surviving partner. King and White, an accounting firm, had been accountants for the Walnut *Kernel* for about ten years before the deaths of Lyman, Sr., and Alda and continued to render accounting services after Lyman, Sr., and Alda died. When King and White were not paid, they sued Lyman, Jr., and the estates of Lyman, Sr., and Alda. The agents of the estates argued that the estates were not liable because the son lacked the authority to employ an accounting firm and only had the authority to wind up the partnership business. King and White argued that Lyman, Jr., had the authority to hire them on behalf of the partnership because the newspaper had been continued to preserve its asset value as a going business so that it could be sold and that this was part of the winding up of the business.

ISSUE   Did Lyman, Jr., as surviving partner, have the authority to hire the accountants on behalf of the partnership and thereby make the estates of the deceased partners liable to the accountants?

DECISION   No. The court concluded that the accountants' services did not constitute services during the winding up process. The court said:

> The services were a continuation of the accounting services pursuant to the ordinary course of the operation of the business. . . . It is probably true that there might have been advantages to the partnership to sell the business as a going business, but the indefinite continuation of the partnership business is contrary to the requirements for winding up of the affairs upon dissolution. . . . The record reflects the fact that the surviving partner was not taking action to wind up the partnership as was his duty.

Distribution of Assets

Order of Claims   After partnership assets are liquidated, the proceeds are distributed to pay any claims against the firm. Claims against the partnership are paid in the following order:

1. claims of partnership creditors
2. claims of partners for loans or advances
3. partners' capital contributions
4. remaining assets distributed as profits and surplus to the partners

If the partnership is solvent, no problems are presented because everyone gets paid. But if the partnership assets are insufficient to pay its debts, the partners must make up the loss in the same proportion as they shared profits. If some of the partners are insolvent but others are able to pay, the firm's creditors are paid by the solvent partners.

In the distribution of the assets of a limited partnership, the limited partners under the ULPA follow creditors but precede general partners, and they receive their share of the profits before the return of their capital contributions. Thus after dissolution the obligations of a limited partnership are paid in the following order:

1. creditors

2. limited partners' share of profits and other compensation

3. limited partners' return of capital contributions

4. loans or advances from general partners

5. profits due to general partners

6. return of general partners' capital contribution

Under the Revised ULPA, loans or advances from partners rank with claims by other creditors, and general and limited partners are treated together rather than ranked separately.

Marshaling of Assets   A partnership creditor has a claim against partnership assets; When partnership assets are insufficient to pay the claim, the creditor has a claim against the individual partners' property. A problem arises when there are both individual and partnership creditors. What are their relative rights to a partner's partnership and individual property? Individual creditors have priority to the partner's individual property, but partnership creditors have priority to partnership property. Under the doctrine called **marshaling of assets,** a partnership creditor must pursue a claim against partnership property before pursuing a partner's individual property. By compelling partnership creditors to exhaust partnership property before pursuing a partner's individual property, the doctrine lets both individual and partnership creditors satisfy their claims if there are substantial assets.

Marshaling of assets doctrine by which creditors must pursue claims against partnership property before pursuing partners' individual property

Continuing the Partnership Business

Depending on the particular business involved, dissolution and subsequent liquidation without the right to continue the partnership business can be economically disastrous to the remaining partners. Consequently, one of the major reasons for having a partnership agreement is to provide for the firm's continuation by the remaining partners despite dissolution. In large accounting and brokerage firms, for example, partners are continually joining and withdrawing from the firm. Technically, these comings and goings dissolve the partnership. But through carefully considered provisions in their partnership agreements, they avoid any termination of activities. A continuation provision in a partnership agreement may allow remaining partners to carry on the partnership by buying out a withdrawing partner. Although this arrangement technically is a dissolution of the partnership, the partnership *business* continues.

Right to Continue   Partners may have the right to continue the partnership business although their agreement contains no continuation provision. As we mentioned earlier, when dissolution is caused by an act that contradicts the agreement, the innocent partners may continue the business by

1. paying the dissolving partner the value of his or her interest minus an amount attributable to any damages resulting from the breach and

2. repaying the wrongful partner for all partnership liabilities.

The value of the partner's interest is generally determined by its market value at dissolution rather than its book value.

The UPA grants the innocent partners the right to continue when there is a wrongful dissolution, but the partners still should provide for the situation in their partnership agreement. Their continuation agreement should include at least:

1. a method for placing a value on the guilty partner's interest

2. an agreed method of reimbursement

3. an agreed method of payment if other than cash.

Continuation by Agreement   The dissolved partnership may be continued by an agreement between the withdrawing and remaining partners at the time of dissolution. It may be provided for in advance by a provision in the partnership agreement. For example, a clause in the partnership agreement may provide:

> In the event of dissolution caused by the retirement of a partner, the remaining partners shall have the right to continue the partnership business under the same name by themselves or with any other persons they may choose; however, they shall pay to the retiring partner the value of his or her interest as of the date of dissolution.

When the dissolution occurs, liquidation consists of bookkeeping and buying out the withdrawing partner.

Providing for the firm's continuation in the partnership agreement requires foresight and care by the partners. They should determine:

1. which events, such as death, retirement, bankruptcy, etc., that cause dissolution may also give rise to the right to continue

2. which partners have the right to continue

3. the method of disposing of the withdrawing partner's interest — for example, purchase by the remaining partners or by an incoming partner

4. the method of paying for the withdrawing partner's interest, such as cash, insurance proceeds, or payments out of future earnings

5. the method of allocating the price of the withdrawing partner's interest.

On the last point, the partners should agree on a valuation method. For example, an appraisal may be good for a real estate partnership but not for a service or professional partnership. The valuation method must be fair, a result of each partner's fiduciary duty of loyalty and of fair dealings among partners. An agreed dollar value, even with periodic adjustments, is not considered fair. Using book value is unfair, unless provisions require periodic reappraisal of assets, such as real estate and inventories. Even a provision using a valuation method that is fair may result in a value that is unfair when implemented. For example, in one case the partnership agreement provided that the surviving partners could use their discretion in valuing the partnership's goodwill. But the partners abused their discretion and stated that the business had no goodwill. The court held that this resulted in an unfair value given to the deceased partner's interest.

The partnership provision calling for the purchase of a withdrawing partner's interest is usually referred to as a buy-sell agreement (see Chapter 30). When the death of a partner is contemplated, the buy-sell agreement usually provides for the purchase of a deceased partner's interest at death and is frequently funded by insurance. In a growing business where the partners have reinvested their profits, the surviving partners may be without immediate funds to pay the deceased partner's interest. The only source of funds for the deceased partner's interest may be the future profits of the business, which then will not be available for reinvestment. In such a situation, the buy-sell provision in the partnership agreement may provide for the funding of the purchase price with insurance. The insurance premiums may be paid by the partners or the partnership. On the death of a partner, the insurance policy proceeds are used to pay the deceased partner's interest.

Continuation's Effect on Existing Liabilities   When a partnership continues, creditors of the former partnership remain as creditors of the continuing partnership. The creditors may enforce their claims against a withdrawing partner, who remains liable for any obligations incurred by the partnership before he or she withdrew from the firm. The remaining partners may relieve the withdrawing partner of existing liabilities, but third parties are not bound by the arrangement unless they agree to the change through a novation.

Continuation's Effect on Later Liabilities   Just as it is important to notify third parties of the partnership's dissolution when it is terminated, it is equally important to provide notice when the business continues. Failure to notify third parties of the dissolution when the business continues may increase the liability of the continuing and former partners. If the continuing partners fail to notify third parties of the partnership's dissolution when a partner withdraws from the firm, the continuing partners may be bound by later acts of their former partner. Conversely, if the business is continued as a corporation, failure to notify former creditors may result in the former partners being held personally liable for new obligations as if they were still partners.

The following case illustrates the liability that may result if the wrong form of notice is given to past creditors of the partnership when the partnership is dissolved and continued.

Credit Bureaus of Merced County, Incorporated v. Shipman

Supreme Court of California
334 P.2d 1036 (1959)

FACTS   Shipman and Davis formed a partnership in 1954 doing business as Shipman and Davis Lumber Company. The partnership was dissolved by agreement on September 20, 1955. A notice of dissolution was published in a newspaper of general circulation in the county where the business was conducted, but actual notice of dissolution was not provided to businesses which had extended credit to the partnership at the time of the dissolution. The dissolution agreement provided that Shipman was to continue the business. After the dissolution, several firms that had extended credit to the partnership before the dissolution extended credit to the continued business. When they were not paid, they assigned their claims to Credit Bureaus of Merced County, Incorporated, which sued both Shipman and Davis. Davis defended on the ground that he was not liable for transactions rendered after the dissolution.

ISSUE   Does a withdrawing partner under these circumstances continue to incur liability on transactions undertaken after dissolution of the partnership involving creditors who previously extended credit to the partnership?

DECISION   Yes. According to the court:

The burden is on a defendant relying on dissolution to prove notice of dissolution. Davis cannot rely on [UPA Section 35] to show actual knowledge. This section provides for publication of notice of dissolution of a partnership. However, as to firms having prior credit dealings with the partnership, actual notice of dissolution is necessary. . . . As to the Merced Hardware account, it is clear that the debts for the items sued upon were all incurred after February 1956. Davis contends that he is not liable for these items of debt because they were incurred after the dissolution of the partnership. . . . [UPA Section 35] provides that after a dissolution a partner can bind the partnership "by any transaction which would bind the partnership if dissolution had not taken place, provided the other party to the transaction: 1. Had extended credit to the partnership prior to the dissolution and had no knowledge or notice of the dissolution."

SUMMARY

Partnership dissolution is the change in the relation of the partners caused by any partner's ceasing to be associated in the carrying on of the partnership. It is distinguished from the winding up of the business. On dissolution, the partnership is not terminated but continues until the winding up is completed.

Partnership dissolution is caused either by the acts of the partners or by operation of law. Partnership dissolution may be caused either by acts of the partners that do or by acts that do not violate the partnership agreement. Acts that do not violate the agreement are:

completion of the partnership term or purpose; the express will or agreement of the partners; or expelling a partner according to the terms of the partnership agreement.

Dissolution of a partnership by operation of law may occur: by any event making it unlawful to carry out the partnership business; by the death, bankruptcy, incapacity or improper conduct detrimental to the business by a partner; when the partnership can only be carried on at a loss; or in other circumstances where dissolution may be necessary and equitable. The causes of dissolution of limited partnerships are similar to those of general partnerships.

After dissolution, the surviving partners who are not bankrupt and who have not wrongfully dissolved the partnership have the right to participate in the winding up of the partnership business. Their authority is limited to doing what is necessary and incidental to winding up the partnership's affairs.

After partnership assets are liquidated, the proceeds are distributed to pay any claims against the partnership in the following order: claims of partnership creditors, claims of partners for loans or services, partners' capital contributions, payment of profits and surplus to the partners. For limited partnerships, order of distribution is the same, except that limited partners are paid their share of profits and their capital contribution after other creditors' claims have been paid but before the general partners are paid.

Under the doctrine of marshaling of assets, a partnership creditor must pursue any claims against partnership property before pursuing a partner's individual property.

The partnership business may continue when the partnership agreement so provides. When the dissolution is caused by the wrongful act of a partner, the innocent partners may continue the partnership by buying out the guilty partner. When the partnership is continued, creditors of the former partnership remain as creditors of the continuing partnership.

REVIEW PROBLEMS

1. Compare partnership dissolution to winding up of partnership business.

2. What may partners do to dissolve a partnership?

3. What are the rights and powers of the partners during the winding up of the partnership business?

4. Dissolution of a partnership need not and usually does not mean that the business of the partnership is discontinued. Why?

5. Frank Gibson, Sarah Jones, and Thomas Dunfee form a partnership that operates the Get Lucky Motel. One day Sarah suffers a heart attack and dies. What effect does her death have on the partnership? Explain.

6. Frank Gibson, Thomas Dunfee, and John Blackburn formed a partnership known as the Ace Manufacturing Company. The partners did not enter into a written or an oral partnership agreement. Gibson and Dunfee contributed

$100,000 cash to the capital of the partnership. Blackburn contributed $10,000. For the first year of operation, Blackburn managed the business. Profits for the first year amounted to $1,200,000. Gibson and Dunfee claimed that they were entitled to a share of the profits based on their capital contributions. Blackburn claimed that he was entitled to a salary for managing the business. The disagreement became so heated that Blackburn left the firm at the end of the first year of operation. On leaving, he demanded to be paid his full interest in the partnership, but he was paid only the $10,000 he originally had contributed. After Blackburn left, the business lost $1,200,000. Gibson and Dunfee intend to wind up the partnership and withdraw their contribution. Blackburn believes that he is entitled to further payment. What are the rights of the parties? Explain.

7. Whitman, McCarty, and Brennan are partners doing business as Aggressive Realty Company, a real estate brokerage agency. Their partnership agreement states that the partnership business is to continue for five years. During the first three years, the partnership suffered losses of $20,000, $30,000, and $35,000, respectively. Conditions in the real estate market were so bad that the partnership could continue doing business only at a loss. Whitman asked McCarty and Brennan to dissolve the partnership at the end of the third year. McCarty and Brennan refused to do so. Can Whitman obtain a dissolution of the partnership? If so, how? Explain.

8. Baker and Corbin were partners in a real estate brokerage business. Both contributed personal services, which were the primary source of profits. Corbin withdrew from the partnership, and Baker continued to run the business. To what extent is Corbin entitled to share in the profits after her withdrawal? Explain.

9. Hugo and Charles were brothers who did business as partners. After several years, Hugo died, and Charles was appointed administrator of his estate. Tax returns disclosed that the partnership business was continued just as it had been before Hugo's death. Hugo's estate received the profits and was charged with the losses of the business. Did Charles have the authority to continue the partnership business after the dissolution of the partnership brought on by Hugo's death, and are the assets of Hugo's estate chargeable with the liabilities of the partnership incurred after Hugo's death?

10. Anderson, Baker, and Chase were partners. Anderson contributed $50,000 in capital and loaned the partnership $40,000. Baker contributed $30,000 in capital. Chase contributed his services. Five years after the partnership was formed, the three partners agreed to dissolve the partnership and wind up the business. The partnership creditors, other than Anderson, have claims of $130,000. After all profits and losses have been recorded, there are $176,000 of assets to be distributed to creditors and partners. How are the proceeds of the partnership to be distributed upon dissolution? Explain.

11. Baker and Corbin were partners doing business as Ace Photographers. When Corbin indicated that she wanted to withdraw from the business, the partners entered into a written dissolution agreement whereby Baker was allowed to continue the business. No notice was given to the firm's creditors. Photo Film, Incorporated, had sold film to Ace Photographers before the dissolution and

continued to do so for several years after the dissolution. Baker ran into financial trouble. He terminated the business and filed for personal bankruptcy. Photo Film had a claim against Ace Photographers for $5,000 for film sold to Ace after the dissolution date. Photo Film, Inc., sued Corbin, claiming that she was liable on the claim. Who wins and why?

12. McCarty and Brennan were partners. Recently, McCarty has noticed that Brennan's memory was slipping more than usual and that he rambled and annoyed customers. McCarty has been thinking of dissolving the partnership and continuing the business as a sole proprietor. The partnership agreement still has several years to go before its termination. What should McCarty do? Explain.

CHAPTER 32

Nature and Formation of Corporations

CHAPTER OBJECTIVES

HISTORICAL PERSPECTIVE

NATURE OF CORPORATIONS

Corporate Characteristics / Corporations and the Constitution / Classes of Corporations

REGULATION OF CORPORATIONS

CORPORATE FORMATION

Preincorporation Activity / Incorporation Procedure / Incomplete Incorporation

DISREGARDING CORPORATE PERSONALITY

SUMMARY

REVIEW PROBLEMS

CHAPTER OBJECTIVES

After reading this chapter, you should be able to:

1. Explain how corporations historically became important.

2. Describe the characteristics of corporations.

3. List the constitutional rights and duties of corporations.

4. Classify corporations.

5. State how and by whom corporations are regulated.

6. List the steps by which corporations are formed.

7. Explain when corporate officers are held liable.

HISTORICAL PERSPECTIVE

The corporation as a form of business organization was well known to the Romans. It was Elizabethan England, however, that gave birth to the modern business corporation. Two forerunners of contemporary corporations were the overseas trading company and the **joint stock company.** (Recall from high-school history the role that joint stock companies like the British East India Company played in colonizing America.)

The United States has evolved into a society dominated by corporations. During the twentieth century, several changes have occurred in the nature of corporations and corporate law. As corporate size has increased, so has the need for **capitalization,** usually obtained through the sale of securities to investors.

Joint stock company unincorporated association that has many characteristics of a corporation but is treated as a partnership at law

Capitalization the ability to raise corporate assets (capital) to operate the corporation

NATURE OF CORPORATIONS

As the discussion of partnership law made clear, partnerships have two distinct disadvantages. The partners share unlimited personal liability for partnership obligations, and a technical dissolution of the partnership results from any change in the partnership relation, such as the retirement or death of one of the partners. These features of personal liability and lack of business continuity add risks to partnerships that potential investors may be unwilling to assume.

The corporation was conceived as a means of avoiding the risks and discontinuities of partnership and of achieving business objectives beyond the reach of individuals. When capital needs are great, risks are high, and the enterprise's duration is long, the corporation is the preferred form of business organization. The corporation is the legal institution that can hold over a period of time the aggregated capital of many, unaffected by the death or withdrawal of individuals.

Corporate Characteristics

The chief attributes of a corporation are:

1. its entity status, sometimes called juristic or corporate personality

2. the limited liability of its owners

3. its continued existence, meaning that a corporation may be established in perpetuity

4. the transferability of its ownership

5. the centralization of its management in its officers and directors rather than in its shareholders/owners.

These corporate characteristics are descriptive only. They are not necessarily found in all corporations. But most corporations share these characteristics. Furthermore, for federal income tax purposes, the presence or absence of these characteristics determines whether an enterprise is taxed as a corporation.

Juristic Personality   The principal characteristic of a corporation that distinguishes it from all other business organizations is its status as a legal entity. Because of that status, the law treats the corporation as a person. This permits the corporation to enter into and execute contracts, own and convey property, and sue and be sued as a separate entity distinct from its owners and managers.

The concept of the corporation as a legal person may seem mysterious. But in fact it is a very practical solution to an important social problem. Because human beings are the subjects of the law's commands, it is necessary for the law to treat the corporation like a person to regulate it for the social and economic good. To imagine life without the concept of the corporation as a legal entity, imagine a transaction between the Ford Motor Company and B. F. Goodrich. Treating the transaction as involving two partnerships would involve millions of people as "partners" with hundreds changing every day. Keeping track of the potentially liable people would be a burdensome task even in a computer society.

Limited Liability   A major consequence of the corporation's status as an entity is the limited liability of its shareholders. Corporate rights and liabilities are not to be confused with those of its owners. Generally, shareholders are not liable for corporate debts beyond the amount of their investment, and the corporation is not liable for the debts of its shareholders. The limited liability includes tort, criminal, and contractual liability. This is a major business incentive for investors because they can avoid personal liability for corporate activities. Similarly, personal creditors of shareholders cannot reach the corporate property, although they may reach the shares of the debtor shareholder.

Continued Existence   Another key advantage of the corporation is its capacity for continuous life, sometimes called *perpetual succession*. Shareholders may come and go with no effect upon the corporate entity. A corporation such as the Ford Motor Company can continue long after its founder and major stockholder has died.

Although in most states corporations enjoy continuous existence, a few jurisdictions, such as Mississippi and Oklahoma, limit the life of a corporation to a certain number of years. Furthermore, the corporation's governing documents may limit its duration if that is deemed desirable by its incorporators.

Transferability of Ownership   Ownership interest in a corporation, which generally takes the form of shares of corporate stock, can be traded readily. This permits investors to place a value on their investment and to **liquidate** it if their investment objectives change. Because ownership interest in a corporation may be transferred by a living shareholder, upon his or her death it is possible to distribute the interest to the shareholder's beneficiaries or heirs. Thus a shareholder may give corporate stock to another after death just as he or she could have given that stock away while alive. When the stockholder dies without leaving a will, the shares pass to those who inherit the estate.

Liquidate to convert shares or other assets of a business or estate into money

Restrictions on the transfer of shares may be written into the corporate governing documents if they are reasonable. This provision usually occurs in corporations with only a few shareholders who wish to limit the corporation's ownership to themselves. Generally they provide that before any stock may be sold it must first be offered to the corporation or other stockholders who have the right to purchase the stock for fair value. Outsiders cannot get an ownership interest in the corporation.

Centralized Management and Control   The final characteristic of a corporation is the separation of its management from its ownership. Shareholders have no direct control over the daily business of the corporation. Although this may be less true of corporations with only a few shareholders, individual shareholders are generally powerless to affect corporate affairs in large organizations with many shareholders. Shareholder control is generally limited to electing the corporation's directors and approving major changes in the corporation's structure and operation.

The corporation is managed by its officers and directors. By statute in most states, the management function is centralized in the board of directors. The board of directors often delegates its duties to several officers, such as a president and vice presidents, whom the board appoints to manage the daily corporate business and to report to the directors for guidance. The only control usually possessed by the shareholders is the power to elect and remove the directors. Shareholders, of course, can achieve power if they join together, but in many large corporations this is often difficult and involves large-scale organization.

Centralized management promotes large-scale organization, not individual rights. The result has been the emergence of an increasingly professional and frequently self-perpetuating class of corporate managers who merely go through the formalities of accounting to shareholders. It would not be unfair to say that the small group running a large corporation accounts only to itself or to a few large shareholders. Considering, however, that management selection is often **meritocratic** and that there is a community of interest and outlook in most instances between management

Meritocratic chosen by virtue of ability

**Disenfranchise-
ment** removal of
the right to vote

and shareholders, the virtual **disenfranchisement** of the shareholder is not as oppressive as it appears. In partial recognition of these realities, corporate law in recent times has sought to protect the shareholder — viewed primarily as investor rather than owner — against fraud and has substantially strengthened the obligations of management to act honestly and to disclose all material facts.

Corporations and the Constitution

Do the rights and protections that the U.S. Constitution extends to "persons," "people," and "citizens" apply to corporations? For example, the Fifth and Fourteenth amendments provide that no "person" shall be "deprived of life, liberty or property, without due process of law," and the Fourteenth Amendment prohibits any state to "deny to any person within its jurisdiction the equal protection of the laws." The Fifth Amendment also provides that no person "shall be compelled in any criminal case to be a witness against himself," and the Fourth Amendment guarantees "the right of the people to be secure in their persons, houses, papers, and effects against unreasonable searches and seizures." Furthermore, Article IV and the Fourteenth Amendment secure the privileges and immunities of the "citizens" of each state and the United States.

The answer to the question depends on the purposes behind these various constitutional provisions.

The U.S. Supreme Court has specifically held that a corporation is a "person," entitled to the equal protection of the law, whose property cannot be taken without legal due process. However, a corporation is not a "person" entitled to the Fifth Amendment's privilege against self-incrimination, although it is considered one of the "people" entitled to the Fourth Amendment's protection against unreasonable searches.

This apparent inconsistency rests on the different purposes underlying these constitutional guarantees. The constitutional provision against self-incrimination is considered essentially a personal one, applying only to natural persons. It is not applicable to corporations because its original purpose was to protect individuals against the use of legal process to obtain self-incriminating testimony. Thus a corporation cannot oppose the **subpoenaing** of its books and records by asserting the privilege. Further, an officer or employee of a corporation cannot withhold testimony or documents on the ground that the corporation would be incriminated, although it would be permissible for such an officer or employee to refuse such evidence on the ground that he or she might be incriminated by its production.

Subpoenaing
process by which a
court orders a
person and certain
books and records
to appear in court
at a particular date
and time

Unlike the privilege against self-incrimination, the Fourth Amendment's protection against unreasonable searches and seizures applies to corporations as well as individuals. However, the protection is not absolute. Only *unreasonable* governmental searches are prohibited. The protection yields in the face of a valid search warrant or subpoena.

In appraising the reasonableness of an intrusion, the courts try to balance the expectation of privacy with the the government's need for information before issuing warrants or subpoenas.

A corporation is not considered a citizen entitled to the protection of the privileges and immunities clauses of the federal Constitution. The consequence is that a corporation may be compelled to comply with the corporation laws of a state in which it intends to do business but in which it is not incorporated. It may even be kept out of the state entirely if the state so wishes, unless the corporation is an interstate business. A state's "doing business" requirements cannot burden interstate commerce because of overriding provisions in the federal Constitution. Thus a state may usually require out-of-state corporations to register and pay fees for the privilege of doing business within the state or to designate an agent within the state for the acceptance of service of legal process.

In the case below, the U.S. Supreme Court, treating the corporation as a "person," resolved the question of whether it possesses freedom of expression under the First Amendment.

First National Bank of Boston v. Bellotti

U.S. Supreme Court
435 U.S. 765 (1978)

First National Bank brought a suit against the Attorney General of Massachusetts (Bellotti) seeking to have Section 8 of the state's criminal statute declared unconstitutional. Section 8 forbade expenditures by corporations to influence the vote on any question submitted to voters other than one materially affecting the property, business, or assets of the corporation. The statute specifically forbade expenditures by corporations to influence votes on tax issues. When the plaintiff and other corporations sought to spend money to publicize their opposition to a referendum which proposed to amend the Constitution to enact a graduated personal income tax, the defendant threatened to enforce Section 8.   FACTS

Does Section 8 reduce the corporation's freedom of expression under the First Amendment to the Constitution?   ISSUE

Yes. The Court ruled that it did. The Court said that the protection of the First Amendment is not lost because its source is a corporation. Further, the "materially affecting" requirement of Section 8 was an impermissible prohibition of speech. It allowed a corporation to speak out on certain referendum subjects — those materially affecting its business — but singled out one ballot question — individual taxation — as prohibitive. The Court said that the legislature was prevented by the Constitution from dictating the subjects about which a person could speak and the speakers who might address a public issue.   DECISION

Classes of Corporations

The corporate form of organization has many dimensions. A corporation may be either public or private, profit or nonprofit, publicly issued or closely held, professional or nonprofessional, foreign or domestic. A comparison of various kinds of corporations that first appear dissimilar often reveals certain shared characteristics.

Public and Private Corporations   A corporation may be broadly classified as either public or private. The distinction refers to its purposes and powers. A public corporation is created and funded by the government to carry out some public purpose. Examples of public corporations include municipal, school, and water districts and various public benefit corporations, such as the U.S. Legal Services Corporation. Many state colleges and universities are organized as public corporations.

Private corporations are all corporations other than those that are public. They are created for private rather than public purposes. The General Motors Corporation is an example of a private corporation.

Certificate of shares formal written document which states that an individual or other legal entity owns a share of a corporation

Profit and Nonprofit Corporations   A corporation for profit is primarily a business corporation, one engaged in commercial enterprises. Thus a corporation for profit is organized to conduct a business with a view to realizing gains to be distributed as dividends among its shareholders. A nonprofit corporation is not organized to make a profit for its members and does not conduct a business. Because they are not organized with a view to distributing gains, nonprofit corporations are usually expressly forbidden by statute to issue **certificates of shares.** They may issue membership certificates. Thus they are sometimes characterized as membership rather than shareholder corporations. Social, philanthropic, religious, and cultural corporations are examples of nonprofit corporations.

Public Issue and Closely Held Corporations   A public issue corporation is one whose stock ownership is diffused and whose management is divorced from its owners. "Going public" is a phrase frequently used to describe the process by which a privately owned firm issues stock to the public. This process is usually accompanied by increased governmental regulation, most notably from the Securities and Exchange Commission (SEC), which administers federal legislation on the issuance and trading of corporate securities.

In contrast to a public issue corporation, in which stock is often widely held and management is normally unrelated to stock ownership, a "close" or "closely held" corporation is one whose stock is not publicly traded and whose stock ownership and management usually intertwine. A close corporation usually has only a few shareholders, most or all of whom participate in its management. Thus it has a striking resemblance to a partnership.

Many corporate concepts and principles created with public issue corporations primarily in mind are not well adapted to close corporations. Although the nature and methods of operation of the two kinds of corporations are different, in the past, state corporate codes generally established the same rules for governing both corporations. Since 1960, a legislative breakthrough has occurred, with many states adding laws designed to meet the problems of close corporations. Even now, however, only a handful of states, most notably Florida, Delaware, and Maryland, have adopted separate statutes for close corporations.

Professional Corporations   Until recently, every state prohibited professionals, such as accountants, architects, doctors, and lawyers, from incorporating their professional practices. A recent trend in some states has been to authorize professionals to practice their professions in the corporate form of organization. An individual or group of people licensed in some kind of professional service may now organize as a corporation in these states. However, restrictions are imposed to protect the public. Thus stock may usually be issued only to duly licensed professionals engaged in the service for which the corporation has been organized.

Foreign and Domestic Corporations   A corporation is domestic to the state where it is created. It is considered foreign in all other states and countries where it does business. Thus a corporation incorporated in Delaware is considered a "foreign" corporation in Ohio. This is true even if the corporation's principal place of business is in Ohio.

REGULATION OF CORPORATIONS

Since the beginning of the Republic, the activities of corporations have been enmeshed in government regulation. Before the middle of the nineteenth century, corporations were generally created pursuant to the granting of a corporate charter or franchise by the state in the form of special legislation. However, as the corporate form of organization became popular, the states enacted general corporate **codes** that governed the creation and operation of corporations.

Although the commerce clause and the necessary and proper clause of the federal Constitution empower the U.S. government to grant corporate charters, the federal government has no corporate code. On occasion, however, the federal government has chartered certain corporations, such as the Postal Service Corporation, by enacting special legislation. Virtually all corporations are the creations of the states. Various federal laws, such as the securities and exchange laws, the tax code, the labor statutes, and the antitrust laws, are noteworthy for their impact upon corporations. These may be viewed as constituting a "federal law of corporations" even though there is no single comprehensive federal corporate code.

> **Codes** published sets of laws set out in bound volumes according to a numbered system, following passage by Congress or the state legislatures

CORPORATE FORMATION

Today thousands of corporations are formed each year without much intellectual effort on the part of the incorporators and without raising any significant legal issues.

Preincorporation Activity

Corporation formation starts with certain preincorporation activity. Before the corporation is formally launched, contracts sometimes must be made, legal relations created, and business activities undertaken with a view to creation of the corporation.

The Promoter   A promoter is someone who undertakes to form a corporation. Corporations do not spring into existence on their own. They result from planning and preliminary work by promoters. It is the promoter who transforms an idea into a business. The promoter plans the development of a corporate business venture, brings together people who are interested in the projected enterprise, organizes and incorporates it, and establishes the newly formed corporation as a fully functioning business. Although promoters are sometimes called "preincorporators," their activities often reach beyond the point of formal incorporation.

The promoter's efforts are largely devoted to making contracts on behalf of the proposed corporation. Sometimes these contracts are self-serving—for instance, when the promoter conveys property to the corporation in exchange for shares of the corporation's stock. Frequently, the contracts are with third persons for materials and services necessary to launch the enterprise. Problems arising from these promoter contracts involve:

1. the duties of promoters toward the unformed corporation and
2. the contractual liabilities of both the promoter and the new corporation to third parties.

Promoter's Duties to the Corporation   Because at the time of the promoter's activities no corporation is yet in being, the promoter is not the corporation's agent. No agency exists because there is no principal. Someone cannot serve another as a self-appointed agent. Nevertheless, a promoter is under certain obligations.

Because they are joint venturers in forming the corporation, all promoters occupy a fiduciary relationship (a relationship based on trust or confidence) with any other co-promoters. Promoters also occupy a fiduciary relationship to the corporation they form. This fiduciary relationship gives the promoter an affirmative duty of fully disclosing to the corporation any dealings with the corporation in which the promoter has a personal interest and, further, a duty to enter any transactions with the corporation in good faith. Thus the promoter may not obtain any secret profits out of transactions with or for the corporation to be formed.

A typical case of promoter liability for failing to fully disclose material information to the corporation occurs when, after organizing the new corporation, the promoter sells to it his own property. If the promoter conveys property to the corporation, he or she must fully disclose any personal interest, the extent of any profit on the transaction, and any other material factors that might affect the corporation's decision whether to purchase. This disclosure must be made either to a board of directors that is not controlled by the promoter or to all existing shareholders.

The usual case of promoter liability for failing to deal in good faith with the corporation is when **watered stock** has been issued to the promoter. The term refers to stock issued by a corporation in excess of any fair and adequate consideration received in exchange for it. It reduces the value of the stock held by other shareholders and further damages creditors of the corporation who may have relied on the belief that the corporation had received assets equivalent in value to the value of the issued shares. Stock watering occurs when promoters cause the overvaluation of their contribution to the corporation, resulting in the issuance of stock by the corporation for less than fair consideration. When there is stock watering, innocent shareholders whose stock has been devalued by the issuance of the watered stock may bring suit on behalf of the corporation to recover the lost value. Further, any injured creditors may force the promoter to pay to the corporation the unpaid value of the shares.

Watered stock issued stock that is represented as fully paid but in fact is not paid up

Preincorporation Contracts   A contract made by the promoter with a third party on behalf of the proposed corporation raises the question of whether the promoter, the corporation, or both are contractually liable. Generally, the promoter remains liable as a party to the contract unless relieved of the liability by the corporation. But the corporation generally is not bound by the contract of the promoter until the corporation assents to the contract.

The usual case of promoter liability on preincorporation contracts occurs when the proposed corporation never comes into existence, or the corporation completely disavows the contract. In such situations, the other party to the contract usually tries to hold the promoter liable. Because the promoter acts for the corporation before its organization, under the general rules of agency law he or she is the principal on the contract. Under agency law, an agent for an undisclosed — or here a nonexistent — principal becomes a party to any contracts made with third parties. Similarly, the promoter is held bound by his or her contracts. If this were not so, any agreement made by the promoter on behalf of the future corporation would be inoperative until after the corporation were formally organized, thereby depriving the third party of any remedy until that time. Personal liability for the promoters on preincorporation contracts is not unfair, because the promoter is in the best position to bring about incorporation and the adoption of the contract by the corporation. Thus it is only fair that the risk that the corporation may not be formed should be the promoter's and not the third party's, even if the third party is advised of the exact state of affairs.

Nevertheless, those dealing with the promoter may look to the corporation and not the promoter for performance of the contract. If the promoter clearly negates liability, the agreement is considered to be a continuing offer to the corporation rather than a contract. If the promoter specifically states that he or she is contracting in the name of the proposed corporation and not individually, the other party must rely entirely on the credit of the proposed corporation and has no claim against the promoter. This is simply a matter of recognizing the intention of the parties.

Generally, a corporation is not liable on a contract made by the promoter for its benefit unless it takes some affirmative action to adopt the contract when it formally comes into existence. Mere incorporation does not of itself render the promoter's contracts binding on the company. There must be some action by the corporation indicating its assent. This adoption may be by express words or writing or may be inferred from the corporation's knowingly accepting the contract's benefits. The reason for this rule of corporation nonliability on preincorporation contracts is to avoid any injustice to the corporation's shareholders and subsequent creditors that would result if the corporation were forced to come into existence burdened with the obligation to perform its promoters' promises. The case below illustrates this general rule of corporate nonliability with regard to promoters' contracts.

Solomon v. Cedar Acres East, Incorporated

Supreme Court of Pennsylvania
317 A.2d 283 (1974)

Solomon, an architect, sought specific performance on work he did for the defendant   FACTS
corporation before it came into existence. His agreement with the promoter of the
corporation was that he would become a 5 percent owner of any future created
corporation that developed the tract of land he worked on. He would also receive 5

percent of the profits of the company. Upon creation of the company, plaintiff sent a bill for architectural services. The defendant refused to honor the agreement that the plaintiff entered into with the promoter, claiming no knowledge of it.

ISSUE   Is the defendant responsible for the contract of its promoter before its incorporation?

DECISION   No. The court ruled that it was not if it did not ratify the agreement following its incorporation. Here the defendant company had no knowledge of the plaintiff's and promoter's agreement to provide for stock issuance and profit sharing. However, the court ruled that Solomon had a right to complete relief against the promoter for services rendered because the latter had admitted in the trial proceedings that the contract was of a personal nature.

Incorporation Procedure

Because corporate existence is a privilege conferred by the state, the proper papers must be filed and certain formalities observed to bring about incorporation. Businesspeople need legal help during this process.

The first step taken in incorporating a business is the selection of the state of incorporation. Once that has been decided, the incorporators must prepare and file the articles of incorporation, along with any fees and taxes, with the secretary of state. If all is in order, the secretary issues a certificate of incorporation, sometimes called the corporate charter. After the issuance of the certificate, an organizational meeting must be held to adopt the corporate bylaws, elect officers, and transact any initial corporate business.

Selecting the State of Incorporation   After determining to incorporate, the first decision to be made is where to incorporate. Most small corporations usually incorporate in the state where they are to be located. If the business is interstate, consideration is sometimes given to other states if the local state corporation and tax laws have restrictions. Delaware is often the first state considered because its legislature and courts generally favor corporate management over dissident minority shareholders. Delaware's corporation statute is considered "liberal" because of its flexibility, which enables management to conduct corporate business with few restrictions.

Delaware is not the only state that may be attractive to incorporators. New Jersey and New York compete with Delaware by offering liberal corporation codes. Today, many corporations are incorporated in these states even though their principal places of business are elsewhere. California has a corporate code that attempts to limit the discretion of corporate management.

One disadvantage of out of state incorporation is that the corporation incurs double taxation in the form of a franchise tax for doing business in the state where it does. Out of state incorporation also subjects the corporation to liability for suits in a jurisdiction removed from its principal place of business. In the event of litigation, there may be an issue of which state's law applies. The general rule is that the law of the incorporating state is applied to issues relating to the internal affairs of the

FIGURE 32-1   Articles of Incorporation of XYZ Corporation

ARTICLE I
Name
The name of this corporation is **XYZ Corporation.**

ARTICLE II
Registered Office and Resident Agent
The registered office of the corporation is **15 Main Street, Kansas City, Kansas.**
The resident agent at that address is **John Doe.**

ARTICLE III
Nature of Business
The nature of the business or purposes to be conducted or promoted are:
To engage in any lawful conduct or activity for which corporations may be organized under the Kansas Corporation Code.

ARTICLE IV
Capital Stock
This corporation is authorized to issue Ten Thousand (10,000) shares of common stock without par value.

ARTICLE V
Incorporators
The names and mailing addresses of the incorporators are as follows:
Dennis Jones — 100 Main Street, Kansas City, Kansas
Mary Jones — 100 Main Street, Kansas City, Kansas

ARTICLE VI
Initial Directors
The powers of the incorporators are to terminate upon the filing of these Articles of Incorporation, and the names and mailing address of the persons who are to serve as directors until the first annual meeting of stockholders or until their successors are elected and qualified are:
Dennis Jones — 100 Main Street, Kansas City, Kansas
Mary Jones — 100 Main Street, Kansas City, Kansas

ARTICLE VII
Bylaws
The power to adopt, repeal and amend the bylaws of this corporation shall reside in the Board of Directors of this corporation.
IN TESTIMONY WHEREOF, we have hereunto set our names this
_____ day of _____ ,

---

corporation. But there is a trend toward making this determination on the basis of whether the state of incorporation has an interest in having its law applied.

Articles of Incorporation   After the state of incorporation is selected, the incorporators must prepare and file the **articles of incorporation,** which are to be submitted, along with any fees, to the secretary of state. Among the items to be included in

Articles of incorporation
the instrument by which a private corporation is formed and organized under the general corporation laws of a state

the articles is the corporation's name. This name must include the word "corporation," "company," "incorporated," or "limited" or an abbreviation of one of those words. Using any word or phrase that indicates that the corporation is organized for any purpose other than the one stated in its articles is prohibited. A corporate name is to be distinguishable in the records of the secretary of state from that of other corporations. If a name is available, incorporators may apply to the secretary of state to reserve the name for 120 days while the corporation is being organized.

Additional information about the corporation's capital structure also must be provided, such as the number and classes of authorized shares. Many states require a minimum stated capital for starting the business (usually $1,000).

The articles also must state the name and address of the corporation's initial registered agent, initial office, and all incorporators. Many states require that there be

FIGURE 32-2   Certificate of Incorporation

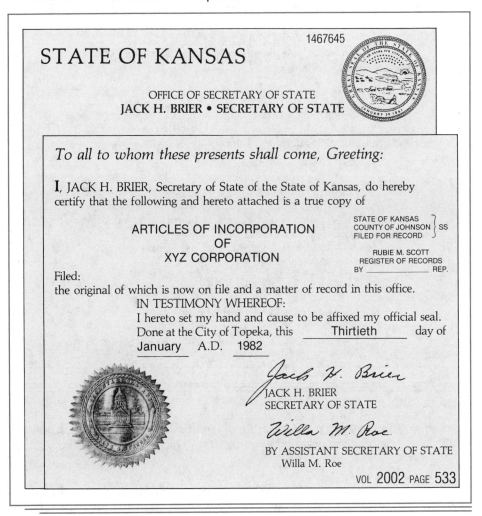

three incorporators and three directors. Some permit the corporation to have only one incorporator and one director, enabling sole proprietors to incorporate their businesses without needlessly involving others.

Organizational Meeting   After issuance of the certificate of incorporation by the secretary of state, an organizational meeting of the board of directors must be held to adopt the bylaws, elect officers, and transact initial corporate business, such as adopting any preincorporation contracts. The corporate bylaws provide private legislation for the regulation and management of corporate affairs and must not conflict with the articles or state law. Unless the articles provide otherwise, adoption of the initial bylaws and any later amendments rests with the board of directors. Many states permit shareholder adoption and amendment of the bylaws.

Incomplete Incorporation

Problems may arise when there has been some defect in the incorporation process, such as a failure by one of the incorporators to sign the articles or a failure to provide the information in the articles as required by statute. Streamlined incorporation procedures make this less of a problem. But when it does occur, it raises the possibility of personal liability for the shareholders. Because the consequences of failing to comply with the technical requirement of incorporation may be so serious, three doctrines have been developed by the courts to shield shareholders from being treated as partners. These doctrines are:

1. de jure incorporation

2. de facto incorporation

3. corporation by estoppel.

De Jure Incorporation   In interpreting the requirements of incorporation statutes, courts generally have held that no useful purpose is served by a strict interpretation that converts every detailed requirement into a prerequisite of corporate existence. If there has been substantial compliance with a statute authorizing the formation of a corporation, a "de jure" corporation results. A de jure corporation is recognized as a corporation for all purposes and to all parties, including the state of incorporation. No one, not even the state, may challenge the organization's corporate status, even if there has been a technical failure to comply with the incorporation procedures.

To obtain de jure status, there must be literal compliance with all mandatory requirements of incorporation and substantial compliance with all directive requirements. What constitutes a mandatory as opposed to a directive requirement is a matter of statutory construction and depends upon the nature of the incorporation defect. Requirements that are merely formalities, such as the requirement that a seal be affixed on the articles, are considered directive only. Their absence is not sufficient to defeat corporate existence. But the more important a requirement is, the more likely it is considered mandatory. Thus the requirement that the articles be filed would be mandatory. Failure to file the articles could not result in de jure corporate status.

De Facto Incorporation   When significant defects prevent a de jure existence, courts may nevertheless recognize the organization as a de facto corporation. In the case of a de facto corporation, third persons cannot take advantage of the defects to charge the shareholders with unlimited liability or to avoid contracts with them. But the state can try to have its charter revoked. This is because the defect is significant enough that the law cannot ignore it, and the state is permitted to take any necessary steps to remedy the situation. A de jure corporation cannot be challenged by anyone, but a de facto corporation can be challenged by the state.

Generally, a de facto corporation results if there is a law in the state under which a corporation might be formed, there has been an attempt in good faith to incorporate under such law, and the organization has conducted business as a corporation. An example of de facto corporate existence might be when articles are drafted in due form and turned over to an attorney who neglects to file them through no fault of the incorporators'. Although there is not sufficient compliance for de jure existence, the de facto corporate status shields the shareholders from personal liability to third parties.

The trend is to eliminate the de facto doctrine because it is believed that modern incorporation statutes are streamlined enough to justify stricter compliance than the doctrine requires. Further, it is believed keeping the de facto doctrine when it is not needed only encourages noncompliance with incorporation procedures.

Incorporation by estoppel when a business is incorporated not by virtue of the appropriate legal steps, but by the way customers, creditors, and others treat the company in the course of doing business with it

Incorporation by Estoppel   When a third person deals with a defectively organized corporation as if it were in fact incorporated, he or she may be prevented from challenging the corporate status of the organization upon later learning of the defective incorporation. It is generally considered to be unfair to allow the third party to hold the shareholders personally liable when he or she originally dealt with the organization as though it were a corporation, knowing that a corporation is an entity of limited liability. But the estoppel theory recognizes the corporation only for the particular third-party transaction. The case below illustrates a court's use of de facto and **estoppel** theories of **incorporation.**

_____ *Timberline Equipment Company, Incorporated v. Davenport* _____

Supreme Court of Oregon
514 P. 2d 1109 (1973)

FACTS   Timberline Equipment Company sought to recover rentals on equipment leased to Davenport, Bennett, and others. The defendants signed articles of incorporation on January 22, 1970. They were defective because they were not in accord with state statutes. Articles of incorporation were finally issued on June 22, 1970. During the period between January 22 and June 22, rental agreements were entered into with the plaintiff. Defendants argued that the rentals were to a de facto corporation, Aero-Fabb

Company, and the plaintiff was estopped from denying the corporate character of the corporation.

Are the rental agreements enforceable against the corporation even though it was legally defective at the time they were entered into?   ISSUE

No. The court ruled that they were not because the principle of de facto corporation no longer existed in Oregon. Its Business Corporation Act was based on the Model Business Corporation Act, which requires the issuance of a certificate of incorporation for a corporation to come into existence. But the court said that the plaintiff could recover against Dr. Bennett personally because he and Davenport signed all checks and assumed to act for the organization during the period in which the rental agreements were entered into.   DECISION

DISREGARDING CORPORATE PERSONALITY

Once incorporation is complete, shareholders reasonably expect to be insulated from liability for the corporation's debts. One of the main purposes of incorporating is to enable the stockholders to engage in a business without incurring any personal liability beyond the loss of their investments. However, if the recognition of the corporate entity results in some injustice, such as defrauding creditors, evading statutory obligations, or defeating public interest, the corporate entity is disregarded. In such a case, personal liability is imposed on the stockholders.

The rapid growth of closely held corporations and diversified corporate organization consisting of a single parent and several subsidiaries has compelled the courts recently to reexamine the entity status of some corporations. Most statutes confer liability on the corporation for corporate debts. As a legal entity, the corporation normally bears sole liability for debts created in its name. However, limited liability protection is a privilege granted to shareholders for the convenience of conducting business in the corporate form. It is a privilege that must be used to promote decent and fair objectives. The corporate entity is disregarded and limited liability lost when the privilege is abused. Shareholders are held personally liable for corporate debts when such a solution is necessary to justice.

Courts have used colorful language in holding shareholders liable. The most common phrase is "piercing the corporate veil," meaning that the corporate entity, which usually effectively veils shareholders from liability on corporate debts, is "pierced" to reach the shareholders and hold them liable. The end result is that shareholder liability is imposed to reach an equitable result.

The question of the status of a corporation often arises when a liability has been incurred in the name of the corporation but the corporation has become insolvent. The creditor, seeking to find a solvent defendant, may sue all or some of the shareholders, arguing that for some reason they should be called upon to pay the corporation's debts. The issue is whether the loss should be imposed on third persons or shareholders. Always treating a corporation as a person would mean that the creditor inevitably suffered the loss. In most cases the result is reasonable because the creditor extended credit to a corporation, which he or she should have known has limited liability. But this result often does not occur when it would be unjust to the creditor, especially involuntary creditors, such as tort victims. Creditors who made contracts with the corporation have more difficulty obtaining shareholder liability because they presumably dealt with the corporation voluntarily and should have known whether the corporation lacked substance.

When control by the stockholders or a parent corporation is carried out in a normal manner, with due regard for all necessary formalities and for the rights of creditors, separate entity status usually is sustained. But when the corporation has no voice in its own affairs, when there is a manipulation of the assets of the corporation and the shareholders, and when corporate and personal activities are inseparable, then the courts look behind the facade and consider the identities as one. In doing this, the courts sometimes say that the corporate entity is merely a "sham" or a mere shadow of the shareholder's personality. Closely held and parent–subsidiary corporations are particularly vulnerable to this attack. Close corporations may fail to follow the formalities of corporate existence, and parent–subsidiaries often share the same directors. Undercapitalized corporations are also targets for "piercing" litigation, because a grossly undercapitalized corporation may be considered a fraud upon creditors. The case below illustrates this point.

DeWitt Truck Brokers, Incorporated v. W. Ray Flemming Fruit Company

U.S. Court of Appeals, Fourth Circuit
540 F. 2d 681 (1976)

FACTS   The DeWitt Company sought to recover hauling charges from Ray Flemming, who was the president of a fruit company for which DeWitt hauled produce. Flemming owned 90 percent of the company. It had one other director. There were no records of board or stockholder meetings, and Flemming was the sole beneficiary of the corporation's profits. DeWitt alleged that he should be able to "pierce the corporate veil" and hold the defendant personally liable. Flemming argued that proof of fraud must be shown to hold him personally liable.

ISSUE   Can the plaintiff "pierce the corporate veil" and hold the defendant personally liable without a showing of fraud?

DECISION   Yes. The court ruled that a showing of fraud was not necessary to hold the defendant liable. It pointed out that under the "alter ego" doctrine the court is concerned with defendant's real relationship to the corporation. If, as in this case, the corporation was undercapitalized, no dividends were paid except to a single individual, no board or shareholder meeting took place, and substantial sums were taken out of the corporation by a single individual, basic fairness required the imposition of individual liability.

_____ SUMMARY _____

Corporations have two distinct advantages over a partnership: freedom from personal liability for its officers, and continuity of function when one or more officers die or depart.
Corporations have five distinct characteristics:

juristic personality

limited liability

continued existence

transferability of ownership

centralized management.

The corporation is a legal entity and is a "person" under the Constitution for some purposes (for example, it is entitled to the Fourteenth Amendment's equal protection of the law), but not for others (for example, it is not entitled to the Fifth Amendment's privilege against self-incrimination).
There are five classes of corporations:

public and private

profit and nonprofit

public issue and closely held

professional

foreign and domestic corporations.

Corporations of all classes may be regulated by federal or state law.
Corporations are usually formed through the efforts of promoters who plan and bring together the people who are interested in the enterprise. The promoter has a fiduciary duty to the unformed corporation. When a promoter enters into a contract on behalf of a proposed corporation, generally he or she is personally liable unless the corporation's board of directors consents to such an agreement after the entity comes into existence. Following preincorporation activity and the selection of a state for location of the business, the articles of incorporation are prepared and submitted with any fees to the secretary of state. An organizational meeting of the board of directors must be held to elect officers and transact initial corporate business.
A corporation comes into existence if there is substantial compliance with a state's incorporation statutes. It is called a de jure corporation. When there are significant defects in the incorporation process, courts have nonetheless recognized the entity as a de facto corporation. Whereas a de jure corporation's existence cannot be attacked by anyone, a de facto corporation can be attacked by the state and its charter revoked. In some cases, courts "pierce the corporate veil" and hold shareholders, officers, and directors personally liable for corporate debts.

REVIEW PROBLEMS

1. What principally distinguishes a corporation from a sole proprietorship or a partnership?

2. Does a corporation have the protection of the Fifth Amendment privilege against self-incrimination? Explain.

3. What is the distinction between a public and private corporation?

4. Are all states required to have the same incorporation laws? Explain.

5. Triplett, his partner, and their secretary acted as incorporators and signed articles of incorporation for Air Capital International, Inc. None served as officers or directors of the corporation. Air Capital violated two sections of the Kansas Corporation statute. The statute provided that articles of incorporation had to be filed with the secretary of state and the registrar of deeds in the county where the corporation's office was located. Air Capital's articles of incoporation were filed with the secretary of state but not with the county registrar of deeds. Thus it never became a legally existing corporation. A second section of the Kansas statute provided that a corporation could not do business until it legally existed. Air Capital did not meet this requirement before it began doing business in 1967. Air Capital, Inc. declared bankruptcy in 1971. The state of Kansas brought action against Triplett, his partner, and their secretary to recover employment taxes due. What result?

6. The Illinois incorporation statute provided that people wishing to form a corporation must "sign, send, and acknowledge" the articles of incorporation before a notary public. Ford and Fisher signed and filed articles of incorporation with the secretary of state but failed to affix any seal to the document. Later the Illinois attorney general brought legal proceedings against the two men, claiming that they were doing business under an illegal corporate certificate, and attempting to revoke the corporate status. What result?

7. Carlton owned the stock of ten taxi corporations, each owning two cabs and carrying the minimum insurance required by state law. Walkovszky was injured in an accident as a result of the negligence of one of the drivers of the cabs. Can Walkovszky successfully sue Carlton and hold him personally liable for his injuries, or must he satisfy any claim he has against the assets of the particular two-cab corporation involved in the accident?

8. Seller entered into a contract for the sale of plants to the Denver Memorial Nursery, Inc. The contract was signed by Parr as Denver's president. Seller knew that the corporation was not yet formed, and the contract recited this fact, but Seller insisted that the contract be executed this way rather than wait until the corporation was organized. The corporation was never formed. Seller sued Parr to hold him personally liable on the contract. What result?

9. A, a promoter of a real estate corporation, B, that was not yet formed, entered into a contract with C for real estate services in buying land. Corporation B was later formed. C sued A for a breach of contract when A refused to pay a commis-

sion to C. A's defense was that C knew that the corporation had not been formed at the time the contract was entered into. What result?

10. Helen Joplin owned a liquor store as a sole proprietorship. Later she sold 25 percent to Henderson. They agreed that a new corporation would be formed with Henderson purchasing 25 percent of the stock, becoming an officer, and drawing a salary of $700. The business was incorporated and operated successfully for three years. Then Henderson proposed a buy out. Joplin refused and fired Henderson. Henderson sued based on a breach of contract. Joplin defended, claiming that preincorporation agreements between directors or shareholders are contrary to public policy and thus void. What result?

11. Before the Bolshevik Revolution in 1917 in Russia, a Russian bank held a balance outstanding to its credit of $66,749.45 in a United States bank. When the Revolution took place, all its assets in the Soviet Union were confiscated by the Bolsheviks, and its stock was canceled. Years later the Russian bank through its shareholders sued a New York bank for the balance outstanding. The defense of the New York bank was that the corporation had been dissolved under Russian law, and thus there existed no legal person or corporation under United States law. It refused to pay the credit balance. What result?

12. A restaurant owner, Zechery, entered into a security agreement for a loan of $11,000 on July 24, 1975. A certificate of incorporation for the restaurant, Roseberry Inn, Inc., was executed on July 24 but was not filed with the Secretary of State until July 30, 1975. When the restaurant failed, the bank sued Roseberry Inn, Inc. and Zechery for repossession of the restaurant equipment, which was security for the loan. Zechery, the defendant, and one of the owners of the Inn argued that the bank could not have acquired a security interest in the equipment because the restaurant was not incorporated and thus did not exist (de jure) at the time the security agreement was executed. What result?

13. Cranson invested in a new corporation, Real Estate Service Bureau, which was about to be created. Cranson would become an officer and director. He was advised by an attorney that the corporation had been incorporated under the law of Maryland. The business of the corporation was conducted through corporate bank accounts, and auditors kept corporate books. Cranson was later elected president of the corporation and as an officer of the corporation had dealings with IBM. Due to an oversight on the part of the attorney, the certificate of incorporation was not filed until after the transactions for typewriters with IBM took place. IBM sued Cranson personally for a balance of $4,334 owed on the typewriters. Cranson claimed that a de facto corporation existed at the time the typewriters were purchased, and thus he was not personally liable. What result?

14. On December 27, 1961, Robertson and Levy entered into an agreement whereby Levy was to form a corporation, Penn Avenue Record Shack, Inc., which was to purchase Robertson's business. The articles of incorporation were submitted to the Supervisor of Corporations of the District of Columbia on December 27, 1961. On January 2, 1962, the articles of incorporation were rejected by the District of Columbia. On January 8, Robertson executed a bill of sale to the Penn Avenue Record Shack, Inc. for all of Robertson's business

assets. Levy, as president of the corporation, issued a note providing for install-ment payments by the corporation to Robertson. The certificate of incorpora-tion was issued on January 17, 1962. When Penn Avenue Record Shack, Inc. ceased doing business in June 1962, Robertson sued Levy personally for the balance owed. Levy, as defendant, argued that there existed a de facto corpora-tion at the time the bill of sale was executed, and thus he was not personally liable. What result?

CHAPTER 33

Financing the Corporation

CHAPTER OBJECTIVES

After studying this chapter, you should be able to:

1. Explain how corporations finance their ongoing operations and expansion through the sale of stocks and bonds.

2. Describe the legal problems in stock subscriptions before and after incorporation.

3. Explain federal and state regulations issuing and trading in securities.

KINDS OF SECURITIES

Securities (see page 408)

The sale of **securities** is the usual method of corporate financing. Most financing comes from investors who receive securities in return for their investments. The security is usually represented by a certificate, such as a share of stock or a bond, that shows the security holder's rights in the corporate business. The two main types of securities are debt securities and equity securities.

Debt Securities

Most state corporation statutes authorize corporations to borrow money, incur liabilities, and issue bonds. Most of these actions do not need shareholder approval. The funds generated by this borrowing must be used only for corporate purposes. Debt securities evidence a debt of the corporation and become corporate liabilities.

Debenture unsecured corporate obligations backed by the general credit of the corporation and its assets

Bond a long-term debt security secured by a lien or mortgage on corporate property

Types of Debt Securities   Debt securities include notes, debentures, and bonds. Notes usually represent short-term borrowing of the corporation. They are payable upon order to a bank or person. Interest payments are due periodically. **Debentures** are unsecured corporate obligations backed by the general credit of the corporation and its assets. If the corporation defaults, creditors attempt to seize the assets. A **bond** (used interchangeably with debentures) is usually a long-term debt security secured by a lien or mortgage on corporate property. Bonds are bearer instruments. Interest payments are made periodically upon submission of coupons by the bondholders.

Debt securities have two important characteristics. They are subject to redemption and conversion. Redemption means the corporation reserves the right to call in and pay off its obligations at any time before they are due, usually at a premium over face value. Debt securities may also be convertible—that is, they may be converted into equity securities (such as common stock) at a certain ratio.

Tax Advantage of Debt Securities   Debt securities offer significant tax advantages for the corporation that issues them. Interest payments on bonds or notes are tax deductible for the corporation, but dividend payments on equity securities (such as common stock) are not. Payments of a debt by a corporation may be considered a nontaxable return on capital for the investor. A redemption of equity securities from a shareholder by the corporation may be taxed as ordinary income. The Internal Revenue Service (IRS) has often investigated corporations' debt structures to determine if they are excessive. If the IRS finds that a debt structure is excessive, it tries to treat the excessive debt as a form of corporate equity for tax purposes. Thus the substantial advantages associated with corporate debt financing have led to considerable litigation. Because the courts have treated each situation as unique, no overriding legal principle has evolved to determine when a corporation's debt is excessive. Courts have considered the ratio of debt to equity as relevant but have rejected a purely quantitative approach.

Equity Securities

Every corporation must issue equity securities, usually called shares or stock. Stockholders (shareholders) own the corporation. Authorization for the issuance of equity is contained in the corporation's articles of incorporation. Unless authorized, the sale of shares is void.

The money raised by the corporation from the sale of stock is the fund out of which the corporation may meet its obligations to creditors. It represents the corporation's stated capital. The corporation is not bound to return to the shareholders their investment before the enterprise is liquidated. The shares usually have no maturity date. Return on the shareholders' investment takes two forms: dividends, which depend on the availability of profits and the discretion of the board of directors; and **capital gains,** which result from the shareholders' ability to sell their stock for a higher price than they originally paid. Shareholders' claims are subordinate to the claims of debt security holders, because debt holders stand as creditors of the corporation, not as its owners. When a corporation is liquidated, shareholders receive only those funds available after all corporate creditors have been paid.

Capital gains
gains from the sale of stock in excess of appraised value or original cost

Common and Preferred Stock   Most states authorize the issuance of more than one class of corporate stock and permit the corporation to vary the rights, preferences, and restrictions among the different classes. The two classes most frequently issued are: (1) common stock and (2) preferred stock.

If the corporation issues only one class of stock, that stock will be **common stock.** Because common stockholders assume the most risk and have the most to gain from the corporate venture, they receive none of the preferences that the holders of other classes of stock may receive. Common stockholders stand behind bondholders and holders of other classes of stock when corporate distributions are made. But common stockholders may participate in the corporate management. (See Chapter 34 for a discussion of the shareholders' role in management.)

Preferred stock is given special rights and preferences when corporate distributions are made. Because of these preferences, preferred shareholders assume less risk than common shareholders. They do not usually participate in corporate management.

Common stock
corporate stock entitling holder to voting rights and dividends, but dividends are paid only after rights of preferred stockholders have been satisfied

Preferred stock
stock which is generally given preference over any other class with regard to payment of dividends and distribution of assets upon liquidation of the corporation

FIGURE 33-1   Stock Certificate

Preferences of any class of stock usually are stated in the articles of incorporation. Thus the extent that preferred stock differs from common stock depends on the provisions of the articles of incorporation where the relative rights and preferences of the shares of each series are outlined as to:

1. the dividend rate to be paid
2. the amount payable to shareholders upon liquidation
3. any redemption rights along with any provisions for **sinking funds** for redeeming preferred shares
4. the conditions for convertible shares
5. any voting rights

Sinking fund assets, usually cash or relatively liquid securities, used by a corporation to redeem its own stocks or bonds

As a practical matter, the special rights and preferences given preferred shareholders by either the articles or the board are printed on the preferred stock certificates.

Preferred stock usually has a stated dividend rate. Although a corporation does not have to pay a dividend in any given year, if it does declare a dividend the preferred shareholders receive the rate stipulated by the articles and are paid before the common shareholders. Preferred shareholders also have superior standing in the distributions of corporate assets upon the corporation's liquidation.

Preferred stock may be made redeemable by the corporation usually at a price fixed by the board of directors. Preferred stock is also convertible into shares of another class or into another type of security, such as a bond.

As noted above, preferred shareholders generally participate less in corporate management than common shareholders. This balances the lower risk assumed by preferred shareholders. Thus preferred stock is generally nonvoting.

Stock Options and Warrants In addition to common and preferred stock, most state statutes authorize the issue of **stock options** and rights. These securities entitle their holders to purchase from the corporation shares of the corporation's stock. If the option is a negotiable instrument giving the owner the right to purchase stock of the corporation at a specified price, it is called a warrant. Warrants are usually issued to make the issue of some other security more attractive. The owner of the warrant is not only guaranteed the right to buy a number of shares but also may trade it freely. Often warrants are issued to present shareholders to prevent a dilution of ownership. Shareholders buy a new issue in the form of warrants and thus get an opportunity to buy the stock at a price lower than its market price.

Stock option In exchange for depositing some consideration, a person retains the option to buy a stock for a limited period of time

Stock options are often issued by a corporation to an officer or employee to compensate him or her for work done or to provide an incentive for further work.

Below is a case illustrating the law as applied to stock options granted to executives as part of a compensation package.

Lieberman v. Koppers Company, Incorporated

Court of Chancery of Delaware
149 A. 2d. 756 (1959)

Lieberman, a stockholder, brought action against the defendant company to have the court declare a deferred compensation plan invalid. The plan provided for the issuance of units in place of options to purchase stock with the value of each unit on date of issue being equal to that of one share of stock on the same date. Each of the employees participating in the plan agreed to remain with the company for five years as a condition of receiving units or until retirement. The plaintiff argued that because the plan provided for compensation based on increased market value of the stock, it was invalid because it bore no reasonable relationship to the value of the services rendered by the corporation and thus constituted a waste of corporate assets.

FACTS

Are the corporate assets being wasted, or do the directors of the corporation have the right to adopt such a plan under the business judgment rule?

ISSUE

The court ruled that since the plan was designed to achieve a legitimate business purpose, that is, to retain qualified executives, it was valid and not a waste of corporate assets. The court stated that services of employees in response to an incentive plan based in part on appreciation of their employer's common stock cannot be said to bear any reasonable relationship to that appreciation.

DECISION

STOCK SUBSCRIPTIONS

A method of corporate financing more common with small corporations than with large is the stock subscription. A stock subscription is an agreement between a corporation and a prospective shareholder by which the corporation agrees to issue shares and the subscriber agrees to pay for them. In most states, an offer by the prospective shareholder and an acceptance by the corporation must exist to bring the stock subscription contract into existence. Stock subscriptions may be executed either before or after incorporation. The issue raised by both preincorporation and postincorporation subscriptions is whether the subscriber attains shareholder status in the corporation. If the subscriber does, he or she is liable for whatever consideration was promised under the subscription agreement in payment for the shares.

Preincorporation Subscriptions

Those interested in forming a business corporation often want to begin financing it before the formal incorporation is complete. One device they use is the preincorporation subscription, by which one or more investors notify the promoter of their intention to purchase shares of a designated class and number in the proposed corporation at an agreed upon sum.

A preincorporation subscription may take many forms. Although a few states, such as Delaware and Kansas, require that stock subscriptions be in writing and signed by the subscriber, most states do not require that a subscription be written. A preincorporation subscription may be an individual transaction, or it may be a class of transactions by a number of people, as when a "subscription list" is signed. The word "subscriber" need not appear, and other language such as "I hereby purchase" may be used. The agreement may include definite provisions of the time and manner of payment of the agreed amount, when the subscriber becomes entitled to a stock certificate, and the legal relations between the subscriber and other shareholders. But usually it gives little or no indication of the intent of the parties with respect to these matters.

Authorities disagree whether a subscriber may withdraw his or her subscription before the corporation comes into existence. The older rule, which still prevails in many states, is that a preincorporation subscription may be withdrawn at any time before acceptance by the corporation. Acceptance cannot occur until the corporation comes into existence. Because no corporation exists when the subscription is executed, the subscription is merely an expression of intent to purchase shares and has no legal effect. Under general contract law, the subscriber's death, insanity, or bankruptcy terminates the subscription offer under the usual rules relating to an unaccepted offer.

Irrevocable may not be recalled or taken back

Newer statutes make preincorporation subscriptions **irrevocable** for a stated period of time, typically six months, unless the subscription agreement provides otherwise or all the subscribers consent to the revocation. Although in some states, by statute acceptance of the subscription offer is held to occur upon incorporation, most statutes require that the corporation actually accept the preincorporation subscription offers. To make a binding subscription contract under these statutes, not only must the corporation be completely organized but it must accept after coming into existence, either expressly by issuing shares to the subscribers or implicitly by recognizing the subscriber as a stockholder.

The realities of corporate finance require an exception to the general principles of contract law. The function of preincorporation subscriptions is to raise capital with which to finance the future corporation. The status of preincorporation subscriptions is of great concern to the new corporation. A practical disadvantage of the rule allowing preincorporation subscriptions to be revoked is that the agreements may disappear. The practical consequences of subscribers' right to revoke is not only uncertainty over the amount of funds a proposed corporation will have available when it incorporates but even the possibility that there will not be enough funds to permit its formal organization. If a subscriber who happens to be one of the major contributors to the proposed corporation revokes his or her subscription, the whole venture may collapse before it gets started.

Postincorporation Subscriptions

When the subscription agreement is made between the subscriber and a corporation already in existence, the subscriber has a binding obligation to purchase, and the corporation to sell, shares of the corporate stock. Ordinary contract principles of offer and acceptance operate here. A stock subscription made with a corporation already in existence is a contract between the subscriber and the corporation. The contract may result either from an offer made by the corporation and accepted by the subscriber or from an offer made by the subscriber and accepted by the corporation.

A postincorporation subscription agreement must be distinguished from an executory contract to purchase stock. A subscription agreement confers shareholder status instantly on the subscriber, even though no stock certificate has yet been issued. Under an executory contract for the purchase of shares, shareholder status is suspended until the contract is fully executed — that is, until a stock certificate has been issued to the purchaser.

Shareholder status under a stock subscription contract does not depend on the issue of a stock certificate. Under a subscription contract, the subscriber is liable for the subscription payment even though the corporation has not delivered the stock certificate. When the subscription is made, the subscriber is instantly vested with all the rights and obligations of a shareholder, even though some shareholder rights, such as voting and receiving dividends, may be suspended until full payment of the subscription price is made.

When the agreement is an executory contract for the purchase of stock, the purchaser does not become a stockholder until the purchase price is fully paid and the stock certificate has been issued. Thus an executory purchaser of shares is relieved of the duty to pay in the event of the corporation's bankruptcy because the corporation cannot perform its duty to deliver shares in a going concern. This rule is simply an application of the contract law principle that a material breach of an executory contract discharges the innocent party of any obligation of performance under the contract.

The problem presented by postincorporation subscriptions and by executory contracts to purchase stock is to distinguish between the two transactions. Because both are contracts, the intent of the parties is controlling. Although not conclusive, calling the contract a "subscription agreement" or a "purchase contract" is highly persuasive. Beyond this, courts look to the nature of the transaction and the rights conferred by the corporation.

Consideration to Be Paid by Subscriber

The issue of shares by a corporation implies that it has received consideration equal in value to the stated value of the shares. Once the corporation has set a formal value on its shares, it cannot sell them below that price. Stockholders who have been issued shares for consideration below the fixed value are liable for any unpaid consideration.

The value of shares to be received as consideration by the corporation is determined by the board of directors. Traditionally, boards of directors have designated the value of shares as the par value or stated value of the stock. The total of the par and stated values of the corporation's issued shares constitutes the stated capital of the corporation.

Par value is the price established by either the articles or the directors below which a share may not be originally issued by the corporation. The dollar value is usually quite low — $1 is typical — but the par value has little practical effect on the issue of shares. Shareholders who do not contribute an amount at least equal to the par value of the stock issued are liable to creditors for the balance. The extent of liability is the difference between the par value and the amount actually contributed. Creditors, including bondholders, may seek to have this amount paid to the corporate treasury or, if there is dissolution and a deficiency, paid to them to satisfy their claims.

State statutes provide that payment for shares may be made with money or other property of any description actually transferred to the corporation or with labor or other services actually rendered to the corporation. Because shares may be issued for a consideration other than cash, a question sometimes arises over whether the corporation received full value for its stock.

Authorities disagree about the valuation of property or services transferred to the corporation in consideration for its shares. A few states follow the "true value" rule. Under this rule, whether a shareholder is liable for any unpaid value depends on whether the assets given in consideration for the shares were actually worth the price of the stock. The shareholder is held liable for any substantial variance between the fair market value of the property or service transferred to the corporation and the price of the stock.

Most states follow the "good faith" rule, which is based on the assumption that people may honestly differ about the value of property and service rendered to a corporation in consideration for its stock. Under this rule, the value set by the corporation is upheld as long as it was honestly made, no fraud or bad faith existed on the part of the directors, and they have exercised the degree of care that an ordinary, prudent person in their position would exercise. The case below is a landmark opinion of the U.S. Supreme Court that originally set forth the "good faith" rule.

─────────── *Cort v. Amalgamating Company* ───────────

United States Supreme Court
119 U.S. 343 (1886)

FACTS   Cort held a judgment against the Amalgamating Company, which was bankrupt. The plaintiff sought to compel the individual stockholders to pay what he alleged was due and unpaid on their shares of the capital stock. The incorporation charter authorized capital stock to be paid in property. Capital stock of $100,000 was paid using the real and personal property of the former partnership the shareholders had done business under. The shares of the new corporation (Amalgamated) were divided in proportion to their interests in the property of the former association, each shareholder estimating the value of the property each contributed. The plaintiff argued that the value they put on the property was illegally and fraudulently arrived at, because all that was contributed was a machine for crushing ore, the right to use a patent, and the charter of the proposed corporation.

Should the plaintiff have been able to execute his judgment compelling the shareholders to pay what he claimed was the unpaid amount due on their shares of capital stock?

ISSUE

No. The Court ruled that the stockholders cannot be compelled to pay the debts of the bankrupt corporation, because there was no evidence that the value put on the property was intentionally and fraudulently made, and that the plaintiff had given credit to Amalgamated on a belief that its stock was fully paid. The Court stated that the patent and machinery had been used in the former association and were immediately serviceable, thus having present value to the company. The Court found the value of the properties to be so near the aggregate capital that there was no showing of bad faith in the evaluation process.

DECISION

GOVERNMENT REGULATION OF SECURITIES

When corporations seek to issue or trade in securities, they must meet the requirements of both federal and state laws.

Federal Regulation

Securities have been defined by the United States Supreme Court as any instrument or transaction in which:

1. a contract or scheme exists and people invest in a common enterprise (such as a mutual fund)

2. the investors have an expectation of profits

3. the profits are derived solely from the efforts of a promoter or third party but not the investor themselves.

Using this definition, the courts have declared a wide range of transactions and instruments to be securities. For example, bonds, stocks, an undivided interest in oil, gas, or mineral rights all have been termed securities. The importance of defining what is a security cannot be overestimated, because if the instrument or transaction is traded publicly between states, it may have to meet the registration requirements of the Securities Act of 1933 (1933 Act) and the Securities Exchange Act of 1934 (Exchange Act).

Securities Act of 1933   This act prescribes rules governing the *issuance* of securities and their registration. It does *not* seek to evaluate the worth of a stock or bond offering made to the public by the issuing corporation (issuer). It seeks only to ensure that the corporation provides full disclosure of all material factors which would affect the average, prudent investor's decision to invest in the issued securities.

When a corporation wishes to issue securities, it files a registration statement with the SEC that contains a **prospectus** and other exhibits and information. A copy of the prospectus must be provided to every purchaser. The additional exhibits and information are kept on file. The SEC staff examines the prospectus and exhibits to see if they include such information as the nature of the registrant's business; properties held; the management, control, and operation of the business; the securities to be offered for sale; and certified financial statements.

Certain types of securities and transactions are exempted from registration under the 1933 Act. Examples are public offerings of securities that do not exceed $1.5 million over a 12-month period, and other small offerings to *accredited* investors, who are generally sophisticated people who do not need the full disclosure protection of the 1933 Act. Also offerings of securities within state boundaries and securities issued by the United States government, nonprofit organizations, and domestic bonds are exempt.

Securities laws exempt transactions by persons other than the issuing corporations, underwriter, or dealer. Transactions involving *no* public offering of securities are also exempt, assuming the number of purchasers does not exceed 35, each offeree has access to the same kind of information that would be available to an investor under the 1933 Act, and no general advertising takes place. This is called a **private placement exemption** and is used by corporations to reward executives and to keep them from moving to other companies.

Congress provided for both civil and criminal liability for the failure of corporations and individuals to meet the requirements of registration under the 1933 Act. Both government (SEC) and private (stockholder) remedies are available under the act. Case law has pointed to certain individuals as most likely to be held liable. For example, losses have been repaid by:

1. the issuer

2. all who signed the registration statement

3. lawyers, engineers, and accountants who participated in the preparation of the registration statement

4. every director

5. every underwriter

The issuing corporation and all those involved in the preparation of a registration statement should therefore exercise great care. It should be noted that all but the issuer are allowed a due diligence defense. This defense requires the individual defendant to show that he or she had reasonable grounds to believe that there were no misstatements or material omissions.

Prospectus a document that must be filed with the Securities Exchange Commission before securities can be sold to the investing public

Private placement exemption an offering of securities to a limited number of relatively sophisticated shareholders, all of whom have access to the same information

The 1933 Act imposes liability on those who commit fraud in connection with the offer or sale of securities when it can be shown that there were *willful* violations of any provision of the act or rules and regulations made by the SEC. The reach of the 1933 Act is illustrated in the case below.

United States v. Naftalin

Supreme Court of the United States
441 U.S. 768 (1979)

Naftalin was president of a registered broker–dealer firm. In July and August 1969, he selected stocks that had peaked in price and were entering declines. He placed five broker orders to sell shares of these stocks, although he did not own the shares he pretended to sell. Gambling that the price of securities would decline before he was requested to deliver them to the broker, he planned to make offsetting purchases through other brokers at lower prices. His profit would be the difference between the price at which he sold and the price at which he covered. He falsely represented that he owned the shares he directed the broker to sell. The market prices of the securities he "sold" did not fall before the delivery date but instead rose sharply. Naftalin could not make covering purchases and never delivered the promised securities to the brokers. The five brokers suffered substantial losses, although those to whom the stocks were sold suffered no losses. The brokers reported the scheme to the SEC. The Justice Department instituted criminal proceedings against Naftalin for violating Section 17 of the Securities Act of 1933. The defendant argued that he committed fraud against the brokers, not Investors. He claimed that Section 17 did not cover brokers but only investors. **FACTS**

Does Section 17 of the 1933 Act cover brokers who are victims of fraud by another broker? **ISSUE**

Yes. The Court decided that brokers were covered by Section 17 of the 1933 Act. The Court stated that the language of the statute required only that fraud occur in the offer or sale of securities. The fraud can occur at any stage of the selling of securities, whether in the initial distribution to broker or in the course of ordinary market trading. **DECISION**

Securities Exchange Act of 1934   This act established the Securities Exchange Commission (SEC) and seeks to ensure fair trading practices for investors and others in the securities market. It sets forth rules governing the *trading,* not the issuance of securities. The Exchange Act covers the following matters:

1. requirements for detailed registration and reporting

2. rules governing the use of proxies

3. provisions governing tender offers

4. provisions relating to short swing profits

5. provisions relating to securities fraud in the marketplace

6. provisions governing corrupt practices of American-based corporations abroad (included in the Foreign Corrupt Practices Act of 1977)

Registration   The Exchange Act requires all publicly held companies regulated by the SEC *to register* two classes of securities: debt and equity. This requirement pertains to all companies with assets of $1 million or more and a class of equity securities having at least 500 shareholders of record. Such securities must be registered or they will not be allowed to be traded on a national securities exchange. Registration of a class of securities under the Exchange Act should not be confused with the registration of an initial offering of nonexempt securities within a class under the 1933 Act. A company registering a class of securities under the Exchange Act must always meet the requirements of the 1933 Act when making an initial public offering that does not meet any of the exemptions noted previously in this chapter.

Since 1934 the SEC has issued rules and prescribed forms for registering classes of securities. Much of the information requested is similar to that required by the 1933 Act. It has sought to integrate the registration requirements of both securities acts.

The SEC also has devised periodic refiling requirements for corporations to ensure that the potential investor has continuing access to information about securities that are being traded on the exchanges. Annual reports (Form 10-K) and quarterly reports (Form 10-Q) have been updated to provide increasing amounts of information for potential investors. Current reports (Form 8-K) can be requested by the SEC and must be filed by the registering company within 15 days if the SEC perceives that a material event has taken place that a reasonably prudent investor should know about to make an investment decision. A significant change in a company's assets or a potential merger have been considered material events.

Proxy an instrument containing the appointment of an agent (usually management) to represent a shareholder who cannot attend the annual meeting

Proxy   A **proxy** is best defined as a writing whereby a holder of registered securities gives permission to another person to vote the stockholder's shares at a stockholders' meeting. In many cases, managers seek proxies from shareholders to defeat a particular issue that has been placed before the board by dissident shareholders. Proxies also are given by shareholders who will not be present for the purpose of electing new directors or preventing a takeover of a company.

Because proxy solicitation often affects the future direction of a corporation, full disclosure is required by the Exchange Act and the SEC. Ten days before mailing a proxy statement to shareholders, the issuing company must file it with the SEC. The SEC often issues informal letters of comment, requiring some changes before proxies are mailed. SEC rules require the solicitor of proxies to furnish shareholders with all material information on the matter being submitted to them for their vote. A form by which shareholders may indicate their agreement or disagreement must be provided as well. In the case of proxies solicited for the purpose of voting for directors, shareholders must receive an annual report.

Often shareholders will request that a certain proposal be placed on the agenda at an annual meeting. Under the Exchange Act and SEC rules, if timely notice is given by the shareholder, management must include such proposals in its proxy statement and allow shareholders to vote for or against it. If management opposes the proposal, it must include a statement in support of the shareholder's proposal, not to exceed 200 words, along with its statement of opposition. Shareholders have used this opportunity, for example, to oppose the making of napalm, to force companies to deal with forms of discrimination, and to deal with company caused pollution of the environment. SEC rules allow management to exclude shareholder proposals for the following reasons:

1. The matter is **moot.**

2. The matter is not significantly related to the issuing company's business.

3. The matter relates to ordinary business operations.

4. The matter would violate state or federal law if included in a proxy proposal passed by the board of directors.

Moot a matter that has already been acted upon before shareholder proposal is set forth

Any issuing company that supplies a proxy statement that is misleading to its shareholders may be held civilly liable (Section 18 of the Exchange Act) to any person who relies on such statements in the buying or selling of registered securities. The SEC is authorized to force compliance with proxy rules by getting injunctions. The U.S. Supreme Court has held that a private right of action exists for damages and other relief.

Tender Offer   A tender offer is an offer by an individual or a corporation to the shareholder of another corporation to purchase a number of shares at a specified price. Tender offers are sometimes referred to as *takeover bids* and usually are communicated in newspaper advertising.

Any person or group that acquires more than 5 percent of a class of securities registered under the Exchange Act is required to file a statement with the SEC and the issuing company within ten days. It must include:

1. the person or group background and the number of share owners

2. its purpose in acquiring the stock

3. the source of funds used to acquire the securities

4. its plans for the targeted company

5. any contracts or understanding with individuals or groups relevant to the targeted company.

It should be noted that if there is a hostile tender offer or takeover bid, the targeted company also must file a statement in its attempt to defeat the takeover.

Short Swing Profits   The Exchange Act prevents directors, officers, and owners of 10 percent of the securities of an issuing corporation that has securities registered with the SEC or a national exchange from realizing profits on stocks by buying and selling within a six-month period. Any such profits must be returned to the corporation. If the corporation fails to sue for recovery of profits, shareholders may file on behalf of the corporation. The SEC seeks to monitor insider short swing profits by requiring officers, directors, and 10 percent owners to file forms with the SEC within ten days of a sale or purchase. Major newspapers also report such buying and selling by insiders.

Insider trading
is the buying or selling of securities by individuals based on nonpublic information where the provider of such information (tipper) has a fiduciary relationship to the issuing corporation and makes a profit on trading in the securities

Securities Fraud   The Exchange Act (Section 10[b]) and SEC Rule 10b-5 have been the grounds for actions against **insider trading** and corporate mismanagement. The SEC rule is a sweeping provision that forbids *any* purchase or sale by *any* person of *any* securities whether a company is registered under the Exchange Act or not. The act forbids the use of interstate mails or any other form of communication:

1. to employ any device, scheme, or artifice to defraud,

2. to make any untrue statement of a material fact necessary in order to make the statements made, in the light of circumstances under which they were made, not misleading, or

3. to engage in any act, practice, or course of business which operates or would operate as a fraud or deceit upon any person, in connection with the purchase or sale of any security.

An example of securities fraud involving corporate mismanagement is illustrated below.

Ernst & Ernst v. Hochfelder

Supreme Court of the United States
425 U.S. 185 (1976)

FACTS   Ernst & Ernst was a "big eight" accounting firm retained by First Securities Company, a small brokerage firm, to audit its books and records, to prepare annual reports for SEC filing, and to respond to questionnaires from the Midwest Stock Exchange.

Hochfelder was a customer of First Securities who invested in a fraudulent securities scheme perpetrated by Leston B. Nay, president of the firm and owner of 92 percent of its stock. Nay induced the respondents to invest funds in special accounts that he said would yield a high rate of return. In fact, there were no accounts, because Nay converted plaintiff's funds to his own use immediately upon receipt. No such accounts were reflected on the books of First Securities nor in filings with the SEC. The fraud came to light in 1968 when Nay committed suicide, leaving a note that described First Securities as bankrupt and the accounts as "spurious." Plaintiff filed an action for damages against Ernst & Ernst, charging that Nay's scheme violated Section 10(b) of the 1934 Act and that Ernst & Ernst had "aided and abetted" Nay's violations through its negligence in failing to conduct proper audits of First Securities. Defendants argued that in the absence of fraud or intentional misconduct, they could not be held liable for damages under Section 10(b) of the 1934 Act and Commission Rule 10(b)-5.

ISSUE   Can the defendant be held liable in a private cause of action for damages in the absence of any allegation of intent to deceive, manipulate, or defraud?

DECISION   No. The Court ruled that the defendants could not be held liable without an allegation and showing of intent to manipulate, deceive, or defraud. The Court stated that in reading the history of Section 10(b) as well as Rule 10(b)-5 it is clear that Congress and the Commission originally intended that there be some element of intent, not negligence alone, to hold defendants liable for fraud.

The person who receives insider information (tippee) is also liable under the Exchange Act for profits made. Both the tipper and tippee must **disgorge** themselves from profits made. The tippee may also be held criminally liable. Courts have found insider trading by partners in a brokerage firm, broker–dealers acting as underwriters, and even an employee of a financial printing firm who worked on documents that involved a contemplated tender offer, as the following case shows.

Disgorge effect of a court order that requires a person found guilty of insider trading to return all profits made on the transaction(s)

Vincent F. Chiarella v. United States

Supreme Court of the United States
445 U.S. 222 (1980)

In 1975 and 1976, Chiarella, a printer, worked as a "markup man" in the composing room of Pandick Press, a New York financial printer. Among documents that the defendant handled were five announcements of corporate takeover bids. The defendant was able to deduce the names of the target companies before the final printing from information contained in the documents. Without disclosing his knowledge, defendant purchased stock in the target companies and sold the shares immediately after the takeover attempts were made public. By this method, the defendant realized a gain of slightly more than $30,000 in the course of 14 months. Subsequently, the SEC began an investigation of his trading activities. In May 1977, the defendant agreed with the SEC to return his profits to the sellers of the shares.

In January 1978, the defendant was indicted on seventeen counts of violating 10(b) of the Securities Exchange Act of 1934 (1934 Act) and SEC Rule 10b-5. He was brought to trial and convicted on all counts. The United States argued that he was an insider within the scope of the 1934 Act and guilty of fraud. The defendant argued that he was not an insider because he had no duty to disclose material, nonpublic information to investors.

FACTS

Did the defendant violate Section 10(b) of the 1934 Act by using material, nonpublic information to trade in securities?

ISSUE

No. The United States Supreme Court said that Chiarella did not and reversed his conviction. The Court stated that the element required to make silence fraudulent, the duty to disclose, was absent. Chiarella was not an agent or fiduciary of the corporations involved. Further, he was not a person in whom the corporations selling securities had placed their trust. The Court concluded that based on the legislative history of Section 10(b)-5, mere possession of nonpublic information without a duty to speak does not constitute fraud.

DECISION

Foreign Corrupt Practices Act of 1977   The Foreign Corrupt Practices Act (FCPA) was enacted because Congress considered corporate bribes to foreign officials to be unethical, harmful to our relations with foreign governments, and unnecessary to American companies doing business overseas.

Passed in 1977, the FCPA applies to all "domestic concerns" whether they do business overseas or not and whether registered with the SEC or not.

The act's *antibribery* provisions prohibit all domestic concerns from offering or authorizing corrupt payments to:

1. a foreign official (or someone acting in an official capacity for a foreign government)

2. a foreign political party official or a foreign political party

3. a candidate for political office in a foreign country.

Recipient a person who receives something of value under the Foreign Corrupt Practice Act of 1977

A payment is corrupt if its purpose is to get the **recipient** to act or refrain from acting so that the American firm can keep or get business. The standard that corporate officials are held to is "knowing" or "has reason to know." If he or she knows or should know that a payment violates the provisions of the act, the official and the company are held liable.

The *accounting* provisions of the act apply only to companies subject to the Securities Acts — that is, only public nonexempt companies. The SEC, in its report to Congress on illegal and questionable payments, requested some reforms. Congress enacted record keeping and internal control provisions. The FCPA requires that all publicly held, registered companies "make and keep books, records, and accounts in reasonable detail" that "accurately and fairly" reflect transactions and disposition of assets. Further, the FCPA requires publicly held companies to maintain systems of internal controls sufficient to provide "reasonable assurances": that transactions are executed in accordance with management's authorization; that transactions are recorded to permit preparation of financial statements in accordance with generally accepted accounting principles; and that at regular intervals management compares records with the actual assets available.

State Regulation

Intrastate goods or securities that are only traded within state boundaries and do not have substantial impact beyond

When Congress enacted the 1933 Securities Act, it specifically preserved the power of the states to regulate securities transactions of an **intrastate** nature. All 50 states have enacted securities statutes. A corporation issuing securities across state boundaries must meet the registration requirements of each of the states in which its securities are sold as well as the federal requirements. The cost and time involved in meeting various state requirements has led to the adoption of the Uniform Securities Act (USA), in whole or in part, by some thirty states.

_____ SUMMARY _____

Corporations finance their operations and expansion through the sale of securities, usually stocks or bonds. In addition, other securities such as stock options and warrants are issued to corporate employees or to corporate officers.

Stock subscriptions made before the incorporation of a business generally must be approved by the board of directors. Subscriptions after incorporation are guided by contract law principles. Payment in consideration for shares of stock may be made by money, by other property actually transferred to the corporation, or by labor or services to the corporation.

Government regulation of securities, including federal and state controls, directly affect the financing of a corporation when it seeks to issue securities, as defined by the 1933 Act and the United States Supreme Court. The 1933 Act regulates the issuance of securities. The 1934 Exchange Act governs the trading in of securities. Corporations must also meet the requirements of both federal and state regulation.

REVIEW PROBLEMS

1. What is the principal difference between equity and debt securities?

2. May preincorporation subscribers withdraw their subscriptions to stock before the corporation comes into existence?

3. What type of consideration may be paid by a subscriber for shares of a company?

4. How does the purpose of the 1933 Securities Act differ from that of the 1934 Exchange Act?

5. Molina attended a meeting with Largosa to discuss the formation of a corporation to sell stereo equipment. At the meeting, Molina signed a subscription form for the purchase of 40 shares at $50 a share, for a total investment of $2,000 in the proposed corporation. The subscription form did not set forth the capital of the proposed corporation nor the extent of Molina's proportionate interest in it. Molina later paid Largosa $2,000 which was deposited in a bank account under the name of the proposed corporation. Shortly after the corporation was officially organized, it failed. Molina sued Largosa to recover his $2,000, contending that because the subscription form did not set forth the total capital of the proposed corporation and his proportionate interest in it, there was no valid subscription contract. What result?

6. The Columbia Straw Paper Company purchased 39 paper mills from Stein for $5 million, for which it issued to Stein $1 million of the corporation's bonds, $1 million of its preferred stock, and $3 million of common stock. The value of the mills was arrived at by analyzing the expected profits to be derived from the property. Columbia later became insolvent, and creditors of the company sued Stein, claiming that the mills he sold to the corporation were not worth $5 million and that the directors acted in bad faith by basing the value of the mills on an extravagant estimation of prospective profits rather than the appraised value of the mills' property. May a corporation make an exchange for its stock on the basis of an estimation of prospective profits to be derived from that property?

7. Maresh, a geologist, owned some oil and gas leases on land in Nebraska. He entered into an oral agreement with Garfield in which Garfield would invest funds for Maresh to drill for oil. Garfield, a businessman, knew a great deal about oil stocks and the securities market. He promised to wire the money to

Maresh, who began drilling immediately. Maresh found out that the land was dry before he received Garfield's money. Garfield refused to invest as he had promised, claiming that the offered lease investment was a security within the meaning of the Securities Act of 1933 and that it had not been registered. What result?

8. Continental Tobacco Company, a manufacturer of cigarettes, sold some unregistered five-year debentures, paying 6 percent common stock, to 38 people between June 1969 and October 1970. Before buying, all investors signed an agreement with Continental that acknowledged receipt of unaudited financial statements, other information about the corporation, access to officers of the company, knowledge of the risk involved, and that they were experienced investors. Purchasers went to meetings in a room where telephones were manned and orders for securities continually came in. One investor called the meetings a "boiler plate operation" where high pressure tactics were used to sell the securities. The SEC brought an action under the 1933 Act, claiming that Continental was guilty of failing to register before selling securities. Continental claimed that it qualified for a private placement exemption. What result?

9. Truckee Showboat, a California corporation, offered to sell its common stock to California residents through the U.S. mails. Its offer to sell was advertised in the Los Angeles *Times* on June 18, 1957, and the offer was made exclusively to California residents. The proceeds of the sale of the stock, minus commission, were to be used to acquire the El Cortez Hotel in Las Vegas, Nevada. Truckee Showboat was incorporated and kept all its records in California. All its directors and officers were Californians. The SEC charged the company with issuing unregistered nonexempt securities under the 1933 Act. Truckee Showboat claimed an intrastate exemption. What result?

10. Livingston was a 20-year employee of Merrill Lynch, a large securities investment firm. Livingston was a securities salesman with the title "account executive." In January 1972, the company gave Livingston and 47 other account executives the title "vice president" as a reward for outstanding sales records. All of their duties and responsibilities were the same as before this recognition. Livingston never acquired any executive duties and never attended board of directors meetings. In November and December 1972, Livingston sold 1,000 shares of Merrill Lynch stock. In March 1973, he repurchased the same number of shares, making a profit of $14,836.37. The company sued for the profits, claiming that Livingston by virtue of his inside information made short swing profits in violation of Section 16(b) of the Securities Exchange Act of 1934. The defendant denied this charge. What result?

11. Mills was a minority shareholder of Electric Auto-Lite Company. Before the merger of Auto-Lite and Mergenthaler into the Mergenthaler Linotype Co., Mergenthaler owned 50 percent of Auto-Lite and dominated its board of directors. American Manufacturing Company in turn had control of Mergenthaler and through it controlled Auto-Lite. Auto-Lite's management at the time of the merger sent out a proxy statement to shareholders of Auto-Lite telling them that their board of directors recommended that they vote for approval of the merger. They failed to include in the proxy statement information as to the fact that Mergenthaler dominated the board and that American Manufacturing through

Mergenthaler controlled Auto-Lite. Mills and other minority shareholders filed a suit claiming that management had sent out a misleading proxy in violation of Section 14 of the Exchange Act of 1934 and that the merger should be set aside. Management and the board of directors of the merged company claimed that there was no material omission in the proxy statement. What result?

12. Lakeside Plastics and Engraving Company (LPE) was a closed corporation incorporated in Minnesota in 1946. It suffered losses until 1952, when it showed a yearly profit but still a large overall deficit. Fields and King in 1946 had each purchased 30 shares, which they held. Myzel, a relative of the Levine family, founders of the company, advised Fields and King in 1954 that the company stock was not worth anything and that the company was going out of business. Both sold their shares to Myzel, who sold them to the Levine family at a substantial profit. Myzel failed to disclose before purchasing the shares that there were increased sales in 1953, a new contract, and profits of $30,000, along with the potential of 1954 sales. Fields, King, and others in separate actions sought damage for violation of 10(b) of the Exchange Act of 1934. What result?

13. A owned oil and gas leases in Ohio. Because he needed cash he sought to sell interests in the leases. He organized three separate corporations for this purpose, and each sold $1 million in securities over a 12-month period. Do the corporations need to register under the 1933 Securities Act, or are they exempt? Explain.

14. A was a journalist for the *Wall Street Journal.* He wrote a column telling of rumors on Wall Street about various companies' health or lack of it. His roommate, B, traded on this information before it was published, because he found drafts of A's columns in the wastebasket in the room where A wrote. B also passed information on to C. The SEC charged A with being a tipper under Section 10(b) of the Exchange Act and B and C with being tippees. Should A, B and C be found guilty of insider trading under Section 10(b)(5) of the 1934 Exchange Act? Explain.

CHAPTER 34

Operating the Corporation

CHAPTER OBJECTIVES

CORPORATE PURPOSES AND POWERS

Corporate Purposes / Corporate Powers

CORPORATE MANAGEMENT

The Role of Shareholders / The Role of the Board of Directors / The Role of Officers and Executives

MANAGEMENT'S FIDUCIARY OBLIGATIONS

Fiduciary Duty to the Corporation / Fiduciary Duty to Shareholders

SUMMARY

REVIEW PROBLEMS

CHAPTER OBJECTIVES

After reading this chapter, you should be able to:

1. Explain the purposes and legal powers of a corporation and the limits of its powers.

2. Define the roles of shareholders, boards of directors, and officers of a corporation.

3. Define the legal rights and duties of shareholders, boards of directors, and officers of a corporation.

4. Discuss the fiduciary duties of management to the corporation.

CORPORATE PURPOSES AND POWERS

Corporate Purposes

The corporation's purpose is its reason for having been organized. It establishes the nature of its business and the range of its permissible activities. Corporations need not be formed for a single purpose only. They may be organized to undertake as many purposes as the incorporators consider desirable. The Revised Model Business Corporation Act (RMBCA) provides that:

> Every corporation incorporated under this Act has the purpose of engaging in *any* lawful business unless a narrower purpose is set forth in the articles of incorporation.

Implicit in this statement also is the requirement that a corporation formed under the general corporate law must have profit as one purpose, because nonprofit corporations are usually organized under a separate statute.

Earlier in the evolution of corporation law, detailed descriptions of corporate purposes were required to be included in the **articles of incorporation.** This rule reflected the general mistrust of unchecked corporate activity. Under modern corporate codes, a generally worded purpose clause may be provided in the articles.

Sometimes incorporators want to limit the activities of the corporation to a particular purpose. When this is the case, a narrow purpose clause may be included in the articles, or a specific prohibition against certain activities may be stated. Because most modern corporate codes permit a "full purpose" clause to be included in the articles, the subject of what is a proper corporate purpose has become less and less important.

Articles of incorporation the instrument by which a private corporation is formed and organized under the general corporation laws of a state

Corporate Powers

Closely related to the subject of corporate purposes is that of corporate powers. Corporate powers are those powers granted to the corporation by articles and statutes to implement its overall objectives. Because corporate purposes and powers are to be compatible, the corporation's powers must be consistent with the corporation's stated purpose.

A corporation's powers may be express or implied. A corporation has express power to perform those acts authorized by the general corporation laws of the state of incorporation and those acts authorized by its articles. Most states have express statutory provisions allowing corporations to sue and be sued, own property, borrow money, and so forth. Corporations also have implied powers to do whatever is reasonably necessary to promote their express powers, unless such acts are expressly prohibited by law. The trend is to interpret broadly what is meant by "reasonably necessary."

Doctrine of *ultra vires* a rule by which corporations are not responsible for transactions not authorized by their charters, articles of incorporation, or laws of their states of incorporation

The *Ultra Vires* Doctrine   Corporate transactions outside the corporation's purposes and powers are *ultra vires* (beyond the power). Under the **doctrine of *ultra vires,*** the corporation is not responsible for transactions that were not authorized by its charter, the articles of incorporation, or the law of the state of incorporation. The older view was that ultra vires acts were void for lack of legal capacity, the reason being that the state had not given the corporation the power to do the particular act. Under this view, the shareholders could not subsequently ratify (approve) the unauthorized corporate act because the transaction was void.

The present view is that ultra vires transactions are voidable. If completely unperformed on both sides, neither party can bring an action on the contract. But if the ultra vires transaction has been fully performed or executed on both sides, either party can bring an action on the contract. The doctrine does not apply to tortious or criminal conduct, because the lack of authorization is not considered an excuse for such conduct.

Two legal consequences attach to an ultra vires transaction:

1. The doctrine may serve as a *basis of liability* asserted by the state or shareholders to enjoin or set aside a corporate act.

2. The doctrine may serve as a *defense to liability* by the corporation arising from an unauthorized transaction, much as a minor can defend against a contract claim by raising the defense of lack of contractual capacity.

This second consequence has been criticized. It lets a corporation benefit from an ultra vires transaction while avoiding any of its burdens.

Because the use of the doctrine as a defense threatens the security of commercial transactions, the doctrine is in decline. Most statutes severely limit the ultra vires doctrine by stating that corporate action may not be challenged on the ground that the corporation lacks or lacked power to act. The RMBCA limits challenges to the corporation's power to act to suits brought by the state attorney general; suits by the corporation against officers or directors for previously authorizing an ultra vires act; and shareholder suits to stop ultra vires acts.

Areas of *Ultra Vires* Application   As we have seen, two legislative developments have resulted in the decline of the doctrine of ultra vires:

1. the elimination of the doctrine as a defense to creditor claims

2. the expansion of permissible corporate powers.

The doctrine is still used where the general corporation statute is silent on the subject. For example, the corporation's right to make charitable contributions is still uncertain in some states. According to the older view, corporations existed solely for the economic benefit of the shareholders. Thus corporate charitable contributions were considered ultra vires unless a benefit to the corporation could be shown. Under this "corporate benefit rule," a corporate contribution to a business college, for example, would have to be supported by showing that the act was intended to create good will between the corporation and the college and that the college might provide the corporation with a pool of potential employees. Some state corporation codes still are silent on the subject of corporate charitable contributions, and so this type of analysis is still necessary. But present provisions in the federal income tax law allowing deductions for charitable contributions, along with current concerns for corporate social responsibility, have resulted in the amendment of three quarters of the states' corporation statutes to allow gifts for the public welfare or for charitable, scientific, or educational purposes.

Another area where the doctrine of ultra vires presently applies is to corporate political activity. Although federal legislation currently regulates this kind of corporate activity, the courts have held that shareholders may not bring private suits under the federal law. Shareholders are limited to state law and the doctrine of ultra vires. The following case illustrates the application of the doctrine of ultra vires in the area of corporate political activity.

------ *Marsili v. Pacific Gas and Electric Company* ------

California Court of Appeals
124 Cal. Rptr. 313 (1975)

Marsili and other stockholders brought suit challenging the propriety of a $10,000   FACTS
contribution made by Pacific Gas and Electric Company (PG&E) to Citizens for San Francisco, an unincorporated association that advocated the defeat of Proposition T appearing on the ballot in the November 2, 1971, election for the city and county of San Francisco. (Proposition T was a nonpartisan proposal that, if adopted, would have prohibited construction in San Francisco of any building more than 72 feet high without earlier approval of the voters.) Plaintiffs argued that the contribution was ultra vires because neither PG&E's articles of incorporation nor the law of California permitted PG&E to make political contributions. The defendant argued that no restriction on management to act on such initiatives as Proposition T appears in its article and thus its contribution was not ultra vires.

Is the $10,000 contribution by PG&E an ultra vires act if it is not expressly permitted   ISSUE
by the articles of incorporation or by state statute?

DECISION   No. The court ruled that no expressed authority for a corporation to contribute to political activity is needed. It said that no restrictions appeared in the articles of incorporation nor under California statute. Whatever transactions are considered reasonably incidental to its business purpose are within the scope of the board of directors' authority. The court said that it believed that the board of directors could reasonably conclude that Proposition T, if adopted, would have an adverse effect on the corporation.

CORPORATE MANAGEMENT

Three groups participate in operating the corporation: the shareholders, the board of directors, and the corporate officers and executives. The following pages examine the management role of each of these groups.

The Role of Shareholders

Shareholders have no direct control over corporate operations. They cannot command the board of directors or the corporate executives to undertake an activity or decide a matter in a particular way. Though ultimate control rests with the shareholders, they usually do not participate actively in corporate affairs. They can take action only by voting during a shareholders' meeting. Shareholder votes at these meetings usually are confined to selecting the membership of the board of directors and approving certain extraordinary transactions. Little more than this minimal involvement is permitted to investors. If they are dissatisfied with their investment, they may sell their stock. But if the corporate management has violated the corporate documents or otherwise incurred a liability toward the investors, the shareholders may bring suit against the responsible parties to recover any loss on behalf of the corporation or to recover any loss to their investment.

Areas of Shareholder Involvement   There are usually two areas of shareholder involvement in corporate affairs:

1. the election of members of the board of directors

2. the approval of certain extraordinary corporate transactions. Under the RMBCA, shareholder participation is restricted to the annual election or removal of corporate directors, loans to employees and directors, sale of the corporation's assets outside the usual course of corporate business, any plan of merger or share exchange and a voluntary **dissolution** of the corporation. Although some statutes require shareholder approval of bylaw amendments, the RMBCA does not. Of course, it is always permissible to increase the areas of shareholder involvement by appropriate provisions in the corporate articles and bylaws.

Dissolution
termination of a
firm's legal existence

Shareholders' Meetings Because they are not agents of the corporation, shareholders cannot act individually. They can act only collectively at shareholders' meetings. The RMBCA requires that an annual shareholders' meeting be held at the times specified in the corporate bylaws. Sometimes it is necessary to have a special meeting of the shareholders for a particular purpose. The RMBCA further permits special meetings to be called by the board of directors, by the holders of more than 5 percent of the shares entitled to vote at the meeting, or by any person authorized to do so in the articles or bylaws.

Most statutes require that notice of any shareholders' meeting be provided to each shareholder of record entitled to vote at such a meeting. The RMBCA stipulates that the notice be in writing, stating the place, day, and hour of the meeting. In the case of a special meeting, the notice also must include the purpose for which the meeting is called. The notice must be delivered between ten and fifty days before the date of the meeting (see Figure 34-1).

FIGURE 34-1 Notice of Special Meeting of Shareowners

October 4, 1985

To the Common Stock Shareowners of
The Toledo Edison Company:

A special meeting of the Shareowners of The Toledo Edison Company ("Toledo Edison") will be held at the principal office of Toledo Edison, Edison Plaza, 300 Madison Avenue, Toledo, Ohio, on November 26, 1985 at 10:00 a.m., Toledo time, for the purpose of acting on the following matters:

1. To consider and vote upon a proposal to approve and adopt an Agreement and Plan of Reorganization between Toledo Edison and The Cleveland Electric Illuminating Company ("CEI") dated June 25, 1985, as amended, which agreement provides for simultaneous mergers of two subsidiaries of Centerior Energy Corporation (the "Holding Company") into Toledo Edison and CEI, respectively, with the result that Toledo Edison and CEI each will become subsidiaries of the Holding Company as described in the accompanying Joint Proxy Statement/Prospectus and the common stock shareowners of Toledo Edison and CEI will become common stock shareowners of the Holding Company; and to approve and adopt an Agreement of Merger among the Holding Company, Toledo Edison and the West Merger Company, a wholly-owned subsidiary of the Holding Company.

2. Any other matters which may properly come before the meeting.

Holders of record of Common Stock at the close of business on September 30, 1985 will be entitled to vote at the meeting.

By order of the Board of Directors,

STRATMAN COOKE, *Secretary*

Waive to surrender a claim, privilege, right, or opportunity

Unless the required notice is **waived,** failure to provide it voids any action taken at the meeting. A waiver may be made by a signed writing or evidenced by conduct, such as attending the meeting without objecting to the lack of notice. The RMBCA permits action to be taken without a shareholders' meeting if written consent specifying the action to be taken is signed by all the shareholders entitled to vote on the matter.

Proxy an instrument containing the appointment of an agent (usually management) to represent a shareholder who cannot attend the annual meeting

A quorum of the shares entitled to vote, represented in person or by **proxy,** must be present before any action can take place at the shareholders' meeting. The RMBCA provides that a majority of the voting shares shall constitute a quorum, unless the articles provide otherwise. But the articles cannot provide for a quorum consisting of less than one third of the voting shares.

The shareholders' meeting usually is conducted according to the provisions of the corporate articles or bylaws, which generally provide that the board chairman or corporate president preside. Minutes of the meeting are recorded by the corporate secretary. Shareholders are entitled to submit and speak on proposals and resolutions during the meeting. Recently, shareholders who are concerned about social issues have used the shareholders' meeting to submit proposals to limit the involvement of their corporations in certain activities, such as investing in countries that violate human rights or practice apartheid (institutionalized racial discrimination).

Because most voting at shareholders' meetings is done by proxy and therefore the result usually is a foregone conclusion, the typical shareholders' meeting is a well-orchestrated occasion designed to fulfill the formalities of corporate law. For this reason, some scholars seriously question the continued practice of requiring an annual shareholders' meeting. In what may be a sign of future development, Delaware no longer requires an annual meeting.

Voting   Shareholders function by voting on matters at the shareholders' meeting. Each share of stock entitles its holder to one vote on each matter submitted to a vote, unless the corporate articles provide for more or less than one vote per share. Thus the holder of 50 shares is generally entitled to cast 50 votes. The RMBCA also authorizes the issuance of nonvoting shares. For example, preferred stock generally has no voting rights. However, even nonvoting stock is entitled to vote on certain extraordinary transactions, such as amendments to the corporate articles, mergers and consolidations, and dissolution of the corporation.

To determine who is entitled to vote, the directors may set a date of record. A person having legal title to the stock on the record date is entitled to vote the shares. A person acquiring legal title to the shares after the record date must obtain the proxy of the record title holder to vote at the shareholders' meeting.

Because a shareholder is entitled to one vote for each share held, the holder of 51 percent of the voting shares has complete control over corporate operations. To assure minority shareholders some voice in corporate affairs, most statutes permit a shareholder to cast as many votes for one candidate for director as there are directors to be elected, multiplied by the shareholder's number of shares. This form of proportional representation — called *cumulative voting* — usually is applied only to the election of directors. In some states, cumulative voting is required by statute and cannot be refused in any election or eliminated in the corporate articles or bylaws. In other states, it can be eliminated in the corporate documents. Under the RMBCA cumulative voting is permitted.

Cumulative voting for directors is controversial. Proponents claim that it is necessary to assure minority voice in corporate affairs. Opponents claim that minority representation means dissent in the boardroom.

A device for diluting the effect of cumulative voting is the staggered election of directors, because the fewer directors to be elected, the greater the number of shares necessary to assure representation. This practice is allowed by the RMBCA. It permits boards consisting of nine or more directors to be divided into two or three classes, with each class being elected to a staggered three-year term. Because the RMBCA allows corporations to eliminate cumulative voting, requiring the staggered election of directors in classes poses no problems. But in states where cumulative voting is required, the staggered election of directors is often prohibited.

A shareholder may vote either in person or by proxy. A proxy is basically a special type of principal – agent relationship and therefore is subject to the rules of agency law (as modified by special state statutes or by federal regulations under Section 14 of the Securities Exchange Act of 1934).

The RMBCA requires that a proxy be in writing. A telegram or cable is sufficient. Some states, like California, require that the proxy be filed with the corporation before or at the shareholders' meeting. A few states allow oral proxies.

Because the proxy is an agency, every appointment of a proxy is revocable. One way a shareholder may revoke a proxy is to attend and vote at the shareholders' meeting. A proxy is not revocable if it is coupled with an interest, meaning that some consideration has been received by the shareholder for his or her delegation of voting rights — for example, an option or pledge to purchase the stock.

Even when proxies are irrevocable, statutes generally limit their duration. The RMBCA provides that the appointment of a proxy is valid for only 11 months after it is made, unless otherwise provided in the proxy. Thus a proxy can extend beyond 11 months only if the writing specifies the date on which it is to expire or the length of time it is to continue in force.

Proxy solicitation by corporate management, competing and attacking groups of shareholders, and even outsiders has become a common and effective method of establishing or maintaining control over a corporation without actually purchasing enough stock to exert control. Section 14 of the Securities Exchange Act of 1934 and Rule 14a of the Securities and Exchange Commission (SEC) regulate proxy solicitation. Their purpose is to protect shareholders from misleading or concealed information in the solicitation of proxies. These proxy rules apply to corporations having more than 500 shareholders and assets of more than $1 million.

Because proxies are revocable, other devices for combining votes for control of the corporation frequently are used. Two such devices are the pooling agreement and the voting trust. A **pooling agreement,** sometimes called a voting agreement, is a contract entered into by several shareholders who mutually promise to vote their shares in a certain manner. In most states, such agreements are specifically enforceable.

A **voting trust** is an agreement among shareholders to transfer their voting rights to a trustee. The trustee is permitted to vote the shares in a block at the shareholders' meeting according to the terms of the trust instrument. Courts are divided on the legality of voting trusts at common law, but most statutes provide for and limit them. Under the RMBCA a voting trust must be in writing. This writing, termed the *voting trust agreement,* must specify the terms and conditions of the voting trust, and a copy of it must be deposited with the corporation. The shareholders must transfer their shares to the trustee and receive in return trust certificates, sometimes called *certifi-*

Pooling agreement agreement by shareholders to place their voting stock in the hands of a committee to be voted in a certain way

Voting trust an agreement among shareholders to transfer their voting rights to a trustee who votes the shares in a block according to the terms of that agreement

cates of beneficial ownership. The RMBCA also limits the life of a voting trust to ten years.

Inspection Rights   For a shareholder to exercise his or her voting rights intelligently, he or she may need access to certain corporate information. Most statutes recognize that those who oppose corporate management must be able to get a list of existing shareholders if they are to succeed in ousting management. Shareholders have an absolute right to examine and copy shareholder lists.

The shareholder also may be able to get information from corporate records. The RMBCA provides that a shareholder has a qualified right to certain corporate information. It requires that the corporate records of account, the minutes of shareholders' and directors' meetings, and a shareholders list are to be kept, usually at the corporation's principal place of business. By sending a written demand five business days before the date on which a shareholder wishes to inspect, he or she may examine any of the relevant corporate records during reasonable working hours. The RMBCA permits an attorney or an agent, who could be an accountant, to accompany the shareholder or to make the inspection for the shareholder if the shareholder wishes. The written demand must be in good faith and for a proper purpose. The right of inspection is limited to three classes of corporate records: minutes of meetings of the board and committees of the board, accounting records, and a record of shareholders.

What is a ''proper purpose'' or a request made in ''good faith'' are issues left for the courts to decide. The following case illustrates the judicial approach to defining these terms.

National Consumers Union v. National Tea Company

Appellate Court of Illinois
302 N.E. 2d 118 (1973)

FACTS   Plaintiffs Jan Schakowsky and the National Consumers Union (NCU), shareholders of defendant, National Tea Company (National), filed a petition to compel National to permit them to examine the books and records of the corporation. Schakowsky was the owner of one share of the corporation for more than six months. NCU also owned one share but for less than six months. Plaintiffs argued that demands for records, minutes, books, and records of account were made in a reasonable manner, in good faith, and for a proper purpose. National argued that NCU was seeking to "sensitize" National to NCU's consumer demands, and NCU expressed no proper purpose for inspecting the documents they wished to examine.

ISSUE   Was the plaintiff's request to inspect the books made in good faith and for a proper purpose?

DECISION   No. The court ruled that plaintiffs did not have a proper purpose for examining the defendants' books. They said that the plaintiffs had a speculative purpose because their past conduct in urging shoppers to boycott National stores was contrary to the best interest of the corporation. The court agreed with the trial court that the plaintiffs were on a "fishing expedition" with the inspection request to further their own consumer goals.

Dividends   A *dividend* is a distribution paid to shareholders because of their stock ownership. It may be in cash, property (including the stock of other corporations), or the stock of the corporation itself. This latter type of dividend is referred to as a *stock dividend.*

The RMBCA prohibits the declaration or payment of a dividend when the corporation is insolvent (unable to pay its debts as they become due) or when such a payment would render the corporation insolvent. Dividends can be lawfully declared and paid only out of the corporation's earned surplus under the traditional approach used in most states. Earned surplus represents the profits realized on operations and investments. However, the RMBCA would permit dividends to be paid out by the board of directors based on financial statements prepared on the basis of accounting principles and practice that are "reasonable" under the circumstances, or on a fair evaluation, or on another method that is reasonable under the circumstances. The RMBCA retains an equity insolvency test but allows directors wider discretion in judging the future ability of the corporation to generate funds and pay debts.

The directors have wide discretion in whether or not to declare a dividend. The directors alone determine the amount of dividends and when they are to be distributed. Shareholders ordinarily have no right to a dividend. A shareholder's "right" to a dividend usually comes about only after a dividend has been declared by a board.

Although courts usually do not disturb the discretion of directors on declaring a dividend, there is an exception to this general rule. When there is a bad faith refusal by the board of directors to declare a dividend, a court may compel a distribution. But courts do not have the power to require a board of directors to declare dividends out of abundant earnings in the absence of fraud or abuse of discretion.

Preemptive Rights   If the articles of incorporation so provide, a shareholder has an option, called a **preemptive right,** that entitles the shareholder to subscribe to a newly authorized issue of shares in the same proportion that his or her present shares bear to all outstanding shares before new shares are offered to the public. Preemptive rights are aimed at preventing the dilution of the shareholder's equity in the corporation against his or her wishes. Under most state statutes now on the books, preemptive rights usually do not apply to treasury shares (meaning shares previously issued and reacquired by the corporation), previously authorized but unsold and unissued shares, or shares that are issued or agreed to be issued upon the conversion of convertible shares. Preemptive rights do not apply to these shares because such shares are not new issues but are part of previous offerings.

Because preemptive rights often interfere with the disposition of large issues of shares, many corporations restrict or eliminate these rights. How preemptive rights may be restricted or eliminated depends on the particular statutory provision governing their application. Some statutes provide that preemptive rights *exist* unless other-

Preemptive right option giving stockholder the right to subscribe to an early authorized issue of shares in the same proportion that is presently held

wise provided in the corporate articles. Other statutes provide that preemptive rights do *not* exist unless expressly provided in the corporate articles.

Transfer of Shares   Generally, a shareholder who is dissatisfied with corporate operations may freely transfer his or her shares to someone else. Such transfers traditionally have been governed by Article 8 of the Uniform Commercial Code as adopted by most states today.

Under Article 8 of the UCC, a stock certificate can be validly transferred only by the delivery of the certificate and its endorsement by the registered owner. The endorsement may be either on the certificate itself or on a separate instrument called a *stock power.* The signature of the registered owner on the back of the certificate constitutes a valid endorsement. An endorsement of the certificate on a stock power alone does not transfer any rights unless the certificate also is delivered to the transferee. When a certificate has been delivered to a purchaser without the necessary endorsement, a transfer has been completed and the purchaser has a specifically enforceable right to compel any necessary endorsement. The effect of a valid transfer is to make the transferee the complete legal and equitable owner of the shares, and the corporation must register the transfer and recognize the transferee as the rightful owner.

Appraisal and Buy-Out Rights of Dissenting Shareholders   Certain kinds of extraordinary transactions, even though lawfully authorized and validly effected, entitle dissenting shareholders to have their shares purchased by the corporation at a fair cash value. This is referred to as the shareholder's *appraisal and buy-out right.* Its purpose is to create a compromise between the overwhelming majority, who desire a fundamental change in the corporate venture, and the insistence of a dissenter not to be forced into a position different from that bargained for when he or she bought the stock.

The RMBCA (Section 13.02) recognizes five extraordinary transactions that give rise to an appraisal and buy-out right:

1. a merger or consolidation

2. a sale or exchange of all or substantially all of the corporate property and assets not in the regular course of business

3. the acquisition of the corporation by another through the exchange of the corporate stock

4. an amendment to the articles of incorporation that materially and adversely affects rights of a dissenter's shares

5. any other corporate action that by virtue of the articles of incorporation, bylaws, or board resolution entitles shareholders to dissent, and be paid for their shares.

Shareholder Suits   Sometimes to enforce a right or to protect an investment, a shareholder resorts to a lawsuit. Although the procedural aspects of shareholder lawsuits are of more concern to lawyers than to businesspeople, some awareness of the basics of shareholder litigation is appropriate.

Shareholder litigation falls into two broad categories:

1. direct suits by shareholders on their own behalf

2. derivative suits on behalf of the corporation

Direct actions by shareholders on their own behalf may be further subdivided into two additional categories:

a. individual actions

b. class actions.

Direct suits by shareholders on their own behalf are limited to the enforcement of claims belonging to the shareholder based on his or her share ownership.

Some examples of shareholder lawsuits that may be brought individually or by class action are suits:

1. to enforce the right to vote

2. to sue for breach of a shareholder agreement

3. to enforce the right to inspect corporate books and records

4. to compel the payment of lawfully declared dividends

5. to protect preemptive rights

6. to compel corporate dissolution.

When the injury to the shareholder's investment results from a wrong to the corporation rather than a wrong directed against the shareholder, a shareholder cannot bring a direct suit on his or her own behalf but must bring a derivative action on behalf of the corporation to enforce a right belonging to the corporation. Any judgment goes directly to the corporation, not to the shareholder who brings the action.

Some examples of derivative suits are these:

1. to recover damages resulting from an ultra vires act

2. to bar corporate officials from breaching their fiduciary duty to the corporation

3. to recover improperly paid dividends

4. to bar outsiders from wronging the corporation or to recover from such a wrong.

The Role of the Board of Directors

Although the shareholders are the owners of the corporation, the board of directors is the supreme power in the management of the corporation. The following pages examine the nature of the board's authority, the appointment of directors to the board, and the formalities of board functions.

Nature of Board Authority   Although the board of directors is charged by statute with the duty of managing the corporation, it is generally recognized that the purpose of the board is only to establish policy and to provide direction to the corporation. Recent legislative developments reflect a trend toward recognizing this reality.

Most state statutes say that the business affairs of the corporation "shall be managed by a board of directors." Recently, many commentators have voiced concern that such language may be interpreted to mean that the directors must become involved in the detailed administration of the corporation's affairs. Although requiring such involvement is reasonable in closely held corporations, recent developments make such an expectation unreasonable in today's complex corporations. One of these developments is the appearance of outside directors, those from outside the corporate management and not otherwise involved with the corporation.

The RMBCA seeks to clarify board responsibility and bring it into accord with the realities of today's corporation, particularly the large, diversified enterprise. It provides that the business and affairs of the corporation be managed *"under the direction"* of a board of directors. The RMBCA eliminates any ambiguity in the role of the board of directors in formulating major management policy as opposed to direct day-to-day management. Only a few state statutes, such as Delaware's and California's, have similar provisions, although a trend exists toward adopting such language.

Generally, the board's responsibility may be broadly described as establishing basic corporate objectives, selecting competent senior executives, monitoring personnel policies and procedures with a view to assuring that the corporation is provided with other competent managers in the future, reviewing the performance of senior executives, and monitoring the corporation's performance. Typical matters over which the board has control include dividends, financing, and corporate policy in the prices of its products, expansion, and labor relations. More specifically, the board of directors is also required or authorized to: call special shareholders meetings, elect corporate officers, declare dividends, recommend dissolution, approve any merger or consolidation, change the registered office or registered agent, allocate to capital surplus consideration received for shares having no par value, cancel reacquired shares, and approve amendments to the corporate bylaws.

Appointment of Directors   The initial directors may be named in the articles of incorporation. These directors may be "dummy directors" who serve only until the first shareholders' meeting and then resign. The RMBCA does not require that the number and names of the directors constituting the initial board be stated in the articles. Except for the first board, the number of directors may be established either by the corporate articles or the bylaws. The effect of this is to permit the directors to keep the power to change the number of directors without seeking shareholder approval. Under the RMBCA, the power to amend the bylaws is vested solely in the board unless reserved to the shareholders by the articles, but amendments to the articles require shareholder approval. By providing for the number of directors only in the bylaws, the directors may reserve for themselves the power to determine their number.

Until recently, most state statutes required a minimum of three directors. But the trend, as illustrated by the RMBCA, is to allow for only one director. This eliminates the need for single shareholder corporations to enlist unnecessary directors.

Although traditionally shareholders elect the directors from among themselves, most statutes specifically provide that directors need not be shareholders of the corporation. Furthermore, few statutes impose age or residency requirements on directors.

Aside from the members of the initial board, directors are elected at the annual shareholders' meeting and usually hold office until the next annual meeting.

Formalities of Board Functions   The general common law rule is that a director may act as a part of the board of directors only at a proper meeting of the board. Under this approach, the board cannot act unless it is formally convened. Informal action is insufficient. The directors must be physically present at the meeting and may not vote by proxy. The idea is to encourage consultation among board members as a group. Today most statutes allow board members to act informally on the written consent of all board members without a meeting. The RMBCA also allows board members to participate in board meetings through a telephone conference call.

Under the RMBCA, board meetings may be held either in or outside the state of incorporation. The time for board meetings is included in the corporate bylaws. Therefore a director is considered to have **constructive notice** of all regular board meetings. Many statutes provide that if there is no provision to the contrary in the bylaws, the directors must be given notice of the time and topic of all specially called meetings. The RMBCA provides only that such notice as required by the bylaws must be given, and it also states that neither the business to be transacted nor the purpose of any special meeting must be specified in the notice unless required by the bylaws. When notice is required by the bylaws, the RMBCA states that a director's attendance at the meeting constitutes a waiver of the required notice, unless the director attends to object to the meeting.

Under the RMBCA, unless the articles or bylaws provide a greater number, a majority of the board members constitutes a quorum for a meeting of the directors. A majority vote of the quorum constitutes a binding act of the board.

The RMBCA permits the articles or bylaws to authorize the board to designate an executive committee or other committees composed of board members to exercise all the authority of the board except in extraordinary matters, such as article amendments, mergers, and the like. Executive committees function between board meetings and are especially useful when the board of directors is large and when consideration of specific matters by the smaller group eases decision making. Finance and audit committees, with duties relating to corporate finance and the selection of auditors, are less common.

Constructive notice knowledge that is not given by expressed writing or conduct but that the law implies a person has

The Role of Officers and Executives

It is generally recognized that the board of directors is not expected to operate the corporate business. The board delegates the day-to-day management to the corporate officers and executives, who are elected by the board and serve at the board's discretion. Unlike most state statutes today, the RMBCA does not require that there be a president, vice president, and treasurer but leaves the number and titles of officers to the bylaws or the board. This consideration is especially important for small corporations. The officers are regarded as agents of the corporation, having the authority conferred by the bylaws or by a board resolution.

MANAGEMENT'S FIDUCIARY
OBLIGATIONS

As we have already observed, those who control and manage modern corporations are protected against interference from shareholders in the handling of corporate affairs. Thus individual shareholders generally are powerless to affect the corporate affairs of large organizations. But this loss of the shareholder's power is not so oppressive as it appears. In partial recognition of these realities, recent corporate and securities law has strengthened the fiduciary obligations of management and of other controlling persons both to the corporation and to the shareholder.

Fiduciary Duty to the Corporation

Directors and officers owe fiduciary duties to the corporation like the fiduciary duties that agents owe principals. These fiduciary duties fall broadly into two categories:

1. the duty of loyalty

2. the duty of care

Duty of Loyalty   Corporate directors and officers occupy a fiduciary relationship with the corporation. It requires the exercise of good faith and loyalty in any dealings with and for the corporation. The basic principle is that corporate directors and officers should not use their positions to make personal profits nor to gain other personal advantages. In principle, this duty of loyalty is similar to the duty of loyalty exercised by agents and partners. But this duty is owed to the corporate entity, not to shareholders. The duty arises most frequently in transactions between the corporation and the corporate official involving possible conflict of interest or when a corporate opportunity comes to the attention of the corporate official.

Conflicts of interest between officers and directors and their corporations may occur whenever a transaction takes place between the corporation and them. The RMBCA does not prohibit a transaction between a director and the corporation in which the director has a financial interest as long as the transaction was fair when authorized or was ratified by the board of directors.

The general rule is that a corporation has first claim to business opportunities and profits that may be regarded as incidental to its business. Such an opportunity is called a *corporate opportunity,* and directors and officers cannot acquire this business opportunity to the harm of the corporation. Seizing a corporate opportunity usually is dealt with by imposing a **constructive trust** on the wrongful director or officer, meaning that he or she is deemed to hold the benefits of the bargain for the corporation.

When an opportunity relevant to the corporation's business comes to the attention of a corporate director or officer, he or she must first offer it to the corporation. Only after a disinterested board determines that the corporation should not pursue the opportunity may the corporate officer or director pursue the matter for his or her own account. But if the corporation is financially unable to take advantage of the opportu-

Constructive trust a trust imposed by a court of law to prevent an injustice

nity, the officer or director need not present it to the corporation. The following case clearly illustrates the corporate opportunity doctrine.

Guth v. Loft, Incorporated

Supreme Court of Delaware
5A. 2d. 503 (1939)

FACTS Loft filed a complaint against Guth and the Pepsi-Cola Company seeking to place in trust for Loft all shares of Pepsi-Cola registered in the name of Guth and Grace (approximately 91 percent of the stock). Guth, president of Loft, a chain of retail stores, bought 91 percent of the shares of Pepsi by borrowing heavily from Loft and used Loft's facilities, employees, and credit. Loft lost profits in its retail stores where Guth replaced Coca-Cola with Pepsi-Cola. Plaintiff claimed that Guth violated his duty of loyalty to Loft. Guth claimed that he had offered Loft's board of directors the opportunity to take over Pepsi-Cola, but they had declined. He also claimed that they had consented to the use of Loft's facilities and resources, but no record of these actions was found in the Loft's board of directors' meetings or by contract.

ISSUE Did Guth violate the duty of loyalty to Loft by not offering Loft's board of directors an opportunity to buy Pepsi-Cola before buying the company himself?

DECISION Yes. The court ruled that he did violate a duty of loyalty and that the opportunity to buy Pepsi-Cola belonged first to Loft. The court said that corporate officers and directors are not permitted to use their positions of trust and confidence to further their private interests. The facts and circumstances showed that Guth's appropriation of the Pepsi-Cola opportunity to himself placed him in a competitive position with Loft with respect to a commodity essential for sale in its stores.

Duty of Care   Corporate officers and directors are charged with affirmative duties concerning the management and control of the business of their corporations, and they are liable for any corporate losses resulting from their negligence. As recently amended, the RMBCA sets forth the duty of care for corporate directors as follows:

a. A director shall discharge his [or her] duties as a director, including his [or her] duties as a member of a committee:

1. in good faith

2. with the care an ordinary prudent person in a like position would exercise

3. in a manner he [or she] reasonably believes to be in the best interests of the corporation.

This is known as the **business judgment rule.**

The RMBCA also lets a director rely on information, opinions, and statements prepared by corporate officials and consultants whom the director reasonably be-

Business judgment rule standard by which courts determine whether corporate directors have acted in good faith and with a duty of care when making judgments on behalf of shareholders

lieves are reliable and competent, and any board committees on which he or she does not serve regarding matters within their designated authority.

The following case illustrates the business judgment rule.

Miller v. American Telephone & Telegraph Company

Third Circuit Court of Appeals
507 F. 2d 759 (1974)

FACTS   Plaintiffs, stockholders in American Telephone and Telegraph Company (AT&T), brought a stockholders' derivative action against AT&T. The suit centered upon the failure of AT&T to collect an outstanding debt of some $1.5 million owed to the company by the Democratic National Committee (DNC) for communication services provided by AT&T during the 1968 Democratic National Convention.

Plaintiffs' complaint alleged that "neither the officers or directors of AT&T have taken any action to recover the amount owed" from on or about August 20, 1968, when the debt was incurred, until May 31, 1972. The failure to collect was alleged to have involved a breach of the defendant directors' duty to exercise diligence in handling the affairs of the corporation and a violation of a federal prohibition on corporate company spending. Defendants argued that there was a failure to state cause of action because collection procedures were within the business judgment of the directors unless it could be shown that there was a breach of a fiduciary duty.

ISSUE   Was the delay in collection of a debt for communicating services from the Democratic National Committee a breach of the fiduciary duty of care by the officers of AT&T?

DECISION   Yes. The court ruled that the failure to collect the $1.5 million was a breach of the fiduciary duty of care owed shareholders and that a cause of action had been stated. The court said that if only a failure to pursue a corporate indebtedness were involved, the sound business judgment rule would provide for a dismissal of the plaintiff's claim. But here the court said that the complaint also alleged a violation of a federal prohibition against corporate political contributions which directly seeks to protect shareholders, and thus stated a cause of action.

Fiduciary Duty to Shareholders

In early court decisions, the directors and officers of a corporation were said to have no fiduciary duty to existing or potential stockholders but solely to the corporation. Recently there has been a trend in decisions finding a duty on the part of officers, directors, employees of the corporation, and employees of investment banking firms retained by the corporation to disclose information obtained as a result of being insiders. At the federal level, the Securities Exchange Act discussed in Chapter 33 addressed itself to disclosure requirements for officers and directors and to what constitutes insider trading.

Although the business judgment rule has given officers and directors freedom in managing a corporation, minority shareholders recently have been filing suits alleging that they have been "frozen out" of the corporation. Minority shareholders often seek injunctions or damages in cases where corporate boards have ratified high salaries for majority or controlling shareholders who are also officers of the corporation. A minority shareholder suit also may result when the board fails to declare dividends and it can be shown that there was not a good faith reason. For example, if the controlling shareholders seek to force the minority to sell their stock by not declaring a dividend or to depress the price of the stock to serve the interest of officers or directors, the courts see a wrongful purpose and a violation of the business judgment rule.

Other circumstances in which minority shareholders have charged oppression involve mergers and amendments to a corporate charter altering voting rights of a class of stock.

SUMMARY

The purposes and power of a corporation are set out expressly in the articles of incorporation and corporation bylaws. Corporations also have implied powers to do what is reasonably necessary to promote their expressed power. When a corporation acts outside its expressed and implied powers, it acts in an ultra vires manner (beyond its power), and such actions are legally void.

Three groups participate in the management of the corporation: the shareholders, board of directors, and officers. Shareholders generally are involved in the election of the board of directors and approval of certain extraordinary transactions, such as the sale of the corporation or the removal of directors. The board of directors represents the shareholders and sets overall policy for the officers and executives, who are charged with carrying it out while supervising the daily operation of the company.

Management has the fiduciary obligation of loyalty and care to the corporation. They also have a duty to existing and potential shareholders to disclose all insider information.

REVIEW PROBLEMS

1. What is the business judgment rule?

2. List the powers of a corporation as set out in the RMBCA.

3. What is meant by the ultra vires doctrine?

4. What rights do shareholders of a corporation have?

5. Biltmore Tissue Corporation was organized in 1932 with an authorized capitalization of 1,000 shares of stock. The adopted bylaws of the corporation contained provisions limiting the number of shares available to each stockholder

and restricting stock transfers both during the life of the stockholder and in case of death. According to the bylaws, if a stockholder wanted to sell or transfer shares, he or she had to give the corporation or other stockbrokers the chance to purchase the stock from the stockholder at the price paid when the stock was originally purchased. If the option was not exercised within 90 days, the stockholder then was free to sell the stock. Henry Kaplan had purchased shares with restrictions of sale and transfer, as detailed above, printed on the stock certificates. When Kaplan died, Biltmore's board of directors voted to exercise its option to repurchase the shares from Kaplan's estate and agreed to pay a sum greater than Kaplan paid for the stock. Those administering Kaplan's estate declined to sell and wanted the stock transferred to the estate. They brought a lawsuit to compel the corporation to transfer the stock according to the estate's wishes, claiming that the limitation on sale and transfer was an unreasonable restraint. They further argued that the ownership in Kaplan could not be coupled with the right of alienation in another person. The corporation argued that due to the restriction of sale and transfer of the stock, it was not prohibiting the transfer of stock but merely putting a reasonable restriction on the transfer. Does the provision in the corporate bylaws, giving the corporation a right or first option to purchase the stock at the price that it originally received for it, amount to an unreasonable restraint on the transfer of the stock?

6. Gilbert, the owner of record of 17 shares of Transamerica Corporation, wrote the management of the company and submitted four proposals that he wanted to be presented for action by shareholders at the next annual stockholders' meeting. The SEC demanded that Transamerica comply with Gilbert's request, but the company refused. The SEC brought an action to forbid Transamerica from making use of any proxy solicited by it for use at the annual meeting, from making use of the mails or any instrumentality of interstate commerce to solicit proxies, or from making use of any soliciting material without complying with the SEC's demands. Transamerica claimed that the shareholder may interest himself or herself only in a subject to which he or she is entitled to vote at a stockholder's meeting when every requirement of state law and of the provisions of the charter and bylaws has been fulfilled. State law states that a certificate of incorporation may set forth provisions that limit, regulate, and define the powers and functions of the directors and stockholders. A bylaw of Transamerica vested in the board of directors the power to decide whether any proposal might be voted on at an annual meeting of stockholders. Three of Gilbert's proposals were:

   to have independent public auditors of the books of Transamerica elected by the stockholders

   to eliminate from a bylaw the requirement that notice of any proposed alteration or amendment of the bylaws be contained in the notice of meetings

   to require an account or a report of the proceedings at the annual meetings to be sent to all stockholders.

   Is Gilbert entitled to make such demands? What are the reasons for and against the proposals made by Gilbert? Will the power of shareholders go to an extreme if small shareholders like Gilbert can exert so much pressure?

7. The directors of Acoustic Products Company concluded that it was essential for the success of the company to purchase the rights to manufacture under certain patents held by the DeForest Radio Company. Acoustic was already involved in the manufacture of phonographs and radios. A contract was entered into between an agent of Acoustic and the major shareholder of DeForest providing that Acoustic could purchase one third of the DeForest stock. This act would increase the possibility for Acoustic to obtain the needed patent rights. The directors of Acoustic could not raise the funds for Acoustic to perform the contract. Thus they personally purchased the DeForest stock. When Acoustic later went bankrupt, the trustee in bankruptcy brought action against the directors, claiming that by purchasing the DeForest shares they had violated the fiduciary duty owed to the corporation. The parties agreed that the acquisition of the rights under the DeForest patents were essential for Acoustic's success. Conceding that there existed a close relation between Acoustic and DeForest, the directors argued that because the company did not have the money to purchase the shares, the directors had violated no duty by purchasing the shares themselves. Who should win? Should the directors suffer financially even though they made their effort to help Acoustic, or is this possibility for suffering by the directors part of the game and necessary to prompt directors to use their best efforts in uncovering financial resources their companies might use to acquire attractive opportunities?

8. Pillsbury had long opposed the Vietnam War. He learned that Honeywell, Incorporated, had a substantial part of its business in the production of munitions used in the war and also that Honeywell had a large government contract to produce antipersonnel fragmentation bombs. Pillsbury was determined to stop this production. He bought one share of Honeywell in his name to get himself a voice in Honeywell's affairs so that he could persuade the company to stop producing munitions. Pillsbury submitted demands to Honeywell, requesting that it produce its original shareholder ledger, current shareholder ledger, and all corporate records dealing with weapons and munitions manufacture. Honeywell refused. Pillsbury brought suit to compel Honeywell to let him inspect the requested records. Pillsbury claimed that he wished to inspect the records to correspond with other shareholders, with the hope of electing to the board one or more directors who represented his viewpoint. Should the court let Pillsbury inspect the records? Does Pillsbury have a proper purpose relevant to his interest as a shareholder? Should a shareholder be allowed to persuade a company to adopt his or her social and political views?

9. A, who owned stock in a gold mining company, B, made a contract with the company to sell his stock. For financial reasons, A later refused to sell and breached his contract. The bylaws of the corporation allowed the executive committee to "conduct the corporation's business." When B sued A, the latter's defense was that the contract was invalid because B's articles of incorporation did not expressly allow the company to purchase its stock from stockholders. Was A's defense valid? Explain.

10. A, president of B company, made a contract with an employee, C, by which C was promised certain retirement benefits. A owned 80 percent of the stock of B and had managed the company independent of the board of directors. When C retired, the board refused to pay the benefits promised him. C sued based on a

breach of contract. B company's defense was that the contract was invalid because it was not approved by the board of directors. What result? Explain.

11. Bio-Lab, Incorporated, was incorporated in 1972 by Morad, Thomson, Coupounas, and Dr. Shaw to form a business in which red blood cells were separated from blood plasma of a paid blood donor. The plasma was then sold to biological manufacturing companies. When disagreement existed among stockholders and members of the board in 1973, Thomson purchased Dr. Shaw's stock, and Morad (42 percent shareholder), Thomson (28 percent) and Coupounas (30 percent) remained on the board. In 1974, Morad, his wife, and Thomson incorporated another blood plasma business, Med-Lab, Inc. He served as president of both Bio-Lab and Med-Lab, working "full time" for both corporations. In May 1976, Coupounas brought suit upon behalf of himself and Bio-Lab against Med-Lab, Inc., Morad, and Thomson, alleging a breach of a fiduciary duty on the behalf of all in forming Med-Lab, Inc. Who won? Explain.

12. Delmarmo Associates owned 13 percent of the shares of New Jersey Engineering and Supply Company. It sought to vote out the management through the use of proxies at the next shareholders' meeting. When it requested the right to inspect New Jersey Engineer's books to obtain a shareholders' list, the corporation denied the request. The corporation's denial was based on the fact that the inspection request was made for purposes of gaining control of New Jersey Engineering. Who won? Explain.

13. Gormley was a manager of a grain elevator business. Following the first year of operation, an audit showed that Gormley had written $87,000 in checks to himself. The audit report to the board recommended that two signatures be required on checks and that Gormley discontinue his practice. Gormley continued to write checks to himself personally, and two years later the grain corporation closed its business owing $400,000 to unsecured creditors. Gormley was convicted of mishandling funds (misappropriation). Speer, a creditor, sued the directors and officers of the defunct corporation, alleging negligence and a breach of a duty of care on the part of the directors. Who won? Explain.

14. Chicago, National League Ball Club, Incorporated, owned and operated the Chicago Cubs, a major league baseball team. Wrigley was 80 percent owner of the corporation's shares and president of the corporation. Schlensky, a minority shareholder, in 1968 filed suit on behalf of the corporation claiming that its profits had been damaged by refusal of Wrigley to install lights in Wrigley Field so that the Cubs could play home games at night like all other major league baseball teams. The Cubs showed operating losses from 1961 to 1965. The plaintiff argued that Wrigley was negligent in failing to exercise due care as an officer and director of the corporation because he allowed his personal opinion that "baseball was a daytime sport" to interfere with the ability of the corporation to make profits. Who won? Explain.

PART V

PROPERTY

CHAPTER 35

Personal Property

CHAPTER OBJECTIVES

PROPERTY AND GOVERNMENT

REAL AND PERSONAL PROPERTY

Real Property / Personal Property / Intangible Personal Property

FIXTURES

Determination of Fixtures / Trade Fixtures

TRANSFER OF TITLE TO PROPERTY

Sale / Gift / Judicial Sale / Abandoned, Lost, and Mislaid Property

CHANGING CONCEPTS OF PROPERTY

SUMMARY

REVIEW PROBLEMS

CHAPTER OBJECTIVES

After reading this chapter, you should be able to:

1. Define real property, personal property, intangible personal property, fixtures, and trade fixtures.

2. Compare and contrast real and personal property, fixtures and trade fixtures.

3. Outline the tests that courts use to determine whether personal property has become a fixture.

4. List and briefly describe the major methods that exist for transferring title to property.

5. Explain how modern law is changing traditional concepts of property.

Property a
bundle of rights
that people have in
things they own

When a person speaks of property, he or she usually refers to something he or she owns — a piano, an automobile, a house. From a legal standpoint, the things themselves are not significant. What is important are the rights the individual has in them. Traditional legal usage defines **property** as the bundle or aggregate of rights that people have in things they own. These include the right to use, sell, or even destroy the thing if the person wishes to do so.

PROPERTY AND GOVERNMENT

The very existence of property depends on government. State and federal laws create and maintain the "bundle of rights" that the legal system refers to as property. The mutual promises of a contract have economic significance because courts award damages if a promise is not kept. A contract is property because society, through law, supports the owner's capacity to control the actions of others through the contract.

Whether something is property is important as far as the Constitution is concerned, because federal and state constitutions prohibit government from taking property without due process of law. More will be said about this in Chapter 37 on real property.

REAL AND PERSONAL PROPERTY

Until about 150 years ago, land was the most important source of wealth and a major determinant of social position both in England and in the United States.

Ownership of land also had political significance, because often only landowners were permitted to vote.

Real Property

One result of the historic importance of land is a distinction in Anglo-American law between land and other forms of wealth. Because of land's economic significance, the early common law provided extensive protection to landowners. A landowner who was thrown off his land could immediately bring an action to recover the land. This was known as a "real action," and it is the reason that land is called **real property** or **real estate.** But a person who lost control of something of economic value other than land, usually a movable item, once could sue only for money. This was known as a "personal action" and the item involved, **personal property.** In modern law, the distinction between real and personal property is still recognized.

Real property or **real estate** land or anything permanently attached to land

Personal property movable property; all property other than real property

Personal Property

Personal property generally is characterized as movable. Historically, personal property consisted of items that had substance. These items were often referred to as goods or **chattels.** In the farming economy that existed in the United States until this century, livestock, farm equipment, and the tools of a person's trade were common examples. Along with land, these items were major forms of wealth. As the nature of the American economy changed, new forms of wealth were created. Today an appreciable amount of wealth is intangible. It consists of rights that a person has that represent value. An intangible right, often referred to as a **chose** (French, "thing") **in action,** is also personal property.

Chattels personal property

Chose in action the right of owners to recover things owned by them but not in their possession

Intangible Personal Property

A stock certificate is an example of intangible personal property. The certificate is evidence of value, although it has no worth in and of itself. The owner of the stock can sell it, use it as security, or give it away. He or she also has numerous rights in relation to the firm, other owners, and creditors. **Intangible property** figures in many business transactions. Patents, copyrights, trademarks, contracts, and stock are examples of intangible property important in business.

As new forms of wealth have been created, personal property has become more like real property in economic significance. This trend has led to a narrowing of the legal distinction between the two, but differences continue to exist and to influence decisions that businesspeople must make.

The distinction between real and personal property raises many insurance, tax, financing, and inheritance questions. In the case that follows, the distinction between the two types of property was important to the outcome of the litigation.

Intangible property documents that represent valuable rights that a person owns

_____ *Barron v. Edwards* _____

Court of Appeals of Michigan
206 N.W. 2d 508 (1973)

FACTS   Barron owned and operated a sod farm. Edwards sold sod. Barron orally agreed to sell 30 acres of sod to Edwards for $350 an acre. The State Highway Department condemned and took title to the farm before Edwards could remove the sod. Barron sued to restrain Edwards from removing the sod, and Edwards counterclaimed for specific performance or, in the alternative, damages. Barron moved to dismiss the counterclaim on grounds that the agreement covered an interest in land and was not enforceable because not in writing.

ISSUE   Was the oral agreement enforceable?

DECISION   The court held that the sod was personal property rather than real property. The applicable statute provided that "goods" includes growing crops and other identified things attached to realty which are capable of severance without material harm.

The court distinguished between *fructus naturales,* which are regarded as realty, and *fructus industriales,* which are regarded as personal property. *Fructus naturales* grow on their own. *Fructus industriales* are cultivated by people. Here the sod owed its existence to yearly fertilizing and cultivation by humans, so it should be treated as personal property even though part of the soil.

The court held that although the sod was personal property, a written agreement was required because the contract involved a sale of goods for over $500. The court returned the case to the trial court to determine if the writing requirement of the Statute had been satisfied.

FIXTURES _____

As the previous case indicates, the classification of property as real or personal has important legal consequences. In many situations, conflicting arguments exist for classifying property one way or the other. Naturally, individuals and firms wish to have property classified in the manner most beneficial to them. This classification problem is further complicated by the fact that the property's designation can change, depending on how it is used.

A common example is items used in home construction, such as a built-in oven. The oven would be personal property when part of a building supplier's inventory. But as part of a dwelling, the built-in oven becomes real property. As we mentioned in Chapter 24, personal property that becomes real property through attachment to land or a building is called a *fixture.*

Severance the transformation of real property into personal property

In some instances, real property is transformed into personal property. This change is often referred to as **severance.** Trees growing in a forest are real property, but if a tree is cut to be milled into lumber or stacked as firewood it becomes personal property. In some states, courts recognize the *doctrine of constructive severance.* In these states, trees standing in a forest are considered personal property as soon as a contract is made selling them to be logged.

Determination of Fixtures

The chief test in determining whether personal property has become a fixture is the intention of the party who attached the item to real property. This intention is not the secret intention of that person, but the intention determined by how the person acted. Other factors that courts consider are how the item is attached and its application and use as a permanent part of the realty. Often attachment and use are considered only as evidence of what was intended. The Wisconsin case that follows indicates the importance of intention. *The Matter of Park Corrugated Box Corporation*, a case that appears later in this chapter, discusses alternative approaches to determining fixtures. In both cases, intention plays a dominant role.

George v. Commercial Credit

U.S. Court of Appeals, Seventh Circuit
440 F. 2d 551 (1971)

Foskett purchased a mobile home on credit. The home was to be placed on land that   FACTS
he owned. When the mobile home was delivered, it was set on cement blocks, hooked up to a septic tank, and connected to electric power lines. Foskett also had the wheels removed. Foskett did not apply for a certificate of title from the motor vehicle department, but he did take out a homeowner's insurance policy on the home.

Subsequently, he executed a real estate mortgage on the property. This mortgage was assigned to Commercial Credit Corporation. Some time later, Foskett filed a petition in bankruptcy, and George was appointed trustee. George contended that the mobile home was a motor vehicle and was therefore personal property. Commercial Credit argued that the mobile home was a fixture. The referee in bankruptcy and the lower court rejected George's argument and he appealed.

Was the mobile home a fixture?   ISSUE

Yes. The court held that the mobile home had become a fixture and thus was   DECISION
included in the security for the real estate mortgage. In determining whether the mobile home was a fixture, the court considered three factors:

1. actual physical attachment to the realty

2. application or adaptation to the use or purpose to which the realty is devoted

3. intention of the person attaching to treat the item as a part of the real estate.

Of the three, intention of the party is the principal consideration. Here, the mobile home was clearly adapted to use as the permanent residence of Foskett and was never moved off his land. The fact that it was physically possible to move the mobile home would not change its classification as a fixture.

Trade Fixtures

The rule that personal property permanently attached to real estate becomes a part of it has serious consequences to tenants. Unless the tenant and owner agree, a tenant making permanent additions to real property may not remove a fixture at the end of the term. This greatly hampers a business from leasing a building if the firm needs to add items — such as display cases or machinery — to operate effectively. Because of this, the legal system differentiates between fixtures and personal property attached to real estate to carry on a trade or business.

Trade fixtures personal property attached to real estate to carry on a trade or business

Items of this latter nature are called **trade fixtures** and generally may be taken by the tenant at the end of the term. Agricultural fixtures are treated in a similar manner. To remove a trade or agricultural fixture, the tenant must restore the premises to its original condition and must remove the item while in possession.

Allowing tenants to remove trade fixtures has social benefits. It encourages both the use of land and efficiency in business. Tenants are more apt to invest in new and improved equipment if they can later remove these items. In a number of states, statutes establish tenants' rights to remove trade fixtures.

Because the doctrine of trade fixtures is important to tenants, parties to a commercial lease should include provisions clearly expressing their intentions. They might agree that the tenant shall not remove items that ordinarily would be trade fixtures. But a lease provision stating the tenant's right to remove items added to carry out its business or trade would clearly show the intention of the parties and would lessen possibilities of disagreement.

The case that follows illustrates the trade fixture doctrine and discusses another approach to determining when an item is a fixture.

Matter of Park Corrugated Box Corporation

U.S. District Court (D.N.J.)
249 F. Supp. 56 (1966)

FACTS   Manufacturers Leasing Corporation petitioned a referee in bankruptcy for an order allowing Manufacturers to reclaim a machine from Park Corrugated Box Corporation, a bankrupt. Manufacturers had sold the machine to Park. Their agreement stated that Manufacturers was to have a security interest in the machine until it was paid for in full. According to New Jersey law, the proper place to file to perfect such a security interest depended on whether the machine was a fixture or a chattel. A security interest for a fixture had to be filed in the county register's office. A security interest in a chattel had to be filed in the office of the secretary of state. Manufacturers had filed in the county register's office, claiming the machine to be a fixture.

ISSUE   Was the machine a fixture?

DECISION   No. The court held that the machine was not a fixture and therefore that Manufacturer's security interest was not perfected. The court used two tests to determine whether a chattel has become a fixture: the "traditional test" and the "institutional doctrine."

Under the "traditional test," the intention of the party making the attachment is the dominant factor. The intention may be inferred from the circumstances surrounding the attachment. Here the machine was only anchored by three leg screws on each side and could easily be removed without material physical damage to the building. In fact, the machine had been moved several times to different sections of the plant.

Under the "institutional doctrine," the test is whether the chattel is permanently essential to the completeness of the structure or its use. In this case, after the machine was removed from the building, the structure still could be used for manufacturing. In fact, the parties' agreement stated that the machine was to be attached so that it could be removed later on.

The court also rejected Manufacturers' claim that the machine was a trade fixture and therefore a fixture. The court held that a fixture is just the opposite of a trade fixture because, by definition, a trade fixture is easily removed.

TRANSFER OF TITLE TO PROPERTY

Sale

Sale is the most important method of transferring title to property. Although the methods of selling both real and personal property have developed along somewhat different lines, both are governed extensively by statute and case law. The sale of goods is the subject of Article 2 of the Uniform Commercial Code, which is discussed in detail in Chapters 15 through 18.

In general the process involved in selling real property is much more formal than that involved in selling goods. Statutes in all states require public recording of the transfer of title to real property if the owner's title is to be valid against claims of third parties who might acquire an interest in the real estate.

Gift

Title to property frequently is transferred by gift. In dollar value, most gifts are made through wills made in anticipation of death.

Gifts by living people are very important. A gift by a living person is usually an *inter vivos* gift. If a living person makes a gift in expectation of impending death, the gift is said to be *causa mortis.* In an *inter vivos* gift, the recipient or donee receives an irrevocable title. In a *causa mortis* gift, the gift may be revoked if the donor does not die.

For a gift by a living person to be valid, the donor must intend to make a gift, and the item must be delivered. In addition, the donee must be willing to accept the gift. Ordinarily this last requirement causes few problems, although the other essential elements of a gift sometimes result in litigation, as the following case illustrates.

Inter vivos gift a gift by a living person

Causa mortis gift a gift made in expectation of impending death

_____ *The Matter of the Estate of Alfred V. Sipe, Deceased* _____

Supreme Court of Pennsylvania
422 A. 2d 826 (1980)

FACTS   Alfred V. Sipe had a savings account at a branch of the Union National Bank. On September 17, 1975, Sipe closed the account and immediately opened a new account in his own name and the name of Mary Drabik, appellant. Instead of having her sign, Sipe signed both his name and hers on the card.

Eighteen months later, Sipe, who was about to enter the hospital, gave the passbook for the joint account to Drabik. Sipe died about six weeks after being released from the hospital. After his release from the hospital, he was in the bank on one occasion with his nephew but did not transact any business.

Eleanor A. Sipe, appellee, administering the estate of Alfred V. Sipe, petitioned for an order directing Drabik to turn over to the estate money she had withdrawn from the joint savings account after Sipe's death. Drabik claims that decedent completed a gift of the savings account. Eleanor Sipe contends that Drabik's failure to sign the signature card was fatal to her case.

ISSUE   Did Alfred V. Sipe make a valid gift of the savings account?

DECISION   Yes. The court held that decedent had made a gift of the savings account. The requirements for a gift are intent, delivery, and acceptance. Appellant's failure to sign the signature card did not negate decedent's intent to make a gift. Decedent clearly asked that a joint account be opened and was given an explanation of the account.

Acceptance of a gift is usually presumed. In this case, the acceptance requirement was met when appellant received the passbook. Delivery was effected, if not when decedent returned the signature card to the bank, when decedent gave the passbook to Drabik.

Judicial Sale

Most courts have the power to order the sale of a defendant's real or personal property to satisfy a judgment. Sometimes the court's order is based on an agreement in which one of the parties has used specific property as a security. Usually the property guarantees payment of the loan or is used to finance the purchase of the property. A real estate mortgage (see Chapter 30) and a security agreement (see Chapter 24) executed by the purchaser of goods are examples. In addition, many states allow designated officials to seize various assets of a defendant and to sell them to satisfy a money judgment. As we have seen in the discussion of bankruptcy, usually state statutes establish a category of property that is exempt from seizure. Generally property necessary to earn a livelihood or sustain life is exempt.

Abandoned, Lost, and Mislaid Property

Abandoned property is that which the owner has voluntarily given up with the intention of surrendering any interest that he or she has. In the event of litigation over supposedly abandoned property, the person claiming title must be able to prove that the owner intended to abandon the property. Merely not using property even for an extended time is not abandonment, although nonuse may be used as evidence showing an intention to abandon. The first person to acquire abandoned property gets title to it.

Lost property and abandoned property are not the same. Lost property is that which the owner had no intention of giving up but has parted with through carelessness or accident. Loss of a diamond that falls out of a ring setting would be an example.

Acquisition of title to lost property differs from the acquisition of title to abandoned property. In most cases, the person who finds lost property acquires an interest that is good against everyone but the true owner. But before the finder acquires title, certain conditions must be met. These conditions vary from state to state.

Some states continue to follow the common law rule. At common law, before the finder of lost property acquired title, he or she was required to make a reasonable search for the true owner. Most states by statute require a finder to notify a designated public official of the finding. If the property is not claimed within a specified period of time — usually six months to a year — the finder acquires the property.

The law considers mislaid property and lost property differently. **Mislaid property** is property that an owner has intentionally placed somewhere and then forgotten. Supposedly when the owner remembers the item, he or she knows where to look for it. As a result, the owner of the place where the property is found and not the finder has the right to the property if it is not claimed by the rightful owner. The law assumes that the owner will return to the place where the item was mislaid. Entrusting the owner of that place with property makes it easier for the true owner to recover his or her property.

For example, Sam, a customer of First Bank, finds a woman's purse on a counter in the lobby. If unclaimed, the purse and its contents become the property of the bank, because the purse apparently was mislaid. If the property had been lost and not mislaid, the result probably would differ. Assume that Sam found the purse on the floor of the lobby and not on the counter. In that event, Sam would acquire title if he took the proper steps, because the purse apparently was lost. But if Sam were an employee of the bank, the bank would be entitled to the purse. An employee who finds lost property while on the job has no right to it as long as the employer has a policy of accepting responsibility for it.

Abandoned property property that an owner has voluntarily given up

Lost property property that an owner has parted with through carelessness or accident

Mislaid property property that an owner has placed somewhere and forgotten

CHANGING CONCEPTS OF PROPERTY

Property is a dynamic concept, continually reshaped by society to meet new economic and social needs. In the United States today, two movements modifying traditional rights associated with property are worth noting. One of these involves the restructuring of property rights in their relationship to civil rights. This movement is embodied in legislation and cases that attempt to assure the fundamental interests of minorities. In most instances, when traditional property rights conflict with basic civil rights, property rights have been limited.

The 1948 U.S. Supreme Court opinion in *Shelly* v. *Kraemer* (see Chapter 1, page 17) exemplifies this trend. This case involved an agreement by certain owners of real estate not to sell or lease their homes to "people of the Negro or Mongolian race." When Shelly, a black, purchased a parcel covered by this restriction, Kraemer and others sued to restrain him from taking possession. The Supreme Court held that state courts could not enforce a private agreement depriving a person of a constitutional right. In effect, the Supreme Court limited the right of Kraemer and the others to restrict the use of their real estate in this manner.

A second direction that the law is taking is to extend property rights to a person's employment or the facilities necessary to practice a chosen profession. Although the movement in this direction is slow, the trend is clear. Recently, status and reputation have been treated as property, as in the following case.

Memphis Development Foundation v. Factors Etc., Incorporated

U.S. Court of Appeals Sixth Circuit
616 F. 2d 956 (1980)

FACTS   Memphis Development Foundation (Foundation) sued to bar Factors Etc., Incorporated, from interfering with Foundation's attempt to erect a large bronze statue of Elvis Presley in downtown Memphis. Foundation solicited donations to pay for the sculpture and gave away 8-inch pewter replicas of the statue to donors of $25 or more.

During his life, Presley had conveyed the exclusive right to exploit the commercial value of his name to Boxcar Enterprises. Factors purchased these rights from Boxcar Enterprises two days after Presley's death. Factors, claiming an exclusive right to profit from Presley's name and likeness, counterclaimed for damages and sought an injunction prohibiting distribution of the replicas.

ISSUE   Does Factors have the exclusive right to profit from Presley's name and likeness?

DECISION   No. The court held that the right to control and profit from the commercial use of a celebrity's name and likeness ends with the death of the celebrity. Foundation therefore could continue to distribute the replicas without interference from Factors.

In declining to recognize an inheritable right of publicity, the court was avoiding a whole set of practical problems. How long would the "property" interest last? Always? For a term of years? Is the right of publicity taxable? At what point does the right collide with the right of free expression guaranteed by the First Amendment? Our legal system usually does not pass on to heirs other similar personal attributes even though the attributes may be shared during life by others or have some commercial value.

The court drew an analogy to the law of defamation, which is designed to protect against the destruction of reputation, including the loss of earning capacity associated with it. There is no right of action for defamation after death.

The court concluded by deciding that whatever minimal benefit to society may result from the added motivation and extra creativity supposedly encouraged by allowing a person to pass on his fame for the commercial use of others does not outweigh the considerations discussed above.

SUMMARY

Property is the bundle of rights that people have in things that they own. These rights are created and maintained by government. American law makes a significant distinction between real property and personal property. Although this distinction is a result of the historic importance of land as a source of wealth, the distinction continues to have important legal consequences today.

Fixtures are items of personal property that have become real property through attachment to land or buildings. Courts have devised a number of tests to determine if an item is a fixture. The chief test is the intention of the person who attached the item, as determined by how that person acted. Trade fixtures are items of personal property that have been attached to real property to carry on a trade or business. They are treated differently by the law from ordinary fixtures. The main difference is that a tenant can remove a trade fixture at the expiration of the tenancy.

Title to property is transferred in a number of different ways. Probably the most important is by sale. Other methods of transferring title are by gift, judicial sale, and finding.

REVIEW PROBLEMS

1. Explain the difference between real and personal property, and indicate some of the legal consequences of this difference.

2. Define intangible personal property and provide some examples of it.

3. Indicate the tests courts use to determine if an item is a fixture.

4. What are the essential elements necessary for making a valid gift?

5. Explain the different legal consequences of classifying an item as a trade fixture as compared with a fixture.

6. Tillotson purchased a drying bin from the B. C. Manufacturing Company. The bin was erected on property owned by the Newman Grove Grain Company. The bin was anchored to a concrete base and became an integral part of the grain corporation's elevator, to which it was attached with loading and unloading ducts, electrical wiring, etc. The Newman Grove Grain Company mortgaged the real estate to the Battle Creek State Bank. Is the bin a fixture? What difference does this make? Explain.

7. Kalyvakis was employed on a passenger vessel. The vessel, the *Olympia,* was docked in New York City. The day that the *Olympia* was to sail Kalyvakis found $3,010 on the floor in the men's room. He turned the money over to his employer. After three years had passed, no one had claimed the money and Kalyvakis asked that it be returned to him. The employer refused on grounds that Kalyvakis had found the money during the course of his employment. Was Kalyvakis entitled to the money? Support your answer.

8. Anne P. Graham and Dennis J. Graham were husband and wife. During their six-year marriage, Anne Graham was employed full time. Her husband worked part time, although his main pursuit was his education. He attended school for approximately three and one half years, acquiring a bachelor of science degree and a master's degree in business. Approximately 70 percent of the family funds were supplied by the wife.

    The Grahams filed a petition for dissolution of marriage. As part of this action, Anne Graham claimed that the master's degree was marital property and subject to division by the court. She asked for $33,134 as her share of this property. Should the degree be treated as property? Discuss.

9. Health Clubs, Inc., contracted to purchase an indoor swimming pool from Stanton. The pool was heated and had a large filtering unit. The heater and filter were easily removable once disconnected. Before Health Clubs, Inc., took possession, Stanton removed both units. When sued, Stanton contended that the units were personal property. Health Clubs, Inc., argued that the units were fixtures. Who is correct? Support your answer.

10. Fishbein purchased a small motel from January. He was to take possession in 30 days. The day after he received a deed to the property, he noticed that January was removing all the furniture. Fishbein sued for a court order to prevent this. He argued that the motel was worthless without the furniture. Would he be successful? Discuss.

11. Milligan owned a farm in Iowa, which he sold to Meyers. Milligan moved into town from the farm, but he left a well drilling rig on the property with the permission of Meyers. The rig was in poor condition, and two of its tires were flat. Milligan told Meyers that the rig was for sale. Several people did come to examine the rig in the weeks following the sale. But the rig was never moved. About two years later, Meyers learned that Milligan had moved to California. The following year Meyers repaired the rig and began to use it. Has Meyers acquired title to the rig? Discuss.

12. Jefferson rented an apartment from Spitzer. Jefferson had a bar built in the recreation room. He also had a refrigerator built into the wall. When his lease expired, Jefferson attempted to remove the bar and the refrigerator. Would he be allowed to do so? Discuss.

CHAPTER 36

Bailment

CHAPTER OBJECTIVES

After reading this chapter, you should be able to:

1. Define bailment, bailor, bailee, conditional sale, and consignment.

2. Explain how the courts traditionally have classified bailments.

3. Outline the legal responsibilities of bailor and bailee for the three bailment classifications.

4. Recognize that the three bailment classifications are convenient for solving legal problems but that the current trend is to consider other factors as well.

Bailment a legal relationship in which one person temporarily holds property owned by another to accomplish an agreed-upon purpose

One legal relationship in which almost everyone becomes involved from time to time is **bailment.** In addition to being important in the daily lives of most individuals, bailments are very common in business transactions.

In a bailment, one person temporarily holds the personal property of another. Usually the property has been placed in the holder's control by agreement between the owner and the holder. The property is to be returned to the owner or disposed of according to the owner's direction when the purpose of the bailment is fulfilled. As we discussed in Chapter 20, the owner who has surrendered the property is called the *bailor.* As we mentioned in Chapter 16, the person who controls it is the *bailee.*

Examples of bailment in commercial transactions include leasing an automobile or equipment, storing goods in a warehouse, and delivering goods to a trucker for shipment. A bailment exists when a person takes an automobile to a garage for repairs or checks a coat in a restaurant. Common personal transactions such as borrowing a friend's golf clubs also create bailments.

Bailments have extensive legal ramifications for both parties, and they also often give rise to difficult legal problems. Because bailments are important in business, the business manager must know the rights and duties of the parties to a bailment and be able to distinguish bailments from other transactions.

ESSENTIAL ELEMENTS

As with most legal relationships, generalizations about bailments are dangerous. Although the following statements about bailments indicate the essential elements of the relationship, each requires a clarification:

1. A bailment's subject matter is personal property.

2. The bailee must have possession of the property.

3. An intention to possess the property must exist or be implied by law.

4. The property must be returned or accounted for when the bailment is complete.

Personal Property

The subject matter of a bailment must be personal property. The property can be either tangible or intangible, but it must be in existence when the bailment is created. The promise of a company to deliver stock to an employee is not a bailment when the only notation of the transaction is an indication on the company's books that the agreement exists. If the stock has been issued, but the company retains the certificates until the employee gets funds to pay applicable taxes, the relationship is a bailment.

Possession

Possession of the goods or chattels by the bailee is a major element in any bailment. Possession generally is determined by the control that the bailee exercises over the property. In most bailments, the property is actually in the bailee's possession, but **constructive possession** is sufficient. For example, most states regard a bank that supplies safe deposit facilities as a bailee in spite of the fact that the bailee does not have control of the bailor's property. The reasoning underlying this rule apparently is that the bank controls admission to the vault where the property is stored.

The case that follows indicates the importance of the control factor in determining whether a parking lot owner is a bailee.

Constructive possession the legal power to exercise control over property not actually in one's possession

FIGURE 36-1 Parking Receipt

XYZ AMUSEMENT PARK

PARKING

134831

THIS CONTRACT LIMITS OUR LIABILITY. READ IT!

This ticket licenses the holder to park ONE MOTOR VEHICLE in parking area at XYZ Amusement Park. XYZ assumes no responsibility for theft, loss, fire, or damage to any Motor Vehicle or any of the contents therein, it being understood that the Driver of the Motor Vehicle has full control of the Motor Vehicle at all times. Only a license to park is granted hereby, and no bailment is created.

Acceptance of this ticket constitutes acknowledgment by holder that holder has read and agrees to the foregoing conditions.

LOCK YOUR VEHICLE

_____ *Central Parking System v. Miller* _____

Supreme Court of Kentucky
586 S.W. 2d 262 (1979)

FACTS   Miller sued to recover the value of wire wheels that had been stolen from his car. The car was parked in a large garage owned by Central Parking. The parking garage was self-service. A machine automatically gave a ticket to the driver, who parked in a place of his or her choice and left the car, taking the keys.

The lower courts held that Central Parking was a bailee for hire and had a legal duty to exercise such ordinary care as a person of reasonable prudence would exercise with respect to his or her own property. Central Parking argued that it was not a bailee.

ISSUE   Is Central Parking a bailee?

DECISION   No. The court stated that when a person parks his automobile in a garage by receiving a ticket from an automated machine, choosing his own place, and taking his keys with him, the garage is not a bailee. The court further stated that Miller must prove specific acts of negligence on the part of Central Parking to recover for the stolen wheels. The judgment of the trial court and the opinion of the court of appeals were reversed.

Agreement

Vendee
purchaser of property

Although many cases indicate that a bailment requires agreement, an express agreement is unnecessary. A bailment can be created by actions indicating that the parties intended to agree, and some courts have found agreements in situations in which they believed that the parties should have agreed.

Return of Property

Conditional sale
a sale in which the buyer obtains possession of the item but the seller retains title until the purchase price is paid

Consignment
bailment in which goods are delivered to a bailee to be sold for the owner

Ordinarily the item bailed or a substitute for the item, usually money, is to be returned or accounted for by the bailee. A transaction in which the recipient of personal property is under no obligation to return or account for it is a sale or a gift. In both a sale and a gift, title passes to the recipient. The distinction between sale and bailment is important, because the legal rights and obligations of a bailee and **vendee** differ markedly.

Delivery of an item to another with payment over a period of time at the end of which the buyer takes title is a **conditional sale,** not a bailment. This transaction (classified as a secured transaction under the UCC) remains a conditional sale even if the seller can retrieve the specific item if payment is not made. But a transaction in which the party to whom property is delivered has an option to purchase or holds the property for sale to another is a bailment. A bailment of this nature is generally referred to as a **consignment.**

LEGAL PRINCIPLES

Before discussing some common legal problems involving bailors and bailees, two fundamental legal maxims must be reviewed. First, like other legal relationships, bailment results from how the parties act. The relationship is not created merely because the parties label their transaction a bailment. If the essential elements exist, a bailment is created no matter how the parties label what they are doing. Second, subject to statute, the rights and obligations of the bailor and bailee are determined by their agreement. Courts look first to the agreement to determine how responsibility is allocated, although an agreement that violates public policy is not enforced.

CLASSIFICATION

In many bailments, the parties either fail to indicate how duties and obligations are to be performed, or they do so inadequately. In these cases, courts have had to work out solutions to the problem of where the equities lie between the parties. One method that has been used is to relate rights and duties to the benefits received by the parties. To make this easier, the following threefold classification of bailments has developed.

Mutual Benefit Bailment

A bailment in which both parties benefit, the most common type of bailment, is the *mutual benefit bailment*. It is especially important in business transactions. Mutual benefit bailments include leaving a suit at the cleaners to be cleaned, leaving a watch at the jewelers to be repaired, and delivering goods to a carrier for shipment.

Bailment for the Sole Benefit of the Bailee

A bailment in which the bailee does not compensate the bailor for the property is often referred to as a *gratuitous bailment* or *bailment for the sole benefit of the bailee.* In this situation, someone lends an item to another, expecting no payment in return. For example, a person might borrow a lawn mower from a neighbor.

Bailment for the Sole Benefit of the Bailor

A bailment in which only the owner benefits is a *bailment for the sole benefit of the bailor.* This type of bailment exists if someone who is not paid holds another's property for safekeeping. For example, a person might agree to store a friend's car in his or her garage as a favor.

Not all legal problems involving bailments can be solved by using these classifications. Recently a number of courts have rejected this system of classification, especially when attempting to decide the bailee's responsibility for care and use of the property, but the classification helps to solve some problems.

In the case that follows, the court held the defendant to a higher standard of care than ordinarily required of a gratuitous bailee.

—— *Nash v. City of North Platte* ——

Supreme Court of Nebraska
288 N.W. 2d 51 (1980)

FACTS   Nash sued the city of North Platte to recover the value of a motorcycle stolen from the city pound. The motorcycle had been seized by the police and was being held by them until they investigated if it had been stolen. The trial court had determined that the city was a gratuitous bailee and required to exercise only slight care in carrying out its duty.

ISSUE   Was the court correct in determining that because this was a gratuitous bailment the defendant had fulfilled its duty by exercising slight care in safeguarding plaintiff's motorcycle?

DECISION   The court held that the determination that the city was a gratuitous bailee required to exercise only slight care was in error. The court stated as follows:

> While the city was not an insurer, it was required to exercise a degree of care which was commensurate with its duty under the circumstances in view of the nature of the property seized.
>
> The evidence shows that the motorcycle was unique in that the plaintiff had spent more than $200 on plating and painting the motor and frame of the motorcycle. The city had stored the motorcycle within a fenced area which had a gate secured by a chain and padlock. The motorcycle itself was not chained or otherwise secured and could be seen by anyone looking into the pound area. The motorcycle was not only attractive to thieves but was relatively portable and could be easily removed from the pound once entry had been gained into the fenced area.
>
> Under the circumstances in this case, we believe the evidence shows as a matter of law that the city failed to exercise the degree of care required by the statute and the city is liable to the plaintiff for failing to "safely keep" the motorcycle which its officers had seized.

BAILOR'S RESPONSIBILITY FOR DEFECTIVE GOODS

In bailments for the sole benefit of the bailee (gratuitous bailments), courts traditionally have required only that the bailor warn the bailee of known dangers exposing the borrower to an unreasonable risk of harm. In a mutual benefit bailment or a bailment for the sole benefit of the bailor, the bailor's responsibility for defective goods is much greater.

Most courts in the United States apply a negligence standard. Thus the bailor is responsible for damages caused by its careless conduct. For example, if the bailment involves a leased item, the injured party (lessee) may recover by showing that the lessor knew of the defect that caused the damage or that the lessor failed to make a proper inspection that would have disclosed the flaw.

Some states recognize an implied warranty of fitness or suitability if the bailee relies upon the bailor's skill and the bailor knows the use for which the property is required. In these states, the bailor's exposure to liability is potentially greater than in states that apply only a negligence standard, because the bailor is responsible in some instances even if not careless — for example, if the bailor makes a reasonable inspection but does not discover a defect that renders the item unfit for the bailee's use. In that the implied warranty of suitability of purpose in a bailment is similar to the Uniform Commercial Code warranty of fitness for a particular purpose, most states allow the bailor to disclaim this warranty in the same manner as a seller.

In *Bona* v. *Graefe,* the case that follows, the court wrestles with the problem of applying new theories of liability in the sale of goods to cases that involve not a sale but a lease. The Maryland court probably reflects the majority opinion in the United States, which imposes a negligence — not a strict liability or implied warranty — standard (see Chapter 19), but many courts would take a different view from Maryland's on the implied warranty of fitness argument.

Bona v. Graefe

Court of Appeals of Maryland
285 A. 2d 607 (1972)

Bona sustained serious injuries when thrown from a runaway golf cart owned by Royce (defendant). Royce had leased the cart to Graefe (defendant), manager of the golf course. Bona was injured when the brakes failed on the cart. Bona sued for breach of warranty and strict liability. **FACTS**

Are breach of warranty and strict liability applicable to bailments or leases? **ISSUE**

No. The court held that breach of warranty and strict liability actions were not applicable to bailments or leases. Both the UCC, which provides for implied warranties, and the Restatement (Torts 2d Sec. 402A), which enunciates strict liability, apply only to one who sells a product. Extension of these principles to bailment agreements should be done by the legislature and not by the courts. **DECISION**

To prevail over a bailor, a bailee must use a negligence action and prove that the bailor failed to use reasonable care in maintaining or inspecting the product.

BAILEE'S RESPONSIBILITY
FOR CARE AND USE

Although the bailee has the bailor's property, the bailee does not guarantee the safety of the property against loss or injury. Almost all courts have stated that a bailee is not an insurer. But a bailee is responsible for any loss caused by its negligence. Traditionally the courts have measured the degree of care that must be exercised by the type of bailment.

In a mutual benefit bailment, the general rule requires the bailee to take ordinary and reasonable care of the subject of the bailment. Liability occurs if the bailee does not exercise the same degree of care that an ordinarily prudent person would use in caring for his or her own property.

Some jurisdictions allow the bailee to escape or limit its liability by agreement with the bailor. But in many states, an agreement of this nature is against public policy and not enforceable. These kinds of agreements are especially apt to be unenforceable if the bargaining power of the bailee is substantially greater than that of the bailor. Because it is possible for the bailee to limit its liability by agreement, the bailor, too, can increase the bailee's responsibility by contract. A common example would be a requirement that the bailee insure the property for the bailor's benefit.

Negligence or the absence of due care is also the standard in a bailment for the sole benefit of the bailor or one that solely benefits the bailee. In each case, however, the degree of care that the bailee must exercise to escape liability differs. In a situation in which only the bailor benefits, the bailee need exercise only slight diligence. Thus the bailee is liable only if its neglect of duty amounts to willfulness and shows a reckless disregard for the rights of others. Conversely, if the bailment is for the sole benefit of the bailee, slight negligence is enough to establish the bailee's responsibility for injury or loss. Courts feel that it is reasonable to expect that a person who borrows another's property will take extraordinary care to protect it. This degree of care has been defined as that which the prudent person would exercise in his or her own affairs of great importance.

Although classification of bailments based upon benefit traditionally has aided courts in determining liability, the current trend is to consider the type of bailment as only one factor in measuring whether conduct is reasonable under the circumstances. Whether a bailee has exercised the proper degree of care is determined by this and factors such as the type of property, the reason for the bailment, custom of the trade, and earlier dealings between the parties.

BAILEE'S USE OF PROPERTY

A bailee who treats the property in a way not authorized by the agreement becomes absolutely liable for any loss or damage. This responsibility exists in spite of the bailee's exercise of due care or of a result that actually benefits the bailor. A bailee who uses the property in an unauthorized manner, stores it someplace other than that agreed upon, or fails to return it according to the contract is liable to the bailor even though injury or loss is caused by an accident or act of God.

In many transactions, the bailee's authority to deal with the property is not expressed clearly by the parties. In these cases, the court must consider a number of factors to determine the bailee's liability. These include:

1. the purpose of the transaction

2. the type of property

3. the relationship between the parties

4. the custom of the business.

In some cases, a bailee who acquires property for repairs cannot allocate this responsibility to another. In others, by considering factors such as the above, a bailee may do so.

SPECIAL SITUATIONS

In many areas of the economy, the law of bailment is based on statute. These statutes evolved as a result of the complexity of modern commercial transactions. Businesses in which legislation has been significant in determining the rights and duties of the parties to a bailment are hotels and motels, common carriers, and warehouses.

Hotels and Motels

The common law regarded hotels and innkeepers as insurers of a guest's person and property. The innkeeper was absolutely liable for the full value of a patron's property unless the innkeeper could establish that any loss was caused by the guest's negligence, by an act of war, or by an act of God. Because travel was dangerous, this extensive liability encouraged hotelkeepers to provide a safe resting place for the guest and security for the guest's possessions. Now that travel conditions have improved, the traditional innkeeper's liability has been modified extensively by statute.

Every state in the United States has enacted some type of legislation that modifies the hotel's responsibility to guests for loss or damage to property. Almost universally these statutes favor the hotel industry. In addition, hotels may limit their liability by their own rules and by contractual disclaimer. But this limitation must not eliminate the hotel's common law duties.

Statutes that limit a hotel's liability require it to provide a safe in which guests can store valuables such as jewelry, money, and documents. The hotel also must furnish adequate notice of the safe's availability. A hotel that does not strictly follow the statutory requirements is not entitled to the benefit of the limitation of liability. If a guest does not use the safe, the hotel has no liability. But even if the guest does leave property in the hotel's safe, the statute allows the hotel to limit liability.

Many items of importance to hotel guests cannot conveniently be protected by a safe. Clothing and personal effects such as watches are examples. At common law, the innkeeper's liability for items of this nature was as absolute as it was for jewelry and other property. Today hotels are liable for loss or damage to clothing only if the loss is the result of the negligence or fraud of the hotel's employees. In the following case, the court is required to interpret the New York statute that modifies the defendant's common law liability.

--- Zaldin v. Concord Hotel ---

Court of Appeals of New York
397 N.E. 2d 370 (1979)

FACTS   The Modells (plaintiffs) were guests at the Concord Hotel. They attended the hotel's nightclub performance, which ended sometime after midnight. The Modells then attempted to store two valuable diamond rings in the safe deposit vault that the hotel provided for its guests. A hotel desk clerk informed them that the vault closed at 11:00 P.M. and could not be opened until morning. During the night, the jewelry was stolen from the Modells' room. When the hotel refused to compensate the Modells for the stolen jewelry, they brought suit against it on a theory of absolute liability.

The hotel's defense was based on a New York statute that provided that a hotel would not be liable for loss of items such as jewelry whenever it provided a vault for safekeeping and posted conspicuous notice of the vault's availability. Both the trial court and an intermediate appellate court determined that the statute protected the hotel. As a result plaintiffs appealed.

ISSUE   Does a statute that limits a hotel's liability "whenever" a safe is provided protect the hotel during the hours when the safe is closed?

DECISION   The court of appeals reversed the lower courts and ruled for the Modells. The court stated that the legislative formula is uncomplicated. It says straightforwardly that whenever a safe is provided, the liability limitations shall be applicable. Conversely, when an innkeeper chooses not to provide a safe for the use of its guests, the innkeeper may not claim statutory protection.

Common Carriers

A firm that offers transportation for pay to the public generally is called a *common carrier*. The services that the common carrier offers may involve the transportation of people, personal property, or both. A common carrier must provide service to all who apply, unless it has a valid reason for refusing to do so. But a common carrier may specialize in a type of service. If it holds itself out as transporting particular kinds of property, it does not have to transport other kinds that are offered to it. Similarly, a common carrier of passengers does not have to transport them to any destinations that they select. Its responsibility is to transport them only to destinations that it usually serves. Although the type of service offered is the determining criterion, in most cases railroads, steamship lines, bus lines, taxicab companies, and truckers are common carriers. Natural gas pipelines are also common carriers.

Carriers are extensively regulated by local, state, and federal governments. Traditionally regulations covered how the carrier performed its obligations as well as the price that the customer paid. The Interstate Commerce Commission (ICC) is the federal agency primarily responsible for regulation of common carriers engaged in interstate commerce.

Transportation of Goods   A common carrier must transport without discrimination all goods that are offered to it as long as the goods are of the type that the carrier ordinarily accepts. For example, a trucking company that ordinarily transports hogs and cattle is not obligated to transport other types of merchandise. The carrier is entitled to compensation for its services and may adopt reasonable rules and regulations dealing with the time, place, and manner of carrying out its tasks.

Common carriers have extensive liability for loss or damage to the goods they transport. This liability generally exceeds that of bailees. Although a carrier is not an absolute insurer for safe delivery of goods, the carrier is liable for loss or damage unless the damage is caused by an act of God, an act of war, an act of the shipper, a public authority, or the nature of the goods. In the case that follows, the common carrier's liability is discussed.

Missouri Pacific Railroad Company v. Elmore and Stahl

United States Supreme Court
377 U.S. 134 (1964)

Elmore and Stahl shipped a carload of melons from Rio Grande City to Chicago via the Missouri Pacific Railroad Company. The melons were in good condition when turned over to the carrier, but they arrived in Chicago damaged. The jury found that the railroad had performed all required transportation service without negligence. But the jury for some unknown reason refused to find that the damage was due solely to the "inherent vice" of the melons. As a result, the court awarded damages to the shipper. The railroad appealed. **FACTS**

Is a common carrier that has exercised reasonable care liable for spoilage if it fails to prove that the cause of spoilage was the natural tendency of the goods to deteriorate? **ISSUE**

The United States Supreme Court held the carrier liable. The Court affirmed the judgment of the trial court, holding as follows: **DECISION**

> The parties agree that the liability of a carrier for damage to an interstate shipment is a matter of federal law controlled by federal statutes and decisions. The Carmack Amendment of 1906, of the Interstate Commerce Act, makes carriers liable "for the full actual loss, damage, or injury . . . caused by" them to property they transport. . . . The statute codified the common law rule that a carrier, though not an absolute insurer, is liable for damage to goods transported by it unless it can show that the damage was caused by "a. the act of God; b. the public enemy; c. the act of the shipper himself; d. public authority; or e. the inherent vice or nature of the goods."

Warehouses

The storage of goods is important to businesses as well as to private individuals. Because of the importance of warehousing, all states have statutes that define the

Warehousing
the business of
storing goods for
hire

rights and duties of the parties in warehousing transactions. One of the most significant of these statutes is Article 7 of the UCC. The UCC defines **warehousing** as the business of storing goods for hire. Many federal statutes also deal with warehouses. Probably the most significant of these is the United States Warehouse Act. It is primarily concerned with storage of agricultural products.

Like a common carrier, a warehouse may be public or private. A public warehouse holds itself out as willing to serve the general public. A private warehouse may limit its clients to one or a few firms. Although the regulatory power of government is more extensive for the public warehouse, the following discussion applies to both public and private warehouses.

Liability of Warehouses   A warehouse is liable to the owner of stored goods for loss or damage only if it fails to exercise reasonable care. Also, the warehouse may limit its liability by including a provision in the storage agreement setting a maximum amount that the owner of the goods may recover. But to do this the warehouse must provide the owner with an opportunity for additional protection at increased rates.

Rights of Warehouses   A warehouse has a lien for reasonable charges against goods stored. These charges include costs such as storage, transportation, and insurance as well as expenses necessary to preserve the goods. The warehouse may enforce the lien by selling the goods in a commercially reasonable manner.

A warehouse does not have to store goods indefinitely, and most warehousing agreements provide a specific period of storage. If the goods are not removed as specified, a warehouse may notify the owner to pay and to move the goods within no less than 30 days. If the owner fails to comply, the warehouse may sell the goods to collect its charges.

SUMMARY

Bailment is a legal relationship in which almost everyone is involved from time to time. A bailment exists if four elements are present: (1) the subject matter must be personal property; (2) the bailee must have possession of the property; (3) the parties either expressly or implicitly must have agreed to the bailee's possession; (4) the bailee must be obligated to return the property or account for it when the purpose of the bailment is accomplished.

Traditionally courts have classified bailments to answer legal questions about the rights and responsibilities of bailor and bailee. The most significant of these classifications for the business manager is the mutual benefit bailment. The other classifications are the bailment for the sole benefit of the bailee and the bailment for the sole benefit of the bailor.

A bailor has legal liability for supplying the bailee with a defective item. If the bailment is for the sole benefit of the bailor or for the benefit of both parties (mutual benefit), the bailor is liable if loss or injury is the result of its careless conduct. If the bailment is for the sole benefit of the bailee, the bailor's only responsibility is to warn the bailee of known dangers.

Although a bailee has the bailor's property, the bailee does not guarantee its safety. A bailee is liable if loss or damage is caused by its negligence. For a mutual benefit bailment, ordinary care is required. If the bailment is one in which only the bailor benefits, the bailee is liable only if its actions show reckless disregard for the bailor's property. Conversely, the bailee must exercise extra care if the bailment is solely for its benefit. In any event, the bailee is absolutely liable if it uses the property in a manner not authorized by the agreement.

REVIEW PROBLEMS

1. Contrast the bailee's liability for loss or injury to bailed property in bailments for the sole benefit of the bailee and sole benefit of the bailor.

2. Briefly explain the difference between a bailment and a conditional sale.

3. Describe the bailor's liability for defective goods in a mutual benefit bailment.

4. Define a common carrier, and briefly indicate the carrier's liability for goods in transit.

5. Amerson wanted to borrow an electric drill from Howell. Howell was aware that the drill had previously shocked three people, none of whom was injured. This information was conveyed to Amerson. In addition, before giving the drill to Amerson, Howell changed the plug and tested the drill, receiving no shock. When Amerson used the drill, he suffered a fatal shock. May Amerson's estate recover from Howell? Discuss.

6. California Artists is a publisher and distributor of Christmas greeting cards. Its policy is to destroy cards that are not sold after two seasons. For a number of years, it delivered boxed cards to Salvage, Inc., a private concern that conducted a dump and salvage operation.
   Material delivered to Salvage was treated in two ways. If a person specified that the material was to be covered with dirt, Salvage would immediately cover it and certify that this had been done. Other material was dumped but subject to salvage. The material not salvaged was covered later. The fee for this was much less than the fee for immediate covering.
   In January 1955, California Artists sent 877,000 cards packaged in cartons to the dump. Its employee was ordered, "Take the cards to the dump and dispose of them." The employee did not indicate that California Artists wanted the cartons covered immediately. The cartons were marked "California Artists."
   Salvage, Inc., sold some of the cartons to McFadden, who planned to sell them. When California Artists learned of this, they brought suit to recover the cards, arguing that Salvage had no right to sell them because it was a bailee for destruction. What might McFadden argue to counter the California Artists' position? Who would win?

7. Dundas owned four horses that were stabled temporarily in an old barn at the fairgrounds. Usually the horses were stabled in a newer barn, but they had been moved with Dundas's knowledge for a short time because of a county fair. The old barn had no telephone, automatic sprinkler system, or smoke or heat detec-

tor. A dry-chemical fire extinguisher was placed at each end of the barn. Owners with horses in the barn were responsible for care and feeding of the horses and for cleaning the stalls. The barn was open for horse owners and the public each day. Owners could remove horses at any time the barn was open and substitute others at their discretion.

A fire occurred in the barn because a 13-year-old boy, whose parents had horses stabled there, was setting off caps and a burning cap set fire to bedding in one of the stalls. Although the boy tried to put out the fire, he was unable to do so. By the time he reached a telephone and fire-fighters arrived, none of the horses could be saved. Dundas sued the county. What is the basis of her action? What defense would the county have? Who would win? Support your answer.

8. Colner had an appointment with Dr. Heller, his dentist. Colner left his coat in the waiting room and went into the office for treatment. No one was in the waiting room when he left it. The office was on the 27th floor of a large commercial building which had excellent security and few thefts. While Colner was being treated, his coat was stolen. Colner sued on grounds that the dentist was a bailee. Was he correct? Support your answer.

9. Lane lent his truck to Tussig, who needed it to deliver some cattle. After the cattle had been delivered, Lane took the truck to a carwash to be cleaned. While Lane was waiting in line for the carwash, a car backed into the truck, causing extensive damage. The driver sped away before Tussig could get his license number. Lane sued Tussig for the damages. Is Tussig held responsible? Support your answer.

10. Singer, a furrier, entered into an agreement to restyle an expensive fur coat for Farmer. The restyling was to follow a pattern selected by Farmer. Singer made several modifications in the design which improved the cut of the coat. But Farmer did not like what Singer had done and refused to accept the coat. Singer sued for the cost of labor and repairs. Farmer counterclaimed for the value of the coat. Who wins? Support your answer.

11. Clancy was a registered guest at the Plaza Hotel. She was the owner of a very expensive fur coat, which she left in her room. The coat was stolen by a thief who was caught after being chased from the hotel. During the chase, the thief dropped the coat in the street, and it was destroyed by automobile traffic. Clancy sued the hotel. Is she successful? Discuss.

12. Ace Trucking Company entered into contracts with three major apple growers in Ohio to transport their produce to Detroit and Chicago. One load of apples being driven to Detroit was damaged. The owner sued Ace, arguing that it was responsible as a common carrier. Was this argument correct? Explain.

13. Bell sold his automobile to Kato. Kato agreed to pay the purchase price over ten months. Title was to revert to Bell if the purchase price was not paid. A legal dispute arose because of damage to the automobile caused by vandals and Kato argued that the transaction was a bailment. Is Kato correct?

CHAPTER 37

Interests in Real Property

CHAPTER OBJECTIVES

SCOPE OF REAL PROPERTY

Fee Simple Estates / Fee Simple Defeasible / Life Estates / Legal Life Estates

LEASEHOLD ESTATES

The Lease as a Contract / Classification by Duration of Term / Classification by Method of Determining Rent / Rights and Duties of the Parties / Termination of Lease

NONPOSSESSORY INTERESTS IN REAL PROPERTY

Easements / Creation of Easements / Profit à Prendre and License / Liens

CO OWNERSHIP

Joint Tenancy / Tenancy in Common / Tenancy by the Entirety / Tenancy in Partnership / Community Property / Condominiums and Cooperatives / Real Estate Investment Trusts

LAND AND THE LAW

SUMMARY

REVIEW PROBLEMS

CHAPTER OBJECTIVES

After reading this chapter, you should be able to:

1. Define estate, fee simple estate, term tenancy, periodic tenancy, easement, co-ownership, lien, community property.

2. Compare fee simple estate, fee simple defeasible, and life estate.

3. Define common law dower and curtesy, and indicate the current legal status of each.

4. Explain the fundamental nature of the lease.

5. Classify leases by duration of term and by method of determining rent.

6. Outline the rights and duties of the parties to a lease in situations not covered by the lease agreements.

7. Compare and contrast easement appurtenant and easement in gross, easement and profit, profit and license.

8. Explain how the common forms of co-ownership differ.

Real property law deals with ownership of land and those things that are permanently attached to it. Because land is an unusual commodity and for centuries has been of great economic importance in the Western world, the legal relationships involving real property are extensive and complicated. This chapter discusses some of them.

SCOPE OF REAL PROPERTY

As traditionally defined by courts and commentators, land ownership encompasses the surface of the earth, everything above that surface, and everything below. The space over which the surface owner has dominion is compared to an inverted pyramid extending upward indefinitely into space and downward to the center of the earth. As air travel became an important means of transportation, the traditional rule gradually has been modified. Today the general rule is that the surface owner's air rights are limited to the space that can be reasonably used and enjoyed.

In cities, landowners, while retaining ownership of the surface, sell the air space above it for the construction of commercial buildings. Ownership of high-rise condominiums is based on divided ownership of air space. In mining regions, the right to extract natural resources is frequently separated from ownership of the surface and leased or sold. In the arid areas of the West, water rights are very often separated from surface ownership of land.

Interests in land may be divided in many different ways. One way, as the previous paragraph indicates, is to divide use and enjoyment of the land itself horizontally in relation to space. Another way is to separate the land from possible rights in it and allow numerous interests to exist simultaneously. This is the basis of the doctrine of estates. This doctrine was important in the historic development of English and American land law and continues to influence real property law today.

The word *estate* as used in real property law indicates the nature, quantity, and quality of an ownership interest. In that an estate refers to an ownership interest, it is or must have the potential for becoming possessory. The extent of an estate is determined by the duration of the interest and the time when the right to possess and enjoy the land begins.

For example, a wife might provide by will that her real property go to her husband for the duration of his life and then to her daughter. Upon the wife's death, both husband and daughter would have existing estates. The husband's estate would be measured by the duration of his life. The daughter's estate could last forever, but it does not begin until her father dies.

Fee Simple Estates

A **fee simple** estate, also called a *fee simple absolute* or simply a *fee,* is the most extensive interest that a person can have in land. This is the type of estate held by most owners of real property. The estate lasts potentially endlessly. It may be transferred to others during the lifetime of the owner. Upon the owner's death, his or her interest does not end but passes by will or the laws of **intestate succession,** if the owner dies without leaving a will. A fee simple is the type of estate held by the wife in the previous example. The only restrictions upon this estate are those imposed by government. If a question exists about the type of estate that is transferred, the courts presume that a fee simple is intended.

Fee simple the most extensive estate that an owner can have in real property

Intestate succession distribution of the assets of a person who dies without a will

Fee Simple Defeasible

A defeasible fee is less extensive than a fee simple, because the **defeasible fee** terminates if certain events occur. But until these events occur, the owner of a defeasible fee possesses the same interests as those of the owner of a fee simple. For example, a defeasible fee might be used if a person wished to give land to a city for recreational purposes. The grantor might execute a deed with the following language: "to the City of Columbus, Georgia, and its successors and assigns so long as the property is used for recreational purposes." If the land is not used for the stated purpose, the city's interest automatically ends and reverts to the grantor or the grantor's heirs. Not all defeasible fees end automatically. Some require the grantor or the grantor's successors to take steps to terminate them. Although the defeasible fee is not used extensively today, it has played a significant role historically in property law.

Defeasible fee an estate that ends when a specified event occurs

Life Estates

    A **life estate** is one whose length is measured by the life of a person, typically the owner but possibly some other person. This latter type of estate is called an **estate *pur autre vie***. Life estates may be created by deed, will, statute, and case law. A life estate may be sold or mortgaged, but the acquiring party's interest ends by the life tenant's death. The following case illustrates the type of legal problem that sometimes arises when a life estate is created.

Sauls v. Crosby

District Court of Appeals of Florida
258 So. 2d 326 (1972)

FACTS   Sauls sold land to Crosby, reserving for herself a life estate. She attempted to cut and sell timber from the property, and Crosby brought an action to prevent her from doing this unless the proceeds were held in trust for him. The trial court agreed that Sauls did not have the right to sell the timber because she was a life tenant.

ISSUE   Does a life tenant have a right to cut and sell timber?

DECISION   No. A life tenant does not have the right to sell timber from the estate. American courts recognize that an ordinary life tenant may cut timber and not be liable for waste if the timber is used for fuel, repairing fences and buildings on the property, for fitting the land for cultivation, or for use as pasture if the inheritance is not damaged.
    The court held that an ordinary life tenant is entitled to the use and enjoyment of the estate during its existence but must not permanently diminish or change the value of the future estate.
    An instrument creating a life tenancy may absolve the tenant of responsibility for waste by stating that the life tenant has the power to consume. Thus there is a sharp distinction between the rights of an ordinary life tenant and those of a life tenant with the power to consume.

Legal Life Estates

    Despite their many possible legal problems, life estates have been used to provide financial security for one spouse upon the death of another. At common law, **dower** and **curtesy** were estates that widows and widowers enjoyed in their spouse's real property by virtue of the marriage.

Dower   At common law, upon the death of her husband, a wife acquired a one

FIGURE 37-1   Relationship among Estates

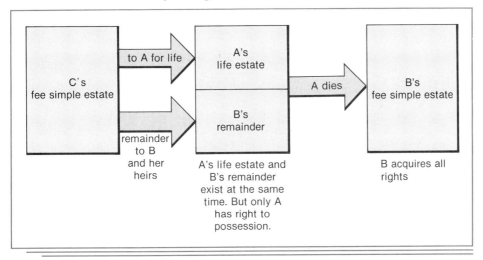

third life interest in lands that he had owned during marriage. Although most states have abolished dower, it continues in a few. In several of these states, dower has been expanded to include the husband, and in others the one third share has been increased to one half. Where dower has been abolished, if the surviving spouse is not provided for by will, state statutes generally allow that person to choose a share in both the real and personal property of the deceased.

Curtesy   At common law, a surviving husband acquired a life interest in all his wife's real property if a child had been born of the marriage. Curtesy has been abolished in most states, but a few still allow the surviving husband a life interest in his deceased wife's realty.

Curtesy an interest acquired by a husband in his wife's real property if a child is born of the marriage

LEASEHOLD ESTATES

Leasehold estates are among the most significant interests that exist today in real property. In business, the lease provides a method for obtaining land with far less capital than fee simple ownership requires. In housing, the lease entails lower immediate costs than fee simple ownership and allows the holder both mobility and freedom to try different life styles.

A leasehold interest is created when the owner of real property, usually referred to as the *landlord* or **lessor,** conveys possession and control of the property to another, called the *tenant* or **lessee,** in exchange for a payment called *rent.* The right of possession granted by the owner is temporary. When the lease ends, possession and control return to the owner.

Lessor the person who rents real property to another

Lessee the tenant

The Lease as a Contract

Conveyance the transfer of an interest in real property

Both real property and contract law apply to leases. Generally at common law, courts applied real property principles to the lease, treating it as a **conveyance** or transfer of land ownership. This was significant to the relationship between the parties for, as long as the tenant was in possession of the land, he or she was required to pay the rent. This rule applied even if the lessor broke promises in the lease or failed to maintain the premises.

In an urban environment, the building or unit of the building rented is more important to the lessee than the land on which the building rests. Thus during this century the trend has been for courts and legislatures to emphasize the contractual aspect of the lease to provide increased protection, especially for residential tenants. The following case illustrates this trend.

Javins v. First National Realty Corporation

U.S. Court of Appeals, D.C. Circuit
428 F. 2d. 1071 (1970)

FACTS   First National Realty Corporation sued Javins and others to recover possession of rented apartments. Each of the defendants had defaulted in payment of rent due. The defendants admitted they had not paid the rent but defended on grounds that approximately 1,500 violations of the District of Columbia housing regulations affected their apartments either directly or indirectly.

ISSUE   Is a landlord required to keep the premises in habitable condition?

DECISION   Yes. Traditional landlord–tenant law, derived from feudal property law, assumed that a lease conveyed to the tenant is an interest in land. This may have been reasonable in a rural, agrarian society, but in the case of the modern apartment dweller, the value of the lease is that it provides a place to live. When American city dwellers, both rich and poor, seek "shelter" today, they seek a well known package of goods and services — a package which includes not merely walls and ceilings, but also adequate heat, light and ventilation, serviceable plumbing facilities, secure windows and doors, proper sanitation, and proper maintenance.

Since a lease contract specifies a particular period of time during which the tenant has a right to use his apartment for shelter, he may legitimately expect that the apartment will be fit for habitation for the time period for which it is rented. Thus we are led by our inspection of the relevant legal principles and precedents to the conclusion that the old common law rule imposing an obligation upon the lessee to repair during the lease term was really never intended to apply to residential urban leaseholds. Contract principles established in other areas of the law provide a more rational framework for the apportionment of landlord–tenant responsibilities; they strongly suggest that a warranty of habitability be implied in all contracts for urban dwellings. A warranty of this nature requires the landlord to make repairs keeping the property in habitable condition.

FIGURE 37-2 Apartment Lease

THIS LEASE Made this _____ day of _____, 19_____, by and between

_____, party of the first part,

hereinafter called lessor, and _____,
party of the second part, hereinafter called lessee.

WITNESSETH: That said lessor hereby leases in its present condition to said lessee the following portion of the

building No. _____ Street, in _____, State of _____,

Apartment _____ on the _____ floor _____ side, _____

for a term of _____, beginning _____

and ending _____, and the said lessee agrees to pay for the use and rent thereof a total

of _____ ($ _____) DOLLARS,

payable at the rate of _____ ($ _____)dollars per month,

for the whole time and to pay the same on the _____ day of each month, in advance, at the office of

The lessee covenants and agrees with the lessor as follows:

1. To take good care of the premises and keep them in good repair, free from filth, danger of fire or any nuisance, and return the same, at the termination of the lease, in as good condition as received by him, usual wear and use, destruction by fire not caused by the negligence of the lessee, and providential destruction excepted.

2. To not sublet or allow any other tenant to come in with or under him or assign this lease or any part thereof by his act, process or operation of law, or in any other manner whatsoever without the written consent of the lessor indorsed on this lease.

3. To make no alteration in the premises without the consent of the lessor in writing, except ordinary repairs as aforesaid; permit the lessor or agent to enter at all reasonable times to view the premises and make such repairs and alterations as said lessor may deem necessary or proper, and within one month before the termination of this lease display a rent sign on said premises and show same to prospective tenants; to not use the premises or permit the use thereof in such manner as to make void or increase the rate of insurance thereon; and to comply with all city ordinances and the laws of this State and save harmless the lessor for or on account of all charges or damages for non-observance thereof.

4. To use the premises only as a private residence, and not display signs or advertisements on the premises, or place or keep anything on the outer window sills, or permit parrots, dogs, cats or other animals therein, keep the entrances and halls free from obstructions and not allow children to play therein or do or permit to be done any other thing that will annoy, embarrass, inconvenience or damage the lessor or other tenants in said building.

It is further agreed by and between the lessor and lessee:

5. The lessor agrees to furnish hot and cold water and heat in season during the term of this lease, unless prevented by circumstances beyond his control. The lessor shall not be held for damages in case of failure to furnish hot and cold water and heat during any portion of the time if beyond his control.

6. If the premises shall be destroyed or so damaged as to become untenantable by fire or other unavoidable casualty, either party may terminate this lease at once by giving written notice of the intention so to do within five (5) days after such casualty.

7. The lessor or his agent shall not be liable for any damages to the lessee, his servants or guests or his or their property occasioned by failure to repair, or from bursting or leaking of the water, gas or plumbing pipes or fixtures in the building, or for damage occasioned by water, snow or ice on the roof or walks, or for damage arising from acts or neglect of the janitor, co-tenants or of the owners or occupants of adjacent property.

8. At the expiration of the term hereby created, or if default be made in the payment of rent after the same is due, or upon the breach of any of the covenants and agreements herein contained, the lessor or his agent shall have the right to enter and take possession of the leased premises, and the lessee agrees to deliver same without process of law, and this lease, at the option of the lessor, shall terminate, but for this cause the obligation of the lessee to pay shall not cease and the lessee shall be liable for any loss or damage to the lessor for his failure to comply with the terms hereof.

9. The covenants herein contained shall run with the premises hereby let and bind the heirs, executors, administrators, assigns and successors of the lessor and lessee respectively and consent of lessor to assignment, and acceptance of rent from assignee of the lessee shall not release the lessee from his obligations to pay rent and comply with the other conditions of this lease.

10. The rules and regulations printed on the back of this lease are made a part of the same as though contained in the body thereof.

_____

_____

_____

_____

IN WITNESS WHEREOF, The parties have hereunto set their hands the day and year above written to duplicate copies.

_____

_____

Classification by Duration of Term

Leased estates are classified in several ways. A traditional classification is by the length of the lease. Major legal differences exist between leases for fixed terms and indefinite terms. A second method of classifying leases is by how the rent is determined. Commercial or income-producing leases are differentiated from residential leases.

Term tenancy a lease that lasts for a fixed period of time

Term Tenancy   A **term tenancy,** sometimes called an *estate for years,* exists for a fixed period. The agreement creating the term establishes particular beginning and ending dates. A lease written to begin on February 1, 1984, and to end on January 31, 1988, is a term tenancy. The term may be as short as a week or a month, but most term tenancies are for a year or more. A few leases have been written with terms of 999 years.

A term tenancy ends automatically at the time designated in the agreement. The owner is not required to notify the tenant of the termination of the lease. Generally in the United States a term tenancy for more than a year must be in writing to be enforceable.

Periodic tenancy a lease that continues for successive periods until terminated by proper notice

Holdover tenancy a tenancy that may be created when a tenant continues to occupy the premises after expiration of the lease

Periodic Tenancy   A **periodic tenancy,** also referred to as a *tenancy from month to month* or *year to year,* is a rental agreement that continues for successive periods until terminated by proper notice from either party.

A periodic tenancy is created in several ways. If a tenant is in possession under a term tenancy unenforceable because it is not in writing, courts generally hold that a periodic tenancy exists. More commonly, the periodic tenancy is created by an express agreement of the parties. Periodic tenancies are also created when a tenant holds over after a term tenancy. The **holdover tenancy** is discussed later in the chapter. The major factor distinguishing the periodic tenancy from the term tenancy is that the periodic tenancy continues until one of the parties gives proper notice that it has ended.

The rules about the time for proper notice varies from state to state. At common law, the general rule was to measure notice by the period of the tenancy. A week to week tenancy required a week's notice; a month to month tenancy required a month's notice. But proper notice for a year to year tenancy was six months. In the United States today, over a quarter of the states have adopted the Uniform Residential Landlord and Tenant Act. This act requires a written notice of ten days for a week to week tenancy and 60 days for a month to month tenancy. Year to year tenancies are not mentioned in the act because they are used almost exclusively for renting agricultural lands.

Tenancy at will an interest in real property that ends at the will of the owner or occupant

Tenancy at Will   A **tenancy at will** is created when the owner of property gives someone permission to occupy it for an unspecified period of time. This type of tenancy may be created by express agreement or by implication. The key factors are that the tenant is lawfully in possession of the property but that the duration of possession is uncertain. For example, a landlord allows a tenant to remain in possession of space in a building scheduled to be torn down until demolition starts.

A tenancy at will ends by any action of either party indicating that he or she no longer wishes to continue it. Many states have passed laws requiring the person wishing to terminate the tenancy to give proper notification to the other. Generally the time required for notification is 30 days. The death of either party or the sale or lease of the property also terminates a tenancy at will.

Tenancy at Sufferance   A **tenancy at sufferance** exists when someone who was a lawful occupant unlawfully occupies another's property. The landlord owes this tenant no duties other than not to injure him or her wantonly or willfully. A tenancy at sufferance may be created if a person who has sold property remains in possession after the time he or she agreed to vacate. The most common example of the tenancy at sufferance is when a person holds over after the expiration of his or her term. This person becomes a holdover tenant if the landlord elects to treat him as such; however, until this decision is made and acted upon, the tenancy is at sufferance.

Tenancy at sufferance a tenancy that exists when a person wrongfully holds over after the expiration of a lease

Holding Over   When a term tenant remains on the premises at the expiration of the term without the owner's consent, the owner has the option of either evicting the tenant or treating the tenant as a holdover. If the owner decides to treat the tenant as a holdover, in most states a periodic tenancy is created. If the original tenancy was for a year or more, almost all states treat the new term as a periodic tenancy for a year. If the original term was for less than a year, the term of holdover tenancy is for a similar period. For example, a month-to-month tenancy is created if the original term tenancy was for a month. An interesting legal problem arises when a tenant holds over after being notified of a rent increase. Most states hold the tenant responsible for the increased rent.

Classification by Method of Determining Rent

A wide range of methods exists for determining the amount of the rent the tenant must pay. In residential leases the rent is usually a fixed amount, but in commercial leases different arrangements often are used to establish the tenant's obligation. These arrangements are primarily the result of the lessor's desire to shift as many economic risks as possible to the tenant. A lessor leasing property for a long term naturally wishes to limit the effect of inflation on rental income. If the rent is a fixed amount and property expenses increase, the owner's income from the property is drastically reduced. Rental payments can be negotiated that protect the owner from this possibility. In other situations, an owner might wish to share in the increased productive use of a parcel of real estate without assuming the risk of investing in a building or a business to use the property. Like protection against inflation, this objective can be met through various types of rental payments. A few of the more common methods for determining rent in commercial leases to accomplish these objectives are the percentage lease, the net lease, and the revaluation or appraisal lease. Many variations and combinations of these basic patterns have been used.

Percentage lease a lease in which the rent is determined by a percentage of sales or profits

Percentage Leases   A **percentage lease** provides the lessor with a rent determined by a fixed percentage of the gross sales or net profits from a business operated on the leased premises. Some percentage leases are written with a fixed minimum rent. Percentage leases protect the lessor against inflation and also provide him or her with a share in the productive use of the property.

Net lease a lease in which the tenant pays a fixed rent plus taxes, insurance, and maintenance expenses

Net Leases   In a **net lease** the tenant pays a fixed rent and in addition agrees to pay the taxes, insurance, and maintenance expenses. A variation of the net lease is the net-net lease. In the net-net lease the tenant agrees to pay all costs attributed to the property. The net lease protects the lessor against inflation.

Revaluation or Appraisal Leases   Some long-term leases provide for adjustment of rental payments based on periodic revaluation of the property. Several different methods of revaluation are used. Revaluation allows the lessor to share in any increase in the value of the land.

Rights and Duties of the Parties

Most problems that arise in a tenancy can be solved by the parties if they have a well-drafted lease. In the lease, landlord and tenant may allocate rights and duties in any manner that they choose as long as what they do is not illegal or against public policy (see Chapter 10). Sometimes parties who enter into a lease do not anticipate a problem. If a dispute arises that is not settled by the lease, the solution must be found in statutory or case law.

Understanding how the law allocates the rights and duties of the parties when there is no agreement in the lease is complicated by the dual nature of the lease and by developments in landlord–tenant law during the past fifty years. The case of *Javins* v. *First National Realty Corp.*, above, illustrates a trend in American law to provide residential tenants with rights not generally available to commercial tenants. This increased protection for residential tenants is also reflected in the statutory law, because many states have expanded the duties of landlords of residential property.

Duty to Repair and Maintain   The allocation of the duty to repair and maintain the premises illustrates the different treatment states sometimes afford commercial and residential leases. At common law, in the absence of agreement, the landlord had a limited duty to repair and maintain the property. If he or she knew of a defect, it had to be corrected before the lease began. No duty existed to maintain the premises except for the common areas of multiunit buildings. A number of states retain the common law rule for commercial leases, but in most states the rule has been modified for residential property. In these states, if residential property is not maintained in habitable condition, tenants have various remedies against landlords. These remedies include revoking the lease, rent abatement, and rent withholding. In a few states, tenants are permitted to make necessary repairs and deduct the cost from the rent.

Use of the Premises   Because a lease is a conveyance as well as a contract, during the term the lessee has the right to possession and control of the property. With few exceptions, the lessor may not enter the premises unless the parties have agreed to the contrary. Thus at common law the landlord's right of access to inspect, to make alterations or repairs, or to show the premises is limited.

Three principal exceptions exist to the rule limiting the landlord's right of access. First, he or she may enter to collect the rent if the lease fails to state where rent shall be paid. Next the Uniform Residential Landlord and Tenant Act and similar state statutes let the landlord inspect the condition of the property and make necessary repairs in emergencies. Inspection requires notice to the tenant and must be done at reasonable times and intervals. Finally, even when there is no statute, the landlord may have access to prevent material damage or loss to the property resulting from tenant's negligence or misconduct.

The tenant may use the property for any reasonable purpose in view of the surrounding circumstances. But the tenant cannot use the property for an illegal purpose, for a purpose that violates public policy, or in a manner that would result in substantial or permanent damage to the property. Most commercial leases limit the use that the tenant can make of the property.

Transfer of Leased Premises   A tenant transfers his or her interest in a leased property by **assignment of lease** or **sublease.** Because the legal consequences of the two types of transfer differ, the parties should be certain that documents controlling the transfer clearly indicate which type they intend.

A transfer is an assignment if the tenant conveys all of his or her remaining interest. Both the new tenant and the landlord are liable to each other according to the terms of the original lease. The original tenant becomes a guarantor that the provisions of the lease are carried out.

A transfer is a sublease if the tenant transfers less than his or her remaining interest. An example is a tenant with a lease running from January 1 to December 31 renting the premises during June and July. Because this transfer is a sublease, neither subtenant nor landlord can sue the other directly for breach of the original lease. If the landlord breaches a lease provision, the subtenant must seek relief by bringing an action against the original tenant on the sublease. If the rent is not paid, the landlord must look to the original tenant.

Assignment of lease a transfer of all of a tenant's remaining interest in the leased premises

Sublease a transfer of less than a tenant's remaining interest in the leased premises

Termination of Lease

Most leases end at a certain time or by agreement of the parties. Many leases contain provisions providing for their termination under certain conditions. A common example is a provision terminating the lease if the premises are destroyed. When there is no provision of this nature, the tenant remains responsible for the rent.

Another example is a provision terminating the lease if the tenant files for bankruptcy. Without this provision, the trustee of the debtor's estate acquires the lease.

A lease is also terminated by **condemnation,** but the tenant is entitled to compensation for the value of the leased property interest. In some instances, statutes provide for the termination of a lease. Generally death does not terminate the obligations of either party, but a few states allow the estate of a decedent to cancel a lease covering the deceased's residence.

Condemnation
the legal proceeding by which the state acquires private property for a public purpose

NONPOSSESSORY INTERESTS IN REAL PROPERTY

Easements

Easement a right to make limited use of another's land

Easement appurtenant an easement that allows the owner of one parcel of land to make limited use of another parcel

Dominant tenement the parcel of land that benefits from use of another parcel

Servient tenement the parcel of land that is subject to use by another parcel

Run with the land the right to use an easement as acquired by the owner of the dominant tenement

Sometimes people have interests in land that are limited to use and do not extend to possession. One example is an **easement.** An easement establishes the right of a person to make limited use of another's property. A common easement is the right to cross another's land with a road or path. Easements are used extensively in the development of land. They are also essential to the operation of utilities and to the mining and gas extraction industries.

Easement Appurtenant   An **easement appurtenant** involves two parcels of land, usually but not necessarily adjoining. The easement allows the possessor of one parcel to benefit by using the other parcel of land (see Figure 37-3). The parcel that benefits is referred to as the **dominant tenement.** The property that is subject to the easement is known as the **servient tenement.** If an easement is appurtenant, any transfer of the dominant tenement includes the easement. The easement appurtenant is said to **run with the land.** The easement cannot be separated and transferred independently of the dominant tenement. Use by the dominant tenement is limited to the terms of the easement.

Unless the document creating the easement indicates that the easement is exclusive, the owner of the servient estate may also use the land upon which the easement has been dedicated. The servient owner's use must not conflict with the purpose and character of the easement. The cost of maintenance is a problem that sometimes arises when an easement has been created without the parties' agreement on how this burden should be allocated. The following case deals with this problem.

Island Improvement Association of Upper Greenwood Lake v. *Ford*

Superior Court of New Jersey, Appellate Division
383 A. 2d 133 (1978)

FACTS   Ford and others were property owners in a private development. Each had an express easement to use roads in the development. Their deeds did not impose any contractual obligation on them to maintain the roads. Title to the roads was held by the private association, the grantor of the deeds to the individual owners. Ford and several other owners refused to make payments to maintain the roads, and the association sued.

Are owners of an easement required to contribute to its maintenance?   ISSUE

Yes. The holders of a dominant estate have an obligation to maintain it as an incident   DECISION
to the beneficial use of the easement. With the benefit ought to come the burden. This is certainly the rule where the easement is solely for the benefit of the dominant estate. There are compelling reasons to apply the rule to this situation even though there may be incidental use of these roads by those who are not the individual landowners.

Easement in Gross   An **easement in gross** exists independently of a dominant tenement. The privileges given by the easement belong to an individual or firm independently of ownership or possession of any specific land. Telephone and electric transmission lines are examples of easements in gross (see Figure 37-3). The right of access over property in such cases does not benefit any particular piece of property.

Easement in gross an easement that does not exist for the benefit of any other particular piece of property

FIGURE 37-3 Easement Appurtenant and Easement in Gross

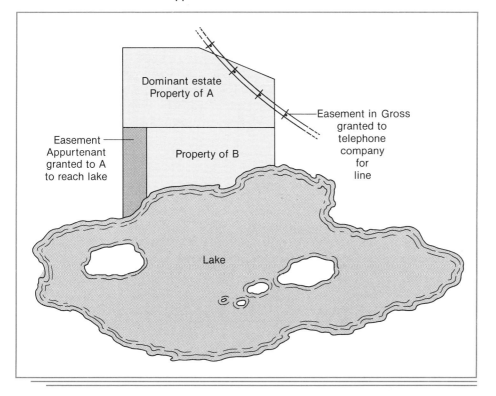

Because of the personal nature of the easement in gross, many American jurisdictions do not allow a noncommercial easement in gross to be transferred. Commercial easements in gross, because of their importance to the public, are transferable.

Creation of Easements

Prescription a method of acquiring a right to use another's land through wrongful use of the land for a certain period of time

Because an easement is an interest in land, it can be created only by a written instrument or by **prescription**. Sometimes courts imply that an easement exists even though no written document is available. One such situation is when a purchaser acquires land to which no access to a public road exists except over land retained by the seller. Courts imply that the seller meant to grant an easement. This type of easement is called a *way of necessity.*

Courts also imply the existence of an easement when a person sells part of his or her land, retaining another part that has been used to benefit the part sold. For instance, A sells several acres of his farm to B. A ditch running across the portion retained by A has been used to drain the acreage purchased by B. An easement for drainage over A's land exists in favor of B if the ditch is obvious and reasonably necessary.

Profit à Prendre and License

Profit à prendre an interest in real property that allows the holder to take something of value from another's land

License a privilege to enter the land of another for a particular purpose

A **profit à prendre** or profit is an interest in real property much like an easement in gross. The distinguishing difference is that the owner of a profit has the right to take something of supposed value from the land. The right to cut and remove timber or to quarry and take gravel are examples of a profit. The profit carries with it the right to enter on the land. Because a profit is an interest in land, it is irrevocable.

A **license** differs from a profit in that the license is merely a personal privilege to enter on another's land for a particular purpose. A license is not an interest in real property. Holding a ticket to an athletic event or occupying a motel room are examples of a license. Most licenses are revocable at the will of the owner of the property. If a license is coupled with an interest in the land, license may not be revoked.

Liens

Lien a security interest in property of another

A **lien** is a very important interest in land. It is a right in another's property that secures payment of a debt or performance of some claim or obligation. Some liens are created by statute, others by agreement of the parties. Liens can exist in both real and personal property. One real property lien with which most people are familiar is the mortgage. Mortgages are discussed in the next chapter.

CO-OWNERSHIP

Another right in land exists when several people own undivided interests in a parcel of land at the same time. Generally in this type of ownership each person is entitled to a specific fraction of the parcel but also shares with the others a single right to possession and profits from the land. This is generally referred to as *concurrent ownership* or **co-ownership.** Co-ownership is often used for holding investment real estate.

Co-ownership ownership of real property by two or more people

Co-ownership was important to the common law, and the various concurrent (existing at the same time) estates that developed at common law remain important today. A number of legal problems are associated with these common law concurrent estates. These problems are reduced or eliminated if several owners use a partnership, corporation, or other arrangement (such as a trust, discussed later in this chapter) to hold title to the property. These devices are becoming increasingly important in real estate, replacing the common law forms of multiple ownership.

Joint Tenancy

The principal feature of a **joint tenancy** is the **right of survivorship.** This means that upon the death of one of the co-owners, that person's interest passes automatically to surviving joint owners. Some state statutes prohibit the creation of a joint tenancy with the right of survivorship. In most states it is still possible to have a joint tenancy, but the person establishing it must clearly indicate that this is the intention.

Joint tenancy co-ownership in which the interest of a deceased co-owner passes automatically to surviving owners

Rights of Joint Tenants   Each co-owner who holds a joint tenancy has an equal right to possession of the entire property. This is referred to as an *undivided interest.* Although a joint tenant may not exclude other joint tenants from possession, the law considers occupancy by one as occupancy by all. If each tenant is to benefit, all must agree to share the property. When agreement cannot be reached, the tenancy must be ended.

Right of survivorship the characteristic of a joint tenancy by which the surviving owners obtain the interest of the deceased co-owner

Termination of Joint Tenancy   A joint tenancy ends if one of the owners sells his or her interest. In some states, a joint tenancy ends if an owner's interest is mortgaged. The joint tenancy also ends if the interest of a joint tenant is sold to satisfy a debt. In any case, a person who acquires the interest of a joint tenant becomes a tenant in common with the remaining co-owners.

Tenancy in Common

A **tenancy in common** is a form of co-ownership in which each owner possesses an undivided fractional interest in a parcel of land. Otherwise each owner's rights are the same as those of a sole owner. Although the joint tenancy was for centuries the favored form of co-ownership, today English and American law favor the tenancy in common. In almost all states, a tenancy in common is implied unless a joint tenancy is clearly indicated by the instrument creating the concurrent estate.

Tenancy in common co-ownership in which each owner possesses an undivided fractional interest in real property but each owner's rights are the same as those possessed by a single owner

Rights of Tenants in Common   Like joint tenants, each tenant in common has an undivided right to possession of the entire parcel. Usually a tenant in common is not responsible to the co-owners for any benefits gained by exclusive occupancy. At the

same time, no tenant in common is entitled to the exclusive use of any part of the land. The result is that problems arise when one co-tenant wrongfully excludes the others or when the property can be practically occupied only by a single tenant.

Under the circumstances, in a number of states, the co-tenants not in occupancy are entitled to a fair compensation for the use of the property. Similar problems arise when a co-tenant not in possession receives benefits from the property more than the other co-owners. These problems can best be solved by agreement among the parties, as can problems involving liability of co-tenants for upkeep and improvements. When agreement cannot be reached, **partition** of property may be the only solution.

Partition the division of real property owned by two or more people

Partition   By partition, a co-owner divides property and ends any interest of other co-owners in the divided portion. Although courts traditionally ordered partition even when no statute authorized them to do so, today partition exists in some form by statute in every state. In a few states, the wording of the statute is broad enough to allow partition when owners are divorced. Many states also make partition available to certain holders of future interests. Under the law of almost all states, co-owners of personal property enjoy the right to partition to the same degree as co-owners of realty.

Tenancy by the Entirety

Tenancy by the entirety co-ownership of real property by husband and wife

Nearly half the states recognize **tenancy by the entirety,** a type of co-ownership existing only between husband and wife. This type of co-ownership is based upon an ancient legal fiction by which the common law regarded husband and wife as a single legal person. One result was that if the two acquired equal interests in real estate by the same instrument, the property was considered owned as an indivisible legal unit. When either died, the survivor remained the property's sole owner. This result is still accepted in modern law. Today a right of survivorship exists for the tenancy by entirety.

A tenancy by the entirety is a more stable type of co-ownership than joint tenancy. Because the spouses are considered a single unit, neither may break the tenancy without the other's consent. A sale by either husband or wife does not end the tenancy nor end the right of survivorship.

Termination of Tenancy by the Entirety   In many jurisdictions, a tenancy by the entirety cannot be terminated by the forced sale of the husband's or wife's interest. If either spouse refuses to pay an individual debt, the creditor cannot attach his or her interest in the property. This rule has been criticized for letting debtors escape responsibility even when they own a valuable asset. In a few states, creditors of the husband, but not of the wife, may reach the income, profits, and title of the property. Whatever interest these creditors acquire is lost if the wife survives. Other states permit the separate creditors of either spouse to sell the share of the debtor, whether husband or wife. If the other spouse survives, the creditor is deprived of his or her interest. If the creditor holds a joint judgment against both spouses, the creditor can attach the estate held by the entirety.

TABLE 37-1   Rights of Co-owners

	Joint Tenancy	Tenancy in Common	Tenancy by the Entirety	Tenancy in Partnership
Right of survivorship	Yes	No	Yes	Yes
Individual interest may be sold	Yes	Yes	No	No
Individual interest may be attached	Yes	Yes	No	No
Individual interest may be mortgaged	State laws differ	Yes	No	No

Tenancies by the entireties are terminated primarily by divorce, when the parties become tenants in common.

Tenancy in Partnership

Most states have adopted the Uniform Partnership Act, which creates the **tenancy in partnership.** This act permits a partnership to buy, hold, and sell real estate in the partnership name. Individual partners share ownership in particular property only as members of the firm. Spouses, heirs, and creditors of individual partners have no rights in partnership property. Although an individual partner may transfer partnership real property, any transfer is made only as an agent for the firm. When a partner dies, that person's share passes to surviving partners.

Tenancy in partnership ownership of real property in the partnership name

Community Property

Community property is a form of co-ownership between husband and wife in which each has a half interest in property acquired during marriage. The property may have been acquired by the work of either spouse. A number of jurisdictions in the United States apply the doctrine of community property to property owned by a husband or wife, including Arizona, California, Idaho, Louisiana, Nevada, New Mexico, Texas, and Washington. Because community property ownership is statutory, each state varies the characteristics of the system to fit its own needs.

Community property is based on a marriage, and husband and wife are regarded as partners. Each co-owns all property acquired by the labor or skill of either while the two are married. This rule applies even though title to a property is individually held by the husband or wife.

Property owned by the husband or wife before marriage and acquired during marriage by gift, inheritance, or will does not become community property. In addition, any real property that either spouse buys with his or her separate property and takes title to in his or her name remains separate property.

Community property co-ownership between husband and wife in which each has a half interest in property acquired during marriage

Condominiums and Cooperatives

Condominium ownership individual ownership in fee simple of a unit in a multiunit structure

Condominiums and **cooperatives** are forms of co-ownership that have become significant factors in the real estate market since World War II. In both cooperatives and condominiums, owners enjoy individual control over designated units in a structure, usually an apartment or office building, while sharing portions of the structure with other owners. This type of ownership generally is found in urban areas where land values are high. Condominium and cooperative ownership is based on statutes, which vary considerably from state to state.

Cooperative ownership individual control of a unit in a multiunit structure based upon a lease obtained by the occupant because of stock owned in the cooperative association

Condominiums   In condominium ownership, a person individually owns part of a building. At the same time, he or she owns as a tenant in common with other condominium owners elements of the real estate necessary for effective use of the entire structure. These elements include land, walls, halls, lobbies, and service facilities, such as elevators, heating, and plumbing systems. Because each unit is owned separately and the owner has an undivided interest in the common elements, a person may sell, mortgage, or lease a unit individually.

Declaration the legal document that creates a condominium

The condominium is created by a **declaration,** a document describing the parcel, units in the structure, and the rights and duties of condominium owners. A set of bylaws regulates the operation and maintenance of the building. Owners of the units share in the costs of maintaining the common elements of the real estate.

The case that follows illustrates one type of problem that arises in condominium ownership.

Ritchey v. Villa Nueva Condominium Association

Court of Appeals, California
146 Cal. Rptr. 695 (1978)

FACTS   Ritchey bought a two-bedroom unit in the Villa Nueva condominium project. He rented the unit to Dorothy Westphol, a woman with two young children. This violated a bylaw of the condominium restricting occupancy to people 18 years old or older. When the condominium association sued to remove Westphol, Ritchey sued seeking an injunction and declaratory relief as well as damages. Ritchey contended that the age restriction was unreasonable in that it discriminated against families with children.

ISSUE   Are age restrictions in condominium documents enforceable?

DECISION   Yes. The court held that age restrictions in condominium documents are enforceable. The United States Congress has adopted several programs to provide housing for the elderly, setting an age minimum of 62 years for occupancy. These represent an implicit legislative finding not only that older adults need inexpensive housing but also that their housing interest and needs differ from those of families with children.

California law provides that restrictions in the bylaws may limit the right of an owner to sell or lease a condominium unit so long as the standards are uniform and objective and are not based upon the race, creed, color, national origin, or sex of the purchaser or lessee. Therefore a restriction upon sale can be based on the age of the vendee or lessee or his or her family.

> The authority of a condominium association necessarily includes the power to issue reasonable regulations governing an owner's use of a unit, to prevent activities which might prove annoying to the general residents. Thus an owners' association can prohibit any activity or conduct that could constitute a nuisance. It may regulate the disposition of refuse, provide for the maintenance and repair of interiors of apartments as well as exteriors, and prohibit or regulate the keeping of pets. Therefore, a reasonable restriction upon occupancy of the individually owned units of a condominium project is not beyond the scope of authority of the owner's association.

Cooperatives In cooperative (often called a co-op) ownership, an individual controls a unit in a building, but the land and building itself are owned by some type of association, often a corporation. The corporation's shareholders are the building's tenants. An individual's right to a particular unit is based on a lease from the association, available only because he or she is a shareholder. The bylaws of the corporation detail the rights and duties of the tenants. Although the building is maintained by the association, maintenance expenses are shared by the shareholder–tenants. Because the individual does not own the unit to which he or she is entitled, individual financing is not available. Most bylaws restrict the individual's right to transfer his or her lease.

Real Estate Investment Trusts

The **trust** is a device that has been used in the United States and England for centuries. In a trust, one person or institution — the *trustee* — is given specific property to manage for the benefit of others. The property may be real or personal. The trust has been an important instrument for law reform and the legal basis for some significant economic innovations. One of these is the **real estate investment trust** (REIT).

A REIT is an organization in which trustees own real estate or loans secured by real estate that they manage for beneficiaries who hold transferable shares representing their respective interests.

REITs developed because they enjoyed some tax advantages over corporations. Income earned by the REIT was not taxable as long as it was distributed to the trust beneficiaries. Of course, the distributed income was taxable to each of them. Income earned by a corporation is taxable both to the corporation and to shareholders when distributed.

Trust a legal relationship in which one person, a trustee, holds title to property which he or she manages for the benefit of another, the beneficiary.

Real estate investment trust an organization in which trustees invest in real estate which they manage for beneficiaries who hold shares representing their interests

LAND AND THE LAW

The variety of interests that can exist in real property illustrate the interrelationships among legal, economic, and social systems. Land always has been a critical factor in economic and social life in the Western world. Its importance is reflected in real estate law. Innovative use of air rights, which is basic to condominium and cooperative ownership, is an example of the dynamism of the legal system. At the same time, the historic interests in real property that continue to be useful to society — such as the concept of estates — are links that join the past and present.

_____ SUMMARY _____

The legal relationships involving real property are extensive and complicated. The reason is that land for centuries has been of great economic importance. Traditionally the surface owner of land also owned to the center of the earth and upward indefinitely into the airspace above. The modern rule limits the surface owner's air rights to air space that can be reasonably used.

Interests in land have been divided in several ways. One way separates the physical land and interests that might exist in it and allows several interests to exist simultaneously. This separation is the basis for the doctrine of estates. The extent of an owner's estate is determined by length of the interest and when the right to possess and enjoy the land begins. For example, a life estate lasts for a person's life. A fee simple estate is one that might last forever.

A leased estate lasts for the duration of the lease agreement. The lease is very important to business because it provides for obtaining land with limited capital. The term tenancy ends automatically at the time designated in a lease. A periodic tenancy continues from period to period, until proper notice of termination is given by either party. Many leases are classified by the method the parties have agreed upon for determining the rent. These types of leases include percentage leases, net leases, and appraisal leases. The rights and duties of the parties to a lease are established by agreement. If a question arises that is not covered by the lease, case or statutory law provides a solution.

Holders of most nonpossessory interests in land may use the property for a particular purpose. Such interests include easements appurtenant, easements in gross, the profit à prendre, and the license. A lien grants a person a security interest in property.

A single parcel of land may be co-owned by several people. At common law, joint tenancy and tenancy in common were the usual forms of co-ownership. In a joint tenancy, the interest of a deceased co-owner passes automatically to the surviving owners. The right of survivorship also exists in the tenancy by the entirety, which is co-ownership by a husband and wife. Today when a number of people own a single piece of land, they usually use a partnership, corporation, or a trust to hold title to the property.

Condominium and cooperative ownership are important and relatively new forms of co-ownership. In both, owners enjoy individual control over designated units in a structure and share common portions of the structure with other occupants. The owner of a condominium has fee simple title to a unit. The cooperative's occupant has a lease to a unit based on the ownership of stock in the cooperative.

REVIEW PROBLEMS

1. Explain the difference between a fee simple absolute and a fee simple defeasible. How are they similar?

2. What is the principal difference between a term tenancy and a periodic tenancy?

3. Define co-ownership. Compare and contrast a joint tenancy and a tenancy in common.

4. Explain the differences between an easement in gross and an easement appurtenant.

5. May conveyed to Tenneco, Incorporated, an easement crossing a portion of his land. Using this easement, Tenneco constructed and put into service an underground natural gas pipeline. Several years later, May constructed a road over a portion of Tenneco's easement. Federal regulations require installation of a protective encasement around pipe where it passes under a street. Tenneco installed the encasement at a cost of $4,903.39 and billed May for this amount. May refused to pay and Tenneco sued. Was Tenneco successful? Discuss.

6. Cushman was developing Blackacre as a residential subdivision. Before Cushman acquired the property, Blackacre was an apricot orchard. A roadway based upon an easement ran from the orchard to a public street. This property subject to the roadway easement was owned by Davis. The road had existed for many years. Its primary use was to move spraying and picking equipment into the orchard ten times each year. Davis also used the road for access to his home and to a water tank. From time to time, others used the road to reach the orchard. Cushman sought to clear title to the easement for access to the subdivision. Davis strenuously objected. Was Cushman successful in his action to clear title?

7. The will of Alma H. Rand contained the following provision:

> That the share of the Estate of Henry Rand of the town of Southport, Lincoln County, State of Maine, shall be left to John Freeman Rand in fee simple with the proviso that he shall never deny access or occupation to the several heirs herein after named during their lifetime.

What kind of estate did John Rand have as a result of this provision? Explain.

8. Luithle and his wife owned real estate as joint tenants. Luithle bought cattle from Schlichenmayer with a worthless check and immediately sold the cattle. Part of the proceeds were used to make a $1,100 mortgage payment on the real property that the couple owned. A short time later, Luithle died. Schlichenmayer sued the wife to recover the $1,100 on grounds that she had been unjustly enriched. Was Schlichenmayer successful? Explain.

9. Cranston leased an apartment from the Buckeye Realty Company. The term of the lease was one year. During June, July, and August, Cranston sublet the apartment to Whitney. Buckeye Realty was aware of the sublease because Whitney paid the rent for June. But Whitney did not pay for July or August. Buckeye

sued Cranston for the rental payments. Cranston defended on grounds that Buckeye accepted Whitney as a subtenant, and only Whitney was liable. Was Cranston correct? Support your answer.

10. Tom owned a unit in a condominium. Red occupied a unit in a cooperative. The apartments were very similar. Red argued that he had a better deal because he did not have to pay real estate taxes but Tom did. Do you agree with Red? Support your answer.

11. Ortlieb rented a building for 15 years. He planned to open a men's clothing store in the building. The owner knew of Ortlieb's plan. In fact, they had discussed it in great detail. Before Ortlieb could open his store, a men's store was opened in an adjacent building. As a result, Ortlieb changed his plans and decided to open an adult bookstore instead. The owner of the building objected to this use, arguing that Ortlieb was limited to using the premises for the stated purpose or something similar. Was the owner correct? Discuss.

12. Pete Brangs and his son, Al, owned real estate as joint tenants. Pete had been involved in a business deal and accumulated a large debt, which he refused to pay because he felt that the creditor had defrauded him. The creditor threatened to attach the real estate if the debt were not paid. Pete believed the creditor could not attach the property because Al had had nothing to do with Pete's business and he and Al were co-owners of the real estate. Was Pete correct? Discuss.

13. Jim and Lucy Monroe, a married couple, lived in a community property state. Jim had not worked for many years because he hated to get up in the morning. Lucy was the sole support of the family. Lucy bought a house and took title in her own name. Six years later, she died, leaving the house to her son. What rights, if any, did Jim have in the property? Support your answer.

14. Anne Crowley purchased a house from Alex Baldwin. The house adjoined an apartment complex that Baldwin was developing. Baldwin promised Crowley that she and future owners of the property would have the use of the pool located in the complex. Crowley lived in the house for several years. During this period she used the pool each summer. When she sold the property, she told the new owners of Baldwin's promise. But Baldwin would not allow them to use the pool. Describe Crowley's interest in the use of the pool. Could Baldwin prevent the new owners from using the pool? Support your answer.

CHAPTER 38

Acquisition, Financing, and Control of Real Property

CHAPTER OBJECTIVES

ADVERSE POSSESSION

Statutes of Limitations / Elements of Adverse Possession / Prescription

EMINENT DOMAIN

PURCHASE AND SALE OF REAL PROPERTY

Anatomy of a Real Estate Sale / Deeds / Essential Elements of a Deed / Recording Statutes

REAL PROPERTY AS SECURITY

The Mortgage Transaction / Lien and Title Theories of Mortgages / Deed of Trust

FORECLOSURE

Judicial Foreclosure / Power of Sale Foreclosure / Due-on-Sale Clause and Foreclosure

CONTROL OF LAND USE

Restrictive Covenants / Zoning

SUMMARY

REVIEW PROBLEMS

CHAPTER OBJECTIVES

After reading this chapter, you should be able to:

1. Explain the elements necessary to establish title by adverse possession.

2. Compare and contrast the types of deeds; lien and title theories of mortgages; mortgages and land installment contracts; mortgages and deeds of trust; judicial foreclosure and power of sale foreclosure.

3. Define eminent domain and its limitations.

4. Outline and discuss the steps in a typical real estate transaction.

5. Describe the control of land use by restrictive covenants and zoning.

The previous chapter explained interests that can exist in real property. This chapter discusses the ways of acquiring title, some methods of financing it, and common methods for its control.

Title or ownership of real property may be acquired in a number of ways. Purchase is the most common. Individuals and sometimes business firms become owners of real property by gift or by inheritance. (Acquisition of real property as a result of the death of the owner is treated in Chapter 39. Gifts are discussed in Chapter 35.) Government or those it authorizes can acquire title to real property by exercising the power of eminent domain. In certain special limited instances, a person or firm can obtain title to property by adverse possession or unauthorized occupancy.

ADVERSE POSSESSION

Adverse possession
acquisition of title to real property by occupying it without the owner's consent for a period of time specified by statute

Obtaining title by **adverse possession** is a legal oddity. It lets a person who is occupying land as a trespasser defeat the rights of the true owner. The justification for this unusual policy is that society benefits when idle land is put to use. The legal system encourages the use of land by giving someone who trespasses a means to establish clear title.

The law balances the encouragement of land use against the protection of private property rights. Because of the importance of protecting private property, a trespasser acquires title only if prescribed conditions are met and certain acts occur. These acts and conditions exist to ensure that the owner has an opportunity to discover challenges to his or her title and a reasonable chance to protect it.

Statutes of Limitations

Basic to all adverse possession claims are state **statutes of limitations.** These statutes establish a period of time during which the rightful owner of land must bring an action to oust the trespasser.

At common law, the owner had to bring suit within 20 years, and several states have adopted this as the limitation period. Although only a handful of states allow the owner more than 20 years to act, a substantial number apply shorter periods. These range from five to eighteen years. Many of the states with short limitation periods are in the sparsely populated western United States. This reflects the public policy underlying adverse possession, which is to encourage land use. In some states, the limitation period is reduced if the trespasser has paid taxes or occupies the land on the basis of a document, such as an invalid deed or will.

A number of states allow occupancy of two or more successive adverse possessors to be added together to establish possession for the necessary period. This is called **tacking,** because the periods are "tacked" together. Although tacking is probably permitted in a majority of states, some jurisdictions limit it to cases involving heirs, spouses, or blood relatives.

Statutes of limitation statutes establishing time within which legal action must be begun

Tacking adding periods of adverse occupancy to establish a claim of adverse possession

Elements of Adverse Possession

Generally five elements must exist for title to be acquired by adverse possession. In addition to proving

1. continuous possession for the statutory period, the claimant must establish that possession is:
2. open and notorious
3. hostile
4. actual, and
5. exclusive

Open and Notorious   Open and notorious acts are those that alert the true owner to claims that are adverse to his or her rights. Although the true owner does not actually have to know what is taking place, the acts must be such that a diligent owner would become aware of them.

Hostile   Acts that are open and notorious are often hostile. The requirement that possession be hostile does not suggest ill will or evil intent but merely that the person in possession of the property claims to occupy as the owner. Most state courts accept that possession is hostile if the occupant claims ownership either by mistake or willfully. A person who enters property with the owner's permission cannot later claim successfully by adverse possession unless he or she repudiates the owner's title.

Actual Possession   Actual possession consists of exercising control over land, making ordinary use of it, and taking the ordinary profit the land is capable of yielding. Courts determine actual possession by looking at the character of the land that is involved. Living on the property is not necessary, unless this is the use that would be expected. In a few states, the adverse possessor must enclose the land to establish a claim.

Exclusive Use   *Exclusive use* means that the claimant has the land for his or her own use. Total exclusion of others is not required, but the adverse possessor must exclude others as would be expected of an owner under the circumstances. Occasional use by others, even the rightful owner, does not negate exclusiveness if the use permitted by the adverse possessor is consistent with his or her claims of ownership. The following case involves the element of exclusive use and several other aspects of adverse possession.

Porter v. Posey

Missouri Court of Appeals
592 S.W. 2d 844 (1979)

FACTS   Plaintiffs purchased property from the Englemeyers. In addition to the property conveyed to them by deed, plaintiffs took possession of a .18 acre tract of land that had been maintained and used by the Englemeyers but which was "owned" by the defendants. The Englemeyers had taken control of this tract 20 years earlier by bulldozing it and building a graveled turnaround on it. The Englemeyers used the tract for access to their property and for overflow parking. At all times, they believed they owned the land.

Just before the plaintiffs took over the land, the defendants had the property surveyed and discovered that the turnaround was on their land. Defendants threatened Mr. Englemeyer with a shotgun and told him to get off the land in dispute. Shortly after the plaintiffs took title to the property from the Englemeyers, the defendants blocked access to the turnaround. Plaintiffs sued to clear title to the disputed tract, claiming that the Englemeyers had acquired title by adverse possession and had transferred their title to the plaintiffs. Defendants claim that the Englemeyers didn't satisfy the open and notorious, hostile, and exclusive elements of adverse possession.

ISSUE   Did the plaintiffs acquire title to the disputed tract of land?

DECISION   Yes. The court tried to determine if the Englemeyers had satisfied the disputed elements of adverse possession. The court said that to be open and notorious, the possession must include acts of ownership sufficient to give the existing owner notice of the claim being made. The Englemeyers satisfied this requirement by bulldozing the land, building the turnaround, and maintaining the land. The defendants' next claim was that the possession was not hostile. The court said, however, that ill will or acrimony is not necessary. Hostile possession is simply an assertion of ownership adverse to that of the true owner, founded on the intent to possess as one's own. This element was sufficiently established by the plaintiffs. Defendants further contended that the possession was not exclusive because others had used the turnaround. The court rejected this argument, saying that possession is exclusive when the claimant occupies the land "for his own use and not for that of another." There was no evidence to indicate that the Englemeyers occupied the land for anyone's benefit other than their own.

Prescription

The previous chapter described the easement, a right to use the land of another for a particular purpose. Most easements are created by written instruments. But an easement also may be created by **prescription,** a legal doctrine similar in several ways to adverse possession. Both are based upon wrongful invasion of the property rights of the true owner, but prescription is based on adverse use, not occupancy. As a result, a person acquiring a prescriptive easement merely acquires a right to *use* another's land, while the successful adverse possessor actually acquires *title.* Another common difference between the two is that it takes less time to acquire an easement by prescription than to acquire title by adverse possession.

Prescription a method of acquiring a right to use another's land through wrongful use of the land for a certain period of time

EMINENT DOMAIN

Eminent domain is the power of the government to acquire private property without the owner's consent. State constitutions and the U.S. Constitution place limitations on this power. Three principal limitations exist:

Eminent domain the power of the government to acquire private property without the owner's consent

The property must be taken for a public purpose.

The owner must be adequately compensated.

The property cannot be taken without due process of law.

Due process guarantees the owner an opportunity to a trial on questions such as the amount of compensation or whether the property is being acquired for public use.

Both the United States and the individual states may delegate the power of eminent domain. They often delegate this power to cities, counties, and public service corporations. Individuals and private corporations may also be authorized to exercise the power of eminent domain.

PURCHASE AND SALE OF REAL PROPERTY

The purchase and sale of real property should be of special interest to business students. Most people participate in several such transactions. The large amounts of money, long-term financial commitments, and technical procedures involved in the sale of real estate make knowledge of these transactions particularly important.

Buying and selling real estate involves several legal areas. Agency and contract law are especially important. Many real estate sales are negotiated by brokers — who are agents — and brokers are involved in leasing, property management, and appraising real estate. The contract is the critical document in a real estate sale, and it governs the relationships between brokers and clients and between landlords and tenants.

Anatomy of a Real Estate Sale

The typical real estate sale in the United States is usually the result of negotiations between buyer and seller, often with the help of a real estate broker. In some areas, especially for residential real estate, a person who wants to buy submits a purchase offer to a seller. Buyers should realize that this document's terms become the contract if the seller accepts. But the seller can reject or make a counteroffer if not satisfied with the purchase offer terms. In this case, the negotiations continue, and a contract on different terms may result.

Another procedure, especially in commercial transactions when agreement seems to have been reached, is for the parties to meet, settle any remaining terms, and execute a contract. For any procedure, all states require that a contract for the sale of real property be in writing to be enforceable.

Equitable title
the right of a buyer to acquire legal title to real property

Equitable Title   When a contract for the sale of real estate is completed, the buyer acquires **equitable title.** This gives the buyer the right to sue for damages or specific performance (see Chapter 18) if the seller refuses to perform. Simultaneously, the seller acquires a right to enforce the contract.

Almost always an interval takes place between the making of the contract and its performance. Customarily the buyer completes the necessary arrangements for financing and examines the seller's title. If the title is defective, the seller has an opportunity to cure defects before the date set for title closing (discussed below).

Risk of Loss   Because the buyer has equitable title between contract signing and title closing, some states make the buyer bear the risk of loss or damage to the property. Thus if the property is damaged by fire, the buyer still must complete the transaction as agreed. But some states reject this rule as unfair, especially when the buyer is not in possession. These states allow the buyer an adjustment in the price to compensate for the loss. But the allocation of the risk of loss should not be left to state law. The problem can and should be settled by the parties in their contract.

Escrow closing a
closing that takes
place through a
third party

Title Closing   Two types of title closing are common in the United States. In most areas, the parties involved in the transaction meet as a group and exchange the funds and documents required to complete the transfer. Ordinarily, buyer, seller, brokers, a representative of the institution financing the sale, and attorneys for each party are present.

In some areas, real estate sales close through a third party called an *escrow agent.* In an **escrow closing,** buyer and seller submit the necessary documents and funds to the escrow agent, who is responsible for seeing that the transaction closes on the terms agreed upon in the contract. When the seller delivers a properly executed deed to the escrow agent and the agent is assured that the seller is passing a good title, the funds and mortgage documents are turned over to the proper parties, and the transaction is completed.

Deeds

Ownership of real property is transferred by an instrument called a **deed**. A deed is a two-party instrument. The person conveying the property is called the *grantor,* and the person to whom the property is conveyed, the *grantee*. Several types of deeds are common in the United States. Ordinarily, the type of deed a seller uses is agreed upon in the sales contract.

Deed a document that transfers ownership of real property

Warranty Deed   A warranty deed conveys title and warrants that the title is good and free of liens and encumbrances. The warranties are also referred to as **covenants**. They provide the purchaser with some protection against claims that might interfere with ownership.

Covenants binding agreements to do something

Although the use and wording of particular covenants vary from one jurisdiction to another, four covenants are common in the United States. One of these is called the *covenant of seisin* or *covenant of right to convey*. By this covenant, the seller guarantees that he or she has good title and the right to transfer it. A second covenant used in many jurisdictions is the *covenant against encumbrances*. In making this covenant, the seller affirms that no encumbrances exist against the property. The *covenant of quiet enjoyment* and the *covenant of general warranty* are guarantees that the buyer will not be evicted from the property by someone with a title superior to the seller's. As a result of these two covenants, the seller agrees to defend the buyer's title against all lawful claims.

Warranty deed covenants do not assure the buyer that the seller has title, but they do provide a right to sue if a covenant is broken. This right is valuable if the seller is solvent and still within the jurisdiction. But a buyer should never rely solely on a warranty deed for title protection.

Bargain and Sale Deed   A bargain and sale deed conveys title but contains no warranties. Although no formal guarantees of title are made, the bargain and sale deed is by nature contractual, and the seller implies that he or she has a title to convey. This deed has a number of variations. It sometimes contains covenants against the seller's acts. If so, the seller guarantees that he or she has done nothing that might adversely affect the title.

Quitclaim Deed   A quitclaim deed merely releases whatever interest the grantor has. Unlike the warranty deed and bargain and sale deed, the transferor by a quitclaim does not purport to convey title. But if the grantor has title, this interest is conveyed as effectively as it would be by a warranty or bargain and sale deed. Quitclaim deeds are commonly used to correct defective titles.

FIGURE 38-1   General Warranty Deed—Ohio Statutory Form

GENERAL WARRANTY DEED

, of   County,

for valuable consideration paid, grant(s), with general warranty covenants, to

, whose tax-mailing address is

,

the following **REAL PROPERTY:** *Situated in the County of*   *in the State*

of Ohio and in the   *of*   :

.

Prior Instrument Reference: Vol.   Page   of the Deed Records of

County, Ohio.   *wife (husband) of the*

Grantor releases all rights of dower therein. Witness   hand(s) this   day

of   , 19   .

Signed and acknowledged in the presence of:

_____   _____
WITNESS

_____   _____
WITNESS

State of Ohio   *County of*   ss.

BE IT REMEMBERED, *That on this   day of   , 19   , before me,*

the subscriber, a   in and for said county, personally came,

the Grantor(s) in the

foregoing Deed, and acknowledged the signing thereof to be   voluntary act and deed.

IN TESTIMONY THEREOF, *I have hereunto subscribed my name and affixed my*

seal on this day and year aforesaid. _____

This instrument was prepared by _____

Essential Elements of a Deed

A deed is a complicated legal instrument that should be drafted by an attorney. To be valid, a deed must contain words of *conveyance* that indicate an intention to convey title. The deed also must identify a competent grantor and grantee, contain a

FIGURE 38-2 Quitclaim Deed

Quitclaim Deed

This Indenture, Made on the _____ *day of* _____ *A.D., One*

Thousand Nine Hundred and _____ *by and between* _____

_____ *of the County of* _____ , *State of* _____ *part* *of the first part, and*

_____ *of the County of* _____ , *State of* _____ *part* *of the second part.*

(Mailing address of said first named grantee is _____ *).*

    WITNESSETH, that the said part _____ *of the first part, in consideration of the sum of*

_____ *DOLLARS,*

to _____ *paid by the said part* _____ *of the second part (the receipt of which is hereby acknowledged)*

do _____ *by these presents REMISE, RELEASE and FOREVER QUIT CLAIM unto the said part* _____ *of the second part,*

the following described lots, tracts or parcels of land, lying, being and situate in the

County of _____ *and State of* _____ , *to-wit: [description]*

    TO HAVE AND TO HOLD THE SAME, with all the rights, immunities, privileges and appurtenances thereto belonging, unto the said part _____ *of the second part and unto* _____ *heirs and assigns forever: so that neither the said part* _____ *of the first part nor* _____ *heirs nor any other person or persons, for* _____ *or in* _____ *name or behalf, shall or will hereinafter claim or demand any right or title to the aforesaid premises or any part thereof, but they and each of them shall, by these presents, be excluded and forever barred.*

    IN WITNESS WHEREOF, the said part _____ *of the first part ha* _____ *hereunto set hand* _____ *and seal* _____ *the day and year above written.*

_____(Seal)

Signed, Sealed and Delivered in Presence of   _____(Seal)

_____   _____(Seal)

_____   _____(Seal)

---

legal description, and be properly signed and executed. A final requirement is a valid delivery and acceptance. Most legal problems involving deeds arise because someone claims the deed has not been properly delivered. The case that follows is an example.

Bennett v. Mings

Court of Civil Appeals of Texas
535 S.W. 2d 408 (1976)

On September 7, 1972, Nellie Mings, a 91-year-old woman, signed a warranty deed   FACTS
conveying land upon which her home was located to her nephew, Cyril C. Bennett. Mrs.

Mings handed the deed to Bennett to put in his safety deposit box. Both parties agreed that the deed would not be recorded until Mrs. Mings's death. In December 1973, at her request, the deed was returned to Mrs. Mings. A few days later, Bennett regained possession of the deed and recorded it. Mrs. Mings testified that she surrendered the deed to Bennett only with the permission that he use the deed for security but that under no circumstances was the deed to be recorded. Bennett testified that he got the deed the second time with permission to record it. The trial court found in favor of Mrs. Mings and ordered the deed canceled. Bennett appealed.

ISSUE   Is there valid delivery of a deed when a grantor gives a grantee possession of the instrument, and the grantee records it?

DECISION   No. The court ruled that for the delivery to be effective, Mrs. Mings must have intended that the deed become immediately operative as a conveyance. Without this intention, handing the deed to the grantee is not enough to pass title. The intent of the grantor is a question for the jury's determination after weighing the evidence. Here the jury was justified in finding that Mrs. Mings did not intend the deed to become operative as a conveyance of her land and home.

Recording Statutes

All states have statutes requiring that important documents affecting the title to real property be entered into the public record. In addition to deeds and mortgages, the statutes generally require that long-term leases, easements, assignments, and similar instruments be recorded. The purpose of these statutes is to notify third parties of interests that exist in a particular piece of land. This recording protects the third party from losses that might happen by acquiring an interest in land subject to unknown claims of another. But the recording statutes do *not* affect the validity of the instrument. An unrecorded deed or mortgage is enforceable between the original parties.

Recording statutes are based on the idea that if a real property interest is not recorded, a person who gets a conflicting interest will have superior rights in the land. For example, if X conveys real property to Y, Y is required to record the deed. If Y does not and X fraudulently conveys to Z, Z may acquire an ownership interest superior to Y's. In order for this to occur, Z must be a **good faith purchaser.** This means that Z must not have knowledge of the sale to Y and must give value for the property.

Good faith purchaser a purchaser without knowledge of a conflicting sale

Constructive Notice   As we discussed in Chapter 34, constructive notice is knowledge that the law implies a person has. Constructive notice exists if a person without actual knowledge could have acquired it by reasonably investigating available sources. If a person acquiring an interest in realty knows something that would lead a reasonable person to make further inquiry, and none is made, the law presumes actual knowledge exists. In addition, any information that might be discovered by a careful check of the record is presumed known. A person with actual or constructive knowledge of an earlier conflicting interest does not acquire his or her interest in good faith. The result is that a person who does not examine the record is penalized, and the recording statutes operate effectively. The following case involves a deed that was not recorded.

Fong v. Batton

District Court of Appeals of Florida
214 So. 2d 649 (1968)

The Fongs conveyed by warranty deed to Batton. The deed contained a *covenant of seisin.* The Fongs had acquired the property 14 years earlier from Donaldson, at which time their deed was recorded. But the public records did not show Donaldson to be the owner, because she had never recorded her deed. Upon finding this flaw in the record, Batton sued for breach of the *covenant of seisin.* The trial court granted plaintiff's motion for summary judgment and awarded her damages. The Fongs appealed.   FACTS

Was there a breach of the *covenant of seisin?*   ISSUE

No. The court held that covenant of seisin is an assurance that a grantor has the very estate in quantity which he purports to convey. Seisin is breached if the grantor has no title at all or if part of the land is in adverse possession. Imperfection in the chain of title is insufficient to sustain a cause of action for breach of the covenant of seisin. The Fongs were only required to convey a marketable title, not a marketable title of record. The recording statute is intended to protect the rights of a bona fide purchaser and not to void an otherwise valid title. An unrecorded link in the chain of title does not create an unmarketable title.   DECISION

REAL PROPERTY AS SECURITY

People often must borrow money for their purchases of a home or commercial real estate. When people have to borrow money, the loan ordinarily is secured by an interest in the property. This security interest gives the lender the right to sell the property and apply the proceeds against the debt if the borrower defaults.

Security interests in real estate are established by mortgages and deeds of trust.

The Mortgage Transaction

Financing based on a mortgage involves two instruments — the mortgage and a promissory note or bond. The mortgage gives the lender a security interest in the real estate. The promissory note or bond contains the terms of the loan and establishes the borrower's personal obligation to pay.

The mortgage and promissory note give the lender alternative remedies in the

Foreclosure a legal action in which security is sold to satisfy a debt that is in default

event of default. Suit may be brought on the note and a personal judgment obtained against the debtor, or the real property may be sold and the proceeds applied against the debt. The latter remedy is called **foreclosure.**

If the lender wins a judgment on the note, the judgment may be collected by attaching other property or by garnisheeing the debtor's wages. If the security when sold does not bring enough to pay the debt, the lender may sue for the difference, using the note. A few states require the lender to choose either to foreclose against the collateral to pay the debt or to sue on the note.

Lien and Title Theories of Mortgages

Modern mortgage law can be traced to the early use of the mortgage in England. At common law a borrower who mortgaged real property as security actually transferred title to the lender. The lender obtained a deed just as if he had purchased the property. As the mortgage was given as security, the title that the lender acquired was not absolute. A provision in the mortgage called the **defeasance clause** provided that, if the debt was paid when due, transfer of title to the lender was voided. Title reverted to the borrower.

Defeasance clause a clause in a mortgage providing that when the debt is paid, the mortgage is canceled

The historical idea that the mortgage conveys title to the mortgagee continues to be used in some states, referred to as *title theory* states. But even in these states, the lender may acquire title but not the right of possession unless the mortgagor defaults.

Most states recognize that in reality a mortgage is a lien, a device to secure a debt. The creditor is primarily interested in having the security sold and the proceeds applied to the debt if the debtor fails to pay or violates some other mortgage provision. States taking this position are called *lien theory* states.

Deed of Trust

Deed of trust a document that conveys title to a trustee who holds it to secure payment of the amount that the buyer owes on the purchase price

In many states, the typical real estate security document involves three parties and is based on the law of trusts. Instead of executing a mortgage, the borrower transfers title to a trustee by a **deed of trust.** The important difference between a mortgage and a deed of trust is that in a trust, legal title to the real estate passes to the trustee.

The trustee holds the property for the benefit of both the borrower and the lender. When the debt secured by the deed of trust is repaid, the trustee returns title to the borrower.

Power of sale provision a clause authorizing the sale of a security if a debt is in default

The trustee may sell the property if the borrower fails to pay or breaches some other condition of the loan agreement. The **power of sale provision** makes foreclosure unnecessary (although the trustee usually can choose that procedure). Because foreclosure can be avoided, applying the security to a defaulted debt is more rapid and economical than going to court. Lawyers in states where the deed of trust is common argue that the ability to sell the security efficiently is the deed of trust's major advantage over the mortgage.

An alternative to mortgages and deeds of trust is the **installment land contract**. In it, the buyer contracts to pay for the property over a period of time. The seller keeps title to the property until the purchase price is paid. The buyer takes possession of the property and collects rents and profits. Installment land contracts in some states are

Installment land contract a contract for the sale of real property in which buyer pays in installments and seller retains title until the debt is paid

FIGURE 38-3   New York Statutory Mortgage Form M

Mortgage

This mortgage, made the .... day of .... , nineteen hundred and .... , between .... , (insert residence) the mortgagor, and .... (insert residence), the mortgagee.

     Witnesseth, that to secure the payment of an indebtedness in the sum of ...... dollars, lawful money of the United States, to be paid on the .... day of .... , nineteen hundred and .... , with interest thereon to be computed from .... , at the rate of .... per centum per annum, and to be paid .... , according to a certain bond or obligation bearing even date herewith, the mortgagor hereby mortgages to the mortgagee (description).

And the mortgagor covenants with the mortgagee as follows:

1. That the mortgagor will pay the indebtedness as hereinbefore provided.

2. That the mortgagor will keep the buildings on the premises insured against loss by fire for the benefit of the mortgagee; that he will assign and deliver the policies to the mortgagee; and that he will reimburse the mortgagee for any premiums paid for insurance made by the mortgagee on the mortgagor's default in so insuring the buildings or in so assigning and delivering the policies.

3. That no building on the premises shall be removed or demolished without the consent of the mortgagee.

4. That the whole of said principal sum and interest shall become due at the option of the mortgagee: after default in the payment of any installment of principal or of interest for .... days; or after default in the payment of any tax, water rate or assessment for .... days after notice and demand; or after default after notice and demand either in assigning and delivering the policies insuring the buildings against loss by fire or in reimbursing the mortgagee for premiums paid on such insurance, as hereinbefore provided; or after default upon request in furnishing a statement of the amount due on the mortgage and whether any offsets or defenses exist against the mortgage debt, as hereinafter provided.

5. That the holder of this mortgage, in any action to foreclose it, shall be entitled to the appointment of a receiver.

6. That the mortgagor will pay all taxes, assessments or water rates, and in default thereof, the mortgagee may pay the same.

7. That the mortgagor within .... days upon request in person or within ..... days upon request by mail will furnish a written statement duly acknowledged of the amount due on this mortgage and whether any offsets or defenses exist against the mortgage debt.

8. That notice and demand or request may be in writing and may be served in person or by mail.

9. That the mortgagor warrants the title to the premises.

In witness whereof this mortgage has been duly executed by the mortgagor.

In presence of:

_____

regulated by statutes designed to protect buyers. These statutes often treat the installment contract as if it were a mortgage. For example, a common provision requires the seller to have the property sold if the buyer defaults, even though the seller has kept title to the property.

FORECLOSURE

Foreclosure, as we have noted, happens when a lender who has advanced funds with real property as security recovers in the event of default. A foreclosure may result in the sale of the property, with the sale price applied to the debt. Any money left after paying the expenses of the sale and the debt is turned over to the borrower. If the sale does not bring enough to pay the debt, in most states the lender can sue for the rest.

Judicial Foreclosure

In the United States foreclosure generally is accomplished by a judicial decree ordering the mortgaged real estate sold to pay the debt. This process is known as *judicial foreclosure* and is what most people have in mind when they use the term "foreclosure." Judicial foreclosure requires a complicated, expensive legal action. Because the procedure results in a court order, due process and the procedural requirements of litigation designed to protect the parties are necessary. In getting the court order and selling the property, the lender must strictly obey the law.

Power of Sale Foreclosure

The legal complications, expense, and delays of judicial foreclosure have encouraged people to find alternatives. Many mortgages allow a mortgagee or third party to sell the real estate without resorting to judicial foreclosure in case of default. The deed of trust also is usually enforced by a sale rather than a judicial order, because the deed gives the trustee the right to sell the security if the borrower defaults.

Statutes in most states provide some protection for the mortgagor whose property is subject to a power of sale foreclosure. These statutes require a public sale, that there be advance notice, usually by advertisement, and that the sale be fairly conducted to get the best price. Trustees are subject to the same statutory regulations in carrying out a power of sale provision. (Trustees also must obey an extensive body of law that regulates fiduciaries generally.)

Due-on-Sale Clause and Foreclosure

Due-on-sale clause a clause in a mortgage that

Many mortgages allow the lender to treat the unauthorized sale of the security as a default. The lender may demand payment of the entire debt if the property is sold. Originally these **due-on-sale clauses** were included in mortgages to provide the lender with an opportunity to evaluate the potential purchaser. As interest rates rose in the mid-1960s, financial institutions began to use the clause to escape from low-interest loans. The clause gave the lender a chance to negotiate a higher rate of interest or to declare the entire balance due and payable.

The following case is one of a number brought in state courts by borrowers arguing that the due-on-sale clause was unenforceable.

requires the borrower to pay the mortgage debt if the property is sold

Occidental Savings and Loan Association v. Venco Partnership

Supreme Court of Nebraska
293 N.W. 2d 843 (1980)

The Occidental Savings and Loan Association (Occidental) brought an action to foreclose a mortgage on property owned by Venco Partnership (Venco). The action was based on the mortgage's due-on-sale clause, which Venco claims is unenforceable because it unreasonably limits its ability to sell the property. Venco further argues that the clause should not be enforced because it violates public policy.

FACTS

Is the due-on-sale clause enforceable?

ISSUE

Yes. The court held that the due-on-sale clause does not unreasonably limit Venco's ability to sell its property. The clause merely speeds up payment of the debt.

DECISION

It is true that the possibility the debt will have to be paid sooner may make it harder for Venco to sell its property as it wishes, but this is not unlike the effect caused by zoning restrictions, building restrictions, or public improvements.

The court then held that a due-on-sale clause is not contrary to public policy. The clause allows a lender to adjust its mortgage loan portfolio in a rising market. This adjustment can be essential to the successful operation of a savings and loan association. The potential failure of savings and loans and the loss of their depositors' funds should be of no less concern to the courts than the inability of a property owner to transfer its mortgage when selling his or her property.

The controversy surrounding the enforcement of the due on sale clause shows how economic developments affect the law. During the 1970s, rapidly rising interest rates in the United States caught savings and loan associations in a financial crunch. They had many outstanding loans at low rates and were experiencing difficulty paying higher rates to depositors. They argued that they needed the due-on-sale clause to help bring their loans up to current market rates. At the same time, owners and real estate sellers contended that the enforcement of the due-on-sale clause depressed real estate sales, because the clause limited the buyer's ability to finance at low rates.

This controversy was further complicated because savings and loan associations are chartered by either state or federal governments. Federally chartered savings and loans are regulated by the Federal Home Loan Bank Board, state savings and loans by state law.

During the 1970s, as mentioned in the previous case, a number of states took the position that the due-on-sale clause could not be enforced because it limited the owner's ability to sell his or her real estate. The clause, they contended, was against public policy because it established a restraint on **alienation.** Federally chartered savings and loans countered by arguing that they were exempted from these state laws because they were regulated by a federal agency. In 1976, the Federal Home Loan Bank Board adopted a regulation providing that a federal savings and loan association had the power to include a due-on-sale clause in its loan instrument.

Alienation the act of selling property to another

The controversy between the Board's authority and state law was settled by a U.S. Supreme Court decision in 1982. In *Fidelity Federal Savings & Loan Association* v. *De La Cuesta* (102 S.Ct. 3014 [1982]), the Court stated that the federal regulation takes precedence over state law. The result of this decision is that in states like California, which had declared the due-on-sale clause a violation of public policy, state savings and loans cannot enforce the clause, but federal savings and loans can. In Nebraska, the jurisdiction involved in the principal case, both state and federal savings and loans may enforce a due-on-sale clause.

CONTROL OF LAND USE

An owner's rights in real property are not absolute. Often these rights are subject to restrictions imposed by government and private agreements. The most common type of public control of land use is zoning. Private agreements limiting land use are called *restrictive covenants.*

Restrictive Covenants

Restrictive covenant an agreement that limits the use of real property

Restrictive covenants are usually placed in a deed by the seller when conveying land to a buyer. The buyer, of course, must have agreed to accept these limitations. Restrictive covenants can be made part of a plan for the development of real property. They are included in the plot plan, which must be filed with the proper authorities.

In developing real property, restrictive covenants are used to ensure that property owners do not suffer a loss in property value because of a neighbor's activity. Restrictive covenants in a residential development might limit the use of land to single family homes or require houses to be more than some minimum square footage. Restrictive covenants also are used when someone sells part of his or her property to make sure that the buyer does not use the land in a way that the seller, who remains as a neighbor, objects to.

Restrictive covenants run with the land. The limitations do not depend on the continued ownership of the buyer who originally agreed to the restriction. In general, enforcement of restrictive covenants has not been favored by courts, because they interfere with the free transfer of property. For a restrictive covenant to run with the land, it must have been the intention of the original grantor and grantee, and the covenant must substantially affect the essential nature of the land.

Restrictive covenants may be ended in several ways. All concerned parties may agree in writing to the termination. This undertaking is difficult if the number involved is large. Covenants can also be terminated by condemnation or by not being enforced when they are violated. The longer violations of covenants are ignored, the less likely a court is to enforce them.

Zoning

Zoning is the division of an area, usually a municipality, into districts to control land use. Zoning ordinances regulate such things as the structure and design of buildings, lot size, and uses to which land may be put. Zoning laws are recent. The notion of comprehensive zoning was first approved by the U.S. Supreme Court in 1926.

Zoning the division of an area into districts to control land use

Although nuisance was the original basis for zoning regulations, today zoning is based on the states' **police power.** On the basis of this power, land use can be regulated to protect the health, safety, and welfare of the public. To be valid, zoning ordinances must not be unreasonable or arbitrary.

Police power the authority of the state to adopt laws that promote the public health, safety, and general welfare

Traditional zoning ordinances divide the municipality into districts for residential, commercial, and industrial uses. Over the years these basic zoning classifications have expanded considerably. As a result, many localities now have 15 to 20 or more zones. Because use within these zones is restricted, land use becomes inflexible. In response to criticism of the traditional zoning process, other techniques for controlling land use have developed since World War II.

Planned Unit Developments (PUDs) are an example of innovative use of the zoning power. In a PUD, zoning regulations are applied to an area larger than the traditional subdivision. The objective of a PUD is to permit mixed use of an area within a development while providing a maximum amount of land for open space. Various types of housing, such as townhouses, apartments, and single-family houses, are permitted within the same tract. Some zoning plans permit commercial as well as residential use. In addition, the plan provides for extensive open areas. A major advantage of the PUD is the flexibility it provides in planning for community growth.

These changes in zoning laws illustrate major changes in real property law since the 1960s. Other changes have been new forms of ownership such as condominiums and cooperatives, new financing and investing techniques, and limits on the rights of owners to use their property to interfere with the civil rights of others. In spite of changes, traditional legal concepts and terms remain important in the field.

SUMMARY

Adverse possession, eminent domain, and purchase are three methods of transferring title to real property. Adverse possession is based on a trespasser claiming title to land because of continuous occupancy for a period established by statute. Unless the rightful owner acts to remove the trespasser within the statutory period, often 20 years, the trespasser acquires title if certain other conditions exist. The claimant must show that possession was open and notorious, hostile, actual, and exclusive.

Eminent domain allows the government to acquire title to private property for public purposes, if the owner is adequately compensated.

Individuals generally get title to real property by purchase. Knowing the legal aspects of buying real property is important to people because substantial amounts of money are involved. In a real estate sale, negotiations usually lead to a contract. Once the contract is signed, the buyer has equitable title and may sue for specific performance if the seller refuses to transfer legal title. Then follows a period before the parties must perform. During this period, the buyer gets financing and examines the seller's title. At the closing, the buyer pays the purchase price and acquires legal title by a deed. Several types of deeds exist. The most common are the warranty deed, the bargain and sale deed, and the quitclaim deed.

Real property often is used as security for a debt. To finance a real estate purchase, buyers often borrow money and use the real estate as security. Financing involves a mortgage or deed of trust. It gives the lender a security interest in the real estate. The other document involved is a promissory note. If the debt is not paid, the lender can foreclose and have the property sold and the proceeds applied against the debt. The most common form of foreclosure is ordered by the courts. Another type of foreclosure is based on a power of sale granted in the mortgage.

The public and some sellers may want to control land use. Sellers can control land use with restrictive covenants in deeds. The state has the power to adopt laws that promote the public health, safety, and general welfare and may pass zoning laws. The extension of public control of land use through zoning has been one of several major developments in real property law during the past 25 years.

REVIEW PROBLEMS

1. Explain the difference between a warranty deed and a bargain and sale deed.

2. What is constructive notice? Explain how constructive notice is related to the operation of the recording statutes.

3. Compare and contrast the lien and title theories of mortgages.

4. What is the difference between a judicial foreclosure and a power of sale foreclosure? How are they similar?

5. List some of the uses of restrictive covenants.

6. Eva Corley, an heir of George Johns, sued the estate of her uncle, J. W. Johns, and beneficiaries under J.W.'s will. She sought to have title to 40 acres willed by J.W. to these beneficiaries invalidated. George Johns had deeded 40 acres to J.W. in 1924. The deed had been found in a trunk belonging to J.W. after his death in 1972. Corley alleged that the deed was invalid, because it had neither been delivered nor recorded. Discuss the validity of Corley's allegations.

7. In 1960, Glass borrowed money from the Veterans Administration (VA) to buy a home. The loan was secured by a mortgage. In 1962, Glass sold the property to Crane, who assumed the indebtedness of Glass. In 1964, Crane defaulted on the debt, and the property was foreclosed. When the property was sold, it did not

bring enough to pay the debt, and the VA sued Glass for the deficiency, amounting to $1,711.34 plus interest. Glass defended on grounds that the debt had been assumed by Crane. Was the VA successful? Discuss.

8. McNaughten's deed contained a restrictive covenant barring the use of the land for purposes such as a "bar, tavern, alehouse, or the like." McNaughten wants to open a restaurant that serves alcoholic beverages. Will he be prohibited from doing so by the restrictive covenant? Support your answer.

9. Fox bought a $90,000 home in a newly developed area. To finance the purchase, he borrowed $80,000 from Central Savings, executing the customary note and mortgage in Central's favor. Some time later a major highway was proposed for the area, and real estate values fell sharply. At about this time, Fox accepted a job in another state. Unable to sell the house or keep up payments, Fox defaulted on the loan. Central Savings then foreclosed. Discuss Fox's potential liability if the home sells at the foreclosure sale for $60,000, with $72,000 remaining on the debt.

10. Cordes, who died in 1946, owned a 420-acre farm in western Illinois. His will divided the farm between his sons, Isaac and James. James built a home on his portion. Isaac's portion contained the family residence. The easiest way to reach James's home was over a lane along the edge of a field belonging to Isaac. This lane was used until 1975, when Isaac died. Isaac's farm was sold to Von Schied, who blocked the lane. James contended that he had an easement by prescription over the land. Do you agree? Discuss.

11. General Motors wished to expand its Detroit plant. The economy of the area was depressed, and the city wanted to help GM get the properties necessary to expand. The city council used the power of eminent domain to acquire several pieces of property in the neighborhood. Local landowners who did not want the plant expanded tried to prevent the transfer of title to GM on grounds that the city did not have the right to acquire this land by eminent domain. Explain on what basis this argument might be made. Do you agree? Discuss.

12. In 1935, Malone gave an easement to his brother Ted. The easement allowed Ted to cross a corner of Malone's land so that Ted could make repairs to a windmill. The easement was recorded, but little use was made of it, and both parties forgot that it existed. In 1972, Malone sold the property to Cudy. Title was transferred by warranty deed. What warranty, if any, has Malone breached? Support your answer.

13. Dawes borrowed $15,000 from her friend Lipski. As security she gave him a mortgage on property that she owned. Lipski did not have the mortgage recorded. When Dawes defaulted on the loan, Lipski tried to foreclose. Dawes argued that he could not do so, because the mortgage was invalid for never having been recorded. Was Dawes correct? Support your answer.

14. Seaquist rented a farm to Bledsoe for 15 years. A lease was executed, but Bledsoe did not have it recorded. Bledsoe occupied the farm. Before the lease expired, Sequist sold the farm to Senska. After title had passed to Senska, he sued to oust Bledsoe from possession. Bledsoe based his defense on the unrecorded lease. Who wins? Support your answer.

15. Latimer borrowed $85,000 at 9½ percent from Wolverine Savings to buy a home. After living in it for four years, Latimer was transferred. During the four years, interest rates had increased rapidly. At the time that Latimer was transferred, they had reached 14½ percent. When Latimer talked with a real estate broker about selling his home, the broker told him that it would be easier to sell if the buyer could assume Latimer's mortgage and take advantage of the 9½ percent interest rate that Latimer was paying Wolverine. When Latimer mentioned this to Wolverine, he was told that his mortgage had a due on sale clause. The clause would make it possible for the bank to prevent the buyer from assuming Latimer's mortgage. Explain the due on sale clause to Latimer.

CHAPTER 39

Wills, Trusts, and Estates

CHAPTER OBJECTIVES

STATE INTESTACY LAWS

WILLS

Requirements for a Valid Will / Revocation of a Will

SPECIAL WILLS

ESTATE ADMINISTRATION

Probate of an Estate / Alternative Methods of Estate Administration

ESTATE PLANNING

Estate Planning and Taxation / Estate Planning and Trusts / Estate Planning and Joint Property / Estate Planning and Insurance / Estate Planning and Custodial Accounts

SUMMARY

REVIEW PROBLEMS

CHAPTER OBJECTIVES

After reading this chapter, you should be able to:

1. Describe the general provisions of state intestacy laws.

2. Identify testamentary capacity, testamentary intent, and statutory execution requirements in the making of a valid will.

3. List the basic steps in the administration of a person's estate.

4. Describe the uses of estate planning.

5. Review how taxation, trusts, joint property, insurance, and custodial accounts are relevant to estate plans.

In this chapter, we are concerned with the laws affecting the disposition of property when the owner of that property dies. The word *estate* means the interest a person has in property, both real property and personal property (see Chapter 28). Thus estate planning occurs during a person's life when he or she arranges for the future distribution of the estate. It is concerned with the distribution of a person's property not only after death but also during a person's lifetime.

This chapter first focuses on the state laws that govern the descent and distribution of a decedent's property. Those laws determine the people who are entitled to receive that property if the decedent did not make a valid will. But because a person may specify, with certain limitations, who shall inherit his or her property by making a valid will, the laws governing the making of a valid will are also examined. The chapter then briefly describes the process, known as **estate administration,** by which property is transferred from the decedent to those entitled to receive that property. Finally, some of the techniques used in estate planning — such as the creating of a trust or the transfer of property to children, parents, or a charity during a person's lifetime — are discussed.

Estate administration the process by which property is transferred from a decedent to those entitled to receive it

STATE INTESTACY LAWS

Intestacy laws laws that govern the distribution of property for people who have not made a valid will

Two sets of state laws govern the inheritance of property. The first set, which comes into effect if a person has not made a valid will, is known as the **intestacy laws.** The second set, which is effective for the **testate distribution** of property, applies when a person has made a valid *last will and testament*. Together these laws determine how a person's estate is to be transferred to those who are to inherit it.

There are significant differences in state inheritance laws, particularly as they relate to community property of married persons. Although no federal laws govern the inheritance of property (although federal tax laws certainly affect estate planning), a uniform law governing the descent and distribution of property has been drafted and submitted to various state legislatures for approval. This law, the Uniform Probate Code, would provide much greater uniformity among the state laws. But only a few states have yet adopted the Uniform Probate Code. Thus our discussion of intestacy laws focuses on the general provisions found in most state statutes.

State intestacy laws govern the handling of the decedent's real and personal property. Because real property descends to a person's **heirs** and personal property is distributed according to state statutes, these laws are generally referred to as **statutes of descent and distribution.**

The law of the state where the decedent's real estate is located determines the heirs to whom the real estate descends. Consequently, if an Indiana decedent owned a Michigan summer cottage, the statutory descent and distribution laws of Michigan determine who inherits that real estate. But because the decedent's personal property is distributed according to the laws of the state where the decedent was **domiciled** — had a legal residence — the furniture in that summer cottage is distributed according to the Indiana descent and distribution statutes.

As a general rule, state intestacy laws provide that a decedent's estate, both real and personal property, be shared by the surviving spouse and children. The spouse's share typically is from one third to one half, if there are children or other descendants of the decedent, such as grandchildren. If no children or grandchildren have survived the decedent, the surviving spouse usually takes the entire estate.

If children and grandchildren have survived the decedent, the question arises of how each is to share in the decedent's estate. If there is no surviving spouse, the entire estate usually is split among the children and grandchildren of the decedent. In determining the descendants' shares, generally the children of a deceased child take the share that that child would have inherited. This method of dividing property is known as *per stirpes* distribution.

Consider the following example. John Adams is married to Jane Adams, and they have three children, A, B, and C (see Figure 39-1). Child C, who died before John Adams, is not a surviving child. But his three children, G, H, and I, are descendants of John Adams. According to typical intestacy laws, John Adams's estate would be divided as follows:

1. A certain share to the surviving spouse, Jane Adams. Usually if more than one child survives the decedent, the spouse receives one third of John Adams's estate.

2. The remaining two thirds to be split in some way among the children and grandchildren *(lineal descendants)* of Adams. According to the *per stirpes* distribution, each surviving child receives an equal share, and the children of the child who did not survive take the share that child would have taken.

In our example, the remaining two thirds of John Adams's estate would be divided as follows:

1. One third of the remaining two thirds (two ninths) to Child A

2. One third of the remaining two thirds (two ninths) to Child B

3. The two ninths that would have gone to Child C instead is split equally among that child's children (Adams's grandchildren) so that G, H, and I

Testate distribution laws that govern the distribution of property of a person who has made a valid last will and testament

Heir a person who receives property of a person who dies without leaving a will

Statutes of descent and distribution laws that provide for the descent of real property and the distribution of personal property

Domicile a person's permanent legal residence

***Per stirpes* distribution** property divided so that each branch or line of a decedent's family shares equally, regardless of the number of recipients

FIGURE 39-1   Per Stirpes Distribution of Estate of John Adams through Intestacy Laws

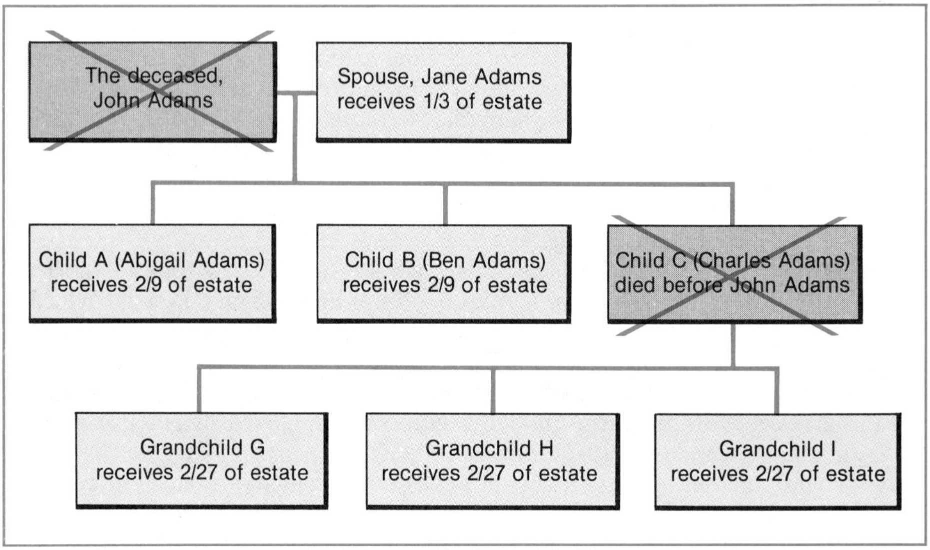

each receive one third of the two ninths share, or two twenty-sevenths of John Adams's estate.

Per capita distribution property divided so that each person who is to receive a share of a decedent's estate receives a like share to the other persons in the same generation

Another method by which property is distributed is on a ***per capita*** basis. Each descendant who is to receive a share of the estate receives a similar amount. Usually the per capita distribution system is used for people of the same generation. Thus it would probably not be used in dividing Adams's property among his children and grandchildren, but it might be used for dividing property among all grandchildren. Assume that neither Adams's spouse nor any children survived him and that there are six grandchildren who survived Adam and Adam's three children, A, B and C. Let's also assume that D and E are children of A, F is a child of B, and G, H, and I are children of C. If the grandchildren shared according to a *per stirpes* distribution, their shares would be different from those in a *per capita* distribution, as Table 39-1 indicates:

TABLE 39-1

	Per Stirpes	Per Capita
Grandchild		
D	⅙ share (½ of A's ⅓)	⅙ share
E	⅙ share (½ of A's ⅓)	⅙ share
F	⅓ share (all of B's ⅓)	⅙ share
G	⅑ share (⅓ of C's ⅓)	⅙ share
H	⅑ share (⅓ of C's ⅓)	⅙ share
I	⅑ share (⅓ of C's ⅓)	⅙ share

In most states, if the decedent leaves neither a spouse nor descendants, the estate is divided among the decedent's parents, if living (known as *ascendants*), and surviving brothers and sisters. In other states, one or more parents may take the entire estate. If there are no people in these categories, the estate usually is distributed to nephews and nieces, because they are blood relatives of the decedent. Most statutes of descent and distribution make no provision for relatives by marriage. The spouse of a child, brother, or parent who is not a blood relative of the decedent usually takes no share of a decedent's estate. Similarly, stepchildren, unless they have been legally adopted, are usually excluded as heirs, because they are not blood relatives. Adopted children generally are regarded as children and heirs of a decedent.

Finally, if there are no descendants, ascendants, or other relatives of the decedent, the intestacy laws provide that the property goes to the state. This provision, known as **escheat,** is rarely applied.

Interpretation of the intestacy laws is shown in the *Warpool* case.

Escheat the passing of property to the state from a person who dies without leaving any close relatives

Warpool v. Flood

Supreme Court of Tennessee
524 S.W.2d 247 (1975)

FACTS

The decedent had one full brother and sister, both of whom died before him. The sister left no children, but the brother had one child who is a full nephew of the decedent. The decedent, who was never married, had no wife or children. His parents died before him. His father had ten children by a previous marriage. All of those children died before the decedent, but some 28 children of those children — nephews, and nieces of the half-brothers and sisters — survive the decedent.

The decedent left no will. The intestacy laws governing the distribution of the decedent's personal property provide that if there is neither a spouse, children, father, or mother of the decedent, then the estate goes "to brothers and sisters, or to the children of such brothers and sisters, representing them, equally."

ISSUE

Do the children of half-brothers and half-sisters of a decedent who died intestate take an equal share of his personal property with the child of a brother or sister of the whole blood.

DECISION

Yes. The court explained that in an earlier case, it had decided that half-brothers and half-sisters shared equally with full brothers and sisters in the personal property of a decedent's estate. The laws that compute the degree of kinship do not distinguish between half blood and whole blood. The court noted that some distinctions between half-blood and whole-blood relatives are made in the laws regarding the descent of real property of a decedent. The legislature was aware of the court's decision in the earlier case, a decision which did not distinguish between whole- and half-blood relatives for the purpose of inheriting personal property.

Further, because the legislature had expressed a clear intent to distinguish the rights of half-blood from those of whole-blood relatives for real property, had it intended to do so for personal property, it would have so provided in the intestacy laws. Because it did not do so, the legislature must have intended to allow the half-brothers and half-sisters to share equally with full brothers and sisters in the distribution of personal property. Their children, taking by representation, also are entitled to share in the distribution of such property.

WILLS

Will a written declaration stating its maker's desires as to the disposition of his or her property after death

As we have seen, if a person does not make a **will** expressing his or her own desires regarding the distribution of property at death, the state intestacy laws determine who inherits the property and how it is divided. Thus the basic reason for preparing a will is to establish one's own plan rather than accept distribution by the state. A will also is used to ensure that persons of one's choice will care for and look after one's children and estate. The naming of a guardian for minor children and of a personal representative for one's property accomplish this purpose. Gifts to charities or the creation of trusts to split the use of property among several people also can be accomplished by a will. Finally, a will usually makes possible the settlement of an estate with a minimum of delay and expense. Accordingly, it is sound business practice for a person to prepare a will and to review its provisions periodically throughout his or her lifetime.

Requirements for a Valid Will

Personal representative the person named by the maker of a will who is to administer and distribute the estate of the decedent

The requirements for a valid will are established by statute. The statutory requirements of the state where a person lives or is a legal resident at the time of death must be met to dispose of personal property by a will. The statutes of the state where a person's real property is located must be complied with to dispose of it by a will. In that statutes vary from state to state, the person who drafts a will must be familiar with the law of the state where the will is to be effective. If the statutory requirements are not complied with, the will usually is not valid, and the person's property passes according to the intestacy laws.

Probate the process by which a will is legally approved as valid and through which the estate is administered until all of the decedent's property has been distributed

Terminology   A will is a written declaration stating its maker's desires about the disposition of his or her property or estate after death. The person making a will is called a *testator* if male and a *testatrix* if female. In this chapter, the term *testator* refers to both a testator and a testatrix. The person named by the testator to look after and administer the estate of the decedent is referred to as the *executor, administrator,* or **personal representative.** This chapter uses the term *personal representative.* Finally, the term **probate** refers to the process by which the will is legally approved as valid and through which the estate is administered until all its property is distributed. If a will is found to be invalid, it is denied probate. In that case, it has no legal effect and does not control the distribution of the testator's estate. Review the effect of the court's decision in the *Pasieka* case below as it relates to the determination of the validity of a will.

Kenney v. Pasieka

Appellate Court of Illinois
260 N.E.2d 766 (1970)

The testator, Frank Pasieka, left a share of his estate to the children of "Frank   FACTS
Pasieka." The decedent, one of his cousins, and a nephew all had that name. The
testator was twice married and left surviving him his second wife and a son by his first
marriage, Ted Pasieka. Ted died after the making of the will in question but before the
death of his father. During his lifetime, the testator took into his home two boys,
Walter and Joseph, both of whom changed their last name to his and lived with him as
sons. Walter never married and has no children. Joseph is married and is the father of
three children, one of whom was named Frank Pasieka.

The decedent's will gave all of his real estate to his son, Ted, for life and provided that,
upon Ted's death, the real estate would become part of the residue of his (Frank's)
estate and would pass "one third thereof to the children of Frank Pasieka; one third to
the children of Joseph Pasieka; and one third to the children of Walter Pasieka." There is
no dispute as to the one third share to the children of Joseph Pasieka, because they do
exist and are entitled to that portion. The difficulty arises in determining which "Frank
Pasieka" the testator intended and what happens to the property given to the children
of Walter Pasieka, because he has no children.

If some provisions of a will are unclear, does some of the property of the decedent   ISSUE
pass to those who would inherit if there were no will?

Yes. The court held that although the presumption is always against intestacy, either   DECISION
in whole or part, a court cannot add provisions to a will in place of those that a testator
has omitted. In interpreting a will, the guiding principle is the intention of the testator.
The question for a court is not what the testator meant to say by the language used, but
what he meant by what he did say. Here the court concluded that it could not
determine what the testator intended for the two thirds of the decedent's estate which
was to go to the children of Frank Pasieka and to the children of Walter Pasieka. Thus
those shares are to be distributed intestate, as if there were no valid will of the testator.

General Requirements   For a will to be valid in most states, it must meet three
requirements. First, the person making the will must have proper testamentary
capacity. A person's capacity to make valid contracts was discussed in Chapter 9. The
testamentary capacity required by inheritance laws, while similar to contractual
capacity, differs from it in several important respects. Second, testamentary intent is
required to make a valid will. The testator must clearly intend that the document
offered will be effective to transfer the property at his or her death. Thus, if a person
intends to transfer property during his lifetime and writes a statement giving stock,
jewelry, or personal property to another, that statement cannot be a will. It does not
indicate the intent to transfer the property effective only with the testator's death.
Third, the testator must comply with the laws on the execution or signing of the will.
Certain formalities in writing, signing, and witnessing a will must be complied with

for the will to be valid. If these requirements are not strictly adhered to, the proposed will is not valid.

Testamentary Capacity   Testamentary capacity requires two elements. The person making a will must be a certain age (usually 18) before signing the will. A person who has not attained that age cannot leave property to another by a will.

Second, the testator must be of "sound mind." The test of a "sound mind" is expressed by courts in different terms, but usually it requires that the testator be aware of three different matters. The testator must know who are the "natural objects of his or her bounty." Usually these "objects" are the testator's family, but they also may be close friends for whom the testator has special concerns. Next the testator must realize the kind and extent of property that he or she proposes to distribute by the will. Finally, the testator must be able to plan for the disposition of that property.

Each of these requirements generally is reviewed in cases where someone's testamentary capacity is questioned. Less mental capacity usually is considered necessary to make a valid will than to manage business affairs or enter into contracts. A person may be feeble, aged, or of low intelligence and still have the required testamentary capacity. In the *Lockwood* case, the court is asked to determine whether a **codicil** (an addition to or alteration of an existing will) is valid. The claim is that it is not valid because Mrs. Lockwood lacked testamentary capacity when she signed the codicil.

Codicil an addition to or alteration of an existing will

Matter of Estate of Lockwood

**California Court of Appeals
62 Cal. Rptr. 230 (1967)**

FACTS   Lockwood executed a will in 1958; there is no question as to its validity. Four days before her death in 1964, at age 89, a codicil was executed. At that time, the decedent was very ill. During these days, Mrs. Lockwood, overcome both physically and mentally by the extremities of age and her many physical ailments, could not communicate with her nurses and old friends. Often, if not continuously, she was in a semi-coma and could not be roused. The codicil revoked her will. The will gave her entire estate to the Rolfes, close friends for many years, who had rendered personal services to her at various times. It substituted a gift of $5,000 to May Delaney and gave the remainder of her estate to her heirs at law, Alan, Audris, and Sharon Swanson, who are appellants here.

ISSUE   Does the evidence show that Mrs. Lockwood was not mentally competent at the time she executed the codicil?

DECISION   Yes. The court held that the decedent, weakened by age, illness, and disease, lacked testamentary capacity at the time she executed the codicil to her will. The court determined testamentary capacity at the time she executed the codicil to her will. The court determined testamentary capacity by examining: 1. whether the decedent had enough mental capacity to understand the nature of her act when she executed the codicil; 2. whether she could remember and understand her relations to the persons who have a claim upon her bounty and whose interests are affected by the provisions of the instrument.

Finally, once it is shown that a person lacked testamentary capacity and that it is caused by a mental disorder of a general and continuous nature, the inference is reasonable that the incompetency continued to exist.

Testamentary Intent   The person making a will must

1. intend to transfer the property and

2. intend that the transfer occur only upon his or her death.

Thus a document that does not clearly show the testator's intent to transfer property is lacking in testamentary intent. Suppose that I have a valuable diamond ring in an envelope and write on the envelope "This ring is for my sister, Susan Sleaford." If the other requirements for a valid will are met, would this document indicate my intent to transfer the property and to have the property transferred at my death?

A second problem with finding proper testamentary intent relates to influences on the testator that may replace his or her intent with that of another. Chapter 8 discussed several problems related to the *genuine assent* required for entering into valid contracts. Similar problems can occur with a testamentary document such as a will. Did fraud, duress, undue influence, or mistake distort the testator's true intent? Although each of these enemies of genuine assent or of valid testamentary intent can make a will invalid, most problems with testamentary intent concern undue influence: Did someone so influence the testator that he or she planned to give away property contrary to what he or she would have done had he or she followed his or her own judgment? The following case concerns this problem of testamentary intent.

_____ *Matter of Estate of Franco* _____

California Court of Appeals
122 Cal. Rptr. 661 (1975)

Caterina Armario contested the last will and testament of her deceased brother, FACTS Carlo Franco. During his life, Carlo was quite close to his sisters and his other relatives. He was a trusting person who was easily influenced by others. Carlo was survived by Caterina, his brother John, and his sister Rosetta Vasella. John, who presumably had the intention of making Carlo upset with Caterina, instigated an incident whereby Carlo did in fact become very angry with Caterina. After this incident, John and his wife took Carlo to John's attorney where Carlo executed his will. With the exception of a $300 gift to Caterina, the will gave all of Carlo's estate to John Franco's two sons to be divided equally between them. John was named executor of the estate. Caterina contends that the will was obtained by undue influence. Under California law, five standards are examined to determine if a will was made under undue influence. These standards reveal whether:

1. the provisions of the will were unnatural

2. the gifts in the will differed from the intentions of the decedent, expressed both before and after its execution

3. the relations between the chief beneficiaries and the decedent gave the beneficiaries a chance to control the act of making the will

4. the decedent's mental and physical condition allowed someone to subvert his freedom of will

5. the chief beneficiaries under the will were active in getting the will executed.

ISSUE   Based on the application of these standards to Carlo Franco's will, had he made it under undue influence?

DECISION   Yes. The court's findings in this case were that Carlo's will was made with undue influence because: 1) the decedent suddenly left almost his entire estate to two nephews he had only seen on five or six occasions during his lifetime even though he had for many years been close to his sister Caterina and to other relatives; 2) before Carlo made his will, he never had expressed a desire to make one. He had told his sister that she would inherit much of his property. 3) After he made this will, he had become disenchanted with his nephews and had expressed a desire to change it; 4) the decedent's mental maturity was that of a 14- to 16-year-old boy, and there was testimony that he was bashful and trusted anyone who was friendly to him; 5) circumstantial evidence allows for the inference that John Franco schemed to have his brother Carlo leave the bulk of his estate to John's two sons and that John and his wife were aware of the scheme and actively participated in Carlo's execution of the will.

Execution of a Will   Most states require that a will be written, signed, and witnessed. A written document is usually required, although some states allow oral wills. A will may be written on a paper bag, a scrap of paper, or a piece of wallpaper. It can be typed or written in ink or crayon. No particular language is required, so long as the testator's intentions can be determined.

A will must be signed by the testator. In some states, statutes specify that the signature be at the end of the will to assure that no pages were later added to the document that was signed. In most states, the statute specifies only that the will be signed but does not state where the signature is to appear.

Similarly, each state by statute and court decision indicates the type of signature that will be effective. Use of nicknames ("Junior"), marks ("X"), or other designations ("Mom") usually are acceptable. As long as testators have indicated by some mark or sign on the document that they approve and intend it to dispose of property at their death, the signature is valid. A person who is unable to sign his or her name or make a mark usually may have another person, at the testator's request and in his or her presence, place the testator's signature on the document.

Finally, a will must be witnessed to be valid. Most states require two witnesses, but a few require three. Witnesses verify that the testator actually signed the document and that, according to the witnesses, he or she had the required testamentary intent and capacity at that time. A witness does not have to read the will to witness it.

Some states require that the witnesses actually see the testator sign the document.

Others require only that the testator in some way acknowledge to the witnesses that the signature is his or hers. Some states also require that the witnesses sign their names to the document in the presence of the testator and in the presence of the other witnesses. The statutes also may require that the witnesses be told that the paper they are signing is a will.

The witnesses to a will usually need not be of a specific age as long as they can understand that they are witnessing a signature. If a witness is an interested person who is to receive some property by the will, some statutes require an additional witness to verify the testator's signature or limit the witness's legacy to the amount he or she would have received had there been no valid will.

Although other requirements may be imposed by some statutes, the writing, signing, and witnessing of the will usually are the only formalities that must be met to make a valid will. The will does not have to be prepared by an attorney, although preparation of a simple will by an attorney is usually not very costly. The will does not usually have to be notarized, although a notary can be a witness. The will does not have to be filed in a specific place in the county of a person's residence or handed over to an attorney. Each of those alternatives exists by statute in some states, but usually they are not requirements. Whoever has the will of a person at the time that person dies is required by law to file it with a court (usually the probate court). Once the will or wills of a person are on file, admission to probate and the validation of the document as the last will and testament of the decedent can be sought.

Revocation of a Will

Because a will is without legal effect until the testator dies, a testator may revoke a will at any time before death. A person usually revokes a will when he or she wants to make a different distribution of the estate. The new will generally includes a clause stating that all earlier wills made by the testator are revoked. In other situations, the testator simply tears up or burns an existing will, leaving property to be distributed under the intestacy laws.

If a person executes a new will or a codicil but does not state that the new revokes the old, the law generally presumes that the intent was to revoke the old will if the new one is totally inconsistent with it. If the new will and the old will are not totally inconsistent, both are read together.

If a person who has written a will changes his or her marital status, some state statutes provide that the will is automatically revoked. In some states, a divorce revokes only that part of a will providing for the former spouse. State statutes usually provide that a person cannot totally disinherit a spouse. Thus a marriage after a will may not totally revoke the will. Instead, the surviving spouse is allowed to take a share of the testator's estate (often one third), even if no provision for the spouse is made in the will.

The birth of a child usually does not revoke a will, but most states provide that a child born after a will has been executed is to receive that portion of the estate that the child would have received had no will been made. But if it appears from the terms of a will that a person does not want that child (or other children who were born before execution of the will) to inherit property, the testator's intentions are honored.

Statutes usually do not provide for a forced share for surviving children in the same way they provide for a surviving spouse.

SPECIAL WILLS

Nuncupative will an oral will made before witnesses

Several special kinds of wills exist. Two of these, the nuncupative will and the holographic will, do not have to meet the same requirements as other wills to be considered valid. The **nuncupative will** is an oral will made before witnesses. Unlike most wills, it need not be in writing. This type of will, valid only in a few states, may be made only when its maker is in a last illness. Even then, there are frequently limitations on the amount and kind of property that may be disposed of under the will.

Holographic will a will written and signed entirely in the handwriting of the person making it

The **holographic will** is a written will, but it is not witnessed. It must be entirely in the handwriting of the testator. Each statutory requirement for holographic wills must be met or a document is not considered valid. For example, if some of the document is printed or typed, it generally is regarded as ineffective and not in compliance with the statutory requirements.

Finally, we note four other special wills. Sometimes a husband and wife want to make similar wills. Although most attorneys advise that each make and sign a separate will, the will of one may be considered the will of the other. Such a will is known as a joint will. Both parties must sign a joint will. The document is first considered for probate when the first party dies and later is considered again when the second party dies. Mutual or reciprocal wills are separate instruments of two or more parties. The wills have reciprocal terms, with each testator giving some property to the other. Because the documents are separate, only one document is considered for probate on the death of one of the testators. But because one party's will was at least in part prepared with the will of another party in mind, the making of reciprocal wills may prohibit the revision of the will of the party who is not the first to die. For this reason, attorneys generally advise clients not to prepare joint or reciprocal wills. They may lose the flexibility to revise their will.

The *statutory will* is prepared on a special document form and witnessed. Statutory wills only recently have been enacted into law in a number of states. They give people will forms to select when they do not want to consult an attorney. In essence, the will is prepackaged. Some states have several different forms, and a person must select from among these. The statutory will must be witnessed to be eligible for probate.

Pour-over will a will that is drafted so that property disposed of by the will pours over into a trust and is managed and governed by its terms

A **pour-over will** is a will which generally is drafted in coordination with a trust agreement. The will, of course, does not take effect until after the death of its maker, but the trust agreement is made effective during that person's lifetime. The trust agreement states how the trustee is to manage property during the person's lifetime and what property is to be added to the trust after the person's death. The pour-over will then is used to transfer to the trustee the property in question after the person's death. Because the trust agreement already has detailed how the property is to be managed and disposed of, the will does not include such provisions in detail. Instead, the property that passes through the will is "poured over" to the existing trust, and its terms then control the disposition of property received. Some people use the pour-over will and trust agreement for privacy, because the will is a matter of public record, but the trust agreement is not.

ESTATE ADMINISTRATION

Whether or not a decedent has made a valid will, there still must be some method by which the decedent's property can be collected, debts and taxes paid, and the estate distributed among those entitled to receive it. The rules and procedures for administering a decedent's estate determine what happens to the property from the moment of the decedent's death until the property and title to it are distributed.

Probate of an Estate

Estates usually are administered according to statutory law and rules of procedure developed and overseen by probate courts.

The first step in the administration, or probate, of a decedent's estate is to determine if the decedent had a valid will. If there is a will, the will should contain the name of the person who the decedent wanted to be responsible for administering the estate — the *personal representative.* If there is no will, one of the decedent's heirs, usually a surviving spouse or child, asks the probate court to be named the personal representative. The court usually appoints such a close heir as personal representative, although in some states the person appointed to administer the estate must live within the state where the court being petitioned is located.

If there is a will, the will must be admitted to probate before it is considered valid. People interested in the will or in the decedent's estate must be notified that there is a petition to admit the will to probate. At the court hearing, proof that the will was executed according to the statutory requirements is given. If anyone questions the execution of the will or either the testamentary intent or the capacity of the decedent, a will contest may develop. In extraordinary cases, such as occurred when billionaire Howard Hughes died, the will contests may take years to resolve. In the usual case, the hearing of the court to probate the will and appoint the personal representative (whether there is a will or not) is simple, uncontested, and quick. If more than one person seeks to be the personal representative, statutory provisions giving preference to close relatives have to be consulted and interpreted by the court.

Once the personal representative has been appointed, the actual administration of the estate begins. Creditors of the decedent are notified, usually by publication in a local newspaper, that they must present their claims against the estate of the decedent within a specified time period (generally six months or less). A monetary award for the support of a surviving spouse while the estate is being administered is then made. The temporary support or allowance paid to the spouse generally takes precedence over all other claims.

Next the personal representative must inventory all the assets in the estate and establish the value of the property. If there are enough assets, the funeral and burial expenses, expenses of the decedent's last illness, estate administration costs, and debts of the decedent then are paid.

Taxes that may be due the state or the federal government must be determined and paid. Estate taxes due to the federal government are assessed against the estate based on its value. Sizable exemptions from the estate taxes, particularly for gifts from spouse to spouse, recently were incorporated in the estate tax laws. For this reason, most estates today do not have significant estate tax liability.

Inheritance taxes due to the state government are assessed on the property received from the decedent. The amount of tax depends not only on the value of the property received but also on the relationship between the decedent and the inheritor. The closer the relationship, the lower the rate of inheritance tax. These taxes are due from the living recipient. But because the testator may have provided by will that the estate was to pay the inheritance tax, it can become liable for this tax. In any event, the taxing authorities can make sure that their taxes are paid before the title to any property is transferred from the estate.

After all administration expenses, taxes, and valid claims or debts have been paid, the personal representative furnishes an accounting to the court and, once it is approved, distributes the remaining property and money to the beneficiaries.

Alternative Methods of Estate Administration

Statutes in a number of states provide several alternatives to administering an estate through the probate procedure. A very simple procedure often may be used for small estates with no unusual amounts or types of property. Often these estates are exempt from the normal probate procedures. Other statutes provide for a probate procedure that can be used if the persons interested in the estate have no objections to it. In this procedure, the beneficiaries and heirs of the decedent are allowed to administer the estate independently with only minimal review by probate court authorities.

Finally, a number of estate planning techniques may minimize the need for estate administration under the probate court. Trusts, life insurance policies, custodial accounts, and joint tenancy agreements are often used. These techniques are discussed in the following pages.

ESTATE PLANNING

Estate planning
the process of
planning for the
future distribution
of a person's estate

Estate planning is the process of planning for the future distribution of a person's estate. The distribution of property during a person's life as well as after death may be planned to meet various objectives. An estate plan cannot simply be chosen and forgotten about. It requires periodic revision as a person's assets increase, marital status changes, and expenses such as those related to rearing and educating children or caring for elderly parents change.

Generally, the primary goal of estate planning is to make sure that the testator's property is distributed to those he or she wants to provide for, when, and in the portion, and how the testator wishes. The estate plan also seeks to minimize the taxes and fees that must be paid from the estate. Paying high taxes not only would interfere with the primary goal but also could force the sale of valuable property, such as a business, that the testator may prefer to pass along intact.

Estate Planning and Taxation

The desire to avoid or minimize taxes due at one's death should not be the primary purpose of estate planning. A person's estate plan should seek instead to meet objectives regarding the distribution of the estate and the care and support of those who are to benefit from it. Only after the objectives of the plan have been determined and the means for attaining them have been examined should attention be focused on the taxation of the estate.

Several taxes affect an estate plan. The two most important are usually the federal estate tax and the state inheritance tax. Both must be paid before the decedent's property may be transferred to heirs or named beneficiaries.

Income taxes also must be paid from the estate for income received by the decedent prior to death. If the estate receives income while it is being administered, further income taxes may be due. One other aspect of income taxation is usually of concern to the estate planner. Because the federal income tax levies a higher rate at higher income levels, splitting the income between two people generally lowers taxes. For example, a person in the 33 percent tax bracket who receives $5,000 annually in stock dividends would owe $1,667 in taxes on that income (omitting any credit or deduction calculation). But if that stock were given to others (such as children or a trust) who were in a 15 percent tax bracket, the tax liability ($750) on that same property would be significantly less.

Trust a legal relationship in which one person, a trustee, holds title to property which he or she manages for the benefit of another, who is either the beneficiary or the trustee

Inter vivos **trust** a trust established by an agreement or deed that takes effect during the lifetime of the person creating it

Estate Planning and Trusts

Under a **trust**, a person has legal title to property but must use that property for the benefit of other people (the beneficiaries). The person who is given legal title to the property (the trustee) is generally instructed how the property is to be used in a written document referred to as a *trust agreement* or *trust deed*. If a person enters into a trust agreement and transfers property to someone else while living, the trust is referred to as a living or *inter vivos* **trust**. If the trust is established by the terms of a person's will, it is referred to as a **testamentary trust**.

A person who creates a living trust (the settlor) may want to retain the power to change the trust agreement to name a new trustee or totally revoke the trust. This type of living trust is a **revocable trust** and, because the creator of the trust can change it, the property in trust usually is taxed as part of the estate of its creator. But because the property has been transferred during the settlor's lifetime, it would not be property that is transferred at the settlor's death. Accordingly, the assets in the trust usually are not subject to probate on the settlor's death.

If a person creates an **irrevocable trust** during his or her lifetime, the property in the trust is legally owned by the trustee. The trust, not the person who created it, must pay taxes on income earned by the trust property. If the settlor of the trust dies after having transferred property to the trustee, generally no estate taxes are assessed against that property, and no probate fees are due for its administration, because the property is not in the estate of the decedent. But the trustee usually charges management fees from the date the trust is established. Most major banks have trust departments staffed by people who provide professional service to the property that the bank holds as trustee.

A testamentary trust found in a will is not effective until the death of the testator. The testamentary trust can be revoked or modified at any time during its creator's lifetime. Because the trust assets are in the control of the testator until death, the trust actually is created by transfer from the executor or personal representative of the decedent's estate to the person named as trustee. In many cases, the creator of a testamentary trust names a bank to act both as the personal representative of the

Testamentary trust a trust established by a person's will and that takes effect on the death of the person creating it

Revocable trust a trust that allows the person creating it to make changes in the terms of the trust; property in a revocable trust is considered property of its creator

Irrevocable trust a trust that is created during a person's life but which cannot be changed by its creator; property in an irrevocable trust is considered to be owned by the trustee

estate and as trustee of the trust. Its powers and directions are those specified by the will creating the trust (as well as some statutory and common law provisions).

One of the benefits of a trust is that it provides for professional property management by the trustee instead of by the person for whom the property is to be used. Another benefit is that the income from property can be given to one person for a limited time (ten years, twenty years, or a lifetime) with instructions that after that time another person is to become owner of the property. In this way, a trust can "skip" a generation, and the person in the skipped generation, who never owned the property, would not have that property subject to estate taxes or property fees at his or her death.

In the following example, George's children are the skipped generation. George Smith has $500,000 that he wants to give to his children and grandchildren. Because George's children are adults and have good jobs and reasonable incomes, George, by means of a trust, will primarily provide for his grandchildren. Assume that George has two children, Alice and Bill, and that each of them has two children. George then has four grandchildren. His *inter vivos* trust agreement would:

1. Give $500,000 to the First National Bank as trustee of the George Smith Trust

2. Provide that the income from the trust be paid annually in equal amounts to his children, Alice and Bill

3. Provide that on the death of either Alice or Bill, their share of the trust (one half for each) be kept in trust for the benefit of their children (grandchildren 1, 2, 3, and 4) until the youngest grandchild attains age 30 and then given to the grandchildren as their own property. (If one of the grandchildren dies before attaining age 30, that share could go to that grandchild's brothers or sisters. If both grandchildren of the same parent die before reaching age 30, their shares would go to the surviving grandchildren.)

Review the *Estate of Hart* case to see how one court interpreted an *inter vivos* irrevocable trust agreement.

Connecticut Bank & Trust Company (Estate of Hart) v. *Hills*

Supreme Court of Connecticut
254 A.2d 453 (1969)

FACTS   The plaintiff, Connecticut Bank & Trust Company, is the trustee of an irrevocable, inter vivos trust established by Helen Hart in 1949. The trustee brought this action to determine if the term "descendant" used in the trust agreement included an adopted son of one of the trust beneficiaries. Income from the trust was paid to the decedent's relatives, Charles and Thomas Hills, until 1966, when Charles Hills died. Charles Hills had no children of his own, but his wife had a son, William, born of an earlier marriage, whom Charles had adopted in 1936. William claims that a trust's use of words such as "descendant" or "issue" include an adopted child when:

1. the adoption took place before the execution of the instrument to be interpreted

2. the testator or settlor regarded the adopted person as the son or daughter of the adoptive parent

3. the testator or settlor never expressed opposition to the adoption.

Is an adopted son a descendant of his father, so that he is entitled to receive his father's share of the income of a trust established by one of his relatives?

No. The court held that there was nothing to indicate that the settlor of the trust, Miss Hart, used the word "descendants" in other than its primary sense and that when so used that term would not include an adopted child such as William. The word "descendant," in its ordinary and primary meaning, connotes lineal relationship by blood. If the settlor had used the term "child" or "children," an adoptive child would ordinarily be entitled to receive the parent's share. Miss Hart was an educated woman, and there is much justification for the conclusion that if she had intended to include William, she would not have chosen the term "descendant," which generally includes only those who have a lineal blood relationship with the primary beneficiaries of the trust.

Estate Planning and Joint Property

Joint property is used in estate planning to transfer property from one person to another by an agreement made during a person's life. Thus joint property is usually not in the probate estate of the first of the two persons to die. That property has been transferred by agreement prior to that person's death to the second person. However, at least some part of the joint property is usually a part of the *taxable* estate of the first person to die.

There are several ways in which the ownership of property may be shared by two or more people. The first method is to establish the two or more persons as **joint tenants** with **rights of survivorship.** The second is to establish them as joint **tenants in common.** The first method is probably the more common. Most states have statutes that provide that bank accounts or securities held in two names usually are held as joint tenants with the right of survivorship. For example, Tom and Jane have a $1,000 savings account in their joint names. If Tom dies before Jane, the $1,000 is owned by Jane. It is not transferred to her by Tom's will nor by the intestacy laws but by the agreement they made while they were both alive.

If Tom and Jane instead hold the savings accounts as tenants in common, both of them own one half, or $500. When Tom dies, $500 is transferred by his will or by the intestacy laws to his heirs or beneficiaries. Thus Jane would still have her $500, but the $500 owned by Tom might be transferred to her or to someone else.

If Tom and Jane are husband and wife, their joint property is sometimes referred to as being owned by them as **tenants by the entirety.** This term is for joint tenants who are spouses and who want the survivor to inherit all their jointly held property.

There are both benefits and drawbacks to holding property jointly. Because both parties have access to the total property, either may use it. One party might withdraw a whole bank account and use it. Although such flexibility is desirable as long as the

Joint tenancy co-ownership in which the interest of a deceased co-owner passes automatically to surviving owners

Right of survivorship the characteristic of a joint tenancy by which the surviving owners obtain the interest of the deceased co-owner

Tenancy in common co-ownership in which each owner possesses an individual fractional interest in real property but each owner's rights are the same as those possessed by a single owner

Tenancy by the entirety co-ownership of real property by husband and wife

parties are amiable, if they are not amiable, this type of ownership may create problems for their joint use of property. Because joint property often is used by husband and wife, another drawback arises over how that property is to be treated if they divorce or one dies. Here it is the estate and income tax laws that cause the problems. Let us look at two possible problem situations.

If two parties own property together and one party dies, the taxing authorities generally presume that the decedent owned the property, and its value is considered part of that person's estate. When the property passes to the surviving party, and that party dies, the property is then included in the estate of that person and is thus subject to double taxation.

A second problem occurs because the property is potentially an asset of both parties. Suppose that a couple jointly owns two automobiles. If either one is involved in an accident, and someone wants to sue for an injury caused by a driver of that automobile, all of the driver's property, both that jointly owned and the property owned solely by the driver, might be awarded to the injured party. But if a person owns one car and the spouse owns another car, neither of them is liable for injuries caused by the driver of a car he or she does not own.

Several advantages are derived from the ownership of property either as joint tenants with rights of survivorship or as tenants by the entirety. Because both parties have access to the entire property during their lives together, one person does not have to get another's consent to use the property. A joint bank account may be signed by either party, a convenience that is desirable in many situations. Second, because the property automatically passes upon the death of the first of the parties to the party who survives, the property is not a part of the probate estate of the first party. The second party usually has quicker access to such property, and no probate fees are due for the administration of the property. Finally, although estate taxes can be a problem for some parties who hold property jointly, the size of estate tax exemptions and the marital deductions allowed for transfers between spouses often mean that estate taxes are not a problem in many estate plans. Joint property does have a viable role in the estate plan of many people.

Estate Planning and Insurance

Life insurance can be used in a variety of ways in estate planning. Ownership of an insurance policy may be established in such a way that the proceeds from the policy at the insured's death are not subject to federal estate taxes. Life insurance usually is not subject to probate expenses, because the benefits stem from the policy and not from any provision in a will or the intestacy laws. In many states, some of the proceeds from insurance policies on the decedent's life also are exempt from state inheritance taxes.

Life insurance is thus often used to provide security for the average person. A variety of policies — whole life, term, endowment, annuity — is available to serve different needs and desires. People who have significant assets in a business often use insurance as a means for transferring those assets to the surviving business associates. The business owns the insurance policy on the partner or key employee, and on that person's death the proceeds from the policy are used by the surviving business associates to purchase the decedent's share and to compensate the estate of the deceased for the decedent's ownership interest in the business.

Estate Planning and Custodial Accounts

The estate tax laws allow one to transfer during one's lifetime a $10,000 gift each year to a single donee or recipient. Thus if George Smith has three children, he can give each of them $10,000 each year ($30,000 total), and the gift does not affect the estate tax or inheritance tax that might be due if that money were transferred at the person's death. Gifts in these amounts can be made during one's lifetime without the donor incurring any tax liability.

If the recipient or donee is a minor, the gift must be given to someone in trust for the child. One of the most common ways to give such gifts is to establish a custodial account. The donor can be the custodian or may name another person as custodian. When the property is transferred from the donor to the custodian, usually the property is no longer in the donor's estate (there can be some tax problems with a transfer from the donor to himself as custodian). If the donor dies, that property is not subject to taxes, either estate or inheritance, or to fees assessed for probate administration. When the property is held for a minor child at least 14 years of age, the income received from the property is subject to income tax assessed on the child and not on the donor or custodian. If the child has little other property, the income may not total enough to subject the child to income taxes.

A custodial account established for a minor child thus allows the donor to remove property from his or her estate, possibly saving estate and inheritance taxes. Furthermore, because the property is owned by the custodian for the child, the income tax liability has been shifted from the donor to the child, and that probably decreases or eliminates some income tax liability. Note that recent tax law changes provide that no shifting of income tax liability occurs if a parent establishes a custodial account and transfers property to it for a child under the age of 14. However, a grandparent or other relative who transfers property to a young child's account will still be able to shift income tax liability on income earned by the property. Probate fees also are saved if the property otherwise would be a part of the donor's estate.

It must be realized, though, that the transfer of property to a custodian for a child legally transfers the ownership of that property to the child. The custodian cannot use it for his or her own benefit. It must be used for the child. Further, once the child attains the age of majority, the balance of the account must be turned over to the child. The control of the property is then in the child's hands, not the donor's. However, if the donor wishes to establish a fund for the child's expenses (such as for a college education) and is willing to use the fund for the child while the child is a minor and to transfer it to the child when he or she attains the age of majority, the custodial account can be a useful tool in the donor's estate plan.

SUMMARY

The laws that affect the disposition of property when a person dies include laws for testate and intestate distribution of property. Testate distribution occurs when a person has made a valid will. Intestacy laws control when no valid will is found. Intestate laws of the place where real estate is located provide for the descent of such property to a person's heirs. Personal property generally is distributed to close relatives. A person inheriting property from one who died might share the inheritance on a *per stirpes* basis or on a *per capita* basis.

To make a valid will, a person must meet three general requirements. The person must have testamentary capacity and testamentary intent, and the formalities of having a written, signed, and witnessed will must be generally complied with. A number of special wills serve special purposes or need not meet all of these requirements. They include the nuncupative and holographic wills.

Estate administration is the management of a decedent's property from the time of the admission of the estate to probate until all property is distributed to heirs and beneficiaries. The probate of an estate is the most common method for its administration, but alternatives to probate exist.

Estate planning is the process of planning for the future distribution of a person's estate. The distribution of property may occur both during the person's life and after death. Estate planning frequently involves tax planning for both federal estate and income taxes. Trusts, which give the legal title to property to one person to hold and use and distribute for the benefit of others, are common parts of estate plans. The joint ownership of property, purchase of insurance, and establishing of custodial accounts also are methods for owning and distributing estate property.

REVIEW PROBLEMS

1. Which basic laws govern the inheritance of property?

2. Which requirements must be met for a will to be valid?

3. What does the term *probate* mean?

4. Is there more to estate planning than the drafting of a valid will? Explain.

5. Birkeland died in 1972. In 1970, he had a document stated to be a will drafted by an attorney. However, contrary to the attorney's instructions, he did not sign it in the attorney's office. He had it sent to him, and he signed it alone. Then, on separate occasions, it was witnessed by two witnesses. Birkeland did not tell either witness that the document was a will, and neither saw him sign his name. One witness said that Birkeland had already signed it, and the other said that he didn't recall if there was any other signature on it. The state statute requires that a will:

   1 □ be signed by the testator

   2 □ be signed in the presence of two attesting witnesses and

   3 □ be acknowledged by the testator to the witnesses as the testator's will.

   Is this will validly executed? Explain.

6. A father wrote a letter to his son containing the following language:

I want to inform you that I bequeathed to you by my last Will the farm in Converville, Virginia, after my wife's death and my own death. I have the Will in my safe here, and it nullifies the one which is in the bank. Be sure and keep this letter.

The son says that the letter is a valid holographic will. The state statute says that a will totally in the handwriting of the testator and signed by him or her can be given effect even if it is not witnessed. Does the letter constitute a will? Can it revoke an earlier will?

7. The decedent executed a will approximately one year before death. In the will, she expressly excluded her husband because "he is financially well off" and her daughter because "she is financially well off and has not visited me for many years." The decedent was 82 when she died. Toward the end of her life, she expressed hostility toward her husband and voiced delusions about his attempts to poison her (which the facts show he did not do). The husband claims that the decedent was unduly influenced by her son, who:

   1 □ took his mother to a lawyer's office to arrange for her to make a will

   2 □ asked the family doctor to witness his mother's will but, when the doctor refused unless the mother were examined by a psychiatrist, declined to take his mother to a psychiatrist

   3 □ was with his mother in the lawyer's office when she conferred about the will and also when she signed it.

   Do these facts constitute undue influence sufficient to set aside the will? Explain.

8. The decedent executed a valid will. Later he remarried but did not execute any other will or codicil. By state statute, the decedent's remarriage after the execution of his will revoked that portion of the will that bequeathed property to his first wife. The decedent's wife at the time of his death (his second wife) claimed that, because the state statute revokes a portion of the decedent's will, it also revokes his choice in that will of his personal representative. She claimed that, as his wife, she should be appointed his personal representative. Do you agree? Explain.

9. Swanson, the decedent, was a legal resident in Georgia at the time of her death. She had executed a will in Georgia. It named an administrator of her estate and disposed of all the property she owned, including some land in Florida. The decedent's stepdaughters, who were beneficiaries under an earlier will, sued in Florida, challenging the decedent's capacity to make a valid will disposing of her Florida property. Can the state of Florida apply its laws to determine the capacity of a Georgia resident to transfer by will her ownership of Florida land?

10. The Hunts, a married couple, were both admitted to a nursing home on June 4, 1979. A few days later, Mrs. Hunt died. Mr. Hunt, who was terminally ill with cancer, was hospitalized on July 5, 1979. Two days later, on July 7, he executed a will. He died the next day, July 8, 1979. Mr. Hunt had been taking a variety of

medications since his cancer had been discovered in October 1978. He had pain medicine available to him every four hours, if needed. He had taken the medicine several times on the day he executed his will. Usually after taking this medicine, Mr. Hunt was incoherent for several hours. Mr. Hunt's doctor saw him several times on the day he died. He testified that at 9:00 A.M. Mr. Hunt was very ill but that by noon he had improved. When he saw him at 5:00 P.M., one hour before the will was signed, he was sitting up in a chair. Did Mr. Hunt have the testamentary capacity needed to make a valid will?

11. Bass died in March 1975, leaving a will dated May 2, 1974, in which he gave all his property to the local Baptist Church, to the exclusion of his wife. His widow objected to the probate of his will, claiming that he lacked testamentary capacity due to his use of drugs and alcohol. The testator had been a heavy drinker for several years and was known in the community as a habitual drunkard. Does the testimony on Bass's alcoholism prove that he lacked testamentary capacity to make a valid will?

12. Grace LaTray died in Montana in January 1978, at the age of 79. Her husband had died the previous year. At the time of her death, she was serving as the representative of his estate. During the last several years of her life, Grace had been chronically ill. She suffered from a number of physical ailments and was receiving medication for several of them at the time of her death. She had suffered a severe stroke, which had paralyzed her left side, about six months before her death. She executed her will while she was in the hospital room. It was witnessed by her attorney, a family member, and a hospital nurse. Does the evidence of decedent's physical infirmities, coupled with her use of many drugs, indicate that she lacked the testamentary capacity needed to execute a valid will?

13. Ritcheson died in July 1971, in Arkansas. In January of that year, he asked his close friend, Peevy, to help him make his will. But Peevy refused and suggested that Ritcheson see a lawyer. In March 1971, Ritcheson was involved in an automobile accident. He remained in poor health from that time until his death. Ritcheson went to Peevy about a week before his death and asked Peevy to call his attorney so that he could have his will made. Ritcheson made some notes on a yellow legal pad for the proposed will. Since the lawyer could not be located that day, Ritcheson left the yellow pad of notes with Peevy. These notes were never again found. A week later, Peevy found Ritcheson dead at his home. On the table beside him, Peevy found a note, entirely in Ritcheson's handwriting, which claimed to dispose of all of Ritcheson's property. In fact, the note did not dispose of some of Ritcheson's property. The note was not signed at the end, nor was it dated. But it did include the decedent's name in the body of the note. Does the document qualify as a holographic will?

14. Ruth Evans claims that her father's will is valid. Other relatives assert that it is not, because Ruth used undue influence over her father. Ruth did arrange for her father to make a will, found an attorney, and accompanied him to the attorney's office for its signing. But the attorney testified that she did not participate in any discussion regarding the terms of the will. The father was found to have acted "senile" at times, but he was also referred to as "stubborn." He insisted on driving his own car and managing some of his own affairs. He confided in his

daughter Ruth and frequently followed her suggestions on things he should do. Should the will of Ruth Evans's father be voided due to her undue influence?

15. Bechtold was adjudged a mental incompetent in a 1973 court proceeding. His sister, Alice Williams, was then appointed his guardian and served in that capacity until his death in 1976. In 1974, Walter executed a last will and testament leaving his entire estate to his sister. No court proceeding was ever held to change Walter's incompetency status to mentally competent. Is Walter's 1974 will valid?

PART VI

GOVERNMENT REGULATION

CHAPTER 40

Insurance

CHAPTER OBJECTIVES

KINDS OF INSURANCE

Life Insurance / Endowment and Annuity Contracts / Accident and Health Insurance / Disability Insurance / Casualty and Fire Insurance / Liability Insurance / No Fault Insurance / Credit Insurance / Title Insurance / Business Interruption Insurance

NATURE OF INSURANCE CONTRACTS

Offer and Acceptance / Insurable Interest / Premiums

DEFENSES OF THE INSURER

Concealment / Misrepresentation / Warranties

INTERPRETATION OF INSURANCE CONTRACTS

Waiver, Estoppel, and Unconscionability / Performance and Termination

INSURANCE FIRMS

Forms of Organization / Brokers and Agents

SUMMARY

REVIEW PROBLEMS

CHAPTER OBJECTIVES

After reading this chapter, you should be able to:

1. Describe the essential characteristics of the basic kinds of insurance.
2. Define such terms as *cash surrender value* and *self* insurance.
3. Explain the general nature of the insurance contract.
4. List the defenses that insurance companies may raise.
5. Discuss how insurance companies are organized.
6. Recognize some of the limits the law imposes on the insurer's right to terminate an insurance contract.

Insurer the person or company who agrees to compensate the insured or the beneficiary for losses caused by specific events

Insured a person whose life or property is insured

Beneficiary a person designated to receive property or money from an insurance company

The term **insurance** is used to refer to a variety of contracts, each of which involves an **insurer** who agrees to pay a sum of money or to give something of value to another person, the **insured** or the **beneficiary,** upon the happening of a contingency or fortuitous event which is beyond the control of the contracting parties. Insurance sales and contracts are regulated by state law pursuant to the terms of the McCarran Act, a federal law enacted in 1945.

Thus each state has its own statutes and administrative regulations. These establish the standards which both domestic and other insurance companies must meet to do business in the state. Most of the state laws are concerned with the solvency of the firms which can be incorporated or licensed in the state. Other provisions specify the conditions under which insurance agents and brokers may be licensed to conduct business.

Because the insurance relationship arises from a contract of insurance between the insurer and the insured, insurance law is best viewed as a part of contract law. Thus the concepts of offer, acceptance, and the other rules relating to contracts generally apply to the insurance contract. Of course, special terms, conditions, and practices affect insurance contracts. This chapter highlights some of these.

KINDS OF INSURANCE

There are many kinds of insurance, and the list that follows is not necessarily comprehensive. The list below refers to the insurance agreements which most often affect private individuals and businesspeople.

Life Insurance

In a **life insurance policy,** the insurer agrees to pay a specific sum of money upon the death of the insured, provided that the fees (premiums) to keep the policy in force have been paid. When the insured person dies, the insurer pays the money to the person designated by the insured, the beneficiary or, if no such person is named, to the estate of the insured. As long as the insured is alive, he or she generally retains the right to change the beneficiary on the insurance policy.

There are several different types of life insurance policies.

Ordinary Life Policies   Ordinary life insurance generally requires the insured to pay premiums throughout his or her life. In addition to the death benefit, the ordinary life policy gives the insured the right to borrow against the policy during his or her life. Thus this policy combines a form of investment or savings with the death benefits. The amount that may be borrowed is limited to the savings portion of the policy, referred to as its **cash surrender value.** As premiums are paid, the cash value generally increases.

Some life insurance policies require premium payments only for a limited period. A person also may fully prepay the premium due on a policy known as a *single premium life insurance policy.* Finally, if the insured cannot continue to pay premiums on an ordinary life insurance policy, he or she usually may convert the policy to an extended term insurance policy (described below) or to a smaller amount of ordinary life insurance.

Term Insurance   *Term insurance* is issued for a limited term. Beyond that term, which may be one or more years, it provides no further insurance for the insured or a named beneficiary. Term insurance is the least expensive form of insurance, because it grants no cash surrender value to the insured. That is, it provides protection but no savings. Some term insurance policies have provisions that allow their owners to convert them at some point to ordinary life or another form of insurance.

Term insurance is a popular alternative for people who want to separate the investment portion of ordinary life insurance from its death benefits or who cannot afford the equivalent protection provided by an ordinary life plan. Employers often provide term insurance to employees for the term of each individual employee's employment.

Universal Life   A *universal life* insurance policy combines the benefits of the term and the ordinary life insurance policies. Essentially, these policies give the insured an opportunity to receive increases in the cash value of the policy that vary with market conditions rather than a smaller company-guaranteed rate. Only that part of the premium necessary to back the death benefit is withheld from the investment program. The rest is available for cash value growth. Some policies also allow the insured to vary the premium and thereby vary the death benefit.

Life insurance policy an insurance policy under which the insurer agrees to pay a specific sum of money to a designated beneficiary on the death of the insured

Cash surrender value the amount of money a whole life insurance policy is worth if surrendered to the company before the death of the insured

Endowment and Annuity Contracts

Endowment and annuity contracts are somewhat like ordinary life insurance contracts. The endowment policy generally pays the insured a lump sum of money at a specified date. The annuity contract pays specific sums to the insured at periodic intervals after the insured reaches a specified age. These policies are often used to fund a child's education or provide additional security during a person's retirement years.

Although annuity contracts are not technically regarded as pure insurance agreements, they are similar to them and therefore are subject to regulation by the state insurance department. Under a fixed annuity, the insured or the beneficiary receives a set sum of money for a set term or for the life of the insured. A variable annuity obligates the insurer to pay a variable sum of money to the insured. The sum varies with the effects of inflation or returns on the insurance company's investments. The assumption is that investment return will parallel the cost of living and therefore that the varying payment will provide a stable amount of purchasing power.

Accident and Health Insurance

Accident and health insurance protects the insured against losses suffered from accidents or sickness. These policies provide for the payment of benefits or the reimbursement of specified expenses if the insured is ill or in an accident. Generally policy limits put a ceiling on the amount of benefits to be paid. Further, some health problems that are chronic or that predate the beginning of the term of a policy may not be covered by the terms of a health insurance policy or are not covered until after a waiting period. This type of insurance is also referred to as *medical insurance,* because it provides the insured with benefits for medical expenses, hospital fees, and doctor bills.

Many employers provide group based health or accident insurance to employees. In group insurance, the insurer offers one master contract for the employer. Its cost per person may be significantly lower than for similar individually based contracts. Many group policies base part of the premiums on the past record of claims from the group.

Disability Insurance

Disability insurance provides income to those who become too ill to continue working in their usual occupation. Generally, disability insurance does not completely replace a person's former income. Because disability insurance benefits are not taxed, as earned income is, usually an amount in disability benefits that is smaller than a person's earlier income generally allows the person to keep on meeting household and other living expenses.

Casualty and Fire Insurance

Casualty insurance protects the insured from loss due to the damage or destruction of personal property by causes other than fire or the elements. This type of insurance is frequently applied to loss or injury due to accident.

Fire insurance protects the policyholder who has insured real or personal property against a loss by fire. The terms of fire insurance policies are standardized by law, but additional coverage is generally available for other forms of damage or to benefit the insured in ways not provided by the standard policy.

Liability Insurance

Liability insurance provides the insured with money to cover losses awarded to others for which the insured has been held liable. The losses may be in the form of injuries to another person or to that person's property. Liability insurance is commonly carried by car owners and by people who own or lease real estate. A related type of insurance covers a professional person who could be held liable for injuries caused to his or her clients, patients, or students. The insurance company agrees to indemnify, or repay, the insured for the amount of his or her liability up to an amount specified in the policy. In many cases, a **deductible amount** first must be paid by the insured before the insurance company pays for the damages assessed against the insured.

Deductible amount a sum to be paid by an insured before an insurer will be liable for any loss suffered by the insured and covered under a policy

No Fault Insurance

No fault insurance is available in states that have laws to compensate victims of automobile or other motor vehicle accidents regardless of the fault or liability of the parties. Generally, the policy provides coverage to the insured, to members of his or her household, to authorized drivers, passengers, and pedestrians who are injured as a result of an accident involving an insured vehicle.

Credit Insurance

Credit insurance protects both the creditor and the debtor by providing for the payment of an indebtedness of the insured in the event of death before the indebtedness has been paid. It is most commonly used to cover a home mortgage or a debt due by a company that might be forced out of business to pay the creditor if a key officer or partner dies.

Title Insurance

Title insurance repays the insured for a loss arising from defects in the title to real estate. Title policies for homeowners generally are written to cover the purchase price of the property. Similar policies for the amount of a mortgage are written for the mortgagee's benefit. (Generally the mortgagee is a bank or other lender of money.) If the seller of the property does not provide a clear title to the property, the purchaser then not only has a right to recover damages from the seller but also from the title insurance company.

Business Interruption Insurance

A business interruption policy provides benefits to cover certain losses. These losses are caused by interruptions in business, such as strikes, property damage from fires or storms, or construction near the place of business that prevents customers from reaching it.

NATURE OF
INSURANCE CONTRACTS

Because insurance companies generally deal in volume and spread their covered risks among a pool of people, their contracts of necessity must be standardized. In fact, laws in many states require substantial standardization in policies covering the same risk for different people. For this reason, insurance contracts are not subject to the same bargaining between parties as are most other contracts.

Offer and Acceptance

Even though insurance agents often contact customers and try to sell insurance policies, by law it is the customer, not the insurance agent, who makes the offer. Thus the contract agreement is reached only after the company accepts the offer, not after the customer has signed approval of policy terms.

If a customer seeks health insurance, the company may condition its acceptance on the results of an up to date physical examination. If the physical examination reveals a history of disease or certain physical problems, the company may reject the offer. It may make a counteroffer and write a different or more expensive policy.

Many insurance problems relate to the authority of the agent to bind the company. If the customer signs an offer, may the agent sign and accept that offer on behalf of the company, or must someone else in the company's home office accept any offers made to the company? An agent generally has authority to bind the company that issues fire or casualty insurance by offering a *binder* that commits the company even before a person in the home office issues the actual policy. But that same agent does not have similar authority to bind the company to issue most life insurance policies.

Because the agent represents the company, the agent's statements affect the terms of the insurance contract. The *Phillips* case raises issues about the terms of an insurance policy.

Ranger Insurance Company v. Phillips

Arizona Court of Appeals
544 P.2d 250 (1976)

FACTS   Boyle was a passenger in a small plane that crashed in 1967. Boyle was killed. The plane was piloted by Bruner, a student pilot, who had logged only 70 hours of flight time, and was owned by Phillips. Ranger had issued a liability insurance policy to Phillips which contained a standard clause limiting those qualified to pilot the insured aircraft. The policy did not cover student pilots. Bruner had a note affixed to his student pilot's license that expressly prohibited him from carrying passengers. But Phillips proved that he told Ranger's agent that he wanted insurance coverage that covered student pilots. The agent assured Phillips and sent Phillips a handwritten note that such coverage would be provided. Later the company deleted the provision for student pilot coverage without informing Phillips. The actual policy was not delivered to Phillips until after the crash. The premiums paid for the insurance issued to Phillips did not reflect coverage for any student pilots.

Did the insurance agent's oral and written statements to Phillips commit the insurer to cover the accident involving the student pilot even if the written policy excluded that person as a covered pilot? ISSUE

Yes. The agent's statements did commit the insurance company. The statements on the student pilot's license did not control the insurance purchased by Phillips from the insurer. Even though Phillips did not pay a premium based on coverage for student pilots, that is what he wanted and what he thought he had received. He never received any notice to the contrary and did not have the policy itself when the accident occurred. Thus the agent's statement, not the written policy itself, represented the true insurance contract between the parties. Despite the provisions on pilot Bruner's license, it is proper for an insurance company to insure against certain risks, even if the risks violate the license provisions of the pilot or FAA regulations. DECISION

Insurable Interest

To eliminate gambling and immoral activities, the law allows only certain people to take out insurance against specific risks. If anyone could purchase a large life insurance policy on a stranger's life or on a stranger's personal property, people might be tempted to purchase such insurance and cause that death or property damage just to collect the insurance benefits. Thus the law requires a person to have an **insurable interest**, such that another person's loss or injury would cause a direct loss or injury to that person.

Insurable interest the right to insure against a loss of goods (or, in some cases, human life)

If you own property or even lease property, you have an insurable interest in it. Shareholders in a closely held corporation have such an interest in the property of the corporation. In life insurance, a close relative, business associate, or creditor of another has an insurable interest in the other person's life. For the purchase of life insurance, the insurable interest must exist at the time the policy is taken out. For other forms of insurance, the insurable interest must exist at the time of the loss.

An insured may take out a life insurance policy on his or her own life and assign the benefits due under the policy to any person, even if that person does not have an insurable interest in the insured's life. Fire and casualty insurance policies may be assigned only with the approval of the insurer.

The concept of an insurable interest is discussed in the following case.

Gendron v. Pawtucket Mutual Insurance Company

Supreme Court of Maine
384 A.2d 694 (1978)

On August 15, 1969, plaintiffs purchased from defendant an insurance policy, effective for three years and in the face amount of $32,000, insuring a gas station they FACTS owned against loss by fire. On December 8, 1971, a fire destroyed the service station. After the purchase of the insurance policy but before the fire, plaintiffs had leased the land and the gasoline service station building on it to the Shell Oil Company for 15 years. The lease provided that Shell would raze and remove the existing gas station within one year and that any new buildings it constructed would belong to Shell.

The lease also provided that Shell was obligated and exclusively entitled to insure the premises to their full insurable value and with loss payable to Shell, against loss by fire.

ISSUE   Did the lease from Grendon to Shell terminate Grendon's insurable interest in the property.

DECISION   No. The existence of an insured's insurable interest in property covered by a contract of insurance is determined by the relationship between the insured and the property insured — more specifically, by whether there is a relationship such that injury to the property will, as a natural consequence, result in a loss to the insured. The question of an insurable interest necessarily involved the insured's relationship to the property insured. Here, plaintiffs had not made an actual transfer of such of their rights in the insured property as would destroy their insurable interest. The mere leasing of property does not destroy its insurable interest. As long as the insured retains legal title to the property, he has an insurable interest in the property.

Premiums

Premiums (payments) for life insurance coverage are paid by the insured over long periods of time. Premiums for casualty, fire insurance, health, and accident insurance generally are paid over short periods. The premiums charged on a life insurance policy are based on mortality rates, guaranteed interest, and expenses.

The mortality rates are based on the experience of insurance companies in the past with rates of death. Premiums also reflect the rate of interest an insurance company can expect to earn on the money it receives in premiums and expenses such as medical examinations, commissions to the agents, and operating expenses.

The premiums charged for many kinds of business and casualty insurance are based primarily on the company's evaluation of the risks it is assuming. Rates charged for certain kinds of casualty and business insurance are regulated by state law. The regulating authority seeks to allow the company to charge rates that are high enough to provide it a reasonable return on its assets but low enough so that people and businesses can afford them.

DEFENSES OF THE INSURER

People who buy insurance may believe that the insurance contract is filled with fine print and that 1,001 defenses are asserted by companies for refusing to pay claims. In fact, in addition to the ordinary defenses used in contract cases, insurance companies use only three defenses to try to avoid paying an otherwise valid claim. The defenses which are commonly used by the insurer are concealment, misrepresentation and breach of warranty.

Concealment

Concealment is the intentional failure of an insured to disclose a material fact to the insurer that would affect the insurer's willingness to accept the risk. For example, if a driver fails to reveal convictions for drunken driving when applying for an automobile insurance policy, the driver has concealed. The essence of concealment is the intentional nondisclosure of a material fact. If an application specifically asks the applicant for information and the applicant provides false information, misrepresentation, not concealment, occurs.

Concealment the intentional failure of an insured to disclose a material fact that would affect the insurer's willingness to accept the risk

Misrepresentation

Misrepresentation occurs when a prospective insured intentionally or innocently misrepresents a material fact that leads an insurer to enter into an insurance contract. The misrepresentation may be oral or written. It may be made on the insurance application form or in written or oral statements made while discussing the insurance contract. A person who states that she is in perfect health when in fact she recently has been treated for a heart condition makes a misrepresentation.

Misrepresentation words or conduct that misleads others as to the material facts of a situation

Only a material misrepresentation provides an insurer with a defense. Further, if the insurer investigates and learns the truth before issuing the insurance policy, it is not relying on the representation made by the applicant. In that case, because the applicant's statement did not induce the insurer to enter into the contract (the insurer knew the statement to be false), the insurer would not have a valid defense to payment of the insurance benefits.

Finally, whether the misrepresentation be innocent or intentional, the insurer has a defense. The principal difference between the innocent and intentional misrepresentation concerns the effect of the misrepresentation on the remedy available to the insurer. The principal remedy available to the insurer is rescission but damages also are available if a misrepresentation is intentional. Rescission returns the parties to their places before making of the contract. Thus the insurer must return all unused premiums, and the insured is without insurance coverage.

To be effective, the insurer's rescission must be made as soon as the misrepresentation is discovered. Statutes generally require that life insurance contracts include an **incontestability clause.** Typically, this clause provides that after a set period (usually one or two years), the insurer may not contest the representations of the insured. One exception exists if a life insurance applicant misrepresents his or her age. Even if the two-year period of incontestability has passed, a contract provision usually limits the amount of benefits payable on the insured's death to the amount that the paid premiums would have bought for a person of the insured's actual age.

The following case illustrates the misrepresentation defense.

Incontestability clause a provision in an insurance policy providing that representations made by an insured may not be contested by the insurer after a set period of time

Smirlock Realty Corporation v. Title Guarantee Company

Court of Appeals of New York
418 N.E.2d 650 (1982)

FACTS   Smirlock Realty purchased property from the Bass Rock corporation. At the time of the purchase, Bass Rock knew that it soon would be entitled to some money from the city, which was condemning the adjoining property and the condemnation affected part of the Bass Rock property. In the contract between Smirlock and Bass Rock, Bass Rock agreed to turn over to Smirlock any proceeds from the condemnation of any of its property.

Smirlock then contracted with Title Guarantee to issue a title insurance policy for the property. Smirlock did not tell Title Guarantee that it knew that part of the property was being condemned, but the pending condemnation was a matter of public record. When Smirlock leased the property to a tenant who wanted to enlarge the warehouse on it, the tenant and Smirlock both discovered that the condemnation had affected more of their property than they thought. Smirlock then sued the title insurance company, which had insured his title to the property. The title policy contract contained a provision that any concealment or misrepresentation by the insured constituted grounds for the cancellation of the policy by the insurer.

ISSUE   Can the title insurance company cancel its policy because of Smirlock's failure to tell it about the condemnation?

DECISION   No. It is true that Smirlock's failure to tell the title insurance company of the condemnation proceeding constituted a misrepresentation of a material fact. But the title insurance company could not rely solely on Smirlock's knowledge regarding the condemnation's affect on his property, because it was a matter of public record.

Title insurance policies are not merely insurance contracts, but essentially warranties made by the insurer based on information available to that insurer. Here the information regarding the condemnation was a matter of public record and should have been known to the insurer. The misrepresentation clause in the insurance contract is there to protect the insurer against the insured's failure to give truthful information that would be available only or primarily to the insured. Because that type of information was not involved in this case, the failure to disclose the condemnation information by the insured is not ground for the insurer to cancel the policy.

Warranties

Warranty (2)
representations in
insurance contracts
which operate as
conditions that
must exist before
the policy is
effective

Warranties are important in insurance contracts because they concern representations within the insurance policy itself. These representations operate as conditions that must exist before the policy is effective or before the insurer's promise to pay benefits is enforceable. If the condition specified fails to occur, the insurer is not obligated to pay. A condition may express the limits of the insurer's liability. For example, a clause stating, "This automobile policy applies only to accidents occurring during the policy period while the automobile is within the United States, its territories, or Canada,'' specifies the time period and the locations of accidents that are and are not covered by the policy. Similarly, a liability policy may provide that:

> The insurer shall not be liable unless suit is brought within 12 months from the date of the occurrence of the loss or of the event giving rise to a claim.

Generally, the trend is away from allowing an insurer to avoid liability on a policy for any breach of a warranty made by the insured. Instead, as in the case of misrepresentation, a breach of warranty must be regarded as material to be given effect. Statutes in some states provide that all statements made by an applicant for life insurance be deemed representations and not warranties. Thus the materiality requirement must be met for the insurer's defense to be valid.

INTERPRETATION OF INSURANCE CONTRACTS

Waiver, Estoppel, and Unconscionability

Sometimes an insurer might assert a defense to paying a claim under the terms of the policy, but because of other factors may not use the defense. A **waiver** is the voluntary relinquishment of a known right, and actions by an insurance agent that waive on behalf of the company some factual concealment by the applicant exemplify the waiver.

Waiver the surrender of a claim, privilege, right, or opportunity

Estoppel, as we have noted in earlier chapters, is the prevention of a person from asserting a position that is inconsistent with his or her actions or conduct when those actions or conduct have been justifiably relied on by the other party. Thus a company that periodically accepts premium payments from an insured that are late by several weeks is estopped later from asserting a similar late payment of premiums as a defense against continuing the insurance coverage.

The concept of unconscionability also affects the defenses available to an insured. Unconscionability is the quality of being shocking to the conscience. As we noted in Chapter 10, when one party has little bargaining power and is faced with a standard contract that cannot be altered and that has been prepared by the other party, the courts may declare the contract or particular parts of it unconscionable and unenforceable.

Performance and Termination

As with contracts generally, most insurance contracts are performed according to their terms. The payment of premiums by the insured and the payment of benefits due by the insurer generally constitutes performance of the insurance contract. Performance terminates the obligations of both the insured and the insurer under the contract. A policy of insurance may also provide that the insurer has the option to cancel the policy after an insured event happens. If cancellation happens before the end of the effective date for which premiums have been paid, the unearned premiums must be returned by the insurer. Cancellation thus is another way of terminating the insurance contract. The *Spindle* case at the end of this section shows how a cancellation clause may be interpreted.

The nonperformance by one party of material terms of a contract generally excuses the other from performing. Clearly, nonpayment of premiums terminates any performance obligation of the insurer. But many insurance contracts have notice clauses that require the insured to notify the insurer within a specified time of a claim that the insurer is obligated to pay. If the insured does not give this notice, the obligation to perform by the insurer may be discharged or excused. But these notice provisions generally are not strictly enforced. Instead, a reasonable time requirement is imposed. Of course, because the notice provision allows the insurance company to begin its investigation of its liability in a timely manner, such provisions benefit the insurer and insured. In the *Milam* case, the court is faced with interpreting the notice provision found in an automobile policy.

Spindle v. Travelers Insurance Companies

California Court of Appeals
136 Cal. Rptr. 404 (1977)

FACTS   Dr. Spindle, a neurosurgeon, is a member of the Southern California Physicians' Council, a nonprofit association. In 1973, the Council issued a policy of malpractice insurance for Dr. Spindle. Dr. Spindle asserts that during the period of negotiation between the Council and the insurer, the insurer represented to the Council that if its members did not have excessive claims filed against them, the members' malpractice policies would be kept in full force and effect.

The insurer notified Dr. Spindle of its intention to cancel his malpractice insurance as of August 3, 1975. Dr. Spindle claims the act of cancellation was intended to coerce and intimidate other members of the Council in their dispute with the insurer over the allowable rate of premium increases.

The contract between the parties clearly provided that no provision restricted the rights of cancellation specified in the policies of insurance issued pursuant to it. Plaintiff's policy also provided for cancellation by the insured upon written notice and by the company upon 30 days' written notice.

ISSUE   Does public policy require that the legal principle of good faith and fair dealing between an insurer and its insured be extended to a limitation on an insurer's right to cancel malpractice insurance policies?

DECISION   Yes. Despite the absence of an expressed "public policy" in California law, it is clear that the right of insurers to cancel insurance policies is not absolute in this state. The Insurance Code limits the grounds upon which an automobile liability or collision policy and property loss policies may be canceled. This and other provisions reflect legislative policy limiting the "absolute" right of insurance policy cancellation.

There is an implied covenant of good faith and fair dealing in every contract. In an insurance contract which the insurer seeks to cancel, that covenant should be examined to determine if bad faith conduct by the insurer is the basis for the cancellation.

The deprivation to this insured of the benefit of his bargain is greater than average because of the lack of competition in the field of malpractice insurance. Plaintiff's amended complaint, therefore, states a cause of action against defendants.

State Farm Mutual Automobile Insurance Company v. Milam

United States District Court of West Virginia
438 F.Supp. 227 (1977)

Carlos Milam, Andrew's father, was the named insured on a policy of automobile liability insurance issued by State Farm Insurance Company. On June 17, 1973, Andrew, then 19 years old and a member of his father's household, was driving a 1971 Ford pickup truck owned by Jarrell when it veered off the highway, striking three pedestrians, killing one, and injuring the other two.

A West Virginia state police officer investigated. Milam had smoked five or six marijuana cigarettes approximately seven hours before the accident. Milam was arrested and charged with negligent homicide and driving while under the influence of drugs. He pleaded guilty to the negligent homicide charge and was sentenced to one year in jail and fined $100. In February 1974, a civil case was filed by one of the injured pedestrians against Andrew Milam as the driver of the car. At the trial, Mrs. Milam first learned that Andrew might have been covered under the insurance policy State Farm had with Carlos Milam. Mrs. Milam immediately telephoned State Farm's agent and informed him of the accident. The insurance policy has a standard clause requiring notice of an event on which a claim is based to be given to the insurer "as soon as practicable."

FACTS

Did the notice to State Farm given by Mrs. Milam comply with the policy's provisions?

ISSUE

Yes, if the notification was given within a reasonable time and the lack of notification did not prejudice the insurer, it is effective.

DECISION

The purpose of a notice provision in policies of automobile liability insurance is to give the insurer an opportunity to make a timely and adequate investigation of the circumstances surrounding the event which resulted in the claim being made against an insured. In order for the insurer to successfully avail itself of the "lack of notice" defense, it must show that it was prejudiced by it. State Farm's rights were not prejudiced by the delay in receiving notice of the June 17, 1973, accident. The West Virginia courts have interpreted the phrase "as soon as practicable" to mean "within a reasonable time, having regard to all of the circumstances."

The explanation or excuse of the Milams for not reporting the accident was that neither had any idea that Carlos Milam's State Farm policy would afford coverage to Andrew while the latter was driving the Jarrell vehicle. We think that as a result of that tendered explanation, the issue of the timeliness of the notice is one of fact. Considering all of the circumstances in this case, we find that notice was given "as soon as practicable."

INSURANCE FIRMS

Forms of Organization

Stock insurance company a corporation established to sell insurance for a profit

There are two major types of insurance organizations: stock companies and mutual companies. A **stock insurance company** is a corporation established to sell insurance for a profit. The corporation is organized like other businesses. It generally has a board of directors, officers, employees, and shareholders. The shareholders may receive corporate profits in the form of dividends declared by the corporation's board of directors. The shareholders are not necessarily customers of the corporation.

Mutual insurance company an insurance company owned by its policyholders

A **mutual insurance company** is owned by the policyholders. By purchasing insurance from the company, the policyholders obtain the right to elect the directors, and they in turn select the officers. Only policyholders may have an ownership interest in a mutual insurance company. A mutual insurance company does not have shareholders, and therefore it does not distribute any profit in the form of dividends.

Brokers and Agents

Because both an agent and a broker are agents of other parties in sales of insurance, you may find it helpful to review Chapter 26. Under the law of agency, an agent is someone who represents another person, the principal, and who is subject to control by the principal.

Insurance agent a person who, on behalf of an insurer, solicits insurance from third parties who become the insured

The **insurance agent** represents the insurance company, which acts as the principal in the selling of insurance to third persons. The insurance agent who contracts with an applicant for insurance does so on behalf of the principal and not in his or her own right. The agent for an insurance company must be appointed by the company he or she represents and must be licensed as a sales agent by the state. An independent agent represents more than one insurer and thus can select from those companies for the insurance needs of the insured.

Insurance broker a person who represents the insured and seeks appropriate policies to cover that person's risk

An **insurance broker** represents the buyer of insurance by placing an order with an insurance company on behalf of that buyer. The broker is the representative or agent for the insured and, like the insurance agent, generally is compensated through commissions paid by the insurance companies. Unlike an agent, the broker does not represent one insurance company but chooses the company to write policies for insured parties. The state licensing requirements imposed on brokers generally are higher than those on insurance agents. Some states allow only agents, not brokers, to write insurance within their boundaries.

SUMMARY

Insurance covers a great number of different types of contracts which distribute risk among a large number of people, the insured, through an insurance company, the insurer. The contracts made by the parties are regulated primarily by state law. The insurance relationship is based on a contract, and the concepts of offer, acceptance, consideration, genuine assent, and other rules which form the basis of contract law are applicable to the insurance contract. Beyond those contract rules, unique concepts such as the insurable interest requirement and the defenses of concealment, breach of warranty, and misrepresentation affect the terms and conditions of an insurance contract. Agents work for insurance companies, whether organized in the stock or mutual form. Brokers represent the insured party.

REVIEW PROBLEMS

1. Describe the primary features and typical uses for whole life insurance, term life insurance, and endowment or annuity life insurance.

2. What type of coverage is generally provided in a health insurance policy? How does a group health insurance policy differ from an individual policy?

3. Why are the rules of offer and acceptance especially important to insurance contracts?

4. Describe the insurer's defense of warranty. What is the significance of the incontestability clause in an insurance contract?

5. What are the essential differences between ordinary life insurance and term life insurance?

6. Why does the law require a person to have an insurable interest to buy life or property insurance on another person or on that person's property?

7. Explain how the insurer can use the defenses of concealment, misrepresentation, and breach of warranty against paying claims.

8. Compare and contrast the role and duties of an insurance agent and insurance broker.

9. Stockberger purchased automobile insurance from Meridian Mutual Insurance Company on several vehicles he owned. Stockberger then purchased an old pickup truck which was neither licensed nor operable. Several months later, in a conversation with Meridian's agent, Stockberger stated that he was repairing the pickup truck and that it would soon be ready to run. When he said that he would need insurance on it, the agent said that once the serial number was obtained, it could be added to the policy.

   The insurance contract on Stockberger's insured vehicles provided automatic coverage to added vehicles owned by the insured if the insured notified the company no later than 30 days after such vehicles were acquired by the insured and additional premiums, if any were due, were paid. Stockberger claims that his conversation with the agent several weeks before the vehicle was made operable, but several months after he acquired it constituted notice to the company and that his pickup truck was automatically insured as of that date because no additional premiums had to be paid to add that vehicle to his existing policy. Do you agree with Stockberger's interpretation of his insurance policy? Explain.

10. Kaplan's automobile insurance policy included liability coverage for damages arising out of the use of any car he owned or drove. Later Kaplan asked the insurance company to delete its liability coverage on the Chevrolet car he owned. While Kaplan was driving a car owned by Kock he was involved in an accident, severely injuring several people. When Kaplan sought to have his insurance company cover his liability for the injuries in that accident, it claimed that his earlier deletion of liability coverage on his Chevrolet, the only car he owned at that time, also deleted liability coverage for his driving another owner's car. Do you agree? Explain.

11. Armstrong purchased a fire insurance policy from the Travelers Insurance Co. The policy promised to pay the insured "the actual cash value" if the property being insured, a farmhouse, were totally destroyed by fire. After a fire destroyed Armstrong's farmhouse, Travelers asserted that the "actual cash value" as used in the policy meant the replacement cost of the farmhouse, less depreciation. Armstrong claimed that because the policy provided that it would indemnify him from loss, the actual cash value means the replacement cost, unaffected by depreciation. Who is correct?

12. Bryant had received property from her mother and had purchased fire insurance on it. Several relatives sued Bryant, claiming the deed from her mother was void because Bryant had exerted undue influence on her mother. Bryant agreed to reconvey title to her mother. A court order to that effect was signed. But before Bryant reconveyed the property, it was destroyed by fire. Bryant claimed that she was entitled to the insurance payments. The insurance company claimed that she did not have an insurable interest in the property at the time of the fire because she no longer owned it. Who wins and why?

13. Gulf Insurance wrote liability insurance for Macalco Incorporated on an airplane it owned and operated. The policy included a standard warranty clause that the insured would comply with all applicable regulations regarding the use of the plane. Insurance was thus provided only when the airplane was being operated by a certified pilot. Macalco's plane crashed and injured several passengers while piloted by a student pilot not certified to carry passengers. After the crash, both the FAA investigation and court testimony showed that pilot error had not caused the crash. Can the insurance company use the breach of its warranty clause by Macalco as a defense against paying? Why?

14. Stuart owned a houseboat and had liability coverage on it with Cincinnati Insurance Company. When he purchased another boat, he asked his wife to call the insurance company and get insurance on it. She called Cincinnati's agent and told him the value of the boat and that the motor, hull, and trailer were to be insured. Nothing was said about adding it to the existing insurance policy on the houseboat. He did, however, state that the company would insure the boat and that the details of the coverage would be discussed later. Several days later, the new boat was damaged. The Stuarts asserted that Cincinnati had issued an oral binder on the boat during the phone conversation and that its liability was based on the value of the new boat and the damage to it. The insurer claimed that because it had not yet worked out the details of the coverage and the premiums due from the Stuarts, no binder had in fact been issued. Further, it asserted, even if there had been a binder, the company's liability was limited to the terms stated

in the existing coverage on the houseboat and not to the full damage suffered on the new boat. Do you agree? Why?

15. In August, Mrs. Englert applied for automobile insurance with the American Family Insurance Company. A policy was issued effective August 9. On September 1, Mrs. Englert received notice that due to the poor driving record of her husband, who might drive the car being insured, her policy would be canceled effective September 16. After Mrs. Englert was involved in an accident on September 3, the insurer discovered that Mrs. Englert's application misrepresented her own and her husband's driving records. Has the insurer waived the right to cancel her policy effective August 9, instead of September 16? Explain.

CHAPTER 41

Fair Employment Practices

After reading this chapter, you should be able to:

1. Explain the federal statutes, executive orders, and administrative regulations that guarantee fairness in employment.

2. Describe the tools for implementing the goals of affirmative action programs.

3. Describe the criticisms of the statutes, regulations, and affirmative action programs.

4. Describe the competing interests involved in implementing affirmative action programs.

STATUTES AND REGULATIONS

Title VII of the 1964 Civil Rights Act

Basic to understanding fair employment practices law is Title VII of the 1964 Civil Rights Act, which was strengthened by the Equal Employment Opportunity Act of 1972. Title VII was enacted as part of a broad civil rights program dealing with discrimination in restaurants and hotels (public accommodations), educational institutions, and federal programs as well as employment. It was one congressional response to the civil rights movement and resulting strife of the 1950s and 1960s.

Title VII makes it unlawful for employers, unions, or employment agencies to make any decision concerning the employment or work status of an individual on the basis of race, sex, religion, or national origin. This prohibition covers private and public employers who have at least 15 employees. One of the few defenses available under Title VII is the bona fide occupational qualification (BFOQ). This provision allows an employer to hire and employ (or a union and employment agency to classify) on the basis of sex, religion, or national origin in limited circumstances when the sex, religion, or national origin of the individual is reasonably relevant to the employment. This defense or exception has been narrowly interpreted by the courts and is discussed more fully later. The BFOQ provision does *not* mention race. Discrimination on the basis of race, if proved, may not be justified by this exception.

Executive Order 11246

In 1965 President Johnson issued Executive Order 11246, and in 1968 President Nixon issued another executive order to amend and strengthen it. Order 11246 prohibits federal contractors who receive more than $10,000 from the federal gov-

TABLE 41.1 Summary of Civil Rights Statutes and Regulations

Statute or Regulation	Purpose
Title VII of the Civil Rights Act of 1964	Makes it unlawful for employers, unions, or employment agencies to make any decision concerning the employment or work status of an individual based on race, sex, religion, or national origin
Executive Order 11246	Prohibits contractors from discriminating against employees or applicants because of race, sex, religion, or national origin. Also requires affirmative action by employers to ensure that applicants are employed without regard to race, sex, religion, or national origin
Equal Pay Act of 1963	Prohibits unequal pay for equal work regardless of sex at managerial levels in state and local government as well as most private industries
National Labor Relations Act	Prohibits employers from refusing to engage in collective bargaining with a union selected by its employees
Age Discrimination in Employment Act of 1967	Prohibits discrimination in employment based on age for people between the ages 40–70

ernment from discriminating against any employee or applicant on the basis of race, sex, religion, or national origin. The executive order also requires employers to take *affirmative action* to ensure that applicants are employed and that employees are treated during employment without regard to their race, sex, religion, or national origin. Specifics of affirmative-action requirements are discussed later in the chapter.

Other Statutes

The Equal Pay Act   The Equal Pay Act of 1963 is an amendment to the Fair Labor Standards Act of 1938, the federal minimum wage and maximum hour law. Amendments to the Equal Pay Act in 1972 and 1974 broadened its coverage so that it mandates equal pay for equal work regardless of sex at professional and managerial levels, in state and local government, as well as in most private industries. The most difficult questions raised under the Equal Pay Act are determining whether male and female workers are actually doing substantially the same work and, if so, whether the difference in pay is based on a factor other than sex. In most instances, the nature of this inquiry demands case by case analysis.

The National Labor Relations Act   The National Labor Relations Act of 1936 deals specifically with the right of employees to engage in or to refrain from collective bargaining. Because once selected, a union becomes the exclusive bargaining representative of the employees, the union has a duty of fair representation. To enforce this duty, the National Labor Relations Board (NLRB) has held that failures of fair representation, including acts of racial and gender discrimination, are unfair labor practices and subject to the usual remedies. Since passage of the 1964 Civil Rights Act (Title VII), the use of this theory has been limited.

State and Local Law   Most states and many communities have their own fair employment practices laws and enforcement agencies that parallel the Title VII provisions. Title VII allows for, and in some instances mandates, **deferral** to these local agencies when the procedures are adequate and the responsibilities similar.

Deferral the putting off of assuming authority or the granting of authority to another body instead

Statutory Purpose and Constitutionality

The policies expressed by these statutes and regulations are both general and specific. Primarily, they reflect the judgment that the most effective way to end physical and economic segregation of women and minority group members is to bring them fully into the business environment. Specifically, the statutes reject employment decisions based on group stereotypes. Employment standards must be job related or justified by business necessity if they have an unequal impact on any **protected group.** The fair employment practices laws imply that artificial barriers should not keep men or women from jobs they can perform.

The policies of the regulations as well as their specific mandates are constitutionally based. For example, the federal statutes are enacted under Congress's power to regulate interstate commerce and under Section 5 of the Fourteenth Amendment. State statutes are enacted under each state's police powers. The authority for the Executive Order is found in the constitutional command that the President "take care that the laws be faithfully executed" and the Fifth Amendment's due process clause, which requires equal protection of citizens by the federal government.

Protected group a group of people specifically intended to fall under a statute or regulation; for example, people 40 to 70 years old fall under the Age Discrimination in Employment Act

Administration and Enforcement

Each statute typically creates an administrative agency for enforcement. Most also encourage and rely on informal means of settling disputes. Title VII created the Equal Employment Opportunity Commission (EEOC), which currently has the power to receive and investigate complaints, pursue informal **conciliation,** and bring suit in its own name against a respondent. The complainant also has the right to sue in federal district court after exhausting administrative remedies. The EEOC also has the power to issue and to publish interpretations of Title VII. Although these guidelines do not have the force of law, they indicate the legal position of the EEOC, which is also likely to be its position in any litigation. Statutory remedies include reinstatement to jobs, back pay awards, injunctions, and other appropriate relief.

Conciliation informal method of bringing together parties to a dispute to settle differences before going to court

A parallel structure has evolved to carry out the mandates of the Executive Order. Primary responsibility is assigned to the Secretary of Labor and the Office of Federal Contract Compliance Programs (OFCCP). However, the secretary may delegate this authority to other agencies and has done so in such cases as schools and hospitals (Health and Human Services) and banks (Treasury). The OFCCP also publishes regulations and interpretive guidelines and seeks informal resolutions of disputes.

Cease and desist order an order to stop doing something permanently

The typical enforcement technique is an administrative hearing and withdrawal of federal funds by the government.

State agencies often have the above powers and also may issue **cease and desist orders** enforceable through appropriate court action.

RACE DISCRIMINATION

The U.S. Constitution protects individual rights and sets the outer limits of permissible government activity. It is also the basis for suits by individuals against the government (or those closely connected with government). Specifically, individuals alleging unlawful discrimination challenge a particular action as a violation of the Fourteenth Amendment's equal protection clause, applicable to the states, or the Fifth Amendment's due process clause, applicable to the federal government. Unlike the statutes discussed above, the equal protection clause is not limited to race or sex discrimination but applies to any sort of irrational discrimination. But race and sex discrimination issues are tested by different standards. Although in general discriminations are valid if they rest on any rational ground, distinctions on the basis of race or sex are not valid unless they rest on "compelling" grounds, in the case of race, or on "substantial" grounds, in the case of sex.

Neutral Standards

Since 1965, the effective date of Title VII, overtly different treatment on the basis of race, sex, religion, or national origin has been increasingly rare. But covert and unintentional discrimination remain problems often difficult to detect or to remedy. Much of the litigation following the enactment of Title VII has been in the area of apparently neutral standards for hiring, promotion, and other conditions of employment that, when applied, have disproportionately adverse effects on protected groups. In such cases, the burden of proof is on the plaintiff to show the unequal impact of applying the standard. When that has been established, the burden then shifts to the defendant to show that the standard in question is job related or justified by business necessity.

For example, suppose that a state requires all its police officers to meet a 5'9" minimum height requirement. A woman presents evidence that approximately 95 percent of the female labor pool is disqualified by the standard. It is then the duty of the defendant to prove that the standard is job related. Given the specific duties of a police officer, is the job performed more effectively by someone at least 5'9" tall? In one case that involved guards at maximum security prisons in Alabama, the U.S. Supreme Court answered no.

Particular problems are raised by testing and educational requirements. Many employers use test results to make decisions about hiring, promoting, and firing workers. Title VII, Section 703(h), provides that it is not unlawful for an employer:

> to give and to act upon the result of any professionally developed ability test, provided that such test, its administration, or action upon the results is not designed, intended, or used to discriminate because of race, color, religion, sex or national origin.

But in many instances, minority group members score low on standardized tests. Some experts argue that these tests are culturally biased and that even a "professionally developed" test may effectively discriminate. In the courts' view, if the complainant can prove that a test has an unequal effect on a protected group, it is then the responsibility of the employer to show that the test is valid both legally and psychologically. For a test to be valid, it must be able to predict with some degree of accuracy whether an applicant will be successful on the particular job for which the test was used. To measure the chances of success on a particular job, one must know what the job requires, what "success" is for the job, and what qualities need to be examined.

Similar issues are raised about educational requirements for employment. On the one hand, Americans have great faith in their educational system. Education is mandatory for a certain number of years and involves a sizable percentage of governmental expenditures. On the other hand, significant segments of the population get less education, either in quality or quantity, than the majority. Therefore the requirement of a diploma for employment may have unequal effects on members of a protected group. If such an effect is shown, the employer must establish the job-relatedness of the requirement. Often the defendant's burden is not as great when the requirement is for a college degree, postgraduate education, or professional training as it is when the requirement is for passing grades on scored tests.

The dimensions of the job-relatedness standard are presently unclear. The central issue appears to be a test of specificity, because notions of simply a "more intelligent" work force have been rejected by the courts. Job-relatedness also has been used to invalidate consideration of arrest records in an employment decision. But the defendant's burden of proof is difficult to assess, because in few cases has the attempt been made. Moreover, the distinction between the concepts of job-relatedness and business necessity remains unclear. At least one court has held that an employment criterion having a disparate impact can be justified only by a showing that the criterion relates to job performance and not by a broader notion of business necessity. Other courts have said that similar criteria may be justified with reference to such business related factors as employee morale and efficiency or the integrity and security of the business.

The inquiry does not necessarily end when the employer proves job-relatedness or business necessity. The court still must determine whether other tests or selection criteria would serve the employer's interest without the undesirable impact. The EEOC places this burden on the employer.

Griggs v. Duke Power Company

Supreme Court of the United States
401 U.S. 424 (1971)

The Duke Power Company's Dam River plant was organized into five operating departments: labor, coal handling, operations, maintenance, and laboratory and test. Blacks were employed only in the labor department, where the highest paying jobs paid less than the lowest paying jobs in the other four operating departments. Promotions were made within each department on the basis of job seniority. Transferees into a department usually began in the lowest position. In 1955, the company instituted a policy of requiring a high school education for initial assignment to any department

FACTS

except labor and for transfer from the coal handling to any "inside" department (Operations, Maintenance, or Laboratory). When the company abandoned its policy of restricting blacks to the labor department in 1965, completion of high school also was made a prerequisite to transfer from labor to any other department. In September 1965 (after the 1964 Civil Rights Act became effective), the company began to permit incumbent employees who lacked a high school education to qualify for transfer from labor or coal handling by passing two professionally prepared general intelligence tests. Neither was intended to measure the ability to learn or to perform a particular job. Griggs and a group of black employees alleged that Duke Power was violating Title VII of the Civil Rights Act of 1964 in requiring a high school diploma or passage of a standardized intelligence test for employment or transfer. The defendant argued that these requirements were not violations of the 1964 act but were used to improve the overall quality of the work force.

ISSUE   Did the company's high school education and standardized test requirements discriminate against black employees and thus violate the Title VII?

DECISION   Yes. The court ruled that the requirements did violate Title VII of the 1964 act. Under the act, practices, procedures, or tests neutral on their face and even neutral in terms of intent could not be maintained if they operated to "freeze" in place the effects of earlier discriminatory practices. The court said that neither the high school completion requirement nor the general intelligence tests was shown to have any meaningful relationship to job performance.

Present Effects of Past Discrimination

Another form of discrimination that fair employment practices laws try to set right is exclusion resulting from past discrimination and the continuing effects of earlier exclusion. For example, previous experience on particular jobs often is used as a selection criterion. If blacks have been excluded from these particular jobs so that they were denied the opportunity to gain the requisite experience, the apparently neutral criterion has an unequal effect. An example of this perpetuation of past discrimination is provided in the *Griggs* case, discussed previously.

The issue of continuing effects of past discrimination is particularly important in connection with seniority systems, which affect, among other things, promotions and layoffs. Past exclusions were, according to the standards of the day, often legal. But their continuing harm affects at least a generation of "locked in" employees.

Seniority systems are among the major achievements of the labor movement in the United States. For the unions, there are several advantages to using seniority to determine issues of promotion and layoff. First, it prevents total domination and favoritism on the part of the employer. Second, seniority adds order and objectivity to dispute resolution. Third, seniority discourages rapid turnover both internally and externally and protects the employee's expectations.

But there are important disadvantages to seniority systems that conflict directly with Title VII principles. Seniority as a determinant of promotions may or may not be job or ability related. More important, a seniority system may have serious continuing consequences for those treated unfairly before the enactment of Title VII.

For example, one problem under seniority systems is promotional opportunities for minority group members hired in limited and segregated positions. Typically, minorities were limited in the past to jobs in only one department segregated from white employees. Seniority was department-based, and transfer to other departments was restricted, if not entirely prohibited. Under Title VII, transfer to other departments still may be limited or prohibited, but all departments are open to new employees. Complaints of discrimination come primarily from the minority group members who were hired before enactment of Title VII or implementation of the company's nondiscrimination policy and who are now frozen into their department. Although the seniority system seems neutral, it has an unequal effect on such a group.

Congress's compromise solution to the problems presented by the present operation of seniority systems is another special section, 703(h), which allows:

> different terms, conditions, or privileges of employment pursuant to a bona fide seniority system . . . provided that such differences are not the result of an intention to discriminate because of race, color, religion, sex or national origin.

Lower federal courts have interpreted this section to require a balance between the protection of existing seniority rights and the need for a realistic remedy for past discrimination. The courts used the phrases "bona fide" and "the result of an intention to discriminate" to invalidate seniority systems that perpetuated discrimination. As a remedy, courts granted blacks artificial seniority, called *constructive seniority,* so that they would be able to get future positions that would have been open to them but for the previous discrimination. In 1977 the Supreme Court reaffirmed the validity of a 1976 decision holding that Section 703(h) allows the award of constructive seniority as a remedy for unlawful employment practices unrelated to the seniority system.

Another problem, critical in times of economic decline, is layoffs. The traditional rule of seniority systems is that the last person hired is the first person fired. In companies where minorities and women were previously excluded but are hired today, the effect of the "last hired, first fired" rule falls heavily on the recently employed minority and female employees. Here again a neutral rule has an adverse effect on protected groups, but the solution is not clear. Minor adjustments in the seniority system do not produce a remedy. While deferring the promotion of a white male may be less onerous than a layoff, to lay off more senior white males in order not to lay off a woman or minority-group member seems to violate the antipreference clause of Title VII, Section 703(j) and to be another form of discrimination in violation of the basic Title VII provision, Section 703(a). No adequate remedy has been found.

In the following case, the U.S. Supreme Court rejected previous interpretations of Section 703(h) and held that it immunized seniority systems that did not originate in racial discrimination even if such systems perpetuated previous discrimination.

Teamsters v. United States

Supreme Court of the United States
431 U.S. 324 (1977)

T.I.M.E.D.C., Incorporated, and the International Brotherhood of Teamsters entered into a collective bargaining agreement which provided that the order in which   FACTS employees could bid for particular jobs within the company would be determined by the seniority held within a particular bargaining unit. Thus, a line driver's seniority, for purposes of bidding for particular runs, took into account only the length of time he had been a line driver at a particular terminal. The practical effect was that a city driver or serviceman who transferred to a line drive job had to forfeit all the seniority he had accumulated in his previous bargaining unit and start at the bottom of the line drivers' "board." It locked minority workers into inferior jobs and perpetuated earlier discrimination by discouraging transfers to jobs as line drivers. The plaintiff (United States) alleged that a seniority system that perpetuates the effects of earlier discrimination could never be "bona fide" or a good defense under Section 703(h). The defendants argued that the seniority system was bona fide because the legislative history of the section showed that Congress intended to immunize pre-1965 seniority systems from the Act.

ISSUE   Was the collective bargaining agreement between the company and the union lawful under Title VII of the Civil Rights Act of 1964?

DECISION   Yes. The Court ruled that the collective bargaining agreement was lawful. It stated that the unmistakable purpose of Section 703(h) was to make clear that the application of a bona fide seniority system would not be unlawful under Title VII. However, the Court pointed out that 703(h) did not immunize all seniority systems. It referred only to bona fide systems that do not show an intention to discriminate.

SEX DISCRIMINATION

Although sex discrimination is prohibited by the same statutes that prohibit racial, religious, and national origin discrimination, there are some fundamental differences in the problems women face. Women constitute 40 percent of the labor force and more than 40 percent of white-collar workers. Women accounted for nearly three fifths of the increase in the labor force in the last decade. Some legislation that is today considered discriminatory against women was actually enacted, in the belief of the legislators, for women's protection. And all of us can recite basic cultural and biological distinctions between men and women. Many of these protective laws and cultural and biological distinctions are used to deny women equal employment opportunity even though the distinctions are irrelevant or the laws unduly restrictive.

In 1978 the median salary for full time, year round work was $16,360 for white men; $12,530 for black men; $9,732 for white women; and $9,020 for black women. The unemployment rates for people age 20 and over for 1979 are also significant: white men, 3.6 percent; black men, 8.4 percent; white women, 5.2 percent; and black women, 10.1 percent. Moreover, even though women constitute more than 40 percent of all white collar workers, only one fifth of managers and administrators are women. Women constitute two fifths of all professional and technical workers. But most of these women are teachers. In fact, women account for 72 percent of all teachers.

One purpose of fair employment practices legislation is to change this statistical picture by questioning widely accepted myths about women workers. One myth is that women as a group are too emotional for leadership positions. Another is that women are physically weak and morally delicate. Women, furthermore, are believed to be less committed than men to careers and therefore unreliable. Finally, there is a belief that women do not ''need'' to work.

To counter these myths, fair employment practices legislation encourages employment decisions to be made on an individual basis, not according to perceived group characteristics. The BFOQ provision of Title VII and parallel laws provide an opportunity to test the validity of these myths.

Bona Fide Occupational Qualification

Section 703(e) of Title VII states:

> Notwithstanding any other provision of this title, 1. it shall not be an unlawful employment practice for an employer to hire and employ employees . . . on the basis of his [or her] . . . sex . . . in those certain instances where . . . sex . . . is a bona fide occupational qualification reasonably necessary to the normal operation of that particular business.

The BFOQ exception also applies to discrimination on the basis of religion and national origin but not to discrimination based on race. This section reflects Congress's belief that in certain situations the sex of an applicant is relevant to job performance. Through its guidelines, the EEOC has narrowly defined these exceptions to include authenticity (model or actor) and sexual function (sperm donor or wet nurse).

Much sex discrimination litigation has involved testing the scope of these exceptions. For example, many states have laws dealing with employment conditions for women. These laws restrict the number of hours a day or a week that women may work, limit by weight the number of pounds women may lift or carry, exclude women from certain occupations, and provide certain minimal benefits (pay, rest periods, seats) that women must have. Under the supremacy clause of the U.S. Constitution, if these state statutes are in conflict with Title VII, federal law prevails. Consequently, courts first must decide whether a state law conflicts with Title VII and then determine the effect on state laws.

The EEOC's guidelines take the position that benefits provided to women by state laws should be extended to men to eliminate discriminatory treatment. Arguably, such action by a court is proper because it avoids holding a statute unconstitutional and is consistent with the legislative intent to protect workers from various hazards. Other state laws that limit or close off opportunities should be considered superseded by Title VII, according to the guidelines. In these cases, extension of the law's application to both sexes would be unworkable, leaving no one legally allowed to do certain work. Here new laws might be passed that provide necessary protections for all workers but no outright prohibitions by sex. A more difficult problem is a third group of laws whose protections may not be perceived as beneficial—for example, maximum hours laws. On the one hand, maximum hours laws protect workers from compulsory overtime. On the other, such laws limit workers' opportunities to take advantage of the premium pay offered for overtime. But it is clear that the mere existence of a relevant state law does not provide an automatic basis for the BFOQ exception.

Another issue raised by the BFOQ provision is its relevance to customer preference. For example, can the fact that a particular business caters to male clients be the
basis for hiring only workers of one sex to deal with these clients? What of the
accounting firm that believes its clients do not take advice from women? Whether
founded on fact or supposition, these beliefs, according to the EEOC's guidelines,
shall not be the basis for a BFOQ exception. There are still unanswered questions
concerning advertising tactics, maintenance of atmosphere and propriety, privacy,
and the need for role models, as well as the practical implications of dictating this
standard to employers. In one sense, the role of the EEOC can best be understood as
educational as well as remedial. In another sense, a narrow functional definition of
the BFOQ provision would indicate that customers' or coworkers' preferences about
the sex of an employee are irrelevant.

The burden of establishing a BFOQ exception falls on the employer. A federal
court of appeals has held that an employer may not exclude women as a class from a
particularly strenuous job without establishing that "all or substantially all women"
could not perform it. However, even this standard may be objectionable, because the
"substantially all" language allows decisions to be based on group rather than individual characteristics. Another court held that the employer must prove that gender
was essential to the job or business before establishing that all or substantially all men
could not perform. Other courts have imposed a more stringent burden of proof,
imposing a functional definition on BFOQs.

Rosenfeld v. Southern Pacific Company

U.S. Court of Appeals
444 F. 2d. 1219 (1971)

FACTS   Leah Rosenfeld applied for the position of agent-telegrapher. The work requirements of the position during the harvesting season demanded ten-hour days and
80-hour weeks, along with heavy physical effort, including the ability to lift objects that
weigh in excess of 25, and in some cases, 50 pounds. When the company denied her the
job, reserving such positions for men only, she brought an action under Title VII, alleging
that she had been discriminated against solely because of her sex. The company argued
that it had not violated Section VII because the arduous nature of the work rendered
women physically unsuited for the job, and appointing a woman to the position would
violate California's labor laws, which limited hours of work for women and restricted
the weight they could lift.

ISSUE   Is the company's policy of reserving the position of agent-telegrapher exclusively for
men a violation of Title VII of the Civil Rights Act of 1964?

DECISION   Yes. The court ruled that the company's policy was a violation of Title VII. It stated
that the company had failed to show that the sexual characteristics of the employee
were crucial to the successful performance of the job and thus not eligible for a BFOQ
exception. Also, the court stated that the objectives of California's labor laws were in
conflict with Title VII of the Civil Rights Act of 1964, and thus by virtue of the
supremacy clause of the United States Constitution were unconstitutional.

DISCRIMINATION
BASED ON RELIGION
AND NATIONAL ORIGIN

Fair employment practices law specifically prohibits discrimination on the basis of religion or national origin. Under Title VII, these prohibitions are subject to the BFOQ exceptions. But in the areas of religion, national origin, race, or sex discrimination, a case raising racial discrimination often includes national origin issues or complaints. But there are several crucial problems in this area of fair employment.

Religious Discrimination

Overt discrimination on the basis of an applicant's or an employer's religion is illegal unless a BFOQ exception is established by the employer. As with sex as a BFOQ, group stereotypes or characteristics commonly associated with a particular religion cannot be the basis of a BFOQ unless factually established by the employer.

Typically the issue of religious discrimination is raised because the religious beliefs of applicants or employees prohibit them from working on a particular day or during a particular time. Thus an employer might refuse to hire an applicant not because he or she was a Seventh-Day Adventist but because that religion forbids its members to work from sundown Friday to sundown Saturday.

The position of the EEOC, through its guidelines, was that a refusal to hire and to accommodate was religious discrimination and that the duty not to discriminate included the obligation to make reasonable accommodations to the religious needs of the employee or applicant. Courts with contrary views held that such a denial was not based on religion but on the unavailability of the employee or applicant at a particular time. Further, these courts held that employers had no obligation to accommodate religious beliefs, usually on the theory that such an accommodation would discriminate against other applicants or employees.

When Congress amended Title VII in 1972, it added to Section 701 subsection (j), which states:

> The term "religion" includes all aspects of religious observances and practices, as well as belief, unless an employer demonstrates that he [or she] is unable to reasonably accommodate to an employee's or prospective employee's religious observance or practice without undue hardship on the conduct of the employer's business.

The extent to which an employer must reasonably accommodate and what constitutes undue hardship are not defined by the statute. In 1977 the Supreme Court took up these issues in *Trans World Airlines, Inc.* v. *Hardison,* which appears below. The case has been criticized for its failure to address the constitutionality of Section 701(j) and its extremely narrow reading of Congress's intent in enacting the 1972 amendment.

Religious discrimination may be an issue in other situations. For example, an employer may require all employees to attend weekly sermonettes, to donate blood, or to contribute money to a union in violation of an employee's religious convictions. It is unclear whether or in what way *Hardison* is applicable to these situations.

The implications of the other 1972 action by Congress relating to religious discrimination are also not straightforward. The 1972 amendment broadened the exemption for religious institutions (Section 702) by exempting them from the religious discrimination prohibitions of Title VII with respect to all employees. Previously Section 702 had exempted only those positions that involved participating in the religious activities of the institution. The impetus for the more pervasive exclusion probably resulted from another Title VII amendment — one that removed the exemption of educational institutions. However, Section 702 raises a significant constitutional question, because the exemption treats religious institutions differently from nonreligious institutions and thus may violate the First Amendment's clause prohibiting government establishment of religion.

Trans World Airlines, Incorporated v. Hardison

Supreme Court of the United States
432 U.S. 63 (1977)

FACTS   Hardison worked as a clerk in a large maintenance and overhaul base of TWA. Because of its essential role, the base had to operate 24 hours a day, 365 days a year. TWA and its union in a collective bargaining agreement agreed that the most junior employees were required to work when the union steward was unable to find enough people to work at a particular time. After transferring to a job where he was lowest in seniority, Hardison notified the manager of the base that because of his religious convictions he would not be able to work from sunset on Friday until sunset on Saturday. The union was not willing to violate the seniority provisions of the collective bargaining agreement, and the company rejected a proposal that Hardison work only a four-day week. The plaintiff was discharged after he failed to report to work for his designated shift on a Friday. Plaintiff argued that the company and the union's failure to accommodate his religious practices, and his discharge, constituted religious discrimination in violation of Title VII. Defendants argued that they made reasonable efforts to accommodate plaintiff's religious practices but could not breach the seniority provisions of their collective bargaining agreement.

ISSUE   Is the company in violation of Title VII of the Civil Rights Act of 1964 by not reasonably accommodating plaintiff's religious practices?

DECISION   No. The Court ruled that TWA and the union had made reasonable efforts to accommodate plaintiff's religious practices. Any further efforts would have worked an undue hardship on the company and breached a valid collective bargaining agreement. The Court stated that without a clear indication from Congress, it did not agree that the statutory obligation of Title VII to accommodate religious needs took precedence over the collective bargaining agreement and the seniority rights of other TWA employees.

National Origin Discrimination

Issues of discrimination on the basis of national origin often are combined with cases involving racial discrimination. Similar problems arise over the validity of tests and educational requirements. National origin discrimination cases often raise such questions as the validity of an English language test or of height and weight standards.

The particular problem raised in national origin cases is whether discrimination on the basis of citizenship is in fact discrimination on the basis of national origin and thus in violation of the fair employment practices laws. In 1973 the U.S. Supreme Court held that, although Congress may have the power to prohibit discrimination on the basis of citizenship, it had not exercised such power in prohibiting discrimination on the basis of national origin. Specifically, the Court stated that a resident alien who was denied employment because she was not a U.S. citizen was not discriminated against on the basis of national origin (which the court interpreted as ancestry) but rather on the basis of citizenship.

AGE DISCRIMINATION

In 1967 Congress enacted the Age Discrimination in Employment Act, outlawing employment discrimination on the basis of age between ages 40 and 65, and a recent amendment raised the upper limit to 70. The act is administered by the EEOC, and its scope, coverage, and procedures are similar to those of the Equal Pay Act. The purpose of the statute is to encourage the making of employment decisions on individual characteristics rather than on stereotypic notions of the effect of age on ability. The statute provides four defenses:

1. Age is a bona fide occupational qualification (BFOQ) reasonably necessary to the normal operation of the particular business.

2. The differentiation is based on reasonable factors other than age.

3. The terms of a bona fide seniority system or any bona fide employee benefit plan (retirement, pension, or insurance) are not a subterfuge.

4. Discharge or discipline has been for good cause.

Although the substance and procedure of the act are nearly identical to those of Title VII, the federal courts appear to apply different standards of proof and liability. The courts have found age discrimination justified by one of the defenses on the basis of less evidence than would satisfy the burden in a Title VII case. Probably the reasons for the distinction lie in the fact that age, at some point, is related to individual ability and that the basis for age discrimination is not hostility but inaccurate perceptions or miscalculated costs. Thus the test formulated by many courts is whether there is a generalization other than age that more accurately predicts ability or whether the employer can adequately test individually without a substantial increase in cost.

DISCRIMINATION IN PUBLIC EMPLOYMENT

Today most public employees are protected from discrimination on the basis of race, sex, religion, or national origin by fair employment practices laws, particularly Title VII of the Civil Rights Act of 1964. Before 1972, public employees' rights were protected, if at all, by separate legislation and constitutional doctrines. The Constitution remains an important source of law in employment decisions, although its protections are broader in some respects and narrower in others than Title VII or other fair employment practices laws.

The Constitution and its protections apply to public employees, although the precise effect of its applicability changes from case to case. Therefore, it is impossible to list in detail what the Constitution prohibits or allows in the employment field. What an individual may do, however, is to acquaint himself or herself with basic constitutional principles and study cases to discover how courts modify the principles to deal with the unique employer – employee relationship.

AFFIRMATIVE ACTION PROGRAMS

Affirmative action programs are designed to put equal employment opportunity laws into effect. Such programs reduce reliance on case-by-case enforcement, provide faster, more effective relief, and generally make equal employment opportunity a reality, not merely rhetoric. The key to affirmative action programs is the employers' mandatory self-evaluation of all terms and conditions of employment.

Affirmative action obligations have two focuses. First, employers must eliminate all present discriminatory practices and conditions. That is, they must comply with equal opportunity laws. They must eliminate discriminatory tests, non – job related employment requirements, and other apparently neutral standards that, although seemingly nondiscriminatory, have discriminatory effects when applied. Second, employers must take further affirmative steps to increase female and minority-group participation in their work forces. This latter obligation is a remedy for the present effects of past discrimination.

Authority for affirmative action programs derives from two primary sources — Executive Order 11246 as amended and Title VII of the 1964 Civil Rights Act as amended. The executive order is administered by the Secretary of Labor, who may (and does) delegate the authority to require and review affirmative action plans to other federal agencies. Title VII (like similar state laws) gives the courts broad powers to remedy discrimination, with the result that a court may order a particular defendant to engage in affirmative action. The EEOC often requires an affirmative action plan as part of its conciliation efforts.

In specific situations, affirmative action rules may be quite complex. Basically, affirmative action programs require employers to evaluate their present work force to see if women and minority group members are present in all positions in appropriate numbers. Appropriateness is determined by the number of women and minorities available and seeking work within the recruitment area. Specifically, there must be:

1. an evaluation of the employer's present work force — the numbers of men, whites, and minority group members at all levels

2. an analysis of all recruitment and selection procedures

3. an analysis of those people applying for and accepting employment, applying for and receiving promotion, and terminating

4. data to determine the recruitment area's labor force characteristics — total population, work force population, training, unemployment

Once collected, these data may detail areas of unequal employment. It is then the obligation of the employer to examine these areas, to determine if the employment of women or minorities is inhibited by any internal or external factor, and, if so, to remedy the situation. With these data, goals and timetables can be set by the employer. Goals reflect employers' decisions concerning how many women and minority group members are necessary for adequate balance, and timetables reflect employers' predictions of when these goals will be attained.

Several criticisms are aimed at affirmative action programs. Some argue that *goal* is just another word for *quota,* and some employers act as if the distinction were only semantic. However, legally there is a difference. A good faith effort to meet affirmative action responsibility is a defense against not reaching a goal. Additionally, "goal" takes into account the availability of qualified workers.

A second criticism is that affirmative action results in lower quality among employees. But if an employer takes into account valid qualifications, quality stays high. Affirmative action may actually raise the quality of a particular work force because the application pool and perceptions of women and minorities both expand.

A third criticism is that affirmative action is in fact unfair to white males, dictating reverse discrimination.

The sanctions both for not having an affirmative action plan when required and for not putting into effect an existing program may be quite severe. They may include withdrawal of all federal funds. Such a sanction is imposed only after an administrative hearing on the merits. Withdrawing funds is necessary on the grounds that it would be a violation of the Fifth Amendment's due process clause for the federal government to continue to finance an organization that discriminates.

The *basic* aim of the regulations is to require employers to review their employment policies and to ensure that decisions are made on the basis of individual capacities rather than on stereotyped images or artificial standards.

_____ SUMMARY _____

Title VII of the Civil Rights Act of 1964, Executive Order 11246, the Equal Pay Act of 1963, and the National Labor Relations Act have provided the major legal thrusts against discrimination in employment. The Equal Opportunity Employment Commission and the Labor Department's Office of Contract Compliance have been the major enforcement agencies. State, city, and county laws and regulations governing employment discrimination are also important for employers to be aware of.

Race discrimination is in and of itself illegal. Often cases of race discrimination do not show an intent on the part of the employer to discriminate, but the effect of a company's hiring pattern may fall unequally on one race. Plaintiffs must show the adverse effect is a result of apparently neutral criteria. The employer must show that the criteria for hiring were job related or part of a business necessity.

Sex discrimination is not per se illegal but may be justified by the employer using a bona fide occupational defense. Generally, the employer must show (1) that it is impractical to find members of one sex who possess the abilities of the other sex, and (2) that these abilities are necessary for the performance of the job. Title VII of the Civil Rights Act also forbids discrimination based on religion or national origin. The Age Discrimination in Employment Act forbids discrimination based on age for those between the ages of 40 and 70. BFOQ and seniority defenses exist for employers when charged with these forms of discrimination.

Affirmative action programs required of federal contractors and subcontractors under Executive Order 11246 have been a source of some concern for employers. Employers must make good faith efforts to meet goals and timetables for hiring minorities. Failure to meet such goals may result in a contractor's loss of government funds.

REVIEW PROBLEMS

1. Title VII of the 1964 Civil Rights Act forbids discrimination based on race and sex. Explain the standards used by the courts in deciding whether discrimination exists in each case.

2. Define a BFOQ.

3. What is the purpose of the Age Discrimination in Employment Act?

4. What do affirmative action programs require employers to do?

5. Marie Fernandez was employed by the Wynn Oil Company from February 1968 to February 4, 1977. During that time, she held various positions, including that of administrative assistant to the executive vice president reporting directly to Wynn's director of worldwide marketing. Wynn has extensive operations outside the United States. Much of its business, in fact, takes place in Latin America and Southeast Asia. Fernandez applied for and was denied a promotion to the position of director of international marketing. She sued Wynn, alleging that it discriminated against her on the basis of sex in violation of Title VII. Wynn defended by claiming that it was legally entitled to discriminate on the basis of sex in hiring for the position of director of international marketing because sex is a bona fide occupational qualification for the position. It argued that it would not consider any woman for the position because of the feeling among Wynn's customers and distributors that it would be undesirable to deal with a woman in a high management position. It contended that many of Wynn's South American distributors and customers, for instance, would be offended by a woman conducting business meetings in her hotel room. The offensive nature of this conduct stems from prevailing cultural customs and mores in Latin America. Will

Wynn be successful in establishing sex as a BFOQ for the position of director of international marketing? Explain.

6. Buck Green, who is black, applied for employment as a clerk at the Missouri Pacific Railroad Company's personnel office in the corporate headquarters in St. Louis, Missouri. In response to a question on the application form, Green disclosed that he had been convicted in December 1967 for refusing military induction. He stated that he had served 21 months in prison until paroled in 1970. After reviewing the application form, Missouri Pacific's personnel officer informed Green that he was not qualified for employment at Missouri Pacific because of his conviction and prison record. Missouri Pacific followed an absolute policy of refusing consideration to any person convicted of a crime other than a minor traffic offense. Green sued Missouri Pacific, seeking relief under Title VII. At trial, Green introduced statistical evidence showing that Missouri Pacific's policy operated automatically to exclude from employment 53 of every 1,000 black applicants but only 22 of every 1,000 white applicants. The rejection rate for blacks was two and one half times that of whites under Missouri Pacific's policy. At trial, Missouri Pacific proffered the following reasons for following its policy:

1 □ fear of cargo theft

2 □ employees' handling of company funds

3 □ bonding qualifications

4 □ possible impeachment of an employee as a witness

5 □ possible liability for hiring people with known violent tendencies

6 □ employment disruption caused by recidivism and

7 □ a lack of moral character of persons with convictions.

Will Green be successful in his suit against Missouri Pacific? Explain.

7. Handy Dan's Barber Shop employed 15 barbers, of whom 11 were Spanish-surnamed Americans, 2 were black, and 2 were white. Handy Dan's maintained a longstanding rule forbidding its Spanish-surnamed American barbers from speaking Spanish to each other in the presence of English-speaking patrons. Three Spanish-surnamed barbers were discharged pursuant to this policy. Did Handy Dan's violate Title VII? What additional information would be helpful for determining whether a violation existed? If Handy Dan's had employed only 14 barbers, would it have been in violation of Title VII?

8. Jelleff Associates, a woman's specialty store that catered to mature women, began reducing personnel because of poor business conditions and excessive payroll expenses. By discharging its older employees (those over 40) and expanding its product line, the company hoped to appeal to a younger market. In terminating one employee, the company gave as its reason the fact that "business was falling off." Another was terminated after being advised that "business was slow." The terminated employees sued Jelleff Associates, claiming that it had violated the Age Discrimination in Employment Act. What result?

9. Weiner, a disgruntled taxpayer, filed suit to set aside the award of a contract to the second lowest bidder. The contract was for the installation of heating and air conditioning equipment in classrooms being constructed by the Cuyahoga Community College with federal funding. The college contended that the lowest bid was not acceptable because the contractor would not promise to refrain from discriminatory hiring practices. The lowest bid had been submitted by a contractor who would make a reasonable effort to hire blacks. The bidder who was awarded the contract promised the college that blacks would be represented in all crafts employed on the project. It was the taxpayer's contention that the promise made by the lowest bidder was consistent with state and federal law and that it was unlawful and unconstitutional abuse of discretion for the college to reject the bid. Who won? Explain.

10. Phillips applied for a job as assembly trainee with Martin Marietta Corporation. She was denied the position because the company was not hiring women with preschool children. At the time that she applied, 70 to 75 percent of those applying were women, and 75 to 80 percent of those hired were women. The company employed men with preschool children. Has Martin violated Title VII? Discuss.

11. Sanchez is a 50-year-old black female worker in a large department store in Columbus, Ohio. She is a fitter in the women's wear department. She earns $150 a week. Cranchford, a white male, worked as a fitter in the men's wear department for $200 a week. Both Sanchez and Cranchford joined the company on the same day. Cranchford was fired for refusing on religious grounds to work on Saturdays. Sanchez requested a transfer to Cranchford's vacant position. Sanchez was the worker with the most experience, which under company rules governed who received a transfer. Sanchez was denied the transfer. List the legal issues involved in this case.

12. Six firefighters challenged a Baltimore provision that established retirement age at lower than 70. They claimed that these provisions violated provisions of the Age Discrimination in Employment Act. The city argued that age is a BFOQ for the position of firefighters, and the city's retirement provisions were valid. It argued that Congress by statute had selected age 55 as the retirement age for most federal firefighters, and thus as a matter of law it constitutes a BFOQ for state and local firefighters. Who won? Explain.

13. Western Airlines required that its flight engineers, who were members of the cockpit crew but did not operate flight controls unless the pilot and co-pilot were incapacitated, retire at age 60. A Federal Aviation Administration (FAA) regulation prohibits pilots and co-pilots from serving after age 60. A group of flight engineers forced to retire at age 60 and pilots who at age 60 were denied reassignment as flight engineers brought suit against Western Airlines, contending that the age 60 retirement requirements for flight engineers was in violation of the Age Discrimination in Employment Act. The airline defended, arguing that a BFOQ existed because its age 60 retirement requirement was "reasonably necessary" for the safe operation of the airlines. Who won? Explain.

CHAPTER 42

Government Regulation of Business Behavior

CHAPTER OBJECTIVES

After reading this chapter, you should be able to:

1. Explain how government regulation of business behavior plays a significant role in business decision making.

2. Describe the role of administrative agencies in government regulation.

3. Compare the social and economic regulation of business.

4. Explain the significance of antitrust laws as a form of economic regulation.

AN INTRODUCTION TO THE DEBATE OVER GOVERNMENT REGULATION

Recent court decisions interpreting the commerce clause of the U.S. Constitution have extended federal government influence over business activities affecting interstate commerce. Congress also has created many administrative agencies to regulate business activities. This trend has stimulated the present national debate over whether government regulates business too much or too little.

Those who argue that there is too much regulation say that the president and Congress should get government "off the back" of business and let the laws of supply and demand dictate prices and production. They urge deregulation of business and elimination of some federal and state regulatory agencies.

Those who argue in favor of government regulation note that it is the role of Congress and of the regulatory agencies it has established to protect the public interest. Pointing out that corporations are created to serve only the narrow interests of their stockholders, they argue that without government regulation, the public interest would not be served in many instances, particularly where business actively affects the community, the state, or the nation. Keep this debate in mind while reading the material in this chapter.

THE ROLE OF ADMINISTRATIVE AGENCIES

Definition and Nature

Almost every type of business enterprise in the United States falls within the scope of one or more administrative agencies, such as the Federal Trade Commission

(FTC), Interstate Commerce Commission (ICC), Federal Communications Commission (FCC), and Security and Exchange Commission (SEC). Our political system operates so extensively through administrative agencies that they have been called a "fourth branch of government," and the United States has been described as an "administrative state." **Administrative agencies** may be defined as governmental bodies, other than the courts and legislatures, that carry out the administrative tasks of government and affect the rights of private parties through adjudication or rule making.

Administrative agencies government bodies that carry out the administrative tasks of government through rule making

Administrative agencies are found at every level of government, but they differ considerably in size. In general, federal agencies are highly structured, staffed with hundreds or thousands of employees. State and local agencies tend to be smaller and more loosely organized. As a result, state and local agencies are more informal, and much important business is carried out behind the scenes by people who are personally acquainted with the problems and the parties or their representatives. People in state and local agencies also usually know others in government and can informally interact with them. They may work in the same office building, share other facilities, and have a background of common participation in state and local party politics.

Administrative agencies affect the rights of private parties in many ways. Some, such as parole boards or the Immigration and Naturalization Service of the U.S. Department of Justice, are concerned with matters involving rights as basic as liberty itself. Others, such as state workers' compensation boards, determine claims for large sums of money. The Interstate Commerce Commission and state public utility commissions fix rates that influence profits in sizable segments of the economy. A principal function of other agencies is to police certain types of activities, such as the sale of liquor, by granting licenses and permits. Many of these same agencies also attempt to protect the public by prohibiting certain actions under threat of fine or suspension of license.

Sometimes an agency has the power to bring criminal actions against those who violate a statute that the agency has been authorized to enforce. The fields in which agencies operate are extensive, and their influence in our society is far reaching.

Independent and Executive Administrative Agencies

There are two general classifications of administrative agencies: independent and executive. Several of the largest and most influential federal agencies are not part of any department of the executive branch. The ICC, FTC, SEC, and NLRB are examples of independent agencies that are very important to the business community. In some states major administrative agencies are independent of the chief executive. Many state constitutions provide for the election of important administrative officers, such as the attorney general and the state treasurer, and deny the governor the right to remove even appointed department heads except for cause.

But some well known federal agencies are parts of executive departments. For example, both the Food and Drug Administration and the Social Security Administration are parts of the U.S. Department of Health and Human Services. The Federal Aviation Administration (FAA) is a part of the Department of Transportation. Most local and state agencies are also organized within larger executive departments. On a day-to-day basis, this does not make much difference because the agencies operate without interference from the other components of the executive branch, but when agencies are organized within the executive branch, greater potential for direct control exists. Many major policy decisions within the jurisdictional power of the agencies may be influenced by the chief executive and his staff.

Reasons for Growth

With the growth of federal legislation that we have noted, Congress found it necessary to set up agencies to carry out the details of the statutes enacted. Thus in passing the Federal Communication Act of 1933, Congress created the FCC. A second reason for creating the agencies was the need for special skills to deal with complex and technical details that demand attention.

A third reason that Congress created administrative agencies was to keep a large number of complex cases out of the already overcrowded federal courts. To the extent that the ICC can settle disputes over trucking routes, for example, it keeps trucking cases out of court. Fourth, as one legal scholar notes, the desire of Congress to make legislative changes that will not be interpreted away by conservative courts may be a prime reason for the growth of the administrative process. For example, when Congress enacted the 1964 and 1965 Civil Rights Acts it also created the Equal Employment Opportunity Commission. Congress was changing social policy with these statutes, and it wanted an administrative agency that would implement the legislation as Congress intended.

WORK OF
ADMINISTRATIVE AGENCIES

Adjudication

Probably the best-known function of administrative agencies is judicial in nature. In many instances both state and federal agencies find facts and apply rules and regulations to these facts just as a court would. In carrying out this judicial function, the federal agencies generally use procedures similar to those used by the courts. This result is probably due to the influence of the large number of legally trained people who are involved in some way with agency adjudication. In addition, the Administrative Procedure Act requires almost all federal agencies to meet certain standards in their procedures. As a result of these factors, generally there is considerable similarity in the enforcement procedures of federal agencies, and state agencies frequently follow similar patterns. Thus we can examine the procedures of an agency such as the FTC and obtain an idea how the judicial function is performed in agencies in general.

In adjudication proceedings, the FTC, like most administrative agencies, follows a procedure of "investigation-complaint-hearing-order." However, because of limited resources, the FTC tries to prevent disputes from reaching the hearing state. As a result, more than 90 percent of the investigations of violations do not result in hearings.

Many cases are administratively closed by the FTC because investigation fails to turn up enough evidence to substantiate a violation or because the public interest does not warrant the lengthy and costly investigation needed to develop the facts necessary to establish a case that will be adequate based on the evidence presented (a *prima facie* case). In a substantial number of cases where evidence of a violation does exist, the FTC disposes of the case before a hearing by consent order procedure.

Both the FTC and the respondent (corporation, partnership, or individual) benefit from the consent order procedure. The FTC obtains a binding **cease and desist order** with little cost and without having to worry about appeal. Respondents benefit because the agreement is for settlement purposes only and does not constitute an admission of guilt. As a result, the order cannot be used in a damage action brought against them, and they avoid the cost of litigation and the public disclosures that might stem from a formal hearing.

Cease and desist order an order to stop doing something permanently

If settlement attempts are unsuccessful, an initial hearing is conducted by an administrative law judge. The procedures used are similar to those used by the federal courts, although the rules of evidence are relaxed.

Within 90 days after the completion of the hearing, the administrative law judge files an initial decision, which becomes the decision of the FCC unless appealed. Any party to the proceeding may appeal the administrative law judge's decision to the FTC, or the FTC may review the decision on its own. In the event of appeal or review, briefs are generally submitted by the parties and oral arguments are heard unless the FTC feels that they are not necessary. In rendering its decision, the FTC has broad power to modify the administrative law judge's decision, including findings of fact.

Limited judicial review of the FTC order to cease and desist is permitted in an appeals court. Most appeals are taken on questions of law, although the Administrative Procedure Act allows review of agency decisions that are "arbitrary and capricious," or an abuse of the agency's discretion, as well as those decisions or procedures that violate the Constitution or exceed the agency's statutory authority.

Rule Making

When a pronouncement affecting the rights and duties of a number of people is made by an agency, the agency acts as a legislature. The power to make rules and regulations of this kind, which may be as binding as laws passed by legislative bodies, has been delegated to the agency by the legislature. The only important difference between an agency rule and a law enacted by a legislative body is that the former may be slightly more susceptible to attack in the courts because the rule was not made by elected officials. Let us consider examples of the rule making authority of some administrative agencies.

After the stock market collapse in 1929, Congress passed legislation in 1934 to protect the public buying and selling of securities on national exchanges. The Securities Exchange Act of 1934 created the SEC, which was given the job of enforcing and administering the Act. The SEC has adopted many rules designed to protect buyers of securities. One of these rules requires broker–dealers who extend credit to customers to furnish information about the credit charges. Both initial and periodic disclosures are necessary. As a result, Congress decided that it would be unnecessary to make the 1968 Truth in Lending Act apply to loans made by brokers to customers buying securities on credit, because the SEC regulation already provided ample legal protection. The SEC rules have the same legal effect as if these actions had been taken by Congress.

Administrative Activities

The acts of administrative agencies of most interest from the legal standpoint are those that involve rule making or adjudication. Agencies, however, act in many ways that are neither judicial nor legislative in nature. They carry out many statutory directives and have countless functions that defy classification. Many of these acts are purely administrative, although they may involve the rights and duties of many citizens, thousands of transactions, and millions of dollars. In many cases, these acts are informal and are usually not reviewed by a court. Even when the possibility of judicial review of action exists, many people affected do not believe that review is practical and accept the agency's action without formal protest.

Many examples of administrative acts can be cited. Agencies often are responsible for the allocation of funds and the granting of licenses. They make tests, manage government property, and supervise inmates in institutions. Agencies clear vessels to leave ports and classify grain. Agencies grant patents, collect taxes, and oversee educational institutions. Agencies frequently conduct investigations, sometimes at the request of the executive or the legislature, sometimes on their own initiative. Some agencies are responsible for law enforcement and prosecution. Others plan, approve, or disapprove the plans of others. Most of the countless jobs that are necessary in the administration of government are done by people in administrative agencies.

Many of these administrative acts are politically, economically, and socially significant and clearly relate to important issues of public policy. The SEC decision in the late 1960s to investigate the selling of mutual funds was an administrative act of this type. As a result of this investigation, the commission proposed sweeping legislation curtailing certain practices in the industry. When the FTC decided in 1972 to bring a legal action against the major sellers of ready to eat cereals, alleging that they were involved in an illegal restraint of trade, the decision to file suit, although administrative in nature, had a potentially great effect on many other areas of the economy. This suit was dropped by the commission in 1981, ostensibly for failure to find anticompetitive conduct. Many believe that it was a political decision by appointees of a new administration that favored less regulation.

CLASSIFICATIONS OF
GOVERNMENT REGULATION

Social Regulation

Government regulation that is addressed *primarily* to individual welfare and perceived social problems is classified as *social*. Since the early 1960s, this form of regulation has grown extensively. Concerns over discrimination in employment and public accommodations brought the 1964 and 1965 Civil Rights Act and later, the establishment of Equal Employment Opportunity Commission (EEOC) to enforce these laws. Concern over clean air and water brought new legislation and the Environmental Protection Agency (EPA) to enforce such laws. The Occupational, Safety and Health Administration (OSHA) was established by Congress when concern over safety of employees in the workplace came to the forefront. Other agencies such as the Consumer Product Safety Commission (CPSC) and the Food and Drug Administration (FDA) were established to enforce legislation that affected social and political life.

Economic Regulation

Economic regulation generally has been designed to affect selected industries to prevent certain forms of business conduct considered bad for the economy. It can be argued that most forms of business regulation have been used to make the laws of supply and demand function correctly. For example, as the reader shall see, Section 2 of the Sherman Act seeks to prevent forms of business conduct that would tend to prevent competition and prevent the free operation of the laws of supply and demand.

INTRODUCTION TO THE ANTITRUST LAWS

Historically, this nation's economy was founded on the concept that government would not interfere in the activities of individual sellers freely competing in the marketplace. Underlying this classical economic theory was the assumption that there would be many sellers in the marketplace and a free flow of information between sellers and buyers. In the late 1800s and early 1900s, business power in several industries (particularly oil) became concentrated in one or two companies. Public demand to break up these "trusts" resulted in the passage of federal antitrust laws and some state statutes. (See Table 42-1 for a summary of these statutes and the business behavior they regulate. They are frequently referred to throughout the chapter.)

While concentrating on such business conduct as price fixing, conspiracies to restrain trade, and other anticompetitive behavior, this chapter also looks at how industry structure affects competition. When "industry structure" is mentioned, the reader should know that the concern of antitrust enforcement agencies generally is with the number and size of sellers. If the industry has only four domestic sellers, like the auto industry, is it more or less competitive? Should one include foreign competition in talking about the number of sellers and how competitive the industry may be?

Enforcement of the Antitrust Laws

Actions under the antitrust laws may be initiated in one of the following:

1. by the Department of Justice in the regular court system
2. by administrative agencies through especially established procedures

TABLE 42-1   Federal Antitrust Statutes Regulating Business Behavior

Structurally Oriented	Behaviorally Oriented
Sherman Act (1890), Section 2 prohibits monopolies and attempts or conspiracies to monopolize.	Sherman Act (1890), Section 1 condemns combinations and conspiracies in restraint of trade, including vertical and horizontal price fixing, group boycotts, division of markets.
Clayton Act (1914), Section 7 prohibits mergers, the effect of which may be substantially to lessen competition or to tend to create a monopoly. Amended (1950) by Celler-Kefauver Act, which clarifies application of Section 7 to acquisitions of assets.	Clayton Act (1914), Section 2 prohibits price discrimination, substantially lessening sellers' level competition (primarily line violations). Amended (1936) by Robinson-Patman Act, which prohibits price discrimination, substantially lessening buyers' (and below) level competition (secondary line violations).
	Clayton Act (1914), Section 3 prohibits exclusive dealing and tying arrangements, the effect of which may be to substantially lessen competition.
	Federal Trade Commission Act (1914), Section 5 prohibits unfair methods of competition, establishes and defines powers of FTC. Amended (1938) by Wheeler-Lea Act, which prohibits unfair trade practices, false advertising.

3. by private citizens in civil suits to obtain compensation for injuries they have suffered as a result of violations of the antitrust laws. This action can be taken by a group of citizens in the form of a *class* action or by the state attorney general of a state on behalf of a group of taxpaying citizens. Triple damages are awarded, meaning a jury or court verdict is automatically *tripled.*

The Department of Justice has a special Antitrust Division, headed by an Assistant Attorney General, responsible for enforcing the Sherman Act and, together with the Federal Trade Commission (FTC), for enforcing the Clayton Act. In addition, the Antitrust Division has special powers relating to the antitrust actions of federal administrative agencies. The FTC is the most important agency in this field. It has exclusive jurisdiction to enforce the Federal Trade Commission Act and with the Department of Justice may enforce the Clayton Act. In addition, the FTC has authority to enforce a number of other statutes relating to labeling and export trade. In jointly enforcing the Clayton Act, the Department of Justice and the FTC try to coordinate their efforts to prevent wasteful duplication. For example, the FTC has taken primary responsibility for enforcing the Robinson-Patman Act.

These public agencies make use of three basic remedies:

1. injunctions
2. criminal sanctions
3. fines

An injunction may prohibit a specified action (for example, distributing pricing information by a trade association), or it may require affirmative action on the part of the party against whom the order applies (for example, getting rid of certain assets).

Violation of the Sherman Act is a felony and may result in a term of prison up to three years. Although the imposition of prison terms in Sherman Act proceedings has received considerable publicity when it has occurred, the number of instances actually has been small. The Sherman Act also provides for fines of $100,000 on each count for an individual and $1 million on each count for a corporation.

Business Behavior Regulated by the Antitrust Laws

Price Fixing and Conspiracies in Restraint of Trade   Section 1 of the Sherman Act (summarized in Table 42-1) prohibits contracts, combinations, or conspiracies that restrain interstate trade. The U.S. Supreme Court has used two standards to determine which acts violate Section 1. The court has set out a *rule of reason* standard, noting that only *unreasonable* restraints of trade are illegal. The court has instructed lower courts and regulatory agencies to weigh the procompetitive effects of a particular business restraint against the anticompetitive effects to determine its reasonableness. Such factors as the nature of the business, the history of the restraint, the reason why businesses adopted it, and other factors peculiar to the business are to be considered. Certain other business activities or restraints are treated as illegal per se (in and of themselves). Once shown to exist, they are illegal, and no balancing of the pro- and anticompetitive effects is allowed into evidence to prove their reasonableness.

The courts with few exceptions have applied a per se standard to price fixing. Agreements fixing prices have always appealed to business people because they reduce, even eliminate, the risks of economic loss. Suppose that competitors A, B, and C, the major manufacturers of generators, agree to take turns offering low bids. Each is assured a portion of the available market, and each knows that price competition and its risks of monetary losses are eliminated. Artificially high prices can be charged and greater profits made. Of course, those who buy generators must pay more than they would in a competitive market. Similar results would follow in a broader based industry if the majority of firms were to agree to charge the same price or at least agree that no one would charge less than a specified price. Price fixing of this kind — among competitors operating on the same level of the marketing structure — is referred to as **horizontal price fixing.**

Horizontal price fixing price fixing among competitors at the same level of a market

Price fixing also occurs — in fact, is probably more easily achieved — between firms at different levels of the distribution system for particular goods. Price agreements between wholesalers and retailers, manufacturers and dealers, franchisors and franchisees are examples of **vertical price fixing.** The parties to price fixing agreements of this type are not competitors, but what they do affects competition.

Vertical price fixing price fixing between firms at different levels of the distribution system for particular goods

In the important case that follows, the Supreme Court emphasized the significance it continues to attach to the per se rule as applied to price fixing arrangements.

Arizona v. Maricopa County Medical Society

U.S. Supreme Court
457 U.S. 332 (1982)

Respondent foundations for medical care were organized by respondent, Maricopa County Medical Society, and another medical society to promote fee-for-service medicine and to provide the community with a competitive alternative to existing health   FACTS insurance plans. The foundations, by agreement of their member doctors, established the maximum fees the doctors could claim in full payment for health services provided to policyholders of specified insurance plans. The state of Arizona filed a complaint against respondents in federal district court, alleging that they were engaged in an illegal price fixing conspiracy in violation of Section 1 of the Sherman Act. Defendants claim they are professionals and that their plan is procompetitive because it provides a unique form of insurance that does not exist which allows for lower premiums.

ISSUE   Has Section 1 of the Sherman Act been violated by competing physicians setting maximum fees for full payment for health services rendered?

DECISION   Yes. The Court ruled that such price fixing agreements were per se illegal. The Court said that agreements such as those set by the doctors provided the same economic rewards to all regardless of their skill, their experience, their training, or their willingness to use innovative procedures in individual patients' cases. It stated that such restraints on prices would discourage entry into the geographic market and deter experimentation and new development. The Court said it made no difference that the parties to the price fixing agreement were professionals. Also the Court noted that lower insurance premiums were already provided in the state without a price fixing agreement by doctors.

Horizontal and Vertical Territorial and Customer Limitations   One device for reducing competition is an agreement between business rivals to divide markets geographically. Each of two or more competitors agrees not to sell in a designated territory. Courts have frequently referred to these agreements as **horizontal territorial limitations.** Similarly, business competitors sometimes agree to allocate customers. Where horizontal territorial limitations and customer allocations are carried out, the seller who is left in the market generally can get higher prices and provide less service because of its monopoly position. Because territorial sales restrictions and customer allocation have few redeeming features, they consistently have been held to be per se violations of antitrust laws. In *United States* v. *Topco Associates, Incorporated*, which follows, the Supreme Court ruled that market allocations were per se illegal even when a group of small- and medium-sized grocery chains with 6 percent of the market created a joint subsidiary to market private label products in competition with large supermarket chains such as A&P and Safeway.

> **Horizontal territorial limitations** an agreement between business rivals to divide markets geographically

Agreements that limit territories in which sales can be made are frequently entered into by manufacturers and dealers or by distributors who sell the manufacturer's product. These **vertical territorial limitations** generally provide an exclusive territory for a single or small number of dealers in a particular product. Both the manufacturer and the dealer–distributor benefit from these territorial restraints. Many argue that limitations of this kind benefit society as well because they increase competition between companies at the same level of the distribution system. For example, franchises frequently contain provisions limiting the territory in which the franchisee can operate.

> **Vertical territorial limitations** restraints placed by manufacturers on retailers as to where they can sell the manufacturer's product from

A corollary of the agreement that allots a specific territory to a seller is the agreement allocating customers. These two often go hand in hand because a territorial restriction prohibiting sales outside a specified area limits the customers with whom the seller may deal. But customer restrictions go beyond territorial allocations. It is not unusual for a manufacturer to reserve a particular buyer for direct sales, prohibiting distributors and dealers from selling to that buyer. The Supreme Court in the case below ruled that *vertical* restrictions (unlike *horizontal*) were to be judged by a *rule of reason* standard.

Continental Television, Incorporated v. GTE Sylvania

U.S. Supreme Court
433 U.S. 36 (1977)

GTE Sylvania (Plaintiff) manufactures and sells television sets. Before 1962, Sylvania sold its televisions to independent or company owned distributors, who resold to a large and diverse group of retailers. Prompted by a decline in its market share to 1 to 2 percent of the national market, Sylvania adopted a franchise plan.   FACTS

Sylvania phased out its wholesale distributors and sold directly to a smaller and more select group of franchised retailers. Each franchisee could sell only from the location at which he was franchised. A franchise did not constitute an exclusive territory. Sylvania retained the right to modify the number of franchises in an area. The revised marketing strategy was successful. But dissatisfied with its sales in San Francisco, Sylvania decided to establish an additional San Francisco retailer (Young Brothers), who would be in competition with Continental (defendant and petitioner-appellant in this case), because the Young Brothers would be only one mile away. Continental then canceled a large Sylvania order and placed an order with Phillips, one of Sylvania's competitors. Sylvania denied a request by Continental to establish a Sylvania franchise in Sacramento. When Continental advised Sylvania it was going ahead with its Sacramento plan and moving Sylvania merchandise to Sacramento, Sylvania terminated its franchise agreement and filed a complaint seeking recovery of money owed and merchandise held by Continental. Continental cross claimed in the same suit that the franchise agreement limiting retail locations selling Sylvania goods was a per se violation of Section 1 of the Sherman Act.

Is the franchise agreement limiting Continental's right to sell Sylvania goods in another location without the permission of Sylvania a per se violation of the Sherman Act?   ISSUE

No. The Court said that vertical limitations such as these were not per se illegal restraints of trade, but had to be judged by a rule of reason. The Court said that no showing had been made in this case or in other cases that vertical restrictions have or are likely to have such a "pernicious effect on competition" that they had no redeeming virtues. The Court pointed to scholarly writings showing that efficiency and competition between distributors are promoted by vertical territorial and customer restraints.   DECISION

Monopoly   Monopoly in its purest economic sense involves a single firm without any effective competition. Not only is no other firm producing the same product, but no other firm produces a product that consumers could switch to if the monopolist's prices are too high. The foregoing definition is far too restrictive for an antimonopoly statute because a firm could have the ability to act unilaterally and create market restraints without falling within the economic definition of a monopoly. Consequently, a *legal* definition of monopoly has been developed by the courts as they have interpreted the language of Section 2 of the Sherman Act. Section 2, summarized in Table 42-1, reads as follows:

> Every person who shall monopolize, or attempt to monopolize, or combine or conspire with any other person or persons, to monopolize any part of the trade or commerce among the several States, or with foreign nations, shall be deemed guilty of a felony, and, on conviction thereof, shall be punished by fine not exceeding $1 million if a corporation, or, if any other person, $100,000, or by imprisonment not exceeding three years.

As its language clearly indicates, Section 2 prohibits three types of activities:

1. monopolization,

2. attempts to monopolize, and

3. combinations or conspiracies to monopolize.

Most actions under Section 2 have been against single firms charged with monopolization. Suits based on attempts or conspiracies to monopolize are much more difficult to win, because they require proof of a specific intent.

In analyzing monopoly cases, the courts have set out guidelines, discussed below, as a basis for decision making. They can be helpful to business managers in making decisions also, especially in light of the harsh penalties for violations of Section 2 of the Sherman Act. The guidelines call for the court to look at the following criteria when determining whether a firm has monopolized the market:

1. the relevant *product* market

2. the relevant *geographic* market

3. whether the firm in the relevant product and geographic market has *overwhelming market power*

4. whether there is a *general intent* to monopolize.

In the landmark case excerpted below, the Supreme Court dealt with these criteria.

United States v. Grinnell Corporation

Supreme Court of the United States
384 U.S. 563 (1966)

FACTS   The United States charged Grinnell with monopolizing the accredited central-station protection business by using its subsidiaries to obtain a dominant market position. Grinnell manufactured plumbing supplies and fire sprinkler systems. It also owned 76 percent of the stock of ADT, 89 percent of the stock of AFA, and 100 percent of the stock of Holmes. ADT provided both burglary and fire protection services; Holmes provided burglary services alone; AFA supplied only fire-protection service. Each offered a central-station service under which hazard-detecting devices installed on the protected premises automatically transmitted an electric signal to a central station. The three companies that Grinnell controlled had over 87 percent of the business.

Has Grinnell violated Section 2 of the Sherman Act by monopolizing the accredited central-station protection business?   ISSUE

Yes. The Court said that a monopoly did exist. It rejected the defendant's argument that the relevant *product* market was not the entire accredited central-station services in their entirety because each of the services (burglary, fire, guards) is distinct and interchangeable. The Court said that it was dealing only with a single service use provided by the component units: the protection of property through a central station that reviews signals. The central station has no substitute and is not interchangeable.   DECISION

Attempt to Monopolize   Section 2 of the Sherman Act forbids *attempts* to monopolize as well as monopolization. In other words, a company does not have to be successful in monopolizing a market. Conduct that brought a corporation close to monopolization and showed an intent to monopolize was all that was required by the Supreme Court in early cases. Today most authorities agree that an attempt to monopolize requires:

1. specific intent

2. predatory or anticompetitive conduct to attain the purpose

3. a dangerous probability of success

A "dangerous probability of success" is usually shown through direct proof of the market power that the firm has attained. "Predatory pricing" has been the focus of much academic and case analysis of monopoly and price discrimination situations. Courts generally have agreed that pricing above marginal or variable costs is not predatory, and thus no specific intent can be shown to support charges that a firm tried to monopolize.

The question is at what point in a firm's pricing policy prices become predatory. In light of the fact that an attempt to monopolize is punishable as a felony with heavy criminal penalties, the answer to this question has some significance for businesspeople. The standard most popular with the courts states that when a firm sets its price *below marginal cost* (or average variable cost used as a substitute), it is engaged in predatory pricing because it no longer seeks to maximize profits but to eliminate an economically viable competitor.

Mergers   A **merger** is the acquisition by one corporation of the assets or stock of another independent corporation wherein the acquired corporation comes to be controlled by the acquirer. Mergers have had an important effect on the nature of industrial organization. They have accounted for much of the current concentration in many industries. Many mergers take place in the United States each year. In the fiscal year 1981, 2,314 mergers took place in the United States, up 53 percent over the

Merger the acquisition by one corporation of the assets or stock of another independent corporation

previous year. DuPont's acquisition of Conoco and Sohio's of Kennecott Copper were the most prominent. The increase in mergers in 1981 was largely due to the Reagan Administration's more relaxed approach to enforcement of Section 7 of the Clayton Act. Also, undervalued stocks, particularly in the oil industry, led companies to believe that it was cheaper to acquire a company than to finance internal expansion, especially at high interest rates. Finally, a number of companies divested themselves of subsidiaries purchased in the late 1950s and early 1960s that were no longer viable profit centers.

On the basis of the economic interrelationships between the firms involved, mergers may be classified into three basic types — horizontal, vertical, and conglomerate. A *horizontal merger* involves two competing firms at the same level of the distribution structure. A *vertical merger* involves two firms at different levels of the distribution structure that deal with the same basic product or process. A *conglomerate merger* results when noncompeting, nonrelated firms merge. The acquisition by RCA of the Hertz Rental Car Company is an example of a conglomerate merger.

Courts use several criteria to determine whether a particular merger is lawful under Section 7 of the Clayton Act (summarized in Table 42-1):

1. the relevant product and geographic market

2. the potential effect of the proposed merger in that market.

In applying these criteria, the court has always found it important to distinguish vertical from horizontal and conglomerate mergers. In some cases, as in the one excerpted below, both vertical and horizontal aspects of a merger exist.

Brown Shoe Company v. United States

Supreme Court of the United States
370 U.S. 294 (1962)

FACTS   The government challenged the acquisition of the G. R. Kinney Company by Brown Shoe on the grounds that the merger violated Section 7 of the Clayton Act. Brown was the third-largest retail shoe seller (over 1,230 outlets) and the fourth-largest shoe manufacturer, while Kinney was the eighth-largest seller (over 350 outlets) and the twelfth-largest manufacturer.

ISSUE   Does the merger of Brown and Kinney violate Section 7 of the Clayton Act?

DECISION   Yes. The Court said that both the vertical and horizontal aspects of the merger violated Section 7. As to the vertical aspect of the merger (Brown Shoe and Kinney's retailers), the Court stated that the product market is that recognized by the public, that is men's, women's, and children's shoes. The relevant geographic market was the nation. The Court said that the probable effect of the vertical aspect of the merger would be to lessen competition at the retail level in men's, women's, and children's shoes. As to the horizontal aspects of the merger, the court determined that the relevant product market was retail shoe departments of general stores and retail shoe stores selling men's, women's, or children's shoes. The geographic market was cities with populations of 10,000 people or more. The probable effect of the merger would be to increase the market share of Brown in the relevant geographic markets, tending to lessen competition under Section 7 of the Clayton Act.

Price Discrimination   In an economy based on freedom and competition, inexperienced business managers might expect that they would be permitted to price their products as the economics of production, distribution, and profit dictate. Not so. Management responsible for determining prices must make its decisions within the framework of extensive federal and state regulations that restrict choices.

One of the most important statutory provisions influencing pricing decisions is Section 2 of the Clayton Act as amended by the Robinson-Patman Act. This legislation tries to foster competition by prohibiting price discrimination in certain instances. Selling physically identical products at different prices can be anticompetitive in many situations. To be found illegal, price discrimination must occur in *interstate commerce* between a seller and different purchasers of commodities of *like grade and quality,* and the effect of such discrimination by the seller must be *to substantially lessen competition* or tend to create a monopoly. Congress enacted the law in 1936 to protect small businesses from huge sellers coming into a market and cutting prices on a product below cost for the sole purpose of driving out small sellers.

One situation, frequently referred to as "primary" or "seller's level" competition, involves competition between sellers and their rivals. The strategy likely to violate Section 2 of the Clayton Act is **whipsawing.** When, for example, the price cutting seller operates in several geographic markets, it can cut prices in one while maintaining its prices in another. This gives it an unfair advantage when competing with a seller that operates only in a single geographic market. Unable to maintain its price, the latter has no way of keeping up its profits. But the former can make up at least a portion of its losses by profits earned in other areas. After eliminating one regional competitor by selective price cutting, the firm functioning in several regions can then turn its attention to another and so on until all regional competitors have been eliminated.

Cases of blatant whipsawing are rare, and selective price cutting can be done for legitimate economic motives — for example, when a firm wishes to secure a market share in a new geographic market area. The courts have had some difficulty balancing legitimate economic interests with the price discrimination laws when a national firm invades a market area that is dominated by a regional firm.

The major defense of large sellers for their selective price cutting or discrimination among purchasers is that they were meeting the competition.

Whipsawing
when a seller cuts prices in one market while maintaining price in another with the intent of driving out competitors in the first market

SUMMARY

This chapter has introduced the reader to government regulation as carried out by administrative agencies. The agencies regulate through adjudicating individual cases, through industrywide rule making, and through various administrative activities.

Government regulation is classified as social or economic, depending on whether its goal is to affect individuals directly in a social and political context or industry and firms in an economic context. One form of economic regulation is antitrust laws against forms of industry and firm behavior. Vertical and horizontal price fixing, monopoly conduct, mergers, and price discrimination all are subject to antitrust laws.

REVIEW PROBLEMS

1. What are the three major ways in which administrative agencies regulate business?

2. What is the difference between social and economic regulation?

3. Who enforces our antitrust laws?

4. What is the difference between vertical and horizontal mergers?

5. The Federal Communications Commission set forth rules prohibiting cable television systems from broadcasting first-run feature films that were less than ten but more than three years old. Home Box Office appealed this rule and other restrictions to the District of Columbia Circuit Court of Appeals, claiming that this exercise of the commission's rule making authority was arbitrary and capricious and that it restricted competition. The commission claimed that the regulations were needed to prevent siphoning by cable companies of copyrighted material broadcast over the air. Were the regulations arbitrary and capricious? Who wins?

6. From 1958 until 1961, Utah Pie Company, a local producer, was the leading seller of frozen pies in the Salt Lake City market. Because of the advantage of its location, the company usually could maintain the lowest prices in a market in which the major competitive weapon was price. During a four-year period, Utah Pie was challenged at one time or another by each of three major competitors, all of which operated in several other markets. Evidence showed that each of these competitors sold frozen pies in the Salt Lake market at prices lower than they charged for pies of like grade and quality in other markets considerably closer to their plants. Evidence also indicated that in several instances, one or more of them had sold at prices below actual cost and that one of the competitors had sent an industrial spy into Utah's plant. During the period, price levels went down substantially. In 1958, Utah had been selling pies for $4.15 a dozen. Some 44 months later, Utah was selling similar pies for $2.75 a dozen. As a result of the actions of Pet Milk, Carnation, and Continental, the three major competitors, Utah Pie brought an action for triple damages, charging each with a violation of Section 2(a) of the Clayton Act as amended by the Robinson-Patman Act. What result?

7. The Philadelphia National Bank and Girard Trust Bank were the second and third largest of the 42 commercial banks with head offices in the metropolitan area consisting of the city of Philadelphia and three adjoining counties. Philadel-

phia National had assets of over $1 billion. Girard had assets of over $750 million. The boards of directors of the banks approved a merger. If they merged, the resulting bank would be the largest in the four-county Philadelphia area. The two banks viewed the merger as strengthening their hand in competing with other large banks in the northeastern United States. The government filed suit, alleging that the proposed merger was in violation of Section 7 of the Clayton Act and asking that the court bar it. What result?

8. Reynolds Metal Company was the largest producer of aluminum foil in the world. In 1956 it acquired Arrow Brands, Incorporated, then engaged in converting aluminum and selling it nationally to wholesale florist supply houses. Arrow purchased its raw aluminum from Reynolds, converted it, and, before its acquisition by Reynolds, accounted for 33 percent of the converted foil sold to the florist industry. Eight other firms also supplied converted aluminum to the florist industry, and some bought from Reynolds. The FTC sued under Section 7, claiming that aluminum foil in the florist trade was the relevant market. Reynolds argued that all trades that required specialized use of aluminum were the relevant product market. What result?

9. Beginning in 1959, four major distributors of stainless steel pipe and tubing who sold in Washington, Oregon, California, Idaho, and Utah began to experience substantial price competition from eastern mills and from small local jobbers, who sold but did not stock pipe and tubing. Upon the invitation of Tubesales Corporation, the dominant and largest distributor, a series of meetings was held to discuss mutual problems. The government claimed that at these meetings the parties agreed to reduce discounts to nonstocking jobbers from 10 percent to 5 percent and to reduce the freight factor in their prices. As a result, new price lists embracing lower freight rates were drawn up by Tubesales and hand delivered to the others. All four distributors were charged with violations of Section 1 of the Sherman Act. What result?

10. In 1864 and 1870, Congress granted the Northern Pacific Railway Company approximately 40 million acres of land to help in the financing and constructing of a railroad to the northwest. The grant consisted of alternate sections of land in a belt 20 miles wide on each side of the track. The granted lands were of various kinds. By 1949, the railroad had sold about 37 million acres of its holdings and leased most of the rest. In a large number of sales and leases, the railroad had inserted "preferential routing" clauses that compelled the owner or lessee to ship over Northern Pacific lines all commodities produced on the land. The preferential routing clause applied only if Northern Pacific's rates were equal to those of competing carriers. In 1949, the government sued under Section 1 of the Sherman Act, seeking a declaration that the preferential routing clauses were unlawful as unreasonable restraints of trade because they constituted tying arrangements. What result?

11. A group of Carvel franchisees operating stores selling soft ice cream products sued Carvel Corporation for triple damages. They alleged that Carvel engaged in illegal exclusive dealing and tying arrangements by requiring the franchisees:

1 □ to refrain from selling non-Carvel products

2 ▢ to buy from Carvel or those it designated certain supplies that ultimately would be part of the final product sold (the franchisees were allowed to purchase equipment and paper goods from other sources subject to quality control specifications)

3 ▢ to follow "suggested" resale prices.

What result?

12. Sealy manufactures box springs and mattresses. Licensees only obtain the right to manufacture and sell Sealy products. Sealy assigned each of its licensees a place to manufacture and a geographic area for promoting Sealy products. Sealy also negotiated separate agreements directly with others. Each licensee would then provide a retailer in its area with Sealy products at a price set by Sealy and a retailer in their separate agreements. One of its licensees sued, claiming violation of Section 1 of the Sherman Act because Sealy was using unreasonable horizontal and vertical restraints. What result?

13. Kennecott Copper Corporation, holding 33 percent of the copper market, acquired Peabody Coal Company, which held 10 percent of the coal market. Both were leaders in their respective markets. Kennecott also owned a small coal company. There were high barriers to entry in the coal industry, and copper supplies were dwindling for Kennecott at the time of purchase. The FTC charged Kennecott with a violation of Section 7 of the Clayton Act, noting that Kennecott would have entered the coal industry on its own due to dwindling copper reserves. The FTC charged that a potential entrant into the coal industry was eliminated when this acquisition took place. What result?

14. United Shoe Machinery Company produced 75 percent of all shoe machines. The company *leased* these machines for ten-year periods and provided free maintenance and repair. It refused to *sell* machines and required all its lessees to operate the leased machines at full capacity. The Justice Department sued United Shoe, charging that it monopolized the shoe machinery market in violation of Section 2 of the Sherman Act. The company claimed that its market share was gained from its superior business acumen and attempts to protect its patents and reputation. What result?

CHAPTER 43

Accountant's Liability

CHAPTER OBJECTIVES

After reading this chapter, you should be able to:

1. Explain when an accountant may be liable to a client for breach of contract.

2. Describe the professional standards for an accountant's work and how those standards relate to legal liability.

3. List the types of opinions an accountant may give about financial documents.

4. Identify the liability of an accountant to a client for negligence.

5. Describe the circumstances under which an accountant may be liable to a third party who relies upon the accountant's work product.

6. State whether the IRS may obtain personal records given to an accountant preparing a tax return.

7. Identify the liability of accountants under securities laws and other federal statutes.

8. Explain the circumstances under which an accountant may be found criminally liable.

Accountants' liability is an important topic in business law today. Increasingly, accounting firms are sued when there have been financial misdealings resulting in bankruptcy or violations of the securities laws. It is important that both certified public accountants (CPAs) and managers understand the legal principles that govern the accountant–client relationship.

There are several ways in which public accountants can incur liability in the practice of their profession. Failure to meet the standards of an employment contract exposes an accountant to contract liability. Theories of intentional tort and negligence (discussed in Chapters 3 and 4) also may provide the basis for a suit against an accountant who has performed improperly. In addition to common law actions, various federal and state statutes impose both civil and criminal liability on accountants.

An accountant's potential liability to third parties, once tightly restricted, has been expanded in recent years. An accountant's exposure to criminal liability also has expanded. This chapter traces the legal developments affecting accountants and their profession.

LIABILITY TO CLIENTS

Accountants' common law civil liability to clients may be grounded in contract or in tort. The choice of theories on which to sue may be especially important when the statute of limitations for contract actions differs from that for tort actions. In many contract suits and in all tort actions, the plaintiff is required to show that the defendant accountant failed to satisfy a required standard of care.

The Role of GAAP and GAAS

The American Institute of Certified Public Accountants (AICPA), the professional association of CPAs, has set forth principles and standards to guide accountants in their practice. Accountants are expected to comply with generally accepted accounting principles **(GAAP)** and generally accepted auditing standards **(GAAS).** Evidence of compliance or noncompliance with these principles may be used to determine whether the accountant exercised the degree of skill and care required.

Although compliance with GAAP and GAAS may substantially reduce the likelihood that an accountant is subject to liability, compliance is not in itself a complete defense. Thus the Second Circuit Court of Appeals in *U.S.* v. *Simon* (1970) in affirming the convictions of accountants who had apparently adhered to GAAP, stated:

> Generally accepted accounting principles instruct an accountant what to do in the usual case where he has no reason to doubt that the affairs of the corporation are being honestly conducted. Once he has reason to believe that this basic assumption is false, an entirely different situation confronts him.

GAAP acronym for generally accepted accounting principles

GAAS acronym for generally accepted auditing standards followed by the accounting profession

Contract Liability

An accountant's liability to a client is usually based in some way on the contract with the client. Violation of the agreement's terms can give rise to an action for breach of contract. A breach of contract action may be based on violations of either the express or implied terms of the contract.

If an accountant expressly agrees to prepare and file a client's tax returns by April 15 and then misses the deadline, an express term of the agreement has been violated. The accountant may be held liable to the client for any penalties resulting from the late filing.

If the accountant commits careless errors that cause the client to suffer losses, the client again has an action in breach of contract. This right holds even though the contract is silent regarding the standard of care to which the accountant must adhere. Every accountant is implicitly bound, in the performance of a contract, to exercise that degree of skill and competence commonly exercised by members of the profession.

An accountant is also, of course, implicitly bound to perform his or her services without fraud. In the following case, an accounting firm was held liable for breach of contract because its employee had helped defraud its client.

Opinion (accountant's) a representation to those who may be expected to rely on the financial statements

Unqualified opinion (accountant's) a representation that a company's statements are a fair reflection of its finances

_____ *Matter of F. W. Koenecke and Sons, Incorporated* _____

U.S. Court of Appeals, Seventh Circuit
605 F.2d 924 (1979)

FACTS   F. W. Koenecke and Sons, a cigarette distributor, shut down in February 1969, after declaring bankruptcy. Shortly before the firm shut down, company president Robert Koenecke caused $315,000 in checks to be drawn on the corporation's account. The checks were payable to Mr. Koenecke and to Clifford Kohler, the sales manager. Glenn Heyman, the company's trustee in bankruptcy, retained the accounting firm of James T. Wilkes to complete the company's books for February and March. Wilkes put staff accountant Alex Birnie in charge of the matter. Apparently unknown to Wilkes, Birnie was also employed by Koenecke. Birnie made false entries into the books to conceal the fact that $315,000 had been paid to Koenecke and Kohler. After discovering the fraud two years later, Heyman sued Wilkes. Wilkes argued that it should not be held liable for the misdeeds of Birnie.

ISSUE   Did Wilkes breach its contract to complete the books when its employee, Birnie, defrauded the client?

DECISION   Yes. The court ruled in favor of the plaintiff Heyman, saying that Birnie's fraudulent conduct could be imputed to Wilkes because Wilkes put Birnie in the position to defraud the client while apparently acting within his authority. The court ruled that the contract obligated Wilkes to correct any false entries in the client's books or, at the very least, to refrain from defrauding the client. Because Wilkes—through its employee Birnie—had failed in these contractual obligations, the firm could be held liable for breach of contract.

The Effect of Accountants' Opinions

Qualified opinion (accountant's) a statement to the effect that a representation is affected by material uncertainty or deviation from GAAP

Adverse opinion (accountant's) a statement to the effect that financial statements do not fairly represent a company's financial condition

After auditing a company's financial statements, an accountant issues an **opinion.** An accountant's opinion is a representation to those who can reasonably be expected to rely on the financial statements.

By expressing an **unqualified opinion,** an accountant represents that the company's financial statements fairly reflect the company's financial picture. That is, the balance sheet properly presents the firm's financial position, the income statement fairly represents the results of the firm's operations, and changes in financial position are accurately depicted. An unqualified opinion requires that the financial statements reflect the consistent application of GAAP. An accountant who cannot express an unqualified opinion is required to issue either a **qualified opinion,** which can be made necessary by material uncertainty or deviations from GAAP; an **adverse opinion,** which states that the financial statements do not fairly present the firm's position in conformance with the GAAP; or a **disclaimer of opinion,** which is issued when the accountant lacks enough information to form an opinion on the accuracy of the audited statements.

Accountants sometimes may prepare or analyze financial documents without conducting a full audit. In such circumstances, accountants rely on the client's financial records without investigating their accuracy. The AICPA has developed the concepts of **compilations** and **reviews** to protect accountants from unwarranted reliance on such documents. In a compilation, the accountant puts information supplied by the client into the form of financial statements. The compilation should be accompanied by a report explaining that no audit has been performed and that the accuracy of the information cannot be assured. Each page of the compiled financial statements should contain a printed reference directing the reader to the disclaiming report. A review involves a limited analysis of financial statements that have been prepared by the client. In a review, the accountant expresses limited assurance that the financial statements are not materially misleading. In an accompanying report, which must be referred to on each page of the statements, the accountant states that the analysis conducted in the review was substantially less than that for a proper audit.

Although qualifications and disclaimers may limit an accountant's liability in certain tort actions, they do not in themselves relieve the accountant of contractual obligations. This principle is illustrated in *Ryan* v. *Kanne,* the following case. The "unaudited statement" disclaimer used in that case was a forerunner of the current compilation and review disclaimers.

Disclaimer of opinion (accountant's) a statement that there is insufficient information to guarantee the accuracy of the audit

Compilation an accountant's basing financial statements solely on information supplied by the client

Review (accountant's) the providing of a limited analysis of financial statements prepared by a client

---

Ryan v. Kanne

Supreme Court of Iowa
170 N.W.2d 395 (1969)

FACTS

James Kanne hired accountants to update his financial statements at a creditor's request. The accountants, who knew that certain creditors would use the "Accounts Payable — Trade" account to determine the feasibility of acquiring Kanne's businesses, apparently agreed to determine the proper balance of that account to within $5,000. After examining Kanne's books, the accountants issued a balance sheet with the words "Unaudited Statement" printed on the top as a disclaimer. It became apparent that the balance sheet contained an inaccurate entry for the "Accounts Payable — Trade" account. A later reaudit by another firm showed that the original accountants had misstated the account by $33,689.22. After Kanne and his creditors refused to pay for the original audit, the accountants sued them for the value of their services. Kanne and his creditors counterclaimed for damages resulting from the accountants' errors. The trial court awarded $3,439.67 to the accountants and $38,685.81 to Kanne and his creditors. The accountants appealed.

ISSUE

Did the accountants' "unaudited statement" disclaimer relieve them of liability for errors?

DECISION

No. The court ruled that the disclaimer would not relieve the accountants of responsibility for their errors. The accountants specifically contracted to determine the "Accounts Payable — Trade" account to within $5,000. The accountants failed to exercise the required level of skill and care in estimating the account, and they could not avoid their contractual obligation simply by issuing a disclaimer.

TORT LIABILITY

In a contract action against an accountant, the parties' rights and obligations are primarily determined by their own agreement. The parties' rights and liabilities in a tort action are determined by common law or by statute. Recall from Chapter 4 that tort liability is founded on the breach of duties imposed by society. The breach may be unintentional, as in the case of negligence, or deliberate, as with fraud. We will consider accountants' liability for both unintentional and intentional torts.

Negligence

As in other negligence actions, a client suing an accountant for negligence must establish:

1. that the accountant owed the client a *duty of care*

2. that the accountant *breached* this duty

3. that the client suffered an *injury*

4. that the accountant's breach was the *proximate cause* of the client's injury.

The accountant's duty of care to a client generally originates in the contract between them. Like other professionals, accountants have a general duty to perform services with the level of skill, care, knowledge, and judgment usual among members of the profession in the particular locality, in accordance with accepted professional standards and in good faith.

The following case illustrates the application of the above principles to accountants' malpractice suits. In the *Rockler* case, the alleged malpractice stemmed from tax-planning services offered by the defendant accountants.

Vernon J. Rockler & Company v. *Glickman, Isenberg, Lurie & Company*

Supreme Court of Minnesota
273 N.W.2d 647 (1978)

FACTS　　Vernon J. Rockler and Company was a securities broker. Rockler held its securities in three separate accounts: an investment account, in which securities were held as capital assets; an inventory account, for trading securities with the public; and a "short sales" inventory account, which kept track of securities which Rockler had sold but had not yet purchased.

Profits on the sale of securities held in the investment account for more than six months were taxed at the capital gains rate, lower than the normal tax rate.

In 1968, with stock prices rising, Mr. Rockler, the firm's president, consulted the Glickman accounting firm about the possibility of using securities in the investment account to cover short sales. Rockler hoped to be able to do this without losing the favorable tax treatment allowed to securities in the investment account. The Glickman firm advised Mr. Rockler that he would probably be able to retain the tax benefits if he moved securities from the investment account to the short sales inventory account but that there were safer means of preserving the tax advantages. Rockler transferred securities from its investment account to its short sales account to cover short sales.

The IRS audited Rockler's 1969 income tax return, and disallowed the capital gains treatment of the transferred securities and assessed a higher tax liability against Rockler. Rockler sued Glickman for malpractice.

Is accountant Glickman guilty of malpractice by virtue of his incorrect advice to Rockler? **ISSUE**

No. The court ruled that Glickman had not committed malpractice. Accountants, like other professionals, owe their clients a duty of reasonable care. To recover for malpractice, a client must establish not only a duty but a breach of that duty, damages, and that the breach of duty was a proximate cause of the damages. Here the court ruled that Glickman's inconclusive advice did not reasonably warrant Rockler's reliance and could not be said to have been the proximate cause of Rockler's damages. Failing to establish an essential element of malpractice, Rockler could not prevail. **DECISION**

Accountants, like other professionals, must undergo extensive training before qualifying for professional practice. In areas that involve such specialized training, courts often ask plaintiffs to provide expert testimony to establish what the defendant's required standard of care was and how it was breached. Recall that a plaintiff in a negligence action may prevail without offering sufficient evidence to support each element of his case. Plaintiffs often find themselves in the difficult position of having to find accountants to testify against other accountants. Professionals have often been accused of perpetrating a "conspiracy of silence" to protect each other from malpractice liability. In accounting, the existence of such universally accepted standards as GAAP and GAAS sometimes may reduce the need for expert testimony to establish a case for malpractice. Still, expert testimony often is needed to properly interpret such standards and the ways in which they should be applied.

Other Torts

Accountants may also, of course, be held liable to their clients for intentional torts. Perhaps the most common action is one alleging fraud. Fraud involves a material misrepresentation of fact, made with knowledge of its falsity and with intent to deceive. To collect damages for fraud, a plaintiff must prove personal reliance on the misrepresentation and that the reliance caused injury. Because accountants' opinions are representations, they may be used as the basis for fraud actions.

Liability of Tax Preparers

Accountants may expose themselves to contract or tort liability in the preparation of clients' tax returns. Accountants may be held liable for damages resulting from the late filing of clients' returns, from negligent misstatement of tax liability, and from erroneous tax advice. In one case, an accountant was held liable for breach of contract for refusing to either file or return the client's tax returns until the bill was paid. The court noted that the accountant could also have been held liable for the tort of **nonfeasance,** for failing to attempt to perform as promised.

Nonfeasance
making no attempt to fulfill an obligation

In preparing taxes, as in an accountant's other duties, an accountant is required to exercise the degree of care, skill, and competence exercised by others in the profession. Breach of this duty can leave the accountant liable for compensatory damages, which are commonly penalties and interest assessed against the client because of the tax preparer's mistake. Tax preparers sometimes are also required to compensate clients for fees paid to attorneys or other accountants to straighten out the tax preparer's error.

A tax preparer also may be subject to civil and criminal liability under the provisions of the Internal Revenue Code. This is discussed later in the chapter.

LIABILITY TO PRODUCE CLIENT RECORDS

The Supreme Court has upheld the right of an authorized government agency to obtain an accountant's records in the investigation of a client. The Court has thus held that the accountant–client relationship, unlike the attorney–client relationship, is not a privileged one. It is now settled that requiring delivery of an accountant's records to an appropriate government agency does not violate the client's constitutional right against compulsory self-incrimination. This doctrine is set forth in the *Couch* case, which follows.

Couch v. United States

U.S. Supreme Court
409 U.S. 322 (1973)

FACTS   In a tax investigation of a restaurant owner, the IRS summoned the records of her accountant. The restaurant owner had been giving the records to her accountant for many years for the purpose of having her tax returns prepared. After the summons was issued, she sought to prevent the records from being turned over to the IRS, claiming that enforcing the summons would violate her Fifth Amendment right against compulsory self-incrimination. She also argued that the accountant–client relationship has the privilege of confidentiality.

ISSUE   Are records given by a client to an accountant protected against compulsory disclosure?

DECISION   No. The Court ruled in favor of the United States, holding that one's constitutional privilege against compulsory self-incrimination is not violated by compelling one's accountant to produce documents that might be incriminating. The privilege against self-incrimination applies to the person, not to the possibly incriminating information. Here the restaurant owner was not compelled to produce anything. Her accountant was compelled to produce records voluntarily given to him by the restaurant owner. Also the Court noted that no confidential accountant–client privilege was recognized under federal law.

The *Couch* case upheld the right of the IRS to summon from an accountant records owned by a client. It would seem to follow from that holding that the IRS would have similar access to the work papers an accountant uses to evaluate a client's tax liability.

Yet despite the *Couch* ruling, the U.S. Court of Appeals for the Second Circuit devised a doctrine of **accountant's work product** immunity from disclosure. In the 1982 case of *U.S.* v. *Arthur Young and Co.,* which follows, the Second Circuit held that protecting the confidentiality of accountants' work was necessary to promote full disclosure by clients to accountants. This disclosure, the court reasoned, was necessary to protect the integrity of the securities markets, which depended on complete and accurate information from their participants. The court thus developed a doctrine for accountants similar to the work product immunity that applies to attorneys.

Accountant's work product background notes and work relating to a job for a client

But the doctrine of accountants' work product immunity had a short life. In 1982 the Supreme Court granted the government's petition for *certiorari.* In its opinion below, the Court relied on the *Couch* decision to reject the doctrine of work product immunity.

_____ *United States v. Arthur Young and Company* _____

United States Supreme Court
52 LW 4355 (1984)

The accounting firm of Arthur Young and Company served as an independent auditor for the Amerada Hess Corporation. One of Arthur Young's functions was to evaluate the adequacy of Amerada's reserve account for contingent tax liabilities. The reserve account was required to cover tax liabilities that might later be assessed by the IRS over and above those reflected on the corporation's return. After a routine IRS audit revealed questionable financial practices by the corporation, the IRS began a criminal investigation of its tax returns and issued a summons to Arthur Young commanding that it hand over its Amerada files, including work papers. At Amerada's request, Arthur Young refused to honor the summons. The IRS sued to enforce the summons. Arthur Young urged the Court to recognize a doctrine of accountants' work product immunity, by which accountants could not be compelled to release the workpapers which they use to prepare audits. Arthur Young argued that such a doctrine was necessary to promote full disclosure by companies to their accountants. Such disclosure to accountants, who prepare the statements required by the Securities Exchange Commission, would be necessary to ensure that the securities markets received the information they need to operate efficiently.

FACTS

Is a policy of holding accountants' work papers immune needed to insure that clients will make full disclosure to accountants?

ISSUE

DECISION   No. The Court ruled in favor of the United States, rejecting the doctrine of accountants' work product immunity. The *Couch* case was cited for the proposition that no privilege of confidentiality was recognized for the accountant–client relationship. The Court concluded that no such privilege was needed to promote full disclosure by firms to their accountants. Accountants, as independent professionals, are already obliged to take whatever investigative steps are necessary to properly verify their clients' financial positions. When accountants cannot get enough information to verify their clients' financial statements properly, they are required to qualify their opinions. Because such qualifications do not put a company's operations in a good light, companies have the incentive to provide accountants with the information needed to issue an unqualified opinion.

LIABILITY TO THIRD PARTIES

Clients are not the only parties that rely on accountants' work. A potential creditor relies on a company's financial statements to evaluate the riskiness of a contemplated loan. A potential purchaser of a firm examines its balance sheet to determine the value of the assets and the extent of the liabilities that would be assumed. A potential buyer of a firm's securities uses the firm's prospectus and other financial data to make the purchase decision. A potential assignee of a debt wants to determine the collectibility of that debt before exchanging something of value for the assignment.

In deciding how far to extend an accountant's liability to third parties, the law must reconcile valid conflicting interests. On the one hand, it would appear that the efficient operation of credit markets, securities markets, and other markets would require that participants be entitled to rely on the relevant information available to them. If participants in these markets are forced to assume the risks associated with inaccurate information, they demand compensation for that risk in the marketplace. An economist would argue that it is most efficient to place the risk on the party with the power to control the risk. In our case, the accountant would be one of the parties best able to control the risks to third parties of inaccurate information.

On the other hand, the accountant might not be able to bear the risk of liability to every third party that could conceivably be hurt by reliance on a financial document prepared by the accountant. For one thing, there is no clear way to control the number of people who rely on particular financial documents, because clients are the ones that distribute the documents. If a negligent mistake could leave an accountant liable to thousands of unknown third parties, the accountant clearly would be assuming an unreasonable risk. Accountants could, of course, insure against such risk, but the cost of such extensive coverage — whether borne by accountants or their clients — might be prohibitive.

Privity of contract the concept that only parties to a contract may use the contract as a basis for suit

For many years, the law placed more emphasis on the need to limit accountants' liability to third parties than on the need to protect third parties from the negligent mistakes of accountants. Thus an accountant's liability for negligence was limited to those with contractual relationships with the accountant — those in **privity of contract** with the accountant. Over the last several decades, the privity requirement has been steadily eroded in most areas of the law. Since the 1960s, the privity doctrine has been weakened with regard to accountants.

Privity and the Ultramares Doctrine

The proposition that an accountant's negligence liability is limited to those in privity with the accountant was set forth in the classic case of *Ultramares Corporation* v. *Touche,* from which the **Ultramares doctrine** originated.

Ultramares doctrine the theory that accountants are not liable to third parties for ordinary negligence

--------- *Ultramares Corporation v. Touche* ---------

Court of Appeals of New York
174 N.E. 441 (1931)

Touche, Niven and Company performed accounting services for Fred Stern and Company, a rubber dealer. In February 1924, Touche issued a balance sheet which showed Stern's net worth to be over $1 million. Touche certified that the balance sheet presented a "true and correct view" of Stern's financial position as of December 31, 1923. In reality, Stern was insolvent. The firm's net worth was misrepresented by falsified entries in Stern's books. The Ultramares Corporation loaned a large amount of money to Stern, relying on the balance sheet. Although Touche was not specifically aware that Ultramares would rely on the balance sheet, it was aware that Stern would use the balance sheet for the purpose of securing credit. Stern went bankrupt in January 1925. Ultramares sued Touche for negligence in the preparation of Stern's balance sheet.

FACTS

Should accountants be held liable to third parties for work that has been negligently prepared?

ISSUE

No. The court rules that Touche could not be held liable to Ultramares for negligence. Chief Justice Cardozo reasoned that if accountants could be held liable in negligence to third parties, a "thoughtless slip or blunder" potentially could expose the accountant to liability from unlimited and undefined classes of plaintiffs. This, Cardozo concluded, would place an unreasonable burden on the accounting profession. Cardozo also argued that permitting such a recovery would leave a negligent accountant in essentially the same position as an accountant who had committed fraud. Cardozo implied that such a ruling would effectively give certain third parties the same rights against accountants that clients have.

DECISION

Gross Negligence and Fraud

A third party who can show that the accountant acted fraudulently can recover from the accountant in spite of lack of privity. Some courts have allowed recovery against accountants by third parties who have established gross negligence, without requiring any other evidence to support the inference of fraud. These courts have not made it clear that the recovery is based on fraud and not on gross negligence. This manipulation of the relationship between fraud and gross negligence has been heavily criticized by legal scholars.

The Erosion of the Privity Requirement

Since the late 1960s, the "assault on the citadel of privity" has spread into the area of accountant's liability. Courts in many jurisdictions now allow a third party plaintiff to recover against an accountant for ordinary negligence.

These courts have not totally ignored Justice Cardozo's warnings against exposing accountants to unlimited liability. Most of the courts subscribing to the new philosophy require the third party plaintiff to belong to a *limited class* of people whose reliance on the accountant's work was *actually foreseen* by the accountant. Indeed, in almost every case in which the third party was allowed to recover, the *particular* third party's reliance actually had been foreseen by the accountant.

Rusch Factors, Incorporated v. *Levin* was one of the first cases to articulate the modern, expanded view of accountants' liability to third parties.

Rusch Factors, Incorporated v. Levin

U.S. District Court for the District of Rhode Island
284 F.Supp. 85 (1968)

FACTS   A corporation sought loans from Rusch Factors, Incorporated, in 1963 and 1964. As a precondition to making the loans, Rusch required the corporation to present certified financial statements. The defendant accountant, Levin, prepared these statements for the corporation. The statements showed the corporation to be solvent, even though it was actually insolvent. Relying on the statements, Rusch loaned the corporation more than $337,000. The corporation later went into receivership, and Rusch was unable to collect a large part of its loan. Rusch sued Levin for negligent misrepresentation.

ISSUE   Should accountants be held liable to third parties whom they specifically know will rely on their statements?

DECISION   Yes. The court ruled in favor of the plaintiff, Rusch Factors. Distinguishing this case from *Ultramares* v. *Touche,* the court contended that the plaintiff here was not a member of an "undefined, unlimited class of remote" parties to which Justice Cardozo was unwilling to subject accountants to negligence liability. Here the accountant actually foresaw Rusch's reliance on the financial statements. The court ruled that accountants could be held liable in negligence for errors relied upon by actually foreseen and limited classes of persons. The court hinted that in the future it might consider holding accountants responsible in negligence to limited classes of third parties whose reliance is foreseeable, though not necessarily foreseen.

The *Rusch* court, in support of its argument for broader accountants' liability to third parties, cited tentative drafts of the Restatement (Second) of Torts. This Restatement since has been finalized. Section 552, dealing with information negligently supplied for the guidance of others, provides:

1. One who, in the course of his business, profession or employment, or in any other transaction in which he has a pecuniary interest, supplies false information for the guidance of others in their business transactions, is subject to liability for pecuniary loss caused to them by their justifiable reliance upon the information, if he fails to exercise reasonable care or competence in obtaining or communicating the information.

2. Except as stated in Subsection (3), the liability stated in Subsection (1) is limited to loss suffered:
   a. by the person or one of a limited group of persons for whose benefit and guidance he intends to supply the information or knows that the recipient intends to supply it; and
   b. through reliance upon it in a transaction that he intends the information to influence or knows that the recipient so intends or in a substantially similar transaction.

3. The liability of one who is under a public duty to give the information extends to loss suffered by any of the class of persons for whose benefit the duty is created, in any of the transactions in which it is intended to protect them.

At least one court has extended accountants' liability to third parties even further. The Supreme Court of New Jersey ruled that an accountant could be held liable in negligence to those whom the accountant should *reasonably foresee* as recipients of the accountant's work for authorized business purposes. Plaintiffs in that case relied on a firm's financial statements in deciding to acquire a controlling interest in the firm. The defendant accountants had audited the financial statements for submission to the SEC. The accountants had failed to detect several falsifications that masked the firm's poor financial condition. Plaintiffs sued the defendant accountants after the acquired firm went bankrupt. In denying defendants' motion for partial summary judgment, the court did not require plaintiffs to show that they were part of a limited class whose reliance on the statements was actually foreseen by the accountants. The "reasonably foreseeable" standard adopted by the court is similar to the standard that applies to most types of negligence actions.

STATUTORY LIABILITY

In addition to common law theories of liability, various federal and state statutes provide a basis for accountants' liability. We will confine our discussion to the federal statutes.

The statutes with the greatest effect on accountants are the Securities Act of 1933 and the Securities and Exchange Act of 1934. Accountants may be brought under the jurisdiction of these acts through their work on financial statements, annual reports, registration statements, and proxy statements.

Recall that Section 11 of the 1933 act provides a civil remedy for securities buyers who have been injured by their reliance on misinformation in the registration statement. Accountants may be held liable under this section for materials that they prepare or certify. Accountants who aid and abet a securities fraud are subject to liability under Section 17.

Accountants who make misstatements in proxy statements may be held liable under Section 14(a) of the 1934 act or under SEC Rule 14a-9. Accountants who make false statements in tender offers may be held liable under Section 14(e) of the 1934 act. Courts have held that knowledge of falsity with intent to deceive is required to hold an accountant liable under both sections.

Accountants' liability under the 1934 act is typically founded on Section 10(b), which grants an implied civil remedy to buyers or sellers of securities who have been damaged by fraud. In the landmark case of *Ernst and Ernst* v. *Hochfelder,* the Supreme Court ruled that a plaintiff would have to establish that the defendant acted with knowledge to prevail in a Section 10(b) action. In the absence of guidance from the Supreme Court, many circuits have held that reckless conduct is enough to satisfy the knowledge requirement of *Ernst.*

CRIMINAL LIABILITY

The federal securities statutes contain criminal as well as civil sanctions. Section 24 of the 1933 act, as amended, provides for a maximum $10,000 fine or five-year jail sentence, or both, for people who willfully violate any section of the act. The penalties also apply to anyone who willfully makes an untrue statement of material fact — or omits pertinent information — in a registration statement. Section 32(a) of the 1934 act prescribes identical sanctions for willful violators of the statute. Criminal liability for accountants can derive from their preparation and filing of annual reports, quarterly reports, and proxy statements.

Accountants also may be subject to criminal liability under the Internal Revenue Code, the Federal False Statements Act, the Federal Mail Fraud Act, and the Conspiracy statute.

Accountants who assist in the fraudulent preparation of a tax return can be subject to a $100,000 fine under Section 7206(2) of the Internal Revenue Code. The section also provides for a maximum prison term of three years.

The Federal False Statements Act makes it a crime to knowingly and willfully make false statements to any federal department or agency. Violators can be subject to a $10,000 fine, five years in jail, or both. An accountant's liability under the act would commonly be based on work on documents filed with the SEC. Audit reports for the financial statements in annual reports, quarterly reports, registration statements, and proxy statements are prime examples. The financial statements themselves are representations of the audited company, but statements in the audit reports are attributed to the accountant.

The Federal Mail Fraud Statute makes it a crime to use the mail to perpetrate a fraudulent scheme. The law carries a maximum $1,000 fine, five-year prison sentence, or both. Courts have interpreted the statute to allow for each mailing to constitute a separate offense. An accountant can be exposed to liability under this statute by certifying financial statements that he or she knows (or should know) to be false and when he or she knows that the statements will be mailed for the purpose of fraud.

Conspiracy liability can be incurred when parties agree to violate any of the above statutes. To be convicted of conspiracy, one need only be party to a criminal agreement in which one of the parties overtly acts to further the crime. The crime need not have been successful nor have been completed by the time it was discovered. A convicted conspirator can face a fine of up to $10,000, a jail term of up to five years, or both.

SUMMARY

Accountants may be liable to their clients in suits either in contract or in tort. Liability in contract is based on a breach of either the express or implied terms of the contract. The liability depends on the type of activity that the accountant is hired to perform and the type of opinion that the accountant renders. Neither compliance with the standards of the profession nor a disclaimer of liability absolutely protects an accountant from suit.

A suit in tort ordinarily is based on a claim that the accountant failed to exercise the level of skill and care that would be typical of members of the profession in that particular place. Accountants also may be sued for the intentional tort of fraud whenever they act with intent to deceive.

The accountant–client relationship is not a privileged one, and the government may require an accountant to produce client records. The records are not protected by the client's right against self-incrimination nor by a theory of work product immunity.

Accountants' liability to third parties who rely on their work is a controversial issue involving many important policy questions. The classic case of *Ultramares* limited an accountant's liability to third parties to cases of gross negligence or fraud. Some courts have gone beyond the *Ultramares* principle and impose liability to those whom the accountant foresaw as relying upon the documents.

Accountants also may be liable to injured parties under the federal securities laws, if they acted with intent to deceive. Criminal liability is possible under a number of federal statutes, including the Internal Revenue Code, the securities acts, and the Federal False Statements Act.

REVIEW PROBLEMS

1. Discuss the role of GAAP and GAAS in determining whether an accountant is subject to liability.

2. Describe the differences among a qualified opinion, an adverse opinion, and a disclaimer of opinion.

3. Why are an accountant's records and work papers relating to a client who is the subject of an IRS investigation subject to subpoena by the IRS?

4. When may a third party recover against an accountant?

5. Guarante–Harrington Associates was a limited partnership engaged in trading securities. According to the partnership agreement, partners could withdraw portions of their interest only at the end of a fiscal year upon 30 days' notice. Guarante and Harrington, the general partners, withdrew $2 million of their capital investment in violation of the agreement. From examining the partnership's audit report and tax returns, which were prepared by Anderson, one could not discover that the $2 million withdrawal was made in violation of the agreement. White, a limited partner, claimed to have suffered damages resulting from his use of the partnership's negligently prepared tax returns to prepare his own tax returns. He sued Anderson. Can Anderson avoid liability by claiming that it did not foresee that White would rely on the partnership's tax return to prepare his own?

6. The accounting partnership of James, Guinn, and Head audited the financial statements of Paschal, who owned various automobile glass businesses. James knew that the Shatterproof Glass Corporation would rely on the audited statements in deciding whether to loan money to Paschal's enterprises. James issued an unqualified opinion that the financial statements, which showed Paschal's businesses to be solvent, were accurate. The businesses actually were insolvent. Shatterproof loaned money to Paschal and lost $400,000. How do you think the court in *Rusch Factors, Inc.* v. *Levin* would have ruled if Shatterproof sued James? Do you think the court in *Ultramares Corp.* v. *Touche* would have ruled differently?

7. Accountants prepared and certified a financial statement for their client, who used the statement to convince a bank to lend it money. The accountants made several major errors in the statement. In addition, they delayed sending out an explanatory letter—which they believed should have been read by anyone using the statement—for about 30 days. The bank, which was not in privity of contract with the accountants, claimed to have suffered damages as a result of the accountants' negligence. Assume that you have been hired to represent the bank in a lawsuit against the accountants. If your jurisdiction recognizes the lack of privity as a bar to accountants' negligence actions, what theory should you pursue?

8. Between 1971 and 1973, Summers bought 9,500 shares of Land & Leisure, Incorporated, common stock at a total cost of $54,000. Summers later concluded that his purchases of stock had been fraudulently induced. In purchasing the stock, Summers claimed to have relied on a 1971 stock prospectus containing financial statements certified by Arthur Young and Company. He alleged that the financial statements were misleading and sued Arthur Young and others. Arthur Young argued that the suit should be dismissed because Summers could not hold it liable for stock purchases made after July 1972, because by then the prospectus had become "stale" and Summers was no longer entitled to rely on it. Is there merit in Arthur Young's argument?

9. Ernst & Ernst, an accounting firm, certified financial statements for American City Bank. The accountants knew that the bank would show the financial statements to prospective lenders of $2 million that the bank needed to raise, but they did not know who would eventually lend the money. Continental, an insurance company, reviewed the financial statements and agreed to lend the

money. The bank later became insolvent, and Continental was not repaid. Continental sued the accountants in Wisconsin federal court, alleging that they negligently certified the financial statements, which misrepresented the bank's financial health. The court followed the rule that accountants could only be held liable to third parties who were part of a "limited class whose reliance on the accountants' work is specifically foreseen." According to this rule, can Ernst & Ernst be held liable to Continental? As a matter of general policy, should accounting firms be held liable on facts such as these?

10. Cooke, an optical equipment manufacturer, engaged Hurwitz to perform accounting services and give investment advice. On Hurwitz's suggestion, Cooke at various times made loans to Maynaugh, another client of Hurwitz's. In 1973, when Hurwitz was preparing Maynaugh's financial statements for the previous year, Hurwitz learned facts that should have indicated to him that Cooke's loans to Maynaugh might not be collectible. Hurwitz later prepared Cooke's financial statements, in which he failed to indicate that the loans to Maynaugh were questionable. Maynaugh eventually went bankrupt. Cooke sued Hurwitz to recover his losses on the loans. Assuming that the loans became uncollectible in 1972, may Cooke recover?

11. Mrs. Levine filed for divorce from Mr. Levine. The court appointed the accounting firm of Wiss and Co. to be "impartial expert" to value Mr. Levine's interest in Unicorp. The valuation was to serve as the basis for an equitable distribution of Mr. Levine's property. After the accountants assessed the value of Mr. Levine's interest in the firm, Mr. and Mrs. Levine reached a property settlement. Mr. Levine later concluded that the accountants had negligently misvalued his interest in Unicorp and that the incorrect assessment had caused him to accept a settlement less favorable than he otherwise could have obtained. After the court denied his motion to abandon the settlement, Mr. Levine sued the accountants. Should Mr. Levine be able to recover from the accountant, given the fact that he voluntarily agreed to the settlement? Explain.

12. Safranek, an accountant, prepared financial statements for Agri-Products, Inc. The statements were expressly marked "unaudited" and contained an express disclaimer of opinion. Seedkem, Inc., relied on the financial statements in lending $700,000 to Agri-Products. Seedkem later learned that the financial statements were inaccurate, allegedly due to Safranek's negligence in preparing them. If Seedkem were to sue Safranek, what would result in a jurisdiction that followed *Ultramares*? Would the result be any different in a state that followed the more modern trend? Explain.

APPENDIX A
THE CONSTITUTION OF THE UNITED STATES OF AMERICA

Preamble

We the People of the United States, in Order to form a more perfect Union, establish Justice, insure domestic Tranquility, provide for the common defence, promote the general Welfare, and secure the Blessings of Liberty to ourselves and our Posterity, do ordain and establish this Constitution for the United States of America.

Article I

SECTION 1. All legislative Powers herein granted shall be vested in a Congress of the United States, which shall consist of a Senate and House of Representatives.

SECTION 2. (1) The House of Representatives shall be composed of Members chosen every second Year by the People of the several States, and Electors in each State shall have the Qualifications requisite for Electors of the most numerous Branch of the State Legislature.

(2) No Person shall be a Representative who shall not have attained to the Age of twenty five Years, and been seven Years a Citizen of the United States, and who shall not, when elected, be an Inhabitant of that State in which he shall be chosen.

(3) Representatives and direct Taxes shall be apportioned among the several States which may be included within this Union, according to their respective Numbers, which shall be determined by adding to the whole Number of free Persons, including those bound to Service for a Term of Years, and excluding Indians not taxed, three fifths of all other Persons.] The actual Enumeration shall be made within three Years after the first Meeting of the Congress of the United States, and within every subsequent Term of ten Years, in such Manner as they shall by Law direct. The Number of Representatives shall not exceed one for every thirty Thousand, but each State shall have at Least one Representative; and until such enumeration shall be made, the State of New Hampshire shall be entitled to chuse three, Massachusetts eight, Rhode Island and Providence Plantations one, Connecticut five, New York six, New Jersey four, Pennsylvania eight, Delaware one, Maryland six, Virginia ten, North Carolina five, South Carolina five, and Georgia three.

The clause of this paragraph inclosed in brackets was amended, as to the mode of apportionment of representatives among the several states, by the Fourteenth Amendment, §2, and as to taxes on incomes without apportionment, by the Sixteenth Amendment.

(4) When vacancies happen in the Representation from any State, the Executive Authority thereof shall issue Writs of Election to fill such Vacancies.

(5) The House of Representatives shall chuse their Speaker and other Officers; and shall have the sole Power of Impeachment.

SECTION 3. (1) The Senate of the United States shall be composed of two Senators from each State, [chosen by the Legislature thereof,] for six Years; and each Senator shall have one Vote.

This paragraph and the clause of following paragraph inclosed in brackets were superseded by the Seventeenth Amendment.

(2) Immediately after they shall be assembled in Consequence of the first Election, they shall be divided as equally as may be into three Classes. The Seats of the Senators of the first Class shall be vacated at the Expiration of the Second Year, of the second Class at the Expiration of the fourth Year, and of the third Class at the Expiration of the sixth Year, so that one third may be chosen every second Year; [and if Vacancies happen by Resignation, or otherwise, during the Recess of the Legislature of any State, the Executive thereof may make temporary Appointments until the next Meeting of the Legislature, which shall then fill such Vacancies.]

(3) No Person shall be a Senator who shall not have attained to the Age of thirty Years, and been nine Years a Citizen of the United States, and who shall not, when elected, be an Inhabitant of that State for which he shall be chosen.

(4) The Vice President of the United States shall be President of the Senate, but shall have no Vote, unless they be equally divided.

(5) The Senate shall chuse their other Officers, and also a President pro tempore, in the Absence of the Vice President, or when he shall exercise the Office of President of the United States.

(6) The Senate shall have the sole Power to try all Impeachments. When sitting for that Purpose, they shall be on Oath or Affirmation. When the President of the United States is tried, the Chief Justice shall preside: And no Person shall be convicted without the Concurrence of two thirds of the Members present.

(7) Judgment in Cases of Impeachment shall not extend further than to removal from Office, and disqualification to hold and enjoy an Office of honor, Trust, or Profit under the United States: but the Party convicted shall nevertheless be liable and subject to Indictment, Trial, Judgment, and Punishment, according to Law.

SECTION 4. (1) The Times, Places and Manner of holding Elections for Senators and Representatives, shall be prescribed in each State by the Legislature thereof; but the Congress may at any time by Law make or alter such Regulations, except as to the Places of chusing Senators.

(2) The Congress shall assemble at least once in every Year, and such Meeting shall [be on the first Monday in December,] unless they shall by Law appoint a different Day.

The part included in brackets was changed by Section 2 of the Twentieth Amendment.

SECTION 5. (1) Each House shall be the Judge of the Elections, Returns, and Qualifications of its own Members, and a Majority of each shall constitute a Quorum to do Business; but a smaller Number may adjourn from day to day, and may be authorized to compel the Attendance of absent Members, in such Manner, and under such Penalties as each House may provide.

(2) Each House may determine the Rules of its Proceedings, punish its Members for disorderly Behavior, and, with the Concurrence of two thirds, expel a Member.

(3) Each House shall keep a Journal of its Proceedings, and from time to time publish the same, excepting such Parts as may in their Judgment require Secrecy; and the Yeas and Nays of the Members of either House on any question shall, at the Desire of one fifth of those Present, be entered on the Journal.

(4) Neither House, during the Session of Congress, shall, without the Consent of the other, adjourn for more than three days, nor to any other Place than that in which the two Houses shall be sitting.

SECTION 6. (1) The Senators and Representatives shall receive a Compensation for their Services, to be ascertained by Law, and paid out of the Treasury of the United States. They shall in all Cases, except Treason, Felony and Breach of the Peace, be privileged from Arrest during their Attendance at the Session of their respective Houses, and in going to and returning from the same; and for any Speech or Debate in either House, they shall not be questioned in any other Place.

(2) No Senator or Representative shall, during the Time for which he was elected, be appointed to any civil Office under the Authority

of the United States, which shall have been created, or the Emoluments whereof shall have been increased during such time; and no Person holding any Office under the United States, shall be a Member of either House during his Continuance in Office.

SECTION 7. (1) All Bills for raising Revenue shall originate in the House of Representatives; but the Senate may propose or concur with Amendments as on other Bills.

(2) Every Bill which shall have passed the House of Representatives and the Senate, shall, before it become a Law, be presented to the President of the United States; If he approve he shall sign it, but if not he shall return it, with his Objections to the House in which it shall have originated, who shall enter the Objections at large on their Journal, and proceed to reconsider it. If after such Reconsideration two thirds of that House shall agree to pass the Bill, it shall be sent together with the Objections, to the other House, by which it shall likewise be reconsidered, and if approved by two thirds of that House, it shall become a Law. But in all such Cases the Votes of both Houses shall be determined by Yeas and Nays, and the Names of the Persons voting for and against the Bill shall be entered on the Journal of each House respectively. If any Bill shall not be returned by the President within ten Days (Sundays excepted) after it shall have been presented to him, the Same shall be a Law, in like Manner as if he had signed it, unless the Congress by their Adjournment prevent its Return in which Case it shall not be a Law.

(3) Every Order, Resolution, or Vote, to Which the Concurrence of the Senate and House of Representatives may be necessary (except on a question of Adjournment) shall be presented to the President of the United States; and before the Same shall take Effect, shall be approved by him, or being disapproved by him, shall be repassed by two thirds of the Senate and House of Representatives, according to the Rules and Limitations prescribed in the Case of a Bill.

SECTION 8. (1) The Congress shall have Power To lay and collect Taxes, Duties, Imposts and Excises, to pay the Debts and provide for the common Defence and general Welfare of the United States; but all Duties, Imposts and Excises shall be uniform throughout the United States;

(2) To borrow money on the credit of the United States;

(3) To regulate Commerce with foreign Nations, and among the several States, and with the Indian Tribes;

(4) To establish an uniform Rule of Naturalization, and uniform Laws on the subject of Bankruptcies throughout the United States;

(5) To coin Money, regulate the Value thereof, and of foreign Coin, and fix the Standard of Weights and Measures;

(6) To provide for the Punishment of counterfeiting the Securities and current Coin of the United States;

(7) To Establish Post Offices and Post Roads;

(8) To promote the Progress of Science and useful Arts, by securing for limited Times to Authors and Inventors the exclusive Right to their respective Writings and Discoveries;

(9) To constitute Tribunals inferior to the Supreme Court;

(10) To define and punish Piracies and Felonies committed on the high Seas, and Offenses against the Law of Nations;

(11) To declare War, grant Letters of Marque and Reprisal, and make Rules concerning Captures on Land and Water;

(12) To raise and support Armies, but no Appropriation of Money to that Use shall be for a longer Term than two Years;

(13) To provide and maintain a Navy;

(14) To make Rules for the Government and Regulation of the land and naval Forces;

(15) To provide for calling forth the Militia to execute the Laws of the Union, suppress Insurrections and repel Invasions;

(16) To provide for organizing, arming, and disciplining, the Militia, and for governing such Part of them as may be employed in the Service of the United States, reserving to the States respectively, the Appointment of the Officers, and the Authority of training the Militia according to the discipline prescribed by Congress;

(17) To exercise exclusive Legislation in all Cases whatsoever, over such District (not exceeding ten Miles square) as may, by Cession of particular States, and the Acceptance of Congress, become the Seat of the Government of the United States, and to exercise like Authority over all Places purchased by the Consent of the Legislature of the State in which the Same shall be, for the Erection of Forts, Magazines, Arsenals, dock-Yards, and other needful Buildings;—And

(18) To make all Laws which shall be necessary and proper for carrying into Execution the foregoing Powers, and all other Powers vested by this Constitution in the Government of the United States, or in any Department or Officer thereof.

SECTION 9. (1) The Migration or Importation of Such Persons as any of the States now existing shall think proper to admit, shall not be prohibited by the Congress prior to the Year one thousand eight hundred and eight, but a Tax or duty may be imposed on such Importation, not exceeding ten dollars for each Person.

(2) The privilege of the Writ of Habeas Corpus shall not be suspended, unless when in Cases of Rebellion or Invasion the public Safety may require it.

(3) No Bill of Attainder or *ex post facto* Law shall be passed.

(4) No Capitation, or other direct, Tax shall be laid, unless in Proportion to the Census or Enumeration herein before directed to be taken.

See also the Sixteenth Amendment.

(5) No Tax or Duty shall be laid on Articles exported from any State.

(6) No Preference shall be given by any Regulation of Commerce or Revenue to the Ports of one State over those of another: nor shall Vessels bound to, or from, one State be obliged to enter, clear, or pay Duties in another.

(7) No money shall be drawn from the Treasury, but in Consequence of Appropriations made by Law; and a regular Statement and Account of the Receipts and Expenditures of all public Money shall be published from time to time.

(8) No Title of Nobility shall be granted by the United States: And no Person holding any Office of Profit or Trust under them, shall, without the Consent of the Congress, accept of any present, Emolument, Office, or Title, or any kind whatever, from any King, Prince, or foreign State.

SECTION 10. (1) No State shall enter into any Treaty, Alliance, or Confederation; grant Letters of Marque and Reprisal; coin Money; emit Bills of Credit; make any Thing but gold and silver Coin a Tender in Payment of Debts; pass any Bill of Attainder, *ex post facto* Law, or Law impairing the Obligation of Contracts, or grant any Title of Nobility.

(2) No State shall, without the Consent of the Congress, lay any Imposts or Duties on Imports or Exports, except what may be absolutely necessary for executing it's inspection Laws: and the net Produce of all Duties and Imposts, laid by any State on Imports or Exports, shall be for the Use of the Treasury of the United States; and all such Laws shall be subject to the Revision and Controul of the Congress.

(3) No State shall, without the Consent of Congress, lay any Duty of Tonnage, keep Troops, or Ships of War in time of Peace, enter into any Agreement or Compact with another State, or with a foreign Power, or engage in War, unless actually invaded, or in such imminent Danger as will not admit of delay.

Article II

SECTION 1. (1) The executive Power shall be vested in a President of the United States of America. He shall hold his Office during the Term of four Years, and, together with the Vice President, chosen for the same Term, be elected, as follows:

(2) Each State shall appoint, in such Manner as the Legislature thereof may direct, a Number of Electors, equal to the whole Number of Senators and Representatives to which the State may be entitled in the Congress; but no Senator or Representative or Person holding an Office of Trust or Profit under the United States, shall be appointed an Elector.

(3) [The Electors shall meet in their respective States, and vote by Ballot for two Persons, of whom one at least shall not be an Inhabitant of the same State with themselves. And they shall make a List of

all the Persons voted for, and of the Number of Votes for each; which List they shall sign and certify, and transmit sealed to the Seat of the Government of the United States, directed to the President of the Senate. The President of the Senate shall, in the Presence of the Senate and House of Representatives, open all the Certificates, and the Votes shall then be counted. The Person having the greatest Number of Votes shall be the President, if such Number be a Majority of the whole Number of Electors appointed; and if there be more than one who have such Majority, and have an equal Number of Votes, then the House of Representatives shall immediately chuse by Ballot one of them for President; and if no Person have a Majority, then from the five highest on the List the said House shall in like Manner chuse the President. But in chusing the President, the Votes shall be taken by States the Representation from each State having one Vote; A quorum for this Purpose shall consist of a Member or Members from two thirds of the States, and a Majority of all the States shall be necessary to a Choice. In every Case, after the Choice of the President, the Person having the greatest Number of Votes of the Electors shall be the Vice President. But if there should remain two or more who have equal Votes, the Senate shall chuse from them by Ballot the Vice President.]

This paragraph, inclosed in brackets, was superseded by the Twelfth Amendment.

(4) The Congress may determine the Time of chusing the Electors, and the Day on which they shall give their Votes; which Day shall be the same throughout the United States.

(5) No person except a natural born Citizen, or a Citizen of the United States, at the time of the Adoption of this Constitution, shall be eligible to the Office of President; neither shall any Person be eligible to that Office who shall not have attained to the Age of thirty five Years, and been fourteen Years a Resident within the United States.

(6) In case of the removal of the President from Office, or of his Death, Resignation or Inability to discharge the Powers and Duties of the said Office, the Same shall devolve on the Vice President, and the Congress may by Law provide for the Case of Removal, Death, Resignation or Inability, both of the President and Vice President, declaring what Officer shall then act as President and such Officer shall act accordingly, until the Disability be removed, or a President shall be elected.

(7) The President shall, at stated Times, receive for his Services, a Compensation, which shall neither be increased nor diminished during the Period for which he shall have been elected, and he shall not receive within that Period any other Emolument from the United States, or any of them.

(8) Before he enter on the Execution of his Office, he shall take the following Oath or Affirmation: "I do solemnly swear (or affirm) that I will faithfully execute the Office of President of the United States, and will to the best of my Ability, preserve, protect and defend the Constitution of the United States."

SECTION 2. (1) The President shall be Commander in Chief of the Army and Navy of the United States, and of the militia of the several States, when called into the actual Service of the United States; he may require the Opinion, in writing, of the principal Officer in each of the Executive Departments, upon any Subject relating to the Duties of their respective Offices, and he shall have Power to grant Reprieves and Pardons for Offenses against the United States, except in Cases of Impeachment.

(2) He shall have Power, by and with the Advice and Consent of the Senate to make Treaties, provided two thirds of the Senators present concur; and he shall nominate, and by and with the Advice and Consent of the Senate, shall appoint Ambassadors, other public Ministers and Consuls, Judges of the supreme Court, and all other Officers of the United States, whose Appointments are not herein otherwise provided for, and which shall be established by Law; but the Congress may by Law vest the Appointment of such inferior Officers, as they think proper, in the President alone, in the Courts of Law, or in the Heads of Departments.

(3) The President shall have Power to fill up all Vacancies that may

happen during the Recess of the Senate, by granting Commissions which shall expire at the End of their next Session.

SECTION 3. He shall from time to time give to the Congress Information of the State of the Union, and recommend to their Consideration such Measures as he shall judge necessary and expedient; he may, on extraordinary Occasions, convene both Houses, or either of them, and in Case of Disagreement between them, with Respect to the Time of Adjournment, he may adjourn them to such Time as he shall think proper; he shall take Care that the Laws be faithfully executed, and shall Commission all the Officers of the United States.

SECTION 4. The President, Vice President and all civil Officers of the United States, shall be removed from Office on Impeachment for, and Conviction of, Treason, Bribery, or other high Crimes and Misdemeanors.

Article III

SECTION 1. The judicial Power of the United States, shall be vested in one supreme Court, and in such inferior Courts as the Congress may from time to time ordain and establish. The Judges, both of the supreme and inferior Courts, shall hold their Offices during good Behaviour, and shall, at stated Times, receive for their Services a Compensation, which shall not be diminished during their Continuance in Office.

SECTION 2. (1) The judicial Power shall extend to all Cases, in Law and Equity, arising under this Constitution, the Laws of the United States, and Treaties made, or which shall be made, under their Authority; — to all Cases affecting Ambassadors, other public Ministers and Consuls; — to all Cases of admiralty and maritime Jurisdiction; — to Controversies to which the United States shall be a Party; — to Controversies between two or more States; — between a State and Citizens of another State;* — between Citizens of different States; — between Citizens of the same State claiming Lands under the Grants of different States, and between a State, or the Citizens thereof, and foreign States, Citizens or Subjects.

(2) In all Cases affecting Ambassadors, other public Ministers and Consuls, and those in which a State shall be a Party, the supreme Court shall have original Jurisdiction. In all the other Cases before mentioned, the supreme Court shall have appellate Jurisdiction, both as to Law and Fact, with such Exceptions, and under such Regulations as the Congress shall make.

(3) The Trial of all Crimes, except in Cases of Impeachment, shall be by Jury; and such Trial shall be held in the State where the said Crimes shall have been committed; but when not committed within any State, the Trial shall be at such Place or Places as the Congress may by Law have directed.

SECTION 3. (1) Treason against the United States, shall consist only in levying War against them, or, in adhering to their Enemies, giving them Aid and Comfort. No Person shall be convicted of Treason unless on the Testimony of two Witnesses to the same overt Act, or on Confession in open Court.

(2) The Congress shall have Power to declare the Punishment of Treason, but no Attainder of Treason shall work Corruption of Blood, or Forefeiture except during the Life of the Person attainted.

Article IV

SECTION 1. Full Faith and Credit shall be given in each State to the public Acts, Records, and judicial Proceedings of every other State. And the Congress may by general Laws prescribe the Manner in which such Acts, Records and Proceedings shall be proved, and the Effect thereof.

SECTION 2. (1) The Citizens of each State shall be entitled to all Privileges and Immunities of Citizens in the several States.

(2) A Person charged in any State with Treason, Felony, or other Crime, who shall flee from Justice, and be found in another State, shall on demand of the executive Authority of the State from which

* This clause has been affected by the Eleventh Amendment.

he fled, be delivered up, to be removed to the State having Jurisdiction of the Crime.

(3) [No Person held to Service or Labour in one State, under the Laws thereof, escaping into another, shall, in Consequence of any Law or Regulation therein, be discharged from such Service or Labour, but shall be delivered up on Claim of the Party to whom such Service or Labour may be due.]

This paragraph has been superseded by the Thirteenth Amendment.

SECTION 3. (1) New States may be admitted by the Congress into this Union; but no new State shall be formed or erected within the Jurisdiction of any other State; nor any State be formed by the Junction of two or more States, or Parts of States, without the Consent of the Legislatures of the States concerned as well as of the Congress.

(2) The Congress shall have Power to dispose of and make all needful Rules and Regulations respecting the Territory or other Property belonging to the United States; and nothing in this Constitution shall be so construed as to Prejudice any Claims of the United States, or of any particular State.

SECTION 4. The United States shall guarantee to every State in this Union a Republican Form of Government, and shall protect each of them against Invasion; and on Application of the Legislature, or of the Executive (when the Legislature cannot be convened) against domestic Violence.

Article V

The Congress, whenever two thirds of both Houses shall deem it necessary, shall propose Amendments to this Constitution, or, on the Application of the Legislatures of two thirds of the several States, shall call a Convention for proposing Amendments, which, in either Case, shall be valid to all Intents and Purposes, as part of this Constitution, when ratified by the Legislatures of three fourths of the several States, or by Conventions in three fourths thereof, as the one or the other Mode of Ratification may be proposed by the Congress; Provided that no Amendment which may be made prior to the Year One thousand eight hundred and eight shall in any Manner affect the first and fourth Clauses in the Ninth Section of the first Article; and that no State, without its Consent, shall be deprived of its equal Suffrage in the Senate.

Article VI

(1) All Debts contracted and Engagements entered into, before the Adoption of this Constitution shall be as valid against the United States under this Constitution, as under the Confederation.

(2) This Constitution, and the Laws of the United States which shall be made in Pursuance thereof; and all Treaties made, or which shall be made, under the Authority of the United States, shall be the supreme Law of the Land; and the Judges in every State shall be bound thereby, any Thing in the Constitution or Laws of any State to the Contrary notwithstanding.

(3) The Senators and Representatives before mentioned, and the Members of the several State Legislatures, and all executive and judicial Officers, both of the United States and of the several States, shall be bound by Oath or Affirmation, to support this Constitution; but no religious Test shall ever be required as a Qualification to any Office or public Trust under the United States.

Article VII

The Ratification of the Conventions of nine States shall be sufficient for the Establishment of this Constitution between the States so ratifying the Same.

Done in Convention by the Unanimous Consent of the States present the Seventeenth Day of September in the Year of Our Lord one thousand seven hundred and Eighty seven and of the Indepen-

dence of the United States of American the Twelfth. IN WITNESS whereof We have hereto subscribed our Names,

Go. Washington — Presidt.
and deputy from Virgina

New Hampshire		
John Langdon		Nicholas Gilman
Massachusetts		
Nathaniel Gorham		Rufus King
Connecticut		
Wm. Saml. Johnson		Roger Sherman
New York		
Alexander Hamilton		
New Jersey		
Wil: Livingston		Wm. Paterson
David Brearley		Jona: Dayton
Pennsylvania		
B. Franklin		Thos. FitzSimons
Thomas Mifflin		Jared Ingersoll
Robt. Morris		James Wilson
Geo. Clymer		Gouv Morris
Delaware		
Geo: Read		Richard Bassett
Gunning Bedford Jun		Jaco: Broom
John Dickinson		
Maryland		
James McHenry		Danl. Carroll
Dan of St Thos. Jenifer		
Virginia		
John Blair		James Madison, Jr.
North Carolina		
Wm. Blount		Hu Williamson
Richd. Dobbs Spaight		
South Carolina		
J. Rutledge		Charles Pinckney
Charles Cotesworth Pinckney		Pierce Butler
Georgia		
William Few		Abr Baldwin
	Attest	William Jackson
		Secretary

Amendments to the Constitution of the United States

AMENDMENT I [1791]

Congress shall make no law respecting an establishment of religion, or prohibiting the free exercise thereof; or abridging the freedom of speech, or of the press; or the right of the people peaceably to assemble, and to petition the Government for a redress of grievances.

AMENDMENT II [1791]

A well regulated Militia being necessary to the security of a free State, the right of the people to keep and bear Arms, shall not be infringed.

AMENDMENT III [1791]

No Soldier shall, in time of peace be quartered in any house, without the consent of the Owner, nor in time of war, but in a manner to be prescribed by law.

AMENDMENT IV [1791]

The right of the people to be secure in their persons, houses, papers, and effects, against unreasonable searches and seizures, shall not be violated, and no Warrants shall issue, but upon probable cause, supported by Oath or affirmation, and particularly describing the place to be searched, and the persons or things to be seized.

AMENDMENT V [1791]

No person shall be held to answer for a capital, or otherwise infamous crime, unless on a presentment or indictment of a Grand Jury, except in cases arising in the land or naval forces, or in the Militia, when in actual service in time of War or public danger; nor shall any person be subject for the same offence to be twice put in jeopardy of life or limb, nor shall be compelled in any criminal case to be a witness against himself, nor be deprived of life, liberty, or property, without due process of law; nor shall private property be taken for public use, without just compensation.

AMENDMENT VI [1791]

In all criminal prosecutions, the accused shall enjoy the right to a speedy and public trial, by an impartial jury of the State and district wherein the crime shall have been committed; which district shall have been previously ascertained by law, and to be informed of the nature and cause of the accusation; to be confronted with the witnesses against him; to have compulsory process for obtaining Witnesses in his favor, and to have the Assistance of Counsel for his defence.

AMENDMENT VII [1791]

In Suits at common law, where the value in controversy shall exceed twenty dollars, the right of trial by jury shall be preserved, and no fact tried by jury shall be otherwise reexamined in any Court of the United States, than according to the rules of the common law.

AMENDMENT VIII [1791]

Excessive bail shall not be required, nor excessive fines imposed, nor cruel and unusual punishments inflicted.

AMENDMENT IX [1791]

The enumeration in the Constitution, of certain rights, shall not be construed to deny or disparage others retained by the people.

AMENDMENT X [1791]

The powers not delegated to the United States by the Constitution, nor prohibited by it to the States, are reserved to the States respectively, or to the people.

AMENDMENT IX [1798]

The Judicial power of the United States shall not be construed to extend to any suit in law or equity, commenced or prosecuted against one of the United States by Citizens of another State, or by Citizens or Subjects of any Foreign State.

AMENDMENT XII [1804]

The electors shall meet in their respective states and vote by ballot for President and Vice-President, one of whom, at least, shall not be an inhabitant of the same state with themselves; they shall name in their ballots the person voted for as President, and in distinct ballots the person voted for as Vice-President, and they shall make distinct lists of all persons voted for as President, and of all persons voted for as Vice-President, and of the number of votes for each, which lists they shall sign and certify, and transmit sealed to the seat of the government of the United States, directed to the President of the Senate;— The President of the Senate shall, in the presence of the Senate and House of Representatives, open all the certificates and the votes shall then be counted;— The person having the greatest number of votes for President, shall be the President, if such number be a majority of the whole number of Electors appointed; and if no person have such majority, then from the persons having the highest numbers not exceeding three on the list of those voted for as President, the House of Representatives shall choose immediately, by ballot, the President. But in choosing the President, the votes shall be taken by states, the representation from each state having one vote; a quorum for this purpose shall consist of a member or members from two-thirds of the states, and a majority of all the states shall be necessary to a choice. [And if the House of Representatives shall not choose a President whenever the right of choice shall devolve upon them before the fourth day of March next following, then the Vice-President shall act as President, as in the case of the death or other constitutional disability of the President.] The person having the greatest number of votes as Vice-President, shall be the Vice-President, if such number be a majority of the whole number of Electors appointed, and if no person have a majority, then from the two highest numbers on the list, the Senate shall choose the Vice-President; a quorum for the purpose shall consist of two-thirds of the whole number of Senators, and a majority of the whole number shall be necessary to a choice. But no person constitutionally ineligible to the office of President shall be eligible to that of Vice-President of the United States.

The part included in brackets has been superseded by section 3 of the Twentieth Amendment.

AMENDMENT XIII [1865]

SECTION 1. Neither slavery nor involuntary servitude, except as a punishment for crime whereof the party shall have been duly convicted, shall exist within the United States, or any place subject to their jurisdiction.

SECTION 2. Congress shall have power to enforce this article by appropriate legislation.

AMENDMENT XIV [1868]

SECTION 1. All persons born or naturalized in the United States, and subject to the jurisdiction thereof, are citizens of the United States and of the State wherein they reside. No State shall make or enforce any law which shall abridge the privileges or immunities of citizens of the United States; nor shall any State deprive any person of life, liberty, or property, without due process of law; nor deny to any person within its jurisdiction the equal protection of the laws.

SECTION 2. Representatives shall be apportioned among the several States according to their respective numbers, counting the whole number of persons in each State, excluding Indians not taxed. But when the right to vote at any election for the choice of electors for President and Vice President of the United States, Representatives in Congress, the Executive and Judicial officers of a State, or the members of the Legislature thereof, is denied to any of the male inhabitants of such State, being twenty-one years of age, and citizens of the United States, or in any way abridged, except for participation in rebellion, or other crime, the basis of representation therein shall be reduced in the proportion which the number of such male citizens shall bear to the whole number of male citizens twenty-one years of age in such State.

SECTION 3. No person shall be a Senator or Representative in Congress, or elector of President and Vice President, or hold any office, civil or military, under the United States, or under any State, who, having previously taken an oath, as a member of Congress, or as an officer of the United States, or as a member of any State legislature, or as an executive or judicial officer of any State, to support the Constitution of the United States, shall have engaged in insurrection or rebellion against the same, or given aid or comfort to the enemies thereof. But Congress may by a vote of two-thirds of each House, remove such disability.

SECTION 4. The validity of the public debt of the United States, authorized by law, including debts incurred for payment of pensions and bounties for services in suppressing insurrection or rebellion, shall not be questioned. But neither the United States nor any State shall assume or pay any debt or obligation incurred in aid of insurrection or rebellion against the United States, or any claim for the loss or emancipation of any slave; but all such debts, obligations and claims shall be held illegal and void.

SECTION 5. The Congress shall have power to enforce, by appropriate legislation, the provisions of this article.

AMENDMENT XV [1870]

SECTION 1. The right of citizens of the United States to vote shall not be denied or abridged by the United States or by any State on account of race, color, or previous condition of servitude.

SECTION 2. The Congress shall have power to enforce this article by appropriate legislation.

AMENDMENT XVI [1913]

The Congress shall have power to lay and collect taxes on incomes, from whatever source derived, without apportionment among the several States, and without regard to any census or enumeration.

AMENDMENT XVII [1913]

The Senate of the United States shall be composed of two Senators from each State, elected by the people thereof, for six years; and each Senator shall have one vote. The electors in each State shall have the qualifications requisite for electors of the most numerous branch of the State legislatures.

When vacancies happen in the representation of any State in the Senate, the executive authority of such State shall issue writs of election to fill such vacancies: *Provided,* That the legislature of any State may empower the executive thereof to make temporary appointments until the people fill the vacancies by election as the legislature may direct.

This amendment shall not be so construed as to affect the election or term of any Senator chosen before it becomes valid as part of the Constitution.

AMENDMENT XVIII [1919]

SECTION 1. [After one year from the ratification of this Article the manufacture, sale, or transportation of intoxicating liquors within, the importation thereof into, or the exportation thereof from the United States and all territory subject to the jurisdiction thereof for beverage purposes is hereby prohibited].

SECTION 2. [The Congress and the several States shall have concurrent power to enforce this article by appropriate legislation].

SECTION 3. [This article shall be inoperative unless it shall have been ratified as an amendment to the Constitution by the legislatures of the several States, as provided in the Constitution, within seven years from the date of the submission hereof to the States by the Congress].

The eighteenth amendment was repealed by the twenty-first amendment to the Constitution of the United States.

AMENDMENT XIX [1920]

The right of citizens of the United States to vote shall not be denied or abridged by the United States or by any State on account of sex.

Congress shall have power to enforce this Article by appropriate legislation.

AMENDMENT XX [1933]

SECTION 1. The terms of the President and Vice President shall end at noon on the 20th day of January, and the terms of Senators and Representatives at noon on the 3d day of January, of the years in which such terms would have ended if this article had not been ratified; and the terms of their successors shall then begin.

SECTION 2. The Congress shall assemble at least once in every year, and such meeting shall begin at noon on the 3d day of January, unless they shall by law appoint a different day.

SECTION 3. If, at the time fixed for the beginning of the term of the President, the President-elect shall have died, the Vice President-elect shall become President. If the President shall not have been chosen before the time fixed for the beginning of his term, or if the President elect shall have failed to qualify, then the Vice President-elect shall act as President until a President shall have qualified; and the Congress may by law provide for the case wherein neither a President-elect nor a Vice President-elect shall have qualified, declaring who shall then act as President, or the manner in which one who is to act shall be selected, and such person shall act accordingly until a President or Vice President shall have qualified.

SECTION 4. The Congress may by law provide for the case of the death of any of the persons from whom the House of Representatives may choose a President whenever the right of choice shall have devolved upon them, and for the case of the death of any of the persons from whom the Senate may choose a Vice President whenever the right of choice shall have devolved upon them.

SECTION 5. Sections 1 and 2 shall take effect on the 15th day of October following the ratification of this article.

SECTION 6. This article shall be inoperative unless it shall have been ratified as an amendment to the Constitution by the legislatures of three-fourths of the several States within seven years from the date of its submission.

AMENDMENT XXI [1933]

SECTION 1. The eighteenth article of amendment to the Constitution of the United States is hereby repealed.

SECTION 2. The transportation or importation into any State, Territory, or possession of the United States for delivery or use therein of intoxicating liquors, in violation of the laws thereof, is hereby prohibited.

SECTION 3. This article shall be inoperative unless it shall have been ratified as an amendment to the Constitution by conventions in the several States, as provided in the Constitution, within seven years from the date of the submission hereof to the States by the Congress.

AMENDMENT XXII [1951]

SECTION 1. No person shall be elected to the office of the President more than twice, and no person who has held the office of President, or acted as President, for more than two years of a term to which some other person was elected President shall be elected to the office of President more than once. But this Article shall not apply to any person holding the office of President when this Article was proposed by the Congress, and shall not prevent any person who may be holding the office of President, or acting as President, during the term within which this Article becomes operative from holding the office of President or acting as President during the remainder of such term.

SECTION 2. This Article shall be inoperative unless it shall have been ratified as an amendment to the Constitution by the legislatures of three-fourths of the several States within seven years from the date of its submission to the States by the Congress.

AMENDMENT XXIII [1961]

SECTION 1. The District constituting the seat of Government of the United States shall appoint in such a manner as the Congress may direct:

A number of electors of President and Vice President equal to the whole number of Senators and Representatives in Congress to which the District would be entitled if it were a State, but in no event more than the least populous state; they shall be in addition to those appointed by the States, but they shall be considered, for the purposes of the election of President and Vice President, to be electors appointed by a State; and they shall meet in the District and perform such duties as provided by the twelfth article of amendment.

SECTION 2. The Congress shall have power to enforce this article by appropriate legislation.

AMENDMENT XXIV [1964]

SECTION 1. The right of citizens of the United States to vote in any primary or other election for President or Vice President, for electors for President or Vice President, or for Senator or Representative in Congress, shall not be denied or abridged by the United States or any State by reason of failure to pay any poll tax or other tax.

SECTION 2. The Congress shall have power to enforce this article by appropriate legislation.

AMENDMENT XXV [1967]

SECTION 1. In case of the removal of the President from office or of his death or resignation, the Vice President shall become President.

SECTION 2. Whenever there is a vacancy in the office of the Vice President, the President shall nominate a Vice President who shall take office upon confirmation by a majority vote of both Houses of Congress.

SECTION 3. Whenever the President transmits to the President pro tempore of the Senate and the Speaker of the House of Representatives his written declaration that he is unable to discharge the powers and duties of his office, and until he transmits to them a written declaration to the contrary, such powers and duties shall be discharged by the Vice President as Acting President.

SECTION 4. Whenever the Vice President and a majority of either the principal officers of the executive departments or of such other body as Congress may by law provide, transmit to the President pro tempore of the Senate and the Speaker of the House of Representatives their written declaration that the President is unable to discharge the powers and duties of his office, the Vice President shall immediately assume the powers and duties of the office as Acting President.

Thereafter, when the President transmits to the President pro tempore of the Senate and the Speaker of the House of Representatives his written declaration that no inability exists, he shall resume the powers and duties of his office unless the Vice President and a majority of either the principal officers of the executive department or of such other body as Congress may by law provide, transmit within four days to the President pro tempore of the Senate and the Speaker of the House of Representatives their written declaration that the President is unable to discharge the powers and duties of his office. Thereupon Congress shall decide the issue, assembling within forty-eight hours for that purpose if not in session. If the Congress, within twenty-one days after receipt of the latter written declaration, or, if Congress is not in session, within twenty-one days after Congress is required to assemble, determines by two-thirds vote of both Houses that the President is unable to discharge the powers and duties of his office, the Vice President shall continue to discharge the same as Acting President; otherwise, the President shall resume the powers and duties of his office.

AMENDMENT XXVI [1971]

SECTION 1. The right of citizens of the United States, who are eighteen years of age or older, to vote shall not be denied or abridged by the United States or by any State on account of age.

SECTION 2. The Congress shall have power to enforce this article by appropriate legislation.

UNIFORM COMMERCIAL CODE
Selected Sections
[1972 Amendments]

ARTICLE ONE — GENERAL PROVISIONS

PART 1

Short Title, Construction, Application and Subject Matter of the Act

§ **1-101.   Short Title.**—This Act shall be known and may be cited as Uniform Commercial Code.

§ **1-102.   Purposes; Rules of Construction; Variation by Agreement.**—
(1) This Act shall be liberally construed and applied to promote its underlying purposes and policies.
(2) Underlying purposes and policies of this Act are
(a) to simplify, clarify and modernize the law governing commercial transactions;
(b) to permit the continued expansion of commercial practices through custom, usage and agreement of the parties;
(c) to make uniform the law among the various jurisdictions.
(3) The effect of provisions of this Act may be varied by agreement, except as otherwise provided in this Act and except that the obligations of good faith, diligence, reasonableness and care prescribed by this Act may not be disclaimed by agreement but the parties may by agreement determine the standards by which the performance of such obligations is to be measured if such standards are not manifestly unreasonable.
(4) The presence in certain provisions of this Act of the words "unless otherwise agreed" or words of similar import does not imply that the effect of other provisions may not be varied by agreement under subsection (3).
(5) In this Act unless the context otherwise requires
(a) words in the singular number include the plural, and in the plural include the singular;
(b) words of the masculine gender include the feminine and the neuter, and when the sense so indicates words of the neuter gender may refer to any gender.

§ **1-103.   Supplementary General Principles of Law Applicable.**—Unless displaced by the particular provisions of this Act, the principles of law and equity, including the law merchant and the law relative to capacity to contract, principal and agent, estoppel, fraud, misrepresentation, duress, coercion, mistake, bankruptcy, or other validating or invalidating cause shall supplement its provisions.

§ **1-104.   Construction Against Implicit Repeal.**—This Act being a general act intended as a unified coverage of its subject matter, no part of it shall be deemed to be impliedly repealed by subsequent legislation if such construction can reasonably be avoided.

§ **1-105.   Territorial Application of the Act; Parties' Power to Choose Applicable Law.**—
(1) Except as provided hereafter in this section, when a transaction bears a reasonable relation to this state and also to another state or nation the parties may agree that the law either of this state or of such other state or nation shall govern their rights and duties. Failing such agreement this Act applies to transactions bearing an appropriate relation to this state.
(2) Where one of the following provisions of this Act specifies the applicable law, that provision governs and a contrary agreement is effective only to the extent permitted by the law (including the conflict of laws rules) so specified:
Rights of creditors against sold goods. Section 2-402.
Applicability of the Article on Bank Deposits and Collections. Section 4-102.
Bulk transfers subject to the Article on Bulk Transfers. Section 6-102.
Applicability of the Article on Investment Securities. Section 8-106.
Perfection provisions of the Article on Secured Transactions. Section 9-103.

§ **1-106.   Remedies to Be Liberally Administered.**—
(1) The remedies provided by this Act shall be liberally administered to the end that the aggrieved party may be put in as good a position as if the other party had fully performed but neither consequential or special nor penal damages may be had except as specifically provided in this Act or by other rule of law.
(2) Any right or obligation declared by this Act is enforceable by action unless the provision declaring it specifies a different and limited effect.

§ **1-107.   Waiver or Renunciation of Claim or Right After Breach.**—Any claim or right arising out of an alleged breach can be discharged in whole or in part without consideration by a written waiver or renunciation signed and delivered by the aggrieved party.

§ 1-108. **Severability.**—If any provision or clause of this Act or application thereof to any person or circumstances is held invalid, such invalidity shall not affect other provisions or applications of the Act which can be given effect without the invalid provision or application, and to this end the provisions of this Act are declared to be severable.

§ 1-109. **Section Captions.**—Section captions are parts of this Act.

PART 2

General Definitions and Principles of Interpretation

§ 1-201. **General Definitions.**—Subject to additional definitions contained in the subsequent Articles of this Act which are applicable to specific Articles or Parts thereof, and unless the context otherwise requires, in this Act:

(1) "Action" in the sense of a judicial proceeding includes recoupment, counter-claim, set-off, suit in equity and any other proceedings in which rights are determined.

(2) "Aggrieved party" means a party entitled to resort to a remedy.

(3) "Agreement" means the bargain of the parties in fact as found in their language or by implication from other circumstances including course of dealing or usage of trade or course of performance as provided in this Act (Sections 1-205 and 2-208). Whether an agreement has legal consequences is determined by the provisions of this Act, if applicable; otherwise by the law of contracts (Section 1-103). (Compare "Contract".)

(4) "Bank" means any person engaged in the business of banking.

(5) "Bearer" means the person in possession of an instrument, document of title, or certificated security payable to bearer or indorsed in blank.

(6) "Bill of lading" means a document evidencing the receipt of goods for shipment issued by a person engaged in the business of transporting or forwarding goods, and includes an airbill. "Airbill" means a document serving for air transportation as a bill of lading does for marine or rail transportation, and includes an air consignment note or air waybill.

(7) "Branch" includes a separately incorporated foreign branch of a bank.

(8) "Burden of establishing" a fact means the burden of persuading the triers of fact that the existence of the fact is more probable than its non-existence.

(9) "Buyer in ordinary course of business" means a person who in good faith and without knowledge that the sale to him is in violation of the ownership rights or security interest of a third party in the goods buys in ordinary course from a person in the business of selling goods of that kind but does not include a pawnbroker. [All persons who sell minerals or the like (including oil and gas) at wellhead or minehead shall be deemed to be persons in the business of selling goods of that kind.] "Buying" may be for cash or by exchange of other property or on secured or unsecured credit and includes receiving goods or documents of title under a pre-existing contract for sale but does not include a transfer in bulk or as security for or in total or partial satisfaction of a money debt.

(10) "Conspicuous": A term or clause is conspicuous when it is so written that a reasonable person against whom it is to operate ought to have noticed it. A printed heading in capitals (as NON-NEGOTIABLE BILL OF LADING) is conspicuous. Language in the body of a form is "conspicuous" if it is in larger or other contrasting type or color. But in a telegram any stated term is "conspicuous". Whether a term or clause is "conspicuous" or not is for decision by the court.

(11) "Contract" means the total legal obligation which results from the parties' agreement as affected by this Act and any other applicable rules or law. (Compare "Agreement".)

(12) "Creditor" includes a general creditor, a secured creditor, a lien creditor and any representative of creditors, including an assignee for the benefit of creditors, a trustee in bankruptcy, a receiver in equity and an executor or administrator of an insolvent debtor's or assignor's estate.

(13) "Defendant" includes a person in the position of defendant in a cross-action or counterclaim.

(14) "Delivery" with respect to instruments, documents of title, chattel paper, or certificated securities means voluntary transfer of possession.

(15) "Document of title" includes a bill of lading, dock warrant, dock receipt, warehouse receipt or order for the delivery of goods, and also any other document which in the regular course of business or financing is treated as adequately evidencing that the person in possession of it is entitled to receive, hold and dispose of the document and the goods it covers. To be a document of title a document must purport to be issued by or addressed to a bailee and purport to cover goods in the bailee's possession which are either identified or are fungible portions of an identified mass.

(16) "Fault" means wrongful act, omission or breach.

(17) "Fungible" with respect to goods or securities means goods or securities of which any unit is, by nature or usage of trade, the equivalent of any other like unit. Goods which are not fungible shall be deemed fungible for the purposes of this Act to the extent that under a particular agreement or document unlike units are treated as equivalents.

(18) "Genuine" means free of forgery or counterfeiting.

(19) "Good faith" means honesty in fact in the conduct or transaction concerned.

(20) "Holder" means a person who is in possession of a document of title or an instrument or a certificated investment security drawn, issued, or indorsed to him or his order or to bearer or in blank.

(21) To "honor" is to pay or to accept and pay, or where a credit so engages to purchase or discount a draft complying with the terms of the credit.

(22) "Insolvency proceedings" includes any assignment for the benefit of creditors or other proceedings intended to liquidate or rehabilitate the estate of the person involved.

(23) A person is "insolvent" who either has ceased to pay his debts in the ordinary course of business or cannot pay his debts as they become due or is insolvent within the meaning of the federal bankruptcy law.

(24) "Money" means a medium of exchange authorized or adopted by a domestic or foreign government as a part of its currency.

(25) A person has "notice" of a fact when

(a) he has actual knowledge of it; or

(b) he has received a notice of notification of it; or

(c) from all the facts and circumstances known to him at the time in question he has reason to know that it exists.

A person "knows" or has "knowledge" of a fact when he has actual knowledge of it. "Discover" or "learn" or a word or phrase of similar import refers to knowledge rather than to reason to know. The time and circumstances under which a notice or notification may cease to be effective are not determined by this Act.

(26) A person "notifies" or "gives" a notice or notification to another by taking such steps as may be reasonably required to inform the other in ordinary course whether or not such other actually comes to know of it. A person "receives" a notice or notification when

(a) it comes to his attention; or

(b) it is duly delivered at the place of business through which the contract was made or at any other place held out by him as the place for receipt of such communications.

(27) Notice, knowledge or a notice or notification received by an organization is effective for a particular transaction from the time when it is brought to the attention of the individual conducting that transaction, and in any event from the time when it would have been brought to his attention if the organization had exercised due diligence.

(28) "Organization" includes a corporation, government or governmental subdivision or agency, business trust, estate, trust, partnership or association, two or more persons having a joint or common interest, or any other legal or commercial entity.

(29) "Party", as distinct from "third party", means a person who has engaged in a transaction or made an agreement within this Act.

(30) "Person" includes an individual or an organization (See Section 1-102).

(31) "Presumption" or "presumed" means that the trier of fact must find the existence of the fact presumed unless and until evidence is introduced which would support a finding of its nonexistence.

(32) "Purchase" includes taking by sale, discount, negotiation, mortgage, pledge, lien, issue or re-issue, gift or any other voluntary transaction creating an interest in property.

(33) "Purchaser" means a person who takes by purchase.

(34) "Remedy" means any remedial right to which an aggrieved party is entitled with or without resort to a tribunal.

(35) "Representative" includes an agent, an officer of a corporation or association, and a trustee, executor or administrator of an estate, or any other person empowered to act for another.

(36) "Rights" includes remedies.

(37) "Security interest" means an interest in personal property or fixtures which secures payment or performance of an obligation. The retention or reservation of title by a seller of goods notwithstanding shipment or delivery to the buyer (Section 2-401) is limited in effect to a reservation of a "security interest". The term also includes any interest of a buyer of accounts [or] chattel paper which is subject to Article 9. The special property interest of a buyer of goods on identification of such goods to a contract for sale under Section 2-401 is not a "security interest", but a buyer may also acquire a "security interest" by complying with Article 9. Unless a lease or consignment is intended as security, reservation of title thereunder is not a "security interest" but a consignment is in any event subject to the provisions on consignment sales (Section 2-326). Whether a lease is intended as security is to be determined by the facts of each case; however,

(a) the inclusion of an option to purchase does not of itself make the lease one intended for security, and

(b) an agreement that upon compliance with the terms of the lease the lessee shall become or has the option to become the owner of the property for no additional consideration or for a nominal consideration does make the lease one intended for security.

(38) "Send" in connection with any writing or notice means to deposit in the mail or deliver for transmission by any other usual means of communication with postage or cost of transmission provided for and properly addressed and in the case of an instrument to an address specified thereon or otherwise agreed, or if there be none to any address specified thereon or otherwise agreed, or if there be none to any address reasonable under the circumstances. The receipt of any writing or notice within the time at which it would have arrived if properly sent has the effect of a proper sending.

(39) "Signed" includes any symbol executed or adopted by a party with present intention to authenticate a writing.

(40) "Surety" includes guarantor.

(41) "Telegram" includes a message transmitted by radio, teletype, cable, any mechanical method of transmission, or the like.

(42) "Term" means that portion of an agreement which relates to a particular matter.

(43) "Unauthorized" signature or indorsement means one made without actual implied or apparent authority and includes a forgery.

(44) "Value". Except as otherwise provided with respect to negotiable instruments and bank collections (Sections 3-303, 4-208 and 4-209) a person gives "value" for rights if he acquires them

(a) in return for a binding commitment to extend credit or for the extension of immediately available credit whether or not drawn upon and whether or not a charge-back is provided for in the event of difficulties in collection; or

(b) as security for or in total or partial satisfaction of a pre-existing claim; or

(c) by accepting delivery pursuant to a pre-existing claim; or

(d) generally, in return for any consideration sufficient to support a simple contract.

(45) "Warehouse receipt" means a receipt issued by a person engaged in the business of storing goods for hire.

(46) "Written" or "writing" includes printing, typewriting or any other intentional reduction to tangible form.

§ **1-202. Prima Facie Evidence by Third Party Documents.**—A document in due form purporting to be a bill of lading, policy or certificate of insurance, official weigher's or inspector's certificate, consular invoice, or any other document authorized or required by the contract to be issued by a third party shall be prima facie evidence of its own authenticity and genuineness and of the facts stated in the document by the third party.

§ **1-203. Obligation of Good Faith**—Every contract or duty within this Act imposes an obligation of good faith in its performance or enforcement.

§ **1-204. Time; Reasonable Time; "Seasonably".**—

(1) Whenever this Act requires any action to be taken within a reasonable time, any time which is not manifestly unreasonable may be fixed by agreement.

(2) What is a reasonable time for taking any action depends on the nature, purpose and circumstances of such action.

(3) An action is taken "seasonably" when it is taken at or within the time agreed or no time agreed at or within a reasonable time.

§ **1-205. Course of Dealing and Usage of Trade.**—

(1) A course of dealing is a sequence of previous conduct between the parties to a particular transaction which is fairly to be regarded as establishing a common basis of understanding for interpreting their expressions and other conduct.

(2) A usage of trade is any practice or method of dealing having such regularity of observance in a place, vocation or trade as to justify an expectation that it will be observed with respect to the transaction in question. If it is established that such usage is embodied in a written trade code or similar writing the interpretation of the writing is for the court.

(3) A course of dealing between parties and any usage of trade in the vocation of trade in which they are engaged or of which they are or should be aware give particular meaning to and supplement or qualify terms of an agreement.

(4) The express terms of an agreement and an applicable course of dealing or usage of trade shall be construed wherever reasonable as consistent with each other; but when such construction is unreasonable express terms control both course of dealing and usage of trade and course of dealing controls usage of trade.

(5) An applicable usage of trade in the place where any part of performance is to occur shall be used in interpreting the agreement as to that part of the performance.

(6) Evidence of a relevant usage of trade offered by one party is not admissible unless and until he has given the other party such notice as the court finds sufficient to prevent unfair surprise to the latter.

§ **1-206. Statute of Frauds for Kinds of Personal Property Not Otherwise Covered.**—

(1) Except in the cases described in subsection (2) of this section a contract for the sale of personal property is not enforceable by way of action or defense beyond five thousand dollars in amount or value of remedy unless there is some writing which indicates that a contract for sale has been made between the parties at a defined or stated price, reasonably identifies the subject matter, and is signed by the party against whom enforcement is sought or by his authorized agent.

(2) Subsection (1) of this section does not apply to contracts for the sale of goods (Section 2-201) nor of securities (Section 8-319) nor to security agreements (Section 9-203).

§ **1-207. Performance or Acceptance Under Reservation of Rights.**—A party who with explicit reservation of rights performs or promises performance or assents to performance in a manner demanded or offered by the other party does not thereby prejudice the rights reserved. Such words as "without prejudice", "under protest" or the like are sufficient.

§ **1-208. Option to Accelerate at Will.**—A term providing that one party or his successor in interest may accelerate payment or performance or require collateral or additional collateral "at will" or "when he deems himself insecure" or in words of similar import shall be construed to mean that he shall have power to do so only if he in good faith believes that the prospect of payment or performance is impaired. The burden of establishing lack of good faith is on the party against whom the power has been exercised.

ARTICLE TWO—SALES

PART 1

Short Title, General Construction and Subject Matter

§ **2-101. Short Title.**—This Article shall be known and may be cited as Uniform Commercial Code—Sales.

§ **2-102. Scope; Certain Security and Other Transactions Excluded From This Article.**—Unless the context otherwise requires, this Article applies to transactions in goods; it does not apply to any transaction which although in the form of an unconditional contract to sell or present sale is intended to operate only as a security transaction nor does this Article impair or repeal any statute regulating sales to consumers, farmers or other specified classes of buyers.

§ **2-103. Definitions and Index of Definitions.**—

(1) In this Article unless the context otherwise requires

    (a) "Buyer" means a person who buys or contracts to buy goods.

    (b) "Good faith" in the case of a merchant means honesty in fact and the observance of reasonable commercial standards of fair dealing in the trade.

    (c) "Receipt" of goods means taking physical possession of them.

    (d) "Seller" means a person who sells or contracts to sell goods. . . .

§ **2-104. Definitions: "Merchant"; "Between Merchants"; "Financing Agency."**—

(1) "Merchant" means a person who deals in goods of the kind or otherwise by his occupation holds himself out as having knowledge or skill peculiar to the practices or goods involved in the transaction or to whom such knowledge or skill may be attributed by his employment of an agent or broker or other intermediary who by his occupation holds himself out as having such knowledge or skill.

(2) "Financing agency" means a bank, finance company or other person who in the ordinary course of business makes advances against goods or documents of title or who by arrangement with either the seller or the buyer intervenes in ordinary course to make or collect payment due or claimed under the contract for sale, as by purchasing or paying the seller's draft or making advances against it or by merely taking it for collection whether or not documents of title accompany the draft. "Financing agency" includes also a bank or other person who similarly intervenes between persons who are in the position of seller and buyer in respect to the goods (Section 2-707).

(3) "Between merchants" means in any transaction with respect to which both parties are chargeable with the knowledge or skill of merchants.

§ **2-105. Definitions: Transferability; "Goods"; "Future" Goods; "Lot"; "Commercial Unit".**—

(1) "Goods means all things (including specially manufactured goods) which are movable at the time of identification to the contract for sale other than the money in which the price is to be paid, investment securities (Article 8) and things in action. "Goods" also includes the unborn young of animals and growing crops and other identified things attached to realty as described in the section on goods to be severed from realty (Section 2-107.)

(2) Goods must be both existing and identified before any interest in them can pass. Goods which are not both existing and identified are "future" goods. A purported present sale of future goods or of any interest therein operates as a contract to sell.

(3) There may be a sale of a part interest in existing identified goods.

(4) An undivided share in an identified bulk of fungible goods is sufficiently identified to be sold although the quantity of the bulk is not determined. Any agreed proportion of such a bulk or any quantity thereof agreed upon by number, weight or other measure may to the extent of the seller's interest in the bulk be sold to the buyer who then becomes an owner in common.

(5) "Lot" means a parcel or a single article which is the subject matter of a separate sale or delivery, whether or not it is sufficient to perform the contract.

(6) "Commercial unit" means such a unit of goods as by commercial usage is a single whole for purposes of sale and division of which materially impairs its character or value on the market or in use. A commercial unit may be a single article (as a machine) or a set of articles (as a suite of furniture or an assortment of sizes) or a quantity (as a bale, gross, or carload) or any other unit treated in use of in the relevant market as a single whole.

§ **2-106. Definitions: "Contract"; "Agreement"; "Contract for Sale"; "Sale"; "Present Sale"; "Conforming" to Contract; "Termination"; "Cancellation".**—

(1) In This Article unless the context otherwise requires "contract" and "agreement" are limited to those relating to the present or future sale of goods. "Contract for sale" includes both a present sale of goods and a contract to sell goods at a future time. A "sale" consists in the passing of title from the seller to the buyer for a price (Section 2-401). A "present sale" means a sale which is accomplished by the marking of the contract.

(2) Goods or conduct including any part of a performance are "conforming" or conform to the contract when they are in accordance with the obligations under the contract.

(3) "Termination" occurs when either party pursuant to a power created by agreement or law puts an end to the contract otherwise than for its breach. On "termination" all obligations which are still executory on both sides are discharged but any right based on prior breach or performance survives.

(4) "Cancellation" occurs when either party puts an end to the contract for breach by the other and its effect is the same as that of "termination" except that the cancelling party also retains any remedy for breach of the whole contract or any unperformed balance.

§ **2-107. Goods to Be Severed From Realty: Recording.**—

(1) A contract for the sale of minerals or the like [(including oil and gas)] or a structure or its materials to be removed from realty is a contract for the sale of goods within this Article if they are to be severed by the seller but until severance a purported present sale thereof which is not effective as a transfer of an interest in land is effective only as a contract to sell.

(2) A contract for the sale apart from the land of growing crops or other things attached to realty and capable of severance without material harm thereto but not described in subsection (1) [or of timber to be

cut] is a contract for the sale of goods within this Article whether the subject matter is to be severed by the buyer or by the seller even though it forms part of the realty at the time of contracting, and the parties can by identification effect a present sale before severance.

(3) The provision of this section are subject to any third party rights provided by the law relating to realty records, and the contract for sale may be executed and recorded as a document transferring an interest in land and shall then constitute notice to third parties of the buyer's rights under the contract for sale.

PART 2

Form, Formation and Readjustment of Contract

§ 2-201.　Formal Requirements; Statute of Frauds.—

(1) Except as otherwise provided in this section a contract for the sale of goods for the price of $500 or more is not enforceable by way of action or defense unless there is some writing sufficient to indicate that a contract for sale has been made between the parties and signed by the party against whom enforcement is sought or by his authorized agent or broker. A writing is not insufficient because it omits or incorrectly states a term agreed upon but the contract is not enforceable under this paragraph beyond the quantity of goods shown in such writing.

(2) Between merchants if within a reasonable time a writing in confirmation of the contract and sufficient against the sender is received and the party receiving it has reason to know its contents, it satisfies the requirements of subsection (1) against such party unless written notice of objection to its contents is given within ten days after it is received.

(3) A contract which does not satisfy the requirements of subsection (1) but which is valid in other respects is enforceable

(a) if the goods are to be specially manufactured for the buyer and are not suitable for sale to others in the ordinary course of the seller's business and the seller, before notice of repudiation is received and under circumstances which reasonably indicate that the goods are for the buyer, has made either a substantial beginning of their manufacture or commitments for their procurement; or

(b) if the party against whom enforcement is sought admits in his pleading, testimony or otherwise in court that a contract for sale was made, but the contract is not enforceable under this provision beyond the quantity of goods admitted; or

(c) with respect to goods for which payment has been made and accepted or which have been received and accepted (Sec. 2-606).

§ 2-202.　Final Written Expression: Part or Extrinsic Evidence.—

Terms with respect to which the confirmatory memoranda of the parties agree or which are otherwise set forth in a writing intended by the parties as a final expression of their agreement with respect to such terms as are included therein may not be contradicted by evidence of any prior agreement or of a contemporaneous oral agreement but may be explained or supplemented

(a) by course of dealing or usage of trade (Section 1-205) or by course of performance (Section 2-208); and

(b) by evidence of consistent additional terms unless the court finds the writing to have been intended also as a complete and exclusive statement of the terms of the agreement.

§ 2-203.　Seals Inoperative.—

The affixing of a seal to a writing evidencing a contract for sale or an offer to buy or sell goods does not constitute the writing a sealed instrument and the law with respect to sealed instruments does not apply to such a contract or offer.

§ 2-204.　Formation in General.—

(1) A contract for sale of goods may be made in any manner sufficient to show agreement, including conduct by both parties which recognizes the existence of such a contract.

(2) An agreement sufficient to constitute a contract for sale may be found even though the moment of its making is undetermined.

(3) Even though one or more terms are left open a contract for sale does not fail for indefiniteness if the parties have intended to make a contract and there is a reasonably certain basis for giving an appropriate remedy.

§ 2-205.　Firm Offers.—

An offer by a merchant to buy or sell goods in a signed writing which by its terms gives assurance that it will be held open is not revocable, for lack of consideration, during the time stated or if no time is stated for a reasonable time, but in no event may such period of irrevocability exceed three months; but any such term of assurance on a form supplied by the offeree must be separately signed by the offeror.

§ 2-206.　Offer and Acceptance in Formation of Contract.—

(1) Unless otherwise unambiguously indicated by the language or circumstances

(a) an offer to make a contract shall be construed as inviting acceptance in any manner and by any medium reasonable in the circumstances.

(b) an order or other offer to buy goods for prompt or current shipment shall be construed as inviting acceptance either by a prompt promise to ship or by the prompt or current shipment of conforming or non-conforming goods, but such a shipment of non-conforming goods does not constitute an acceptance if the seller seasonably notifies the buyer that the shipment is offered only as an accommodation to the buyer.

(2) Where the beginning of a requested performance is a reasonable mode of acceptance an offeror who is not notified of acceptance within a reasonable time may treat the offer as having lapsed before acceptance.

§ 2-207. Additional Terms in Acceptance or Confirmation.—

(1) A definite and seasonable expression of acceptance or a written confirmation which is sent within a reasonable time operates as an acceptance even though it states terms additional to or different from those offered or agreed upon, unless acceptance is expressly made conditional on assent to the additional or different terms.

(2) The additional terms are to be construed as proposals for addition to the contract. Between merchants such terms become part of the contract unless:

(a) the offer expressly limits acceptance to the terms of the offer;

(b) they materially alter it; or

(c) notification of objection to them has already been given or is given within a reasonable time after notice of them is received.

(3) Conduct by both parties which recognizes the existence of a contract is sufficient to establish a contract for sale although the writings of the parties do not otherwise establish a contract. In such case the terms of the particular contract consist of those terms on which the writings of the parties agree, together with any supplementary terms incorporated under any other provisions of this Act.

§ 2-208. Course of Performance or Practical Construction.—

(1) Where the contract for sale involves repeated occasions for performance by either party with knowledge of the nature of the performance and opportunity for objection to it by the other, any course of performance accepted or acquiesced in without objection shall be relevant to determine the meaning of the agreement.

(2) The express terms of the agreement and any such course of performance, as well as any course of dealing and usage of trade, shall be construed whenever reasonable as consistent with each other; but when such construction is unreasonable, express terms shall control course of performance and course of performance shall control both course of dealing and usage of trade (Section 1-205).

(3) Subject to the provisions of the next section on modification and waiver, such course of performance shall be relevant to show a waiver or modification of any term inconsistent with such course of performance.

§ 2-209. Modification, Rescission and Waiver.—

(1) An agreement modifying a contract within this Article needs no consideration to be binding.

(2) A signed agreement which excludes modification or rescission except by a signed writing cannot be otherwise modified or rescinded, but except as between merchants such a requirement on a form supplied by the merchant must be separately signed by the other party.

(3) The requirements of the statute of frauds section of this Article (Section 2-201) must be satisfied if the contract as modified is within its provisions.

(4) Although an attempt at modification or rescission does not satisfy the requirements of subsection (2) or (3) it can operate as a waiver.

(5) A party who has made a waiver affecting an executory portion of the contract may retract the waiver by reasonable notification received by the other party that strict performance will be required of any term waived, unless the retraction would be unjust in view of a material change of position in reliance on the waiver.

§ 2-210. Delegation of Performance; Assignment of Rights.—

(1) A party may perform his duty through a delegate unless otherwise agreed or unless the other party has a substantial interest in having his original promisor perform or control the acts required by the contract. No delegation of performance relieves the party delegating of any duty to perform or any liability for breach.

(2) Unless otherwise agreed all rights of either seller or buyer can be assigned except where the assignment would materially change the duty of the other party, or increase materially the burden or risk imposed on him by his contract, or impair materially his chance of obtaining return performance. A right to damages for breach of the whole contract or a right arising out of the assignor's due performance of his entire obligation can be assigned despite agreement otherwise.

(3) Unless the circumstances indicate the contrary a prohibition of assignment of "the contract" is to be construed as barring only the delegation to the assignee of the assignor's performance.

(4) An assignment of "the contract" or of "all my rights under the contract" or an assignment in similar general terms is an assignment of rights and unless the language or the circumstances (as in an assignment for security) indicate the contrary, it is a delegation of performance of the duties of the assignor and its acceptance by the assignee constitutes a promise by him to perform those duties. This promise is enforceable by either the assignor or the other party to the original contract.

(5) The other party may treat any assignment which delegates performance as creating reasonable grounds for insecurity and may without prejudice to his rights against the assignor demand assurances from the assignee (Section 2-609).

PART 3

General Obligation and Construction of Contract

§ 2-301. General Obligations of Parties.—The obligation of the seller is to transfer and deliver and that of the buyer is to accept and pay in accordance with the contract.

§ 2-302. Unconscionable Contract or Clause.—

(1) If the court as a matter of law finds the contract or any clause of the contract to have been unconscionable at the time it was made the court may refuse to enforce the contract, or it may enforce the remainder of the contract without the unconscionable clause, or it may so limit the application of any unconscionable clause as to avoid any unconscionable result.

(2) When it is claimed or appears to the court that the contract or any clause thereof may be unconscionable the parties shall be afforded a reasonable opportunity to present evidence as to its commercial setting, purpose and effect to aid the court in making the determination.

§ 2-303. Allocation or Division of Risks.—Where this Article allocates a risk or a burden as between the parties "unless otherwise agreed," the agreement may not only shift the allocation but may also divide the risk or burden.

§ 2-304. Price Payable in Money, Goods, Realty, or Otherwise.—

(1) The price can be made payable in money or otherwise. If it is payable in whole or in part in goods each party is a seller of the goods which he is to transfer.

(2) Even though all or part of the price is payable in an interest in realty the transfer of the goods and the seller's obligations with reference to them are subject to this Article, but not the transfer of the interest in realty or the transferor's obligations in connection therewith.

§ 2-305. Open Price Term.—

(1) The parties if they so intend can conclude a contract for sale even though the price is not settled. In such a case the price is a reasonable price at the time for delivery if:

(a) nothing is said as to price; or

(b) the price is left to be agreed by the parties and they fail to agree; or

(c) the price is to be fixed in terms of some agreed market or other standard as set or recorded by a third person or agency and it is not so set or recorded.

(2) A price to be fixed by the seller or by the buyer means a price for him to fix in good faith.

(3) When a price left to be fixed otherwise than by agreement of the parties fails to be fixed through fault of one party the other may at his option treat the contract as cancelled or himself fix a reasonable price.

(4) Where, however, the parties intend not to be bound unless the price be fixed or agreed and it is not fixed or agreed there is no contract. In such a case the buyer must return any goods already received or if unable so to do must pay their reasonable value at the time of delivery and the seller must return any portion of the price paid on account.

§ 2-306. Output, Requirements and Exclusive Dealings.—

(1) A term which measures the quantity by the output of the seller or the requirements of the buyer means such actual output or requirements as may occur in good faith, except that no quantity unreasonably disproportionate to any stated estimate or in the absence of a stated estimate to any normal or otherwise comparable prior output or requirements may be tendered or demanded.

(2) A lawful agreement by either the seller or the buyer for exclusive dealing in the kind of goods concerned imposes unless otherwise agreed an obligation by the seller to use best efforts to supply the goods and by the buyer to use best efforts to promote their sale.

§ 2-307. Delivery in Single Lot or Several Lots.—Unless otherwise agreed all goods called for by a contract for sale must be tendered in a single delivery and payment is due only on such tender but where the circumstances give either party the right to make or demand delivery in lots the price if it can be apportioned may be demanded for each lot.

§ 2-308. Absence of Specified Place for Delivery.—Unless otherwise agreed

(a) the place for delivery of goods is the seller's place of business or if he has none his residence; but

(b) in a contract for sale of identified goods which to the knowledge of the parties at the time of contracting are in some other place, that place is the place for their delivery; and

(c) documents of title may be delivered through customary banking channels.

§ 2-309. Absence of Specific Time Provisions; Notice of Termination.—

(1) The time for shipment or delivery of any other action under a contract if not provided in this Article or agreed upon shall be a reasonable time.

(2) Where the contract provides for successive performances but is indefinite in duration it is valid for a reasonable time but unless otherwise agreed may be terminated at any time by either party.

(3) Termination of a contract by one party except on the happening of an agreed event requires that reasonable notification be received by the other party and an agreement dispensing with notification is invalid if its operation would be unconscionable.

§ 2-310. Open Time for Payment or Running of Credit; Authority to Ship Under Reservation.—Unless otherwise agreed

(a) payment is due at the time and place at which the buyer is to receive the goods even though the place of shipment is the place of delivery; and

(b) if the seller is authorized to send the goods he may ship them under reservation, and may tender the documents of title, but the buyer may inspect the goods after their arrival before payment is due unless such inspection is inconsistent with the terms of the contract (Section 2-513); and

(c) if delivery is authorized and made by way of documents of title otherwise than by subsection (b) then payment is due at the time and place at which the buyer is to receive the documents regardless of where the goods are to be received; and

(d) where the seller is required or authorized to ship the goods on credit the credit period runs from the time of shipment but post-dating the invoice or delaying its dispatch will correspondingly delay the starting of the credit period.

§ 2-311. Options and Cooperation Respecting Performance.—

(1) An agreement for sale which is otherwise sufficiently definite (subsection (3) of Section 2-204) to be a contract is not made invalid by the fact that it leaves particulars of performance to be specified by one of the parties. Any such specification must be made in good faith and within limits set by commercial reasonableness.

(2) Unless otherwise agreed specifications relating to assortment of the goods are at the buyer's option and except as otherwise provided in subsections (1) (c) and (3) of Section 2-319 specifications or arrangements relating to shipment are at the seller's option.

(3) Where such specification would materially affect the other party's performance but is not seasonably made or where one party's cooperation is necessary to the agreed performance of the other but is not seasonably forthcoming, the other party in addition to all other remedies

(a) is excused for any resulting delay in his own performance; and

(b) may also either proceed to perform in any reasonable manner or after the time for a material part of his own performance treat the failure to specify or to cooperate as a breach by failure to deliver or accept the goods.

§ 2-312. Warranty of Title and Against Infringement; Buyer's Obligation Against Infringement.—

(1) Subject to subsection (2) there is in a contract for sale a warranty by the seller that

(a) the title conveyed shall be good, and its transfer rightful; and

(b) the goods shall be delivered free from any security interest or other lien or encumbrance of which the buyer at the time of contracting has no knowledge.

(2) A warranty under subsection (1) will be excluded or modified only by specific language or by circumstances which give the buyer reason to know that the person selling does not claim title in himself or that he is purporting to sell only such right or title as he or a third person may have.

(3) Unless otherwise agreed a seller who is a merchant regularly dealing in goods of the kind warrants that the goods shall be delivered free of the rightful claim of any third person by way of infringement or the like but a buyer who furnishes specifications to the seller must hold the seller harmless against any such claim which arises out of compliance with the specifications.

§ 2-313. Express Warranties by Affirmation, Promise, Description, Sample.—

(1) Express warranties by the seller are created as follows:

(a) Any affirmation of fact or promise made by the seller to the buyer which relates to the goods and becomes part of the basis of the bargain creates an express warranty that the goods shall conform to the affirmation or promise.

(b) Any description of the goods which is made part of the basis of the bargain creates an express warranty that the goods shall conform to the description.

(c) Any sample or model which is made part of the basis of the bargain creates an express warranty that the whole of the goods shall conform to the sample or model.

(2) It is not necessary to the creation of an express warranty that the seller use formal words such as "warrant" or "guarantee" or that he have a specific intention to make a warranty, but an affirmation merely of the value of the goods or a statement purporting to be merely the seller's opinion or commendation of the goods does not create a warranty.

§ 2-314. Implied Warranty: Merchantability; Usage of Trade.—

(1) Unless excluded or modified (Section 2-316), a warranty that the goods shall be merchantable is implied in a contract for their sale if the seller is a merchant with respect to goods of that kind. Under this section the serving for value of food or drink to be consumed either on the premises or elsewhere is a sale.

(2) Goods to be merchantable must be at least such as

(a) pass without objection in the trade under the contract description; and

(b) in the case of fungible goods, are of fair average quality within the description; and

(c) are fit for the ordinary purposes for which such goods are used; and

(d) run, within the variations permitted by the agreement, of even kind, quality and quantity within each unit and among all units involved; and

(e) are adequately contained, packaged, and labeled as the agreement may require; and

(f) conform to the promises or affirmations of fact made on the container or label if any.

(3) Unless excluded or modified (Section 2-316) other implied warranties may arise from course of dealing or usage of trade.

§ 2-315. Implied Warranty: Fitness for Particular Purpose.—Where the seller at the time of contracting has reason to know any particular purpose for which the goods are required and that the buyer is relying on the seller's skill or judgment to select or furnish suitable goods, there is unless excluded or modified under the next section an implied warranty that the goods shall be fit for such purpose.

§ 2-316. Exclusion or Modification of Warranties.—

(1) Words or conduct relevant to the creation of an express warranty and words or conduct tending to negate or limit warranty shall be construed wherever reasonable as consistent with each other; but subject to the provisions of this Article on parol or extrinsic evidence (Section 2-202) negation or limitation is inoperative to the extent that such construction is unreasonable.

(2) Subject to subsection (3), to exclude or modify the implied warranty of merchantability or any part of it the language must mention merchantability and in case of a writing must be conspicuous, and to exclude or modify any implied warranty of fitness the exclusion must be by a writing and conspicuous. Language to exclude all implied warranties of fitness is sufficient if it states, for example, that "There are no warranties which extend beyond the description on the face hereof."

(3) Notwithstanding subsection (2)

(a) unless the circumstances indicate otherwise, all implied warranties are excluded by expressions like "as is," "with all faults" or other language which in common understanding calls the buyer's attention to the exclusion of warranties and makes plain that there is no implied warranty; and

(b) when the buyer before entering into the contract has examined the goods or the sample or model as fully as he desired or has refused to examine the goods there is no implied warranty with regard to defects which an examination ought in the circumstances to have revealed to him; and

(c) an implied warranty can also be excluded or modified by course of dealing or course of performance or usage of trade.

(4) Remedies for breach of warranty can be limited in accordance with the provisions of this Article on liquidation or limitation of damages and on contractual modification of remedy (Sections 2-718 and 2-719).

§ **2-317. Cumulation and Conflict of Warranties Express or Implied.**—Warranties whether express or implied shall be construed as consistent with each other and as cumulative, but if such construction is unreasonable the intention of the parties shall determine which warranty is dominant. In ascertaining that intention the following rules apply:

(a) Exact or technical specifications displace an inconsistent sample or model or general language of description.

(b) A sample from an existing bulk displaces inconsistent general language of description.

(c) Express warranties displace inconsistent implied warranties other than an implied warranty of fitness for a particular purpose.

§ **2-318. Third Party Beneficiaries of Warranties Express or Implied.**—A seller's warranty whether express or implied extends to any natural person who is in the family or household of his buyer or who is a guest in his home if it is reasonable to expect that such person may use, consume or be affected by the goods and who is injured in person by breach of the warranty. A seller may not exclude or limit the operation of this section.

§ **2-319. F.O.B. and F.A.S. Terms.**—

(1) Unless otherwise agreed the term F.O.B. (which means "free on board") at a named place, even though used only in connection with the stated price, is a delivery term under which

(a) when the term is F.O.B. the place of shipment, the seller must at that place ship the goods in the manner provided in this Article (Section 2-504; and bear the expense and risk of putting them into the possession of the carrier; or

(b) when the term is F.O.B. the place of destination, the seller must at his own expense and risk transport the goods to that place and there tender delivery of them in the manner provided in this Article (Section 2-503);

(c) when under either (a) or (b) the term is also F.O.B. vessel, car or other vehicle, the seller must in addition at his own expense and risk load the goods on board. If the term is F.O.B. vessel the buyer must name the vessel and in an appropriate case the seller must comply with the provisions of this Article on the form of bill of lading (Section 2-323).

(2) Unless otherwise agreed the term F.A.S. vessel (which means "free alongside") at a named port, even though used only in connection with the stated price, is a delivery term under which the seller must

(a) at his own expense and risk deliver the goods alongside the vessel in the manner usual in that port or on a dock designated and provided by the buyer; and

(b) obtain and tender a receipt for the goods in exchange for which the carrier is under a duty to issue a bill of lading.

(3) Unless otherwise agreed in any case falling within subsection (1) (a) or (c) or subsection (2) the buyer must seasonably give any needed instructions for making delivery, including when the term is F.A.S. or F.O.B. the loading berth of the vessel and in an appropriate case its name and sailing date. The seller may treat the failure of needed instructions as a failure of cooperation under this Article (Section 2-311). He may also at his option move the goods in any reasonable manner preparatory to delivery or shipment.

(4) Under the term F.O.B. vessel or F.A.S. unless otherwise agreed the buyer must make payment against tender of the required documents and the seller may not tender nor the buyer demand delivery, of the goods in substitution for the documents.

§ **2-320. C.I.F. and C. & F. Terms.**—

(1) The term C.I.F. means that the price includes in a lump sum the cost of the goods and the insurance and freight to the named destination.

(2) Unless otherwise agreed and even though used only in connection with the stated price and destination, the term C.I.F. destination or its equivalent requires the seller at his own expense and risk to

(a) put the goods into the possession of a carrier at the port for shipment and obtain a negotiable bill or bills of lading covering the entire transportation to the named destination; and

(b) load the goods and obtain a receipt from the carrier (which may be contained in the bill of lading) showing that the freight has been paid or provided for; and

(c) obtain a policy or certificate of insurance, including any war risk insurance, of a kind and on terms then current at the port of shipment in the usual amount, in the currency of the contract, shown to cover the same goods covered by the bill of lading and providing for payment of loss to the order of the buyer or for the account of whom it may concern; but the seller may add to the price the amount of the premium for any such war risk insurance; and

(d) prepare an invoice of the goods and procure any other documents required to effect shipment or to comply with the contract; and

(e) forward and tender with commercial promptness all the documents in due form and with any indorsement necessary to perfect the buyer's rights.

(3) Unless otherwise agreed the term C. & F. or its equivalent has the same effect and imposes upon the seller the same obligations and risks as a C.I.F. term except the obligation as to insurance.

(4) Under the term C.I.F. or C. & F. unless otherwise agreed the buyer must make payment against tender of the required documents and the seller may not tender nor the buyer demand delivery of the goods in substitution for the documents.

§ 2-321. C.I.F. or C. & F.: "Net Landed Weights"; "Payment on Arrival"; Warranty of Condition or Arrival.—Under a contract containing a term C.I.F. or C. & F.

(1) Where the price is based on or is to be adjusted according to "net landed weights," "delivered weights," "out turn" quantity or quality or the like, unless otherwise agreed the seller must reasonably estimate the price. The payment due on tender of the documents called for by the contract is the amount so estimated but after final adjustment of the price a settlement must be made with commercial promptness.

(2) An agreement described in subsection (1) or any warranty of quality or condition of the goods on arrival places upon the seller the risk of ordinary deterioration, shrinkage and the like in transportation but has no effect on the place or time of identification to the contract for sale or delivery or on the passing of the risk of loss.

(3) Unless otherwise agreed where the contract provides for payment on or after arrival of the goods the seller must before payment allow such preliminary inspection as is feasible; but if the goods are lost delivery of the documents and payment are due when the goods should have arrived.

§ 2-322. Delivery "Ex-Ship".—

(1) Unless otherwise agreed a term for delivery of goods "ex-ship" (which means from the carrying vessel) or in equivalent language is not restricted to a particular ship and requires delivery from a ship which has reached a place at the named port of destination where goods of the kind are usually discharged.

(2) Under such a term unless otherwise agreed

(a) the seller must discharge all liens arising out of the carriage and furnish the buyer with a direction which puts the carrier under a duty to deliver the goods; and

(b) the risk of loss does not pass to the buyer until the goods leave the ship's tackle or are otherwise properly unloaded.

§ 2-323. Form of Bill of Lading Required in Overseas Shipments; "Overseas."—

(1) Where the contract contemplates overseas shipment and contains a term C.I.F. or C. & F. or F.O.B. vessel, the seller unless otherwise agreed must obtain a negotiable bill of lading stating that the goods have been loaded on board or, in the case of a term C.I.F. or C. & F., received for shipment.

(2) Where in a case within subsection (1) a bill of lading has been issued in a set of parts, unless otherwise agreed if the documents are not to be sent from abroad the buyer may demand tender of the full set; otherwise only one part of the bill of lading need be tendered. Even if the agreement expressly requires a full set

(a) due tender of a single part is acceptable within the provisions of this Article on cure of improper delivery (subsection (1) of Section 2-508); and

(b) even though the full set is demanded, if the documents are sent from abroad the person tendering an incomplete set may nevertheless require payment upon furnishing an indemnity which the buyer in good faith deems adequate.

(3) A shipment by water or by air or a contrct contemplating such shipment is "overseas" insofar as by usage of trade or agreement it is subject to the commercial, financing or shipping practices characteristic of international deep water commerce.

§ 2-324. "No Arrival, No Sale" Term.—Under a term "no arrival, no sale" or terms of the like meaning, unless otherwise agreed

(a) the seller must properly ship conforming goods and if they arrive by any means he must tender them on arrival but he assures no obligation that the goods will arrive unless he has caused the non-arrival; and

(b) where without fault of the seller the goods are in part lost or have so deteriorated as no longer to conform to the contract or arrive after the contract time, the buyer may proceed as if there had been casualty to identified goods (Section 2-613).

§ 2-325. "Letter of Credit" Term; "Confirmed Credit."—

(1) Failure of the buyer seasonably to furnish an agreed letter of credit is a breach of the contract for sale.

(2) The delivery to seller of a proper letter of credit suspends the buyer's obligation to pay. If the letter of credit is dishonored, the seller may on seasonable notification to the buyer require payment directly from him.

(3) Unless otherwise agreed the term "letter of credit" or "banker's credit" in a contract for sale means an irrevocable credit issued by a financing agency of good repute and, where the shipment is overseas, of good international repute. The term "confirmed credit" means that the credit must also carry the direct obligation of such an agency which does business in the seller's financial market.

§ 2-326. Sale on Approval and Sale or Return; Consignment Sales and Rights of Creditors.—

(1) Unless otherwise agreed, if delivered goods may be returned by the buyer even though they conform to the contract, the transaction is

(a) a "sale on approval" if the goods are delivered primarily for use, and

(b) a "sale or return" if the goods are delivered primarily for resale.

(2) Except as provided in subsection (3), goods held on approval are not subject to the claims of the

buyer's creditors until acceptance; goods held on sale or return are subject to such claims while in the buyer's possession.

(3) Where goods are delivered to a person for sale and such person maintains a place of business at which he deals in goods of the kind involved, under a name other than the name of the person making delivery, then with respect to claims of creditors of the person conducting the business the goods are deemed to be on sale or return. The provisions of this subsection are applicable even though an agreement purports to reserve title to the person making delivery until payment or resale or uses such words as "on consignment" or "on memorandum." However, this subsection is not applicable if the person making delivery

(a) complies with an applicable law providing for a consignor's interest or the like to be evidenced by a sign, or

(b) establishes that the person conducting the business is generally known by his creditors to be substantially engaged in selling the goods of others, or

(c) complies with the filing provisions of the Article on Secured Transactions (Article 9).

(4) Any "or return" term of a contract for sale is to be treated as a separate contract for sale within the statute of frauds section of this Article (Section 2-201) and as contradicting the sale aspect of the contract within the provisions of this Article on parol or extrinsic evidence (Section 2-202).

§ 2-327. Special Incidents of Sale on Approval and Sale or Return.—

(1) Under a sale on approval unless otherwise agreed

(a) although the goods are identified to the contract the risk of loss and the title do not pass to the buyer until acceptance; and

(b) use of goods consistent with the purpose of trial is not acceptance but failure seasonably to notify the seller of election to return the goods is acceptance, and if the goods conform to the contract acceptance of any part is acceptance of the whole; and

(c) after due notification of election to return, the return is at the seller's risk and expense but a merchant buyer must follow any reasonable instructions.

(2) Under a sale or return unless otherwise agreed

(a) the option to return extends to the whole or any commercial unit of the goods while in substantially their original condition, but must be exercised seasonably; and

(b) the return is at the buyer's risk and expense.

§ 2-328. Sale by Auction.—

(1) In a sale by auction if goods are put up in lots each lot is the subject of a separate sale.

(2) A sale by auction is complete when the auctioneer so announces by the fall of the hammer or in other customary manner. Where a bid is made while the hammer is falling in acceptance of a prior bid the auctioneer may in his discretion reopen the bidding or declare the goods sold under the bid on which the hammer was falling.

(3) Such a sale is with reserve unless the goods are in explicit terms put up without reserve. In an auction with reserve the auctioneer may withdraw the goods at any time until he announces completion of the sale. In an auction without reserve, after the auctioneer calls for bids on an article or lot, that article or lot cannot be withdrawn unless no bid is made within a reasonable time. In either case a bidder may retract his bid until the auctioneer's announcement of completion of the sale, but a bidder's retraction does not revive any previous bid.

(4) If the auctioneer knowingly receives a bid on the seller's behalf or the seller makes or procures such a bid, and notice has not been given that liberty for such bidding is reserved, the buyer may at his option avoid the sale or take the goods at the price of the last good faith bid prior to the completion of the sale. This subsection shall not apply to any bid at a forced sale.

PART 4

Title, Creditors and Good Faith Purchasers

§ 2-401. Passing of Title; Reservation for Security; Limited Application of This Section.—Each provision of this Article with regard to the rights, obligations and remedies of the seller, the buyer, purchasers or other third parties applies irrespective of title to the goods except where the provision refers to such title. Insofar as situations are not covered by the other provisions of this Article and matters concerning title become material the following rules apply:

(1) Title to goods cannot pass under a contract for sale prior to their identification to the contract (Section 2-501), and unless otherwise explicitly agreed the buyer acquires by their identification a special property as limited by this Act. Any retention or reservation by the seller of the title (property) in goods shipped or delivered to the buyer is limited in effect to a reservation of a security interest. Subject to these provisions and to the provisions of the Article on Secured Transactions (Article 9), title to goods passes from the seller to the buyer in any manner and on any conditions explicitly agreed on by the parties.

(2) Unless otherwise explicitly agreed title passes to the buyer at the time and place at which the seller completes his performance with reference to the physical delivery of the goods, despite any reservation of a security interest and even though a document of title is to be delivered at a different time or place; and in particular and despite any reservation of a security interest by the bill of lading.

(a) if the contract requires or authorizes the seller to send the goods to the buyer but does not require him to deliver them at destination, title passes to the buyer at the time and place of shipment; but

(b) if the contract requires delivery at destination, title passes on tender there.

(3) Unless otherwise explicitly agreed where delivery is to be made without moving the goods,

(a) if the seller is to deliver a document of title, title passes at the time when and the place where he delivers such documents; or

(b) if the goods are at the time of contracting already identified and no documents are to be delivered, title passes at the time and place of contracting.

(4) A rejection or other refusal by the buyer to receive or retain the goods, whether or not justified, or a justified revocation of acceptance revests title to the goods in the seller. Such revesting occurs by operation of law and is not a "sale."

§ 2-402. Rights of Seller's Creditors Against Sold Goods.—

(1) Except as provided in subsections (2) and (3), rights of unsecured creditors of the seller with respect to goods which have been identified to a contract for sale are subject to the buyer's rights to recover the goods under this Article (Sections 2-502 and 2-716).

(2) A creditor of the seller may treat a sale or an identification of goods to a contract for sale as void if as against him a retention of possession by the seller is fraudulent under any rule of law of the state where the goods are situated, except that retention of possession in good faith and current course of trade by a merchant-seller for a commercially reasonable time after a sale or identification is not fraudulent.

(3) Nothing in this Article shall be deemed to impair the rights of creditors of the seller

(a) under the provisions of the Article on Secured Transactions (Article 9); or

(b) where identification to the contract or delivery is made not in current course of trade but in satisfaction of or as security for a preexisting claim for money, security or the like and is made under circumstances which under any rule of law of the state where the goods are situated would apart from this Article constitute the transaction a fraudulent transfer or voidable preference.

§ 2-403. Power to Transfer; Good Faith Purchase of Goods; "Entrusting."—

(1) A purchaser of goods acquires all title which his transferor had or had power to transfer except that a purchaser of a limited interest acquires rights only to the extent of the interest purchased. A person with voidable title has power to transfer a good title to a good faith purchaser for value. When goods have been delivered under a transaction of purchase the purchaser has such power even though

(a) the transferor was deceived as to the identity of the purchaser, or

(b) the delivery was in exchange for a check which is later dishonored, or

(c) it was agreed that the transaction was to be a "cash sale," or

(d) the delivery was procured through fraud punishable as larcenous under the criminal law.

(2) Any entrusting of possession of goods to a merchant who deals in goods of that kind gives him power to transfer all rights of the entruster to a buyer in ordinary course of business.

(3) "Entrusting" includes any delivery and any acquiescence in retention of possession regardless of any condition expressed between the parties to the delivery or acquiescence and regardless of whether the procurement of the entrusting or the possessor's disposition of the goods have been such as to be larcenous under the criminal law.

(4) The rights of other purchasers of goods and of lien creditors are governed by the Articles on Secured Transactions (Article 9), Bulk Transfers (Article 6) and Documents of Title (Article 7).

PART 5

Performance

§ 2-501. Insurable Interest in Goods; Manner of Identification of Goods.—

(1) The buyer obtains a special property and an insurable interest in goods by identification of existing goods as goods to which the contract refers even though the goods so identified are non-conforming and he has an option to return or reject them. Such identification can be made at any time and in any manner explicitly agreed to by the parties. In the absence of explicit agreement identification occurs

(a) when the contract is made if it is for the sale of goods already existing and identified;

(b) if the contract is for the sale of future goods other than those described in paragraph (c), when goods are shipped, marked or otherwise designated by the seller as goods to which the contract refers;

(c) when the crops are planted or otherwise become growing crops or the young are conceived if the contract is for the sale of unborn young to be born within twelve months after contracting or for the sale of crops to be harvested within twelve months or the next normal harvest season after contracting whichever is longer.

(2) The seller retains an insurable interest in goods so long as title to or any security interest in the goods remains in him and where the identification is by the seller alone he may until default or insolvency or notification to the buyer that the identification is final substitute other goods for those identified.

(3) Nothing in this section impairs any insurable interest recognized under any other statute or rule of law.

§ 2-502. Buyer's Right to Goods on Seller's Insolvency.—

(1) Subject to subsection (2) and even though the goods have not been shipped a buyer who has paid a part or all of the price of goods in which he has a special property under the provisions of the immediately preceding section may on making and keeping good a tender of any unpaid portion of their price recover them from the seller if the seller becomes insolvent within ten days after receipt of the first installment on their price.

(2) If the identification creating his special property has been made by the buyer he acquires the right to recover the goods only if they conform to the contract for sale.

§ 2-503. Manner of Seller's Tender of Delivery.—

(1) Tender of delivery requires that the seller put and hold conforming goods at the buyer's disposition and give the buyer any notification reasonably necessary to enable him to take delivery. The manner, time and place for tender are determined by the agreement and this Article, and in particular

(a) tender must be at a reasonable hour, and if it is of goods they must be kept available for the period reasonably necessary to enable the buyer to take possession; but

(b) unless otherwise agreed the buyer must furnish facilities reasonably suited to the receipt of the goods.

(2) Where the case is within the next section respecting shipment tender requires that the seller comply with its provisions.

(3) Where the seller is required to deliver at a particular destination tender requires that he comply with subsection (1) and also in any appropriate case tender documents as described in subsections (4) and (5) of this section.

(4) Where goods are in the possession of a bailee and are to be delivered without being moved

(a) tender requires that the seller either tender a negotiable document of title covering such goods or procure acknowledgment by the bailee of the buyer's right to possession of the goods; but

(b) tender to the buyer of a nonnegotiable document of title or of a written direction to the bailee to deliver is sufficient tender unless the buyer seasonably objects, and receipt by the bailee of notification of the buyer's rights fixes those rights as against the bailee to honor the non-negotiable document of title or to obey the direction remains on the seller until the buyer has had a reasonable time to present the document or direction, and a refusal by the bailee to honor the document or to obey the direction defeats the tender.

(5) Where the contract requires the seller to deliver documents

(a) he must tender all such documents in correct form, except as provided in this Article with respect to bills of lading in a set (subsection (2) of Section 2-323); and

(b) tender through customary banking channels is sufficient and dishonor of a draft accompanying the documents constitutes non-acceptance or rejection.

§ 2-504. Shipment by Seller.—

Where the seller is required or authorized to send the goods to the buyer and the contract does not require him to deliver them at a particular destination, then unless otherwise agreed he must

(a) put the goods in the possession of such a carrier and make such a contract for their transportation as may be reasonable having regard to the nature of the goods and other circumstances of the case; and

(b) obtain and promptly deliver or tender in due form any document necessary to enable the buyer to obtain possession of the goods or otherwise required by the agreement or by usage of trade; and

(c) promptly notify the buyer of the shipment.

Failure to notify the buyer under paragraph (c) or to make a proper contract under paragraph (a) is a ground for rejection only if material delay or loss ensues.

§ 2-505. Seller's Shipment Under Reservation.—

(1) Where the seller has identified goods to the contract by or before shipment:

(a) his procurement of a negotiable bill of lading to his own order or otherwise reserves in him a security interest in the goods. His procurement of the bill to the order of a financing agency or of the buyer indicates in addition only the seller's expectation of transferring that interest to the person named.

(b) a non-negotiable bill of lading to himself or his nominee reserves possession of the goods as security but except in a case of conditional delivery (subsection (2) of Section 2-507) a non-negotiable bill of lading naming the buyer as consignee reserves no security interest even though the seller retains possession of the bill of lading.

(2) When shipment by the seller with reservation of a security interest is in violation of the contract for sale it constitutes an improper contract for transportation within the preceding section but impairs neither the rights given to the buyer by shipment and identification of the goods to the contract nor the seller's powers as a holder of a negotiable document.

§ 2-506. Rights of Financing Agency.—

(1) A financing agency by paying or purchasing for value a draft which relates to a shipment of goods acquires to the extent of the payment or purchase and in addition to its own rights under the draft and any document of title securing it any rights of the shipper in the goods including the right to stop delivery and the shipper's right to have the draft honored by the buyer.

(2) The right to reimbursement of a financing agency which has in good faith honored or purchased the draft under commitment to or authority from the buyer is not impaired by subsequent discovery of defects with reference to any relevant document which was apparently regular on its face.

§ 2-507. Effect of Seller's Tender; Delivery on Condition.—

(1) Tender of delivery is a condition to the buyer's duty to accept the goods and, unless otherwise agreed, to his duty to pay for them. Tender entitles the seller to acceptance of the goods and to payment according to the contract.

(2) Where payment is due and demanded on the delivery to the buyer of goods or documents of title, his right as against the seller to retain or dispose of them is conditional upon his making the payment due.

§ 2-508.   Cure by Seller of Improper Tender or Delivery; Replacement.—

(1) Where any tender or delivery by the seller is rejected because non-conforming and the time for performance has not yet expired, the seller may seasonably notify the buyer of his intention to cure and may then within the contract time make a conforming delivery.

(2) Where the buyer rejects a non-conforming tender which the seller had reasonable grounds to believe would be acceptable with or without money allowance the seller may if he seasonably notifies the buyer have a further reasonable time to substitute a conforming tender.

§ 2-509.   Risk of Loss in the Absence of Breach.—

(1) Where the contract requires or authorizes the seller to ship the goods by carrier

(a) if it does not require him to deliver them at a particular destination, the risk of loss passes to the buyer when the goods are duly delivered to the carrier even though the shipment is under reservation (Section 2-505); but

(b) if it does require him to deliver them at a particular destination and the goods are there duly tendered while in the possession of the carrier, the risk of loss passes to the buyer when the goods are there duly so tendered as to enable the buyer to take delivery.

(2) Where the goods are held by a bailee to be delivered without being moved, the risk of loss passes to the buyer

(a) on his receipt of a negotiable document of title covering the goods; or

(b) on acknowledgment by the bailee of the buyer's right to possession of the goods; or

(c) after his receipt of a non-negotiable document of title or other written direction to deliver, as provided in subsection (4) (b) of Section 2-503.

(3) In any case not within subsection (1) or (2), the risk of loss passes to the buyer on his receipt of the goods if the seller is a merchant; otherwise the risk passes to the buyer on tender of delivery.

(4) The provisions of this section are subject to contrary agreement of the parties and to the provisions of this Article on sale on approval (Section 2-327) and on effect of breach on risk of loss (Section 2-510).

§ 2-510.   Effect of Breach on Risk of Loss.—

(1) Where a tender or delivery of goods so fails to conform to the contract as to give a right of rejection the risk of their loss remains on the seller until cure or acceptance.

(2) Where the buyer rightfully revokes acceptance he may to the extent of any deficiency in his effective insurance coverage treat the risk of loss as having rested on the seller from the beginning.

(3) Where the buyer as to conforming goods already identified to the contract for sale repudiates or is otherwise in breach before risk of their loss has passed to him, the seller may to the extent of any deficiency in his effective insurance coverage treat the risk of loss as resting on the buyer for a commercially reasonable time.

§ 2-511.   Tender of Payment by Buyer; Payment by Check.—

(1) Unless otherwise agreed tender of payment is a condition to the seller's duty to tender and complete any delivery.

(2) Tender of payment is sufficient when made by any means or in any manner current in the ordinary course of business unless the seller demands payment in legal tender and gives any extension of time reasonably necessary to procure it.

(3) Subject to the provisions of this Act on the effect of an instrument on an obligation (Section 3-802), payment by check is conditional and is defeated as between the parties by dishonor of the check on due presentment.

§ 2-512.   Payment by Buyer Before Inspection.—

(1) Where the contract requires payment before inspection non-conformity of the goods does not excuse the buyer from so making payment unless

(a) the non-conformity appears without inspection; or

(b) despite tender of the required documents the circumstances would justify injunction against honor under the provisions of this Act (Section 5-114).

(2) Payment pursuant to subsection (1) does not constitute an acceptance of goods or impair the buyer's right to inspect or any of his remedies.

§ 2-513.   Buyer's Right to Inspection of Goods.—

(1) Unless otherwise agreed and subject to subsection (3), where goods are tendered or delivered or identified to the contract for sale, the buyer has a right before payment or acceptance to inspect them at any reasonable place and time and in any reasonable manner. When the seller is required or authorized to send the goods to the buyer, the inspection may be after their arrival.

(2) Expenses of inspection must be borne by the buyer but may be recovered from the seller if the goods do not conform and are rejected.

(3) Unless otherwise agreed and subject to the provisions of this Article on C.I.F. contracts (subsection (3) of Section 2-321), the buyer is not entitled to inspect the goods before payment of the price when the contract provides

(a) for delivery "C.O.D." or on other like terms; or

(b) for payment against documents of title, except where such payment is due only after the goods are to become available for inspection.

(4) A place or method of inpspection fixed by the parties is presumed to be exclusive but unless otherwise expressly agreed it does not postpone identification or shift the place for delivery or for passing the risk of loss. If compliance becomes impossible, inspection shall be as provided in this section unless the place or method fixed was clearly intended as an indispensable condition failure of which avoids the contract.

§ 2-514. When Documents Deliverable on Acceptance; When on Payment.—Unless otherwise agreed documents against which a draft is drawn are to be delivered to the drawee on acceptance of the draft if it is payable more than three days after presentment; otherwise, only on payment.

§ 2-515. Preserving Evidence of Goods in Dispute.—In furtherance of the adjustment of any claim or dispute

(a) either party on reasonable notification to the other and for the purpose of ascertaining the facts and preserving evidence has the right to inspect, test and sample the goods including such of them as may be in the possession or control of the other; and

(b) the parties may agree to a third party inspection or survey to determine the conformity or condition of the goods and may agree that the findings shall be binding upon them in any subsequent litigation or adjustment.

PART 6

Breach, Repudiation and Excuse

§ 2-601. Buyer's Rights on Improper Delivery.—Subject to the provisions of this Article on breach in installment contract (Section 2-612) and unless otherwise agreed under the sections on contractual limitations of remedy (Sections 2-718 and 2-719), if the goods or the tender of delivery fail in any respect to conform to the contract, the buyer may

(a) reject the whole; or

(b) accept the whole; or

(c) accept any commercial unit or units and reject the rest.

§ 2-602. Manner and Effect of Rightful Rejection.—

(1) Rejection of goods must be within a reasonable time after their delivery or tender. It is ineffective unless the buyer seasonably notifies the seller.

(2) Subject to the provisions of the two following sections on rejected goods (Sections 2-603 and 2-604)

(a) after rejection any exercise of ownership by the buyer with respect to any commercial unit is wrongful as against the seller; and

(b) if the buyer has before rejection taken physical possession of goods in which he does not have a security interest under the provisions of this Article (subsection (3) of Section 2-711), he is under a duty after rejection to hold them with reasonable care at the seller's disposition for a time sufficient to permit the seller to remove them; but

(c) the buyer has no further obligations with regard to goods rightfully rejected.

(3) The seller's rights with respect to goods wrongfully rejected are governed by the provisions of this Article on Seller's remedies in general (Section 2-703).

§ 2-603. Merchant Buyer's Duties as to Rightfully Rejected Goods.—

(1) Subject to any security interest in the buyer (subsection (3) of Section 2-711), when the seller has no agent or place of business at the market or rejection a merchant buyer is under a duty after rejection of goods in his possession or control to follow any reasonable instructions received from the seller with respect to the goods and in the absence of such instructions to make reasonable efforts to sell them for the seller's account if they are perishable or threaten to decline in value speedily. Instructions are not reasonable if on demand indemnity for expenses is not forthcoming.

(2) When the buyer sells goods under subsection (1), he is entitled to reimbursement from the seller or out of the proceeds for reasonable expenses of caring for and selling them, and if the expenses include no selling commission then to such commission as is usual in the trade or if there is none to a reasonable sum not exceeding ten per cent on the gross proceeds.

(3) In complying with this section the buyer is held only to good faith and good faith conduct hereunder is neither acceptance nor conversion nor the basis of an action for damages.

§ 2-604. Buyer's Options as to Salvage of Rightfully Rejected Goods.—Subject to the provisions of the immediately preceding section on perishables if the seller gives no instructions within a reasonable time after notification of rejection the buyer may store the rejected goods for the seller's account or reship them to him or resell them for the seller's account with reimbursement as provided in the preceding section. Such action is not acceptance or conversion.

§ 2-605. Waiver of Buyer's Objections by Failure to Particularize.—

(1) The buyer's failure to state in connection with rejection a particular defect which is ascertainable by reasonable inspection precludes him from relying on the unstated defect to justify rejection or to establish breach

(a) where the seller could have cured it if stated seasonably; or

(b) between merchants when the seller has after rejection made a request in writing for a full and final written statement of all defects on which the buyer proposes to rely.

(2) Payment against documents made without reservation of rights precludes recovery of the payment for defects apparent on the face of the documents.

§ 2-606. What Constitutes Acceptance of Goods.—

(1) Acceptance of goods occurs when the buyer

(a) after a reasonable opportunity to inspect the goods signifies to the seller that the goods are conforming or that he will take or retain them in spite of their non-conformity; or

(b) fails to make an effective rejection (subsection (1) of Section 2-602), but such acceptance does not occur until the buyer has had a reasonable opportunity to inspect them; or

(c) does any act inconsistent with the seller's ownership; but if such act is wrongful as against the seller it is an acceptance only if ratified by him.

(2) Acceptance of a part of any commercial unit is acceptance of that entire unit.

§ 2-607. Effect of Acceptance; Notice of Breach; Burden of Establishing Breach After Acceptance; Notice of Claim or Litigation to Person Answerable Over.—

(1) The buyer must pay at the contract rate for any goods accepted.

(2) Acceptance of goods by the buyer precludes rejection of the goods accepted and if made with knowledge of a nonconformity cannot be revoked because of it unless the acceptance was on the reasonable assumption that the non-conformity would be seasonably cured but acceptance does not of itself impair any other remedy provided by this Article for non-conformity.

(3) Where a tender has been accepted

(a) the buyer must within a reasonable time after he discovers or should have discovered any breach notify the seller of breach or be barred from any remedy; and

(b) if the claim is one for infringement or the like (subsection (3) of Section 2-312) and the buyer is sued as a result of such a breach he must so notify the seller within a reasonable time after he receives notice of the litigation or be barred from any remedy over for liability established by the litigation.

(4) The burden is on the buyer to establish any breach with respect to the goods accepted.

(5) Where the buyer is sued for breach of a warranty or other obligation for which his seller is answerable over

(a) he may give his seller written notice of the litigation. If the notice states that the seller may come in and defend and that if the seller does not do so he will be bound in any action against him by his buyer by any determination of fact common to the two litigations, then unless the seller after seasonable receipt of the notice does come in and defend he is so bound.

(b) if the claim is one for infringement or the like (subsection (3) of Section 2-312) the original seller may demand in writing that his buyer turn over to him control of the litigation including settlement or else be barred from any remedy over and if he also agrees to bear all expense and to satisfy any adverse judgment, then unless the buyer after seasonable receipt of the demand does turn over control the buyer is so barred.

(6) The provisions of subsections (3), (4) and (5) apply to any obligation of a buyer to hold the seller harmless against infringement or the like (subsection (3) of Section 2-312).

§ 2-608. Revocation of Acceptance in Whole or in Part.—

(1) The buyer may revoke his acceptance of a lot or commercial unit whose non-conformity substantially impairs its value to him if he has accepted it

(a) on the reasonable assumption that its non-conformity would be cured and it has not been seasonably cured; or

(b) without discovery of such nonconformity if his acceptance was reasonably induced either by the difficulty of discovery before acceptance or by the seller's assurances.

(2) Revocation of acceptance must occur within a reasonable time after the buyer discovers or should have discovered the ground for it and before any substantial change in condition of the goods which is not caused by their own defects. It is not effective until the buyer notifies the seller of it.

(3) A buyer who so revokes has the same rights and duties with regard to the goods involved as if he had rejected them.

§ 2-609. Right to Adequate Assurance of Performance.—

(1) A contract for sale imposes an obligation on each party that the other's expectation of receiving due performance will not be impaired. When reasonable grounds for insecurity arise with respect to the performance of either party the other may in writing demand adequate assurance of due performance and until he receives such assurance may if commercially reasonable suspend any performance for which he has not already received the agreed return.

(2) Between merchants the reasonableness of grounds for insecurity and the adequacy of any assurance offered shall be determined according to commercial standards.

(3) Acceptance of any improper delivery or payment does not prejudice the aggrieved party's right to demand adequate assurance of future performance.

(4) After receipt of a justified demand failure to provide within a reasonable time not exceeding thirty days such assurance of due performance as is adequate under the circumstances of the particular case is a repudiation of the contract.

§ 2-610. Anticipatory Repudiation.—When either party repudiates the contract with respect to a performance not yet due the loss of which will substantially impair the value of the contract to the other, the aggrieved party may

(a) for a commercially reasonable time await performance by the repudiating party; or

(b) resort to any remedy for breach (Section 2-703 or Section 2-711), even though he has notified the repudiating party that he would await the latter's performance and has urged retraction; and

(c) in either case suspend his own performance or proceed in accordance with the provisions of this Article on the seller's right to identify goods to the contract nonwithstanding breach or to salvage unfinished goods (Section 2-704).

§ 2-611. Retraction of Anticipatory Repudiation.—

(1) Until the repudiating party's next performance is due he can retract his repudiation unless the aggrieved party has since the repudiation cancelled or materially changed his position or otherwise indicated that he considers the repudiation final.

(2) Retraction may be by any method which clearly indicates to the aggrieved party that the repudiating party intends to perform, but must include any assurance justifiably demanded under the provisions of this Article (Section 2-609).

(3) Retraction reinstates the repudiating party's rights under the contract with due excuse and allowance to the aggrieved party for any delay occasioned by the repudiation.

§ 2-612. "Installment Contract"; Breach.—

(1) An "installment contract" is one which requires or authorizes the delivery of goods in separate lots to be separately accepted, even though the contract contains a clause "each delivery is a separate contract" or its equivalent.

(2) The buyer may reject any installment which is non-conforming if the nonconformity substantially impairs the value of that installment and cannot be cured or if the non-conformity is a defect in the required documents; but if the non-conformity does not fall within subsection (3) and the seller gives adequate assurance of its cure the buyer must accept that installment.

(3) Whenever non-conformity or default with respect to one or more installments substantially impairs the value of the whole contract there is a breach of the whole. But the aggrieved party reinstates the contract if he accepts a non-conforming installment without seasonably notifying of cancellation or if he brings an action with respect only to past installments or demands performance as to future installments.

§ 2-613. Casualty to Identified Goods.—

Where the contract requires for its performance goods identified when the contract is made, and the goods suffer casualty without fault of either party before the risk of loss passes to the buyer, or in a proper case under a "no arrival, no sale" term (Section 2-324) then

(a) if the loss is total the contract is avoided; and

(b) if the loss is partial or the goods have so deteriorated as no longer to conform to the contract the buyer may nevertheless demand inspection and at his option either treat the contract as avoided or accept the goods with due allowance from the contract price for the deterioration or the deficiency in quantity but without further right against the seller.

§ 2-614. Substituted Performance.—

(1) Where without fault of either party the agreed berthing, loading, or unloading facilities fail or an agreed type of carrier becomes unavailable or the agreed manner of delivery otherwise becomes commercially impracticable but a commercially reasonable substitute is available, such substitute performance must be tendered and accepted.

(2) If the agreed means or manner of payment fails because of domestic or foreign governmental regulation, the seller may withhold or stop delivery unless the buyer provides a means or manner of payment which is commercially a substantial equivalent. If delivery has already been taken, payment by the means or in the manner provided by the regulation discharges the buyer's obligation unless the regulation is discriminatory, oppressive or predatory.

§ 2-615. Excuse by Failure of Presupposed Conditions.—

Except so far as a seller may have assumed a greater obligation and subject to the preceding section on substituted performance:

(a) Delay in delivery or non-delivery in whole or in part by a seller who complies with paragraphs (b) and (c) is not a breach of his duty under a contract for sale if performance as agreed has been made impracticable by the occurrence of a contingency the non-occurrence of which was a basic assumption on which the contract was made or by compliance in good faith with any applicable foreign or domestic governmental regulation or order whether or not it later proves to be invalid.

(b) Where the causes mentioned in paragraph (a) affect only a part of the seller's capacity to perform, he must allocate production and deliveries among his customers but may at his option include regular customers not then under contract as well as his own requirements for further manufacture. He may so allocate in any manner which is fair and reasonable.

(c) The seller must notify the buyer seasonably that there will be delay or non-delivery and, when allocation is required under paragraph (b), of the estimated quota this made available for the buyer.

§ 2-616. Procedure on Notice Claiming Excuse.—

(1) Where the buyer receives notification of a material or indefinite delay or an allocation justified under the preceding section he may by written notification to the seller as to any delivery concerned, and where the prospective deficiency substantially impairs the value of the whole contract under the provisions of this Article relating to breach of installment contracts (Section 2-612), then also as to the whole,

(a) terminate and thereby discharge any unexecuted portion of the contract; or

(b) modify the contract by agreeing to take his available quota in substitution.

(2) If after receipt of such notification from the seller the buyer fails so to modify the contract within a reasonable time not exceeding thirty days the contract lapses with respect to any deliveries affected.

(3) The provisions of this section may not be negated by agreement except in so far as the seller has assumed a greater obligation under the preceding section.

PART 7

Remedies

§ 2-701. Remedies for Breach of Collateral Contracts Not Impaired.—

Remedies for breach of any obligation or promise collateral or ancillary to a contract for sale are not impaired by the provisions of this Article.

§ 2-702. Seller's Remedies on Discovery of Buyer's Insolvency.—

(1) Where the seller discovers the buyer to be insolvent he may refuse delivery except for cash including payment for all goods theretofore delivered under the contract, and stop delivery under this Article (Section 2-705).

(2) Where the seller discovers that the buyer has received goods on credit while insolvent he may reclaim the goods upon demand made within ten days after the receipt, but if misrepresentation of solvency has been made to the particular seller in writing within three months before delivery the ten day limitation does not apply. Except as provided in this subsection the seller may not base a right to reclaim goods on the buyer's fraudulent or innocent misrepresentation of solvency or of intent to pay.

(3) The seller's right to reclaim under subsection (2) is subject to the rights of a buyer in ordinary course or other good faith purchaser or lien creditor under this Article (Section 2-403). Successful reclamation of goods excludes all other remedies with respect to them.

§ 2-703. Seller's Remedies in General.—Where the buyer wrongfully rejects or revokes acceptance of goods or fails to make a payment due on or before delivery or repudiates with respect to a part or the whole, then with respect to any goods directly affected and, if the breach is of the whole contract (Section 2-612), then also with respect to the whole undelivered balance, the aggrieved seller may

    (a) withhold delivery of such goods;

    (b) stop delivery by any bailee as hereafter provided (Section 2-705);

    (c) proceed under the next section respecting goods still unidentified to the contract;

    (d) resell and recover damages as hereafter provided (Section 2-706);

    (e) recover damages for non-acceptance (Section 2-708) or in a proper case the price (Section 2-709);

    (f) cancel.

§ 2-704. Seller's Right to Identify Goods to the Contract Notwithstanding Breach or to Salvage Unfinished Goods.—

(1) An aggrieved seller under the preceding section may

    (a) identify to the contract conforming goods not already identified if at the time he learned of the breach they are in his possession or control;

    (b) treat as the subject of resale goods which have demonstrably been intended for the particular contract even though those goods are unfinished.

(2) Where the goods are unfinished an aggrieved seller may in the exercise of reasonable commercial judgment for the purposes of avoiding loss and of effective realization either complete the manufacture and wholly identify the goods to the contract or cease manufacture and resell for scrap or salvage value or proceed in any other reasonable manner.

§ 2-705. Seller's Stoppage of Delivery in Transit or Otherwise.—

(1) The seller may stop delivery of goods in the possession of a carrier or other bailee when he discovers the buyer to be insolvent (Section 2-702) and may stop delivery of carload, truckload, planeload or larger shipments of express or freight when the buyer repudiates or fails to make a payment due before delivery or if for any other reason the seller has a right to withhold or reclaim the goods.

(2) As against such buyer the seller may stop delivery until

    (a) receipt of the goods by the buyer; or

    (b) acknowledgment to the buyer by any bailee of the goods except a carrier that the bailee holds the goods by the buyer; or

    (c) such acknowledgment to the buyer by a carrier by reshipment or as warehouseman; or

    (d) negotiation to the buyer of any negotiable document of title covering the goods.

(3) (a) To stop delivery the seller must so notify as to enable the bailee by reasonable diligence to prevent delivery of the goods.

    (b) After such notification the bailee must hold and deliver the goods according to the directions of the seller but the seller is liable to the bailee for any ensuing charges or damages.

    (c) If a negotiable document of title has been issued for goods the bailee is not obliged to obey a notification to stop until surrender of the document.

    (d) A carrier who has issued a non-negotiable bill of lading is not obliged to obey a notification to stop received from a person other than the consignor.

§ 2-706. Seller's Resale Including Contract for Resale.—

(1) Under the conditions stated in Section 2-703 on seller's remedies, the seller may resell the goods concerned or the undelivered balance thereof. Where the resale is made in good faith and in a commercially reasonable manner the seller may recover the difference between the resale price and the contract price together with any incidental damages allowed under the provisions of this Article (Section 2-710), but less expenses saved in consequence of the buyer's breach.

(2) Except as otherwise provided in subsection (3) or unless otherwise agreed resale may be at public or private sale including sale by way of one or more contracts to sell or of identification to an existing contract of the seller. Sale may be as a unit or in parcels and at any time and place and on any terms but every aspect of the sale including the method, manner, time, place and terms must be commercially reasonable. The resale must be reasonably identified as referring to the broken contract, but it is not necessary that the goods be in existence or that any or all of them have been identified to the contract before the breach.

(3) Where the resale is at private sale the seller must give the buyer reasonable notification of his intention to resell.

(4) Where the resale is at public sale

    (a) only identified goods can be sold except where there is a recognized market for a public sale of futures in goods of the kind; and

(b) it must be made at a usual place or market for public sale if one is reasonably available and except in the case of goods which are perishable or threaten to decline in value speedily the seller must give the buyer reasonable notice of the time and place of the resale; and

(c) if the goods are not to be within the view of those attending the sale the notification of sale must state the place where the goods are located and provide for their reasonable inspection by prospective bidders; and

(d) the seller may buy.

(5) A purchaser who buys in good faith at a resale takes the goods free of any rights of the original buyer even though the seller fails to comply with one or more of the requirements of this section.

(6) The seller is not accountable to the buyer for any profit made on any resale. A person in the position of a seller (Section 2-707) or a buyer who has rightfully rejected or justifiably revoked acceptance must account for any excess over the amount of his security interest, as hereinafter defined (subsection (3) of Section 2-711).

§ 2-707. "Person in the Position of a Seller."—

(1) A "person in the position of a seller" includes as against a principal an agent who has paid or become responsible for the price of goods on behalf of his principal or anyone who otherwise holds a security interest or other right in goods similar to that of a seller.

(2) A person in the position of a seller may as provided in this Article withhold or stop delivery (Section 2-705) and resell (Section 2-706) and recover incidental damages (Section 2-710).

§ 2-708. Seller's Damages for Nonacceptance or Repudiation.—

(1) Subject to subsection (2) and to the provisions of this Article with respect to proof of market price (Section 2-723), the measure of damages for non-acceptance or repudiation by the buyer is the difference between the market price at the time and place for tender and the unpaid contract price together with any incidental damages provided in this Article (Section 2-710), but less expenses saved in consequence of the buyer's breach.

(2) If the measure of damages provided in subsection (1) is inadequate to put the seller in as good a position as performance would have done then the measure of damages is the profit (including reasonable overhead) which the seller would have made from full performance by the buyer, together with any incidental damages provided in this Article (Section 2-710), due allowance for costs reasonably incurred and due credit for payments or proceeds of resale.

§ 2-709. Action for the Price.—

(1) When the buyer fails to pay the price as it becomes due the seller may recover, together with any incidental damages under the next section, the price

(a) of goods accepted or of conforming goods lost or damaged within a commercially reasonable time after risk of their loss has passed to the buyer; and

(b) of goods identified to the contract if the seller is unable after reasonable effort to resell them at a reasonable price or the circumstances reasonably indicate that such effort will be unavailing.

(2) Where the seller sues for the price he must hold for the buyer any goods which have been identified to the contract and are still in his control except that if resale becomes possible he may resell them at any time prior to the collection of the judgment. The net proceeds of any such resale must be credited to the buyer and payment of the judgment entitles him to any goods not resold.

(3) After the buyer has wrongfully rejected or revoked acceptance of the goods or has failed to make a payment due or has repudiated (Section 2-610), a seller who is held and entitled to the price under this section shall nevertheless be awarded damages for non-acceptance under the preceding section.

§ 2-710. Seller's Incidental Damages.—

Incidental damages to an aggrieved seller include any commercially reasonable charges, expenses or commissions incurred in stopping delivery, in the transportation, care and custody of goods after the buyer's breach, in connection with return or resale of the goods or otherwise resulting from the breach.

§ 2-711. Buyer's Remedies in General, Buyer's Security Interest in Rejected Goods.—

(1) Where the seller fails to make delivery or repudiates or the buyer rightfully rejects or justifiably revokes acceptance then with respect to any goods involved, and with respect to the whole if the breach goes to the whole contract (Section 2-612), the buyer may cancel and whether or not he has done so may in addition to recovering so much of the price as has been paid

(a) "cover" and have damages under the next section as to all the goods affected whether or not they have been identified to the contract; or

(b) recover damages for non-delivery as provided in this Article (Section 2-713).

(2) Where the seller fails to deliver or repudiates the buyer may also

(a) if the goods have been identified recover them as provided in this Article (Section 2-502); or

(b) in a proper case obtain specific performance or replevy the goods as provided in this Article (Section 2-716).

(3) On rightful rejection or justifiable revocation of acceptance a buyer has a security interest in goods in his possession or control for any payments made on their price and any expenses reasonably incurred in their inspection, receipt, transportation, care and custody and may hold such goods and resell them in like manner as an aggrieved seller (Section 2-706).

§ 2-712. "Cover"; Buyer's Procurement of Substitute Goods.—

(1) After a breach within the preceding section the buyer may "cover" by making in good faith and without unreasonable delay any reasonable purchase of or contract to purchase goods in substitution for those due from the seller.

(2) The buyer may recover from the seller as damages the difference between the cost of cover and the contract price together with any incidental or consequential damages as hereinafter defined (Section 2-715), but less expenses saved in consequence of the seller's breach.

(3) Failure of the buyer to effect cover within this section does not bar him from any other remedy.

§ 2-713. Buyer's Damages for Non-Delivery or Repudiation.—

(1) Subject to the provisions of this Article with respect to proof of market price (Section 2-723), the measure of damages for non-delivery or repudiation by the seller is the difference between the market price at the time when the buyer learned of the breach and the contract price together with any incidental and consequential damages provided in this Article (Section 2-715), but less expenses saved in consequence of the seller's breach.

(2) Market price is to be determined as of the place for tender or, in cases of rejection after arrival or revocation of acceptance, as of the place of arrival.

§ 2-714. Buyer's Damages for Breach in Regard to Accepted Goods.—

(1) Where the buyer has accepted goods and given notification (subsection (3) of Section 2-607) he may recover as damages for any non-conformity of tender the loss resulting in the ordinary course of events from the seller's breach as determined in any manner which is reasonable.

(2) The measure of damages for breach of warranty is the difference at the time and place of acceptance between the value of the goods accepted and the value they would have had if they had been as warranted, unless special circumstances show proximate damages of a different amount.

(3) In a proper case any incidental and consequential damages under the next section may also be recovered.

§ 2-715. Buyer's Incidental and Consequential Damages.—

(1) Incidental damages resulting from the seller's breach include expenses reasonably incurred in inspection, receipt, transportation and care and custody of goods rightfully rejected, and any commercially reasonable charges, expenses or commissions in connection with effecting cover and any other reasonable expense incident to the delay or other breach.

(2) Consequential damages resulting from the seller's breach include

(a) any loss resulting from general or particular requirements and needs of which the seller at the time of contracting had reason to know and which could not reasonably be prevented by cover or otherwise; and

(b) injury to person or property proximately resulting from any breach of warranty.

§ 2-716. Buyer's Right to Specific Performance or Replevin.—

(1) Specific performance may be decreed where the goods are unique or in other proper circumstances.

(2) The decree for specific performance may include such terms and conditions as to payment of the price, damages, or other relief as the court may deem just.

§ 2-717. Deduction of Damages From the Price.—The buyer on notifying the seller of his intention to do so may deduct all or any part of the damages resulting from any breach of the contract from any part of the price still due under the same contract.

§ 2-718. Liquidation or Limitation of Damages; Deposits.—

(1) Damages for breach by either party may be liquidated in the agreement but only at an amount which is reasonable in the light of the anticipated or actual harm caused by the breach, the difficulties of proof of loss, and the inconvenience or nonfeasibility of otherwise obtaining an adequate remedy. A term fixing unreasonably large liquidated damages is void as a penalty.

(2) Where the seller justifiably withholds delivery of goods because of the buyer's breach, the buyer is entitled to restitution of any amount by which the sum of his payments exceeds

(a) The amount to which the seller is entitled by virtue of terms liquidating the seller's damages in accordance with subsection (1), or

(b) in the absence of such terms, twenty per cent of the value of the total performance for which the buyer is obligated under the contract or $500, whichever is smaller.

(3) The buyer's right to restitution under subsection (2) is subject to offset to the extent that the seller establishes

(a) a right to recover damages under the provisions of this Article other than subsection (1), and

(b) the amount or value of any benefits received by the buyer directly or indirectly by reason of the contract.

(4)Where a seller has received payment in goods their reasonable value or the proceeds of their resale shall be treated as payments for the purposes of subsection (2); but if the seller has notice of the buyer's breach before reselling goods received in part performance, his resale is subject to the conditions laid down in this Article on resale by an aggrieved seller (Section 2-706).

§ 2-719. Contractual Modification or Limitation of Remedy.—

(1) Subject to the provisions of subsections (2) and (3) of this section and of the preceding section on liquidation and limitation of damages,

(a) the agreement may provide for remedies in addition to or in substitution for those provided in this Article and may limit or alter the measure of damages recoverable under this Article, as by limiting the buyer's remedies to return of the goods and repayment of the price or to repair and replacement of non-conforming goods or parts; and

(b) resort to a remedy as provided is optional unless the remedy is expressly agreed to be exclusive, in which case it is the sole remedy.

(2) Where circumstances cause an exclusive or limited remedy to fail of its essential purpose, remedy may be had as provided in this Act.

(3) Consequential damages may be limited or excluded unless the limitation or exclusion is unconscionable. Limitation of consequential damages for injury to the person in the case of consumer goods is prima facie unconscionable but limitation of damages where the loss is commercial is not.

§ 2-720.   Effect of "Cancellation" or "Rescission" on Claims for Antecedent Breach.—Unless the contrary intention clearly appears, expressions of "cancellation" or "rescission" of the contract or the like shall not be construed as a renunciation or discharge of any claim in damages for an antecedent breach.

§ 2-721.   Remedies for Fraud.—Remedies for material misrepresentation or fraud include all remedies available under this Article for non-fraudulent breach. Neither rescission or a claim for rescission of the contract for sale nor rejection or return of the goods shall bar or be deemed inconsistent with a claim for damages or other remedy.

§ 2-722.   Who Can Sue Third Parties for Injury to Goods.—Where a third party so deals with goods which have been identified to a contract for sale as to cause actionable injury to a party to that contract

(a) a right of action against the third party is in either party to the contract for sale who has title to or a security interest or a special property or an insurable interest in the goods; and if the goods have been destroyed or converted a right of action is also in the party who either bore the risk of loss under the contract for sale or has since the injury assumed that risk as against the other;

(b) if at the time of the injury the party plaintiff did not bear the risk of loss as against the other party to the contract for sale and there is no arrangement between them for disposition of the recovery, his suit or settlement is, subject to his own interest, as a fiduciary for the other party to the contract;

(c) either party may with the consent of the other sue for the benefit of whom it may concern.

§ 2-723.   Proof of Market Price: Time and Place.—

(1) If an action based on anticipatory repudiation comes to trial before the time for performance with respect to some or all of the goods, any damages based on market price (Section 2-708 or Section 2-713) shall be determined according to the price of such goods prevailing at the time when the aggrieved party learned of the repudiation.

(2) If evidence of a price prevailing at the times or places described in this Article is not readily available the price prevailing within any reasonable time before or after the time described or at any other place which in commercial judgment or under usage of trade would serve as a reasonable substitute for the one described may be used, making any proper allowance for the cost of transporting the goods to or from such other place.

(3) Evidence of a relevant price prevailing at a time or place other than the one described in this Article offered by one party is not admissible unless and until he has given the other party such notice as the court finds sufficient to prevent unfair surprise.

§ 2-724.   Admissibility of Market Quotations.—Whenever the prevailing price or value of any goods regularly bought and sold in any established commodity market is in issue, reports in official publications or trade journals or in newspapers or periodicals of general circulation published as the reports of such market shall be admissible in evidence. The circumstances of the preparation of such a report may be shown to affect its weight but not its admissibility.

§ 2-725.   Statute of Limitations in Contracts for Sale.—

(1) An action for breach of any contract for sale must be commenced within four years after the cause of action has accrued. By the original agreement the parties may reduce the period of limitation to not less than one year but may not extend it.

(2) A cause of action accrues when the breach occurs, regardless of the aggrieved party's lack of knowledge of the breach. A breach of warranty occurs when tender of delivery is made, except that where a warranty explicitly extends to future performance of the goods and discovery of the breach must await the time of such performance the cause of action accrues when the breach is or should have been discovered.

(3) Where an action commenced within the time limited by subsection (1) is so terminated as to leave available a remedy by another action for the same breach such other action may be commenced after the expiration of the time limited and within six months after the termination of the first action unless the termination resulted from voluntary discontinuance or from dismissal for failure or neglect to prosecute.

(4) This section does not alter the law on tolling of the statute of limitations nor does it apply to causes of action which have accrued before this Act becomes effective.

ARTICLE THREE — COMMERCIAL PAPER

PART 1

Short Title, Form and Interpretation

§ 3-101.   Short Title.—This Article shall be known and may be cited as Uniform Commercial Code—Commercial Paper.

§ 3-102.   Definitions and Index of Definitions.—

(1) In this Article unless the context otherwise requires

(a) "Issue" means the first delivery of an instrument to a holder or a remitter.

(b) An "order" is a direction to pay and must be more than an authorization or request. It must identify the person to pay with reasonable certainty. It may be addressed to one or more such persons jointly or in the alternative but not in succession.

(c) A "promise" is an undertaking to pay and must be more than an acknowledgment of an obligation.

(d) "Secondary party" means a drawer or endorser.

(e) "Instrument" means a negotiable instrument. . . .

§ 3-103. Limitations on Scope of Article.—

(1) This Article does not apply to money, documents of title or investment securities.

(2) The provisions of this Article are subject to the provisions of the Article on Bank Deposits and Collections (Article 4) and Secured Transactions (Article 9).

§ 3-104. Form of Negotiable Instruments; "Draft"; "Check"; "Certificate of Deposit"; "Note."—

(1) Any writing to be a negotiable instrument within this Article must

(a) be signed by the maker or drawer; and

(b) contain an unconditional promise or order to pay a sum certain in money and no other promise, order, obligation or power given by the maker or drawer except as authorized by this Article; and

(c) be payable on demand or at a definite time; and

(d) be payable to order or to bearer.

(2) A writing which complies with the requirements of this section is

(a) a "draft" ("bill of exchange") if it is an order;

(b) a "check" if it is a draft drawn on a bank and payable on demand;

(c) a "certificate of deposit" if it is an acknowledgment by a bank of receipt of money with an engagement to repay it;

(d) a "note" if it is a promise other than a certificate of deposit.

(3) As used in other Articles of this Act, and as the context may require, the terms "draft", "check", "certificate of deposit" and "note" may refer to instruments which are not negotiable within this Article as well as to instruments which are so negotiable.

§ 3-105. When Promise or Order Unconditional.—

(1) A promise or order otherwise unconditional is not made conditional by the fact that the instrument

(a) is subject to implied or constructive conditions; or

(b) states its consideration, whether performed or promised, or the transaction which gave rise to the instrument, or that the promise or order is made or the instrument matures in accordance with or "as per" such transaction; or

(c) refers to or states that it arises out of a separate agreement; or

(d) states that it is drawn under a letter of credit; or

(e) states that it is secured, whether by mortgage, reservation of title or otherwise; or

(f) indicates a particular account to be debited or any other fund or source from which reimbursement is expected; or

(g) is limited to payment out of a particular fund or the proceeds of a particular source, if the instrument is issued by a government or governmental agency or unit; or

(h) is limited to payment out of the entire assets of a partnership, unincorporated association, trust or estate by or on behalf of which the instrument is issued.

(2) A promise or order is not unconditional if the instrument

(a) states that it is subject to or governed by any other agreement; or

(b) states that it is to be paid only out of a particular fund or source except as provided in this Section.

§ 3-106. Sum Certain.—

(1) The sum payable is a sum certain even though it is to be paid

(a) with stated interest or by stated installments; or

(b) with stated different rates of interest before and after default or a specified date; or

(c) with a stated discount or addition if paid before or after the date fixed for payment; or

(d) with exchange or less exchange, whether at a fixed rate or at the current rate; or

(e) with costs of collection or an attorney's fee or both upon default.

(2) Nothing in this Section shall validate any term which is otherwise illegal.

§ 3-107. Money.—

(1) An instrument is payable in money if the medium of exchange in which it is payable is money at the time the instrument is made. An instrument payable in "currency" or "current funds" is payable in money.

(2) A promise or order to pay a sum stated in a foreign currency is for a sum certain in money and, unless a different medium of payment is specified in the instrument, may be satisfied by payment of that number of dollars which the stated foreign currency will purchase at the buying sight rate for that currency on the day on which the instrument is payable or, if payable on demand, on the date of demand. If such an instrument specifies a foreign currency as the medium of payment the instrument is payable in that currency.

§ 3-108. Payable on Demand.—Instruments payable on demand include those payable at sight or on presentation and those in which no time for payment is stated.

§ 3-109. Definite Time.—

(1) An instrument is payable at a definite time if by its terms it is payable

(a) on or before a stated date or at a fixed period after a stated date; or

(b) at a fixed period after sight; or

(c) at a definite time subject to any acceleration; or

(d) at a definite time subject to extension at the option of the holder, or to extension to a further definite time at the option of the maker or acceptor or automatically upon or after a specified act or event.

(2) An instrument which by its terms is otherwise payable only upon an act or event uncertain as to time of occurrence is not payable at a definite time even though the act or event has occurred.

§ 3-110. Payable to Order.—

(1) An instrument is payable to order when by its terms it is payable to the order or assigns of any person therein specified with reasonable certainty, or to him or his order, or when it is conspicuously designated on its face as "exchange" or the like and names a payee. It may be payable to the order of

(a) the maker or drawer; or

(b) the drawee; or

(c) A payee who is not maker, drawer or drawee; or

(d) two or more payees together or in the alternative; or

(e) an estate, trust or fund, in which case it is payable to the order of the representative of such estate, trust or fund or his successors; or

(f) an office, or an officer by his title as such in which case it is payable to the principal but the incumbent of the office or his successors may act as if he or they were the holder; or

(g) a partnership or unincorporated association, in which case it is payable to the partnership or association and may be indorsed or transferred by any person thereto authorized.

(2) An instrument not payable to order is not made so payable by such words as "payable upon return of this instrument properly indorsed."

(3) An instrument made payable both to order and to bearer is payable to order unless the bearer words are handwritten or typewritten.

§ 3-111.—Payable to Bearer.—An instrument is payable to bearer when by its terms it is payable to

(a) bearer or the order of bearer; or

(b) a specified person or bearer; or

(c) "cash" or the order of "cash", or any other indication which does not purport to designate a specific payee.

§ 3-112. Terms and Omissions Not Affecting Negotiability.—

(1) The negotiability of an instrument is not affected by

(a) the omission of a statement of any consideration or of the place where the instrument is drawn or payable; or

(b) a statement that collateral has been given for the instrument or in case of default on the instrument the collateral may be sold; or

(c) a promise or power to maintain or protect collateral or to give additional collateral; or

(d) a term authorizing a confession of judgment on the instrument if it is not paid when due; or

(e) a term purporting to waive the benefit of any law intended for the advantage or protection of any obligor; or

(f) a term in a draft providing that the payee by indorsing or cashing it acknowledges full satisfaction of an obligation of the drawer; or

(g) a statement in a draft drawn in a set of parts (Section 3-801) to the effect that the order is effective only if no other part has been honored.

(2) Nothing in this Section shall validate any term which is otherwise illegal.

§ 3-113. Seal.—An instrument otherwise negotiable is within this Article even though it is under a seal.

§ 3-114. Date, Antedating, Postdating.—

(1) The negotiability of an instrument is not affected by the fact that it is undated, antedated or post-dated.

(2) Where an instrument is antedated or postdated the time when it is payable is determined by the stated date if the instrument is payable on demand or at a fixed period after date.

(3) Where the instrument or any signature thereon is dated, the date is presumed to be correct.

§ 3-115. Incomplete Instruments.—

(1) When a paper whose contents at the time of signing show that it is intended to become an instrument is signed while still incomplete in any necessary respect it cannot be enforced until completed, but when it is completed in accordance with authority given it is effective as completed.

(2) If the completion is unauthorized the rules as to material alteration apply (Section 3-407), even though the paper was not delivered by the maker or drawer; but the burden of establishing that any completion is unauthorized is on the party so asserting.

§ 3-116. Instruments Payable to Two or More Persons.—An instrument payable to the order of two or more persons

(a) if in the alternative is payable to any one of them and may be negotiated, discharged or enforced by any of them who has possession of it;

(b) if not in the alternative is payable to all of them and may be negotiated, discharged or enforced only by all of them.

§ 3-117. Instruments Payable With Words of Description.—An instrument made payable to a named person with the addition of words describing him

(a) as agent or officer of a specified person is payable to his principal but the agent or officer may act as if he were the holder;

(b) as any other fiduciary for a specified person or purpose is payable to the payee and may be negotiated, discharged or enforced by him;

(c) in any other manner is payable to the payee unconditionally and the additional words are without effect on subsequent parties.

§ 3-118. **Ambiguous Terms and Rules of Construction.**—The following rules apply to every instrument:

(a) Where there is doubt whether the instrument is a draft or a note the holder may treat it as either. A draft drawn on the drawer is effective as a note.

(b) Handwritten terms control typewritten and printed terms, and typewritten control printed.

(c) Words control figures except that if the words are ambiguous figures control.

(d) Unless otherwise specified a provision for interest means interest at the judgment rate at the place of payment from the date of the instrument, or if it is undated from the date of issue.

(e) Unless the instrument otherwise specifies two or more persons who sign as maker, acceptor or drawer or indorser and as a part of the same transaction are jointly and severally liable even though the instrument contains such words as "I promise to pay."

(f) Unless otherwise specified consent to extension authorizes a single extension for not longer than the original period. A consent to extension, expressed in the instrument, is binding on secondary parties and accommodation makers. A holder may not exercise his option to extend an instrument over the objection of a maker or acceptor or other party who in accordance with Section 3-604 tenders full payment when the instrument is due.

§ 3-119. **Other Writings Affecting Instrument.**—

(1) As between the obligor and his immediate obligee or any transferee the terms of an instrument may be modified or affected by any other written agreement executed as a part of the same transaction, except that a holder in due course is not affected by any limitation of his rights arising out of the separate written agreement if he had no notice of the limitation when he took the instrument.

(2) A separate agreement does not affect the negotiability of an instrument.

§ 3-120. **Instruments "Payable Through" Bank.**—An instrument which states that it is "payable through" a bank or the like designates that bank as a collecting bank to make presentment but does not of itself authorize the bank to pay the instrument.

§ 3-121. **Instruments Payable at Bank.**—A note or acceptance which states that it is payable at a bank is not of itself an order or authorization to the bank to pay it.

§ 3-122. **Accrual of Cause of Action.**—

(1) A cause of action against a maker or an acceptor accrues

(a) in the case of a time instrument on the day after maturity;

(b) in the case of a demand instrument upon its date or, if no date is stated, on the date of issue.

(2) A cause of action against the obligor of a demand or time certificate of deposit accrues upon demand, but demand on a time certificate may not be made until on or after the date of maturity.

(3) A cause of action against a drawer of a draft or an indorser of any instrument accrues upon demand following dishonor of the instrument. Notice of dishonor is a demand.

(4) Unless an instrument provides otherwise, interest runs at the rate provided by law for a judgment

(a) in the case of a maker acceptor or other primary obligor of a demand instrument, from the date of demand;

(b) in all other cases from the date of accrual of the cause of action.

PART 2

Transfer and Negotiation

§ 3-201. **Transfer: Right to Indorsement.**—

(1) Transfer of an instrument vests in the transferee such rights as the transferor has therein, except that a transferee who has himself been a party to any fraud or illegality affecting the instrument or who as a prior holder had notice of a defense or claim against it cannot improve his position by taking from a later holder in due course.

(2) A transfer of a security interest in an instrument vests the foregoing rights in the transferee to the extent of the interest transferred.

(3) Unless otherwise agreed any transfer for value of an instrument not then payable to bearer gives the transferee the specifically enforceable right to have the unqualified indorsement of the transferor. Negotiation takes effect only when the indorsement is made and until that time there is no presumption that the transferee is the owner.

§ 3-202. **Negotiation.**—

(1) Negotiation is the transfer of an instrument in such form that the transferee becomes a holder. If the instrument is payable to order it is negotiated by delivery with any necessary indorsement; if payable to bearer it is negotiated by delivery.

(2) An indorsement must be written by or on behalf of the holder and on the instrument or on a paper so firmly affixed thereto as to become a part thereof.

(3) An indorsement is effective for negotiation only when it conveys the entire instrument or any unpaid residue. If it purports to be of less it operates only as a partial assignment.

(4) Words of assignment, condition, waiver, guaranty, limitation or disclaimer of liability and the like accompanying an indorsement do not affect its character as an indorsement.

§ 3-203. Wrong or Misspelled Name.—Where an instrument is made payable to a person under a misspelled name or one other than his own he may indorse in that name or his own or both; but signature in both names may be required by a person paying or giving value for the instrument.

§ 3-204. Special Indorsement; Blank Indorsement.—

(1) A special indorsement specifies the person to whom or to whose order it makes the instrument payable. Any instrument specially indorsed becomes payable to the order of the special indorsee and may be further negotiated only by his indorsement.

(2) An indorsement in blank specifies no particular indorsee and may consist of a mere signature. An instrument payable to order and indorsed in blank becomes payable to bearer and may be negotiated by delivery alone until specially indorsed.

(3) The holder may convert a blank indorsement into a special indorsement by writing over the signature of the indorser in blank any contract consistent with the character of the indorsement.

§ 3-205. Restrictive Indorsements.—an indorsement is restrictive which either

    (a) is conditional; or

    (b) purports to prohibit further transfer of the instrument; or

    (c) includes the words "for collection", "for deposit", "pay any bank", or like terms signifying a purpose of deposit or collection; or

    (d) otherwise states that it is for the benefit or use of the indorser or of another person.

§ 3-206. Effect of Restrictive Indorsement.—

(1) No restrictive indorsement prevents further transfer or negotiation of the instrument.

(2) An intermediary bank, or a payor bank which is not the depositary bank, is neither given notice nor otherwise affected by a restrictive indorsement of any person except the bank's immediate transferor or the person presenting for payment.

(3) Except for an intermediary bank, any transferee under an indorsement which is conditional or includes the words "for collection", "for deposit", "pay any bank", or like terms (subparagraphs (a) and (c) of Section 3-205) must pay or apply any value given by him for or on the security of the instrument consistently with the indorsement and to the extent that he does so he becomes a holder for value. In addition such transferee is a holder in due course if he otherwise complies with the requirements of Section 3-302 on what constitutes a holder in due course.

(4) The first taker under an indorsement for the benefit of the indorser or another person (subparagraph (d) of Section 3-205) must pay or apply any value given by him for or on the security of the instrument consistently with the indorsement and to the extent that he does so he becomes a holder for value. In addition such taker is a holder in due course if he otherwise complies with the requirements of Section 3-302 on what constitutes a holder in due course. A later holder for value is neither given notice nor otherwise affected by such restrictive indorsement unless he has knowledge that a fiduciary or other person has negotiated the instrument in any transaction for his own benefit or otherwise in breach of duty (subsection (2) of Section 3-304).

§ 3-207. Negotiation Effective Although It May Be Rescinded.—

(1) Negotiation is effective to transfer the instrument although the negotiation is

    (a) made by an infant, a corporation exceeding its powers, or any other person without capacity; or

    (b) obtained by fraud, duress or mistake of any kind; or

    (c) part of an illegal transaction; or

    (d) made in breach of duty.

(2) Except as against a subsequent holder in due course such negotiation is in an appropriate case subject to rescission, the declaration of a constructive trust or any other remedy permitted by law.

§ 3-208. Reacquisition.—Where an instrument is returned to or required by a prior party he may cancel any indorsement which is not necessary to his title and reissue or further negotiate the instrument, but any intervening party is discharged as against the reacquiring party and subsequent holders not in due course and if his indorsement has been cancelled is discharged as against subsequent holders in due course as well.

PART 3

Rights of a Holder

§ 3-301. Rights of a Holder.—The holder of an instrument whether or not he is the owner may transfer or negotiate it and, except as otherwise provided in Section 3-603 on payment or satisfaction, discharge it or enforce payment in his own name.

§ 3-302. Holder in Due Course.—

(1) A holder in due course is a holder who takes the instrument

    (a) for value; and

    (b) in good faith; and

    (c) without notice that it is overdue or has been dishonored or of any defense against or claim to it on the part of any person.

(2) A payee may be a holder in due course.

(3) A holder does not become a holder in due course of an instrument:

(a) by purchase of it at judicial sale or by taking it under legal process; or

(b) by acquiring it in taking over an estate; or

(c) by purchasing it as part of a bulk transaction not in regular course of business of the transferor.

(4) A purchaser of a limited interest can be a holder in due course only to the extent of the interest purchased.

§ 3-303. **Taking for Value.**—A holder takes the instrument for value

(a) to the extent that the agreed consideration has been performed or that he acquires a security interest in or a lien on the instrument otherwise than by legal process; or

(b) when he takes the instrument in payment of or as security for an antecedent claim against any person whether or not the claim is due; or

(c) when he gives a negotiable instrument for it or makes an irrevocable commitment to a third person.

§ 3-304. **Notice to Purchaser.**—

(1) The purchaser has notice of a claim or defense if

(a) the instrument is so incomplete, bears such visible evidence of forgery or alteration, or is otherwise so irregular as to call into question its validity, terms or ownership or to create an ambiguity as to the party to pay; or

(b) the purchaser has notice that the obligation of any party is voidable in whole or in part, or that all parties have been discharged.

(2) The purchaser has notice of a claim against the instrument when he has knowledge that a fiduciary has negotiated the instrument in payment of or as security for his own debt or in any transaction for his own benefit or otherwise in breach of duty.

(3) The purchaser has notice that an instrument is overdue if he has reason to know

(a) that any part of the principal amount is overdue or that there is an uncured default in payment of another instrument of the same series; or

(b) that acceleration of the instrument has been made; or

(c) that he is taking a demand instrument after demand has been made or more than a reasonable length of time after its issue. A reasonable time for a check drawn and payable within the states and territories of the United States and the District of Columbia is presumed to be thirty days.

(4) Knowledge of the following facts does not of itself give the purchaser notice of a defense or claim

(a) That the instrument is antedated or postdated;

(b) that it was issued or negotiated in return for an executory promise or accompanied by a separate agreement, unless the purchaser has notice that a defense or claim has arisen from the terms thereof;

(c) that any party has signed for accommodation;

(d) that an incomplete instrument has been completed, unless the purchaser has notice of any improper completion;

(e) that any person negotiating the instrument is or was a fiduciary;

(f) that there has been default in payment of interest on the instrument or in payment of any other instrument, except one of the same series.

(5) The filing or recording of a document does not of itself constitute notice within the provisions of this Article to a person who would otherwise be a holder in due course.

(6) To be effective notice must be received at such time and in such manner as to give a reasonable opportunity to act on it.

§ 3-305. **Rights of Holder in Due Course.**—To the extent that a holder is a holder in due course he takes the instrument free from

(1) all claims to it on the part of any person; and

(2) all defenses of any party to the instrument with whom the holder has not dealt except

(a) infancy, to the extent that it is a defense to a simple contract; and

(b) such other incapacity, or duress, or illegality of the transaction, as renders the obligation of the party a nullity; and

(c) such misrepresentation as has induced the party to sign the instrument with neither knowledge nor reasonable opportunity to obtain knowledge of its character or its essential terms; and

(d) discharge in insolvency proceedings; and

(e) any other discharge of which the holder has notice when he takes the instrument.

§ 3-306. **Rights of One Not Holder in Due Course.**—Unless he has the rights of a holder in due course any person takes the instrument subject to

(a) all valid claims to it on the part of any person; and

(b) all defenses of any party which would be available in an action on a simple contract; and

(c) the defenses of want or failure of consideration, non-performance of any condition precedent, non-delivery, or delivery for a special purpose (Section 3-408); and

(d) the defense that he or a person through whom he holds the instrument acquired it by theft, or that payment or satisfaction to such holder would be inconsistent with the terms of a restrictive indorsement. The claim of any third person to the instrument is not otherwise available as a defense to any party liable thereon unless the third person himself defends the action for such party.

§ 3-307. **Burden of Establishing Signatures, Defenses and Due Course.**—

(1) Unless specifically denied in the pleadings each signature on an instrument is admitted. When the

effectiveness of a signature is put in issue

    (a) the burden of establishing it is on the party claiming under the signature; and

    (b) the signature is presumed to be genuine or authorized except where the action is to enforce the obligation of a purported signer who has died or become incompetent before proof is required.

    (2) When signatures are admitted or established, production of the instrument entitles a holder to recover on it unless the defendant establishes a defense.

    (3) After it is shown that a defense exists a person claiming the rights of a holder in due course has the burden of establishing that he or some person under whom he claims is in all respects a holder in due course.

PART 4

Liability of Parties

§ 3-401. Signature.—

(1) No person is liable on an instrument unless his signature appears thereon.

(2) A signature is made by use of any name, including any trade or assumed name, upon an instrument, or by any word or mark used in lieu of a written signature.

§ 3-402. Signature in Ambiguous Capacity.—Unless the instrument clearly indicates that a signature is made in some other capacity it is an indorsement.

§ 3-403. Signature by Authorized Representative.—

(1) A signature may be made by an agent or other representative, and his authority to make it may be established as in other cases of representation. No particular form of appointment is necessary to establish such authority.

(2) An authorized representative who signs his own name to an instrument

    (a) is personally obligated if the instrument neither names the person represented nor shows that the representative signed in a representative capacity;

    (b) except as otherwise established between the immediate parties, is personally obligated if instrument names the person represented but does not show that the representative signed in a representative capacity, or if the instrument does not name the person represented but does show that the representative signed in a representative capacity.

(3) Except as otherwise established the name of an organization preceded or followed by the name and office of an authorized individual is a signature made in a representative capacity.

§ 3-404. Unauthorized Signatures.—

(1) Any unauthorized signature is wholly inoperative as that of the person whose name is signed unless he ratifies it or is precluded from denying it; but it operates as the signature of the unauthorized signer in favor of any person who in good faith pays the instrument or takes it for value.

(2) Any unauthorized signature may be ratified for all purposes of this Article. Such ratification does not of itself affect any rights of the person ratifying against the actual signer.

§ 3-405. Imposters; Signature in Name of Payee.—

(1) An indorsement by any person in the name of a named payee is effective if

    (a) an imposter by use of the mails or otherwise has induced the maker or drawer to issue the instrument to him or his confederate in the name of the payee; or

    (b) a person signing as or on behalf of a maker or drawer intends the payee to have no interest in the instrument; or

    (c) an agent or employee of the maker or drawer has supplied him with the name of the payee intending the latter to have no such interest.

(2) Nothing in this Section shall affect the criminal or civil liability of the person to indorsing.

§ 3-406. Negligence Contributing to Alteration or Unauthorized Signature.—Any person who by his negligence substantially contributes to a material alteration of the instrument or to the making of an unauthorized signature is precluded from asserting the alteration or lack of authority against a holder in due course or against a drawee or other payor who pays the instrument in good faith and in accordance with the reasonable commercial standards of the drawee's or payor's business.

§ 3-407. Alteration.—

(1) Any alteration of an instrument is material which changes the contract of any party thereto in any respect, including any such change in

    (a) the number of relations of the parties; or

    (b) an incomplete instrument, by completing it otherwise than as authorized; or

    (c) the writing as signed, by adding to it or by removing any part of it.

(2) As against any person other than a subsequent holder in due course

    (a) alteration by the holder which is both fraudulent and material discharges any party whose contract is thereby changed unless that party assents or is precluded from asserting the defense;

    (b) no other alteration discharges any party and the instrument may be enforced according to its original tenor, or as to incomplete instruments according to the authority given.

(3) A subsequent holder in due course may in all cases enforce the instrument according to its original tenor, and when an incomplete instrument has been completed, he may enforce it as completed.

§ 3-408. Consideration.—Want or failure of consideration is a defense as against any person not having the rights of a holder in due course (Section 3-305), except that no consideration is necessary for an instrument or obligation thereon given in payment of or as security for an antecedent obligation of any kind. Nothing in this Section shall be taken to displace any statute outside this Act under which a promise is enforceable notwithstanding lack or failure of consideration. Partial failure of consideration is a defense pro tanto whether or not the failure is in an ascertained or liquidated amount.

§ 3-409. Draft Not an Assignment.—

(1) A check or other draft does not of itself operate as an assignment of any funds in the hands of the drawee available for its payment, and the drawee is not liable on the instrument until he accepts it.

(2) Nothing in this Section shall affect any liability in contract, tort or otherwise arising from any letter of credit or other obligation or representation which is not an acceptance.

§ 3-410. Definition and Operation of Acceptance.—

(1) Acceptance is the drawee's signed engagement to honor the draft as presented. It must be written on the draft, and may consist of his signature alone. It becomes operative when completed by delivery or notification.

(2) A draft may be accepted although it has not been signed by the drawer or is otherwise incomplete or is overdue or has been dishonored.

(3) Where the draft is payable at a fixed period after sight and the acceptor fails to date his acceptance the holder may complete it by supplying a date in good faith.

§ 3-411. Certification of a Check.—

(1) Certification of a check is acceptance. Where a holder procures certification the drawer and all prior indorsers are discharged.

(2) Unless otherwise agreed a bank has no obligation to certify a check.

(3) A bank may certify a check before returning it for lack of proper indorsement. If it does so the drawer is discharged.

§ 3-412. Acceptance Varying Draft.—

(1) Where the drawee's proffered acceptance in any manner varies the draft as presented the holder may refuse the acceptance and treat the draft as dishonored in which case the drawee is entitled to have his acceptance cancelled.

(2) The terms of the draft are not varied by an acceptance to pay at any particular bank or place in the continental United States, unless the acceptance states that the draft is to be paid only at such bank or place.

(3) Where the holder assents to an acceptance varying the terms of the draft each drawer and indorser who does not affirmatively assent is discharged.

§ 3-413. Contract of Maker, Drawer and Acceptor.—

(1) The maker or acceptor engages that he will pay the instrument according to its tenor at the time of his engagement or as completed pursuant to Section 3-115 on incomplete instruments.

(2) The drawer engages that upon dishonor of the draft and any necessary notice of dishonor or protest he will pay the amount of the draft to the holder or to any indorser who takes it up. The drawer may disclaim this liability by drawing without recourse.

(3) By making, drawing or accepting the party admits as against all subsequent parties including the drawee the existence of the payee and his then capacity to indorse.

§ 3-414. Contract of Indorser; Order of Liability.—

(1) Unless the indorsement otherwise specifies (as by such words as "without recourse") every indorser engages that upon dishonor and any necessary notice of dishonor and protest he will pay the instrument according to its tenor at the time of his indorsement to the holder or to any subsequent indorser who takes it up, even though the indorser who takes it up was not obligated to do so.

(2) Unless they otherwise agree indorsers are liable to one another in the order in which they indorse, which is presumed to be the order in which their signatures appear on the instrument.

§ 3-415. Contract of Accommodation Party.—

(1) An accommodation party is one who signs the instrument in any capacity for the purpose of lending his name to another party to it.

(2) When the instrument has been taken for value before it is due the accommodation party is liable in the capacity in which he has signed even though the taker knows of the accommodation.

(3) As against a holder in due course and without notice of the accommodation oral proof of the accommodation is not admissible to give the accommodation party the benefit of discharges dependent on his character as such. In other cases the accommodation character may be shown by oral proof.

(4) An indorsement which shows that it is not in the chain of title is notice of its accommodation character.

(5) An accommodation party is not liable to the party accommodated, and if he pays the instrument has a right of recourse on the instrument against such party.

§ 3-416. Contract of Guarantor.—

(1) "Payment guaranteed" or equivalent words added to a signature mean that the signer engages that if the instrument is not paid when due he will pay it according to its tenor without resort by the holder to any other party.

(2) "Collection guaranteed" or equivalent words added to a signature mean that the signer engages that if the instrument is not paid when due he will pay it according to its tenor, but only after the holder has reduced his claim against the maker or acceptor to judgment and execution has been returned unsatisfied, or

after the maker or acceptor has become insolvent or it is otherwise apparent that it is useless to proceed against him.

(3) Words of guaranty which do not otherwise specify guarantee payment.

(4) No words of guaranty added to the signature of a sole maker or acceptor affect his liability on the instrument. Such words added to the signature of one of two or more makers or acceptors create a presumption that the signature is for the accommodation of the others.

(5) When words of guaranty are used presentment, notice of dishonor and protest are not necessary to charge the user.

(6) Any guaranty written on the instrument is enforceable notwithstanding any statute of frauds.

§ 3-417. Warranties on Presentment and Transfer.—

(1) Any person who obtains payment or acceptance and any prior transferor warrants to a person who in good faith pays or accepts that

(a) he has a good title to the instrument or is authorized to obtain payment of acceptance on behalf of one who has a good title; and

(b) he has no knowledge that the signature of the maker or drawer is unauthorized, except that this warranty is not given by a holder in due course acting in good faith

(i) To a maker with respect to the maker's own signature; or

(ii) To a drawer with respect to the drawer's own signature, whether or not the drawer is also the drawee; or

(iii) to an acceptor of a draft if the holder in due course took the draft after the acceptance or obtained the acceptance without knowledge that the drawer's signature was unauthorized; and

(c) the instrument has not been materially altered, except that this warranty is not given by a holder in due course acting in good faith

(i) to the maker of a note; or

(ii) To the drawer of a draft whether or not the drawer is also the drawee; or

(iii) to the acceptor of a draft with respect to an alteration made prior to the acceptance if the holder in due course took the draft after the acceptance, even though the acceptance provided "payable as originally drawn" or equivalent terms; or

(iv) to the acceptor of a draft with respect to an alteration made after the acceptance.

(2) Any person who transfers an instrument and receives consideration warrants to his transferee and if the transfer is by indorsement to any subsequent holder who takes the instrument in good faith that

(a) he has a good title to the instrument or is authorized to obtain payment or acceptance on behalf of one who has a good title and the transfer is otherwise rightful; and

(b) all signatures are genuine or authorized; and

(c) the instrument has not been materially altered; and

(d) no defense of any party is good against him; and

(e) he has no knowledge of any insolvency proceeding instituted with respect to the maker or acceptor or the drawer of an unaccepted instrument.

(3) By transferring "without recourse" the transferor limits the obligation stated in subsection (2) (d) to a warranty that he has no knowledge of such a defense.

(4) A selling agent or broker who does not disclose the fact that he is acting only as such gives the warranties provided in this Section, but if he makes such disclosure warrants only his good faith and authority.

§ 3-418. Finality of Payment or Acceptance.—

Except for recovery of bank payments as provided in the Article on Bank Deposits and Collections (Article 4) and except for liability for breach of warranty on presentment under the preceding section, payment or acceptance of any instrument is final in favor of a holder in due course, or a person who has in good faith changed his position in reliance on the payment.

§ 3-419. Conversion of Instrument; Innocent Representative.—

(1) An instrument is converted when

(a) a drawee to whom it is delivered for acceptance refuses to return it on demand; or

(b) any person to whom it is delivered for payment refuses on demand either to pay or to return it; or

(c) it is paid on a forged indorsement.

(2) In an action against a drawee under subsection (1) the measure of the drawee's liability is the face amount of the instrument. In any other action under subsection (1) the measure of liability is presumed to be the face amount of the instrument.

(3) Subject to the provisions of this Act concerning restrictive indorsements a representative, including a depositary or collecting bank, who has in good faith and in accordance with the reasonable commercial standards applicable to the business of such representative dealt with an instrument or its proceeds on behalf of one who was not the true owner is not liable in conversion or otherwise to the true owner beyond the amount of any proceeds remaining in his hands.

(4) An intermediary bank or payor bank which is not a depositary bank is not liable in conversion solely by reason of the fact that proceeds of an item indorsed restrictively (Section 3-205 and 3-206) are not paid or applied consistently with the restrictive indorsement of an indorser other than its immediate transferor.

PART 5

Presentment, Notice of Dishonor and Protest

§ 3-501. When Presentment, Notice of Dishonor, and Protest Necessary or Permissible.—

(1) Unless excused (Section 3-511) presentment is necessary to charge secondary parties as follows:

(a) presentment for acceptance is necessary to charge the drawer and indorsers of a draft where the draft so provides, or is payable elsewhere than at the residence or place of business of the drawee, or its date of payment depends upon such presentment. The holder may at his option present for acceptance any other draft payable at a stated date;

(b) presentment for payment is necessary to charge any indorser;

(c) in the case of any drawer, the acceptor of a draft payable at a bank or the maker of a note payable at a bank, presentment for payment is necessary, but failure to make presentment discharges such drawer, acceptor or maker only as stated in Section 3-502 (1) (b).

(2) Unless excused (Section 3-511)

(a) notice of any dishonor is necessary to charge any indorser;

(b) in the case of any drawer, the acceptor of a draft payable at a bank or the maker of a note payable at a bank notice of any dishonor is necessary, but failure to give such notice discharges such drawer, acceptor or maker only as stated in Section 3-502 (1) (b).

(3) Unless excused (Section 3-511) protest of any dishonor is necessary to charge the drawer and indorsers of any draft which on its face appears to be drawn or payable outside of the states and territories of the United States and the District of Columbia. The holder may at his option make protest of any dishonor of any other instrument and in the case of a foreign draft may on insolvency of the acceptor before maturity make protest for better security.

(4) Notwithstanding any provision of this Section, neither presentment nor notice of dishonor nor protest is necessary to charge an indorser who has indorsed an instrument after maturity.

§ 3-502. Unexcused Delay; Discharge.—

(1) Where without excuse any necessary presentment or notice of dishonor is delayed beyond the time when it is due

(a) Any indorser is discharged; and

(b) any drawer or the acceptor of a draft payable at a bank or the maker of a note payable at a bank who because the drawee or payor bank becomes insolvent during the delay is deprived of funds maintained with the drawee or payor bank to cover the instrument may discharge his liability by written assignment to the holder of his rights against the drawee or payor bank in respect of such funds, but such drawer, acceptor or maker is not otherwise discharged.

(2) Where without excuse a necessary protest is delayed beyond the time when it is due any drawer or indorser is discharged.

§ 3-503. Time of Presentment.—

(1) Unless a different time is expressed in the instrument the time for any presentment is determined as follows:

(a) where an instrument is payable at or a fixed period after a stated date any presentment for acceptance must be made on or before the date it is payable;

(b) where an instrument is payable after sight it must either be presented for acceptance or negotiated within a reasonable time after date or issue whichever is later;

(c) where an instrument shows the date on which it is payable presentment for payment is due on that date;

(d) where an instrument is accelerated presentment for payment is due within a reasonable time after the acceleration;

(e) with respect to the liability of any secondary party presentment for acceptance or payment of any other instrument is due within a reasonable time after such party becomes liable thereon.

(2) A reasonable time for presentment is determined by the nature of the instrument, any usage of banking or trade and the facts of the particular case. In the case of an uncertified check which is drawn and payable within the United States and which is not a draft drawn by a bank the following are presumed to be reasonable periods within which to present for payment or to initiate bank collection:

(a) with respect to the liability of the drawer, thirty days after date or issue whichever is later; and

(b) with respect to the liability of an endorser, seven days after his indorsement.

(3) Where any presentment is due on a day which is not a full business day for either the person making presentment or the party to pay or accept, presentment is due on the next following day which is a full business day for both parties.

(4) Presentment to be sufficient must be made at a reasonable hour, and if at a bank during its banking day.

§ 3-504. How Presentment Made.—

(1) Presentment is a demand for acceptance or payment made upon the maker, acceptor, drawee or other payor by or on behalf of the holder.

(2) Presentment may be made

(a) by mail, in which event the time of presentment is determined by the time of receipt of the mail; or

(b) through a clearing house; or

(c) at the place of acceptance or payment specified in the instrument or if there be none at the place of business or residence of the party to accept or pay. If neither the party to accept or pay nor anyone authorized to act for him is present or accessible at such place presentment is excused.

(3) It may be made

(a) to any one of two or more makers, acceptors, drawees or other payors; or

(b) to any person who has authority to make or refuse the acceptance or payment.

(4) A draft accepted or a note made payable at a bank in the continental United States must be presented at such bank.

(5) In the cases described in Section 4-210 presentment may be made in the manner and with the result stated in that section.

§ 3-505. Rights of Party to Whom Presentment is Made.—

(1) The party to whom presentment is made may without dishonor require

    (a) exhibition of the instrument; and

    (b) reasonable identification of the person making presentment and evidence of his authority to make it if made for another; and

    (c) that the instrument be produced for acceptance or payment at a place specified in it, or if there be none at any place reasonable in the circumstances; and

    (d) a signed receipt on the instrument for any partial or full payment and its surrender upon full payment.

(2) Failure to comply with any such requirements invalidates the presentment but the person presenting has a reasonable time in which to comply and the time for acceptance or payment runs from the time of compliance.

§ 3-506. Time Allowed for Acceptance or Payment.—

(1) Acceptance may be deferred without dishonor until the close of the next business day following presentment. The holder may also in a good faith effort to obtain acceptance and without either dishonor of the instrument or discharge of secondary parties allow postponement of acceptance for an additional business day.

(2) Except as longer time is allowed in the case of documentary drafts drawn under a letter of credit, and unless an earlier time is agreed to by the party to pay, payment of an instrument may be deferred without dishonor pending reasonable examination to determine whether it is properly payable, but payment must be made in any event before the close of business on the day of presentment.

§ 3-507. Dishonor; Holder's Right of Recourse; Term Allowing Re-Presentment.—

(1) An instrument is dishonored when

    (a) a necessary or optional presentment is duly made and due acceptance or payment is refused or cannot be obtained within the prescribed time or in case of bank collections the instrument is seasonably returned by the midnight deadline (Section 4-301); or

    (b) presentment is excused and the instrument is not duly accepted or paid.

(2) Subject to any necessary notice of dishonor and protest, the holder has upon dishonor an immediate right of recourse against the drawers and indorsers.

(3) Return of an instrument for lack of proper indorsement is not dishonor.

(4) A term in a draft or an indorsement thereof allowing a stated time for representment in the event of any dishonor of the draft by nonacceptance if a time draft or by nonpayment if a sight draft gives the holder as against any secondary party bound by the term an option to waive the dishonor without affecting the liability of the secondary party and he may present again up to the end of the stated time.

§ 3-508. Notice of Dishonor.—

(1) Notice of dishonor may be given to any person who may be liable on the instrument by or on behalf of the holder or any party who has himself received notice, or any other party who can be compelled to pay the instrument. In addition an agent or bank in whose hands the instrument is dishonored may give notice to his principal or customer or to another agent or bank from which the instrument was received.

(2) Any necessary notice must be given by a bank before its midnight deadline and by any other person before midnight of the third business day after dishonor or receipt of notice of dishonor.

(3) Notice may be given in any reasonable manner. It may be oral or written and in any terms which identify the instrument and state that it has been dishonored. A misdescription which does not mislead the party notified does not vitiate the notice. Sending the instrument bearing a stamp, ticket or writing stating that acceptance or payment has been refused or sending a notice of debit with respect to the instrument is sufficient.

(4) Written notice is given when sent although it is not received.

(5) Notice to one partner is notice to each although the firm has been dissolved.

(6) When any party is in insolvency proceedings instituted after the issue of the instrument notice may be given either to the party or to the representative of his estate.

(7) When any party is dead or incompetent notice may be sent to his last known address or given to his personal representative.

(8) Notice operates for the benefit of all parties who have rights on the instrument against the party notified.

§ 3-509. Protest; Noting for Protest.—

(1) A protest is a certificate of dishonor made under the hand and seal of a United States consul or vice consul or a notary public or other person authorized to certify dishonor by the law of the place where dishonor occurs. It may be made upon information satisfactory to such person.

(2) The protest must identify the instrument and certify either that due presentment has been made or the reason why it is excused and that the instrument has been dishonored by non-acceptance or nonpayment.

(3) The protest may also certify that notice of dishonor has been given to all parties or to specified parties.

(4) Subject to subsection (5) any necessary protest is due by the time that notice of dishonor is due.

(5) If, before protest is due, an instrument has been noted for protest by the officer to make protest, the protest may be made at any time thereafter as of the date of the noting.

§ 3-510. Evidence of Dishonor and Notice of Dishonor.—The following are admissible as evidence and create a presumption of dishonor and of any notice of dishonor therein shown:

    (a) a document regular in form as provided in the preceding section which purports to be a protest;

(b) the purported stamp or writing of the drawee, payor bank or presenting bank on the instrument or accompanying it stating that acceptance or payment has been refused for reasons consistent with dishonor;

(c) any book or record of the drawee, payor bank, or any collecting bank kept in the usual course of business which shows dishonor, even though there is no evidence of who made the entry.

§ 3-511. Waived or Excused Presentment, Protest or Notice of Dishonor or Delay Therein.—

(1) Delay in presentment, protest or notice of dishonor is excused when the party is without notice that it is due or when the delay is caused by circumstances beyond his control and he exercises reasonable diligence after the cause of the delay ceases to operate.

(2) Presentment or notice or protest as the case may be is entirely excused when

(a) the party to be charged has waived it expressly or by implication either before or after it is due; or

(b) such party has himself dishonored the instrument or has countermanded payment or otherwise has no reason to expect or right to require that the instrument be accepted or paid; or

(c) by reasonable diligence the presentment or protest cannot be made or the notice given.

(3) Presentment is also entirely excused when

(a) the maker, acceptor or drawee of any instrument except a documentary draft is dead or in insolvency proceedings instituted after the issue of the instrument; or

(b) acceptance or payment is refused but not for want of proper presentment

(4) Where a draft has been dishonored by nonacceptance a later presentment for payment and any notice of dishonor and protest for nonpayment are excused unless in the meantime the instrument has been accepted.

(5) A waiver of protest is also a waiver of presentment and of notice of dishonor even though protest is not required.

(6) Where a waiver of presentment or notice of protest is embodied in the instrument itself it is binding upon all parties; but where it is written above the signature of an indorser it binds him only.

PART 6

Discharge

§ 3-601. Discharge of Parties.—

The extent of the discharge of any party from liability on an instrument is governed by the sections on

(a) payment or satisfaction (Section 3-603); or

(b) tender of payment (Section 3-604); or

(c) cancellation or renunciation (Section 3-605); or

(d) impairment of right of recourse or of collateral (Section 3-606); or

(e) reacquisition of the instrument by a prior party (Seciton 3-208); or

(f) fraudulent and material alteration (Section 3-407); or

(g) certification of a check (Section 3-411); or

(h) acceptance varying a draft (Section 3-412); or

(i) unexcused delay in presentment or notice of dishonor or protest (Section 3-502).

(2) Any party is also discharged from his liability on an instrument to another party by any other act or agreement with such a party which would discharge his simple contract for the payment of money.

(3) The liability of all parties is discharged when any party who has himself no right of action or recourse on the instrument

(a) reacquires the instrument in his own right; or

(b) is discharged under any provisions of this Article, except as otherwise provided with respect to discharge for impairment of recourse or of collateral (Section 3-606).

§ 3-602. Effects of Discharge Against Holder in Due Course.—No discharge of any party provided by this Article is effective against a subsequent holder in due course unless he has notice thereof when he takes the instrument.

§ 3-603. Payment or Satisfaction.—

(1) The liability of any party is discharged to the extent of his payment or satisfaction to the holder even though it is made with knowledge of a claim of another person to the instrument unless prior to such payment or satisfaction the person making the claim either supplies indemnity deemed adequate by the party seeking the discharge or enjoins payment or satisfaction by order of a court of competent jurisdiction in an action in which the adverse claimant and the holder are parties. This subsection does not, however, result in the discharge of the liability

(a) of a party who in bad faith pays or satisfies a holder who acquired the instrument by theft or who (unless having the rights of a holder in due course) holds through one who so acquired it; or

(b) of a party (other than an intermediary bank or a payor bank which is not a depositary bank) who pays or satisfies the holder of an instrument which has been restrictively indorsed in a manner not consistent with the terms of such restrictive indorsement.

(2) Payment of satisfaction may be made with the consent of the holder by any person including a stranger to the instrument. Surrender of the instrument to such a person gives him the rights of a transferee (Section 3-201).

§ 3-604. Tender of Payment.—

(1) Any party making tender of full payment to a holder when or after it is due is discharged to the extent

of all subsequent liability for interest, costs and attorney's fees.

(2) The holder's refusal of such tender wholly discharges any party who has a right of recourse against the party making the tender.

(3) Where the maker or acceptor of an instrument payable otherwise than on demand is able and ready to pay at every place of payment specified in the instrument when it is due, it is equivalent to tender.

§ 3-605. Cancellation and Renunciation.—

The holder of an instrument may even without consideration discharge any party

(a) in any manner apparent on the face of the instrument or the indorsement, as by intentially cancelling the instrument or the party's signature by destruction or mutilation, or by striking out the party's signature; or

(b) by renouncing his rights by a writing signed and delivered or by surrender of the instrument to the party to be discharged.

(2) Neither cancellation nor renunciation without surrender of the instrument affects the title thereto.

§ 3-606. Impairment of Recourse or of Collateral.—

(1) The holder discharges any party to the instrument to the extent that without such party's consent the holder

(a) without express reservation of rights releases or agrees not to sue any person against whom the party has to the knowledge of the holder a right of recourse or agrees to suspend the right to enforce against such person the instrument or collateral or otherwise discharges such person, except that failure or delay in effecting any required presentment, protest or notice of dishonor with respect to any such person does not discharge any party as to whom presentment, protest or notice of dishonor is effective or unnecessary; or

(b) unjustifiably impairs any collateral for the instrument given by or on behalf of the party or any person against whom he has a right of recourse.

(2) By express reservation of rights against a party with a right of recourse the holder preserves

(a) all his rights against such party as of the time when the instrument was originally due; and

(b) the right of the party to pay the instrument as of that time; and

(c) all rights of such party to recourse against others.

PART 7

Advice of International Sight Draft
(omitted)

PART 8

Miscellaneous

§ 3-801. omitted.

§ 3-802. Effect of Instrument on Obligation for Which It Is Given.—

(1) Unless otherwise agreed where an instrument is taken for an underlying obligation

(a) the obligation is pro tanto discharged if a bank is drawer, maker or acceptor of an instrument and there is no recourse on the instrument against the underlying obligor; and

(b) in any other case the obligation is suspended pro tanto until the instrument is due or if it is payable on demand until its presentment. If the instrument is dishonored action may be maintained on either the instrument or the obligation; discharge of the underlying obligor on the instrument also discharges him on the obligation.

(2) The taking in good faith of a check which is not postdated does not of itself so extend the time on the original obligation as to discharge a surety.

§ 3-803. Notice to Third Party.—Where a defendant is sued for breach of an obligation for which a third person is answerable over under this Article he may give the third person written notice of the litigation, and the person notified may then give similar notice to any other person who is answerable over to him under this Article. If the notice states that the person notified may come in and defend and that if the person notified does not do so he will in any action against him by the person giving the notice be bound by any determination of fact common to the two litigations, then unless after seasonable receipt of the notice the person notified does come in and defend he is so bound.

§ 3-804. Lost, Destroyed or Stolen Investments.—The owner of an instrument which is lost, whether by destruction, theft or otherwise, may maintain an action in his own name and recover from any party liable thereon upon due proof of his ownership, the facts which prevent his production of the instrument and its terms. The court may require security indemnifying defendant against loss by reason of further claims on the instrument.

§ 3-805. Instruments Not Payable to Order or to Bearer.—This Article applies to any instrument whose terms do not preclude transfer and which is otherwise negotiable within this Article but which is not payable to order or to bearer, except that there can be no holder in due course of such an instrument.

PART I

General Provisions and Definitions

§ **4-101.** **Short Title.**—This Article shall be known and may be cited as Uniform Commercial Code—Bank Deposits and Collections.

§ **4-102.** **Applicability.**—

(1) To the extent that items within this Article are also within the scope of Articles 3 and 8, they are subject to the provisions of those Articles. In the event of conflict the provisions of this Article govern those of Article 3 but the provisions of Article 8 govern those of this Article.

(2) The liability of a bank for action or non-action with respect to any item handled by it for purposes of presentment, payment or collection is governed by the law of the place where the bank is located. In the case of action or non-action by or at a branch or separate office of a bank, its liability is governed by the law of the place where the branch or separate office is located.

§ **4-103.** **Variation by Agreement; Measure of Damages; Certain Action Constituting Ordinary Care.**—

(1) the effect of the provisions of this Article may be varied by agreement except that no agreement can disclaim a bank's responsibility for its own lack of good faith or failure to exercise ordinary care or can limit the measure of damages for such lack or failure; but the parties may by agreement determine the standards by which such responsibility is to be measured if such standards are not manifestly unreasonable.

(2) Federal reserve regulations and operating letters, clearing house rules, and the like, have the effect of agreements under subsection (1), whether or not specifically assented to by all parties interested in items handled.

(3) Action or non-action approved by this Article or pursuant to Federal Reserve regulations or operating letters constitutes the exercise of ordinary care and, in the absence of special instructions, action or non-action consistent with clearing house rules and the like or with a general banking usage not disapproved by this Article, prima facie constitutes the exercise of ordinary care.

(4) The specification or approval of certain procedures by this Article does not constitute disapproval of other procedures which may be reasonable under the circumstances.

(5) The measure of damages for failure to exercise ordinary care in handling an item is the amount of the item reduced by an amount which could not have been realized by the use of ordinary care, and where there is bad faith it includes other damages, if any, suffered by the party as a proximate consequence.

§ **4-104.** **Definitions and Index of Definitions.**—

(1) In this Article unless the context otherwise requires

(a) "Account" means any account with a bank and includes a checking, time, interest or savings account;

(b) "Afternoon" means the period of a day between noon and midnight.

(c) "Banking day" means that part of any day on which a bank is open to the public for carrying on substantially all of its banking functions;

(d) "Clearing house" means any association of banks or other payors regularly clearing items;

(e) "Customer" means any person having an account with a bank or for whom a bank has agreed to collect items and includes a bank carrying an account with another bank;

(f) "Documentary draft" means any negotiable or non-negotiable draft with accompanying documents, securities or other papers to be delivered against honor of the draft;

(g) "Item" means any instrument for the payment of money even though it is not negotiable but does not include money;

(h) "Midnight deadline" with respect to a bank is midnight on its next banking day following the banking day on which it receives the relevant item or notice or from which the time for taking action commences to run, whichever is later;

(i) "Property payable" includes the availability of funds for payment at the time of decision to pay or dishonor;

(j) "Settle" means to pay in cash, by clearing house settlement, in a charge or credit or by remittance, or otherwise as instructed. A settlement may be either provisional or final;

(k) "Suspends payments" with respect to bank means that it has been closed by order of the supervisory authorities, that a public officer has been appointed to take it over or that it ceases or refuses to make payments in the ordinary course of business.

(2) Other definitions applying to this Article and the sections in which they appear are:

"Collecting bank"	Section 4-105.
"Depositary bank"	Section 4-105.
"Intermediary bank"	Section 4-105.
"Payor bank"	Section 4-105.
"Presenting bank"	Section 4-105.
"Remitting bank"	Section 4-105.

(3) The following definitions in other Articles apply to this Article:

"Acceptance"	Section 3-410.
"Certificate of deposit"	Section 3-104.

"Certification"	Section 3-411.
"Check"	Section 3-104.
"Draft"	Section 3-104.
"Holder in due course"	Section 3-302.
"Notice of dishonor"	Section 3-508.
"Presentment"	Section 3-504.
"Protest"	Section 3-509.
"Secondary party"	Section 3-102.

(4) In addition Article 1 contains general definitions and principles of construction and interpretation applicable throughout this Article.

§ 4-105. "Depository Bank"; "Intermediary Bank"; "Collecting Bank"; "Payor Bank"; "Presenting Bank"; "Remitting Bank"—In this Article unless the context otherwise requires:

(a) "Depository bank" means the first bank to which an item is transferred for collection even though it is also the payor bank.

(b) "Payor bank" means a bank by which an item is payable as drawn or accepted;

(c) "Intermediary bank" means any bank to which an item is transferred in course of collection except the depositary or payor bank;

(d) "Collecting bank" means any bank handling the item for collection except the payor bank;

(e) "Presenting bank" means any bank presenting an item except a payor bank;

(f) "Remitting bank" means any payor or intermediary bank remitting for an item.

§ 4-106. Separate Office of a Bank.—A branch or separate office of a bank [maintaining its own deposit ledgers] is a separate bank for the purpose of computing the time within which and the place at or to which action may be taken or notices or orders shall be given under this Article.

Note: The brackets are to make it optional with the several states whether to require a branch to maintain its own deposit ledgers in order to be considered to be a separate bank for certain purposes under Article 4. In some states "maintaining its own deposit ledgers" is a satisfactory test. In others branch banking practices are such that this test would not be suitable.

§ 4-107. Time of Receipt of Items.—

(1) For the purpose of allowing time to process items, prove balances and make the necessary entries on its books to determine its position for the day, a bank may fix an afternoon hour of two P.M. or later as a cut-off hour for the handling of money and items and the making of entries on its books.

(2) Any item or deposit of money received on any day after a cut-off hour so fixed or after the close of the banking day may be treated as being received at the opening of the next banking day.

§ 4-108. Delays.—

(1) Unless otherwise instructed, a collecting bank in a good faith effort to secure payment may, in the case of specific items and with or without the approval of any person involved, waive, modify or extend time limits imposed or permitted by this Act for a period not in excess of an additional banking day without discharge of secondary parties and without liability to its transferor or any prior party.

(2) Delay by a collecting bank or payor bank beyond time limits prescribed or permitted by this Act or by instructions is excused if caused by interruption of communication facilities, suspension of payments by another bank, war, emergency conditions or other circumstances beyond the control of the bank provided it exercises such diligence as the circumstances require.

PART 2

Collection of Items: Depositary and Collecting Banks

§ 4-201. Presumption and Duration of Agency Status of Collecting Banks and Provisional Status of Credits; Applicability of Article; Item Indorsed "Pay Any Bank".—

(1) Unless a contrary intent clearly appears and prior to the time that a settlement given by a collecting bank for an item is or becomes final (subsection (3) of Section 4-211 and Section 4-212 and 4-213) the bank is an agent or sub-agent of the owner of the item and any settlement given for the item is provisional. This provision applies regardless of the form of indorsement or lack of indorsement and even though credit given for the item is subject to immediate withdrawal as of right or is in fact withdrawn; but the continuance of ownership of an item by its owner and any rights of the owner to proceeds of the item are subject to rights of a collecting bank such as those resulting from outstanding advances on the item and valid rights of setoff. When an item is handled by banks for purposes of presentment, payment and collection, the relevant provisions of this Article apply even though action of parties clearly establishes that a particular bank has purchased the item and is the owner of it.

(2) After an item has been indorsed with the words "pay any bank" or the like, only a bank may acquire the rights of a holder

(a) until the item has been returned to the customer initiating collection; or

(b) until the item has been specially endorsed by a bank to a person who is not a bank.

§ 4-202. Responsibility for Collection; When Action Seasonable.—

(1) A collecting bank must use ordinary care in

(a) presenting an item or sending it for presentment; and

(b) sending notice of dishonor or non-payment or returning an item other than a documentary draft to the bank's transferor [or directly to the depositary bank under subsection (2) of Section 4-212] *(see note to Section 4-212)* after learning that the item has not been paid or accepted, as the case may be; and

    (c) settling for an item when the bank receives final settlement; and

    (d) making or providing for any necessary protest; and

    (e) notifying its transferor of any loss or delay in transit within a reasonable time after discovery thereof.

(2) A collecting bank taking proper action before its midnight deadline following receipt of an item, notice or payment acts seasonably; taking proper action within a reasonably longer time may be seasonable but the bank has the burden of so establishing.

(3) Subject to subjection (1) (a), a bank is not liable for the insolvency, neglect, misconduct, mistake or default of another bank or person or for loss or destruction of an item in transit or in the possession of others.

§ 4-203. **Effect of Instructions.**—Subject to the provisions of Article 3 concerning conversion of instruments (Section 3-419) and the provisions of both Article 3 and this Article concerning restrictive indorsements only a collecting bank's transferor can give instructions which affect the bank or constitute notice to it and a collecting bank is not liable to prior parties for any action taken pursuant to such instructions or in accordance with any agreement with its transferor.

§ 4-204. **Methods of Sending and Presenting; Sending Direct to Payor Bank—**

(1) A collecting bank must send items by reasonably prompt method taking into consideration any relevant instructions, the nature of the item, the number of such items on hand, and the cost of collection involved and the method generally used by it or others to present such items.

(2) A collecting bank may send

    (a) any item direct to the payor bank;

    (b) any item to any non-bank payor if authorized by its transferor; and

    (c) any item other than documentary drafts to any non-bank payor, if authorized by Federal Reserve regulation or operating letter, clearing house rule or the like.

§ 4-205. **Supplying Missing Indorsement; No Notice From Prior Indorsement.—**

(1) A depositary bank which has taken an item for collection may supply any indorsement of the customer which is necessary to title unless the item contains the words "payee's indorsement required" or the like. In the absence of such a requirement a statement placed on the item by the depositary bank to the effect that the item was deposited by a customer or credited to his account is effective as the customer's indorsement.

(2) An intermediary bank, or payor bank which is not a depositary bank, is neither given notice nor otherwise affected by a restrictive indorsement of any person except the bank's immediate transferor.

§ 4-206. **Transfer Between Banks—**Any agreed method which identifies the transferor bank is sufficient for the item's further transfer to another bank.

§ 4-207. **Warranties of Customer and Collecting Bank on Transfer or Presentment of Items; Time for Claims.—**

(1) Each customer or collecting bank who obtains payment or acceptance of an item and each prior customer and collecting bank warrants to the payor bank or other payor who in good faith pays or accepts the item that

    (a) he has a good title to the item or is authorized to obtain payment or acceptance on behalf of one who has a good title; and

    (b) he has no knowledge that the signature of the maker or drawer is unauthorized, except that this warranty is not given by any customer or collecting bank that is a holder in due course and acts in good faith

      (i) to a maker with respect to the maker's own signature; or

      (ii) to a drawer with respect to the drawer's own signature, whether or not the drawer is also the drawee; or

      (iii) to an acceptor of an item if the holder in due course took the item after the acceptance or obtained the acceptance without knowledge that the drawer's signature was unauthorized; and

    (c) the item has not been materially altered, except that this warranty is not given by any customer or collecting bank that is a holder in due course and acts in good faith

      (i) to the maker of a note; or

      (ii) to the drawer of a draft whether or not the drawer is also the drawee; or

      (iii) to the acceptor of an item with respect to an alteration made prior to the acceptance if the holder in due course took the item after the acceptance, even though the acceptance provided "payable as originally drawn" equivalent terms; or

      (iv) to the acceptor of an item with respect to an alteration made after the acceptance.

(2) Each customer and collecting bank who transfers an item and receives a settlement or other consideration for it warrants to his transferee and to any subsequent collecting bank who takes the item in good faith and

    (a) he has a good title to the item or is authorized to obtain payment or acceptance on behalf of one who has a good title and the transfer is otherwise rightful; and

    (b) all signatures are genuine or authorized; and

    (c) the item has not been materially altered; and

    (d) no defense of any party is good against him; and

    (e) he has no knowledge of any insolvency proceeding instituted with respect to the maker or acceptor or the drawer of an unaccepted item.

In addition each customer and collecting bank so transferring an item and receiving a settlement or other consideration engages that upon dishonor and any necessary notice of dishonor and protest he will take up the item.

(3) The warranties and the engagement to honor set forth in the two preceding subsections arise notwithstanding the absence of endorsement or words of guaranty or warranty in the transfer or presentment and a collecting bank remains liable for their breach despite remittance to its transferor. Damages for breach of such warranties or engagement to honor shall not exceed the consideration received by the customer or collecting bank responsible plus finance changes and expenses related to the item, if any.

(4) Unless a claim for breach of warranty under this section is made within a reasonable time after the person claiming learns of the breach, the person liable is discharged to the extent of any loss caused by the delay in making claim.

§ 4-208. Security Interest of Collecting Bank in Items, Accompanying Documents and Proceeds.—

(1) A bank has a security interest in an item and any accompanying documents or the proceeds of either

(a) in case of an item deposited in an account to the extent to which credit given for the item has been withdrawn or applied;

(b) in case of an item for which it has given credit available for withdrawal as of right, to the extent of the credit given whether or not the credit is drawn upon and whether or not there is a right of charge-back; or

(c) if it makes an advance on or against the item.

(2) When credit which has been given for several items received at one time or pursuant to a single agreement is withdrawn or applied in part the security interest remains upon all the items, any accompanying documents or the proceeds of either. For the purpose of this section, credits first given are first withdrawn.

(3) Receipt by a collecting bank of a final settlement for an item is a realization on its security interest in the item, accompanying documents and proceeds. To the extent and so long as the bank does not receive final settlement for the item or give up possession of the item or accompanying documents for purposes other than collection, the security interest continues and is subject to provisions of Article 9 except that

(a) no security agreement is necessary to make the security interest enforceable (subsection (1)(b) of Section 9-203); and

(b) no filing is required to perfect the security interest; and

(c) the security interest has priority over conflicting perfected security interests in the item, accompanying documents or proceeds.

§ 4-209. When Bank Gives Value for Purposes of Holder in Due Course.—For purposes of determining its status as a holder in due course, the bank has given value to the extent that it has a security interest in an item provided that the bank otherwise complies with the requirements of Section 3-302 on what constitutes a holder in due course.

§ 4-210. Presentment by Notice of Item Not Payable by, Through or at a Bank; Liability of Secondary Parties.—

(1) Unless otherwise instructed, a collecting bank may present an item not payable by, through or at a bank by sending to the party to accept or pay a written notice that the bank holds the item for acceptance or payment. The notice must be sent in time to be received on or before the day when presentment is due and the bank must meet any requirement of the party to accept or pay under Section 3-505 by the close of the bank's next banking day after it knows of the requirement.

(2) Where presentment is made by notice and neither honor nor request for compliance with a requirement under Section 3-505 is received by the close of business on the day after maturity or in the case of demand items by the close of business on the third banking day after notice was sent, the presenting bank may treat the item as dishonored and charge any secondary party by sending him notice of the facts.

§ 4-211. Media of Remittance; Provisional and Final Settlement in Remittance Cases.—

(1) A collecting bank may take in settlement of an item

(a) a check of the remitting bank or of another bank on any bank except the remitting bank; or

(b) a cashier's check or similar primary obligation of a remitting bank which is a member of or clears through a member of the same clearing house or group as the collecting bank; or

(c) appropriate authority to charge an account of the remitting bank or of another bank with the collecting bank; or

(d) if the item is drawn upon or payable by a person other than a bank, a cashier's check, certified check or other bank check or obligation.

(2) If before its midnight deadline the collecting bank properly dishonors a remittance check or authorization to charge on itself or presents or forwards for collection a remittance instrument or of on another bank which is of a kind approved by subsection (1) or has not been authorized by it, the collecting bank is not liable to prior parties in the event of the dishonor of such check, instrument or authorization.

(3) A settlement for an item by means of a remittance instrument or authorization to charge is or becomes a final settlement as to both the person making and the person receiving the settlement

(a) if the remittance instrument or authorization to charge is of a kind approved by subsection (1) or has not been authorized by the person receiving the settlement and in either case the person receiving the settlement acts seasonably before its midnight deadline in presenting, forwarding for collection or paying the instrument or authorization,—at the time the remittance instrument or authorization is finally paid by the payor by which it is payable;

(b) if the person receiving the settlement has authorized remittance by a non-bank check or obligation or by a cashier's check or similar primary obligation of or a check upon the payor or other remitting bank which is not of a kind approved by subsection (1)(b),—at the time of the receipt of such remittance check or obligation; or

(c) if in a case not covered by subparagraphs (a) or (b) the person receiving the settlement fails to seasonably present, forward for collection, pay or return a remittance instrument or authorization to it to charge before its midnight deadline,—at such midnight deadline.

§ 4-212. Right of Charge-Back or Refund.—

(1) If a collecting bank has made provisional settlement with its customer for an item and itself fails by reason of dishonor, suspension of payments by a bank or otherwise to receive a settlement for the item which is or becomes final, the bank may revoke the settlement given by it, charge back the amount of any credit given for the item to its customer's account or obtain refund from its customer whether or not it is able to return the items if by its midnight deadline or within a longer reasonable time after it learns the facts it returns the item or sends notification of the facts. These rights to revoke, chargeback and obtain refund terminate if and when a settlement for the item received by the bank is or becomes final (subsection (3) of Section 4-211 and subsections (2) and (3) of Section 4-213).

[(2) Within the time and manner prescribed by this section and Section 4-301, an intermediary or payor bank, as the case may be, may return an unpaid item directly to the depositary bank and may send for collection a draft on the depositary bank and obtain reimbursement. In such case, if the depositary bank has received provisional settlement for the item, it must reimburse the bank drawing the draft and any provisional credits for the item between banks shall become and remain final.]

Note: *Direct return is recognized as an innovation that is not yet established bank practice, and therefore, Paragraph 2 has been bracketed. Some lawyers have doubts whether it should be included in legislation or left to development by agreement.*

(3) A depositary bank which is also the payor may charge-back the amount of an item to its customer's account or obtain refund in accordance with the section governing return of an item received by a payor bank for credit on its books (Section 4-301).

(4) The right to charge-back is not affected by

(a) prior use of the credit given for the item; or

(b) failure by any bank to exercise ordinary care with respect to the item but any bank so failing remains liable.

(5) A failure to charge-back or claim refund does not affect other rights of the bank against the customer or any other party.

(6) If credit is given in dollars as the equivalent of the value of an item payable in a foreign currency the dollar amount of any charge-back or refund shall be calculated on the basis of the buying sight rate for the foreign currency prevailing on the day when the person entitled to the charge-back or refund learns that it will not receive payment in ordinary course.

§ 4-213. Final Payment of Item by Payor Bank; When Provisional Debits and Credits Become Final; When Certain Credits Become Available for Withdrawal.—

(1) An item is finally paid by a payor bank when the bank has done any of the following, whichever happens first:

(a) paid the item in cash; or

(b) settled for the item without reserving a right to revoke the settlement and without having such right under statute, clearing house rule or agreement; or

(c) completed the process of posting the item to the indicated account of the drawer, maker or other person to be charged therewith; or

(d) made a provisional settlement for the item and failed to revoke the settlement in the time and manner permitted by statute, clearing house rule or agreement.

Upon a final payment under subparagraphs (b), (c) or (d) the payor bank shall be accountable for the amount of the item.

(2) If provisional settlement for an item between the presenting and payor banks is made through a clearing house or by debits or credits in an account between them, then to the extent that provisional debits or credits for the item are entered in accounts between the presenting and payor banks or between the presenting and successive prior collecting banks seriatim, they become final upon final payment of the item by the payor bank.

(3) If a collecting bank receives a settlement for an item which is or becomes final (subsection (3) of Section 4-211, subsection (2) of Section 4-213) the bank is accountable to its customer for the amount of the item and any provisional credit given for the item in an account with its customer becomes final.

(4) Subject to any right of the bank to apply the credit to an obligation of the customer, credit given by a bank for an item in an account with its customer becomes available for withdrawal as of right.

(a) in any case where the bank has received a provisional settlement for the item,—when such settlement becomes final and the bank has had a reasonable time to learn that the settlement is final;

(b) in any case where the bank is both a depositary bank and a payor bank and the item is finally paid,—at the opening of the bank's second banking day following receipt of the item.

(5) A deposit of money in a bank is final when made but, subject to any right of the bank to apply the deposit to an obligation of the customer, the deposit becomes available for withdrawal as of right at the opening of the bank's next banking day following receipt of the deposit.

§ 4-214. Insolvency and Preference.—

(1) Any item in or coming into the possession of a payor or collecting bank which suspends payment and which item is not finally paid shall be returned by the receiver, trustee or agent in charge of the closed bank to the presenting bank or the closed bank's customer.

(2) If a payor bank finally pays an item and suspends payments without making a settlement for the item with its customer or the presenting bank which settlement is or becomes final, the owner of the item has a preferred claim against the payor bank.

(3) If a payor bank gives or a collecting bank gives or receives a provisional settlement for an item and thereafter suspends payments, the suspension does not prevent or interfere with the settlement becoming final if such finality occurs automatically upon the lapse of certain time or the happening of certain events (subsection (3) of Section 4-211, subsections (1) (d), (2) and (3) of Section 4-213).

(4) If a collecting bank receives from subsequent parties settlement for an item which settlement is or becomes final and suspends payments without making a settlement for the item with its customer which is or becomes final, the owner of the item has a preferred claim against such collecting bank.

PART 3

Collection of Items: Payor Banks

§ 4-301. Deferred Posting; Recovery of Payment by Return of Items; Time of Dishonor.—
(1) Where an authorized settlement for a demand item (other than a documentary draft) received by a payor bank otherwise than for immediate payment over the counter has been made before midnight of the banking day of receipt the payor bank may revoke the settlement and recover any payment if before it has made final payment (subsection (1) of Section 4-213) and before its midnight deadline it
    (a) returns the item; or
    (b) sends written notice of dishonor or nonpayment if the item is held for protest or is otherwise unavailable for return.

(2) If a demand item is received by a payor bank for credit on its books it may return such item or send notice of dishonor and may revoke any credit given or recover the amount thereof withdrawn by its customer, if it acts within the time limit and in the manner specified in the preceding subsection.

(3) Unless previous notice of dishonor has been sent an item is dishonored at the time when for purposes of dishonor it is returned or notice sent in accordance with this section.

(4) An item is returned:
    (a) as to an item received through a clearing house, when it is delivered to the presenting or last collecting bank or the clearing house or is sent or delivered in accordance with its rules; or
    (b) in all other cases, when it is sent or delivered to the bank's customer or transferor or pursuant to his instructions.

§ 4-302. Payor Bank's Responsibility for Late Return of Item.—In the absence of a valid defense such as breach of a presentment warranty (subsection (1) of Section 4-207), settlement effected or the like, if an item is presented on and received by a payor bank the bank is accountable for the amount of
    (a) a demand item other than a documentary draft whether properly payable or not if the bank, in any case where it is not also the depositary bank, retains the item beyond midnight of the banking day of receipt without settling for it or, regardless of whether it is also the depositary bank, does not pay or return the item or send notice of dishonor until after its midnight deadline; or
    (b) any other properly payable item unless within the time allowed for acceptance or payment of that item the bank either accepts or pays the item or returns it and accompanying documents.

§ 4-303. When Item Subject to Notice, Stop-Order, Legal Process or Setoff; Order in Which Items May Be Charged or Certified.—
(1) Any knowledge, notice or stop-order received by, legal process served upon or setoff exercised by a payor bank, whether or not effective under other rules of law to terminate, suspend or modify the bank's right or duty to pay an item or to charge its customer's account for the item, comes too late to so terminate, suspend or modify such right or duty if the knowledge, notice, stop-order or legal process is received or served and a reasonable time for the bank to act thereon expires or the setoff is exercised after the bank has done any of the following;
    (a) accepted or certified the item;
    (b) paid the item in cash;
    (c) settled for the item without reserving a right to revoke the settlement and without having such right under statute, clearing house rule or agreement;
    (d) completed the process of posting the item to the indicated account of the drawer, maker or other person to be charged therewith or otherwise has evidenced by examination of such indicated account and by action its decision to pay the item; or
    (e) become accountable for the amount of the item under subsection (1) (d) of Section 4-213 and Section 4-302 dealing with the payor bank's responsibility for late return of items.

(2) Subject to the provisions of subsection (1) items may be accepted, paid, certified or charged to the indicated account of its customer in any order convenient to the bank.

PART 4

Relationship Between Payor Bank and Its Customer

§ 4-401. When Bank May Charge Customer's Account.—

(1) As against its customer, a bank may charge against his account any item which is otherwise properly payable from that account even though the charge creates an overdraft.

(2) A bank which in good faith makes payment to a holder may charge the indicated account of its customer according to

(a) the original tenor of his altered item; or

(b) the tenor of his completed item, even though the bank knows the item has been completed unless the bank has notice that the completion was improper.

§ 4-402. Bank's Liability to Customer for Wrongful Dishonor.—A payor bank is liable to its customer for damages proximately caused by the wrongful dishonor of an item. When the dishonor occurs through mistake liability is limited to actual damages proved. If so proximately caused and proved damages may include damages for an arrest or prosecution of the customer or other consequential damages. Whether any consequential damages are proximately caused by the wrongful dishonor is a question of fact to be determined in each case.

§ 4-403. Customer's Right to Stop Payment; Burden of Proof of Loss.—

(1) A customer may by order to his bank stop payment of any item payable for his account but the order must be received at such time and in such manner as to afford the bank a reasonable opportunity to act on it prior to any action by the bank with respect to the item described in Section 4-303.

(2) An oral order is binding upon the bank only for fourteen calendar days unless confirmed in writing within that period. A written order is effective for only six months unless renewed in writing.

(3) The burden of establishing the fact and amount of loss resulting from the payment of an item contrary to a binding stop payment order is on the customer.

§ 4-404. Bank Not Obligated to Pay Check More Than Six Months Old.—A bank is under no obligation to a customer having a checking account to pay a check, other than a certified check, which is presented more than six months after its date, but it may charge its customer's account for a payment made thereafter in good faith.

§ 4-405. Death or Incompetence of Customer.—

(1) A payor or collecting bank's authority to accept, pay or collect an item or to account for proceeds of its collection if otherwise effective is not rendered ineffective by incompetence of a customer of either bank existing at the time the item is issued or its collection undertaken if the bank does not know of an adjudication of incompetence. Neither death nor incompetence of a customer revokes such authority to accept, pay, collect or account until the bank knows of the fact of death or of an adjudication of incompetence and has reasonable opportunity to act on it.

(2) Even with knowledge a bank may for ten days after the date of death pay or certify checks drawn on or prior to that date unless ordered to stop payment by a person claiming an interest in the account.

§ 4-406. Customer's Duty to Discover and Report Unauthorized Signature or Alteration.—

(1) When a bank sends to its customer a statement of account accompanied by items paid in good faith in support of the debit entries or holds the statement and items pursuant to a request or instructions of its customer or otherwise in a reasonable manner makes the statement and items available to the customer, the customer must exercise reasonable care and promptness to examine the statement and items to discover his unauthorized signature or any alteration on an item and must notify the bank promptly after discovery thereof.

(2) If the bank establishes that the customer failed with respect to an item to comply with the duties imposed on the customer by subsection (1) the customer is precluded from asserting against the bank

(a) his unauthorized signature or any alteration on the item if the bank also establishes that it suffered a loss by reason of such failure; and

(b) an unauthorized signature or alteration by the same wrongdoer on any other item paid in good faith by the bank after the first item and statement was available to the customer for a reasonable period not exceeding fourteen calendar days and before the bank receives notification from the customer of any such unauthorized signature or alteration.

(3) The preclusion under subsection (2) does not apply if the customer establishes lack of ordinary care on the part of the bank in paying the item(s).

(4) Without regard to care or lack of care of either the customer or the bank a customer who does not within one year from the time the statement and items are made available to the customer (subsection (1)) discover and report his unauthorized signature or any alteration on the face or back of the item or does not within three years from that time discover and report any unauthorized indorsement is precluded from asserting against the bank such unauthorized signature or endorsement or such alteration.

(5) If under this section a payor bank has a valid defense against a claim of a customer upon or resulting from payment of an item and waives or fails upon request to assert the defense the bank may not assert against any collecting bank or other prior party presenting or transferring the item a claim based upon the unauthorized signature or alteration giving rise to the customer's claim.

§ 4-407. Payor Bank's Right to Subrogation on Improper Payment.—If a payor bank has paid an item over the stop payment order of the drawer or maker or otherwise under circumstances giving a basis for objection by the drawer or maker, to prevent unjust enrichment and only to the extent necessary to prevent loss to the bank by reason of its payment of the item, the payor bank shall be subrogated to the rights

(a) of any holder in due course on the item against the drawer or maker; and

(b) of the payee or any other holder of the item against the drawer or maker either on the item or under the transaction out of which the item arose; and

(c) of the drawer or maker against the payee or any other holder of the item with respect to the transaction out of which the item arose.

Collection of Documentary Drafts

§ 4-501.   Handling of Documentary Drafts; Duty to Send for Presentment and to Notify Customer of Dishonor.—A bank which takes a documentary draft for collection must present or send the draft and accompanying documents for presentment and upon learning that the draft has not been paid or accepted in due course must seasonably notify its customer of such fact even though it may have discounted or bought the draft or extended credit available for withdrawal as of right.

§ 4-502.   Presentment of "On Arrival" Drafts.—When a draft or the relevant instructions require presentment "on arrival", "when goods arrive" or the like, the collection bank need not present until in its judgment a reasonable time for arrival of the goods has expired. Refusal to pay or accept because the goods have not arrived is not dishonor; the bank must notify its transferor of such refusal but need not present the draft again until it is instructed to do so or learns of the arrival of the goods.

§ 4-503.   Responsibility of Presenting Bank for Documents and Goods; Report of Reasons for Dishonor; Referee in Case of Need.—Unless otherwise instructed and except as provided in Article 5 a bank presenting a documentary draft

(a) must deliver the documents to the drawee on acceptance of the draft if it is payable more than three days after presentment; otherwise, only on payment; and

(b) upon dishonor, either in the case of presentment for acceptance or presentment for payment, may seek and follow instructions from any referee in case of need designated in the draft or if the presenting bank does not choose to utilize his services it must use diligence and good faith to ascertain the reason for dishonor, must notify its transferor of the dishonor and of the results of its effort to ascertain the reasons therefor and must request instructions.

But the presenting bank is under no obligation with respect to goods represented by the documents except to follow any reasonable instructions seasonably received; it has a right to reimbursement for any expense incurred in following instructions and to prepayment of or indemnity for such expenses.

§ 4-504.   Privilege of Presenting Bank to Deal With Goods; Security Interest for Expenses.—

(1) A presenting bank which, following the dishonor of a documentary draft, has seasonably requested instructions but does not receive them within a reasonable time may store, sell, or otherwise deal with the goods in any reasonable manner.

(2) For its reasonable expenses incurred by action under subsection (1) the presenting bank has a lien upon the goods or their proceeds, which may be forclosed in the same manner as an unpaid seller's lien.

ARTICLE FIVE—LETTERS OF CREDIT

§ 5-101.   Short Title.—This Article shall be known and may be cited as Uniform Commercial Code—Letters of Credit.

§ 5-102.   Scope.—

(1) This Article applies

(a) to a credit issued by a bank if the credit requires a documentary draft or a documentary demand for payment; and

(b) to a credit issued by a person other than a bank if the credit requires that the draft or demand for payment be accompanied by a document of title; and

(c) to a credit issued by a bank or other person if the credit is not within subparagraphs (a) or (b) but conspicuously states that it is a letter of credit or is conspicuously so entitled.

. . . [The remaining portion of this article omitted as it contains materials not usually covered in Business Law.]

ARTICLE SIX—BULK TRANSFERS

§ 6-101.   Short Title.—This Article shall be known and may be cited as Uniform Commercial Code—Bulk Transfers.

§ 6-102.   "Bulk Transfer"; Transfers of Equipment; Enterprises Subject to This Article; Bulk Transfers Subject to This Article.—

(1) A "bulk transfer" is any transfer in bulk and not in the ordinary course of the transferor's business of a major part of the materials, supplies, merchandise or other inventory (Section 9-109) of an enterprise subject to this Article.

(2) A transfer of a substantial part of the equipment (Section 9-109) of such an enterprise is a bulk transfer if it is made in connection with a bulk transfer of inventory, but not otherwise.

(3) The enterprises subject to this Article are all those whose principal business is the sale of merchandise from stock, including those who manufacture what they sell.

(4) Except as limited by the following section all bulk transfers of goods located within this State are subject to this Article.

§ 6-103. Transfers Excepted From This Article.—The following transfers are not subject to this Article:

(1) Those made to give security for the performance of an obligation;

(2) General assignments for the benefit of all the creditors of the transferor, and subsequent transfers by the assignee thereunder;

(3) Transfers in settlement or realization of alien or other security interests;

(4) Sales by executors, administrators, receivers, trustees in bankruptcy, or any public offer under judicial process;

(5) Sales made in the course of judicial or administrative proceedings for the dissolution or reorganization of a corporation and of which notice is sent to the creditors of the corporation pursuant to order of the court or administrative agency;

(6) Transfers to a person maintaining a known place of business in this State who becomes bound to pay the debts of the transferor in full and gives public notice of that fact, and who is solvent after becoming so bound;

(7) A transfer to a new business enterprise organized to take over and continue the business, if public notice of the transaction is given and the new enterprise assumes the debts of the transferor and he receives nothing from the transaction except an interest in the new enterprise junior to the claims of creditors;

(8) Transfers of property which is exempt from execution.

§ 6-104. Schedule of Property, List of Creditors.—

(1) Except as provided with respect to auction sales (Section 6-108), a bulk transfer subject to this Article is ineffective against any creditor of the transferor unless:

(a) The transferee requires the transferor to furnish a list of his existing creditors prepared as stated in this section; and

(b) The parties prepare a schedule of the property transferred sufficient to identify it; and

(c) The transferee preserves the list and schedule for six months next following the transfer and permits inspection of either or both and copying therefrom at all reasonable hours by any creditor of the transferor, or files the list and schedule in *(a public office to be here identified).*

(2) The list of creditors must be signed and sworn to or affirmed by the transferor or his agent. It must contain the names and business addresses of all creditors of the transferor, with the amounts when known, and also the names of all persons who are known to the transferor to assert claims against him even though such claims are disputed.

(3) Responsibility for the completeness and accuracy of the list of creditors rests on the transferor, and the transfer is not rendered ineffective by errors or omissions therein unless the transferee is shown to have had knowledge.

§ 6-105. Notice to Creditors.—In addition to the requirements of the preceding section, any bulk transfer subject to this Article except one made by auction sale (Section 6-108) is ineffective against any creditor of the transferor unless at least ten days before he takes possession of the goods or pays for them, whichever happens first, the transferee gives notice of the transfer in the manner and to the persons hereafter provided (Section 6-107).

[§ 6-106. Application of the Proceeds.—In addition to the requirements of the two preceding sections:

(1) Upon every bulk transfer subject to this Article for which new consideration becomes payable except those made by sale at auction it is the duty of the transferee to assure that such consideration is applied so far as necessary to pay those debts of the transferor which are either shown on the list furnished by the transferor (Section 6-104) or filed in writing in the place stated in the notice (Section 6-107) within thirty days after the mailing of such notice. This duty of the transferee runs to all the holders of such debts, and may be enforced by any of them for the benefit of all.

(2) If any of said debts are in dispute the necessary sum may be withheld from distribution until the dispute is settled or adjudicated.

(3) If the consideration payable is not enough to pay all of the said debts in full distribution shall be made pro rata.]

Note: *This section is bracketed to indicate division of opinion as to whether or not it is a wise provision, and to suggest that this is a point on which State enactments may differ without serious damage to the principle of uniformity.*

In any State where this section is omitted, the following parts of sections, also bracketed in the text, should also be omitted, namely:

Section 6-107(2)(e).

6-108(3)(c).

6-109(2).

In any State where this section is enacted, these other provisions should be also.

§ 6-107. The Notice.—

(1) The notice to creditors (Section 6-105) shall state:

(a) that a bulk transfer is about to be made; and

(b) the names and business addresses of the transferor and transferee, and all other business names and addresses used by the transferor within three years last past so far as known to the transferee; and

(c) whether or not all the debts of the transferor are to be paid in full as they fall due as a result of the transaction, and if so, the address to which creditors should send their bills.

(2) If the debts of the transferor are not to be paid in full as they fall due or if the transferee is in doubt on that point then the notice shall state further:

(a) the location and general description of the property to be transferred and the estimated total of the transferor's debts;

(b) the address where the schedule of property and list of creditors (Section 6-104) may be inspected;

(c) whether the transfer is to pay existing debts and if so the amount of such debts and to whom owing;

(d) whether the transfer is for new consideration and if so the amount of such consideration and the time and place of payment; and

[(e) if for new consideration the time and place where creditors of the transferor are to file their claims.]

(3) The notice in any case shall be delivered personally or sent by registered mail to all the persons shown on the list of creditors furnished by the transferor (Section 6-104) and to all other persons who are known to the transferee to hold or assert claims against the transferor.

§ 6-108. Auction Sales; "Auctioneer".—

(1) A bulk transfer is subject to this Article even though it is by sale at auction, but only in the manner and with the results stated in this section.

(2) The transferor shall furnish a list of his creditors and assist in the preparation of a schedule of the property to be sold, both prepared as before stated (Section 6-104).

(3) The person or persons other than the transferor who direct, control or are responsible for the auction are collectively called the "auctioneer". The auctioneer shall:

(a) receive and retain the list of creditors and prepare and retain the schedule of property for the period stated in this Article (Section 6-104);

(b) give notice of the auction personally or by registered mail at least ten days before it occurs to all persons shown on the list of creditors and to all other persons who are known to him to hold or assert claims against the transferor; [and]

[(c) assure that the net proceeds of the auction are applied as provided in this Article (Section 6-106).]

(4) Failure of the auctioneer to perform any of these duties does not affect the validity of the sale or the title of the purchasers, but if the auctioneer knows that the auction constitutes a bulk transfer such failure renders the auctioneer liable to the creditors of the transferor as a class for the sums owing to them from the transferor up to but not exceeding the net proceeds of the auction. If the auctioneer consists of several persons their liability is joint and several.

§ 6-109. What Creditors Protected.—

(1) The creditors of the transferor mentioned in this Article are those holding claims based on transactions occurring before the bulk transfer, but creditors who become such after notice to creditors is given (Sections 6-105 and 6-107) are not entitled to notice.

[(2) Against the aggregate obligation imposed by the provisions of this Article concerning the application of the proceeds (Section 6-106 and subsection (3)(c) of 6-108) the transferee or auctioneer is entitled to credit for sums paid to particular creditors of the transferor, not exceeding the sums believed in good faith at the time of the payment to be properly payable to such creditors.]

§ 6-110. Subsequent Transfers.—When the title of a transferee to property is subject to a defect by reason of his noncompliance with the requirements of this Article, then:

(1) a purchaser of any such property from such transferee who pays no value or who takes with notice of such noncompliance takes subject to such defect, but

(2) a purchaser for value in good faith and without such notice takes free of such defect.

§ 6-111. Limitation of Actions and Levies.—No action under this article shall be brought nor levy made more than six months after the date on which the transferee took possession of the goods unless the transfer has been concealed. If the transfer has been concealed, actions may be brought or levies made within six months after its discovery.

Note to Article 6: *Section 6-106 is bracketed to indicate division of opinion as to whether or not it is a wise provision and to suggest that this is a point on which State enactments may differ without serious damage to the principal of uniformity.*

In any State where Section 6-106 is not enacted, the following parts of sections, also bracketed in the text, should also be omitted, namely:

Sec. 6-107(2)(e)
6-108(3)(c)
6-109(2).

In any State where Section 6-106 is enacted, these other provisions should be also.

PART 1

General

§ 7-101. Short Title.—This Article shall be known and may be cited as Uniform Commercial Code—Documents of Title.

. . . [The remaining portion of this article omitted as it contains material not usually covered in Business Law.]

ARTICLE EIGHT—INVESTMENT SECURITIES

PART 1

Short Title and General Matters

§ 8—101. Short Title.—This Article shall be known and may be cited as Uniform Commercial Code—Investment Securities.

§ 8—102. Definitions and Index of Definitions.

(1) In this Article, unless the context otherwise requires:

(a) A "certificated security" is a share, participation, or other interest in property of or an enterprise of the issuer or an obligation of the issuer which is

(i) represented by an instrument issued in bearer or registered form;

(ii) of a type commonly dealt in on securities exchanges or markets or commonly recognized in any area in which it is issued or dealt in as a medium for investment; and

(iii) either one of a class or series or by its terms divisible into a class or series of shares, participations, interests, or obligations.

(b) An "uncertificated security" is a share, participation, or other interest in property or an enterprise of the issuer or an obligation of the issuer which is

(i) not represented by an instrument and the transfer of which is registered upon books maintained for that purpose by or on behalf of the issuer;

(ii) of a type commonly dealt in on securities exchanges or markets; and

(iii) either one of a class or series or by its terms divisible into a class or series of shares, participations, interests, or obligations.

(c) A "security" is either a certificated or an uncertificated security. If a security is certificated, the terms "security" and "certificated security" may mean either the intangible interest, the instrument representing that interest, or both, as the context requires. A writing that is a certificated security is governed by this Article and not by Article 3, even though it also meets the requirements of that Article. This Article does not apply to money. If a certificated security has been retained by or surrendered to the issuer or its transfer agent for reasons other than registration of transfer, other temporary purpose, payment, exchange, or acquisition by the issuer, that security shall be treated as an uncertificated security for purposes of this Article.

(d) A certificated security is in "registered form" if

(i) it specifies a person entitled to the security or the rights it represents; and

(ii) its transfer may be registered upon books maintained for that purpose by or on behalf of the issuer, or the security so states.

(e) A certificated security is in "bearer form" if it runs to bearer according to its terms and not by reason of any indorsement.

(2) A "subsequent purchaser" is a person who takes other than by original issue.

(3) A "clearing corporation" is a corporation registered as a "clearing agency" under the federal securities laws or a corporation:

(a) at least 90 percent of whose capital stock is held by or for one or more organizations, none of which, other than a national securities exchange or association, holds in excess of 20 percent of the capital stock of the corporation, and each of which is

(i) subject to supervision or regulation pursuant to the provisions of federal or state banking laws or state insurance laws,

(ii) a broker or dealer or investment company registered under the federal securities laws, or

(iii) a national securities exchange or association registered under the federal securities laws; and

(b) any remaining capital stock of which is held by individuals who have purchased it at or prior to the time of their taking office as directors of the corporation and who have purchased only so much of the capital stock as is necessary to permit them to qualify as directors.

(4) A "custodian bank" is a bank or trust company that is supervised and examined by state or federal authority having supervision over banks and is acting as custodian for a clearing corporation.

(5) Other definitions applying to this Article or to specified Parts thereof and the sections in which they appear are:

"Adverse claim". Section 8—302.
"Bona fide purchaser". Section 8—302.
"Broker". Section 8—303.
"Debtor". Section 9—105.
"Financial intermediary". Section 8—313.
"Guarantee of the signature". Section 8—402.
"Initial transaction statement". Section 8—408.
"Instruction". Section 8—308.
"Intermediary bank". Section 4—105.
"Issuer". Section 8—201.
"Overissue". Section 8—104.
"Secured Party". Section 9—105.
"Security Agreement". Section 9—105.

(6) In addition, Article 1 contains general definitions and principles of construction and interpretation applicable throughout this Article.

§ 8—103. Issuer's Lien.—A lien upon a security in favor of an issuer thereof is valid against a purchaser only if:

(a) the security is certificated and the right of the issuer to the lien is noted conspicuously thereon; or

(b) the security is uncertificated and a notation of the right of the issuer to the lien is contained in the initial transaction statement sent to the purchaser or, if his interest is transferred to him other than by registration of transfer, pledge, or release, the initial transaction statement sent to the registered owner or the registered pledgee.

§ 8—104. Effect of Overissue; "Overissue".

(1) The provisions of this Article which validate a security or compel its issue or reissue do not apply to the extent that validation, issue, or reissue would result in overissue; but if:

(a) an identical security which does not constitute an overissue is reasonably available for purchase, the person entitled to issue or validation may compel the issuer to purchase the security for him and either to deliver a certificated security or to register the transfer of an uncertificated security to him, against surrender of any certificated security he holds; or

(b) a security is not so available for purchase, the person entitled to issue or validation may recover from the issuer the price he or the last purchaser for value paid for it with interest from the date of his demand.

(2) "Overissue" means the issue of securities in excess of the amount the issuer has corporate power to issue.

§ 8—105. Certificated Securities Negotiable; Statements and Instructions Not Negotiable; Presumptions.

(1) Certificated securities governed by this Article are negotiable instruments.

(2) Statements (Section 8—408), notices, or the like, sent by the issuer of uncertificated securities and instructions (Section 8—308) are neither negotiable instruments nor certificated securities.

(3) In any action on a security:

(a) unless specifically denied in the pleadings, each signature on a certificated security, in a necessary indorsement, on an initial transaction statement, or on an instruction, is admitted;

(b) if the effectiveness of a signature is put in issue, the burden of establishing it is on the party claiming under the signature, but the signature is presumed to be genuine or authorized;

(c) if signatures on a certificated security are admitted or established, production of the security entitles a holder to recover on it unless the defendant establishes a defense or a defect going to the validity of the security;

(d) if signatures on an initial transaction statement are admitted or established, the facts stated in the statement are presumed to be true as of the time of its issuance; and

(e) after it is shown that a defense or defect exists, the plaintiff has the burden of establishing that he or some person under whom he claims is a person against whom the defense or defect is ineffective (Section 8—202).

§ 8—106. Applicability.—The law (including the conflict of laws rules) of the jurisdiction of organization of the issuer governs the validity of a security, the effectiveness of registration by the issuer, and the rights and duties of the issuer with respect to:

(a) registration of transfer of a certificated security;

(b) registration of transfer, pledge, or release of an uncertificated security; and

(c) sending of statements of uncertificated securities.

§ 8—107. Securities Transferable; Action for Price.

(1) Unless otherwise agreed and subject to any applicable law or regulation respecting short sales, a person obligated to transfer securities may transfer any certificated security of the specified issue in bearer form or registered in the name of the transferee, or indorsed to him or in blank, or he may transfer an equivalent uncertificated security to the transferee or a person designated by the transferee.

(2) If the buyer fails to pay the price as it comes due under a contract of sale, the seller may recover the price of:

(a) certificated securities accepted by the buyer;

(b) uncertificated securities that have been transferred to the buyer or a person designated by the buyer; and

(c) other securities if efforts at their resale would be unduly burdensome or if there is no readily available market for their resale.

§ 8—108. Registration of Pledge and Release of Uncertificated Securities.—A security interest in an uncertificated security may be evidenced by the registration of pledge to the secured party or a person designated by him. There can be no more than one registered pledge of an uncertificated security at any time. The registered owner of an uncertificated security is the person in whose name the security is registered, even if the security is subject to a

registered pledge. The rights of a registered pledgee of an uncertificated security under this Article are terminated by the registration of release.

PART 2

Issue—Issuer

§ 8—201. "Issuer."

(1) With respect to obligations on or defenses to a security, "issuer" includes a person who:

(a) places or authorizes the placing of his name on a certificated security (otherwise than as authenticating trustee, registrar, transfer agent, or the like) to evidence that it represents a share, participation, or other interest in his property or in an enterprise, or to evidence his duty to perform an obligation represented by the certificated security;

(b) creates shares, participations, or other interests in his property or in an enterprise or undertakes obligations, which shares, participations, interests, or obligations are uncertificated securities;

(c) directly or indirectly creates fractional interests in his rights or property, which fractional interests are represented by certificated securities; or

(d) becomes responsible for or in place of any other person described as an issuer in this section.

(2) With respect to obligations on or defenses to a security, a guarantor is an issuer to the extent of his guaranty, whether or not his obligation is noted on a certificated security or on statements of uncertificated securities sent pursuant to Section 8—408.

(3) With respect to registration of transfer, pledge, or release (Part 4 of this Article), "issuer" means a person on whose behalf transfer books are maintained.

§ 8—202. Issuer's Responsibility and Defenses; Notice of Defect or Defense.

(1) Even against a purchaser for value and without notice, the terms of a security include:

(a) if the security is certificated, those stated on the security;

(b) if the security is uncertificated, those contained in the initial transaction statement sent to such purchaser or, if his interest is transferred to him other than by registration of transfer, pledge, or release, the initial transaction statement sent to the registered owner or registered pledgee; and

(c) those made part of the security by reference, on the certificated security or in the initial transaction statement, to another instrument, indenture, or document or to a constitution, statute, ordinance, rule, regulation, order or the like, to the extent that the terms referred to do not conflict with the terms stated on the certificated security or contained in the statement. A reference under this paragraph does not of itself charge a purchaser for value with notice of a defect going to the validity of the security, even though the certificated security or statement expressly states that a person accepting it admits notice.

(2) A certificated security in the hands of a purchaser for value or an uncertificated security as to which an initial transaction statement has been sent to a purchaser for value, other than a security issued by a government or governmental agency or unit, even though issued with a defect going to its validity, is valid with respect to the purchaser if he is without notice of the particular defect unless the defect involves a violation of constitutional provisions, in which case the security is valid with respect to a subsequent purchaser for value and without notice of the defect. This subsection applies to an issuer that is a government or governmental agency or unit only if either there has been substantial compliance with the legal requirements governing the issue or the issuer has received a substantial consideration for the issue as a whole or for the particular security and a stated purpose of the issue is one for which the issuer has power to borrow money or issue the security.

(3) Except as provided in the case of certain unauthorized signatures (Section 8—205), lack of genuineness of a certificated security or an initial transaction statement is a complete defense, even against a purchaser for value and without notice.

(4) All other defenses of the issuer of a certificated or uncertificated security, including nondelivery and conditional delivery of a certificated security, are ineffective against a purchaser for value who has taken without notice of the particular defense.

(5) Nothing in this section shall be construed to affect the right of a party to a "when, as and if issued" or a "when distributed" contract to cancel the contract in the event of a material change in the character of the security that is the subject of the contract or in the plan or arrangement pursuant to which the security is to be issued or distributed.

§ 8—203. Staleness as Notice of Defects or Defenses.

(1) After an act or event creating a right to immediate performance of the principal obligation represented by a certificated security or that sets a date on or after which the security is to be presented or surrendered for redemption or exchange, a purchaser is charged with notice of any defect in its issue or defense of the issuer if:

(a) the act or event is one requiring the payment of money, the delivery of certificated securities, the registration of transfer of uncertificated securities, or any of these on presentation or surrender of the certificated security, the funds or securities are available on the date set for payment or exchange, and he takes the security more than one year after that date; and

(b) the act or event is not covered by paragraph (a) and he takes the security more than 2 years after the date set for surrender or presentation or the date on which performance became due.

(2) A call that has been revoked is not within subsection (1).

§ 8—204. Effect of Issuer's Restrictions on Transfer.—A restriction on transfer of a security imposed by the issuer, even if otherwise lawful, is ineffective against any person without actual knowledge of it unless:

(a) the security is certificated and the restriction is noted conspicuously thereon; or

(b) the security is uncertificated and a notation of the restriction is contained in the initial transaction statement sent to the person or, if his interest is transferred to him other than by registration of transfer, pledge, or release, the initial transaction statement sent to the registered owner or the registered pledgee.

§ 8—205. Effect of Unauthorized Signature on Certificated Security or Initial Transaction Statement.

—An unauthorized signature placed on a certificated security prior to or in the course of issue or placed on an initial transaction statement is ineffective, but the signature is effective in favor of a purchaser for value of the certificated security or a purchaser for value of an uncertificated security to whom the initial transaction statement has been sent, if the purchaser is without notice of the lack of authority and the signing has been done by:

(a) an authenticating trustee, registrar, transfer agent, or other person entrusted by the issuer with the signing of the security, of similar securities, or of initial transaction statements or the immediate preparation for signing of any of them; or

(b) an employee of the issuer, or of any of the foregoing, entrusted with responsible handling of the security or initial transaction statement.

§ 8—206. Completion or Alteration of Certificated Security or Initial Transaction Statement.

(1) If a certificated security contains the signatures necessary to its issue or transfer but is incomplete in any other respect:

(a) any person may complete it by filling in the blanks as authorized; and

(b) even though the blanks are incorrectly filled in, the security as completed is enforceable by a purchaser who took it for value and without notice of the incorrectness.

(2) A complete certificated security that has been improperly altered, even though fraudulently, remains enforceable, but only according to its original terms.

(3) If an initial transaction statement contains the signatures necessary to its validity, but is incomplete in any other respect:

(a) any person may complete it by filling in the blanks as authorized; and

(b) even though the blanks are incorrectly filled in, the statement as completed is effective in favor of the person to whom it is sent if he purchased the security referred to therein for value and without notice of the incorrectness.

(4) A complete initial transaction statement that has been improperly altered, even though fraudulently, is effective in favor of a purchaser to whom it has been sent, but only according to its original terms.

§ 8—207. Rights and Duties of Issuer With Respect to Registered Owners and Registered Pledgees.

(1) Prior to due presentment for registration of transfer of a certificated security in registered form, the issuer or indenture trustee may treat the registered owner as the person exclusively entitled to vote, to receive notifications, and otherwise to exercise all the rights and powers of an owner.

(2) Subject to the provisions of subsections (3), (4), and (6), the issuer or indenture trustee may treat the registered owner of an uncertificated security as the person exclusively entitled to vote, to receive notifications, and otherwise to exercise all the rights and powers of an owner.

(3) The registered owner of an uncertificated security that is subject to a registered pledge is not entitled to registration of transfer prior to the due presentment to the issuer of a release instruction. The exercise of conversion rights with respect to a convertible uncertificated security is a transfer within the meaning of this section.

(4) Upon due presentment of a transfer instruction from the registered pledgee of an uncertificated security, the issuer shall:

(a) register the transfer of the security to the new owner free of pledge, if the instruction specifies a new owner (who may be the registered pledgee) and does not specify a pledgee;

(b) register the transfer of the security to the new owner subject to the interest of the existing pledgee, if the instruction specifies a new owner and the existing pledgee; or

(c) register the release of the security from the existing pledge and register the pledge of the security to the other pledgee, if the instruction specifies the existing owner and another pledgee.

(5) Continuity of perfection of a security interest is not broken by registration of transfer under subsection (4)(b) or by registration of release and pledge under subsection (4)(c), if the security interest is assigned.

(6) If an uncertificated security is subject to a registered pledge:

(a) any uncertificated securities issued in exchange for or distributed with respect to the pledged security shall be registered subject to the pledge;

(b) any certificated securities issued in exchange for or distributed with respect to the pledged security shall be delivered to the registered pledgee; and

(c) any money paid in exchange for or in redemption of part or all of the security shall be paid to the registered pledgee.

(7) Nothing in this Article shall be construed to affect the liability of the registered owner of a security for calls, assessments, or the like.

§ 8—208. Effect of Signature of Authenticating Trustee, Registrar, or Transfer Agent.

(1) A person placing his signature upon a certificated security or an initial transaction statement as authenticating trustee, registrar, transfer agent, or the like, warrants to a purchaser for value of the certificated security or a purchaser for value of an uncertificated security to whom the initial transaction statement has been sent, if the purchaser is without notice of the particular defect, that:

(a) the certificated security or initial transaction statement is genuine;

(b) his own participation in the issue or registration of the transfer, pledge, or release of the security is within his capacity and within the scope of the authority received by him from the issuer; and

(c) he has reasonable grounds to believe the security is in the form and within the amount the issuer is authorized to issue.

(2) Unless otherwise agreed, a person by so placing his signature does not assume responsibility for the validity of the security in other respects.

Transfer

§ 8—301. Rights Acquired by Purchaser.

(1) Upon transfer of a security to a purchaser (Section 8—313), the purchaser acquires the rights in the security which his transferor had or had actual authority to convey unless the purchaser's rights are limited by Section 8—302(4).

(2) A transferee of a limited interest acquires rights only to the extent of the interest transferred. The creation or release of a security interest in a security is the transfer of a limited interest in that security.

§ 8—302. "Bona Fide Purchaser"; "Adverse Claim"; Title Acquired by Bona Fide Purchaser.

(1) A "bona fide purchaser" is a purchaser for value in good faith and without notice of any adverse claim:

(a) who takes delivery of a certificated security in bearer form or in registered form, issued or indorsed to him or in blank;

(b) to whom the transfer, pledge, or release of an uncertificated security is registered on the books of the issuer; or

(c) to whom a security is transferred under the provisions of paragraph (c), (d)(i), or (g) of Section 8—313(1).

§ 8—303. "Broker".—"Broker" means a person engaged for all or part of his time in the business of buying and selling securities, who in the transaction concerned acts for, buys a security from, or sells a security to, a customer. Nothing in this Article determines the capacity in which a person acts for purposes of any other statute or rule to which the person is subject.

§ 8—304. Notice to Purchaser of Adverse Claims.

(1) A purchaser (including a broker for the seller or buyer, but excluding an intermediary bank) of a certificated security is charged with notice of adverse claims if:

(a) the security, whether in bearer or registered form, has been indorsed "for collection" or "for surrender" or for some other purpose not involving transfer; or

(b) the security is in bearer form and has on it an unambiguous statement that it is the property of a person other than the transferor. The mere writing of a name on a security is not such a statement.

(2) A purchaser (including a broker for the seller or buyer, but excluding an intermediary bank) to whom the transfer, pledge, or release of an uncertificated security is registered is charged with notice of adverse claims as to which the issuer has a duty under Section 8—403(4) at the time of registration and which are noted in the initial transaction statement sent to the purchaser or, if his interest is transferred to him other than by registration of transfer, pledge, or release, the initial transaction statement sent to the registered owner or the registered pledgee.

(3) The fact that the purchaser (including a broker for the seller or buyer) of a certificated or uncertificated security has notice that the security is held for a third person or is registered in the name of or indorsed by a fiduciary does not create a duty of inquiry into the rightfulness of the transfer or constitute constructive notice of adverse claims. However, if the purchaser (excluding an intermediary bank) has knowledge that the proceeds are being used or the transaction is for the individual benefit of the fiduciary or otherwise in breach of duty, the purchaser is charged with notice of adverse claims.

§ 8—305. Staleness as Notice of Adverse Claims.—An act or event that creates a right to immediate performance of the principal obligation represented by a certificated security or sets a date on or after which a certificated security is to be presented or surrendered for redemption or exchange does not itself constitute any notice of adverse claims except in the case of a transfer:

(a) after one year from any date set for presentment or surrender for redemption or exchange; or

(b) after 6 months from any date set for payment of money against presentation or surrender of the security if funds are available for payment on that date.

§ 8—306. Warranties on Presentment and Transfer of Certificated Securities; Warranties of Originators of Instructions.

(1) A person who presents a certificated security for registration of transfer or for payment or exchange warrants to the issuer that he is entitled to the registration, payment, or exchange. But, a purchaser for value and without notice of adverse claims who receives a new, reissued, or re-registered certificated security on registration of transfer or receives an initial transaction statement confirming the registration of transfer of an equivalent uncertificated security to him warrants only that he has no knowledge of any unauthorized signature (Section 8—311) in a necessary indorsement.

(2) A person by transferring a certificated security to a purchaser for value warrants only that:

(a) his transfer is effective and rightful;

(b) the security is genuine and has not been materially altered; and

(c) he knows of no fact which might impair the validity of the security.

(3) If a certificated security is delivered by an intermediary known to be entrusted with delivery of the security on behalf of another or with collection of a draft or other claim against delivery, the intermediary by delivery warrants only his own good faith and authority, even though he has purchased or made advances against the claim to be collected against the delivery.

(4) A pledgee or other holder for security who redelivers a certificated security received, or after payment and on order of the debtor delivers that security to a third person, makes only the warranties of an intermediary under subsection (3).

(5) A person who originates an instruction warrants to the issuer that:

(a) he is an appropriate person to originate the instruction; and

(b) at the time the instruction is presented to the issuer he will be entitled to the registration of transfer, pledge, or release.

(6) A person who originates an instruction warrants to any person specially guaranteeing his signature (subsection 8—312(3)) that:

(a) he is an appropriate person to originate the instruction; and

(b) at the time the instruction is presented to the issuer

(i) he will be entitled to the registration of transfer, pledge, or release; and

(ii) the transfer, pledge, or release requested in the instruction will be registered by the issuer free from all liens, security interests, restrictions, and claims other than those specified in the instruction.

(7) A person who originates an instruction warrants to a purchaser for value and to any person guaranteeing the instruction (Section 8—312(6)) that:

(a) he is an appropriate person to originate the instruction;

(b) the uncertificated security referred to therein is valid; and

(c) at the time the instruction is presented to the issuer

(i) the transferor will be entitled to the registration of transfer, pledge, or release;

(ii) the transfer, pledge, or release requested in the instruction will be registered by the issuer free from all liens, security interests, restrictions, and claims other than those specified in the instruction; and

(iii) the requested transfer, pledge, or release will be rightful.

(8) If a secured party is the registered pledgee or the registered owner of an uncertificated security, a person who originates an instruction of release or transfer to the debtor or, after payment and on order of the debtor, a transfer instruction to a third person, warrants to the debtor or the third person only that he is an appropriate person to originate the instruction and, at the time the instruction is presented to the issuer, the transferor will be entitled to the registration of release or transfer. If a transfer instruction to a third person who is a purchaser for value is originated on order of the debtor, the debtor makes to the purchaser the warranties of paragraphs (b), (c)(ii) and (c)(iii) of subsection (7).

(9) A person who transfers an uncertificated security to a purchaser for value and does not originate an instruction in connection with the transfer warrants only that:

(a) his transfer is effective and rightful; and

(b) the uncertificated security is valid.

(10) A broker gives to his customer and to the issuer and a purchaser the applicable warranties provided in this section and has the rights and privileges of a purchaser under this section. The warranties of and in favor of the broker, acting as an agent are in addition to applicable warranties given by and in favor of his customer.

§ 8—307. Effect of Delivery Without Indorsement; Right to Compel Indorsement.—If a certificated security in registered form has been delivered to a purchaser without a necessary indorsement he may become a bona fide purchaser only as of the time the indorsement is supplied; but against the transferor, the transfer is complete upon delivery and the purchaser has a specifically enforceable right to have any necessary indorsement supplied.

§ 8—308. Indorsements; Instructions.

(1) An indorsement of a certificated security in registered form is made when an appropriate person signs on it or on a separate document an assignment or transfer of the security or a power to assign or transfer it or his signature is written without more upon the back of the security.

(2) An indorsement may be in blank or special. An indorsement in blank includes an indorsement to bearer. A special indorsement specifies to whom the security is to be transferred, or who has power to transfer it. A holder may convert a blank indorsement into a special indorsement.

(3) An indorsement purporting to be only of part of a certificated security representing units intended by the issuer to be separately transferable is effective to the extent of the indorsement.

(4) An "instruction" is an order to the issuer of an uncertificated security requesting that the transfer, pledge, or release from pledge of the uncertificated security specified therein be registered.

(5) An instruction originated by an appropriate person is:

(a) a writing signed by an appropriate person; or

(b) a communication to the issuer in any form agreed upon in a writing signed by the issuer and an appropriate person.

If an instruction has been originated by an appropriate person but is incomplete in any other respect, any person may complete it as authorized and the issuer may rely on it as completed even though it has been completed incorrectly.

(6) "An appropriate person" in subsection (1) means the person specified by the certificated security or by special indorsement to be entitled to the security.

(7) "An appropriate person" in subsection (5) means:

(a) for an instruction to transfer or pledge an uncertificated security which is then not subject to a registered pledge, the registered owner; or

(b) for an instruction to transfer or release an uncertificated security which is then subject to a registered pledge, the registered pledgee.

(8) In addition to the persons designated in subsections (6) and (7), "an appropriate person" in subsections (1) and (5) includes:

(a) if the person designated is described as a fiduciary but is no longer serving in the described capacity, either that person or his successor;

(b) if the persons designated are described as more than one person as fiduciaries and one or more are no longer serving in the described capacity, the remaining fiduciary or fiduciaries, whether or not a successor has been appointed or qualified;

(c) if the person designated is an individual and is without capacity to act by virtue of death, incompetence, infancy, or otherwise, his executor, administrator, guardian, or like fiduciary;

(d) if the persons designated are described as more than one person as tenants by the entirety or with right of survivorship and by reason of death all cannot sign, the survivor or survivors;

(e) a person having power to sign under applicable law or controlling instrument; and

(f) to the extent that the person designated or any of the foregoing persons may act through an agent, his authorized agent.

(9) Unless otherwise agreed, the indorser of a certificated security by his indorsement or the originator of an instruction by his origination assumes no obligation that the security will be honored by the issuer but only the obligations provided in Section 8—306.

(10) Whether the person signing is appropriate is determined as of the date of signing and an indorsement made by or an instruction originated by him does not become unauthorized for the purposes of this Article by virtue of any subsequent change of circumstances.

(11) Failure of a fiduciary to comply with a controlling instrument or with the law of the state having jurisdiction of the fiduciary relationship, including any law requiring the fiduciary to obtain court approval of the transfer, pledge, or release, does not render his indorsement or an instruction originated by him unauthorized for the purposes of this Article.

§ 8—309. Effect of Indorsement Without Delivery.—An indorsement of a certificated security, whether special or in blank, does not constitute a transfer until delivery of the certificated security on which it appears or, if the indorsement is on a separate document, until delivery of both the document and the certificated security.

§ 8—310. Indorsement of Certificated Security in Bearer Form.—An indorsement of a certificated security in bearer form may give notice of adverse claims (Section 8—304) but does not otherwise affect any right to registration the holder possesses.

§ 8—311. Effect of Unauthorized Indorsement or Instruction.—Unless the owner or pledgee has ratified an unauthorized indorsement or instruction or is otherwise precluded from asserting its ineffectiveness:

(a) he may assert its ineffectiveness against the issuer or any purchaser, other than a purchaser for value and without notice of adverse claims, who has in good faith received a new, reissued, or re-registered certificated security on registration of transfer or received an initial transaction statement confirming the registration of transfer, pledge, or release of an equivalent uncertificated security to him; and

(b) an issuer who registers the transfer of a certificated security upon the unauthorized indorsement or who registers the transfer, pledge, or release of an uncertificated security upon the unauthorized instruction is subject to liability for improper registration (Section 8—404).

§ 8—312. Effect of Guaranteeing Signature, Indorsement or Instruction.

(1) Any person guaranteeing a signature of an indorser of a certificated security warrants that at the time of signing:

(a) the signature was genuine;

(b) the signer was an appropriate person to indorse (Section 8—308); and

(c) the signer had legal capacity to sign.

(2) Any person guaranteeing a signature of the originator of an instruction warrants that at the time of signing:

(a) the signature was genuine;

(b) the signer was an appropriate person to originate the instruction (Section 8—308) if the person specified in the instruction as the registered owner or registered pledgee of the uncertificated security was, in fact, the registered owner or registered pledgee of the security, as to which fact the signature guarantor makes no warranty;

(c) the signer had legal capacity to sign; and

(d) the taxpayer identification number, if any, appearing on the instruction as that of the registered owner or registered pledgee was the taxpayer identification number of the signer or of the owner or pledgee for whom the signer was acting.

(3) Any person specially guaranteeing the signature of the originator of an instruction makes not only the warranties of a signature guarantor (subsection (2)) but also warrants that at the time the instruction is presented to the issuer:

(a) the person specified in the instruction as the registered owner or registered pledgee of the uncertificated security will be the registered owner or registered pledgee; and

(b) the transfer, pledge, or release of the uncertificated security requested in the instruction will be registered by the issuer free from all liens, security interests, restrictions, and claims other than those specified in the instruction.

(4) The guarantor under subsections (1) and (2) or the special guarantor under subsection (3) does not otherwise warrant the rightfulness of the particular transfer, pledge, or release.

(5) Any person guaranteeing an indorsement of a certificated security makes not only the warranties of a signature guarantor under subsection (1) but also warrants the rightfulness of the particular transfer in all respects.

(6) Any person guaranteeing an instruction requesting the transfer, pledge, or release of an uncertificated security makes not only the warranties of a special signature guarantor under subsection (3) but also warrants the rightfulness of the particular transfer, pledge, or release in all respects.

(7) No issuer may require a special guarantee of signature (subsection (3)), a guarantee of indorsement (subsection (5)), or a guarantee of instruction (subsection (6)) as a condition to registration of transfer, pledge, or release.

(8) The foregoing warranties are made to any person taking or dealing with the security in reliance on the guarantee, and the guarantor is liable to the person for any loss resulting from breach of the warranties.

§ 8—313. When Transfer to Purchaser Occurs; Financial Intermediary as Bona Fide Purchaser; "Financial Intermediary".

(1) Transfer of a security or a limited interest (including a security interest) therein to a purchaser occurs only:

(a) at the time he or a person designated by him acquires possession of a certificated security;

(b) at the time the transfer, pledge, or release of an uncertificated security is registered to him or a person designated by him;

(c) at the time his financial intermediary acquires possession of a certificated security specially indorsed to or issued in the name of the purchaser;

(d) at the time a financial intermediary, not a clearing corporation, sends him confirmation of the purchase and also by book entry or otherwise identifies as belonging to the purchaser

(i) a specific certificated security in the financial intermediary's possession;

(ii) a quantity of securities that constitute or are part of a fungible bulk of certificated securities in the financial intermediary's possession or of uncertificated securities registered in the name of the financial intermediary; or

(iii) a quantity of securities that constitute or are part of a fungible bulk of securities shown on the account of the financial intermediary on the books of another financial intermediary;

(e) with respect to an identified certificated security to be delivered while still in the possession of a third person, not a financial intermediary, at the time that person acknowledges that he holds for the purchaser;

(f) with respect to a specific uncertificated security the pledge or transfer of which has been registered to a third person, not a financial intermediary, at the time that person acknowledges that he holds for the purchaser;

(g) at the time appropriate entries to the account of the purchaser or a person designated by him on the books of a clearing corporation are made under Section 8—320;

(h) with respect to the transfer of a security interest where the debtor has signed a security agreement containing a description of the security, at the time a written notification, which, in the case of the creation of the security interest, is signed by the debtor (which may be a copy of the security agreement) or which, in the case of the release or assignment of the security interest created pursuant to this paragraph, is signed by the secured party, is received by

(i) a financial intermediary on whose books the interest of the transferor in the security appears;

(ii) a third person, not a financial intermediary, in possession of the security, if it is certificated;

(iii) a third person, not a financial intermediary, who is the registered owner of the security, if it is uncertificated and not subject to a registered pledge; or

(iv) a third person, not a financial intermediary, who is the registered pledgee of the security, if it is uncertificated and subject to a registered pledge;

(i) with respect to the transfer of a security interest where the transferor has signed a security agreement containing a description of the security, at the time new value is given by the secured party; or

(j) with respect to the transfer of a security interest where the secured party is a financial intermediary and the security has already been transferred to the financial intermediary under paragraphs (a), (b), (c), (d), or (g), at the time the transferor has signed a security agreement containing a description of the security and value is given by the secured party.

(2) The purchaser is the owner of a security held for him by a financial intermediary, but cannot be a bona fide purchaser of a security so held except in the circumstances specified in paragraphs (c), (d)(i), and (g) of subsection (1). If a security so held is part of a fungible bulk, as in the circumstances specified in paragraphs (d)(ii) and (d)(iii) of subsection (1), the purchaser is the owner of a proportionate property interest in the fungible bulk.

(3) Notice of an adverse claim received by the financial intermediary or by the purchaser after the financial intermediary takes delivery of a certificated security as a holder for value or after the transfer, pledge, or release of an uncertificated security has been registered free of the claim to a financial intermediary who has given value is not effective either as to the financial intermediary or as to the purchaser. However, as between the financial intermediary and the purchaser the purchaser may demand transfer of an equivalent security as to which no notice of adverse claim has been received.

(4) A "financial intermediary" is a bank, broker, clearing corporation, or other person (or the nominee of any of them) which in the ordinary course of its business maintains security accounts for its customers and is acting in that capacity. A financial intermediary may have a security interest in securities held in account for its customer.

§ 8—314. Duty to Transfer, When Completed.

(1) Unless otherwise agreed, if a sale of a security is made on an exchange or otherwise through brokers:

(a) the selling customer fulfills his duty to transfer at the time he:

(i) places a certificated security in the possession of the selling broker or a person designated by the broker;

(ii) causes an uncertificated security to be registered in the name of the selling broker or a person designated by the broker;

(iii) if requested, causes an acknowledgment to be made to the selling broker that a certificated or uncertificated security is held for the broker; or

(iv) places in the possession of the selling broker or of a person designated by the broker a transfer instruction for an uncertificated security, providing the issuer does not refuse to register the requested transfer if the instruction is presented to the issuer for registration within 30 days thereafter; and

(b) the selling broker, including a correspondent broker acting for a selling customer, fulfills his duty to transfer at the time he:

(i) places a certificated security in the possession of the buying broker or a person designated by the buying broker;

(ii) causes an uncertificated security to be registered in the name of the buying broker or a person designated by the buying broker;

(iii) places in the possession of the buying broker or of a person designated by the buying broker a transfer instruction for an uncertificated security, providing the issuer does not refuse to register the requested transfer if the instruction is presented to the issuer for registration within 30 days thereafter; or

(iv) effects clearance of the sale in accordance with the rules of the exchange on which the transaction took place.

(2) Except as provided in this section or unless otherwise agreed, a transferor's duty to transfer a security under a contract of purchase is not fulfilled until he:

(a) places a certificated security in form to be negotiated by the purchaser in the possession of the purchaser or of a person designated by the purchaser;

(b) causes an uncertificated security to be registered in the name of the purchaser or a person designated by the purchaser; or

(c) if the purchaser requests, causes an acknowledgment to be made to the purchaser that a certificated or uncertificated security is held for the purchaser.

(3) Unless made on an exchange, a sale to a broker purchasing for his own account is within subsection (2) and not within subsection (1).

§ 8—315. Action Against Transferee Based Upon Wrongful Transfer

(1) Any person against whom the transfer of a security is wrongful for any reason, including his incapacity, as against anyone except a bona fide purchaser, may:

(a) reclaim possession of the certificated security wrongfully transferred;

(b) obtain possession of any new certificated security representing all or part of the same rights;

(c) compel the origination of an instruction to transfer to him or a person designated by him an uncertificated security constituting all or part of the same rights; or

(d) have damages.

(2) If the transfer is wrongful because of an unauthorized indorsement of a certificated security, the owner may also reclaim or obtain possession of the security or a new certificated security, even from a bona fide purchaser, if the ineffectiveness of the purported indorsement can be asserted against him under the provisions of this Article on unauthorized indorsements (Section 8—311).

(3) The right to obtain or reclaim possession of a certificated security or to compel the origination of a transfer instruction may be specifically enforced and the transfer of a certificated or uncertificated security enjoined and a certificated security impounded pending the litigation.

§ 8—316. Purchaser's Right to Requisites for Registration of Transfer, Pledge, or Release on Books—Unless otherwise agreed, the transferor of a certificated security or the transferor, pledgor, or pledgee of an uncertificated security on due demand must supply his purchaser with any proof of his authority to transfer, pledge, or release or with any other requisite necessary to obtain registration of the transfer, pledge, or release of the security; but if the transfer, pledge, or release is not for value, a transferor, pledgor, or pledgee need not do so unless the purchaser furnishes the necessary expenses. Failure within a reasonable time to comply with a demand made gives the purchaser the right to reject or rescind the transfer, pledge, or release.

§ 8—317. Creditors' Rights

(1) Subject to the exceptions in subsections (3) and (4), no attachment or levy upon a certificated security or any share or other interest represented thereby which is outstanding is valid until the security is actually seized by the officer making the attachment or levy, but a certificated security which has been surrendered to the issuer may be reached by a creditor by legal process at the issuer's chief executive office in the United States.

(2) An uncertificated security registered in the name of the debtor may not be reached by a creditor except by legal process at the issuer's chief executive office in the United States.

(3) The interest of a debtor in a certificated security that is in the possession of a secured party not a financial intermediary or in an uncertificated security registered in the name of a secured party not a financial intermediary (or in the name of a nominee of the secured party) may be reached by a creditor by legal process upon the secured party.

(4) The interest of a debtor in a certificated security that is in the possession of or registered in the name of a financial intermediary or in an uncertificated security registered in the name of a financial intermediary may be reached by a creditor by legal process upon the financial intermediary on whose books the interest of the debtor appears.

(5) Unless otherwise provided by law, a creditor's lien upon the interest of a debtor in a security obtained pursuant to subsection (3) or (4) is not a restraint on the transfer of the security, free of the lien, to a third party for new value; but in the event of a transfer, the lien applies to the proceeds of the transfer in the hands of the secured party or financial intermediary, subject to any claims having priority.

(6) A creditor whose debtor is the owner of a security is entitled to aid from courts of appropriate jurisdiction, by injunction or otherwise, in reaching the security or in satisfying the claim by means allowed at law or in equity in regard to property that cannot readily be reached by ordinary legal process.

§ 8—318. No Conversion by Good Faith Conduct—An agent or bailee who in good faith (including observance of reasonable commercial standards if he is in the business of buying, selling, or otherwise dealing with securities) has received certificated securities and sold, pledged, or delivered them or has sold or caused the transfer or pledge of uncertificated securities over which he had control according to the instructions of his principal, is not liable for conversion or for participation in breach of fiduciary duty although the principal had no right so to deal with the securities.

§ 8—319. Statute of Frauds—A contract for the sale of securities is not enforceable by way of action or defense unless:

(a) there is some writing signed by the party against whom enforcement is sought or by his authorized agent or broker, sufficient to indicate that a contract has been made for sale of a stated quantity of described securities at a defined or stated price;

(b) delivery of a certificated security or transfer instruction has been accepted, or transfer of an uncertificated security has been registered and the transferee has failed to send written objection to the issuer within 10 days after receipt of the initial transaction statement confirming the registration, or payment has been made, but the contract is enforceable under this provision only to the extent of the delivery, registration, or payment;

(c) within a reasonable time a writing in confirmation of the sale or purchase and sufficient against the sender under paragraph (a) has been received by the party against whom enforcement is sought and he has failed to send written objection to its contents within 10 days after its receipt; or

(d) the party against whom enforcement is sought admits in his pleading, testimony, or otherwise in court that a contract was made for the sale of a stated quantity of described securities at a defined or stated price.

§ 8—320. Transfer or Pledge Within Central Depository System

(1) In addition to other methods, a transfer, pledge, or release of a security or any interest therein may be effected by the making of appropriate entries on the books of a clearing corporation reducing the account of the transferor, pledgor, or pledgee and increasing the account of the transferee, pledgee, or pledgor by the amount of the obligation or the number of shares or rights transferred, pledged, or released, if the security is shown on the account of a transferor, pledgor, or pledgee on the books of the clearing corporation; is subject to the control of the clearing corporation; and

(a) if certificated,

(i) is in the custody of the clearing corporation, another clearing corporation, a custodian bank, or a nominee of any of them; and

(ii) is in bearer form or indorsed in blank by an appropriate person or registered in the name of the clearing corporation, a custodian bank, or a nominee of any of them; or

(b) if uncertificated, is registered in the name of the clearing corporation, another clearing corporation, a custodian bank, or a nominee of any of them.

(2) Under this section entries may be made with respect to like securities or interests therein as a part of a fungible bulk and may refer merely to a quantity of a particular security without reference to the name of the registered owner, certificate or bond number, or the like, and, in appropriate cases, may be on a net basis taking into account other transfers, pledges, or releases of the same security.

(3) A transfer under this section is effective (Section 8—313) and the purchaser acquires the rights of the transferor (Section 8—301). A pledge or release under this section is the transfer of a limited interest. If a pledge or the creation of a security interest is intended, the security interest is perfected at the time when both value is given by the pledgee and the appropriate entries are made (Section 8—321). A transferee or pledgee under this section may be a bona fide purchaser (Section 8—302).

(4) A transfer or pledge under this section is not a registration of transfer under Part 4.

(5) That entries made on the books of the clearing corporation as provided in subsection (1) are not appropriate does not affect the validity or effect of the entries or the liabilities or obligations of the clearing corporation to any person adversely affected thereby.

§ 8—321. Enforceability, Attachment, Perfection and Termination of Security Interests

(1) A security interest in a security is enforceable and can attach only if it is transferred to the secured party or a person designated by him pursuant to a provision of Section 8—313(1).

(2) A security interest so transferred pursuant to agreement by a transferor who has rights in the security to a transferee who has given value is a perfected security interest, but a security interest that has been transferred solely under paragraph (i) of Section 8—313(1) becomes unperfected after 21 days unless, within that time, the requirements for transfer under any other provision of Section 8—313(1) are satisfied.

(3) A security interest in a security is subject to the provisions of Article 9, but:

(a) no filing is required to perfect the security interest; and

(b) no written security agreement signed by the debtor is necessary to make the security interest enforceable, except as provided in paragraph (h), (i), or (j) of Section 8—313(1). The secured party has the rights and duties provided under Section 9—207, to the extent they are applicable, whether or not the security is certificated, and, if certificated, whether or not it is in his possession.

(4) Unless otherwise agreed, a security interest in a security is terminated by transfer to the debtor or a person designated by him pursuant to a provision of Section 8—313(1). If a security is thus transferred, the security interest, if not terminated, becomes unperfected unless the security is certificated and is delivered to the debtor for the purpose of ultimate sale or exchange or presentation, collection, renewal, or registration of transfer. In that case, the security interest becomes unperfected after 21 days unless, within that time, the security (or securities for which it has been exchanged) is transferred to the secured party or a person designated by him pursuant to a provision of Section 8—313(1).

PART 4

Registration

§ 8—401. Duty of Issuer to Register Transfer, Pledge, or Release

(1) If a certificated security in registered form is presented to the issuer with a request to register transfer or an instruction is presented to the issuer with a request to register transfer, pledge, or release, the issuer shall register the transfer, pledge, or release as requested if:

(a) the security is indorsed or the instruction was originated by the appropriate person or persons (Section 8—308);

(b) reasonable assurance is given that those indorsements or instructions are genuine and effective (Section 8—402);

(c) the issuer has no duty as to adverse claims or has discharged the duty (Section 8—403);

(d) any applicable law relating to the collection of taxes has been complied with; and

(e) the transfer, pledge, or release is in fact rightful or is to a bona fide purchaser.

(2) If an issuer is under a duty to register a transfer, pledge, or release of a security, the issuer is also liable to the person presenting a certificated security or an instruction for registration or his principal for loss resulting from any unreasonable delay in registration or from failure or refusal to register the transfer, pledge, or release.

§ 8—402. Assurance that Indorsements and Instructions Are Effective

(1) The issuer may require the following assurance that each necessary indorsement of a certificated security or each instruction (Section 8—308) is genuine and effective:

(a) in all cases, a guarantee of the signature (Section 8—312(1) or (2)) of the person indorsing a certificated security or originating an instruction including, in the case of an instruction, a warranty of the taxpayer identification number or, in the absence thereof, other reasonable assurance of identity;

(b) if the indorsement is made or the instruction is originated by an agent, appropriate assurance of authority to sign;

(c) if the indorsement is made or the instruction is originated by a fiduciary, appropriate evidence of appointment or incumbency;

(d) if there is more than one fiduciary, reasonable assurance that all who are required to sign have done so; and

(e) if the indorsement is made or the instruction is originated by a person not covered by any of the foregoing, assurance appropriate to the case corresponding as nearly as may be to the foregoing.

(2) A "guarantee of the signature" in subsection (1) means a guarantee signed by or on behalf of a person reasonably believed by the issuer to be responsible. The issuer may adopt standards with respect to responsibility if they are not manifestly unreasonable.

(3) "Appropriate evidence of appointment or incumbency" in subsection (1) means:

(a) in the case of a fiduciary appointed or qualified by a court, a certificate issued by or under the direction or supervision of that court or an officer thereof and dated within 60 days before the date of presentation for transfer, pledge, or release; or

(b) in any other case, a copy of a document showing the appointment or a certificate issued by or on behalf of a person reasonably believed by the issuer to be responsible or, in the absence of that document or certificate, other evidence reasonably deemed by the issuer to be appropriate. The issuer may adopt standards with respect to the evidence if they are not manifestly unreasonable. The issuer is not charged with notice of the contents of any document obtained pursuant to this paragraph (b) except to the extent that the contents relate directly to the appointment or incumbency.

(4) The issuer may elect to require reasonable assurance beyond that specified in this section, but if it does so and, for a purpose other than that specified in subsection (3)(b), both requires and obtains a copy of a will, trust, indenture, articles of co-partnership, by-laws, or other controlling instrument, it is charged with notice of all matters contained therein affecting the transfer, pledge, or release.

§ 8—403. Issuer's Duty as to Adverse Claims

(1) An issuer to whom a certificated security is presented for registration shall inquire into adverse claims if:

(a) a written notification of an adverse claim is received at a time and in a manner affording the issuer a reasonable opportunity to act on it prior to the issuance of a new, reissued, or re-registered certificated security, and the notification identifies the claimant, the registered owner, and the issue of which the security is a part, and provides an address for communications directed to the claimant; or

(b) the issuer is charged with notice of an adverse claim from a controlling instrument it has elected to require under Section 8—402(4).

(2) The issuer may discharge any duty of inquiry by any reasonable means, including notifying an adverse claimant by registered or certified mail at the address furnished by him or, if there be no such address, at his residence or regular place of business that the certificated security has been presented for registration of transfer by a named person, and that the transfer will be registered unless within 30 days from the date of mailing the notification, either:

(a) an appropriate restraining order, injunction, or other process issues from a court of competent jurisdiction; or

(b) there is filed with the issuer an indemnity bond, sufficient in the issuer's judgment to protect the issuer and any transfer agent, registrar, or other agent of the issuer involved from any loss it or they may suffer by complying with the adverse claim.

(3) Unless an issuer is charged with notice of an adverse claim from a controlling instrument which it has elected to require under Section 8—402(4) or receives notification of an adverse claim under subsection (1), if a certificated security presented for registration is indorsed by the appropriate person or persons the issuer is under no duty to inquire into adverse claims. In particular:

(a) an issuer registering a certificated security in the name of a person who is a fiduciary or who is described as a fiduciary is not bound to inquire into the existence, extent, or correct description of the fiduciary relationship; and thereafter the issuer may assume without inquiry that the newly registered owner continues to be the fiduciary until the issuer receives written notice that the fiduciary is no longer acting as such with respect to the particular security;

(b) an issuer registering transfer on an indorsement by a fiduciary is not bound to inquire whether the transfer is made in compliance with a controlling instrument or with the law of the state having jurisdiction of the fiduciary relationship, including any law requiring the fiduciary to obtain court approval of the transfer; and

(c) the issuer is not charged with notice of the contents of any court record or file or other recorded or unrecorded document even though the document is in its possession and even though the transfer is made on the indorsement of a fiduciary to the fiduciary himself or to his nominee.

(4) An issuer is under no duty as to adverse claims with respect to an uncertificated security except:

(a) claims embodied in a restraining order, injunction, or other legal process served upon the issuer if the process was served at a time and in a manner affording the issuer a reasonable opportunity to act on it in accordance with the requirements of subsection (5);

(b) claims of which the issuer has received a written notification from the registered owner or the registered pledgee if the notification was received at a time and in a manner affording the issuer a reasonable opportunity to act on it in accordance with the requirements of subsection (5);

(c) claims (including restrictions on transfer not imposed by the issuer) to which the registration of transfer to the present registered owner was subject and were so noted in the initial transaction statement sent to him; and

(d) claims as to which an issuer is charged with notice from a controlling instrument it has elected to require under Section 8—402(4).

(5) If the issuer of an uncertificated security is under a duty as to an adverse claim, he discharges that duty by:

(a) including a notation of the claim in any statements sent with respect to the security under Sections 8—408(3), (6), and (7); and

(b) refusing to register the transfer or pledge of the security unless the nature of the claim does not preclude transfer or pledge subject thereto.

(6) If the transfer or pledge of the security is registered subject to an adverse claim, a notation of the claim must be included in the initial transaction statement and all subsequent statements sent to the transferee and pledgee under Section 8—408.

(7) Notwithstanding subsections (4) and (5), if an uncertificated security was subject to a registered pledge at the time the issuer first came under a duty as to a particular adverse claim, the issuer has no duty as to that claim if transfer of the security is requested by the registered pledgee or an appropriate person acting for the registered pledgee unless:

(a) the claim was embodied in legal process which expressly provides otherwise;

(b) the claim was asserted in a written notification from the registered pledgee;

(c) the claim was one as to which the issuer was charged with notice from a controlling instrument it required under Section 8—402(4) in connection with the pledgee's request for transfer; or

(d) the transfer requested is to the registered owner.

§ 8—404. Liability and Non-Liability for Registration

(1) Except as provided in any law relating to the collection of taxes, the issuer is not liable to the owner, pledgee, or any other person suffering loss as a result of the registration of a transfer, pledge, or release of a security if:

(a) there were on or with a certificated security the necessary indorsements or the issuer had received an instruction originated by an appropriate person (Section 8—308); and

(b) the issuer had no duty as to adverse claims or has discharged the duty (Section 8—403).

(2) If an issuer has registered a transfer of a certificated security to a person not entitled to it, the issuer on demand shall deliver a like security to the true owner unless:

(a) the registration was pursuant to subsection (1);

(b) the owner is precluded from asserting any claim for registering the transfer under Section 8—405(1); or

(c) the delivery would result in overissue, in which case the issuer's liability is governed by Section 8—104.

(3) If an issuer has improperly registered a transfer, pledge, or release of an uncertificated security, the issuer on demand from the injured party shall restore the records as to the injured party to the condition that would have obtained if the improper registration had not been made unless:

(a) the registration was pursuant to subsection (1); or

(b) the registration would result in overissue, in which case the issuer's liability is governed by Section 8—104.

§ 8—405. Lost, Destroyed, and Stolen Certificated Securities

(1) If a certificated security has been lost, apparently destroyed, or wrongfully taken, and the owner fails to notify the issuer of that fact within a reasonable time after he has notice of it and the issuer registers a transfer of the security before receiving notification, the owner is precluded from asserting against the issuer any claim for registering the transfer under Section 8—404 or any claim to a new security under this section.

(2) If the owner of a certificated security claims that the security has been lost, destroyed, or wrongfully taken, the issuer shall issue a new certificated security or, at the option of the issuer, an equivalent uncertificated security in place of the original security if the owner:

(a) so requests before the issuer has notice that the security has been acquired by a bona fide purchaser;

(b) files with the issuer a sufficient indemnity bond; and

(c) satisfies any other reasonable requirements imposed by the issuer.

(3) If, after the issue of a new certificated or uncertificated security, a bona fide purchaser of the original certificated security presents it for registration of transfer, the issuer shall register the transfer unless registration would result in overissue, in which event the issuer's liability is governed by Section 8—104. In addition to any rights on the indemnity bond, the issuer may recover the new certificated security from the person to whom it was issued or any person taking under him except a bona fide purchaser or may cancel the uncertificated security unless a bona fide purchaser or any person taking under a bona fide purchaser is then the registered owner or registered pledgee thereof.

§ 8—406. Duty of Authenticating Trustee, Transfer Agent, or Registrar

(1) If a person acts as authenticating trustee, transfer agent, registrar, or other agent for an issuer in the registration of transfers of its certificated securities or in the registration of transfers, pledges, and releases of its uncertificated securities, in the issue of new securities, or in the cancellation of surrendered securities:

(a) he is under a duty to the issuer to exercise good faith and due diligence in performing his functions; and

(b) with regard to the particular functions he performs, he has the same obligation to the holder or owner of a certificated security or to the owner or pledgee of an uncertificated security and has the same rights and privileges as the issuer has in regard to those functions.

(2) Notice to an authenticating trustee, transfer agent, registrar or other agent is notice to the issuer with respect to the functions performed by the agent.

§ 8—407. Exchangeability of Securities

(1) No issuer is subject to the requirements of this section unless it regularly maintains a system for issuing the class of securities involved under which both certificated and uncertificated securities are regularly issued to the category of owners, which includes the person in whose name the new security is to be registered.

(2) Upon surrender of a certificated security with all necessary indorsements and presentation of a written request by the person surrendering the security, the issuer, if he has no duty as to adverse claims or has discharged the duty

(Section 8—403), shall issue to the person or a person designated by him an equivalent uncertificated security subject to all liens, restrictions, and claims that were noted on the certificated security.

(3) Upon receipt of a transfer instruction originated by an appropriate person who so requests, the issuer of an uncertificated security shall cancel the uncertificated security and issue an equivalent certificated security on which must be noted conspicuously any liens and restrictions of the issuer and any adverse claims (as to which the issuer has a duty under Section 8—403(4)) to which the uncertificated security was subject. The certificated security shall be registered in the name of and delivered to:

(a) the registered owner, if the uncertificated security was not subject to a registered pledge; or

(b) the registered pledgee, if the uncertificated security was subject to a registered pledge.

§ 8—408. Statements of Uncertificated Securities

(1) Within 2 business days after the transfer of an uncertificated security has been registered, the issuer shall send to the new registered owner and, if the security has been transferred subject to a registered pledge, to the registered pledgee a written statement containing:

(a) a description of the issue of which the uncertificated security is a part;

(b) the number of shares or units transferred;

(c) the name and address and any taxpayer identification number of the new registered owner and, if the security has been transferred subject to a registered pledge, the name and address and any taxpayer identification number of the registered pledgee;

(d) a notation of any liens and restrictions of the issuer and any adverse claims (as to which the issuer has a duty under Section 8—403(4)) to which the uncertificated security is or may be subject at the time of registration or a statement that there are none of those liens, restrictions, or adverse claims; and

(e) the date the transfer was registered.

(2) Within 2 business days after the pledge of an uncertificated security has been registered, the issuer shall send to the registered owner and the registered pledgee a written statement containing:

(a) a description of the issue of which the uncertificated security is a part;

(b) the number of shares or units pledged;

(c) the name and address and any taxpayer identification number of the registered owner and the registered pledgee;

(d) a notation of any liens and restrictions of the issuer and any adverse claims (as to which the issuer has a duty under Section 8—403(4)) to which the uncertificated security is or may be subject at the time of registration or a statement that there are none of those liens, restrictions, or adverse claims; and

(e) the date the pledge was registered.

(3) Within 2 business days after the release from pledge of an uncertificated security has been registered, the issuer shall send to the registered owner and the pledgee whose interest was released a written statement containing:

(a) a description of the issue of which the uncertificated security is a part;

(b) the number of shares or units released from pledge;

(c) the name and address and any taxpayer identification number of the registered owner and the pledgee whose interest was released;

(d) a notation of any liens and restrictions of the issuer and any adverse claims (as to which the issuer has a duty under Section 8—403(4)) to which the uncertificated security is or may be subject at the time of registration or a statement that there are none of those liens, restrictions, or adverse claims; and

(e) the date the release was registered.

(4) An "initial transaction statement" is the statement sent to:

(a) the new registered owner and, if applicable, to the registered pledgee pursuant to subsection (1);

(b) the registered pledgee pursuant to subsection (2); or

(c) the registered owner pursuant to subsection (3).

Each initial transaction statement shall be signed by or on behalf of the issuer and must be identified as "Initial Transaction Statement".

(5) Within 2 business days after the transfer of an uncertificated security has been registered, the issuer shall send to the former registered owner and the former registered pledgee, if any, a written statement containing:

(a) a description of the issue of which the uncertificated security is a part;

(b) the number of shares or units transferred;

(c) the name and address and any taxpayer identification number of the former registered owner and of any former registered pledgee; and

(d) the date the transfer was registered.

(6) At periodic intervals no less frequent than annually and at any time upon the reasonable written request of the registered owner, the issuer shall send to the registered owner of each uncertificated security a dated written statement containing:

(a) a description of the issue of which the uncertificated security is a part;

(b) the name and address and any taxpayer identification number of the registered owner;

(c) the number of shares or units of the uncertificated security registered in the name of the registered owner on the date of the statement;

(d) the name and address and any taxpayer identification number of any registered pledgee and the number of shares or units subject to the pledge; and

(e) a notation of any liens and restrictions of the issuer and any adverse claims (as to which the issuer has a duty under Section 8—403(4)) to which the uncertificated security is or may be subject or a statement that there are none of those liens, restrictions, or adverse claims.

(7) At periodic intervals no less frequent than annually and at any time upon the reasonable written request of the registered pledgee, the issuer shall send to the registered pledgee of each uncertificated security a dated written statement containing:

(a) a description of the issue of which the uncertificated security is a part;

(b) the name and address and any taxpayer identification number of the registered owner;

(c) the name and address and any taxpayer identification number of the registered pledgee;

(d) the number of shares or units subject to the pledge; and

(e) a notation of any liens and restrictions of the issuer and any adverse claims (as to which the issuer has a duty under Section 8—403(4)) to which the uncertificated security is or may be subject or a statement that there are none of those liens, restrictions, or adverse claims.

(8) If the issuer sends the statements described in subsections (6) and (7) at periodic intervals no less frequent than quarterly, the issuer is not obliged to send additional statements upon request unless the owner or pledgee requesting them pays to the issuer the reasonable cost of furnishing them.

(9) Each statement sent pursuant to this section must bear a conspicuous legend reading substantially as follows: "This statement is merely a record of the rights of the addressee as of the time of its issuance. Delivery of this statement, of itself, confers no rights on the recipient. This statement is neither a negotiable instrument nor a security."

ARTICLE NINE—SECURED TRANSACTIONS

PART 1

Short Title, Applicability and Definitions

§ 9-101. Short Title.—This Article shall be known and may be cited as Uniform Commercial Code—Secured Transactions.

§ 9-102. Policy and [Subject Matter] of Article.—

(1) Except as otherwise provided in Section 9-103 on multiple state transactions and in Section 9-104 on excluded transactions, this Article applies so far as concerns any personal property and fixtures within the jurisdiction of this State

(a) to any transaction (regardless of its form) which is intended to create a security interest in personal property or fixtures including goods, documents, instruments, general intangibles, chattel paper of accounts and also

(b) to any sale [or] accounts or chattel paper.

(2) This Article applies to security interests created by contract including pledge, assignment, chattel mortgage, chattel trust, trust deed, factor's lien, equipment trust, conditional sale, trust receipt, other lien or title retention contract and lease or consignment intended as security. This Article does not apply to statutory liens except as provided in Section 9-310.

(3) The application of this Article to a security interest in a secured obligation is not affected by the fact that the obligation is itself secured by a transaction or interest to which this Article does not apply.

§ 9-103* [Perfection of Security Interests in Multiple State Transactions—

(1) Documents, instruments and ordinary goods.

(a) This subsection applies to documents and instruments and to goods other than those covered by a certificate of title described in subsection (2), mobile goods described in subsection (3), and minerals described in subsection (5).

(b) Except as otherwise provided in this subsection, perfection and the effect of perfection or nonperfection of a security interest in collateral are governed by the law of the jurisdiction where the collateral is when the last event occurs on which is based the assertion that the security interest is perfected or unperfected.

(c) If the parties to a transaction creating a purchase money security interest in goods in one jurisdiction understand at the time that the security interest attaches that the goods will be kept in another jurisdiction, then the law of the other jurisdiction governs the perfection and the effect of perfection or non-perfection of the security interest from the time it attaches until thirty days after the debtor receives possession of the goods and thereafter if the goods are taken to the other jurisdiction before the end of the thirty-day period.

(d) When collateral is brought into and kept in this state while subject to a security interest perfected under the law of the jurisdiction from which the collateral was removed, the security interest remains perfected, but if action is required by Part 3 of this Article to perfect the security interest,

(i) if the action is not taken before the expiration of the period of perfection in the other jurisdiction or the end of four months after the collateral is brought into this state, whichever period first expires, the security interest becomes unperfected at the end of that period and is thereafter deemed to have been unperfected as against a person who became a purchaser after removal;

(ii) if the action is taken before the expiration of the period specified in sub-paragraph (i), the security interest continues perfected thereafter;

(iii) for the purpose of priority over a buyer of consumer goods (subsection (2) of Section 9-307), the period of the effectiveness of a filing in the jurisdiction from which the collateral is removed is governed by the rules with respect to perfection in subparagraphs (i) and (ii).

(2) Certificate of title.

(a) This subsection applies to goods covered by a certificate of title issued under a statute of this state or of another jurisdiction under the law of which indication of a security interest on the certificate is required as a condition of perfection.

(b) Except as otherwise provided in this subsection, perfection and the effect of perfection or nonperfection of the security interest are governed by the law (including the conflict of laws rules) of the jurisdiction issuing the certificate until four months after the goods are removed from that jurisdiction and thereafter until the goods are registered in another jurisdiction, but in any event not beyond surrender of the certificate. After the expiration of that period, the goods are not covered by the certificate of title within the meaning of this section.

(c) Except with respect to the rights of a buyer described in the next paragraph, a security interest, perfected in another jurisdiction otherwise than by notation on a certificate of title, in goods brought into this state and thereafter covered by a certificate of title issued by this state is subject to the rules stated in paragraph (d) of subsection (1).

(d) If goods are brought into this state while a security interest therein is perfected in any manner under the law of the jurisdiction from which the goods are removed and a certificate of title is issued by this state and the certificate does not show that the goods are subject to the security interest or that they may be subject to security interests not shown on the certificate, the security interest is subordinate to the rights of a buyer of the goods who is not in the business of selling goods of that kind to the extent that he gives value and receives delivery of the goods after issuance of the certificate and without knowledge of the security interest.

(3) Accounts, general intangibles and mobile goods.

(a) This subsection applies to accounts (other than an account described in subsection (5) on minerals) and general intangibles and to goods which are mobile and which are of a type normally used in more than one jurisdiction, such as motor vehicles, trailers, rolling stock, airplanes, shipping containers, road building and construction machinery and commercial harvesting machinery and the like, if the goods are equipment or are inventory leased or held for lease by the debtor to others, and are not covered by a certificate of title described in subsection (2).

(b) The law (including the conflict of laws rules) of the jurisdiction in which the debtor is located governs the perfection and the effect of perfection or non-perfection of the security interest.

(c) If, however, the debtor is located in a jurisdiction which is not a part of the United States, and which does not provide for perfection of the security interest by filing or recording in that jurisdiction, the law of the jurisdiction in the United States in which the debtor has its major executive office in the United States governs the perfection and the effect of perfection or non-perfection of the security interest through filing. In the alternative, if the debtor is located in a jurisdiction which is not a part of the United States or Canada and the collateral is accounts or general intangibles for money due or to become due, the security interest may be perfected by notification to the account debtor. As used in this paragraph, "United States" includes its territories and possessions and the Commonwealth of Puerto Rico.

(d) A debtor shall be deemed located at his place of business if he has one, at his chief executive office if he has more than one place of business, otherwise at his residence. If, however, the debtor is a foreign air carrier under the Federal Aviation Act of 1958, as amended, it shall be deemed located at the designated office of the agent upon whom service of process may be made on behalf of the foreign air carrier.

(e) A security interest perfected under the law of the jurisdiction of the location of the debtor is perfected until the expiration of four months after a change of the debtor's location to another jurisdiction, or until perfection would have ceased by the law of the first jurisdiction, whichever period first expires. Unless perfected in the new jurisdiction before the end of that period, it becomes unperfected thereafter and is deemed to have been unperfected as against a person who became a purchaser after the change.

(4) Chattel paper. The rules stated for goods in subsection (1) apply to a possessory security interest in chattel paper. The rules stated for accounts in subsection (3) apply to a non-possessory security interest in chattel paper, but the security interest may not be perfected by notification to the account debtor.

(5) Minerals. Perfection and the effect of perfection or non-perfection of a security interest which is created by a debtor who has an interest in minerals or the like (including oil and gas) before extraction and which attaches thereto as extracted, or which attaches to an account resulting from the sale thereof at the wellhead or minehead are governed by the law (including the conflict of laws rules) of the jurisdiction where in the well head or minehead is located.

(6) Uncertificated securities. The law (including the conflict of laws rules) of the jurisdiction of organization of the issuer governs the perfection and the effect of perfection or nonperfection of a security interest in uncertificated securities.

*[This section 9-103 has been completely rewritten]

§ 9-104. Transactions Excluded From Article.—This Article does not apply

(a) to a security interest subject to any statute of the United States such as the Ship Mortgage Act, 1920, to the extent that such statute governs the rights of parties to and third parties affected by transactions in particular types of property; or

(b) to a landlord's lien; or

(c) to a lien given by statute or other rule of law for services or materials except as provided in Section 9-310 on priority of such liens; or

(d) to a transfer of a claim for wages, salary or other compensation of an employee, or

(e) to a transfer by a government or governmental subdivision or agency; or

(f) to a sale of accounts or chattel paper as part of a sale of the business out of which they arose, or an assignment of accounts or chattel paper which is for the purpose of a collection only, or a transfer of a right to payment under a contract to an assignee who is also to do the performance under the contract or a transfer of a single account to an assignee in whole or partial satisfaction of a preexisting indebtedness; or

(g) to a transfer of an interest or claim in or under any policy of insurance, except as provided with respect to proceeds (Section 9-306) and priorities in proceeds (Section 9-312); or

(h) to a right represented by a judgment; (other than a judgment taken on a right to payment which was collateral); or

(i) to any right of set-off; or

(j) except to the extent that provision is made for fixtures in Section 9-313, to the creation or transfer of an interest in or lien on real estate, including a lease or rents thereunder; or

(k) to a transfer in whole or in part of any claim arising out of tort; or

(l) to a transfer of an interest in any deposit account (Subsection (1) of Section 9-105), except as provided with respect to proceeds (Section 9-106) and priorities in proceeds (Section 9-312).

§ 9-105. Definitions and Index of Definitions.—

(1) In this Article unless the context otherwise requires:

(a) "Account debtor" means the person who is obligated on an account, chattel paper, contract right or general intangible;

(b) "Chattel paper" means a writing or writings which evidence both a monetary obligation and a security interest in or a lease of specific goods. When a transaction is evidenced both by such a security agreement or a lease and by an instrument or a series of instruments, the group of writings taken together constitutes chattel paper;

(c) "Collateral" means the property subject to a security interest, and includes accounts, contract rights and chattel paper which have been sold;

(d) "Debtor" means the person who owes payment or other performance of the obligation secured, whether or not he owns or has rights in the collateral, and includes the seller of accounts, contract rights or chattel paper. Where the debtor and the owner of the collateral are not the same person, the term "debtor" means the owner of the collateral in any provision of the Article dealing with the collateral, the obligor in any provision dealing with the obligation, and may include both where the context so requires;

[(e) "Deposit account" means a demand, time, savings, passbook or like account maintained with a bank, savings and loan association, credit union or like organization, other than an account evidenced by a certificate of deposit;]

[(f)] "Document" means document of title as defined in the general definitions of Article 1 (Section 1-201), [and a receipt of the kind described in subsection (2) of Section 7-201;]

[(g) "Encumbrance" includes real estate mortgages and other liens on real estate and all other rights in real estate that are not ownership interests.]

[(h)] "Goods" includes all things which are movable at the time the security interest attaches or which are fixtures (Section 9-313), but does not include money, documents, instruments, accounts, chattel paper, general intangibles, or minerals or the like (including oil and gas) before extraction. "Goods" also includes standing timber which is to be cut and removed under a conveyance or contract for sale, the unborn young of animals, and growing crops.

[(i)] "Instrument" means a negotiable instrument (defined in Section 3-104), or a certificated security (defined in Section 8-102) or any other writing which evidences a right to the payment of money and is not itself a security agreement or lease and is of a type which is in ordinary course of business transferred by delivery with any necessary indorsement or assignment;

[(j) "Mortgage" means a consensual interest created by a real estate mortgage, a trust deed on real estate, or the like;]

[(k) An advance is made "pursuant to commitment" if the secured party has bound himself to make it, whether or not a subsequent event of default or other event not within his control has relieved or may relieve him from his obligation.]

[(l)] ["Security agreement" means an agreement which] creates or provides for a security interest;

[(m)] "Secured party" means a lender, seller or other person in whose favor there is a security interest, including a person to whom accounts, (contract rights) or chattel paper have been sold. When the holders of obligations issued under an indenture of trust, equipment trust agreement or the like are represented by a trustee or other person, the representative is the secured party;

[(n) "Transmitting utility" means any person primarily engaged in the railroad, street railway or trolley bus business, the electric or electronics communications transmission business, the transmission of goods by pipeline, or the transmission or the production and transmission of electricity, steam, gas or water, or the provision of sewer service.]

(2) Other definitions applying to this Article and the sections in which they appear are: . . .

§ 9-106. Definitions: "Account"; "Contract Right"; "General Intangibles."—"Account" means any right to payment for goods sold or leased or for services rendered which is not evidenced by an instrument or chattel paper [whether or not it has been earned by performance.] "General intangibles" means any personal property (including things in action) other than goods, accounts, chattel paper, documents, instruments [and money] . . .

§ 9-107. Definitions: "Purchase Money Security Interest."—A security interest is a "purchase money security interest" to the extent that it is

(a) taken or retained by the seller of the collateral to secure all or part of its price; or

(b) taken by a person who by making advances or incurring an obligation gives value to enable the debtor to acquire rights in or the use of collateral if such value is in fact so used.

§ 9-108. When After-Acquired Collateral Not Security for Antecedent Debt.—Where a secured party makes an advance, incurs an obligation, releases a perfected security interest, or otherwise gives new value

which is to be secured in whole or in part by after-acquired property his security interest in the after-acquired collateral shall be deemed to be taken for new value and not as security for an antecedent debt if the debtor acquires his rights in such collateral either in the ordinary course of his business or under a contract of purchase made pursuant to the security agreement within a reasonable time after new value is given.

§ 9-109. Classification of Goods; "Consumer Goods"; "Equipment"; "Farm Products"; "Inventory."—Goods are

(1) "consumer goods" if they are used or brought for use primarily for personal, family or household purposes;

(2) "equipment" if they are used or bought for use primarily in business (including farming or a profession) or by a debtor who is a non-profit organization or a governmental subdivision or agency or if the goods are not included in the definitions of inventory, farm products or consumer goods;

(3) "farm products" if they are crops or livestock or supplies used or produced in farming operations or if they are products of crops or livestock in their unmanufactured states (such as ginned cotton, woolclip, maple syrup, milk and eggs), and if they are in the possession of a debtor engaged in raising, fattening, grazing or other farming operations. If goods are farm products they are neither equipment nor inventory;

(4) "inventory" if they are held by a person who holds them for sale or lease or to be furnished under contracts of service or if he has so furnished them, or if they are raw materials, work in process or materials used or consumed in a business. Inventory of a person is not to be classified as his equipment.

§ 9-110. Sufficiency of Description.—For the purposes of this Article any description of personal property or real estate is sufficient whether or not it is specific if it reasonably identifies what is described.

§ 9-111. Applicability of Bulk Transfer Laws.—The creation of a security interest is not a bulk transfer under Article 6 (see Section 6-103).

§ 9-112. Where Collateral Is Not Owned by Debtor.—Unless otherwise agreed, when a secured party knows that collateral is owned by a person who is not the debtor, the owner of the collateral is entitled to receive from the secured party any surplus under Section 9-502(2) or under Section 9-504(1), and is not liable for the debt or for any deficiency after resale, and he has the same right as the debtor

(a) to receive statements under Section 9-208;

(b) to receive notice of and to object to a secured party's proposal to retain the collateral in satisfaction of the indebtedness under Secton 9-505;

(c) to redeem the collateral under Section 9-506;

(d) to obtain injunctive or other relief under Section 9-507(1) Section 9-507 (1); and

(e) to recover losses caused to him under Section 9-208(2).

§ 9-113. Security Interests Arising Under Article on Sales.—A security interest arising solely under the Article on Sales (Article 2) is subject to the provisions of this Article except that to the extent that and so long as the debtor does not have or does not lawfully obtain possession of the goods

(a) no security agreement is necessary to make the security interest enforceable; and

(b) no filing is required to perfect the security interest; and

(c) the rights of the secured party on default by the debtor are governed by the Article on Sales (Article 2).

§ 9-114. Consignment—

(1) A person who delivers goods under a consignment which is not a security interest and who would be required to file under this Article by paragraph (3) (c) of Section 2-326 has priority over a secured party who is or becomes a creditor of the consignee and who would have a perfected security interest in the goods if they were the property of the consignee, and also has priority with respect to identifiable cash proceeds received on or before delivery of the goods to a buyer, if

(a) the consignor complies with the filing provision of the Article on Sales with respect to consignments (paragraph (3) (c) of Section 2-326) before the consignee receives possession of the goods; and

(b) the consignor gives notification in writing to the holder of the security interest if the holder has filed a financing statement covering the same types of goods before the date of the filing made by the consignor; and

(c) the holder of the security interest receives the notification within five years before the consignee receives possession of the goods; and

(d) the notification states that the consignor expects to deliver goods on consignment to the consignee, describing the goods by item or type.

(2) In the case of a consignment which is not a security interest and in which the requirements of the preceding subsection have not been met, a person who delivers goods to another is subordinate to a person who would have a perfected security interest in the goods if they were the property of the debtor.]*

*This section new in 1972.

PART 2

Validity of Security Agreement and Rights of Parties Thereto

§ 9-201. General Validity of Security Agreement.—Except as otherwise provided by this Act a security agreement is effective according to its terms between the parties, against purchasers of the collateral and against creditors. Nothing in this Article validates any charge or practice illegal under any statute or regulation thereunder governing usury, small loans, retail installment sales, or the like or extends the application of any such statute or regulation to any transaction not otherwise subject thereto.

§ 9-202. Title to Collateral Immaterial.—Each provision of this Article with regard to rights, obligations and remedies applies whether title to collateral is in the secured party or in the debtor.

§ 9-203. [Attachment and] Enforceability of Security Interest; Proceeds; Formal Requisites.—

[(1) Subject to the provisions of Section 4-208 on the security interest of a collecting bank, Section 8-321 on security interests in securities and Section 9-113 on a security interest arising under the Article on Sales, a security interest is not enforceable against the debtor or third parties with respect to the collateral and does not attach unless

(a) the collateral is in the possession of the secured party pursuant to agreement, or the debtor has signed a security agreement which contains a description of the collateral and in addition, when the security interest covers crops growing or to be grown or timber to be cut, a description of the land concerned; and

(b) value has been given; and

(c) the debtor has rights in the collateral.

(2) A security interest attaches when it becomes enforceable against the debtor with respect to the collateral. Attachment occurs as soon as all of the events specified in subsection (1) have taken place unless explicit agreement postpones the time of attaching.

(3) Unless otherwise agreed a security agreement gives the secured party the rights to proceeds provided by Section 9-306.]

[(4)] A transaction, although subject to this Article, is also subject to the "Consumer Finance Act" . . . "The Retail Installment Sales Act" . . . and in the case of conflict between the provisions of this Article and any such statute, the provisions of such statute control. Failure to comply with any applicable statute has only the effect which is specified therein.

§ 9-204. When Security Attaches; After-Acquired Property; Future Advances.—

[(1) Except as provided in subsection (2), a security agreement may provide that any or all obligations covered by the security agreement are to be secured by after-acquired collateral.

(2) No security interest attaches under an after-acquired property clause to consumer goods other than accessions (Section 9-314) when given as additional security unless the debtor acquires rights in them within ten days after the secured party gives value.]

[(3)] Obligations covered by a security agreement may include future advances or other value whether or not the advances or value are given pursuant to commitment [subsection (k) of Section (1) of Section 9-105).]

§ 9-205. Use or Disposition of Collateral Without Accounting Permissible.—A security interest is not invalid or fraudulent against creditors by reason of liberty in the debtor to use, commingle or dispose of all or part of the collateral (including returned or repossessed goods) or to collect or compromise accounts, contract rights or chattel paper, or to accept the return of goods or make repossessions, or to use, commingle or dispose of proceeds, or by reason of the failure of the secured party to require the debtor to account for proceeds or replace collateral. This Section does not relax the requirements of possession where perfection of a security interest depends upon possession of the collateral by the secured party or by a bailee.

§ 9-206. Agreement Not to Assert Defenses Against Assignee; Modification of Sales Warranties Where Security Agreement Exists.—

(1) Subject to any statute or decision which establishes a different rule for buyers of consumer goods, an agreement by a buyer that he will not assert against an assignee any claim or defense which he may have against the seller is enforceable by an assignee who takes his assignment for value, in good faith and without notice of a claim or defense, except as to defenses of a type which may be asserted against a holder in due course of a negotiable instrument under the Article on Commercial Paper (Article 3). A buyer who as part of one transaction signs both a negotiable instrument and a security agreement makes such an agreement.

(2) When a seller retains a purchase money security interest in goods the Article on Sales (Article 2) governs the sale and any disclaimer, limitation or modification of the seller's warranties.

§ 9-207. Rights and Duties When Collateral Is in Secured Party's Possession.—

(1) A secured party must use reasonable care in the custody and preservation of collateral in his possession. In the case of an instrument or chattel paper reasonable care includes taking necessary steps to preserve rights against prior parties unless otherwise agreed.

(2) Unless otherwise agreed, when collateral is in the secured party's possession

(a) reasonable expenses (including the cost of any insurance and payment of taxes or other charges) incurred in the custody, preservation, use or operation of the collateral are chargeable to the debtor and are secured by the collateral;

(b) the risk of accidental loss or damage is on the debtor to the extent of any deficiency in any effective insurance coverage;

(c) the secured party may hold as additional security any increase or profits (except money) received from the collateral, but money so received, unless remitted to the debtor, shall be applied in reduction of the secured obligation;

(d) the secured party must keep the collateral identifiable but fungible collateral may be commingled;

(e) the secured party may repledge the collateral upon terms which do not impair the debtor's right to redeem it.

(3) A secured party is liable for any loss caused by his failure to meet any obligation imposed by the preceding subsections but does not lose his security interest.

(4) A secured party may use or operate the collateral for the purpose of preserving the collateral or its value or pursuant to the order of a court of appropriate jurisdiction or, except in the case of consumer goods, in the manner and to the extent provided in the security agreement.

§ 9-208. Request for Statement of Account or List of Collateral.—

(1) A debtor may sign a statement indicating what he believes to be the aggregate amount of unpaid indebtedness as of a specified date and may send it to the secured party with a request that the statement be approved or corrected and returned to the debtor. When the security agreement or any other record kept by the secured party identifies the collateral a debtor may similarly request the secured party to approve or correct a list of the collateral.

(2) The secured party must comply with such a request within two weeks after receipt by sending a written correction or approval. If the secured party claims a security interest in all of a particular type of collateral owned by the debtor he may indicate that fact in his reply and need not approve or correct an itemized list of such collateral. If the secured party without reasonable excuse fails to comply he is liable for any loss caused to the debtor thereby; and if the debtor has properly included in his request a good faith statement of the obligation or a list of the collateral or both, the secured party may claim a security interest only as shown in the statement against persons misled by his failure to comply. If he no longer has an interest in the obligation or collateral at the time the request is received he must disclose the name and address of any successor in interest known to him and he is liable for any loss caused to the debtor as a result or failure to disclose. A successor in interest is not subject to this Section until a request is received by him.

(3) A debtor is entitled to such a statement once every 6 months without charge. The secured party may require payment of a charge not exceeding $10 for each additional statement furnished.

PART 3

Rights of Third Parties; Perfected and Unperfected

Security Interests; Rules of Priority

§ 9-301. Persons Who Take Priority Over Unperfected Security Interests; [Rights of] "Lien Creditor".—

(1) Except as otherwise provided in subsection (2), an unperfected security interest is subordinate to the rights of

(a) persons entitled to priority under Section 9-312;

(b) a person who becomes a lien creditor before [the security interest] is perfected;

(c) in the case of goods, instruments, documents, and chattel paper, a person who is not a secured party and who is a transferee in bulk or other buyer not in ordinary course of business, [or is a buyer of farm products in the ordinary course of business] to the extent that he gives value and receives delivery of the collateral without knowledge of the security interest and before it is perfected;

(d) in the case of accounts, contract rights, and general intangibles, a person who is not a secured party and who is a transferee to the extent that he gives value without knowledge of the security interest and before it is perfected.

(2) If the secured party files with respect to a purchase money security interest before or within ten days after the [debtor receives possession of the] collateral, he takes priority over the rights of a transferee in bulk or of a lien creditor which arise between the time the security interest attaches and the time of filing.

(3) A "lien creditor" means a creditor who has acquired a lien on the property involved by attachment, levy or the like and includes as assignee for benefit of creditors from the time of assignment, and a trustee in bankruptcy from the date of the filing of the petition or a receiver in equity from the time of appointment. Unless all the creditors represented had knowledge of the security interests such a representative of creditors is a lien creditor without knowledge even though he personally has knowledge of the security interest.

[(4) A person who becomes a lien creditor while a security interest is perfected takes subject to the security interest only to the extent that it secures advances made before he becomes a lien creditor or within 45 days thereafter or made without knowledge of the lien or pursuant to a commitment entered into without knowledge of the lien.]

§ 9-302. When Filing is Required to Perfect Security Interest; Security Interests to Which Filing Provisions of This Article Do Not Apply.—

(1) A financing statement must be filed to perfect all security interests except the following:

(a) a security interest in collateral in possession of the secured party under Section 9-305;

(b) a security interest temporarily perfected in instruments or documents without delivery under Section 9-034 or in proceeds for a 10 day period under Section 9-306;

[(c) a security interest created by an assignment of a beneficial interest in a trust of a decedent's estate;]

(d) a purchase money security interest in consumer goods; but filing is required [for a motor vehicle required to be registered; and fixture filing is required for priority over conflicting interests in fixtures to the extent provided in Section 9-313;]

(e) an assignment of accounts or contract rights which does not alone or in conjunction with other assignments to the same assignee transfer a significant part of the outstanding accounts or contract rights of the assignor;

(f) a security interest of a collecting bank (Section 4-208) or in securities (Section 8-321) or arising under the Article on Sales (see Section 9-113) or covered in subsection (3) of this section;

[(g) an assignment for the benefit of all the creditors of the transferor, and subsequent transfers by the assignee thereunder.]

(2) If a secured party assigns a perfected security interest, no filing under this Article is required in order to continue the perfected status of the security interest against creditors of and transferees from the original debtor.

[(3) The filing of a financing statement otherwise required by this Article is not necessary or effective to perfect a security interest in property subject to

(a) a statute or treaty of the United States which provides for a national or international registration or a national or international certificate of title or which specifies a place of filing different from that specified in this Article for filing of the security interest; or

(b) the following statutes of this state; [[list any certificate of title statute covering automobiles, trailers, mobile homes, boats, farm tractors, or the like, and any central filing statute*.]]; but during any period in which collateral is inventory held for sale by a person who is in the business of selling goods of that kind, the filing provisions of this Article (Part 4) apply to a security interest in that collateral created by him as debtor; or

(c) a certificate of title statute of another jurisdiction under the law of which indication of a security interest on the certificate is required as a condition of perfection (subsection (2) of Section 9-103).

(4) Compliance with a statute or treaty described in subsection (3) is equivalent to the filing of a financing statement under this Article, and a security interest in property subject to the statute or treaty can be perfected only by compliance therewith except as provided in Section 9-103 on multiple state transactions. Duration and renewal of perfection of a security interest perfected by compliance with the statute or treaty are governed by the provisions of the statute or treaty; in other respects the security interest is subject to this Article.

*Note: *It is recommended that the provisions of certificate of title acts for perfection of security interests by notation on the certificates should be amended to exclude coverage of inventory held for sale.*]

§ 9-303. When Security Interest Is Perfected; Continuity of Perfection.—

(1) A security interest is perfected when it has attached and when all of the applicable steps required for perfection have been taken. Such steps are specified in Sections 9-302, 9-304, 9-306. If such steps are taken before the security interest attaches, it is perfected at the time when it attaches.

(2) If a security interest is originally perfected in any way permitted under this Article and is subsequently perfected in some other way under this Article, without an intermediate period when it was unperfected, the security interest shall be deemed to be perfected continuously for the purposes of this Article.

§ 9-304. Perfection of Security Interest in Instruments, Documents and Goods Covered by Documents; Perfection by Permissive Filing; Temporary Perfection Without Filing or Transfer of Possession.—

(1) A security interest in chattel paper or negotiable documents may be perfected by filing. A security interest in money or instruments (other than certificated securities or instruments which constitute part of chattel paper) can be perfected only by the secured party's taking possession, except as provided in subsections (4) and (5) of this section and subsections (2) and (3) of Section 9—306 on proceeds.

(2) During the period that goods are in the possession of the issuer of a negotiable document therefor, a security interest in the goods is perfected by perfecting a security interest in the document, and any security interest in the goods otherwise perfected during such period is subject thereto.

(3) A security interest in goods in the possession of a bailee other than one who has issued a negotiable document therefor is perfected by issuance of a document in the name of the secured party or by the bailee's receipt of notification of the secured party's interest or by filing as to the goods.

(4) A security interest in instruments (other than certificated securities) or negotiable documents is perfected without filing or the taking of possession for a period of 21 days from the time it attaches to the extent that it arises for new value given under a written security agreement.

(5) A security interest remains perfected for a period of 21 days without filing where a secured party having a perfected security interest in an instrument (other than a certificated security), a negotiable document or goods in possession of a bailee other than one who has issued a negotiable document therefor

(a) makes available to the debtor the goods or documents representing the goods for the purpose of ultimate sale or exchange or for the purpose of loading, unloading, storing, shipping, transshipping, manufacturing, processing or otherwise dealing with them in a manner preliminary to their sale or exchange, but priority between conflicting security interests in the goods is subject to subsection (3) of Section 9—312; or

(b) delivers the instrument to the debtor for the purpose of ultimate sale or exchange or of presentation, collection, renewal or registration of transfer.

(6) After the 21 day period in subsections (4) and (5) perfection depends upon compliance with applicable provisions of this Article.

§ 9—305. When Possession by Secured Party Perfects Security Interest Without Filing—

A security interest in letters of credit and advices of credit (subsection (2)(a) of Section 5—116), goods, instruments (other than certificated securities), money, negotiable documents, or chattel paper may be perfected by the secured party's taking possession of the collateral. If such collateral other than goods covered by a negotiable document is held by a bailee, the secured party is deemed to have possession from the time the bailee receives notification of the secured party's interest. A security interest is perfected by possession from the time possession is taken without a relation back and continues only so long as possession is retained, unless otherwise specified in this Article. The security interest may be otherwise perfected as provided in this Article before or after the period of possession by the secured party.

§ 9-306. "Proceeds"; Secured Party's Rights on Disposition of Collateral

(1) ["Proceeds" includes whatever is received upon the sale, exchange, collection or other disposition of collateral or proceeds. Insurance payable by reason of loss or damage to the collateral is proceeds, except to the extent that it is payable to a person other than a party to the security agreement.] Money, checks, [deposit accounts,] and the like are "cash proceeds". All other proceeds are "non-cash proceeds".

(2) Except where this Article otherwise provides, a security interest continues in collateral notwithstanding sale, exchange or other disposition thereof unless [the disposition was] authorized by the secured party in the security agreement or otherwise, and also continues in any identifiable proceeds including collections received by the debtor.

(3) The security interest in proceeds is a continuously perfected security interest if the interest in the original collateral was perfected but it ceases to be a perfected security interest and becomes unperfected ten days after receipt of the proceeds by the debtor unless

[(a) a filed financing statement covers the original collateral and the proceeds are collateral in which a security interest may be perfected by filing in the office or offices where the financing statement has been filed and, if the proceeds are acquired with cash proceeds, the description of collateral in the financing statement indicates the types of property constituting the proceeds; or]

[(b) a filed financing statement covers the original collateral and the proceeds are identifiable cash proceeds; or]

[(c) the security interest in the proceeds is perfected before the expiration of the ten day period. [Except as provided in this section, a security interest in proceeds can be perfected only by the methods or under the circumstances permitted in this Article for original collateral of the same type.]

(4) In the event of insolvency proceeding instituted by or against a debtor, a secured party with a perfected security interest in proceeds has a perfected security interest [only in the following proceeds:]

(a) in identifiable non-cash proceeds[,] [and in separate deposit accounts containing only proceeds;]

(b) in identifiable cash proceeds in the form of money which is [neither] commingled with other money [nor] deposited in a [deposit] account prior to the insolvency proceedings;

(c) in identifiable cash proceeds in the form of checks and the like which are not deposited in a [deposit] account prior to the insolvency proceedings; and

(d) in all cash and [deposit] accounts of the debtor [in which] proceeds have been commingled [with other funds,] but the perfected security interest under this paragraph (d) is

(i) subject to any right of set-off; and

(ii) limited to an amount not greater than the amount of any cash proceeds received by the debtor within ten days before the institution of the insolvency proceedings [less the sum of (I) the payments to the secured party on account of cash proceeds received by the debtor during such period and (II) the cash proceeds received by the debtor during such period to which the secured party is entitled under paragraphs (a) through (c) of this subsection (4).]

(5) If a sale of goods results in an account or chattel paper which is transferred by the seller to a secured party, and if the goods are returned to or are repossessed by the seller or the secured party, the following rules determine priorities:

(a) If the goods were collateral at the time of sale for an indebtedness of the seller which is still unpaid, the original security interest attaches again to the goods and continues as a perfected security interest if it was perfected at the time when the goods were sold. If the security interest was originally perfected by a filing which is still effective, nothing further is required to continue the perfected status; in any other case, the secured party must take possession of the returned or repossessed goods or must file.

(b) An unpaid transferee of the chattel paper has a security interest in the goods against the transferor. Such security interest is prior to a security interest asserted under paragraph (a) to the extent that the transferee of the chattel paper was entitled to priority under Section 9-308.

(c) An unpaid transferee of the account has a security interest in the goods against the transferor. Such security interest is subordinate to a security interest asserted under paragraph (a).

(d) A security interest of an unpaid transferee asserted under paragraph (b) or (c) must be perfected for protection against creditors of the transferor and purchasers of the returned or repossessed goods.

§ 9-306.01. Debtor Disposing of Collateral and Failing to Pay Secured Party Amount Due under Security Agreement; Penalties for Violation.—

(1) It is unlawful for a debtor under the terms of a security agreement (a) who has no right of sale or other disposition of the collateral or (b) who has a right of sale or other disposition of the collateral and is to account to the secured party for the proceeds of any sale or other disposition of the collateral, to sell or otherwise dispose of the collateral and willfully and wrongfully to fail to pay the secured party the amount of said proceeds due under the security agreement.

(2) An individual convicted of a violation of this Section shall be punished by imprisonment in the penitentiary for not less than one year nor more than ten years.

(3) A corporation convicted of a violation of this Section shall be punished by a fine of not less than two thousand dollars nor more than ten thousand dollars.

(4) In the event the debtor under the terms of a security agreement is a corporation or a partnership, any officer, director, manager, or managerial agent of the debtor who violates this Section or causes the debtor to violate this Section shall, upon conviction thereof, be punished by imprisonment in the penitentiary for not less than one year nor more than ten years.

§ 9-307. Protection of Buyers of Goods.—

(1) A buyer in ordinary course of business (subsection (9) of Section 1-201) other than a person buying farm products from a person engaged in farming operations takes free of a security interest created by his seller even though the security interest is perfected and even though the buyer knows of its existence.

(2) In the case of consumer goods, a buyer takes free of a security interest even though perfected if he buys without knowledge of the security interest, for value and for his own personal, family or household purposes or his own farming operations unless prior to the purchase the secured party has filed a financing statement covering such goods.

[(3) A buyer other than a buyer in ordinary course of business (subsection (1) of this section) takes free of a security interest to the extent that it secures future advances made after the secured party acquires knowledge of the purchase, or more than 45 days after the purchase, whichever first occurs, unless made pursuant to a commitment entered into without knowledge of the purchase and before the expiration of the 45 day period.]

§ 9-308.* Purchase of Chattel Paper and Instruments—

[A purchaser of chattel paper or an instrument who gives new value and takes possession of it in the ordinary course of his business has priority over a security interest in the chattel paper or instrument

(a) which is perfected under Section 9-304 (permissive filing and temporary perfection) or under Section 9-306 (perfection as to proceeds) if he acts without knowledge that the specific paper or instrument is subject to a security interest; or

(b) which is claimed merely as proceeds of inventory subject to a security interest (Section 9-306) even though he knows that the specific paper or instrument is subject to the security interest.]

*This section was redrafted in 1972.

§ 9—309. Protection of Purchasers of Instruments, Documents and Securities—

Nothing in this Article limits the rights of a holder in due course of a negotiable instrument (Section 3-302) or a holder to whom a negotiable document of title has been duly negotiated (Section 7—501) or a bona fide purchaser of a security (Section 8—302) and the holders or purchasers take priority over an earlier security interest even though perfected. Filing under this Article does not constitute notice of the security interest to such holders or purchasers.

§ 9-310. Priority of Certain Liens Arising by Operation of Law.—

When a person in the ordinary course of his business furnishes services or materials with respect to goods subject to a security interest, a lien upon goods in the possession of such person given by statute or rule of law for such materials or services takes priority over a perfected security interest unless the lien is statutory and the statute expressly provides otherwise.

§ 9-311. Alienability of Debtor's Rights: Judicial Process.—

The debtor's rights in collateral may be voluntarily or involuntarily transferred (by way of sale, creation of a security interest, attachment, levy, garnishment or other judicial process) notwithstanding a provision in the security agreement prohibiting any transfer or making the transfer constitute a default.

§ 9-312. Priorities Among Conflicting Security Interests in the Same Collateral.—

[(1) The rules of priority stated in other sections of this Part and in the following sections shall govern when applicable: Section 4-208 with respect to the security interests of collecting banks in items being collected, accompanying documents and proceeds; Section 9-103 on security interests related to other jurisdictions; Section 9-114 on consignments.]

(2) A perfected security interest in crops for new value given to enable the debtor to produce the crops during the production season and given not more than three months before the crops become growing crops by planting or otherwise takes priority over an earlier perfected security interest to the extent that such earlier interest secures obligations due more than six months before the crops become growing crops by planting or otherwise, even though the person giving new value had knowledge of the earlier security interest.

[(3) A perfected purchase money security interest in inventory has priority over a conflicting security interest in the same inventory and also has priority in identifiable cash proceeds received on or before the delivery of the inventory to a buyer if

(a) the purchase money security interest is perfected at the time the debtor receives possession of the inventory; and

(b) the purchase money secured party gives notification in writing to the holder of the conflicting security interest if the holder had filed a financing statement covering the same types of inventory (i) before the date of the filing made by the purchase money secured party, or (ii) before the beginning of the 21 day period where the purchase money security interest is temporarily perfected without filing or possession (subsection (5) of Section 9-304); and

(c) the holder of the conflicting security interest receives the notification within five years before the debtor receives possession of the inventory; and

(d) the notification states that the person giving the notice has or expects to acquire a purchase money security interest in inventory of the debtor, describing such inventory by item or type.]

(4) A purchase money security interest in collateral other than inventory has priority over a conflicting security interest in the same collateral [or its proceeds] if the purchase money security interest is perfected at the time the debtor receives possession of the collateral or within 10 days thereafter.

(5) In all cases not governed by other rules stated in this section (including cases of purchase money security interests which do not qualify for the special priorities set forth in subsections (3) and (4) of this section), priority between conflicting security interests in the same collateral shall be determined [according to the following rules:

(a) Conflicting security interests rank according to priority in time of filing or perfection. Priority dates from the time a filing is first made covering the collateral or the time the security interest is first perfected, whichever is earlier, provided that there is no period thereafter when there is neither filing nor perfection.

(b) So long as conflicting security interests are unperfected, the first to attach has priority.]

[(6) For the purposes of subsection (5) a date of filing or perfection as to collateral is also a date of filing or perfection as to proceeds.

(7) If future advances are made while a security interest is perfected by filing, the taking of possession, or under Section 8—321 on securities, the security interest has the same priority for the purposes of subsection (5) with respect to the future advances as it does with respect to the first advance. If a commitment is made before or while the security interest is so perfected, the security interest has the same priority with respect to advances made pursuant thereto. In other cases a perfected security interest has priority from the date the advance is made.

§ 9-313. Priority of Security Interests in Fixtures.—

[(1) In this section and in the provisions of Part 4 of this Article referring to fixture filing, unless the context otherwise requires

(a) goods are "fixtures" when they become so related to particular real estate that an interest in them arises under real estate law

(b) a "fixture filing" is the filing in the office where a mortgage on the real estate would be filed or recorded of a financing statement covering goods which are or are to become fixtures and conforming to the requirements of subsection (5) of Section 9-402

(c) a mortgage is a "construction mortgage" to the extent that it secures an obligation incurred for the construction of an improvement on land including the acquisition cost of the land, if the recorded writing so indicates.

(2) A security interest under this Article may be created in goods which are fixtures or may continue in goods which become fixtures, but no security interest exists under this Article in ordinary building materials incorporated into an improvement on land.

(3) This Article does not prevent creation of an encumbrance upon fixtures pursuant to real estate law.

(4) A perfected security interest in fixtures has priority over the conflicting interest of an encumbrancer or owner of the real estate where

(a) the security interest is a purchase money security interest, the interest of the encumbrancer or owner arises before the goods become fixtures, the security interest is perfected by a fixture filing before the goods become fixtures or within ten days thereafter, and the debtor has an interest of record in the real estate or is in possession of the real estate; or

(b) the security interest is perfected by a fixture filing before the interest of the encumbrancer or owner is of record, the security interest has priority over any conflicting interest of a predecessor in title of the encumbrancer or owner, and the debtor has an interest of record in the real estate or is in possession of the real estate; or

(c) the fixtures are readily removable factory or office machines or readily removable replacements of domestic appliances which are consumer goods, and before the goods become fixtures the security interest is perfected by any method permitted by this Article; or

(d) the conflicting interest is a lien on the real estate obtained by legal or equitable proceedings after the security interest was perfected by any method permitted by this Article.

(5) A security interest in fixtures, whether or not perfected, has priority over the conflicting interest of an encumbrancer or owner of the real estate where

(a) the encumbrancer or owner has consented in writing to the security interest or has disclaimed an interest in the goods as fixtures; or

(b) the debtor has a right to remove the goods as against the encumbrancer or owner. If the debtor's right terminates, the priority of the security interest continues for a reasonable time.

(6) Notwithstanding paragraph (a) of subsection (4) but otherwise subject to subsections (4) and (5), a security interest in fixtures is subordinate to a construction mortgage recorded before the goods become fixtures if the goods become fixtures before the completion of the construction. To the extent that it is given to refinance a construction mortgage, a mortgage has this priority to the same extent as the construction mortgage.

(7) In cases not within the preceding subsections, a security interest in fixtures is subordinate to the conflicting interest of an encumbrancer or owner of the related real estate who is not the debtor.]

[(8)] When the secured party has priority over all owners and encumbrancers of the real estate, he may, on default, subject to the provisions of Part 5, remove his collateral from the real estate but he must reimburse any encumbrancer or owner of the real estate who is not the debtor and who has not otherwise agreed for the cost of repair of any physical injury, but not for any diminution in value of the real estate caused by the absence of the goods removed or by any necessity for replacing them. A person entitled to reimbursement may refuse permission to remove until the secured party gives adequate security for the performance of this obligation.

§ 9-314. Accessions.—

(1) A security interest in goods which attaches before they are installed in or affixed to other goods takes priority as to the goods installed or affixed (called in this section "accessions") over the claims of all persons to the whole except as stated in subsection (3) and subject to Section 9-315(1).

(2) A security interest which attaches to goods after they become part of a whole is valid against all persons subsequently acquiring interests in the whole except as stated in subsection (3) but is invalid against any person with an interest in the whole at the time the security interest attaches to the goods who has not in writing consented to the security interest or disclaimed an interest in the goods as part of the whole.

848

(3) The security interests described in subsections (1) and (2) do not take priority over

   (a) a subsequent purchaser for value of any interest in the whole; or

   (b) a creditor with a lien on the whole subsequently obtained by judicial proceedings; or

   (c) a creditor with a prior perfected security interest in the whole to the extent that he makes subsequent advances

if the subsequent purchase is made, the lien by judicial proceedings obtained or the subsequent advance under the prior perfected security interest is made or contracted for without knowledge of the security interest and before it is perfected. A purchaser of the whole at a foreclosure sale other than the holder of a perfected security interest purchasing at his own foreclosure sale is a subsequent purchaser within this Section.

(4) When under subsections (1) or (2) and (3) a secured party has an interest in accessions which has priority over the claims of all persons who have interests in the whole, he may on default subject to the provisions of Part 5 remove his collateral from the whole but he must reimburse any encumbrancer or owner of the whole who is not the debtor and who has not otherwise agreed for the cost of repair of any physical injury but not for any diminution in value of the whole caused by the absence of the goods removed or by any necessity for replacing them. A person entitled to reimbursement may refuse permission to remove until the secured party gives adequate security for the performance of this obligation.

§ 9-315. Priority When Goods Are Commingled or Processed.—

(1) If a security interest in goods was perfected and subsequently the goods or a part thereof have become part of a product or mass, the security interest continues in the product or mass if

   (a) the goods are so manufactured, processed, assembled or commingled that their identity is lost in the product or mass; or

   (b) a financing statement covering the original goods also covers the product into which the goods have been manufactured, processed or assembled.

In a case to which paragraph (b) applies, no separate security interest in that part of the original goods which has been manufactured, processed or assembled into the product may be claimed under Section 9-314.

(2) When under subsection (1) more than one security interest attaches to the product or mass, they rank equally according to the ratio that the cost of the goods to which each interest originally attached bears to the cost of the total product or mass.

§ 9-316. Priority Subject to Subordination.—Nothing in this Article prevents subordination by agreement by any person entitled to priority.

§ 9-317. Secured Party Not Obligated on Contract of Debtor.—The mere existence of a security interest or authority given to the debtor to dispose of or use collateral does not impose contract or tort liability upon the secured party for the debtor's acts or omissions.

§ 9-318. Defenses Against Assignee; Modification of Contract After Notification of Assignment; Term Prohibiting Assignment Ineffective; Identification and Proof of Assignment.—

(1) Unless an account debtor has made an enforceable agreement not to assert defenses or claims arising out of a sale as provided in Section 9-206 the rights of an assignee are subject to

   (a) all the terms of the contract between the account debtor and assignor and any defense or claim arising therefrom; and

   (b) any other defense or claim of the account debtor against the assignor which accrues before the account debtor receives notification of the assignment.

(2) So far as the right to payment [or a part thereof] under an assigned contract [has not been fully earned by performance,] and notwithstanding notification of the assignment, any modification of or substitution for the contract made in good faith and in accordance with reasonable commercial standards is effective against an assignee unless the account debtor has otherwise agreed but the assignee acquires corresponding rights under the modified or substituted contract. The assignment may provide that such modification or substitution is a breach by the assignor.

(3) The account debtor is authorized to pay the assignor until the account debtor receives notification that the [amount due or to become due] has been assigned and that payment is to be made to the assignee. A notification which does not reasonably identify the rights assigned is ineffective. If requested by the account debtor, the assignee must seasonably furnish reasonable proof that the assignment has been made and unless he does so the account debtor may pay the assignor.

(4) A term in any contract between an account debtor and an assignor [is ineffective if it] prohibits assignment of an account [or prohibits creation of a security interest in a general intangible for money due or to become due or requires the account debtor's consent to such assignment or security interest.]

PART 4

FILING

§ 9-401. Place of Filing; Erroneous Filing; Removal of Collateral

First Alternative Subsection (1)

(1) The proper place to file in order to perfect a security interest is as follows:

   [(a) when the collateral is timber to be cut or is minerals or the like (including oil and gas) or accounts subject to subsection (5) of Section 9-103, or when the financing statement is filed as a fixture filing

(Section 9-313) and] the collateral is goods which are or are to become fixtures, then in the office where a mortgage on the real estate would be filed or recorded;

(b) in all other cases, in the office of the Secretary of State.

Second Alternative Subsection (1)

(1) The proper place to file in order to perfect a security interest is as follows:

(a) when the collateral is equipment used in farming operations, or farm products, or accounts, [contract rights] or general intangibles arising from or relating to the sale of farm products by a farmer, or consumer goods, then in the office of the........in the county of the debtor's residence or if the debtor is not a resident of this state then in the office of the........in the county where the goods are kept, and in addition when the collateral is crops [growing or to be grown] in the office of the........in the county where the land [on which the crops are growing or to be grown] is located;

(b) when the collateral is [timber to be cut or is minerals or the like (including oil and gas) or accounts subject to subsection (5) of Section 9-103, or when the financing statement is filed as a fixture filing (Section 9-313) and the collateral is goods which are or are to become fixtures,] then in the office where a mortgage on the real estate would be filed or recorded;

(c) in all other cases, in the office of the Secretary of State.

Third Alternative Subsection (1)

(1) The proper place to file in order to perfect a security interest is as follows:

(a) when the collateral is equipment used in farming operations, or farm products, or accounts, [contract rights] or general intangibles arising from or relating to the sale of farm products by a farmer, or consumer goods, then in the office of the........in the county of the debtor's residence or if the debtor is not a resident of this state then in the office of the........in the county where the goods are kept, and in addition when the collateral is crops growing or to be grown in the office of the........in the county where the land [on which the crops are growing or to be grown] is located;

(b) when the collateral is [goods which at the time the security interest attaches are or are to become fixtures] timber to be cut or is minerals or the like (including oil and gas) or accounts subject to subsection (5) of Section 9-103, or when the financing statement is filed as a fixture filing (Section 9-313) and the collateral is goods which are or are to become fixtures, then in the office where a mortgage on the real estate [concerned] would be filed or recorded;

(c) in all other cases, in the office of the Secretary of State and in addition, if the debtor has a place of business in only one county of this state, also in the office of........of such county, or, if the debtor has no place of business in this state, but resides in the state, also in the office of........of the county in which he resides.

Note: *One of the three alternatives should be selected as subsection (1).*

(2) A filing which is made in good faith in an improper place or not in all of the places required by this section is nevertheless effective with regard to any collateral as to which the filing complied with the requirements of this Article and is also effective with regard to collateral covered by the financing statement against any person who has knowledge of the contents of such financing statement.

(3) A filing which is made in the proper place in this State continues effective even though the debtor's residence or place of business or the location of the collateral or its use, whichever controlled the original filing, is thereafter changed.

(4) [The] rules stated in Section 9-103 determine whether filing is necessary in this State.

[(5) Notwithstanding the preceding subsections, and subject to subsection (3) of Section 9-302, the proper place to file in order to perfect a security interest in collateral, including fixtures, of a transmitting utility is the office of the Secretary of State. This filing constitutes a fixture filing (Section 9-313) as to the collateral described therein which is or is to become fixtures.

(6) For the purposes of this section, the residence of an organization is its place of business if it has one or its chief executive office if it has more than one place of business.]

Note: *Subsection (6) should be used only if the state chooses the Second or Third Alternative Subsection (1).*

§ 9-402. Formal Requisites of Financing Statement; Amendments; Mortgage as Financing Statement.—

(1) A financing statement is sufficient if it [gives the names of the debtor and the secured party,] is signed by the debtor, gives an address of the secured party from which information concerning the security interest may be obtained, gives a mailing address of the debtor and contains a statement indicating the types, or describing the items, of collateral. A financing statement may be filed before a security agreement is made or a security interest otherwise attaches. When the financing statement covers crops growing or to be grown [or goods which are or are to become fixtures,] the statement must also contain a description of the real estate concerned. [When the financing statement covers timber to be cut or covers minerals or the like (including oil and gas) or accounts subject to subsection (5) of Section 9-103, or when the financing statement is filed as a fixture filing (Section 9-313) and the collateral is goods which are or are to become fixtures, the statement must also comply with subsection (5).] A copy of the security agreement is sufficient as a financing statement if it contains the above information and is signed by [the debtor. A carbon, photographic or other reproduction of a security agreement or a financing statement is sufficient as a financing statement if the security agreement so provides or if the original has been filed in this state.]

(2) A financing statement which otherwise complies with subsection (1) is sufficient [when] it is signed by the secured party [instead of the debtor] if it is filed to perfect a security interest in

(a) collateral already subject to a security interest in another jurisdiction when it is brought into this state, [or when the debtor's location is changed to this state.] Such a financing statement must state that the collateral was brought into this state [or that the debtor's location was changed to this state] under such circumstances; [or]

(b) proceeds under Section 9-306 if the security interest in the original collateral was perfected. Such a financing statement must describe the original collateral; [or

(c) collateral as to which the filing has lapsed; or

(d) collateral acquired after a change of name, identity or corporate structure of the debtor (subsection (7).]

(3) A form substantially as follows is sufficient to comply with subsection (1):

Name of debtor (or assignor) ....

Address ....

Name of secured party or assignee) ....

Address ....

1. This financing statement covers the following types (or items) of property:
   (Describe) ....
2. (If collateral is crops) The above described crops are growing or are to be grown on:
   (Describe Real Estate) ....
[3. (If applicable) The above goods are to become fixtures on*]

*Where appropriate substitute either "The above timber is standing on...." or "The above minerals or the like (including oil and gas) or accounts will be financed at the wellhead or minehead of the well or mine located on...."

[(Describe Real Estate) ....
and this financing statement is to be filed [for record] in the real estate records. (If the debtor does not have an interest of record) The name of a record owner is] ....
4. (If [proceeds or] products of collateral are claimed) Products of the collateral are also covered.

(use ....
whichever   Signature of Debtor (or Assignor)
is ....
applicable)   Signature of Secured Party (or Assignee)

(4) [A financing statement may be amended by filing a writing signed by both the debtor and the secured party. An amendment does not extend the period of effectiveness of a financing statement.] If any amendment adds collateral, it is effective as to the added collateral only from the filing date of the amendment. [In this Article, unless the context otherwise requires, the term "financing statement" means the original financing statement and any amendments.

(5) A financing statement covering timber to be cut or covering minerals or the like (including oil and gas) or accounts subject to subsection (5) of Section 9-103, or a financing statement filed as a fixture filing (Section 9-313) where the debtor is not a transmitting utility, must show that it covers this type of collateral, must recite that it is to be filed [for record] in the real estate records, and the financing statement must contain a description of the real estate [sufficient if it were contained in a mortgage of the real estate to give constructive notice of the mortgage under the law of this state.] If the debtor does not have an interest of record in the real estate, the financing statement must show the name of a record owner.

(6) A mortgage is effective as a financing statement filed as a fixture filing from the date of its recording if (a) the goods are described in the mortgage by item or type, (b) the goods are or are to become fixtures related to the real estate described in the mortgage, (c) the mortgage complies with the requirements for a financing statement in this section other than a recital that it is to be filed in the real estate records, and (d) the mortgage is duly recorded. No fee with reference to the financing statement is required other than the regular recording and satisfaction fees with respect to the mortgage.

(7) A financing statement sufficiently shows the name of the debtor if it gives the individual, partnership or corporate name of the debtor, whether or not it adds other trade names or the names of partners. Where the debtor so changes his name or in the case of an organization its name, identity or corporate structure that a filed financing statement becomes seriously misleading, the filing is not effective to perfect a security interest in collateral acquired by the debtor more than four months after the change; unless a new appropriate financing statement is filed before the expiration of that time. A filed financing statement remains effective with respect to collateral transferred by the debtor even though the secured party knows of or consents to the transfer.]

[(8)] A financing statement substantially complying with the requirements of this section is effective even though it contains minor errors which are not seriously misleading.

§ 9-403. What Constitutes Filing; Duration of Filing; Effect of Lapsed Filing; Duties of Filing Officer.—

(1) Presentation for filing of a financing statement and tender of the filing fee or acceptance of the statement by the filing officer constitutes filing under this Article.

[(2) Except as provided in Subsection (6)] a filed financing statement is effective for a period of five years from the date of filing. The effectiveness of a filed financing statement lapses on the expiration of [the five] year period unless a continuation statement is filed prior to the lapse. [If a security interest perfected by filing exists at the time insolvency proceedings are commenced by or against the debtor, the security interest remains perfected until termination of the insolvency proceedings and thereafter for a period of sixty days or until expiration of the five year period, whichever occurs later.] Upon lapse the security interest becomes unperfected, [unless it is perfected without filing. If the security interest becomes unperfected upon lapse, it is deemed to have been unperfected as against a person who became a purchaser or lien creditor before lapse.]

(3) A continuation statement may be filed by the secured party [(i) within six months before and sixty days after a stated maturity date of five years or less, and (ii) otherwise] within six months prior to the expiration of the five year period specified in subsection (2). Any such continuation statement must be signed by the secured party, identify the original statement by file number and state that the original statement is still effective. [A continuation statement signed by a person other than the secured party of record must be accompanied by a separate written statement of assignment signed by the secured party of record and complying with subsection (2) of Section 9-405, including payment of the required fee.] Upon timely filing of the continuation statement, the effectiveness of the original statement is continued for five years after the last date to which the filing was effective whereupon it lapses in the same manner as provided in subsection (2) unless another continuation statement is filed prior to such lapse. Succeeding continuation statements may be filed in the same manner to continue the effectiveness of the original statement. Unless a statute on disposition of public records provides otherwise, the filing officer may remove a lapsed statement from the files and destroy it [immediately if he has retained a microfilm or other photographic record, or in other cases after one year after the lapse. The filing officer shall so arrange matters by physical annexation of financing statements to continuation statements or other related filings, or by other means, that if he physically destroys the financing statements of a period more than five years past, those which have been continued by a continuation statement or which are still effective under subsection (6) shall be retained.]

[(4) Except as provided in subsection (7) a] filing officer shall mark each statement with a [consecutive] file number and with the date and hour of filing and shall hold the statement [or a microfilm or other photographic copy thereof] for public inspection. In addition the filing officer shall index the statements according to the name of the debtor and shall note in the index the file number and the address of the debtor given in the statement.

[(5) The uniform fee for filing and indexing and for stamping a copy furnished by the secured party to show the date and place of filing for an original financing statement or for a continuation statement shall be $........if the statement is in the standard form prescribed by the [Secretary of State] and otherwise shall be $........, plus in each case, if the financing statement is subject to subsection (5) of Section 9-402, $........The uniform fee for each name more than one required to be indexed shall be $........The secured party may at his option show a trade name for any person and an extra uniform indexing fee of $........shall be paid with respect thereto.

(6) If the debtor is a transmitting utility (subsection (5) of Section 9-401) and a filed financing statement so states, it is effective until a termination statement is filed. A real estate mortgage which is effective as a fixture filing under subsection (6) of Section 9-402 remains effective as a fixture filing until the mortgage is released or satisfied of record or its effectiveness otherwise terminates as to the real estate.

(7) When a financing statement covers timber to be cut or covers minerals or the like (including oil and gas) or accounts subject to subsection (5) of Section 9-103, or is filed as a fixture filing, [it shall be filed for record and] the filing officer shall index it under the names of the debtor and any owner of record shown on the financing statement in the same fashion as if they were the mortgagors in a mortgage of the real estate described, and, to the extent that the law of this state provides for indexing of mortgages under the name of the mortgagee, under the name of the secured party as if he were the mortgagee thereunder, or where indexing is by description in the same fashion as if the financing statement were a mortgage of the real estate described.]

§ 9-404. Termination Statement.—

[(1) If a financing statement covering consumer goods is filed on or after........, then within one month or within ten days following written demand by the debtor after there is no outstanding secured obligation and no commitment to make advances, incur obligations or otherwise give value, the secured party must file with each filing officer with whom the financing statement was filed, a termination statement to the effect that he no longer claims a security interest under the financing statement, which shall be identified by file number. In other cases whenever there is no outstanding] secured obligation and no commitment to make advances, incur obligations or otherwise give value, the secured party must on written demand by the debtor send the debtor, [for each filing officer with whom the financing statement was filed,] a [termination] statement [to the effect] that he no longer claims a security interest under the financing statement, which shall be identified by file number. A termination statement signed by a person other than the secured party of record must be accompanied by a [separate written] statement [of assignment signed] by the secured party of record [complying with subsection (2) of Section 9-405, including payment of the required fee.] If the affected secured party fails to [file such a termination statement as required by this subsection, or to] send such a termination statement within ten days after proper demand therefor he shall be liable to the debtor for one hundred dollars, and in addition for any loss caused to the debtor by such failure.

(2) On presentation to the filing officer of such a termination statement he must note it in the index. [If he has received the termination statement in duplicate, he shall return one copy of the termination statement to the secured party stamped to show the time of receipt thereof. If the filing officer has a microfilm or other photographic record of the financing statement, and of any related continuation statement, statement of assignment and statement of release, he may remove the originals from the files at any time after receipt of the termination statement, or if he has no such record, he may remove them from the files at any time after one year after receipt of the termination statement.]

[(3) If the termination statement is in the standard form prescribed by the Secretary of State,] the uniform fee for filing and indexing [the] termination statement shall be $........, [and otherwise shall be $........, plus in each case an additional fee of $........for each name more than one against which the termination statement is required to be indexed.]

Note: *The date to be inserted should be the effective date of the revised Article 9.*

§ 9-405.   Assignment of Security Interest; Duties of Filing Officer; Fees.—

(1) A financing statement may disclose an assignment of a security interest in the collateral described in the [financing] statement by indication in the [financing] statement of the name and address of the assignee or by an assignment itself or a copy thereof on the face or back of the statement. On presentation to the filing officer of such a financing statement the filing officer shall mark the same as provided in Section 9-403(4). The uniform fee for filing, indexing and furnishing filing data for a financing standard form prescribed by the Secretary of State and otherwise shall be $........, plus an additional fee of $........for each name more than one against which the financing statement is required to be indexed.]

(2) A secured party may assign of record all or a part of his rights under a financing statement by the filing [in the place where the original financing statement was filed] of a separate written statement of assignment signed by the secured party of record and setting forth the name of the secured party of record and the debtor, the file number and the date of filing of the financing statement and the name and address of the assignee and containing a description of the collateral assigned. A copy of the assignment is sufficient as a separate statement if it complies with the preceding sentence. On presentation to the filing officer of such a separate statement, the filing officer shall mark such separate statement with the date and hour of the filing. He shall note the assignment on the index of the financing statement [or in the case of a fixture filing, or a filing covering timber to be cut, or covering minerals or the like (including oil and gas) or accounts subject to subsection (5) of Section 9-103, he shall index the assignment under the name of the assignor as grantor and, to the extent that the law of this state provides for indexing the assignment of a mortgage under the name of the assignee. The uniform fee for filing, indexing and furnishing filing data about such a separate statement of assignment shall be $........if the statement is in the standard form prescribed by the Secretary of State and otherwise shall be $........, plus in each case an additional fee of $........for each name more than one against which the statement of assignment is required to be indexed. Notwithstanding the provisions of this subsection, an assignment of record of a security interest in a fixture contained in a mortgage effective as a fixture filing (subsection (6) of Section 9-402) may be made only by an assignment of the mortgage in the manner provided by the law of this state other than this Act.]

(3) After the disclosure or filing of an assignment under this section, the assignee is the secured party of record.

§ 9-406.   Release of Collateral; Duties of Filing Officer; Fees.—

A secured party of record may by his signed statement release all or a part of a collateral described in a filed financing statement. The statement of release is sufficient if it contains a description of the collateral being released, the name and address of the debtor, the name and address of the secured party, and the file number of the financing statement. [A statement of release signed by a person other than the secured party of record must be accompanied by a separate written statement of assignment signed by the secured party of record and complying with subsection (2) of Section 9-405, including payment of the required fee.] Upon presentation of such a statement [of release] to the filing officer he shall mark the statement with the hour and date of filing and shall note the same upon the margin of the index of the filing of the financing statement. The uniform fee for filing and noting such a statement of release shall be $........[if the statement is in the standard form prescribed by the [Secretary of State] and otherwise shall be $........,plus in each case an additional fee of $........for each name more than one against which the statement of release is required to be indexed.

[§ 9-407.   Information From Filing Officer.]*—

[(1) If the person filing any financing statement, termination statement, statement of assignment, or statement release, furnishes the filing officer a copy thereof, the filing officer shall upon request note upon the copy the file number and date and hour of the filing of the original and deliver or send the copy to such person.]

[(2) Upon request of any person, the filing officer shall issue his certificate showing whether there is on file on the date and hour stated therein, any presently effective financing statement naming a particular debtor and any statement of assignment thereof and if there is, giving the date and hour of filing of each such statement and the names and addresses of each secured party therein. The uniform fee for such a certificate shall be $........if the request for the certificate is in the standard form prescribed by the [Secretary of State] and otherwise shall be $........ Upon request the filing officer shall furnish a copy of any filed financing statement or statement of assignment for a uniform fee of $........per page.]

*This section optional.

§ 9-408.   Financing Statements Covering Consigned or Leased Goods.—

*A consignor or lessor of goods may file a financing statement using the terms "consignor," "consignee," "lessor," "lessee" or the like instead of the terms specified in Section 9-402. The provisions of this Part shall apply as appropriate to such a financing statement but its filing shall not of itself be a factor in determining whether or not the consignment or lease is intended as security (Section 1-201(37)). However, if it is determined for other reasons that the consignment or lease is so intended, a security interest of the consignor or lessor which attaches to the consigned or leased goods is perfected by such filing.

*This section new in 1972.

Default

§ **9-501.** **Default; Procedure When Security Agreement Covers Both Real and Personal Property.—**

(1) When a debtor is in default under a security agreement, a secured party has the rights and remedies provided in this Part and except as limited by subsection (3) those provided in the security agreement. He may reduce his claim to judgment, foreclose or otherwise enforce the security interest by any available judicial procedure. If the collateral is documents the secured party may proceed either as to the documents or as to the goods covered thereby. A secured party in possession has the rights, remedies and duties provided in Section 9-207. The rights and remedies referred to in this subsection are cumulative.

(2) After default, the debtor has the rights and remedies provided in this Part, those provided in the security agreement and those provided in Section 9-207.

(3) To the extent that they give rights to the debtor and impose duties on the secured party, the rules stated in the subsections referred to below may not be waived or varied except as provided with respect to compulsory disposition of collateral [(subsection (3) of Section 9-504 and] Section 9-505) and with respect to redemption of collateral (Section 9-506) but the parties may by agreement determine the standards by which the fulfillment of these rights and duties is to be measured if such standards are not manifestly unreasonable:

(a) subsection (2) of Section 9-502 and subsection (2) of Section 9-504 insofar as they require accounting for surplus proceeds of collateral;

(b) subsection (3) of Section 9-504 and subsection (1) of Section 9-505 which deal with disposition of collateral;

(c) subsection (2) of Section 9-505 which deals with acceptance of collateral as discharge of obligation;

(d) Section 9-506 which deals with redemption of collateral; and

(e) subsection (1) of Section 9-507 which deals with the secured party's liability for failure to comply with this Part.

(4) If the security agreement covers both real and personal property, the secured party may proceed under this Part as to the personal property or he may proceed as to both the real and the personal property in accordance with his rights and remedies in respect to the real property in which case the provisions of this Part do not apply.

(5) When a secured party has reduced his claim to judgment the lien of any levy which may be made upon his collateral by virtue of any execution based upon the judgment shall relate back to the date of the perfection of the security interest in such collateral. A judicial sale, pursuant to such execution, is a foreclosure of the security interest by judicial procedure within the meaning of this Section, and the secured party may purchase at the sale and thereafter hold the collateral free of any other requirements of this Article.

§ **9-502.** **Collection Rights of Secured Party.—**

(1) When so agreed and in any event on default the secured party is entitled to notify an account debtor or the obligor on an instrument to make payment to him whether or not the assignor was theretofore making collections on the collateral, and also to take control of any proceeds to which he is entitled under Section 9-306.

(2) A secured party who by agreement is entitled to charge back uncollected collateral or otherwise to full or limited recourse against the debtor and who undertakes to collect from the account debtors or obligors must proceed in a commercially reasonable manner and may deduct his reasonable expenses of realization from the collections. If the security agreement secures an indebtedness, the secured party must account to the debtor for any surplus, and unless otherwise agreed, the debtor is liable for any deficiency. But, if the underlying transaction was a sale of accounts or chattel paper, the debtor is entitled to any surplus or is liable for any deficiency only if the security agreement so provides.

§ **9-503.** **Secured Party's Right to Take Possession After Default.—**Unless otherwise agreed a secured party has on default the right to take possession of the collateral. In taking possession a secured party may proceed without judicial process if this can be done without breach of the peace or may proceed by action.

If the security agreement so provides the secured party may require the debtor to assemble the collateral and make it available to the secured party at a place to be designated by the secured party which is reasonably convenient to both parties. Without removal a secured party may render equipment unusable, and may dispose of collateral on the debtor's premises under Section 9-504.

§ **9-504.** **Secured Party's Right to Dispose of Collateral After Default; Effect of Disposition.—**

(1) A secured party after default may sell, lease or otherwise dispose of any or all of the collateral in its then condition or following any commercially reasonable preparation or processing. Any sale of goods is subject to the Article on Sales (Article 2). The proceeds of disposition shall be applied in the order following to

(a) the reasonable expenses of retaking, holding, preparing for sale [or lease,] selling, [leasing] and the like and, to the extent provided for in the agreement and not prohibited by law, the reasonable attorneys' fees and legal expenses incurred by the secured party;

(b) the satisfaction of indebtedness secured by the security interest under which the disposition is made;

(c) the satisfaction of indebtedness secured by any subordinate security interest in the collateral if written notification of demand therefor is received before distribution of the proceeds is completed. If requested by the secured party, the holder of a subordinate security interest must seasonably furnish reasonable proof of his interest, and unless he does so, the secured party need not comply with his demand.

(2) If the security interest secures an indebtedness, the secured party must account to the debtor for any surplus, and, unless otherwise agreed, the debtor is liable for any deficiency. But if the underlying transaction was a sale of accounts or chattel paper, the debtor is entitled to any surplus or is liable for any deficiency only if the security agreement so provides.

(3) Disposition of the collateral may be by public or private proceedings and may be made by way of one or more contracts. Sale or other disposition may be as a unit or in parcels and at any time and place and on any terms but every aspect of the disposition including the method, manner, time, place and terms must be commercially reasonable. Unless collateral is perishable or threatens to decline speedily in value or is of a type customarily sold on a recognized market, reasonable notification of the time and place of any public sale or reasonable notification of the time after which any private sale or other intended disposition is to be made shall be sent by the secured party to the debtor, if he has not signed after default a statement renouncing or modifying his right to notification of sale. In the case of consumer goods no other notification need be sent. In other cases notification shall be sent to any other secured party from whom the secured party has received (before sending his notification to the debtor or before the debtor's renunciation of his rights) written notice of a claim of an interest in the collateral. The secured party may buy at any public sale and if the collateral is of a type customarily sold in a recognized market or is of a type which is the subject of widely distributed standard price quotations he may buy at private sale.

(4) When collateral is disposed of by a secured party after default, the disposition transfers to a purchaser for value all of the debtor's rights therein, discharges the security interest under which it is made and any security interest or lien subordinate thereto. The purchaser takes free of all such rights and interests even though the secured party fails to comply with the requirements of this Part or of any judicial proceedings

(a) in the case of a public sale, if the purchaser has no knowledge of any defects in the sale and if he does not buy in collusion with the secured party, other bidders or the person conducting the sale; or

(b) in any other case, if the purchaser acts in good faith.

(5) A person who is liable to a secured party under a guaranty, indorsement, repurchase agreement or the like and who receives a transfer of collateral from the secured party or is subrogated to his rights has thereafter the rights and duties of the secured party. Such a transfer of collateral is not a sale or disposition of the collateral under this Article.

§ 9-505. Compulsory Disposition of Collateral; Acceptance of the Collateral as Discharge of Obligation.—

(1) If the debtor has paid 60 percent of the cash price in the case of a purchase money security interest in consumer goods or 60 percent of the loan in the case of another security interest in consumer goods, and has not signed after default a statement renouncing or modifying his rights under this Part a secured party who has taken possession of collateral must dispose of it under Section 9-504 and if he fails to do so within ninety days after he takes possession the debtor at his option may recover in conversion or under Section 9-507(1) on secured party's liability.

(2) In any other case involving consumer goods or any other collateral a secured party in possession may, after default, propose to retain the collateral in satisfaction of the obligation. Written notice of such proposal shall be sent to the debtor [if he has not signed after default a statement renouncing or modifying his rights under this subsection. In the case of consumer goods no other notice need be given. In other cases notice shall be sent to any other secured party from whom the secured party has received (before sending his notice to the debtor or before the debtor's renunciation of his rights) written notice of a claim of an interest in the collateral. If the secured party receives objection in writing from a person entitled to receive notification within twenty-one days after the notice was sent, the secured party must dispose of the collateral under Section 9-504.] In the absence of such written objection the secured party may retain the collateral in satisfaction of the debtor's obligation.

§ 9-506. Debtor's Right to Redeem Collateral.—

At any time before the secured party has disposed of collateral or entered into a contract for its disposition under Section 9-504 or before the obligation has been discharged under Section 9-505(2) the debtor or any other secured party may unless otherwise agreed in writing after default redeem the collateral by tendering fulfillment of all obligations secured by the collateral as well as the expenses reasonably incurred by the secured party in retaking, holding, and preparing the collateral for disposition, in arranging for the sale, and to the extent provided in the agreement and not prohibited by law, his reasonable attorneys' fees and legal expenses.

§ 9-507. Secured Party's Liability for Failure to Comply With This Part.—

(1) If it is established that the secured party is not proceeding in accordance with the provisions of this Part disposition may be ordered or restrained on appropriate terms and conditions. If the disposition has occurred the debtor or any person entitled to notification or whose security interest has been made known to the secured party prior to the disposition has a right to recover from the secured party any loss caused by a failure to comply with the provisions of this Part. If the collateral is consumer goods, the debtor has a right to recover in any event an amount not less than the credit service charge plus 10 percent of the principal amount of the debt or the time price differential plus 10 percent of the cash price.

(2) The fact that a better price could have been obtained by a sale at a different time or in a different method from that selected by the secured party is not of itself sufficient to establish that the sale was not

made in a commercially reasonable manner. If the secured party either sells the collateral in the usual manner in any recognized market therefor or if he sells at the price current in such market at the time of his sale or if he has otherwise sold in conformity with reasonable commercial practices among dealers in the type of property sold he has sold in a commercially reasonable manner. The principles stated in the two preceding sentences with respect to sales also apply as may be appropriate to other types of disposition. A disposition which has been approved in any judicial proceeding or by any bona fide creditors' committee or representative of creditors shall conclusively be deemed to be commercially reasonable, but this sentence does not indicate that any such approval must be obtained in any case nor does it indicate that any disposition not so approved is not commercially reasonable.

Part I

Preliminary Provisions

§ 1. **Name of Act.**—This Act may be cited as Uniform Partnership Act.

§ 2. **Definition of Terms.**—In this Act, "Court" includes every court and judge having jurisdiction in the case.

"Business" includes every trade, occupation, or profession.

"Person" includes individuals, partnerships, corporations, and other associations.

"Bankrupt" includes bankrupt under the Federal Bankruptcy Act or insolvent under any state insolvent act.

"Conveyance" includes every assignment, lease, mortgage, or encumbrance.

"Real property" includes land and any interest or estate in land.

§ 3. **Interpretation of Knowledge and Notice.**—(1) A person has "knowledge" of a fact within the meaning of this Act not only when he has actual knowledge thereof, but also when he has knowledge of such other facts as in the circumstances shows bad faith.

(2) A person has "notice" of a fact within the meaning of this Act when the person who claims the benefit of the notice:

(a) States the fact to such person, or

(b) Delivers through the mail, or by other means of communication, a written statement of the fact to such person or to a proper person at his place of business or residence.

§ 4. **Rules of Construction.**—(1) The rule that statutes in derogation of the common law are to be strictly construed shall have no application to this Act.

(2) The law of estoppel shall apply under this Act.

(3) The law of agency shall apply under this Act.

(4) This Act shall be so interpreted and construed as to effect its general purpose to make uniform the law of those states which enact it.

(5) This Act shall not be construed so as to impair the obligations of any contract existing when the Act goes into effect, nor to affect any action or proceedings begun or right accrued before this Act takes effect.

§ 5. **Rules for Cases not Provided for in this Act.**—In any case not provided for in this Act the rules of law and equity, including the law merchant, shall govern.

Part II

Nature of a Partnership

§ 6. **Partnership Defined.**—(1) A partnership is an association of two or more persons to carry on as co-owners a business for profit.

(2) But any association formed under any other statute of this state, or any statute adopted by authority, other than the authority of this state, is not a partnership under this act, unless such association would have been a partnership in this state prior to the adoption of this act; but this act shall apply to limited partnerships except in so far as the statutes relating to such partnerships are inconsistent herewith.

§ 7. **Rules for Determining the Existence of a Partnership.**—In determining whether a partnership exists, these rules shall apply:

(1) Except as provided by § 16 persons who are not partners as to each other are not partners as to third persons

(2) Joint tenancy, tenancy in common, tenancy by the entireties, joint property, common property, or part ownership does not of itself establish a partnership, whether such co-owners do or do not share any profits made by the use of the property.

(3) The sharing of gross returns does not of itself establish a partnership, whether or not the persons sharing them have a joint or common right or interest in any property from which the returns are derived.

(4) The receipt by a person of a share of the profits of a business is prima facie evidence that he is a partner in the business, but no such inference shall be drawn if such profits were received in payment:

(a) As a debt by installments or otherwise.

(b) As wages of an employee or rent to a landlord,

(c) As an annuity to a widow or representative of a deceased partner,

(d) As interest on a loan, though the amount of payment vary with the profits of the business.

(e) As the consideration for the sale of a good-will of a business or other property by installments or otherwise.

§ 8. **Partnership Property.**—(1) All property originally brought into the partnership stock or subsequently acquired by purchase or otherwise, on account of the partnership, is partnership property.

(2) Unless the contrary intention appears, property acquired with partnership funds is partnership property.

(3) Any estate in real property may be acquired in the partnership name. Title so acquired can be conveyed only in the partnership name.

(4) A conveyance to a partnership in the partnership name, though without words of inheritance, passes the entire estate of the grantor unless a contrary intent appears.

Part III

Relations of Partners to Persons Dealing With the Partnership

§ 9. **Partner Agent of Partnership as to Partnership Business.**—(1) Every partner is an agent of the partnership for the purpose of its business, and the act of every partner, including the execution in the partnership name of any instrument, for apparently carrying on in the usual way the business of the partnership of which he is a member binds the partnership, unless the partner so acting has in fact no authority to act for the partnership in the particular matter, and the person with whom he is dealing has knowledge of the fact that he has no such authority.

(2) An act of a partner which is not apparently for the carrying on of the business of the partnership in the usual way does not bind the partnership unless authorized by the other partners.

(3) Unless authorized by the other partners or unless they have abandoned the business, one or more but less than all the partners have no authority to:

(a) Assign the partnership property in trust for creditors or on the assignee's promise to pay the debts of the partnership,

(b) Dispose of the good-will of the business,

(c) Do any other act which would make it impossible to carry on the ordinary business of a partnership,

(d) Confess a judgment,

(e) Submit a partnership claim or liability in arbitration or reference.

(4) No act of a partner in contravention of a restriction on authority shall bind the partnership to persons having knowledge of the restriction.

§ 10. **Conveyance of Real Property of the Partnership.**—(1) Where title to real property is in the partnership name, any partner may convey title to such property by a conveyance executed in the partnership name; but the partnership may recover such property unless the partner's act binds the partnership under the provisions of paragraph (1) of §9 or unless such property has been conveyed by the grantee or a person claiming through such grantee to a holder for value without knowledge that the partner, in making the conveyance, has exceeded his authority.

(2) Where title to real property is in the name of the partnership, a conveyance executed by a partner, in his own name, passes the equitable interest of the partnership, provided the act is one within the authority of the partner under the provisions of paragraph (1) of §9.

(3) Where the title to real property is in the name of one or more but not all the partners, and the record does not disclose the right of the partnership, the partners in whose name the title stands may convey title to such property, but the partnership may recover such property if the partners' act does not bind the partnership under the provisions of paragraph (1) of §9, unless the purchaser or his assignee, is a holder for value, without knowledge.

(4) Where the title to real property is in the name of one or more or all the partners, or in a third person in trust for the partnership, a conveyance executed by a partner in the partnership name, or in his own name, passes the equitable interest of the partnership, provided the act is one within the authority of the partner under the provisions of paragraph (1) of §9.

(5) Where the title to real property is in the names of all the partners a conveyance executed by all the partners passes all their rights in such property.

§ 11. **Partnership Bound by Admission of Partner.**—An admission or representation made by any partner concerning partnership affairs within the scope of his authority as conferred by this Act is evidence against the partnership.

§ 12. **Partnership Charged with Knowledge of or Notice to Partner.**—Notice to any partner of any matter relating to partnership affairs, and the knowledge of the partner acting in the particular matter, acquired while a partner or then present to his mind, and the knowledge of any other partner who reasonably could and should have communicated it to the acting partner, operate as notice to or knowledge of the partnership, except in the case of a fraud on the partnership committed by or with the consent of that partner.

§ 13. **Partnership Bound by Partner's Wrongful Act.**—Where, by any wrongful act or omission of any partner acting in the ordinary course of the business of the partnership or with the authority of his co-partners, loss or injury is caused to any person, not being a partner in the partnership, or any penalty is incurred, the partnership is liable therefor to the same extent as the partner so acting or omitting to act.

§ 14. **Partnership Bound by Partner's Breach of Trust.**—The partnership is bound to make good the loss:

(a) Where one partner acting within the scope of his apparent authority receives money or property of a third person and misapplies it; and

(b) Where the partnership in the course of its business receives money or property of a third person and the money or property so received is misapplied by any partner while it is in the custody of the partnership.

§ 15. **Nature of Partner's Liability.**—All partners are liable:

(a) Jointly and severally for everything chargeable to the partnership under §§13 and 14.

(b) Jointly for all other debts and obligations of the partnership; but any partner may enter into a separate obligation to perform a partnership contract.

§ 16. **Partner by Estoppel.**—(1) When a person, by words spoken or written or by conduct, represents himself, or consents to another representing him to any one, as a partner in an existing partnership or with one or more persons not actual partners, he is liable to any such person to whom such representation has been made, who has, on the faith of such representation, given credit to the actual or apparent partnership, and if he has made such representation or consented to its being made in a public manner he is liable to such person, whether the representation has or has not been made or communicated to such person so giving credit by or with the knowledge of the apparent partner making the representation or consenting to its being made:

(a) When a partnership liability results, he is liable as though he were an actual member of the partnership.

(b) When no partnership liability results, he is liable jointly with the other persons, if any, so consenting to the contract or representation as to incur liability, otherwise separately.

(2) When a person has been thus represented to be a partner in an existing partnership, or with one or more persons not actual partners, he is an agent of the persons consenting to such representation to bind them to the same extent and in the same manner as though he were a partner in fact, with respect to persons who rely upon the representation. Where all the members of the existing partnership consent to the representation, a partnership act or obligation results; but in all other cases it is the joint act or obligation of the person acting and the persons consenting to the representation.

§ 17. **Liability of Incoming Partner.**—A person admitted as a partner into an existing partnership is liable for all the obligations of the partnership arising before his admission as though he had been a partner when such obligations were incurred, except that this liability shall be satisfied only out of partnership property.

Part IV

Relations of Partners to One Another

§ 18. **Rules Determining Rights and Duties of Partners.**—The rights and duties of the partners in relation to the partnership shall be determined, subject to any agreement between them, by the following rules:

(a) Each partner shall be repaid his contributions, whether by way of capital or advances to the partnership property and share equally in the profits and surplus remaining after all liabilities, including those to partners, are satisfied; and must contribute towards the losses, whether of capital or otherwise, sustained by the partnership according to his share in the profits.

(b) The partnership must indemnify every partner in respect of payments made and personal liabilities reasonably incurred by him in the ordinary and proper conduct of its business, or for the preservation of its business or property.

(c) A partner, who in aid of the partnership makes any

payment or advance beyond the amount of capital which he agreed to contribute, shall be paid interest from the date of the payment or advance.

(d) A partner shall receive interest on the capital contributed by him only from the date when repayment should be made.

(e) All partners have equal rights in the management and conduct of the partnership business.

(f) No partner is entitled to remuneration for acting in the partnership business, except that a surviving partner is entitled to reasonable compensation for his services in winding up the partnership affairs.

(g) No person can become a member of a partnership without the consent of all the partners.

(h) Any difference arising as to ordinary matters connected with the partnership business may be decided by a majority of the partners; but no act in contravention of any agreement between the partners may be done rightfully without the consent of all the partners.

§ 19. **Partnership Books.**—The partnership books shall be kept, subject to any agreement between the partners, at the principal place of business of the partnership, and every partner shall at all times have access to and may inspect and copy any of them.

§ 20. **Duty of Partners to Render Information.**—Partners shall render on demand true and full information of all things affecting the partnership to any partner or the legal representative of any deceased partner or partner under legal disability.

§ 21. **Partner Accountable as a Fiduciary.**—(1) Every partner must account to the partnership for any benefit, and hold as trustee for it any profits derived by him without the consent of the other partners from any transaction connected with the formation, conduct, or liquidation of the partnership or from any use by him of its property.

(2) This section applies also to the representatives of a deceased partner engaged in the liquidation of the affairs of the partnership as the personal representatives of the last surviving partner.

§ 22. **Right to an Account.**—Any partner shall have the right to a formal account as to partnership affairs:

(a) If he is wrongfully excluded from the partnership business or possession of its property by his co-partners.

(b) If the right exists under the terms of any agreement,

(c) As provided by §21,

(d) Whenever other circumstances render it just and reasonable.

§ 23. **Continuation of Partnership Beyond Fixed Term.**—(1) When a partnership for a fixed term or particular undertaking is continued after the termination of such term or particular undertaking without any express agreement, the rights and duties of the partners remain the same as they were at such termination, so far as is consistent with a partnership at will.

(2) A continuation of the business by the partners or such of them as habitually acted therein during the term, without any settlement or liquidation of the partnership affairs, is prima facie evidence of a continuation of the partnership.

Part V

Property Rights of a Partner

§ 24. **Extent of Property Rights of a Partner.**—The property rights of a partner are (1) his rights in specific partnership property, (2) his interest in the partnership, and (3) his right to participate in the management.

§ 25. **Nature of a Partner's Right in Specific Partnership Property.**—(1) A partner is co-owner with his partners of specific partnership property holding as a tenant in partnership.

(2) The incidents of this tenancy are such that:

(a) A partner, subject to the provisions of this Act and to any agreement between the partners, has an equal right with his partners to possess specific partnership property for partnership purposes; but he has no right to possess such property for any other purpose without the consent of his partners.

(b) A partner's right in specific partnership property is not assignable except in connection with the assignment of rights of all the partners in the same property.

(c) A partner's right in specific partnership property is not subject to attachment or execution, except on a claim against the partnership. When partnership property is attached for a partnership debt the partners, or any of them, or the representatives of a deceased partner, cannot claim any right under the homestead or exemption laws.

(d) On the death of a partner his right in specific partnership property vests in the surviving partner or partners, except where the deceased was the last surviving partner, when his right in such property vests in his legal representative. Such surviving partner or partners, or the legal representative of the last surviving partner, has no right to possess the partnership property for any but a partnership purpose.

(e) A partner's right in specific partnership property is not subject to dower, curtesy, or allowances to widows, heirs, or next of kin.

§ 26. **Nature of Partner's Interest in the Partnership.**—A partner's interest in the partnership is his share of the profits and surplus, and the same is personal property.

§ 27. **Assignment of Partner's Interest.**—(1) A conveyance by a partner of his interest in the partnership does not of itself dissolve the partnership, nor, as against the other partners in the absence of agreement, entitle the assignee, during the continuance of the partnership to interfere in the management or administration of the partnership business or affairs, or to require any information or account of partnership transactions, or to inspect the partnership books; but it merely entitles the assignee to receive in accordance with his contract the profits to which the assigning partner would otherwise be entitled.

(2) In case of a dissolution of the partnership, the assignee is entitled to receive his assignor's interest and may require an account from the date only of the last account agreed to by all the partners.

§ 28. **Partner's Interest Subject to Charging Order.**—(1) On due application to a competent court by any judgment creditor of a partner, the court which entered the judgment, order, or decree, or any other court, may charge the interest of the debtor partner with payment of the unsatisfied amount of such judgment debt with interest thereon; and may then or later appoint a receiver of his share of the profits, and of any other money due or to fall due to him in respect of the partnership, and make all other orders, directions, accounts and inquiries which the debtor partner might have made, or which the circumstances of the case may require.

(2) The interest charged may be redeemed at any time before foreclosure, or in case of a sale being directed by the court may be purchased without thereby causing a dissolution:

(a) With separate property, by any one or more of the partners, or

(b) With partnership property, by any one or more of the partners with the consent of all the partners whose interests are not so charged or sold.

(3) Nothing in this Act shall be held to deprive a partner of his right, if any, under the exemption laws, as regards his interest in the partnership.

Part VI

Dissolution and Winding Up

§ 29. Dissolution Defined.—The dissolution of a partnership is the change in the relation of the partners caused by any partner ceasing to be associated in the carrying on as distinguished from the winding up of the business.

§ 30. Partnership Not Terminated by Dissolution.—On dissolution the partnership is not terminated, but continues until the winding up of partnership affairs is completed.

§ 31. Causes of Dissolution.—Dissolution is caused:
(1) Without violation of the agreement between the partners:
    (a) By the termination of the definite term or particular undertaking specified in the agreement,
    (b) By the express will of any partner when no definite term or particular undertaking is specified,
    (c) By the express will of all the partners who have not assigned their interests or suffered them to be charged for their separate debts, either before or after the termination of any specified term or particular undertaking,
    (d) By the explusion of any partner from the business bona fide in accordance with such a power conferred by the agreement between the partners;
(2) In contravention of the agreement between the partners, where the circumstances do not permit a dissolution under any other provision of this section, by the express will of any partner at any time;
(3) By any event which makes it unlawful for the business of the partnership to be carried on or for the members to carry it on in partnership;
(4) By the death of any partner;
(5) By the bankruptcy of any partner or the partnership;
(6) By decree of court under §32.

§ 32. Dissolution by Decree of Court.—(1) On application by or for a partner the court shall decree a dissolution whenever:
    (a) A partner has been declared a lunatic in any judicial proceeding or is shown to be of unsound mind,
    (b) A partner becomes in any other way incapable of performing his part of the partnership contract,
    (c) A partner has been guilty of such conduct as tends to affect prejudicially the carrying on of the business,
    (d) A partner wilfully or persistently commits a breach of the partnership agreement, or otherwise so conducts himself in matters relating to the partnership business that it is not reasonably practicable to carry on the business in partnership with him.
    (e) The business of the partnership can only be carried on at a loss,
    (f) Other circumstances render a dissolution equitable.
(2) On the application of the purchaser of a partner's interest under §§27 or 28:
    (a) After the termination of the specified term or particular undertaking,
    (b) At any time if the partnership was a partnership at will when the interest was assigned or when the charging order was issued.

§ 33. General Effect of Dissolution on Authority of Partner.—Except so far as may be necessary to wind up partnership affairs or to complete transactions begun but not then finished, dissolution terminates all authority of any partner to act for the partnership,
(1) With respect to the partners,
    (a) When the dissolution is not by the act, bankruptcy or death of a partner; or
    (b) When the dissolution is by such act, bankruptcy or

death of a partner, in cases where §34 so requires.
(2) With respect to persons not partners, as declared in §35.

§ 34. Right of Partner to Contribution From Co-partners After Dissolution.—Where the dissolution is caused by the act, death or bankruptcy of a partner, each partner is liable to his co-partners for his share of any liability created by any partner acting for the partnership as if the partnership had not been dissolved unless:
    (a) The dissolution being by act of any partner, the partner acting for the partnership had knowledge of the dissolution, or
    (b) The dissolution being by the death or bankruptcy of a partner, the partner acting for the partnership had knowledge or notice of the death or bankruptcy.

§ 35. Power of Partner to Bind Partnership to Third Persons After Dissolution.—(1) After dissolution a partner can bind the partnership except as provided in Paragraph (3)
    (a) By any act appropriate for winding up partnership affairs or completing transactions unfinished at dissolution;
    (b) By any transaction which would bind the partnership if dissolution had not taken place, provided the other party to the transaction:
        (I) Had extended credit to the partnership prior to dissolution and had no knowledge or notice of the dissolution; or
        (II) Though he had not so extended credit, had nevertheless known of the partnership prior to dissolution, and, having no knowledge or notice of dissolution, the fact of dissolution had not been advertised in a newspaper of general circulation in the place (or in each place if more than one) at which the partnership business was regularly carried on.
(2) The liability of a partner under paragraph (1b) shall be satisfied out of partnership assets alone when such partner had been prior to dissolution:
    (a) Unknown as a partner to the person with whom the contract is made; and
    (b) So far unknown and inactive in partnership affairs that the business reputation of the partnership could not be said to have been in any degree due to his connection with it.
(3) The partnership is in no case bound by any act of a partner after dissolution:
    (a) Where the partnership is dissolved because it is unlawful to carry on the business, unless the act is appropriate for winding up partnership affairs; or
    (b) Where the partner has become bankrupt; or
    (c) Where the partner has no authority to wind up partnership affairs; except by a transaction with one who:
        (I) Had extended credit to the partnership prior to dissolution and had no knowledge or notice of his want of authority; or
        (II) Had not extended credit to the partnership prior to dissolution, and, having no knowledge or notice of his want of authority, the fact of his want of authority has not been advertised in the manner provided for advertising the fact of dissolution in paragraph (1bII).
(4) Nothing in this section shall affect the liability under §16 of any person who after dissolution represents himself or consents to another representing him as a partner in a partnership engaged in carrying on business.

§ 36. Effect of Dissolution on Partner's Existing Liability.—(1) The dissolution of the partnership does not of itself discharge the existing liability of any partner.
(2) A partner is discharged from any existing liability upon dissolution of the partnership by an agreement to that effect between himself, the partnership creditor and the person or partnership continuing the business; and such agreement may be inferred from the course of dealing between the creditor having knowledge of the dissolution and the person or partnership continuing the business.

(3) Where a person agrees to assume the existing obligations of a dissolved partnership, the partners whose obligations have been assumed shall be discharged from any liability to any creditor of the partnership who, knowing of the agreement, consents to a material alteration in the nature or time of payment of such obligations.

(4) The individual property of a deceased partner shall be liable for all obligations of the partnership incurred while he was a partner but subject to the prior payment of his separate debts.

§ 37. **Right to Wind Up.**—Unless otherwise agreed the partners who have not wrongfully dissolved the partnership or the legal representative of the last surviving partner, not bankrupt, has the right to wind up the partnership affairs; provided, however, that any partner, his legal representative or his assignee, upon cause shown, may obtain winding up by the court.

§ 38. **Rights of Partners to Application of Partnership Property.** —(1) When dissolution is caused in any way, except in contravention of the partnership agreement, each partner as against his co-partners and all persons claiming through them in respect of their interests in the partnership, unless otherwise agreed, may have the partnership property applied to discharge its liabilities, and the surplus applied to pay in cash the net amount owing to the respective partners. But if dissolution is caused by expulsion of a partner, bona fide under the partnership agreement and if the expelled partner is discharged from all partnership liabilities, either by payment or agreement under §36 (2), he shall receive in cash only the net amount due him from the partnership.

(2) When dissolution is caused in contravention of the partnership agreement the rights of the partners shall be as follows:

(a) Each partner who has not caused dissolution wrongfully shall have:

(I) All the rights specified in paragraph (1) of this section, and

(II) The right, as against each partner who has caused the dissolution wrongfully, to damages for breach of the agreement.

(b) The partners who have not caused the dissolution wrongfully, if they all desire to continue the business in the same name, either by themselves or jointly with others, may do so, during the agreed term for the partnership and for that purpose may possess the partnership property, provided they secure the payment by bond approved by the court, or pay to any partner who has caused the dissolution wrongfully, the value of his interest in the partnership at the dissolution, less any damages recoverable under clause (2aII) of the section, and in like manner indemnify him against all present or future partnership liabilities.

(c) A partner who has caused the dissolution wrongfully shall have:

(I) If the business is not continued under the provisions of paragraph (2b) all the rights of a partner under paragraph (1), subject to clause (2aII), of this section,

(II) If the business is continued under paragraph (2b) of this section the right as against his co-partners and all claiming through them in respect of their interests in the partnership, to have the value of his interest in the partnership, less any damages caused to his co-partners by the dissolution, ascertained and paid him in cash, or the payment secured by bond approved by the court, and to be released from all existing liabilities of the partnership; but in ascertaining the value of the partner's interest the value of the good-will of the business shall not be considered.

§ 39. **Rights Where Partnership is Dissolved for Fraud or Misrepresentation.**—Where a partnership contract is rescinded on the ground of the fraud or misrepresentation of one of the parties thereto, the party entitled to rescind is, without prejudice to any other right, entitled:

(a) To a lien on, or right of retention of, the surplus of the partnership property after satisfying the partnership liabilities to third persons for any sum of money paid by him for the purchase of an interest in the partnership and for any capital or advances contributed by him; and

(b) To stand, after all liabilities to third persons have been satisfied, in the place of the creditors of the partnership for any payments made by him in respect of the partnership liabilities; and

(c) To be indemnified by the person guilty of the fraud or making the representation against all debts and liabilities of the partnership.

§ 40. **Rules for Distribution.**—In settling accounts between the partners after dissolution, the following rules shall be observed, subject to any agreement to the contrary:

(a) The assets of the partnership are:

(I) The partnership property,

(II) The contributions of the partners necessary for the payment of all the liabilities specified in clause (b) of this paragraph.

(b) The liabilities of the partnership shall rank in order of payment, as follows:

(I) Those owing to creditors other than partners,

(II) Those owing to partners other than for capital and profits,

(III) Those owing to partners in respect of capital,

(IV) Those owing to partners in respect of profits.

(c) The assets shall be applied in the order of their declaration in clause (a) of this paragraph to the satisfaction of the liabilities.

(d) The partners shall contribute, as provided by §18 (a) the amount necessary to satisfy the liabilities; but if any, but not all, of the partners are insolvent, or, not being subject to process, refuse to contribute, the other partners shall contribute their share of the liabilities, and, in the relative proportions in which they share the profits, the additional amount necessary to pay the liabilities.

(e) An assignee for the benefit of creditors or any person appointed by the court shall have the right to enforce the contributions specified in clause (d) of this paragraph.

(f) Any partner or his legal representative shall have the right to enforce the contributions specified in clause (d) of this paragraph, to the extent of the amount which he has paid in excess of his share of the liability.

(g) The individual property of a deceased partner shall be liable for the contributions specified in clause (d) of this paragraph.

(h) When partnership property and the individual properties of the partners are in possession of a court for distribution, partnership creditors shall have priority on partnership property and separate creditors on individual property, saving the rights of lien or secured creditors as heretofore.

(i) Where a partner has become bankrupt or his estate is insolvent the claims against his separate property shall rank in the following order:

(I) Those owing to separate creditors,

(II) Those owing to partnership creditors,

(III) Those owing to partners by way of contribution.

§ 41. **Liability of Persons Continuing the Business in Certain Cases.**—(1) When any new partner is admitted into an existing partnership, or when any partner retires and assigns (or the representative of the deceased partner assigns) his rights in partnership property to two or more of the partners, or to one or more of the partners and one or more third persons, if the business is continued without liquidation of the partnership affairs, creditors of the first or dissolved partnership are also creditors of the partnership so continuing the business.

(2) When all but one partner retire and assign (or the representative of a deceased partner assigns) their rights in partnership property to the remaining partner, who continues the business without liquidation of partnership affairs, either alone or with others, creditors of the dissolved partnership are also creditors of the person or partnership so continuing the business.

(3) When any partner retires or dies and the business of the dissolved partnership is continued as set forth in paragraphs (1) and (2) of this section, with the consent of the retired partners or the representative of the deceased partner, but without any assignment of his right in partnership property, rights of creditors of the dissolved partnership and of the creditors of the person or partnership continuing the business shall be as if such assignment had been made.

(4) When all the partners or their representatives assign their rights in partnership property to one or more third persons who promise to pay the debts and who continue the business of the dissolved partnership, creditors of the dissolved partnership are also creditors of the person or partnership continuing the business.

(5) When any partner wrongfully causes a dissolution and the remaining partners continue the business under the provisions of §38 (2b), either alone or with others, and without liquidation of the partnership affairs, creditors of the dissolved partnership are also creditors of the person or partnership continuing the business.

(6) When a partner is expelled and the remaining partners continue the business either alone or with others, without liquidation of the partnership affairs, creditors of the dissolved partnership are also creditors of the person or partnership continuing the business.

(7) The liability of a third person becoming a partner in the partnership continuing the business, under this section, to the creditors of the dissolved partnership shall be satisfied out of partnership property only.

(8) When the business of a partnership after dissolution is continued under any conditions set forth in this section the creditors of the dissolved partnership, as against the separate creditors of the retiring or deceased partner or the representative of the deceased partner, have a prior right to any claim of the retired partner or the representative of the deceased partner against the person or partnership continuing the business, on account of the retired or deceased partner's interest in the dissolved partnership

or on account of any consideration promised for such interest or for his right in partnership property.

(9) Nothing in this section shall be held to modify any right of creditors to set aside any assignment on the ground of fraud.

(10) The use by the person or partnership continuing the business of the partnership name, or the name of a deceased partner as part thereof, shall not of itself make the individual property of the deceased partner liable for any debts contracted by such person or partnership.

§ 42. Rights of Retiring or Estate of Deceased Partner When the Business is Continued.—When any partner retires or dies, and the business is continued under any of the conditions set forth in §41 (1, 2, 3, 5, 6), or §38 (2b), without any settlement of accounts as between him or his estate and the person or partnership continuing the business, unless otherwise agreed, he or his legal representative as against such persons or partnership may have the value of his interest at the date of dissolution ascertained, and shall receive as an ordinary creditor an amount equal to the value of his interest in the dissolved partnership with interest, or, at his option or at the option of his legal representative, in lieu of interest, the profits attributable to the use of his right in the property of the dissolved partnership; provided that the creditors of the dissolved partnership as against the separate creditors, or the representative of the retired or deceased partner, shall have priority on any claim arising under this section, as provided by §41 (8) of this Act.

§ 43. Accrual of Actions.—The right to an account of his interest shall accrue to any partner, or his legal representative, as against the winding up partners or the surviving partners or the person or partnership continuing the business, at the date of dissolution, in the absence of any agreement to the contrary.

Part VII

Miscellaneous Provisions

§ 44. When Act Takes Effect.—This Act shall take effect on the . . . . . . day of . . . . . . one thousand nine hundred and . . . . .

§ 45. Legislation Repealed.—All Acts or parts of Acts inconsistent with this Act are hereby repealed.

APPENDIX D
UNIFORM LIMITED PARTNERSHIP ACT (1976)

Article 1

General Provisions

§ 101. Definitions.—As used in this Act, unless the context otherwise requires:

(1) "Certificate of limited partnership" means the certificate referred to in Section 201, and the certificate as amended.

(2) "Contribution" means any cash, property, services rendered, or a promissory note or other binding obligation to contribute cash or property or to perform services, which a partner contributes to a limited partnership in his capacity as a partner.

(3) "Event of withdrawal of a general partner" means an event that causes a person to cease to be a general partner as provided in Section 402.

(4) "Foreign limited partnership" means a partnership formed under the laws of any State other than this State and having as partners one or more general partners and one or more limited partners.

(5) "General partner" means a person who has been admitted to a limited partnership as a general partner in accordance with the partnership agreement and named in the certificate of limited partnership as a general partner.

(6) "Limited partner" means a person who has been admitted to a limited partnership as a limited partner in accordance with the partnership agreement and named in the certificate of limited partnership as a limited partner.

(7) "Limited partnership" and "domestic limited partnership" mean a partnership formed by 2 or more persons under the laws of this State and having one or more general partners and one or more limited partners.

(8) "Partner" means a limited or general partner.

(9) "Partnership agreement" means any valid agreement, written or oral, of the partners as to the affairs of a limited partnership and the conduct of its business.

(10) "Partnership interest" means a partner's share of the profits and losses of a limited partnership and the right to receive distributions of a partnership assets.

(11) "Person" means a natural person, partnership, limited partnership (domestic or foreign), trust, estate, association, or corporation.

(12) "State" means a state, territory, or possession of the United States, the District of Columbia, or the Commonwealth of Puerto Rico.

§ 102. Name.—The name of each limited partnership as set forth in its certificate of limited partnership:

(1) shall contain without abbreviation the words "limited partnership";

(2) may not contain the name of a limited partner unless (i) it is also the name of a general partner or the corporate name of a corporate general partner, or (ii) the business of the limited partnership had been carried on under that name before the admission of that limited partner;

(3) may not contain any word or phrase indicating or implying that it is organized other than for a purpose stated in its certificate of limited partnership;

(4) may not be the same as, or deceptively similar to, the name of any corporation or limited partnership organized under the laws of this State or licensed or registered as a foreign corporation or limited partnership in this State; and

(5) may not contain the following words [here insert prohibited words].

§ 103. Reservation of Name.—

(a) The exclusive right to the use of a name may be reserved by:

(1) any person intending to organize a limited partnership under this Act and to adopt that name;

(2) any domestic limited partnership or any foreign limited partnership registered in this State which, in either case, intends to adopt that name;

(3) any foreign limited partnership intending to register in this State and adopt that name; and

(4) any person intending to organize a foreign limited partnership and intending to have it register in this State and adopt that name.

(b) The reservation shall be made by filing with the Secretary of State an application, executed by the applicant, to reserve a specified name. If the Secretary of State finds that the name is available for use by a domestic or foreign limited partnership, he shall reserve the name for the exclusive use of the applicant for a period of 120 days. Once having so reserved a name, the same applicant may not again reserve the same name until more than 60 days after the expiration of the last 120-day period for which that applicant reserved that name. The right to the exclusive use of a reserved name may be transferred to any other person by filing in the office of the Secretary of State a notice of the transfer, executed by the applicant for whom the name was reserved and specifying the name and address of the transferee.

§ 104. Specified Office and Agent.—Each limited partnership shall continuously maintain in this State:

(1) an office, which may but need not be a place of its business in this State, at which shall be kept the records required by Section 105 to be maintained; and

(2) an agent for service of process on the limited partnership, which agent must be an individual resident of this State, a domestic corporation, or a foreign corporation authorized to do business in this State.

§ 105. Records to be Kept.—Each limited partnership shall keep at the office referred to in Section 104(1) the following: (1) a current list of the full name and last known business address of each partner set forth in alphabetical order, (2) a copy of the certificate of limited partnership and all certificates of amendment thereto, together with executed copies of any powers of attorney pursuant to which any certificate has been executed, (3) copies of the limited partnership's federal, state and local income tax returns and reports, if any, for the 3 most recent years, and (4) copies of any then effective written partnership agreements and of any financial statements of the limited partnership for the 3 most recent years. Those records are subject to inspection and copying at the reasonable request, and at the expense, of any partner during ordinary business hours.

§ 106. Nature of Business.—A limited partnership may carry on any business that a partnership without limited partners may carry on except [here designate prohibited activities].

§ 107. Business Transactions of Partner with Partnership.—Except as provided in the partnership agreement, a partner may lend money to and transact other business with the limited partnership and, subject to other applicable law, has the same rights and obligations with respect thereto as a person who is not a partner.

Article 2

Formation: Certificate of Limited Partnership

§ 201. Certificate of Limited Partnership.—
(a) In order to form a limited partnership two or more persons must execute a certificate of limited partnership. The certificate shall be filed in the office of the Secretary of State and set forth:

(1) the name of the limited partnership;

(2) the general character of its business;

(3) the address of the office and the name and address of the agent for service of process required to be maintained by Section 104;

(4) the name and the business address of each partner (specifying separately the general partners and limited partners);

(5) the amount of cash and a description and statement of the agreed value of the other property or services contributed by each partner and which each partner has agreed to contribute in the future;

(6) the times at which or events on the happening of which any additional contributions agreed to be made by each partner are to be made;

(7) any power of a limited partner to grant the right to become a limited partner to an assignee of any part of his partnership interest, and the terms and conditions of the power;

(8) if agreed upon, the time at which or the events on the happening of which a partner may terminate his membership in the limited partnership and the amount of, or the method of determining, the distribution to which he may be entitled respecting his partnership interest, and the terms and conditions of the termination and distribution;

(9) any right of a partner to receive distributions of property, including cash from the limited partnership;

(10) any right of a partner to receive, or of a general partner to make, distributions to a partner which include a return of all or any part of the partner's contribution;

(11) any time at which or events upon the happening of which the limited partnership is to be dissolved and its affairs wound up,

(12) any right of the remaining general partners to continue the business on the happening of an event of withdrawal of a general partner; and

(13) any other matters the partners determine to include therein.

(b) A limited partnership is formed at the time of the filing of the certificate of limited partnership in the office of the Secretary of State or at any later time specified in the certificate of limited partnership if, in either case, there has been substantial compliance with the requirements of this section.

§ 202. Amendment to Certificate.—(a) A certificate of limited partnership is amended by filing a certificate of amendment thereto in the office of the Secretary of State. The certificate shall set forth:

(1) the name of the limited partnership;

(2) the date of filing the certificate; and

(3) the amendment to the certificate.

(b) Within 30 days after the happening of any of the following events, an amendment to a certificate of limited partnership reflecting the occurrence of the event or events shall be filed:

(1) a change in the amount or character of the contribution of any partner, or in any partner's obligation to make a contribution:

(2) the admission of a new partner;

(3) the withdrawal of a partner; or

(4) the continuation of the business under Section 801 after an event of withdrawal of a general partner.

(c) A general partner who becomes aware that any statement in a certificate of limited partnership was false when made or that any arrangements or other facts described have changed, making the certificate inaccurate in any respect, shall promptly amend the certificate, but an amendment to show a change of address of a limited partner need be filed only once every 12 months.

(d) A certificate of limited partnership may be amended at any time for any other proper purpose the general partners determine.

(e) No person has any liability because an amendment to a certificate of limited partnership has not been filed to reflect the occurrence of any event referred to in subsection (b) of this Section if the amendment is filed within the 30-day period specified in subsection (b).

§ 203. Cancellation of Certificate.—A certificate of limited partnership shall be cancelled upon the dissolution and the commencement of winding up of the partnership or at any other time there are no limited partners. A certificate of cancellation shall be filed in the office of the Secretary of State and set forth:

(1) the name of the limited partnership;

(2) the date of filing of its certificate of limited partnership;

(3) the reason for filing the certificate of cancellation;

(4) the effective date (which shall be a date certain) of cancellation if it is not to be effective upon the filing of the certificate; and

(5) any other information the general partners filing the certificate determine.

§ 204. Execution of Certificates.—
(a) Each certificate required by this Article to be filed in the office of the Secretary of State shall be executed in the following manner:

(1) an original certificate of limited partnership must be signed by all partners named therein;

(2) a certificate of amendment must be signed by at least one general partner and by each other partner designated in the certificate as a new partner or whose contribution is described as having been increased; and

(3) a certificate of cancellation must be signed by all general partners;

(b) Any person may sign a certificate by an attorney-in-fact, but a power of attorney to sign a certificate relating to the admission, or increased contribution, of a partner must specifically describe the admission or increase.

(c) The execution of a certificate by a general partner constitutes an affirmation under the penalties of perjury that the facts stated therein are true.

§ 205. Amendment or Cancellation by Judicial Act.—If a person required by Section 204 to execute a certificate of amendment or cancellation fails or refuses to do so, any other partner, and any assignee of a partnership interest, who is adversely affected by the failure or refusal, may petition the [here designate the proper court] to direct the amendment or cancellation. If the court finds that the amendment or cancellation is proper and that any person so designated has failed or refused to execute the certificate, it shall order the Secretary of State to record an appropriate certificate of amendment or cancellation.

§ 206. Filing in Office of Secretary of State.—
(a) Two signed copies of the certificate of limited partnership and of any certificates of amendment or cancellation (or of any judicial decree of amendment or cancellation) shall be delivered to the Secretary of State. A person who executes a certificate as an agent or fiduciary need not exhibit evidence of his authority as a prerequisite to filing. Unless the Secretary of State finds that any certificate does not conform to law, upon receipt of all filing fees required by law he shall:

(1) endorse on each duplicate original the word "Filed" and the day, month and year of the filing thereof;

(2) file one duplicate original in his office; and

(3) return the other duplicate original to the person who filed it or his representative.

(b) Upon the filing of a certificate of amendment (or judicial decree of amendment) in the office of the Secretary of State, the certificate of limited partnership shall be amended as set forth therein, and upon the effective date of a certificate of cancellation (or a judicial decree thereof), the certificate of limited partnership is cancelled.

§ 207. Liability for False Statement in Certificate.—If any certificate of limited partnership or certificate of amendment or cancellation contains a false statement, one who suffers loss by reliance on the statement may recover damages for the loss from:

(1) any person who executes the certificate, or causes another to execute it on his behalf, and knew, and any general partner who knew or should have known, the statement to be false at the time the certificate was executed; and

(2) any general partner who thereafter knows or should have known that any arrangement or other fact described in the certificate has changed, making the statement inaccurate in any respect within a sufficient time before the statement was relied upon reasonably to have enabled that general partner to cancel or amend the certificate, or to file a petition for its cancellation or amendment under Section 205.

§ 208. Notice.—The fact that a certificate of limited partnership is on file in the office of the Secretary of State is notice that the partnership is a limited partnership and the persons designated therein as limited partners are limited partners, but it is not notice of any other fact.

§ 209. Delivery of Certificates to Limited Partners.—Upon the return by the Secretary of State pursuant to Section 206 of a certificate marked "Filed", the general partners shall promptly deliver or mail a copy of the certificate of limited partnership and each certificate to each limited partner unless the partnership agreement provides otherwise.

Article 3

Limited Partners

§ 301. Admission of Additional Limited Partners.—(a) After the filing of a limited partnership's original certificate of limited partnership, a person may be admitted as an additional limited partner:

(1) in the case of a person acquiring a partnership interest directly from the limited partnership, upon the compliance with the partnership agreement or, if the partnership-agreement does not so provide, upon the written consent of all partners; and

(2) in the case of an assignee of a partnership interest of a partner who has the power, as provided in Section 704, to grant the assignee the right to become a limited partner, upon the exercise of that power and compliance with any conditions limiting the grant or exercise of the power.

(b) In each case under subsection (a), the person acquiring the partnership interest becomes a limited partner only upon amendment of the certificate of limited partnership reflecting that fact.

§ 302. Voting.—Subject to Section 303, the partnership agreement may grant to all or a specified group of the limited partners the right to vote (on a per capita or other basis) upon any matter.

§ 303. Liability to Third Parties.—(a) Except as provided in subsection (d), a limited partner is not liable for the obligations of a limited partnership unless he is also a general partner or, in addition to the exercise of his rights and powers as a limited partner, he takes part in the control of the business. However, if the limited partner's participation in the control of the business is not substantially the same as the exercise of the powers of a general partner, he is liable only to persons who transact business with the limited partnership with actual knowledge of his participation in control.

(b) A limited partner does not participate in the control of the business within the meaning of subsection (a) solely by doing one or more of the following:

(1) being a contractor for or an agent or employee of the limited partnership or of a general partner;

(2) consulting with and advising a general partner with respect to the business of the limited partnership;

(3) acting as surety for the limited partnership;

(4) approving or disapproving an amendment to the partnership agreement; or

(5) voting on one or more of the following matters:

(i) the dissolution and winding up of the limited partnership;

(ii) the sale, exchange, lease, mortgage, pledge, or other transfer of all or substantially all of the assets of the limited partnership other than in the ordinary course of its business;

(iii) the incurrence of indebtedness by the limited partnership other than in the ordinary course of its business;

(iv) a change in the nature of the business; or

(v) the removal of a general partner.

(c) the enumeration in subsection (b) does not mean that the possession or exercise of any other powers by a limited partner constitutes participation by him in the business of the limited partnership.

(d) A limited partner who knowingly permits his name to be used in the name of the limited partnership, except under circumstances permitted by Section 102(2)(i), is liable to creditors who extend credit to the limited partnership without actual knowledge that the limited partner is not a general partner.

§ 304. Person Erroneously Believing Himself Limited Partner.—(a) Except as provided in subsection (b), a person who makes a contribution to a business enterprise and erroneously but in good faith believes that he has become a limited partner in the enterprise is not a general partner in the enterprise and is not bound by its obligations by reason of making the contribution, receiving distributions from the enterprise, or exercising any rights of a limited partner, if, on ascertaining the mistake, he

(1) causes an appropriate certificate of limited partnership or a certificate of amendment to be executed and filed; or

(2) withdraws from future equity participation in the enterprise.

(b) A person who makes a contribution of the kind described in subsection (a) is liable as a general partner to any third party who transacts business with the enterprise (i) before the person withdraws and an appropriate certificate is filed to show withdrawal, or (ii) before an appropriate certificate is filed to show his status as a limited partner and, in the case of an amendment, after expiration of the 30-day period for filing an amendment relating to the person as a limited partner under Section 202, but in either case only if the third party actually believed in good faith that the person was a general partner at the time of the transaction.

§ 305. Information.—Each limited partner has the right to:

(1) inspect and copy any of the partnership records required to be maintained by Section 105; and

(2) obtain from the general partners from time to time upon reasonable demand (i) true and full information regarding the state of the business and financial condition of the limited partnership, (ii) promptly after becoming available, a copy of the limited partnership's federal, state and local income tax returns for each year, and (iii) other information regarding the affairs of the limited partnership as is just and reasonable.

Article 4

General Partners

§ 401. Admission of Additional General Partners.—After the filing of a limited partnership's original certificate of limited partnership, additional general partners may be admitted only with the specific written consent of each partner.

§ 402. Events of Withdrawal.—Except as approved by the specific written consent of all partners at the time, a person ceases to be a general partner of a limited partnership upon the happening of any of the following events:

(1) the general partner withdraws from the limited partnership as provided in Section 602;

(2) the general partner ceases to be a member of the limited partnership as provided in Section 702;

(3) the general partner is removed as a general partner in accordance with the partnership agreement;

(4) unless otherwise provided in the certificate of limited partnership, the general partner: (i) makes an assignment for the benefit of creditors; (ii) files a voluntary petition in bankruptcy; (iii) is adjudicated a bankrupt or insolvent; (iv) files a petition or answer seeking for himself any reorganization, arrangement, composition, readjustment, liquidation, dissolution or similar relief under any statute, law, or regulation; (v) files an answer or other pleading admitting or failing to contest the material allegations of a petition filed against him in any proceeding of this nature; or (vi) seeks, consents to, or acquiesces in the appointment of a trustee, receiver, or liquidator of the general partner or of all or any substantial part of his properties;

(5) unless otherwise provided in the certificate of limited partnership, the general partner, [120] days after the commencement of any proceeding against the general partner seeking reorganization, arrangement, composition, readjustment, liquidation, dissolution or similar relief under any statute, law, or regulation, the proceeding has not been dismissed, or if within [90] days after the appointment without his consent or acquiescence of a trustee, receiver, or liquidator of the general partner or of all or any substantial part of his properties, the appointment is not vacated or stayed or within [90] days after the expiration of any such stay, the appointment is not vacated;

(6) in the case of a general partner who is a natural person,

   (i) his death; or

   (ii) the entry by a court of competent jurisdiction adjudicating him incompetent to manage his person or his estate;

(7) in the case of a general partner who is acting as a general partner by virtue of being a trustee of a trust, the termination of the trust (but not merely the substitution of a new trustee);

(8) in the case of a general partner that is a separate partnership, the dissolution and commencement of winding up of the separate partnership;

(9) in the case of a general partner that is a corporation, the filing of a certificate of dissolution, or its equivalent, for the corporation or the revocation of its charter; or

(10) in the case of an estate, the distribution by the fiduciary of the estate's entire interest in the partnership.

§ 403. General Powers and Liabilities.—Except as provided in this Act or in the partnership agreement, a general partner of a limited partnership has the rights and powers and is subject to the restrictions and liabilities of a partner in a partnership without limited partners.

§ 404. Contributions by General Partner.—A general partner of a limited partnership may make contributions to the partnership and share in the profits and losses of, and in distributions from, the limited partnership as a general partner. A general partner also may make contributions to and share in profits, losses, and distributions as a limited partner. A person who is both a general partner and a limited partner has the rights and powers, and is subject to the restrictions and liabilities, of a general partner and, except as provided in the partnership agreement, also has the powers, and is subject to the restrictions, of a limited partner to the extent of his participation in the partnership as a limited partner.

§ 405. Voting.—The partnership agreement may grant to all or certain identified general partners the right to vote (on a per

capita or any other basis), separately or with all or any class of the limited partners, on any matter.

Article 5

Finance

§ 501. Form of Contribution.—The contribution of a partner may be in cash, property, or services rendered, or a promissory note or other obligation to contribute cash or property or to perform services.

§ 502. Liability for Contribution.—(a) Except as provided in the certificate of limited partnership, a partner is obligated to the limited partnership to perform any promise to contribute cash or property or to perform services, even if he is unable to perform because of death, disability or any other reason. If a partner does not make the required contribution of property or services, he is obligated at the option of the limited partnership to contribute cash equal to that portion of the value (as stated in the certificate of limited partnership) of the stated contribution that has not been made.

(b) Unless otherwise provided in the partnership agreement, the obligation of a partner to make a contribution or return money or other property paid or distributed in violation of this Act may be compromised only by consent of all the partners. Notwithstanding the compromise, a creditor of a limited partnership who extends credit, or whose claim arises, after the filing of the certificate of limited partnership or an amendment thereto which, in either case, reflects the obligation, and before the amendment or cancellation thereof to reflect the compromise, may enforce the original obligation.

§ 503. Sharing of Profits and Losses.—The profits and losses of a limited partnership shall be allocated among the partners, and among classes of partners, in the manner provided in the partnership agreement. If the partnership agreement does not so provide, profits and losses shall be allocated on the basis of the value (as stated in the certificate of limited partnership) of the contributions made by each partner to the extent they have been received by the partnership and have not been returned.

§ 504. Sharing of Distributions.—Distributions of cash or other assets of a limited partnership shall be allocated among the partners, and among classes of partners, in the manner provided in the partnership agreement. If the partnership agreement does not so provide, distributions shall be made on the basis of the value (as stated in the certificate of limited partnership) of the contributions made by each partner to the extent they have been received by the partnership and have not been returned.

Article 6

Distribution and Withdrawal

§ 601. Interim Distributions.—Except as provided in this Article, a partner is entitled to receive distributions from a limited partnership before his withdrawal from the limited partnership and before the dissolution and winding up thereof:

(1) to the extent and at the times or upon the happening of the events specified in the partnership agreement; and

(2) if any distribution constitutes a return of any part of his contribution under Section 608(c), to the extent and at the times or upon the happening of the events specified in the certificate of limited partnership.

§ 602. Withdrawal of General Partner.—A general partner may withdraw from a limited partnership at any time by giving written notice to the other partners, but if the withdrawal violates the partnership agreement, the limited partnership may recover from the withdrawing general partner damages for breach of the partnership agreement and offset the damages against the amount otherwise distributable to him.

§ 603. Withdrawal of Limited Partner.—A limited partner may withdraw from a limited partnership at the time or upon the happening of events specified in the certificate of limited partnership and in accordance with the partnership agreement. If the certificate does not specify the time or the events upon the happening of which a limited partner may withdraw or a definite time for the dissolution and winding up of the limited partnership, a limited partner may withdraw upon not less than 6 months' prior written notice to each general partner at his address on the books of the limited partnership at its office in this State.

§ 604. Distribution Upon Withdrawal.—Except as provided in this Article, upon withdrawal any withdrawing partner is entitled to receive any distribution to which he is entitled under the partnership agreement and, if not otherwise provided in the agreement, he is entitled to receive, within a reasonable time after withdrawal, the fair value of his interest in the limited partnership as of the date of withdrawal based upon his right to share in distributions from the limited partnership.

§ 605. Distribution in Kind.—Except as provided in the certificate of limited partnership, a partner, regardless of the nature of his contribution, has no right to demand and receive any distribution from a limited partnership in any form other than cash. Except as provided in the partnership agreement, a partner may not be compelled to accept a distribution of any asset in kind from a limited partnership to the extent that the percentage of the asset distributed to him exceeds a percentage of that asset which is equal to the percentage in which he shares in distributions from the limited partnership.

§ 606. Right to Distribution.—At the time a partner becomes entitled to receive a distribution, he has the status of, and is entitled to all remedies available to, a creditor of the limited partnership with respect to the distribution.

§ 607. Limitations on Distribution.—A partner may not receive a distribution from a limited partnership to the extent that, after giving effect to the distribution, all liabilities of the limited partnership, other than liabilities to partners on account of their partnership interests, exceed the fair value of the partnership assets.

§ 608. Liability Upon Return of Contribution.—(a) If a partner has received the return of any part of his contribution without violation of the partnership agreement or this Act, he is liable to the limited partnership for a period of one year thereafter for the amount of the returned contribution, but only to the extent necessary to discharge the limited partnership's liabilities to creditors who extended credit to the limited partnership during the period the contribution was held by the partnership.

(b) If a partner has received the return of any part of his contribution in violation of the partnership agreement or this Act, he is liable to the limited partnership for a period of 6 years thereafter for the amount of the contribution wrongfully returned.

(c) A partner receives a return of his contribution to the extent that a distribution to him reduces his share of the fair value of the net assets of the limited partnership below the value (as set forth in the certificate of limited partnership) of his contribution which has not been distributed to him.

Article 7

Assignment of Partnership Interests

§ 701. Nature of Partnership Interest.—A partnership interest is personal property.

§ 702. Assignment of Partnership Interest.—Except as provided in the partnership agreement, a partnership interest is assignable in whole or in part. An assignment of a partnership interest does not dissolve a limited partnership or entitle the assignee to become or to exercise any rights of a partner. An assignment entitles the assignee to receive, to the extent assigned, only the distribution to which the assignor would be entitled. Except as provided in the partnership agreement, a partner ceases to be a partner upon assignment of all his partnership interest.

§ 703. Rights of Creditor.—On application to a court of competent jurisdiction by any judgment creditor of a partner, the court may charge the partnership interest of the partner with payment of the unsatisfied amount of the judgment with interest. To the extent so charged, the judgment creditor has only the rights of an assignee of the partnership interest. This Act does not deprive any partner of the benefit of any exemption laws applicable to his partnership interest.

§ 704. Right of Assignee to Become Limited Partner.—(a) An assignee of a partnership interest, including an assignee of a general partner, may become a limited partner if and to the extent that (1) the assignor gives the assignee that right in accordance with authority described in the certificate of limited partnership, or (2) all other partners consent.

(b) An assignee who has become a limited partner has, to the extent assigned, the rights and powers, and is subject to the restrictions and liabilities, of a limited partner under the partnership agreement and this Act. An assignee who becomes a limited partner also is liable for the obligations of his assignor to make and return contributions as provided in Article 6. However, the assignee is not obligated for liabilities unknown to the assignee at the time he became a limited partner and which could not be ascertained from the certificate of limited partnership.

(c) If an assignee of a partnership interest becomes a limited partner, the assignor is not released from his liability to the limited partnership under Sections 207 and 502.

§ 705. Power of Estate of Deceased or Incompetent Partner.—If a partner who is an individual dies or a court of competent jurisdiction adjudges him to be incompetent to manage his person or his property, the partner's executor, administrator guardian, conservator, or other legal representative may exercise all the partner's rights for the purpose of settling his estate or administering his property, including any power the partner had to give an assignee the right to become a limited partner. If a partner is a corporation, trust, or other entity and is dissolved or terminated, the powers of that partner may be exercised by its legal representative or successor.

Article 8

Dissolution

§ 801. Nonjudicial Dissolution.—A limited partnership is dissolved and its affairs shall be wound up upon the happening of the first to occur of the following:

(1) at the time or upon the happening of events specified in the certificate of limited partnership;

(2) written consent of all partners;

(3) an event of withdrawal of a general partner unless at the time there is at least one other general partner and the certificate of limited partnership permits the business of the limited partnership to be carried on by the remaining general partner and that partner does so, but the limited partnership is not dissolved and is not required to be wound up by reason of any event of withdrawal if, within 90 days after the withdrawal, all partners agree in writing to continue the business of the limited partnership and to the appointment of one or more additional partners if necessary or desired; or

(4) entry of a decree of judicial dissolution under Section 802.

§ 802. Judicial Dissolution.—On application by or for a partner the [here designate the proper court] court may decree dissolution of a limited partnership whenever it is not reasonably practicable to carry on the business in conformity with the partnership agreement.

§ 803. Winding Up.—Except as provided in the partnership agreement, the general partners who have not wrongfully dissolved a limited partnership or, if none, the limited partners, may wind up the limited partnership's affairs; but the [here designate the proper court] court may wind up the limited partnership's affairs upon application of any partner, his legal representative, or assignee.

§ 804. Distribution of Assets.—Upon the winding up of a limited partnership, the assets shall be distributed as follows:

(1) to creditors, including partners who are creditors, to the extent permitted by law, in satisfaction of liabilities of the limited partnership other than liabilities for distributions to partners under Section 601 or 604;

(2) except as provided in the partnership agreement, to partners and former partners in satisfaction of liabilities for distributions under Section 601 or 604; and

(3) except as provided in the partnership agreement, to partners *first* for the return of their contributions and *secondly* respecting their partnership interests, in the proportions in which the partners share in distributions.

Article 9

Foreign Limited Partnerships

§ 901. Law Governing.—Subject to the Constitution of this State, (1) the laws of the state under which a foreign limited partnership is organized govern its organization and internal affairs and the liability of its limited partners, and (2) a foreign limited partnership may not be denied registration by reason of any difference between those laws and the laws of this State.

§ 902. Registration.—Before transacting business in this State, a foreign limited partnership shall register with the Secretary of State. In order to register, a foreign limited partnership shall submit to the Secretary of State, in duplicate, an application for registration as a foreign limited partnership, signed and sworn to by a general partner and setting forth:

(1) the name of the foreign limited partnership and, if different, the name under which it proposes to register and transact business in this State;

(2) the state and date of its formation;

(3) the general character of the business it proposes to transact in this State;

(4) the name and address of any agent for service of process on the foreign limited partnership whom the foreign limited partnership elects to appoint; the agent must be an individual resident of this state, a domestic corporation, or a foreign corporation having a place of business in, and authorized to do business in, this State;

(5) a statement that the Secretary of State is appointed the agent of the foreign limited partnership for service of process if no agent has been appointed under paragraph (4) or, if appointed, the agent's authority has been revoked or if the agent cannot be found or served with the exercise of reasonable diligence;

(6) the address of the office required to be maintained in the State of its organization by the laws of that State or, if not so required, of the principal office of the foreign limited partnership; and

(7) if the certificate of limited partnership filed in the foreign limited partnership's state of organization is not required to include the names and business addresses of the partners, a list of the names and addresses.

§ 903. Issuance of Registration.—

(a) If the Secretary of State finds that an application for registration conforms to law and all requisite fees have been paid, he shall:

(1) endorse on the application the word "Filed", and the month, day and year of the filing thereof;

(2) file in his office a duplicate original of the application; and

(3) issue a certificate of registration to transact business in this State.

(b) The certificate of registration, together with a duplicate original of the application, shall be returned to the person who filed the application or his representative.

§ 904. Name.—A foreign limited partnership may register with the Secretary of State under any name (whether or not it is the name under which it is registered in its state of organization) that includes without abbreviation the words "limited partnership" and that could be registered by a domestic limited partnership.

§ 905. Changes and Amendments.—If any statement in the application for registration of a foreign limited partnership was false when made or any arrangements or other facts described have changed, making the application inaccurate in any respect, the foreign limited partnership shall promptly file in the office of the Secretary of State a certificate, signed and sworn to by a general partner, correcting such statement.

§ 906. Cancellation of Registration.—A foreign limited partnership may cancel its registration by filing with the Secretary of State a certificate of cancellation signed and sworn to by a general partner. A cancellation does not terminate the authority of the Secretary of State to accept service of process on the foreign limited partnership with respect to [claims for relief] [causes of action] arising out of the transactions of business in this State.

§ 907. Transaction of Business Without Registration.—(a) A foreign limited partnership transacting business in this State may not maintain any action, suit, or proceeding in any court of this State until it has registered in this State.

(b) The failure of a foreign limited partnership to register in this State does not impair the validity of any contract or act of the foreign limited partnership or prevent the foreign limited partnership from defending any action, suit, or proceeding in any court of this State.

(c) A limited partner of a foreign limited partnership is not liable as a general partner of the foreign limited partnership solely by reason of having transacted business in this State without registration.

(d) A foreign limited partnership, by transacting business in this State without registration, appoints the Secretary of State as its agent for service of process with respect to [claims for relief] [causes of action] arising out of the transaction of business in this State.

§ 908. Action by [Appropriate Official.]—The [appropriate official] may bring an action to restrain a foreign limited partnership from transacting business in this State in violation of the Article.

Article 10

Derivative Actions

§ 1001. Right of Action.—A limited partner may bring an action in the right of a limited partnership to recover a judgment in its favor if general partners with authority to do so have refused to bring the action or if an effort to cause those general partners to bring the action is not likely to succeed.

§ 1002. Proper Plaintiff.—In a derivative action, the plaintiff must be a partner at the time of bringing the action and (1) at the time of the transaction of which the complains or (2) his status as a partner had devolved upon him by operation of law or pursuant to the terms of the partnership agreement from a person who was a partner at the time of the transaction.

§ 1003. Pleading.—In a derivative action, the complaint shall set forth with particularity the effort of the plaintiff to secure initiation of the action by a general partner or the reasons for not making the effort.

§ 1004. Expenses.—If a derivative action is successful, in whole or in part, or if anything is received by the plaintiff as a result of a judgment, compromise or settlement of an action or claim, the court may award the plaintiff reasonable expenses, including reasonable attorney's fees, and shall direct him to remit to the limited partnership the remainder of those proceeds received by him.

Article 11

Miscellaneous

§ 1101. Construction and Application.—This Act shall be so applied and construed to effectuate its general purpose to make uniform the law with respect to the subject of this Act among states enacting it.

§ 1102. Short Title.—This Act may be cited as the Uniform Limited Partnership Act.

§ 1103. Severability.—If any provision of this Act or its application to any person or circumstance is held invalid, the invalidity does not affect other provisions or applications of the Act which can be given effect without the invalid provision or application, and to this end the provisions of this Act are severable.

§ 1104. Effective Date, Extended Effective Date and Repeal.— Except as set forth below, the effective date of this Act is   and the following Acts [list prior limited partnership acts] are hereby repealed:

(1) The existing provisions for execution and filing of certificates of limited partnerships and amendments thereunder and cancellations thereof continue in effect until [specify time required to create central filing system], the extended effective date, and Sections 102, 103, 104, 105, 201, 202, 203, 204 and 206 are not effective until the extended effective date.

(2) Section 402, specifying the conditions under which a general partner ceases to be a member of a limited partnership, is not effective until the extended effective date, and the applicable provisions of existing law continue to govern until the extended effective date.

(3) Sections 501, 502, and 608 apply only to contributions and distributions made after the effective date of this Act.

(4) Section 704 applies only to assignments made after the effective date of this Act.

(5) Article 9, dealing with registration of foreign limited partnerships, is not effective until the extended effective date.

§ 1105. Rules for Cases Not Provided for in This Act.—In any case not provided for in this Act the provisions of the Uniform Partnership Act govern.

Contents of 1983 Revised Model Business Corporation Act Cross-Referenced to Contents of 1969 Model Business Corporation Act
(Sections marked with an * are not included in this appendix)

Section No. in 1983 Act	Section Title	Section No. in 1969 Act
	Chapter 1. General provisions	
	Subchapter A. Short title and reservation of power	
1.01	Short title	1
1.02*	Reservation of power to amend or repeal	149
	Subchapter B. Filing documents	
1.20*	Filing requirements	new
1.21*	Forms	142
1.22*	Filing, service, and copying fees	128, 129
1.23*	Effective date of filing	new
1.24*	Correcting filed document	new
1.25*	Filing duty of secretary of state	new
1.26*	Appeal from secretary of state's refusal to file document	140
1.27*	Evidentiary effect of copy of filed document	141
1.28*	Certificate of good standing	new
1.29*	Penalty for signing false document	136
	Subchapter C. Secretary of State	
1.30*	Powers	139
	Subchapter D. Definitions	
1.40*	Act definitions	2
1.41*	Notice	new
1.42*	Number of shareholders	new
	Chapter 2. Incorporation	
2.01	Incorporators	53
2.02	Articles of incorporation	54
2.03*	Incorporation	55, 56
2.04*	Liability for preincorporation transactions	146
2.05	Organization of corporation	57
2.06	Bylaws	27 sent. 1, 3
2.07	Emergency bylaws	27A part
	Chapter 3. Purposes and powers	
3.01	Purposes	3
3.02	General powers	4
3.03*	Emergency powers	27A part
3.04	Ulta vires	7
	Chapter 4. Name	
4.01	Corporate name	8
4.02	Reserved name	9
4.03*	Registered name	10, 11
	Chapter 5. Office and agent	
5.01*	Registered office and registered agent	12
5.02*	Change of registered office or registered agent	13 part
5.03*	Resignation of registered agent	13 part
5.04*	Service on corporation	14

Section No. in 1983 Act	Section Title	Section No. in 1969 Act
11.06*	Effect of merger or share exchange	76
11.07*	Merger or share exchange with foreign corporation	77
	Chapter 12. Sale of assets	
12.01	Sale of assets in regular course of business and mortgage of assets	78
12.02	Sale of assets other than in regular course of business	79
	Chapter 13. Dissenters' rights	
	Subchapter A. Right to dissent and obtain payment for shares	
13.01	Definitions	81(a)
13.02	Right to dissent	80(a), (c), (d)
13.03*	Dissent by nominees and beneficial owners	80(b)
	Subchapter B. Procedure for exercise of dissenters' rights	
13.20	Notice of dissenters' rights	81(b), (d) sent. 2
13.21*	Notice of intent to demand payment	81(c)
13.22	Notice of how to demand payment	81(d) sents. 1, 3, 4
13.23	Duty to demand payment	81(e) sent. 1
13.24	Share restrictions	81(e) sent. 2, 3
13.25	Payment	81(f) (3)
13.26*	Failure to make payment	81(f) (1), (2)
13.27*	After-acquired shares	81(j) (1)
13.28	Procedure if shareholder dissatisfied with payment or offer	81(g), (j) (2)
	Subchapter C. Judicial appraisal of shares	
13.30	Court action	81(j)(3), (h)
13.31	Court costs and counsel fees	81(i)
	Chapter 14. Dissolution	
	Subchapter A. Voluntary dissolution	
14.01*	Dissolution by incorporators or initial directors	82
14.02	Dissolution by directors and shareholders	84(a)–(c)
14.03*	Articles of dissolution	83, 84(d), 92, 93
14.04*	Revocation of dissolution	88–91
14.05*	Effect of dissolution	87
14.06*	Known claims against dissolved corporation	87(a)
14.07*	Unknown claims against dissolved corporation	105
	Subchapter B. Administrative dissolution	
14.20*	Grounds for administrative dissolution	95
14.21*	Procedure for administrative dissolution	new
14.22*	Reinstatement following administrative dissolution	new
14.23*	Appeal from denial of reinstatement	new
	Subchapter C. Judicial dissolution	
14.30*	Grounds for judicial dissolution	94(b), (c), 97(a)–(d)
14.31*	Procedure for judicial dissolution	96, 97, 98
14.32*	Receivership or custodianship	98, 99, 101
14.33*	Decree of dissolution	100, 102, 103
	Subchapter D. Miscellaneous	
14.40*	Deposit with state treasurer	104
	Chapter 15. Foreign corporations	
	Subchapter A. Certificate of authority	
15.01*	Authority to transact business required	106
15.02*	Consequences of transacting business without authority	124
15.03*	Application for certificate of authority	110, 111
15.04*	Amended certificate of authority	118

§ 1.01. Short Title

This Act shall be known and may be cited as the "[name of state] Business Corporation Act."

§ 2.01. Incorporators

One or more persons may act as the incorporator or incorporators of a corporation by delivering to the secretary of state articles of incorporation.

§ 2.02. Articles of Incorporation

(a) The articles of incorporation must set forth:

(1) a corporate name for the corporation that satisfies the requirements of section 4.01;

(2) the number of shares the corporation is authorized to issue;

(3) the address of the corporation's initial registered office and the name of its initial registered agent at that office; and

(4) the name and address of each incorporator.

(b) The articles of incorporation may set forth:

(1) the names and addresses of the individuals who are to serve as the initial directors;

(2) provisions not inconsistent with law regarding:

(i) the purpose or purposes for which the corporation is organized;

(ii) managing the business and regulating the affairs of the corporation;

(iii) defining, limiting, and regulating the powers of the corporation, its directors, and shareholders;

(iv) a par value for authorized shares or classes of shares; and

(3) any provision that under this Act is required or permitted to be set forth in the bylaws.

(c) The articles of incorporation need not set forth any of the corporate powers enumerated in this Act.

§ 2.05. Organization of Corporation

(a) After incorporation:

(1) if initial directors are named in the articles of incorporation, the initial directors shall hold an organizational meeting, at the call of a majority of the directors, to complete the organization of the corporation by appointing officers, adopting bylaws, and carrying on any other business brought before the meeting;

(2) if initial directors are not named in the articles, the incorporator or incorporators shall hold an organizational meeting at the call of a majority of the incorporators:

(i) to complete the organization of the corporation; or

(ii) to elect directors who shall complete the organization of the corporation.

(b) Action required or permitted by this Act to be taken by incorporators at an organizational meeting may be taken without a meeting if the action taken is evidenced by one or more written consents describing the action taken and signed by each incorporator.

(c) An organizational meeting may be held in or out of this state.

§ 2.06. Bylaws

(a) The incorporators or initial directors of a corporation shall adopt initial bylaws for the corporation.

(b) The bylaws of a corporation may contain any provision for managing the business and regulating the affairs of the corporation that is not inconsistent with law or the articles of incorporation.

§ 2.07. Emergency Bylaws

(a) Unless the articles of incorporation provide otherwise, the directors of a corporation may adopt bylaws to be effective only in an emergency defined in subsection (d). The emergency bylaws, which are subject to amendment or repeal by the shareholders, may make all provisions necessary for managing the corporation during the emergency, including:

(1) procedures for calling a meeting of the board;

(2) quorum requirements for the meeting; and

(3) designation of additional or substitute directors.

(b) All provisions of the regular bylaws consistent with the emergency bylaws remain effective during the emergency. The emergency bylaws are not effective after the emergency ends.

(c) Corporate action taken in good faith in accordance with the emergency bylaws:

(1) binds the corporation; and

(2) may not be used to impose liability on a corporate director, officer, employee, or agent.

(d) An emergency exists for purposes of this section if a quorum of the corporation's directors cannot readily be assembled:

(1) because of attack on the United States or on the location where the corporation conducts its business or where its directors or shareholders customarily meet;

(2) because of nuclear disaster; or

(3) because of some other catastrophic event.

§ 3.01. Purposes

(a) Every corporation incorporated under this Act has the purpose of engaging in any lawful business unless a narrower purpose is set forth in the articles of incorporation.

(b) A corporation engaging in a business that is subject to regulation under another statute of this state may incorporate under this Act only if permitted by, and subject to all limitations of, the other statute.

§ 3.02. General Powers

Unless its articles of incorporation provide otherwise, every corporation has the same powers as an individual to do all things necessary or convenient to carry out its business and affairs, including without limitation power:

(1) to have perpetual duration and succession in its corporate name;

(2) to sue and be sued, complain and defend in its corporate name;

(3) to have a corporate seal, which may be altered at will, and to use it, or a facsimile of it, by impressing or affixing it or in any other manner reproducing it;

(4) to make and amend bylaws, not inconsistent with its articles of incorporation or with the laws of this state, for managing the business and regulating the affairs of the corporation;

(5) to purchase, receive, lease, or otherwise acquire, and own, hold, improve, use, and otherwise deal with, real or personal property, or any legal or equitable interest in property, wherever located;

(6) to sell, convey, mortgage, pledge, lease, exchange, and otherwise dispose of all or any part of its property;

(7) to purchase, receive, subscribe for, or otherwise acquire; own, hold, vote, use, sell, mortgage, lend, pledge, or otherwise dispose of; and deal in and with shares or other interests in, or

obligations of, other domestic or foreign corporations, associations, partnerships (without regard to their purpose or purposes), and individuals, the United States, a state, or a foreign government;

(8) to make contracts and guarantees, incur liabilities, borrow money, issue its notes, bonds, and other obligations, and secure any of its obligations by mortgage or pledge of any of its property, franchises, or income;

(9) to lend money, invest and reinvest its funds, and receive and hold real and personal property as security for repayment;

(10) to be a promoter, partner, member, associate, or manager of any partnership, joint venture, trust, or other entity;

(11) to conduct its business, locate offices, and exercise the powers granted by this Act within or without this state;

(12) to elect directors and appoint officers, employees, and agents of the corporation, define their duties, fix their compensation, and lend them money and credit;

(13) to pay pensions and establish pension plans, pension trusts, profit sharing plans, share bonus plans, share option plans, and benefit and incentive plans for any or all of its current or former directors, officers, employees, and agents;

(14) to make donations for the public welfare or for charitable, scientific, or educational purposes;

(15) to transact any lawful business that will aid governmental policy;

(16) to make payments or donations, or do any other act, not inconsistent with law, that furthers the business and affairs of the corporation.

§ 3.04. Ultra Vires

(a) Except as provided in subsection (b), the validity of corporate action may not be challenged on the ground that the corporation lacks or lacked power to act.

(b) A corporation's lack of power to act may be challenged:

(1) in a proceeding by a shareholder against the corporation to enjoin the act;

(2) in a proceeding by the corporation, directly, derivatively, or through a receiver, trustee, or other legal representative, against an incumbent or former director, officer, employee, or agent of the corporation; or

(3) in a proceeding by the Attorney General under section 14.30.

(c) In a shareholder's proceeding under subsection (b)(1) to enjoin an unauthorized corporate act, the court may enjoin or set aside the act, if equitable and if all affected persons are parties to the proceeding, and may award damages for loss (other than anticipated profits) suffered by the corporation or another party because of enjoining the unauthorized act.

§ 4.01. Corporate Name

(a) A corporate name:

(1) must contain the word "corporation," "incorporated," "company," or "limited," or the abbreviation "corp.," "inc.," "co.," or "ltd."; and

(2) may not contain language stating or implying that the corporation is organized for a purpose other than that permitted by section 3.01 and its articles of incorporation.

(b) Except as authorized by subsections (c) and (d), a corporate name must be distinguishable upon the records of the secretary of state from:

(1) the corporate name of a corporation incorporated or authorized to transact business in this state;

(2) a corporate name reserved or registered under section 4.02 or 4.03; and

(3) the fictitious name adopted by a foreign corporation authorized to transact business in this state because its real name is unavailable.

(c) A corporation may apply to the secretary of state for authorization to use a name that is not distinguishable upon his records from one or more of the names described in subsection (b). The

Secretary of State shall authorize use of the name applied for if:

(1) the other corporation consents to the use in writing and submits an undertaking in form satisfactory to the secretary of state to change its name to a name that is distinguishable upon the records of the secretary of state from the name of the applying corporation; or

(2) the applicant delivers to the secretary of state a certified copy of the final judgment of a court of competent jurisdiction establishing the applicant's right to use the name applied for in this state.

(d) A corporation may use the name (including the fictitious name) of another domestic or foreign corporation that is used in this state if the other corporation is incorporated or authorized to transact business in this state and the proposed user corporation:

(1) has merged with the other corporation;

(2) has been formed by reorganization of the other corporation; or

(3) has acquired all or substantially all of the assets, including the corporate name, of the other corporation.

§ 4.02. Reserved Name

(a) A person may apply to the secretary of state to reserve the exclusive use of a corporate name, including a fictitious name for a foreign corporation whose corporate name is not available. If the secretary of state finds that the corporate name applied for is available, he shall reserve the name for the applicant's exclusive use for a nonrenewable 120-day period.

(b) The owner of a reserved corporate name may transfer the reservation to another person by delivering to the secretary of state a signed notice of the transfer that states the name and address of the transferee.

§ 6.01. Authorization Generally

(a) Each corporation may create and issue the number of shares of each class stated in its articles of incorporation.

(b) If classes of shares are authorized, the articles of incorporation must describe the designations, preferences, limitations, and relative rights of each class.

(c) The articles of incorporation may limit or deny the voting rights of or provide special voting rights for the shares of any class except to the extent prohibited by this Act.

(d) The articles of incorporation may authorize:

(1) the redemption at the option of the corporation or shareholder of:

(i) classes of preferred shares that have a preference over any other class of shares in the assets of the corporation upon liquidation; and

(ii) classes of common shares, whether or not they have a preference over other classes of common shares, if there exists at least one class of voting common shares not subject to redemption;

(2) the redemption at the option of the shareholder of shares of an investment corporation regulated under federal law; and

(3) the redemption at the option of the corporation of common shares issued by:

(i) a corporation that is subject to governmental regulation or regulation by a national securities exchange, if the regulation requires some or all of the shareholders to possess prescribed qualifications or limits the permissible holdings of shareholders and redemption is necessary to prevent loss or allow reinstatement of benefits or entitlements;

(ii) a professional corporation, if the redemption complies with [section 23 of the Model Professional Corporation Supplement].

§ 6.02. Classes of Preferred Shares

(a) If the articles of incorporation so provide, a corporation may issue classes of preferred shares:

(1) subject to the right or duty of the corporation to redeem the shares under section 6.01(d) at a price fixed in accordance with the articles of incorporation;

(2) entitling the holders of the shares to cumulative, non-cumulative, or partially cumulative dividends;

(3) having preference over any other class of shares in the payment of dividends;

(4) having preference over any other class of shares in the assets of the corporation upon liquidation;

(5) convertible into shares of any other class or into shares of any series of the same or any other class, except a class having a prior or superior right to the payment of dividends or in the assets upon liquidation.

(b) Subsection (a)'s description of the designations, preferences, limitations, and relative rights of share classes is not exhaustive.

§ 6.03. Series Within a Class

(a) If the articles of incorporation so provide, a corporation may issue the shares of any preferred class in series.

(b) The articles may authorize the board of directors to create one or more series within a preferred class of shares and determine the designation, relative rights, preferences, and limitations of each series in accordance with the requirements of this section and the articles of incorporation.

(c) Each series of a class must be given a unique designation.

(d) All shares of the same class must provide identical relative rights, preferences, and limitations except with respect to:

(1) dividend rates;

(2) redeemability, including the redemption price, terms, and conditions;

(3) repurchase obligations of the corporation for all or part of a series at the option of the holders of another class;

(4) the amount payable per share upon liquidation;

(5) sinking fund provisions for the redemption or repurchase of shares;

(6) convertibility, including the terms and conditions of conversion;

(7) voting rights.

(e) Before issuing any shares of a series created under subsection (b), the corporation must deliver to the secretary of state articles of amendment, which are effective without shareholder action, that set forth:

(1) the name of the corporation;

(2) a copy of the resolution creating the series showing the date it was adopted; and

(3) a statement that the resolution was duly adopted by the board.

§ 6.20. Subscription for Shares

(a) A subscription for shares entered into before incorporation is irrevocable for six months unless the subscription agreement provides a longer or shorter period or all the subscribers agree to revocation.

(b) A subscription agreement entered into after incorporation is a contract between the subscriber and corporation.

(c) The board of directors may determine the payment terms of subscriptions for shares, whether entered into before or after incorporation, unless the subscription agreement specifies them. The board's call for payment on subscriptions must be uniform as to all shares of the same class or series.

(d) If a subscriber defaults in payment under the agreement, the corporation may collect the amount owed as any other debt. The bylaws may prescribe other penalties for nonpayment but a subscription and the installments already paid on it may not be forfeited unless the corporation demands the amount due by written notice to the subscriber and it remains unpaid for at least 20 days after the effective date of the notice.

(e) If a subscription for unissued shares is forfeited for nonpayment, the corporation may sell the shares subscribed for. If the shares are sold for more than the amount due on the subscription, the corporation shall pay the excess, after deducting the expense of sale, to the subscriber or his representative.

§ 6.21. Issuance of Shares

(a) The powers granted in this section are subject to restriction by the articles of incorporation.

(b) Shares may be issued at a price determined by the board of directors, or the board may set a minimum price or establish a formula or method by which the price may be determined.

(c) Consideration for shares may consist of cash, promissory notes, services performed, contracts for services to be performed, or any other tangible or intangible property. If shares are issued for other than cash, the board of directors shall determine the value of the consideration received as of the time the shares are issued.

(d) Shares issued when the corporation receives the consideration determined by the board are validly issued, fully paid, and nonassessable.

(e) A good faith judgment of the board of directors as to the value of the consideration received for shares is conclusive.

(f) The corporation may place shares issued for a contract for future services or a promissory note in escrow, or make other arrangements to restrict the transfer of the shares, and may credit distributions in respect of the shares against their purchase price, until the services are performed or the note is paid. If the services are not performed or the note is not paid, the shares escrowed or restricted and the distributions credited may be cancelled in whole or part.

§ 6.22. Liability of Subscribers and Shareholders

(a) A subscriber for or holder of shares of a corporation is not liable to the corporation or its creditors with respect to the shares except to pay the subscription price or the consideration determined for them under section 6.21.

(b) If shares are issued for promissory notes, for contracts for services to be performed, or before subscriptions are fully paid, a transferee of the shares is not liable to the corporation or its creditors for the unpaid balance but the transferor remains liable.

§ 6.23. Share Exchanges, Dividends, and Splits

(a) The powers granted in this section are subject to restriction by the articles of incorporation.

(b) If authorized by its board of directors, and subject to the limitation of subsection (c), a corporation may, without requiring consideration:

(1) issue its own shares to its shareholders in exchange for or in conversion of its outstanding shares; or

(2) issue its own shares pro rata to its shareholders or to the shareholders of one or more classes or series to effectuate share dividends or splits.

(c) Shares of one class or series may not be issued to the shareholders of another class or series unless (1) the articles of incorporation so authorize, (2) the holders of at least a majority of the outstanding votes of the class or series to be issued consent in writing to or vote affirmatively for the issue, or (3) there are no holders of the class or series to be issued.

§ 6.24. Share Rights and Options

(a) The powers granted in this section are subject to restriction by the articles of incorporation.

(b) A corporation may create and issue rights or options entitling their holders to purchase shares of any class, or any series within a class, in forms, on terms, at times, and for prices prescribed by the corporation's board of directors. Rights or options may be issued together with or independently of the corporation's issue and sale of its shares or other securities and may be issued as incentives to directors, officers, or employees of the corporation or any of its subsidiaries.

(c) A good faith judgment of the board of directors as to the value of the consideration received for rights or options entitling their holders to purchase shares is conclusive.

§ 6.27. Restriction on Transfer or Registration of Shares and Other Securities

(a) The articles of incorporation, bylaws, an agreement among shareholders, or an agreement between shareholders and the corporation may impose restrictions on the transfer or registration of transfer of shares of the corporation. A restriction does not affect shares issued before the restriction was adopted unless the holders of the shares are parties to the restriction agreement or voted in favor of the restriction.

(b) A restriction on the transfer or registration of transfer of shares is valid and enforceable against the holder or a transferee of the holder if the restriction is authorized by this section and is noted conspicuously on the front or back of the certificate or is contained in the information statement required by section 6.26(b). Unless so noted, a restriction is not enforceable against a person without knowledge of the restriction.

(c) A restriction on the transfer or registration of transfer of shares is authorized:

(1) to maintain the corporation's status when it is dependent on the number or identity of its shareholders;

(2) to preserve exemptions under federal or state securities law;

(3) for any other reasonable purpose.

(d) A restriction on the transfer or registration of transfer of shares may:

(1) obligate the shareholder first to offer the corporation or other persons (separately, consecutively, or simultaneously) an opportunity to acquire the restricted shares;

(2) obligate the corporation or other persons (separately, consecutively, or simultaneously) to acquire the restricted shares;

(3) require the corporation, the holders of any class of its shares, or another person to approve the transfer of the restricted shares, if the requirement is not manifestly unreasonable;

(4) prohibit the transfer of the restricted shares to designated persons or classes of persons, if the prohibition is not manifestly unreasonable.

(e) For purposes of this section, "shares" includes a security convertible into or carrying a right to subscribe for or acquire shares.

§ 6.30. Shareholders' Preemptive Rights

(a) The shareholders of a corporation do not have a preemptive right to acquire the corporation's unissued shares except to the extent the articles of incorporation so provide.

(b) A statement included in the articles of incorporation that "the corporation elects to have preemptive rights" (or words of similar import) means that subsections (c) through (f) apply except to the extent the articles of incorporation expressly provide otherwise.

(c) If the articles of incorporation provide for preemptive rights, the shareholders of a corporation have a preemptive right, granted on uniform terms and conditions prescribed by the board of directors to provide a fair and reasonable opportunity to exercise the right, to acquire proportional amounts of the corporation's unissued shares upon the decision of the board of directors to issue them.

(d) A shareholder may waive his preemptive right. A waiver evidenced by a writing is irrevocable even though it is not supported by consideration.

(e) There is no preemptive right:

(1) to acquire shares issued as incentives to directors, officers, or employees under section 6.24;

(2) to acquire shares issued to satisfy conversion or option rights;

(3) to acquire shares authorized in articles of incorporation that are issued within six months from the effective date of incorporation;

(4) to acquire shares sold otherwise than for money;

(5) for holders of shares of any class preferred or limited as to entitlement to dividends or assets;

(6) for holders of common shares to acquire shares of any class preferred or limited as to obligations or entitlement to dividends or assets unless the shares are convertible into common shares or carry a right to subscribe for or acquire common shares.

(f) Shares subject to preemptive rights that are not acquired by shareholders may be issued to any person for a period of one year after being offered to shareholders at a consideration set by the board of directors that is not lower than the consideration set for the exercise of preemptive rights. An offer at a lower consideration or after the expiration of one year is subject to the shareholders' preemptive rights.

§ 6.31. Corporation's Power to Acquire Own Shares

(a) A corporation may acquire its own shares.

(b) If a corporation acquires its own shares, they constitute authorized but unissued shares unless the articles of incorporation prevent reissue, in which event the acquired shares are cancelled and the number of authorized shares is reduced by the number of shares acquired.

(c) If the number of authorized shares is reduced by an acquisition, the corporation must deliver to the secretary of state, not later than the due date of its next annual report, articles of amendment, which are effective without shareholder action, that set forth:

(1) the name of the corporation;

(2) the number of acquired shares cancelled, itemized by class and series; and

(3) the total number of authorized shares, itemized by class and series, remaining after cancellation of the acquired shares.

§ 6.40. Distributions to Shareholders

(a) Subject to restriction by the articles of incorporation and the limitation in subsection (c), a board of directors may authorize and the corporation may make distributions to its shareholders.

(b) If the directors do not fix the record date for determining shareholders entitled to a distribution (other than one involving a repurchase or reacquisition of shares), it is the date the board authorizes the distribution.

(c) No distribution may be made if, after giving it effect:

(1) the corporation would not be able to pay its debts as they become due in the usual course of business; or

(2) the corporation's total assets would be less than the sum of its total liabilities plus (unless the articles of incorporation permit otherwise) the maximum amount payable at the time of distribution to shareholders having preferential rights in liquidation.

(d) A board may base a determination that a distribution may be made under subsection (c) either on financial statements prepared on the basis of accounting practices and principles that are reasonable in the circumstances or on a fair valuation or other method that is reasonable in the circumstances.

(e) The effect of a distribution under subsection (c) is measured:

(1) in the case of distribution by purchase, redemption, or other acquisition of the corporation's shares, as of the earlier of (i) the date money or other property is transferred or debt incurred by the corporation or (ii) the date the shareholder ceases to be a shareholder with respect to the acquired shares;

(2) in all other cases, as of (i) the date of its authorization if payment occurs within 120 days after the date of authorization or (ii) the date of payment if payment occurs more than 120 days after the date of authorization.

(f) A corporation's indebtedness to a shareholder incurred by reason of a distribution made in accordance with this section is at parity with the corporation's indebtedness to its general, unsecured creditors except to the extent subordinated by agreement.

§ 7.01. Annual Meeting

(a) A corporation shall hold a shareholders' meeting annually at a time stated in or fixed in accordance with the bylaws.

(b) Annual shareholders' meetings may be held in or out of this state at the place stated in or fixed in accordance with the bylaws. If no place is stated in or fixed in accordance with the bylaws, annual meetings shall be held at the corporation's principal office.

(c) The failure to hold an annual meeting at the time stated in or fixed in accordance with a corporation's bylaws does not affect the validity of any corporate action.

§ 7.02. Special Meeting

(a) A corporation shall hold a special shareholders' meeting:

(1) on call of its board of directors or the individual or individuals authorized to do so by the articles of incorporation or bylaws; or

(2) if the holders of at least five percent of all the votes entitled to be cast at a proposed special meeting sign and deliver to the corporation's secretary one or more written demands for the meeting describing the purpose or purposes for which it is to be held.

(b) If not otherwise fixed under section 7.07, the record date for determining shareholders entitled to demand a special meeting is the date the first shareholder signs the demand.

(c) Special shareholders' meetings may be held in or out of this state at the place stated or fixed in accordance with the bylaws. If no place is stated or fixed in accordance with the bylaws, special meetings shall be held at the corporation's principal office.

(d) Only business within the purpose or purposes described in the meeting notice required by section 7.05 (c) may be conducted at a special shareholders' meeting.

§ 7.04. Action Without Meeting

(a) Action required or permitted by this Act to be taken at a shareholders' meeting may be taken without a meeting and without action by the directors if the action is taken by all the shareholders entitled to vote on the action. The action must be evidenced by one or more written consents describing the action taken, signed by all the shareholders entitled to vote on the action, and delivered to the secretary of the corporation for inclusion in the minutes or filing with the corporate records.

(b) If not otherwise determined under section 7.07, the record date for determining shareholders entitled to take action without a meeting is the date the first shareholder signs the consent under subsection (a).

(c) A consent signed under this section has the effect of a meeting vote and may be described as such in any document.

(d) If this Act requires that notice of proposed action be given to nonvoting shareholders and the action is to be taken by unanimous consent of the voting shareholders, the corporation must give its nonvoting shareholders written notice of the proposed action at least 10 days before it is to be taken. The written consent or consents must recite that this notice was given.

§ 7.05. Notice of Meeting

(a) An officer of the corporation shall notify its shareholders of the date, time, and place of each annual and special shareholders' meeting no fewer than 10 nor more than 50 days before the meeting date. Unless this Act or the articles of incorporation require otherwise, the corporation is required to give notice only to shareholders entitled to vote at the meeting.

(b) Unless this Act or the articles of incorporation require otherwise, notice of an annual meeting need not include a description of the purpose or purposes for which the meeting is called.

(c) Notice of a special meeting must include a description of the purpose or purposes for which the meeting is called.

(d) If not otherwise fixed under section 7.07, the record date for determining shareholders entitled to notice of and to vote at an annual or special shareholders' meeting is the close of business on the day before the notice is mailed to the shareholders.

(e) Unless the bylaws require otherwise, if an annual or special shareholders' meeting is adjourned to a different date, time, or place, notice need not be given of the new date, time, or place if the new date, time, or place is announced at the meeting before adjournment. If a new record date for the adjourned meeting is or must be fixed under section 7.07, however, notice of the adjourned meeting must be given under this section to the shareholders of record on the new record date.

§ 7.06. Waiver of Notice

(a) A shareholder may waive any notice required by this Act, the articles of incorporation, or bylaws before or after the date and time stated in the notice. The waiver must be in writing, be signed by the shareholder entitled to the notice, and be delivered to the secretary of the corporation for inclusion in the minutes or filing with the corporate records.

(b) A shareholder's attendance at a meeting:

(1) waives objection to lack of notice or defective notice of the meeting, unless the shareholder at the beginning of the meeting objects to holding the meeting or transacting business at the meeting;

(2) waives objection to consideration of a particular matter at the meeting that is not within the purpose or purposes described in the meeting notice, unless the shareholder objects to considering the matter when it is presented.

§ 7.07. Record Date

(a) The bylaws may fix or provide the manner of fixing the record date for determining the shareholders entitled to notice of a shareholders' meeting, to demand a special meeting, to vote, or to take any other action. If the bylaws do not fix or provide for fixing a record date, the directors of the corporation may fix a future date as the record date.

(b) A record date fixed under this section may not be more than 60 days before the meeting or action requiring a determination of shareholders.

(c) A determination of shareholders entitled to notice of or to vote at a shareholders' meeting is effective for any adjournment of the meeting unless the board fixes a new record date, which it must do if the meeting is adjourned to a date more than 120 days after the record date fixed for the original meeting.

(d) If a court orders a meeting adjourned to a date more than 120 days after the record date, it may provide that the original record date continues in effect or it may fix a new record date.

§ 7.20. Shareholders' List for Meeting

(a) After fixing a record date for a meeting, a corporation shall prepare an alphabetical list of the names of all its shareholders who are entitled to notice of a shareholders' meeting. The list must be arranged by class of shares and showing the address of and number of shares held by each shareholder.

(b) The shareholders' list must be available for inspection by any shareholder, beginning two business days after notice of the meeting for which the list was prepared is given and continuing through the meeting, at the corporation's principal office or at a place identified in the meeting notice in the city where the meeting will be held. A shareholder, his agent, or attorney is entitled on written demand to inspect and copy the list, during regular business hours and at his expense, during the period it is available for inspection.

(c) The corporation shall make the shareholders' list available at the meeting, and any shareholder, his agent, or attorney is entitled to inspect and copy the list at any time during the meeting or any adjournment.

(d) If the corporation refuses to allow a shareholder, his agent, or attorney to inspect and copy the shareholders' list before or at the meeting, the [name or describe] court in the county where the corporation's principal office (or if none in this state its registered office) is located, on application of the shareholder, may summarily order the inspection and copying at the corporation's expense and may postpone the meeting for which the list was prepared until the inspection and copying are complete.

(e) Refusal or failure to prepare or make available the shareholders' list does not affect the validity of action taken at the meeting.

§ 7.21. Voting Entitlement of Shares

(a) Except as provided in subsections (b) and (c) or unless the articles of incorporation provide otherwise, each outstanding share, regardless of class, is entitled to one vote on each matter voted on at a shareholders' meeting. Only shares are entitled to vote.

(b) Absent special circumstances, the shares of a corporation are not entitled to vote if they are owned, directly or indirectly, by a second corporation, domestic or foreign, and the first corporation owns, directly or indirectly, a majority of the shares entitled to vote for directors of the second corporation.

(c) Redeemable shares are not entitled to vote after notice of redemption is mailed to the holders and a sum sufficient to redeem the shares has been deposited with a bank, trust company, or other financial institution under an irrevocable obligation to pay the holders the redemption price on surrender of the shares.

§ 7.22. Proxies

(a) A shareholder may vote his shares in person or by proxy.

(b) A shareholder may appoint a proxy to vote or otherwise act for him by signing an appointment form, either personally or by his attorney-in-fact.

(c) An appointment of a proxy is effective when received by the secretary or other officer or agent authorized to tabulate votes. An appointment is valid for 11 months unless a longer period is expressly provided in the appointment form.

(d) An appointment of a proxy is revocable by the shareholder unless the appointment form conspicuously states that it is irrevocable and the appointment is coupled with an interest. Appointments coupled with an interest include the appointment of:

(1) a pledgee;

(2) a person who purchased or agreed to purchase the shares;

(3) a creditor of the corporation who extended it credit under terms requiring the appointment;

(4) an employee of the corporation whose employment contract requires the appointment; or

(5) a party to a voting agreement created under section 7.31.

(e) The death or incapacity of the shareholder appointing a proxy does not affect the right of the corporation to accept the proxy's authority unless notice of the death or incapacity is received by the secretary or other officer or agent authorized to tabulate proxy votes before the proxy exercises his authority under the appointment.

(f) An appointment made irrevocable under subsection (d) is revoked when the interest with which it is coupled is extinguished.

(g) A transferee for value of shares subject to an irrevocable appointment may revoke the appointment if he did not know of its existence when he acquired the shares and the existence of the irrevocable appointment was not noted conspicuously on the certificate representing the shares or on the information statement for shares without certificates.

(h) Subject to section 7.24 and to any express limitation on the proxy's authority appearing on the face of the appointment form, a corporation is entitled to accept the proxy's vote or other action as that of the shareholder making the appointment.

§ 7.24. Corporation's Acceptance of Votes

(a) If the name signed on a vote, consent, waiver, or proxy appointment corresponds to the name of a shareholder, the corporation if acting in good faith is entitled to accept the vote, consent, waiver, or proxy appointment and give it effect as the act of the shareholder.

(b) If the name signed on a vote, consent, waiver, or proxy appointment does not correspond to the name of its shareholder, the corporation if acting in good faith is nevertheless entitled to accept the vote, consent, waiver, or proxy appointment and give it effect as the act of the shareholder if:

(1) the shareholder is an entity and the name signed purports

to be that of an officer or agent of the entity;

(2) the name signed purports to be that of an administrator, executor, guardian, or conservator representing the shareholder and, if the corporation requests, evidence of fiduciary status acceptable to the corporation has been presented with respect to the vote, consent, waiver, or proxy appointment;

(3) the name signed purports to be that of a receiver or trustee in bankruptcy of the shareholder and, if the corporation requests, evidence of this status acceptable to the corporation has been presented with respect to the vote, consent, waiver, or proxy appointment;

(4) the name signed purports to be that of a pledgee, beneficial owner, or attorney-in-fact of the shareholder and, if the corporation requests, evidence acceptable to the corporation of the signatory's authority to sign for the shareholder has been presented with respect to the vote, consent, waiver, or proxy appointment;

(5) two or more persons are the shareholder as cotenants or fiduciaries and the name signed purports to be the name of at least one of the coowners and the person signing appears to be acting on behalf of all the coowners.

(c) The corporation is entitled to reject a vote, consent, waiver, or proxy appointment if the secretary or other officer or agent authorized to tabulate votes, acting in good faith, has reasonable basis for doubt about the validity of the signature on it or about the signatory's authority to sign for the shareholder.

(d) The corporation and its officer or agent who accepts or rejects a vote, consent, waiver, or proxy appointment in good faith and in accordance with the standards of this section are not liable in damages to the shareholder for the consequences of the acceptance or rejection.

(e) Corporate action based on the acceptance or rejection of a vote, consent, waiver, or proxy appointment under this section is valid unless a court of competent jurisdiction determines otherwise.

§ 7.30. Voting Trusts

(a) Shareholders may create a voting trust, conferring on a trustee the right to vote or otherwise act for them, by signing an agreement setting out the provisions of the trust (which may include anything consistent with its purpose) and transferring their shares to the trustee. When a voting trust agreement is signed, the trustee shall prepare a list of the names and addresses of all owners of beneficial interests in the trust, together with the number and class of shares each transferred to the trust, and deliver copies of the list and agreement to the corporation's principal office.

(b) A voting trust becomes effective on the date the shares subject to the trust are registered in the trustee's name. A voting trust is valid for not more than 10 years after its effective date unless extended under subsection (c).

(c) All or some of the parties to a voting trust may extend it for additional terms of not more than 10 years each by signing an extension agreement and obtaining the voting trustee's written consent to the extension. An extension agreement must be executed during the 12-month period immediately preceding expiration of the voting trust it is intended to extend. The voting trustee must deliver copies of the extension agreement and list of beneficial owners to the corporation's principal office. An extension agreement binds only those parties signing it.

§ 7.31. Voting Agreements

(a) Two or more shareholders may provide for the manner in which they will vote their shares by signing an agreement for that purpose. A voting agreement created under this section is not subject to the provisions of section 7.30.

(b) A voting agreement created under this section is specifically enforceable.

§ 7.40. Procedure in Derivative Proceedings

(a) A person may not commence a proceeding in the right of a domestic or foreign corporation unless he was a shareholder of the corporation when the transaction complained of occurred or unless he became a shareholder through transfer by operation of law from one who was a shareholder at that time.

(b) A complaint in a proceeding brought in the right of a corporation must be verified and allege with particularity the demand made, if any, to obtain action by the directors and either that the demand was refused or ignored or why he did not make the demand. Whether or not a demand for action was made, if the corporation commences an investigation of the changes made in the demand or complaint, the court may stay any proceeding until the investigation is completed.

(c) A proceeding commenced under this section may not be discontinued or settled without the court's approval. If the court determines that a proposed discontinuance or settlement will substantially affect the interest of the corporation's shareholders or a class of shareholders, the court shall direct that notice be given the shareholders affected.

(d) On termination of the proceeding the court may require the plaintiff to pay any defendant's reasonable expenses (including counsel fees) incurred in defending the proceeding if it finds that the proceeding was commenced without reasonable cause.

(e) For purposes of this section, "shareholder" includes a beneficial owner whose shares are held in a voting trust or held by a nominee on his behalf.

§ 8.01. Requirement for and Duties of Board

(a) Except as provided in subsection (c), each corporation must have a board of directors.

(b) All corporate powers shall be exercised by or under the authority of, and the business and affairs of the corporation managed under the direction of, its board.

(c) A corporation having 50 or fewer shareholders may dispense with or limit the authority of a board of directors by describing in its articles of incorporation who will perform some or all of the duties of a board.

§ 8.02. Qualifications of Directors

The articles of incorporation or bylaws may prescribe qualifications for directors. A director need not be a resident of this state or a shareholder of the corporation unless the articles of incorporation or bylaws so prescribe.

§ 8.03. Number and Election of Directors

(a) A board of directors must consist of one or more individuals, with the number specified in or fixed in accordance with the articles of incorporation or bylaws.

(b) If a board of directors has power to fix or change the number of directors, the board may increase or decrease by 30 percent or less the number of directors last approved by the shareholders, but only the shareholders may increase or decrease by more than 30 percent the number of directors last approved by the shareholders.

(c) The bylaws may establish a variable range for the size of the board by fixing a minimum and maximum number of directors. If a variable range is established, the number of directors may be fixed or changed from time to time, within the minimum and maximum, by the shareholders or the board. After shares are issued, only the shareholders may change a variable-range board size or change from a fixed to a variable-range board size or vice versa.

(d) Directors are elected at the first annual shareholders' meeting and at each annual meeting thereafter unless their terms are staggered under section 8.06.

§ 8.05. Terms of Directors Generally

(a) The terms of the initial directors of a corporation expire at the first annual shareholders' meeting.

(b) The terms of all other directors expire at the next annual shareholders' meeting following their election unless their terms are staggered under section 8.06.

(c) A decrease in the number of directors does not shorten an incumbent director's term.

(d) The term of a director elected to fill a vacancy expires at the next shareholders' meeting at which directors are elected.

(e) Despite the expiration of a director's term, he continues to serve until his successor is elected and qualifies or until there is a decrease in the number of directors.

§ 8.06. Staggered Terms for Directors

If there are nine or more directors, the articles of incorporation may provide for staggering their terms by dividing the total number of directors into two or three groups, with each group containing one-half or one-third of the total, as near as may be, and specifying that the terms of directors in the first group expire at the first annual shareholders' meeting after their election, that the terms of the second group expire at the second annual shareholders' meeting after their election, and that the terms of the third group, if any, expire at the third annual shareholders' meeting after their election.

§ 8.08. Removal of Directors by Shareholders

(a) The shareholders may remove a director with or without cause unless the articles of incorporation provide that directors may be removed only for cause.

(b) If a director is elected by a class of shareholders, he may be removed only by the shareholders of that class.

(c) If cumulative voting is authorized, a director may not be removed if the number of votes, or if he was elected by a class of shareholders the number of votes of that class, sufficient to elect him under cumulative voting is voted against his removal.

(d) A director may be removed by the shareholders only at a meeting called for the purpose of removing him and the meeting notice must state that the purpose, or one of the purposes, of the meeting is removal of the director. Except as provided in subsection (c), a director may be removed only if the number of votes cast to remove him would be sufficient to elect him at a meeting to elect directors.

(e) An entire board of directors may be removed under this section.

§ 8.10. Vacancy on Board

(a) Unless the articles of incorporation provide otherwise, if a vacancy occurs on a board of directors, including a vacancy resulting from an increase in the number of directors:

(1) the board of directors may fill the vacancy; or

(2) if the directors remaining in office constitute fewer than a quorum of the board, they may fill the vacancy by the affirmative vote of a majority of all the directors remaining in office.

(b) If the vacant office was held by a director elected by a class of shareholders, only the holders of that class of shares are entitled to vote to fill the vacancy if it is filled by the shareholders.

(c) A vacancy that will occur at a specific future date (by reason of a resignation effective at a future date under section 8.07(b) or otherwise) may be filled before the vacancy occurs if the new director does not take office until the vacancy occurs.

§ 8.20. Meetings

(a) A board of directors may hold regular or special meetings in or out of this state.

(b) Unless the articles of incorporation or bylaws provide otherwise, a board may permit one or more directors to participate in a regular or special meeting by, or conduct the meeting through the use of, any means of communication by which all directors participating may simultaneously hear each other during the meeting. A director participating in a meeting by this means is deemed to be present in person at the meeting.

§ 8.21 Action Without Meeting

(a) Unless the articles of incorporation or bylaws provide otherwise, action required or permitted by this Act to be taken at a board of directors' meeting may be taken without a meeting if the action is taken by all members of the board. The action must be evidenced by one or more written consents describing the action taken, signed by each director, and delivered to the secretary of the board for inclusion in the minutes or filing with the corporate records.

(b) Action taken under this section is effective when the last director signs the consent, unless the consent specifies a different effective date.

(c) A consent signed under this section has the effect of a meeting vote and may be described as such in any document.

§ 8.22. Notice of Meeting

(a) Unless the articles of incorporation or bylaws provide otherwise, regular meetings of the board may be held without notice of the date, time, place, or purpose of the meeting.

(b) Unless the articles of incorporation or bylaws provide for a longer or shorter period, special meetings of the board must be preceded by at least two days' notice of the date, time, and place of the meeting. The notice need not describe the purpose of the special meeting unless required by the articles of incorporation or bylaws.

§ 8.23. Waiver of Notice

(a) A director may waive any notice required by this Act, the articles of incorporation, or bylaws before or after the date and time stated in the notice. The waiver must be in writing, signed by the director entitled to the notice, and delivered to the secretary of the corporation for inclusion in the minutes or filing with the corporate records.

(b) A director's attendance at or participation in a regular or special meeting waives any required notice of the meeting unless the director at the beginning of the meeting objects to holding the meeting or transacting business at the meeting and does not thereafter vote for or assent to action taken at the meeting.

§ 8.24. Quorum and Voting

(a) Unless the articles of incorporation or bylaws require a greater number, a quorum of a board of directors consists of:

(1) a majority of the fixed number of directors if the corporation has a fixed board size; or

(2) a majority of the number of directors prescribed, or if no number is prescribed the number in office immediately before the meeting begins, if the corporation has a variable-range board size.

(b) The articles of incorporation may authorize a quorum of a board of directors to consist of no fewer than one-third of the fixed or prescribed number of directors determined under subsection (a).

(c) If a quorum is present when a vote is taken, the affirmative vote of a majority of directors present is the act of the board unless the articles of incorporation or bylaws require the vote of a greater number of directors.

(d) A director who is present at a meeting of the board or a committee of the board when corporate action is taken is deemed to have assented to the action taken unless: (1) he objects at the beginning of the meeting to holding it or transacting business at the meeting; (2) he requests that his dissent from the action taken be entered in the minutes of the meeting; or (3) he gives written notice of his dissent to the presiding officer of the meeting before its adjournment or to the secretary of the corporation immediately after adjournment of the meeting. The right of dissent is not available to a director who votes in favor of the action taken.

§ 8.25. Committees

(a) If the articles of incorporation or bylaws so provide, a board of directors may create one or more committees and appoint members of the board to serve on them. Each committee may have two or more members, who serve at the pleasure of the board.

(b) The creation of a committee and appointment of members to it must be approved by the greater of (1) a majority of all the directors in office when the action is taken or (2) the number of directors required by the articles of incorporation or bylaws to take action under section 8.24.

(c) Sections 8.20 through 8.24, which govern meetings, action without meetings, notice and waiver of notice, and quorum and voting requirements of the board of directors, apply to committees and their members as well.

(d) To the extent specified by the board of directors or in the articles of incorporation or bylaws, each committee may exercise the board's authority under section 8.01.

(e) A committee may not, however:

(1) authorize distributions;

(2) approve or recommend to shareholders action that this Act requires to be approved by shareholders;

(3) fill vacancies on the board or on any of its committees;

(4) adopt, amend, or repeal the bylaws;

(5) approve a plan of merger not requiring shareholder approval;

(6) authorize or approve reacquisition of shares, except according to a general formula or method prescribed by the board; or

(7) authorize or approve the issuance or sale or contract for sale of shares, or determine the designation and relative rights, preferences, and limitations of a series of shares, except that the board may direct a committee (or another person or persons) to fix the specific terms of the issuance or sale or contract for sale.

(f) The creation of, delegation of authority to, or action by a committee does not alone constitute compliance by a director with the standards of conduct described in section 8.30.

§ 8.30. General Standards for Directors

(a) A director shall discharge his duties as a director, including his duties as a member of a committee:

(1) in good faith;

(2) with the care an ordinarily prudent person in a like position would exercise under similar circumstances; and

(3) when exercising his business judgment, with the belief, premised on a rational basis, that his decision is in the best interests of the corporation.

(b) In discharging his duties a director is entitled to rely on information, opinions, reports, or statements, including financial statements and other financial data, if prepared or presented by:

(1) one or more officers or employees of the corporation whom the director reasonably believes to be reliable and competent in the matters presented;

(2) legal counsel, public accountants, or other persons as to matters the director reasonably believes are within the person's professional or expert competence; or

(3) a committee of the board of which he is not a member, as to matters within its jurisdiction, if the director reasonably believes the committee merits confidence.

(c) A director is not acting in good faith if he has knowledge concerning the matter in question that makes reliance otherwise permitted by subsection (b) unwarranted.

(d) Subject to compliance with section 8.31 if a director has an interest in a transaction:

(1) the director is not liable for the performance of the duties of his office if he acted in compliance with this section; and

(2) a person alleging a violation of this section has the burden of proving the violation.

(e) Subject to compliance with other provisions of this Act and other applicable law, a proceeding to enjoin, modify, rescind, or reverse a business decision, based on an alleged violation of this section, may not prevail if the directors who made the decision discharged their duties in compliance with this section.

§ 8.31. Director or Officer Conflict of Interest

(a) If a transaction is fair to a corporation at the time it is authorized, approved, or ratified, the fact that a director or officer of the corporation has a direct or indirect interest in the transaction is not a ground for invalidating the transaction or for imposing liability on that director or officer.

(b) In a proceeding contesting the validity of a transaction in which a director or officer has an interest, the person asserting validity has the burden of proving fairness unless:

(1) the material facts of the transaction and the director's or officer's interest were disclosed or known to the board of directors or a committee of the board and the board or committee authorized, approved, or ratified the transaction by the vote of a requisite quorum of directors who had no interest in the transaction; or

(2) the material facts of the transaction and the director's or officer's interest were disclosed to the shareholders entitled to vote and they authorized, approved, or ratified the transaction by the vote of a requisite quorum of shareholders who had no interest in the transaction.

(c) The presence of, or votes entitled to be cast by, the director or officer who has a direct or indirect interest in the transaction may be counted in determining whether a quorum is present but may not be counted when the board of directors, a committee of the board, or the shareholders vote on the transaction.

(d) For purposes of this section, a director or officer has an indirect interest in a transaction if an entity in which he has a material financial interest or in which he is an officer, director, or general partner is a party to the transaction. A vote or consent of that entity is deemed to be a vote or consent of the director or officer for purposes of subsection (c).

§ 8.32. Loans to Directors

(a) Except as provided by subsection (c), a corporation may not lend money to or guarantee the obligation of a director of the corporation unless:

(1) the particular loan or guarantee is approved by vote of the holders of at least a majority of the votes represented by the outstanding voting shares of all classes, except the votes of the benefited director; or

(2) the corporation's board of directors determines that the loan or guarantee benefits the corporation and either approves the specific loan or guarantee or a general plan authorizing loans and guarantees.

(b) The fact that a loan or guarantee is made in violation of this section does not affect the borrower's liability on the loan.

(c) This section does not apply to loans and guarantees authorized by statute regulating any special class of corporations.

§ 8.40. Required Officers

(a) A corporation has the officers described in its bylaws or appointed by the board of directors in accordance with the bylaws.

(b) A duly appointed officer may appoint one or more assistant officers if authorized by the board of directors.

(c) The board shall delegate to one of the officers responsibility for preparing minutes of the directors' and shareholders' meetings and for authenticating records of the corporation. The officer with this responsibility is deemed to be the secretary of the corporation for purposes of this Act.

(d) The same individual may simultaneously hold more than one office in a corporation.

§ 8.41. Duties of Officers

Each officer has the authority and shall perform the duties set forth in the bylaws or, to the extent consistent with the bylaws, the duties prescribed in a resolution of the board of directors or by direction of an officer authorized by the board to prescribe the duties of other officers.

§ 8.42. Standards of Conduct for Officers

(a) An officer with discretionary authority shall discharge his duties under that authority:

(1) in good faith;

(2) with the care an ordinarily prudent person in a like position would exercise under similar circumstances; and

(3) when exercising his business judgment, with the belief, premised on a rational basis, that his decision is in the best interests of the corporation.

(b) In discharging his duties an officer is entitled to rely on information, opinions, reports, or statements, including financial statements and other financial data, if prepared or presented by:

(1) one or more officers or employees of the corporation whom the officer reasonably believes to be reliable and competent in the matters presented; or

(2) legal counsel, public accountants, or other persons as to matters the officer reasonably believes are within the person's professional or expert competence.

(c) An officer is not acting in good faith if he has knowledge concerning the matter in question that makes reliance otherwise permitted by subsection (b) unwarranted.

(d) Subject to compliance with section 8.31 if an officer has an interest in a transaction:

(1) an officer is not liable for the performance of the duties of his office if he acted in compliance with this section; and

(2) a person alleging a violation of this section has the burden of proving the violation.

(e) Subject to compliance with other provisions of this Act and other applicable law, a proceeding to enjoin, modify, rescind, or reverse a business decision, based on an alleged violation of this section, may not prevail if the officer who made the decision discharged his duty in compliance with this section.

§ 8.43. Resignation and Removal of Officers

(a) An officer may resign at any time by giving written notice to the corporation. A resignation is effective when the notice is given unless the notice specifies a future effective date. If a resignation is made effective at a future date and the corporation accepts the future effective date, its board of directors may fill the pending vacancy before the effective date if the board provides that the successor does not take office until the effective date.

(b) A board of directors may remove any officer at any time with or without cause.

§ 8.50. Subchapter Definitions

In this subchapter:

(1) "Corporation" includes any domestic or foreign predecessor entity of a corporation in a merger or other transaction in which the predecessor's existence ceased upon consummation of the transaction.

(2) "Director" means an individual who is or was a director of a corporation or an individual who, while a director of a corporation, is or was serving at the corporation's request as a director, officer, partner, trustee, employee, or agent of another foreign or domestic corporation, partnership, joint venture, trust, employee benefit plan, or other enterprise. A director is considered to be serving an employee benefit plan at the corporation's request if his duties to the corporation also impose duties on, or otherwise involve services by, him to the plan or to participants in or beneficiaries of the plan.

(3) "Expenses" include counsel fees.

(4) "Liability" means the obligation to pay a judgment, settlement, penalty, fine (including an excise tax assessed with respect to an employee benefit plan), or reasonable expenses incurred with respect to a proceeding.

(5) "Official capacity" means: (i) when used with respect to a director, the office of director in a corporation; and (ii) when used with respect to an individual other than a director, as contemplated in section 8.56, the office in a corporation held by the officer or the employment or agency relationship undertaken by the employee or agent on behalf of the corporation. "Official capacity" does not include service for any other foreign or domestic corporation or any partnership, joint venture, trust, employee benefit plan, or other enterprise.

(6) "Party" includes an individual who was, is, or is threatened to be made a named defendant or respondent in a proceeding.

(7) "Proceeding" means any threatened, pending, or completed action, suit, or proceeding, whether civil, criminal, administrative, or investigative and whether formal or informal.

§ 10.02. Amendment by Directors

Unless the articles of incorporation provide otherwise, a corporation's board of directors may adopt one or more amendments to the corporation's articles of incorporation without shareholder action:

(1) to extend the duration of the corporation if it was incorporated at a time when limited duration was required by law;

(2) to delete the names and addresses of the initial directors;

(3) to delete the name and address of the initial registered agent or registered office, if a statement of change is on file with the secretary of state;

(4) to split the issued and unissued authorized shares if the corporation has only one class of shares and, if the shares have a par value, to reduce proportionately the par value;

(5) to change the corporate name by substituting the word "corporation," "incorporated," "company," "limited," or the abbreviation "corp.," "inc.," "co.," or "ltd.," for a similar word or abbreviation in the name, or by adding, deleting, or changing a geographical attribution for the name; or

(6) to make any other change expressly permitted by this Act to be made without shareholder action.

§ 10.03. Amendment by Directors and Shareholders

(a) A corporation's board of directors may propose one or more amendments to the articles of incorporation for action by the shareholders.

(b) To be adopted:

(1) the board must recommend the amendment to the shareholders unless the board determines that because of conflict of interest or other special circumstances it should make no recommendation and communicates the basis for its determination to the shareholders with the amendment; and

(2) the shareholders must approve the amendment.

(c) The board may condition its submission of the proposed amendment on any basis.

(d) The corporation shall notify each shareholder, whether or not entitled to vote, of the proposed shareholders' meeting in accordance with section 7.05. The notice must also state that the purpose, or one of the purposes, of the meeting is to consider the proposed amendment and contain or be accompanied by a copy or summary of the amendment.

(e) Unless this Act or the articles of incorporation require a greater vote:

(1) if the amendment would create dissenters' rights, the amendment to be adopted must be approved by a majority of all votes entitled to be cast on the amendment;

(2) all other amendments to be adopted must be approved by the holders of a majority of all votes cast on the amendment.

§ 10.04. Shareholder Class Voting on Amendments

(a) The holders of the outstanding shares of a class are entitled to vote as a class (if shareholder voting is otherwise required) on a proposed amendment if the amendment would:

(1) increase or decrease the aggregate number of authorized shares of the class;

(2) effect an exchange or reclassification of all or part of the shares of the class;

(3) effect an exchange, or create the right of exchange, of all or part of the shares of the class into the shares of another class;

(4) change the designation, relative rights, voting rights, preferences, or limitations of all or part of the shares of the class;

(5) change the shares of all or part of the class into the same or a different number of shares of the same class or another class;

(6) create a new class of shares having rights or preferences prior, superior, or substantially equal to the shares of the class, or increase the rights, preferences, or number of authorized shares of any class having rights or preferences prior, superior, or substantially equal to the shares of the class;

(7) in the case of a preferred class of shares, divide the shares

into a series, designate the series, and determine (or authorize the board of directors to determine) variations in the relative rights and preferences between the shares of the series;

(8) limit or deny an existing preemptive right of all or part of the shares of the class; or

(9) cancel or otherwise affect dividends on all or part of the shares of the class that have accumulated but not yet been declared.

(b) If a proposed amendment would affect a series of a class of shares in one or more of the ways described in subsection (a), the holders of that series are entitled to vote as a separate class on the proposed amendment.

(c) If a proposed amendment that entitles two or more series to vote as separate classes under subsection (b) would affect two or more series of a class of shares in the same or a substantially similar way, the holders of the shares of all the series so affected must vote as a single class on the proposed amendment.

(d) A class or series of shares is entitled to the voting rights granted by this section although the articles of incorporation provide that the shares are nonvoting shares.

§ 10.20. Amendment by Directors or Shareholders

(a) A corporation's board of directors may amend or repeal the corporation's bylaws unless:

(1) the articles of incorporation reserve this power exclusively to the shareholders in whole or part; or

(2) the shareholders in amending or repealing a particular bylaw provide expressly that the directors may not amend or repeal that bylaw.

(b) A corporation's shareholders may amend or repeal the corporation's bylaws even though the bylaws may also be amended or repealed by its board of directors.

11.03. Action on Plan by Shareholders

(a) After adopting a plan of merger or share exchange, the board of directors of each corporation party to the merger, and the board of directors of the corporation whose shares will be acquired in the share exchange, shall submit the plan of merger (except as provided in subsection (g)) or share exchange for action by its shareholders.

(b) To be authorized:

(1) the board must recommend the plan of merger or share exchange to the shareholders unless the board determines that because of conflict of interest or other special circumstances it should make no recommendation and communicates the basis for its determination to the shareholders with the plan; and

(2) the shareholders must approve the plan.

(c) The board may condition its submission of the proposed merger or share exchange on any basis.

(d) The corporation shall notify each shareholder, whether or not entitled to vote, of the proposed shareholders' meeting in accordance with section 7.05. The notice must also state that the purpose, or one of the purposes, of the meeting is to consider the plan of merger or share exchange and contain or be accompanied by a copy or summary of the plan.

(e) Unless this Act, the articles of incorporation, or the board require a greater vote, the plan of merger or share exchange to be authorized must be approved by the holders of a majority of all the votes entitled to be cast on the plan.

(f) Voting by a class or series of shares is required:

(1) on a plan of merger if the plan contains a provision that, if contained in a proposed amendment to articles of incorporation, would entitle the class or series to vote as a class or series on the proposed amendment under section 10.04;

(2) on a plan of share exchange if the class or series is included in the exchange.

(g) Action by the shareholders of the surviving corporation on a plan of merger is not required if:

(1) the articles of incorporation of the surviving corporation

will not differ (except in name) from its articles before the merger;

(2) each shareholder of the surviving corporation whose shares were outstanding immediately before the effective date of the merger will hold the same number of shares, with identical designations, preferences, limitations, and relative rights, immediately after;

(3) the number of voting shares outstanding immediately after the merger, plus the number of voting shares issuable on conversion of other securities or on exercise of rights and warrants issued pursuant to the merger, will not exceed by more than 20 percent the total number of voting shares of the surviving corporation outstanding immediately before the merger; and

(4) the number of participating shares outstanding immediately after the merger, plus the number of participating shares issuable on conversion of other securities or on exercise of rights and warrants issued pursuant to the merger, will not exceed by more than 20 percent the total number of participating shares outstanding immediately before the merger.

(h) As used in subsection (g):

(1) "Participating shares" means shares that entitle their holders to participate without limitation in distributions.

(2) "Voting shares" means shares that entitle their holders to vote unconditionally in elections of directors.

(i) After a merger or share exchange is authorized, and at any time before articles of merger or share exchange are filed, the planned merger or share exchange may be abandoned, subject to any contractual rights, without further shareholder action.

§ 12.01. Sale of Assets in Regular Course of Business and Mortgage of Assets

(a) A corporation may sell, lease, exchange, or otherwise dispose of all, or substantially all, of its property in the usual and regular course of business, or mortgage, pledge, or dedicate to the repayment of indebtedness (whether with or without recourse) any or all of its property whether or not in the usual and regular course of business, on the terms and conditions and for the consideration determined by the board of directors.

(b) Unless the articles of incorporation require it, approval by the shareholders of a transaction described in subsection (a) is not required.

§ 12.02. Sale of Assets Other Than in Regular Course of Business

(a) A corporation may sell, lease, exchange, or otherwise dispose of all, or substantially all, of its property (with or without the good will), otherwise than in the usual and regular course of business, on the terms and conditions and for the consideration determined by the corporation's board of directors, if the board adopts and its shareholders approve the proposed transaction.

(b) To be authorized:

(1) the board must recommend the proposed transaction to the shareholders unless the board determines that because of conflict of interest or other special circumstances it should make no recommendation and communicates the basis for its determination to the shareholders with the proposed transaction; and

(2) the shareholders must approve the transaction.

(c) The board may condition its submission of the proposed transaction on any basis.

(d) The corporation shall notify each shareholder, whether or not entitled to vote, of the proposed shareholders' meeting in accordance with section 7.05. The notice must also state that the purpose, or one of the purposes, of the meeting is to consider the sale, lease, exchange, or other disposition of all, or substantially all, the property of the corporation and contain or be accompanied by a description of the transaction.

(e) Unless the articles of incorporation or the board require a greater vote, the transaction to be authorized must be approved by the holders of a majority of all the votes entitled to be cast on the transaction.

(f) After a sale, lease, exchange, or other disposition of property is authorized, the transaction may be abandoned, subject to any contractual rights, without further shareholder action.

(g) A transaction that constitutes a distribution is governed by section 6.40 and not by this section.

§ 13.01. Definitions
In this chapter:

(1) "Corporation" means the issuer of the shares held by a dissenter before the corporate action, or the surviving or acquiring corporation by merger or share exchange of that issuer.

(2) "Dissenter" means a shareholder who is entitled to dissent from corporate action under section 13.02 and who exercises that right when and in the manner required by sections 13.20 through 13.28.

(3) "Fair value," with respect to a dissenter's shares, means the value of the shares immediately before the effectuation of the corporate action to which the dissenter objects, excluding any appreciation or depreciation in anticipation of the corporate action unless exclusion would be inequitable.

(4) "Interest" means interest from the effective date of the corporate action until the date of payment, at the average rate currently paid by the corporation on its principal bank loans or, if none, at a rate that is fair and equitable under all the circumstances.

(5) "Shareholder" includes a beneficial owner of shares held by a nominee.

§ 13.02. Right to Dissent
(a) A shareholder of a corporation is entitled to dissent from, and obtain payment for his shares in the event of, any of the following corporate actions:

(1) consummation of a plan of merger to which the corporation is a party if (i) shareholder approval is required for the merger by section 11.03 or the articles of incorporation or (ii) the corporation is a subsidiary that is merged with its parent under section 11.04;

(2) consummation of a plan of share exchange to which the corporation is a party as the corporation whose shares will be acquired;

(3) consummation of a sale or exchange of all, or substantially all, of the property of the corporation other than in the usual and regular course of business, including a sale in dissolution, but not including a sale pursuant to court order or a sale for cash pursuant to a plan by which all or substantially all of the net proceeds of the sale will be distributed to the shareholders within one year after the date of sale;

(4) an amendment of the articles of incorporation that materially and adversely affects rights in respect of a dissenter's shares because it:

(i) alters or abolishes a preferential right of the shares;

(ii) creates, alters, or abolishes a right in respect of redemption, including a provision respecting a sinking fund for the redemption or repurchase, of the shares;

(iii) alters or abolishes a preemptive right to acquire shares or other securities;

(iv) excludes or limits the right to vote on any matter, or to cumulate votes, other than a limitation by dilution through issuance of shares or other securities with similar voting rights; or

(5) any other corporate action taken pursuant to a shareholder vote if the articles of incorporation, bylaws, or a resolution of the board of directors provides that shareholders are entitled to dissent and obtain payment for their shares.

(b) A shareholder entitled to dissent and obtain payment for his shares under this chapter may not challenge the corporate action creating his entitlement unless the action is unlawful or fraudulent with respect to the shareholder or the corporation.

§ 13.20. Notice of Dissenters' Rights
(a) If proposed corporate action creating dissenters' rights under section 13.02 is submitted to a vote at a shareholders' meeting, the meeting notice must state that shareholders are or may be entitled to assert dissenters' rights under this chapter and be accompanied by a copy of this chapter.

(b) If proposed corporate action creating dissenters' rights under section 13.02 is taken without a vote of shareholders, the corporation shall notify in writing all shareholders entitled to assert dissenters' rights that the action was taken and send them the notice described in section 13.22.

§ 13.22. Notice of How to Demand Payment
(a) If proposed corporate action creating dissenters' rights under section 13.02 is authorized at a shareholders' meeting, the corporation shall notify in writing all shareholders who satisfied the requirements of section 13.21 how to demand payment for their shares.

(b) The subsection (a) notice must:

(1) state where the payment demand must be sent and where and when certificates for certificated shares must be deposited;

(2) inform holders of uncertificated shares to what extent transfer of the shares will be restricted after the payment demand is received;

(3) supply a form for demanding payment that includes the date of the first announcement to news media or to shareholders of the terms of the proposed corporate action and requires that the person asserting dissenters' rights certify whether he acquired beneficial ownership of the shares before or after that date;

(4) set a date by which the corporation must receive the payment demand, which date may not be fewer than 30 nor more than 60 days after the effective date of the subsection (a) notice; and

(5) be accompanied by a copy of this chapter.

§ 13.23. Duty to Demand Payment
(a) A shareholder notified of how to demand payment for his shares under section 13.22 must demand payment, certify that he acquired beneficial ownership of the shares either before or after the first announcement date, and deposit his certificates in accordance with the terms of the notice.

(b) A shareholder who does not demand payment or deposit his share certificates where required, each by the date set in the demand notice, is not entitled to payment for his shares under this chapter.

§ 13.24. Share Restrictions
(a) The corporation may restrict the transfer of uncertificated shares from the date the demand for their payment is received until the proposed corporate action is effectuated or the restrictions released under section 13.26.

(b) The person for whom dissenters' rights are asserted as to uncertificated shares retains all other rights of a shareholder until these rights are modified by effectuation of the proposed corporate action.

§ 13.25. Payment
(a) As soon as the proposed corporate action is effectuated, or upon receipt of a payment demand if the action has already been effectuated, the corporation shall pay each dissenter who complied with section 13.23 the amount the corporation estimates to be the fair value of his shares, plus accrued interest.

(b) The payment must be accompanied by:

(1) the corporation's balance sheet as of the end of a fiscal year ending not more than 16 months before the date of payment, an income statement for that year, a statement of changes in shareholders' equity for that year, and the latest available interim financial statements, if any;

(2) a statement of the corporation's estimate of the fair value of the shares;

(3) a statement of the dissenter's right to demand payment under section 13.28; and

(4) a copy of this chapter.

§ 13.28. Procedure if Shareholder Dissatisfied with Payment or Offer
(a) A dissenter may notify the corporation in writing of his own

estimate of the fair value of his shares and amount of interest due, and demand payment of the difference between his estimate and the corporation's payment under section 13.25, or reject the corporation's offer under section 13.27 and demand payment of the fair value of his shares and interest due, if:

(1) the dissenter believes that the amount paid under section 13.25 or offered under section 13.27 is less than the fair value of his shares or that the interest due is incorrectly calculated; or

(2) the corporation does not make payment and does not return the deposited certificates or release the transfer restrictions imposed on uncertificated shares within 60 days after the date set for demanding payment.

(b) A dissenter waives his right to demand payment under this section unless he notifies the corporation of his demand in writing under subsection (a) within 30 days after the corporation made or offered payment for his shares.

§ 13.30. Court Action

(a) If a demand for payment under section 13.28 remains unsettled, the corporation shall commence a proceeding within 60 days after receiving the payment demand and petition the [name or describe] court to determine the fair value of the shares and accrued interest. If the corporation does not commence the proceeding within the 60-day period, it shall pay each dissenter whose demand remains unsettled the amount demanded.

(b) The corporation shall commence the proceeding in the county where its principal office, or if none in this state its registered office, is located. If the corporation is a foreign corporation without a registered office in this state, it shall commence the proceeding in the county in this state where the registered office of the domestic corporation merged with or whose shares were acquired by the foreign corporation was located.

(c) The corporation shall make all dissenters (whether or not residents of this state) whose demands remain unsettled parties to the proceeding as in an action against their shares and all parties must be served with a copy of the petition. Nonresidents may be served by registered or certified mail or by publication as provided by law.

(d) The jurisdiction of the court in which the proceeding is commenced under subsection (b) is plenary and exclusive. The court may appoint one or more persons as appraisers to receive evidence and recommend decision on the question of fair value. The appraisers have the powers described in the order appointing them, or in any amendment to it. The dissenters are entitled to the same discovery rights as parties in other civil proceedings.

(e) Each dissenter made a party to the proceeding is entitled to judgment (1) for the amount, if any, by which the court finds the fair value of his shares, plus interest, exceeds the amount paid by the corporation or (2) for the fair value, plus accrued interest, of his after-acquired shares for which the corporation elected to withhold payment under section 13.27.

§ 13.31. Court Costs and Counsel Fees

(a) The court in an appraisal proceeding commenced under section 13.30 shall determine all costs of the proceeding, including the reasonable compensation and expenses of appraisers appointed by the court, and shall assess the costs against the corporation. The court may assess costs against all or some of the dissenters, in amounts the court finds equitable, to the extent the court finds the dissenters acted arbitrarily, vexatiously, or not in good faith in demanding payment under section 13.28.

(b) The court may also assess the fees and expenses of counsel and experts for the respective parties, in amounts the court finds equitable:

(1) against the corporation and in favor of any or all dissenters if the court finds the corporation did not substantially comply with the requirements of sections 13.20 through 13.28; or

(2) against either the corporation or a dissenter, in favor of any other party, if the court finds that the party against whom the

fees and expenses are assessed acted arbitrarily, vexatiously, or not in good faith with respect to the rights provided by this chapter.

(c) If the court finds that the services of counsel for any dissenter were of substantial benefit to other dissenters similarly situated, and that the fees for those services should not be assessed against the corporation, the court may award to these counsel reasonable fees to be paid out of the amounts awarded the dissenters who were benefited.

§ 14.02. Dissolution by Directors and Shareholders

(a) A corporation's board of directors may propose dissolution for action by the shareholders.

(b) To be authorized:

(1) the board must recommend dissolution to the shareholders unless the board determines that because of conflict of interest or other special circumstances it should make no recommendation and communicates the basis for its determination to the shareholders; and

(2) the shareholders must approve dissolution.

(c) The board may condition its submission of the proposal for dissolution on any basis.

(d) The corporation shall notify each shareholder, whether or not entitled to vote, of the proposed shareholders' meeting in accordance with section 7.05. The notice must also state that the purpose, or one of the purposes, of the meeting is to consider dissolving the corporation.

(e) Unless the articles of incorporation or the board require a greater vote, dissolution is authorized if approved by the holders of a majority of all votes entitled to be cast at the meeting.

§ 16.01. Corporate Records

(a) A corporation shall keep as permanent records minutes of all meetings of its shareholders and board of directors, a record of all actions taken by the shareholders or directors without a meeting, and a record of all actions taken by a committee of the board of directors in place of the board on behalf of the corporation.

(b) A corporation shall maintain appropriate accounting records.

(c) A corporation or its agent shall maintain a record of its shareholders, in a form that permits preparation of a list of the names and addresses of all shareholders, in alphabetical order by class of shares showing the number and class of shares held by each.

(d) A corporation shall maintain its records in written form or in another form capable of conversion into written form within a reasonable time.

(e) A corporation shall keep the following records at its principal office:

(1) its articles or restated articles of incorporation and all amendments to them currently in effect;

(2) its bylaws or restated bylaws and all amendments to them currently in effect;

(3) resolutions adopted by its board of directors creating one or more series of shares, and fixing their relative rights, preferences, and limitations, if shares issued pursuant to those resolutions are outstanding;

(4) the minutes of all shareholders' meetings, and records of all action taken by shareholders without a meeting, for the past three years;

(5) all written communications to shareholders generally within the past three years, including the financial statements furnished for the past three years under section 16.20;

(6) a list of the names and business addresses of its current directors and officers; and

(7) a copy of its most recent annual report supplied the secretary of state under section 16.22.

§ 16.02. Inspection of Records by Shareholders

(a) Subject to section 16.03 (c), a shareholder of a corporation is entitled to inspect and copy, during regular business hours at the corporation's principal office, any of the records of the corporation described in section 16.01 (e) if he gives the corporation written notice of his demand at least five business days before the date on which he wishes to inspect and copy.

(b) A shareholder of a corporation is entitled to inspect and copy, during regular business hours at a reasonable location specified by the corporation, any of the following records of the corporation if the shareholder meets the requirements of subsection (c) and gives the corporation written notice of his demand at least five business days before the date on which he wishes to inspect and copy:

(1) excerpts from minutes of any meeting of the board of directors, records of any action of a committee of the board while acting in place of the board on behalf of the corporation, minutes of any meeting of the shareholders, and records of action taken by the shareholders or directors without a meeting, to the extent not subject to inspection under section 16.02(a);

(2) accounting records of the corporation; and

(3) the record of shareholders.

(c) A shareholder may inspect and copy the records identified in subsection (b) only if:

(1) his demand is made in good faith and for a proper purpose;

(2) he describes with reasonable particularity his purpose and the records he desires to inspect; and

(3) the records are directly connected with his purpose.

(d) The right of inspection granted by this section may not be abolished or limited by a corporation's articles of incorporation or bylaws.

(e) This section does not affect:

(1) the right of a shareholder to inspect records under section 7.20 or, if the shareholder is in litigation with the corporation, to the same extent as any other litigant;

(2) the power of a court, independently of this Act, to compel the production of corporate records for examination.

§ 16.03. Scope of Inspection Right

(a) A shareholder's agent or attorney has the same inspection and copying rights as the shareholder he represents.

(b) The right to copy records includes, if reasonable, the right to receive copies made by photographic, xerographic, or other means.

(c) The corporation may impose a reasonable charge, covering the costs of labor and material, for providing copies of any documents the shareholder is entitled to inspect. The charge may not exceed the estimated cost of production or reproduction of the records.

(d) The corporation may comply with a shareholder's demand to inspect the record of shareholders under section 16.02 (b)(3) by providing him with a list of its shareholders that was compiled no earlier than the date of the shareholder's demand.

§ 16.04 Court-Ordered Inspection

(a) If a corporation does not allow a shareholder who complies with section 16.02 (a) to inspect and copy any records required by that subsection to be available for inspection, the [name or describe court] in the county where the corporation's principal office, or if none in this state its registered office, is located may summarily order inspection and copying of the records demanded at the corporation's expense upon application of the shareholder.

(b) If a corporation does not within a reasonable time allow a shareholder to inspect and copy any other record, the shareholder who complies with section 16.02(b) and (c) may apply to the [name or describe court] in the county where the corporation's principal office, or if none in this state its registered office, is located for an order to permit inspection and copying of the records demanded. The court shall dispose of an application under this subsection on an expedited basis.

(c) If the court orders inspection and copying of the records demanded, it shall also order the corporation to pay the shareholder's costs (including reasonable counsel fees) incurred to obtain the order unless the corporation proves that it refused inspection in good faith because it had a reasonable basis for doubt about the right of the shareholder to inspect the records demanded.

(d) If the court orders inspection and copying of the records demanded, it may impose reasonable restrictions on the use or distribution of the records by the demanding shareholder.

Glossary

Abandoned property   property that an owner has voluntarily given up

Acceleration clause   a clause that advances the date for payment

Acceptance   a drawee's agreement to honor a draft, resulting in primary liability

Acceptor   a drawee who has agreed to pay a draft when it is due

Accommodation party   a person who lends his or her name and credit to an instrument

Accord and satisfaction   a contract with new consideration to discharge an earlier contract

Account   a right to payment for goods sold or leased or for a service

Accountant's work product   background notes and work relating to a job for a client

Account debtor   an installment purchaser whose contract has been assigned to a finance company by the seller

Account receivable   a claim against a debtor for goods sold or services rendered

Accounts receivable financing   the financial lender advances money secured by accounts receivable

Adequacy   economic value of a consideration

Adjudication   the pronouncing of a formal judgment for one party or the other in a lawsuit

Administrative agencies   government bodies that carry out the administrative tasks of government through rule making

Adversary principle   the principle that places the responsibility for developing or defending a case upon the parties and not on some designated legal official

Adverse opinion (accountant's)   a statement to the effect that financial statements do not fairly represent a company's financial condition

Adverse possession   acquisition of title to real property by occupying it without the owner's consent for a period of time specified by statute

affidavit   a written statement of fact sworn to be true by the person who signs it

Affirmative defense   an answer that asserts that plaintiff has no legal claim

Age of majority   the age at which a person attains legal competency and loses minor status

Agency   a legal relationship in which one person, an agent, is authorized to act for another, a principal

Agent   a person authorized to act for another in a legal relationship

Aggrieved party   one who is the victim of another's repudiation

Alienation   the act of selling property to another

Ancillary agreements   agreements that are attendant to or aid the principal agreement

Answer   a document outlining the defendant's defense; part of the pleadings

Anticipatory breach   the breaking of an agreement before the duty of performance

Anticipatory repudiation   notification, before the fact, of an intention not to perform

Appellate court   a court that reviews the decisions of a lower court

Articles of incorporation   the instrument by which a private corporation is formed and organized under the general corporation laws of a state

Assignee   the person receiving a contract's rights

Assignment   the transfer of rights or benefits of a contract

Assignment of lease   a transfer of all of a tenant's remaining interest in the leased premises

Assignor   the person transferring a contract's rights

Assumption of risk   the voluntary exposure to a known and appreciated danger

Assurance of performance   legal promise that party will carry out a contract

Attachment   the procedure through which a secured party establishes a security interest in collateral against a debtor

Bailee   one who holds goods under the instructions of the owner

Bailment   a legal relationship in which one person temporarily holds property owned by another to accomplish an agreed-upon purpose

Bailor   the owner of bailed property

Bearer instrument   an instrument not payable to the order of a specified person

Bearer paper   an instrument payable to the order of a specified bearer

Beneficiary   a person designated to receive property or money from an insurance company

Bequest   a gift by will of personal property

Bilateral contract   a contract involving an exchange of promises

Bilateral mistake   an error made by both parties to a contract

Bill of lading   a document of title issued by a carrier

Blank endorsement   an endorsement that does not specify a particular payee

Blue laws   laws that outlaw certain sales or transactions on Sundays

Bond   a long-term debt security secured by a lien or mortgage on corporate property

Breach   the full or partial violation of the terms of a contract

Briefs   written documents presenting the legal arguments

Bulk transfer   a sale in bulk, not in the ordinary course of business

Burden of proof   the necessity of proving certain facts in dispute on an issue

Business judgment rule   standard by which courts determine whether corporate directors have acted in good faith and with a duty of care when making judgments on behalf of shareholders

Buy-sell agreement   an agreement among partners to buy the interest of any partner who withdraws from the partnership

C & F   term meaning that price of goods includes transportation only

Capacity   the ability or competence to do something at law

Capital gain or loss   profit or loss resulting from the sale or exchange of a capital asset

Capital gains   gains from the sale of stock in excess of appraised value or original cost

Capitalization   the ability to raise corporate assets (capital) used to operate the corporation

Cash surrender value   the amount of money a whole life insurance policy is worth if surrendered to the company before the death of the insured

Causa mortis **gift**   a gift made in expectation of impending death

Cease and desist order   an order to stop doing something permanently

Certificate of incorporation   an instrument by which a private corporation is formed; generally must be filed with the Secretary of State of the state a company is to be incorporated in

Certificate of deposit (CD)   an instrument acknowledging that a bank has received money and promises to repay it

Certificate of shares   formal written document which states that an individual or other legal entity owns a share of a corporation

Certification   a guarantee by a financial institution to pay an instrument when presented

Certiorari   a judicial procedure in which a higher court directs a lower court to send up the record of a case for appellate review

Challenge   the right of parties in a lawsuit to object to a particular person serving as a juror; usually must be for a reason

Charging order   a court order given to a judgment creditor so that a partnership will stand charged with paying a partner's debt out of the partner's interest

Chattel paper   writings that evidence both a money debt and a security interest

Chattels   personal property

Check   a special form of draft drawn on a bank

Chose in action   the right of owners to recover things owned by them but not in their possession

C.I.F.   term meaning that price of goods includes insurance and transportation

Civil case   a case brought by a private individual trying to resolve a private right

Closing   the final steps in a sale of real estate, when the buyer pays for the property and the seller delivers the deed

Codes   published sets of laws set out in bound volumes according to a numbered system, following passage by Congress or the state legislatures

Codicil   an addition to or alteration of an existing will

Codification   the process of enacting judge-made law into statute

Collateral   property securing a debt or obligation

Commercial impracticability   the doctrine that may allow for cancellation of a contract when it becomes commercially impracticable to perform

Commercial paper   written promises or obligations to pay money

Commercial unit   a quantity in which goods are commonly sold

Common law   law derived from court decisions

Common stock   corporate stock entitling holder to voting rights and dividends, but dividends are paid only after rights of preferred stockholders have been satisfied

Community property   co-ownership between husband and wife in which each has a half interest in property acquired during marriage

Comparative negligence   a defense that weighs the relative negligence of the parties and adjusts the award accordingly

Compilation   an accountant's basing financial statements solely on information supplied by the client

Composition agreement   an agreement between a debtor and many creditors to reorganize debt payments

Concealment   the intentional failure of an insured to disclose a material fact that would affect the insurer's willingness to accept the risk

Conciliation   informal method of bringing together parties to a dispute to settle differences before going to court

Condemnation   the legal proceeding by which the state acquires private property for a public purpose

Condition precedent   a clause in a contract that provides for the happening of some event or the performance of some act before the contract becomes binding

Condition subsequent   a clause in a contract that provides for the release or discharge of an obligation upon the happening of a certain event

Conditional restrictive endorsement an endorsement that imposes a condition on the right of an endorsee to collect

Conditional sale a sale in which the buyer obtains possession of the item but the seller retains title until the purchase price is paid; classified as a secured transaction under the UCC

Condominium ownership individual ownership in fee simple of a unit in a multiunit structure

Conflict of law rules general principles used to determine which laws should be referred to when a conflict exists between the laws of several states

Conforming the quality of meeting the exact specifications and quantity agreed upon by the parties

Consequential damages losses that are an indirect result of a contract breach

Consideration a legal obligation incurred as the bargained exchange for a promise

Consignment bailment in which goods are delivered to a bailee to be sold for the owner

Constructive notice knowledge that is not given by expressed writing or conduct but that the law implies a person has

Constructive possession the legal power to exercise control over property not actually in one's possession

Constructive trust a trust imposed by a court of law to prevent an injustice

Consumer Credit Contract an instrument that shows or embodies a debt by a consumer, missing from a purchase money loan

Consumer goods any tangible, personal property normally used for personal, family, or household purposes

Continuation statement a document publicly filed to renew a financing statement

Contract an agreement that courts will recognize and enforce

Contract implied in fact a contract created by the actions of the parties

Contract implied by law a contract created by a court although the parties never intended to contract

Contributory negligence a defense to a negligence claim that states conduct by the plaintiff contributed to the plaintiff's injury

Conveyance the transfer of an interest in real property

Cooperative ownership individual control of a unit in a multiunit structure based upon a lease obtained by the occupant because of stock owned in the cooperative association

Co-ownership ownership of real property by two or more people

Copyright a right granted by statute to an author or originator of a literary or artistic production whereby the author is invested for a limited time with the right to sell or license to sell his or her creation

Corporation business entity created for the primary purpose of making a profit

Course of dealing a sequence of previous conduct between parties to a transaction

Course of performance situations in which more than one performance is contemplated by a contract

Convenants binding agreements to do something

Cover obtain goods to substitute for those not delivered

Counterclaim an answer that asserts that defendant has a claim against the plaintiff

Creditor beneficiary a third party whose benefit from a contract is in payment of a legal duty owed by the promise

Crime an act or failure to act that the government has made punishable by imprisonment, fine, or death

Crimes *malum in se* crimes that require conscious wrongdoing

Crimes *malum prohibitum* crimes that do not require criminal intent

Criminal case a case brought by the state against a defendant who has violated a law enacted to protect society from harm

Curtesy an interest acquired by a husband in his wife's real property at the time of their marriage

Debenture unsecured corporate obligations backed by the general credit of the corporation and its assets

Declaration the legal document that creates a condominium

Deductible amount a sum to be paid by an insured before an insurer will be liable for any loss suffered by the insured and covered under a policy

Deed a document that transfers ownership of real property

Deed of trust a document that conveys title to a trustee who holds it to secure payment of the amount that the buyer owes on the purchase price

Defeasance clause a clause in a mortgage providing that when the debt is paid, the mortgage is canceled

Defeasible fee an estate that ends when a specified event occurs

Defendant a person being sued

Deferral the putting off of assuming authority or the granting of authority to another body instead

Delegated powers the powers the states constitutionally delegated to the federal government

Delegation the transfer of contractual duties

Denial an answer that asserts that some of the claims in the complaint are not true

Deposition an attorney's interrogation of a person sworn to tell the truth

Destination contract an agreement in which seller is responsible for delivering goods to the buyer's city

Dicta statements made by a court in a prior case that later courts need not follow because the statements were not necessary to the result

Discharge to release a party from obligations in a contract

Disclaimer of opinion (accountant's) a statement that

there is insufficient information to guarantee the accuracy of the audit

Disclosed principal a principal whose existence and identity is known to the third party

Discovery procedures methods for obtaining information about a case from an opposing party

Disenfranchisement removal of the right to vote

Disgorge effect of a court order that requires a person found guilty of insider trading to return all profits made on the transaction(s)

Dishonor a refusal to accept or to pay after a proper request

Dissolution termination of a firm's legal existence

Distributed actually paid out as dividends

Diversity jurisdiction power of federal courts to hear cases in which opposing parties are residents of different states

Doctrine of *Ultra vires* a rule by which corporations are not responsible for transactions not authorized by their charters, articles of incorporation, or laws of their states of incorporation

Document of title an instrument indicating the holder's right to obtain possession of the goods covered

Domicile a person's permanent legal residence

Dominant tenement the parcel of land that benefits from use of another parcel

Donee beneficiary a third party whose benefit from a contract is a gift from the promisee

Dower an interest that a widow acquires in real property that her husband owned during their marriage

Draft a written order to pay money

Drawee the person to whom an order to pay a draft is directed

Drawer the person who orders a drawee to pay a draft

Due on sale clause a clause in a mortgage that requires the borrower to pay the mortgage debt if the property is sold

Due process fundamental fairness in administration of justice

Duress an unlawful use of acts or threats by one person to force another person to perform an act (i.e., make a contract) that they otherwise would not have performed

Easement a right to make limited use of another's land

Easement appurtenant an easement that allows the owner of one parcel of land to make limited use of another parcel

Easement in gross an easement that does not exist for the benefit of any other particular piece of property

Eminent domain the power of the government to acquire private property without the owner's consent

Endorsement the signature of an endorser written for the purpose of transferring an instrument

Enterprise liability the principle that the manufacturer or seller of a defective product is responsible to the consumer injured because of that defect

Entrustment delivery and acceptance of goods

Equitable estoppel general legal doctrine used to achieve fairness by holding a party to an act that someone has justifiably relied on

Equitable title the right of a buyer to acquire legal title to real property

Equity fairness and justice, as opposed to statutory or case law, as a basis for a decision

Escheat the passing of property to the state from a person who dies without any close relatives

Escrow closing a closing that takes place through a third party

Estate the interest that a person has in real or personal property

Estate administration the process by which property is transferred from a decedent to those entitled to receive it

Estate planning the process of planning for the future distribution of a person's estate

Estate *pur autre vie* a life estate measured by the life of someone other than the owner

Estoppel term which refers to the inability of an individual based on justice and fairness to assert legal rights, especially when another individual has been induced to act based on conduct or silence of the former's representation

Exculpatory clause a provision that relieves or limits a party's liability for nonperformance of a contract

Executed contract a contract that has been fully performed

Executory promise a promise that has not yet been fulfilled

Express contract a contract formed by the oral or written words of the parties

Express warranty a guarantee regarding the quality, character, or suitability of goods that arises by action or words of the seller

Ex-ship term meaning that seller pays freight to designated port where buyer obtains the goods

Extension agreement an arrangement wherein a creditor agrees to a longer repayment period and the debtor agrees to pay the debt in full

Extortion conduct which seeks to compel or coerce payments in an unlawful manner

Factoring the financial lender advances money and purchases the firm's accounts receivable

F.A.S. free alongside a ship

Federal question a case in which the result depends upon interpretation of the Constitution, a federal statute, treaty, or federal regulation

Fee simple the most extensive estate that an owner can have in real property

Felony the most serious category of crime

Fiduciary a person holding a legal relationship of trust in which he or she acts primarily for the benefit of another in certain matters

Fiduciary relationship a relationship based on trust or confidence

Financing statement a publicly recorded document that indicates a secured party's interest in collateral

Firm offer an offer that cannot be revoked for a certain time

Fixtures   personal property that has become real property through attachment to real estate

Floating lien   a secured party's lien in both present and future property acquired by the debtor

F.O.B.   free on board a carrier, typically a truck or train

Forbearance   an agreement to refrain from something that a person could otherwise do

For collection endorsement   an endorsement that uses words such as "for collection" or "pay any bank"

For deposit endorsement   an endorsement that uses the words "for deposit"

Foreclosure   a legal action in which security is sold to satisfy a debt that is in default

Fraud   intentional misrepresentation of fact

Fraud in the execution   a universal defense so basic that a victim never actually assented to a contract

Fraud in the inducement   fraud in the material facts that causes a victim to assent to a contract

Full faith and credit clause   a provision in the Constitution requiring each state to recognize the judgments, public acts, and records of every other state

Full warranty   a warranty that meets all of the standards imposed by the FTC act

Fungible goods   goods that are indistinguishable and interchangeable

GAAP   acronym for *g*enerally *a*ccepted *a*ccounting *p*rinciples

GAAS   acronym for *g*enerally *a*ccepted *a*uditing *s*tandards followed by the accounting profession

Garnishment   a legal proceeding in which a debtor's assets, held by another person, are applied to pay a debt

General jurisdiction   the power of a court to hear all types of cases

General verdict   a verdict in which the jury finds either for plaintiff or defendant

Good faith purchaser   a purchaser without knowledge of a conflicting sale

Goods   tangible, movable items

Guarantor   a person who agrees to pay an instrument under certain circumstances

Heir   a person who receives property of a person who dies without leaving a will

Holder   a person to whom an instrument has been negotiated

Holder in due course   a holder of an instrument who took it in good faith, for value, and without notice of any claims or defenses against it

Holder through a holder in due course   someone who takes a negotiable instrument after a holder in due course has possessed it

Holdover tenancy   a tenancy that may be created when a tenant continues to occupy the premises after expiration of the lease

Holographic will   a will written and signed entirely in the handwriting of the person making it

Horizontal price fixing   price fixing among competitors at the same level of a market

Horizontal territorial limitations   an agreement between business rivals to divide markets geographically

Identification   marking of goods as objects of a particular transaction

Illusory promise   one which makes performance entirely discretionary for the promisor

Impaired claim   a claim that would receive less than full value under a reorganization plan

Implied warranty of fitness for a particular purpose   a guarantee by a seller who knows both the particular purpose for which the purchaser needs the goods and that the purchaser is relying on the seller to select goods for that purpose

Implied warranty of merchantability   a promise made by a merchant's conduct in selling a good that the product is fit for the ordinary purposes for which it is used

Impossibility   a doctrine in contract law that allows for a cancellation when a contract becomes legally impossible to perform

Incidental beneficiary   a third party whose benefit from a contract is not intended by the contracting parties

Incidental damages   expenses resulting from handling of goods made necessary by other party's breach

Incompetence   a declared inability to perform a required duty

Incontestability clause   a provision in an insurance policy providing that representations made by an insured may not be contested by the insurer after a set period of time

Incorporation by estoppel   when business is incorporated not by virtue of the appropriate legal steps, but by the way customers, creditors, and others treat the company in the course of doing business with it

Indemnify   reimburse; repay

Indemnity   reimbursement

Insider   someone with information not available to people outside the corporation concerning the value of a corporation's securities

Insider trading   the buying or selling of securities by individuals based on nonpublic information where the provider of such information (tipper) has a fiduciary relationship to the issuing corporation and makes a profit on trading in the securities

Insolvent   the financial condition of a person or business that cannot pay its debts as they become due

Installment land contract   a contract for the sale of real property in which buyer pays in installments and seller retains title until the debt is paid

Insurable interest   the right to insure against a loss of goods (or, in some cases, human life)·

Insurance agent   a person who, on behalf of an insurer, solicits insurance from third parties who become the insured

Insurance broker   a person who represents the insured and seeks appropriate policies to cover that person's risk

Insured   a person whose life or property is insured

Insurer   the person or company who agrees to compensate the insured or the beneficiary for losses caused by specific events

Intangible property   documents that represent valuable rights that a person owns

Integration agreements   clauses stating that all previous negotiations are merged into the final contract

Intended beneficiary   any third party who receives rights under a contract

Interrogatories   written questions answered under oath

Inter vivos **gift**   a gift to a living person

Inter vivos **trust**   a trust established by an agreement or deed that takes effect during the lifetime of the person creating it

Intestacy laws   laws that govern the distribution of property for people who have not made a valid will

Intestate succession   distribution of the assets of a person who dies without a will

Intrastate   goods or securities that are only traded within state boundaries and do not have substantial impact beyond

Irrevocable   may not be recalled or taken back

Irrevocable agency   an agency which cannot be ended by the principal

Irrevocable trust   a trust that is created during a person's life but which cannot be changed by its creator; property in an irrevocable trust is considered to be owned by the trustee

Issuance   the first delivery of an instrument to a holder

Issue   delivery of an instrument by the drawer or maker to the payee

Joint stock company   unincorporated association that has many characteristics of a corporation but is treated as a partnership at law

Joint tenancy   co-ownership in which the interest of a deceased co-owner passes automatically to surviving owners

Journal entry   official document reflecting what happened at trial

Judgment   the decision of a court about the rights and claims of litigants

Judgment debtor   a defendant against whom a judgment has been rendered and who remains unsatisfied

Jurisdiction   the geographic area, persons, and subject matter over which a particular court has the power to make decisions

Lapse   a passage of time within which a party has a right to exercise a right

Last shot doctrine   the principle that the last document exchanged before performance contains the terms of the contract

Law   principles that govern conduct and can be enforced in the courts

Lay testimony   testimony given by a nonprofessional person; for example, a person who is not a psychiatrist testifies about someone's mental condition

Legal detriment   legal obligation stemming from a contract agreement to take on a duty or give up a right

Legislation   laws made by a legislative body

Lessee   the tenant

Lessor   the person who rents real property to another

License   a privilege to enter the land of another for a particular purpose

Lien   a security interest in property of another

Lien creditor   a creditor with a claim against specific property in the debtor's estate

Life estate   an ownership interest in land that lasts for a person's lifetime

Life insurance policy   an insurance policy under which the insurer agrees to pay a specific sum of money to a designated beneficiary on the death of the insured

Limited jurisdiction   a court that has the power to hear only certain types of cases

Limited partnership   an agreement between two or more people to conduct a business daily, and one or more special partners who will contribute capital but not participate in management, and not be held liable for the debts of the partnership

Limited warranty   any warranty covered by the FTC Act that does not meet the standards for a full warranty

Liquidate   to convert shares or other assets of a business or estate into money

Liquidated damages   those which are specified in a contract

Liquidated damages clause   a clause that specifies the amount that will be paid if a party breaches a contract

Liquidating partner   the partner chosen by other partners to oversee the winding up of the business

Liquidation   a bankruptcy proceeding that erases all debts of the bankrupt after all of his or her property has been collected and distributed to claimants

Litigants   parties to a lawsuit

Litigation   contested legal action

Long-arm jurisdiction   power a state court acquires over a nonresident defendant who has done business in the state or who has certain other "minimal contacts" with the state

Lost property   property that an owner has parted with through carelessness or accident

Main purpose doctrine   policy that states when the promisor benefits from accepting secondary liability, an oral promise is enforceable

Maker   the party to a note who promises to pay a sum of money

Market price   cost of a good at a particular place and time

Marshaling of assets   doctrine by which creditors must pursue claims against partnership property before pursuing partners' individual property

Material alteration   a later change of commercial paper that significantly changes the contract of a party

Merger   the acquisition by one corporation of the assets or stock of another independent corporation

Meritocratic   chosen by virtue of ability

Misdemeanors   crimes that are less serious than felonies

Mislaid property   property that an owner has placed somewhere and forgotten

Misrepresentation   words or conduct that misleads others as to the material facts of a situation

Mistake   a state of mind not in accord with the facts

Mitigation   the obligation to lessen damages

Moot   a matter that has already been acted upon before shareholder proposal is set forth

Mortgage   an interest in property created by a writing providing security for the payment of a debt

Motion   an application to a court for an order

Motion for a directed verdict   a request by one party that a court order a verdict in its favor because the other party has failed to prove facts necessary to win its case

Mutual insurance company   an insurance company owned by its policy holders

Necessaries   items which, based on a minor's station in life, are required for his or her general welfare

Negligence   conduct that creates an unreasonable risk of harm to another; a tort; a civil wrong

Negotiable instrument   an instrument in writing and signed, containing an unconditional order or promise to pay a specific amount of money to order or bearer at a definite time or on demand

Negotiation   the transfer of an instrument to a third party

Net lease   a lease in which the tenant pays a fixed rent plus taxes, insurance, and maintenance expenses

No arrival, no sale   term meaning that seller retains risk of loss during shipment but is not liable for accidents in transit

Nonconforming goods   goods which differ from specifications of a contract

Nondischargeable claims   claims for which a debtor remains liable even after other claims are discharged

Nonfeasance   making no attempt to fulfill an obligation

Nonfeasibility   impracticability

No-replacement clause   a term in a contract stating that no variances are acceptable

Novation   an agreement in which a third party agrees to perform the duties of one contracting party, so that the replaced party no longer has any contract obligation

Nullify   to treat an act or proceeding as not taking place or having no legal effect

Nuncupative will   an oral will made before witnesses

Obligee   the person who receives the performance of the obligor

Obligor   the person who has the duty of performing so that someone (assignor or assignee) will have a contract right

Offeree   one who accepts an offer

Offeror   one who makes an offer

Opinion (accountant's)   a representation to those who may be expected to rely on the financial statements

Option contract   a contract which mandates that an offer be kept open for a set period of time

Order instrument   an instrument payable to the order of a specified person

Origin contract   an agreement in which seller is responsible for delivering the goods from seller's place of business

Output contract   one in which a producer agrees to sell the entire production of an item to a particular buyer

Overdraft   a check written for an amount of money in excess of the amount on deposit

Overdue   an instrument that has not been paid by its maturity date

Parol evidence rule   a rule that excludes as unenforceable terms or promises not contained in a final and complete written contract

Partnership   an association of two or more people to carry on as co-owners of a business for profit

Partnership dissolution   the relation caused by any partner ceasing to be associated in the carrying on of the partnership business

Partnership property   property that belongs to the partnership as opposed to property that belongs to a partner in his or her individual capacity

Part performance   condition in which an oral agreement is enforceable if one party already has taken substantial action in reliance on the promise of another

Partial performance   carrying out as much of the contract as is possible under the circumstances

Partition   the division of real property owned by two or more people

Past consideration   the bargained-for performance has already occurred

Payee   the person to whom an instrument originally is issued

Per capita distribution   property divided so that each person who is to receive a share of a decedent's estate receives a like share to the other persons in the same generation

Percentage lease   a lease in which the rent is determined by a percentage of sales or profits

Perfection   the process by which the secured party establishes priority in the debtor's collateral against the competing claims of third parties

Perfect tender rule   policy by which goods that fail to conform in any respect may be rejected by the buyer

Periodic tenancy   a lease that continues for successive periods until terminated by proper notice

Per se   Latin for "by itself," something forbidden in and of itself

Personal defenses   defenses that cannot be asserted against a holder in due course

Personal jurisdiction power of a court to hear a case involving a specific defendant

Personal property moveable property; all property other than real property

Personal representative the person named by the maker of a will who is to administer and distribute the estate of the decedent

Per stirpes **distribution** property divided so that each branch or line of a decedent's family shares equally, regardless of the number of recipients

Petit jury a jury, traditionally of 12 people, used for the trial of a civil or criminal case

To petition to request a court to consider a matter

Petition (complaint) a document outlining the plaintiff's claim; part of the pleadings

Plaintiff a person who brings a lawsuit

Pleadings the first stage in a civil case

Police power the authority of the state to adopt laws that promote the public health, safety, and general welfare

Pooling agreement agreement by shareholders to place their voting stock in the hands of a committee to be voted in a certain way

Postdated the condition of a check delivered before its date

Pour-over will a will that is drafted so that property disposed of by the will pours over into a trust and is managed and governed by its terms

Power of attorney written authorization creating an agency

Power of sale provision a clause authorizing the sale of a security if a debt is in default

Precedent a previous decision relied upon by a court for authority in making a current decision

Preemptive right option giving stockholder the right to subscribe to an early authorized issue of shares in the same proportion that is presently held

Preemptory challenge the right of parties in a lawsuit to object without giving a reason to a particular person serving as a juror

Preexisting duty rule the rule by which no legal detriment is incurred if a party already is obligated to perform by an earlier contract or law

Preference the payment of money or transfer of property to a creditor that gives creditor priority over other creditors

Preferred stock stock which is generally given preference over any other class with regard to payment of dividends and distribution of assets upon liquidation of the corporation

Prescription a method of acquiring a right to use another's land through wrongful use of the land for a certain period of time

Presentment submission of commercial paper for acceptance or payment

Pretrial conference a meeting presided over by a judge in which parties try to eliminate problems that might arise at trial

Prima facie determined to be so without more information needed

Primary liability condition in which a promisor is directly liable to a creditor

Primary liability an unconditional obligation to pay according to the terms of commercial paper

Principal a person who agrees to let an agent act on his or her behalf

Private placement exemption an offering of securities to a limited number of relatively sophisticated shareholders, all of whom have access to the same information

Privilege a particular benefit or advantage held by a person over and above the rights held by others

Privileges and immunities clause a provision in the Constitution prohibiting states from adopting legislation that discriminates against citizens of other states

Privity of contract the concept that only parties to a contract may use the contract as a basis for suit

Probate the process by which a will is legally approved as valid and through which the estate is administered until all of the decedent's property has been distributed

Product liability cases cases involving defective products, whether on warranty, misrepresentation, strict liability or negligence theories

Profit à prendre an interest in real property that allows the holder to take something of value from another's land

Promisee a person who receives a promise

Promisor a person who makes a promise to a promisee

Promissory estoppel doctrine used to insure fairness in situations in which one party has justifiably relied on the promise of another

Property a bundle of rights that people have in things they own

Prospectus a document that must be filed with the Securities Exchange Commission before securities can be sold to the investing public

Protected group a group of people specifically intended to fall under a statute or regulation; for example, people 40 to 70 years old fall under the Age Discrimination in Employment Act

Proximate the quality of being a direct and natural sequence between a breach of duty and an injury

Proximate cause the direct and natural sequence between the breach of duty and injury

Proxy an instrument containing the appointment of an agent (usually management) to represent a shareholder who cannot attend the annual meeting

Puffing mere sales talk

Purchase Money Loan a cash advance to a consumer in exchange for which the consumer pays a finance charge; the cash is used to buy goods

Qualified endorsement an obligation of the unqualified endorser to pay an instrument if the party primarily obligated to pay fails to pay when the note comes due

Qualified opinion (accountant's) a statement to the effect that a representation is affected by material uncertainty or deviation from GAAP

Ratification   the later approval by the principal if an earlier, unauthorized act by someone claiming to act as an agent

Reaffirmed debt   an agreement that a debt, having been legally discharged in bankruptcy, is again legally valid

Real estate investment trust   an organization in which trustees invest in real estate which they manage for beneficiaries who hold shares representing their interests

Real property or **real estate**   land or anything permanently attached to land

Recipient   a person who receives something of value under the Foreign Corrupt Practice Act of 1977

Recital of consideration   a statement of what the consideration is and an indication that it has been given in exchange

Recklessness   intended harm, but harm more serious than the defendant expected

Recourse   a turning to or a seeking of aid

Regular income proceeding   a bankruptcy proceeding that allows an individual with a regular income to readjust his or her debts without being declared a bankrupt; a plan for payment of the debts in full or in part must be approved by the court

Regulatory statutes   licensing laws requiring a fee for a permit to engage in a business or activity; primarily concerned with regulating permit seekers

Reorganization   a bankruptcy proceeding that allows a business debtor to stay in business while reorganizing its debts; some portion of outstanding debts are paid to creditors while the remainder is erased

Replevin   legal process of obtaining property that is in another's hands

Requirements contract   one in which a buyer agrees to purchase all of its requirements for an item from a particular supplier

Rescission   cancellation or abrogation of an agreement

Res ipsa loquitur   Latin for ''the thing speaks for itself''; legal doctrine permitting establishment of an inference of negligence from the evidence of the act itself

Respondeat superior   Latin for ''let the superior respond''; legal doctrine by which an employer is held liable for the torts of an employee committed within the scope of employment

Restitution   the return of whatever one has received under terms of an agreement

Restrictive covenant   an agreement that limits the use of real property

Retained powers   those powers that the states did not delegate to the federal government

Revenue statutes   licensing laws requiring a fee for a permit; primarily concerned with raising revenue

Review (accountant's)   the providing of a limited analysis of financial statements prepared by a client

Revocable trust   a trust that allows the person creating it to make changes in the terms of the trust; property in a revocable trust is considered property of its creator

Revocation   recall of an offer by the offeror

Right of survivorship   the characteristic of a joint tenancy by which the surviving owners obtain the interest of the deceased co-owner

Run with the land   the right to use an easement as acquired by the owner of the dominant tenement

Sale   passing of title from seller to buyer of goods

Sale on approval   term for goods intended for use by the buyer but that may be returned

Sale or return   term for goods intended for resale by the buyer but that may be returned

Sanction   a penalty or punishment provided as a means of enforcing obedience to the law

Search Warrant   a written court order that gives police the right to search a particular place

Seasonably   within an appropriate time based on industry standards

Secondary liability   (1) conditional commitment to pay commercial paper only after the party primarily liable fails to pay

(2) a condition in which a promisor is liable only after the original debtor has defaulted

Secured creditor   a creditor who acquires a security interest in personal property

Security   an instrument or transaction in which people invest in a common enterprise in expectation of profits derived solely from the efforts of a promoter or third party

Securities   instruments or transactions in which people invest in a common enterprise in expectation of profits derived solely from the efforts of a promoter or third party

Security agreement   an agreement that creates or provides a security interest

Security interest   an interest in personal property or fixtures which secures payment of an obligation

Security interest   a pledge by a debtor of property or other materials of value to make his or her promise of payment under a contract enforceable by a creditor in the event of a breach

Servient tenement   the parcel of land that is subject to use by another parcel

Severance   the transformation of real property into personal property

Severed   separated or divided from property (land or anything permanently attached to it)

Sinking fund   assets, usually cash or relatively liquid securities, used by a corporation to redeem its own stocks or bonds

Special endorsement   an endorsement that specifies to whom or to whose order an instrument is payable

Special verdict   a verdict in which the jury answers specific questions of fact submitted to it by the court

Specific performance   judicially compelled fulfillment of exact terms of contract

Stale check   a check presented more than six months after its date

Stare decisis   the doctrine that courts follow principles derived from previous cases involving similar facts

Status quo   the existing state of things

Statute   a law

Statute of limitations   statutes establishing time within which legal action must be begun

Statutes of descent and distribution   provide laws that for the descent of real property and the distribution of personal property

Statutory law   law based upon statutes enacted by government bodies

Statutory liens   a claim created by statute to secure payment of a debt

Stay of proceedings   the effect of a filing for bankruptcy to freeze other legal proceedings involving the debtor; those proceedings stay as they were at the time the petition in bankruptcy is filed

Stock option   in exchange for depositing some consideration, a person retains the option to buy a stock for a limited period of time

Stock insurance company   a corporation established to sell insurance for a profit

Strict liability   tort theory that permits liability without regard to fault

Sublease   a transfer of less than a tenant's remaining interest in the leased premises

Subpoenaing   process by which a court orders a person and certain books and records to appear in court at a particular date and time

Substantial performance   a state in which all material terms of an agreement have been met, and only insignificant matters remain

Substitute limited partner   a person who takes the place of a limited partner

Substitute performance   change actions so as to meet contract requirements

Sufficiency   presence of a legal detriment in exchange for a promise

Summons   a document that notifies the defendant that an action is being brought against him or her

Surety   one who undertakes to pay money or to do any other act, in the event that his or her principal fails to do so

Survivorship   the right of a person to property by reason of having survived another person who had an interest in it

Tacking   adding periods of adverse occupancy to establish a claim of adverse possession

Tenancy at sufferance   a tenancy that exists when a person wrongfully holds over after the expiration of a lease

Tenancy at will   an interest in real property that ends at the will of the owner or occupant

Tenancy by the entirety   co-ownership of real property by husband and wife

Tenancy in common   co-ownership in which each owner possesses an undivided fractional interest in real property but each owner's rights are the same as those possessed by a single owner

Tenancy in partnership   ownership of real property in the partnership name

Term tenancy   a lease that lasts for fixed period of time

Testamentary trust   a trust established by a person's will and that takes effect on the death of the person creating it

Testate distribution   laws that govern the distribution of property of a person who has made a valid last will and testament

Title   the right to possess goods

Tort   a civil wrong other than a breach of contract

Trade fixtures   personal property attached to real estate to carry on a trade or business

Trademark   a distinct mark of authenticity by which a product of a manufacturer may be distinguished from all others

Trial court   the court in which evidence is presented and witnesses testify

Trial de novo   a new trial

Tribunal   court

Trust   a legal relationship in which one person, a trustee, holds title to property which he or she manages for the benefit of another who is either the beneficiary or trustee

Trust endorsement   an endorsement that states that is is for the benefit or the use of the endorser or another person

Trustee in bankrupty   someone who represents a debtor's estate by collecting property, investigating the debtor's financial status, and reporting to the court about its distribution

Tying agreement   in antitrust law, a refusal by a manufacturer to sell a primary product (tying) unless the retailer or franchisee agrees to buy a secondary product (tied)

Ultramares doctrine   the theory that accountants are not liable to third parties for ordinary negligence

Unallocated   not distributed or assigned

Unconscionable contract   an agreement that shocks the conscience and it is so unfair and unreasonable that it should not be enforced

Undisclosed principal   a principal whose existence is unknown to the third party

Undue influence   the wrongful persuasion of a person to do something that he or she would not do if left to act alone

Unenforceable contract   an agreement this is valid but which may not be enforced because it is illegal

Unfair Trade Practice   an act in violation of the Federal Trade Commission Act

Unforeseen difficulties   unanticipated factors that substantially change expectations under a contract

Unilateral contract   a contract that involves a promise in return for action

Unilateral mistake   an error made by only the party to a contract

Universal defenses   defenses that may be asserted against a holder in due course

Unqualified opinion (accountant's)   a representation that a company's statements are a fair reflection of its finances

Unsecured creditor   a person who has no claim on any specific property of the debtor and who is paid from the general assets that are not tied to any specific debts

Usage of trade   the regular and usual method of dealing in a place, vocation or trade

Usury contracts   contracts illegal because the amount of interest charged for the use of money exceeds the amount permitted by law

Valid contract   a contract in which all the elements necessary to create a contract have been complied with

Vendee   purchaser of property

Verdict   a jury's answer to the question of fact that the court has submitted to them

Vertical price fixing   price fixing between firms at different levels of the distribution system for particular goods

Vertical territorial limitations   restraints placed by manufacturers on retailers as to where they can sell the manufacturer's product from

Vicarious liability   indirect liability; used in agency law to describe a principal's tort liability to third parties

Void contract   a contract that is not enforceable by anyone

Void title   a title which never had any legal meaning in the eyes of the law

Voidable contract   a contract that may not be enforceable under certain circumstances

Voidable title   a title which possesses a legal standing but may lose such at the option of one of the parties

Voting trust   an agreement among shareholders to transfer their voting rights to a trustee who votes the shares in a block according to the terms of that agreement

Wagering contract   an agreement to pay a designated amount of money or property when the uncertain outcome of an event is determined

Waived   to surrender a claim, privilege, right, or opportunity

Waiver   the surrender of a claim, privilege, right or opportunity

Warehouse receipt   a document of title issued by a warehouse

Warehousing   the business of storing goods for hire

Warranty   (1) guarantee that a product is free from certain defects
(2) representations in insurance contracts which operate as conditions that must exist before the policy is effective

Warranty of title   a guarantee that the owner has good title to the goods as against all other people

Watered stock   issued stock that is represented as fully paid but in fact is not paid up

Whipsawing   when a seller cuts prices in one market while maintaining price in another with the intent of driving out competitors in the first market

White collar crime   crime committed in commercial context, often by managers and professionals

Will   a written declaration stating its maker's desires as to the disposition of his or her property after death

Winding up   the process of terminating and liquidating the partnership business

Within the Statute   required by the Statute to be in writing

Without recourse   does not give the assignee any right or recourse to the assignor if the obligor does not pay his or her account; burden of collection is on the assignee

With recourse   commits the assignor to repurchase the right that was the subject of the assignment; ultimate burden of collection is on the assignor

Zoning   the division of an area into districts to control land use

Case Index

Italic type indicates cases excerpted in text; roman type indicates cases otherwise cited.

SUBJECT INDEX

About the Authors

Douglas Whitman is Professor at the School of Business Administration of the University of Kansas. He received his B.A. from Knox College, his M.B.A. from the University of Kansas, J.D. from the University of Missouri, and LL.M. from the University of Missouri. He has written articles on advertising law and products liability, and has published in *St. John's Law Review; Southwestern Law Journal* (at Southern Methodist Law School); *The University of California, Davis Law Review; The University of Pittsburgh Law Review Journal of Product Liability;* and *American Business Law Journal.* His articles have also been reprinted in *The Advertising Law Anthology, The Personal Injury Desk Book, The Corporate Counsel's Annual,* and by The American Trial Lawyer's Association. He has also written articles for the Advertising Compliance Service.

F. William McCarty is Professor in the Department of Finance and Commercial Law at Western Michigan University. A specialist in international business law, administrative law, and estate planning, Professor McCarty received his J.D. degree from the University of Michigan. He is the author of numerous articles and books, including *Modern Business Law: Contracts; Modern Business Law: Legal Environment;* and *Legal Environment: An Introduction to the American Legal Environment.*

Frank F. Gibson is a Professor of Business Law and Legal Environment in the College of Administrative Science of The Ohio State University, where he has taught since 1966. He also serves as Associate Director of the Center for Real Estate Education and Research. He was formerly Editor-in-Chief of *The American Business Law Journal,* and currently serves as Secretary-Treasurer of the American Business Law Association.

Thomas W. Dunfee is the Joseph Kolodny Professor of Social Responsibility at the Wharton School, University of Pennsylvania. He received the J.D. degree in 1966 and the LL.M. in 1969 from the New York University School of Law. He is Chairman of the Department of Legal Studies and also has an appointment in marketing at the Wharton School. He has served as Editor-in-Chief of *The American Business Law Journal* for three years. He is the author of many books on the subject of business law and has published widely in academic journals, including *The Northwestern Law Review* and *The American Business Law Journal.* He also has wide experience acting as consultant to corporations, government agencies, and trade associations.

Bartley A. Brennan is Professor and chair of the Department of Legal Studies, Bowling Green State University. He is a graduate of the School of Foreign Service, Georgetown University (B.S., International Economics) and The College of Law, State University of New York at Buffalo (J.D.). He was a Volunteer in the United States Peace Corps, was employed by the Office of Opinions and Review of the Federal Communications Commission, and worked in the General Counsel's office of a private corporation. He has received appointments as a visiting Associate Professor, The Wharton School, The University of Pennsylvania, and as a Research

Fellow, Ethics Resource Center, Washington, D.C. He is author of articles dealing with government regulation.

John D. Blackburn is an Associate Professor of Business law at The Ohio State University. He received his B.S. degree from Indiana University and his J.D. degree from The University of Cincinnati. He has served on the faculties of The University of Cincinnati, Indiana University, and The Wharton School, University of Pennsylvania. He has published articles and books in the field of labor law, including *The Legal Environment of Business, Labor Relations: Law, Practice, and Policy.*